THE UNITED STATES AIR FORCE IN SOUTHEAST ASIA

Tactical Airlift

by

Ray L. Bowers

OFFICE OF AIR FORCE HISTORY
UNITED STATES AIR FORCE
WASHINGTON, D.C., 1983

The Author

Ray Bowers wrote this history during 1969–1977 while assigned to the Office of Air Force History, Washington, D.C., where he served as supervisory historian of the Special Histories Branch. He holds a B.S. degree from the U.S. Naval Academy (1950) and an M.A. in history from the University of Wisconsin, Madison (1960). From 1960 to 1967, he was a member of the history department, U.S. Air Force Academy, where he directed instruction in the military history program. His Air Force flying career included duty as chief navigator, 345th Tactical Airlift Squadron (C–130) in 1967–1968, where he participated in major Southeast Asian operations such as the Khe Sanh and the Tet Offensive resupply efforts. He has written or edited many publications in military history, and he presented "Air Power in Southeast Asia, A Tentative Appraisal" at the 1978 military history symposium at the Air Force Academy. He retired from active duty as a colonel in 1977, and now serves as publications officer with the Carnegie Institution of Washington.

United States Air Force
Historical Advisory Committee

(As of December 31, 1982)

Lt. General Charles G. Cleveland,
   USAF
Commander, Air University

Dr. Edward L. Homze
University of Nebraska

Dr. Alfred F. Hurley,
   Brig. General, USAF (Ret.)
North Texas State University

Maj. General Robert E. Kelley,
   USAF
Superintendent, USAF Academy

Dr. Joan Kennedy Kinnaird
Trinity College

Dr. David E. Place,
The General Counsel, USAF

General Bryce Poe, II,
   USAF (Ret.)

Dr. David A. Shannon
University of Virginia

Foreword

Throughout the War in Southeast Asia, American and Vietnamese forces relied heavily on tactical airlift to satisfy the logistical demands of the conflict. While doctrine normally dictated the use of railroads and roads first to move supplies, there was simply no way other than aircraft to move quickly the necessary volume of men and materiel over difficult terrain that was subject to frequent interdiction by the enemy. Tactical airlift had to support simultaneously the full range of U.S. and Vietnamese activities: irregular forces, covert operations, remote outposts, and full-scale conventional operations involving thousands of men. And the support had to be provided despite shortages of aircraft and crews, bureaucratic inefficiency, and chronic scheduling problems.

The successful accomplishment of the mission was a testament to the skill and determination of those who flew and supported the thousands of transport sorties so vital to the allied effort. Theirs was a record of continual ingenuity and innovation in tactics, techniques, organization, and equipment. In total tonnage moved, Air Force tactical airlift in Southeast Asia very quickly exceeded previous efforts in the China–Burma–India theater in World War II, the Berlin Airlift, or the Korean War.

Tactical airlift matured in Vietnam. American airlift personnel worked with the French prior to their pull-out in the mid-1950s, and started assisting South Vietnamese in the years just prior to the massive American involvement. Tactics were developed, and then changed constantly in an effort to adapt to current military situations. Sometimes the old procedures did not apply. For example, the dropping of paratroops, long a staple of tactical airlift, was only marginally successful and in 1966 was largely abandoned in favor of helicopter-borne assault forces. But the early involvement in airborne assault did provide experience in supporting a seemingly endless variety of missions and helped shape the future of the airlift mission.

Few tactical airlift missions in Vietnam could be called routine; weather, terrain, enemy action, and the usual snafus saw to that. Tactical airlift forces lost 122 aircraft and 229 crewmembers in Vietnam, many while attempting to deliver critical cargo to friendly units surrounded or besieged by enemy forces. Some crewmembers earned prestigious decorations, including the Medal of Honor, for their performance in the face of enemy fire; others died lonely deaths from causes that will probably go forever unrecorded. But as this book consistently documents, the cargo virtually always got through when it was within the realm of possibility.

A positive theme throughout the war was the cooperation between tactical airlift and its primary user, the U.S. Army. Army personnel grumbled about late deliveries and the occasionally inaccurate airdrop of supplies, but with the exception of the siege of An Loc in 1972 the complaints were surprisingly minor. In the case of An Loc, Army personnel were sharply critical of the Air Force for the length of time it took to devise successful airdrop methods in the face of an unprecedented antiaircraft threat. Yet even this criticism became muted when new and successful tactics were introduced. The key to the successful Army-Air Force relationship was the willingness at all levels of command in both services to exchange information, to work together, and to appreciate the other service's problems. The lessons learned in Vietnam ought to have a major impact at the inter-service management level in any future conflict.

For those with a taste for the unusual there is a chapter on unorthodox operations which documents for the first time the use of tactical airlift to support secret missions throughout Southeast Asia; included was the novel use of A–1 fighter-bombers to drop supplies in drogue-retarded napalm tanks, while other A–1s bombed the surrounding jungle to disguise the true nature of the mission. Also revealed are details on the use of C–130s as bombers and reconnaissance aircraft, and the insertion and extraction of special forces sent to harass North Vietnamese operations on the Ho Chi Minh Trail.

Finally, the reader will be challenged to examine and to assimilate a wealth of detail, and to assemble a cogent picture of tactical airlift across a broad operational spectrum. One thing emerges with clarity from this book: tactical airlift in Vietnam triumphed over enormous obstacles. It will forever be to the credit of tactical airlift forces that few friendly units were overrun because tactical airlift failed to deliver the material when victory or defeat hinged on supply from the air.

RICHARD H. KOHN
Chief, Office of Air Force History

Preface

This book presents as its principal theme the United States Air Force's use of one form of air power, tactical airlift aviation, in a changing limited warfare situation. The book's language and content are tailored for readers belonging to two overlapping groups—students of war and professional military officers. Several questions are central: how was tactical airlift to perform in Southeast Asia, what was actually achieved, and by what methods?

The conflict took its shape from the interaction of two systems of war. Most of the time the war was without fronts and exhibited many of the classic features of guerrilla conflict. Communist forces were skilled in camouflaged movement and supply—a necessary accommodation to allied air power. The communist ability to infiltrate major military and paramilitary units and supply areas almost anywhere in Southeast Asia was never adequately checked by the allies. The Americans replied with their own air mobility, seeking out the enemy and subjecting him to the killing effects of air power and artillery. Both the allies and the communists periodically undertook multiregimental regional operations, the allies concentrating forces quickly by air, the communists doing so by patient and covert overland movement. Both sides sought to dominate the "hearts and minds" of the civilian population; but neither fully succeeded, the unfortunate citizenry generally thinking and acting in terms of personal survival. In the end conventional military superiority settled matters.

Air transport gave the allies in Vietnam a powerful tool for mobility and supply, permitting major operations in remote areas on short notice. Airlift also made it possible to economize on defensive forces by affording a fast means of reinforcing threatened regions, either from off shore or from other parts of Vietnam. Transports routinely sustained isolated garrisons, when necessary by parachute. Finally, the transport force conducted a countrywide passenger and logistics service and made immediate deliveries of needed spare parts to repair grounded aircraft.

This volume focuses on the operations of the Air Force airlift system in Vietnam and its three principal transport aircraft types. In the years before 1965 there were four squadrons of C–123 Providers in Vietnam operating primarily on behalf of South Vietnamese forces and the U.S. Army Special Forces. Beginning in 1965 the four-engine C–130 Hercules dominated the huge airlift effort to support the U.S. Army and Marines in Vietnam. Late in 1966 the Air Force acquired smaller C–7 Caribous from the U.S. Army, and these aircraft thereafter served in diverse and useful roles. The supplies hauled by Air Force transports in Vietnam far exceeded the combined payloads airlifted in the Korean War, the Berlin Airlift, and in the very active China-Burma-India theater of World War II. This book also examines briefly airlift activities in Southeast Asia of the U.S. Army and the Marine Corps, the contract firms, the Vietnamese Air Force, the air forces of the other allies, and the North Vietnamese. The strategic airlift operations of the U.S. Air Force's Military Airlift Command, however, are outside the scope of this book.

I have tried to convey the story of the airlifters themselves—the men who worked and flew to keep the airlift system going. I have sought to picture the nature of cockpit duty, the perspiration in aerial port work in high-volume operations at forward sites, the urgency of the hundreds of details at squadron level, and the dilemma of the leader tempering his zeal for the mission with the knowledge that one accident resulting from poor judgment could cost a hundred lives.

The book is also a history of ideas. It examines the troop carrier concept as it evolved from the 1950s to shape the force in Vietnam and discusses its aircraft, organization, state of training, tactics, and roles. In the early war years, reacting to the Army's theories of airmobile warfare and expansion of its organic helicopter arm, the Air Force moved vigorously to improve its own airlift capabilities. This Air Force tactical airlift mission became the foundation for important Air Force roles in a new system of combat-zone tactics. Part of the process also entailed the inevitable erosion of the traditional parachute assault idea. And ultimately from the airlift experience in Vietnam emerged fresh ideas that influenced Air Force and U.S. Army doctrine of the mid-1970s. This history was initially written as three separate studies successively treating the periods through 1964, 1968, and 1975, each roughly corresponding to a major era in American foreign and military policy. The present text, condensed from these earlier versions, follows the same structure. Chapters are organized topically for the convenience of researchers interested only in certain aspects of tactical airlift. Discussions of managerial and organizational matters are kept to the bare essentials, especially after the creation of the 834th Air Division which became the basic administrative structure. I have used the pages thus conserved to give relatively full accounts of certain combat and logistical operations, in the belief that these are of historical significance and not simply of technical value. Even so, only the more important and representative actions are detailed, once the essential operational patterns became established. Discussions of the use of transport aircraft in the war for Laos and in other special uses are treated independently in Part III.

A bibliographic note is added at the back of the book. Two archival repositories containing diverse materials were most fruitful—the Washington National Records Center at Suitland, Md., and the Albert F. Simpson Historical Research Center at Maxwell Air Force Base, Ala. Also central to my research were direct contacts with perhaps one hundred individuals, all veterans of airlift activities in Vietnam. The paucity of documentation for the years before 1965 dictated that available material be mined to the fullest and that further information be gathered through interviews. Beginning with 1967 the problem became one of overabundance. To have examined every relevant document would have extended the project several years. My selective research for the later years concentrated primarily on the study of command histories, interviews, and End of Tour reports deposited at Maxwell Air Force Base, reports of Air Force advisors working with the Vietnamese Air Force, after-action or postmission reports on particular operations, and collections of documents microfilmed by Project CHECO (Contemporary Historical Examination of Current Operations) or gathered by individual CHECO authors.

As research deepened, categorical conclusions became more difficult. I am nevertheless willing to stand behind several broad generalizations. I feel that the American airlifters proved their professional expertise in flying operations, and that many exhibited great dedication and imagination. The personal courage of aircrews and ground crews was unblemished and at times magnificent. Leadership from the 834th Air Division command and staff apparatus was strong. Bureaucratic inanities were not absent, but on balance the airlift effort was managed and executed intelligently. Probably the most serious failing was the Air Force's tardiness in developing an adequate aerial port apparatus, a key to efficiency in high-volume airlift operations. Cooperation in the field among the services was generally good, marked after 1964 by a spirit of compromise among the separate service staffs in Washington. I feel that the absence of heavy-lift helicopters from the centrally managed airlift system was unfortunate, though not ruinous. Helicopter and fixed-wing transport capabilities were effectively meshed in combat situations in spite of, not because of, separate systems for airlift requests and allocations. Also regrettable was the inadequacy of prewar doctrine for joint use of forward airheads, compromising the safety of crews and troop loads, until a systematic joint effort was organized in 1968 among officers serving in Vietnam. Past rivalries among the services accounted for both the unsatisfactory helicopter arrangement and the forward airhead difficulties.

The air transport vehicle (including the helicopter) proved an unsurpassed instrument for combat-zone transportation in Southeast Asia. The final years of the war, however, made clear the vulnerability of transports to relatively cheap surface-to-air missiles. Whether this will inhibit future use of airlift craft over hostile terrain will depend on developments in equipment and tactics. With this reservation I am convinced that the combat-zone airlift function deserves future funding and technical development, to improve craft payload, vertical flight, and defensive qualities. Whether such aircraft belong in the Army, or in the Air Force's Military Airlift Command, or should be under the control of theater and tactical air force commanders, are not crucial issues. Effective airlift operations can be carried out under any of these arrangements if commanders and staffs cooperate in a common purpose.

I began work on this book upon my assignment to Office of Air Force History in the spring of 1969 while the war in Southeast Asia was far from over. My explorations never ceased to be an adventure. Although supervisory and other tasks created frequent and sometimes prolonged intrusions, this study has occupied better than half my work during the past eight years. I am in debt to my colleagues for their help on countless small matters, to my supervisors for their understanding, to the many individuals who gave their time and information in interviews, to those who read and commented upon early versions of the text, to the administrators of the various repositories for help in getting to the needed materials, and especially to the infinitely good-humored Elizabeth Schwartzmann, who typed and gave perceptive suggestions on the endless drafts.

Lawrence J. Paszek, Senior Editor in the Office of Air Force History, designed and managed the publication of this work from raw manuscript through distribution. I am also grateful to Anne Shermer for the selection and placement of photography; to S. Duncan Miller and Eugene P. Sagstetter, editors for the study; and to Ann Caudle and Bobbi Levien, who painstakingly scrutinized the manuscript, galleys, and page proofs for the ever-elusive error. The photography was selected primarily from the Defense Audiovisual Agency, unless otherwise indicated; the art from the USAF Art Collection. My gratitude is further extended to James Watson of the Typography and Design Division, U.S. Government Printing Office for his role in the layout and design of *Tactical Airlift*.

Ray L. Bowers

EDITOR'S ACKNOWLEDGEMENT

The Office of Air Force History has benefitted consistently from the advice and suggestions of Dana Bell, historian and curator at the National Air and Space Museum. As in previous publications, his keen eye continues to improve the focus of presentation in our aviation art and photography. Many thanks.

LJP

DEDICATION

To the officers and men of a future U.S. Air Force, that they may know the frailties and aspirations of those who have gone before.

Contents

	Page
The Author	iii
Foreword	v
Preface	vii
Photographs	xv
Maps and Charts	xxiii

Part One: The Counterinsurgency Years, 1946–1964

I.	The French War in Indochina	3
II.	The Troop Carrier Idea, 1954–1961	25
III.	Farm Gate and the Air Commando Tradition	47
IV.	The Dirty Thirty and the Vietnamese Air Force Transport Arm	67
V.	Mule Train—The First Year	83
VI.	The Airlift System, 1963–1964	115
VII.	Air Supply of Special Forces	149

Part Two: The Years of the Offensive, 1965–1968

VIII.	The Entry of the C–130, 1965–1966	169
IX.	Search and Destroy	203
X.	The Airlift System in Growth, 1966–1967	241
XI.	Junction City and the Battles of 1967	269
XII.	The Khe Sanh Campaign	295
XIII.	Tet and the Battles of 1968	317
XIV.	The Air Force Caribous	353

Part Three: Other Applications

XV.	The Auxiliary Roles	379
XVI.	Airlift in Irregular Warfare	417
XVII.	The War for Laos	439

Part Four: The Years of Withdrawal, 1969–1975

XVIII.	The Airlift System, 1969–1971	467
XIX.	The Campaigns of 1969–1971, Cambodia and the Panhandle	493

		Page
XX.	The Caribou Force, 1969–1972	521
XXI.	The Easter Offensive—The Battle of An Loc	539
XXII.	The Easter Offensive—The Countrywide Response	559
XXIII.	The Advisory Role and the Vietnamese Air Force Airlift Arm	581
XXIV.	Return to Cold War in Southeast Asia	605
XXV.	The 1975 Denouement	631
XXVI.	Reflections	649

Appendices

1. 2d Air Division Organization, July 1963 663
2. 315th Air Division Organization, June 1964 665
3. Pacific Airlift Organization, March 1968 667
4. Peak Theater Airlift Force Posture, March 31, 1968 . . . 669
5. Theater Airlift Force Posture, March 31, 1972 671
6. Agreement between Chief of Staff, U.S. Army and Chief of Staff, U.S. Air Force, 6 April 1966 673
7. Workload, USAF Airlift Forces in Vietnam 675
8. Workload, Combined Forces in Vietnam, 1965–1972 (Cargo Only, Monthly Average Tonnages) 683
9. Workload, PACAF Forces in Western Pacific, 1969–1972 . 685
10. Workload, 315th Air Division, 1965–1968 687
11. USAF Transports Lost in SEA (Excludes Rescue Aircraft) . 689
12. Historic Theater Airlifts (Passengers and Cargo) 691

Notes 693
Glossary 807
Bibliographic Note 829
Index 835

Photographs

	Page
French Air Force C–47s at Do Son airfield	6
A C–119 Flying Boxcar on loan to French forces; loading a C–119 with cargo for Dien Bien Phu	12
Chinese, French, and American personnel unload a C–124 at Saigon; French military personnel board a Tactical Air Command C–124	13
Painting French markings on a USAF C–119; maintenance specialists work on a flak-damaged C–119; French parachutists being dropped during an attack on a Vietminh stronghold	14
Generals Otto P. Weyland and Earle E. Partridge	15
Gen. Earle E. Partridge visits men being airlifted back to France	22
Evacuating the wounded after the fall of Dien Bien Phu	23
Gen. Curtis E. LeMay	33
President John F. Kennedy, Robert S. McNamara, and Gen. Lyman L. Lemnitzer	43
Brig. Gen. Theodore R. Milton	48
VNAF C–47 transports in formation over Tay Ninh; Air Commandos A1C Richard B. Costello, Capt. William H. Brandt, and SSgt. Russell D. Lapray; Vietnamese paratroopers hooking up; members of the Vietnamese airborne brigade at Tan Son Nhut	56
Dirty Thirty insignia	66
C–47s on the flight line, Tan Son Nhut; Capt. Robeson S. Moise; Captains Ty Lewis, Harold Sweet, and Bill Blackburn; VNAF officer and Capt. Joseph Grant with the Dirty Thirty insignia	76
Viet Cong prisoners unload sacks of rice	87
A hard-surface airfield at Ban Me Thuot	89
Gen. Emmett O'Donnell with VNAF officers	96
Vietnamese Army paratroopers board C–123s; Vietnamese soldiers en route to the drop zone	100

	Page
U.S. Army Caribou in Vietnam	110
Gen. Paul D. Harkins	111
Thai airmen unload a USAF C–124	112
A C–124 delivers a trailer truck loaded with supplies to Takhli Air Base	113
Col. David T. Fleming	118
A1C Theodore R. MacDonald and Capt. William L. Lawter maintain radio contact with a C–123	119
Maj. Gen. Rollen H. Anthis talks with Vietnamese paratroopers; USAF maintenance specialists at work on a C–123 engine; Vietnamese paratroopers jump from C–123s over Tay Ninh	130
Three C–123s on a Vietnamese paratroop training mission over Vung Tau; Nguyen Cao Ky; new aerial port detachment at Qui Nhon	131
Containerized delivery; low-altitude parachute extraction system; a normal cargo drop	142
Robert S. McNamara	145
The rugged central highlands of Vietnam	148
Gen. Jacob E. Smart and Lt. Gen. William C. Westmoreland; Special Forces members release a live cow dropped by parachute at Phu Tuc; C–47 crews support U.S. Army Special Forces	156
An Army Special Forces team contacts a village chief and his assistant; Montagnards disembark from an American transport; Gen. Maxwell D. Taylor, Maj. Gen. Victor H. Krulak, and Maj. Gen. Rollen H. Anthis	157
Air Force C–130 Hercules	170
American dependents leave the Republic of Vietnam	171
A C–130 lifts off a membrane runway at a Vietnam outpost; maintenance work on a C–130; transports from the 315th Air Division lined up on the taxi strip at Tan Son Nhut	178
Combat control team communicates with the airlift control center; traffic managers at the Joint Operations Center check the progress of a C–123; smoke marker from the air; combat controllers mark the paradrop zone	188

	Page
U.S. Army Caribou in Vietnam	110
Gen. Paul D. Harkins	111
Thai airmen unload a USAF C–124	112
A C–124 delivers a trailer truck loaded with supplies to Takhli Air Base	113
Col. David T. Fleming	118
A1C Theodore R. MacDonald and Capt. William L. Lawter maintain radio contact with a C–123	119
Maj. Gen. Rollen H. Anthis talks with Vietnamese paratroopers; USAF maintenance specialists at work on a C–123 engine; Vietnamese paratroopers jump from C–123s over Tay Ninh	130
Three C–123s on a Vietnamese paratroop training mission over Vung Tau; Nguyen Cao Ky; new aerial port detachment at Qui Nhon	131
Containerized delivery; low-altitude parachute extraction system; a normal cargo drop	142
Robert S. McNamara	145
The rugged central highlands of Vietnam	148
Gen. Jacob E. Smart and Lt. Gen. William C. Westmoreland; Special Forces members release a live cow dropped by parachute at Phu Tuc; C–47 crews support U.S. Army Special Forces	156
An Army Special Forces team contacts a village chief and his assistant; Montagnards disembark from an American transport; Gen. Maxwell D. Taylor, Maj. Gen. Victor H. Krulak, and Maj. Gen. Rollen H. Anthis	157
Air Force C–130 Hercules	170
American dependents leave the Republic of Vietnam	171
A C–130 lifts off a membrane runway at a Vietnam outpost; maintenance work on a C–130; transports from the 315th Air Division lined up on the taxi strip at Tan Son Nhut	178
Combat control team communicates with the airlift control center; traffic managers at the Joint Operations Center check the progress of a C–123; smoke marker from the air; combat controllers mark the paradrop zone	188

	Page
Loaded cargo pallets share the flight line with a C–130; the terminal at Tan Son Nhut; forklift being used to unload a C–124	193
Gen. Hunter Harris with Lt. Gen. Joseph Moore; Lt. Gen. William W. Momyer congratulates Capt. Richard A. Fritz, TSgt. Charles L. Peterson, and SSgt. William J. Slough; Army specialists clear mines from a field at An Khe; C–130 crashes near Qui Nhon	198
Vietnam War Art (Anon., Courtesy U.S. Air Force Art Collection)	202
President Lyndon B. Johnson; C–130s wait to transport the 1st Cavalry Division to An Khe	210
Gen. Earle G. Wheeler; Gen. John P. McConnell; members of the 1st Air Cavalry Division board a C–130 for movement to An Khe	211
U.S. Army paratroopers jump from a C–130, 1966; C–130 Hercules takes off from a dirt strip at Nhon Co; soldiers of the 173rd Airborne Brigade rig pallets of supplies	220
C–130 transports at Tay Ninh during Operation Birmingham	226
An Air Force loadmaster directs the loading of 1st Infantry Division troops and equipment; Lt. Ken R. Lawrence checks his instruments en route to Tay Ninh; USAF CH–3C helicopter prepares to transport a 105-mm howitzer to the front lines during Operation Mastiff	227
Air Force construction team replaces pierced steel planking with N9–M1 aluminum matting	231
Army CH–54 Flying Crane; CH–47 Chinook on a search and destroy mission; off-loading fuel drums from a USAF CH–3C	234
Airlift support personnel discuss incoming flights at Da Nang; an Army controller uses USAF equipment at a forward operating base; USAF combat control team directs the paradrop of Army troops	244
C–123 crash near a Special Forces camp	250
C–130 destroyed by Communist mortar fire	251
An adjustable 25K–loader; cargo netting placed over a stack of tires	254
A1C Richard D. Dover logs in the arrival of a C–130; Gen. Hunter Harris; passenger terminal at Tan Son Nhut; cargo ready for shipment	255
Two airmen rig cargo and parachute extraction equipment	260

	Page
Cargo extraction over An Khe	261
Dr. Harold Brown and Lt. Gen. Joseph H. Moore; pierced steel planking forms a runway	264
Aviation fuel is pumped from a fuel bladder; loading fuel drums	265
Brig. Gen. William G. Moore talks with officers taking part in Operation Attleboro; a C–123 squeezes between a bunker and an old French villa	272
Dust never settled at Dau Tieng during Operation Attleboro	273
Airlift of 173rd Airborne Brigade from Dak To to Phu Hiep	280
Members of the 173rd Airborne Brigade, moments after jumping from a C–130; a C–130 paradrops supplies and equipment to Army forces	281
Sgt. Joseph F. Mack and Capt. Joseph K. Glenn receive Silver Stars and Distinguished Flying Crosses from Gen. John P. McConnell	287
A C–123 touches down on the Khe Sanh runway	298
U.S. Army and Air Force riggers load cargo on a C–123 for paradrop to troops at Khe Sanh; Maj. Jimmy Dennis pilots a C–130 to the paradrop zone; Air Force and Navy jets put down a line of defensive fire to protect a C–130 departing from Khe Sanh	308
An Army rigger aboard a USAF C–130 attaches a static line to a hook-up cable; supplies are dropped into the beleaguered outpost of Khe Sanh	309
Marine crews move quickly to recover cargo dropped by transport aircraft; Marines recover ammunition pallets that overshot the drop zone; the trailing hook of the C–130 cargo load catches on the arresting cable stretched across the Khe Sanh runway	310
Lt. Col. Joe M. Jackson receives the Medal of Honor from President Lyndon B. Johnson	318
Members of the 82nd Airborne Division board a MAC C–141 at Pope AFB	326
UH–1D helicopter is loaded onto a C–133 bound for Vietnam	327
Ruins of a C–45 aircraft after a mortar and rocket attack; ruins of a warehouse at the 8th Aerial Port; second aerial port building suffered slight damage; firemen battle the blaze of a C–47	331
Capt. Ross E. Kramer	337

	Page
An Air Force Caribou takes off from A Luoi	341
Ammunition is loaded aboard a USAF C–7A for support of Operation Delaware	342
Caribou crew chief tells the pilot the way is clear to taxi for take off; an Army officer briefs Army and Air Force personnel on the Caribou transfer; Lt. Col. John F. Yelton is briefed by Maj. Maynard A. Austin	356
Sgt. William T. Brown discusses the C–7A engine with Cadet James D. Haas	362
Lt. Gen. William W. Momyer	363
C–124 Globemaster delivers a CH–34 helicopter at Da Nang; USAF C–135 Stratolifter at Da Nang; C–141 Starlifter on the flight line at Tan Son Nhut	386
Interior view of the C–5 Galaxy; arc lamps mounted under a C–123 provide a constant light source; a C–47 Skytrain ready to take off for a flare-drop mission	387
AC–47 Dragonship crewmen tend their miniguns; USAF AC–119 "Shadow" gunship in flight over Nha Trang Air Base; Sgt. John E. Bradley checks the miniguns on an AC–119	390
C–123 under the Ranch Hand sign at Nha Trang; C–123s support Boi Loi woods-burning mission	391
Patients on stanchions are secured in place by Capt. Nicholas J. Perotto and A1C Stanley M. Danna; transferring patients to a C–141 for the trip to the States; SSgt. Billy E. Neeley prepares an intravenous bottle	398
Air America headquarters, Udorn AB, Thailand	402–403
Three airmen load surrender leaflets into a distribution chute	406
RAAF crews leave their aircraft upon arrival at Tan Son Nhut	413
An Australian UH–1D helicopter used to support the 2nd Royal Australian Army Regiment, Vietnam	414
Troops of the Korean Tiger Division board a USAF C–130 at Qui Nhon Air Base	415
Capt. James P. Fleming	426
Thai troops and Special Forces advisors board a CH–3E	427

	Page
USAF C–123 lands at a camp near Plei Djereng; Army UH–1C transports supplies to Nui Ba Den; A1C Gary W. Harwell marks the drop zone for a C–130	436
A low altitude parachute extraction delivery over Bu Dop; aerial view of a Special Forces camp	437
Long Tieng, Laos, January 16, 1972; nighttime firing of tracers by an AC–119K; left side of an AC–119K gunship	460
Site of an aircraft accident near Gia Nghia, Vietnam	478
Wreckage of a C–130 at Kham Duc, Vietnam	479
Sgt. Dannie B. Needham checks a valve on a fuel bladder	481
U.S. military personnel board a commercial airliner at the Da Nang Aerial Port; aerial view of a C–5 Galaxy; Mr. B. J. Lewis shows TSgt. Phillip Lewis how to search for illicit materials	489
Rescue—1969 Style (Art by Frances Walter, Courtesy U.S. Air Force Art Collection)	492
A C–130 begins a sharp climb after take-off at Kham Duc; combat control team backs its jeep onto a C–130; combat controllers coordinate air traffic at Kham Duc	496
Capt. Palmer G. Arnold receives the Silver Star from Vice President Spiro T. Agnew and Vice President Nguyen Cao Ky	503
President Nguyen Van Thieu and Vice President Nguyen Cao Ky	509
Secretary of Defense Melvin Laird, Gen. George S. Brown, and U.S. Ambassador Ellsworth Bunker	518
USAF C–7B Caribou at Phu Cat Air Base	529
Col. Wilbert Turk receives a visit from Gen. John P. McConnell and Maj. Gen. Royal N. Baker	534
Capt. Edward N. Brya	543
C–141 Aircraft Unloading (Art by Douglas D. Smith, Courtesy U.S. Air Force Art Collection)	558
A C–130 makes a nighttime stop at Da Nang	560
The first C–119 transferred to the Vietnamese Air Force	584
VNAF C–123 comes in for a landing	588

	Page
TSgt. William Brazier instructs VNAF students on the maintenance of the C–123 engine	589
Operation Homecoming (Art by Maxine McCaffrey, Courtesy U.S. Air Force Art Collection)	604
C–141 at Clark Air Base, Philippines receives a red cross; Maj. James E. Marrott at the controls of the first C–141 flown into Hanoi; a jubilant ex-POW deplanes at Clark; Operation Homecoming command post at Scott Air Force Base	610
Vietnamese refugees aboard a C–141 en route to Clark Air Base .	640
A USAF airman carries refugee children from a C–141	641

Maps and Charts

	Page
Southeast Asia	facing p. 1
Southeast Asia, 1954	4
Northern Indochina, 1954	15
Aircraft Performance, Basic Mission	34
The Pacific	36
South Vietnam: Farm Gate and Vietnam Air Force Operations	51
South Vietnam: Mule Train, 1962–64	99
Parachute Assaults, 1963–64	127
Special Forces Locations Receiving Airdrops, October 1–17, 1963	155
Western Pacific Area	172
South Vietnam, 1965–67	175
C–130 Airlift Force in Vietnam	176
Tactical Airlifts, Summer 1965	205
Ia Drang Campaign, October–November 1965	210
173d Brigade Movements, 1965–66	217
Odyssey of the 1/101st Brigade, Spring and Summer, 1966	221
Operations Northwest of Saigon, 1966	226
Locations of 45 Aerial Ports in Vietnam, July 1967	254
Saigon Plain	273
Junction City	280
The Highlands, 1966	283
The Northern Provinces, 1966	289
Khe Sanh, 1968	296
Khe Sanh Combat Base	298
Common Service Airlift System Bases and Operations, 1968	320

	Page
A Shau Valley, Spring 1968	334
Principal Air Deliveries, 1968	348
Caribou Bases and Operations, 1967–68	361
Southeast Asia: Auxiliary Roles	381
Special Forces Activity, South Vietnam, 1965–68	418
Helicopter Performance, Basic Mission	427
Southeast Asia: Communist Airlift	433
The War in Laos	444
Contract Airlift Fleets for Laos	447
Location of Units, excluding Vietnam	474
Location of Units, within Vietnam	475
Location of Aerial Port Units as of June 1970	488
The War in 1968–70	494
Support for 1st Cavalry Division	498
The Border Highlands, 1970	501
Southern Incursions, 1970	503
834th Air Division Support of Cambodian Operations, April 30–June 30, 1970	504
Airlifts into Cambodia	506
The Northern Provinces, Lam Son 719	511
Caribou Operations in South Vietnam	524
Caribou Operations in the Highlands	528
The An Loc Campaign	541
Summary of An Loc Supply, 1972	555
The 1972 Campaigns	562
Kontum Region, 1972	569
C–130 Airdrop Sorties, Easter Offensive	574
South Vietnam, 1972	585
Programmed and Actual Vietnamese Air Force Levels	587

	Page
Southeast Asia, 1972–73	607
South Vietnam, 1972–73	614
Commodity Movements into Cambodia, July 1974	626
Cambodia	628
The 1975 Campaign	634

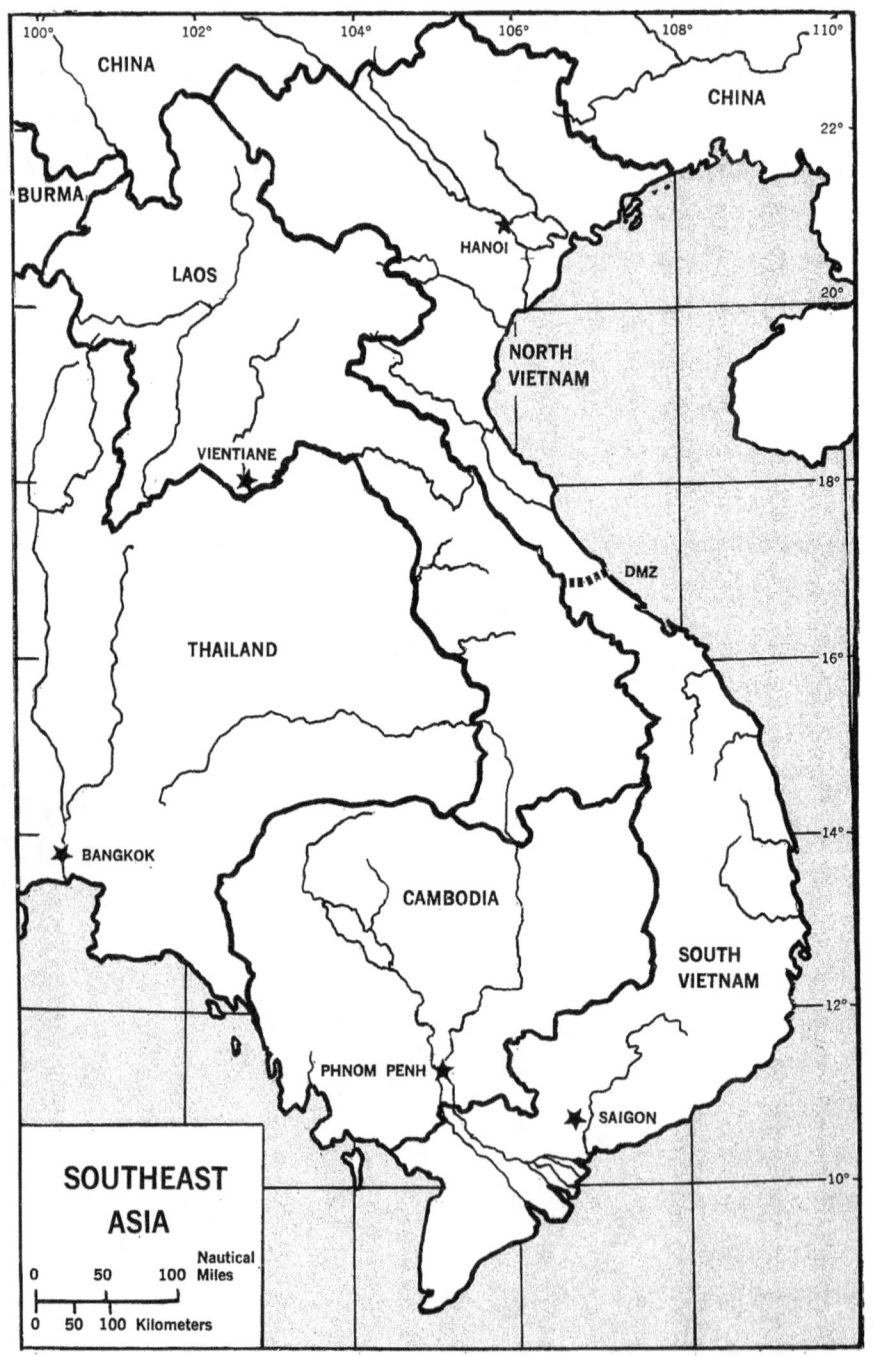

Part One:
The Counterinsurgency Years, 1946-1964

I. The French War in Indochina

The joyless war of the French in Indochina passed into history at Geneva in 1954. Through eight years of a "war without fronts," French Union Forces, comprising French troops, Foreign Legionnaires, loyal Indochinese, North Africans, and Senegalese, controlled only the ground on which they stood. The Viet Minh used the classic tactics of the insurgent, moving at will across the terrain of Indochina and avoiding battle except on terms of its own choosing. Espousing nationalism, the Viet Minh won support from the peasantry, a source of manpower for carrying on the war. Sustained in the later years by weapons and materiel from Communist China, the Viet Minh confronted the French with a nearly impossible military situation.

An important potential asset for the French was their total superiority in the air. With command of the air came the ability to use that medium for transportation, observation, and the delivery of firepower. Handicapping strike and reconnaissance aircraft, however, was the geography of Indochina—its spaciousness, forests, and climate—which afforded the guerrilla army opportunities for dispersion and concealment. Geography, however, suggested important uses for air transport. Airlift gave the French army freedom from dependence on surface communications, whether in maintaining isolated garrisons or in operating offensively in enemy-dominated regions. A decade later, the Americans would employ air transport in essentially the same ways, fighting essentially the same enemy in the same arena.

With President Harry S Truman's May 1950 decision to assist the French, America undertook an almost entirely advisory and logistical military role in Indochina.[1] The U.S. Air Force's contribution was primarily on behalf of the French airlift arm and included provision of transports, spare parts and equipment, instructors, and temporary maintenance detachments. Air Force transport units based in the Pacific made regular deliveries of military materiel to Indochina and on very rare occasions flew sorties between points within the country.

Throughout the war years, French forces occupied several principal enclaves. A chain of defensive positions guarded the Red River flatlands in

TACTICAL AIRLIFT

the north, including the cities of Hanoi and Haiphong, the Bac Mai and Gia Lam airfields at Hanoi, and the Cat Bi and Do Son fields outside Haiphong. A second major French concentration lay around Saigon and included the Tan Son Nhut and Bien Hoa airfields. French forces also garrisoned perimeters about lesser centers at Tourane (later called Da Nang), and Nha Trang. Overland movement outside these enclaves invited ambush by day and was suicidal at night. Based inside these protected areas were the French air transport squadrons, primarily at Tan Son Nhut, Do Son, and Nha Trang.

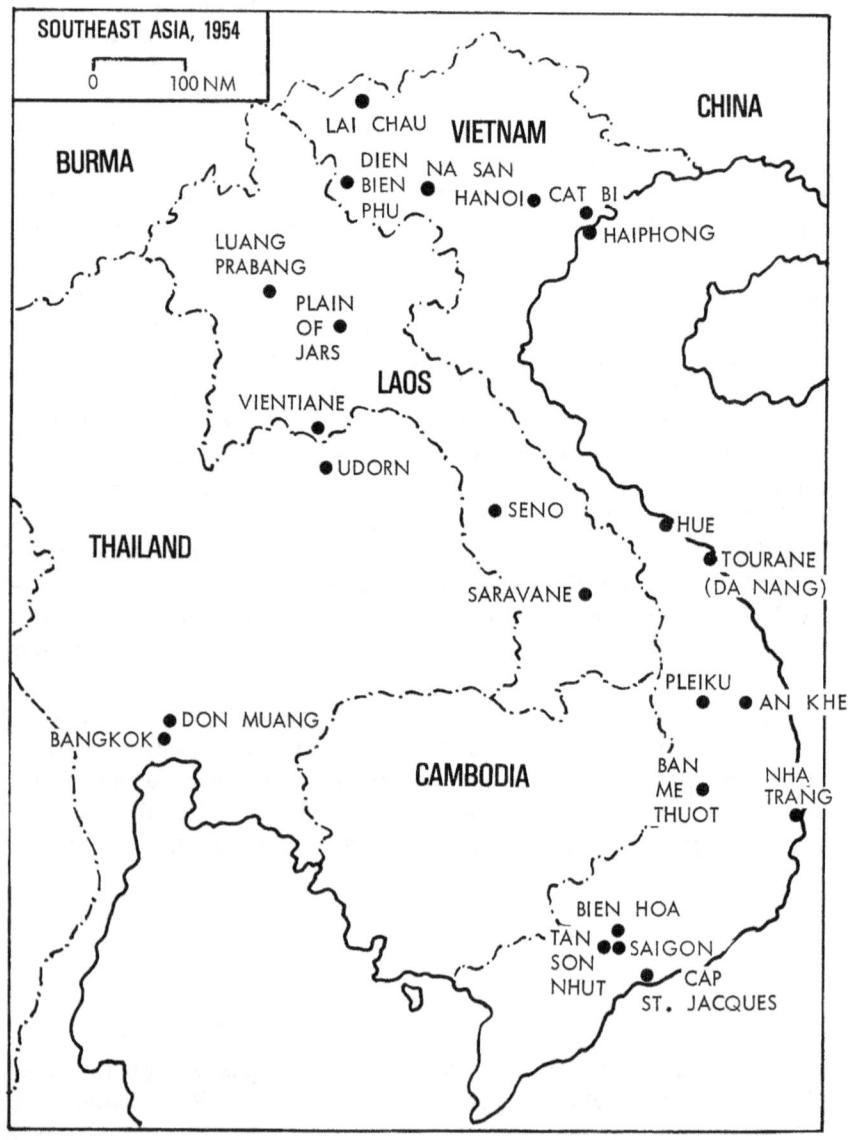

THE FRENCH WAR

In the less populated highlands of Vietnam and over much of Laos, the French garrisoned numerous camps and posts. They conceived these sites as rallying points for opponents of the Viet Minh, among the mountain people, and as bases to support patrol activity by French-led counterguerrilla troops. The garrisons were supplied primarily by transport aircraft operating from the larger coastal bases. Few of the isolated posts had landing strips, so that airdrop became the customary delivery method. Over seventy drop zones in the interior were in routine use by 1953.[2]

These fixed defensive positions tended to tie down more than half the French manpower. Under American pressure, the French organized and expanded a Vietnamese National Army, intending that the loyalist soldiery man the fortified posts, thus releasing French troops for offensive roles. French motorized units, equipped with tanks, trucks, and artillery, were stationed at major bases and were prepared for fast movement into the interior. Communist ambushes in early 1954 ripped apart one such unit, Mobile Group 100, within the Pleiku-An Khe-Ban Me Thuot triangle of southern Vietnam, exemplifying the futility of French roadbound supply efforts against an enemy capable of off-road movement.[3]

In contrast, airborne mobility inherent in parachute troops and transport aircraft promised worthwhile tactical possibilities. An Airborne Forces Command was organized in 1949 with headquarters, training, and support facilities at Saigon and Hanoi. The well-trained paratroop force expanded in size throughout the war, exceeding eight thousand men by the end of the conflict.

The paratroop battalions proved their tactical skills in more than 150 operations of varied dimensions. Few parachute operations, however, could damage an enemy indifferent to pressure on communications. Usually Viet Minh forces faded away from the objective area, offering little resistance either to the paratroops or to ground forces. Paratroops could strike instantly but once on the ground they had no greater mobility than conventional forces, and deep strikes raised the major problem of retrieving the paratroops after completion of their mission.* Paratroops were sometimes used in defensive situations, making approximately sixty reinforcement jumps into or near isolated posts under attack. Several times, airborne units jumped into areas chosen to protect the withdrawal of other forces. Occasionally, where suitable airstrips existed at threatened points, transports landed the troopers.[4]

Another means for challenging the Viet Minh in the interior was the *Base Aero-Terrestre*, situated in a remote area and built around a heavy-

---

*Parachute assaults spearheaded each of the main French offensives from Hanoi—sweeps in 1947 into the northern hills, and the later Hoa Binh and Lorraine operations. An example of the independent raid was Operation Hirondelle near the Chinese border in 1953, wherein three battalions destroyed communist war materiel before withdrawing overland sixty miles for naval pickup.

TACTICAL AIRLIFT

Americans, continually pressed by the French to provide more transport aircraft, first priority lay in reforming the sagging French maintenance system. Toward this end, members of the U.S. Far East Air Forces turned their energies during 1952 and became involved in an Indochina airlift activity which increased steadily until the 1954 armistice.

American maintenance and supply teams from Air Force units based in the Pacific arrived in Vietnam during late 1952 and sought to improve French Air Force logistics. Both nations viewed this cooperation as temporary, with French self-sufficiency the eventual goal. A stream of American mobile training teams gave further assistance. Six such teams arrived from the United States for six-month tours during 1953. The logistics and training teams moderately improved French maintenance, despite frictions when American confidence rubbed against French pride.[10]

Air Force officials repeatedly recommended against complying with French requests for additional C–47s, believing that more transports would be unusable unless maintained by American personnel. The idea of lending Air Force transports to the French for short periods met few objections. During the summer of 1952, the French asked for sufficient transports to drop three paratroop battalions (about twenty-four hundred men). In view of the urgent need to achieve battlefield victories, and despite the past ineffectiveness of large paratroop operations, American officials yielded to French entreaties. U.S. Ambassador Donald R. Heath in Saigon informed Washington on August 15, 1952:

> Actually, even if the offensive spirit of command and troops were at highest pitch, no effective offensive could be undertaken against the Viet Minh because French-Viet forces lack the indispensable element to force the elusive enemy to battle—namely, sufficient planes for more massive air drops of parachute battalions.[11]

Consequently, the Air Force, on September 20, 1952, directed the Far East Air Forces to provide twenty-one C–47s on a four-month loan. The aircraft were to be delivered to the coastal base at Nha Trang, along with spare parts and would thereafter be operated by French crews and would display French markings, although the United States would retain ownership. Simultaneously, the French were to shift twenty-nine C–47s from Europe,* to bring the transport fleet in Indochina up to 102 planes. An Air Force supply team flew to Nha Trang on October 6 to assist in organizing the spare parts and equipment to be provided by the Americans.[12]

The 1952 loan project began with misfortune. On October 20 a tropical storm damaged ten C–47s that had just arrived at Nha Trang. Repairs

---

* Most were received from the Belgian Air Force, then reequipping with newer aircraft.

were made promptly, using parts airlifted from Clark Field in the Philippines. Several weeks later, the French maintenance force, overwhelmed with the additional C–47s, urgently requested the assistance of American mechanics. Deeming emergency maintenance "vital to the holding of Na San," Ambassador Heath urged "immediately favorable action." On December 20, 1952, Air Force headquarters directed the Far East Air Forces to provide a maintenance team with a strength "adequate for the balance of the loan time of USAF C–47 aircraft." A team of approximately twenty-eight men was promptly dispatched and remained at Nha Trang until the following summer.[13]

Although the 102-ship C–47 fleet had been conceived primarily for use in parachute assaults, in practice the ships were used for heavy-volume work. The Viet Minh offensives in late 1952 against Na San and a smaller base at Lai Chau necessitated some one hundred resupply flights daily. Twenty French battalions in Laos, meanwhile, became entirely dependent on air supply as a result of fresh communist attacks against Luang Prabang and the Plain of Jars. Although disappointed by an absence of French offensive operations, the Americans accepted that circumstances required continuation of the C–47 loan beyond February. The loan period was extended, the French returning eight ships in April 1953 and the remainder in August.[14]

The idea of using C–119 Flying Boxcars for airdrops in Indochina was appealing. The twin-boom aircraft had been designed for an airdrop role, and its rear cargo door and elevated tail section made it possible to release an entire cargo load in a single pass. French officials as early as 1951 requested some C–119s, evaluating the work capacity of the craft as double that of the C–47 and stating that the 119s would operate strictly in airdrop work from major airfields.[15]

The Far East Air Forces C–119 fleet in 1953 consisted of approximately 103 craft, all assigned to the 483d Troop Carrier Wing at Ashiya Air Base, Japan, commanded by Col. Maurice F. Casey. The wing flew regularly in Korea, and maintained a majority of its aircraft for short-notice paratroop assaults. Colonel Casey with several wing officers visited Indochina in early spring 1953, looking into possible operating problems. The group visited air bases throughout Vietnam, Laos, and Cambodia. Casey reported widespread inadequacies in ground radio equipment and instrument flight facilities, and described the language problems and hazardous terrain likely to face American crews. Casey asserted that the Gia Lam Airfield at Hanoi, the most likely C–119 operating base, needed paved taxiways and parking space, since the loose gravel covering these areas was hazardous to C–119 propellers. As for the possibility of providing the C–119s on a loan basis, Casey asserted that French crewmen could easily be cross-trained to fly these aircraft and demonstrated this by giving several French pilots informal transition instruction at the Saigon airfield.

Colonel Casey himself preferred that the wing's aircraft be flown by his own crews, but he made no written recommendation in the matter.[16]

Gen. Mark W. Clark, USA, commander of the U.S. Far East Command, after personally visiting Indochina on March 26, 1953, requested permission to dispatch two C–119s with American Air Force crews primarily to land armored vehicles at interior points in Laos. Clark repeated his request on April 18 but changed the concept of employment as a result of Colonel Casey's report, envisioning the C–119s being used for airdrops and for routine missions between major air terminals. The Joint Chiefs of Staff decided against supporting these proposals and opposed the use of Air Force aircrews. An urgent recommendation by Adm. Arthur W. Radford, USN, Commander in Chief, U.S. Pacific Command, to lend six C–119s to the French for operation by civilian crews, gained speedy Joint Chiefs and presidential approval in the last week of April.[17]

Pilot checkouts began promptly at Clark. Crews from the 483d Wing gave ground and flight instruction to crewmen from the French Air Force and to a group of civilian pilots recruited in the Far East under contract to a private airline, Civil Air Transport, Inc. Checkouts were completed on the flight to Vietnam and the six C–119s landed at Gia Lam on May 4–5, 1953. Eighteen ground crewmen from the 483d Wing accompanied the aircraft to instruct and assist in maintenance. The American aircrews remained at Hanoi flying about eighty missions during the three months of Project Swivel Chair. The French and Civil Air Transport crews flew all operational missions. The project shifted to Cat Bi in early June, because of runway deterioration at Gia Lam. A second group of French pilots received C–119 training with U.S. Air Force units in Europe and replaced the civilian pilots in late June.[18]

Neither Gen. Otto P. Weyland, commanding the Far East Air Forces, nor Maj. Gen. Chester E. McCarty, commander of the 315th Air Division (the theater airlift headquarters), was pleased with the continuation of Swivel Chair. Both officers foresaw growing maintenance problems for the 483d Wing and shortages of airlift between Japan and Korea. General McCarty, while visiting in Vietnam, asserted that the Swivel Chair aircraft were being wastefully employed and that no significant heavy drops had materialized. French Air Force officials, although pleased with the payload of the C–119, its airdrop qualities, and its ease of loading, were nevertheless unhappy over runway damage at Cat Bi, a result of the ship's heavy weight. Through an agreement negotiated by the U.S. mission in Saigon with Gen. Henri E. Navarre, the new French Commander in Indochina, the C–119s and the 483d Wing's personnel left Indochina on July 28, 1953. Also by agreement, the Far East Air Forces maintained six C–119s on ten-hour alert, ready if needed for heavy drops in Indochina. French crews, further, were to receive periodic C–119 refresher flights.[19]

Released from the demands of the Korean War by the armistice of

July 27, 1953, the Americans assumed the burden of new commitments to bolster French airlift capabilities. Instead of using C–119s for sustained duty, the Americans under Project Iron Age agreed to hold available twenty-two C–119s for short-term loan, sufficient in number to increase French paratroop assault capabilities to an equivalent of one hundred C–47s. According to the 483d Wing Operation Plan 4–53 of October 9, the aircraft were to arrive at Cat Bi within seventy-two hours for loan periods of approximately five days. American Air Force crews were to ferry the aircraft to Vietnam and would return the ships to Japan as soon as the specified drops were completed. To General McCarty, this would prevent "champagne and ice runs" by the French. Although the planes would bear French markings, 483d personnel in their own uniforms would perform all maintenance and technical supply functions.[20]

Training French Air Force aircrews in the C–119 was resumed at Clark on September 23, with 483d Wing aircraft, instructors, and maintenance personnel. The goal was a capability to operate in Indochina with twenty-two aircraft. Civil Air Transport crewmen, meanwhile, received additional training at Ashiya, and were "exceptionally well qualified," according to Colonel Casey, who himself instructed in the flight program. Many Civil Air pilots were former Air Force or Navy officers and one was a former member of the 483d. The lure of high pay, adventure, and the Far East apparently accounted for their latest choice of occupation.[21]

The expanded training program, the planning for Iron Age, and a presidential decision to provide another twenty-five C–47s (bringing permanent strength in Indochina in December to one hundred aircraft)[22] all reflected the Eisenhower administration's willingness to support the French airlift effort. Behind the American policy was satisfaction with General Navarre's aggressive plans and the belief that air transport offered an important asset for the campaigns ahead.

General Navarre's decision to establish a *Base Aero-Terrestre* at Dien Bien Phu was rooted in Viet Minh threats against Laos. From the airhead, Navarre reasoned, French units could interdict communist forces in Laos and, should the Viet Minh decide to concentrate against the airhead, a setpiece battle would develop wherein French air and artillery firepower could be decisive. Accordingly on the morning of November 20, 1953, two paratroop battalions jumped from sixty French Air Force C–47s and seized the valley of Dien Bien Phu. Viet Minh troops fled or were quickly overcome, and a second wave of troopers jumped unopposed in the afternoon.[23]

A C-119 Flyng Boxcar on loan to French forces.

Loading a C-119 with cargo for Dien Bien Phu, May 1954.

Chinese, French, and American personnel unload a C–124 at Saigon, August 1954.

French military personnel board a Tactical Air Command C–124 Globemaster at Orly Field, Paris, bound for Indochina, May 3, 1954.

Painting French markings on a USAF C–119.

USAF maintenance specialists work on a flak-damaged C–119 as a Senegalese guard stands by, Haiphong Air Base, May 1954.

French parachutists being dropped during an attack on a Vietminh stronghold, November 1954.

Generals Otto P. Weyland and Earl E. Partridge, former Far East Air Forces commanders, at a joint retirement ceremony, July 1959.

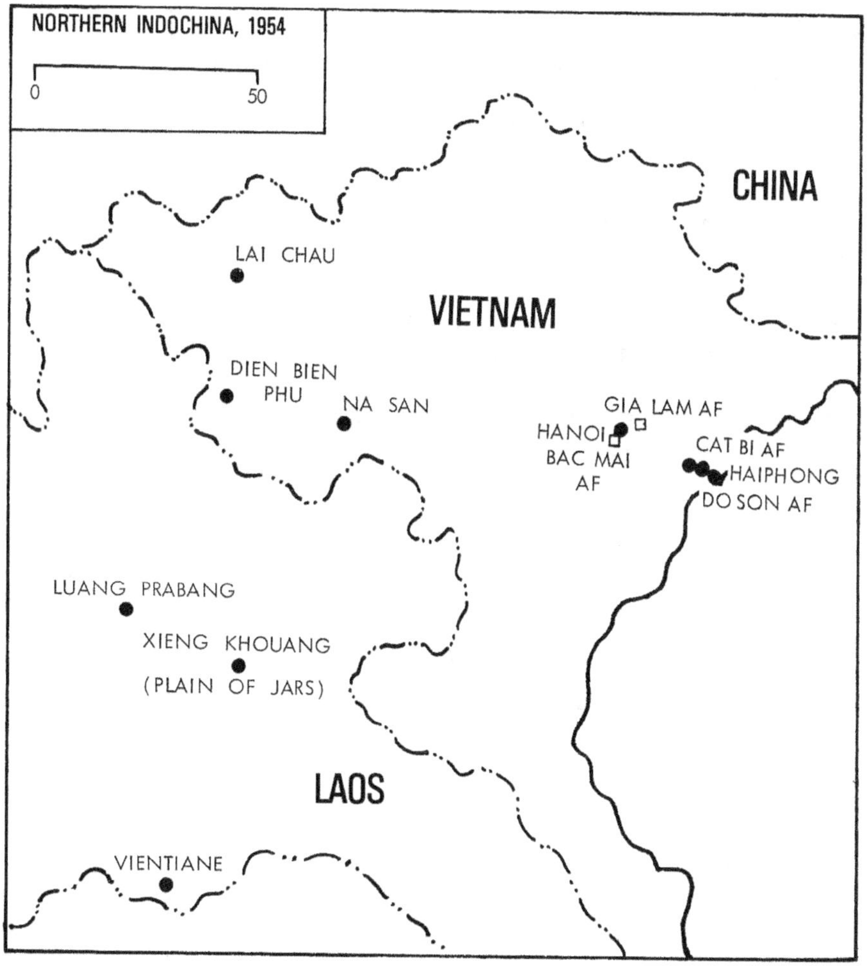

TACTICAL AIRLIFT

Engineer troops promptly began renovating the old airstrip primarily by hand labor. French aircrews attempted two drops of 17,000-pound bulldozers urgently needed by the engineers at Dien Bien Phu. Several 483d Wing C-119s were flown to Cat Bi for this purpose. On the first try on November 23, the bulldozer fell away from its parachute and was smashed. Two days later, a second dozer was successfully dropped. Colonel Casey noted that this was the heaviest single item ever dropped in the Far East. Meanwhile, other French crews completed training in heavy drops at Cat Bi and at Clark Field and made four drops at Dien Bien Phu on December 3.[24]

The first C-47 landed at the rebuilt Dien Bien Phu strip on November 25 amid clouds of red dust. Later, the engineers covered the runway with pierced steel planking. The 150 miles separating Dien Bien Phu from Hanoi meant that each C-47 did well to make two trips daily. The seventy daily deliveries sufficed for essential resupply, but permitted little space for airlift of construction materials needed for defensive positions. Items airlanded during December included 155-mm artillery weapons and ten disassembled light tanks.[25]

Fifteen C-119s of the 483d Wing arrived at Cat Bi on December 5, the first ships requested by General Navarre specifically under the Iron Age plan. The craft were loaned for the stated purpose of dropping 1,070 tons of materiel (mainly barbed wire and ammunition) at Dien Bien Phu. The planes again bore French insignia and were flown by French aircrews. The American detachment was asked to provide twelve ships each day. The planes rotated to Ashiya for inspections and major repairs, returning to Cat Bi carrying spare parts, replacement crewmen, or parachutes. The original tonnage commitment was completed on December 21, but the aircraft remained at Cat Bi to meet a fresh requirement for another 930 tons of barbed wire and stakes.[26]

During the winter, French forces at Pleiku and the Plain of Jars became entirely dependent upon air resupply, further straining French airlift capabilities. The Iron Age commitments were successively renewed, so that the original idea of short-term loans became meaningless. The number of airplanes provided daily rose to seventeen in January, then dropped again to twelve late in the month. Each ship flew one or two missions per day and each averaged over three hours flying time. An eight-man U.S. Army detachment from Ashiya prepared parachutes and loaded aircraft at Cat Bi. By mid-March the Iron Age C-119s had dropped fifty-seven hundred tons during 965 sorties.[27]

Although the Iron Age C-119s were used primarily for the Dien Bien Phu drops, the French sometimes employed them for drops and landings elsewhere, for example, at the hard-pressed base at Luang Prabang. The 119s also flew twice-weekly courier missions between Cat Bi and Saigon, moving critical supplies and hospital patients. The French also used the

THE FRENCH WAR

C–119s as napalm bombers at Dien Bien Phu, claiming good results. The Americans had discouraged this use, citing unsatisfactory trials in Korea. One ship loaded with napalm crashed on takeoff from Cat Bi on March 23.[28]

General Weyland and other officials opposed proposals to use American Air Force crews for certain C–119 missions and the Joint Chiefs of Staff noted that "practically all supply flights involve flying over enemy-held territory." Several members of the 483d Wing, however, visited Dien Bien Phu, including Colonel Casey who landed with a maintenance team to recover a C–119 forced down for repairs. A few wing pilots arranged privately to accompany one or two drop missions from Cat Bi, although this practice was officially frowned upon. Otherwise, the 483d crews flew only on engineering test and pilot checkout flights in the Cat Bi area, and on daily support flights between Cat Bi and Clark Field. American Civilian Air Transport crewmen returned to C–119 cockpits early in March to supplement the French Air Force crews.[29]

Airdrome facilities at Cat Bi were barely adequate. The main runway was eight thousand feet long, constructed of asphalt and concrete, with steel matting in places. Continuous repairs were necessary to arrest runway deterioration. Air traffic control was unsatisfactory—pilots reported several near-collisions close to the airfield, and during overcast weather takeoffs were possible only at fifteen-minute intervals. American Air Force control tower operators assisted at Cat Bi during April and May, but preparations for installing an American ground controlled approach radar were interrupted by the end of the campaign.[30]

The maintenance detachment from the 483d Wing kept the Cat Bi planes in good flying condition, aided by the aircraft rotation system and ample supplies of spare parts. Concerned with heading off future French recriminations, Colonel Casey leaned over backwards to satisfy French officers, and requested written confirmations of the number of C–119s in commission daily. The 483d detachment by April numbered 121 men most of whom served sixty-day tours. Enlisted men lived in eight-man huts, officers commuted by jeep from a Haiphong hotel. Colonel Casey installed an American mess hall, arranged for food and fresh water from Clark Field, personally chose all supervisors, and insisted on tight discipline. The flavor of combat too was present since Viet Minh commandos damaged a C–119 and several other aircraft in a night attack in March. Most of the Americans found their weeks at Cat Bi memorable and, for Casey, this was the "highlight experience" of his military career.[31]

A lesser venture, also benefiting the French airlift effort, resulted from a French request for American maintenance personnel to support two squadrons of C–47s and one squadron of B–26 Invaders. Upon presidential direction, the Air Force on January 30, 1954, ordered the Far East Air Forces to form a provisional maintenance unit, to be in place in Indochina

TACTICAL AIRLIFT

by February 5. The message closed with the admonition, "imperative this group perform effectively." General Weyland had opposed the proposal, but directed fast and early action to select and prepare the men. Far East Air Forces officers in discussions with the French chose Tourane as location for the B–26s and Do Son for the C–47 group.[32]

A provisional unit* was formed from Air Force air depot wings in Japan, Korea, and at Clark Field. Some forty-four aircraft loads of support equipment were loaded at Clark aboard C–54 Skymasters, C–119s, and C–124 Globemasters. The C–47 element, consisting of seven officers and 113 airmen, left Clark the morning of February 5, landing at Cat Bi and moving to Do Son by vehicle. The detachment received its first C–47s for maintenance on February 9. By the end of the month, the Americans at Do Son had worked six thousand man-hours, completing nine periodic inspections.

Living and work facilities at Do Son proved adequate and parts shortages were met by making available Air Force spares. Most Americans shuddered at the condition of the French aircraft, some flying with over a hundred malfunctions and many filthy from carrying livestock. Maj. Kenneth F. Knox, the American commander at Do Son, watched one French mechanic stand on an engine while loosening a spark plug with a sledgehammer. He later conceded that the French were well motivated, but privately resolved not to fly with them. French officers, though, officially complained that the Americans worked too slowly. Total flying time nonetheless increased. During May and June, the C–47s flew twenty-one thousand hours, compared with twelve thousand hours in January and February.[33]

Overwater airlift missions by Far East Air Forces transports during 1954 were planned increasingly to assist Southeast Asia. Periodic emergency shipments from Japan of various ordnances—flares, smoke bombs, bomb clusters—were met by diverting 315th Air Division C–119s and C–124s from other tasks. During the critical weeks before the fall of Dien Bien Phu, aircraft of the 315th not already on loan to the French spent nearly half their flying hours in support of the Indochina war. Clark Field became the airlift hub, amid routes from Japan and the continental United States. Because of deteriorating runways in Vietnam, the C–124s usually operated only as far as Clark, hauling military materiel including ammunition, aircraft parts, and parachutes and rigging for airdrops.† Surface and air shipments from the United States similarly converged at the Philippines.

---

* The unit was first designated 642d Field Maintenance Squadron, but was redesignated FEALOGFOR (Far East Air Logistics Force), Field Maintenance Squadron, Provisional, soon after its arrival in Indochina.

† Thirteen C–124s of Tactical Air Command hauled one thousand troops from France and North Africa to Tourane via Karachi and Ceylon, starting on April 20.

THE FRENCH WAR

Final movement into Vietnam was by C–119s and C–54s of the 315th Air Division.

A C–119 could fly the one thousand miles from Clark to Haiphong in six hours. In mid-April, the 816th Troop Carrier Squadron of the 483d Wing moved to Clark with fifteen C–119s, tasked to make six round trips daily to Indochina. The 119s were flown to Ashiya periodically for maintenance, blending into the rotation system set up for Iron Age. Cargo handling personnel at Clark, some of them shifted from other jobs, worked double shifts, breaking down cargo for separate destinations, preparing shipping forms, and loading aircraft.[34]

The situation at Dien Bien Phu became increasingly desperate after mid-March. The degeneration of the airlift effort, and indeed of the whole battle from the French viewpoint, directly resulted from the close-in Viet Minh artillery and antiaircraft fire. The communists spent three months preparing, hauling guns and ammunition over mountain trails to camouflaged, dug-in positions almost impervious to French fire. Shelling in March destroyed a C–47 while landing and demolished a parked C–119 that had been forced to land for repairs. Airlanded supply virtually ceased except for an occasional C–47 at night. Communist gunners, however, soon discovered the night tactic and destroyed three C–47s during March 26 and 27. A last C–47 took off the night of March 27, loaded with patients; another landed but was destroyed on the ground the next night. Drop zones also came under shellfire, making recovery of the dropped materiel a hazardous business.[35]

Subsequently during the campaign, reinforcements, a few at a time, parachuted in at night. More than six hundred men with no previous parachute training thus jumped blindly toward the center of the camp. Communist fire made daytime low-level supply drops suicidal. High-altitude drops proved inaccurate, mainly because of the unreliability in the delay parachute-opening mechanism. A chute opening at ten thousand feet, for example, would drift with the wind for six minutes. When low clouds covered the drop zone, crews sometimes aimed with the aid of a tethered meteorological balloon. The recovery rate of supply packages declined as the defended area grew smaller in size. Most of the thirty-five Iron Age C–119s damaged by ground fire were hit in the last weeks of the battle for Dien Bien Phu. Five received major damage, generally from 37-mm explosive shells. Civil Air Transport pilots denounced the French failure to prevent the Viet Minh fire and pointed out that their contract required "no combat flying." A legendary civilian pilot and former Air Force officer, James "Earthquake" McGovern, piloted the only C–119 actually shot down at Dien Bien Phu. The bulky and bearded American was lost with four crewmen on May 6, on his forty-fifth mission over the valley.[36]

The Cat Bi 119s averaged twenty-three sorties nightly during mid-April. On several nights supplies dropped by the C–119s and C–47s exceeded two hundred tons, the quantity needed by the fifteen thousand-man garrison for one day's combat. When choices became necessary, food took priority behind ammunition and medical supplies, and the garrison spent the final month on half rations. Loadings climbed above two hundred tons again during the final fortnight, but only a fraction actually reached the defenders. In a last effort on May 6, twenty-five C–47s and twenty-five C–119s dropped 196 tons and the next day C–47 drops continued despite low clouds which precluded C–119 flights. Nevertheless, during the evening of May 7, Dien Bien Phu fell.[37]

The pattern of events at Dien Bien Phu was unmistakable in the communist siege of Khe Sanh fourteen years later. American officers in 1968 scrutinized the history of the earlier affair. Citing the reasons for the Dien Bien Phu defeat, the Americans listed first the "inadequate logistics support caused by an insecure line of communications and insufficient airlift."[38] This assessment is open to challenge. Without question, the French airlift force was deficient in equipment, techniques, and personnel. Still, air-delivered tonnages roughly equaled the eight thousand tons of weapons, fuel, and ammunition brought overland by the Viet Minh. Given the inability of the French air and artillery forces to destroy the communist guns, it is doubtful that a larger airlift arm could have long deferred the outcome.

In late May the Iron Age C–119 detachment moved from Cat Bi to the French base at Tourane. Increasing Viet Minh activity in the Red Delta and runway wear at Cat Bi necessitated the shift. The new location lay equidistant between Hanoi and Saigon, and was a full hour's flying time nearer to Clark Field. The airfield was adjacent to the city and port of Tourane, affording easy transfer of seaborne cargo. The larger of two usable runways was seventy-nine hundred feet long and two hundred feet wide, and was constructed of concrete and asphalt. Many buildings were new, but hangars were small.

Between sixteen and eighteen C–119s were kept at Tourane through early June to furnish twelve operational aircraft daily, capable of twenty-four three-hour sorties. The aircraft occasionally received hostile fire in the landing pattern at Tourane, and tracers and artillery could be seen close to the base nightly. Stray bullets occasionally struck buildings, although the field was surrounded by a perimeter of strong points and barbed wire. Friendly naval and artillery fire sometimes passed overhead en route to targets on the south and west perimeter. Pilots and crew chiefs of the 483d were kept at Tourane on three-week rotations and were available to fly out aircraft if required. A night evacuation became essential in late June and the aircraft were removed to Tan Son Nhut and Clark. All planes returned the next day, after the base had withstood a determined perimeter attack. Earlier in the month, Viet Minh guerrillas beyond the base perimeter had seized three enlisted men and two U.S. Army parachute riggers. The five were released in good health on August 31 after six weeks of captivity.

The 483d maintenance personnel occasionally flew to other bases to recover aircraft grounded for maintenance. When an engine change was required, an Air Force C–119 crew would fly to the marooned aircraft with a spare engine, a mobile A-frame to hoist it, and a four-man engine-change crew. Normally, the relief trip would return to Tourane the same day with the defective engine, leaving the maintenance crew and an engineering test pilot to work through the night and to return the next day with the repaired transport. Aircraft were recovered by Americans in this way from Laotian bases at Vientiane, Seno, Xiangkhoang, and Saravane. Once, while the repairmen slept off-base at Saravane, communist infiltrators apparently entered the American aircraft, but did no serious damage. Lt. Col Donald C. Pricer, commander of the 483d detachment, flew the relief plane on most of these occasions.[39]

American Air Force officials invoking the original Iron Age plan, insisted that the French justify all aircraft loans by naming specific tasks and tonnage requirements. General McCarty, concerned about the continuing drain on 315th Air Division capabilities, again charged that the French were using the C–119s wastefully, flying missions which could be handled by C–47s. The Joint Chiefs of Staff on July 12 directed the Far East Air Forces to remove eight aircraft and a proportionate number of personnel, leaving only eight C–119s at Tourane, including four with American markings that were kept in readiness for possible personnel evacuation. The provisional squadron reported eighty-five persons on duty on July 30, half the total of two weeks earlier.

The departure of the last C–119 from Tourane on September 7 closed out the 483d Wing role in Indochina. The wing had maintained operations for nine months in a theater more than two thousand miles from its home base. French and Civil Air Transport crews parachuted 14,800 tons of cargo in 2,750 C–119 sorties. Three C–119s were destroyed but no American Air Force lives were lost.[40]

The American C–47 maintenance detachment at Do Son closed officially on June 29, and a detachment of four C–46 commandos and crews belonging to the 315th Troop Carrier Wing in Japan also departed. The C–46s had been kept at Do Son since mid-May in readiness to evacuate the C–47 mechanics in the event of a Viet Minh attack. To assure operability, each C–46 flew every few days, often on missions to Tourane or Cat Bi. One C–46 crashed on landing at Do Son on June 14.[41]

A few chores remained for the 315th Air Division. Division C–124s hauled five hundred French wounded from Tan Son Nhut to Japan during the early summer. Medical flight crews were from the 6481st Medical Air Evacuation Group, a unit also under the 315th Air Division. Military Air Transport Service planes completed the movement of patients to Europe

At Tokyo International Airport, Gen. Earle E. Partridge visits men being airlifted back to France during Operation Wounded Warrior.

during Operation Wounded Warrior.[42] In late July and August, the C-124s hauled 106 tons of tents from military supply depots in Japan for use by refugees in Indochina. It briefly appeared that U.S. airlift forces might be called upon to assist in moving Vietnamese refugees from North Vietnam. Possible large-scale air movements were studied, including a Hanoi to Cat Bi emergency shuttle. In actuality, of the nine hundred thousand refugees from the north, over two hundred thousand left by air, nearly all by civil airlines. Ships and crews from the 483d Wing made only a few trips from Gia Lam to Tourane, lifting out diplomatic personnel.[43]

Transport aviation had been important in the French conduct of the war, linking the enclaves and permitting supply of forces in the interior. Although these contributions were valuable, the French transport force was too small, its equipment too obsolete, and its methods too outmoded to realize the true potential of airlift. Too much was asked of the airlift forces at Dien Bien Phu, despite extraordinary U.S. Air Force assistance. The battle also exposed weaknesses in existing airdrop methods, in particular the inaccuracy of high-altitude drops and the difficulty of recovering loads on the ground under fire.

A fundamental lesson learned was that last-minute efforts to prop

THE FRENCH WAR

Courtesy: John Schlight

Evacuating the wounded after the fall of Dien Bien Phu, June 1954.

up an unsound airlift system are a poor substitute for prior and sustained development based on appropriate doctrine. Transport airplanes are only a part of the whole airlift system. Sustained airlift operations required a corps of highly trained personnel, ample spare parts and high-quality aircraft maintenance, trained aerial port units with suitable equipment, and an overall airlift control agency for efficient allocation and scheduling. In most of these areas the French Air Force was seriously weak.

II. The Troop Carrier Idea, 1954-1961

The years following Dien Bien Phu were important ones for the Air Force troop carrier arm. Doctrines were developed and forces created which later were applied in South Vietnam. New tactical transports—the C–123 and the C–130—began their careers in the active force. Techniques and equipment were developed for short-field assault landings, for airdrops of heavy equipment, and for increased range. Most crucial in its influence on the later war effort was the decision, made in 1956, that the Air Force airlift helicopter force should be disbanded; most transport helicopters thereafter belonged to the ground forces for operation outside the centralized theater airlift system.

Air Force transports and crews visited Southeast Asia only occasionally, although their presence elsewhere in the western Pacific became the foundation for planning speedy and large troop interventions. The crisis in Laos beginning in 1959 forced renewed American attention to the region and required intermittent use of airlift forces based in the United States and in the Pacific.

Interest in applying air transport to problems of counterinsurgency warfare became strong in 1961, reflecting White House response to a deteriorating situation in South Vietnam. Decisions later in the year resulted in the arrival in Vietnam of varied American air units, predominantly helicopter and fixed-wing transport units, intended to improve the airborne mobility of South Vietnamese troops. These deployments began the long history of Air Force airlift operations in South Vietnam.

Air transport attained a foremost role in theater military operations during the Second World War. Airborne assault seemingly offered commanders combat zone mobility beyond anything known in military history. During the Normandy invasion parachute and glider infantry provided an important margin for Allied success. More often than not, however, results of airborne operations were disappointing—troop carrier transports were not equipped for precise navigation, and paratroop units once on the ground (lacking vehicles and heavy weapons) became immobile and vulnerable. Fulfillment of the promise of vastly improved airborne mobility remained for the future.

The war also made clear that transport aircraft could be enormously valuable in sustained high-volume air supply. During the final months of the war in Europe, Allied transports (primarily C–47s) helped overcome saturated ground transportation by airlifting large tonnages of rations, gasoline, and munitions to forward areas. Airlift was even more vital in Burma, where the rugged and jungle-covered land offered the Japanese cover in moving against Allied surface communications.[1]

The Korean War furnished similar evidence. Two parachute assault operations in the first year proved technically successful, but were of only minor strategic consequence. More significant were airlandings of combat units and supplies at Kimpo Air Base shortly after the Inchon landings, and air supply in North Korea during the ensuing advance and withdrawal. Although supply drops to isolated positions continued through the war, it was during the final two years that the transport force settled into an intensive and sustained high-volume effort. Emphasis was on higher aircraft utilization, improved maintenance, efficiency in cargo handling, and tight operational control. Such businesslike matters were the trademark of Maj. Gen. William H. Tunner, former commander during the Berlin airlift and during 1950–51 chief of all Far East-based transports. Tunner's command—designated the 315th Air Division in early 1951—by its existence reflected the Air Force's belief in centralized management and control of airlift forces. Centralization encouraged systematic attention to emerging problems, and allowed the transport fleet to be allocated to the most necessary tasks.[2]

An Air Force-wide project sought to codify prevailing air doctrine toward the end of the Korean War. The task of reconciling all points of view was not easy, but in the case of doctrine for theater airlift, the result was clear and enduring. Drafts prepared by the Eighteenth Air Force, a troop carrier command within the Tactical Air Command (TAC), evolved into final form as Air Force Manual (AFM) 1–9, Theater Airlift Operations, July 1, 1954. The manual listed tasks for theater airlift forces as: logistic airlift operations, aeromedical evacuation, airborne operations, and special airlift operations. Although many TAC officers believed that airborne assaults would be infrequent in the future, the manual asserted that "troop carrier forces are combat type forces: they participate in offensive action against the enemy during an airborne operation."

The manual defined the term "logistical airlift operations" broadly to include "unit deployments" as well as airdrop supply. Unit deployments were airlanded movements of complete combat units to meet changing tactical situations, like the 1950 hauls into Kimpo. The manual recognized that "when units are air transportable they become more mobile, and . . . constitute a threat to the enemy because they can be deployed quickly and at will."

The prominence awarded the unit deployment idea reflected the trend away from parachute assault. Parachute operations required specially trained troops, were costly in materials and personnel injuries, and introduced forces piecemeal into combat. By contrast, improvements in the air transportability of equipment promised air mobility for "general" as opposed to "airborne" forces. Army studies suggested that to make essential items air transportable, light self-propelled antitank guns or light tanks could substitute for heavier tanks, towed weapons could replace their self-propelled counterparts, and engineer battalions could be equipped with lighter construction equipment. Air Force tactical fighter units, too, could be airlifted as units; in 1952 the 315th Air Division moved the personnel and equipment of an entire fighter-bomber wing from Japan to Korea.

AFM 1–9 was clear on one point. Theater troop carrier resources belonged under centralized control, normally within a numbered troop carrier air force. This view followed closely the broader Air Force doctrine found in Air Force Manual 1–2 that, because of the inherent flexibility of the air weapon and its ability to concentrate effort, air forces should not be partitioned among different commands. The troop carrier air force, according to AFM 1–9, would be under the direct authority of theater air commanders, who were responsible neither to tactical air force nor to ground force commanders, much as the 315th Air Division operated outside the Fifth Air Force which was under the Far East Air Forces. Priorities among airlift users would be established by the theater commander through an air transportation board with triservice representation, as in Korea, keeping this function outside the air component structure. A control center within the troop carrier headquarters would make daily schedules and control flight movements, while liaison officers from the airlift users would coordinate daily requests and assure that units and materiel were ready for movement at the proper time and place. The control center would prepare flight itineraries for each mission, showing loads and times for each sortie, and distribute this information in the form of daily operations orders to troop carrier and aerial port units.[3]

Thus by 1954 Air Force doctrine for troop carrier aviation remained firmly rooted in the experience of World War II and Korea. The versatility and usefulness of air transportation were understood and were reflected amply in the official view. AFM 1–9 remained in effect for twelve years, until superseded midway during the Southeast Asia war.

AFM 1–9 was published as an unclassified document, and thus gave little indication of the Air Force's growing interest in tactical nuclear warfare. The national theory of war, or "new look" in defense policy, emerged after 1953 partly in reaction to the prolonged and distasteful stalemate in Korea. For the Air Force troop carrier forces the classic theater airlift roles became overshadowed by new responsibilities supporting the nuclear strike effort. A TAC symposium in 1955 and the report of Exercise Sagebrush the same year acknowledged the "de-emphasis of mass airborne operations in this thermonuclear age." Furthermore, sustained theater supply of ground forces seemed almost irrelevant in a war wherein initial strikes could be decisive. Troop carrier aircraft in Europe and the Far East were accordingly held in constant readiness for prestrike movements of weapons and strike aircraft under plans made necessary because of various political restrictions. An Air Force-wide troop carrier conference in 1956 declared that "support by combat airlift for the retaliatory effort is and will be the paramount responsibility."[4]

Since high-performance strike aircraft of the era could operate only from lengthy, paved runways, there seemed little point to designing transports for landings and takeoffs at short, unimproved strips. Representatives from United States Air Forces in Europe, attending the 1956 conference, therefore insisted that funds should not be wasted for heavy landing gear and extra engine power. Later that same year, the TAC operations analysis directorate, forecasting the next fifteen years of tactical airlift evolution, reaffirmed the importance of air logistics in an atomic war, and denied the desirability of short-field capabilities promised by the new technology.[5]

Reaction to the new look soon appeared. Leading theorists of military affairs, including Robert Osgood, Bernard Brodie, and Henry A. Kissinger, challenged the emphasis on nuclear capabilities in military planning. The Rockefeller Report, prepared during 1957 by a group of scholars and scientists, agreed that while all-out war remained the gravest danger, it was not the most likely threat. From the top ranks of the Army came pressure for improvements in conventional forces and in the long-range airlift needed to move those forces globally. Early interventions in "brush-fire" situations, they argued, offered the hope of heading off bigger confrontations. Recurrent crises over Berlin, Taiwan, Southeast Asia, and the Middle East seemed to vindicate these views, and the new look was recognized as capable of much flexibility in dealing with these and other crises.[6]

A parallel idea was the composite air strike force concept. A composite air strike force was a tailored force of fighters, bombers, reconnaissance, and troop carrier craft, capable of fast movement from the United States to overseas trouble spots. Transportation of ground crews, equipment, and supplies required considerable airlift. The payload and range capabilities of the newer four-engine troop carrier craft of TAC were suited for the strike force support role, and exercises and contingency plans of the late 1950s were so developed. The larger job of hauling ground force units overseas remained for the long-range transports of MATS.* The troop carriers ordinarily augmented the theater airlift forces in logistics or assault work, while the MATS crews returned to the United States for second trips. The divisions of tasks were not rigid, and assignments could be adjusted according to need. The traditional distinctions between strategic and tactical transports thus dimmed. It appeared a contradiction that a troop carrier force built for a role in supporting theater ground force operations now performed its foremost roles on behalf of the strike forces.[7]

---

* Military Air Transport Service, reorganized January 1, 1966, as Military Airlift Command (MAC).

Combat zone airlift methods were also in a transitional period during the 1950s. Parachute assaults remained a part of joint field exercises expertly staged from Air Force transports by the Army's still-vigorous paratroop arm, but newer ideas emerging within the Army suggested other forms of battlefield air mobility might be more effective. The possibilities offered by helicopters were glimpsed during the Korean War, and were afterwards publicized by senior officers. Maj. Gen. James M. Gavin,* in a 1954 article, called for use of air vehicles in classic cavalry roles. In his 1958 book, *War and Peace in the Space Age*, he urged conversion of the airborne divisions into sky-cavalry formations, though retaining parachute capability. Field Manual (FM) 57-35 described the movement of combat elements by Army-owned aircraft in battlefield "airmobile operations." Such tactics could apply to varied situations, ranging from nuclear battlefields to counterguerrilla situations.[8]

The Air Force, too, appreciated the possibilities for new forms of battlefield airlift. The assault aircraft idea emerged after World War II from projects to install engines on glider airframes. Such powered gliders were seen as inexpensive but rugged craft, with slow landing speeds, able to make repeated deliveries to airheads seized by paratroop assault. The Air Force selected the XC-123, designed by Chase Aircraft Company Inc., from its XCG-20 glider. Some three hundred twin-engine C-123Bs were built by Fairchild Engine and Airplane Corporation at Hagerstown, Maryland, and deliveries to TAC began in 1955. Assault aircraft operations appeared in the joint exercises, but the concept weakened, partly because of the vulnerability of the C-123 Provider in hostile areas. Consequently, these aircraft were gradually shifted to logistic tasks in support of strike aircraft units. Upon assignment of some C-123s to the Air Force Reserve and with further reductions programmed for 1957 in the active force, it appeared that the plane was to become the Air Force's first and only fixed-wing assault airplane. The eventuality seemed certain in 1960 when the Army stated its wish that the Air Force buy more long-range transports instead of craft equipped with the latest technology for short-field work.[9]

Even more short-lived was the Air Force's helicopter assault transport force. As early as 1949, design studies led TAC to the conclusion that troop carrier helicopters merited vigorous development. Severe fund limitations prohibited action at that time, along with Air Staff preference for fixed-wing assault craft. The Korean War spurred Air Force approval of a TAC requirement for an assault helicopter group. TAC received its first H-19s early in 1952, diverted from other commands. The 8th Helicopter Flight was attached to the conventional troop carrier wing at Sewart Air Force Base, Tennessee.[10]

---

* General Gavin became Assistant Chief of Staff for Operations and Plans, Army Staff, and left the Army in 1958 over the issue of readiness for limited war.

TACTICAL AIRLIFT

The rotary-wing vehicle adapted easily to existing troop carrier doctrine. The ability of the helicopter to land in inaccessible places promised a new flexibility in airborne assault and in short-haul logistical work. The helicopter could launch an attack despite low ceilings, required no parachute jump skills of its crews or passengers, and could land forces in compact groups. Helicopters could pick up casualties from advanced positions, vastly improving the aeromedical evacuation system, and promised worthwhile capabilities for covert operations. Future helicopter wings were to be organized under a theater troop carrier commander. By the end of 1955, five squadrons had been activated, with the projection of a force of nine squadrons (three groups) of assault helicopters.[11]

In the belief that helicopters should be directly responsible to the unit supported and thus under the command of the ground commanders, the Army remained committed to the idea of maintaining its own cavalry helicopter arm. Under roles agreements of 1951 and 1952, Army aircraft requirements were to be developed for airlifts "within the combat zone." Air Force troop carrier forces were responsible for lifts "from exterior points to within the combat zone." In planning joint exercises, Army officers consistently opposed use of Air Force helicopters beyond this function and, in early December 1954, the Department of the Army notified the Air Force that it had no requirement for combat zone support by Air Force troop carrier helicopter squadrons. The position had been stated previously, and it now amounted to withdrawal of Army support for the three programmed Air Force helicopter assault groups. On January 17, 1955, the Air Force chief of staff, in a memorandum addressed to the Army chief of staff, defended the Air Force tactical helicopter role. The memorandum reasoned that the helicopter was in reality "just another aircraft" for airborne operations and logistical air support—an air vehicle which would be particularly useful in dispersed operations on nuclear battlefields. The Army reply the following month bluntly reasserted that it would not support the use of Air Force assault helicopter groups to meet Army requirements.[12]

The Air Force a year later conceded with reluctance "that the Army is the primary user of rotary-wing aircraft, and should have its own rotary-wing capability." Further, it stated that the Army should be authorized to use its own helicopters in airborne operations and in aeromedical evacuation "within the combat zone." TAC assault helicopter squadrons were converted to helicopter support squadrons, with a primary mission of providing logistic support for Air Force units in the United States and within overseas theaters.[13]

The Air Force helicopter troop carrier arm thus passed into history, although a single squadron operated in the Far East theater airlift system until 1960. Given the range and payload limitations of existing helicopters, the loss of this Air Force role seemed less than critical. For the future, however, General McCarty, commander of the TAC troop carrier units, warned that technical improvements in helicopters would eventually result in "real airlift potential that definitely should be integrated with and assigned to the Theater Combat Airlift Force."[14] His view went unheeded; a decade later, many American transport helicopters in South Vietnam worked outside a centralized airlift system, denying to the user a worthwhile flexibility.

By September 1960 the Army had fifty-five hundred helicopter and fixed-wing aircraft, an increase of eight hundred in four years. Plans called for a further expansion to eighty-eight hundred within a decade including procurement by 1964 of more than 250 CV–2 Caribou fixed-wing transports, to be built by de Havilland Aircraft of Canada. The Caribou was of modest size, but could operate easily into and out of short and unpaved strips. Simple in design, the ship was powered by two fourteen-cylinder reciprocating engines, and handled an average payload of about two and a half tons—roughly half the amount carried by the C–123. The Army envisioned organizing the Caribous into sixteen-ship companies, assigning one to each army and army corps, primarily for forward area transport.[15]

Army officers defended the organic aviation arm, citing the need for fast responsiveness on future battlefields; aircrews would live with the ground forces, and would be familiar with the tactics of ground warfare as well as with the immediate combat situation. After retiring as Army chief of staff, Gen. Maxwell D. Taylor wrote in 1959 that the Air Force had for decades neglected its responsibilities to the Army, and that new weapons and equipment for tactical air support and airlift should be organic within the Army. The official Army view was that of Field Manual 55–4, December 1959, which was that a centralized theater airlift system would consist of Air Force transport aircraft and operate under allocations established by a joint agency under the theater commander. Army airlift forces (i.e., the Caribous) would be separately controlled, primarily under priorities and allocations established by the Army, and would be attached to the operational control of particular ground commanders when needed for tactical missions. The guidance of FM 55–4 became doctrine for American forces in South Vietnam until 1967.[16]

Air Staff opposition to Army expansion in aviation appeared backed by solid rationale. The vulnerability to enemy action of slow-flying craft and the difficulties in moving short-range aircraft overseas in emergencies were the main Air Force objections. But the heart of the Air Force position rested on the conviction that:

> Because of fear of losing control of a separate Army air service, the Army is not capitalizing on the inherent flexibility of air power. It still wants to use aircraft as artillery pieces having them always on call at all levels of command.[17]

To the Air Staff, decentralized control of airlift resources meant unnecessarily large forces, ineffective use of maintenance skills, and a grievous loss of flexibility. On no other matter in troop carrier doctrine was the Air Force position as clear as that of centralized Air Force control.

Disagreements among the services over cargo handling, drop-zone management, medical evacuation, and other tactical airlift roles influenced planning for joint exercises. The question of who should exert air traffic control about the airhead was especially loaded, since whoever controlled the airspace would be in a position to determine the entire pattern of tactical air operations. Clear-cut resolution of the issue was important for the safety of aircrews and passengers. The assault airstrip was likely to be a marginal facility to begin with, and intense traffic would require the most skilled controller. The prospect of large numbers of Army helicopters operating alongside Air Force troop carrier aircraft demanded a centralized and workable traffic control system, one familiar to both Air Force and Army pilots. Airhead traffic control in exercises was usually settled by temporary compromises; often, Air Force personnel operated a control facility, but with unsatisfactory radio communications with Army aircraft and vehicle traffic. During one exercise, two aircraft—one Army and one Air Force—landed simultaneously at opposite ends of the runway. A joint agreement and a refined system for forward airhead traffic control remained unrealized.[18]

Beginning in late 1960, under Chief of Staff Gen. Thomas D. White, the Air Staff resolved upon a new approach toward Army aviation. Instead of basing its positions on legalistic arguments, the Air Force intended to adapt to the battlefield an airmobility idea, performing its own appropriate missions. General White requested the Air Staff to prepare for closer working relations with the Army, and he agreed with Gen. George H. Decker, Army chief of staff, to "resolve long-standing doctrinal divergencies." Preliminary discussions began toward this end.[19]

The apparent trend toward compromise was overshadowed by the appointment of Robert S. McNamara as Secretary of Defense in January 1961. The new secretary made clear his resolve to wield full authority, and relied upon his civilian-dominated staff for systematic analysis of problems. A new pattern for decisionmaking resulted, moderating the effects if not the depth of interservice rivalry. Knowing McNamara's practice of subjecting questions to cost-effectiveness comparisons, the Air Force took heart in its argument stressing centralization in airlift management. At the same time, the Kennedy administration's focus upon limited warfare capabilities, and the emergence from retirement of Maxwell Taylor as presidential military adviser, promised sympathetic appraisal of the Army's organic air establishment. Selection of Gen. Curtis E. LeMay as the new Air Force chief of staff in early 1961 implied strong Air Force representations in all matters. Within this context, conflict between the Army's airmobility ideas and the

TROOP CARRIER IDEA

Air Force Chief of Staff Gen. Curtis E. LeMay during a tour of Vietnam, 1962.

Air Force's concepts for troop carrier aviation continued, conditioning and being conditioned by events in Vietnam.

A prototype four-engine C–130, designed and built by Lockheed Aircraft Corporation, first flew in 1954. Testing and development were rapid and, despite delays caused by propeller problems, the first model joined TAC for squadron service in December 1956. Its turboprop engines gave the C–130 Hercules revolutionary performance: greater speed, range, and takeoff qualities than the C–119, and double the latter's payload. The C–130 accommodated a family of load-bearing platforms developed after World War II, designed for airdrops of heavy equipment. In addition, numerous features were tailored for its tactical transport role including a rear-opening ramp that allowed straight-in loading at truckbed or ground height. The C–130 became for the next two decades the workhorse of the Air Force's tactical airlift fleet.[20]

In 1959 the Air Force completed its planned force of twelve C–130A squadrons, six in TAC, three in Europe, and three in the Far East. The aircraft was equipped with external fuel tanks needed to combat adverse winds during transoceanic missions. A further development of the C–130A, designated the C–130B, first flew in November 1958. The B-model had more powerful engines, a new propeller, extra external fuel capacity, and a

TACTICAL AIRLIFT

beefed-up landing gear that raised the aircraft's allowable gross weight. A later modification, the C–130E entered the fleet in the early 1960s.[21]

The long history of the C–130 in the Far East began in December 1957, with the arrival in Japan of a single TAC Hercules to survey routes and base facilities. In the months that followed, the three squadrons of the 483d Troop Carrier Wing at Ashiya exchanged their C–119 Flying Boxcars for new C–130 Hercules, and the air and ground crews were assisted in their transitional training by TAC personnel. In addition, two TAC C–130A squadrons in April 1958 were made temporarily a part of a composite air strike force responding to the Taiwan Strait crisis. While operating from Clark and Ashiya, respectively, the TAC squadrons took over most of the theater airlift tasks, leaving the 483d Wing free to concentrate on conversion training. By the end of 1960, the permanently-assigned

AIRCRAFT PERFORMANCE, BASIC MISSION*

	Takeoff Weight	Fuel Weight	Payload	Takeoff run (over 50 ft obstacle)	Cruise speed (knots)	Range (NM)
C-47D	33,000	4,355	9,485	5,100	141	1,026
C-123B	57,800	13,700	11,043	4,670	142	1,891
C-123K	60,000	12,476	10,948	2,802	141	1,573
C-119G	72,700	13,344	15,858	5,470	162	1,415
Caribou (C-7A)	28,500	2,880	6,219	1,200	132	544
C-124A	198,000	35,344	59,800	7,230	193	1,740
C-130A	124,200	29,379	33,810	3,830	290	1,900
C-130B	135,000	29,389	36,270	4,330	293	1,847
C-130E	152,914	33,772	44,679	5,410	291	1,787

Note: The above data affords only general indication as to capability for any particular task. Reductions and tradeoffs in loading fuel and cargo drastically affect performance capabilities, as do variations in allowance for safety and economy. The principal improvements in the C–130B and C–130E, over the C–130A, were in systems reliability and overall gross weight. The C–123K emerged in the 1960s and is discussed in a later chapter.

* *USAF Standard Aircraft/Missile Characteristics* (Brown Book), Aeronautical Systems Division, USAF, Vol II, 1975.

squadrons shifted to new bases—one to Tachikawa Air Base, Japan, and two to Naha Air Base, Okinawa. Few members of the 483d regretted leaving uncharming Ashiya for the glitter of Tokyo or the warmer breezes of Okinawa.[22]

The 315th Air Division theater airlift headquarters, established in Japan during the Korean War, remained in existence. Organized directly under PACAF* and separate from the Fifth Air Force, the 315th preserved the concept of central theater airlift control. Day-to-day airlift priorities and allocations were determined within the regional Joint Military Transportation Board, located in Japan. The board was replaced in March 1961 by the Western Pacific Transportation Office (WTO) located at Tachikawa and charged by CINCPAC with "responsibility for insuring the optimum utilization of airlift . . . for tactical, training, and logistical support of PACOM forces." The western Pacific area extended from Eniwetok to Calcutta, within which the 315th provided intratheater lift "to supplement the services provided by the MATS." With senior officer representatives from all three services, the transportation office received airlift forecasts and justifications a month in advance, either approving or disapproving requests and levying tasks directly upon the 315th. Each month the air division forecast anticipated airframe and flying hour capabilities, along with detailed reports of the past month's flying.[23]

The 315th Air Division also had operational control over two dozen C–124 Globemasters stationed at Tachikawa, an air base belonging to MATS. The massive and ungainly appearing C–124s lacked the speed and shortfield utility of the C–130 Hercules, but they could carry certain engines, weapons, and vehicles too bulky for the latter. The air division also controlled four C–54 Skymasters, used mainly to lift medical patients between Far East bases. In late 1961 a decision was made to add a fourth C–130 squadron. This acknowledged the long-held PACAF contention that airlift was a primary limiting factor restricting theater war capabilities. The new squadron arrived in June 1962.[24]

Three principal tasks dominated peacetime flying in the Far East: individual and tactical training, intratheater airlift for air and ground forces in Japan, Korea, and Okinawa, and joint exercises with U.S. and allied forces. A fixed number of aircraft were kept on constant alert on Okinawa, ready to airlift nuclear and conventional weapons and components to strike units. Aircrews found themselves with little leisure time, but were rewarded with flight missions to the Philippines, Hong Kong, and Bangkok. One crew was much envied, after visiting "that most exotic, delightful, and mysterious city of the Pacific—San Francisco."[25]

---

* The Far East Air Forces in 1957 merged into the Pacific Air Forces (PACAF), located in Hawaii, under a unified Commander in Chief, Pacific Command, or CINCPAC.

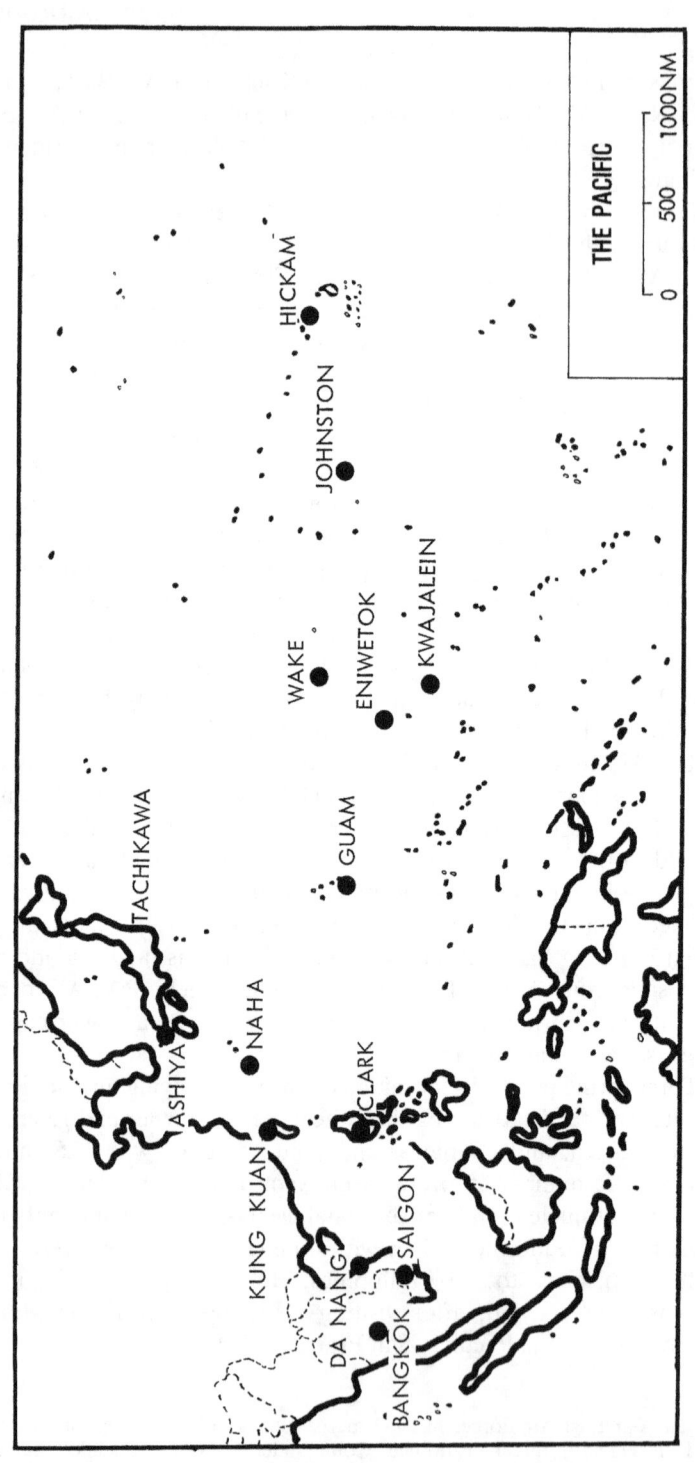

Transpacific crossings meanwhile became routine for the C–130 crews. By developing Eniwetok as a staging base in place of Kwajalein, it became possible under most conditions to fly from Hawaii to the Philippines with only a single stop en route. Facilities at Eniwetok were slowly improved, and stocking of C–130 equipment and spare parts at Clark Field was increased. During Exercise Mobile Yoke in 1960, twenty TAC transports maintained a ninety-five percent incommission rate at Clark, flying regular round-trip missions to Kung Kuan Air Base in Taiwan and to Bangkok.[26]

C–130 aircrewmen were generally young. Aircraft commanders were predominantly captains or majors in their early thirties, and most navigators were lieutenants in their twenties. Normal family life was nearly impossible, given the frequent absences from home during joint exercises and overseas deployments. C–130 crews knew the pressures of the unit operational readiness inspection, the rigors of survival training at Stead Air Force Base, Nevada, and the pallidness of a cold egg and cheese sandwich in a flight lunch. Crews used the term, "TAC sunset," watching dawn toward the end of an eighteen-hour day. A 1961 survey conducted at Sewart Air Force Base indicated that the average C–130 aircrew workweek was sixty-two hours, and that individuals were away from home forty-one percent of the time. Few air or ground crewmen could hope for fast promotions or future career diversity. Disillusioned, many returned to civilian life, compounding the problems of inexperience and overwork in the squadrons. Those men who stayed became the nucleus for an expanding C–130 force during the Southeast Asia years.[27]

During the fighting at Dien Bien Phu, the U.S. Joint Chiefs took the position that "Indochina is devoid of decisive military objectives," and warned against intervention by significant American forces. Military planners, nevertheless, examined possible actions, foreseeing important roles for the Air Force theater airlift force. One proposal suggested shifting a full wing of transports (C–119s and C–46s) from Japan to Clark, and further staging to Tourane and Haiphong for in-country airlift work. Three squadrons of C–124 Globemasters, meanwhile, would augment the Pacific force, primarily for overwater hauling. In a separate study, the Army Staff determined that an adequate intervention force would require airlift to drop one assault division.[28]

After Geneva, the United States and the SEATO powers* retained

---

* The Southeast Asia Treaty Organization (SEATO) was established in September 1954, to manifest collective security in the region and further the American plans to send external forces into the region. The U.S. Joint Chiefs in late 1955, although recognizing that the main threat in South Vietnam was infiltration and internal subversion, directed CINCPAC to develop a plan for "swift and decisive intervention" in case of overt aggression from the North. The chiefs believed that a U.S. Army regimental combat team could be airlifted at once to Tourane (later renamed Da Nang) to stop the communist invasion above 16° latitude; other forces would meanwhile move by air and sea to points farther south. An Air Force medium troop carrier wing would operate from the airfield at Cap Saint Jacques (later called Vung Tau). The resulting CINCPAC Operation Plan (OPlan) 46–56 followed these proposals, prescribing the introduction of a brigade task force of eight thousand personnel and five thousand tons of materiel, all to be airlifted in two days from bases elsewhere in the Pacific. The task would require maximum effort by the 315th Air Division and substantial augmentation by transports and personnel from MATS.[29]

The Kingdom of Laos became a valuable buffer insulating South Vietnam, Cambodia, and Thailand from the north, a "tripwire" which could trigger SEATO assistance in case of a Chinese or North Vietnamese invasion. CINCPAC OPlan 32 (L)–59, for example, called for the airlift of two Marine battalions from Okinawa to Vientiane and Seno as an immediate reaction force, preceding the introduction of a larger joint task force. Variations to this plan included the possible use of American Army units based in Hawaii and readiness for parachute assault operations. In all cases, the force in Laos would be supplied by air, pending the development of overland transport lines. Again, the plan required the full use of the 315th Air Division, assisted by C–130s and C–124s from the United States. During late summer of 1959, the air division increased its readiness for possible introduction of Marine battalions.[30]

Actual missions to Southeast Asia were infrequent. Ships and crews landed occasionally at the major airports, supporting embassy and military assistance activities. The 315th task forces flew to Thailand annually in conjunction with the principal SEATO exercises. Shortly before the spring 1958 elections in Laos, C–119s and C–130s delivered over 1,000 tons of supplies to widespread locations in that country.[31]

But conflict within Laos brought a pointed American response. During the first week of January 1961, C–130s of the 315th Air Division and a TAC C–130 squadron converged on Clark Field preparing for possible transport of marines. The 315th returned to normal mission activity after a

---

objective "to prevent the area from passing into or becoming economically dependent on the Communist bloc." Remaining outside the alliance were South Vietnam and Laos, although both accepted SEATO protection under a special protocol to the original Manila treaty. The United States and its SEATO allies were barred by the Geneva agreements from stationing forces in either South Vietnam or Laos.

few days, but the TAC squadron remained in the Far East until early March; meanwhile, another TAC squadron arrived in Okinawa to participate in American and SEATO exercises scheduled for February. In conjunction with the exercises, the air division established several command posts in upper Thailand.[32] A renewed diplomatic crisis in March brought fresh marines and theater transports to Clark and another TAC C–130 squadron arrived at Clark on the fourteenth. The C–130s made numerous overwater hauls to Thailand, delivering munitions and weaponry for transfer to Laotian forces. Also airlifted to Udorn were sixteen H–34 helicopters for operational use by contract aircrews.[33]

The Laotian situation deteriorated further in late April. C–130s made direct deliveries to Seno and Vientiane. CINCPAC on the twenty-sixth ordered airborne troops to Clark, and American leaders examined the feasibility of moving troops into Laos against the communist opposition. Secretary of Defense McNamara stated that the communists could easily halt the thirty-six daily transport sorties that were needed to sustain a force at Vientiane. American military officers were less pessimistic. Admiral Arleigh A. Burke, Chief of Naval Operations, pointed out that the task force, if necessary, could retreat into Thailand and be reinforced by air at Udorn. On April 26, after prolonged meetings in the White House, CINCPAC received instructions to develop a fresh plan for deploying one brigade to northeast Thailand and another to Da Nang as a show-of-force threatening intervention in Laos. Tension eased soon afterwards following a military cease-fire in Laos and the opening of a new Geneva Conference on May 12, 1961.[34]

The 1961 Laotian crisis confirmed the importance of the Philippines as an essential air gateway to Southeast Asia. During the year, PACAF called for improved staging facilities at Clark Field, proposing stockage of equipment (including materiel for an airborne battle group) and development of a camp site for six thousand troops. The Army instead urged that a full division be positioned in the Clark area to reduce airlift requirements for any Southeast Asia troop movements. A serious constraint in planning was the inadequacy of Southeast Asian airfields particularly in Laos where only the Seno and Vientiane runways could even marginally handle C–130s and C–124s. Furthermore, both these fields if used would require continuing and heavy maintenance. The solution seemed to be to improve runways in Laos and northern Thailand, and to increase supply stocks in Thailand, actions already begun.[35]

Speedy air access by U.S. forces to Southeast Asia remained a feature of American military planning. But after the spring of 1961, a greater question arose: how should American strength be applied to stem the gradual deterioration inside South Vietnam? Air Force researchers looked closely at historical uses of the aircraft in counterinsurgency, grafting conclusions onto established doctrine. Potential roles for air transport in low-grade conflict seemed great in support of military and paramilitary forces and for nation-building activities.

This Air Force counterinsurgency potential was soon to be tested. Poverty and disunity in South Asia had provided fertile soil for revolutionary activity. Moderate governments in emerging areas were vulnerable to the classic weapons of the insurgent: subversion, propaganda, terror, and guerrilla warfare. To the Soviets these conditions, if nurtured and brought under communist leadership, promised a fresh path toward the old goal of world revolution. Nikita S. Khrushchev, speaking before the Party Congress in Moscow on January 6, 1961, reaffirmed Soviet determination to support "wars of liberation" among the former colonial peoples.

President John F. Kennedy quickly picked up the challenge, and on February 1, 1961, directed Secretary of Defense McNamara to study ways of developing counterinsurgency forces. McNamara twice referred the matter to the Joints Chiefs of Staff and on the second occasion asserted that "the development by the United States of counter-guerrilla forces is a critical requirement in the defense of the Free World and . . . should be pressed with all possible vigor." President Kennedy's address to Congress on March 28 made clear his continued concern over indirect aggression, guerrilla conflict, and small wars. In reaction to this unmistakable White House pressure, "counterinsurgency" became a favored topic for discussion and thought among American officers.[36]

The U.S. Air Force had little firsthand experience in counterinsurgency. During the second World War, Allied transport aircraft served in the opposite role, supporting friendly guerrilla and unconventional warfare troops inside enemy territory. Airlift provided the guerrillas with transportation to and from operating areas, and a means of supply. After the Korean War, Air Force unconventional warfare units (air supply and communication wings) were reduced in number and in 1957 eliminated entirely. Conventional troop carrier units were, thereafter, required to maintain capabilities for unconventional warfare missions. In practice, however, this included nothing more than those skills developed for normal airdrop and assault work.[37]

The Air Force examined historical examples of counterinsurgency operations—the experiences of the British in Malaya and of the French in Indochina and Algeria. In the Malayan campaign (1948–1960), fixed-wing transports moved troops and supplies between bases, and made supply drops to offensive patrols. Helicopters lifted troops and made medical evacuations. The official British history concluded that air transport was the Royal Air Force's most important role in the campaign. The French in Algeria (1954–1962) used fixed-wing transports to land and drop supplies in interior operating areas. More than one hundred helicopters performed fast troop movements, either in response to enemy attacks or in planned offensive efforts.[38]

The U.S. Air Force on April 14, 1961, activated under TAC the 4400th Combat Crew Training Squadron (CCTS) at Hurlburt Field, Florida. Its training mission was conducted under cover. The unit was expected to fly operations against guerrillas, either as an overt Air Force operation or in some undefined covert capacity. The capability of operating at austere locations with simple and rugged aircraft was uppermost. To Col. Benjamin H. King, first commander of the 4400th, the main mission was to "get on with the problem . . . get the outfit together, learn how to fly the airplanes, learn how to maintain them, and get your supplies set up."[39]

Like the American air commando force in Burma during 1944,* the new special warfare unit possessed an integral airlift capability, organized and controlled separately from any conventional theater airlift force. An obvious choice for the airlift arm of the 4400th was the C–47, which had served in Malaya, Indochina, and Algeria. The C–47 Skytrain was less versatile than the C–123 Provider, but was widely used by foreign governments. This was an important advantage which enabled the 4400th crews to work with foreign personnel in training or operations, and strengthened their cover story in the event of covert actions. C–47 airlift squadrons had been assigned overseas for some years, and hundreds of these Gooney Birds (as the aircraft was popularly known) still served in supporting roles. The 4400th was authorized sixteen C–47s, eight B–26s, and eight T–28s, and initial planning called for equal numbers of spare aircraft to be kept in ready storage.

Known by its nickname, Jungle Jim, the 4400th launched into a summer of hard work. Its 125 officers and 235 airmen were volunteers, and had been put through rigid psychological screening. The flavor of eliteness, self-reliance, and personal dedication was strong. The men were taught French and Spanish, the use of infantry weapons, hand-to-hand combat, psychological warfare, and parachuting. C–47 aircrews worked hardest at their most demanding tasks—night penetrations and supply of friendly guerrillas or Special Forces. Other missions included day penetrations and drops, medical evacuations, leaflet and loudspeaker operations, and forward field operations. Crews learned to refuel from fifty-five-gallon drums, and each ship carried a hand pump for this purpose. Each Gooney Bird was equipped with ultra high frequency (UHF), very high frequency (VHF), and high frequency (HF) radios, exhaust flame dampeners, attachments for jet-assisted takeoffs, loudspeakers, and litter supports.† In a combat readiness test conducted by TAC in September 1961, the C–47 crews scored well ahead of the strike aircraft sections, operating success-

---

* The 1st Air Commando Group was tailored to support British Maj. Gen. Orde C. Wingate's 1944 air invasion of Burma, and included light transport, C–47, glider, and strike aircraft.

† Thus modified, the ships were designated SC–47s; the S stood for "search."

fully in very difficult weather. The 4400th achieved operational readiness in September.[40]

The Air Force thus easily expanded its doctrine to fit the new preoccupation with limited warfare. When in late June 1961 President Kennedy asked for an inventory of paramilitary assets, urging the Joint Chiefs to assume "dynamic and imaginative leadership" in this area, the Air Force pointed to its Jungle Jim unit with satisfaction. The older doctrines for employing troop carrier aviation remained—doctrines of airborne warfare, theater logistics, unit mobility, and strike force support. Now, the Air Force believed that the C–123s and C–130s also had capabilities valuable in a low-level conflict. The effectiveness with which the troop carrier forces operated in Southeast Asia after 1961 verified the flexibility and essential soundness, if not the precision, of prewar tactical airlift and employment doctrine.[41]

The limited warfare doctrines current in 1961 were tailored to the worsening situation in South Vietnam, where the communists were intensifying their vicious campaign of propaganda and intimidation. Several hundred village leaders were assassinated monthly, confronting the government of President Ngo Dinh Diem in Saigon with insoluble problems in nation-building. The citizenry—poorly protected from terrorists and without deep loyalties to a class-ridden and frequently corrupt regime—gave the insurgents a logistics, recruiting, and intelligence-gathering base.[42]

Following the Geneva accords, Americans gradually took over from the French responsibility for training and equipping South Vietnamese military forces. A Military Assistance Advisory Group, Vietnam (MAAGV), limited to 342 men by the Geneva accords, administered the military programs. In early 1960 the U.S. Joint Chiefs agreed that the emphasis in training within the South Vietnamese forces should be changed "from conventional to anti-guerrilla warfare." Soon thereafter, U.S. Army Special Forces teams entered Vietnam as instructors. During fiscal 1961, South Vietnam was the fifth ranking recipient of U.S. military and economic aid.[43]

The Saigon regime appeared very much aware of the importance of air transport for improving national communications and combating insurgency. A national plan for airfield construction received the personal attention of President Diem, so that by 1961 he could claim that his country had the most advanced aviation infrastructure in Southeast Asia. The airlift arm of the Vietnamese Air Force (VNAF) consisted of two squadrons at Tan Son Nhut, each authorized sixteen C–47s. The civil airline, Air Vietnam, also operated C–47s, which helped to overcome deficiencies in the nation's surface communications which had been disrupted by insurgency.[44]

President Kennedy's affirmation on May 11, 1961, that the United States would seek to prevent communist domination of South Vietnam by initiating "on an accelerated basis, a series of mutually supporting actions

Courtesy: John F. Kennedy Library
President John F. Kennedy with Robert S. McNamara (left) and JCS Chairman Gen. Lyman L. Lemnitzer (center), May 1962.

of a military, political, economic, psychological, and covert character," confirmed the direction of the nation's policy. The Air Staff for the moment held that the present situation was one which could be "met adequately by indigenous capability." Any active Air Force role, the staff held, should "be limited to provision of a light transport squadron (C–123 or C–47) and recce [reconnaissance] as required." During the next months, proposals to introduce American airlift forces were listened to as American leaders sensed the usefulness of air transport in the counterinsurgency, but sought to keep Americans with weapons out of combat. By year's end, several decisions resulted in the dispatch to Vietnam of men and aircraft from the American services. The desire to improve the air mobility of the Vietnamese ground forces was one of the several objectives of the diverse assistance package.[45]

The first American air transport unit to arrive in Vietnam was a flight of four SC–47 aircraft and their crews from the Jungle Jim squadron. Secretary McNamara on September 5, 1961, announced to his service secretaries his wish to make Vietnam "a laboratory for the conduct of sublimited war." In a memorandum prepared in the Air Staff plans directorate dated September 19, 1961, Secretary of the Air Force Eugene M. Zuckert recommended to McNamara that a small force of C–47s, B–26s, and

T–28s from the 4400th be dispatched to assist the Vietnamese Air Force "in developing new techniques and equipment for use against the Vietcong." McNamara termed the proposal "attractive" and, after seeking concurrence by the Joint Chiefs of Staff, on October 11 obtained the President's decision to send the force, subject to Vietnamese President Diem's concurrence, "for the initial purpose of training Vietnamese forces." The detachment, known as Farm Gate, included four SC–47s, four RB–26s, eight T–28s, and 151 personnel. It departed for Bien Hoa in November.[46]

The idea of sending a much larger force of American Air Force transports was taken up by the Department of Defense, the Joint Chiefs, and the services in a joint study on possible actions in South Vietnam. Their joint report of October assessed the capabilities of the Vietnamese C–47 squadrons, and concluded that the VNAF lacked the capability to absorb additional transport aircraft, except on the basis of a long-range military assistance program. Use of American aircraft for logistic support missions would permit the Vietnamese C–47s to concentrate on combat support. The need for additional airlift was further emphasized by a panel in Saigon, headed by the British counterinsurgency specialist, Robert G. K. Thompson. After listing the principal deficiencies of South Vietnam, the Thompson group placed at the head of the list the lack of transport aircraft, pointing out that "it will be essential during the next six months for units up to battalion strength to be able to operate in the Highlands, particularly along the Laos frontier, away from their bases, for periods of up to six weeks."[47]

Further impetus for increased airlift capability came from a group headed by General Taylor, then serving as presidential military representative, following an October visit to Vietnam. Taylor stated that improvement of the Vietnamese C–47 force would be "slow and painful," and recommended the addition of air transport through contract with Air America and by the introduction of U.S. Army helicopter units. In a joint memorandum prepared for the President, dated November 11, McNamara and Secretary of State Dean Rusk proposed a series of immediate actions to support the Saigon regime. The proposal incorporated many of General Taylor's views. Listed first was a recommendation for "increased airlift to the GVN [Government of Vietnam] forces, including helicopters, light aviation, and transport aircraft, manned to the extent necessary by U.S. uniformed personnel and under U.S. operational control." President Kennedy approved the recommendation after discussing the memorandum with the National Security Council and then authorized that President Diem be so advised.[48]

But questions remained: how many transports should be deployed and of what type? The previous May, PACAF had raised the possibility of pulling together a squadron of C–47 aircraft and crews then scattered in support roles among active units. However, the creation of a flying unit of members unknown to their leaders or to one another appeared unsound. Alternatively, to dispatch a significantly larger C–47 element from the Jungle Jim squadron would cripple tactical development at Hurlburt. The best alternative appeared clear. Five squadrons of C–123s were still in TAC. These squadrons had few operational commitments and were scheduled for inactivation. Replying to an Air Staff query on the matter, PACAF in late November recommended, and CINCPAC concurred, that one squadron of C–123s should move to Clark Air Base en route to Southeast Asia. McNamara, meeting with the Joint Chiefs on December 4, gave final approval for movement of sixteen aircraft to Clark, subject to the concurrence of the Secretary of State. The Secretary of Defense asked for an early departure date, urging that the first aircraft arrive in the Philippines by December 20. Under Project Mule Train, eight C–123s left for Clark on the 11th.[49]

Another transport candidate was the Army's fixed-wing CV–2 Caribou, which was well suited for operations in Southeast Asia because of its short- and rough-field takeoff and landing capabilities. A single Caribou had been tested in Vietnam during the second half of 1961 and had proved "extremely valuable and useful." The Army in December informed CINCPAC that a Caribou company could be moved into Vietnam early the next year. But CINCPAC on December 14 rejected the Caribous, since the C–123 Providers along with a company of Army U–1 Otters had already been requested and these aircraft met immediate fixed-wing transport needs.[50]

The single Vietnamese Air Force helicopter squadron demonstrated only an insignificant trooplift capability. Lt. Gen. Lionel C. McGarr, USA, chief of MAAGV, in early 1961 cautioned President Diem that the unit should be used operationally, not administratively, and suggested that a small infantry force be kept alerted to respond by helicopter to guerrilla attacks. General McGarr also concluded that a larger rotary-wing capability was needed, and on October 25, 1961, he recommended that two U.S. Army helicopter companies be assigned to Vietnam. The Taylor report supported McGarr's view and suggested that U.S. Army units provide "much needed airlift." Two Army companies, equipped with H–21 Work Horse helicopters, sailed from the United States on November 22; five days later, McNamara dispatched a third H–21 company. A squadron of U.S. Marine helicopters followed in April 1962, also to provide mobility for Vietnamese troops.[51]

A host of other U.S. military actions ensued in late 1961, bolstering the Vietnamese armed forces, improving facilities in Vietnam, and enlarging the American military presence. A few of these actions involved airlift activity. Project Ranch Hand introduced six TAC C–123s, modified to spray chemical defoliants along roadways. PACAF C–124s and C–130s during November airlifted men and equipment from elsewhere in the Pacific theater to form the 2d ADVON, the new Air Force advanced echelon headquarters in Saigon. Named its commander, and Chief, Air Force Section, MAAGV, was Brig. Gen. Rollen H. Anthis, an officer with considerable tactical air and air transport experience. Various subsidiary units under the 2d ADVON were also airlifted into Southeast Asia, including air base squadron detachments at Bien Hoa, Don Muang (Bangkok), and Tan Son Nhut.[52]

As the year 1961 ended, attention of the troop carrier forces of the United States Air Force had shifted to a preoccupation with Southeast Asia. Secretary McNamara in December stated that South Vietnam had "number one priority" and would receive whatever resources were needed, other than U.S. combat troops.[53] Twenty years had elapsed since the United States became involved in a greater Pacific war. For much of that period, the ability of the nation's airlift forces to deploy military power into Southeast Asia had reinforced America's policy of wakeful detachment. Now once again, seven years after Dien Bien Phu, U.S. troop carrier planes and personnel moved into Vietnam. This time their stay in that beautiful but unhappy land would be prolonged for over a decade.

III. Farm Gate and the Air Commando Tradition

The first Air Force transport unit to operate in Vietnam was the Farm Gate C–47 Skytrain element, which arrived at Bien Hoa from Hurlburt in November 1961. Its main task was the supply of isolated military camps throughout Vietnam and this required the sharpest skills in airdrop and airlanding work. Classic techniques for forward area supply, known to Skytrain crewmen in Burma, Korea, and among the French in Indochina, again came into use.

The term, air commando, was officially adopted for Jungle Jim and Farm Gate personnel in 1962. The name connoted informality of discipline, but total dedication. The air commandos had little use for red tape, mediocre leaders, or "standardization." They said what they thought and performed to the limit of their endurance. The enthusiasm and resourcefulness thus unleashed accounted for the remarkable accomplishments of the Farm Gate airlifters; if the aircraft were old and tired, the men who flew and maintained them decidedly were not.

The Farm Gate C–47 element remained small, expanding only to seven aircraft by 1964. And by that time its effort became overshadowed by the large tonnages airlifted by the fleet of Air Force C–123s in Vietnam. Shortly thereafter, use of the Air Force C–47s for gunship, psychological, and administrative courier roles ended their tactical airlift mission. But during the earlier years, the work of the Farm Gate C–47s represented a significant and imaginative application of air transport to the problem of the insurgency.

Two days after President Kennedy's October 11, 1961, decision to dispatch a Jungle Jim task force to Vietnam, a team of officers including the comander of the 4400th, Colonel King, met in Hawaii with Brig. Gen. Theodore R. Milton, commander of the Thirteenth Air Force in the Philippines, and the Pacific Command staff. After explaining the capabilities of Jungle Jim, King's group and General Milton moved on to Saigon, there winning an "enthusiastic" initial response. The MAAGV chief, General McGarr, at once asked that the deploying force be enlarged. Colonel King visited Bien Hoa, Da Nang, and Nha Trang, looking over these bases as

TACTICAL AIRLIFT

Brig. Gen. Theodore R. Milton, Thirteenth Air Force Commander, in 1962.

possible operating locations. He recommended and McGarr approved Bien Hoa as an operating site, because of its relatively central location and nearness to the various headquarters at Saigon. During the discussions, the idea of training the Vietnamese Air Force was never mentioned; the Jungle Jim mission appeared to be purely operational—to respond to the needs of the American ambassador and the military forces in the country.

Returning to Hawaii, Colonel King met with the PACAF staff on October 28, and secured agreements on field kitchen arrangement, ground transportation, refueling, and ammunition supply, all of which were to be provided by PACAF. The Farm Gate element, it was understood, would deploy with organizational maintenance personnel and equipment, supply personnel and "flyaway" spare parts kits, as well as medical, communications, administrative, and combat control team personnel. On November 4 a team deployed from Tachikawa to Bien Hoa to erect a tent camp for the anticipated Farm Gate force.[1]

Four SC–47 aircraft left Hurlburt on November 5, 1961, with King at the controls of the first aircraft and Capt. Richard Tegge as navigator. The four crews had been selected from among the 4400th's most highly qualified personnel. Despite the extra fuel capacity of the SC types, the leg from California to Hawaii so depended on favorable winds that the Alaska route had been chosen. The long haul halfway around the world at 120 knots, in itself proved something of a challenge to airmanship and stamina. The longest leg was the fifteen-hour overland flight from Malmstrom Air Force Base, Montana, to Elmendorf Air Force Base, Alaska. One crew made an unplanned but safe landing at White Horse, in the Canadian Yukon. All remained an extra day at Elmendorf, waiting for an engine to be changed on King's aircraft. Leaving Elmendorf on the eighth, the four planes island-hopped to Adak in the Aleutians, Midway, Wake, Guam, and Clark. Crews navigated independently by long-standing loran and celestial techniques, flying at intervals of approximately twenty minutes. The four ships rendezvoused over the Philippine coast, and flew over Clark in formation before landing on November 13. Having logged over seventy-five hours of flying time in eight days, the crews rested forty-eight hours at Clark, meeting there the T–28 pilots who had traveled (along with the T–28s themselves) by MATS heavy airlift. The four SC–47s arrived at Bien Hoa without ceremony on November 16, 1961, met by the main ground echelon. In-country missions began the first week.[2]

The Farm Gate mission as officially stated by Secretary McNamara and President Kennedy had been limited to training and the development of methods. In reality the concept of operations was far broader. PACAF on December 4 proposed employment in actual operations. For the C–47s this meant "aerial resupply, airdrops of Vietnamese paratroopers, tactical intelligence collection, psychological warfare, and other missions as required." Tasks included the resupply of approximately two dozen border patrol bases, each eventually possessing a landing strip capable of handling a C–47. CINCPAC on December 20 clarified a recent ruling by McNamara: Farm Gate's basic mission was to work out tactics and techniques; operational flights were authorized, however, "provided a Vietnamese is on board for purpose of receiving combat or combat support training."[3]

To the Farm Gate C–47 crewmen, the requirement for a combined crew looked like a purely political matter, since no Vietnamese C–47 trainees in need of training were on hand. To satisfy the proviso, unskilled Vietnamese enlisted personnel were carried on certain "combat" flights. Later, Vietnamese navigators proved useful on Farm Gate night flare missions. Although it was claimed with some validity that Farm Gate served as an example of professional air power for the Vietnamese, the C–47 section performed no direct training of the Vietnamese Air Force. All Farm Gate planes had the red-and-yellow VNAF insignia in place of American markings. In reality the mission was operational, with a secondary experimental purpose.[4]

The Farm Gate unit was officially designated Detachment 2, 4400th Combat Crew Training Squadron, to perform missions under the nominal operational control of 2d ADVON. Colonel King, however, believed from earlier personal conversations with General LeMay that he was supposed to answer directly to the American ambassador and the Central Intelligence Agency (CIA) representative in Vietnam on matters concerning covert projects. King therefore accepted requests for C–47 supply flights directly from the air attaché, the CIA, and the Agency for International Development (AID). Although these missions were carried out skillfully, relations became strained between King and General Anthis, the ADVON commander. In King's words, Anthis "crawled my frame several times," over a lack of coordination in such mission activity, a problem compounded by difficulties in communications between Bien Hoa and Saigon. Colonel King in late December privately advised his successor, Lt. Col. Robert L. Gleason, to seek better relations with the ADVON. Frictions lessened as the lines of authority firmed. Outside agencies thereafter made airlift mission requests to the logistics directorate of MACV,* and the 2d ADVON command center assigned all Farm Gate C-47 missions. Administratively, Detachment 2 remained an element of the 4400th at Hurlburt, with especially close ties in matters developing new tactics and equipment.[5]

Through its existence apart from the other American and allied airlift units in Vietnam, the Farm Gate element appeared to contradict the Air Force's doctrine of centralized airlift control. As events developed, however, Farm Gate principally served the requirements of the Army's Special Forces and its own needs, work which easily distinguished the element's duties from the tasks of the other airlift units. Furthermore, the habitual allocation (or dedication) of the C-47s could be changed overnight at the ADVON should the aircraft be needed for other roles. Crews felt that some missions and loads were a waste of time, and saw occasional examples of wasteful duplication in itineraries among the C-47s, C-123s, and the Army transports. Such cases loomed large to crewmen who felt their energies wasted, but these were relatively infrequent. An indisputable weakness, albeit less personal to the crewmen, was the absence of close mission control during the flying day; crews could be diverted from their planned itineraries only by ad hoc radio or telephone procedures.[6]

The war's first combat loss among Air Force airlift forces occurred on February 11, 1962. A Farm Gate SC-47 crashed and burned near Bao Loc, killing the eight Americans and one Vietnamese on board. The plane had left Bien Hoa, landed at Tan Son Nhut, and had taken off with a load of propaganda leaflets for dispersal along a scheduled flight route to Da Nang. Hostile fire was suspected, but the actual cause of the crash remains undetermined. The aircraft had apparently been flying at low altitude along a valley in clear weather.[7]

To replace the lost ship, TAC upon Colonel King's recommendation dispatched a standard C-47, stripped of loudspeakers and other extra

---

* The Military Assistance Command, Vietnam (MACV) was a subordinate unified command established in January 1962 under CINCPAC. The 2d ADVON headquarters functioned as the Air Force component command of MACV, and became the 2d Air Division on October 8, 1962.

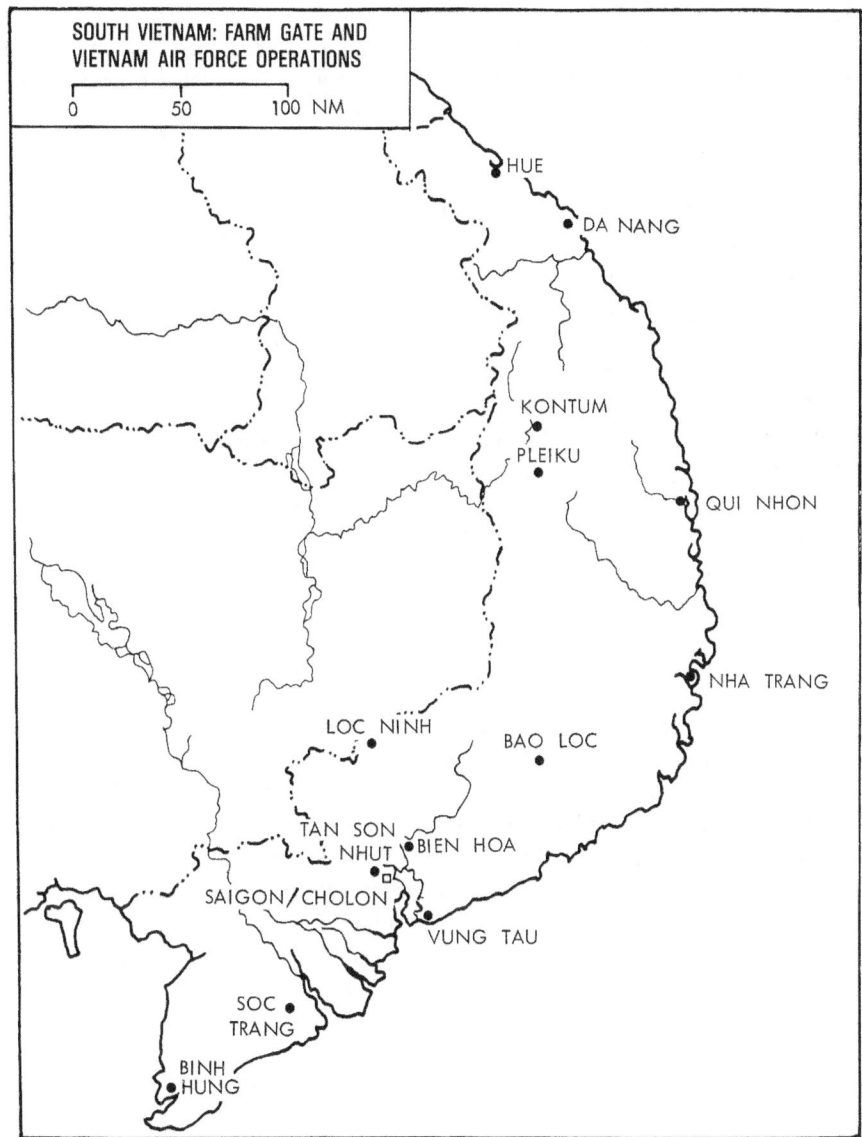

equipment found on the SC models. Thereafter, Farm Gate crews called this aircraft "the light one," preferring its performance, maneuverability, and payload over the characteristics of its three heavier cousins. When in January 1963 the detachment received two additional C–47s, both were lighter versions.[8]

Aircrew replacements, arriving for six-month rotational tours, came directly from the Jungle Jim squadron at Hurlburt. At Bien Hoa, the newcomers received briefings on the intelligence situation and flying matters.

TACTICAL AIRLIFT

Each recent arrival flew first a few missions with an instructor to major airfields and accompanied a night flare mission. More rigorous work then followed and each new crewman flew daily with his instructor on resupply missions to isolated points. The checkout ended when the newcomer attained full qualification in the demanding shortfield and airdrop skills.

Expansion and reorganization of Jungle Jim in Florida, meanwhile, reflected President Kennedy's continued interest in counterinsurgency warfare. Replacing the 4400th CCTS* in the spring of 1962 was a new entity called the Special Air Warfare Center (SAWC) with two subordinate groups. The 1st Air Commando Group had three operational squadrons, one of which flew C-47s and C-46 Commandos. The 1st Combat Applications Group had the role of developing doctrine, tactics, and equipment for field operations. Farm Gate became a detachment of the 1st Air Commando Group. Secretary McNamara late in 1962 approved expansion of the commando group to wing status, which included a squadron of C-47, C-46, and U-10B Super Couriers. The squadron had no transport helicopters, despite Air Force recommendations that it should.[9]

Flying in Vietnam differed markedly from routine transport work in the United States. The limited system for air traffic control and the scarcity of precision navigation aids made the use of instrument flight rules clearance procedures impractical and entailed long delays and communications frustrations. Most C-47 flights were therefore conducted under liberalized visual flight rule procedures, by which aircrews remained themselves responsible for staying clear of clouds and other aircraft. Pilots cruised either above or below cloud layers, and penetrated broken layers by spiraling through holes. Ground controlled approach landing patterns, under control of ground radar, and instrument letdowns using low frequency radio beacons were almost never attempted; indeed, the skills in instrument flying which so dominated proficiency training in the U.S. Air Force found little application in Farm Gate C-47 operations.

Accurate navigation constituted a serious problem in view of the remote location of many supply points, the mountainous terrain, and the usually poor weather. Several low frequency radio beacons offered limited navigational assistance, but the basic technique remained mapreading supplemented by dead reckoning. Pilots and copilots assisted the navigator,

---

* The 4400th CCTS became the 4400th CCTG in March 1962, with three subordinate squadrons, among them the 4400th Air Transport Squadron. SAWC was activated on April 27, 1962.

whose outside visibility was very restricted. The navigator's celestial and loran equipment were of no use during the short in-country flights and the driftmeter provided only wind (not fixing) information. The challenge of locating an isolated mountain camp after descending through a break in the clouds, often taxed every grain of crew experience and wit; at such times, the search was performed as quickly as possible, to reduce exposure to enemy fire while beneath the clouds at low altitude.

Farm Gate operation officers maintained lists of airfields approved for C–47 use, generally those having at least twenty-five hundred feet of landing surface. Except in emergencies when waivers could be granted by the Farm Gate commander at Bien Hoa, aircraft were not scheduled into unapproved fields. Few remote strips had control towers or communications facilities, and careful identification was necessary to ensure that the field was secure and usable. A low pass over the landing area permitted visual inspection for possible hazards and afforded a final check of runway direction and field identification. Usually, personnel on the ground would set out green smoke grenades, signifying that the camp was not under attack and also indicating the wind direction.

The favored technique for C–47 shortfield landings in Vietnam involved a high and steep, power-off approach, maintaining an airspeed of eighty knots until final roundout and then the heavy use of brakes after touchdown. The steep angle of descent reduced exposure to hostile small-arms fire on final approach. Nearby trees or high terrain, crosswinds, or intermittent visibility complicated landings. Pilots were urged to practice their precision shortfield skills at every opportunity, even though landings were seldom made on strips of less than twenty-five hundred feet in length.

Rough surfaces were as much a problem as field dimensions. Airstrips used by the C–47s might be of clay, laterite (a reddish hard soil common in the area), grass, or covered with pierced steel planking (PSP) or asphalt, in various states of repair. Ruts and loose objects menaced landing gear and exposed surfaces. Propeller damage during landings was a common occurrence, tempering use of those tail-high landing-roll techniques taught at Hurlburt for shortfield work.

Night landings were attempted only in emergencies, since the forward landing points lacked fixed runway lighting. Shielded flashlights for marking landing areas had been used in training with the Special Forces in the United States, but these were hard to spot unless perfectly pinpointed. Cans of burning gasoline, laid out alongside the strip, proved more satisfactory in Vietnam. Experiments in making landings using the light of flares previously dropped by the landing aircraft, proved understandably chancy. The Farm Gate detachment requested that the problem be further investigated at Hurlburt.

Airdrop missions called for imaginative methods. Prior to takeoff, aircrews plotted exact drop-zone locations and studied information folders, which sometimes included aerial photos. Approaching the drop zone, the crew attempted FM radio contact with personnel below. If this failed, the appearance of properly colored smoke or panel signals on the ground signified readiness below to receive loads. Drop altitude was normally between 150 and 350 feet, the lower the better for accuracy, provided parachutes had time to deploy properly. Night drops were made only in rare emergencies, although crews were routinely urged to note camp layouts and landmarks in case of night missions.

Drop mission loads usually consisted of twelve bundles, each weighing up to two hundred pounds. Bundles rested on pallets which could be shoved over the roller conveyers on the floor of the aircraft. Those crew members—navigators, Vietnamese observers, and maintenance men along for the ride—not needed in actually flying the plane, helped the loadmasters in manhandling the pallets to the side cargo door. Crews flew rectangular patterns over the drop zones, kicking out one or two bundles on each pass. The altitude and shape of the pattern depended on terrain and the possibility of hostile ground fire; supply locations in mountainous areas sometimes required very careful flying within the valleys, particularly when marginal weather prevailed. The exact release point was determined purely by aircrew judgment, taking consideration of whatever wind information was available to them and could be adjusted according to the results of the previous passes. Accuracy was often important; some of the smaller drop zones were located entirely within fortified perimeters. The driftmeter was tested as a sighting device for lining up during the run, but was not used on actual deliveries.

The Farm Gate airlifters experimented with methods for freefall delivery of cargo; these were new techniques, untried previously at Hurlburt. Half-filled "blivet bags" containing fifty pounds of rice could be dropped from C–47s flying at forty feet, and the bags would skip along the ground on impact without breaking. Within weeks after arriving at Bien Hoa, the first aircrews used this technique for deliveries in the delta region south of Saigon. The method proved ideal for delivering goods to one extremely small drop zone bordered by water. Other nonfragile items such as bundles of sandbags or barbed wire were freedropped, using higher altitudes (about fifteen hundred feet) to reduce rolling on impact. Freefall techniques not only improved accuracy, but reduced the expense and effort of preparing materials for drops. Farm Gate or Vietnamese Air Force strike aircraft normally accompanied transports on drop missions and suppressed hostile ground fire.

Although clouds, low ceilings, and poor visibility were chronic problems and frequently caused mission delays, air aborts because of weather were virtually unknown. On one occasion a Farm Gate crew, hauling an emergency load of ammunition to a Special Forces camp, found the camp completely covered by ground fog. After orbiting the area for two hours and unsuccessfully seeking radio contact and a way to penetrate the undercast, the crew spotted the smoke trail of a flare, apparently fired from below. The crew turned quickly, pushing out the ammunition packages at the spot of the flare's smoke. The aircrew learned the next day that the entire load had been recovered; one package landed exactly on target.[10]

The early view expressed by McNamara and Zuckert, that Farm Gate was to represent a kind of laboratory for developing new techniques and equipment for counterinsurgency warfare, proved only marginally valid for the airlifters. Most of the airlift tactics employed in Vietnam by the C–47s had been worked out previously at Hurlburt and the results in Vietnam were those of emphasis, not technique. Although developments in tactics for night flare work were significant, in airlift work proper the problem for Farm Gate lay not so much in developing new techniques, but in relearning and becoming skilled in the old.

On the other hand, the diverse developmental projects ranged from inflight pickup of personnel from the C–47 and C–46 to airdrop supply from A–1E strike aircraft. Much attention went to the problem of locating drop or landing zones in darkness or bad weather. Several aircraft were equipped with Decca navigation sets (a British product employing ground stations) for this purpose. Another approach was to place electronic aids on drop (or landing) zones. Several radio beacons were tested as was the tactical landing approach radar (TALAR), which emitted a narrow beam signal for reception in the aircraft. As in Jungle Jim's operational activities, developmental work rested heavily upon the initiative and resourcefulness of individual officers and airmen; and adherence to formal and prescribed procedures was distinctly secondary.[11]

Although the camp supply role in the early years was the most prominent and most demanding task, it consumed less than half the total Farm Gate C–47 flying hours. Other tasks varied and some were outside the usual air transport functions. These uses reflected the adaptability of the transport and foreshadowed the varied usages of larger and more numerous Air Force transports in Vietnam in later years.

The Farm Gate C–47s flew occasional practice paratroop missions with the Vietnamese airborne brigade and its training establishment near Saigon. Actual parachute assault missions were rare, but included two drops of sizable Vietnamese Special Forces units. On June 4, 1963, five American and four Vietnamese Air Force C–47s dropped 232 troops in a raid against a suspected Viet Cong station ten miles east of Bien Hoa. The drop zone was marked by a Farm Gate U–10, and the American carriers released their troops accurately. Vietnamese aircraft, which had flown from Tan Son Nhut to Bien Hoa for loading, made their drops twenty minutes later, also with technical success. Reconnaissance of the drop-zone area, including photos taken by Farm Gate less than forty-eight hours before the mission, proved extremely valuable in mission prepara-

VNAF C-47 transports in formation over Tay Ninh, 1963.

In the Air Commando tradition, A1C Richard B. Costello (left), loadmaster, Capt. William H. Brandt, pilot, and flight mechanic SSgt. Russell D. Lapray wear the Australian commando hat. Their C-123 is in the background, 1965.

Vietnamese paratroopers hooking up.

Members of the Vietnamese airborne brigade at Tan Son Nhut, 1962.

tion. Tactically, the raid was a limited success; a close-range firefight developed four hours after the drop, and an enemy staging area consisting of several buildings was captured, along with foodstuffs and equipment. A similar venture, Hurricane III, was less auspiciously executed on June 26, 1963; approximately 242 Vietnamese Special Forces paratroops jumped from three Farm Gate and seven Vietnamese Air Force C–47s into a location eight miles from the earlier site. The Americans dropped pathfinder personnel ahead of the main force and provided the first two-ship element in the stream. All aircraft again marshaled at Bien Hoa. All jumps were accurate, except for the initial Vietnamese element which landed in trees. The jumpers were shot at during descent, though none were wounded. The operation was marred by bitterness during the mission briefing, apparently resulting from Vietnamese displeasure over the dominant American role in planning and leading the drop. An American Air Force liaison officer who had coordinated the mission recommended that Farm Gate not participate with the Vietnamese Air Force in such ventures or that the Vietnamese should lead the formation. Although good relations generally prevailed between the Vietnamese Special Forces and the Farm Gate unit, no further airborne raids involving Farm Gate materialized.[12]

The idea of operating Farm Gate strike aircraft from other locations in Vietnam had been discussed almost from the start of the Farm Gate operation. The concept gained strength during the summer of 1962, following complaints by senior Army personnel in Vietnam over delays in fulfilling requests for air strikes because of the distances between Bien Hoa and target areas. The Thirteenth Air Force on September 6 recommended that deployed air strike teams (DASTs) be positioned at Pleiku and Soc Trang, for support of the II Corps and the delta areas, respectively. Each strike team consisted of five or six T–28s or B–26s, with a C–47 for flare work and internal airlift support. The strike team concept supported the Farm Gate augmentation proposals first considered by the Joint Chiefs of Staff in December, and two C–47s sent in January 1963 were justified principally in terms of this new role. The 2d Air Division soon afterwards reported that these aircraft had been sent and were operating out of Soc Trang, Pleiku, and Da Nang.[13]

Movement of materiel and support personnel between Bien Hoa and the operating locations became a routine responsibility for the Farm Gate airlift section. Scheduled C–47 courier flights operated twice weekly to the strike aircraft locations at Soc Trang and Da Nang, while less regular flights supported Farm Gate detachments at Pleiku and Nha Trang. In general, administrative flying was not burdensome. By 1964, C–47s flew two round trips daily, linking Bien Hoa with 2d Air Division headquarters at Tan Son Nhut. More popular among the aircrews were troop recreation flights every two weeks to Hong Kong or Bangkok.[14]

Psychological warfare operations from the outset were an essential

TACTICAL AIRLIFT

part of the operational concept for Farm Gate. In the first weeks, crews experimented with loudspeaker and leaflet-dispensing techniques, and on December 20, 1961, tried these in conjunction with rice drops by Vietnamese Air Force C–47s. Observers on the ground reported that reactions among the populace ranged from indifference to great excitement. The loss of a crew in February 1962 led to high-level review of the psychological warfare role. Eight days after the crash, Secretary McNamara asked Pacific Command and MACV leaders why only one Vietnamese was on board. The secretary contended that the Vietnamese should fly such missions, and that he did not wish to expose American personnel to such risks. The Farm Gate loudspeaker and amplifier planes were accordingly transferred to the Vietnamese Air Force.[15]

The development of a night flareship-airstrike capability became an important Farm Gate contribution. In flareship work, C–47 crews released parachute flares from an overhead orbit, illuminating friendly outposts under attack and permitting visual airstrikes. A practice range near Bien Hoa was used for experimentation and training, and the methods thus worked out were eventually adopted by the three units engaged in flare-dropping—the Farm Gate and VNAF C–47s, and the U.S. Air Force C–123s at Tan Son Nhut. The Farm Gate flareship role gradually declined. Whereas in 1962 a Farm Gate C–47 flew nightly, a year later their contribution amounted to a single ship on ground standby at Bien Hoa.[16]

The idea of using the transport in attack or bombing roles led to further tests in January 1963 when a C–47 dropped twenty-pound fragmentation bombs from its doorway. More promising was the installation in the C–47 of side-firing 7.62-mm miniguns at Eglin Air Force Base, Florida. A test team arrived in Vietnam nearly two years later and installed the guns and sighting equipment on two Bien Hoa C–47s. The gunship proved successful in night outpost defense, reducing delays and problems of communications between flare and strike aircraft. The use of the C–47 for the gunship-flareship role later entirely overshadowed its airlift role.[17]

Another aircraft, the U–10 Super Courier (or Helio Courier)—a single-engine, fixed-wing aircraft—gave Farm Gate a light airlift capability. The plane had space for four passengers or could carry seventy cubic feet of cargo. Its maximum payload with full fuel was 550 pounds. Personnel or cargo could be airdropped, and the ship could operate into dirt strips shorter than a thousand feet. Unable to meet General McGarr's request to send U–10s (then still designated as the L–28) in 1961, the Air Force promptly contracted for delivery of fourteen U–10s to the 4400th early the next year. After training and experimentation at Jungle Jim, four U–10s were sent to Southeast Asia in August 1962. Their mission included visual reconnaissance, forward air control, and light airlift, the last to include liaison air transport and the movement of personnel and materials for psychological operations.

The four U–10Bs quickly proved their usefulness in airlift work. They flew frequently to Binh Hung, a hamlet in the southernmost peninsula of Vietnam which was defended by the local citizens led by the renowned Father Hoa. Previously the C–47s had supported the hamlet through airdrops. Only a part of the dirt airstrip was usable because of rough terrain at one end. Other missions to remote sites often involved hauling medical or civic action personnel and supplies. Emergency medical evacuations were often performed, sometimes (according to air commando lore) after Army helicopters had declined to try the missions. One U–10 pilot landed at an outpost during a night battle to remove a captured Viet Cong officer for immediate interrogation. On another occasion, personnel were landed on an eight hundred-foot segment of dirt road. The U–10s thus represented a valuable supplement to the heavier haul capabilities of the Farm Gate C–47s, both for routine, forward area, and emergency airlift tasks.

A formal operational test of the U–10B in Vietnam in early 1963 concluded that the aircraft was excellent in the airlift and psychological warfare roles, but barely satisfactory for visual reconnaissance and unsuitable for forward air control, owing to its restricted cockpit visibility. Particularly attractive was the superiority of the U–10 over the C–47 for loudspeaker work, because of the ship's slow speed of flight and low engine noise. During May 1963, equipment intended originally for the C–47s was installed on additional U–10s to support the U.S. Army's psychological warfare program. To improve the U–10's responsiveness to Army requests, the aircraft was sent regularly from Bien Hoa to bases further north. Whereas airlift and administrative sorties amounted to more than half of its monthly workload in the summer of 1963, the sortie rate declined to ten percent by January 1964, and the Farm Gate U–10 element became known as the psychological warfare section.[18]

In recognition of their dedication and their relatively informal discipline, both Farm Gate and Jungle Jim crews were officially designated in 1962 as air commandos. The early air commandos at Bien Hoa were high in morale and enthusiasm. All were volunteers for duty with Jungle Jim, and all shared the hard training experiences at Hurlburt. Flying personnel trained as complete crews, and in most cases stayed together in Vietnam, where distinctions of rank further eroded. Informally (but strongly) disciplined, all shared a strong desire for getting things done. Rules and established practices seldom interfered with mission accomplishment.

Until 1963, manning was limited at Bien Hoa where there was only one overworked flying crew for each C–47. The workweek was normally seven days in length and there were no holidays or weekends. The zest for flying remained strong, if for no other reason than it was cooler and cleaner in the air. C–47 aircrews were especially pleased because they landed each day at localities throughout the country and were largely removed from close supervision. They felt a keen rivalry with the American C–123 units at Tan Son Nhut, and even claimed superior tonnage and passenger-haul performances. The Farm Gate airlifters were proud of their own freewheeling dedication, and some believed that the C–123 aircrews lacked determination in flying their missions and were being stifled by unimaginative and formal methods.[19]

Air commando leaders encouraged individual initiative and responsibility both from inclination and necessity. The C–47 section chief was usually the senior aircraft commander and he flew daily, leaving little time for meetings or paperwork. His office space was nonexistent. Leadership pointed in the direction of mission achievement with only nodding emphasis on adherence to flying regulations. If compromises with flying safety occasionally happened, no C–47 accidents resulted, reflecting the competence and judgment of the individual aircrews. Rules limiting an individual's consecutive hours of flying duty existed on paper, but in Farm Gate units they took second place to on-the-spot personal judgment. Air commando leaders respected the importance and the morale value of the Australian tropical hat, which became a symbol of air commando eliteness and individuality. Though banned by a four-star general visiting Bien Hoa in 1962, the tropical hat soon returned.[20]

A sense of wartime was present, although the C–47 aircrews did not experience the heavy losses and associated morale problems found among the strike aircraft sections. Enemy small-arms fire became a gradually increasing concern for the C–47 crews, who chose flight patterns about drop zones and airstrips with care. Records of battle damage were kept only incompletely, showing only that four C–47s received hits in 1962 and eight in 1963. Typical hits were from .30-caliber fire and these occurred most often in the delta country southwest of Saigon.

Accustomed to speaking out on all occasions, Farm Gate officers in their End of Tour Reports fervently criticized various matters, ranging from shortages of personal flying gear to a lack of current intelligence information, except by word of mouth among crews. An important handicap was the absence of permanently installed FM radios in the C–47s, necessitating use of a hand-carried set for communication with personnel on drop zones. Farm Gaters condemned rivalries between the U.S. Army and the Air Force over preponderance in tactical air roles. They agreed, however, that interservice relationships were excellent at the working level.[21]

The style of the air commandos was also distinctive in maintenance of their aging aircraft. One consideration in creating Jungle Jim was to simplify maintenance and move away from the complex methods demanded by the Air Force's newer aircraft. Although the C–130, for example, could land and take off at primitive sites, sustained operation at any location depended on bulky ground support equipment: auxiliary power sources, air conditioning and starting systems, and specialized test equipment. Returning to simpler planes, the air commandos relied heavily on the skill and resourcefulness of the individual crew chief while reducing the amount of materiel and the variety of special skills needed to assist him.

The extraordinary dedication of the Farm Gate maintenance men was beyond question, and this was reflected in their excellent aircraft incommission rates during the early months. Among C–47 aircrews, respect for the achievements of the mechanics, who kept the elderly craft airworthy, was profound. Operational ready rates remained high, while the men labored under conditions of high humidity and temperature and lacked many basic work facilities. Coordination between aircrews and ground crews was unusually close, and with only four C–47s assigned, pilots were personally acquainted with the maintenance history of each aircraft. Maintenance men often flew along on operational missions, gaining satisfaction from observing the results of their labors. Aircrews were usually pleased to welcome them aboard, for they represented precious assistance in case of a breakdown away from home base.[22]

During the second half of 1962, a heavy and sustained flying effort began to reveal fundamental weaknesses in the undermanned maintenance system. A Thirteenth Air Force operations staff visitor to Bien Hoa during the first week of November 1962 reported that maintenance standards and safety were being compromised in meeting the demanding flying schedule. Maintenance men were working long hours, seven days a week, with grossly inadequate quality control supervision. All aircraft appeared covered with dust and a film, and auxiliary aircraft equipment was improperly stored. The C–47s had been overflying programmed hours from the outset and were for the past five months exceeding eighty hours monthly per aircraft, contrary to the fifty-hour allocation upon which spare parts and support manning were based. That the fleet remained operational at all under these conditions was remarkable.[23]

To correct the immediate problem, forty-three maintenance men were dispatched to Bien Hoa on temporary assignment from Japan, pending action by the Air Force to increase manning. Additional men were selected with preference given to individuals experienced on the Farm Gate aircraft. A subsequent proposal to perform C–47 periodic inspections at Clark instead of Bien Hoa was rejected by PACAF, because of the flying time required for the round trip to Clark, and the desirability of keeping the dock personnel at Bien Hoa where they were available for unscheduled repairs. Aircraft were sometimes moved to the Philippines, however, for some unscheduled maintenance jobs and for major C–47 inspection and repair under contract with Philippines Air Lines.[24]

The austere living conditions encountered by the first Farm Gaters at Bien Hoa gradually improved, and the dirt-floored tent camp gave way to a cantonment of some seventy frame buildings, each with a wood floor, corrugated roof, and wooden side louvers. The "Bien Hoa huts" were reasonably comfortable, and set the pattern for construction of most of the later bases in Vietnam. Food at the military mess facility was unappetizing and the Vietnamese water-pumping system periodically broke down, necessitating the rationing of water. The abundant insect population of Bien Hoa made it necessary to sleep under mosquito netting, while the chronic heat and humidity quickly gave one's bedding a moldy aura. Officer aircrew members contrasted these primitive conditions with those of their C–123 counterparts in Saigon, who lived in Vietnamese hotels in that yet unspoiled city. Some nonflying personnel spoke of a feeling of imprisonment with the Bien Hoa cantonment and not everyone relished the compulsory calisthenics held at six in the morning. Uniformly applauded, however, were the irregular Saturday evening C–47 flights to Saigon, leaving in late afternoon and returning at midnight, which permitted a taste of the bright lights for twenty privileged passengers. Refinements such as movies, a library, officers' and airmen's clubs, chapel, and post office began to appear at Bien Hoa in 1963 and thereafter.[25]

The Farm Gate commandos of 1962 were conscious of their heritage from World War II, and events during the night of July 20, 1963, reviewed their tradition of achievement. Shortly before midnight, a ground alert SC–47 at Bien Hoa took off to drop flares in the delta. Six men were aboard, commanded by the pilot, Capt. Warren P. Tomsett. About 0200, the joint operations center (JOC) at Saigon radioed Captain Tomsett, asking whether he could attempt a rescue pickup at Loc Ninh, a thirty-six hundred-foot strip in the jungle border country north of Saigon. Tomsett took up the new heading, relinquishing the flare mission to a Vietnam Air Force C–47. Locating Loc Ninh in the blackness of the jungle was itself a worthy achievement, given the complete absence of radio aids. Arriving in the vicinity, the crew spotted several dim fires (paper soaked in gasoline and jammed on sticks) which roughly outlined the landing surface.

The Loc Ninh strip had been used in daylight by Farm Gate crews. The high trees at both ends and the rise at the middle of the runway made landing tricky under any circumstances. Captain Tomsett's first approach was too high and too fast, but on the second attempt, using full flaps and sharply reduced power, his landing was successful. Six wounded Vietnamese soldiers were lifted aboard by their comrades, using stretchers improvised from parachutes. During the critical takeoff moments later, a section of instrument panel lighting failed, necessitating dependence on a pocket flashlight. Small-arms fire could be seen on both sides of the aircraft, but the darkened aircraft was not hit. An American Special Forces medic who came aboard at Loc Ninh cared for the wounded.

The mission was without doubt an exceptional one, requiring extreme pilot skill along with the dedication of each crewmember. Probably other Farm Gate crews would have attempted the mission, and most, but perhaps not all (in the judgment of Tomsett's fellow pilots), would have succeeded.

General LeMay presented the crew the Mackay Trophy* at Hurlburt on July 9, 1964.[26]

Well before the end of their third year at Bien Hoa, however, it was clear that the eliteness and special ways of the air commandos did not adequately fit the actual situation. The flying mission, as it had actually evolved, did not demand the special training in low-level and covert work given to the original Jungle Jim squadron. Meanwhile, the air commando force in Florida encountered difficulty attracting volunteers, and by mid-1963 one-half of the newcomers were nonvolunteers. Few career air commandos remained at Hurlburt who had not previously served in Vietnam at least one six-month tour.

Tactical Air Command in April 1963 published a plan converting Farm Gate to a permanently manned unit, drawing upon personnel from the Air Force at large. Responsibility for providing tactical training remained with SAWC, and the first class of permanent assignees arrived at Hurlburt in late June. A mix of temporary and permanent assignees prevailed at Bien Hoa until year's end. Also, it was decided to double aircrew and maintenance manning, and to plan for higher sortie rates. Organizationally, the C–47 section at Bien Hoa became part of the 1st Air Command Squadron (Composite) under the 34th Tactical Wing, both organized on July 8, 1963, and placed under PACAF jurisdiction.[27]

It soon became evident at Bien Hoa that the flying skills of the newcomers were generally below those of the veteran Jungle Jim crews. This had been to a lesser extent true of the replacement crews under the temporary assignment system, and formal standardization-evaluation flight checks were prescribed for each new crewman. By 1964, however, instructor pilots were voicing serious misgivings about the declining flying proficiency. Pilots who had never flown aircraft with conventional landing gear might receive as little as sixteen hours of left seat (first pilot) flying time at Hurlburt. A C–47 instructor charged that "their landings and ground handling of the aircraft were substandard even on long, hard surface runways. They would definitely be unable to cope with crosswind landings on short, narrow, dirt strips." Addressing these conditions, leaders found it necessary to abandon the informal ways of the past. Formal training requirements, written regulations, and standard procedures became an essential part of the unit's activity as in other Air Force units in Vietnam.[28]

The double manning decision proved surprisingly damaging to aircrew morale. With twelve crews available to fly six ships, crewmen found them-

---

* The Mackay Trophy is awarded annually for "the most meritorious flight of the year." Since its inception in 1912, winners have included Rickenbacker, Arnold, Doolittle, Foulois, and Yeager. A C–47 first figured in the award in 1947, for a mission on the Greenland icecap.

selves with considerable spare time, and it was felt that flying proficiency was being lost. The 2d Air Division opposed any change, calculating arithmetically the total demand from missions, the ground-alert system, and necessary training. Otherwise, morale remained high, aided by the practice of giving high effectiveness reports and through a generous policy for awarding Air Medals.[29]

A tactical group battle damage study in late 1963 determined that a C–47 crewman serving a one-year tour had a probability of sixty-three percent of experiencing at least one battle damage. During the first half of 1964, recorded episodes of hits occurred at double the earlier rate. One aircraft took six hits only five miles from Bien Hoa. Viet Cong commandos penetrated the fencing at Nha Trang on the night of September 23, 1963, seriously damaging two parked Farm Gate C–47s. Engine failure during takeoff at Tan Son Nhut caused the destruction of another on January 22, 1964. No Americans were injured in any of these episodes since the February 1962 crash.[30]

The conversion to permanently assigned maintenance personnel was accompanied by major revisions in maintenance concepts. A separate consolidated maintenance squadron under the 34th Tactical Group removed the maintenance function from the operational squadrons. Simultaneously, the highly systematized methods prescribed by Air Force Manual 66–1 were put into effect, entailing rigid maintenance planning and scheduling. A few shortcomings persisted—three or four mechanics still shared a single toolbox. But the increases in manning, tightened supervision, and standardization in procedures soon brought measurable improvement. Operational readiness rates during 1964 held well over eighty percent against fifty-nine percent during the spring and summer of 1963. Maintenance man-hours stood at 10.5 per flying hour, against an AFM 66–1 standard of 10.0.

In maintenance, as in flying operations, the individualistic flavor of the past yielded to a more highly organized system, one designed to produce sustained results at reasonable efficiency. Through the entire period, the C–47 upheld its reputation for reliability and simplicity of maintenance. Although major mechanical problems afflicted the other Farm Gate types, the veteran Gooney Birds performed well, whether under the original Farm Gate system or AFM 66–1.[31]

The supply operation out of Nha Trang on behalf of the remote Special Forces camps continued until the end of 1964. Most of the time, two ships and three crews (each with an extra loadmaster) were kept at Nha Trang, permitting four round-trip missions each day. It was, nevertheless, apparent that the C–123 was superior to the C–47 both for airdrop and shortfield work; several of the C–47 pilots had themselves stated this in their End of Tour Reports. As administrative courier work increased on behalf of the various Air Force detachments in Vietnam, and after one ship was stationed at Bangkok for similar service in Thailand, the use of the C–47s for Special Forces support came to an end. The event was regretted by many of the C–47 crewmen, who took satisfaction in their demanding and colorful roles.[32]

With the passing of the camp-supply mission, the elitist aura of the air commando airlifters vanished. The small all-volunteer force of dedicated, if somewhat unruly professionals, had done all that was possible. The air commando name was not abandoned and was instead adopted by the large force of C–123 crews in Vietnam; but henceforth it was time for the application of Air Force standards.

IV. The Dirty Thirty and the Vietnamese Air Force Transport Arm

A decision to place U.S. Air Force pilots in Vietnamese transport cockpits was a temporary measure, intended to meet pressing Vietnamese pilot shortages. For the members of the Air Force Pilot Augmentation Group—the "Dirty Thirty" as they became known even in official circles—the assignment to Vietnam proved to be an unusual and memorable experience. The Americans discovered that the Vietnamese transport pilots were highly skilled, often more so than the Americans in the type of flying required in Vietnam. A camaraderie developed among them and they soon overcame differences of habit and outlook. Those Americans who took the trouble discovered a richness in the culture and language of the Vietnamese. The Dirty Thirty operation, beginning in the spring of 1962 and ending before Christmas 1963, probably changed the course of the war very little. But as a unique venture in allied cooperation at cockpit level, the endeavor was a success. The idea of organizing aircrews and squadrons of combined nationality was tried only occasionally thereafter, and then only in response to special needs. Whether further binational efforts might have significantly advanced the overall American-Vietnamese effort remains unproven.

The Vietnamese Air Force was established in 1950 to supplement the French Air Force in the war against the Viet Minh. French instructors used their native language, and provided pilot training at Nha Trang. The graduates were used as fillers in French units or assigned to all-Vietnamese units equipped with light airplanes. Individuals destined for multiengine transports and bombers received further training in France and North Africa. Vietnamese Air Force ground crewmen were assigned as trainees to French units, where they performed menial maintenance tasks. Vietnamese officers assumed all command responsibilities from the French in 1955.[1]

Expansion of the VNAF was modest during the late 1950s, and shortages of skilled aircrews and ground crews reflected a lack of technical orientation among the Vietnamese population. With the arrival of the Military Assistance and Advisory Group, Vietnam, U.S. Air Force personnel worked to improve the VNAF logistically by reorganizing their maintenance along American lines, installing systems for determining stock levels and requirements, and arranging for translations of technical publications. The Vietnamese maintenance and supply capabilities gradually improved, but remained below American standards. Selected Vietnamese were trained in air and ground specialties in the United States. By 1961 the VNAF included some 4,400 personnel and was organized into six operational squadrons, but remained far inferior in stature and influence to the Vietnamese Army which numbered 147,000 men.[2]

The first VNAF transport squadron was formed in the summer of 1955, and consisted of sixteen C–47s and nine qualified aircrews. Their yellow-and-red insignia replaced the old French Air Force markings. A second C–47 squadron was created in April 1957, and by the fall of the following year both were rated combat ready. Both squadrons operated from Tan Son Nhut, under the 1st Transport Group. Transition training consumed nearly half the group's flying effort, and the number of proficient crews reached twenty-three in 1961, not including those assigned to the civil airline, Air Vietnam. Flying skills were good and not a single accident marred the eighteen thousand hours of flying in 1961. Maintenance improved slowly. The C–47 flying rate rose from twenty-five hours monthly in 1957 to nearly twice that figure. The group acquired skill in parachute assault work, performing frequent training missions with the Army's airborne brigade, but actual combat assaults against the Viet Cong were rare. Routine transportation tasks, along with continued training, dominated flying activity. The two C–47 squadrons nevertheless represented an important resource that linked the regime to its people and was capable of moving troop units quickly into regions contested by the guerrillas.[3]

As U.S. air units arrived in Vietnam in early 1962, American leaders introduced long-term programs for Vietnamese Air Force expansion, looking toward future American withdrawal. A limiting factor in such plans was the shortage of Vietnamese pilots. Additional aircraft could be made available to the Vietnamese quickly, and logistical support could be facilitated by means of contract maintenance arrangements, but the only lasting solution for pilot shortages lay in training programs whose effect would be years in the future. In February 1962 the VNAF had only 225 trained pilots to fill the 271 cockpit and staff positions requiring flying officers. The problem repeatedly emerged during Secretary McNamara's monthly conferences in Hawaii and various approaches were discussed, including the use of American or third-country pilots in VNAF cockpits.[4]

General Anthis, in his capacity as chief of the Air Force Section of MAAGV, decided to place thirty U.S. Air Force pilots in the Vietnamese 1st Transport Group as one of several actions he took to expand the Vietnamese Air Force in early 1962. Placing American and Vietnamese pilots in the same cockpit had been proposed by Air Force Maj. Charles P. Barnett, who had served since 1960 as MAAGV advisor with the transport group and had himself flown regularly with the Vietnamese. The thirty Americans were designated as copilots and were integrated into Vietnamese C–47 aircrews. This allowed transfer of a number of Vietnamese pilots to T–28 strike aircraft which were being delivered to Nha Trang. The decision followed a Farm Gate C–47 crash and invited fewer adverse political reactions than using Americans in fighter cockpits. And it agreed with McNamara's wish to reduce American exposure to combat hazards. The Americans arrived in April 1962, immediately releasing eighteen Vietnamese copilots for the Nha Trang program. For the Americans (and this was not foreseen), the assignment provided unusual insight into the strengths and weaknesses of the Vietnamese airlift force, and indeed of the Vietnamese society.[5]

The original thirty Air Force pilots had been chosen the previous month under quotas levied upon the commands by Air Force, "for special category assignment to MAAG Vietnam." The selectees were to be fully and currently qualified to fly C–47s. Since little else was known about the assignment, few men volunteered. Several of those selected had been listed on recent manpower reports as surplus pilots within their commands. Some had considerable experience in the venerable C–47, although several required copilot qualification training after reaching Vietnam, particularly those who came from the Strategic Air Command (SAC). Perhaps one out of four had previous Tactical Air Command troop carrier experience. Nearly all were captains, except for Major Barnett who became chief of the group; most were aged thirty or more and several had flown in World War II.

Few of the copilots had more than a week or two to prepare for the assignment, and many moved their wives and children to new homes. Travel across the Pacific was by MATS contract carrier. The men arrived at Tan Son Nhut in several groups over a three-day period beginning in mid-April. Several pilots stationed in Japan served temporarily with the group until all stragglers were on hand. The first arrivals stayed in tents at Tan Son Nhut, but shortly all moved into the stucco-and-tile Dong Khanh Hotel in Cholon, a suburb of Saigon, where the second floor was leased to the Americans. An initial briefing at the downtown officers' club described the general situation in Vietnam, after which Major Barnett outlined the nature of the job ahead. The group then went by bus to Tan Son Nhut, where they met and spent several hours talking with their Vietnamese counterparts. Each American was assigned to one of the two Vietnamese squadrons, and each was detailed to fly initially with a particular Vietnamese pilot, after consideration of individual flying experience and language skill.

Although Major Barnett urged that the Americans share first-pilot responsibilities with the Vietnamese, General Anthis insisted that the Americans publicly be known to be serving as copilots, as laid down in the guiding directives. Several American officers were at first dissatisfied with this secondary role, especially since many Vietnamese were second lieutenants and all were youthful in appearance. The obvious flying experience of the Vietnamese, however, soon overcame the early American doubts. As mutual confidence developed among individuals, pilots of the nationalities routinely exchanged seats for part of each day's flying, allowing the Americans to perform many takeoffs and landings from the left seat. This practice was encouraged for its harmonious effect by the transport group commander, Lt. Col. Nguyen Cao Ky. As a result, those Americans not previously qualified as first pilots in the C-47 became so by the end of their tours. With the rarest exceptions, however, the Vietnamese officer remained officially in command of the aircraft.[6]

Dissimilar habits of flying continued to divide the groups. American pilots since World War II had been nurtured on concepts of flying safety. Energetic officers at all Air Force command levels served as flying safety officers, whose job it was to spearhead programs for reducing all conceivable hazards to flight. Also, the Air Force emphasized instrument-flying techniques, taught on the ground using elaborate training equipment and practiced in the air on nearly all flights. Flying by instruments became second nature for most American pilots, and rigid adherence to the procedures prescribed by instrument-flying rules and flying safety regulations became automatic. All this was wholly different from the flying techniques encountered by the Americans assigned to the VNAF transport group.

The Vietnamese never attempted an instrument approach if they could make a visual one. Upon reaching the vicinity of their destination, Vietnamese pilots invariably sought the slightest break in a cloud cover, making a tight downward spiral to get underneath the overcast for a visual landing. Radical aircraft maneuvers sometimes resulted, and the possibility of an inflight collision when flying in rain or near clouds was ever present. The Vietnamese, experienced in recognizing particular landmarks near the different airfields, could locate and approach the landing places accurately in limited visibility. The Americans at first were appalled by their seeming recklessness, but most came to realize that usually this was a safer way of doing the job, given the unreliability of most radio approach aids, the absence of heavy air traffic, and the experience and training of the Vietnamese in this way of flying. Very soon, the Americans themselves were doing the same things.

Less defensible was the custom among Vietnamese pilots of placing a cardboard panel across the windshield whenever the sun became an annoyance, shutting off forward visibility. Few American copilots became accustomed to flying blind in clear weather. Too, Americans at first were startled by the Vietnamese technique when taxiing close to another aircraft of having several crewmen stand on the wing of the parked ship, weighing it down sufficiently to permit vertical clearance. But this unorthodox method seemed to work well enough. Another source of concern among the Americans was that Vietnamese Air Force flying regulations, which supposedly governed all flying activity, were written only in Vietnamese and were unintelligible to the Americans.

The contrasting approaches to flying led to only one serious incident. It occurred during the early months and followed open criticisms by several of the understandably nervous Americans. Colonel Ky called a meeting in an attempt to reduce tensions. Officers of both groups aired their complaints and the Vietnamese had as many as the Americans. The confrontation had a salutary effect, contributing to the development of the fine relationships which marked future Dirty Thirty operations. The Americans became more tactful in offering advice on instrument flying and ground controlled approach work. The best approach they found was example, asking permission first and then demonstrating smooth techniques.

The early arrangement whereby each American flew only with a particular crew soon gave way in one squadron to a system of separate scheduling. Each copilot flew daily except after a night mission or alert duty, averaging about sixty hours per month. Ordinarily, a pilot wore his flying clothing to a breakfast before daylight at the downtown Five Oceans officers' hotel, arriving at the aircraft for a dawn takeoff. After six hours or so of flying and ramp time, the crew returned to Saigon for lunch and a siesta, usually followed in midafternoon by another flight mission. There was very little flying from noon Saturday until Monday, and no night missions except for flare work.

Within the American group, the less experienced members looked to the veterans for guidance. Information passed informally among them on hazards, facilities, and recommended techniques at the various airstrips and drop zones. The Air Force's traditional monthly flying safety meetings were faithfully organized by Capts. John A. Herschkorn, Jr., and Pat Kernan, spreading information on various incidents and observations of the past month. The Vietnamese were aware of this ritual among the Americans, but they never emulated it. No system existed for one American to administer a flight check to another. The Americans could ask a Vietnamese pilot how a Dirty Thirty officer was performing in the air, but the answer was invariably favorable since the Vietnamese disliked criticizing anyone. When replacements for the original Thirty began to arrive from the United States early in 1963, each newcomer was scheduled for one or two missions as an extra crewmember. The newcomer would then fly as copilot with Major Barnett and finally with the Vietnamese squadron commander, who gave instructions and checked on the American's ability to land the aircraft.

The Americans had few responsibilities during mission preparation. The Vietnamese navigator received the weather briefing and did the flight planning, while the flight mechanic inspected the aircraft. The American officer usually went by himself to the aircraft, met the rest of the crew there, and learned the planned itinerary. In keeping with the responsibilities of the copilot, the American handled the throttles, raised the landing gear, positioned the flaps, read the checklist (when used), and carried on radio conversations to English-speaking controllers. Although the Vietnamese pilots and some of their navigators spoke understandable English, the Vietnamese customarily spoke on the interphone in their own language. The American copilot thus was left to guess what was being discussed and his anxieties increased with the tone of urgency in the conversation.

In dividing tasks among the crewmembers, the Vietnamese carefully defined the responsibilities and status of the navigator, radio operator, and particularly the flight mechanic. The latter customarily started the engines, and he himself performed the final engine check or runup just prior to takeoff. The pilot watched while the flight mechanic did these things, and only rarely did he overrule the mechanic's judgment. If engine difficulties occurred during flight, the mechanic would take over control of the malfunctioning engine. This was a questionable practice since most Vietnamese engineers' arms were too short to reach easily the prop-feathering buttons. Most Americans became very watchful during takeoffs, lest a feathering button be accidentally or hastily activated by an excited Vietnamese engineer.

Several Dirty Thirty members witnessed the crash of a C–47 at Kontum in July 1962. As the ship lifted from the airstrip in the rain, smoke appeared in one of the nacelles. The propeller could be seen feathering, but almost at once the prop resumed turning as if the crew were attempting to restart. The aircraft stalled in a turn at the field's boundary and landed on its back. There were no survivors. Among those on board was Capt. William Bunker, the first and only American to lose his life as a member of the Dirty Thirty.

The Vietnamese pilots were well practiced at making steep, power-off approaches into short airstrips. The Dirty Thirty had little experience in this kind of work, being accustomed to power-on approaches into long, hard-surfaced runways. Capt. Kendall G. Lorch, after making a difficult power-off landing, was congratulated by his obviously pleased Vietnamese aircraft commander. The Vietnamese officer clapped the American on the shoulder and praised him with: "Oh, you made that landing just like a Frenchman."

The Vietnamese Air Force C–47s routinely made supply drops at isolated posts. Sometimes, four ships joined on drop missions, each aircraft making individual passes from a rectangular orbit. Several Vietnamese army men handled the loads inside the aircraft and pushed the bundles to the doorways for jettison. Vietnamese ground officers and American advisors on several occasions complained about drop inaccuracy; it appeared that Vietnamese crews often dropped while flying too far above the ground or too fast, decreasing accuracy and increasing breakage. At times surface wind calculations were ignored and aircrews failed to observe and correct for impact errors. Those American copilots with troop carrier experience gave cautious advice, bringing about some improvement.

The Vietnamese navigators, knowing the terrain and the weather conditions of the country, became expert in finding their way in limited visibility. They easily located remote drop zones and in several paratroop assault operations outperformed the American C–123 force, mainly because of their greater familarity with local landmarks. The Vietnamese pilot used a low frequency radio beacon both for homing and lines of position, an item long discarded by American aircrews. Aural-null techniques, whereby a crewman obtained reliable bearings without the use of automatic direction finding equipment, had to be relearned by the American copilots. Reliance on the simple magnetic compass required an awareness of its idiosyncrasies which were beyond the understanding of the Dirty Thirty. Oddly enough, the Vietnamese scheduled occasional medium-altitude and overwater-navigation training missions, allowing the navigator to practice celestial navigation, a skill seemingly of little value in the existing conflict. The transport group also operated a C–47 as a flying classroom for the Vietnamese Air Force navigator school.

The efforts of the American Farm Gate force toward night strikes led to the regular use of the Vietnamese Air Force C–47s as flareships. The Vietnamese joined in procedural tests in mid-1962, and soon afterwards their C–47s undertook nightly flare responsibilities. One ship orbited above Saigon each evening, ready to fly to any outpost under attack; a second aircraft took over the duty at midnight. A third remained on ground alert at Tan Son Nhut, while a fourth stood by. Throughout 1963, flareships and crews were kept at Da Nang and Pleiku, and rotated every six or seven days from Tan Son Nhut. The Dirty Thirty copilots flew on all flare missions. Their presence was especially useful in handling radio communications with American forward air controllers and strike pilots. A Vietnamese navigator would talk to the outpost below, and would translate the situation on the ground for the Dirty Thirty officer. The latter would then pass on the information to an American strike pilot and controller, and the Dirty Thirty copilot would coordinate the ensuing flare and strike runs. Interference and difficulties in making contact using the portable frequency modulation (FM) radios and the VHF set made radio communication at best frustrating, and the role of the American copilot in overcoming handicaps of language was often crucial.

Hostile small-arms fire could be encountered anywhere in Vietnam. Bullet holes tended to concentrate in the aircrafts' aft sections. Once, a serious situation occurred during a training mission when a bullet severed the rudder control cable, necessitating use of differential engine power for directional control of the aircraft during the landing. Outpost supply missions often met with fire, especially when terrain permitted only a single direction of approach. The psychological warfare leaflet-drop missions were the most hazardous, although these usually were accompanied by fighter escort and were flown at treetop level. Aircraft occasionally returned with their bottoms stained by foliage. At least two C–47s had engines shot out on leaflet missions. Loudspeaker missions were safer; they were flown in the single loudspeaker–equipped aircraft, known unofficially as the "sing along." The Dirty Thirty made their own survival kits, which contained equipment for use after bailout or crash landing. They consisted of materials obtained locally; official kits later were obtained and placed in the planes.

Aircraft maintenance proved eminently satisfactory. The C–47 was well known to the Vietnamese mechanics, many of whom had trained in the United States. American maintenance advisors worked closely with the Vietnamese, aiding them also in procurement of equipment and spare parts. The Vietnamese maintenance sections operated on a twenty-four-hour schedule, working into the night when necessary to prepare aircraft for the next day's missions. Most planes were back in flying status by early evening. The Americans were mildly surprised at the apparent carelessness of the Vietnamese aircrews in performing engine runup checks. The wet climate caused water in the leads and plugs, and ignition (mag drop) checks often were well out of tolerance. The aircrew would take off anyway, and the dubious Americans admitted that the engine seemed to function well in the air. Sometimes the Vietnamese abbreviated or simply omitted these checks.

With few exceptions, the Vietnamese scheduled their C–47s centrally from Saigon, although without a formal system of priorities and allocations. Airlift missions were of several types. Airline passenger routes were flown from Saigon, with stops at Qui Nhon, Da Nang, Hue, and Pleiku. All sorts of people including women, children, and priests would get on and off at each point, but the official nature of their business was unclear to the Americans. Army combat units sometimes were moved, the aircraft shuttling them between locations for several days. Supply missions were at times aromatic, involving the delivery of livestock on the hoof, since refrigeration was nonexistent in the countryside. On one occasion, a six hundred-pound steer was paradropped. The C–47s sometimes carried senior officers on trips to the corps headquarters, entailing long waits and inconvenience for the aircrew. But by custom a general officer distributed pocket money to each crewmember, including the American copilot. All things considered, the Dirty Thirty officers judged that the Vietnamese used their airlift arm for necessary and useful activities.[7]

From the first, the Vietnamese officers were pleasant to the Americans and many lasting friendships were formed, particularly with Americans who appreciated local food and customs. Nearly all the Vietnamese pilots spoke some English, but with accents not readily understood by Americans. Hand signals for use in the cockpit were worked out, and many Americans took courses in Vietnamese or learned a little Pidgin French. Basic communication was English, however, as the Vietnamese improved in their use of it and the Americans became accustomed to the accents. The two national groups came together frequently in evening gatherings at Saigon restaurants, usually instigated by Colonel Ky. On some occasions, the Americans provided or participated in the entertainment. A few American officers received invitations to visit the clean if modestly furnished homes of the Vietnamese officers. On missions away from Tan Son Nhut, the Americans ate with the Vietnamese crewmen. And at Da Nang, where crews staged for a week of flare alert duty, the Americans often chose to stay in the Vietnamese billets rather than in the American tent compound. Certain Dirty Thirty members became known among the Vietnamese for their skill in flying, or for their willingness to fly extra missions. Some Americans became interested in Saigon charity projects.

There was a strong tendency among the Dirty Thirty to think of themselves as part of the Vietnamese Air Force. Most were quite ready to join the Vietnamese crewmen in criticizing the "Americans"—meaning the American C–123 crews at Tan Son Nhut—for mistakes during combined assault operations. The Vietnamese pilots were both likable and well educated; some had lived in the north during boyhood, and others had relatives in the Diem government. When tardiness or lackadaisical performance occurred among Vietnamese crewmembers, the Americans kept their criticisms within their own circle, understanding that for the Vietnamese the war was no mere career diversion which would end in twelve months.

In the official chain of command, the Pilot Augmentation Group was placed under an Air Force senior advisor to the transport group (Major Barnett), who in turn was under the operations branch of the Air Force Section of MAAGV. Major Barnett was thus the official link to higher American agencies, and his daily activities reflected the administrative and coordinating responsibilities. Within the Dirty Thirty group there was little formal organization. Two rooms near the Vietnamese squadron area served as a combination office and ready room for the Americans, manned around the clock by a duty officer from the Thirty. Squadron and flight commanders existed on paper, but in practice the leaders tended to be those whose experience and temperament qualified them.

One of these leaders was Capt. Robert "Bear" Barnett, who was later killed in a B–57 accident in Vietnam. Barnett was a gregarious character of seemingly inexhaustible energy. He arranged group photographs, designed the Dirty Thirty emblem, scrounged for survival gear, organized entertainments, and challenged Colonel Ky to shooting matches. Dirty Thirty veterans ten years later generally agreed that it was primarily "Bear" Barnett who inspired the group pride which came to mark them. The nominal chief, Maj. Charles P. Barnett, gave free rein to informality but supervisory control became tighter under his successor, Maj. Raymond E. Nicholson. The unconventional style of the Thirty, however, diminished little.

C-47s on the flightline, Tan Son Nhut, 1962.

(1)   (2)

Dirty Thirty pilots: (1) Capt. Robeson S. Moise and (2) Captains Ty Lewis, (left) Harold Sweet, and Bill Blackburn (right).

VNAF officer and Capt. Joseph Grant with the Dirty Thirty insignia, Tan Son Nhut.

DIRTY THIRTY

The origin of the Dirty Thirty name is unclear. One legend has it that the nickname came from an Army officer's comment at the unscrubbed appearance of the Dirty Thirty members lunching at the Five Oceans after a morning of flying. Actually, living conditions in the Dong Khahn Hotel and in the Hong Kong Hotel were far from primitive, although cold-water showers were a frequent (and sometimes useful) shock. Flying clothing shortages led to the wearing of unofficial paraphernalia, including pieces of civilian clothing, scrounged weapons, and survival gear. Replacements arriving in 1963 were forewarned to bring extra suits. The Thirty nevertheless relished their nickname, along with their distinctive though unofficial insignia. The emblem featured the profile of a goat, a creature said to represent both the Vietnamese symbol of fertility and the American symbol of odor. Others pointed out that the Vietnamese referred to the Americans as goats who ate from tin cans.

Morale among the men was high, sustained by group solidarity and satisfaction with the flying job. Occasional flights to Singapore, Kuala Lumpur, Bangkok, and Hong Kong were pleasant breaks and were sought by both the Vietnamese and the Americans. Mail and pay reached the Americans through the Military Assistance Advisory Group (MAAG) in Saigon. Medically, the Thirty proved a hardy lot except for periodic gastrointestinal troubles which seemed to afflict everyone whether on Vietnamese or American diets. None of the Thirty contracted hepatitis. Each individual received one Air Medal but Vietnamese awards could not be accepted. Flying time was not listed as "combat" on individual flying records. The greatest morale boosters and unfailing occasions for noisy celebrations were the successive reductions in tour length (originally eighteen months), down to fifteen months, and finally to one year. The replacement of the original Thirty over several months in early 1963 produced no change in the spirit and performance of the unit.[8]

If the Thirty seemed forgotten in matters of equipment, certainly their reputation was widely known. *Aviation Week* reported in August 1962 that the men were "meeting their responsibilities with dignity, patience, and excellent results." The troop information journal of the Air Force included an informative six-page article on the Thirty, and senior Air Force officers occasionally visited the group, among them General Anthis and Gen. Walter C. Sweeney, Jr., the commander of TAC. Some of the Dirty Thirty were introduced to local public officials at outlying airfields: Capt. Robeson S. Moise met President Diem and the American ambassador while on the ground at Can Tho. Each man received an invitation to the ambassador's 1962 Christmas party, and many attended affairs held by the air attaché office.[9]

A central figure who contributed immeasurably to the harmony surrounding the Dirty Thirty venture was the energetic commander of the Vietnamese Air Force Air Transport Group, Ky. Softspoken and sincere in manner, Ky was liked and admired by the Thirty. Trained under the French, Ky himself flew regularly, usually on the more demanding missions. Dirty Thirty members who shared his cockpit found him a flying "artist." Ky later revealed that he had misgivings at the start of the venture, recalling that during an earlier tour at the U.S. Air Force Air Command and Staff School, his pride of nationality and mistrust of foreigners caused him to become narrow-minded toward Americans. Nevertheless, Ky displayed sensitivity in countless considerate actions toward the Americans, episodes which belied his later ignoble public image in the United States. As head of the Vietnamese Air Force in 1964, Ky requested that Major Nicholson, the second chief of the Dirty Thirty, be reassigned as his personal advisor. Nicholson was not sent, but the incident suggested that the Dirty Thirty experience may have aided indirectly in later relations between the allies, when Ky's role in his country's politics enlarged.[10]

The Buddhist agitation which disturbed South Vietnam in mid-1963 raised concern in American circles that the Dirty Thirty members might be photographed transporting Buddhist prisoners. Acting on instructions from the MAAG staff, Major Nicholson instructed his officers to quit any mission when Buddhist prisoners were brought on board. More than once, an American copilot remained behind, to be picked up later. During the crisis culminating in the overthrow of President Diem on November 1, the Dirty Thirty were confined to their hotel, where they watched their Vietnamese associates making flaredrops over the city. The Americans resumed their flying duties soon after the coup.

The decision to close down the Dirty Thirty operation was made well before November 1963. Withdrawal of the American copilots was part of a one thousand-man reduction of U.S. forces in Vietnam, undertaken as a gesture toward ultimate American departure. In deciding to end the Dirty Thirty operation, a temporary reduction of Vietnamese Air Force C–47 capability was anticipated, though it was expected that Vietnamese graduates from pilot training programs would restore the unit to full strength by the next summer.

Maj. Jacob H. Rodenbough served as Dirty Thirty chief during the final weeks, having replaced Major Nicholson unexpectedly in the fall. Inexperienced Vietnamese copilots at the time arrived as replacements for the Thirty, and it was necessary for the newcomers to fly on missions with the most qualified Vietnamese instructors. The resulting overload among the Vietnamese pilots brought a decision to use two American pilots on certain night flare missions, without a Vietnamese pilot on board. Only the most qualified Americans were thus used, always with a Vietnamese navigator aboard the aircraft. Dirty Thirty members had not previously held aircraft commander responsibilities, though a few were granted the honorary title.

On December 4, 1963, two dozen Dirty Thirty officers waited to board an American Air Force jet transport at Tan Son Nhut bound for home. Two officers remained in Vietnam to serve as advisors with the 43d Air Transport Group, as the First Group was redesignated. The departing Americans wore Vietnamese Air Force pilot wings recently awarded to them by Colonel Ky at a special ceremony; many displayed handlebar mustaches. Several Vietnamese pilots attended the ceremony, constituting a sufficient if quiet honor. Most of the Americans returned to preferred assignments, including several who had requested duty in Europe or Japan. Collectively, the two Dirty Thirty groups had logged more than twenty-thousand flying hours in Vietnam.[11]

One perceptive Dirty Thirty member, Capt. Kenneth M. MacCammond, afterwards outlined the significant achievements of the group. First were the direct accomplishments—the participation by the Americans in airlift and flare operations, and their role in releasing Vietnamese pilots for strike aircraft work. The second was a less tangible but a more lasting contribution—helping the Vietnamese to acquire the kind of air discipline necessary later when large numbers of American planes began to use the same airspace, increasing operations at night and by instruments, and by example suggesting the position of the military officer in a democracy.

Finally, to Captain MacCammond, the Dirty Thirty experience offered perspectives on insurgency warfare potentially valuable to American commanders and planners. General Anthis on several occasions, according to one Dirty Thirty veteran, urged the members to "keep our eyes and ears open and learn everything we can about counterinsurgency warfare." MacCammond and others had followed Anthis' advice, exploiting their unusual vantage point to seek out the nature of the conflict. No final report or debriefing program was ever undertaken, however, to bring together the lessons of the Dirty Thirty venture. Except among the individuals themselves, most of whom were scattered in unrelated assignments, the store of experience and the outlook was by and large lost to the Air Force.[12]

The members of the Pilot Augmentation Group were not the first Americans in war to share cockpits with Asian allies. American airmen had been mixed with Thai C–47 crews during the Korean War, and others had flown with the Chinese late in World War II. In Vietnam, however, the Americans came not as cadres, but as partners. The Dirty Thirty venture verified the ability of the American airman to work and fly in close partnership with allies of different culture and outlook. MacCammond and Capt. Harold L. Sweet listed as the keys to successful relationships of this kind: an adventurous palate, the energy to learn a new language, an honest curiosity in the history and symbols of a different culture, competence in one's own work, and perhaps most of all the total absence of superior attitudes in personal dealings. That the Dirty Thirty members, haphazardly chosen and without guidance on such matters from higher authority, by

TACTICAL AIRLIFT

and large understood and followed these guidelines reflected favorably on the nature of American democratic society.

Plans for expansion of the Vietnamese Air Force reflected the strong American desire to withdraw American forces from Vietnam. Secretary McNamara repeatedly expressed the intent to "Vietnamize" the war effort (although the word was not yet in official use). American Air Force officers, however, understood the organizational and human prerequisites for meaningful VNAF growth. During a three-hour conference in Saigon in April 1962, for example, President Diem and General LeMay revealed very different outlooks—Diem pressed for additional aircraft, while LeMay stressed that the president could get more out of the craft he already possessed.[13]

Two issues shaped planning for the future Vietnamese airlift arm. Most significant was the question of priorities—whether to focus available trained manpower into fighter or transport units. McNamara in the spring of 1963 challenged the existing program as too heavy in fighters and too light in transports and helicopters; a year later, the secretary stated that Vietnamese pilots assigned to transport units should be shifted to fighter units, letting Americans absorb a greater airlift role. A second factor was the Vietnamese wish to acquire C–123s, a proposal first raised by Diem in 1962, since the 123 had better payload, airdrop, and shortfield qualities than the C–47. U.S. Air Force officials agreed with Diem's logic, but held that the Air Force needed its C–123s for duty in Vietnam and in the future air commando structure. Shifting outlooks and other considerations produced many changes in programming for the future force, but in actuality the transport force remained at two squadrons and the conversion to C–123s was delayed for nearly a decade after it was first proposed.[14]

Most of the members of the Vietnamese Air Force joining the C–47 squadrons as replacements for the Dirty Thirty were recent graduates of flying schools in the United States. Recruitment of pilot candidates had been difficult due to the limited education of the Vietnamese youth, the severe security investigation required by the Diem regime, and the need for English language familiarity. After further training in English, a total of 166 students completed undergraduate pilot training during 1963 and 1964, including two hundred hours of flying in the T–28. Those selected for assignment to the transport squadrons underwent further training in the C–47. By mid-May 1964 the Vietnamese Air Force reported a total of ninety-four C–47 pilots and copilots, but approximately twenty short of the full cockpit and staff authorization.[15]

Americans found little to criticize in the technical competence of the Vietnamese C–47 aircrews. An inspection team from the Thirteenth Air Force in January 1964 contrasted the "superb" work of the C–47s in flareship roles with the ineffective performance of the Vietnamese fighter squadrons. On other occasions, however, the Americans charged the Vietnamese airlifters with a lack of dedication. A senior MACV officer, in a conversation with Vietnamese defense officials, complained of the inactivity of the Vietnamese C–47s on weekends. Though the Vietnamese seemed to agree with the Americans, reform was not forthcoming. Citing an example of apparent dereliction of duty by a Vietnamese flareship crew, Col. Winston P. Anderson, director of operations for the 2d Air Division, pointed out to General Anthis that the Americans had to continue "pushing" the Vietnamese. The U.S. Air Force was aware that its own reputation was in part at stake in the performance of the Vietnamese Air Force. Replying to a criticism of the Vietnamese combat motivation by General Earle G. Wheeler, Army chief of staff, the American Air Force pointed out that similar observations could be made of the Vietnamese army.[16]

Air Force officers tried to assure critics that the Vietnamese C–47s were used only for worthwhile purposes. General LeMay asked PACAF in early 1962 to look into reports by Air Staff visitors that the transports were hauling officials and their families. Special concern was given to the C–47 flareships kept at Da Nang and Pleiku, where the Vietnamese army corps commanders habitually used the aircraft for other purposes. The problem came to the surface during an attempt to rescue the crew of a downed U.S. Army helicopter in December 1963. The flareship, supposedly on alert at Pleiku, was discovered by the Americans to be flying on a "personal junket"; a U.S. Air Force C–123 flareship arrived on the scene too late and two American lives were lost. Vietnamese Air Force headquarters subsequently ordered that the alert flareships not be diverted for personal use under any circumstances, but it remained difficult for Vietnamese junior officers to resist the orders of the very senior corps commanders.[17]

Senior Vietnamese officers put off all American proposals to combine Vietnamese and American transport efforts under a single scheduling and allocations apparatus. For the Americans, centralization promised better efficiency and would strengthen the Air Force case for bringing the U.S. Army Caribous into a consolidated system. The Vietnamese joined in a combined movements allocation board in mid-1963, but this led to no significant merger of effort. The Vietnamese contributed only a single C–47 daily for a predetermined itinerary under the control of the American airlift system. Col. Lyle D. Lutton, Jr., recent commander of the United States' C–123 force in Vietnam, addressed the problem in a 1963 article prepared for a professional Air Force journal. He charged that repeated American efforts to consolidate airlift requirements encountered "a disappointing lack of interest and recognition from Vietnamese officialdom in eliminating duplication of effort." The PACAF staff returned Colonel Lutton's article with the statement that criticism of the Vietnamese Air Force should be deleted or moderated "for political reasons."[18]

Attempted consolidation began by late 1963, when the Vietnamese airlift scheduling officers (each of whom spoke good English) worked at desks not far from the U.S. Air Force controllers. The Americans could thus informally ascertain whether scheduled Vietnamese aircraft could carry items in American aerial ports; conversely, the Americans sometimes helped out the Vietnamese by squeezing an extra sortie on top of a day's schedule. Since the overall Vietnamese capability was in any event relatively small, a further merger was not pressed strongly by the Americans; more immediately important was the matter of enlarging the total airlift capability of the C–47s, primarily by training more aircrews.[19]

By 1964 the Vietnamese Air Force took pride in the development of its fixed wing airlift arm. Although the total lift capacity was small by comparison with the tonnages hauled by the much larger fleet of American transports in the Far East, the Vietnamese C–47 units represented a technically skilled cadre upon which to base future growth. Relations between the Vietnamese and the Americans were satisfactory, and were clearly strengthened by the success of the Dirty Thirty venture. Vietnamese reluctance to yield control of their transports to a combined agency dominated by the Americans was understandable and even justifiable, recognizing that one day the Vietnamese would stand alone.

V. Mule Train—The First Year

A single squadron of Tactical Air Command C–123 Providers arrived in Vietnam in January 1962 as part of Project Mule Train. A second squadron followed in midyear. The C–123 squadrons were neither elite volunteer units like Farm Gate nor improvisations like the Dirty Thirty detachment. Both C–123 units were squadrons of the professional peacetime Air Force, accustomed to conventional methods of flying and management. In Vietnam, however, the C–123 aircrews faced the same primitive operating environment confronting the C–47 crewmen, and quickly learned to apply the same essential techniques.

Although ranking low in prestige in an Air Force dominated by newer and more powerful aircraft, the early C–123s and their crews performed well in Vietnam. Their contributions foreshadowed much larger numbers of transports that were to operate later in Vietnam, while the apparatus for managing their operations became the nucleus for the future system of scheduling and control.

Since the beginning of its Air Force service in 1955, the C–123 had proved conclusively its safety and reliability. The aircraft's conservative design and engineering simplicity minimized mechanical problems and its incommission rates consistently surpassed those of the C–130 and the C–124. The 464th Troop Carrier Wing at Pope Air Force Base, North Carolina, operated the five C–123 squadrons still in active status in late 1961. The unit had experienced only one fatal accident in three years.[1]

The C–123B's characteristics were sound if unspectacular. The cargo compartment held sixty troops, or a wide variety of vehicles and cargo. A hydraulically operated rear ramp and numerous high-strength tiedown fittings facilitated cargo loading. Welded tubular steel construction around the cockpit, and heavy compression members elsewhere, offered crash protection—a vestige of the plane's origins as a glider. The 123 was not pressurized and usually cruised at 5,000 feet and 140 knots true airspeed. The aircraft could haul a maximum eight-ton payload twelve hundred miles round trip, an adequate range for transoceanic missions.[2]

One of the C–123's most prominent features was its shortfield landing capability. During an assault landing the aircraft began a relatively flat, power-on approach with flaps lowered fully. Upon crossing the final obstacle, the pilot further reduced power until touchdown. Reverse-pitch propellers and an antiskid braking system aided to cut short the landing roll. Ground-roll distance for a well-executed landing was under one thousand feet, but an additional eight hundred feet were required to clear a fifty-foot obstacle during descent. Landings in crosswinds were hazardous, but TAC decided against a wider landing-gear modification, believing that the C–123 was obsolescent.[3]

The powerplant for the C–123B consisted of two eighteen-cylinder, air-cooled Pratt and Whitney reciprocating engines. Data from suitability testing in 1955 indicated unsafe margins in case of loss of one engine during takeoff, and the Fairchild firm began planning to add auxiliary jet engines. General McCarty in 1955 made it plain that "if the aircraft will not perform any better than indicated on these charts, we want jet augmentation or we don't want the aircraft at all." The C–123J, tested at Edwards in 1958, incorporated two turbojet engines in wingtip pods. It achieved a significant safety margin for single-engine flight and reduced takeoff distances slightly, but the financial costs prohibited modification of the fleet.[4]

Another shortcoming lay in the C–123's airdrop qualities. The size and strength of the rear ramp limited cargo bundles to two thousand pounds, although several bundles could be released in succession over an elongated drop zone. Early models of the aircraft had no provision for a navigator, whose role in air drops was essential. A navigator's seat was later added in the forward part of the cargo compartment behind the copilot, and rudimentary navigation equipment was installed. The navigator's outside visibility, which was important for low-level and airdrop work, was poor.[5]

Most aircrews and ground crews of the 464th Wing were veterans in the C–123. Their skills in airlanded assault and supply techniques were well honed, and they repeatedly earned praise for their work in major joint exercises in the United States. Each aircrew consisted of two pilots and a flight mechanic; one navigator was generally assigned for every four crews.[6]

The Mule Train deployment order followed by two days McNamara's final decision to relocate the C–123. By Operation Order 19–6, December 6, 1961, TAC directed the 464th Wing to send a C–123 squadron of sixteen aircraft with its support personnel for 120 days temporary duty in the Far East. Airmen and officers at Pope had already learned of the impending move at a general meeting addressed by Col. William T. Daly and by Lt. Col. Floyd K. Shofner, commanders respectively of the 464th Wing and the 346th Troop Carrier Squadron. The operation was labeled "a classified training exercise to Clark Air Base," but most individuals surmised that Southeast Asia was to be their ultimate destination. The 346th Squadron, probably the wing's most competent squadron, was chosen for the venture along with sufficient support personnel to operate "as a tactical airlift force." Squadron personnel who were not eligible or not qualified for the operation were replaced by individuals from other wing units. In addition, aircrew loadmasters, previously assigned to aerial port squadrons, were shifted to the 346th. In all, 243 persons were to be sent.

Preparations were hasty, since the first eight aircraft were scheduled to depart on December 10. During their final days at Pope, the aircrews planned the overseas flights and attended lectures on survival, long-range cruise control, and the operation of the newly installed auxiliary fuel and oil tanks. Each aircraft was flown on a seven-hour long-range test mission. And each crew underwent a proficiency check flight. Crewmen felt this was unnecessary, since all of them had been previously judged "combat ready." Finally, fifty-six tons of equipment were prepared for Military Air Transport Service airlift to the Far East.[7]

Final briefing for the movement was held on Saturday, December 9. After a twenty-four-hour delay caused by poor weather, the first eight aircraft led by Colonel Shofner left Pope. The second group, although scheduled to take off a day later, remained at Pope over the Christmas holidays and departed on January 2. This flight was led by the squadron operations officer, Maj. Wayne J. Witherington. The first eight planes arrived at Clark a week later. The Pacific crossing was fatiguing but uneventful, with landings at Hickam, Wake, and Guam. The aircraft flew in loose formations of three, minimizing the chance for error by navigators more accustomed to a different kind of flying. Newly installed loran sets provided regular lines of position which, when combined with sun observations, gave accurate fixes. Overall the ferry operations were safe, if slow, and set the pattern for future C–123 transoceanic flights.[8]

The first group of C–123s remained at Clark for two weeks. The aircrews recuperated from the long Pacific flight and attended intelligence and theater operations briefings given by the Thirteenth Air Force staff. On December 30, four ships were ordered to Vietnam and their crews made final preparations. Three days later, led by Colonel Shofner, the planes were flown to Tan Son Nhut. The crews arrived without ceremony and, finding no arrangement for billeting, made their ways to downtown Saigon hotels. The C–123s began airlift operations on January 3, 1962.[9]

Defining how the Mule Train force was to be used, American officials emphasized tactical applications over logistical. Mule Train's primary mission, according to an early Pacific Air Forces concept, and reflected thereafter in Air Staff memoranda, was to provide "tactical airlift support of South Vietnamese armed forces." A secondary mission was to perform airlift logistical support for 2d Air Division advanced echelon activities in Southeast Asia. Specific tasks designated by Pacific Air Forces included troop drops, assault landings, supply drops, aeromedical evacuation, and air resupply, in that order. Adm. Harry D. Felt, USN, Commander in Chief, Pacific Command, told Secretary McNamara during a mid-December 1961 conference in Hawaii that the C–123s would be used in combat support roles, as opposed to routine transportation services; McNamara explicitly approved these roles. Army Chief of Staff General Decker, in Senate hearings on January 26, 1962, stated that American airlift forces

TACTICAL AIRLIFT

were in Vietnam to provide tactical mobility for Vietnamese ground forces.[10]

Air Force officers—bred on AFM 1–9 and existing airlift doctrine—also understood the much broader applicability of airlift forces, beyond narrowly defined tactical roles. The Pacific Air Forces staff, for example, described the potential for a true "air logistic system" for South Vietnam. Air transport, the staff believed, could be particularly valuable in Southeast Asia, "because of the proven vulnerability of rail and road networks and the high manpower and equipment costs of providing safe passage thereon." Airlift could supply isolated strongpoints and support offensive sweeping operations, affording freedom from surface supply. The meager size of the initial Mule Train force prevented full implementation of these ideas, but it was clear that the Pacific Air Force had not forgotten established doctrine.[11]

Proposals for operating the C–123s from Clark or for apportioning the aircraft among the regional senior advisors in Vietnam quickly led to the development of a concept of centralized countrywide control. On December 28, 1961, a team of 315th Air Division officers arrived at Tan Son Nhut, for the purpose of developing a plan for introducing the Mule Train force. Col. Lopez J. Mantoux, deputy commander of the division, soon joined the group to provide overall guidance. As airlift specialists, the officers of the 315th understood the need for aerial port and mission control systems for any sustained operation, but this need was overshadowed by the emphasis on tactical employment and by the immediate question of how to handle the C–123 entry. The team recommended introduction of twelve aircraft during January and a daily commitment of six, each to be utilized for four flying hours. A route structure and an all-weather capability would be gradually developed as the aircrews gained familiarity with operating conditions. Consistent with AFM 1–9, the team recommended creation of a joint agency to allocate airlift priorities, anticipating that tactical missions would in all cases receive the highest priority. Personnel from the 315th Air Division, on January 2, 1962, formed the airlift branch of the Vietnamese Air Force/2d ADVON joint operations center at Tan Son Nhut and thereafter undertook to manage C–123 daily mission activity.[12]

Early missions were almost entirely logistical. Cargo usually consisted of foodstuffs and relatively small items. Wheeled loads, such as jeeps and power generators, were commonly carried; helicopter rotor blades and other materiel were frequently hauled between Saigon and Qui Nhon in support of the U.S. Army helicopter company at the latter location. Personnel lifts supported the installation of Air Force radar and communications equipment for the tactical air control system (TACS). No training or advisory role existed, and there was no rule requiring Vietnamese personnel on board. The C–123s were marked with American insignia, and the

Viet Cong prisoners unload sacks of rice from a C–123 during a Mule Train resupply mission, June 1962.

aircrews wore military clothing. The four aircraft and their crews at Tan Son Nhut were joined on January 2 by two additional ships and aircrews weekly until the desired strength of twelve was reached late in the month.

During January, Mule Train aircraft flew a total of 548 hours, without accident or hazardous incident. No mission was canceled for lack of ready aircraft. During February, operations settled into a routine whereby seven ships flew daily missions of approximately four flying hours in length. Two aircraft and crews (with maintenance personnel) were positioned at Da Nang for operations in the northern region. Four were rotated to Clark for major maintenance. Briefing the Chief of Staff in March, the Air Staff reported that the early performance of the Mule Train unit had "exceeded expectations."[13]

The Mule Train squadron encountered essentially the same operating problems faced by the Vietnamese and American C–47 crews. There was no lavish apparatus of ground radar, navigation aids, communications, and instrument approach facilities such as the airmen in the United States were used to. A dozen low frequency radio beacons located at the major airfields gave some navigational assistance, but the Americans considered the signals too unreliable for instrument landing approaches. Attempts to obtain instrument clearances, moreover, usually led to communications troubles

TACTICAL AIRLIFT

and wasteful delays. It therefore seemed equally safe and far more convenient to fly under visual flight rules, whereby the crew was responsible for its own traffic clearance. When cloud penetration was unavoidable, the recently installed TACS radars at Saigon, Da Nang, and Pleiku provided informal traffic advisory assistance. The C–123 crews quickly became accustomed to visual flying techniques long practiced by the Vietnamese—the spiraling climb or descent through a break in an overcast, the cruise either just above or just below a cloud layer, the visual approach and landing in conditions of marginal visibility. All crew members joined in looking out for other aircraft. These methods, strange to airmen accustomed to rigid instrument procedures, continued to characterize troop carrier operations in Vietnam throughout the next decade.

Vietnamese controllers, using VHF and UHF radio communications regulated takeoffs and landings at the major fields. Most of the controllers spoke English, although their transmissions often had to be repeated, either by a tower operator or by a C–123 copilot. The system was generally satisfactory, except when traffic became particularly heavy, then American controllers joined the Vietnamese, especially at the often saturated Tan Son Nhut tower. Navigation facilities gradually improved with the installation of omnidirectional radio stations at Da Nang and Nha Trang, and tactical air navigation stations at Tan Son Nhut, Pleiku, and Da Nang. Precision ground controlled approach equipment for instrument landing approaches was placed in operation at Tan Son Nhut, and later at Soc Trang, Vung Tau, and Da Nang.[14]

A dozen hard-surface airfields became the nucleus for the Mule Train route structure. These were generally located about main population centers and military bases, and had been used by the C–47s of Air Vietnam and the Vietnamese Air Force. C–123 scheduled passenger runs and military logistics missions linked Da Nang, Tan Son Nhut, Nha Trang, Bien Hoa, Pleiku, Ban Me Thuot, Hue, Da Lat, Soc Trang, Qui Nhon, and Vung Tau, and virtually every Mule Train sortie took off or landed at one of these airfields. These air stations made up a chain of primary fields, affording an adequate skeleton for a countrywide airlift system. Coverage was least satisfactory in the Mekong Delta country in the south, where soft ground made construction difficult.[15]

Aircrews generally flew about three of every four days. Their itineraries allowed the aircraft to return to Tan Son Nhut by nightfall. Aircrews made every effort to return to Saigon each evening, since sleeping and messing facilities elsewhere were rare. Mechanical breakdowns away from Tan Son Nhut were infrequent; a stranded crew needing maintenance assistance usually got word back to Mule Train operations through another aircraft or by land telephone. A crew flew the prescribed itinerary, checking in with the control towers where these existed, but flight following and close mission control from Tan Son Nhut were nearly impos-

A hard-surface airfield at Ban Me Thuot, 1963.

sible. Communications problems became vexing when a crew could find no cargo for pickup after landing at the specified airfield. To retrace the situation by land telephone through the joint operations center consumed many hours of valuable crew and aircraft time.[16] Another concern was the underuse of cargo space. The Mule Train squadron hauled 1,996 tons of passengers and cargo during 921 sorties in February and March, an average of a little better than two tons per sortie, compared with the aircraft capacity of five or six tons. Several factors explained the low usage figures, including the difficulty of making available large cargo loads for the smaller locations and the lack of backhaul cargo at many points. Nevertheless, in order to raise the allowable maximum payload of the C–123s, some two thousand pounds of unnecessary gear, including heaters and anti-icing accumulators, were removed from the aircraft in April. Restrictions were temporarily imposed reducing takeoff margins for the sake of heavier payloads. Colonel Shofner warned against this trend, judging that "eventually equipment would falter and an accident would result."[17]

Another measure to increase the overall airlift capacity followed the February crash of a Ranch Hand spray C–123 and the consequent decision to halt defoliation operations. Two Ranch Hand aircraft and their crews returned to the United States and were replaced by airlift C–123s and crews, thus increasing the size of the Mule Train force to eighteen. Spray equipment was removed from the several remaining Ranch Hand planes, allowing their use for airlift work.[18]

The use of the aerial spray crews in airlift work, however, was not successful. The original Mule Train squadron (the 346th) was a highly skilled group and had received a Tactical Air Command flying safety award for accident-free flying during 1961. The initial squadron's crew members were proud that to the spring of 1962 not a single Mule Train aircraft had been so much as scratched in Vietnam. By contrast, although many of the Ranch Hand people originally came from the 464th Wing, the skills demanded for spray tasks were different from those needed for tactical airlift. On April 20, 1962, a Ranch Hand aircraft and crew took off from Da Nang on a cargo-haul sortie to Dong Ha, near the demilitarized zone. Thirty miles from their destination, with good ceiling and visibility, the crew spotted an 1,100-foot north-south airstrip northwest of Hue and misidentified it as the Dong Ha 3,900-foot east-west runway. No navigator was aboard and available maps of the area were poor, but the mistake was unjustifiable. The pilot managed to land successfully, but quickly became apprehensive as a crowd began to congregate about the aircraft. He then attempted a downwind takeoff, but the ship failed to get off the ground. Although the crew escaped from the crash with no serious injuries, the plane was demolished.

An important reform followed. Lt. Gen. Thomas S. Moorman, vice commander of Pacific Air Forces, firmly reminded the Thirteenth Air Force of the need for "increased supervision, stringent standardization, improved training programs, flying safety consciousness, and discipline." General Anthis accordingly directed that the Ranch Hand detachment be merged with the C–123 airlift organization to facilitate closer supervision and the development of appropriate operational procedures. The loose leadership and control which worked so well in the Farm Gate and Mule Train units invited trouble when a unit such as Ranch Hand attempted unfamiliar tasks.[19]

The unblemished Mule Train accident record ended on May 2, 1962, with the failure of the left main wheel of a C–123 attempting to take off at Tan Son Nhut with a load of Vietnamese troops and cargo. The pilot successfully halted the aircraft on the runway, all persons escaped without injury, and the ensuing fire was extinguished by a local crash crew. A second C–123 wheel failure occurred nearly three weeks later as the aircraft was taxiing on rough pierced steel planking. As a consequence of these two accidents, installation of redesigned wheel assemblies in all C–123s began promptly.[20]

The threat of Viet Cong antiaircraft fire was of only minor concern in routine airlift work. Aircrews ordinarily flew at least twenty-five hundred feet above the ground, and when possible chose offshore routes. The first confirmed report of small-arms fire against a Mule Train C–123 took place in February during an airdrop mission in the A Shau Valley, but the first hits occurred the next month when one aircraft was holed in the elevator and another in the right engine, both by small-caliber weapons. Exposure was greatest at low altitudes—during takeoffs, landings, and airdrops. The delta area was most dangerous, although small-arms fire was occasionally encountered near each of the major air bases. Following the first confirmed report of fire, Colonel Shofner requested armorplating for installation in the cockpit floor and aircrews sometimes improvised additional seat protection by using heavy personnel flak suits. On July 10 A1C Howard W. Wright became the first C–123 member to be wounded by Viet Cong ground fire. He was hit in the right thigh while the aircraft was descending at Tan Son Nhut.[21]

The idea of moving a second C–123 squadron to Vietnam came up at the Secretary of Defense Conference of February 19, 1962, in Hawaii. During a discussion of the matter, General Anthis assured Secretary McNamara that the C–123 was proving to be a most suitable transport for operations in Vietnam. In a message to CINCPAC, dated March 12, MACV officially recommended the sending of a second unit, citing as the basis for their recommendation high Mule Train flying during the summer. The Air Staff challenged the need for more transport aircraft in Vietnam, and also opposed a separate MACV request for a U.S. Caribou company. The MACV logistics section on May 22 asserted that Mule Train capabilities were becoming saturated, and indicated that transports would be placed on daily strip alert for tactical missions. Four days later, the Joint Chiefs of Staff directed movement of another sixteen C–123s to the Pacific.[22]

The deployment order came as no surprise to the air and ground crews of the 777th Troop Carrier Squadron at Pope Air Force Base which had been selected for the move. Aircraft had already received Mule Train modifications, so that final preparations for the move could be advanced for departure on May 28. The movement to the Far East was designated as Sawbuck II*, and resembled in execution the earlier Mule Train moves. Five MATS transports hauled the ground crewmen, although one aircraft island-hopped with the Providers and carried an enroute maintenance team. The first Provider echelon reached Clark on June 8; four aircraft and crews then went on to Bangkok on the eleventh to provide air transport service in Thailand while awaiting the arrival of a Caribou company. The remaining twelve 123s flew to Da Nang during the next four days.

In view of the crowding at Tan Son Nhut, Da Nang was selected as a second operating base in Vietnam. The latter possessed good airfield facilities, seaport facilities, and a location favorable for operating over the northern part of South Vietnam. The 777th aircraft at Da Nang, like Mule Train, were placed under the operational control of the 2d ADVON through the Joint Chief's airlift branch. The Bangkok C–123 detachment came under the operational control of the Air Force component commander, in Thailand. Administratively, all Mule Train, Ranch Hand, and Sawbuck II personnel were organized under the Tactical Air Force Squadron, Provisional 2, based at Pope with members assigned temporary

---

* Sawbuck I was an earlier move of a reconnaissance detachment to the west coast, and one C–123 to PACAF.

duty in Southeast Asia. For the purpose of consolidating maintenance and supply, the Sawbuck II ground crews were moved to Tan Son Nhut in September. Aircraft and crews thereafter rotated to Da Nang.[23]

Originally, Mule Train manpower planning provided for four-month duty tours for both aircrews and ground crews. The first group of replacements left Pope on March 21, 1962, by MATS airlift to take the place of forty-seven Mule Train members. Similar rotations followed during the next three months, resulting in a complete turnover of the original group. But, citing the experience of the French that aircrews became more proficient and useful the longer they stayed in Indochina, PACAF gained approval for lengthened tours of six months. During the summer PACAF and TAC further recommended that the C-123 units be permanently assigned to the Pacific, with individual tours a year or more in duration. An Air Force policy remained in effect, however, that South Vietnam should be an "experience-gaining opportunity for as many Air Force officers as possible."[24]

Several accidents in the second half of 1962 suggested a need for tighter supervision. A Sawbuck II crew left Tan Son Nhut for Ban Me Thuot in mid-July under visual flight rules. About fifty miles from their destination, the crew descended through a cloud break in order to complete the flight underneath the layer. They were unable to remain in the clear while circling only 500 feet above the rolling terrain and began to climb into the clouds. At about 3,300 feet, the plane flew into a hillside. Fortunately, tall trees cushioned the impact and the four-man crew (no navigator was aboard) survived the crash and for three days remained at the site until evacuated by a helicopter. An accident board determined that the primary cause for the loss of the aircraft was poor pilot judgment in "attempting to maintain VFR in mountainous terrain in deteriorating weather." This was a cursory if safe verdict, and ignored the fact that the accident was a consequence of the kind of marginal visual flights made daily by C-123 crews. More significant were the board's observations on the need for better maps and on improved traffic control in Vietnam.[25]

Two landing accidents occurred in late October. On the twenty-fourth, an aircraft trying to land at Quang Ngai touched down 180 feet short of the runway, resulting in major damage to the main landing gear and aft fuselage. Misjudgment by the pilot and the crew's failure to compute performance data were deemed the causes. Five days later, another C-123 crashed during an attempted landing at a new airfield under construction at Dak To. The landing gear folded upon hitting a large rock lip not visible from the air. The aircraft had been scheduled to land on the older Dak To dirt field, but this was not made clear in the mission order; furthermore, the new field was incorrectly shown as "usable" in the published air facilities chart. The pilot, Capt. Richard S. Dowell, had not made a previous landing at Dak To, in violation of a recent ruling requiring a ride to the field. An accident board assessed the primary cause of the accident as faulty supervision. The wreckage became a permanent landmark at Dak To.[26]

Whereas the early Mule Train crews and their replacements had been veterans of C–123 and troop carrier aviation, a decline in the quality of newcomers became evident in late 1962. Many pilots were new to the C–123, having been recently drawn from the Air Force at large and put through a training program at Pope. Colonel Daly, commander of 464th Wing at Pope, warned his superiors that accidents overseas were likely to become more frequent.[27] A Thirteenth Air Force operations team visited Vietnam during the first week of November and further warned that the existing information folders on airfields and drop zones were "outdated, inadequate, and a detriment rather than an aid to aircrews." To tighten overall supervision of flying practices, the operations team recommended creation of a C–123 standardization-evaluation flight at Tan Son Nhut. The idea was not new, since nearly every flying unit in the Air Force had such a flight which consisted of several experienced and able aircrew personnel responsible for developing and publishing flight procedures and for seeing that line crews and flight instructors adhered to these procedures. Acting independently, Colonel Daly had dispatched to Vietnam "two of my finest standardization-evaluation Captains, Cooper and Taddiken." As another measure, General Anthis informed PACAF that 179 C–123 flying hours were to be used during November solely for training.[28]

But squadron commanders were faced with a real dilemma. Traditionally, air leaders were expected to stir up a strong sense of mission dedication among their men, encouraging crews to overcome all obstacles to "hack the mission." In Mule Train, and indeed in all airlift ventures in Vietnam, seldom did the importance of a single sortie justify unusual compromises in air safety. On the other hand, to adhere rigidly to standing regulations would seriously hamper daily deliveries. The solution lay in a commonsense approach—strongly warning crewmen against taking unjustified risks and unsafe shortcuts, but leaving the decision in an operational situation to the judgment of the aircraft commander.

Flight-line maintenance at Tan Son Nhut was at first of high quality. The 346th Squadron maintenance men had years of experience in working on the C–123, and had adequate spare parts in the flyaway kit brought from Pope. The base supply office at Clark, however, proved unable to avoid a depletion of the flyaway kit stocks. Cannibalization of aircraft and the arrival of a second set of kits with Sawbuck II provided some relief, but aircraft grounded due to parts shortages reached a horrendous twenty-five percent in June. Strenuous attention to the problem during the summer, however, enabled the base supply offices at Clark and Tan Son Nhut to meet the demand. Meanwhile, maintenance personnel worked seven days a week to meet the increasing flying requirement of seventy-two hours per aircraft in June, above the fifty hours initially established. But unrepaired malfunctions began to accumulate. Increasingly, the practice became to schedule an aircraft for missions despite numerous malfunctions, no one of which was sufficient to ground the plane. Gradually, the entire fleet deteriorated in this way. However, given the high qualification of the aircrews and their judgment in aborting when necessary, flying safety remained unimpaired. A Mule Train pilot described the C–123s in late 1962 as follows:[29]

> We operated when we had good engines and when we had good flight instruments on at least one side of the instrument panel. Beyond that we took almost anything that could fly. We didn't get very sophisticated about cracks in the gear and magnafluxing the wing spars and that sort of thing. If it was tied together we flew it, because the 123 is a very durable and rugged little machine. And the maintenance people did the very best they could to prevent any real serious flaws becoming unnoticed. But as far as the niceties—all the radios didn't often work, some of the flight instruments often failed because of the heat and humidity.[30]

Living arrangements for the maintenance troops at Tan Son Nhut were abysmal. The tent cantonment was dirty, overcrowded, and inundated with mud. There was no hot water for showers. Unscreened tents were located next to the flight line, where engine noise made sleep difficult. Menus at the field mess were austere, refrigeration was limited, and rats and roaches were plentiful. Few individuals escaped gastrointestinal afflictions. Conditions at the Spartan tent camp at Da Nang were somewhat better. Scarcely improving morale among the enlisted men was the knowledge that officer aircrew members lived in pleasant downtown billets, dined in restaurants, and received generous per diem allowances. For their part, pilots and navigators, who warmly praised the flight-line improvisations and the dedication of the ground crewmen, denounced the contrast in living arrangements. That these deplorable conditions influenced maintenance efficiency, if not also the quality of work, is beyond question.[31]

Senior officers visiting Vietnam during the year praised the dedication and ability of the men of Mule Train. Aircrew officers were generally junior in rank (only three field grade officers accompanied the original Mule Train deployment), but they were highly experienced in flying. One Mule Train officer, Capt. Benjamin N. Kraljev, Jr., had flown over Dien Bien Phu in an Iron Age C–119 in 1954. They were also dependable in judgment, and functioned well under loose supervision. Within the unit, leadership emerged from the instructor pilots—Capts. Charles West, Carl Wyrick, William Richards, and their successors—men whose competence and energy established the pattern for the others. Although a few individuals adopted an immature flamboyance, the workload never suffered. As in Farm Gate, the satisfaction of having a clearcut task each day and performing it well was strong. The standards of professional airmanship established by the early C–123 crews in Vietnam were never excelled by those that followed.[32]

The Air Force's determination to establish a tactical mobility role for the C–123 became apparent in a plan, submitted to the Joint Chiefs of Staff February 20, 1962, which outlined the Air Force's approach to counterinsurgency in Vietnam. Basic to this proposal was the recommendation that quick reaction force packages be formed, to consist of paratroop units of the Vietnamese army and of allied transport and helicopter aircraft. The reaction force packages were to be positioned at major airstrips and were to be prepared to react to Viet Cong attacks on outposts and villages. The paper picked nine quick reaction locations to blanket the country effectively.

The paper proposed that a typical reaction unit include a battalion of paratroops, one-third of whom would be kept on alert. At Tan Son Nhut, Vietnamese Air Force C–47s and H–34s would provide the alert airlift arm. Positioned at each of the other sites would be five U.S. Air Force C–123s and ten U.S. Army H–34s, along with five American-operated T–28s for strike and escort support. The suitability of the C–123 for the quick reaction role had been demonstrated by its ability to operate "out of short unprepared fields with a payload of 60 combat troops." Further, airborne troops could be dropped by parachute or airlanded, according to the situation.

The plan required the placement of simple communications equipment at each village and seemed compatible with the strategic hamlet program being implemented for the security of the rural population. The paper also called for various psychological warfare and civic action measures. In sum, the Air Force proposal became "a virtual blueprint for the whole counterinsurgency program." General LeMay urged that it become the basis for American and South Vietnamese strategy and he appreciated the fact that the effort might begin in one or two regions, then expand gradually over the whole country and eventually become entirely a South Vietnamese operation.[33]

The emerging rivalry between the American services made unqualified Joint Chiefs endorsement improbable. On March 2 the chiefs agreed to refer the plan, along with a dissenting Army memorandum, to the Joint Staff for comment and to CINCPAC for "appropriate study and consideration." With characteristic energy, General LeMay moved to prevent stagnation of the quick reaction force idea. General Taylor spoke to Secretary McNamara about the proposal and sent him a copy of the plan. A communication for the President also had been prepared, but was halted in the Office of the Secretary of the Air Force on the understanding that General LeMay had already taken up the matter with President Kennedy. Copies of the plan were provided to PACAF, the Thirteenth Air Force, the 2d ADVON, and to Brig. Gen. John A. Dunning, who as head of plans and policy was the senior Air Force officer in MACV. Similar proposals for rapid reaction force packages had been simultaneously developed by 2d ADVON, but had met opposition at MACV because of the bare sufficiency of forces for current activities. In his April meeting with President Diem, General LeMay received Diem's strong endorsement for the quick reaction plan in combination with the strategic hamlet idea, while the Air Staff continued to urge Gen. Emmett O'Donnell, PACAF commander, to nudge CINCPAC toward active support.[34]

Interim arrangements to initiate the plan began in March. The 2d ADVON reported that five hundred Vietnamese paratroopers were placed on alert status during daylight hours in Saigon, along with five Vietnamese Air Force C–47s on forty-minute standby. An American C–123 was kept on alert and another in backup status. A Mule Train alert crew stayed in tents on base, remaining on duty through the night for possible flareship missions. For movement of the Fire Brigade paratroop force, it was anticipated that the alert aircraft would be augmented by additional C–47s and C–123s as available. A written plan also provided for the recall of Mule Train mission aircraft operating near Saigon, able theoretically to take off again within two hours.[35]

The alert paratroop battalion at Tan Son Nhut made an emergency

Gen. Emmett O'Donnell, PACAF commander, with VNAF officers at Saigon International Airport, April 1963.

move to Da Nang in mid-March and six Mule Train aircraft joined in the effort. In drawing the 123s away from their normal air logistic duties even for several days, the operation produced an immediate swelling of backlog cargo awaiting movement. Although it was clear that any permanent expansion of the C-123 alert responsibility would bring undesirable increases in cargo backlogs, General LeMay during his April visit pressed for such action as a step toward full implementation of the quick reaction plan. Soon after arrival of the second C-123 squadron in June, the C-123 alert force was increased to six aircraft, five at Tan Son Nhut and one at Da Nang.[36]

The quick reaction concept depended heavily upon the effectiveness of parachute assault, but neither the physical geography of South Vietnam nor the experience of the French airborne forces in Indochina were encouraging. The Air Staff, in submitting the plan to the Joint Chiefs, pointed out these handicaps. Cleared areas for drop zones were rare in the forested highlands which dominate the northern two-thirds of South Vietnam. The Mekong Delta lowlands comprising much of the south were frequently flooded. Most promising for paratroop operations were the semiforested plains within a sixty-mile arc to the north and west of Saigon, an area known for considerable Viet Cong activity. The location about Saigon of the Vietnamese airborne forces, the Vietnamese C-47s, and the Mule Train C-123s, strengthened the possibilities for ventures within this area and all of the significant parachute operations in 1962 occurred there.[37]

Aircrew techniques for delivering paratroops accurately to drop zones had advanced only slightly from those of the second World War. Technical procedures for loading and discharging jumpers from C-123s had been refined by TAC, and thousands of training and exercise missions had been flown over the eastern United States. A systematic method for calculating the exact jump point once the drop zone was visually located, called the computed air release point (CARP), had been adapted from the experiences of the Royal Canadian Air Force. This calculation used known parachute ballistics and prevailing wind conditions. The most fundamental problem of the aircrew remained unsolved, however, that of locating and identifying an unfamiliar drop zone, especially during conditions of darkness or poor visibility. The C-123 had no electronic aids on board designed to assist the navigator in locating drop zones. This omission was justifiable in view of the aircraft's basic simplicity and its intended airland assault role, but memory of misplaced paratroopers in Sicily and Normandy was inauspicious for the tasks ahead.

Since the navigator's outside visiblity from his station behind the pilots was poor, C-123 copilots were supposed to furnish position information to the navigator. Mapreading became an important part of the copilot's training at Pope and in the flying in Vietnam. Even though the aircrew had located the initial point for the run-in to the drop zone, precise and positive identification of the zone itself still remained. The zones were usually located in flat featureless areas and were difficult to spot from low altitude even in good weather with the aid of photographs. The two pilots and the navigator strained forward during the final two minutes, attempting to glimpse the objective early enough to permit final corrections. Air Force pathfinder teams were trained to parachute ahead of the main force to mark drop zones with flares and smoke. Such combat control teams were organized within the aerial port squadrons, but were not used in the early Vietnamese parachute operations. In practice, placing paratroops accurately depended primarily upon the eyes and wits of the aircrews.[38]

The Vietnamese army paratroopers were members of the Vietnamese airborne brigade and were organized into six battalions. The battalions rotated duties, so that while one stood on quick reaction alert, one or two of the others might be engaged in jump proficiency training, while the remainder participated in field operations, either as a central reserve or as an infantry force attached to other units. The quick reaction battalion remained at Tan Son Nhut, available to take off in a few hours. The American C–123 aircrews respected the Vietnamese paratroopers, who received jump pay totaling only fifty cents per actual jump. Their devotion to duty was sometimes demonstrated when they practiced parachute landings by dropping in full gear off the back of trucks.[39] One American pilot described the Vietnamese trooper thus:

> He stands about five feet two or three, he has to walk stiff-legged and on tiptoe because his gun butt's dragging the ground, he's got cooking pots strapped to him plus maybe a few live chickens, but he'd have a big smile on his face before he goes out . . . . I think if anybody's ever seen a Vietnamese paratrooper in the back end of a C–47 . . . why you'd have a great deal of admiration for him.[40]

A parachute assault of the 5th Airborne Battalion near the Cambodian border west of Saigon on January 21, 1962, revealed the capabilities of the Vietnamese airborne and troop carrier forces and was of interest to American officials as a possible model for the future. The operation was planned well in advance and was designed to surprise the Viet Cong forces believed to be in the area. The battalion jumped from Vietnamese Air Force C–47s, landing on and securing the prescribed drop zone. The jump was coordinated with the surface movement of four other battalions, and the five-day timetable went as planned. Contact with the enemy was slight, however, and the Joint Chiefs of Staff termed the results "disappointing." The Americans suspected that the enemy had withdrawn because of the heavy air reconnaissance and air strikes preceding the assault, and criticized the troopers for the time lost while they collected their parachutes before moving against the Viet Cong. On February 20, six Mule Train C–123s again joined the Vietnamese C–47s and the U.S. Army H–21s and stood by for possible drops into the same drop zone. In the meantime

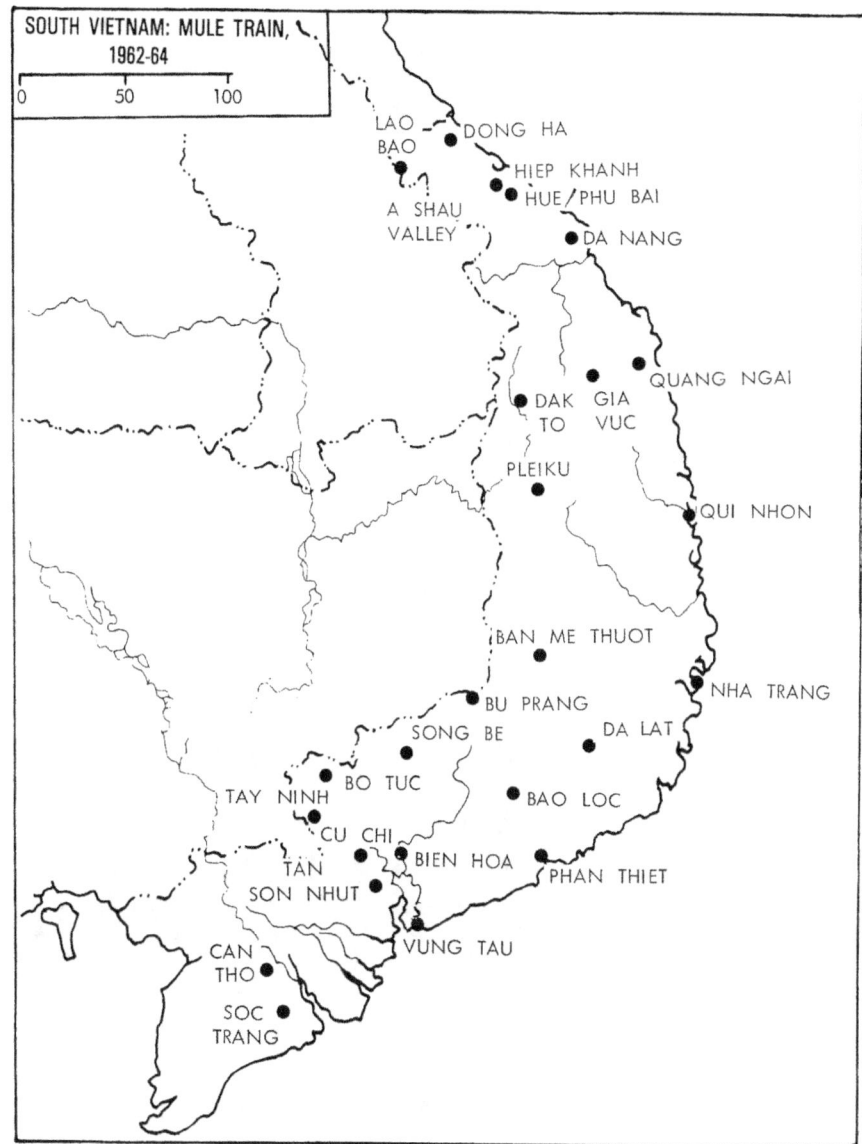

South Vietnamese ground forces maneuvered in the area attempting unsuccessfully to flush out the enemy.[41]

The first C–123 combat drop occurred two weeks later, in relief of an outpost at Bo Tuc in Northern Tay Ninh Province, five miles from the Cambodian border. The post came under heavy Viet Cong attack during the night of March 4/5 and received air strike support the next morning. Shortly after noon, the joint operations center airlift branch received a paratroop mission request, and three C–123s with troops from the 5th

Vietnamese Army paratroopers board USAF C–123s at Tan Son Nhut for a training mission, May 1962.

Vietnamese soldiers en route to the drop zone.

Airborne Battalion took off immediately. Two of the aircraft flew a second sortie to Bo Tuc and the five flights delivered a total of 198 troopers, including several American advisors. The airdrops were unopposed and the forces neither received nor inflicted casualties. Further reinforcements were airlanded in the area the next day. The operation demonstrated that while airborne reinforcements might save an outpost, they could not force an enemy to fight against his will.[42]

Dissatisfaction with the comparative inactivity of the Mule Train force in the airborne assault role became the basis for a March 17 Pacific Air Forces message, dispatched from General O'Donnell's office to the Thirteenth Air Force and subsequently redirected to the 2d ADVON. It read in part:

> C-123s were deployed to South Vietnam for tactical use. To date, these aircraft have been primarily utilized in their secondary role of logistical carriers. As a result, the U.S. Army is attempting to justify the introduction of other aircraft with the primary function of tactically airlifting ground forces into objective areas . . . . The purpose of these suggestions is to solicit and increase tactical usage of the C-123 by ARVN units through creating a market, if necessary, in the combat support role.[43]

The message urged that strenuous effort be made to identify potential assault strips and drop zones in Vietnam, and that training missions be flown to these places, thus refining navigation and approach methods and introducing both Vietnamese and U.S. Army personnel to the versatility of the C-123. The Joint Chiefs in July recommended that several Air Force air liaison officers recently assigned to assist the Vietnamese corps and division staffs develop opportunities for "selling assault transport." The orientation of the liaison officers hitherto had been largely toward the tactical air strike role and ground commanders were encouraged to request the use of the airborne brigade, a force of "3,000 rough and ready troops," thus bringing the troop carrier arm into action.[44]

The first combined assault involving both American and Vietnamese troop carrier aircraft took place on June 28, 1962. A dozen Vietnamese Air Force C-47s joined sixteen C-123s in dropping paratroops thirty-five miles north of Saigon, near a location that had been under Viet Cong attack the previous evening. The decision to drop came shortly after dawn and in the haste premission planning was cut short, contributing to subsequent confusion during the flight. The aerial rendezvous between the American and Vietnamese formations began smoothly, but the run-in was ragged because of the differing speeds and maneuverabilities of the two aircraft. Further, an unexpectedly low ceiling necessitated a last-minute change in drop altitude and additional delay resulted in the area when the leaders of the American and Vietnamese formations disagreed on identification of the drop zone. The jumpers were nevertheless dropped with accuracy, although tactical success on the ground was slight. After the operation, representatives from Mule Train met with Vietnamese pilots and U.S. Air Force liaison officers to work out better mission procedures. It was agreed that in future operations a Vietnamese navigator would fly in the lead C-123 to assist the Americans in locating the drop zone.[45]

This measure proved valuable during the next paratroop mission two weeks later when a ground convoy was ambushed by Viet Cong in an area of rubber plantations thirty-eight miles north of Saigon. The attack was broken off after ten minutes, but airborne forces were dropped three and a half hours later in hopes of blocking the enemy retirement. This was exclusively a C-123 operation and involved over twenty aircraft. A second blocking force was introduced by helicopter. Again, identification of the drop zone was a problem, since the area lacked distinctive geographical features. A Vietnamese officer in the first C-123 assisted the lead navigator, Capt. Charles R. Blake, in locating the area. General Sweeney, the TAC commander, witnessed the jump from the air. After the parachute assault, reinforcements were airlanded at a nearby dirt strip. All landings were unopposed and contact with Viet Cong forces after the initial ambush was negligible. The force was withdrawn by air on the third day.[46]

C-123s, C-47s, and H-21s joined on September 24 in a coordinated assault against several Viet Cong-controlled villages near Cu Chi, twenty miles northwest of Saigon. Poor weather delayed the five hundred-troop paradrop, and the single available radio frequency soon became cluttered. A helicopter commander remarked afterwards that the troops could have moved faster by foot.[47]

On November 20, five C-123s and twelve Vietnamese C-47s each dropped 250 troops, reopening operations in Zone D, the forested Viet Cong haven north of Bien Hoa. The Americans were supposed to drop ahead of the C-47s, but they were unable to locate the drop zone because of extremely poor visibility. The trailing Vietnamese nevertheless released the paratroops successfully over the correct area, obliging the Americans to continue their efforts. The C-123s airdropped the men on the fourth and fifth passes, but missed the objective by one kilometer. Simultaneously during the first week of the Zone D operation, the C-123s completed 154 airlanded sorties and the C-47s, 77, hauling troops and equipment between Saigon and the Phuoc Long airstrip seventy miles to the north. Twenty C-47s executed a second paratroop assault a week later with little confusion; five men were killed during the landing and in crossing a nearby minefield, but there was no contact with the enemy.[48]

The five-aircraft C-123 quick reaction alert force at Tan Son Nhut achieved no significant successes. The alert aircrews stayed in their barracks near the flight line, while the paratroop battalion remained in varying states of readiness according to circumstances; five Vietnamese C-47s also stood by during daylight hours. Practice missions proved the quick reaction force's capability to deliver paratroops seventy-five minutes after a request. A joint operations plan which outlined procedures for the Fire Brigade alert force and prescribed various alert postures, was published on October 17, 1962, and signed by General Anthis and senior officers of the VNAF and the Vietnamese army. The plan provided that the assault force would ordinarily consist of 360 paratroops—50 to be carried in each of the five C–123s, and 22 in each of five C–47s. The faster C–123s would drop first, thus averting the possibility of an overrun by the trailing element. Another 140 troops along with cargo were to be delivered within three hours by a second flight.

Although the text of the October plan stated that the procedure would be expanded, and while every Friday six C–123s made practice troop drops, American officials nevertheless questioned the quick reaction concept. Actual launches had been infrequent, and friction developed from the reluctance of the Vietnamese to infringe on their lunch or siesta habits. On one occasion during General Sweeney's July visit, to demonstrate the Vietnamese unwillingness to respond, the American alert force took off and overflew an objective area empty. Most troubling was the apparent weakness of the parachute assault method itself against an enemy difficult to locate and able to avoid battle at will. At year's end, plans for organizing an additional airborne battalion were canceled, reflecting MACV's evaluation of the "past employment of airborne battalions, and success of current military operations using helicopters."[49]

Air Force doctrine for theater operations stressed the concept of a centralized airlift system, along the lines developed in the Korean War and prescribed in AFM 1–9 in 1953. In addition, the many joint exercises of the 1950s had convinced TAC troop carrier officers not only that airlift organization should be centralized, but that the airlift control apparatus should be separated from the joint operations center, where communications resources and attention were dominated by the tactical air strike function. The exact form of the airlift system varied considerably from one exercise to another, but it generally included a troop carrier headquarters with a central control post, functioning through combat airlift support units (CALSUs) located at the principal operating airfields. As an extension of the troop carrier headquarters, each support unit had operations and communications personnel, who briefed troop carrier crews and coordinated with aerial port and other local agencies. Similar functions at forward airfields and landing zones were performed by smaller teams called movement control centers (MCC). The support units and control centers were not permanent, but came into existence only for particular exercises. They did however provide experience in tactical airlift management to many troop carrier officers. The ideal of an integrated airlift system with central management of aircraft, aerial ports, and control agencies, was strong in the minds of most TAC and 315th Air Division airlift officers. Centralized control in the Air Force view promised not only efficiency in management but also flexibility in usage, allowing airlift forces to be directed to the most urgent theaterwide tasks. Conflict with the U.S. Army's preference for decentralized control for the sake of improved responsiveness and battlefield cooperation remained a fundamental issue for a number of years.[50]

Airlift arrangements during the first months in Vietnam bore little resemblance to those set forth in AFM 1-9 and developed through joint exercises. A joint airlift allocations board existed only nominally above the joint operations centers for setting monthly airlift priorities. This initially seemed to be an unimportant omission, since the tempo of ground operations was slow and the Vietnamese were not accustomed to shipping by air. An American-manned air traffic coordinating office (ATCO) passed daily logistical shipment requests to the joint operations centers, identifying requests as routine or priority.

The joint operations center's airlift branch became the principal agency for daily air transportation management and the immediate point of contact for the Mule Train squadron. The coordinating office prepared schedules and attempted to follow missions using information telephoned from the Mule Train operations center. The latter could communicate with aircrews only by short-range radio. The temporary duty officers from the 315th Air Division who manned the airlift branch were replaced in early March by four officers assigned from the United States for eighteen-month tours with the 2d ADVON. Only one of the four had a background in airlift work. All four regularly worked fourteen to sixteen hours a day during March and April. However, the increasing pace of briefings, staff actions, and daily mission coordination allowed neither the time nor development of understanding to meet deepening problems confronting the airlift effort. In a letter to General Anthis dated May 12, Colonel Shofner complained of the many last-minute changes to the daily mission orders and he recommended that "the highest qualified airlift people available be assigned as ATCO and airlift duty officers." In the meantime, the Thirteenth Air Force had requested relief of three airlift branch officers, because of their "substandard performance, and . . . no experience in airlift operations." Personnel from the 315th Air Division returned to man again the airlift branch. These officers, although unfamiliar with the C-123, appreciated the operational limitations which confronted troop carrier operations. Major Witherington and his assistants discovered with gratitude that questions of cargo and fuel load, existing weather limitations, and airstrip conditions could now be intelligently discussed and appraised with the joint operations center.⁵¹ Unfortunately, the fundamental airlift deficiencies were too deep seated for correction by so limited a reform.

Dissatisfaction with the airlift operation was soon expressed. The American senior ground force advisor at Pleiku in a March 12 letter to MACV listed examples of unsatisfactory support—airlift delays, for example, apparently caused foodstuffs to spoil before reaching Pleiku. Some personnel complained of waiting several days at Tan Son Nhut for air transportation to Pleiku, and others were unable to get transportation at Da Nang for Saigon. Officers at Nha Trang stated that it had taken eight days to deliver a rebuilt T–28 engine from Bien Hoa to Nha Trang, while the aircraft remained out of commission. Aircrews confirmed that wasteful delays were common and when they arrived at destinations they often had to hunt out receivers for their cargo, or make impromptu arrangements for offloading and reloading. Cargo and passengers were often not ready when the C–123 arrived, apparently because no one on the ground realized that a mission was due. Only at Tan Son Nhut and Da Nang, where in December 1961 local coordination was by combat airlift support unit detachments from the 315th Air Division, were terminal operations reasonably efficient.⁵²

Some complaints apparently were colored by service rivalry, and others reflected a lack of knowledge or initiative among users. Nevertheless, the existence of serious weaknesses was obvious in mid-April to a PACAF team under Brig. Gen. Travis M. Hetherington studying the situation. The group visited Tan Son Nhut and five other points normally served by C–123s and reported that the Mule Train operation itself was being conducted in a "highly professional manner," but that "a very definite problem" existed in the airlift area, citing many of the prevailing inefficiencies. The Hetherington findings were confirmed during a visit by General LeMay during April 18–20, which included an inspection of the Mule Train aircraft and crews. The operations section of LeMay's report, prepared by Brig. Gen. Jamie Gough, bluntly asserted that "there is no effective airlift system," and recommended that an officer experienced in theater airlift operations be sent temporarily to the 2d ADVON "to set up an airlift system." Col. George M. Foster, PACAF director of transportation, who was known to Gough since both had served with the 484th Wing at Ashiya, was selected. Colonel Foster initiated a series of measures which culminated in a major reorganization in the fall.⁵³

The difficulties appeared to lie in two areas: insufficient aerial port facilities and an inadequate apparatus for communications and aircraft control. Systematic attention to these problems required a further clarification of responsibilities and possibly a major reorganization. One proposal considered within PACAF in May was to place the C–123 operation under the direct management of the 315th Air Division, thus exploiting the airlift expertise and facilitating possible use of the division's C–130s in

Southeast Asia. General Milton, commanding the Thirteenth Air Force, recommended a lesser reform, calling for the creation of a deputy for airlift within 2d ADVON with a small staff of about twelve men, "to give us the professional supervision this operation requires without creating another little empire." Milton's view incorporated MACV's wish to retain full operational control.[54]

The final arrangement, decided upon in September after lengthy staff coordination in Saigon and Hawaii, entailed major reform. A new combat cargo group was to be established in Southeast Asia, manned by permanently assigned personnel. The combat cargo group would establish operational control over Air Force troop carrier and aerial port units in Vietnam and Thailand. Pending activation of permanent units, PACAF on September 21 set up temporary units at Tan Son Nhut—the 6492d Combat Cargo Group (Troop Carrier), Provisional, and 6493d Aerial Port Squadron, Provisional. Colonel Mantoux, who had planned the initial Mule Train mission in January, arrived at Tan Son Nhut to take command of the 6492d. More than twenty officers and men from the 315th Air Division worked in the combat group headquarters during the fall, pending arrival of the permanent staff. The 315th personnel, in General Anthis' opinion, represented the division's "most professional and dedicated airlift specialists."[55]

Detailed procedures, responsibilities, and organization for a "U.S. military airlift system within Southeast Asia" was established by MACV Directive 42 and its enclosure, initially dated October 11, 1962, and reissued under the original date with added clarifications of command lines. The apparatus, known afterwards as the Southeast Asia Airlift System (SEAAS) clearly reflected past trends in Air Force doctrine. The directive provided that the combat cargo group would replace the old joint operations center airlift branch, both as an airlift staff agency in the 2d ADVON and in exercising mission control over Vietnam-based transports. As later amended, the group would also function as a coordinating agency for C-130s based elsewhere while transiting Southeast Asia, would maintain cognizance of MATS trips, and would maintain liaison with Vietnamese and Thai airlift agencies. An aerial port squadron and its detachments, under the combat cargo group, were to receive and manifest cargo and passengers, load and unload aircraft, and store cargo in transit. The group also was to function as the headquarters for the aerial port and C-123 squadrons and perform normal command and administrative roles. The combat cargo group thus appeared jurisdictionally competent to build and operate an expanding theater airlift system.[56]

Reform of the MACV transportation allocations system had begun the previous spring when Brig. Gen. Frank A. Osmanski, USA, MACV's logistics chief, directed his staff to plan an agency within the logistics section to undertake this function. Directive 42 stipulated that a movements branch of MACV's logistics section as recommended by General Osmanski, would function as a joint airlift allocations board and would in effect represent the MACV or theater commander. Airlift users were to forecast needs to the logistics section twenty-five days before each new month. The combat control group was then to estimate its capabilities. Ten days later, allocations were to be decided in a meeting, chaired by the logistics chief, to develop a tentative schedule for the following month. Flexibility was essential and additional requests could be made at any time, preferably at least two days before shipment. Requesters assigned priorities to each shipment, ranging from priority one (emergency) through priority four (not urgent). Within the same priority, the items longest in the system moved first. But the directive set up no specific procedures for immediate responses to emergency or tactical requests. General Anthis made it clear that he expected the combat cargo organization to be responsive in emergencies to the tactical air control system through the joint operations center outside the apparatus of the movements branch.[57]

The 315th Troop Carrier Group (Combat Cargo) and 8th Aerial Port Squadron activated on December 8, 1962, replaced the provisional units. The 315th Group had a strength of twenty-seven officers and twenty-one airmen, all of whom were on permanent assignment. Group headquarters was organized into sections for operations, materiel, plans, training, standardization-evaluation, safety, and administration. The manning document included spaces for the transport movement control detachments at Tan Son Nhut, Da Nang, and Don Muang. Although the 315th Group was an element of the 315th Air Division, the group's responsibilities included developing tactics and techniques and providing technical advice on airlift matters. Operational command of the group rested with the Commander, MACV, who in theory exercised control through his Air Force component command, the 2d Air Division. Certain administrative activities, including pay, messing, and court-martial jurisdiction, along with periodic maintenance and supply support at Clark, remained the responsibility of the Thirteenth Air Force. TAC, however, continued to provide air and ground crews for the C–123 squadrons.[58]

As the first commander of the 315th Group, Colonel Mantoux, formerly the deputy commander of the air division and commander of the 6492d Combat Cargo Group, brought with him the outlook of an airlift specialist, one inclined to think in terms of efficiency in sustained airlift operations. In contrast, General Anthis and his immediate staff were more consciously involved in defending the Air Force's roles and missions in Vietnam. These divergent viewpoints, according to Mantoux's later recollections, led to no major differences in policy, nor did Anthis reject any specific proposals made by Mantoux. Years later, recalling that his position between Anthis and the 315th Air Division was sometimes awkward, Mantoux wrote: "As I look back on it, it really does not seem to have been any problem, yet when things were rough and tempers frayed, it seemed to be one." In essence, the interests of all commands pointed toward the same objective—the achievement of a high-efficiency airlift system, one capable of both sustained logistics and responsive tactical service.[59]

Transport movement control detachments were established at four additional locations in late 1962: Qui Nhon, Nha Trang, Can Tho, and Pleiku. Communications between the combat cargo group and the new detachments was based principally on the very unreliable Vietnamese telephone system, a wholly unsatisfactory means for immediate operational purposes. Improvements were anticipated with the approval later in the year of secure teletype circuits to link a proposed airlift communications center at Tan Son Nhut with the control detachments. In addition, in a letter of October 25, 1962, the cargo group requested installation of radio equipment at the control detachment locations. The equipment would operate on a common troop carrier frequency, thus permitting the detachments to communicate with individual aircraft. If and when implemented, the integrated teletype radio apparatus was to link aircraft, detachments, and the cargo group in a reliable and fast network. For the moment, however, the chronic annoyances of an inadequate communications system remained. But the apparatus of the transport movement control detachments, functioning as satellites of the combat cargo control headquarters, established a pattern for the much larger airlift control system which followed.[60]

Monthly statistics of airlift activity demonstrated improving efficiency. With C–123 flying hours remaining relatively constant at nineteen hundred hours monthly, combined cargo and passenger tonnage thereafter rose in every successive month, from twenty-three hundred tons in June to thirty-nine hundred tons in November 1962. During the last three months of the year, tonnage utilization (cargo and passenger tonnage per sortie) was 2.9 tons as compared to 2.4 tons for the previous quarter. The average sortie duration also increased, indicating still more favorable ton-mile trends.[61]

In the United States the controversy over tactical air roles came to a head in 1962. After several months of study by his systems analysis office, Secretary McNamara in a memorandum of April 19, 1962, called upon the Secretary of the Army for "fresh and perhaps unorthodox concepts which will give us a significant increase in mobility." Four months later, an Army board under the chairmanship of Lt. Gen. Hamilton H. Howze, USA, arrived at "a single general conclusion: adoption by the Army of the airmobile concept." The board further recommended the creation of air assault divisions, equipped with large numbers of aircraft to haul troops into battle and provide fire support. Separately organized air transport brigades, equipped with heavier helicopters and Caribou transports, would distribute supplies to forward points. American Air Force transports, the Howze group proposed, would make "wholesale movements to bases as far forward as possible," linking these sites with the Army's transport craft to form an all-air line of communication.[62]

To the Air Force, the Howze recommendations boiled down to what the Army had long wanted—a tactical air force of its own. An Air Force board, chaired by Lt. Gen. Gabriel P. Disosway, vice commander of TAC, met during the summer of 1962 and arrived at the conclusion that although improvements in Army mobility were needed, the approach should be to develop "existing and proven" Air Force capabilities. Air Force transports, for example, could make deliveries to forward airstrips, and a single C–130 could haul six times the tonnage of a Caribou. Finally, the Disosway board asserted that helicopters were too slow and vulnerable for assault penetrations, and restated the Air Force conviction that centralized control was a necessity for theater air forces. Seeking reconciliation of their different approaches, McNamara on November 14 charged the two services with "the task of finding ways by which we can take full advantage of aviation." The Air Force replied ten days later, agreeing that there should be field tests of the Army's concepts and stating that it was devoting itself to "imaginative approaches" toward airlift support of the Army.[63]

The issues arising from the Howze board recommendations clearly influenced service positions regarding Southeast Asia. Maj. Gen. Sam W. Agee, the Air Force's director of operations, wrote that the Army was trying "to wrest a large part, if not all, of the airlift missions in Vietnam from the Air Force." He feared that arrangements in Vietnam could "have a long-term adverse effect on the U.S. military posture that could be more important than the battle presently being waged with the Viet Cong." Senior Air Force officers after visiting Vietnam acknowledged that the Army's transport helicopters were performing a useful service, but they unsuccessfully urged that the aircraft should be controlled centrally under the joint operations center. The Air Force's position on the Caribous, endlessly restated and defended, was essentially twofold: the service was against sending Caribou units to Vietnam, and it was in favor of placing the Caribous, once they had reached Vietnam, under centralized airlift system control. PACAF, the Thirteenth Air Force, and the 2d Air Division all supported this viewpoint.[64]

In its opposition to the introduction of Caribou units, the Air Force insisted that the C–123 could do most jobs better. The C–123 could haul more than double the Caribou's payload over three times the distance, and had twice the volume of cargo space. Although the C–123 required considerably more runway for takeoff (1,750 feet compared to 1,020 feet for

TACTICAL AIRLIFT

U.S. Army Caribou in Vietnam, 1962.

the Caribous), the difference with the Caribou narrowed when the C-123 carried only enough fuel and cargo to equalize range and payload. The C-123 had a compensating advantage when landing on wet surfaces, since the Caribou had not yet been equipped with reversible-pitch propellers.[65]

In May 1962 MACV, in restating earlier requests for the assignment of a Caribou unit, asserted its intention to use the Caribous in "an integrated . . . logistics airlift system." Four aircraft would be committed daily to the centralized control agency.[66] Approval for movement of Caribous to Thailand followed, and the first of eighteen left Fort Benning, Georgia, on May 31. The 1st Aviation Company flew across the North Atlantic, Europe, and the Middle East, and the first element reached Bangkok on June 17 while the last arrived three weeks later, five days late. Although the trip was slow, it was faster than movement by ship and avoided the burden of disassembling and crating each aircraft. The Caribous and aircrews operated initially from Korat, primarily on nonscheduled logistics missions on behalf of American forces in Thailand.[67]

Eight of the Korat-based Caribous moved to Vietnam the next July, directed by the MACV commander, Gen. Paul D. Harkins, USA, to conduct a field test. Admiral Felt accepted entry of the Caribou into Vietnam "on a temporary basis for test purposes." Six of the aircraft were positioned for direct support of the U.S. Army senior advisors at Da Nang, Pleiku, and Tan Son Nhut, and two operated from Tan Son Nhut in direct support of MACV. Their employment was principally in unscheduled and airlanded operations. The flying hour usage was high and soon led to shortages of spare parts, reminiscent of the early Mule Train problems.[68]

But the Caribous quickly proved their usefulness. During a ten-day period in July, the two Da Nang aircraft hauled troops and equipment for

Army Gen. Paul D. Harkins, MACV commander, 1962.

the establishment of a new camp at Lao Bao, in the extreme northwest of South Vietnam. The two Caribous made two or three sorties daily, hauling into a strip plainly inaccessible to the C–123s.[69]

The remaining Caribous in Thailand moved to Vietnam in December and the company headquarters transferred to Vung Tau. MACV's joint operations section justified the realignment by citing declining activity in Thailand, a need for more airlift in Vietnam, and the desire of the Army "to evaluate effectiveness of the Caribou company in a counterinsurgency role." All aircraft thereafter operated from Vung Tau, except for those supporting the corps advisors at Da Nang and Pleiku. The intention to place some Caribous under the airlift system for scheduling and control was repeatedly stated, but in practice the Army generally disregarded the idea. The issue continued into 1963 and reappeared during the discussion of the new MACV national campaign plan and the associated air transport buildup.

The payload and range capabilities of the C–130 Hercules and the C–124 Globemasters were well suited for long-range lift tasks. During 1962, the transports controlled by the 315th Air Division delivered supplies regularly to Southeast Asia, supplementing seaborne deliveries and air shipments by MATS. An early task was Project Barn Door, the air movement to Vietnam of heavy equipment and personnel for a tactical air control system. Preparations included sending on December 26, 1961, an

TACTICAL AIRLIFT

airlift support unit to Clark, including maintenance, communications, aerial port, and command post personnel. The division committed twenty transports for the Barn Door project.

These missions began on January 2–3, 1962, with the delivery of seven loads to Tan Son Nhut. Subsequent flow was heaviest to Da Nang, where a heavy radar site and an air support operations center were to be established. A movement control team was sent to Da Nang on January 6 and erected its own tent encampment. Before returning to Clark nine days later, the Da Nang team handled seventy-three transport aircraft arrivals. Offloading of the aircraft often took only thirty minutes, although refueling delays were sometimes lengthy. An omnirange radio facility at Da Nang made possible instrument landings in the prevailing difficult weather. The heavy runway usage caused noticeable deterioration of taxiways and the loading ramp, but the concrete airstrip proved entirely satisfactory.

Missions to other locations were generally successful, although several aircraft required tire changes at Clark due to cuts incurred on the pierced-steel-planking runways at Bien Hoa and at Pleiku where a C–124 blew a nosewheel tire. The concrete runways at Nha Trang and Tan Son Nhut, however, proved adequate. The transports used altitude block reservations en route and every mission listed on the original flow schedule took off on

Thai airmen unload a USAF C–124 Globemaster at Don Muang Air Base.

A C-124 delivers a trailer truck loaded with supplies to Takhli Air Base, Thailand, May 1962.

the prescribed day. The Barn Door project ended on January 15, after seventy-four C-130 and sixty-eight C-124 sorties. The ability of the theater troop carrier force to operate in Vietnam was successfully demonstrated.[70]

In support of America's firm stand against communist actions in Laos, preliminary movement began with the departure on May 12 of four Okinawa-based C-130 Hercules for Clark to assist in the transfer of F-100 Super Sabres to Thailand. Four fighters and three C-130s landed in Thailand the next day for an "operational visit." Two days later, on May 15, the Joint Chiefs of Staff issued orders sending to Thailand elements of Joint Task Force (JTS) 116, formed under contingency planning for American intervention. Eleven 315th Air Division C-130s took position the next day at Don Muang with maintenance, aerial port, and extra flight crew personnel. Air movement of a Marine battalion landing team from its debarkation point at Bangkok to Udorn, Thailand, commenced at midday, May 17. The C-130s completed eighty-five round trips between Don Muang and Udorn, returning to Okinawa three days later.

Another flow of transports began on the night of May 19/20. Among the first were elements of the JTF 116 headquarters and the 315th Air Division airlift support teams. They were assigned to provide aerial port, communications, and control services at four locations in Thailand. All air division drop and training missions were canceled, and joining in the extended effort were sixteen C-130B transports from TAC, the last of which arrived at Clark on May 24. For fifteen days beginning on May 20, 120 C-130 and 51 C-124 departures cleared Okinawa for Thailand with a refueling stop at Clark. Their payloads averaged twelve tons of men and equipment. Although the Marine combat troops had been airlifted from

Thailand during the summer, the continuing American presence required substantial daily air support.[71]

Clark Air Base remained the principal gateway for transports of both MATS and the 315th Division for air access to Southeast Asia, and overlapping of capabilities and routes was unavoidable. During the summer of 1962, the 315th furnished seven scheduled flights weekly from Clark to Tan Son Nhut, while MATS provided twenty-one. Both commands flew additional unscheduled missions, although MATS normally scheduled flights only to Tan Son Nhut and Don Muang. A CINCPAC proposal in September to discontinue 315th Air Division flights to Southeast Asia in favor of exclusive dependence upon MATS met firm opposition at PACAF. The C-130s were necessary, PACAF held, for munitions hauls to Bien Hoa, for medical evacuations from Nha Trang, and for direct delivery to Air Force tactical units at Da Nang and upper Thailand. The overlapping of routes continued without serious consequences. MATS and the 315th Air Division aerial ports at Clark were consolidated and a single air traffic coordinating office at the air base determined which traffic should be moved by which command.[72]

The Air Force could look back upon the first year of C-123 operations in Vietnam with at least partial satisfaction. Through strenuous efforts, crews demonstrated the usefulness of airlift in a countrywide counterinsurgency effort. The national campaign plan called for even greater dependence on air transport and led to the forecast that the airlift requirement for the next year would be 4.4 million ton-miles per month, twice the existing capability.* A regional airlift system had been formally constituted, marking a step toward the creation of a central managerial structure for the future. Within the airlift squadrons, manning and maintenance patterns changed to reflect the prospect of a sustained effort. Having acquiesced in the idea that the Army needed transport helicopters in Vietnam, the Air Force, though acting positively, had not yet demonstrated its own capability to provide mobility for parachute infantryman. Finally, the Mule Train effort, a modest infusion of American power into Vietnam, had apparently contributed to a measurable decline in Viet Cong military activity. This was first evident in May 1962 and continued throughout the summer and fall.[73]

---

* Twenty-seven C-123s could produce 1.4 million ton-miles per month, eight Caribous could generate 0.3 million ton-miles per month, thirty-two C-47s added 0.5 million ton-miles per month. The Farm Gate C-47s were not included in the MACV calculations.

VI. The Airlift System, 1963-1964

Three developmental trends were detectable during 1963 and 1964. The first was the growth of the Southeast Asia Airlift System that centralized management of in-country transports, aerial ports, and airlift control detachments. As the overall volume of airlift effort increased, two additional C–123 transport squadrons were assigned to Vietnam, raising the total to four. Progress toward greater efficiency was measurable. In its logistical applications, airlift fitted easily into the whole national transportation system, effectively complementing the surface transport modes. But disagreement persisted among the services on the use of the Army Caribou transports within the airlift system.

A second trend was the continuing search for a tactical, as opposed to a logistical, troop carrier role. By supporting the parachute assaults, the Air Force was advocating an obsolete technique, a fact made gradually clear by the indifferent results of successive operations. Difficulties among the C–123 aircrews in executing with precision the paratroop missions constituted an unusual blemish on the Air Force's competence. By the end of 1964, the decline of the parachute assault idea appeared nearly complete, and was overtaken by the troop-carrying helicopter and by the use of the C–123s in airlanded tactical tasks.

A final line of development, which will be treated in the following chapter, was the unusually successful application of C–47s, C–123s, Caribous, and helicopters in supplying isolated camps. This was a separate logistics system operated by the U.S. Army Special Forces.

The national campaign plan, published by MACV in late 1962, provided for a general framework of allied counterinsurgency activities, which included offensive military operations, expansion of the self-defended "strategic hamlets," and border-control measures. In-country transportation channels were to be realigned to reduce the role of Saigon as the point of origin of most shipments. Further, redistribution centers were to be developed at Da Nang, Qui Nhon, Nha Trang, and Can Tho, each of which would receive cargo by water for transshipment by air to interior locations. Air transport was essential for east-west short hauls to forestall a major effort by enemy forces to disrupt or destroy ground lines of communications. The Air Force accepted this general scheme and appreciated the suitability of water transport for most hauls from Saigon to the redistribution centers. But in the plan for east-west airlift patterns, the Air Force saw the specter of a system of local control arrangements under the authority of regional corps commands, arrangements which were anathema to the Air Force's concept of centralized control.[1]

The 2d Air Division worked out several possible force structures, each tailored to meet the airlift requirements of the plan. One scheme called for the operation of C–130s from Vung Tau and Tan Son Nhut; another called for expansion of the C–123 fleet to 109 aircraft. MACV on January 2, 1963, officially requested the early introduction of a third C–123 squadron, with a fourth unit held in reserve in the United States until needed. In March the proposal received approval from the Joint Chiefs and the secretaries largely without the controversy attending the simultaneous proposal for the introduction of additional Caribous (see below). A third C–123 squadron arrived in mid-April, led by the 464th Wing commander, Colonel Daly. Fifteen of the squadron's sixteen C–123s were at Da Nang on April 17. The plan for the fourth squadron provided that it be positioned at Bien Hoa, but some aircraft and crews were to be kept at Nha Trang and Qui Nhon on a rotational basis.[2]

AFM 1–9, Theater Airlift Operations, had cautioned that "airlift should not be considered a substitute for surface transportation," and should be used for routine logistics purposes only to preserve the air fleet for possible tactical or emergency needs. On the other hand, dependence on airlift, according to the national campaign plan, admitted the undeniable ability of the enemy in Vietnam to interdict road movements at virtually any point. General Osmanski, in a letter to his counterpart on the Vietnamese joint general staff, analyzed the costs of protecting ground convoys. Small Viet Cong forces, he argued, should not be allowed to tie down numerous government troops in escort roles. Thus, even relatively routine transport movements might justifiably be performed by air, despite the apparent increased monetary expense, particularly if routes were known to be insecure or if weapons, ammunition, or communications equipment valuable to the communists were to be hauled.[3] Interviewed more than a year later, after a succession of communist ambushes, Osmanski reaffirmed his outlook.

> In a normal theater of operations such as Europe one relies on the five means of transportation in priority—rail, road, pipeline, inland waterways, and finally air. But here, because of VC interdiction of the surface means of transportation we rely on them in reverse order—air first, then on water, there is no pipeline, then on road and least on rail.[4]

The airlift requirements justified in the campaign plan proved vastly exaggerated. South Vietnamese offensive military operations failed to materialize in the dimension envisioned, and road convoys proved less subject to ambush than anticipated in the plan. In a scaled-down plan put in effect in May 1963, monthly airlift tonnage expectations were reduced to 14,500 tons by August, rather than to 36,000 tons per month as originally forecast. For the American airlifters, the tonnage reduction was probably fortunate. Brig. Gen. Theodore G. Kershaw, commander of the 315th Air Division, warned that expansion of airlift was more than a matter of acquiring additional aircraft. He foresaw air and ground congestion at many locations, insufficiency of aerial port facilities at most, difficulties of air approaches during bad weather seasons, and failure of airstrips to withstand sustained C–123 landings. A suspicion remained that the revised tonnage estimate was still too high, for airlift movements during the first five months of 1963 averaged only 3,500 tons monthly.[5]

By mid-1963 the ground transport situation had improved and certain roads, once virtually closed by the threat of ambush, were now used regularly by unescorted or lightly escorted Vietnamese army convoys. The important routes from the coast to the interior points of Pleiku, Ban Me Thuot, and Da Lat remained essentially open through most of the next year, and in the first six months only three ambushes occurred. Petroleum movements by road were generally unhindered. The small railway system, however, remained handicapped by its vulnerability to sabotage at night. Reacting to widespread Viet Cong actions against the railroads in late 1963, CINCPAC asked for a restudy of in-country logistics and he wanted to determine whether less reliance on airlft might result in more effective route security.[6]

In any case, statistics made clear the finite capacity of the existing airlift force. Of the American Military Assistance Program materiel moved out of Saigon in the late summer of 1964, seventy percent of the tonnage went by road, twenty percent by sea, five percent by rail, and only five percent by air. On the other hand, eight percent, approximately eight thousand tons per month, of the domestic military cargo movements during that summer moved by air, i.e., twice the percentage of the previous summer, while approximately twenty-five percent moved by water and the remainder mainly by road. Forty percent of the cargo destined for American receivers, however, went by air. The dominance of airlift in passenger movements is not reflected in the tonnage figures.[7]

The countrywide shipment patterns during these years evolved largely as projected in the national campaign plan. The coastal vessels used for shipment of goods from Saigon to lesser ports proved successful. Like the American airlift system, coastal sealift was organized centrally under MACV overview. In late 1964, the assistance command recommended the creation of a U.S. Army logistics command in Vietnam to reflect the Army's ongoing need for a large-scale logistics effort which could not be supported by the existing naval agency. The Air Staff appreciated MACV's reasoning, but they distrusted the Army's desire to place its own aerial port

TACTICAL AIRLIFT

Col. David T. Fleming, commander of the 315th Troop Carrier Group.

teams at airfields not already served by Air Force port detachments. To the Air Force, it followed that "the next step [forward] be integration of the airlift system into the proposed logistics command." The question awaited the Joint Chiefs' consideration.[8]

Col. Thomas B. Kennedy arrived in Vietnam in May 1963 as the first permanently assigned commander of 315th Troop Carrier Group, Assault. He was a veteran airman, having served in the Berlin and Korea airlifts and most recently was a member of the MATS staff. His group was a "minimal operational and planning headquarters," but nominally under the control of the 315th Air Division and further assigned to the operational command of MACV and 2d Air Division. Kennedy found that the arrangement created some awkward conflicts in loyalty, but he considered his primary responsibility to the 2d Air Division. As described in the 1962 combat cargo group reorganizational plan, the group also was constituted as an airlift staff element for the 2d Air Division, but Kennedy was designated director of air transportation for the division and he maintained appropriate staff relationships with MACV. Col. Charles W. Borders, the operations officer during the second half of 1964, spent much of his time visiting the group's transport movement control, aerial port, and squadron locations, and sought more and better facilities and equipment for them. He experienced excellent relationships with the 2d Air Division, particularly with the division's deputy commander, Col. Allison C. Brooks. Colonel Brooks possessed a strong airlift background, having served formerly in MATS headquarters and as a troop carrier wing commander. Known as the "Gray Fox," Brooks was regarded as a driving force by Borders and was also a close personal friend of Col. David T. Fleming, Kennedy's replacement.[9]

Transport movement controllers A1C Theodore R. MacDonald (left) and Capt. William L. Lawter maintain radio contact with a C-123 on its way to Da Nang, 1963.

The belief implicit in MACV Directive 42 that most airlift movements could be forecast well in advance proved invalid. In practice, most logistical and tactical movements resulted from oncall requests with an advance notice of twenty-four to forty-eight hours on the order. The allocations procedures specified in the directive were therefore overshadowed by the daily process of matching immediate requirements against existing capabilities. Each day, movement requests were consolidated at the desk of a field grade Air Force officer assigned to the movements branch of MACV's logistics section. An officer from the 315th Group would bring up-to-date data showing the backlogs of routine cargo awaiting movement at each location, along with information on the operational status of the troop carrier fleet. When difficult choices had to be made between movements of equally stated priority, the final adjudicator was the logistics officer. The daily schedules were thus established by four in the afternoon, and this permitted aerial ports to prepare loads during the night and to plan missions for the troop carrier units.[10]

Changes to the planned itineraries necessitated by weather, aircraft breakdowns, or emergency requests were managed by the 315th Group. Aircraft engaged in shuttling between Saigon and nearby locations could be readily diverted to different tasks, and quick reaction force alert ships could be alternately used for the local runs. Mission changes were most problematic for the aerial port managers, often involving laborious breakdown of previously prepared loads. Schedules for aircraft operating from Da Nang were ordinarily prepared at that location and published in the group's consolidated "frag order" (the daily mission directive). The most criticized feature of the allocations scheduling system involved the inability of the logistics officer, because of his many other responsibilities, to scrutinize critically users' requests, screening out unjustified requests and exaggerated priorities.[11]

Improvements in communications and in daily mission control anticipated for early 1963 were slow to materialize. Activation of teletype circuits, previously approved for airlift use, was held up in the belief that the airlift system could share the joint operation center's lines used for control of strike aircraft. Teletype service at several points, most notably at Nha Trang, remained unsatisfactory, and the primary means of communication between the six transport movement controls and Tan Son Nhut remained the telephone. An air-ground radio net requested two years earlier was largely in existence by 1964, linking transport control with mission aircraft. Each transport movement control had its own call sign: Pleiku was "Cross Bow," Nha Trang was "Beach Boy," Qui Nhon was "Sea Breeze"; and the practice of contacting transport control on all sorties became fixed among aircrews. A kind of central flight-following procedure thus developed as aircraft arrivals and departures were relayed via telephone by the transport controls to Tan Son Nhut. A fixed high frequency station in the 315th Group's operations center began operation in early 1964, promising direct contact with troop carrier aircraft anywhere in the country. But regular communications were interrupted by atmospheric characteristics and equipment malfunctions, problems which had hampered earlier efforts to link aircrews with the Mule Train operations office. Aircrews neither used the high frequency radios for routine reporting nor monitored the group frequency for possible mission diversions, but instead they relied on communications through mission control. By February 1964 an aircrew could communicate directly with six mission control detachments using the common airlift frequency, or if necessary an aircrew could reach the 315th Group directly using high frequency equipment if conditions permitted. While agreeing that flight-following capabilities had much improved, aircrews and transport movement control personnel remained critical of continuing difficulties and unreliability in communications.[12]

The operations section within the 315th Group became known by mid-1963 as the airlift control center (ALCC), with sections for the scheduling, mission control, and operational planning functions. Working space was limited and the general surroundings very noisy. The control center and each movement control detachment used quick-reference card systems and status boards as aids in mission following. Each was required to use its own initiative to keep the system flowing, rather than consult the control center through the troublesome communications. Inexperience in airlift matters among newly assigned control center and movement control personnel brought recommendations that these individuals be recruited from the C-123 squadrons. For Maj. Horace W. Shewmaker, chief of the Qui Nhon and Nha Trang movement control detachments during 1964, each day brought new crises and communications headaches. He nevertheless judged the overall airlift system to be both productive and efficient, and "capable of expansion without change to its fundamental structure."[13]

In all discussions, Air Force officials remained opposed to deploying more Caribous to Vietnam, and they favored employing those already assigned under a centralized airlift system. The Air Force feared, for example, that a second Caribou company requested by MACV in its national campaign plan would be used to enlarge corps-level airlift establishments to the detriment of overall efficiency and contrary to the rationalized need for an airlift system. Somewhat encouraging was a January 1963 CINCPAC recommendation, that all Caribous should "be included in the established airlift system." The following March, the Joint Chiefs approved the CINCPAC position. The approval was less than an admission of full support, but it afforded legalistic support for future Air Force efforts to bring the Caribou fleet under airlift system control.[14]

Despite 2d Air Division representations at MACV's logistics section, the number of Caribou aircraft under airlift system control remained only a token force. Although by an agreement in January 1963 three planes were to be provided daily, the actual commitment dwindled to fewer than one per day in May and June, as maintenance difficulties reduced the number of incommission aircraft below the corps' allocations. Meanwhile, Air Force airlift staff officers noted that much of the Caribou work under the corps advisors was administrative support, and they quoted Army Caribou pilots who complained of inefficiency. In June Admiral Felt repeated his "desire that all Caribous [should] be included in the overall airlift system." MACV then prepared a new proposal whereby both companies would be in the airlift system, although one would function in direct support of the four corps advisors.[15]

The 61st Aviation Company arrived at Vung Tau in July 1963, having flown by way of the Azores, Spain, and the Middle East. Its aircraft were assigned each day for employment under the respective corps advisors, while according to a provision in an annex to MACV Directive 44, dated July 8, the 1st Aviation Company was to operate within the Southeast Asia Airlift System. By late August, allocations from the 1st Company to the airlift system had reached eight aircraft daily. With a full-time liaison officer from 1st Company serving with the Tan Son Nhut mission control detachment, a significant beginning toward integrated operations appeared at hand.[16]

MACV had remained unenthusiastic over control of the 1st Company by the airlift system, and it offered little resistance to the proposal to withdraw the unit as part of a thousand-man token reduction at the end of 1963. The unit left Vung Tau in December, leaving behind some of its aircraft as spares for the 61st. Thereafter, the planes of the 61st operated from Da Nang, Pleiku, and Vung Tau, generally under corps advisor control. The company provided Special Forces support only in response to a specific mission request. But usage within the airlift system declined and stopped entirely in mid-July 1964. In midyear, however, controversy over the Army transport renewed when General LeMay formally disagreed with a recommendation of the Joint Chiefs that approved return of a second Caribou company to Vietnam. LeMay challenged MACV's employment of the Caribous, and he stated that the aircraft should be a part of the airlift system "for more effective airlift operation."[17]

The usefulness of the Caribous in Vietnam was undeniable. During 1963, despite a declining maintenance rate and shortages of experienced manpower, the 1st Company continually increased the passenger and cargo workload, often operating into locations and under conditions unsuitable for sustained C-123 operations. The installation of reversible-pitch propellers proved successful. Caribou crews made frequent airdrops, generally to Special Forces camps, both by parachute and free fall methods. They also worked on tactics for resupply of forward patrols. Regular missions employing low-level extraction techniques promised better accuracy and economy than by paradrops. Through the low level method, the crew actuated a parachute to extract the palletized cargo. Army test reports also indicated that a new forward-scanning weather avoidance radar "enhanced the effectiveness" of the Caribous in Vietnam. But accidents seemed to occur in bunches, and some aircraft were damaged in shortfield landings and others lost on takeoff.[18]

Assessments of the extent of duplication and waste resulting from the independence of the Caribous from the airlift system remained controversial. Episodes of duplication occurred with sufficient frequency, for example, when C-123s discovered that their loads had been already picked up by opportune Caribou lift. On the other hand, some Air Force liaison officers held the belief that a number of their service's aircraft should be controlled at the corps level. General Anthis was confronted with the problem of satisfying "a customer that is also a competitor;" and General Osmanski recognized that some complaints were made by individuals "adept at trying to trick" the Southeast Asia Airlift System into unfavorable showings. Such conduct among officers in the field was a rare exception, and generally the climate of cooperation was total. Officers at the airlift control center did find members of the nearby MACV Army aviation section wholly committed to the immediate fighting of a war.[19]

A decision was reached in early 1963 to place the C-123 units permanently in Vietnam. This was done to offset the undesirable turnover of personnel caused by the six-month tours, and the inability of the training program at Pope to provide sufficient replacements for the three squadrons. Indeed, the squadron that was sent in 1963 consisted primarily of men going to Vietnam for the second time. The Joint Chiefs concurred on April 12 with the Air Force "to exploit the operational experience of personnel now lost after six months." With the conversion, authorized crew-to-aircraft ratio was set at 1.5 to permit increases in sorties and aircraft utilization.[20]

The Air Force continued to encourage men to volunteer for Southeast Asia, and the selection rule was adopted to assure that "only the best go west." The experience level in the C-123 was low, especially in the 309th and 210th Squadrons at Tan Son Nhut. Tightened supervision, begun in late 1962, increased, although the factor of individual judgment and adaptability remained important. Indeed, one C-123 instructor concluded that his biggest problem lay in getting former bomber and tanker pilots to break away from reliance on prescribed procedures. Weekly meetings discussing weaknesses and solutions were held among the 315th Group standardization personnel and the squadron instructors. The adoption of a twelve-month permanent tour standard quickly built up the average in-country experience among crewmen, but it also brought an annoying increase in paperwork.[21]

C-123 training in the United States remained a topic of continuing review. Cargo airdrops received renewed emphasis as a result of the early Mule Train experience. Upon recommendations from Vietnam in the spring of 1963, tactical training was revised. Corridor stream and night low-level airdrop missions were eliminated; and emphasis shifted to day assault landings, airdrops, and formation flying. Instructor pilots in Vietnam also criticized the inability of newcomers to make landings with heavy loads, which resulted in several near-accidents in 1964. More work in nonstandard and steep landing approaches also appeared desirable, along with additional practice in mapreading navigation at the altitudes ordinarily used in Vietnam. Training of enlisted flight mechanics and loadmasters seemed in some areas to be superficial and this necessitated prolonged checkouts in Vietnam.[22]

The 311th Squadron at Da Nang preserved an air of individuality. Drawn entirely from Pope personnel in 1963, the crewmen were generally younger, lower in rank, and far more experienced in the C-123 than their counterparts at Tan Son Nhut. The work of the 311th included frequent missions to mountain airstrips and drop zones, and operations into the A Shau Valley. Lt. Col. Harry "the Horse" Howton, the commander of the

TACTICAL AIRLIFT

311th, became a legendary figure and his colorful leadership earned him the dedicated effort of his men. He was a favorite subject among reporters and writers visiting Da Nang. And officers of the 315th Group staff spoke of Howton's "own little airline," because of the fact that schedules were drawn up within his unit.[23]

Viet Cong ground fire increased steadily against allied transports. Seventeen C–123s received hits in 1962, seventy in 1963, and more than a hundred in 1964.* At first most hits came from individual small-arms fire, but multiple hits from machineguns became more and more frequent. The communists formed antiaircraft companies, and developed techniques for digging in and concealing gun positions. Transport crews used, hereafter, higher en route altitudes and tighter landing patterns. To supplement the data furnished by the official intelligence system, information on hot areas passed by word of mouth among crewmen. When flying into such areas, crews stayed clear of ridges and made steep descents to remain as low as possible. The simplicity and ruggedness of the C–123 proved assets in such instances. Fighter escort was planned for certain missions and this was a valuable tactic since the communists learned not to open fire in the presence of strike aircraft. During major operations in the A Shau Valley in May 1964, for example, transports and helicopters timed their arrival to take advantage of scheduled air cover. The congestion of transports at the valley airstrips was unavoidable, but this was preferable to operating unescorted. Experience substantiated the conviction that, given proper strike support, the C–123s could operate anywhere in South Vietnam.[24]

Despite the trend of hits between 1962 and 1964, few aircraft losses could be clearly attributed to communist ground fire. Enemy action was suspected, but not confirmed, in the loss of a C–123 before dawn on October 24, 1963, while the Provider was dispensing flares south of Saigon. A year later, ground fire originating from Cambodia destroyed a C–123 while dropping ammunition at the Bu Prang camp. The wreckage lay just inside South Vietnam and all eight crewmen perished. A second C–123 on the same mission also received ground fire.[25]

Carelessness or indiscipline in the air could never be absolutely excluded as factors in aircraft accidents. Intolerable were aircrew actions such as those causing the crash of a 315th Group C–123 in northeast Thailand on April 12, 1963. After a normal takeoff at Nakhon Phanom, the aircraft's crew attempted to snare a red flag mounted on top of a fifty-foot pole. On the second try, the left wing struck a house and the aircraft crashed. Two Thais on the ground were killed along with the four-man

---

* The stated figures include data for UC–123s, which accounted for approximately a third of the above totals. Per sortie, UC–123s were hit at least twice as frequently as the airlift C–123s.

crew; a Thai civilian entered the burning aircraft but he was unsuccessful in his rescue attempt. During the investigation, the board learned that other C–123 crews had also tried to snag the flag. This episode represented an indefensible breach of flying discipline and stained the group's otherwise creditable record of achievement.[26]

In spite of the Nakhon Phanom fiasco, the deteriorating accident rate of late 1962 was reversed. One crew barely avoided disaster when it aborted a landing attempt on the sloping strip at Bao Loc. During its go-round, the aircraft flew through vegetation and extending tree limbs, clogging an oil filter. This necessitated an emergency landing at Bien Hoa. Another crew escaped serious injury in mid-1964 during a landing at Gia Vuc. Apparently as a result of unequal propeller reversal, the aircraft swerved into a barracks and totally burned. Though the plane was the seventh C–123 lost in Southeast Asia, the 315th Group received for that year the PACAF tactical flight safety trophy and the Air Force flying safety plaque, "in view of the hazardous missions flown and the limited airfield and navigational facilities."[27]

Contentment was apparent among troop carrier crewmen, stemming from the diversity of their missions and the readily apparent results of their endeavors. Howton, whose military career included service in the China-Burma-India theater in World War II and later troop carrier operations in Korea, reported that morale was "the highest I have ever encountered." He, like many others, felt that his tour had been "the most challenging and rewarding I have ever had." Most officers believed their Vietnam service would be beneficial to their careers, and many received desirable reassignments upon returning to the United States. The opportunity to earn awards and decorations, and to accumulate "combat support" flying time were important incentives. Flights supporting Special Forces, airdrops, and munitions hauls qualified as combat support, and one Air Medal was awarded for each twenty-five of these (the criteria for this award changed periodically). Personnel shortages became a blessing in part, creating extra work and thus filling the time ordinarily left for family responsibilities. Most crewmen disliked the necessity to lengthen their individual tours beyond twelve months, which was widely done because of shortages in the fall of 1964. After the Bu Prang loss in October, some heldover crewmen asked to be grounded. Supervisors quietly honored some requests, understanding the morale effect of the extensions.[28]

Billeting and messing arrangements for enlisted men at Tan Son Nhut improved little, while overcrowding in the barracks and messhall worsened. Most individuals at Da Nang lived in open-bay barracks furnished with double bunks; noisy conditions made rest next to impossible for individuals on the night work or flying schedule. Other annoyances included the unsuitability of heavy Air Force fatigue clothing and boots, and shortages of vehicles for onbase transportation. Serious health problems were absent, except for occasional cases of hepatitis and attacks of dysentery which seemed to strike everyone periodically.[29]

The enlisted members of the C–123 aircrews deserved special credit, since they shared the risks of the officers along with the privations in pay and living conditions of the other airmen. Loadmaster work was wearisome and sometimes especially dangerous, since these men handled heavy cargo during loadings and drops. The Mule Train loadmasters were relatively junior, bringing with them the enthusiasm and physical stamina of youth. On many crews, the officers pitched in to help offload at places distant from aerial port locations. The tasks of the flight mechanics were ordinarily less exhausting, although for a time Mule Train flight mechanics doubled as ground crewmen. The policy of scheduling each flight mechanic regularly in "his own" aircraft offered valuable familiarity with the peculiarities of each plane, but the notion quickly proved irreconcilable with maintenance efficiency. Recognized for their expert knowledge of aircraft engines and auxiliary systems, able "engineers" could assess malfunctions better than many pilots, and their advice often made possible safe completion of otherwise doubtful missions. The daily airlift accomplishments of the C–123 fleet were thus made possible by the energy and skills of all crewmembers.[30]

The distinctiveness of improvisation continued to mark C–123 maintenance. Much of the work at Tan Son Nhut was conducted outdoors; at night, crews used flashlights or vehicle headlamps. Of five engine changes made in March 1963, the engine shop performed four away from their home base. Over usage and climate contributed to engine and tire failures, dirty oil systems, and corrosion. But the shortages of spare parts and maintenance equipment improved gradually. Aircraft were flown to Clark for periodic inspection work. Days off for the maintenance people were nonexistent and aircrews warmly praised their efforts, marveling at their ability to keep the aircraft flying despite the difficult work conditions and the harsh usage. One C–123 instructor pilot wrote that "the relationship between flight crews and maintenance men is the best I have ever seen."[31]

The wearing effects of heavy usage reduced the incommission rate in May and June 1963, while the squadrons at Tan Son Nhut fell seriously short of their monthly flying quota of sixty hours per aircraft. Several changes, all pointing toward traditional maintenance management, helped reverse the decline. Consolidated aircraft maintenance squadrons were created in July at Tan Son Nhut and Da Nang. All maintenance personnel and equipment from the C–123 and other flying units were absorbed into the new squadrons. The 315th Group thus relinquished its responsibility for maintaining the C–123s. Also put into effect in July were the highly systematized methods of maintenance management procedures. With the

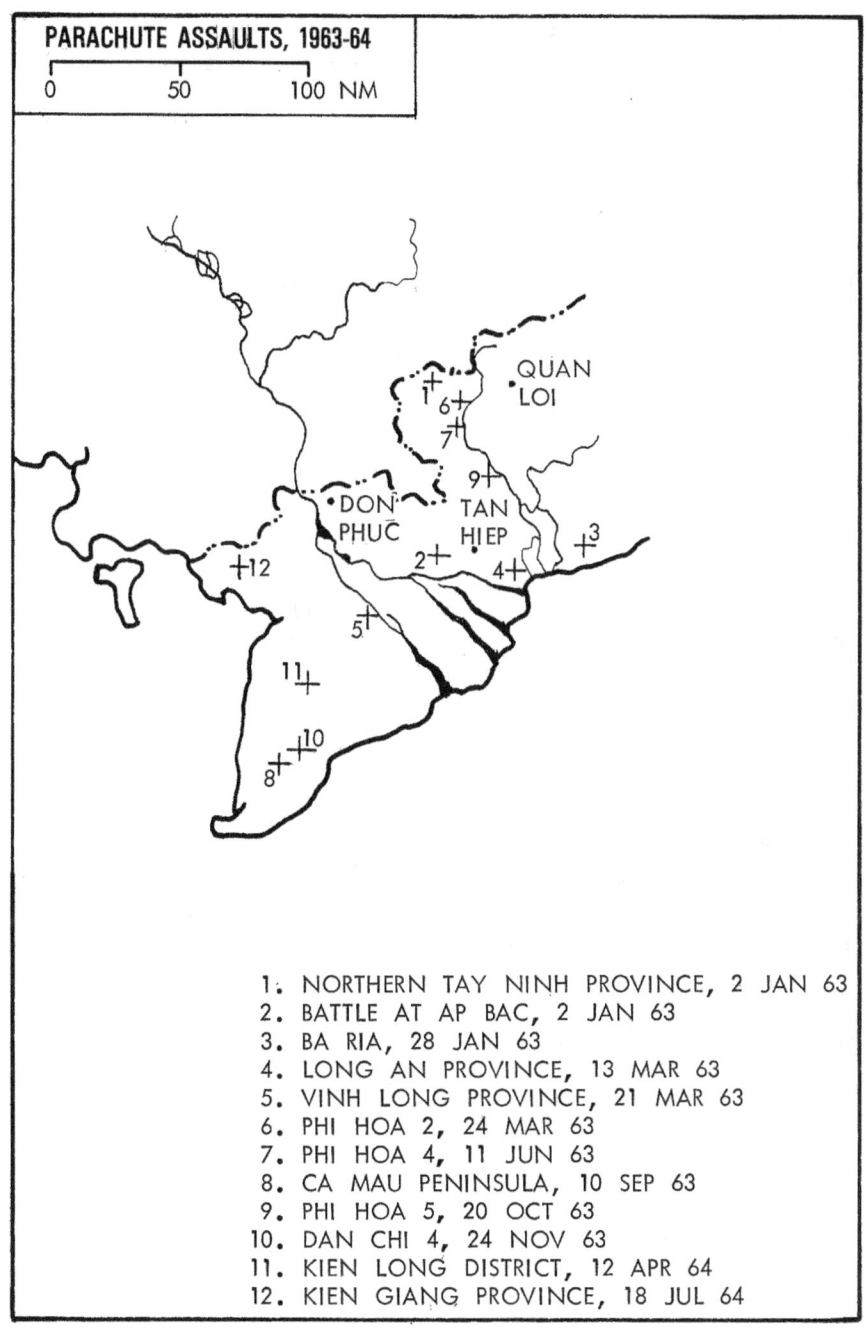

TACTICAL AIRLIFT

conversion to one-year permanent manning and the introduction of newly designed maintenance vans, the changes amounted to a fresh start for C-123 maintenance in Vietnam.[32]

The status of the remaining C-123 force in the United States became anomalous as the 464th Wing resumed its conversions to C-130s. The Air Force in mid-1963 recommended, and the Secretary of Defense later approved, transfer of the C-123s to the special air warfare force, a descendant of Jungle Jim. The C-123s remaining at Pope were moved to Hurlburt along with a nucleus of officers and airmen. They formed the 317th Air Commando Squadron (Troop Carrier), which was activated July 1, 1964. Pipeline C-123 training for Vietnam also shifted to Hurlburt. The C-123 units, thereafter, claimed the air commando tradition, although the eliteness of the early Jungle Jim venture had faded.[33]

The Air Force during 1963 persisted in its efforts to make the parachute assault method work. General Anthis repeatedly informed PACAF that the airlift fleet was primarily an instrument for tactical roles, with logistics employment a secondary mission. If the reverse were true, he said, "we are likely to end up as an airline rather than as an assault airlift force." The Air Force thus went along with the gung ho attitude of U.S. Army advisors, who saw in the paratroops the best fighters in the Vietnamese army.[34]

Two tactical operations in early January 1963 brought together helicopter and parachute mobility. The first effort was a planned morning assault near the Cambodian border, directly north of Tay Ninh City. A parachuted force was to move toward units landed by helicopter, sweeping an area believed to house the principal regional Viet Cong headquarters. Helicopters staged from Quan Loi airstrip, twenty miles east of the objective area. To preserve surprise, preliminary reconnaissance was limited and planning for the airlift was held to a single day.

American C-123 and Vietnamese C-47 crews attended a predawn briefing at Tan Son Nhut. Soon after daylight, seventeen C-123s and twenty C-47s loaded 1,250 paratroops and taxied into line for takeoff. As in most previous assaults, Colonel Ky flew the lead C-47. The join-up and flight to the jump area were uneventful, except for troublesome saturation of radio frequencies. Air strikes hit the drop zones and other targets shortly before drop time. Since the zone was narrow, the C-123s flew individually at five-second intervals. Approaching the area, the lead crew spotted protruding stakes on the ground. Aborting the jump, the transports began to orbit, awaiting a decision by the Vietnamese airborne brigade commander aboard one of the C–123s. Broken clouds made the orbit a hazardous undertaking. After long discussion, the Vietnamese officer decided to jump as planned. Injuries were not numerous and some elements intentionally descended into a nearby wooded area. The prolonged orbit, however, betrayed hopes of surprise and ground operations developed slowly. Twenty-eight hours after the jump the joint operations control duty officer wrote: "Paratroops are in pickup zone and will not leave until chutes are picked up. No wonder we never catch the VC's." The six-day search netted several hundred Viet Cong casualties along with considerable amounts of enemy supplies.[35]

More controversial was the operation conducted on the same day in the Mekong Delta, thirty-five miles southwest of Saigon. This had been planned as a helicopter venture, staged from the Tan Hiep airfield near My Tho. After several unopposed troop lifts in the morning, ten American H–21s attempted an assault at the hamlet of Ap Bac, where they encountered intense fire from concealed enemy positions. Four copters were shot down at the landing zone, along with an American gunship helicopter. In late afternoon, the Vietnamese ground commander called for paratroops. Approximately an hour later, 320 boarded seven Providers in a formation led by Lt. Col. Andrew Johnson.

Approaching the drop zone, confusion again prevailed in the lead aircraft, because the troops below fired flares of colors different from those briefed. Unsure of the meaning of the signal, Johnson refused to drop the men until he received radio clearance. The troops jumped on the third pass over the site. Their jump accuracy was good, but they encountered fire during their assembly on the ground and by next morning had twenty men killed and another thirty-one wounded, including two U.S. Army advisors. Throughout the next day, transports and another paratroop battalion remained ready for further jumps; the battalion was not sent as the intensity of fighting subsided.[36]

Allied reexamination of the events established that there was an absence of strike aircraft during the morning hours, there was a lack of aggressiveness among South Vietnamese troops, and the transport helicopters were obviously vulnerable. General Harkins believed that the drop zone for the paratroop assault had been unwisely chosen. As a demonstration of the readiness of the reaction force, however, the mission had been a success, marred only by the confusion at the site.[37]

The allies later captured a copy of the communist analysis of the Ap Bac battle. The document revealed that the enemy learned of the afternoon drops shortly beforehand by intercepting allied radio communications. The communists watched the three overhead passes by the seven C–123s (the document misidentified the aircraft as C–47s). The sight of the transports

Maj. Gen. Rollen H. Anthis, commander of 2d Air Division, talks with Vietnamese paratroopers waiting to board a USAF transport, October 1963.

USAF maintenance specialists at work on a C-123 engine, 1964.

Vietnamese paratroopers jump from C-123s during a major operation over Tay Ninh Province, March 1963.

Three C–123s on a Vietnamese paratroop training mission over Vung Tau. 1964.

Nguyen Cao Ky, as an air commodore in 1964.

New aerial port detachment at Qui Nhon.

TACTICAL AIRLIFT

and descending paratroops caused some of their new recruits to take refuge in ditches, getting their weapons wet. Other troops fired resolutely on the paratroopers in the air and on the ground, wiping out several elements and forcing local retreats. The document drew several lessons:

(1) Viet Cong commanders should be alert to the possibility of parachute assaults, considering the tactical situation and the presence of a clear drop zone.

(2) The presence of an allied observation plane, followed by the appearance of the C–47s, would signal the assault.

(3) Troops should fire upon descending troopers, preferably in organized barrage starting as soon as parachutes opened and aiming below the knees.

(4) The paratroop commander, with his distinctive colored parachute, should be singled out for fire.

(5) Paratroops were vulnerable when first landing, because of dispersion, unfamiliarity with terrain, and the need to untie weapons.

(6) The defenders should attack, seeking hand-to-hand combat, as soon as the jumpers hit the ground.[38]

More than a thousand troopers jumped from twenty-one C–123s on January 28, 1963, near Ba Ria, north of Vung Tau. Despite reduced maneuverability, an in-trail "V" formation of three aircraft each was used in order to get the entire force on the ground as quickly as possible. Ninety-five percent of the men landed in the short drop zone. Vietnamese Air Force C–47s dropped thereafter. Although to that date the assault was technically the most successful involving American aircraft, no contact with communist forces resulted. Just prior to the airborne phase, an enemy communication was intercepted, instructing the Viet Cong forces in the area to disperse and evade government forces.[39]

Three airborne operations in 1963, each involving the C–123s and the C–47s, appeared to verify the superior accuracy of the Vietnamese in placing troops on designated drop zones. In the three assaults of March 13, 21, and 24, the C–47s placed their loads correctly. Of the troops carried by the C–123s on the 21st, one half missed the zone by three to four miles. Three days later in Tay Ninh Province the C–123s put 100 parachutists, including a U.S. advisor, into the jungle adjacent to the drop zone. This was the largest operation of the series, involving sixteen C–123s, eighteen C–47s, and 1,181 men of the airborne brigade. Two C–123s received hits. The six-day ground operation included heliborne operations and resulted in capture of a Viet Cong munitions factory and food depot, and was considered "exceptionally successful."[40]

On the strength of information indicating an assembly of high Viet Cong officials, an airborne assault was launched the morning of June 11, fifteen miles northeast of Tay Ninh City. Ten C–47s and six C–123s arrived at the target area on schedule in early morning. The C–47s dropped their troops successfully, but because of rainshowers which partly obscured the drop zone, the C–123s turned to Tan Son Nhut. They were recalled to the drop zone when the showers appeared to move away, but again the Americans had trouble finding the area, neglecting the advice of a Vietnamese navigator in the lead C–123. After several passes, the C–123s made their drops; many paratroopers landed away from the drop area and others were confused during their assembly because the 123s had dropped the men using the opposite axis of flight from that planned. The delay between the Vietnamese and American drops proved unfortunate, since it left the men on the ground understrength. Five of the C–123s did receive small-arms hits.[41]

However the September 10 reinforcement jump near Ca Mau in the extreme south of Vietnam was reasonably successful. Although briefing instructions and the actual loading were confused, Capt. Jack V. Cebe-Habersky, assistant air liaison officer to the airborne brigade, guided the transports by radio to the drop zone from an L–19. T–28s made pre-strikes, and ten C–47s and seven C–123s dropped five hundred men "with professional dispatch."[42]

A succession of frustrations reached the bizarre in Operation Phi Hoa 5, on October 20. Fourteen C–123s preceded sixteen C–47s to the drop site near the Parrot's Beak salient of Cambodia, northwest of Saigon. Unable to spot the zone, the Americans turned away for a second run. Again, an American officer in a light aircraft gave verbal instructions and laid down smoke grenades. Approaching the area a second time, an American navigator prematurely actuated the green-light jump signal, causing the poised paratroopers to begin exiting. Other aircraft in the element also began the drop at the sight of the leader's chute, as did the trailing Providers. Before the mistake could be corrected by radio, some 350 men had landed about two miles short of the intended place. Fortunately, contact with the enemy on the ground was negligible; this permitted the jumpers to rejoin, although many parachutes were lost.[43]

The tragic drop on November 24 (Dan Chi 4) confirmed with finality the limitations already plain. The mission was prepared hastily to reinforce forces under heavy attack in the Ca Mau Peninsula. A hurried briefing gave the American crews only thirty minutes to launch aircraft; they were told that the Vietnamese Air Force C–47s would lead, and that the C–123s were to drop on the preceding parachutes. Five C–47s and eight C–123s carried a full battalion. But, because of a lack of warning, no control ship accompanied the transports.

The Vietnamese dropped first and successfully placed their jumpers. The lead American navigator, because of inadequate maps, became disoriented during the run. And the camouflaged parachutes of the earlier jumpers were unrecognizable until the C–123s passed directly overhead. Exiting late, the second wave landed into an area of heavy growth and deep water, well beyond the limits of the zone. Eight men drowned, troop assembly was difficult, and nearly all of the chutes were lost. The jump therefore was halted before all of the men had exited, and those remaining jumped accurately on another pass. Three American aircraft received hits; and, in general, contact on the ground with the Viet Cong forces was negligible.[44]

The next day, Col. Joe B. Lamb of the U.S. Army, an advisor to the airborne brigade, accompanied the brigade commander to investigate the drop. At Ca Mau, Lamb met a senior Vietnamese officer who indicated that he was initiating formal correspondence on the consistently poor performance of the C–123 aircrews. His letter, addressed to Vietnamese Air Force headquarters with an information copy for MACV, referred to the Dan Chi 4 and Phi Hoa 5 operations. He requested "appropriate measures to be taken to avoid above cited deficiencies in future operations." Lamb, meanwhile, compiled for MACV a record of the brigade's airborne operations since January, pointedly highlighting the difficulties involving the C–123s. An American officer warned that the Vietnamese paratroopers might become reluctant to jump from the C–123s, if the errors continued.[45]

Replying to an official letter from General Anthis on the matter, Colonel Kennedy stressed that most of the failures were the result of inadequate information and a lack of time for planning. These could be avoided, Kennedy wrote, had the Vietnamese been more cooperative in mission preparation. Although the quick reaction force operations plan specified procedures for combined operations, each assault, for example, entailed fresh and prolonged adjudication over employed tactics. Kennedy later described the "absolute chaos and disorganization" which prevailed prior to these missions and the last-minute debate on the drop zone location and approach path.[46]

The reforms took several directions. Soon after Dan Chi 4, the 2d Division requested higher command assistance in obtaining expanded scale maps, since "accuracy of airborne assaults was being affected by lack of charts to pinpoint DZ's." New tests led to better techniques for marking drop zones with flares and smoke, and the idea of using an airborne controller in assaults—a notion absent in prewar U.S. doctrine—was affirmed in combined procedures published in 1964. American officers tried to interest the Vietnamese in the special gear used by the British in Malaya for parachuting into trees, hopefully making possible a far wider choice of drop zones. Arrangements for Vietnamese officers to visit Singapore, however, encountered interminable obstacles and were eventually canceled.[47]

Paratroops and transports were marshaled on at least five occasions during 1964, but only two operations were actually carried out. During the morning of April 12, a battalion jumped into the Kien Long district of southernmost Vietnam, after Viet Cong attacks the previous night. Surface winds gusting to twenty knots dragged the men upon landing, injuring 66 of the 584 who had jumped. The two waves landed a half mile from the drop zone. Only intermittent contact with the enemy resulted. Another mission on July 18 was technically more successful. All ten C–47s and a like number of C–123s dropped accurately, but there was no contact with the enemy.[48]

The quick reaction force concept faded along with the parachute assault idea. The Fire Brigade transport force, normally consisting of five C–47s and three C–123s, could lift only two airborne companies—a force too small to challenge the larger Viet Cong formations now appearing. The idea, therefore, gained strength to delay paratroop response until a larger force could be marshaled. More frequently, alert transports were used for unplanned lifts and local paratroop training. The airborne brigade itself organized an "Eagle Flight" force, an alert element ready for immediate helicopter movement. With the paratroops themselves adopting the helicopter assault concept, the parachute approach became obsolescent.[49]

American Air Force officers acknowledged the advantages of helicopter mobility in Vietnam, offering a wide choice of landing zones, the capacity to withdraw or relocate forces, the ease of troop assembly after landing, and the ability to deliver troops not having special jump training. The Air Force, however, pointed out the vulnerability of helicopters to hostile fire, and firmly opposed the idea of arming these aircraft. Maj. Gen. Glen W. Martin, PACAF plans and operations deputy, advised Anthis in June 1963 that arming the helicopter "eliminates its use in a role for which it is better suited, that of helicopter transport." By mid-1964, the bulk of the two-hundred-aircraft U.S. Army helicopter force in Vietnam was deployed under the operational control of the corps senior advisors, with a reserve element placed at Saigon under MACV joint operations control for shifting when needed among the several corps.[50]

As the paratroop assault concept declined, the use of the Provider fleet in airlanded tactical movements became more frequent. Indeed, the helicopter airmobile idea, instead of ending the tactical role for the 123s, produced a host of new applications which sustained or cooperated with forward helicopter operations. The troop capacity, range, and shortfield qualities of the C–123 introduced innumerable possibilities for imaginative employment.

Exemplifying airlanded tactical applications were the continuing C–123 missions into the A Shau Valley, which intensified in late 1963. Operations into the valley recurred often in the subsequent airlift history in Vietnam. Lying near the Laotian border, roughly three miles wide, and traversed along its length by a primitive roadway, the valley offered the communists an avenue from Laos to the hills about Da Nang and points to the south. Three airstrips existed within the valley. A Luoi at the northern end and A Shau at the southern were usable by C–123s, and the former under day conditions only. Ta Bat near the center depended upon C–123 airdrops and Caribou and Marine helicopter landings. Several Vietnamese battalions garrisoned the airfields, while Vietnamese special troops operated about the lesser outposts. The entire region resembled a strategic airhead, in that overland movements were rarely attempted by the single hill road from the coast. Communist forces were able to enter and move about the valley, and transports could expect ground fire at anytime. Weather chronically handicapped air operations, compounded by the total absence of landing aids. Two Da Nang-based 123s routinely shuttled each day into A Luoi; troop rotations, reinforcements, or engineer construction projects brought intermittent increases in the airlift effort. On November 18, for example, after a night of heavy communist attacks, the C–123s brought into A Shau 540 troops and thirty-five tons of munitions. An intensified air resupply effort continued for the next two weeks, until there was a decline in enemy activity and a withdrawal of reinforcements. Confrontation in the valley continued and on one occasion small-arms fire wounded the pilots of a Caribou preparing for takeoff. Lt. Gen. William C. Westmoreland, deputy commander of MACV, was aboard the aircraft at the time and chagrined local authorities closed the valley's three airfields, promising that the garrisons would receive a diet of airdropped basic rations until the insecure situation was corrected.[51]

Another form of C–123 airlanded tactics developed in the Quyet Thang 33/64 operation of March 14–16, 1964, staged in the roadless and partly submerged area where the Mekong River enters Vietnam. The C–123s used the dirt airstrip at Don Phuc, in the heart of the operational area; a command post and artillery forces were lifted in the first morning, simultaneous with the initial helicopter and waterborne assaults. That afternoon, the 123s began to deliver fuel and rocket ordnance for the helicopters; without this effort, the closest replenishment facility was fifty miles away. An air liaison officer present at Don Phuc reported that he was "happy to see the USAF in tactical operations," and that the initiative of the aircrews had enhanced the "sometimes tattered USAF feathers."[52]

Still another form of air mobility exploiting the range of the 123s was adopted for the deployment of an airborne battalion and ranger company from Saigon to Quang Ngai on April 28, 1964. Helicopter assaults out of Quang Ngai began the previous day. The airlift flow plan called for takeoffs at Tan Son Nhut every fifteen minutes; ten C–123s were to haul 360 troops and sixteen tons of cargo, and they were to be followed by ten

Vietnamese Air Force C–47s with 220 troops. On the ground at Quang Ngai, the aircraft were to discharge their loads with engines running to minimize congestion. The plan was executed with only minor deviations, and during the afternoon of the twenty-eighth, the newly arrived force was lifted by helicopter to the battle area. Some of the C–123s made additional trips from Saigon, and others shuttled to and from Da Nang, carrying fuel for the helicopters and T–28s operating from Quang Ngai.[53]

The capabilities of the C–123s to shift forces from one part of Vietnam to another received attention in new contingency plans developed at MACV. Various alternatives were discussed. In one plan, the Providers were to be augmented by C–130s. General Westmoreland, who had assumed the command of MACV in mid-1964 and was himself a former airborne officer, recognized the ability of the transports to make fast division-sized movements. This, he believed, made it possible for the Vietnamese to cope with the major military threats.[54]

The evidence became unmistakable. Not only did the C–123 excel in airlanded tactics, but also there existed an important need for this kind of activity in a "war without fronts." The airlanded tactical applications, although less dramatic than parachute assault operations, correctly foreshadowed the employment of the C–123s and a larger force of C–130s in Vietnam in later years. The ability of the Southeast Asia Airlift System to sustain daily high volume logistics demands, while maintaining readiness for surges in the tactical effort, become the heart of the airlift story.

Essential to an efficient theater airlift system are the management and handling of cargo at the theater airfields. Misdirected or damaged cargo, or unnecessary aircraft-loading delays, sap the resources of a command. Under agreements dating back to 1952, the Air Force held primary responsibility for tactical aerial port activities. The Army retained the obligation to prepare parachutes, platforms, and cargo for airdrops, and kept responsibility for loading aircraft during major unit moves, tasks which might otherwise saturate a local aerial port. Air Force Manual 1–9 established that the Air Force would operate aerial port facilities under the command control of a theater airlift commander, and would assign parent aerial port squadrons and smaller detachments at airfields according to need. Aerial port squadrons of varying size were accordingly organized in TAC and the Air Force Reserve. In addition to managing cargo and passengers at theater airfields, the squadrons provided loadmasters for duty on airdrops and combat control teams. The latter trained as pathfinders for assault drops, but had broad capabilities if stationed at forward airstrips. During Exercise Swift Strike in 1961, the aerial port apparatus was substantial. TAC and Reserve port personnel served as cargo handling teams at five airfields, while six combat control teams deployed to forward locations. The apparatus became the foundation for the aerial port system later adopted in Southeast Asia.[55]

Newly established aerial port detachments operated in early 1962 at Tan Son Nhut, Da Nang, and Pleiku, manned with personnel from the Japan-based 7th Aerial Port Squadron. Elsewhere in Vietnam, cargo handling depended largely on the resourcefulness and energy of the aircrew and local personnel. A team of senior PACAF officers determined in April that at many sites supplies were "constantly being misplaced or lost." At Nha Trang, for example, an Air Force communication team commander felt obliged to meet every incoming aircraft to assure that his supplies reached him.[56]

Three port detachments were added during the spring—two in Thailand and one at Nha Trang. At the six ports, operations were hampered by equipment and facility limitations. Critical shortages "affecting the mission" were listed and the assets of the entire theater screened. Forklifts, used for moving and hoisting loads into the rear doorway of the C–123s, frequently broke down under heavy usage; repairs usually depended on the resourcefulness of inadequately trained mechanics at the scene. Aircrews often complained of errors in the weight of cargo shown on loading documents, a potential cause for major accidents.[57]

The aerial port apparatus under the 6493d Aerial Port Squadron (Provisional), set up in late 1962, included 135 permanently assigned personnel, fifteen others in temporary assignments, and sixty-one Vietnamese and Thai nationals used for unskilled tasks. Most were assigned to the major ports at Tan Son Nhut and Bangkok. With activation of the 8th Aerial Port Squadron in early December 1962, this unit became the model for future growth. The 8th was an assigned unit of the 315th Group and under its operational control. MATS air terminal detachments at the major airfields remained separate entities, until they merged with the 8th in October 1963.[58]

Gradual improvements in facilities and equipment diminished the need for improvisation and ingenuity at the ports. Hot lines were installed linking the aerial port's space control office at Tan Son Nhut to both the joint operations center and base operations office at the 315th Group, and to the freight and passenger holding areas. The link thus formed an independent communications network for terminal operations.

Overtime was common and days off rare among aerial port members, as the monthly tonnages increased. Port detachments in Vietnam handled over 5,000 tons in January and 6,500 tons in May. The Tan Son Nhut facility was by far the busiest, handling 3,700 tons in May, compared with

1,500 at Da Nang, 700 at Pleiku, and 600 at Nha Trang. At Tan Son Nhut, cargo brought in by air or sea to Saigon was repacked into smaller loads and marked for various destinations within Vietnam. Beginning before dawn each morning, the forklifts could be heard installing the repackaged cargo into the holds of the C-123s.

Expansion during 1963 largely followed the traffic forecasts of the national campaign plan. New port detachments, designated as redistribution centers, opened at Qui Nhon and Can Tho in May. A detachment moved to Bien Hoa from Thailand in June. Port squadron strength reached 150 in June, nearly a twofold increase in a six-month period; the national campaign plan provided for further increases to raise the personnel strength to five hundred. Since the Air Force had few individuals experienced in tactical aerial port work, numerous low-ranking airmen from supply and associated specialties were assigned to the 8th Squadron. Local on-the-job-training programs generally made such newcomers quickly productive. Especially attractive was the idea of increasing the use of local nationals, promising not only early cuts in Air Force manpower, but also providing a pool of trained people able to carry on after the American departure. A PACAF team had so recommended in June 1963, and suggested that a suitable ratio might be one military supervisor for every four Vietnamese employees. An enlarged program for training Vietnamese civilians was accordingly introduced.[59]

The Air Force's Project 463L, a universal cargo handling system for the C-130 Hercules aircraft, promised faster and more efficient cargo handling along with improved methods as well for the C-123, and for other strategic transports of MATS. The C-130s had a dual rail system installed capable of receiving standard aluminum pallets. Cargo could be loaded on the pallets at the aerial ports, and moved planeside by small trailers or forklifts, and loaded by the latter. At major ports, self-propelled platforms or "K-loaders," facilitated fast loading of multiple pallets. Both C-123s and C-130s if necessary could make fast offloadings by unlocking the pallets, taxiing forward, and allowing the pallets to roll out. Equipment for the 463L system began to arrive in the Pacific in late 1963; in spite of the endless shortage of aluminum pallets and the chronic problems with equipment maintenance, the system proved enormously valuable.[60]

Shortages of materiel handling equipment persisted. For example, only eighteen forklifts were on hand in Vietnam in May 1963, including four heavy-duty type—three were located at Tan Son Nhut and one at Da Nang. The absence of forklifts at outpost locations sometimes necessitated time-consuming hand loading or offloading, while the difficulty of keeping forklifts in commission never ended. Scales for weighing cargo remained generally unavailable throughout 1964, necessitating "educated guesswork" in keeping loads within safe limits and resulting in the loss of considerable lift capacity because of unnecessary safety margins.[61]

TACTICAL AIRLIFT

Aerial port workloads increased in proportion to overall airlift activity. The effort at Qui Nhon built up rapidly under the redistribution concept of the national campaign plan; and the creation of a Special Forces logistics center at Nha Trang resulted in major cargo increases at that port. On June 20, 1964, the 8th Squadron announced that its detachments in Thailand and Vietnam had handled 357 tons of cargo, a new single-day record. A new detachment was placed at Vung Tau in December, where the problems initially were as great as elsewhere. Rainstorms regularly converted the cargo area into mud, and on one occasion knocked down the port tent. At year's end, personnel manning for the eight aerial ports in Vietnam stood at three hundred, including fifty local civilians. The creation of additional detachments came under discussion, but the 8th Squadron recommended that detachments be placed only at locations handling at least 150 tons per month.[62]

At the end of 1964, the aerial port apparatus in Vietnam had moved away from its shabby beginnings. The port system had been neglected during the Mule Train operation, mainly because the sustained and expanding nature of the airlift operation had not been foreseen and the focus was upon tactical roles. Crews and users occasionally complained about unsatisfactory port service, but it was clear that a countrywide structure, capable of major expansion, had been created.

The non-Vietnamese based transport force continued its previous roles. Hauls to Southeast Asia increased only moderately, from a monthly average of 427 tons in 1962 to 530 tons during the first half of 1964. These figures reflect also the increasing use of sealift and MATS transports. The C–130s usually carried high-priority engine and aircraft parts, mail, passengers, and humanitarian supplies. The C–124 Globemasters also hauled various engines, generators, and weapons, too bulky for the 130s.* Introduction of a special sea service ended the routine use of C–130s for hauls of aviation munitions from the Philippines to Vietnam. The four Pacific C–130 squadrons thus focused on three peacetime activities: individual and unit training; airlift for forces in Japan, Korea, and Okinawa; and joint exercises with American and allied forces. Eleven C–130s were kept on ground alert at Kadena Air Base, Okinawa, ready to move nuclear components and weapons to strike force bases. During August 1963, over

---

* One of the two C–124 squadrons of the 1503d Air Transport Wing (MATS) moved to Hickam in June 1964 as a measure to improve U.S. gold flow. The 22d Troop Carrier Squadron remained at Tachikawa under 315th Air Division.

seventy Air Force C–130s and C–124s, and Marine KC–130s assembled on Okinawa, and prepared for possible air evacuation of American civilians from Vietnam. Various contingency plans depended heavily upon the theater transports. One plan, for example, forecast the use of paratroop assaults in conjunction with amphibious landings against objectives in Vietnam.[63]

The idea of placing C–130 units in Vietnam first appeared in 1962. A 2d ADVON study concluded that the limited volume of airlift activity and the generally poor runway conditions made introduction of the C–130 undesirable, although the matter could be reexamined in the future. Thereafter, the 315th Air Division held a position against in-country basing of the 130s, citing the inefficiency of using long-range transports for frequent thirty-minute hauls and the inability of most airfields in Vietnam to withstand their sustained use. PACAF in late 1962 established the conditions for the limited use of the Hercules within Vietnam. The 315th Group in Vietnam could request deviations from C–130 route schedules. Approval rested with the air division. Also, C–130 aircrews were directed to check in with local terminal agencies upon landing in Vietnam, to assure "effective utilization of available space on the aircraft." Thus until late 1964, use of the C–130s within Vietnam followed four modes: (1) by advance request through the logistics section to the MACV Western Pacific Transportation Office; (2) by placing loads on aircraft scheduled to make a second in-country stop en route to out-country locations; (3) by request to the 315th Air Division for diversions; and (4) emergency diversions, primarily medical evacuations.[64]

Of extreme importance, these events affected the development of the C–130 force in the United States. Largely in reaction to the Army's argument for airmobile warfare, the Air Force pressed ahead with projects designed to improve the tactical capabilities of its C–130s. Meanwhile, the Air Force tested in field exercises the ability of its transports to deploy and sustain ground armies through an all-air line of communications. This experience helped earn for the Air Force a standoff in the service fight and helped shape the future employment of the C–130s in Vietnam.

Although excellent airdrop characteristics had been designed into the C–130, weakness remained in making drops in bad weather. During the 1950s a systematic method for computing parachute ballistics and descent winds was introduced, and combat control team personnel received intensive training as pathfinders on drop zones. A special task force set up at Sewart Air Force Base, Tenn., in early 1963 completed the testing of a new system of in-trail, low-level formation tactics, designed to overcome all but the lowest ceilings and to minimize exposure to hostile ground fire. All TAC and PACAF C–130s accordingly received Doppler radar equipment with an automatic position computer, designed to assist the navigator in his

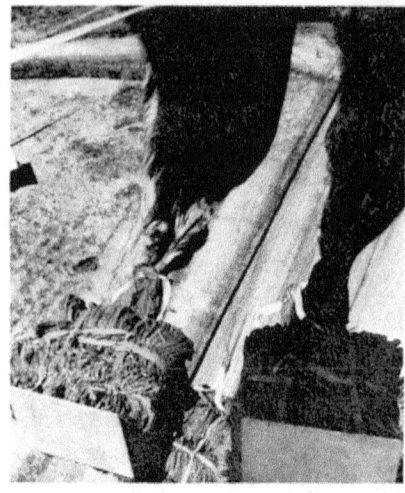

Airlifters in Vietnam employed a variety of delivery systems.

Containerized delivery, 1964.

Low-altitude parachute extraction system.

Parachute of a normal cargo drop dwarfs a Special Forces member.

rigorous low-level tasks. A requisite for reliable drops, however, remained visual sighting of the drop zone.[65]

An alternative to the paradrop method was the extraction of loads from transports flying just above the ground. The ground proximity extraction system (GPES) consisted of a hook-and-cable arrangement. The aircraft flew low so that its hook (connected to the cargo) snagged a ground cable stretched across the path of flight. Water-twister energy absorbers, attached to the steel cable, decelerated the load after extraction. The system resembled that used for arresting aircraft landing on carriers. A Sewart task force tested the extraction system, and about eighty-five C–130 attempts averaging four tons per extraction, were performed during Exercise Swift Strike III in 1963. A demonstration at Tan Son Nhut in March 1963 was unimpressive, as the hook failed to engage on the first two passes. The ground proximity system promised precision delivery of heavy loads, but required prepositioning of ground equipment and recovery of heavy platforms for reuse. Its reliability unproven, the extraction equipment was removed from Vietnam in June 1963.[66]

In early 1964, a self-contained extraction system known as the low-altitude parachute extraction system (LAPES) was tested at Eglin. A C–130 could deliver three eight thousand-pound loads in successive passes and each load was pulled from the aircraft by an extraction parachute released by the aircrew. Landing-gear wheels remained extended while performing the drop, thus avoiding damage in case an aircraft accidently contacted the ground. In a later exercise, LAPES was used to deliver GPES ground equipment, proving the greater utility of the former. Both LAPES and GPES were tested with C–123s, but a crash during GPES delivery ended the effort, except for light loads.[67]

A continuous goal was to improve the ability of the C–130 to operate into short and unimproved airstrips. Assault-landing techniques were refined in troop carrier units and the Joint Chiefs directed the extraordinary effort be made to qualify all C–130 crews for assault work. Airlanded operations at forward positions became a feature of the successive joint exercises during the period. Tests for modifying the C–130 fleet with various landing-gear improvements, an antiskid braking system, more powerful engines, and a structural beefup prompted agreement within TAC that these were worthy of long-term and future funding.[68]

Later, airlift commanders bringing with them their TAC knowledge for using the C–130s in forward areas stressed the importance of the 1963–1964 joint exercises in the United States. But disagreement among the services continued in late 1964, and several developments appeared irreversible. One was the acceptance of the Army's helicopter airmobile idea, strengthened by the acknowledged usefulness of the helicopters in Vietnam. Another was the undeniable competence of the Air Force's

TACTICAL AIRLIFT

C–130 force for theater and many forward supply tasks.[69] The strong airlift system in Vietnam represented another fait accompli, essentially mirroring the Air Force's doctrine of centralization and ruling out any compromise negating the existence of the Southeast Asia Airlift System. Ambiguities persisted, however. There remained the question of the role of the Army's Caribous and the Air Force's cargo helicopters, the latter revived for the 1964 tests. Subsequent Air Force programs for expanding the C–130 force to thirty-two squadrons reflected the immediate desire to strengthen transoceanic capabilities, but the ultimate effect was to enlarge the force available for heavy use within Vietnam. Meanwhile, the evolving airlift control methods and the improved forward area capabilities of the C–130 could be expected to influence future airlift activities in Vietnam.[70]

The incidents in the Gulf of Tonkin on August 2 and 4, 1964, brought a strong American response, including air strikes against North Vietnam. Air Force strike aircraft (F–100s and B–57s) were sent for the first time to bases in South Vietnam, while Japan-based fighters moved to Thailand. The Tactical Air Command dispatched three fighter squadrons across the Pacific, along with forty-four C–130s under Project One Buck.

The One Buck C–130s were drawn from the 314th, 463d, and 516th Troop Carrier Wings, located respectively at Sewart, Langley, and Dyess Air Force Bases. The transfer order came during the night of August 4/5, and the first aircraft took off before dawn. The Pacific crossings were performed routinely. The 130s hauled support personnel and equipment for themselves and some of the fighter units. Theater missions under the 315th Air Division's operational control began on August 10. One C–130B squadron operated from Clark and another from Naha. But twelve C–130Es of the 516th returned to Dyess on the eleventh, after each aircraft had flown at least one mission to Vietnam.[71]

The two new squadrons quickly reduced the backlog of accumulated cargo resulting during the Southeast Asia buildup. In two weeks, beginning on August 5, two thousand tons of cargo were airlifted from Clark in more than three hundred flights. Maintenance and aerial port personnel, along with additional communications and control center personnel, shifted from elsewhere within the 315th Air Division to Clark. Also, for three weeks, all Japan-based C–124s operated from Clark. Heavy rains, billeting shortages, and inadequate equipment for cargo handling at Clark contributed to the hectic state of affairs.[72]

Shortly before the Tonkin Gulf affair MACV had concluded that the

Secretary of Defense Robert S. McNamara at Tan Son Nhut, 1964.

Southeast Asia Airlift System was saturated and requested a fourth C-123 squadron. Since the beginning of the year the C-123s had consistently flown above the allotted sixty aircraft hours monthly, and sapped any capability for future increases. As an interim measure, MACV requested the temporary assignment to the 2d Air Division of four C-130s, "until C-123s are in place." During late July, several 315th Air Division 130s operated from Tan Son Nhut for periods of approximately four days, but on August 8 (one day after McNamara had approved the placement of a fourth C-123 squadron) the Joint Chiefs directed CINCPAC to assign eight C-130s to Vietnam for a four- to six-month tour. A somewhat different arrangement, favored by 315th Air Division and concurred in by MACV, was actually put in effect, although the same result was achieved. All C-130s continued to operate from their offshore locations, but they were applied to in-country backlogs by scheduling or diverting overwater missions to make multiple stops within Vietnam. The scheme avoided the need for a substantial C-130 support establishment within Vietnam, and afforded flexibility in meshing intratheater and in-country schedules. Operational control remained with the 315th Division. Frequently, aircraft and crews remained overnight in Vietnam, and on several occasions they deployed there for tours of about four days in duration. On some days during the fall and winter, as many as twenty-five C-130 and C-124 aircraft operated in Southeast Asia. In the view of the air division, the arrangement

TACTICAL AIRLIFT

afforded "a rapid response and surge capability far beyond that of an assigned force of eight C-130 aircraft positioned in RVN."[73]

Secretary McNamara's decision to assign a fourth C-123 squadron caught TAC midway in its transfer of the C-123s from Pope to Hurlburt. No unit was fully manned nor ready to depart. The first eight aircraft and crews left Hurlburt for Vietnam on September 23, and were followed four weeks later by a second similar flight. The crewmen were primarily those who had recently completed pipeline training. The new unit was designated the 19th Air Commando Squadron and was activated October 1, 1964, at Tan Son Nhut.[74]

Widespread flooding in November and December blocked surface travel over much of Vietnam and necessitated hundreds of humanitarian relief airlifts. Flooding was most severe about Quang Ngai, but emergency deliveries extended as far north as Da Nang and as far south as Phan Thiet. Additional C-130 missions were scheduled and a special arrangement was put into effect, allowing the Tan Son Nhut airlift control center to schedule all C-130s transiting Vietnam to make an additional "up-country" stop without consultation with the 315th Air Division. Heavy clouds and wet runways daily challenged the aircrews as sortie totals climbed. The airlift system accepted the extra mission load without change to its normal mode of operation, although saturation of ramp space and aerial ports at some points reduced efficiency. The system retained its capacity for responsiveness and, when an unexpected unit movement arose during the morning takeoffs on November 17, nine C-123s shifted over to the new task with little confusion.[75]

The intensive flying activity of the early weeks gradually declined for the One Buck crews. A rotational system was introduced and during December the Dyess wing became responsible for replacing aircraft and crews at Naha, and the Sewart wing at Clark. Weekly, one C-130E aircraft and two aircrews arrived as replacements. Maintenance personnel served two-month tours at the Far East locations. The Pacific C-130 force thus stabilized at four permanent and two rotational squadrons.[76]

By the end of 1964, the Air Force had proven its organizational skills, having established in South Vietnam a productive, responsive, and expansible airlift system. The excellent qualities of the C-123 for combat-zone employment had been proven, and C-130s had been employed on a small scale without difficulty. Transport aviation plainly afforded a superb means for moving and sustaining military forces in Vietnam; it also appeared, however, that airlift could neither force the enemy to fight in unfavorable circumstances nor compel the loyalty of the South Vietnamese people to their government. The year 1964 brought political uncertainty to Vietnam and a rising tempo of Viet Cong activity, causing MACV to conclude that "the motivation differential apparently has shifted significantly in favor of the Viet Cong."[77]

The rugged central highlands of Vietnam.

VII. Air Supply of Special Forces

The hills and plateaus of the central highlands occupied most of the interior of South Vietnam, reaching from the Saigon plain to the northern border of the country. From the air, the highlands had a great natural beauty, a rugged terrain blanketed by the greenest of grasses and forests. Narrow waterways cut toward the sea; villages and signs of cultivation were scattered. The airman landing in the highlands often found dry and relatively cool air, a welcome change from the humidity of Saigon.

About five percent of South Vietnam's population lived in the area. Many were tribal peoples, Montagnards, accustomed to primitive agricultural methods and resentful toward Vietnamese rule and colonization. Communist forces easily crisscrossed the region's long and indistinct borders with Laos and Cambodia. The highlands thus became a vast neutral arena within which the communists could train and equip combat forces, evading or offering combat at will. The desirability of challenging the Viet Cong in the interior thus appeared clear to allied planners, aware of the success of small unit techniques against guerrillas in Malaya.

Transportation though presented special problems. Before 1961, certain South Vietnamese posts in the mountains could be reinforced only by man-carried supplies. But supply parties were frequently ambushed, and many posts had to be abandoned.[1] Nevertheless, encouraged by the Americans, the Saigon government in late 1961 planned major military activities in the highlands using U.S. Army Special Forces teams as both local organizers and instructors. Partly from the example of the British in Malaya, the new camps were to be supplied principally by air.

Support of the Special Forces camps had been a major aspect of the earlier Farm Gate C–47 Skytrain operation. Later, the American C–123 Providers assisted in the supply effort and, as airlift requirements steadily increased, they undertook an increasing share of the load. New techniques for air supply were developed and new airfields came into being. The supply of remote camps became, by the end of 1964, the most significant contribution of the Air Force transports in Vietnam.

During 1961 the Americans urged the Saigon government to try a new approach in the highlands. Their general idea was to win the loyalty of the tribesmen and to give them weapons for use against the communists. Although Diem hesitated to arm the Montagnards, pilot operations for the Civilian Irregular Defense Group (CIDG) project began in late 1961. U.S. Army Special Forces troops, the Green Berets, whose potential for counterinsurgency held the personal interest of President Kennedy, were active in the field effort. Twelve-man Special Forces detachments (known as A–teams) went to selected villages, lived among the tribesmen, and won their cooperation by providing medical care, firearms, and the initiative for starting civic improvement projects. At each camp, local CIDG forces were recruited, equipped, and trained for self-defense. The hope was that each camp or area development center would become a nucleus for self-defense forces in nearby hamlets and for a regional strike force capable of offensive counterguerrilla action. The program proposed to make the highlands dangerous for the communists without introducing large numbers of non-Montagnard troops.[2]

In December 1961, American and South Vietnamese Special Forces troops entered the relatively well-populated plain about Ban Me Thuot and launched a pilot CIDG effort. Their success was immediate. By mid-1962, self-defense forces existed in some seventy lightly fortified villages, and a four hundred-man mobile strike force was in being. Secretary McNamara reported to the President that as a result of the enterprise thirty Viet Cong had been killed and sixty had defected; on the other hand, CIDG recruits had lost in combat only one of their two thousand weapons. At year's end, twenty-eight Special Forces A–teams were present in Vietnam, most of them engaged in the CIDG program in the highlands. Over twenty thousand self-defense and strike force troops had been trained. The results fortified American determination to expand the program.[3]

The CIDG program came under the direction of the combined studies division (CSD), a CIA operational agency located in Saigon under the supervision of the American ambassador. The operations center could communicate by radio with the Special Forces camps, facilitating its operational control of the teams. American logistical support for the program was handled entirely apart from the procurement and distribution of materiel for the Vietnamese army. Air shipment originated either at the division's supply depot in Saigon or from a forward supply facility established at Da Nang. The division controlled its own small air transport force, primarily composed of civilian contract aircraft. The Farm Gate C–47s and occasionally the Mule Train C–123s supplemented the non-military transports for shipments out of Saigon, while the C–123 detachment at Da Nang served the camps in the northern region.[4]

The Farm Gate airlifters from the start worked harmoniously in the CIDG program, building upon the earlier cooperation between Jungle Jim and the Special Forces in the United States. For the C–47 crews, the flying day usually began with a short flight from Bien Hoa to Tan Son Nhut.

SUPPLY OF SPECIAL FORCES

Vietnamese laborers moved the cargo from the warehouse and loaded the aircraft under American supervision. Each bundle was marked with its accurate weight, unlike much air cargo shipped in Vietnam. During the fall of 1962, Capt. James Hampton, a Farm Gate copilot, spearheaded the construction of elevated loading platforms in an old hangar, thus permitting loadings at Bien Hoa and eliminating some of the flights to Tan Son Nhut. During 1962 the Farm Gate C–47s spent about one-fourth of their total effort, approximately 650 sorties, in behalf of the Special Forces. The C–123 contribution, meanwhile, gradually increased and by year's end roughly matched that of Farm Gate.[5]

A continuing issue was the question of using organic Army transports for the CIDG and Special Forces supply effort. During 1962 the Army proposed the creation of a Special Forces aviation brigade in the United States, and a unit equipped with Caribous, helicopters, and other craft was formed on a test basis at Fort Bragg, North Carolina. MACV in October recommended to CINCPAC that twenty-four Army aircraft (including four Caribous) be assigned as organic aircraft to Special Forces in Vietnam for emergency supply operations. General Anthis vigorously opposed the recommendation, citing the capabilities of Farm Gate and Mule Train, and the acknowledged satisfaction with the Air Force's past performance. CINCPAC on November 2 rejected the MACV recommendation, raising as an alternative the possibility of introducing additional Air Force aircraft. Admiral Felt during a conference at Saigon on January 10, 1963, reaffirmed his strong opposition to the creation of a "private air force" for the Special Forces.[6]

With the transfer of the CIDG project from CIA to Army control, the Special Forces logistics system went through a changeover period in early and mid-1963. The coastal base at Nha Trang was selected as a site for a new headquarters designated the U.S. Army Special Forces (Provisional), Vietnam,* and for a Special Forces logistics support center. While hangar construction and depot stockage proceeded at Nha Trang, the C–123s and C–47s gradually took over the workload of the nonmilitary transports in hauling CSD materiel from Saigon.[7] The average monthly tonnages hauled for the defense group project during the first half of 1963 reveal the shifting effort:[8]

	Airland	*Airdrop*
315th Troop Carrier Group (C–123)	1036	52
Farm Gate (C–47)	297	199
CSD (nonmilitary aircraft phased out in May, a four-month average)	51	13
Army (Caribou)	126	2

---

* Henceforth called Special Forces, Vietnam, in this study.

TACTICAL AIRLIFT

Although the C–123s thus claimed a larger share of the overall workload, Farm Gate C–47s flew twenty-five hundred Special Forces support sorties in 1963, more than triple the 1962 figure and approximately half the unit's total sortie effort for the year.[9]

The logistics support center moved from Saigon to Nha Trang during June 1963, occupying four newly constructed warehouses. The CIDG and Special Forces logistics pipeline, activated on July 1, began with procurement of items in the United States or in the Far East. Materiel moved to the Army's counterinsurgency support office in Okinawa, for further shipment by sea, and offloading at Nha Trang. Certain high-priority cargo moved into Vietnam by C–130. Although truck or boat convoys were sometimes used, over eighty percent of the materiel left Nha Trang by American military air transportation.

The teams in the field made known their supply needs by radio, and response was good. Packaged weapons, ammunition, and supplies, kept at Nha Trang and the forward supply points, were available for next-day air delivery. Standard bundles were rigged for immediate loading for emergency drops and, if necessary, the composition of bundles could be altered slightly at the last minute.

In some respects the logistics system seemed wasteful, because of its loose accountability and indeed of the almost exclusive reliance on expensive air delivery. On the other hand, the wish to hold down the American presence argued against placing storekeeper and aircraft maintenance men at field locations, and against the use of escorted land convoys. The air logistics apparatus thus fit the physical and psychological coloration of the CIDG venture, well exploiting the special characteristics of air transport.[10]

Agreement on a pattern of future irregular defense group air resupply was reached at a Saigon meeting on March 7, 1963. Present were the MACV logistics chief and the respective commanders of the 315th Group and Special Forces, Vietnam. The Air Force representatives agreed to provide a regular airlift allocation of twenty tons daily, primarily using the C–123s of the 315th Group, but supplemented by Farm Gate for limited loads and for airdrops into small drop zones. Any additional airlift requirements would be handled by routine request, allocation, and scheduling procedures under MACV Directive 42. The 315th Group was to give the Special Forces confirmation of the next day's mission schedule by noon daily, a commitment strongly desired by the Special Forces to allow teams time to prepare to receive loads. The scheduling information was to be obtained through a newly designated transport liaison officer, a qualified airlift specialist to be attached to the Special Forces at Nha Trang.[11] Agreeing to make available sufficient ships and crews to meet the daily twenty-ton commitment, the Air Force began a rotational system, keeping two Farm Gate C–47s and three 315th Group C–123s at Nha Trang. For

SUPPLY OF SPECIAL FORCES

PACAF, the Special Forces support effort had "the highest priority in RVN."[12]

The transport liaison officer at Nha Trang proved useful for local coordination and mutual understanding. In addition, a 315th Group transport movement control detachment, established on July 1, 1963, served as a control post and agency for further coordination at Nha Trang. Approximately six overworked temporary duty officers and men manned the control post until permanently assigned personnel arrived during 1964. The control post remained open sixteen hours a day, using adequate if cramped working space provided by the Special Forces. Each mission originating at Nha Trang required close control, particularly airdrops, since errors in coordination could easily result in a failure to complete delivery at the receiving end. The control detachment maintained folders containing photographs and descriptions of the various drop zones and landing strips, and briefed aircrews for each mission. Like most detachments in Vietnam, the Nha Trang control post was inconvenienced by unreliable outside communications, receiving notices of inbound aircraft from other points usually after the planes had landed. The control personnel sometimes accompanied supply flights, which made them more conscious of problems in the field and in the air.[13]

Ramp space at Nha Trang for parking and loading aircraft was limited. An additional ramp space was completed only in late 1964, with further construction programmed for the accommodation of a full C-123 squadron. Aircraft loadings were mostly performed by Vietnamese, but supervised by the small Air Force aerial port detachment and Special Forces personnel.[14]

The high competence of the troop carrier aircrews engaged in Special Forces work was indisputable. Supervisors assigned only the more able pilots of the 315th Group to Nha Trang rotation, recognizing the hazardous and demanding nature of many irregular defense group missions. Pilots new to Vietnam flew routine missions out of Tan Son Nhut for several months. Only when they were deemed sufficiently skilled did the newcomers enter the Nha Trang rotation, accompanying an instructor or highly qualified pilot. Certified only after several missions, they then became eligible for subsequent rotational duty. Many individuals advanced to instructor status midway through their tour in Vietnam. Similarly, newly assigned C-47 pilots joined the Nha Trang rotation only in the final stages of their in-country checkout.[15]

An aircrew at Nha Trang typically flew two missions daily, each involving a round trip to a detachment location. Missions sometimes involved small deliveries to two or three different points. Except for an occasional flare mission or a night emergency supply request, flying was entirely a daytime endeavor, since defense group sites lacked lights for night landings. The noon meal, usually a sandwich or an inflight ration, was gulped down whenever possible. At the forward locations, periods of heat and dust alternated with drizzle and mud, so that airmen appreciated a hot shower and cold brew upon returning to Nha Trang each evening.

Missions generally entailed the most demanding techniques. Those aspects marking routine airlift work in Vietnam—the reliance on the aircrew's judgment and resourcefulness, the absence of instrument and navigation aids, and the communications difficulties—all of these were intensified in Special Forces work. The C–123s regularly landed at airstrips having less than two thousand feet of runway, and at other sites they encountered an assortment of hazards. Navigators customarily accompanied both airland and drop missions, performing dead-reckoning navigation, plotting radio bearings, and working with the pilots in mapreading.[16]

A crew's rotational tour at Nha Trang varied in length from several days to as long as three weeks. Crewmen found the duty both pleasant and professionally satisfying. Billeting arrangements varied from time to time, but were excellent in the American MAAG compound near the beach. There, coastal breezes offered a relief not found in Saigon and Bien Hoa. Aircrews concluded that the Air Force kitchen was unsanitary and the dining hall too crowded. They therefore often dined in the French seafood restaurants in town or at the Special Force's mess. Relations between the airlifters and the Green Berets were excellent, and the latter generously shared their resources, including five Army vehicles lent to the Nha Trang airlift detachment for local transportation. The Air Force ingratiated itself by bringing privately purchased copies of recent magazines and newspapers to the camps, and by giving briefings to Special Forces personnel newly arrived in Vietnam. The aircrews stressed their service's emergency airlift and air strike resources available at the field. Special Forces officers often warmly praised the work of the airlifters, and each came to recognize the voice of the other during their radio communications.[17]

Airlanded delivery was preferable to delivery by parachute. Parachute drops had several disadvantages, among them the need for special rigging, the possibility of breakage or loss, and the inconvenience for ground personnel in recovering loads. Thus, where airstrips were sufficiently long and the surface dry, cargo was delivered by landing. Caribous landed at places inaccessible to the C–123s and C–47s, but the loss of two Caribous on soft strips at Buon Mi Ga and Tra My in 1963 indicated that there was need for more judicious employment. When the Caribous were unable to land, Special Forces logistics personnel often requested helicopter delivery from U.S. Army regional advisors. Distance and weight of cargo often

SUPPLY OF SPECIAL FORCES

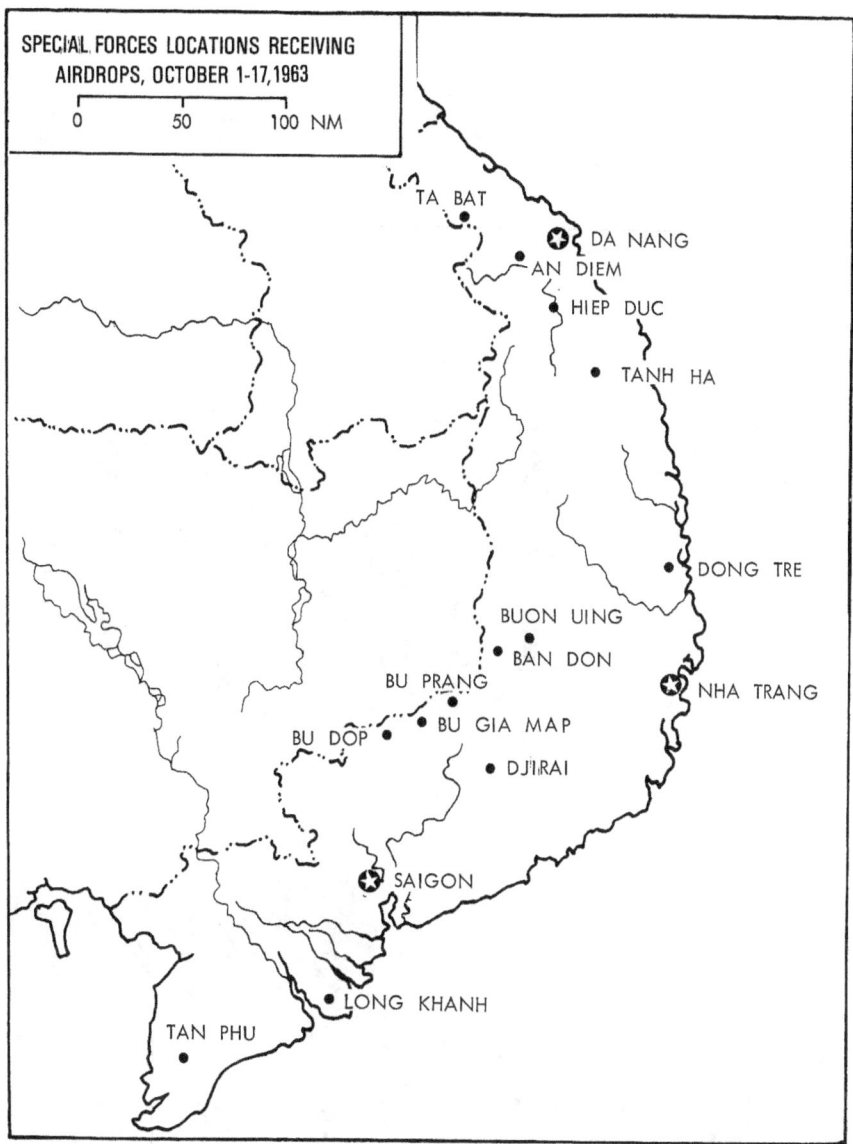

made helicopter use impractical, however, and often all helicopters were fully committed to other tasks. The work which remained was left for airdrop by fixed-wing transports. The Farm Gate C-47s performed most of the drop missions out of Nha Trang, while the C-123s concentrated upon their specialty of delivering heavier loads into short fields. The C-123s at Da Nang, however, engaged in considerable airdropping to the northern camps. On rare occasions, when a single very heavy item was to be airdropped, such as a bulldozer, a C-130 flew to Vietnam for the mission.[18]

155

Gen. Jacob E. Smart, PACAF commander, (left) and Army Lt. Gen. William C. Westmoreland on the flight line at Tan Son Nhut, 1964.

Special Forces members release a live cow dropped by parachute at Phu Tuc.

Courtesy: U.S. Army

C-47 crews supporting U.S. Army Special Forces.

Courtesy: U.S. Army

An Army Special Forces team contacts a village chief and his assistant (left). Soldiers in "tiger suits" are Vietnamese members of the strike force.

Courtesy: U.S. Army

Montagnards disembark from an American transport near the strategic hamlet of Buon Chay, January 1973.

Gen. Maxwell D. Taylor, chairman of the Joint Chiefs of Staff, on a tour of Tan Son Nhut, 1963. General Taylor is accompanied by Maj. Gen. Victor H. Krulak, Special Assistant to the JCS (left), and Maj. Gen. Rollen H. Anthis, commander, 2nd Air Division (right).

TACTICAL AIRLIFT

Although the Farm Gate C-47 unit was from the start well prepared for supply drop work, neither the Mule Train aircraft nor their crews were initially ready to undertake cargo drops. Except for a small test project, the only such C-123 air activity at Pope had been the drop of paratroops. During their first month in Vietnam, the Mule Train crews went through a fast retraining program designed to revive their techniques for dropping moderate-sized cargo loads.[19]

U.S. Army advisors supervised Vietnamese personnel in packaging materials for airdrop and rigging of parachutes. During flight the aircrew loadmaster had responsibility for the cargo, but two or three Special Forces troops or Vietnamese assistants helped in pushing out the bundles. Loads generally included ammunition, foodstuffs, and other essential items. When dropping livestock, the larger animals were bundled into crude wicker baskets fitted with parachutes, and went out over the tailgate along with everything else; the unusual sight of the creatures descending by parachute occasioned many comments.[20]

Drop accuracy was important, since the zones were small, often only a limited clearing within a fortified perimeter. Cargo falling into the jungle was frequently captured by the Viet Cong. For accuracy, C-123 crews released cargo from comparatively low altitudes, about four hundred feet. Computed ballistics solutions were thus unimportant and accuracy depended mainly upon the visual judgment of the pilot. The navigator assisted in identifying the drop zone and in providing wind information. The parachute was supposed to open slightly above ground level, pulling the load upright just before impact and thus reducing impact shock.* After each release, the pilot climbed to about one thousand feet, then returned to the initial point for the next pass. Alertness was vital to avoid terrain hazards and pilots learned to vary patterns. One C-123 received fourteen hits on its sixth pass over a drop zone, after it had made five unchallenged runs over the same path. The family of tactics developed in Vietnam were taught in the Pope and Hurlburt training programs.[21]

These methods helped to reduce exposure of transport aircraft to hostile fire. But in addition, Vietnamese fighter planes usually escorted drop missions, deterring, and often silencing Viet Cong ground fire. Coordination of fighter and airlift schedules was sometimes a problem, and transport crews complained that the escort fighters were sometimes too far away to respond when needed. A new tactic was adopted in early 1964. Two fighters flew crossing patterns in front of and below the transport while two other fighters orbited behind. Upon encountering fire, the transport crew immediately dispatched smoke bombs or flares and marked the location for

---

* Both C-47s and C-123s also made successful low-level free-fall drops of clothing, rice, and construction materials.

SUPPLY OF SPECIAL FORCES

the fighters. The 315th Group crews fastened flare pistols to the side of their aircraft, and fired the pistols by attached lanyards.[22]

The absence of FM radios in the transport cockpits precluded radio communication between aircrews and the irregular defense group locations. The latter possessed battery powered sets similar to those provided to the Vietnamese army. A small number of PRC–10 and PRC–25 receiver-transmitter radios became available for makeshift use in the transports. Battery unreliability, problems in manual tuning, and confusion over frequencies were frequent. Vietnamese radio operators sometimes accompanied missions, but knowing little English they were of only slight help. Visual signals at the drop zone sometimes sufficed—colored smoke by day, and signal fires at night. The Viet Cong learned to display decoy lights at night, and thus added to the difficulty of night drops. As a consequence, loads were occasionally dropped with gross inaccuracy. Permanent installation of airborne FM equipment was programmed for a later date, but Air Force crewmen remained sharply critical of the incompatibility in radio equipment which prevented airdrop crews from communicating with men on the ground.[23]

Most of the time, Special Forces personnel warmly praised the work of the transport crews. The Farm Gate C–47s were consistently successful in their drops. The C–123s received occasional criticism because of errors in crew coordination, cargo handling, or in drop-zone identification. Restraining straps and hooks broke on several occasions, causing premature releases. Loads could be destroyed if crews released from too low an altitude to permit full chute deployment; more often damage resulted from faulty rigging. Errors were most likely to occur on emergency missions when briefings and mission preparation were curtailed. U.S. Army Caribou crews, flying Special Forces drops out of Da Nang in 1963, met with similar problems. Caribou drop tactics were similar to those of the C–123s, including the pullup at release and the free-fall method. Rivalry with the Army aircraft helped to stimulate efforts within the 315th Group and the 2d Air Division to overcome the C–123 difficulties.[24]

Subsequent developmental projects in Vietnam and in the United States brought improvements to airlift capabilities. Most focused on the kinds of rigorous tasks required of Special Forces missions, and some promised improvements benefiting the whole range of C–123 and C–47 work.

Of much potential significance was the YC–123H, an adaptation of the C–123B, with improved qualities for shortfield and forward area work. Senior Air Force officers visited Vietnam in early 1962 and reported that the standard C–123B was "ideal for this type of warfare," but they took note of the aircraft's limited engine power, which held down the size of safe payloads, particularly in mountainous areas. The visitors also criticized the relatively high landing pressure which precluded operations on the softer strips. The YC–123H incorporated auxiliary jet engines on pylons mounted outboard of the main engines, a drag parachute to reduce landing roll, and wider-track landing gear with larger tires and wheels. These changes improved the aircraft's ability to deliver ten-ton payloads to short strips. But flight-testing in the United States in the fall of 1962 indicated that the improvements fell short of full expectations, and the Air Staff tentatively recommended against costly retrofit of the C-123 fleet.

A single YC-123H was flown to Vietnam in January 1963 for additional testing. During a ten-week period of evaluation, the aircraft was integrated into airlift system scheduling, and was used daily in whatever activities best suited operational needs. Its increased payload capability was regularly exploited, and many 315th Group pilots were most pleased with the advantages of the improved landing gear in crosswinds and on soft fields. Takeoff ground roll with maximum payload was cut almost in half. The test aircraft returned to the United States in May, and was destroyed in an accident later in the year.[25]

Official assessments of the H-model were generally favorable. Midway through the test period, the 2d Air Division advised the Air Staff that the aircraft was doing "excellent work." In a message dated April 5, 1963, prepared by Col. Leon M. Tannenbaum, the 315th Group commander, General Anthis judged the YC-123H capable of satisfying the need for shortfield transport capabilities. Further, the H-model could deliver in four sorties tonnage equivalent to seven C-123 or fifteen Caribou flights. The final test report prepared by the 2d Air Division stated that the aircraft was "capable of fulfilling the majority of airlift requirements likely to be encountered in the RVN," and recommended acquiring sufficient H-models for three squadrons. However, Harkins and Osmanski at MACV officially disagreed, and concluded that the need for the H-model was insufficient since few airfields in Vietnam could support sustained heavyweight deliveries. On December 23, 1963, at a time when forces in Vietnam were being reduced, the Air Staff determined that "the USAF has no further interest in modification of C-123B to YC-123H configuration."[26]

Another project sought to provide the air transport fleet with all-weather paradrop capability in South Vietnam. Much effort was devoted to tests of the British-designed Decca navigation system, consisting of a chain of one master and two slave ground stations that furnished the aircrew continual positioning information. The airborne equipment gave a pen-and-ink tracing across a terrain chart located in the cockpit. Ground stations were installed in late 1962 near Vung Tau, Phan Thiet, and Tay Ninh, and eighteen C-123s received the airborne components, as well as a small number of C-47s, B-26s, and helicopters.[27]

But Decca results were disappointing. Aircrews had trouble receiving the signals, malfunctions were frequent, and readings were sometimes grossly erroneous. The accuracy rate of 113 feet average was acceptable on those rare occasions when actual drops were possible, but this happened only within a one hundred-mile range of the ground stations. Testing in the United States with C–130s produced similar results. The final Decca failure occurred in September 1963 during a C–123 demonstration flight for the new PACAF commander, Gen. Jacob E. Smart. The mission encountered a series of equipment malfunctions, and the general retired to the rear cabin in apparent disgust. The Joint Chiefs ruled in August 1964 that the Air Force should continue to operate the ground chain, primarily for use by Army helicopters for whom the equipment was of some marginal value.[28]

In contrast to the failure of the Decca system, the tactical air navigation (tacan) stations in Vietnam and Thailand gave convenient and reliable navigation assistance in instrument weather. In the tacan system, the aircraft transmitted an interrogator pulse to a ground station, and received back range and bearing information. Tacan was widely used by transport and strike aircraft crews as an aid to navigation, but its accuracy was inadequate for blind airdrops.[29] In addition, other devices investigated were an airborne doppler system tested in Caribous and helicopters, radar beacons and reflectors evaluated with the airborne radar of the 315th Air Division C–130s in 1962, a tactical version of loran-C and shoran. The idea of transmitting radio signals from drop zones claimed attention. The Sarah homer, tested by the 315th Air Division in 1963, proved quite satisfactory for this role except that signals became reduced in wooded terrain. Fifty lightweight radio beacons had been issued the previous year to Vietnamese units served primarily by the Caribous, but tests of two newer types of radio beacons as aids in locating airstrips and drop zones began the following year. None of this equipment received full endorsement or entered into general use. The idea of using ground controlled approach radar for guiding drops was not investigated, although such units were in use at the major airfields. The all-weather airdrop problem, recognized since World War II, but a chronic victim of deficient funding, remained essentially unsolved.[30]

A byproduct of the CIDG program was an improved net of forward airfields stretched over most of South Vietnam. Outlines of the airfield system were already evident in 1961, when the Diem regime undertook a construction program and recognized the importance of aviation in nation-building. In existence at the time were improved fields near the major cities and in outlying areas maintained formerly by French plantation owners.

TACTICAL AIRLIFT

The national airport plan of 1960 called for the construction of seventy-nine airfields capable of receiving C–47 Skytrains, and for 1961 the regime optimistically claimed the existence of sixty fields, of which thirteen were paved. Many were surfaced with laterite, a locally found hard crusty soil of reddish color, which could be easily shaped and compacted. Dry laterite could support aircraft as large as the C–130 Hercules, although its load-bearing qualities degenerated rapidly during the wet season. In selecting locations for new CIDG area development centers, the presence of an airstrip was often a foremost consideration.[31]

The Americans recognized the importance of forward airfields in theater operations. Reflecting problems in forward airfield construction and repair during the Korean War, AFM 1–9 called for an airfield apparatus extending to forward zones and dedicated exclusively for air transport use if possible. In subsequent joint exercises, the American services explored the use of rapidly prepared airstrips in offensive assault operations, and the Army's Corps of Engineers developed a family of air transportable construction equipment for this purpose. A defense department and Joint Chiefs of Staff study group, foreseeing possible major ground operations in the interior areas of Vietnam, called for the construction of additional airstrips in late 1961.[32]

However, American funding for airfield construction in Vietnam during the next two years provided mainly for improvements in existing fields. The Vietnamese civilian directorate of air bases, meanwhile, slowly expanded the number of C–47 fields under the national airport plan. The Vietnamese army had a separate construction program which focused directly on airfields for supply of military units. In the nine-month period ending with July 1963, the Vietnamese army engineers opened eighteen new or rehabilitated strips with runways varying in length from thirteen hundred to forty-five hundred feet and constructed of packed earth, although at times further surfaced with laterite or gravel. At a few locations, pierced steel or aluminum planking was laid down over laterite, giving the fields wet-weather capabilities. Among the irregular defense group support strips built in the central highlands by the Vietnamese engineers were those at Dak Pek, Cung Son, and Mang Buk. Americans noted that modern earth classification techniques were neglected, but the firm and usually well-drained soils of the highlands eliminated most design and construction pitfalls. The main problem was finding flat areas with unobstructed approaches. Unsatisfactory field design in the Mekong Delta area, however, led to a series of airstrip failures, and even asphalt surfaces became spongy and rutted under constant C–123 usage because of the softer subsoils.[33]

Nearly all forward airfields lacked sufficient ramp parking space. If two aircraft were scheduled into the same field, one often had to wait aloft while the other completed offloading at the end of the runway. Some of the fields, especially those in mountainous areas near Laos, could be approached only with difficulty. At Kham Duc near the Laotian border southwest of Da Nang, a steep hill blocked one end of the runway, so that landings had to be executed in one direction and takeoffs in the other, regardless of wind conditions. A project to lower the hill by bulldozer began in 1963. Fifty miles to the north, the A Shau airstrip lay amid hilltops often obscured by clouds. This necessitated precarious low-level approaches down the length of the valley. Dak To, south of Kham Duc, had claimed a C–123 and its crew in 1963. All three locations—Dak To, Kham Duc, and A Shau—supported Special Forces A-teams and all three sites earned at an early date unpleasant reputations among troop carrier airmen.[34]

The question of the number of airfields usable by each type of transport became entwined with service disputes over roles and capabilities. Early lists of airfields usable by C–123s sometimes considered only strip length, neglecting sustained load-bearing capacity. Whether or not a particular airfield was suitable usually depended on the degree of safety and the extent of usage envisioned. During March 1962, a Mule Train crew led by Capt. Carl Wyrick, with two officers from the 315th Air Division, flew survey missions to dozens of airstrips in Vietnam, including some of very doubtful suitability. The survey classified about 75 fields as "usable" by the C–123s. An earlier survey team had been less optimistic and used more stringent criteria, and its report had been rejected by General Anthis. In August 1963, of the 175 airfields in South Vietnam listed by MACV, the C–123s were actually using 68, most of which exceeded two thousand feet in length. Thereafter, the number of fields actually used by this aircraft increased by fifty percent each year, reflecting expansion of the CIDG effort and the continuing airfield construction program. Many of these airstrips became important in later years, serving as airheads for sustained allied offensive ground and airmobile operations.[35]

The volume of Special Forces air transport activity gradually expanded as the number of CIDG camps increased in 1964. Each new twelve-man detachment required airlift of about 60 tons of equipment and supplies during its first six weeks, followed by 17 tons per month thereafter. Airlifted tonnages reached 2,147 during July 1964 and 2,410 tons the next October. The July figure included 495 tons delivered by parachute and free-fall drop, nearly double the amount dropped a year earlier. Of the July tonnage, sixty-one percent was loaded at Nha Trang, twenty-four percent at Da Nang, ten percent at Saigon, and four percent at Can Tho. Compared with the 2,147 tons airlifted in July, land and water shipments within the Special Forces system totaled 282 and 107 tons respectively. The truck hauls were mainly out of Pleiku, while water movements were primarily between Nha Trang and Da Nang, and from Can Tho to delta camps.

TACTICAL AIRLIFT

Nearly all cargo reaching the Special Forces distribution system now arrived at Nha Trang by sea from Okinawa or by coastal vessel from Saigon, and less than one percent entered Vietnam by air.[36]

Like the irregular defense group program, the associated airlift effort had important civic action aspects. The American transports were highly visible, threatened no harm, and represented a source of food and medicines. They even served as a kind of a civil airline because of a liberal American policy of allowing civilians to ride as passengers. Ships returning empty to Nha Trang and Da Nang often carried passengers approved by the local district chief.[37]

The Special Forces and civilian defense groups gained an additional mission starting in late 1963, when they were made responsible for screening and reconnoitering the Laotian and Cambodian border areas. Border surveillance sites, previously established under the combined studies division, were converted to the CIDG system, and the personnel assigned to the latter were to be trained by Vietnamese Special Forces teams, assisted by Americans. During 1964, the civilian defense group's border control role gradually supplanted the group's earlier emphasis upon building local self-defense units, and a pronounced shift of locations took place. By year's end, most A–teams were positioned near the western border to screen the southern third of the country. Their results were not impressive. One company-sized CIDG patrol unit existed for each twenty-eight miles of border, and they were spread too thin either to halt enemy infiltration or to provide more than fragmentary intelligence.[38]

Another reorientation grew from the appealing idea of using CIDG teams for offensive long-range patrol activity, entering areas previously safe for the Viet Cong. Defense teams could operate either independently or as reconnaissance forces in advance of helicopter-borne rangers or infantry. Such efforts within the borders of Vietnam were disappointing in 1963 and 1964, but the idea was pressed strongly by Secretary McNamara and Gen. Maxwell D. Taylor during their 1964 visits to Saigon. This idea was further plainly reflected in a letter of instructions sent by the new 5th Special Forces Group to all operational detachments on November 3, 1964. The letter stated that CIDG strike forces should seek "continuous offensive counterguerrilla operations."[39]

Airdrop supply of offensive strike force patrols presented special problems due to the extremely irregular terrain found in many parts of the highlands and the scarcity of cleared spaces for use as drop zones. The supply activity required highly accurate airdrop methods, a pickup capability, containers for free-fall delivery, and inexpensive disposable parachutes. The Caribous dominated in this role throughout 1964, because their smaller cargo capacity better matched the loads required. Although patrols could often not be seen from the air because of the jungle canopy, communication by radio was generally possible. The patrol usually displayed

SUPPLY OF SPECIAL FORCES

smoke to mark the drop zone, preferably a stream bed or open ridge, though on occasions drops were made into the trees. Crews refined accuracy by adjusting the release point on successive passes.[40]

Although Army Pentagon officials pressed the government for an authorization of their own air arm within the Army's Special Forces structure, until late 1964 Caribou transports in Vietnam were not dedicated for Special Forces use. The aircraft were generally scheduled by the respective corps senior advisors, who made planes available to Special Forces only upon particular mission request or on an opportune basis. Special Forces personnel, including the commander of Special Forces, Vietnam, expressed dissatisfaction with this arrangement, since the Caribous were sometimes unavailable and were in any case subject to cancellation. Late cancellations were especially undesirable, since at some camps personnel had to make short but dangerous overland trips to rendezvous with the aircraft. Special Forces logistics officers thus preferred to depend on the C-123s and C-47s. As a result, the customary service positions were oddly reversed. The Air Force provided a dedicated airlift service, while the Army made its aircraft available through a daily allocations process.[41]

During November 1964, one Australian and three U.S. Army Caribou aircraft moved to Nha Trang from the 92d Aviation Company at Qui Nhon to supplement the Air Force rotational force. The Caribou augmentation had been requested by the Special Forces command, claiming the Caribou superior for landing on wet surfaces during the rainy season, and for delivering supplies by low-level inflight extraction (LOLEX). Approximately fifteen airfields normally serviced by the C-123, but "rendered useless by rain," were deemed accessible to the Caribou throughout the year. At Nha Trang, the Air Force transport movement control and the Army Caribou detachment pooled communications resources, combining mission scheduling and ensuing functions. A senior Air Force movement control officer in the combined activity quickly came to appreciate the shortfield capability of the Caribou, viewing its role as complementary with the C-123's ability to haul ten thousand-pound generators and the 2½-ton trucks widely used throughout Vietnam. During December the Air Force C-47s withdrew from Special Forces supply work, and the C-123 force at Nha Trang was simultaneously increased to seven.[42]

The success of the overall CIDG effort remains questionable. American confidence in the venture was high, as reflected in the spring 1964 decisions to double U.S. Special Forces manpower in Vietnam and to convert from six-month temporary duty to one-year permanent assignments. The revolt of Montagnard troops at five camps near Ban Me Thuot in September 1964, however, not only slowed the momentum of the CIDG strike team program, but also suggested serious weaknesses in the whole CIDG effort.[43] The defense group's strength at year's end was 21,500, located at forty-four sites.

TACTICAL AIRLIFT

Assessments were more clearcut in evaluating the role of transport aviation in supporting the CIDG program. The employment of the C–123 in Special Forces supply was easily that aircraft's most rewarding use and was an inexpensive byproduct of the larger roles for which the Providers had come to Vietnam. In no other Southeast Asia activity did air transport make a more direct or vital contribution. The dependence of the Special Forces teams on air transportation was nearly total, given the scarcity of roads and the skill of the enemy in ambush. If interservice disputes tinged the Special Forces supply mission, the main effect was to strengthen Air Force determination to provide the best possible service.[44] For most troop carrier airmen, the experiences in Special Forces work were the most vivid and satisfying of their military careers. The daily airmanship and dedication of the Air Force and Army aircrews in camp supply defy overstatement.

Part Two:
The Years of the Offensive, 1965-1968

VIII. The Entry of the C-130, 1965-1966

American leaders during the winter of 1964–1965 reached the consensus that this nation's policy was failing in Vietnam. They introduced a new policy in February 1965 stressing a measured application of air power against North Vietnam. Further decisions followed during the spring and summer placing U.S. Army and Marine combat units in South Vietnam and employing them in mobile offensive operations. The enemy, too, increased his involvement, and North Vietnamese formations appeared in the south in increasing numbers, practicing a system of camouflaged tactics and logistics made obligatory as a response to allied air power. The "war without fronts" in South Vietnam thus continued and brought with it a growing air mobility for allied ground troops.

The American buildup increased air transport requirements both for lifts within South Vietnam and for hauls into Southeast Asia. The Air Force met this need in three ways: by increasing the offshore C–130 force, by increasing flying rates for each unit, and by seeking improvements in managerial efficiency. The four squadrons of C–123s continued to operate into South Vietnam, but the use of the C–130 force within the country became a dominant feature of these years.

The C–130 Hercules proved remarkedly adaptable for in-country tasks, vastly increasing the overall Southeast Asia Airlift System capacity and extending operations regularly into the night. A fundamental decision was reached to base the C–130 units offshore and to rotate aircraft and crews to operating locations in Vietnam. This decision was reviewed periodically but survived these reassessments. And the arrangement proved workable, if beset by problems. By 1966 these aircraft regularly landed at forward airstrips, operating near the limits of the ship's safety margins.

The airlift control system readily accommodated the C–130s, but in other respects the expansion brought serious inefficiencies. Slowness in enlarging aerial port capacities was reminiscent of the earlier period of C–123 expansion, and the ports struggled to overcome insufficiencies of manpower, equipment, and facilities. Members of the airlift squadrons strove to meet unrealistic expectations, often putting forth Herculean efforts. Accident rates spiraled. The apparent need for reform led in late 1966 to the creation of the 834th Air Division, the agency for future airlift system management.

TACTICAL AIRLIFT

Air Force C-130 Hercules.

The fast-moving developments in early 1965 taxed the full capabilities of the six-squadron C-130 force in the Pacific.[1] Four C-130A squadrons were permanently assigned in Japan, three at Naha under the 6315th Operations Group and one at Tachikawa directly under the 315th Air Division. Rotational squadrons from the Tactical Air Command remained after August 1964 at Clark and Naha. President Lyndon B. Johnson on February 7 ordered the evacuation of American military and government dependents from Vietnam, "to clear the decks and make absolutely clear our continued determination." Twenty-two 315th Air Division C-130s were placed on alert at Clark on February 9 in readiness for the operation. The actual evacuation, however, was arranged by the Saigon embassy and carried out largely by chartered commercial airlift. The 2d Air Division later reported that military transports evacuated 376 persons while over one thousand moved by commercial means. The scene at Da Nang was especially sober, where dependents boarded an Air Force C-130 for Hong Kong, while planeloads of marines arrived from Okinawa. McNamara congratulated the military establishment for its limited part in the evacuation.[2]

The President also announced on February 7 his decision to send a U.S. Marine light antiaircraft missile battalion to Vietnam. The unit was to be equipped with rocket-propelled Hawk missiles, to protect strike aircraft at Da Nang against communist air attack. The 315th Air Division in fifty-

ENTRY OF THE C-130

American dependents leave the Republic of Vietnam after the president's evacuation order, February 10, 1965.

two C-130 flights on the seventh and eighth of February lifted 309 passengers and 315 tons of missiles, launchers, power vans, and other equipment, hauling these direct from Okinawa to Da Nang. The theater paratroop force, the Army's 173d Airborne Brigade, was held for several days on a two-hour alert for possible air movement from Okinawa. Other airlifts followed, hauling personnel and equipment of tactical fighter units to Southeast Asia.³

The presence of substantial allied air units at Da Nang led to a decision in late February to introduce two U.S. Marine reinforced battalions for base defense. This decision accorded with repeated recommendations made during that month by the Joint Chiefs of Staff, CINCPAC, and General Westmoreland, and had the reluctant concurrence of Ambassador Maxwell Taylor who sensed that the arrival of United States infantry units implied America's assumption of the ground war. The use of the 173d Brigade instead of the Marines had been considered but rejected in part because of CINCPAC's desire to preserve the theater's airborne assault

TACTICAL AIRLIFT

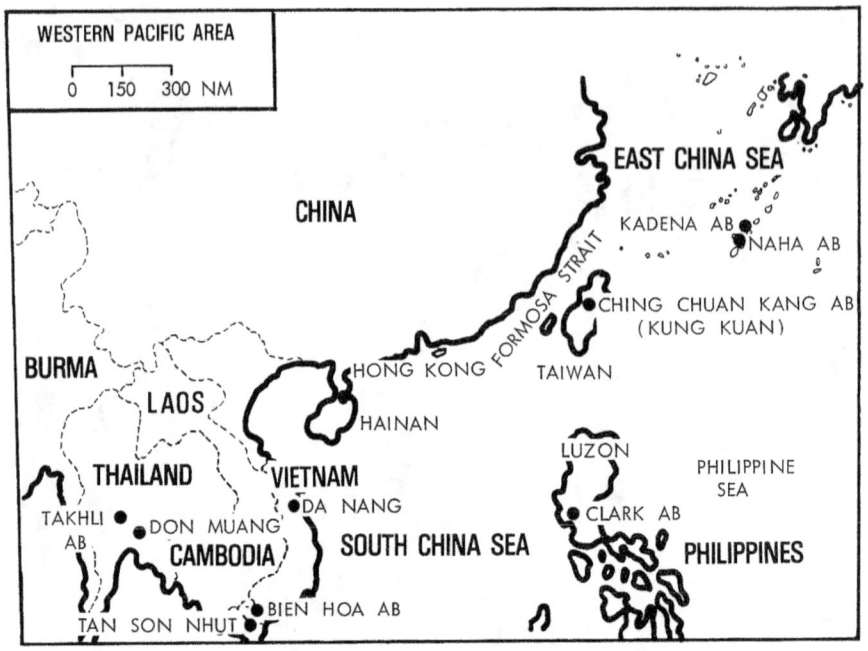

capability. The Joint Chiefs advised on February 27 that the deployment had been approved and, by message dated March 7, directed CINCPAC to commence the movements.[4]

One Marine battalion landing team stationed afloat off Da Nang splashed ashore on the morning of March 8. Twenty-four Marine helicopters landed at Da Nang the next morning from an offshore carrier, and several Marine KC–130 tanker-transports brought in helicopter unit personnel from Okinawa. The 315th Air Division undertook the larger task of hauling the second battalion landing team from Okinawa.

The landing team airlift was performed expertly and without serious difficulty. The 315th Air Division, providing seventy-six C–130 aircraft, began the move on the morning of the seventh upon receipt of CINCPAC's directive. During the following night the first troop elements moved from their billeting areas. They and their equipment were then organized into C–130 loads. After a delay of three hours, while awaiting final clearance from Saigon, the first Hercules took off from Naha after sunrise. The stream followed at thirty-minute intervals between individual aircraft. The flow halted after the thirteenth Hercules arrived, when MACV advised that Da Nang could no longer accommodate the simultaneous arrival of the battalions. After telephone clearance from General Westmoreland, the airlift resumed again shortly after midnight on the morning of the tenth. Two days later the entire landing team had arrived, except for tanks and low-

ENTRY OF THE C-130

priority vehicles. The surface vehicles were moved by sea to Da Nang. In all, Air Force C-130s delivered 1,030 combat-equipped troops and six hundred tons of cargo, and flew over nine hundred hours. Congestion and delays on the ground at Da Nang proved to be the only significant technical flaw. A few transports received very light ground fire, but only one aircraft reported a harmless hit. The Marine headquarters sent a glowing letter of recognition and praised the airlift.[5]

The 173d Airborne Brigade became the first U.S. Army unit committed to Vietnam, being brought in by the 315th Air Division in early May 1965. The decision to commit the unit grew from President Johnson's conviction that "something new" had to be added to South Vietnam, namely a brigade force for the Vung Tau-Bien Hoa region. The brigade's initial mission was security, but it was expected to expand into active counterinsurgency operations, an activity conferred as well upon the Marines about Da Nang. The Air Staff, keenly aware of the need for base defense at Bien Hoa, supported the Joint Chiefs' decision favoring the deployment. The air movement of the 173d from Okinawa confirmed the capabilities of the 315th Air Division to carry out such tasks.[6]

On April 14 CINCPAC had first alerted the 173d Brigade to prepare to move two battalions to Vietnam by airlift; on the same day PACAF received a warning to prepare sufficient aircraft for the lift. The brigade headquarters and one battalion were scheduled to go to Bien Hoa and the second battalion was to land at Vung Tau. An Australian brigade would join the 173d at Bien Hoa in June. The 173d was advised to maintain its parachute capability for possible in-country employment. The 6315th Operations Group performed detailed planning under the basic directive, 315th Air Division Operation Order (OpOrd) 373-65. A 150-sortie airlift effort was proposed, to extend over three days. Diplomatic arrangements with the South Vietnamese were completed on May 1, and an advance party flew from Okinawa to Saigon two days later.[7]

The C-130 stream took off from Okinawa at midnight on the fifth. Crews and aircraft from the 315th Air Division participated. By seven in the morning, thirty-eight sorties had taken off from Naha and Kadena. Landings at Bien Hoa began in daylight after a flight of over six hours, and within three hours a brigade operations center was set up at the airfield. During the air movement eleven hundred tons of equipment and eighteen hundred troops were delivered in 142 aircraft loads to Bien Hoa and Vung Tau. Of these flights, eighty-one C-130 and five C-124 missions landed at Bien Hoa. The remaining brigade elements arrived by sea at the Saigon and Vung Tau ports between May 12 and June 1.[8]

The paratroops thus joined the Marines as the vanguard of American field forces in Vietnam. The theater troop carrier forces never again executed offshore, brigade-size unit deployments, although the capability for doing so remained prominent in contingency planning. Later ground units

TACTICAL AIRLIFT

arrived in Vietnam generally by sea and occasionally by strategic airlift. The presence of the 173d in Vietnam marked a new phase in the long partnership between the Pacific troop carrier and the airborne arms. Past joint airborne training imperfectly resembled the kinds of air mobility now possible, but traditional bonds strengthened interservice cooperation in scores of future unit air movements within Vietnam.

Since the previous summer, offshore-based C-130s had flown missions in South Vietnam under various arrangements. During a four-month period that included February 1965, C-130s flew 1,024 hours and lifted fifty-two hundred tons of cargo and passengers on flights entirely within Vietnam. During a brief mission in February, set up for the purpose of hauling aviation ordnance to Qui Nhon, the 315th Air Division for the first time temporarily relinquished daily scheduling authority for the C-130s to the airlift control center of the 315th Group at Tan Son Nhut. Further intensification of ground combat the following month additionally burdened the overworked C-123 force, necessitating greater use of the C-130s. A temporary assignment of four C-130s to Tan Son Nhut stretched into May and early June. Itineraries again were laid out by the control center using only airfields approved for C-130 use by the air division; the latter, however, retained nominal operational control through an on-the-scene C-130 mission commander.[9]

The desirability of making more permanent arrangements appeared clear. A MACV fact sheet prepared in March emphasized that more air transport was needed to avoid tying down allied troops in highway security. The paper supported General Westmoreland's formal recommendation to CINCPAC that a partial squadron of eight C-130s be positioned in-country for sustained operations. The 315th Air Division continued to oppose the idea of permanent in-country assignment. It insisted that the past arrangements had kept backlogs low in Vietnam, and made the 130s available for overwater missions and contingencies elsewhere.[10]

Both viewpoints appeared satisfied with the arrival on June 4 at Tan Son Nhut of four C-130s for operations of "indefinite" duration. These aircraft joined those formerly assigned for "temporary" duty. The newly arrived aircraft were accompanied by extra maintenance personnel and aircrews needed for the sustained operations. This action admitted that the shuttle system was to be a continuing thing. It also recognized that Hercules aircraft and crews would continue to rotate from offshore bases, and their presence in Vietnam would be adjusted to according to need. By June 23 the in-country force consisted of nine C-130s, six at Tan Son Nhut for

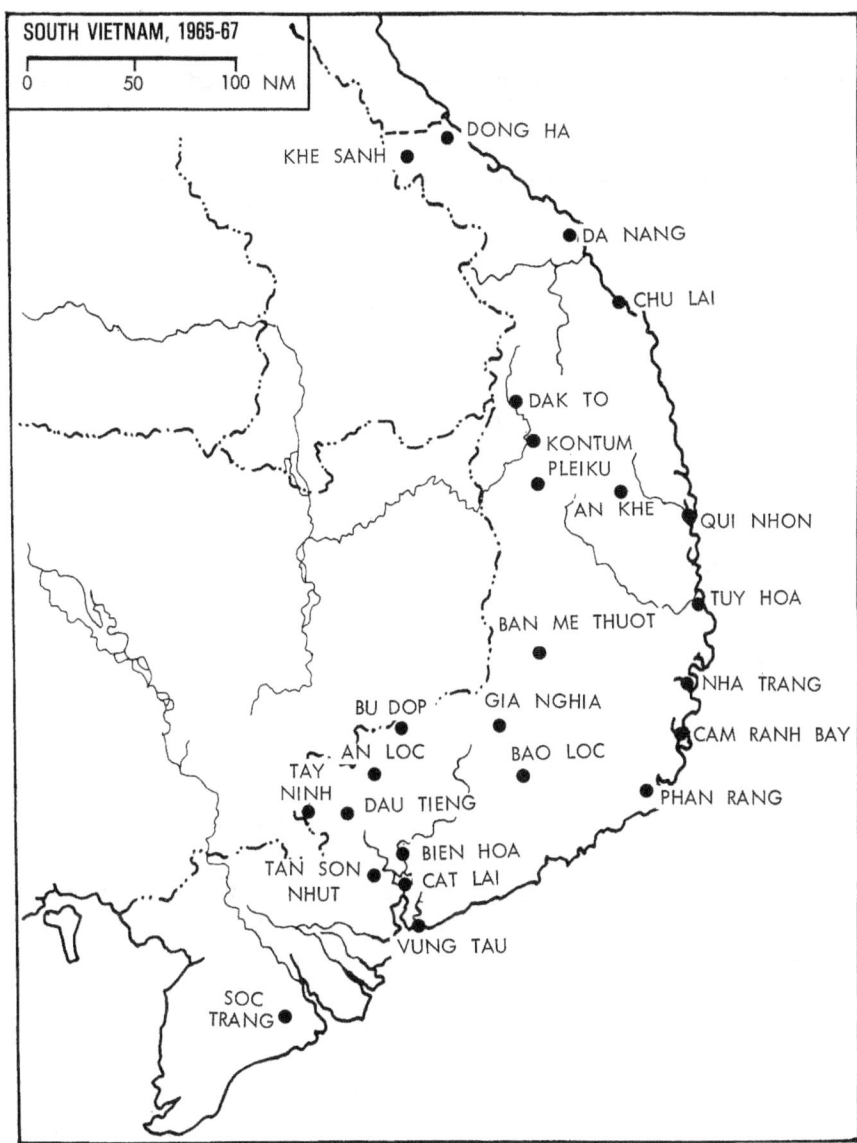

indefinite usage and three for specific lift requirements from Qui Nhon to airfields in the interior.[11]

While in Vietnam the shuttle C–130s operated as a part of the Southeast Asia Airlift System, but under MACV operational direction through the airlift control center. The number of aircraft in Vietnam varied according to immediate mission requirements as determined by MACV. The trend was clearly upward although expansion was limited by shortages of ramp space, base facilities, and by aerial port inadequacies. New detach-

TACTICAL AIRLIFT

ments of C–130s were placed at Nha Trang and Vung Tau during the fall. A decision to construct a major logistics air terminal at Cam Ranh Bay had been made the previous summer, a decision which reflected a recognition of the site's excellent natural harbor and of its obvious potential for development as an air base. By October the construction of a ten thousand-foot aluminum matting runway and a small parking ramp permitted the base's all-weather use, and a C–130E shuttle force began operations two months later. The total in-country C–130 force increased from fifteen to thirty-two aircraft by the end of 1965. Those C–130As formerly used for flareship work out of Da Nang entered the Cam Ranh Bay rotation in May 1966.[12]

C–130 Airlift Force in Vietnam

	Dec 31, 1965	Nov 1, 1966
Tan Son Nhut	14 C–130B	23 C–130B
Vung Tau	5 C–130E	(closed in March 1966)
Nha Trang	8 C–130E	8 C–130E
Cam Ranh Bay	5 C–130E	13 C–130A
	32	44

Operations offices for administration and command of the C–130 detachments were set up at Tan Son Nhut and other locations manned by temporary duty personnel from the 315th Air Division and offshore C–130 units. These elements assigned missions to crews and aircraft, provided intelligence and operational information, managed sundry details in getting missions launched, and coordinated with local base units. Upon airlift control center request, the element at Tan Son Nhut had sole in-country authority to waive airfield criteria and crew flying restrictions. This element was redesignated in late 1965 as Det 5, 315th Air Division, and increased its manning by adding thirty permanent and two hundred temporary duty maintenance men. By mid-1966 the detachment had expanded to five hundred men. At other locations gradual improvements in facilities for the detachments' maintenance, parking, and billeting resulted from combinations of self-effort, locally coordinated arrangements, and contract construction.[13]

Maintenance tasks at the shuttle locations in Vietnam were kept to a minimum in order to hold down the size of the ground force. Detachment activities consisted principally of postflight inspections; changes of wheels, engines, and props; routine servicing; and replacement of individual components. Certain minor malfunctions were left for offshore repair. Aircraft seldom remained in Vietnam longer than two weeks, thus permitting inspection work offshore at intervals of 125 flying hours. The 315th Air Division advised that shuttle aircraft likely to be out of commission for more than twenty-four hours should be repaired by cannibalizing other aircraft or replacing the planes from off shore. Maintenance men from offshore units served at the shuttle locations for tours of thirty to sixty days, and augmented the small cadres of permanently assigned individuals. A crew chief left the flight line only after ten or twelve hours of hard work.[14]

To the C-130 aircrews, operations in Vietnam appeared both inefficient and unsafe. Many professional airmen, accustomed to the highly regulated methods common to TAC and to interisland work, were dubious of the style of flying practiced in Vietnam and of methods well known to the C-123 and C-47 airlifters. Hazardous taxi conditions seemed universal not only at the overcrowded larger airfields, but at forward sites where runways and taxi strips were freely used by vehicles, helicopters, and the local populace. Aircrews questioned the practice of postponing minor repair work until the aircraft had rotated offshore. Ramp delays while awaiting aerial port or refueling service were chronic and radio communication saturation added to the frustrations. Delays in taking off from Saigon because of heavy traffic were common. Scheduling at times seemed inefficient, especially when an aircrew returned with no load to Tan Son Nhut, only to depart empty for pickup elsewhere.[15]

One C-130 squadron commander convincingly describes the mess of the Tan Son Nhut shuttle, documenting his report with written statements from his aircraft commanders and with a detailed account of his own flight experience of September 29, 1965. After rising at five in the morning and obtaining with difficulty motor transportation, the crew arrived at Tan Son Nhut nearly three hours later only to learn informally that their aircraft might be out of commission. The crew prepared for the flight anyway, arriving planeside at 0900 to find the aircraft ready to go but with no cargo. After waiting two hours, and in the meantime trying to locate their missing load, the pilot hitchhiked back to C-130 operations where the duty officers expressed surprise that the crew had not yet departed. After arranging for the loading, the pilot returned to discover another aircraft parked in front of his ship and blocking his path to the new loading area. Loading was finally completed in the early afternoon. After a routine delivery to Qui Nhon, the aircraft developed maintenance problems which prevented takeoff until it was too dark to continue to Kontum with a load of tactical emergency cargo. After sixteen hours, the crew returned to their quarters in Saigon having made only one delivery of ordinary cargo. While conceding that this frustrating day was not entirely typical, the squadron commander concluded that many of the events were normal. Such conditions, he wrote, tempted aircrews to seek shortcuts and to take unsound risks.[16]

Shuttle aircrews especially criticized the unsatisfactory arrangements for housing, messing, and ground transportation. C-130 crewmen often spent hours searching for hotel rooms and sometimes slept in their aircraft or in hotel lobbies. By 1966 crews were able to stay in local "villas" near

A C–130 lifts off a membrane runway at a Vietnam outpost.

Maintenance work on a Hercules at an in-country location, 1966.

Transports from the 315th Air Division lined up on the taxi strip at Tan Son Nhut, 1965.

the base, but these were not air conditioned and the lack of sanitation was scored by the air division's surgeon. Meals were often taken at Tan Son Nhut at a flight line trailer, the "Roach Coach," which served hot dogs, fruit juice, and coffee. At Nha Trang, the crews stayed in an open-bay barracks. Heat, noise, and cleaning activity made proper rest all but impossible for men on the night-flying schedule. At Cam Ranh Bay aircrews resided in tents or open-bay barracks. The continuing conditions of frustration and inadequate rest hardly squared with the responsibilities of the crews, on whose judgment rested the safety of their passengers.[17]

The wings based outside of Vietnam understood that crewmen were dangerously overworked. One unit reported that many aircrews were not getting any rest days during their ten-day cycles in Vietnam, and another reported that some crews had to be returned to Vietnam after only nineteen hours at their home station. Replying to a senatorial inquiry in February 1966, PACAF and the 2d Air Division denied that "crews in Vietnam sometimes fly at the point of exhaustion." The reply cited a recent reform reducing the allowable workday for aircrews in Vietnam to twelve hours. Another constructive measure was an increase in the shuttle force manning, thus allowing occasional rest days for crewmen in Vietnam.[18]

The carrying capacity of the C–130 proved an enormous asset for the Southeast Asia Airlift System. Further, the introduction of this aircraft allowed around-the-clock operations. This was feasible because the aircraft's navigational radar permitted operations during periods of darkness and marginal weather. Ground aids for safer flight were now more widely available in Vietnam, including ground controlled approach radar for landings, a radar advisory service for inflight warning of the approach of other aircraft, and tacan radio equipment for instantaneous navigational fixing. Airfields at Nha Trang, Qui Nhon, and Cam Ranh Bay received improved night lighting. The C–130 effort thus evolved into a high-volume, twenty-four-hour, air logistics service linking the main airfields. Operations to marginal forward strips remained principally work for the C–123s. A division message, dated August 1, 1965, confirms this trend, prescribing that highly qualified, "short-stop" C–130 pilots could operate only into strips exceeding in length the "computer ground run distance plus 1,000 feet." This in effect barred the C–130s from airfields having runways less than thirty-five hundred feet in length and promised to hamper employment of the Hercules force in the large-scale offensive ventures for which the U.S. Army was preparing. Behind the air division's conservative policy was concern for safety as well as awareness that the tonnage capacity of the C–130 could be only partly used in shortfield work.[19]

Pilots and supervisors returning from the TAC rotational units in late summer 1965 informed TAC headquarters that C–130 assault capability developed in recent years was not being fully exploited in Vietnam. They called for a revised concept of operations to include "direct support of army combat operations." Soon afterwards the Air Force asked PACAF to examine the use of "the full potential of tactical assault airlift" in Southeast Asia. The 2d Air Division vice commander on October 29, 1965, added that the C–130 capability for using unprepared surfaces two thousand feet long had been proven in the past and that if the Air Force "wanted to lose the airlift task to the Army, we were headed in the right direction." The 315th Air Division modified its policy on November 10, authorizing operations into all fields within the performance limitations of the aircraft. The flights had to be specifically approved by the Det 5 commander after he considered the urgency of the tactical situation and the capabilities of a particular aircrew. PACAF on November 26 concurred in the deletion of the one thousand-foot runway safety margin. An intensified training program ensued at the offshore bases to strengthen the skills of the designated short-stop pilots and to increase their numbers. The decision to use the C–130s for shortfield work, coupled with efforts to improve selected forward strips to meet the minimum Hercules landing-takeoff capability, paved the way for the application of this aircraft to battles of the future.[20]

An inquiry by Secretary McNamara revived the question of in-country basing. The MACV staff had leaned toward the idea and, on July 10, 1966, Lt. Gen. William W. Momyer, the Seventh Air Force commander,* proposed to PACAF in-country assignment of a C–130 wing with "clear-cut and standardized lines of command and control" and with full in-country maintenance capability. General Momyer repeated his recommendation in September, further stressing the need for fullest possible familiarity among aircrews with the places and methods encountered in Vietnam. The Seventh Air Force staff accordingly began planning for a four-squadron wing at Cam Ranh Bay. After discussing the question with General Westmoreland in October, Secretary McNamara ordered the Joint Chiefs of Staff to develop a plan for stationing two C–130 squadrons in Vietnam.[21]

The positions of the various commands on this issue were by now firm, so that the resulting staff work and discussions amounted to reaffirmations of old positions. The 315th Air Division, PACAF, and the Pacific Command had consistently supported basing out of Vietnam and the increasing use of C–130s for in-country work, first by using transiting aircraft then by temporary augmentations and finally by the shuttle system. The shuttle arrangement had numerous advantages: reducing the need for in-country logistics support, maintenance facilities and ramp space, and allowing for the movement of cargo from abroad by aircraft rotating into Vietnam. Shuttled C–130s produced higher daily flying rates while in-country than was possible with permanently assigned units, since heavy

---

* The 2d Air Division became the Seventh Air Force on April 1, 1966.

maintenance and crew training were done out of the country. Finally, weakening the view that in-country basing would enhance aircrew familiarity with operating conditions, crewmen assigned to the Naha, Clark, and Tachikawa squadrons served Far East tours of up to thirty-six months, far longer than the twelve months prescribed for individuals assigned in Vietnam. Air Staff support for out-of-country basing was crucial, and this idea was reaffirmed in meetings within the Air Staff board structure and before the Joint Chiefs. Clearly the acceptance of the idea reflected the absence of specific failings in the shuttle system. In forwarding the requested plan to McNamara on November 19, 1966, the Joint Chiefs of Staff joined CINCPAC in recommending continued basing out of Vietnam. In a memorandum to the Joint Chiefs, dated December 5, Secretary McNamara concurred. He was swayed by the high construction costs and the economic impact permanently assigned Hercules squadrons would have on Vietnamese currency.[22]

Secretary McNamara's decision became final although the pros and cons of out-of-country basing remained a popular topic for debate among airlifters. Morale remained satisfactory among C-130 air and ground crewmen, aided by a late 1966 command decision to count each shuttle cycle of fifteen days or more toward an official Southeast Asia tour. Those aircrews assigned at Mactan Isle Airfield, Philippines, and Ching Chuan Kang Air Base, Taiwan, were buoyed by the expectation of returning home in thirteen months; those with families at Clark, Naha, and Tachikawa lived an odd existence, alternating periods of combat duty in Vietnam with normal family life.

In August 1966, for the first time, the C-130s hauled more tonnage in Vietnam than the combined total shifted by the C-123s, Caribous, and Vietnamese C-47s. But in the next three months, C-130 tonnages remained well below the MACV forecast of haul requirements. The conclusion reached within the 315th Air Division was that the MACV forecast of sixty thousand tons monthly had been inflated. In reality tonnages had been limited by the availability of air transport. Tactical operations had been shaped to fit the existing in-country transport force, relying more heavily on road transport than might otherwise have been the case. In its monthly operational report for July, the U.S. Army operational headquarters for the central provinces—Headquarters II Field Force, Vietnam—reported steadily increasing shortages of Air Force airlift, increasingly frequent cases of postponed and incomplete movements, and a need to tighten airlift priorities among ground force tacticians.[23]

The growing role of the C-130s in South Vietnam necessitated major expansion of the force based offshore. Additional temporarily assigned rotational (rote) squadrons arrived from TAC in April 1965, easing the overcommitment of the existing squadrons. The augmentations were authorized for a duration of ninety days, "subject to reexamination," but the deployments stretched through the summer as theater airlift requirements grew. Each of four parent wings in TAC rotated personnel and aircraft to and from the Far East, and maintained the strength of their deployed squadrons. C–130 strength in the Pacific held at eight squadrons through August 1965:

815th TCS	HQ 315th AD	C–130A	at Tachikawa
21st TCS	6315th Ops Gp	C–130A	at Naha
35th TCS	6315th Ops Gp	C–130A	at Naha
817th TCS	6315th Ops Gp	C–130A	at Naha
314th TCW (one rote sq)	from Sewart	C–130B/E	at Clark
516th TCW (one rote sq)	from Dyess	C–130E	at Naha
436th TCW (one rote sq)	from Langley	C–130B	at Clark
464th TCW (one rote sq)	from Pope	C–130E	at Kadena

In the meantime, further expansion was directly linked to an enlargement of the American role in the ground war. General Westmoreland's attention to offensive and mobile tactics against communist main forces and base areas promised a larger role for air transport. During Phase I of the ground war, conceived as a strategic defensive period extending roughly through 1965, MACV had recommended four additional C–130 squadrons. MACV's calculations assumed that each American airborne brigade would require one air movement and twenty days of air supply each month, that ten Vietnamese battalions would move by air each month, and that eight battalions in the highlands would require continuing air resupply.[24]

But the expansion of the offshore fleet to twelve C–130 squadrons was accomplished simultaneously with conversion of all squadrons to a permanent change of station, ending the temporary augmentations from TAC. An intricate shift schedule was developed predicated on the availability of beddown bases in the Pacific. The 314th Troop Carrier Wing was based on Taiwan with three E–model squadrons. The wing received its aircraft from three of the rotational detachments already in the Pacific and its manpower from the three respective parent wings. Each squadron operated temporarily with interim locations, then they moved to Kung Kuan Air Base in early 1966. Facilities there were still far from adequate and many men had to live off base in rented quarters while tents used as offices often collapsed during heavy rains. The chronic damp wind made the winter chilly. Kung Kuan was renamed Ching Chuan Kang Air Base on March 20, and was thereafter known throughout the theater by its initials, CCK.

The buildup of the 463d Wing in the Philippines on Mactan Island was less painful although the wing headquarters and two squadrons found facilities on the island base scarcely lavish. A rotational squadron arrived in August 1965 and found workmen still fitting canvas tops on newly erected wood-frame quarters; the crewmen pitched in amid rainshowers to get the area ready for occupancy. The tents proved quite livable and were equipped with electricity and modest furnishings. The C-130 A-model force remained at Naha and Tachikawa, but they acquired a fifth squadron from the United States in November 1965.[25]

The shuffling of units during the fall and winter of 1965-1966 established the C-130 basing which prevailed through much of the war. Until a temporary augmentation two years later, theater C-130 strength remained at twelve squadrons identified and located as follows:

Unit	Former Location	New Base	Date Arrived
463d TCW (C-130B)		Mactan	Nov 23, 1965
774th TCS	Langley AFB	Mactan	Nov 23, 1965
773d TCS	Clark (rote)	Clark	Nov 23, 1965
29th TCS	Forbes AFB	Clark	Jan 30, 1966
772d TCS	Langley AFB (interim rote to Mactan)	Mactan	Feb 12, 1966
314th TCW (C-130E)		Kung Kuan	Jan 22, 1966
50th TCS	Clark (rote)	Kung Kuan	Jan 23, 1966
345th TCS	Naha (rote)	Kung Kuan	Mar 20, 1966
776th TCS	Kadena (rote)	Kung Kuan	Apr 1, 1966
6315th Ops Gp (C-130A), redesignated 374th TCW, Aug 8, 1966			
41st TCS	Lockbourne AFB	Naha	Nov 21, 1965
21st TCS	Naha	None	None
35th TCS	Naha	None	None
817th TCS	Naha	None	None
815th TCS, HQ 315th AD	Tachikawa	None	None

One way to increase total airlift capacity without introducing more aircraft was by increasing the flying hour rate. Such action required additional air and ground crews, greater supplies of spare parts, and increased funding. Normal C-130 usage prior to 1965 stood at 1.5 hours per airframe daily. During the spring of 1965 actual usage in the eight squadrons in PACAF climbed above 2.0 hours. Under Project Fast Fly, which began September 15, 1965, C-130A and C-130B rates were to increase from 1.5 to 2.5 hours effective October 1. PACAF and TAC C-130E rates were to increase in progressive steps, reaching 5.0 hours daily by July 1, 1966. Maintenance manning tables were enlarged, and all units were to implement a six-day work week, an increase of half a day. Existing aircrew authorizations (one and a half crews per assigned aircraft) also were raised to two for A- and B-model units and to three for the C-130E. Project Fast Fly more than doubled the hours flown by the twelve-squadron C-130 fleet from 8,640 hours monthly under the former rates to eighteen thousand hours monthly.[26]

But the Fast Fly rates were not easily achieved. Harsh operating conditions in Vietnam intensified the maintenance burden. Short sorties required frequent landings, some of them on rough strips which caused stress on landing gears, brakes, hydraulic systems, propellers, and engines. And the consumption of tires was extreme. During the first twelve days of 1966, the Tan Son Nhut detachment reported ninety-four main landing-gear tire changes. And frequent engine starts contributed to a large number of starter failures.

The C–130A units were especially troubled by maintenance problems. The older A–models required thirty maintenance man-hours per flying hour compared with the eighteen man-hours necessary for the E–models. To ease the maintenance workloads the A–models were used mainly in less rigorous overwater flying. But repeated propeller reversal malfunctions, resulting in at least one serious accident in Vietnam, brought a restriction in April 1966 against their landing on unpaved strips or on airfields less than four thousand feet in length. In contrast, the B–models consistently flew more than their allocations even though nearly all flying was within Vietnam. The 314th Wing built up to the Fast Fly rate slightly behind schedule, being troubled by delays in moving into Kung Kuan. The wing reached the 5.0 daily hour rate on schedule in July 1966, and for this it earned a letter of commendation from PACAF. The E–models at Nha Trang averaged 6.5 hours daily by virtue of around-the-clock operations and maintenance. Behind the remarkable C–130 flying rates stood the sweat and skill of several thousand overworked and unsung ground crewmen, many of them relatively new to the aircraft.[27]

The expansion to twelve squadrons and the Fast Fly increases, along with the need to replace all personnel at Ching Chuan Kang and Mactan every thirteen months, brought an increased requirement for trained C–130 aircrews. TAC in late 1965 expanded the program of the 442d Combat Crew Training Group at Sewart Air Force Base, and established replacement training units at each of the five TAC troop carrier wings. The 442d gave introductory training in the C–130 to pilots and flight engineers. Replacement training units provided introductory training to navigators and loadmasters and tactical training to all crewmen. By June 1966 a total of ninety C–130s were assigned to the training group and the replacement units. The program functioned on a seven-day workweek, produced over five hundred qualified crews during 1966, and essentially caught up with the demand created by Fast Fly.[28]

The unavoidable decline in C–130 experience among crewmen was of concern especially in view of the increasingly demanding missions in Vietnam. Whereas in mid-1965 the 315th Air Division aircrewmen averaged over one thousand total hours in the aircraft, graduates of the stateside training program had only 165 hours. Many of the officers entering the pipeline were older men, creating a topheavy rank structure in the Pacific squadrons. At the end of 1966, for example, the 50th Squadron at Ching Chuan Kang Air Base had seventeen lieutenant colonels and twenty-two majors. Although new to the C–130, many of these men were veteran flyers whose experience dated back to World War II. The majority of the aircraft commanders over the age of forty—the so-called "Grey Berets"— relished these flying duties after years of staff or administrative work. Most proved entirely capable of performing rigorous duty in Vietnam.[29]

Looking ahead to the possible introduction of American ground units along the full length of South Vietnam, the MACV staff in 1965 recognized the need for the development of an east-west distribution system of "logistical islands." The U.S. Army 1st Logistical Command, activated on April 1, 1965, established logistical support commands at the principal seaports, each responsible for port clearance, supply depot, and line-haul (over fifty miles) trucking functions. The result was the establishment of four logistical islands, served by Army support commands at Saigon, Cam Ranh Bay, and Qui Nhon, and by the naval component command at Da Nang.[30]

Land transportation was hampered by the deterioration of many highways from heavy use, flooding, and enemy demolition. General Westmoreland directed in 1966 that land routes be opened and used to the greatest possible extent. Highway movements accordingly increased although they were dedicated exclusively for shipment within each of the logistical islands. Most road hauls were short, connecting ports and depots with nearby base camps. Railroad shipments remained insignificant, since the communists easily destroyed the restored rail-line segments.[31]

Water lines of communication were used where possible. Coastal shipping linked the Cam Ranh Bay depot with satellite locations at Phan Rang, Nha Trang, and Tuy Hoa. Vessels served the region north of Da Nang while the delta waterways afforded broad access to shallow-draft craft. Substantial tonnages were moved by water between the deep-draft ports, linking the separate logistical islands.[32]

Since land haul was preferred for movement within the logistical islands, and sealift between them, the role of airlift (apart from its tactical applications) became a backup for the other modes of transportation, handling tasks for which surface movement was too slow. Logistical airlift included the movement of most mail, high-value or emergency items, perishable foods, and passengers, both across and within the logistical islands. Daily scheduled flights linked the major bases administratively and permitted reduction of the normal aerial port cargo backlogs. Airlift deliveries of general cargo to base areas and operating locations, some of which were inaccessible by surface, blended into the tactical role.[33]

Data compiled by MACV and U.S. Army units give further indication of the relationships among the transportation modes. In-country cargo and passenger movements in the first three months of 1966, expressed in thousands of tons were as follows:

TACTICAL AIRLIFT

By land		1,694.2
U.S. trucks	1,301.7	
Vietnamese trucks	372.5	
rail	20.0	
By sea		261.3
U.S. landing ship, tank (LST)	105.9	
barges	127.1	
Vietnamese navy	28.3	
By air		310.2
SEAAS	151.2	
VNAF	12.0	
U.S. Army	147.0 (including helicopters)	

The figures fail to reflect the greater distances involved in the work of the Southeast Asia Airlift System and the LSTs.[34]

Under arrangements inherited from the earlier period, the mode of transport by which a particular shipment moved was in effect determined by the daily allocations of airlift at MACV's movements branch. Several officers of the 315th Group in June 1965 called attention to the absence of any combined movements board, whose existence was supposedly directed by MACV. Staff officers from Air Force headquarters also challenged the logic of the existing arrangement.[35] A MACV joint movements transportation board, including representatives from the MACV staff agenices and the U.S. component commands, began meeting on March 21, 1966, for the purpose of allocating common service sea and air transportation. The group gathered each month thereafter. The board balanced users' forecasts of tonnage lift requirements with existing capabilities by encouraging them to reduce requests or by taking action to acquire additional transport means.[36]

For day-to-day management a MACV traffic management agency was created in September 1965 under logistics section supervision, "to better utilize available air, sea, and land transportation resources." Organized within this agency was a directorate of movements which included branches or centers for land movement, sealift, and airlift. Each center received transportation requests daily, allocated capabilities according to MACV priorities, and controlled flow of cargo traffic to respective operators. Manned principally by an Army transportation unit and augmented by individuals from the other services, the traffic management agency became fully operational by mid-March 1966.[37]

The agency together with the joint movements transportation board undertook the managerial role previously attempted by the logistics section. The new arrangement approximated those prescribed in existing doctrine, and promised to assure a rational division of tasks among the separate transportation modes. Operation of the Southeast Asia Airlift System remained an Air Force responsibility under allocations of the theater commander through the transportation board. Organic Army air transport and Vietnamese Air Force C-47 capabilities remained outside the central allocations process.

The C-130s adapted easily to the Southeast Asia Airlift System's control apparatus. MACV's traffic agency had two functions: it guided the flow of cargo into the aerial ports for routine movement; and it ruled upon requests for special and emergency lifts, passing them to the control center as specific mission requirements. Inexperience among men assigned to the airlift control center was a handicap. At one time, the commander, his deputy, and a majority of assigned officers lacked any previous experience in airlift work. Col. George L. Hannah, Jr., commander of the 315th Air Commando Group,* had a businesslike objective:

> I expect the ALCC to be able to tell me at any time the location, mission, and status of every aircraft in our entire fleet. . . . No aircraft will depart for any location unless it has been so directed by ALCC or through the appropriate agency. . . .[38]

The several airlift control element agencies, formerly called traffic management detachments, continued to function as extensions of the control center at the principal airlift operating locations. Yet the struggle to overcome inadequate communications and work facilities continued undiminished, as the expanding sortie effort brought an infinite variety of daily headaches in expediting the flow of aircraft. Manning was limited and only 92 spaces were approved of the 209 recommended for the control center and control elements in the summer of 1965. This made a twenty-four-hour operation difficult. Rather than spread available strength too thin, the number of control elements was held to seven in the spring of 1966.[39]

The task of extending the airlift control apparatus to forward locations often fell to the Air Force combat controllers. Three twenty-four-man combat control teams arrived in Vietnam soon after October 1965 (a temporary duty team had served at An Khe the previous summer). The teams split into elements of four to eight men which were sent to forward strips with the first transport. Their standard equipment included a radio vehicle, a homing beacon, and runway lighting equipment. Such teams were usually accompanied by a qualified troop carrier pilot designated as mis-

---

*The 315th Troop Carrier Group was renamed the 315th Air Commando Group, Troop Carrier, and the 309th, 310th, and 311th Squadrons became air commando squadrons, effective March 8, 1965. The group was raised to wing status on March 8, 1966.

The USAF airlift control system at work:

A "Blue Beret" combat control team communicates with the airlift control center.

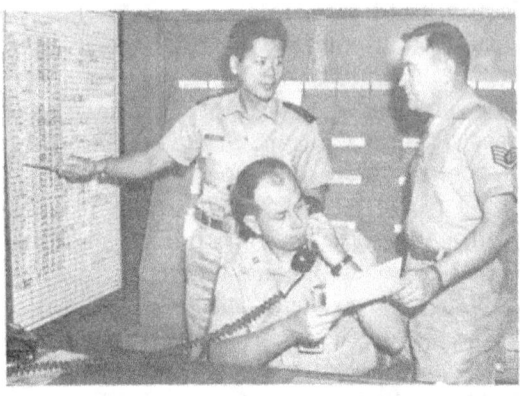

Traffic managers at the Joint Operations Center, Tan Son Nhut, check the flight progress of a C-123.

A smoke marker from air.

Combat controllers mark the paradrop zone with smoke and red cloth panels.

sion commander. They established radio communications with the control center and assisted in coordinating airlift activities with local units. Air traffic control responsibilities were often performed by U.S. Army teams, although arrangements to exploit the equipment and talents of both Army and combat control teams were flexible. One team officer reported that the Marines and a cavalry division were sometimes cocky, but when traffic became heavy the combat control team was welcome. Although these duties were less dramatic than the parachute tasks for which the teams trained, the elite Blue Berets assured the mission commander and the airlift crews of their resourceful support.[40]

A major barrier to efficient control was poor communications. Colonel Howton, commanding the 311th Squadron at Da Nang, compared Southeast Asia communications to the pony express era, noting that teletype messages from the control center sometimes took twelve hours to reach his hands. Especially gnawing were the delays in installing ARC–44 FM radios in the C–123s; this modification, needed for contact with ground force units, stretched into 1966. The same difficulty accompanied introduction of the C–130s, necessitating the use of jury-rigged PRC–25 FM sets.[41]

Measurements of the efficiency of the airlift effort reinforced the criticism of the C–130 aircrews. Data for June 1966 reveals sixteen hundred examples of mission delay, most of them caused by maintenance, loading, and air traffic difficulties. The total time delay equated to the work of several aircraft. To allow more comprehensive analyses of SEAAS effectiveness, an automated reporting system was implemented on October 1, 1966. Aircrews were required to keep detailed records of each sortie and each load and submit an airlift operating report after each day's flying for computer storage and analysis. This annoying bookkeeping task fell to the navigator.[42]

A system of priority designations identified movement requests above the routine. Those missions—designated tactical emergency, emergency supply, or combat essential—claimed whatever aircraft were available and, if necessary, a ship was diverted from its scheduled itinerary. Tactical emergency lifts usually supported ground force units; emergency supply and combat essential could entail lifts of petroleum products and ammunition for ground forces or aircraft parts and ordnance. PACAF data indicated that in April and May 1966 the airlift system completed on time fifty-three of fifty-nine tactical emergency missions and 358 of 389 emergency supply.[43]

But the same operational data failed to convey numerous cases of ground force dissatisfaction with the airlift system's service. Complaints were often traceable to unsatisfactory information flow between airlift users and providers. A battalion commander waiting with his unit for late transports was seldom tolerant, even if he later learned that delays had been unavoidable or caused by higher priority lifts. An Air Force air liaison officer with the cavalry division described specific instances when transports arrived late to pick up units, or in insufficient number, or not at all. Sometimes, notification that mission requests had been turned down never reached cavalry officers. Certain C–130 aircrews seemed uncooperative, and one battalion commander described the C–123 crews which lifted his unit as "ragged, unpredictable, and . . . invariably late." The air liaison officer summarized the picture as "how not to accomplish an airlift mission in support of military operations." The intensity of feeling was sufficient to prompt a remonstrance to the Air Force in early 1966 by Gen. Harold K. Johnson, Army chief of staff.[44]

A Seventh Air Force memorandum of July 31, 1966, directly considered the problem. The memo recommended that qualified airlift officers be assigned as members of the respective tactical air control parties to ground force units down to brigade level. These tactical airlift liaison officers would serve as airlift advisors and coordinators, overcoming in the most forthright way the gap in information flow. Despite reservations by the logistics section over the use of liaison officers below the division level, a test plan was published by MACV on October 25 requiring that airlift liaison officers be assigned to brigades effective November 1.

The Seventh Air Force memorandum also proposed changes in the emergency airlift request procedures. Under the existing system, according to the memo, excessive delays occurred during passage of emergency requests upward through successive ground force command levels; a similar situation had prevailed in the close air support request net several years earlier. The memo recommended that emergency lift requests pass from the brigade or division directly to the corps-level direct air support center, using the existing air support net communications. Ground commanders at division and field force level would monitor such requests, intervening only to disapprove or modify requests. The support center, which included Army representation, would transmit requests to the MACV command center or traffic management agency for approval and would simultaneously warn the control center to start preliminary mission planning. The proposal became the basis for tests.[45]

The idea of creating a new air division to be under Southeast Asia Airlift System management was first conceived during the introduction of the C–130 shuttle system in 1965. The concept received renewed attention when the Secretary of Defense decided to transfer the Caribous to the Air Force. As the plan developed during May and June 1966, the air division would absorb the airlift control center from the 315th Wing, would possess as assigned units the new Caribou wing, the C–123 wing, and an aerial port group, and would exert operational control over the C–130 shuttle force. General Momyer, who took command of the Seventh Air Force on July 1, 1966, sought and gained MACV approval for the formation of the airlift air division, which he "considered essential for effective management and control of the rapidly expanding in-country airlift mission." The new command, designated the 834th Air Division, was activated at Tan Son Nhut on October 15, 1966, with an authorized headquarters strength of ninety-three.[46]

The creation of the air division was consistent with earlier troop carrier doctrine which prescribed centralized management of airlift forces under the theater joint commander. Yet to be worked out was the nature of airlift system autonomy from other tactical air control agencies, although the emergency airlift request methods soon to be tested suggested close integration. The new air division appeared to be competent to deal with internal problems of the airlift system, while its general officer billet assured stronger representations with other organizations. The birth of the 834th, the forthcoming tests of the new emergency net, the tactical air liaison officer idea, and the actions toward integration of the Caribou force, together represented a major overhaul of the airlift system. Rounding out the reforms of late 1966 were the reorganization and enlargement of the aerial port network.

The aerial port workload in Vietnam increased from thirty thousand tons monthly in the first half of 1965 to one hundred and forty thousand tons in June 1966. This rise grossly outstripped the ability of the aerial port system to function with efficiency. Criticisms of aerial port performance became widespread both among aircrews impatient over mission delays and in official reports of supervisors and inspecting officers. The men of the aerial port units lived and worked under primitive conditions, struggled with inadequate equipment and facilities, were chronically overworked, and received few rewards save personal satisfaction. Their problems were similar to those encountered in the buildup of 1962–63.[47]

The seven aerial port detachments in Vietnam at the start of 1965 expanded to thirty-five by year's end, organized under the 8th Aerial Port Squadron at Tan Son Nhut, the 14th at Cam Ranh Bay, and the 15th at Da Nang.* Personnel strength to December was less than half the 1,995 number judged necessary to meet the immediate workload. Increases in manning were slowed by delays in gaining approval of spaces and in acquiring personnel once authorized. Several increments of temporary duty personnel provided partial relief. Work schedules at Da Nang, for example, were twelve hours on and twelve hours off, but aircraft turnaround times remained an unacceptable ninety minutes. The 2d Air Division appealed to higher commands asserting that the "grossly inadequate" aerial port manning was "stifling" airlift capability. Furthermore, few of the men actually on hand had previous experience in air terminal work. Generally, the several aerial port squadrons of TAC had been small and were manned

---

* The 14th and 15th Aerial Port Squadrons were formed December 1, 1965.

mainly for the airdrop role. One expedient was the "Road Show," a team which gave intensive cargo handling instruction at the different locations in Vietnam.[48]

Construction of pavement, fencing, and buildings proceeded slowly. New port detachments scrounged to make improvements, often contending with alternating cycles of dust and mud. At Kontum the new detachment arrived in July 1965 to discover general disarray. Expensive pallets were being used by the Vietnamese for bunkers and walkways, petroleum drums and cargo nets were scattered about, and security and property accounting were being neglected. At An Khe, the small detachment rigged a terminal from two shipping containers connected by a pierced steel planking porch and fenced with sandbags. At Ban Me Thuot, where the airfield was considered unsafe after dark, a tent served as the only storage point. Shortages of ramp and storage space plagued even the older locations. Loaded pallets were often stored in the open on unpaved surfaces, and protected only by plastic sheeting. Aside from the extemporizations, construction seldom began until three months after official approval. PACAF later acknowledged that part of the problem was the low priorities set on aerial port construction in favor of "hard core projects."[49]

Except at the largest terminals, there was little need in Vietnam for the heavier equipment recently developed under Project 463L. A typical cargo loading in Vietnam was by simple hydraulic forklift which raised loaded cargo pallets to aircraft bed height. Loading of palletized cargo was a simple and fast process involving a forklift operator, an aircrew loadmaster, and two or three helpers to push the pallets along the aircraft's dual rails. Vehicles could be driven up the inclined ramp and secured by chains to permanent fixtures. Aircraft interiors could be converted in minutes for passengers or patients by rigging canvas seats or litter brackets.

The daily aerial port routine at the major terminals followed common patterns. Cargo entered the port system from depots regulated by traffic management regional offices and local cargo air traffic coordinating offices (both manned principally by the Army). Cargo arrival at the port during evening hours was preferred when mission activity was light. Port workers then readied priority shipments for early movement; other cargo became backlog, kept on hand to permit full utilization of opportune space. Specialized aerial port workers palletized the cargo according to destination, building up pallet loads to optimum weight and volume. Palletizing was usually night-shift work and was followed by preparation of pallet documents in time for load planning about four hours before mission time. The load planner selected those pallets to be shipped on particular missions, attempting to develop a good aircraft load while considering shipment priorities and aircraft balance. A light pallet or loose mail might be identified for placement on the C–130's rear ramp. If a full five-pallet load for a particular destination was not available, other pallets might be selected

Loaded cargo pallets share the flight line with a C-130.

The terminal at Tan Son Nhut, 1965.

Forklift being used to unload a C-124.

for transshipment. A completed planning worksheet was then used to set out the appropriate pallets in readiness for loading and for final preparation of documents. Supervising the loading and actual flow of traffic was an aerial port duty officer aided by a radio dispatcher and a vehicle-borne "ramp tramp" coordinator.[50]

Ramp safety was a matter for particular concern given the urge for speed, the customary fatigue among individuals, and the inexperience among port personnel. The fingers and feet of cargo handlers were especially vulnerable; forklift drivers could easily damage the aircraft sides during loading, or might run down people at night. Ammunition and petroleum handling necessitated extra safety measures.

A chronic problem, never fully resolved, was the unsatisfactory reliability of the forklift. On November 15, 1965, for example, of seventy-seven forklifts in Vietnam only thirty-two were in commission. Several factors appeared at work: harsh usage, spare parts shortages, lack of maintenance skills, and certain design flaws. Maintenance teams from the United States and preventive maintenance training barely kept pace with the intensifying problem. Late in 1965 the 315th Group asked for and received manpower assistance from the Army for handloading aircraft. In November 1966 only 134 of 236 assigned forklifts (347 were authorized) were in commission.[51]

Another problem was a theater-wide shortage of the 88- by 108-inch pallets. An abundance of pallets was desirable to permit aerial ports to prepare backlog cargo for opportune transportation. Each pallet was precisely dimensioned, cost four hundred dollars, and was made of aluminum facing on a balsa wood core. Careless handling could spoil a pallet's alignment with the dual rails or cause dents or bending thereby necessitating repair at the maintenance facility in Japan. Contributing to their attrition was the usefulness of pallets for bunker construction at forward airheads. PACAF requests for more pallets began in October 1964. Aircrews were enjoined to pick up empty pallets when delivering loaded ones, a difficult matter during tactical movements. Long-awaited relief came abruptly during late 1965 and January 1966 with the delivery of eighteen hundred pallets.[52]

During 1966 the aerial port squadrons and the larger detachments unofficially organized five-man mobility teams. These teams were sent to forward locations during tactical operations, taking with them forklifts and assorted field equipment. In July, for example, the 8th Squadron dispatched eight teams to six different locations. At the forward airhead the aerial port team joined the mission commander, the combat control team, and (after 1966) the tactical airlift liaison officer to make up a tailored airlift support element. Mobility sections were later formally organized in each of the three aerial port squadrons for this role.[53]

Promotions and awards were slow for aerial port personnel. The Da

Nang unit in 1964 and 1965, for example, failed to receive a single promotion. The men's morale and enthusiasm remained high, however, and commanders attributed this to the airmen's awareness of the need for their efforts. A form of recognition came in September 1966 upon presentation of the National Defense Transportation Association Award to the 8th Aerial Port Squadron for its outstanding service while operating "under combat conditions, in a hostile environment, coupled with shortages of materiel and personnel."[54]

The in-country C-123 airlift force remained at four squadrons* and proposals for expansion of the fleet were thwarted by the limited Air Force inventory of these aircraft. Statistical data shows the impressive and increasing accomplishments by the Providers, reflecting their higher flying hour rates and the gradual improvements in airlift system management. Monthly tonnages lifted by the air fleet doubled during the period of January 1965 to September 1966, and the quarterly average increased from thirty-one thousand tons to sixty-six thousand tons. Missions between major airfields across the corps areas became fewer; shorter hauls into locations unsuitable for the C-130s became more frequent.[55]

Personnel shortages after 1964 created hardships on the crewmen. Although ninety-six aircrews were authorized in January 1965, only fifty-six were assigned to the four squadrons. An increased flow of aircrew replacements from Hurlburt gradually eased the shortage, and for the first time the four C-123 squadrons attained full operational accreditation in July 1966.† The average flying experience of the newcomers remained low since many second lieutenants entered the pipeline at Hurlburt directly from flying training.[56]

Increases in the flying rate overextended maintenance capabilities. Programmed daily flying increased from two to three hours per aircraft during 1965, but during most months actual flying exceeded these amounts, at times by more than twenty-five percent. Deterioration in the C-123 operational-ready rate followed, and by year's end the force was unable to achieve the 3.0 flying standard. Colonel Hannah officially concluded that C-123 maintenance was "totally unacceptable and almost at the point of being dangerous." A series of maintenance squadron reforms

---

* The 310th Squadron moved to Nha Trang in April 1964, ending its rotation from Tan Son Nhut; the defoliation unit merged with the 309th Squadron in early 1965.

† Reorganization of the Special Air Warfare Center on December 1, 1965, brought into being at Hurlburt the 4410th Combat Crew Training Wing.

were introduced including postmission critiques by pilots, daily maintenance staff meetings, and generally tighter supervision. Incommission rates improved in early 1966 although flying remained slightly under the 3.0 programmed hours.[57]

Missions into short airstrips and mountainous areas placed a premium on engine reliability. It became increasingly apparent that the engines lacked the ability to develop full power. Analyses pointed to no single cause. A change of spark plugs often brought immediate improvement but engine malfunctions often reappeared after a mission or two. Several crashes highlighted the problem. One squadron commander instructed his pilots to insist on peak performance in engine checks prior to departing on missions.[58]

A renewed proposal from Fairchild-Hiller Aircraft Company for adding auxiliary jet engines to the C-123s promised greater safety during takeoffs and improved capacity for forward area work. The idea had been tested successfully on the YC-123H. The directorate of operational requirements and development plans at Air Force headquarters in July 1965 invited recommendations from the commands. The 2d Air Division enthusiastically endorsed the modification idea, noting that with the addition of the jets the aircraft could take off from most remote strips even with one reciprocating engine inoperative. With all four engines operating, the maximum payload could be increased under typical conditions from five to over eight tons; on the other hand takeoff distance with the increased load could be reduced from 1,400 to 920 feet. The 315th Air Division, PACAF, and the Special Air Warfare Center approved a modification program for 120 aircraft that began late in 1966. This included the installation of two J-85 jet engines, antiskid brakes, and a cockpit stall-warning device. The retrofit was scheduled at the Fairchild plant at Hagerstown.[59]

The air and ground crewmen serving one-year tours in the C-123 units were a cross section of the peacetime air force. Most worked hard, responding to circumstances with energy and initiative. The air commando name remained, but use of the Australian commando hat and squadron scarves was prohibited throughout the Air Force in 1966. Crowded enlisted housing and messing facilities at Tan Son Nhut and Da Nang continued to jeopardize proper rest and diet, but there were no serious problems of health and morale.[60]

In addition to the problems of terrain, weather, and limited facilities known to C-123 and C-130 aircrews in the earlier years, the expanded war added new hazards. Crowding at forward airstrips also used by Army helicopters and vehicles necessitated constant watchfulness when landing and taxiing. Congested airspace raised the danger of inflight collision, especially in the vicinity of airfields. Friendly artillery fire and air strikes posed further potential dangers for the transport crews, while preventive measures against possible enemy fire required little emphasis.

Of approximately seventy identifiable episodes involving significant damage to C–123 and C–130 aircraft during 1965 and the first ten months of 1966, one-third occurred during landings away from the home base. Each assault landing contained an element of uncertainty because of the narrow safety margin against possible mechanical failure or imprecision in pilot technique. Runway overruns and eroded shoulders resulted in major accidents. Such landing accidents seldom resulted in the loss of life or in the total destruction of an aircraft but they often necessitated months of major repair work. Three fatal C–130 accidents occurred during the period, and each was complicated by bad weather. The first C–130 and crew lost in Southeast Asia went down during a go-around at Korat, Thailand, on April 24, 1965. Five months later, four aircrewmen died when a Hercules came down into the water while attempting to land at Qui Nhon, a place known for its tricky crosswinds. Three men were killed on a night flight to Pleiku on March 29, 1966, when the aircraft touched down short of the runway. Five other aircraft were lost during landings at An Loc, Tuy Hoa, Qui Nhon, (all were C–123 crashes), and at An Khe (a C–130 crash). Especially ill-fated was the hillside strip at An Loc where six C–123 landing accidents were recorded during these years. Several accidents resulted from collisions with helicopters sitting adjacent to active air strips. One C–123 while landing at Dau Tieng struck a Chinook helicopter on one side of the runway and an HU–1D helicopter on the other.[61]

Less forgiving, although far rarer, were takeoff accidents resulting from engine failures. Four planes were destroyed in this way. The first, a C–123, occurred at a delta airstrip but all seventy-five men aboard survived the rice-paddy crash landing. Two months later a C–130 pilot elected to attempt a takeoff from Chu Lai despite a known engine problem. Two passengers died in the fire which resulted from loss of control during the takeoff roll. Engine failures caused two C–123 crashes on takeoff at the beginning of 1966 and forty-six Americans died in the second of these accidents, at An Khe.[62]

Yet more chilling was the possibility of navigational error when flying in poor visibility near mountainous terrain. The C–123s were especially vulnerable, lacking navigational radar and used frequently for deliveries in the highlands. In mid-1965, a C–123 of the 310th Squadron flew into a mountain while attempting airdrops in marginal weather south of Pleiku. None of the nine crewmen survived. Eighty-one Vietnamese paratroops and the four-man crew were killed in December when a C–123 flying in limited visibility from Pleiku to Tuy Hoa disintegrated on a cliffside. No

Gen. Hunter Harris (right), commander of Pacific Air Forces, with Lt. Gen. Joseph Moore, 2nd Air Division commander, 1965.

Lt. Gen. William W. Momyer (right) congratulates C–123 crewmembers Capt. Richard A. Fritz, TSgt. Charles L. Peterson (center) and SSgt. William J. Slough for averting a crash on March 1, 1966.

Army specialists clear mines from a field adjacent to the An Khe airstrip, August 1965.

Courtesy: U.S. Army

This C–130 crashed into the water while attempting to land at Qui Nhon, September 1965.

navigator was aboard. A Ching Chuan Kang-based C–130, off course while returning from Vietnam, crashed in the mountains of Taiwan. North of An Khe a midair collision between a C–123 flareship and an A–1E on the night of January 12/13, 1966, took the lives of six crewmen.[63]

The six C–130s and ten C–123s thus lost in flying accidents, along with an eleventh C–123 struck by a Vietnamese aircraft while parked at Da Nang, exceeded the total destroyed by enemy action for the same period. This compared with a total of eleven C–123s lost to all causes in Southeast Asia during the three previous years. The loss of eight aircraft in accidents during the ten weeks ending in late January 1966 represented a level of attrition intolerable even under the prevailing operating conditions. Commanders moved to reverse the trend. The 315th Air Division charged that crews were not complying with time-tested directives and insisted that supervisors at all levels act against "complacency and nonprofessional performance" in flying. Gen. Hunter Harris, Jr., PACAF commander, on a visit with a C–130 unit on Okinawa, "did not appear overly concerned about the accident rate, implying losses could be expected," but he quickly dispelled this impression after the three January accidents near An Khe. The 315th Group took stern measures against the practice of flying visually in extremely marginal weather, and prescribed substantial margins for safe terrain clearance. Col. Robert T. Simpson, who assumed command of the 315th Wing in mid-1966, attacked the accident rate with a widely displayed slogan: "Our mission is not so urgent or pressing that we cannot afford time to accomplish it safely."[64]

The specific measures taken for improving operational safety were built upon the standardization-evaluation systems long established in the C–123 and C–130 units. Additionally, airfield folders were improved and made available to the new C–130 detachments. Each C–123 pilot recorded his landings at each airfield for reference in future mission scheduling. The twelve-hour maximum crew duty day was maintained more rigidly although it could be extended to sixteen hours during conditions of urgency. The reduction in operational losses by mid-1966 became apparent; major C–123 accidents totaled six during the first half of the year and declined to zero during the next four months.[65]

Less successful were efforts to curb the lesser mishaps which were typical of operations at forward airheads shared with the Army. A MACV directive, dated May 9, 1966, prescribed joint planning conferences and fixed traffic control responsibilities under an airfield control officer designated by the ground force commander. Air Force crews, nevertheless, learned to be extremely watchful for uncontrolled Army helicopter flying, for choppers parked close to landing strips, and for vehicles and pedestrians using runways at will. The absence of common radio frequencies for communication between airlift crews and Army agencies was regrettable. It

TACTICAL AIRLIFT

was partly overcome by combat control team efforts to advise aircrews of helicopter and artillery activity.[66]

Communist ground fire remained a lesser, though significant consideration for airlifters. The number of C-123 airlift mssions receiving hits averaged five monthly through 1966, but peaked to fifteen in April 1966. The first C-130 to be shot down by the enemy crashed on December 21, 1965. The 314th Wing aircraft had been preparing to land at Tuy Hoa with a load of thirteen tons of jet fuel. Ground fire brought down a second C-130 near Pleiku three weeks later and a C-123 flareship near An Khe in mid-May 1966. Hostile action was suspected in crashes of a C-123 between Khe Sanh and Dong Ha in early February and a C-130 twenty miles south of Cam Ranh Bay in early October. No crewmembers survived the five crashes.[67]

A PACAF bulletin, published May 23, 1965, listed techniques for reducing vulnerability to ground fire, during steep landing approaches or when flying within 3,000 feet of the ground. Units were urged to practice ground controlled approaches using steep (4½-degree) glide slopes. Assessing methods for escaping in case of enemy air intercept, PACAF recommended that transport crews enter clouds and make sharp turns; an alternate tactic would be flight at treetop level with frequent turns. But MACV considered the possibility of enemy air action remote and opposed use of U.S. Army light antiaircraft Redeye missiles, concerned that these might fall into communist hands. A welcome improvement was the capability, attained after diligent effort among the C-123 units, to airdrop five tons in a single pass and end exposure of the aircraft in multiple runs over hot areas.[68]

Communist attacks on allied airfields further threatened the transport fleet. A Viet Cong demolition squad supported by mortar fire penetrated Da Nang Air Base in the early hours of July 1, 1965, destroying two C-130s and two Vietnamese Air Force C-47s, and damaging three C-123s, eighteen C-47s, a C-130, and numerous other aircraft. Communist sappers penetrated An Khe Airfield after midnight on April 20, 1966, damaging two parked C-130s with satchel charges and small-arms fire and leveling the aerial port office area. Similar attacks were conducted against Nha Trang, Pleiku, and countless lesser strips, posing added concern for airlift crews on the night schedule.[69]

Two instances of attempted sabotage occurred in mid-1966. In one case, a handgrenade was discovered rigged to the aircraft ramp during a C-130 flight from Dak To with one hundred passengers. The grenade exploded after being thrown from the aircraft. A second occurrence resulted in the destruction of a Caribou by an undetected explosive device while the aircraft was parked at Vung Tau. Sabotage was suspected as well in other unexplained crashes including the June explosion of a MAC C-130 after it had departed from Cam Ranh Bay and the October loss of a similar aircraft south of that base. The events suggested caution in employing local persons in aerial port work. Transport crews thereafter searched carefully for explosive devices before takeoffs, especially after hauling Vietnamese passengers.[70]

Communist action thus permanently removed from the Air Force aircraft inventory seven C–130s and six C–123s during these years, including a C–130 lost over North Vietnam. Thirty transports were lost between March 1965 and the end of the following year. This number scarcely dented the nation's capacity to wage war but it was sufficient to disrupt planning and required caution when employing the force in more dangerous combat situations.

The shuttle system in Vietnam evolved as a practical and uniquely tailored accommodation to immediate circumstances. Equally important with the specific details of organization was organizational flexibility. Further reforms improved efficiency and responsiveness, but by the fall of 1966 the basic pattern for future airlift management had been tested and found satisfactory. A final development, which will be examined in the next chapter, was the application of the expanded in-country airlift force in the tactics and strategy of the ground war.

(Anon., Courtesy U.S. Air Force Art Collection)

Vietnam War Art

IX. Search and Destroy

American leaders hoped that our vigorous intervention in South Vietnam, accompanied by a bombing campaign against the north, would convey to the enemy the hopelessness of his cause and lead to a satisfactory negotiated settlement. For the ground war in the south the Americans adopted a mobile strategy designed to destroy the enemy's forces and disrupt his base areas. Air Force transports moved battalions and brigades to forward operational areas, supplied them during airmobile offensive operations, and withdrew them for rest or fresh ventures elsewhere. Airlift made possible offensive operations independent of vulnerable road communications and allowed allied units to reinforce quickly promising or dangerous situations. The strategy left for Vietnamese units the continuing role of occupation or pacification of the countryside upon which ultimate success might depend.

The campaigns of 1965–66 capped the continuing controversies over Army air mobility. Expanded combat operations afforded a freedom of action for the favored theories of both services, demanding more air transport of every kind. Air Force C–123s and C–130s linked with the Army's helicopters and Caribous in the central highland battles of the 1st Cavalry Division, in the movements about Vietnam of the U.S. airborne brigades, and in the offensive efforts over the plain about Saigon. The division of roles remained flexible, accommodating the immediate situation. Events in Vietnam thus hastened the resolution of doctrinal differences at the higher level and culminated in a 1966 agreement to transfer all Caribou aircraft to the Air Force. The Air Force in turn renounced its claims to a helicopter airlift arm.

The allied war situation in February 1965 was in serious disarray. Conditions grew worse in the central provinces of South Vietnam where, according to MACV staff assessments, the Viet Cong had "virtual control" of large areas. Overland routes from the coast to Pleiku and Kontum remained blocked as well as the coastal road above Nha Trang. Although Viet Cong movements were largely screened from the allies, three North Vietnamese regiments began gradual shifts southward through the hill country north and east of Pleiku. As the crisis deepened, Air Force C–123s were called upon repeatedly to lift supplies over routes normally served by road, to haul in reinforcements, and to provide flareship support for posts under attack. To the American transport crewmen the urgency of their missions was obvious.[1]

Airlift became more crucial with the intensified communist attacks starting in May. In late spring, in three separate operations, C–123s moved relief forces to Phuoc Binh, Dong Xoai, and Quang Ngai in response to enemy attacks. The last operation overtaxed the 123 fleet and necessitated a special four-ship C–130 augmentation from off shore in early June.

More dramatic was the three-day airlift into Cheo Reo southeast of Pleiku, which began with a tactical emergency operation in the evening of June 30. South Vietnamese paratroop reinforcements heavily engaged the North Vietnamese forces. In the initial four hours a C–123 landed every eight minutes and the fleet delivered sixteen hundred troops with their equipment and ammunition. Another one thousand men were lifted in over the next two days along with 290 tons of cargo. The Hercules assisted in the operation and hauled in 105-mm artillery and ammunition from Pleiku. Radio communications for air traffic control were lacking until the arrival of combat team personnel the second day. The transports landed by night using flareship illumination and makeshift runway lighting. On July 4–5, the troops were extracted to Pleiku and Kontum principally by C–123. Immediately following the Cheo Reo operation, an air movement began into Dak To under similar conditions. These combined efforts, including resupply and extractions, within a ten-day period required over six hundred C–123 sorties and included the movement of over ten thousand troops.

Meanwhile, the closing of Highway 19 between the coast and Pleiku necessitated continued air resupply into Pleiku and entailed over two hundred C–130 sorties from Qui Nhon during June. Road convoys in mid-July eventually punched through to Pleiku after a clearing operation by fourteen South Vietnamese battalions with the assistance of C–130 and C–123 transport of men and materiel. These and other airlifts, according to Col. Theodore C. Mataxis, a U.S. Army senior advisor in II Corps, provided the margin that permitted the Vietnamese to hold their own during the critical period.[2]

Reviving earlier tactics, the communists besieged a border civilian irregular defense camp at Duc Co west of Pleiku in early August, and attacked an overland relief column. C–123s made airdrops along the highway, resupplied the blocked convoy, and dropped rice and medical supplies into the Duc Co camp. A U.S. advisor at the camp judged the effort only "marginally effective" because of breakage, inaccuracy, and the frequent failure of radio communications. Airlanded deliveries into Duc Co by the C–123s, however, earned an Army officer's admiration although he observed that cargo handling and control were unsatisfactory. One aircraft received mortar damage and over twenty small-arms hits during a

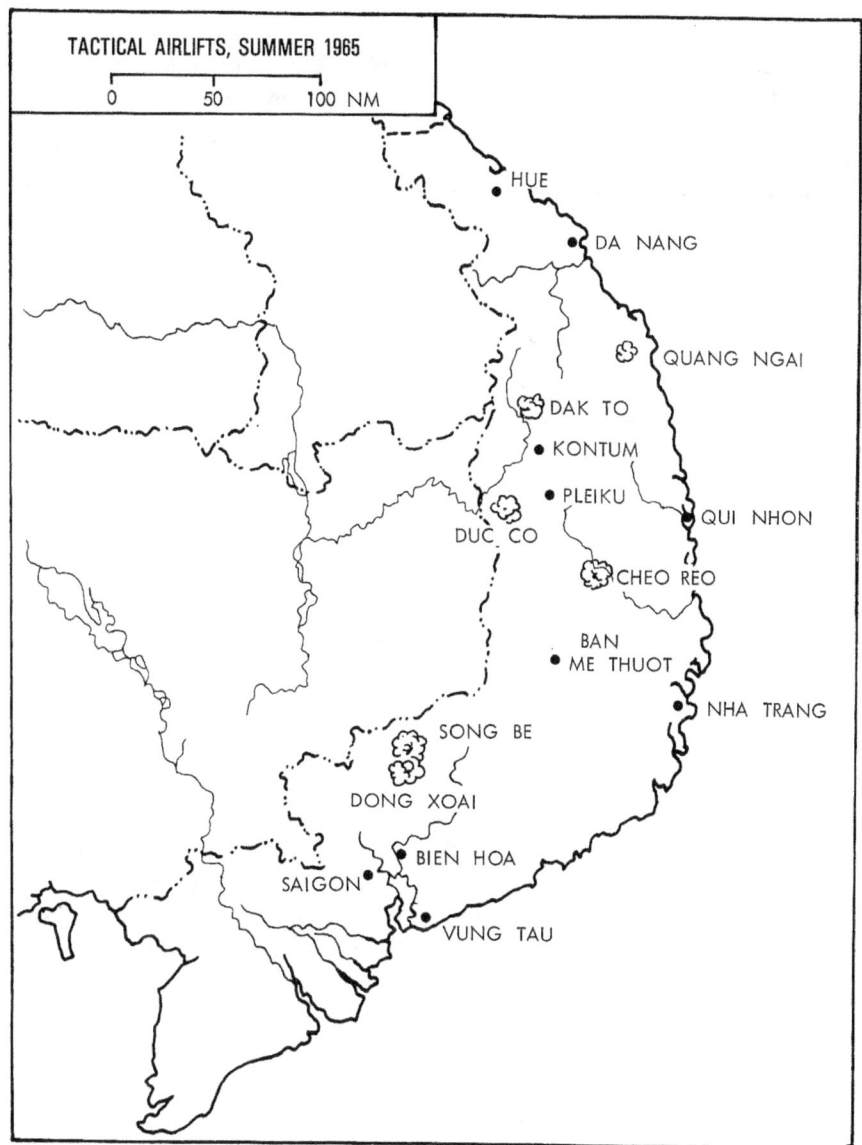

medical evacuation. Two Vietnamese airborne battalions entered Duc Co by helicopter and then were followed by a third. Following this action the Hercules and Providers began moving combat elements of the U.S. 173d Airborne Brigade from Bien Hoa to Pleiku. The two-day effort required 150 sorties. Air Force aerial port personnel in the meantime worked almost continuously to receive the troops and vast quantities of equipment at the two Pleiku airfields. After three weeks of patrolling about Kontum, the brigade returned to Bien Hoa by C–130.[3]

TACTICAL AIRLIFT

The summer tactical airlifts combined U.S. troop carrier forces in airlanded operations with Vietnamese units. The 1965 operations were characterized mainly by C–130 participation and by airlifting of the large units. Not until August were American ground units involved. The feasibility of still greater tactical mobility efforts was nevertheless clear. Whether or not the troop carrier force would be thus employed rested on decisions of basic U.S. military strategy makers for Vietnam. Their choice was essentially whether or not to seize the initiative on the ground against an enemy skilled in dispersal, camouflage, and evasion.

The offensive approach was steadfastly advocated by General Westmoreland. In his June 13 message to CINCPAC he postulated the employment of U.S. forces together with the Vietnamese airborne and marine battalions in offensive search-and-destroy operations against hardcore communist units in their base areas. The bulk of the South Vietnamese army would thus be left to face the guerrillas in populated areas. A Joint Staff study group, in a July 14 report, recommended pressure against enemy main force units "to run them into the ground and destroy them." The study group was uncertain that methods could be found to destroy permanently communist battalions, but it asserted that enemy forces could be attacked, their base areas occupied, and friendly areas of strength established. The report identified a substantial need for air resupply during such operations, estimating daily requirements for an airmobile division in combat of up to six hundred tons. MACV Directive 525–4, dated September 17, 1965, outlined the command's policy for a concept of operations. A foremost objective was the attainment of the offensive, principally by repetitive search-and-destroy operations in Viet Cong base areas, thereby forcing the enemy away from the population centers. Although operations in 1965 were viewed as strategically defensive, offensive and mobile efforts were to be undertaken as much as possible. Air transport would move units and supplies to support these ventures, and whenever possible they would be supplemented by land communications.[4]

An alternative to the offensive approach became known as the coastal enclave strategy. Its advocates recommended limiting American intervention to the occupation of certain populated regions, denying the enemy victory, and setting the stage for political accommodation or a revitalization of South Vietnamese efforts. Under this strategy, air transport forces would supplement access by sea to the several enclaves. Air officers found some elements agreeable and PACAF on June 8 urged limiting American troop roles to the defense of enclaves and air bases "from which we can operate our air." The enclave strategy came to public attention in a February 1966 Harper's article by retired Lt. Gen. James M. Gavin, USA, who recommended more limited roles in the south and cessation of the air campaign in the north. Gen. John P. McConnell, who replaced General

LeMay as Chief of Staff in early 1965, joined the Joint Chiefs in opposing Gavin's proposals, seeing in them an abandonment of national objectives.[5]

President Johnson's approval to send the new airmobile division gave tacit sanction to the offensive idea for it was patently illogical to choose the airmobile unit for static roles. In April McNamara approved the permanent organization of the 1st Cavalry Division (Airmobile) as part of a sixteen-division Army force structure over the official dissent of McConnell who had urged further testing of airmobile methods. The Joint Chiefs, less General McConnell, advised McNamara that the division would offer "unique potential combat characteristics . . . in low-and mid-intensity combat situations." Air transport considerations became central in discussions of where and how to employ the cavalry in Vietnam.[6]

The feasibility of placing an American division in the Pleiku area came under discussion in March 1965 following a visit to Vietnam by General Johnson. Receiving formal encouragement from the Joint Chiefs and General Westmoreland, Johnson in a memorandum of March 29 indicated the Army's intent to nominate the airmobile division for deployment to the highlands. Appended to the memorandum was a paper envisioning the air movement into the interior of the division's three brigades to be deployed respectively to Pleiku, Kontum, and Dak To. Combat operations were to be "directed toward the destruction of insurgent forces through offensive operations." The port of Qui Nhon was designated as a forward depot for the division with maximum reliance on Air Force resupply and troop movement. Although land resupply using Highway 19 was seen as a useful supplement, the air link would "free the combat commander from reliance on a land logistical tail with its inherent disadvantage of fixed forward supply installations." Daily supply requirements for the airmobile division were estimated at 585 tons plus an additional 262 tons for supporting forces.[7]

The Air Staff examined the feasibility of the concept and identified four C–130-capable airfields—Pleiku Old, Pleiku New, Kontum, and Catecka—each of which might receive 125 tons of air supply daily. This equated to a force size of sixteen C–130s to be based at Tan Son Nhut and to fly four hours each daily. Ten Air Force helicopters could operate from the four C–130 airheads, redistributing 150 tons daily over an average radius of twenty miles. The Air Staff, after forwarding these computations to the Joint Chiefs in a memorandum of March 24, nevertheless opposed the Army proposal because of the risks involved and in particular raised the question of the consequences if the airfields were lost. PACAF saw in the exposed situation at Pleiku "the basis for another Dien Bien Phu." PACAF also rebutted recent Army suggestions that Caribous could handle communications to the highlands, and the command noted that the daily eight hundred-ton requirement equated to 141 Caribou round trips in contrast to 29 for C–130s. In the end the Air Staff rejected the use of an airmobile division and proposed the employment of airmobile forces based on the utilization of a conventional infantry division supported by Air Force CH–3s.[8]

The Air Force proposal was opposed by Adm. U. S. G. Sharp, USN, CINCPAC, who repeatedly cited the need for the establishment of secure seaport enclaves at Qui Nhon and Nha Trang as essential to operations inland. Agreeing, General Westmoreland in mid-June pressed for an early movement of two brigades into the interior with a third to be positioned at An Khe primarily for protection of the highway network. To Westmoreland, Highway 19 and the interior plateau seemed a proper arena for battle. The site was away from populated areas, likely to attract the enemy, and suitable for the mobility and firepower of an airmobile division. Further, highway communications to Pleiku could be backed up by a C–130 squadron "on a contingency basis" as well as by C–123s, Caribous, and organic Chinook helicopters. The Air Staff, meanwhile, opposed sending an "untrained, untested division into the highlands" claiming that the Air Force role in prospective communications operations needed resolution. McNamara on June 16 decided upon initial coastal employment for all three brigades although General Wheeler, Joint Chiefs chairman, pointed out that once the division was in-country it was subject to movement dictated by MACV. Final authorization by President Johnson for movement of the 1st Cavalry Division (Airmobile) to Vietnam came on July 28.[9]

Three U.S. Army brigades preceded the 1st Cavalry Division into Vietnam. The 173d Airborne Brigade entered by air in May, and a brigade of the 1st Infantry Division came ashore at Vung Tau in mid-July.* A second airborne brigade arrived at Cam Ranh Bay in late July, and the U.S. Marine force in the northern provinces reached a strength of twelve battalions in August. Thus the full Phase I force was in place with only the 1st Cavalry and the remainder of the 1st Infantry Division scheduled to come in September and October respectively.[10]

The structure of the new airmobile division reflected the latest technical and doctrinal developments within the Army. The division initially had eight infantry battalions, three with a parachute capability. It was authorized 434 aircraft, nearly all of which were helicopters and were to be used primarily for troop mobility. Most of the aircraft were placed within two assault helicopter battalions, a cavalry squadron, and a thirty-nine-ship aerial rocket battalion. Within the division, but organized separately for general support, were several dozen heavier CH–47 Chinook helicopters.

---

* One battalion of 1st Infantry Division arrived in Vietnam earlier for security duty at Cam Ranh Bay. The battalions landing at Vung Tau were shuttled by air to Bien Hoa.

SEARCH AND DESTROY

The Caribous were not an integral part of the division but had been attached since 1964.[11]

An advance party of the 1st Cavalry Division assembled at Nha Trang on August 25. Accompanied by nine hundred troops of the 101st, vehicles, and considerable equipment, the group moved by C–130 to the new base camp location at An Khe. There the newcomers hacked out bivouac areas, a defense perimeter, and an oversized heliport. The site lay in a bowl thirty miles inland from Qui Nhon on Highway 19. Earlier in the summer C–123s had landed over two hundred tons of airstrip construction materials, and in recent operations six allied battalions cleared and erected strong points along the road from Qui Nhon. The main body of the division arrived at Qui Nhon by sea in September and proceeded to An Khe by helicopter or road. Eighteen Caribou aircraft and crews of the 17th Aviation Company flew across the Pacific, arriving at Vung Tau for eventual basing at Pleiku.[12]

The Air Force airlift support of the cavalry division in the first weeks at An Khe was inauspicious. Highway 19 served as a secure line of communications from Qui Nhon, easily handling the daily two hundred-ton resupply effort required as a result of the light scale of combat. Cavalry helicopters and Caribous made retail distribution out of An Khe to field units in nearby regions. The division, however, requested a daily priority allocation or dedication of C–123 and C–130 sorties primarily for moving helicopter parts and mail from Saigon. MACV rejected the request stating that the existing airlift request and allocation system should be used. The division accordingly forwarded airlift requests to the U.S. Army corps-level command at Nha Trang, and worked through the airlift coordinator of the Air Force tactical air control party attached to the division.* Cargo saturation at Tan Son Nhut and high-priority mission requests caused frequent mission delays and cancellations so that the division dispatched Caribous to Saigon for pickups. Another difficulty discouraging the use of C–130s to An Khe was the rough condition of the pierced steel planking landing surface, which despite repairs caused frequent cuts and blowouts of landing-gear tires. An Air Force combat control team detachment handled cargo at An Khe until replaced by a three-man aerial port team equipped with a single forklift. Army personnel assisted in offloadings.[13]

The likelihood of future cavalry operations in the Pleiku region was generally understood, although the ability of the Caribous and Chinooks to make heavier and sustained deliveries over the greater distances yet remained to be proven. Concerned with establishing Air Force responsibili-

---

* I Field Force, Vietnam, at Nha Trang was the American command corresponding to the Vietnamese II Corps. II Field Force, Vietnam, at Bien Hoa corresponded to the III Corps. Both field forces were under Headquarters United States Army, Vietnam (USARV).

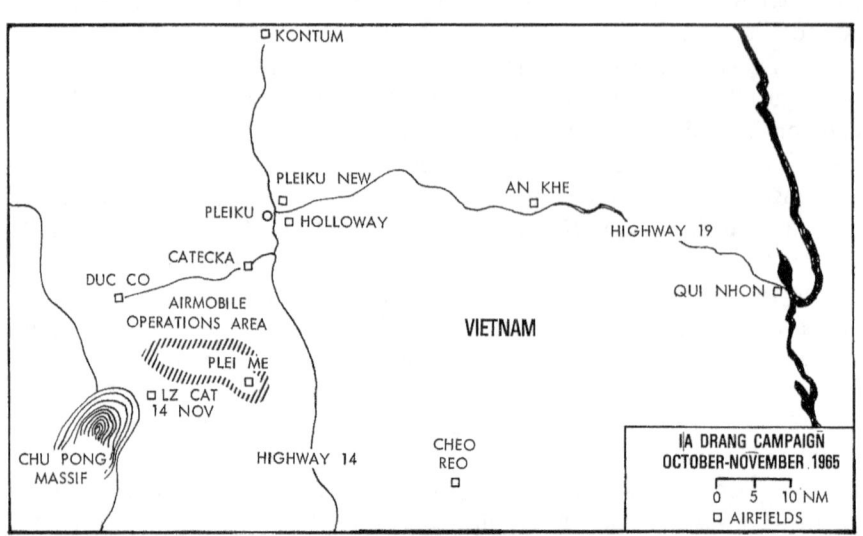

President Lyndon B. Johnson, 1966.

At Nha Trang, C–130s wait to transport the 1st Cavalry Division to An Khe, August 25, 1965.

Gen. Earle G. Wheeler as Army Chief of Staff, 1963.

Gen. John P. McConnell, Air Force Chief of Staff, 1968.

Courtesy: U.S. Army
Members of the 1st Air Cavalry Division board a C–130 for air movement to An Khe.

211

ties toward the airmobile division, General McConnell in July obtained General Johnson's agreement that each service would establish teams to join in examining air strike and airlift requirements. Under Project New Focus teams were dispatched to visit Vietnam in the fall. Air Force staff papers continued to view reservedly the idea of an all-air line of communications to Pleiku, but insisted that any airlift logistics support for airmobile forces in the highlands was an Air Force task. General Johnson, in his congressional testimony in mid-October, reasserted the Army's preference for using Caribou-Chinook aircraft for communications. He cited the vulnerability of the C–130, its airstrip requirements, and the inconvenience of handling its large loads at forward points.[14]

The early entry of the cavalry division into the interior plateau was triggered by communist pressure against the civilian irregular defense camp at Plei Me, approximately thirty miles south of Pleiku. There had been no warning of enemy intentions. Attacks by fire and small-unit penetrations began in early evening on October 19. Two North Vietnamese regiments, meanwhile, took position several miles to the north in readiness to ambush any overland relief forces. The camp defenders received immediate help from strike aircraft and C–123 flareships which encountered heavy antiaircraft fire. Two Vietnamese ranger companies flew from Qui Nhon to Pleiku by C–123 the next day and moved to the vicinity of Plei Me by helicopter the morning of the twenty-first. A Vietnamese armored convoy simultaneously set out by road from Pleiku. The overland column included units stationed near Pleiku and an infantry battalion flown from Kontum in four C–130 sorties. Lead elements reached Plei Me on the twenty-fifth, but the trucks carrying the task force's fuel and ammunition were attacked and destroyed by the enemy. Rear elements of the relief force returned to Pleiku.[15]

The Air Force's C–123s and Army Caribous made daily drops of ammunition and rations at the camp. All C–123 missions originated from Nha Trang and were flown by the 310th Air Commando Squadron. Requests for air supply, following the usual channel procedures for the Special Forces, were radioed from the camp to the 5th Special Forces Group at Nha Trang. Landings were impossible at Plei Me because of runway damage and continued enemy fire. On October 20, the first day of drops, four C–123s received a total of twenty hits; one aircraft was forced to divert to Pleiku. From October 22 to 25, nineteen C–123s received hits. During some of the missions, escort fighters sprayed the ridges on either side of the approach path while the defenders released white-phosphorous smoke. No hits were received when these actions were taken. Airdrop tactics were extemporized to minimize exposure to fire using lower than standard approach altitudes between 200 and 350 feet. The small size of the Plei Me camp, a triangle with sides two hundred twenty yards in length, necessitated that aircrews make repeated drop runs. Their accuracy was satisfactory and the loss rate of supplies was 1.6 percent. At least five deliveries were made at night using flareship illumination. During October 22–25, C–123s dropped 118 tons during twenty-five sorties while the Caribous delivered 38 tons in sixteen sorties from Nha Trang and Pleiku. Drops continued through the twenty-eighth of that month following the arrival of an armored task force which increased supply requirements while the road remained closed.[16]

General Westmoreland visited An Khe on October 20 and that evening the division staff made plans for the possible movement of a battalion task force to Pleiku. The selected battalion was placed on alert along with eight Caribou aircraft. The battalion moved on the morning of the twenty-third using the Caribous and the division's helicopters. A second battalion with artillery elements and the 1st Brigade headquarters followed later in the day. The movement continued into the next day while certain units helicoptered from Pleiku to the landing zones chosen for artillery positions to support the Plei Me relief force. The firebases were thereafter sustained by CH–47 Chinook lifts of fuel, guns, and munitions.

During the continuous operations on the twenty-fifth, Caribous and Chinooks labored to get supplies to Pleiku, lifting 513 tons from An Khe, Qui Nhon, and Nha Trang. But fuel supplies at Pleiku fell to seven thousand gallons on the twenty-sixth in contrast to a daily consumption rate of seventy thousand gallons. The next morning it appeared that only eighteen of the thirty Chinooks could be in commission. Enlargement of the airlink became an absolute necessity later the same day when Westmoreland decided to seek out and destroy the enemy forces retreating from Plei Me. Additional battalions moved from An Khe to join in the three weeks of aggressive airmobile warfare which followed. The Ia Drang Valley campaign, which extended to November 28, was the first confrontation between American and North Vietnamese forces and was viewed by American Army officers as the first combat test of airmobile tactics.[17]

Two questions remained unresolved: how early was airlift system assistance requested, and how quickly did the Air Force respond. In the early stages Pleiku had been viewed as a supply venture of modest dimension within the capabilities of the Caribou and Chinook fleets, not unlike the planned operations in the coastal region which the highlands campaign unexpectedly replaced. Maj. Gen. Harry W. O. Kinnard, USA, commander of the 1st Cavalry Division, indicated that he at once started through "multiple channels" to secure Air Force lift to Pleiku but that airlift system assistance began slowly. The 2d Air Division indicated that the airlift request was received on October 27. The following evening the MACV command center learned of the "critical" status of JP–4 [jet fuel] at Pleiku through a call from the logistics section at the Nha Trang headquarters. Air delivery of fifty thousand gallons was requested for the morning of the twenty-ninth. During the night the MACV center coordinated with the logistics section and with the Army on immediate airlift of empty five hundred-gallon containers (bladders) from Pleiku to Tan Son Nhut for refilling. Departures of fuel-carrying C–130s for Pleiku began before dawn. Consumption continued to outpace supply and by the evening of the twenty-ninth the division reported "zero gallons of JP–4 on hand to support operations."[18]

Once under way the C–130 petroleum lift was impressive. Within three days, deliveries reached three-quarters of the daily rate originally requested. Lt. Col. John R. Stoner, chief of the tactical air control party, flew to Pleiku early in the resupply effort and observed the 130s arriving at short intervals. Each ship offloaded ten to fifteen 500-gallon bladders while the engines turned and the aircraft remained on the ground only for a few minutes. In contrast each Caribou or Chinook could carry only two 500-gallon bladders of fuel, while a C–123 handled four.[19]

The C–130 streams from Saigon and Qui Nhon hauled considerable ammunition as well as fuel. Initially, all C–130 deliveries went to the six thousand-foot Pleiku New airfield just north of the city. Most of the fuel bladders deposited at this site were then lifted by Chinooks to helicopter forward operating locations at Du Co and Catecka. Other cargo offloaded at Pleiku New was taken by truck to Camp Holloway, the old airfield east of the city. The camp had been the home of the first deployed brigade and was heavily used by Caribous and helicopters. The crowded parking and taxi facilities, the steep runway slope, and the concern for runway deterioration explained the Army's decision to make Pleiku New a C–130 terminal. Holloway was temporarily closed in September because of runway damage and only an occasional 130 landed at the airfield.

A four thousand-foot dirt strip known as Catecka Tea Plantation, ten miles south of Pleiku, became the principal refueling point for the cavalry helicopters through most of the Ia Drang battle. Early in the operation the C–130s and C–123s also began delivering fuel to Catecka, drastically reducing transshipments from Pleiku New. Airstrip construction and maintenance requirements at Catecka proved negligible, and ruts caused by the 130s were smoothed by towing fuel bladders behind a vehicle. Dry weather was essential and any significant rainfall would assuredly have halted the C–130 airlift. The 1st Cavalry Division reported later that the Air Force transport stream into Catecka "was certainly one of the biggest Godsends of the whole exercise—otherwise we would have had to grind to a halt for a lack of fuel." An Air Force combat control team assisted Army personnel in cargo handling and traffic control at Catecka. Backhauls of casualties from Catecka were most often to Qui Nhon.[20]

An attractive alternative to the air supply link was the possibility of running convoys over Highway 19 from Qui Nhon. Korean troops in the coastal section held the road open as far as An Khe, but the 1st Cavalry Division's limited vehicle inventory and the full commitment of its infantry forces elsewhere discouraged the idea of further clearing the road. The division, in a reply to a higher command inquiry in early November, stated that it would begin this effort when two infantry battalions became available. Highway 19 was opened and a ground route established a week later although the airlift effort into the highlands continued in heavy volume.[21]

Air cavalry units continued to press the enemy in the Ia Drang area south and west of Pleiku. On November 14 a helicopter assault against the enemy's Chu Pong Mountain redoubt astride the Cambodian border triggered three days of vicious enemy attacks against the American landing zone. C–123s landed at the Duc Co civilian defense camp late in the battle to supplement the effort. At the end of the battle the 1st Cavalry Division estimated that the enemy had been badly defeated and his losses were equivalent to a full regiment killed. The remnants were driven into Cambodia. But the retirement of the Americans to An Khe at the end of November left the area again to the enemy.[22]

The air supply system had indisputably been vital in the tactical success of the Pleiku campaign. The 2d Air Division reported that during late October and much of November the Southeast Asia Airlift System delivered fifty-four hundred tons in direct support of the 1st Cavalry Division. The daily average was 186 tons. Of the total tonnage fifty-eight percent was petroleum. The full lift represented sixteen percent of the entire airlift system in-country workload during the period and consumed one-fourth of the flying time. No 1st Cavalry Division requests had been rejected although the quantity of petroleum products delivered on most days fell moderately short of the desired amount. General Kinnard on the other hand stated that the division received from external points 2,920 tons by organic air and 1,446 tons overland during a period of thirty-five days. The daily shipments for the division therefore came to three hundred tons. In the meantime support for other users was in turn reduced, and backlog cargo awaiting movement at aerial ports throughout Vietnam increased fifty percent during the battle.[23]

The Pleiku campaign did much to clarify future relationships between Army airmobile and Air Force troop carrier forces. Air Force opposition to the airmobile concept softened. General Harris advised General McConnell that the cavalry division had done "a highly commendable job" despite a demonstrated lack of staying power. Colonel Stoner returned to the United States in March for a series of debriefings and discussions at Air Force headquarters. In a television interview Stoner persuasively stated that the airmobile division had been used dramatically and effectively in Vietnam, and that it had proven its ability at Ia Drang to find and fight the enemy when no other formation could.[24]

Colonel Stoner felt that the campaign had strengthened among officers of the cavalry division an appreciation for Air Force capabilities, and increased the Army's willingness to seek Air Force assistance. Any lingering

TACTICAL AIRLIFT

ground force contention that organic aircraft were essential for high-volume air supply operations was clearly ended. In his narrative assessment of lessons learned, which he prepared for the Army staff, General Kinnard recommended that an additional Chinook company be sent for logistics support. He cited the performance of the four attached CH–54 Flying Crane helicopters in recovering damaged aircraft and making retail deliveries of heavy loads. Kinnard's broader view, however, was that airmobile units must plan to rely heavily on Air Force support both for firepower and resupply. He argued that Air Force airlift should be counted on to bring supplies forward to brigade base areas. Kinnard emphasized to the New Focus teams then in Vietnam that his Chinooks and Caribous were needed for tactical employment and minimum essential distribution, and that his division's need for Air Force lift probably exceeded that of any other formation. He judged the division's own retail distribution capability as limited to a distance of twenty-five miles and disagreed specifically with an Army study which envisioned retail distribution over a 150-mile radius. Circulated within the division during December and published in January was a formal "lessons learned" report reflecting the same conclusions. Plainly, doctrinal divergencies of the two services had narrowed.[25]

The two American airborne brigades in Vietnam fit easily into partnership with the troop carrier arm. After its arrival in May, the 173d began small-unit clearing operations about Vung Tau and Bien Hoa, and in late June entered the enemy base area north of Saigon. Meanwhile, the 3,700-man 1st Brigade of the 101st Airborne Division arrived at Cam Ranh Bay on July 29. They were met by Ambassador Taylor and General Westmoreland, both former commanders of the 101st. A few days earlier, Westmoreland had conveyed to Sharp his concept for employing in offensive and reaction operations the paratroop brigades as strategic reserve forces. The base camp for the 173d would remain at Bien Hoa while the 1st Brigade would operate from a coastal location, initially near Nha Trang. An Army staff document, furnished to McConnell in July, sketched how the airborne units could move from base camps to the plateau region about Pleiku. This paper showed how the brigades could move either by Army helicopters (with intermediate refueling) or by C–123 and C–130 lift.[26]

The air movement of the 173d to Pleiku coincided with the Duc Co fighting, and the move plainly reflected the application of the general reserve mission concept. After returning to Bien Hoa the brigade began a succession of offensive endeavors, supported by helicopters, Caribous, trucks, and more and more by Air Force transports. During the second

SEARCH AND DESTROY

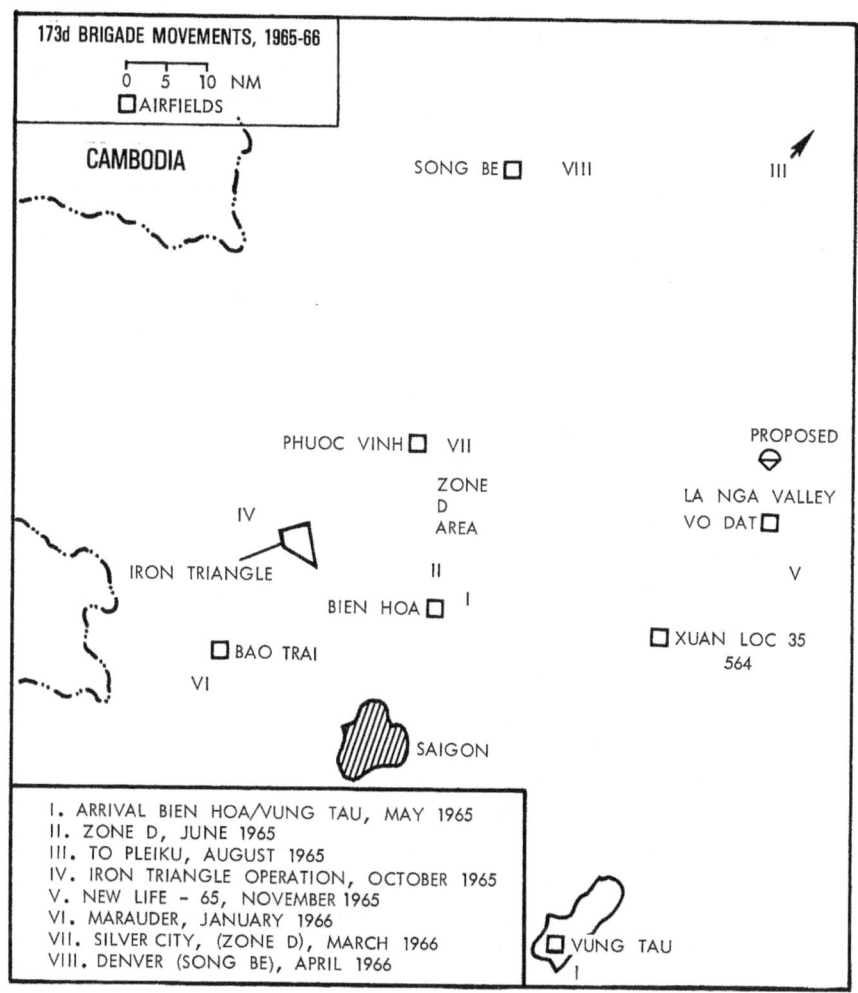

week of October 1965 the brigade entered and swept the Iron Triangle region twenty miles north of Saigon that had been considered inviolate enemy territory. The Brigade's initial movement was overland but resupply was primarily by air to avoid exposure of ground convoys to ambush by an alerted enemy. Because of the absence of an airstrip at the forward supply point within the Iron Triangle, the logistical system depended on airdrops, extractions, and helicopters. C–123s made nine heavy-equipment drops during the operation, but the brigade preferred extraction delivery by Caribou because of better accuracy, less damage to loads, and less exposure to enemy fire. Being advised that the C–130s in Vietnam were unprepared to make extraction deliveries, the brigade commander after the operation recommended that steps be taken to achieve this capability in view of the C–130's payload superiority over the Caribou's.[27]

The operation was also highlighted by a five-ship emergency airdrop to a unit of the 173d isolated by enemy forces and in critical need of ammunition and food. On the morning of October 10, five 19th Air Commando Squadron crews took off from Tan Son Nhut loaded with bundles for individual release in successive passes over the small drop zone. Planned fire-suppression support was absent. The C–123 crews dropped from in-trail formation at altitudes of three hundred to six hundred feet and met with severe ground fire on every pass. One crew was forced to depart after dropping one bundle because their navigator was severely wounded. Each of the remaining aircraft was hit during its initial run. The flight leader received the most serious damage and had to steer by rudder and differential engine power after loss of most aileron control. Alterations in the flight path brought little relief from enemy fire. The four crews continued the mission until all bundles were delivered and successfully recovered. Three crews flew through the gauntlet seven times.[28]

The troop carrier role was substantially greater in the brigade's November air invasion of the valley about Vo Dat located forty miles east of Bien Hoa. The region had been recovered from the jungle, settled the previous decade, and was now rich in rice production. Communist cadres since 1964 had administered the local population. Planning called for a heliborne seizure of the Vo Dat airstrip on November 23 by the Australian battalion attached to the 173d. Fixed-wing transports would then deliver vehicles, artillery, forklifts, and reinforcements. Two days later two American battalions of the 173d were to execute a parachute assault at the opposite (north) side of the valley. Additional battalions from the U.S. 1st Infantry Division were to move by road from Saigon. But suspecting that the parachute operation had become known to the enemy, the brigade commander on short notice moved up the schedule and directed that all three battalions land on the Vo Dat strip. The plan for a parachute assault was abandoned.

Events moved quickly on November 21. Forty UH–1D helicopters landed the first wave at Vo Dat shortly after nine in the morning. The field was quickly secured and cleared of mines, and the first C–130 landed an hour later carrying an Air Force combat control team to direct air traffic. Six Hercules had been diverted into Bien Hoa the previous afternoon to wait in readiness for shuttling between Bien Hoa and Vo Dat. By evening of the first day, thirty-five C–130 and fifteen Caribou flights had flown in four batteries of artillery, battalion and brigade command posts, and varied equipment. All landings were unopposed, and the overhead air cover was not needed in support of the transports. C–130 crews had spotted firing to the right of the runway but chose approach paths to avoid suspected points of danger. Missions resumed at dawn the next day.

Favored by dry weather, the short laterite strip at Vo Dat proved satisfactory. The field had no permanent buildings or facilities and could

SEARCH AND DESTROY

accommodate only two aircraft simultaneously for offloading. The operation was hampered by forklift breakdowns at Bien Hoa, but air movements proceeded sufficiently to permit gradual release of shuttling aircraft during the afternoon.

Overland communications with Vo Dat were established on November 23, as troopers moved out over the valley. The operation ended on December 17 with the withdrawal of units by air and road.

The brigade judged that the operation represented a model counterinsurgency effort and exemplified its methods for destroying guerrilla strength. The area had been reclaimed in time for the rice harvest and medical civic action had benefited the population. Three Vietnamese battalions remained behind to maintain government control. Over the three-week period, the endeavor had been sustained largely by resupply. The brigade reported that the C-130s had hauled to Vo Dat a total of twenty-five hundred tons in 237 sorties. Another seven hundred tons had been delivered by Army transport and motor convoy. Retail distribution from the airstrip to units in the valley was by truck and helicopter.[29]

Operation Marauder, beginning on January 1, 1966, featured the C-123s in an air transport venture into the strip at Bao Trai twenty-five miles west of Bien Hoa. After deployment by helicopter and vehicle from Bien Hoa, all resupply during the eight-day operation was by air. Tactical movements and resupply forward from Bao Trai were by helicopter and road. The brigade expressed dissatisfaction with its failure to receive all the C-123 lifts it had requested, and with the lack of information on flight cancellations which might permit alternate arrangements for moving the more critical loads. The same complaints reappeared during March in the brigade's daily reports during Operation Silver City into Zone D. Initial positioning of supplies was again by vehicle convoy followed by air supply to Phuoc Vinh. Brigade logistics officers spent the morning of March 9 trying to find out why the C-123s requested six days earlier had not appeared. The fiasco recurred the next morning. In both cases, urgent calls produced several aircraft for afternoon service, but the confusion scarcely built future confidence and illustrated why most ground force officers preferred to depend on organic lift. The operation ended on March 23. During Silver City the Air Force delivered 585 tons in 112 sorties. Tactically, the brigade considered the operation its most successful to date.[30]

In Operations Marauder and Silver City the initial movements of troops and supplies had been by truck or helicopter. Fixed-wing airlift performed air resupply thus eliminating the need for the ground forces to protect a surface communications line. This pattern was broken in Operation Denver which began on April 10, 1966. During a four-day period the entire brigade was lifted to the Song Be airstrip fifty miles north of Bien Hoa. The brigade had only two days to prepare vehicles, artillery, and

U.S. Army paratroopers jump from a C–130, 1966.

C–130 Hercules takes off from a dirt strip at Nhon Co.

Courtesy: U.S. Army

Soldiers of the 173rd Airborne Brigade rig pallets of supplies to be airlifted to the 503rd Infantry Regiment during Operation Silver City, March 21, 1966.

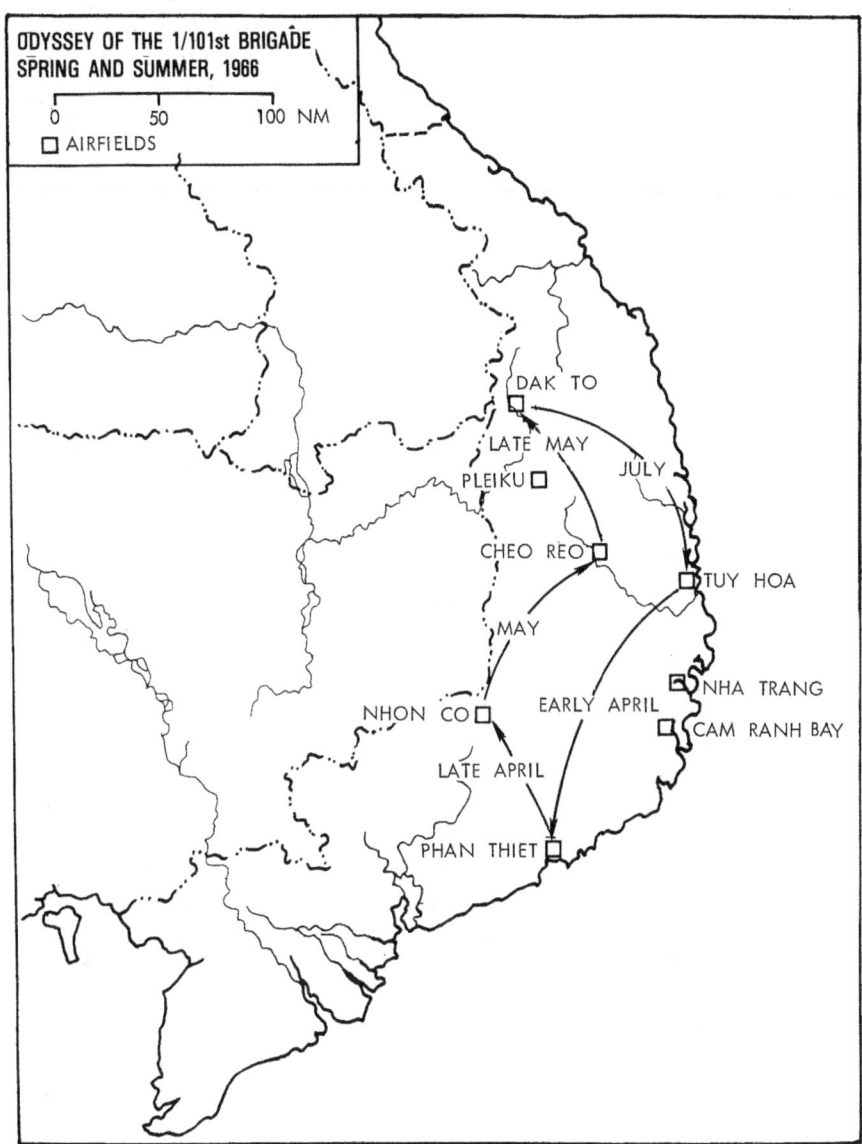

supplies, but the air move by 129 C–130 flights was handled without serious difficulty. The brigade operated for two weeks about Song Be and staged numerous lesser movements by helicopter. The unit was sustained by an average daily air resupply of sixty tons. The brigade returned to Bien Hoa by C–130 on April 22–23. Unit airlifts to and from Song Be became routine for the Hercules in subsequent years, and the airstrip there became a focal point for supporting allied forces in the border areas of northern III Corps.[31]

TACTICAL AIRLIFT

By the spring of 1966 the 1st Brigade of the 101st Airborne Division fought in many of the same areas as the 173d. The 1st operated about An Khe and Qui Nhon, moved to Bien Hoa in December, and after January performed search-and-destroy missions in the coastal provinces south of Qui Nhon. Its movements to and from operating locations were principally by C–123, C–130, and coastal LST. Early in 1966 supply lines were established by road from the ports at Cam Ranh Bay and Nha Trang to the brigade base camp at Phan Rang. From there supplies moved by Caribou, C–130, C–123, and LST to the operating locations. Further distribution was then made by helicopter.[32]

During the spring and summer the 1st Brigade made five successive movements to new operating areas, each move entirely by airlift. Their odyssey began with the movements from Tuy Hoa to Phan Thiet on April 8. Air supply deliveries thereafter from Nha Trang to Phan Thiet averaged eighty tons daily and sustained the brigade in its sweeps of the region. The airstrip at Phan Thiet had been built by the Japanese in World War II, and was judged "marginal" for the C–130 and "totally unsafe" in darkness.[33]

The C–130s on April 26 began to lift the brigade to the central highlands airstrip at Nhon Co seventy miles northwest of Phan Thiet. Engineer and aerial port elements had arrived the previous week, but plans for prepositioning supplies on the twenty-fifth were canceled because of emergency airlift missions elsewhere. Army planners were forced to juggle the planned flow of troop units, equipment, and supplies, and to keep within the forty-five-sortie-per-day limit established because of the limited ramp facilities at Nhon Co. The airstrip consisted of laterite with many exposed sharp rocks causing on the average fifteen C–130 tire changes daily during the first week. Tire-change teams worked at each terminal. The deployment was completed on May 1. Subsequent supply was entirely by air, mainly from Nha Trang, and averaged seventy-five tons per day for the next two weeks. Rainfall coupled with heavy usage further damaged the strip and in mid-May, after three of four consecutive aircraft had tire blowouts during landing, the Air Force mission commander temporarily closed the field to C–130s. In the same month the brigade participated in helicopter assault and sweep missions staged from Nhon Co, and intercepted and mauled a North Vietnamese battalion near Bu Gia Map.

The night operations into Nhon Co brought into question the difference in outlook between troop carrier officers and the Army's tactical and logistical planners. Replying to ground force requests for night missions, the airlifters insisted that operations into marginal strips that depended on smudge pot lighting were unsafe, and such flights were therefore justifiable only in actual combat emergencies. Scheduled nonemergency missions into Nhon Co were thus generally limited to the daylight only, although occasional C–130s landed at night. A similar disagreement grew from the Air Force's reluctance to operate into the Bu Gia Map strip because of its muddy and soft surface. In a test landing of an empty C–130, the aircraft sank twelve inches into the soft ground. Several other C–130s landed at Bu Gia Map in mid-May with reduced loads, but Caribous were mainly used for the unit withdrawals. The Air Force's adherence to these unpopular positions in face of obvious ground force disappointments spoke well for the courage and judgment of middle-level troop carrier leaders.[34]

The movement of the brigade from Nhon Co to Cheo Reo, situated in the highlands between Ban Me Thuot and Pleiku, began on May 19. An average of eight Hercules were used daily during the eight-day effort, which was hampered by a continuous tire-damage problem, persistent low ceilings, and the need for each aircraft to leave the flow periodically for refueling. Despite repair efforts the runway surface at Cheo Reo deteriorated quickly until the strip was described by the Air Force mission commander as "a piece of junk." The brigade meanwhile delayed its planned search-and-destroy mission because of a newly detected enemy buildup west and north of Pleiku. One battalion moved to Pleiku as a reserve for that reason and in a six-day lift, beginning with May 29, two battalions flew to the airfield at Dak To. There the brigade fought its sternest test in relief of besieged Tou Morong. The shift from Dak To to Tuy Hoa took place between July 15 and 21.[35]

The Vietnamese airborne brigade made similar air movements serving as a nationwide reserve force under the control of the Joint General Staff in Saigon. American advisors thought highly of the Vietnamese paratroops and Westmoreland called them "the best troops in-country." During the first eight months of 1966, Air Force transports moved at least twelve general reserve battalions (including paratroops, marines, and rangers) into or out of the airfields at Bong Son, Quang Ngai, and Qui Nhon along the central coast. Twelve C–130s assisted in moving Vietnamese marines from Saigon to Da Nang during the political disturbances in April, joined by four Military Airlift Command C–133 Cargomasters which lifted armored elements. Vietnamese paratroop battalions fought beside American units in the II Corps highlands and about Saigon.[36]

Parachute assaults were few. U.S. Army advisors serving with the airborne brigade urged that the parachute capability be used, but the tactical advantages remained unclear. On September 14, 1965, two Vietnamese airborne battalions of 1,125 troopers jumped from fifteen C–130s, seizing a drop zone just north of Lai Khe near Saigon. The mission was flown using the in-trail formation tactics recently developed in TAC, and was executed with precision despite heavy rainshowers and low ceilings in the area. The drop followed a B–52 Stratofortress strike and was coordinated with a helicopter assault by the 173d Brigade. Four days of light ground contact followed. On several occasions Air Force combat control teams jumped from C–123s into secure zones near Saigon, preceding Vietnamese battalion jumps from C–130s. The tactic seemed questionable. The teams arrived ahead of the main force, compromised surprise, and ended air strike preparation of the drop zone. The practice missions nevertheless served to improve procedures for combined operations involving the C–130s.[37]

The American airborne units in Vietnam made no parachute assaults throughout 1966 other than to participate in proficiency jumps and occasional small unit operations. Interest in potential parachute operations arose within MACV, however, as expanding troop levels diluted existing helicopter lift capacity. Encouraged by Westmoreland to consider using the parachute capability, MACV on September 7, 1966, asked the Seventh Air Force and the U.S. Army to study the problems of two-battalion drop; the memo listed as paratroop assets the 173d, the 1st, and one battalion of the 1st Cavalry Division.[38]

The troop carrier airborne partnership combined well with the prevailing offensive strategy. Throughout 1966 the 173d and 1st Brigades crisscrossed the central areas of South Vietnam. The C–130 aircraft demonstrated their capability to lift combat units to relatively primitive airstrips, and to perform sustained air resupply of active combat operations. Techniques and coordination improved so that difficulties encountered during one operation were avoided in the next. But limitations persisted and, in particular, traffic saturation, forward airfield deficiencies, weather, and darkness created major problems. Whether hit-and-run airlanded operations of this sort, tactically and technically successful, could seriously weaken the will of a determined enemy remained to be proven.

Troops of the main body of the U.S. 1st Infantry Division, called the Big Red One, debarked at Vung Tau in October 1965. The unit quickly became acquainted with the Southeast Asia Airlift System and over eleven thousand men were moved from Vung Tau to Bien Hoa by C–130s in a five-day shuttle beginning October 25. The division's units moved to five separate base camps to the north of Saigon. In a similar fashion two brigades of the 25th Infantry Division arrived at Vung Tau in early 1966 and proceeded by air to Bien Hoa and Saigon. The base camp for the 25th's brigades was at Cu Chi to the northwest of Saigon. Thus, in addition to the 173d Brigade at Bien Hoa, by the spring of 1966 five U.S. Army conventional infantry brigades were stationed in semipermanent locations all within fifteen miles of Bien Hoa. An insecure road system connected the base camps to one another and to Saigon, and resupply depended upon large and frequent vehicle convoys supplemented by occasional airlift. During November 1965, for example, while expanding the 1st Division's complex, over twenty-two thousand tons moved by road in contrast to only 181 tons by air. Each of the base camps had airstrips suitable for C–123 landings, and in December these aircraft began daily deliveries of perishables.[39]

Guidance on the future employment of these brigades was furnished

SEARCH AND DESTROY

by General Westmoreland in a December 7, 1965, message to the subordinate commands. He directed his forces to join in a "war of attrition" exploiting superior mobility and firepower to destroy enemy forces while defending friendly installations with as few units as possible. Westmoreland assured that the necessary airlift would be allocated for such ventures and promised that the Southeast Asia Airlift System would have a major role in the coming operations over the area to the north and west of Saigon as far as the Cambodian border. Heavy use of transports for lifting and resupplying the infantry brigades in tactical operations represented an attempt to achieve air mobility with units not specifically conceived and tailored for this purpose.[40]

Operation Mastiff, a two-brigade offensive effort by the 1st Infantry Division along the upper Saigon River, began on February 21, 1966, and foreshadowed future tactical airlift uses. Two days prior to the start of the attack the 2d Brigade moved by C–123s from Bien Hoa to Dau Tieng. The Air Force and Army aircraft then positioned other units at Phu Loi, the principal helicopter base camp, located several miles west of Bien Hoa. Once the assault was launched, and until the twenty-seventh of the month, all resupply was accomplished by air. The C–123s flew eighty-two sorties delivering petroleum products and ammunition. Several Air Force CH–3 helicopters joined the Army aircraft in displacing artillery and making field resupply. Although the Dau Tieng strip was unable to receive C–130s, the division commander judged that the airlink was adequate and that the brigade movement had been a "high point in combined airlift."[41]

Two months later invasion of Tay Ninh Province during Operation Birmingham, which involved all three brigades of the 1st Infantry Division, was launched and initially resupplied principally by air. Initial plans called for seventy-five C–130 D-day sorties to the airstrip west of Tay Ninh City. They were to haul in five infantry battalions, five artillery batteries, and two brigade headquarters. Estimates that the airstrip could accommodate only sixty sorties per day required alteration of the plan. Some Army units were prepositioned by C–123s at Dau Tieng, others were landed on D-day at another nearby dirt strip (Soui Da), and still others entered the battle area by road convoy. When the attack began on April 24, the first four C–130s arrived at Tay Ninh in five-second in-trail formation. The aircraft landed with textbook precision at thirty-second intervals and deposited four hundred troops. Nine planes, originating from base camps at Lai Khe, Phu Loi, and Phuoc Vinh, flew fifty-six sorties to Tay Ninh on the first day, and the mission commander noted that the field could readily have accepted seventy-five sorties. The weather was ideal, several instances of tire damage causing the only delays. Ground fire struck one aircraft wounding two men. In subsequent weeks the division was resupplied through Tay Ninh.

During the planning stage it was assumed that all resupply into Tay

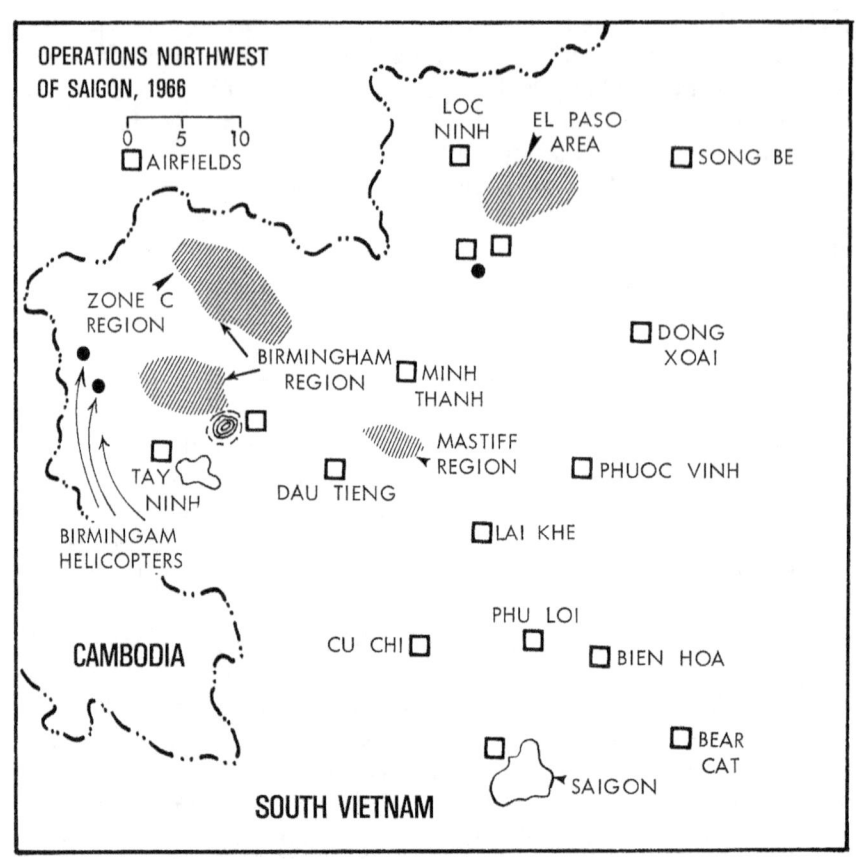

C–130 transports at Tay Ninh during Operation Birmingham.

An Air Force loadmaster directs the loading of 1st Infantry Division troops and equipment being airlifted during Operation Birmingham, April 24, 1966.

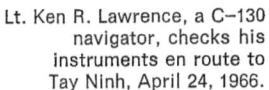
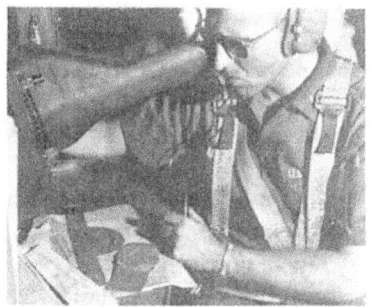

Lt. Ken R. Lawrence, a C-130 navigator, checks his instruments en route to Tay Ninh, April 24, 1966.

A USAF CH-3C helicopter prepares to transport a 105-mm howitzer to the front lines during Operation Mastiff, March 1966.

Ninh was to be accomplished by air and primarily by C–130s. MACV therefore requested that additional C–130s be positioned in country to meet the predicted supply requirements of 465 tons daily. This requirement was stated by the Army on June 25. In reality during the last six days of April a daily average of 424 tons was airlifted to Tay Ninh. Air supply continued around the clock while flarepots and portable lamps provided runway illumination during hours of darkness. Nevertheless, partly because of artillery consumption well beyond predicted amounts, the backlog of materiel awaiting air movement for Tay Ninh rose to 1,220 tons. Landlines of supply to Tay Ninh were accordingly opened on May 1 and the level of offensive activity simultaneously reduced to permit a buildup of supplies at Tay Ninh. Airlift limitations also ruled out the introduction of the 1st Brigade into the Birmingham area, a move which had been considered at MACV. For the first week of May, tonnages hauled by road convoy approximated the amount airlifted. The inadequacy of existing bridges for heavy fuel carriers led to a division of efforts. The trucks hauled ammunition and the 130s lifted petroleum. However, final distribution of supplies to field units was principally by Army helicopter. Caribou courier aircraft linked each base camp with Tay Ninh, and they averaged fourteen sorties daily under the operational control of the infantry division transportation office.

The hitherto dry and dusty weather season ended abruptly with the onset of the monsoons and three inches of rainfall between May 4 and 7. The rains brought slight runway deterioration at Tay Ninh but, more seriously, they necessitated the closing of the road from Cu Chi. Supply thereafter was entirely by air, although at a volume lower than before as the campaign entered its final stages. The operation ended with the return of the last units to base camps on May 17. The 315th Air Division reported that a total of 679 C–130 and 266 C–123 sorties had supported the operation, lifting ninety-five hundred troops and ninety-seven hundred tons of cargo. The 1st Division claimed the destruction of numerous communist supply caches along the Cambodian border, but the unit disappointingly brought to battle only a single enemy battalion.[42]

The use of Air Force transports with the U.S. infantry brigades in Operations Mastiff and Birmingham exemplified the concept of joint applications. Variants of this notion were apparent during an early April assault east of Saigon. C–130s hauled units and equipment to Vung Tau for helicopter pickup, and C–123s delivered to three smaller airstrips within the immediate objective area.[43] The C–123 arm dominated the airlift contribution in the El Paso series in the border areas north of Saigon, which extended through the summer. The focal points of operations were three airstrips about An Loc and Loc Ninh, all of which were marginal for use during the wet summer monsoons. Supporting El Paso were more than five thousand C–123 sorties which meshed with helicopter and surface modes and with periodic C-130 lifts into Loc Ninh. Army officers lauded the daily availability of the Caribous under 1st Division control, thus implying a lack of responsiveness in Air Force lift.[44]

A major innovation, which facilitated use of air resupply in tactical operations, was the Army's system of forward distribution. At the start of an operation the 1st Logistical Command sent a tailored forward support activity unit consisting of depot personnel to a selected forward base. The site usually adjoined a C-130 or C-123 airstrip; there supply personnel received air and ground deliveries and maintained two- to five-day stockage levels. At given times forward support activities might function at several bases, each supporting a different tactical venture. Placement of a forward support contingent at a forward airstrip facilitated breakdown of air-delivered loads at that transshipment point. Brigade task forces could thus be air-resupplied, bypassing divisional depots. Where C-123 or C-130 airstrips existed forward of the support element, as in the case of airdrops, the support activity was entirely bypassed.

Most campaigns of 1966 and later in the II and III Corps regions were supported basically in this way. The system possessed flexibility at every level and reflected the peculiar conditions of the conflict—the absence of fixed fronts, organic vehicle limitations, the rapid shifting of units and supply lines, and the focus on airlift. The capabilities of Air Force air transport were thus exploited to their safe limit. The Air Force doctrinal view, that its transports should deliver as far forward as possible, was in fact applied.[45]

The availability of suitable airstrips in the objective area usually determined the pattern for using Air Force transports. But there were three critical factors: airfield dimensions (runway length and width and cleared overrun distance); surfacing (weight limit, durability under prolonged heavy use, and wet weather features); and layout-parking space, taxiways, and absence of ground obstacles. Construction standards established in mid-1966 prescribed a surfaced runway of 3,500 feet, a 150-foot-square turnaround area at each end, taxiways, and an all-weather parking apron, 300 by 1,200 feet in dimension. Such an airstrip should accommodate 120 C-130 sorties in two days (this was time to introduce a reinforced brigade) followed by sustained air resupply.[46]

American airfield construction efforts in 1965 focused on the major jet-capable bases at Chu Lai, Cam Ranh Bay, and Phan Rang. The U.S. Army 8th Engineer Battalion (a unit of the 1st Cavalry Division) built the airfield at An Khe, and thereby developed skills and techniques in forward airstrip construction which were later applied elsewhere. By year's end fourteen construction battalions of the Army, Navy, and Marines, along with twenty-two thousand contractor personnel, the latter entirely engaged in fixed-base projects, were present in Vietnam. The Air Force in the past possessed no organic capability for runway or air base construction and instead requested engineer unit or contract construction through the other services. Red Horse squadrons, newly organized Air Force civil engineer heavy repair units with a secondary capability for constructing "expedient airfields," were sent to Vietnam in early 1966. These squadrons, however, worked on the main bases only and left the Air Force airlifters throughout the war dependent on the other services for construction and repair of forward airfields.[47]

A Seventh Air Force-U.S. Army working group in May 1966 prepared a master plan for forward airfield development. An important condition in this planning was the primary requirement for airfields capable of handling the C-130 Hercules. This allayed earlier Air Force concern that the Army preferred smaller but more numerous strips. Upon approving the group's recommendations, MACV ruled that priority in construction during the summer of that year should go to the western highland region and to the provinces adjacent to Cambodia near Saigon. Twenty fields were identified for improvement. Among those with the highest priority were Kontum and Plei Me in the highlands, Son Be and Loc Ninh north of Saigon, and Dong Ha, Quang Ngai, Khe Sanh, and An Hoa in the northern provinces.[48]

The airfield program soon encountered problems in acquiring suitable runway surfacing materials. The destructive effect of pierced steel planking on C-130 tires was well known, and its use was largely confined to the construction of parking areas and taxiways. Slightly better was M8A-1 steel matting, a refinement of pierced steel planking without the pierced holes. The matting was relatively cheap and easily procured but rough for landing and taxiing aircraft. The Army, with its interest in airmobility, developed T-17 membrane, a rubberlike nylon fabric laid down in sheets and pinned to the undersurface. The membrane could be laid down quickly to waterproof a dirt strip in one day. Most suitable of all were several types of aluminum matting laid in blocks and offering a smooth surface with good wet-weather traction until worn. One type of aluminum matting was AM-2 developed by the Navy, but nearly half the world supply of this construction material had been used in building the field at Chu Lai. Improved versions of aluminum matting, developed by the Army and known as XM-18 and XM-19, were slightly lighter and more usable on softer subsoils than AM-2. But the aluminum matting was expensive, scarce, and in demand for jet and fixed logistics airfields.[49]

A rigorous test of the membrane was made after the use of the pierced steel planking landing surface at An Khe resulted in repeated tire damage

SEARCH AND DESTROY

Upgrading the airfield at Tan Son Nhut, an Air Force construction team replaces pierced steel planking with new N9–M1 aluminum matting, August 1965.

to C–130s. This compromised airlift system support for the 1st Cavalry Division. In late May and June of 1966 the main field, pending repairs, was closed to C–130s, necessitating the use of the alternate airstrip of T–17 membrane. During a two-week period this alternate runway handled 216 C–130, 700 Caribou, and 38 C–123 landings. A six-man maintenance crew kept the field open, inspecting for and patching tears in the membrane after each C–130 landing. Although rainfall was slight, the C–130s repeatedly made ruts eight to twelve inches deep. This required frequent roller and vibratory compaction work that in itself proved damaging to the membrane. Nevertheless, the durability of such surfacing exceeded previous expectations, thus assuring its usefulness for forward operations if given proper maintenance. In August aluminum matting was placed temporarily over the membrane at An Khe during the asphalting of the main runway. This arrangement was also tried at Phan Rang and in both cases splits in the membrane allowed moisture to saturate the subsurface, resulting in abrupt pavement failure.[50]

Allocations of scarce aluminum matting, which affected the pace of airfield expansion, were reviewed continually by Secretary McNamara. To reduce the engineer workload, MACV in August 1966 directed the upgrading of the pierced steel strip at Khe Sanh as a backup for Dong Ha in support of border operations. This work replaced the planned airfield at Quang Tri. Dong Ha and Khe Sanh received the highest priorities in airfield upgrading and large amounts of steel matting were allocated for each. The sharp and protruding edges of the matting installed at Dong Ha, however, brought a speedy decision on September 19 to substitute aluminum matting which had been programmed for use elsewhere. Engineers at

231

Khe Sanh received the entire supply of aluminum matting by airlift from Qui Nhon and Da Nang. Both aluminum airstrips were completed in early October prior to the monsoon season. Westmoreland expressed his satisfaction with this accomplishment.[51]

The site at Cheo Reo posed a significant problem for MACV construction officers. Located in the highlands between Pleiku and Tuy Hoa, Cheo Reo had been the scene of heavy fighting in the summer of 1965, and was viewed as a suitable airhead for offensive operations the following year. Westmoreland repeatedly emphasized the necessity for upgrading the field prior to heavy C–130 usage, and a U.S. Army engineer company and a Vietnamese engineer battalion arrived there in mid-March. The Americans undertook rehabilitation of the existing airstrip and expansion of the parking aprons. They completed their work on April 21 in time for the arrival of the 1st Brigade. The Vietnamese battalion meanwhile labored on the construction of a more permanent asphalt strip adjacent to the old bed. But the rehabilitation program proved insufficient even for the calculated one-time, one-brigade operation. With the departure of the 1st Brigade, Cheo Reo remained closed to C–130s and C–123s until the completion of the Vietnamese army's construction project later in the summer.[52]

A systematic program for inspecting airfields was essential in order to furnish aircrews, tactical planners, and engineers with up-to-date information on conditions at each airstrip. Qualified transport pilots, sometimes accompanied by ground force and engineer personnel, made survey visits after each upgrading project prior to tactical lifts or upon reports of deterioration. Information was collected by the 315th Group and disseminated monthly to interested agencies. By October 1966 a permanent airfield survey team was established within the Seventh Air Force. Earlier a system for identifying fields by number prefixed with the letter "V" was started, ending confusion about the use of duplicate or similar names at different locations. Airfields were categorized according to suitability for different aircraft, thus minimally safe strips were Type I, substandard fields were Type II, and adequate fields were Type III. The shortest length for a Type I C–130 strip was twenty-five hundred feet and for Type I C–123 laterite strips was nineteen hundred feet.[53]

In October 1966 MACV listed 66 airfields in use by C–130s of which 16 were Type III and 28 Type II; 116 were designated for C–123s, including 17 Type III and 67 Type II. The T–17 membrane was favored for use at C–123 strips while steel matting proved most useful for parking and taxi areas at base area strips and for overlaying T–17 in forward areas. Planners attempted to keep quantities of membranes in reserve for short-notice tactical needs. Little interest was demonstrated in permanent construction. A MACV airfield evaluation committee, created under the master plan in June, each month identified and listed in priority order fields requiring repair or upgrade. Anticipating accelerated production of surfac-

SEARCH AND DESTROY

ing materials, MACV's goal of placing fixed-wing fields within sixteen miles of any objective appeared within reach.[54]

Throughout 1965 there was a substantial convergence of service views on the role of airlift in future air-ground warfare. Army Gen. Paul D. Adams, commander of Strike Command (STRICOM), concluded that Air Force C–130s should deliver cargo as far forward as possible, that airstrips capable of handling this plane should be prepared where feasible, and that further distribution forward of the C–130 airhead should be by ground force helicopters. The final report by the STRICOM joint task force evaluating airmobile concepts, dated June 30, 1965, reached the same views and further concluded that the Caribou was inferior for either the large or small deliveries. Army Brig. Gen. John Norton, reporting from Vietnam in November 1965 and named to command the 1st Cavalry Division the next spring, informed the Army staff that the fullest possible use of Air Force lift was essential and that the Air Force would not thereby infringe on Army roles. Army people, Norton reported, felt that "the Air Force is doing a terrific job," and all wanted "more C–123s and C–130s to do the jobs these aircraft are best suited for." Norton's findings diverged from those of STRICOM in one respect. Despite their limitations the Caribous proved enormously valuable in Vietnam, performed tasks otherwise requiring Chinooks, and freed the medium helicopters for tasks they alone could perform.[55]

The question of an Air Force helicopter airlift arm reappeared in 1965. An Air Staff committee in January proposed an Air Force-wide structure including six heavy helicopter squadrons of CH–3Cs or equivalent which would remain within the structure until replaced in future years by units equipped with vertical-flight transports. Air Force Secretary Zuckert, in a memorandum to McNamara dated March 18, 1965, proposed clarification of service roles and recommended that the Air Force own and operate all "cargo coded rotary wing resources" including the CH–3C, CH–47 (Chinook), and CH–54 (Flying Crane) for assault airlift and air supply functions. The memorandum added that the Air Force heavy helicopters would function in conjunction with lighter Army utility helicopters to link the C–130 airhead with units being supplied.[56]

The question of sending a CH–3C force to Vietnam had been raised in the spring of 1965 by the Air Staff and General McConnell during their discussions of air supply capabilities into the Pleiku area. Col. David T. Fleming, as 2d Air Division director of air transport, initiated a request in June 1965 for the procurement of twenty-five Air Force CH–3C helicop-

Courtesy: U.S. Army
An Army CH–54 Flying Crane.

A CH–47 Chinook on a search and destroy mission in Tay Ninh Province, November 1966.

Off-loading fuel drums from a USAF CH–3C.

ters and aircrews for use within the airlift system and for delivery to assault zones and Special Forces camps. Beddown at as many as five operating bases was envisioned. CINCPAC and the Joint Chiefs of Staff in August recommended approval. A MACV planning paper of September 1 stated that the CH–3s, if sent, would be used for hauling combat control teams, airfield survey teams and casualties, and for supplying sites lacking suitable drop zones.[57]

Upon approving the use of CH–3Cs on September 15, Deputy Secretary of Defense Cyrus R. Vance noted that the stated mission appeared to be an Army function, and he qualified his decision as contingent on further clarification of the matter or transfer of the CH–3C unit to the Army. A week later, McConnell replied on behalf of the Joint Chiefs. He advised that the CH–3C unit would be used to support Air Force activities and to supply remote sites in Laos, and he omitted any reference to conventional ground force support. McConnell also informed the Air Staff that he had reached "an informal understanding" with Vance that the Air Force would not attempt to deliver supplies to the Army by helicopter. The concession was made in the interest of preserving accord with Vance and McNamara, since the latter opposed an Air Force helicopter arm and had been twice challenged in force and budget actions earlier in the year. Thereafter, the Air Force advocated a limited helicopter role, although it continued to hope for the development of a vertical-flight, fixed-wing craft. The Air Force's interim objectives included the development of new delivery modes for fixed-wing transports such as a low-altitude parachute extraction system and the improvement of assault strip construction capability. Requesting the purchase of additional CH–3s in November, the Air Force omitted reference to possible use of this aircraft in air supply operations for ground force support.[58]

The outcome of these discussions was the official creation of the 20th Helicopter Squadron at Tan Son Nhut on October 8, 1965. The unit was authorized a complement of fourteen CH–3s (the number reduced from twenty-five because of limited resources) and the aircraft were drawn mainly from the TAC unit at Eglin Air Force Base, Florida, and from new production. The unit's mission, according to the Seventh Air Force, was:

> To support various Air Force combat activities, such as the communications sites, Tactical Air Control System, air liaison officers, airfield construction, aeromedical evacuations, counterinsurgency operations, and to support/augment search and rescue forces in SEA if required. The unit will also be responsive to priority requirements of MACV.

Airlift activity commenced in December, and sorties increased to a monthly average of 990 during the first three months of 1966. The CH–3s operated from the main base at Tan Son Nhut and from operating locations at Da Nang and Cam Ranh Bay. Operational control was initially vested in the

TACTICAL AIRLIFT

local base support unit at each site, but shifted to the 14th Air Commando Wing at Nha Trang in early 1966. Planning and staff supervisory control was centered in the airlift branch of the 2d Air Division. Control by the 315th Wing or within the airlift system was thus entirely absent, which was consistent with the clarification of roles.[59]

The unit was soon occupied in tasks beyond its mission statement. Responding to a Marine request in January 1966, the 20th enlarged its Da Nang detachment to eight craft. For two months the Air Force helicopters performed medium lift support for Marine operations south of Chu Lai, completing nearly six hundred varied cargo and troop lifts. Six of the Da Nang craft returned to Nha Trang in March, promptly commencing extensive support of U.S. Army operations west of Tuy Hoa. Tasks authorized by the 2d Air Division were limited to displacement and resupply of artillery elements, loads beyond the capability of available Army helicopters, and the transport of heavy items such as ammunition, rations, and water. The Nha Trang flight flew nearly four hundred sorties in March in behalf of the Army including retrieval of two downed UH–1s. Meanwhile, the Tan Son Nhut CH–3s served successfully in Operation Mastiff, and in April MACV arranged with the Seventh Air Force that first priority for use of these ships was to be for support of ground force operations, pending arrival of additional CH–47 Chinooks. In June General Westmoreland requested a specific allocation of CH–3 flying hours for the same purpose.[60]

The critical shortages of Chinooks temporarily ended doctrinal rigidity. The trend toward using them in air supply and troop movements with the Army ended, however, upon transfer of the 20th to Nha Trang in June and employment of the unit in unconventional warfare roles. Guidance from Air Force headquarters at the beginning of 1967 reconfirmed the Air Force position that its helicopters should not compete with Army helicopters, but should plainly establish their role in special air warfare.[61]

Equally sensitive was the issue of the Army's fixed-wing Caribou fleet. In a letter to Westmoreland dated April 7, 1965, Maj. Gen. Joseph H. Moore, commander of the Seventh Air Force, renewed the proposal that the two companies of CV–2 Caribous then in Vietnam should be employed under the Southeast Asia Airlift System, promising better customer services and reduced aerial port duplication. Moore envisioned no major basing changes but recommended scheduling by the airlift control centers under MACV priorities. Westmoreland, having requested an additional three Caribou companies in July for the Phase I expansion to raise the total to six,* rejected the idea of centralized control and indicated that each company was to support either a corps area, the Special Forces, or MACV.

---

* A third was due with the 1st Cavalry Division.

The Air Force raised no opposition to the augmentation, appreciating that more Caribous were needed. The first of the three companies arrived in November and at the end of 1965 Caribou strength in Vietnam was eighty-eight craft. Although General McConnell renewed the question of placing the Caribou force under the airlift system's control, agreement was limited to a MACV proviso that Caribou pilots should advise Air Force aerial ports when unused cargo or passenger space was anticipated. The Air Force meanwhile held firmly against a new Army proposal to procure 120 CV-7 Buffalo aircraft.* The Air Force viewed the turboprop aircraft as a costly duplication of the jet-modified C-123.[62]

Negotiations resulting in the transfer of all Caribou and Buffalo aircraft to the Air Force was managed privately by the two chiefs of staff. McConnell had begun his tenure determined to do something about service differences on tactical aviation, and he later recalled that his observations on the Army's low usage rate of the Caribou became the catalyst for their discussions. Private conversations with General Johnson began in late 1965. Brig. Gen. Richard A. Yudkin, Deputy Director of Plans for Advanced Planning, who assisted McConnell in preparing the negotiating sessions, had the impression that the meetings were encouraged by the influence of Joint Chiefs Chairman Wheeler and by his desire to avoid resolution of the matter by the Secretary of Defense or by the Joint Chiefs of Staff (where the other services could exert influence).

McConnell and Johnson met frequently, but according to their own schedules, and they exchanged memoranda sometimes through handwritten notes. After each session McConnell "debriefed" a small number of Air Staff officers, informing them of the decisions reached or the direction being taken. The chief rarely asked for substantive advice although Yudkin and his associates prepared backup data for each meeting, and on one occasion produced eight different texts for possible agreement, each carefully analyzed in its individual folder. At one point, Johnson charged that the airlift system lacked responsiveness in meeting emergency airlift requests. To this the Air Force replied on March 9, 1966, by offering: (1) to place liaison officers as low as battalion level if necessary, (2) to institute a system of emergency requests using the tactical air control system net, and (3) to accept the idea of ground force mission control under temporary circumstances. The Air Staff on the same date cautioned officers in the Pacific to avoid actions which might stiffen Westmoreland against Caribou transfer. McConnell and Johnson drafted the final agreement in pencil in the latter's office. McConnell recalled that both chiefs informed their staffs

---

* Only a few CV-7s were procured for test, although one served successfully in South Vietnam. A McNamara ruling, deferring Buffalo procurement on December 11, 1965, later became permanent.

that only constructive comments were wanted, and that "if anyone attempted to change the meaning of what we agreed to, he was fired." The imminence of final agreement became clear when on March 25 Vance advised the Joint Chiefs that any Caribou and Buffalo aircraft to be procured in the future would be assigned to the Air Force.[63]

The formal agreement was signed by McConnell and Johnson on April 6, 1966. Its main provision was that the Army would transfer all Caribous* and Buffalos to the Air Force by January 1, 1967, and relinquish its claims for future fixed-wing tactical airlift craft. Johnson in turn gained assurance that the Army would be consulted in future force structure and developmental decisions and that Air Force Caribou, Buffalo, and C–123 aircraft might be "attached" to Army divisions or subordinate commands. The Air Force made a final renunciation of its helicopter supply role, but reserving the right to operate helicopters for rescue and special air warfare. Both services agreed to continue joint development of vertical takeoff craft.[64]

For some Army officers the loss of the Caribous in return for empty guarantees of the status quo in helicopters was a bitter defeat. A current of opinion resisted the claim of the superiority of the heavier C–130 for supply work in a combat zone. Of some consolation was the promise of easement in the Army's shortage of pilots. Nor did the Air Force, which had long challenged the usefulness of the Caribou, now receive the agreement with enthusiasm, appreciating the manpower and funding resources the new Caribou squadrons would require. Yudkin legalistically felt it was unwise for the Air Force to renounce any air vehicle (i.e., the helicopter) needed for a military task. Both chiefs merit credit for enforcing a sensible agreement on their lukewarm subordinates and for creating a climate of cooperation during the transfer period which followed. Final resolution as to how the Air Force Caribou arm in Vietnam was to be used—whether under central control or "attached" to particular users—remained to be determined.[65]

The implications of the agreement reached years into the future and influenced the history of airlift in Southeast Asia as well as that of the whole military airlift establishment. Given the climate of opinion in the Office of the Secretary of Defense, it is difficult to see how McConnell as the advocate of the Air Force positions could have achieved more. Army ownership of the medium helicopters in Vietnam appeared to be working well, exploiting fully the capabilities of those vehicles. The idea of placing some of these craft within the Southeast Asia Airlift System, while still appealing to airlifters, remained beyond consideration. At the least McConnell kept open the path for future Air Force ownership of vertical and

---

* Under the Air Force the CV–2 Caribou would be known as the C–7 Caribou.

shortfield transports. Beyond this, assessment of the wisdom of the Caribou transfer awaited the performance of the Air Force in its utilization of these craft in the months and years to come.

By late 1966 the search-and-destroy strategy had reached full fruition. The Americans correctly assessed that the crescendo of offensives would soon give pause to the enemy. MACV planners looked ahead to larger and more productive ventures in the Saigon plain region during the winter dry monsoon, relying yet more heavily on troop carrier forces for mobility and resupply. The Army's occasional dissatisfaction with Air Force airlift support in tactical operations, along with the impending Caribou transfer, led to a series of major reforms within the airlift system. These subjects will be examined in the next chapter. These reforms became an important turning point for the Southeast Asia Airlift System, and resulted in the creation of a structure for improved effectiveness in future campaigns.

X. The Airlift System in Growth, 1966-1967

For the Common Service Airlift System (CSAS), formerly the Southeast Asia Airlift System, the fifteen months beginning with the formation of the 834th Air Division in October 1966 was a period of relative stability and orderly growth. Airlifted tonnage increased by two-thirds, an increase made possible by expanding the in-country C–130 shuttle force. The new air division headquarters provided close daily management of the airlift effort, pressed for better equipment and facilities, and for the development of improved tactical methods. Aircrews and squadron supervisors who had served in earlier periods generally agreed that efficiency seemed better than in the past as evidenced by more suitable loads and by speedier turnarounds. Better facilities and greater systematization dimmed somewhat an earlier reputation for expediency.

An important trend was the improvement in ground force satisfaction with the Air Force airlift service. This reflected both better performance by the common service system and the presence of tactical airlift liaison officers with ground force units. The touted new emergency airlift request system proved relatively unimportant since the continuing work of the liaison officers often headed off the necessity for emergency requests. And resolution of the most important airlift issues dividing the Army and Air Force left a climate of healthy competition.

Selected to command the new 834th Air Division was Brig. Gen. William G. Moore, Jr., an officer with broad military experience and long associations with troop carrier development in TAC. Moore had commanded the 314th Troop Carrier Wing in 1962–63 and had served simultaneously as the chief of the Close Look task group. His more recent command of STRICOM forces during joint airborne exercises enlarged his expertise and reputation as a troop carrier leader. Some years later Moore told interviewers "I love TAC, I love those C–130s, and I love that [tactical airlift] mission." Aware during the summer of 1966 of plans for the creation of the 834th, Moore energetically sought this new command, and won the recommendation of several senior officers. The TAC chief, General Disosway, soon afterwards learned that Moore was recruiting selected officers within TAC for his new command. Disosway told Moore to stop this, insisting tongue in cheek that generals were supposed to be able to get results with inexperienced people. Two other officers, arriving soon after Moore, had major responsibilities. Col. Hugh E. Wild arrived from MAC to become deputy to Moore and troubleshooter for aerial port and cargo handling matters, and Col. Louis P. Lindsay became the 834th director of operations.[1]

The air division headquarters possessed the customary directorates including operations, materiel, intelligence, and personnel. Under Lindsay's direction came the airlift control center which included divisions for airfield surveys, aerial port traffic, and joint planning for airborne or unit move missions. The principal focal points for daily airlift management, however, were the scheduling and command post sections within the control center. In the center converged the various mission requirements channels including the new emergency request system through MACV combat operations center (COC), the unit move and special mission requirements from the traffic management agency, and the cargo awaiting movement as reported daily by the aerial ports. The airlift control center scheduling officers laboriously converted these inputs into daily schedules, attempting to follow the formal priority system. The latter system, however, failed to discriminate between the mass of routine (Priority One) requests, so that schedulers often relied on the stated required delivery dates in order to establish priority.

The resulting schedule became a necessary starting point for the mission day. Command post duty officers followed and controlled the process of mission execution; officers worked shifts and individuals handled C–130s, C–123s, and C–7 Caribous respectively. Duty officers faced numerous pressures—pointed inquiries from senior officers, pleas from mission commanders and liaison officers in the field, unofficial word that a particular shipment was "hot," and unending changes to itineraries necessitated by bad weather, aircraft breakdowns, or unforeseen delays. Reconciliation of all considerations was often impossible. Duty officers soon learned to be cautious in reacting to preliminary information on emergency requests, a feature which was desired in the new emergency request system. They found it better to wait for final approval lest missions already in progress be unnecessarily dislocated. Despite the many handicaps, however, the airlift control center provided much flexibility in the daily employment of the force, although the desirability of an automatic data processing system for scheduling and mission following seemed obvious. A formal request for an automatic system was first submitted in April 1967.[2]

Control center activity expanded in proportion to the increasing workload of the force. Office and command post space was gradually enlarged, and a new specially designed building was constructed near the loading ramp and the aerial port at Tan Son Nhut. The control center also undertook the direct daily scheduling of the C–123s at Da Nang and Nha Trang, whose itineraries had previously been worked out locally. The hope was that the capabilities of the detached C–123s could be better meshed with those of transiting C–130s and C–123s. The airlift control elements at the several main airfields represented extensions of the control center. The thirteen airlift control elements in operation in late 1967 remained organizationally separate from the local aerial port detachments; proposals for merging the elements with the ports were made with the hope of improving local coordination. During heavy operations away from the established control element sites, field grade pilots from the airlift squadrons served as mission commanders. Beginning in late 1967 a pool of temporary-duty mission commanders remained at Tan Son Nhut available for field duty under airlift control center control.[3]

Air Force combat control team personnel assisted and sometimes substituted for the mission commander at a forward location. All permanently assigned control team members (seventy-two in number) were stationed at Tan Son Nhut and were organized as part of the aerial port group. At one stage in early 1967, eleven of the twelve six-man control team elements were stationed at field locations. MACV prescribed that Air Force combat control team elements should be relieved by Army controllers before the eleventh day of each new operation, but in actuality combat control team assignments often stretched longer. Before each day's flying, airlift crews jotted down the location of each element along with its radio frequency and call sign. Past shortages in radio equipment had eased although calls for more advanced models were widespread. The control teams (commonly called Tailpipes) became valuable assets during the countless lifts into outlying places helping to assure mission safety, speeding traffic flow, and coordinating with local agencies and the airlift control center.[4]

Efficient and responsive airlift required rapid information flow, harnessing the simultaneous efforts of the transport detachments, aerial ports, airlift control elements, combat control teams, and aircrews. Although communications remained troublesome during daily operations, facilities steadily improved aided as Moore notes by the clout of his general officer rank. Since the agencies involved in airlift seldom dealt with those engaged in air strike work, and since air transport sorties outnumbered those of the other Air Force agencies in South Vietnam, justification for retaining the separate airlift control communications net was compelling. Independent communications reflected tendencies toward broader autonomy. The airlift control center had been physically separate from the Seventh Air Force tactical air control center at Tan Son Nhut since late 1965, and the two centers had little common business except in flareship work and in arranging strike escort for airdrops. Radar sites of the tactical air control system assisted airlift crews flying through congested airspace during marginal weather, apparently without a need for higher organizational ties. The considerable autonomy enjoyed by the airlifters in Vietnam came close to contradicting a fundamental point of Air Force doctrine, that of integrated control of all theater air forces. Moore, supported by TAC, successfully

Airlift support personnel discuss incoming flights at Da Nang Air Base. From left to right are: SMSgt. James L. Andrews, A1C Johnnie M. Moore, and A2C J. W. Graham.

An Army controller uses Air Force communications equipment at a forward operating base during Operation Cedar Falls, 1967.

A USAF combat control team directs the paradrop of U.S. Army troops, October 1966.

defended the existing arrangement in an August meeting at Air Force headquarters. Subordination of the airlift control center to the tactical air control center remained only nominal, but each day the airlift control officers delivered a copy of their schedules to the tactical center so they could be officially dispatched by the latter. Official documents carefully reiterate that the airlift control center was "subordinate to and operationally connected" to the tactical center.[5]

The emergency request procedures conceived in 1966 proved only moderately successful in tests during Operation Attleboro later in the same year. The elapsed time for ninety-one emergency requests, from the moment of submission until the MACV command operations center approved, averaged 1.7 hours. Time from combat operations center approval (or cargo-available time, if later) until aircraft readiness for loading averaged 3.1 hours. The saturation of direct air support center communications with air strike information made it difficult to keep requesters informed of the status of airlift needs, in the absence of direct exchange of information between requesters and the airlift control center. This weakness led to the conclusion, unsuccessfully pressed by the 834th, that a separate airlift request radio net was needed. To avoid keeping aircraft and crews on ground alert, the airlift control center followed past practice and filled emergency requests by diverting planes from planned itineraries. The principal ground force user during Attleboro, the II Field Force, concluded that the new system was "responsive, efficient, and flexible" and ought to be continued.[6]

The emergency request procedures remained in effect although they were made increasingly unnecessary by the generally improving liaison between airlifters and ground force customers. Of approximately thirty thousand airlift sorties in August 1967, for example, less than one percent were emergency priority. At times the Air Force was itself the heaviest user of priority airlift and the urgency was often the need to resupply air controller detachments at forward strips. Momyer in February 1967 warned his command to become more stringent when applying the combat essential priority or a higher classification.[7]

Of greater significance were the tactical airlift liaison officers. In late 1966 the tactical liaison idea was tested and thirty airlift officers, many of them assigned to the offshore C–130 wings, now served with U.S. Army brigades, divisions, etc., in Vietnam. In preliminary briefings at the 834th each liaison officer learned his principal role. He was to be a staff officer within the ground force unit, capable of planning and managing tactical air movements and resupply operations. His effectiveness would depend upon his own ability to develop working relationships with his hosts. An enlisted radio or operations specialist accompanied each liaison officer.[8]

Lt. Col. Thomas M. Sadler, upon whose recommendations the airlift liaison experiment had been initiated, served as a liaison officer at the field force headquarters at Nha Trang. He reported that throughout the II Corps area "the very act of being in the field" promoted goodwill and a spirit of cooperation. During priority missions he functioned as an expediter, watching against oversights and improving the whole climate of information. In other cases, however, the greatest value of the tactical airlift liaison officer lay in encouraging the timely use of lower priority mission requests thus making emergency missions unnecessary. Satisfaction with this experiment was therefore general except in those brigades which at the moment were not dependent upon airlift and where the liaison parties were without a role. Most evaluators concluded that assignment of liaison officers to particular brigades was unwise. They suggested that several officers should be detailed to each division and be available for temporary duty with whichever brigades were combat active.[9]

On paper the role of the airlift liaison officer seemed superfluous and overlapped with the functions of the mission commander, the combat control team, the air liaison officer, and the prescribed request and control nets. Yet, given the frictions of theater operations and in the context of past ground force dissatisfaction, his presence with ground units seemed absolutely justifiable to all Air Force officials. Praise for the continuing work of the temporarily assigned liaison officers throughout the winter reinforced this conclusion. When higher approval of permanent manpower spaces seemed in jeopardy, General Momyer sent a message to PACAF insisting that the validity and necessity of the liaison concept had been proven. He said that for the first time tactical airlift rapid response was comparable with fighter and reconnaissance support. Momyer also rejected an arrangement calling for the use of liaison personnel not airlift-qualified, and he offered to send Moore to Hawaii to present the case. Manpower spaces were accordingly realigned, and the temporary duty liaison officers were replaced with permanently assigned men. By late 1967 the liaison officer apparatus was in full operation and received credit from Air Staff visitors for drastically reducing airlift response time. Further, a decision to provide each tactical liaison officer with a radio jeep gave him direct access to the airlift control center and in effect compensated for the weaknesses in the emergency airlift request system communications.[10]

Expansion of the airlift system paralleled the growth in surface transport capabilities but the proportionate contribution of airlift changed very little. American cargo movements within Vietnam in 1967, measured in thousands of short tons, were as follows:

Trucks (line-haul, over 50 miles)	2,525
Trucks (local and port clearance)	11,387
Rail	216
Common service sealift	1,823
CSAS airlift	984
Army and Marine helicopters	827

Expansion was most notable in line-haul trucking reflecting a resolve at MACV headquarters to open up land routes for civilian use and to conserve airlift. Line-haul traffic was heaviest along Highway 19 to Pleiku, along the central coast, and radially out of Saigon. In cargo ton-miles, airlift contributed approximately twenty percent and sealift thirty percent of the total. Vietnamese transport agencies added only small amounts; their Skytrains, for example, lifted only a tenth of the tonnage airlifted by the Americans on behalf of Vietnamese forces.[11]

The U.S. Army remained the heaviest user of common service airlift (sixty-seven percent by tonnage in 1967), followed by the Vietnamese forces (thirteen percent), U.S. Air Force (nine percent), Navy and Marines (nine percent), and the Agency for International Development (two percent). Allocations of airlift and sealift were decided by the MACV joint movements transportation board, but the process became relatively meaningless since forecasts of requirements usually approximated the existing lift capabilities. The board meetings shifted from monthly to quarterly in January 1967, but this still allowed review of the main in-country transportation problems. Both the transportation board and the continuously functioning MACV traffic management agency preferred to meet deficits in airlift capability by arranging for additional C-130s, thus avoiding refusals of particular requests. The picture began to change in late 1967 after several months of sharply rising airlift requirements. The traffic agency warned users to evaluate future requests for airlift more stringently.[12]

By the end of 1967, combined C-130 and C-123 accomplishments monthly exceeded by two-thirds those of fifteen months earlier. The expanding workload threatened to outstrip aerial port, communications, and ground service facilities, but statistical measurements of overall efficiency remained stable. Indeed, recorded mission delays for C-130s and C-123s declined steadily while tons delivered per flying hour and per sortie gradually improved. The airlifters claimed a milestone on June 12, 1967, when tonnage lifted in Vietnam (since January 1965) surpassed the nearly two million tons credited to American transports during the Berlin airlift. Having previously exceeded the tonnages airlifted in the China-Burma-India theater and during the Korean War, the Vietnam airlift became history's largest thus far.[13]

The in-country C-130 force fluctuated in size, varying with the immediate tactical and unit movement requirements. But the general trend was upward; forty-four aircraft in December 1966 expanded in number to sixty-five a year later. The C-130 detachment at Nha Trang was reassigned on May 1 upon completion of additional facilities at Cam Ranh Bay, but a new detachment was established at Tuy Hoa in October pending the completion of the construction of more revetments at Cam Ranh Bay. The Tan Son Nhut and Cam Ranh Bay units, hitherto detachments of the 315th Air Division, were assigned effective August 15, 1967, to the 834th and received their command and maintenance cadres from the latter. The in-country force reached a strength of seventy-two aircraft on January 4, 1968:[14]

Det 1, 834th Air Division, Tan Son Nhut	27 C-130Bs
Det 2, 834th Air Division, Cam Ranh Bay	35 C-130As and C-130Es
Task Force A, 315th Air Division, Tuy Hoa	10 C-130Es
Total	72

The C-130 offshore fleet remained fixed at twelve squadrons although calculations indicated that another squadron would be needed to support the 525,000 troop level approved for Vietnam in 1968.* The question of assigning these aircraft permanently to Vietnam reemerged, and the idea was favored by Westmoreland, Momyer, and the 834th. Moore also accepted the proposal primarily because of his expectation of improved maintenance. But an important barrier to approval was allocation of additional manpower spaces required beyond the ceiling instituted by the Secretary of Defense. The PACAF commander, Gen. John D. Ryan, upon rejecting the Seventh Air Force proposals for in-country basing, noted that the permanent cadres were to be established at Tan Son Nhut and Cam Ranh Bay and this should improve control and management. The 315th Air Division meanwhile gave assurances of its ability to send additional ships rapidly into Vietnam if needed.[15]

The 315th Wing, three of its C-123 squadrons (the 309th, 310th, and 311th), and its consolidated maintenance squadrons, moved to the coastal base at Phan Rang in the early summer of 1967. The shift was intended to reduce congestion at Tan Son Nhut and to facilitate centralization of maintenance. The 311th in addition retained a ten-ship detachment at Da Nang, preserving the mission capability in the northern provinces. The Phan Rang facilities with a ten thousand-foot concrete runway soon became one of the best in Vietnam. The air base generated little air cargo, however, so that overall common service airlift system efficiency suffered. One-fourth of all C-123 departures from Phan Rang were empty, and squadrons moving supplies to this base experienced a decline in their lift tonnages to 2.31 tons per operational sortie, nearly twenty percent below the June figure.[16]

---

* All troop carrier wings were in 1967 renamed tactical airlift wings and troop carrier squadrons became tactical airlift squadrons. The 315th Air Commando Wing (with C-123s) and its squadrons were not affected.

Personnel shortages sometimes pushed aircrewmen close to physical and psychological exhaustion. Combat-ready C–123 airlift crews declined in number to sixty-four at the beginning of 1967 (ninety crews had been authorized), and the assigned strength of C–130 pilots reached a low of 345 in midyear (the authorization was 444). The need for officers as mission commanders, in the command post, and elsewhere in liaison and supervisory roles, further cut into pilot strength. The work overload at Phan Rang at one point caused the temporary physical disqualification of a dozen flight engineers. Waivers of individual monthly flying limits were common in all units. The result was a virtual seven-day workweek for most crewmen and minimal rest between missions for aircrews while in Vietnam.[17]

Increasingly, older officers occupied cockpit positions. The 345th Squadron at Ching Chuan Kang, for example, had twenty lieutenant colonels assigned, most of whom had entered the pipeline after years of nonflying assignments. The average age of aircraft commanders in the 463rd Wing was in the early forties. Although the rigors of airlift duty in Vietnam were undeniable, neither the stamina nor the initiative of the older men came into question. To reduce flying training, PACAF accepted the idea that all crews need not possess tactical (airdrop) qualifications. And to improve crew coordination and mission safety, a policy of scheduling by integral crews was established although this was applied wisely with considerable flexibility. More rigid was the policy that navigators should fly on all C–130 sorties within Vietnam, even though perhaps half the total flying was in daylight and during clear weather. To PACAF's inquiries on the subject, the 834th and 315th Air Divisions as well as each of the C–130 wings maintained that the presence of a navigator provided added safety in darkness or bad weather. Few twelve-hour missions were wholly within daylight hours, and few itineraries were entirely along cloudless routes. Furthermore, the absence of a navigator could make it difficult to divert a crew to another air base, for example, an unplanned patient evacuation to Clark. The potential manpower savings thus appeared inconsequential and full navigator manning was continued.[18]

Whatever the advantage of basing the C–130s offshore, few could argue that the arrangement handicapped aircraft maintenance. Col. Barney L. Johnson, Jr., director of materiel for the 834th Air Division, in May 1967 charged that under the existing system mission delays attributable to maintenance had "risen" to an unacceptable level, and affected more than one-fourth of all in-country missions. There followed the decision to assign permanent maintenance cadres at the C–130 operating locations and to transfer maintenance control to the 834th. This decision reflected an expectation that certain heavier maintenance tasks would be undertaken at Tan Son Nhut and Cam Ranh Bay. Henceforth Johnson's small staff assumed the air division's supervisory role, acting through a chief of maintenance at the two main detachment sites. The 834th pressed for and won

TACTICAL AIRLIFT

Courtesy: U.S. Army
One of the eight C-123 crashes in 1966, near a Special Forces camp.

many improvements in work facilities, and in fact achieved greater maintenance self-sufficiency in-country. Still, the in-country maintenance detachments were troubled by unending personnel turnovers, divided responsibilities, and an absence of personal ties to a unit. The maintenance cadres (thirty-six men) appeared too small but changes were precluded by manning ceilings.[19]

Statistics of maintenance performance were below standard but these figures hid the practice of operating aircraft with numerous uncorrected malfunctions. Cannibalization remained a way of life in Vietnam, averaging four Hercules daily throughout 1967. This prompted an 834th comment that "the aircraft are being supported by cannibalization and not by supply." This pattern was officially denounced in late 1968 when Seventh Air Force inspectors rated the Tan Son Nhut and Cam Ranh maintenance detachments "marginal" and furnished a list of unsatisfactory conditions. These discrepancies ranged from dangerous refueling practices to storing uninspected parts from crashed airplanes with new parts. In contrast the stable and consolidated C-123 maintenance arrangement at Phan Rang produced increased performance, despite the aircraft's age and long history of strenuous use in Vietnam.[20]

Any assessment of the C-130 maintenance system must take heed of the twin goals of heavy flying and a low accident rate. Seldom was an incommission aircraft kept long on the ground either in Vietnam or off shore. The 314th Wing consistently exceeded the 5.0-hour flying rate.

Communist mortar fire destroyed this C–130 at Nha Trang, November 26, 1967.

Other units, authorized a 2.5-hour rate, steadily performed at 3.0. This achievement was accomplished despite persistent problems with landing gear, brakes, props, and other assemblies caused by frequent landings on rough and short airstrips. Behind the achievements of the airlift forces stood the thousands of C–130 and C–123 maintenance men who worked long hours with great dedication to meet the unending pressures for maximum flying efforts.[21]

The flying game in Vietnam remained a tough and challenging business, the possibility for disaster seldom far from sight. The moderate and improving accident rate testified to the competence of the crews and the sturdiness of their aircraft, and reflected the stress placed upon safety by wing and squadron leaders. During 1967, eight Hercules were destroyed in separate accidents. Four of these resulted from materiel failures (flaps, brakes, trim, and engine), reinforcing Moore's desire to achieve closer control of the C–130 maintenance establishment. The other losses were variously associated with the nature of the operating environment—a takeoff accident at An Khe caused by helicopter wash, a night crash into a mountainside near Hue, a collision with a bulldozer at Dak To, and a drop mission accident at Khe Sanh. Five of the eight aircraft lost were B–models from the 463d Wing. Six of the accidents were fatal, and the total loss of life was seventy-six, including fifty-six passengers. Three additional major accidents, each with reparable damage, brought the year's total to eleven, in comparison to eight for the previous year. In proportion to the increase in flying hours the overall rate had improved five percent. C–123 major accidents decreased to five in 1967 compared with eight the previous year. All five resulted in the destruction of the aircraft, three in landing mishaps at forward airstrips—one a prop-reversal failure, another a nosegear collapse at Kham Duc, and the third during a short touchdown at Gia Nghia. One crewman was killed in the destruction of a C–123 while on the ground at Tan Son Nhut when the aircraft was struck by a landing F–105. An entire crew was lost on a hillside near Bao Loc not far from the first Farm Gate C–47 crash in 1962 and under similarly unclear circumstances.[22]

Communist ground-to-air fire remained an annoyance. Airlift C–123s and C–130s receiving hits averaged twenty-two monthly during 1967. Ground fire destroyed only one transport, a C–123, which received multiple .50-caliber hits after takeoff from Dau Tieng in November 1966. The pilot of the aircraft made a safe crash landing. Another C–123 crew counted seventy fragmentation holes from twenty-nine hits of various caliber while returning from an airdrop mission at Cha La. The communists were more successful in attacking aircraft on the ground. Twelve C–123s were damaged during a mortar attack at Da Nang in mid-July although all were reparable; another received over 180 holes while taking off during a mortar attack at the Tonle Cham Special Forces camp. Five C–130s were destroyed by shelling—two in the July Da Nang attack, two at Dak To in November, and another at Nha Trang in late November.[23]

The aerial port system in Vietnam experienced a period of continued expansion after 1966 although at a less frenzied pace than earlier. When the 2d Aerial Port Group headquarters moved to Vietnam, it afforded a clear chain of command under the 834th Air Division for the three port squadrons. The number of port detachments and "operating locations" leveled off in mid-1967 at approximately forty. Cargo handled by the aerial ports rose steadily from 130,000 tons monthly in late 1966 and peaked at 209,000 tons in March 1968. Thereafter it stabilized at about 180,000 tons per month. The efficiency of the port detachments improved slightly during the period, including the percentage of on-time departures and the average pallet loading. One aircrew officer, who had flown a previous airlift tour in 1965, observed that aerial port effectiveness had vastly improved and that most of the time loads were ready and waiting for the transports upon their arrival. Cam Ranh Bay surpassed Tan Son Nhut as the principal air cargo point of origin in December 1967, while Da Nang remained third followed in delivery order by Bien Hoa, Nha Trang, and Qui Nhon.[24]

Manpower authorizations remained level at twenty-five hundred spaces throughout 1967, and they scarcely reflected the growing workload. The authorizations were well below the nominal formula of seventy-five tons per man per month. Temporary-duty augmentees from off shore helped bridge several periods of saturation. Inexperience remained a severe handicap. Any reserve of aerial port experience in the Air Force had been previously consumed by the need to replace all persons in Vietnam every twelve months. The workloads of individuals could be grueling, and sometimes they labored sixteen consecutive hours in dust, mud, or rain. An Air Staff visitor in late 1967 reported a serious lack of motivation among aerial port enlisted men. He recommended an infusion of enthusiastic junior officers, perhaps recent Air Force Academy graduates. Moore cautioned against selling short his men. Certainly few had performed aerial port work before and most hoped never to do it again. Nevertheless, the men understood the importance of their mission and individually they did their jobs well.[25]

Established in late 1966 under the 2d Aerial Port Group was a traffic management office within the airlift control center to serve in the daily management of the airlift system. The management office monitored aerial port backlogs and special movements on a twenty-four-hour basis, and worked closely with the control center schedulers and duty officers. The management officers attempted to maintain communications with port squadrons and detachments, sought to "take the pulse" of operations and to assure that shipments were ready at the proper time and place. The office also became the nucleus for alerting combat control teams and aerial port mobility teams for field developments. The office was redesignated the directorate of traffic operations in January 1968, and continued its former role. The aerial port group also performed staff visits to each squadron, detachment, and operating location.[26]

Improvement in aerial port facilities continued. Many dirt storage areas, vulnerable to alternating cycles of dust and mud, received hard-surfacing. The 2d Group reported that in the twelve months beginning with October 1966 over eighty thousand square feet of covered air freight terminal space was erected; meanwhile, seven times that amount of open cargo-holding space was in use. Passenger terminal buildings were built at such points as Kontum, Dong Ha, and Tuy Hoa. And fencing and lighting improvements promised to reduce pilferage. Aerial port construction requirements still suffered in competition with the needs of other combat and support units, but improvements had been made. Helpful in winning approval for aerial port construction was the 834th Air Division, now that the most pressing needs of other units were satisfied.[27]

Strong action by Moore and the staffs of the 834th Air Division and the Seventh Air Force brought definite improvement to the deplorable condition of materiel-handling equipment, i.e., forklifts and vehicle loaders. Upon visiting the Seventh Air Force materiel control center, Moore

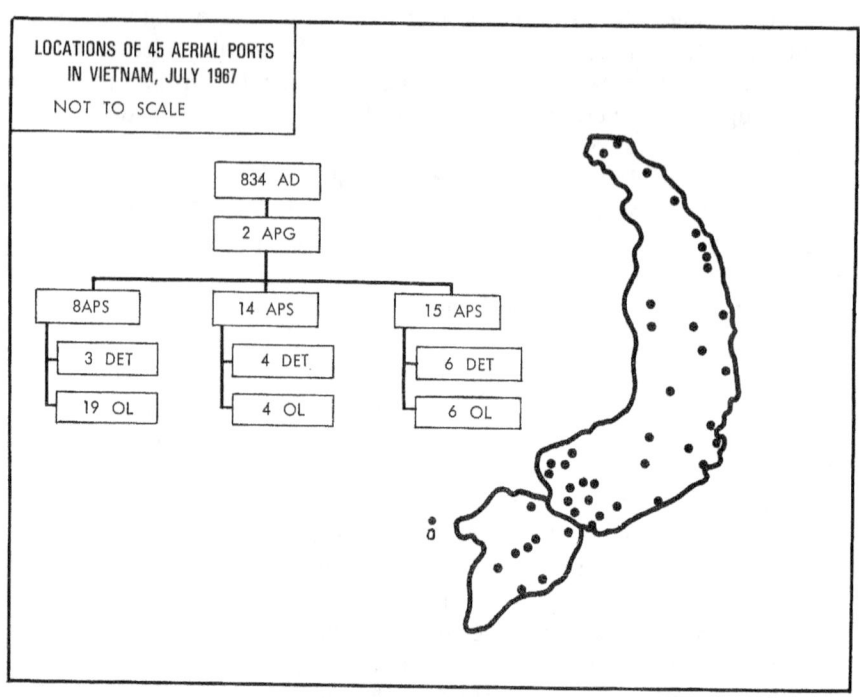

The adjustable 25K-loader has roller tracks, cutting the unloading time for this C–135 from hours to minutes, Tan Son Nhut, 1966.

Placing cargo netting over a stack of aircraft tires are A1C Jesus M. Cruz (left) and SSgt. Robert C. Kendig, Tuy Hoa Aerial Port, 1968.

Parking ramp coordinator A1C Richard D. Dover logs in the arrival of a C–130 at Bien Hoa Aerial Port, July 1966.

Gen. Hunter Harris, 1966.

The passenger terminal at Tan Son Nhut, 1966.

Cargo ready for shipment, 1967.

TACTICAL AIRLIFT

discovered that although out-of-commission strike aircraft were lavishly monitored, the status of equipment was largely neglected. Upon Moore's urging, Momyer in late 1966 informed General Harris that the poor condition and shortage of the equipment was affecting the ability of the ports to provide satisfactory airlift service in Vietnam. Momyer solicited the support of PACAF, Air Force Logistics Command, and Air Force headquarters to correct this matter. Harris promised to increase authorizations and to provide strong help in several proposed areas. Equipment and spare parts began to arrive by air shipment from the United States, and Moore succeeded in acquiring additional items from Military Airlift Command units through informal arrangements. Other measures focused on maintenance. A component repair program opened at Clark, contract overhaul began in Bangkok, and parts stockages were increased. Especially beneficial were visits by temporary-duty maintenance teams from the Air Force Logistics Command and PACAF. The number of incommission forklifts for example rose from 134 in November 1966 to 234 the following spring. For the time being, the 2d Group accepted the viewpoint that materiel handling equipment maintenance responsibility should remain outside the aerial port structure and remain within the respective host base vehicle repair units. During late 1967 the debilitating effects of heavy and strenuous usage began to outstrip the efforts toward improved maintenance, indicating that forklift life expectancy in Vietnam was well less than the eight years used in programming replacement items.[28]

Recommendations were widespread for better designed handling equipment, especially with tougher hydraulic systems, transmissions, and axles for rough terrain work, and with radiators and tires protected against damage by shrapnel. Early in 1968 several dozen forklifts designed for adverse terrain arrived in Vietnam, replacing standard and rough terrain lifts at forward locations. The new diesel-powered equipment quickly gained recognition for its superiority. But the lifts had large, air-filled tractor-type tires and were therefore vulnerable to shrapnel.[29]

The problem of pallets, nets, and tiedown chains being sequestered away from the airlift system received considerable attention. The ingenuity of ground troops and local civilians in finding uses for these materials seemed unlimited. The 834th did not favor a system of hand-receipt accountability. Instead, in strongly worded statements the air division urged aircrews and port personnel to locate this equipment. Teams from aerial port squadrons traveled to forward locations to search for and recover misappropriated pallets. Transports occasionally landed empty at forward points simply to pick up stacks of recovered pallets. The pallet repair facility at Tachikawa was enlarged, and provisions were made for minor repair capabilities in the field. It was obvious that without constant emphasis the situation would again quickly deteriorate. A cheaper expendable cargo pallet was officially requested by the Seventh Air Force in 1968.[30]

AIRLIFT SYSTEM IN GROWTH

Accurate knowledge of the weight of each item of cargo was directly related to safety of flight, and was the subject of several formal operational requirement actions. Weighing facilities were available at only four Vietnam bases in early 1967; elsewhere aerial ports had to accept weights stated by shippers or resort to guesswork. Stated weights during unit movements were often notoriously inaccurate, since ground force vehicles were frequently loaded down with unspecified supplies. By late 1967, five-ton capacity scales were installed or programmed for fourteen locations, and early the next year pit scales capable of weighing vehicles and K–loaders were installed at several points. For loading elsewhere, several trailer-mounted C–130 transportable electronic scales were tested. The scales gave direct and accurate readings, although they were inclined to malfunction. An alternative method incorporating a direct attachment to the forklift's hydraulics appeared promising in tests offshore, but the device had not yet been employed in Vietnam.[31]

Air Force aerial ports maintained only a small capacity for rigging parachutes and loads for airdrops, generally only sufficient in number to permit aircrew and combat control team training. Until 1966 the rigging of parachutes and loads for airdrops in Vietnam was done by the agencies being supported, principally the Special Forces and the Vietnamese airborne brigade. The same agencies performed aircraft loading under the supervision of aircrew loadmasters. Airdrops were in decline in late 1965 because of landing-strip improvements at many Special Forces camps and because of the availability of more Caribous and Chinooks. Nevertheless, Westmoreland directed that planning be undertaken for a substantial and sustained airdrop resupply capability which envisioned operations in the northern provinces. A capacity for rigging 250 tons per day was established, an amount sufficient to resupply a brigade task force. The MACV airdrop resupply plan, published March 7 and revised July 15, 1966, established procedures for forming a provisional unit at Tan Son Nhut and for consolidating rigger personnel from in-country airborne and quartermaster units. The unit formed in June 1966 while awaiting the arrival at Cam Ranh Bay of the 109th Quartermaster Company (Aerial Delivery). The latter had materials and manpower sufficient to rig 250 tons daily for fourteen continuous days without reusing items. Rigging skills improved steadily after improper work caused several malfunctions during early 1967 drops. The company opened a second facility at Bien Hoa later in the year, seeking an overall rigging capacity of five hundred tons daily. Augmentations from off shore brought capacity to six hundred tons during the expanded drop effort in 1968. Air Force officers warmly praised the work of the Army riggers, and both Moore and his successor recommended against shifting this important function to the Air Force.[32]

Each of the squadrons under the 2d Aerial Port Group organized several aerial port mobility teams, designed to deploy to smaller airstrips during unit movements and tactical resupply operations. Teams typically consisted of approximately six persons, and each team was equipped with one or two adverse terrain forklifts. During January 1968, for example, 108 port mobility personnel were simultaneously deployed to thirteen different locations. Mobility teams generally included the unit's best qualified and most dedicated individuals who were disciplined and had high morale. The teams served in nearly all significant field operations during this period including Khe Sanh, Delaware, and the later battles in 1968. One airlift mission commander, who lived and worked in the mud with several teams, reported:

> I have never seen a group that [was] so highly motivated, so keen to do a job under the most adverse circumstances that you can imagine. They will put up with anything. They will work, and work continuously to keep this thing going.[33]

The indispensable aerial port contribution in Vietnam was accomplished with little guidance from prewar doctrine. Those who served in these units were forced to overcome the exigencies of their inexperience, insufficient manning, inadequate equipment, and low priorities in acquiring better facilities. The National Defense Transportation Association bestowed its annual award, both in 1967 and 1968, upon the squadrons of the 2d Group thus rendering them much-needed recognition. For the future the demonstrated need for greater preparedness brought an expansion of the aerial port function in the Air Force Reserve forces. Reserve aerial port units provided much of the manpower for the 1968 expansion in Korea following the Pueblo incident, and over the next four years the units expanded from twelve squadrons to a strength of thirty-nine squadrons and twenty-nine flights. It thus appeared that the Air Force had taken note of the troubles in aerial port mobilization in Vietnam.[34]

The development of improved equipment and techniques for the most part took place in the United States. Feedback from Vietnam was strong, however, both through the established system of formal operational requirements and by virtue of the wide Southeast Asia experience among TAC personnel. Within TAC developmental activity was centralized at the Tactical Air Warfare Center on Eglin Air Force Base. The center was originally formed in late 1963 and reorganized two years later to include a deputy for assault airlift systems. An entirely new command—the Air Force Tactical Airlift Center—came into being on September 1, 1966, at Pope Air Force Base primarily to seek new concepts, equipment, and procedures. Most of the airlift projects under way at Eglin were transferred to the new command.[35]

A new airdrop method, the container delivery system (CDS), permitted drops of substantial loads from a relatively low altitude of six hundred feet thus improving accuracy and marginal weather capability. Cargo weighing over a ton could be rigged inside a canvas container and placed on a plywood platform. A C-130 crew could release simultaneously sixteen such packages, a C-123 seven. To release the load at the proper point the pilot raised the aircraft nose eight degrees and added power. Simultaneously, a release parachute severed the load restraint resulting in extraction by gravity. The load reached the ground quickly while a descent parachute gave stability. Early container delivery development took place at the Army Quartermaster School, and the system was first adapted for the C-123. Testing with the C-130 took place in early 1965. During the next year the 315th Air Division crews learned the new method and in early 1967 they joined the C-123s in regular airdrops in Vietnam employing this method. Previously, the 130s were used for drops only when an item weighed more than a ton and required the application of the older heavy drop technique. Until 1972 the vast majority of C-130 cargo drops in Vietnam employed container delivery rigging.[36]

The relatively trouble free development of the container system contrasted with the controversial development of the low-altitude parachute extraction system. The 315th Air Division remained unenthusiastic over this extraction delivery method mainly because of the expensive crew training requirements. Thus the only LAPES-capable units in the Pacific were the temporary-duty squadrons from TAC. In a letter* to the 2d Air Division, dated October 31, 1965, the MACV chief of staff requested measures to employ LAPES within Vietnam if the system proved feasible. An eighteen-man team from TAC, expert in delivery and rigging techniques, arrived at Tachikawa in April 1966. The group trained a cadre of C-130 crewmen and riggers at Tachikawa and in late May assisted in LAPES missions within Vietnam. Their deliveries averaged eight tons, and included extractions of ammunition at artillery sites. Of ten extractions attempted in Vietnam, all but two were successful. One failure occurred at An Khe when a premature pullup caused release twenty-five feet above the ground (five feet was the normal maximum) and resulted in destruction of platform and load. While in Vietnam the TAC group provided instruction in C-123 LAPES techniques and rigging methods.[37]

Ground force reactions were generally favorable, and Westmoreland

---

* The MACV message also requested a capability for PLADS—parachute low-altitude delivery system—designed for precision deliveries of small packages by C-130s. The TAC team gave instruction in PLADS as well as LAPES. PLADS was destined for no major future role in Vietnam, its purpose overtaken by use of Caribous for low-level drops.

TACTICAL AIRLIFT

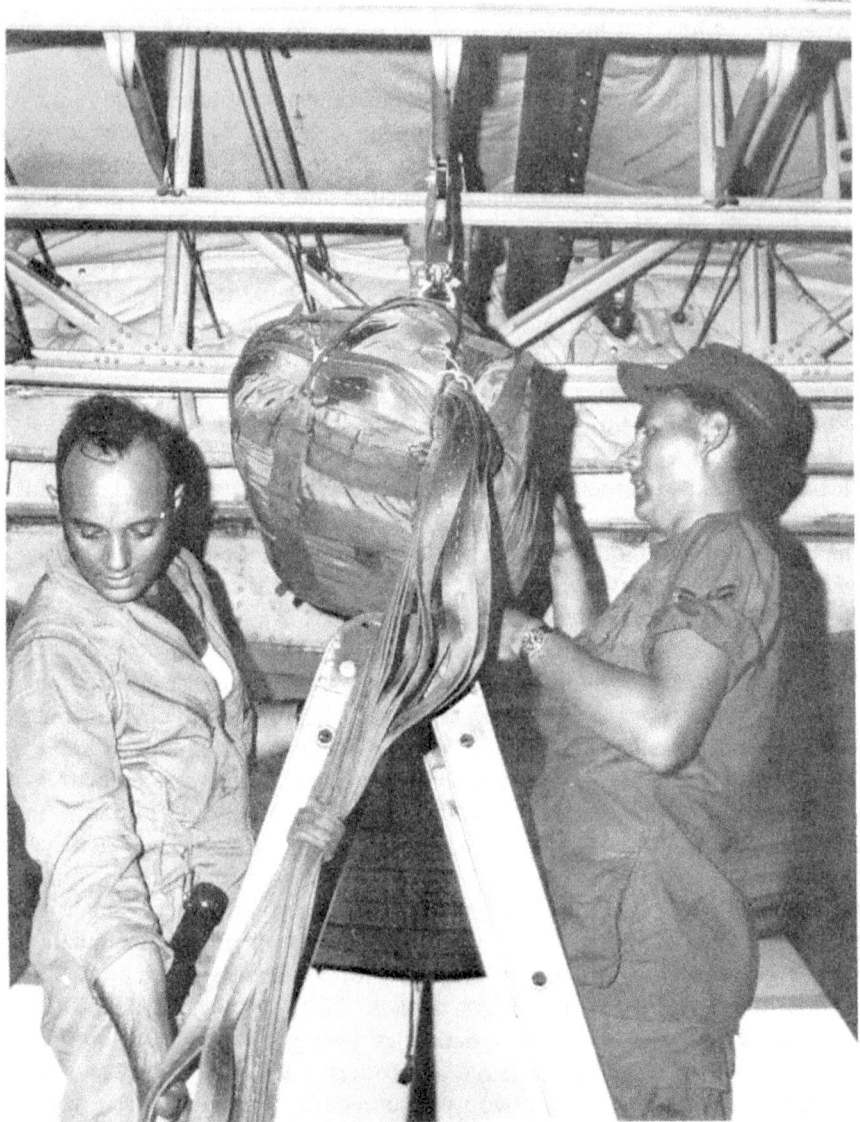

Two airmen aboard a C-130 rig a pallet of cargo and parachute extraction equipment for a low altitude drop, June 1967.

joined the Air Force in recommending that the Army acknowledge its formal acceptance of the extraction system. Army commands in the United States, however, continued to withhold their approval, ostensibly because of system unreliability during testing and because of the absence of previously stated official requirements. Westmoreland in June 1966 nevertheless approved the retention of this capability within Vietnam, and MACV in

AIRLIFT SYSTEM IN GROWTH

Cargo extraction over An Khe, May 1966.

August established a requirement for 290 LAPES hardware units. Meanwhile, training programs within the Pacific Command C–130 squadrons pointed toward qualification of forty-eight crews in the system. Army riggers from the 109th Company also underwent training in the extraction methods.[38]

Responding to a Seventh Air Force study challenging the practicable use of the ejection system in Vietnam, Moore in February pointed out to Momyer that even the most rundown airstrips in Vietnam were capable of receiving the heaviest LAPES deliveries. But unexpected technical troubles appeared during the spring. Two C–130Bs in early June attempted delivery of four platforms at Cat Lai, east of Saigon. One platform was smashed because of a high release, and two loads broke away from their extraction-deceleration parachutes. Improper rigging prevented release of a fourth load. The unfortunate experience brought immediate remedial action, and the following week four platforms were delivered at Cat Lai without malfunction. During the summer fortification materials were delivered at the Bu Dop Special Forces camp. Of thirty-seven LAPES platforms delivered, all but eight extractions were trouble-free. Bulldozers cleared the loads from the extraction zones, and Caribous picked up the dismantled platforms for reuse. During 1967 the LAPES deliveries at Cat Lai, Bu Dop, and Khe Sanh totaled five hundred tons.[39]

The chronic problems associated with all-weather airdrops produced a multiplicity of solutions. Tested at Eglin was a five-pound radar beacon transponder which, when positioned within a drop zone, produced signals on the navigation radar of the C–130. The system offered tactical flexibility, but its drop accuracy averaged only 350 feet. MACV recommended tests of a similar method of positioning small radar reflectors in the drop zone. Another beacon transponder system, Red Chief, was tested during the spring of 1965 during 150 C–47 supply drops in Vietnam with an average accuracy of 180 feet. The Air Staff acted to initiate installation of Red Chief equipment in sixty-eight C–123s in March 1966. Another solution was the adaptation of the loran-D tactical navigation system. The equipment apparently was applicable to air resupply as well as to airstrike work, and ground stations were erected in the Eglin area for testing. The system proved unsatisfactory, however, and the commanders of the Tactical Air Command and the Air Force Systems Command asserted, "beyond any doubt, the present C–130 airlift fleet can only support missions during visual flight conditions."[40]

The search for solutions produced two lines of development which had special significance for the future. In long-range planning the Air Force sought within the C–130 a system entirely self-contained using dual-frequency airborne radar. Repeatedly in 1966 and 1967 the commanders of TAC, Air Force Systems Command, and PACAF called for the installation of the adverse-weather aerial delivery system (AWADS). The Air Staff supported formal operational requirement actions (SOR 216 and SEAOR 98), and after prolonged review amid tight budget limits the Office of the Secretary of Defense in November 1967 approved the Air Force's plan for AWADS development. The appearance of AWADS-equipped C–130s in the Southeast Asia war did not come until 1972.[41]

More immediately available was a blind-drop method which relied on ground radar guidance. Late in 1966 the 311th Air Commando Squadron made fifteen C–123 drops to Special Forces camps in the northern provinces under the guidance of Marine AN/TPQ–10 radar sites. All loads were recovered, but the need to drop from an altitude of six thousand feet to preserve radar contact caused large impact errors. The main problem was to minimize drift during descent. Further refinements of the method were achieved by the Tactical Air Command with the C–130 and various Air Force radars. A time-delay parachute opening mechanism improved accuracy and impact error during twenty-two demonstration drops in Vietnam averaged under two hundred yards. A Tactical Air Command test report in August 1967 noted that both Marine and Air Force radars proved suitable and that an aircrew could fly radar-directed missions without benefit of practice. MACV in late July directed the Seventh Air Force to prepare for radar-guided drops in the northern provinces, and a month later it requested the Seventh to seek Air Force approval of the method as a standard. C-123s and Caribous began ground-directed drops for the Special Forces at the end of August and completed thirteen satisfactory missions in the next three months. Before each drop a dummy load was released to ensure against erroneous map coordinates.[42]

But subsequent developments indicated that the capabilities for aircraft landing at forward strips had improved. Westmoreland reported in August 1967 that the number of usable airfields in South Vietnam had risen to 91 for the C-130, 131 for the C-123, and 174 for the Caribou. Also, sufficient stocks of previously scarce airfield matting were now on hand. Additional steps were taken to reduce airstrip deterioration under heavy usage. Crews were urged to avoid making hard landings and the heavy use of brakes. In the meantime the Seventh Air Force identified certain airstrips for lengthening. The Air Force Flight Dynamics Laboratory sent to the Pacific test data showing that reduced tire pressures could reduce the need for airstrip surfacing. And within the Vietnamese civil aviation budget was a provision for new navigation and radio facilities at Tay Ninh, Kontum, Ban Me Thuot, and elsewhere. The improvement promised safer bad-weather operations. Secretary of the Air Force Dr. Harold Brown, after discussing the matter with Moore in Vietnam, required periodic reports of Air Staff agencies detailing the progress in preparing newly tested portable ground controlled approach units for deployment to Vietnam. Also dispatched to Vietnam were portable airfield lighting sets for use in night operations at forward airstrips. When the lights proved too dim, the forward sites resumed dependence upon the old technique of igniting jet fuel in fifty-five-gallon drums.[43]

The first jet-equipped C-123K arrived at Clark on May 1, 1967. In the next four months an additional twenty-nine arrived. In turn the C-123Bs were ferried to the Fairchild-Hiller plant for modification. The conversion included installation of a J-85 engine pod outboard of each nacelle, heavier flaps, a new stall-warning system, a reinforced landing gear, an antiskid braking system, and extra generators for inflight jet engine starts. Within the 315th Wing reactions to the K-models were overwhelmingly favorable. The jets greatly improved takeoff and climb performance, allowed heavier loads, and reduced exposure to enemy ground fire after takeoff. Moore cited the example of a short airstrip in the delta, where B-models could carry only twenty-five troops per sortie while the K-models could lift fifty-five. Although it was originally believed that the J-85s would be used only ten percent of the flying time actual usage was five times greater. On airdrop missions, for example, the jets were never turned off, assuring greater stability and safety. Conversion of the entire 315th Wing airlift fleet was completed in early 1968.[44]

The airlift of aviation fuels for use by Army helicopters at forward

Secretary of the Air Force Dr. Harold Brown and Lt. Gen. Joseph H. Moore interview an aircrew member, 1966.

Pierced steel planking forms a runway at a remote outpost, dependent on C–123 deliveries, 1966.

Aviation fuel is pumped from the fuel bladder aboard a C-130 into an empty bladder in a storage area at Phan Thiet, September 25, 1966.

Loading fuel drums, 1966.

points increased considerably. The C–130s used several fuel bladder systems. Most valuable for airdrops and for deliveries to locations lacking storage and dispensing systems were the five hundred-gallon collapsible neoprene bladders, a type used during the 1965 Ia Drang attack. In late November 1965 two C–130As arrived at Tan Son Nhut, each equipped with two two thousand-gallon baffled fabric tanks resting on platforms fitted inside the cargo compartment. The associated pumps could offload at five hundred gallons-per-minute. The new system cut down turnaround time and eliminated the need to reload empty bladders. The four tanks were then transferred into two C–130Bs in December, and the aircraft thereafter flew daily out of Tan Son Nhut, one hauling jet fuel and the other aviation gasoline. During the first six weeks of this activity fifteen thousand gallons per day were delivered. An improved system was introduced in September 1966 employing two three thousand-gallon tanks in each C–130. The two thousand-gallon bladders were thereafter used singly with C–123s. A final method, proposed and tested in Vietnam in early 1966, included the use of the aircraft's own fuel tanks, defueling them at the destination. The C–130E was especially suited for this role because of the aircraft's 1,450-gallon external tanks which were ordinarily unfilled during in-country flying. This method placed extra strain on the wing structures especially during hard or assault landings, but was used when necessary to supplement the "bladder birds." C–123s and C–130s delivered over a million gallons of jet fuel to Army fields in November 1966. This role represented one of the most direct contributions to the allied offensive strategy in South Vietnam.[45]

The desire at all Air Force levels to outperform the U.S. Army helicopters became an important driving force for achieving these improvements. The Army's CH–47 Chinooks were impressive rivals of the Air Force in size and operational effectiveness. A joint manual, published on January 1, 1967, loosely described the division of tasks. The Air Force fixed-wing transports and Army helicopters were to be employed in "mutually complementary" roles; the Air Force would "sustain an air line of communications to divisions and brigades and deliver to lower echelons when necessary." Flexibility was thus preserved along with an inevitable and largely constructive competition for tasks.[46]

An Air Force Manual 2–4, Tactical Air Operations—Tactical Airlift, August 10, 1966, superseded AFM 1–9 which, since 1954, was the formal expression of Air Force troop carrier doctrine. The new manual reiterated that tactical airlift forces should be organized under the theater Air Force component commander. Further, centralized control was to be exercised by an airlift control center, through detached airlift control elements and combat control teams. The control center was to be located "adjacent to" or be "operationally connected" to the tactical air control center, allowing integration of airlift operations with the overall air effort. The language apparently left room for autonomous airlift control and communications. Allocations of airlift capability rested with the joint force commander who might form a joint board to assist in this function. The assignment of experienced airlift officers to tactical air control parties, the latter being attached to ground force divisions, was prescribed; it was optional whether the airlift officers should be used at the brigade and lower levels. In a significant departure from the principle of centralized control, and reflecting the recent Caribou agreement, the new manual stated that short-range airlift craft "may be attached to subordinate tactical echelons of the field Army" if the need was determined by the joint or unified commander. The manual further asserted that the Air Force would deliver to brigade level "on a sustained basis" and farther forward as required. AFM 2-4 thus clearly reflected the challenge of the Army's airmobile ideas along with recent experience in Vietnam. The new doctrine was soon tested when the allied campaigns in the Saigon plain, the western highlands, and in the northern provinces of the Republic of Vietnam accelerated.[47]

XI. Junction City and the Battles of 1967

The infusion of American Army forces assured allied tactical supremacy on the ground in South Vietnam. Offensive search-and-destroy operations penetrated communist base areas and promised to break down the enemy's organized military strength and to provide the conditions essential for long-term pacification. Although communist bases in Cambodia remained largely immune, the Americans set out to make the enemy's situation inside South Vietnam impossible and ultimately to weaken his resolve to fight.

Within this strategy the role of tactical airlift followed the pattern seen in Operation Birmingham. The search-and-destroy ventures typically centered around one or more C–130 airstrips which became the focal points for buildup and resupply. Allied helicopters and infantry combed the surrounding region, sought out the enemy, and exposed him to the killing effects of air and artillery firepower. The C–130s played a central role in Operation Junction City, the largest of the search-and-destroy operations to date. This operation opened in February 1967 with the war's first and only American battalion-size parachute assault and featured substantial use of airdrop resupply.

The allies and communists were willing to fight battles in the border regions. The highlands offered enemy units concealment and ready access to Cambodian sanctuaries. Westmoreland believed that the campaigns in remote areas permitted unrestricted use of allied firepower, afforded scope for airmobile tactics, and helped shield pacification activities in the populated regions. The ability of the C–130s to bring in quickly reinforcements and high volume air resupply made possible this forward stance. The period's heaviest fighting took place at Khe Sanh in mid-1967, and at Loc Ninh and Dak To in the fall. In each battle allied forces entered the confrontation by air and while engaged depended heavily upon air resupply. On the political front the period closed with guarded expressions of confidence for the future among American leaders. They were pleased in particular with the orderliness of the Vietnamese national elections in September.

TACTICAL AIRLIFT

Military operations in the Saigon plain in late 1966 revealed the viability of the emerging allied offensive capability and the flexibility of the Air Force airlift force. C–123s and C–130s delivered fuel, munitions, and general cargo in support of the offensive ground operations. The airlifters regularly hauled supplies to relatively primitive airstrips at fire support areas such as Lai Khe and Quan Loi and even to more primitive sites beyond Loc Ninh and Minh Thanh.

Operation Attleboro began quietly in the early fall, but by mid-November the venture required fifty-two C–123 and C–130 sorties daily. The fire support area at Dau Tieng for weeks depended exclusively on Provider air resupply from Bien Hoa and Tan Son Nhut.[1] During one phase of the operation, landings at Dau Tieng were made on the average of one every seven minutes. Several times communist shells closed the strip for repairs, and hostile fire brought down one C–123. Maintenance men of the 315th Wing worked around the clock to keep this maximum effort going. On the ground at Dau Tieng the tactical airlift officer coordinated the flow of arriving aircraft without the benefit of radios or the assistance of combat control teams. In terms of enemy losses in men and materiel the operation was an allied success.[2]

More important, months of planning were devoted to Operation Junction City which was scheduled for late February 1967 and was intended as a massive entrapment of enemy forces in Zone C including northern Tay Ninh Province. During January and February 1967, American forces assumed their positions on three sides of the objective area and established forward logistics bases. Transports in the meantime flew hundreds of sorties in the preparatory effort which included C–130s bringing in over fourteen hundred tons of munitions to Minh Thanh. Further, Westmoreland and the MACV staff planned to lift in forces using all available helicopters, but they desired that a battalion of 173d Airborne Brigade be scheduled to jump from C–130s in the first American parachute assault of the war.[3]

The American inclination to stage a parachute assault somewhere within Vietnam had been evident the previous year. Responding to Westmoreland's pointed inquiries, subordinate Army commanders in October 1966 forwarded to him several proposals for battalion assault jumps in the border areas. MACV ordered practice missions and more than eight hundred paratroopers of the 173d Brigade jumped from sixteen C–130s near Bien Hoa on October 30. A second practice mission followed the next month.[4] Meanwhile, the Air Force demonstrated its readiness to cooperate —ten C–130s and three C–123s joined twenty Vietnamese Air Force C–47s in a two-battalion Vietnamese jump in the southernmost delta in late December. All of the men landed on target with the exception of three C–47 strings who jumped too soon after a mixup in cockpit signals.

Though a practice mission, three American transports were hit by ground fire and a C–123 loadmaster incurred fatal wounds.[5]

The 834th Air Division's OPlan 476–67, 1 January 1967, became the guide for airborne operations in Vietnam, including the Junction City assault. The plan prescribed a battalion drop from twenty-six C–130s. Half of the aircraft would carry troops while the others would haul the battalion's equipment. The 130s were to converge at a marshaling base for loading eight hours prior to takeoff and thus preserve surprise and prolong use of the transports for normal tasks. The Air Force, further, would provide certain aerial port personnel and equipment, although the Army retained responsibility for packaging and rigging cargo. Final inspection of loaded aircraft became a joint responsibility. The 834th retained operational control of the transports under MACV mission directives and named an airlift force commander who would accompany the lead aircraft. The plan additionally prescribed the use of in-trail formation tactics at medium en route altitudes with a descent to drop altitudes during the run-in. This approach was a departure from the low-level tactics developed in Close Look and practiced by all C–130 units. The absence of enemy air interceptors and heavy antiaircraft weaponry made the need for low-level flight purposeless. Finally the plan postulated the usefulness of airborne operations in Vietnam as a means to "achieve tactical surprise by sudden, undetected mass delivery of combat forces into the enemy area."[6]

Pilots and navigators from the out-of-country C–130 wings arrived at Tan Son Nhut on February 18 to assist in planning for the Junction City assault. After a briefing by General Moore they joined the planners of the 834th Air Division to work out tactics, write operation orders, and to prepare route and drop-zone briefing aids. Principals in the planning were two 314th Wing navigators assigned to lead the assault formation. Representatives from the other C–130 units worked primarily on the follow-up equipment drops.

The drop zone in Operation Junction City lay near the main highway at Katum, four miles from the Cambodian border. The site was selected for use as the brigade command post and as an artillery fire support base. To insure secrecy only a handful of ground force officers knew the true objective. Army planners chose a cover drop zone of similar size and characteristics but located fifteen miles farther east. Informed by his own staff that the designated drop zone made little sense, Moore raised the question with the 173d commander. The general only then learned of the existence of a plan for deception and gained agreement that his key planners would receive the correct information. The briefing packages, though prepared, were revised although the route up to the final twenty miles remained unchanged. Finally, recent photographs of the true drop zone and the run-in path were obtained.[7]

The troop carrier and airborne planners worked out details without

Brig. Gen. William G. Moore, 834th Air Division commander, talks with other Air Force and Army officers taking part in Operation Attleboro.

A C–123 squeezes between a bunker and an old French villa at the Dau Tieng airstrip.

Dust never settled at Dau Tieng during Operation Attleboro. USAF C–123s landed every seven minutes on November 6, 1966.

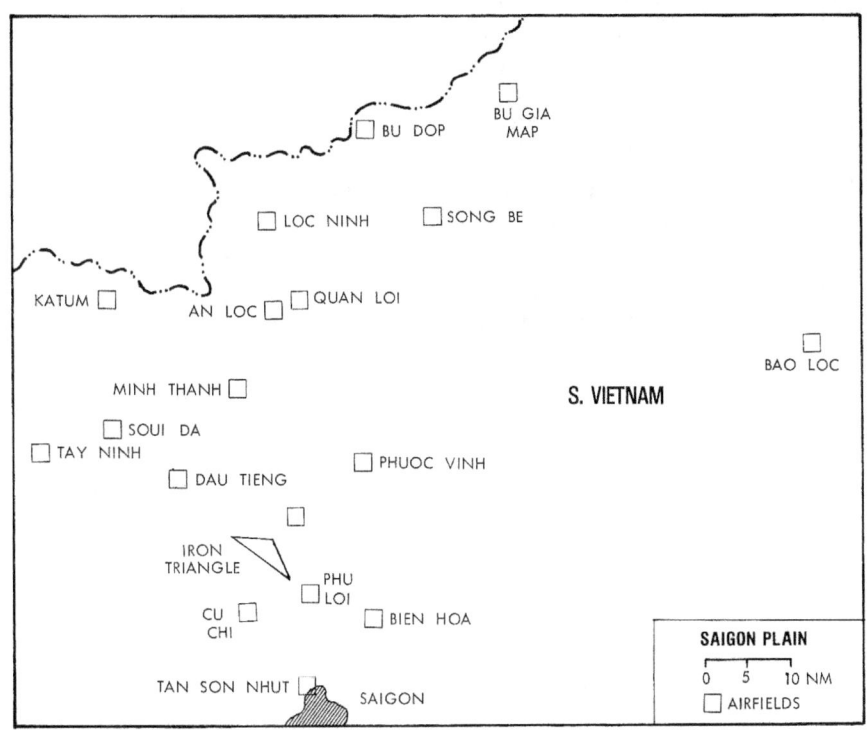

difficulty. The question of the jump altitude was fixed at one thousand feet and each aircraft was to pass over the drop zone within twenty-six seconds. The time was too brief for the safe exit of the sixty-man load. Two passes for the thirteen-ship formation were accordingly planned. Loading plans were so developed that each paratroop company would land in its own sector of the drop zone. Although the possibility of enemy opposition at or near the drop zone was unlikely, nearly two hours of preparatory air strikes were scheduled. Helicopter gunships were to be in proximity of the drop zone during the drops and assembly. The mission for the paratroopers upon landing was perimeter security while the heavy-equipment drops and the initial base consolidation activities continued.

Selected to make the Junction City jump was the 2d Battalion, 503d Infantry, of the 173d Brigade. The unit underwent refresher jump training in early February. On February 21 the men received mission briefing from their commander and were placed in quarantine at Camp Zinn near Bien Hoa. Jump equipment was issued, individual items packed, parachutes fitted and checked. Each aircraft's jumpmaster briefed jump, landing, and emergency procedures. Members of an Air Force combat control team who accompanied the paratroopers had responsibility for guiding the equipment-drop formation.[8]

The C-130 assault force began converging at Bien Hoa after midnight February 22. Ten C-130B* aircraft arrived from Tan Son Nhut in the early morning hours ready to begin loading for the heavy-equipment drops. The four E-models destined to lead the troop-carrying formation arrived from Nha Trang shortly thereafter, followed an hour later by three more B-models from Tan Son Nhut and nine C-130s from Cam Ranh Bay. The troop-carriers were parked tip to tip at the west end of the Bien Hoa ramp. The aircrews, after a predawn breakfast, went by bus to a theater building for mission briefing.

Brig. Gen. John R. Deane, Jr., USA, and General Moore opened the briefing. Subsequent presentations dealt with the flight portion of the assault and the navigational and drop-zone details. Aircrews were surprised to learn of the true site since their earlier preparations had been based on the cover plan. Another last-minute change was the selection of an alternate identification point. A dogleg route was substituted which intercepted the original run-in path several miles closer to the drop zone. After the briefing the navigators reworked their flight plans and studied the Katum site. Copilots and loadmasters returned to the flight line to monitor loading activities.[9]

Meanwhile at Camp Zinn the paratroopers loaded themselves and

---

* References to the different C-130 models in this section simplifies identification of the units participating. The C-130As were from 374th Wing (at Naha) and from Tachikawa, the C-130Bs were from 463d Wing (Philippines), and the C-130Es were from 314th Wing (Taiwan).

their equipment into trucks for the short trip to the aircraft. At the flight line guides with "chalk number" placards led the men through the darkness to the proper aircraft. Individual loads of the paratroopers with the reserve chutes and personal equipment were heavy. Marshaling and loading were performed without confusion. One C–130 copilot noticed General Deane's pearl-handled pistols but was more surprised to see a diminutive American female correspondent wearing battle garb climbing aboard one of the aircraft.[10]

Engine start and runup were performed on schedule. The troop-carrying aircraft taxied first for takeoff. The first aircraft rolled at eight twenty-five in the morning, and the others followed at regular intervals. All aircraft were airborne within three minutes. In the meantime reports of nearby firing delayed the planned turn to an on-course heading.

The planned route took the formation to the south and west of Saigon to the Black Virgin Mountain (Nui Ba Den) just north of Tay Ninh. This indirect path required about thirty minutes of flying time, a procedure believed necessary to permit orderly inflight preparation for the drops by the navigators and loadmasters and to allow for possible adjustment of timing for the run-in. Two navigators shared duties in the lead aircraft, one worked the radar, obtained doppler wind information, and did the table computations, while the second stood behind the pilots and performed mapreading by visual reference with the ground. The two-navigator technique had previously been used in formation lead work, but it was a departure from the method normally practiced whereby pilots gave mapreading assistance to a single navigator. Navigation in any case was simplified by the excellent visibility prevailing throughout the mission. A minor complication resulted when a delay resulted in assuming course, thus requiring the leaders to raise airspeed and to make it difficult for the rear aircraft to take up the correct intervals. The formation maintained absolute radio silence. The identification point was sighted and the planned dogleg successfully negotiated. The run-in began on the planned northeasterly track, and the formation slowed to 125 knots while descending to drop altitude at the prescribed point.

Nearing the drop zone the lead crew could see the final preparatory air strikes and the explosions were audible. An airborne forward air controller spoke to the formation by radio and set off colored smoke bombs at the site. The smoke was helpful in confirming the drop zone.

Each aircraft in the formation generally followed the path of the leaders, although each navigator determined his own alignment and his exact time of release. The first troopers were out at the briefed time and all planes crossed the drop zone at correct twenty-second intervals. Enemy fire was not evident. As the jumpers began landing exactly within the area of the colored smoke, the airborne controller waxed enthusiastic. General Moore, hitherto grim and intent in manner, smiled and lit his cigar in satisfaction.[11]

TACTICAL AIRLIFT

After crossing the drop zone the troop-carriers turned sharply to the right, remained at drop altitude, and returned to the previous run-in track for a second pass. It was important to turn promptly to avoid crossing the Cambodian border and to reduce exposure to possible ground fire. The second pass was completed at ten minutes after nine; again all paratroopers landed on the correct target. Following this drop, the C-130s gained altitude and set course for Tan Son Nhut and Cam Ranh Bay. The lead aircraft with Moore aboard remained in the area to observe the equipment drops.

The troop drops appeared successful without qualification. Weather had remained excellent, hostile fire was negligible, and only one C-130 received a single bullet hole, discovered after landing. The in-trail formation procedures proved a flexible basis for the employed tactics and were used without the slightest confusion. At the drop zone the 173d was well pleased and the commander of the brigade said the drops went exactly as planned. Deane later remarked that his landing was precisely at the intended spot. The brigade reported only eleven injuries, all minor; no troopers were wounded during descent. A total of 780 men made the jump including 510 from the 2d Battalion and 110 from the artillery battery.

The equipment drops were also in most respects successful. The combat control team had jumped in the second pass and immediately marked the desired impact point with smoke. Of the ten cargo-carrying C-130Bs, eight were rigged for conventional heavy-equipment drops and released their loads from an altitude of fifteen hundred feet; two container deliveries followed immediately. The aircraft thus delivered over eighty tons although the loads were limited by the nature of the weapons and equipment dropped. All ten cargo aircraft returned to Bien Hoa for reloading for another container drop. The Air Force aerial port mobility team there readied the planes in forty-five minutes. The early afternoon drops were successfully completed and they averaged well over ten tons per transport. During the course of the day, five cargo carriers received hits; none was seriously damaged.

Load recovery during the operation presented some difficulties. The two container loads were heavily damaged, and witnesses on the ground at the drop site concluded that this was caused by releasing from too low an altitude. Other loads landed in swamp areas at the fringe of the drop zone and could be recovered only by tracked vehicles. The combat control teams tried unsuccessfully to warn the afternoon aircrews to drop well away from the swamp. Seeking better ground-to-air communications, the control team later borrowed a radio from the forward air controller. The recovery of parachute canopies and equipment bags was slow. Many items were lost or damaged as a result, and the littering of the site hampered helicopter landings during the morning. On the other hand, activities within the drop zone proceeded smoothly. Hostile fire occurred only during midmorning, wounding one trooper. Brigade and battalion command posts were fully operational by noon. A senior ground observer sensed in late morning a euphoria and lassitude among the troopers and interpreted this to be a postreaction to the adrenalin generated earlier.[12]

Elsewhere on February 22, in the largest helicopter effort to date, eight infantry battalions assaulted from 250 aircraft along the northern rim of Zone C. Two battalions of the 173d landed several miles from the Katum drop zone. Two other brigades landed at objectives along the border fifteen miles farther west. Meanwhile, two brigades moved overland to form the western cordon above Trai Bi and completed the encirclement of the western Zone C with the 173d.[13]

Airdrops resumed on the twenty-third. All sorties originated at Cam Ranh Bay and all employed the container delivery system. Plans called for airdrops of twelve hundred tons in the first seven days, leaving the riggers of the Army's 109th Quartermaster Company with a surplus capacity of 550 tons for emergencies. The 15th Aerial Port Squadron began loading C–130A transports before sunrise on the twenty-third, and a seven-ship A-model formation departed three hours later. Using standard formation takeoff procedures the seven aircraft joined up off the coast and proceeded to Tay Ninh at about nine thousand feet. Their en route weather was good, but low clouds covered the zone. This latter factor hampered the day's effort. Approaching the objective, the formation descended into the clouds and each plane navigated independently. The flight leader broke out only a mile from the Katum drop zone and was too far to the right to make the drop. Remaining under the clouds, he flew a racetrack course and twice aborted passes because of helicopters below. He finally released on the fourth pass. Meanwhile, a second formation took off from Cam Ranh Bay, consisting of eight B–model C–130s from the Tan Son Nhut detachment. After dropping their cargo, both groups returned to Cam Ranh Bay for reloading.[14]

But problems at the drop zones persisted throughout the day. The weather ruined the integrity of formations, and aircraft were left to mill about individually and to coordinate by radio with an airborne forward air controller and the combat control team. Trying to stay underneath the cloud layer some crews dropped loads from too low an altitude, others found themselves in the clouds during the awkward pullup phase upon release. One Hercules crew misidentified the drop zone and released a half-mile short; another misinterpreted the smoke signals, dropped too soon, and confused the trailing crew. Some afternoon drops supported the 196th Brigade in the northwestern corner of the allied ring. Two loads intended for the brigade landed too far from their drop zone for recovery. Prolonged flying at low level resulted in four instances of battle damage and for several aircraft it was sufficient to prevent the crew from taking off again.

Some airplanes were fired upon from the Cambodian side of the border. But more significantly, in thirty-eight drops during the day a total of 499 tons were delivered, nearly all munitions.[15]

Yet criticisms of the day's results were sharp. Senior Army officers watching a six-ship formation drop at Katum noted that the loads were spread over nearly a mile with five loads landing in swamp areas. A dissatisfied 1st Infantry Division logistician reluctantly agreed at midday to continue the afternoon drop schedule, but he telephoned cancellation of the next day's resupply effort. The aircrews were briefed to move the desired impact point away from the wetlands, but some of the afternoon loads again landed in the difficult areas. Although personnel from the 109th parachuted in to assist in recovering loads, some of the ammunition remained unrecovered the next day, prompting additional requests for more drop-zone workers. Army observers also stated that many C–130 crews released during a very steep pullup, causing the bundles and parachutes to interfere with one another and resulting in damage to loads on impact. Moore acknowledged that it may have been a mistake to assign A–model aircrews to the drops since they were the least qualified in tactical work and until recently had flown only occasionally in Vietnam.[16]

Drops over the next five days continued out of Cam Ranh Bay, averaging nearly one hundred tons daily. B–models were primarily used, landing at Tan Son Nhut each night. Normally, four aircraft dropped for the 173d each morning and four for the 196th each afternoon. Accuracy and mission coordination gradually improved. Defective container webbing (apparently resulting from prolonged storage) caused eight of the twelve confirmed rigging malfunctions. On February 27 two containers of 105-mm ammunition separated from their parachutes in midair, detonating upon contact with the ground and destroying eight other containers which had landed normally. The 196th Brigade reported that the 105-mm ammunition packed in wood boxes generally landed undamaged, but that one-fourth of that dropped in metal "jungle packs" was dented and unusable. Despite these sundry difficulties the 196th judged that the week's drops were "excellent," estimating that sixty-five Chinook sorties had been thus saved for other tasks.[17]

During the first weeks of Junction City, allied troops moved through Zone C, especially the border areas, maneuvering in many cases by helicopter. These forces drove overland to link with the 173d at Katum. A company of Army engineers began work on an airfield at Katum on February 24, clearing a 2,900-foot strip from jungle cover and surfacing it with local laterite. The field was inspected and received its first Hercules on March 3. Construction of a second field began at Prek Klok located south of Katum. The 196th Brigade also improvised the construction of an airstrip. C–130s and C–123s supplemented road communications into Tay Ninh, the main hub for resupply of fire support areas at Trai Bi, French

Fort (just north of the Black Virgin), and Soui Da. C-130s also landed at Soui Da which was surfaced with T-17 membrane. During one stretch of Operation Junction City, eleven of twelve combat control teams worked the three border drop zones while the others coordinated at the area airstrips.[18]

Phase II of the operation began on March 18. Troop units shifted eastward to the construction of a camp and airfield at Tonle Cham, the site formerly designated in the cover plan for the parachute assault. Supplies came through the fire support stations at Minh Thanh and Quan Loi. C-123s and C-130s lifted the 173d out of Junction City on March 15, unloading them at Soui Da. A week later a stream of C-130s returned the brigade from Bien Hoa to Minh Thanh. In the next three weeks, more than four hundred Air Force transport sorties (primarily flown by C-130s) sustained the 173d and other units at Minh Thanh.[19]

Construction at Tonle Cham illustrates the process of forward airfield preparation. The work was done by D Company, 1st Engineer Battalion, a unit from Katum. Jungle clearing began on March 15. Three weeks later, the runway was opened for use and numerous aircraft landed at Tonle Cham during the remainder of Operation Junction City, including twenty-nine C-130s. The newly constructed airstrips at Tonle Cham, Katum, Prek Klok, and Soui Da, made it possible for the American Army to reenter Zone C at will."[20]

The idea of keeping a roving brigade in the western part of Zone C, to remain after departure of the main units, received Westmoreland's approval in mid-March. The 196th Brigade, then operating near Prek Klok, was selected. The brigade was capable of operating entirely without ground communications and was resupplied solely by parachute and helicopter. In four preparatory drops C-130s delivered fifty-eight tons to sites several miles north of French Fort. The brigade began its "floating" operations on March 27 upon closure of the fire support area at French Fort. Brigade forces moved overland toward Katum receiving en route over ninety tons of ammunition, fuel, and water in C-130 drops on March 27 and 28. During an eight-day period commencing March 31, C-130Bs dropped a daily average of seventy-four tons. All loads were container-rigged by the 109th Company at Cam Ranh Bay. From Katum the force moved gradually west, reaching its destination by April 6. Combat control teams accompanied each of the brigade's three battalions and each operated in its own drop zone. These sites changed frequently, occasionally while aircraft were en route. Once an aircrew orbited overhead while the control team marked a roadside field. On other occasions airborne controllers in observation aircraft guided drop ships. At one site combat control personnel cleared a landing zone for Caribou use only.[21]

Needed for duties elsewhere, the 196th moved to Tay Ninh on April 8, ending the floating brigade experiment. Assessments were favorable.

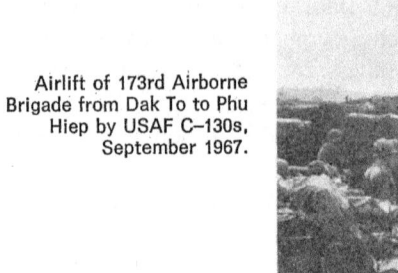

Airlift of 173rd Airborne Brigade from Dak To to Phu Hiep by USAF C-130s, September 1967.

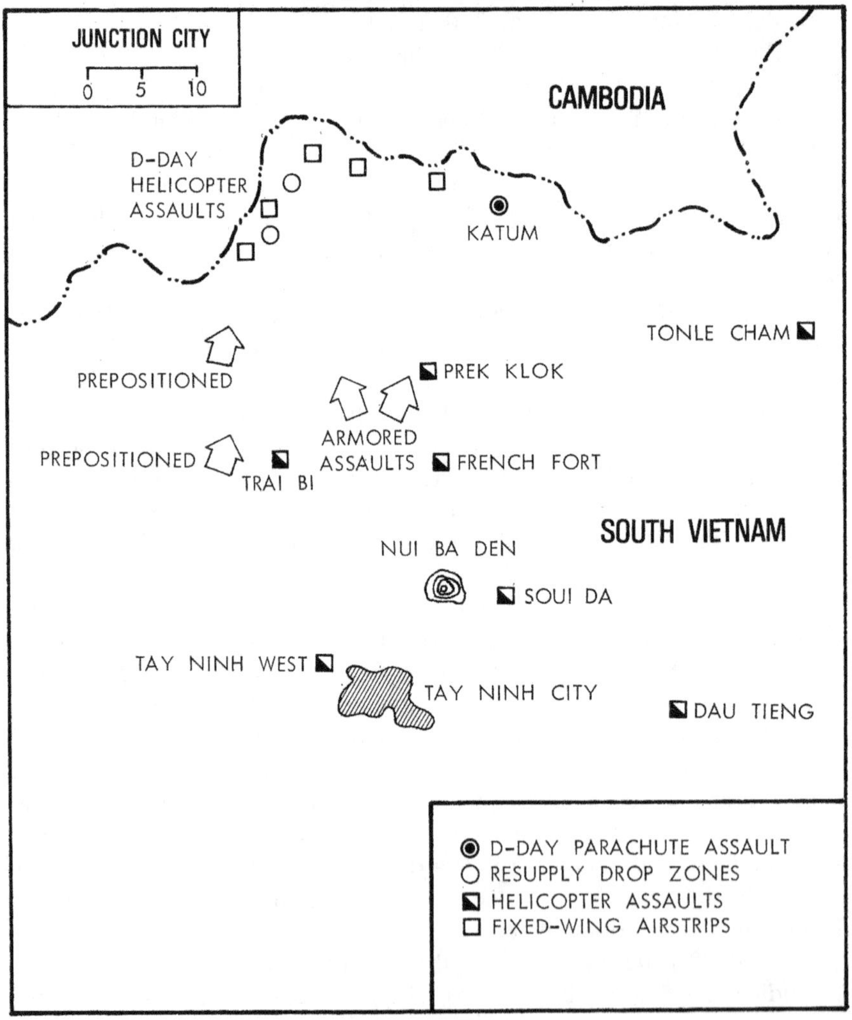

Member of the 173rd Airborne Brigade, moments after jumping from a C-130 over Tay Ninh. The aircraft in the background is an O-1E Bird Dog, used to direct strikes against enemy ground positions.

A C-130 Hercules paradrops supplies and equipment to Army forces during Operation Junction City, February 1967.

Maj. Gen. Shelton E. Lollis, USA, commander of 1st Logistical Command, concluded that such a force could be effectively supplied by airdrops in the future. The presence of the combat control team assured full flexibility, General Lollis observed, while the main limiting factor seemed to be the ability of the receiving unit to absorb large deliveries. The 196th agreed that the mobile brigade could deny the enemy an area such as Zone C, and recommended the inclusion of an armored element, supporting artillery, and additional helicopters. The brigade's evaluation of the C–130 drops was favorable.[22]

For the complete period of Operation Junction City, C–130s dropped over seventeen hundred tons of equipment and supplies. The recurring handling problems at the drop zones—loads damaged or lost, and the annoying need to recover parachutes—indicated that where feasible helicopter delivery was preferable to parachute supply. The paradrop capability was worth preserving, however, and the Army, after reviewing Junction City, pronounced drops an "extremely efficient" method which offered "not only an emergency but also an expedient means of resupply to tactical units." By sharpening the Air Force's and Army's readiness to conduct airdrop resupply, Junction City became an important forerunner of the major parachute resupply ventures in the next year in Vietnam.[23]

The common airlift system met the extra workload of Junction City without difficulty. Countrywide aerial port backlogs rose from three thousand tons on February 21 to more than four thousand tons a week later, but returned to their former level by the end of March. The forty-four-aircraft C–130 shuttle force was not expanded. The effect of Junction City on the overall course of the war remains unclear. Fighting had been generally light. Viet Cong units were forced out of the area, and the principal communist headquarters shifted into Cambodia. A former communist lieutenant colonel later informed the allies that the entire series of Zone C offensives (including Junction City) discouraged them and led to their decision to attempt a general offensive in 1968.[24]

The confrontations in the highland provinces followed consistent patterns. American and South Vietnamese units based in the region kept the enemy off-balance with localized search-and-destroy operations of short duration. Communist units periodically crossed from Cambodia to menace towns and camps in the border provinces. At such times the Hercules brought in reinforcements, landing on the main airstrips at Pleiku, Kontum, and Ban Me Thuot. Allied truck convoys routinely resupplied the interior from the coast, supplemented by airlifts of mail, passengers, and

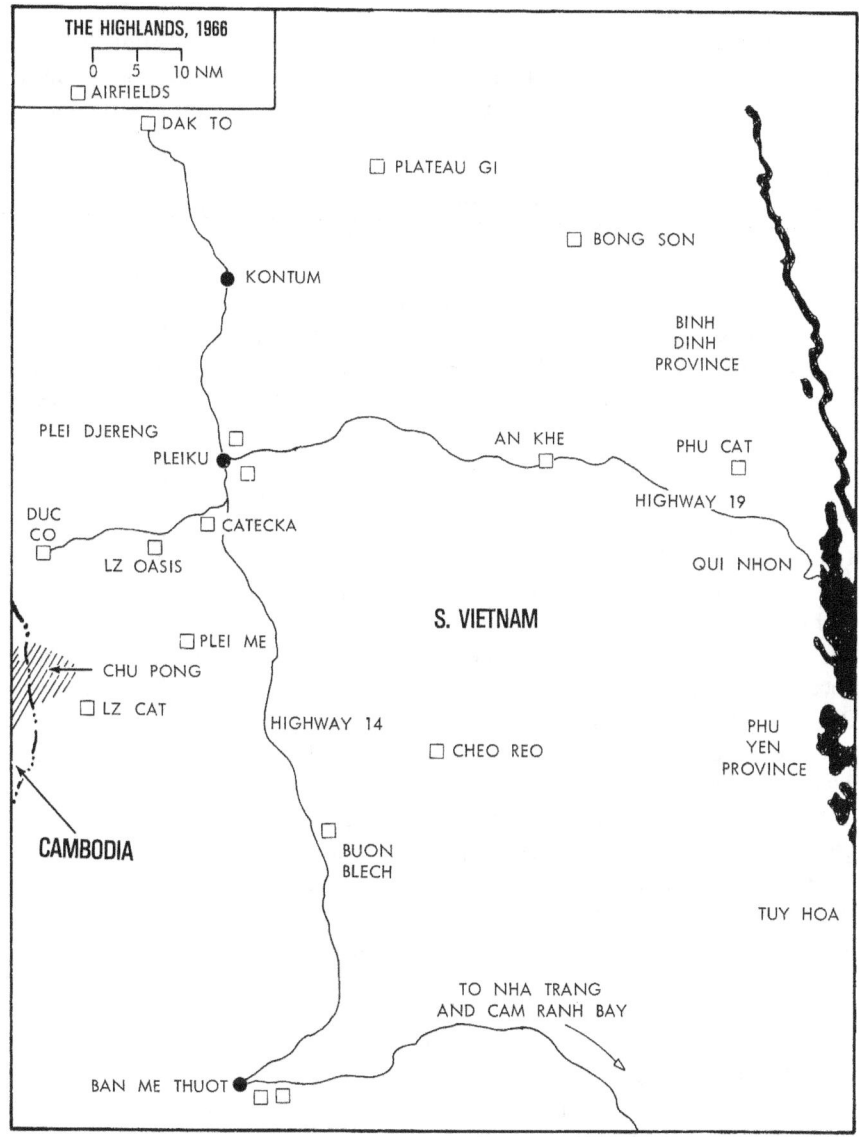

special items. Air transport remained available to support full-scale operations in the event of road interruption.

Fighting in early 1966 took place primarily in the plateau region between Pleiku and Ban Me Thuot. A sustained airlink opened into Ban Me Thuot in February with the deployment by C-130 of a U.S. infantry brigade. The C-130s resupplied around the clock, operating from Cam Ranh Bay and meeting a daily cargo quota of three hundred tons. As the brigade gradually shifted its operations farther north, airlifts intermittently reached them at smaller strips such as Buon Blech and Cheo Reo. The highway deliveries slowly replaced air supply to Ban Me Thuot. Meanwhile, the 1st Cavalry Division returned to the Ia Drang battleground south of Pleiku. Fixed-wing airlift supplemented road and helicopter access into the battle area. C–130s landed at Catecka, Duc Co, and a new airstrip southwest of Catecka—Landing Zone (LZ) Oasis, built and surfaced with T–17 membrane by divisional engineers. Providers and Caribous, supporting a two-brigade air assault into the Chu Pong area, landed on a new dirt strip, LZ Cat, adjacent to the communist-held Chu Pong Massif. Another Ia Drang campaign in August coincided with rains and flooding that hampered road movements and softened landing surfaces. C–123s made airdrops at several places; these were plagued by inaccuracy, numerous rigging malfunctions, and an episode in which falling bundles destroyed two helicopters at LZ Cat. The cavalry division nevertheless deemed the drops "responsive."[25]

Streams of C–130s periodically transported brigade-scale reinforcements in reaction to North Vietnamese movements. The 1st Brigade of the 101st Airborne Division landed at Kontum in December 1966. Two months later the 1st Brigade of the 4th Infantry Division entered the highlands in February 1967, landing at Plei Djereng west of Pleiku. Plei Djereng had been recently opened to C–130 aircraft and it thereafter became a focus for resupply. The 173d Brigade moved from Bien Hoa to Pleiku on May 24–27, 1967. The brigade shifted to the north in mid-June, operating then from a fire support area at Dak To and at times depended exclusively on air resupply. During June transports shifted two Vietnamese airborne battalions to Kontum, and hauled a brigade of the 1st Cavalry Division to Dak To from field operations near the coast. The cavalry battalion completed its move on June 2. The fast troop movement spoke well for the Army's ability to extract its forces from active operations, and to proceed to the nearest C–130 field and then quickly to reenter combat at a new location.[26]

Such unit movements represented hard work for the transport aircrews. Typically, the aircrew reported to the flight line about dawn and then flew to the loading base. The crew usually found an orderly line of waiting army vehicles, trailers, and troops. An Air Force mission commander supervised flight-line activity, coordinating between aircrews and Army personnel. Discussions sometimes became heated when pilots were reluctant to accept loads weighing to the limit of safety. Such difficulties usually passed after the day's first trip, after pilots became reassured of the conditions at their destination and as their aircraft burned off excess fuel. Crews typically spent the full mission day shuttling back and forth between the two points, but diverted every three or four hours to the nearest Air Force base for refueling. Sometimes, crews on other itineraries would contribute one or two sorties to the unit movement shuttle. The pace of the movement was usually determined by the capacity of approach facilities and parking space at destination. Troop carrier crews were rarely informed of the tactical purposes behind the unit moves. There was no mistaking, however, the effects of combat on the mud-covered and uncommunicative infantrymen, the "Grunts," each of whom remained detached through his own fatigue and private thoughts.

The C–130 withdrawal of the 173d from Dak To in September coincided with three days of heavy rain. The airstrip quickly deteriorated requiring major patching by engineer troops. This repair work was important because in late October local reconnaissance confirmed that at least four North Vietnamese regiments were converging through the forested hill country around the town. The second battle of Dak To, fought in November 1967, became a foremost example of the usefulness of the C–130 force within the context of allied strategy.[27]

The 173d returned by C–130 to Dak To in the first week of November. Clouds and rain complicated the airlift at both terminals. As fighting increased in the heights immediately south of the airstrip and in the forest terrain to the west, the flow of reinforcements continued. A Vietnamese airborne battalion arrived from Hue on the fifth and sixth, another from Saigon on the thirteenth, and two more the following week. These latter moves were achieved by Vietnamese Air Force C–47s supplemented by American C–130s. Two battalions from 1st Cavalry Division were sent by C–130 from An Khe in mid-November. Thus, of the fifteen allied battalions in the battle area, most entered by air. Westmoreland later reported that the reinforcements had beaten the enemy to the punch, denying initiative to him.[28]

The consumption of supplies at the Dak To fire support area soared, particularly of artillery ammunition. On November 6, in the hopes of completing a C–130 resupply within forty-eight hours, the MACV command center proposed to commence night landings using emergency runway lighting. An alternative was night delivery to the airstrip at Kontum which was twenty-five miles away. MACV decided to hold off adopting either approach, but shortly before midnight on the eighth, fire support officers at Dak To forecast a zero balance by the next morning. A sustained high-volume daylight airlift followed until a desired three-day supply was attained. A daily allocation of twenty C–130 sorties was thereafter established while other needs were met by emergency requests. Distribution forward of the fire support area to battalion and artillery locations was by helicopter and truck.[29]

Conditions on the ground at Dak To reflected the absence of a joint doctrine for airhead control. During the September operations two C–130s collided with Army trucks; the second collision occurred during takeoff. Another departing C–130 hit a bulldozer in mid-October killing its driver; the aircrew landed safely, but the aircraft was damaged beyond economic repair. These incidents resulted from an absence of paved roads at Dak To and vehicles were obliged to stay close to the runway to avoid the mud. Still more dangerous was the heavy and apparently uncontrolled helicopter traffic which sharply increased during the November battle as helicopter crews shuttled in with fresh loads of supplies, ammunition, and fuel. On November 8, Brig. Gen. Hugh E. Wild, acting commander of the 834th Air Division, informed MACV that the possibility of a C–130 loss must be accepted if operations were to continue into Dak To. His warning brought a decision to continue landings, but at the same time attempts were made to improve helicopter and vehicle traffic control. The absence of further tragedy spoke well for the watchfulness of the C–130 crews aided by an overworked combat control team detachment. The air about Dak To contained not only the smoke of battle but the oaths of irritated C–130 pilots.[30]

At times as many as five C–130s were simultaneously on the ground at Dak To, some waiting for offloading, while others were temporarily blocked from departing the cramped parking area. The ramp and the adjacent ammunition storage area thus offered a fine target for enemy mortar teams, several of which were spotted by allied troops outside the airstrip perimeter. On November 12, several mortar rounds struck the airfield hastening the departure of the aircraft then parked. The attack caused no damage. Despite these warnings the airlifters made no change in their routine. But taking advantage of ranging information which they had gained earlier, communist mortar crews opened fire in early morning three days later, choosing a moment when the last of three C–130s on the ramp had stopped its engines. A fourth aircraft which had just landed took off immediately. About ten mortar rounds hit the parking ramp, destroying two of the C–130s and igniting several fires. A third Hercules received shrapnel damage and leaked fuel. During a lull in the attack, about twenty-five minutes after its beginning, two members of an aircrew ran from shelter to their plane. They started its engines, backed the aircraft away from the others, and taxied away. Their action unquestionably saved all of the aircraft and was lauded by the commander of 4th Infantry Division who witnessed the episode. Capt. Joseph K. Glenn and Sgt. Joseph F. Mack of the 776th Squadron at Ching Chuan Kang received Silver Stars for their heroism. The award was made in person by General McConnell.

Meanwhile, a pallet containing ammunition was still inside one of the other transports and detonated, while the burning fuel on the ramp flowed into the ammunition area. And fresh mortar rounds brought spectacular explosions of the stored ammunition. The explosions continued at intervals well into the night. All Air Force personnel, including the stranded aircrews, the combat control team, and a five-man aerial port mobility team survived the disaster. Lost were thirteen hundred tons of ammunition which represented the entire fire support area stockage, and seventeen thousand gallons of fuel.[31]

Sgt. Joseph F. Mack and Capt. Joseph K. Glenn (center) receive Silver Stars and Distinguished Flying Crosses from Air Force Chief of Staff Gen. John P. McConnell for saving their damaged C-130 during the battle of Dak To.

With the Dak To airstrip closed and supply stocks down to critical levels, extraordinary resupply efforts were clearly required. Airdrops were considered, and drop-rigged loads of munitions were positioned on the ramp at Cam Ranh Bay. Instead, C–130 landings were temporarily shifted to Kontum for overland haul to Dak To. Fast work by Army ordnance disposal personnel cleared the Dak To airstrip, and C–130 landings resumed on the seventeenth, shuttling ammunition in daylight hours only. Only one aircraft was permitted on the ground at a time. The C–130s landed from the east and were met on the opposite end by an aerial port team with its equipment. Offloadings were done rapidly while the engines turned; aircrews took off in minutes toward the east. Meanwhile, ammunition-carrying transports circled overhead awaiting an opportunity to land.[32]

The Dak To campaign climaxed with a vicious five-day fight on Hill 875 to the west. The airlift effort phased down rapidly thereafter. Logistics had been vital and the 1st Logistical Command reported receipt at Dak To of 12,700 tons during November, of which 5,100 arrived by air; the traffic management agency, on the other hand, indicated that the airlift system had delivered 8,600 tons of cargo in support of the operation, including deliveries to Kontum and Pleiku. General Westmoreland, in his public report on the course of the war published in 1968, concluded that "along with the gallantry and tenacity of forces, our tremendously successful air logistics operation was the key to victory."[33]

Throughout the first half of 1966, U.S. Marine forces gradually enlarged their pacification and local offensive activities, extending them well beyond the original enclaves of Da Nang and Chu Lai. Marine battalions further deployed into the demilitarized zone in midyear.[34] Logistics support for the entire I Corps area was channeled through the major sea and air port of Da Nang. Most shipments came by water, but air deliveries were made from off shore by MAC, the 315th Air Division, and the Marine KC–130 unit on Okinawa.*[35]

The isolation of the northern region from the rest of South Vietnam made vital the ability to bring in reinforcements, a role for which the speed, range, and capacity of the C–130 were well suited. A series of MACV plans developed in 1966 provided for airlifting north various combinations of airborne and airmobile brigades. Contingency Plan Oregon conceived the idea of introducing below Da Nang a new U.S. Army division and of freeing Marine units for the growing confrontation on the demilitarized zone. The 834th Air Division calculated that a four-brigade force could be lifted from southern bases to Chu Lai in four days. The effort would require forty-four additional C–130s from overseas as well as fifty percent reduction in normal in-country airlift activity.[36]

Westmoreland decided in April 1967 to deploy Task Force Oregon (later known as the 23d or Americal Division) which required an immediate shift of two brigades. A brigade of the 1st Cavalry Division deployed from nearby regions using its own resources, but the second, the 196th Light, required an airlift of more than three hundred miles. Orders were issued on April 7. Air Force tactical airlift officers worked with the 196th planning the move and setting up the Tay Ninh airstrip for the loading. A combat control team, an aerial port team, and a C–130 maintenance detachment also were moved to Tay Ninh. A tacan aid was installed along with oil-barrel flarepots to supplement the battery-powered lighting.[37]

C–130 operations began on the morning of April 9. The first 196th troops landed at Chu Lai in early afternoon. Flying time from Tay Ninh to Chu Lai was approximately ninety minutes, and with good fortune and an hour or so extension a crew could make three round trips in a twelve-hour

---

* Marine Aerial Refueler Squadron 152 shifted from Iwakuni, Japan, to Futema Marine Corps Airfield (MCAF), Okinawa, August 11, 1965.

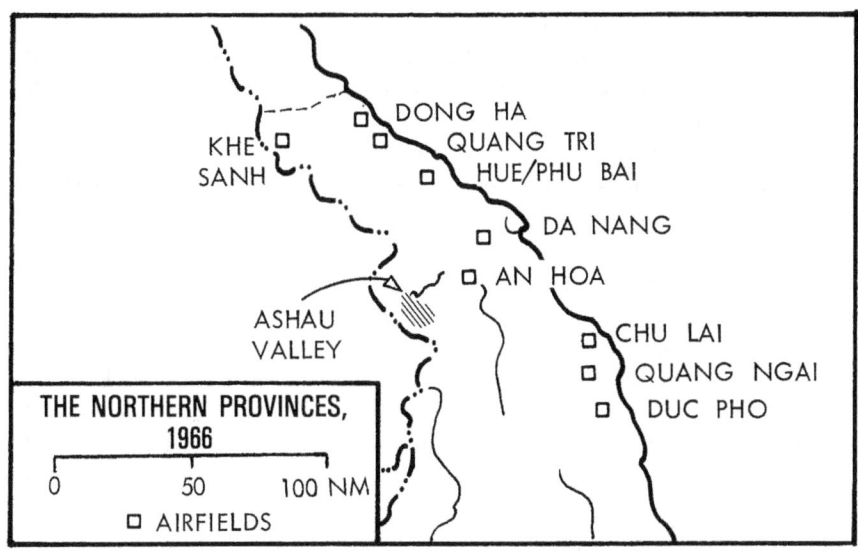

THE NORTHERN PROVINCES, 1966

day. The aircraft refueled at Chu Lai. Sixteen aircraft were kept steadily in the operation except for a six-hour disruption on April 11 caused by a communist mortar attack at Chu Lai. The movement was completed shortly after nightfall on April 14. Over thirty-five hundred troops and four thousand tons of equipment had been hauled during 350 sorties. Twenty additional C–130s and forty-four aircrews from off shore augmented the in-country force so that normal mission activity was undisturbed. A divisional logistics officer reported that the move of the 196th was accomplished very smoothly. The officer cited the "top-notch job" performed by the airlift liaison officers and aerial port personnel at Tay Ninh, and he contrasted the large number of transports available for this move with the sparse airlift support in the past. Later in April, the 130s assisted in the moves of two additional brigades to the Oregon area as well as in the shift of Marine forces northward.[38]

A month later, from off shore, C–130s staged a speedy troop reinforcement of the northernmost Marine position. On May 14, planes and aircrews from each of the island bases converged on Naha for loading. All missions then delivered cargo to Dong Ha. The air transports offloaded with engines running, holding their average ground time to twenty minutes; most flew on to Chu Lai for refueling. On the ground at Dong Ha there were an Air Force mission commander, a C–130 maintenance element, an aerial port team, and a combat control team. The thirteen hundred-mile move of twelve hundred Marines and three hundred tons of equipment was completed forty-four hours after the initial notice to the 315th Air Division. The effort demonstrated the readiness of the offshore C–130 force for emergency operations.[39]

TACTICAL AIRLIFT

If the airlift into the northern provinces was at all times a useful asset, airlift within the region was sometimes critical. Air transport supplemented the often inadequate surface modes for movements between coastal points, and formed the sole lifeline for Special Forces camps in the thinly populated interior. Available for these air transport duties were the Providers of the 311th Air Commando Squadron at Da Nang, detachments of Caribous and Army utility craft, numerous Marine helicopters, Air Force C–130s transiting the region, and several administrative transports organic to the Navy and Marine commands at Da Nang. In addition, the Marines placed a KC–130 detachment at Da Nang on June 1, 1965, rotating their men and aircraft from the parent squadron offshore. While in-country the KC–130s lifted between Da Nang and the main airfields at Chu Lai and Phu Bai (near Hue), refueled strike aircraft aloft, and made occasional airdrops to field units. The detachment usually consisted of three aircraft but was temporarily expanded to eight during the July 1966 movement to Dong Ha.[40]

Airlifters of the separate services joined in the relief efforts during the final desperate hours of the besieged Special Forces camp in the A Shau Valley, sixty miles west of Da Nang and on the main artery for enemy forces entering South Vietnam from Laos. For years C–123s and Caribous had made landings or drops several times weekly to the post and the nearby A Luoi camps, often encountering enemy ground fire and difficult weather conditions. After December 1965, North Vietnamese forces converged on the A Shau camp. Heavy mortar and infantry attacks began after midnight, March 9, 1966, and destroyed the camp's supply area. Low ceilings hampered resupply that day, but during the afternoon two Army Caribous and two C–123s penetrated the overcast to make successful munitions drops. One of the C–123s was badly damaged by gunfire but made it back to Da Nang. This resupply ended after the Caribou drops on the tenth descended into enemy hands and the camp fell to the enemy.[41]

The allied base at Khe Sanh, situated in the hill country in the northwest corner of the republic, was known well to the airlifters. The site had been in use since 1962 as a Special Forces and CIDG camp, and was well situated for launching air-and-ground surveillance operations into the Laotian panhandle. C–130s began landing occasionally in February 1966, and a three thousand-foot runway was completed later in the year. A U.S. Marine company garrisoned the airfield and patrolled the nearby area. In late April 1967 their patrols encountered dug-in communist troops on the heights five miles from the base. Two reinforcing Marine battalions landed at Khe Sanh by helicopter, and KC–130s and C–123s began regular deliveries of rations and munitions. In a four-day fight the Marines took the hill positions at a cost of a hundred men.[42]

After considerable effort, Marine engineers reopened the primitive road between Dong Ha and Khe Sanh (Highway 9), unused since 1964.

However, frequent communist demolitions and an ambush during the summer led to a command decision to rely solely on airlift into Khe Sanh. Unfortunately, summer rainfall and heavy usage by C–130s caused rapid erosion of the runway and the airstrip was closed to aircraft use in late August. The Marine KC–130s thereupon commenced daily drops of food, fuel, and munitions. Air Force C–130s meanwhile undertook the greater task of delivering construction materials for rebuilding the airstrip.[43]

Airdrops of construction materials and extractions at Khe Sanh began on September 6. Each day thereafter, three Air Force C–130s flew container-drop missions and two others delivered supplies by LAPES. Recovery of the latter was simple. An M–48 tank dragged the seven-ton packages away from the extraction zone. Pickup of the container loads was less convenient and drops were halted at two each afternoon to permit recovery before darkness when enemy parties moved onto the undefended drop zone. Caribous in the meantime continued to land at Khe Sanh, picking up used parachutes and LAPES components. Empty LAPES platforms, too large for the Caribous, were carried out by helicopters. The effort of bringing in construction materials ended three days later. Nearly all items were serviceable upon arrival, although several loads broke apart from their LAPES platforms on extraction.[44]

The forces at Khe Sanh remained entirely dependent on air resupply throughout the fall. Marine helicopters and Air Force Caribous continued landing, while Providers and Hercules made drops, primarily to deliver bunker materials, barbed wire, and metal for the erection of fortifications at the nearby Lang Vei camp. Misfortune intervened on October 15 when a C–130E crashed and burned under a low ceiling, three hundred feet short of the runway. Of the six crewmen aboard, only one survived. They had attempted to deliver a load of sandbags by the free-fall drop method, a technique used by Caribous and C–123s, and now authorized for C–130s.[45] The rebuilt Khe Sanh runway opened for Provider use on October 28 and for the C–130s a month later.[46]

The Khe Sanh airdrops were forerunners of a more extensive resupply activity the next year. But in both years their endeavors required the co-operation of Navy suppliers, Army riggers, Air Force airlifters, and the Marines on the ground at Khe Sanh. The 1967 missions introduced the Marines to the capabilities and limitations of drops and extractions, led to refinements in rigging, and gave experience to all in poor-weather operations. Finally, by sustaining the Marines at Khe Sanh and aiding airfield construction, the airlift effort set the stage for the later confrontation at this site.

The increase of allied forces along the demilitarized zone (DMZ) provided extraordinary transportation problems. The northernmost provinces were isolated from Da Nang by a spur of the Annamite Mountains, reaching to the sea below Hue. A winding railway and roadway (Highway

TACTICAL AIRLIFT

1) which traversed the hill mass at the Hai Van Pass was easily blocked by enemy action. During late 1967, truck convoys moved only five thousand tons monthly over the highway and were hampered by road deterioration due to traffic, weather, and sabotage. Rail shipments were negligible and the tracks were hopelessly vulnerable to sabotage. Most transport north from Da Nang was by water, and landing craft delivered fourteen thousand tons monthly to Phu Bai and twenty-three thousand tons to Dong Ha. Marine trucks and helicopters redistributed forward from these points to units to the north and west.[47]

Paralleling the surface lines of communication, Air Force C–123s and C–130s in late 1967 delivered twelve hundred tons to Phu Bai and twenty-two hundred tons to Dong Ha monthly. Communist artillery made a regular target of the Dong Ha base, and airlifters became acquainted with the waterlogged slit trenches and sandbagged shelters beside the offloading ramp. A notice at Da Nang advised pilots to shut down engines while offloading at Dong Ha so that the sound of incoming rounds could be heard. The destruction of vast fuel and ammunition supplies on September 4 confirmed the need for a second air-field along the demilitarized zone, preferably a site outside of enemy artillery range. General Westmoreland in the same evening ordered MACV to find a site near Quang Tri city, suitable for completion of a runway before the onset of the winter monsoon. Construction of the new base began in mid-September. The effort was given "unconditional first priority" in construction materials, and the first Hercules landed on October 23. The Dong Ha ammunition supply facility moved to the new site promptly and both airfields were thereafter used regularly by the transports. Airlift became the primary means for movements of passengers and patients to and from Dong Ha, Quang Tri, and Phu Bai, and became absolutely vital for munitions shipments during the crisis early in the following year.[48]

The 1967 campaigns against Dak To and Khe Sanh suggested that the communists were trying to draw American forces away from the populated regions. The October attacks against the town of Loc Ninh and the nearby CIDG camp fit into the same pattern. The allies airlifted men and materiel into the battle area. Congestion among Hercules transports and helicopters was heavy, and orbiting aircraft were at times forced to depart without landing. Starting with the end of October, the C–130s flew 225 sorties in support of the battle, lifting reinforcements and over three thousand tons of cargo. A similar relief and resupply airlift went into the improved strip at Bu Dop northeast of Loc Ninh.[49]

General Westmoreland planned to concentrate his winter offensive operations in the Saigon plain, taking advantage of that region's characteristic dry season. For the December Operation Yellowstone a thirty-day air supply effort had been planned for Katum. But priority airlift requirements elsewhere forced the intermittent use of road supply convoys, which occasioned unfair criticisms by Army logisticians about the undependability of airlift. Hercules aircrews landing at Katum found dense jungle vegetation growing close to the airstrip on all sides, and an air of insecurity took strength from the rumor that communist-dug tunnels were discovered under the runway.[50] The veracity of this is uncertain. Meanwhile, the 1st Brigade of the 101st Airborne Division returned by C–130 from an expedition to the northern provinces, moving first to Bao Loc and then to Song Be. The Bao Loc field was difficult for pilots to land on because of its severely humped runway slope and the sharp drop off at the western approach end. Other units of the 101st Airborne Division joined the 1st Brigade and they arrived at Bien Hoa in December by strategic airlift from Kentucky.[51]

Westmoreland's offensive plans were disrupted by communist pressure in the far north. The commandant of the Marine Corps addressed President Johnson by memorandum on September 22 advising that the situation in the demilitarized zone was one of "deteriorating weather and increasing enemy pressure." A senior Marine officer in the Pacific warned that unless the casualties due to enemy shelling were curbed matters would "resound all the way back to Dubuque."[52] During January 1968 the entire 1st Cavalry Division shifted to the Hue region, supported by eight hundred Air Force transport sorties. Also moving northward was the 2d Brigade of the 101st, and it was hauled primarily by C–130 from Cu Chi to Phu Bai and to the new Quang Tri strip.[53]

In assessing the course of the war at the end of 1967, the MACV staff calculated that the enemy's casualties were now exceeding his rate of infiltration and recruitment. The staff estimated that the communists could employ large forces only at the edges of their sanctuaries and that future allied pacification programs would therefore be successful. Westmoreland found the enemy "increasingly resorting to desperation tactics in attempting to achieve military/psychological victory." Meeting with the Joint Chiefs in November, he estimated that continued allied military pressure should permit a reduction in American involvement in two years or less. Less encouraging was the evidence in late January 1968 that communist main forces were infiltrating toward Saigon, Hue, Da Nang, and the provincial capitals. This was apparently a sequel to the enemy's attempts to draw allied forces to the border areas.[54]

Although it may not have seemed so to the overworked men, the airlift system was well prepared to meet future tests. Mission control of the airlift force was close but flexible and the aerial port system was well developed. Transport crews knew Vietnam and were familiar with the growing complex of airfields available to the C-130. Airdrop and extraction methods had been improved and rigging capabilities strengthened. On November 29, 1967, Brig. Gen. Burl W. McLaughlin, after a succession of airlift assignments including wing and air division commands in TAC, arrived in Vietnam to assume command of the 834th Air Division.[55] The instruments of airlift fashioned by Moore and his predecessors thus passed into the experienced hands of McLaughlin.

XII. The Khe Sanh Campaign

   Airlift made possible the allied victory of Khe Sanh in 1968. For eleven weeks early in the year, the defenders of this post were exclusively resupplied by air and withstood the attacks of four North Vietnamese regiments. The campaign bore comparison with the classic combat airlifts of Stalingrad, Burma, and Dien Bien Phu. The success at Khe Sanh reflected the application of lessons drawn from past campaigns, the improved technology for tactical airlift now at hand, and the absolute allied air superiority. The outcome of the struggle was a triumph of tactical defense used in intelligent combination with heavy firepower and air lines of communication.
   Fixed-wing transports and helicopters of the Air Force and Marines joined in the air resupply. Favoring the airlift was the close proximity of Khe Sanh to the coastal bases; the site was only thirty minutes by air from Da Nang. The resupply could thus be handled by a small number of transports, generally fewer than ten percent of the in-country airlift force. For the assigned aircrews, however, the missions to Khe Sanh were supreme tests of airmanship. Two factors gave Khe Sanh special significance for the airlifters—weather conditions that often approached the impossible, and the enemy's determined and resourceful use of firepower. Crucial was the ability of the airlifters to perform all-weather paradrops which had been a major weakness of air transport forces. The Common Service Airlift System met the situation primarily by adapting old techniques and hardware in new and imaginative ways.
   The allies became aware of the gathering enemy concentration about Khe Sanh in mid-December 1967. North Vietnamese units, which in the past had moved past the post en route southward without stopping, now began to take up positions in the hills and forests to the north and southwest of the airstrip. Perhaps fifteen thousand combat troops, well-camouflaged and resupplied by trucks through Laos, were present. Communist reconnaissance and probes about the airstrip's perimeter during January left little doubt that a major confrontation was at hand.[1]
   The terrain about Khe Sanh was broken and covered by lush forests or tall elephant grass. Overlooking the airstrip from all directions was a series of mountain peaks, averaging in height about fifteen hundred feet above airstrip elevation and rising to four thousand feet to the north. Overland communications had been severed since mid-1967 because eight bridges were washed out or otherwise destroyed. Engineers estimated that they would need fourteen days to reopen the road assuming no interference from the enemy. Climatological data at MACV indicated that cloud ceil-

TACTICAL AIRLIFT

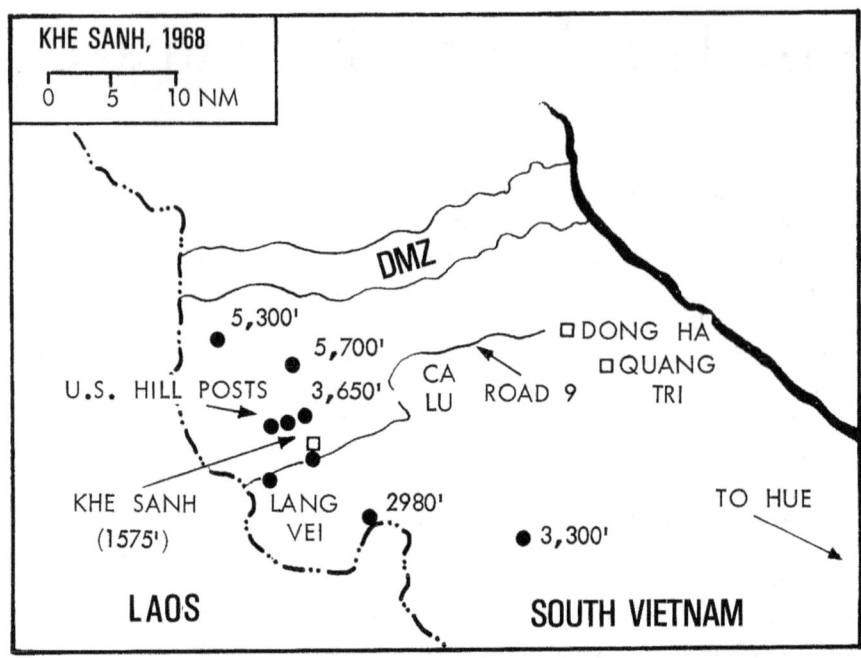

ings below one thousand feet and visibility of less than two and a half miles could be expected at Khe Sanh on more than half of the mornings from November through April; during the same months, however, ceilings usually improved to about three thousand feet in early afternoon.[2]

The nature of the enemy buildup and the geographic situation suggested comparisons with the earlier Dien Bien Phu battle. Both campaigns began at the start of the winter wet season. Both garrisons depended entirely upon air resupply although the shorter distance to Khe Sanh made overland reinforcement and resupply a possibility. Study groups at MACV and Joint Chiefs of Staff judged that the enemy about Khe Sanh would try to reenact the full Dien Bien Phu scenario. A historian at MACV briefed Westmoreland on the 1954 campaign noting that both at Dien Bien Phu, and thus far at Khe Sanh, the defenders had failed "to completely suppress antiaircraft fire which could take a heavy toll of cargo aircraft and helicopters." Westmoreland firmly stood by his decision to hold Khe Sanh, supported in his thinking by the senior Marine officer in Vietnam and by the Joint Chiefs. Offensive relief operations, in Westmoreland's judgment, could safely await favorable weather in the spring.[3]

In early January there were two infantry battalions and an artillery battalion, all from 26th Marine Regiment, at Khe Sanh. Air Force C–130s lifted in a third infantry battalion on the sixteenth.[4]

On January 19 stocks of rations, fuel, and munitions on hand at Khe Sanh were sufficient to meet the consumption demands for thirty days.

Much of the ammunition was dispersed around the artillery firing positions, and over one thousand tons were stored near the east end of the runway in the larger of two munitions dumps. The proposed introduction of a fourth infantry battalion raised new supply questions. The MACV logistics chief informed General Westmoreland on the twentieth that the 185-ton daily supply requirement could be accomplished by fifteen C–130 sorties and that an additional seventy-five sorties were needed if stocks were to be built up to a thirty-five-day level for the expanded force. Since fixed-wing transports had been averaging fifteen landings daily at Khe Sanh, mainly by employing three C–130s in back-and-forth shuttles from Da Nang, an airlift effort of this magnitude appeared feasible.[5]

C–123s and C–130s had sustained smaller allied forces at Khe Sanh in the past. Among the airlifters the site's runway was well known for its approach-and-landing difficulties. Further, the runway sat on an eight hundred-foot rise. Pilots landing from the east had trouble judging heights since ground references were absent. And unpredictable wind patterns often caused the aircraft to sink markedly just before touching down. A burnt-out shell of a crashed C–130 was a constant reminder of the criticality of the approach. The difficulty of making a perfect descent resulted in frequent hard landings and severe use of brakes, thus contributing to the periodic deterioration of the runway's surface.[6]

The hitherto sporadic communist mortar, rocket, and artillery fire against the airstrip and hill positions increased to two hundred rounds on January 19. Continued shelling the next day damaged the fuselage and fuel system of a C–130A. At dawn on the twenty-first, shells detonated the main ammunition dump. Fires and intermittent explosions continued throughout the day, and fourteen hundred tons of munitions, nearly the entire stock of the dump, were destroyed. Also, during the course of the day, communist troops constructed bunkers and foxholes in the terrain between the base and the outlying hills, and dispersed the local defenders of Khe Sanh village.[7]

The loss of the ammunition dump prompted an immediate request for "tactical emergency" air resupply. The 311th Squadron detachment at Da Nang was advised of the mission requirement in late afternoon of the twenty-first. Six C–123s were diverted from other air routes and loaded with ammunition at Da Nang. They arrived at Khe Sanh at twilight, and the base was found shrouded by low clouds. Two thousand feet of the airstrip were unusable, and debris from the day's shelling littered the remainder. Adding to the difficulties was the fact that the runway lights had been knocked out earlier in the day. But, aided by the light of flares fired from Marine artillery, all six aircraft landed successfully. Offloading was rapid while shelling and explosions continued in the munitions area. Meanwhile, Marine helicopters completed their cargo deliveries during the day. No C–130s were scheduled in this day.

Beyond the leveled ammunition dump (foreground), a C–123 touches down on the Khe Sanh runway, January 21, 1968.

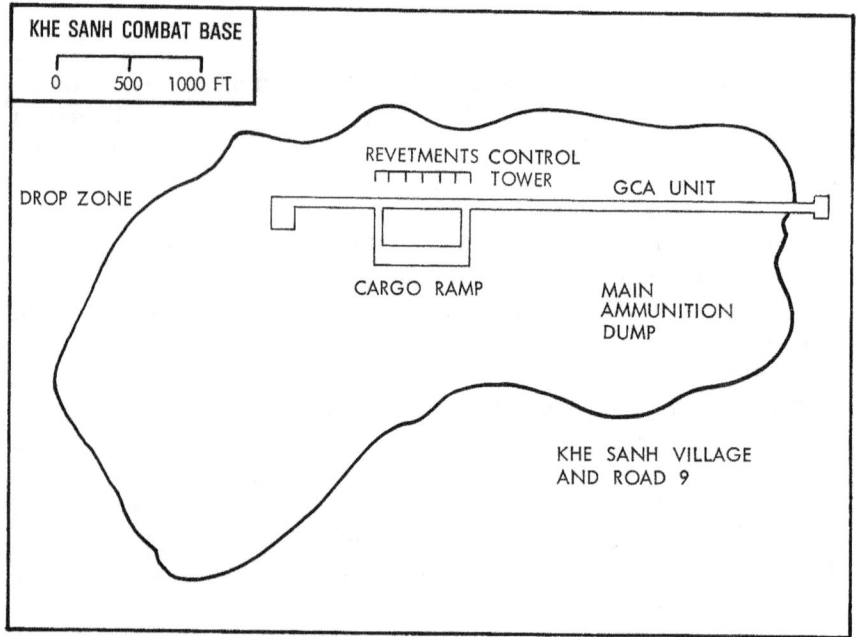

C-123 landings continued into the next day as the garrison reorganized from the previous day's ordeal. These transports brought in over eighty-eight tons of ammunition and other supplies from Da Nang and airlifted civilian refugees on their return flights. The helicopters, meanwhile, hauled in over five hundred members of a fourth Marine infantry battalion. C-130s resumed landing on the twenty-third. But because of the heavy shelling only two aircraft were allowed on the ground simultaneously, and other planes orbited to the east to await their turn at penetrating the cloud cover. Darkness finally halted the landings after a Hercules pulled up after mistakenly lining up its landing approach on the lights of a parked C-130 on the loading ramp.[8]

For the next eight days Air Force deliveries to Khe Sanh averaged 250 tons per day. The C-130s averaged eighteen landings daily in the same period. On the other hand, Caribous and C-123s each averaged two since their activity was held down to permit fullest utilization of the high-payload C-130s. The Caribous ceased even this limited role after the end of the month. The Air Force C-130s delivered on the twenty-seventh a single-day high of 310 tons for the entire campaign. Also, three sorties on that day transported a Vietnamese ranger battalion from Da Nang. Marine KC-130s and helicopters continued to land at Khe Sanh. Statistics on their contributions are fragmentary, but on at least four days helicopters lifted in more than twenty tons, principally hauling from Dong Ha. The CH-46s mainly worked between the Khe Sanh main base and the hill positions, resupplying the outposts and shifting personnel. For the entire month of January, according to Marine statistics, the C-123s and C-130s hauled thirty-six hundred tons into Khe Sanh, and their own CH-53s carried in 565 tons. Favoring the airlifted effort had been the unseasonably good weather, marred only by early-morning ground fog. An important asset at the site was the Marine ground controlled approach unit which made possible landings in ceilings as low as five hundred feet and visibilities down to two miles.[9]

But less auspicious was the enemy's obvious presence on all sides of the base and his growing capability to attack air communications by ground fire. From positions along the normal landing approach east of the airstrip, small communist units set up automatic weapons and directed antiaircraft fire at the descending transports. The sound of their firing served to inform personnel on the ground at Khe Sanh that another transport was inbound. Enemy fire ripped through the fuselage of a C-130 on the twenty-fifth, but the crew managed a safe landing. Crewmen attempted to pinpoint the location of the communist firing positions for F-4 strike aircraft. Transport crews used passive measures, staying in protective clouds as much as possible, and flew steep, tight patterns. Forward air controllers sometimes coordinated fighter strikes to coincide with transport approaches. Many airlifters experienced chilling moments, watching tracers interlacing their flight path into Khe Sanh.[10]

Even more serious was the persistent communist shelling of the airstrip. This typically began while transports were on the ground, apparently an attempt to destroy the aircraft. Craters and debris occasionally forced the temporary closure of the runway. Generally, mortar fire came from within three thousand yards of the base perimeter; the heavier rocket and artillery weapons were dug in well to the west, which was convenient to the communist lines of supply. The Americans tried to silence the shellings with artillery and air strikes, and after firing only a few rounds they forced the communist teams to seek cover. Air transport crews minimized their time on the ground by "speed offloading." This was accomplished by unlocking the dual rails while taxiing gently forward; the loaded pallets thereupon rolled rearward and down the rear ramp. The procedure worked well except that pallets sometimes toppled onto their sides causing extra trouble for forklift operators. C–123 crews were able to reduce their exposure by turning off the runway as quickly as possible and taxiing directly into the parking ramp. The C–130s ordinarily had to roll to the west end for turnaround.[11]

The daily Khe Sanh supply totals were scrutinized in the White House and the information was of direct concern to the President. The airlift control center on February 4 advised its staff that the airlift effort "in the I Corps area, and particularly the Khe Sanh Air Base area, is vital to the U.S. national interest." Flight requirements thus were to be met by 120 percent overscheduling, and missions were not to be diverted outside the region without special authority. Further, the order specified that those C–130s flying north to work out of Da Nang were not to be used for stops at intermediate points. All missions to Khe Sanh carried an "Emergency Resupply" priority.[12]

Despite these decisions, scheduled deliveries into Khe Sanh declined sharply in the first weeks of February. One explanation was poor weather, which prevented landings about forty percent of the time. Warm moist air tended to rise from the valley to the east, causing morning and evening ground fog over the airstrip. Conditions remained overcast around the clock and visibility was seldom better than four miles. Increased enemy shelling also slowed deliveries. Over two hundred rounds impacted on the fourth, fifth, and sixth, respectively, increasing to six hundred rounds on the eighth. The runway was closed for repairs three times during the week. The aboveground activities at Khe Sanh halted while a Provider or Hercules was on the ground in the realization that the transports were "mortar magnets." Several aircraft were damaged by automatic-weapons fire while on the runway. A more serious setback was the destruction of the ground controlled approach unit on February 7. With the equipment inoperable, C–130 landings (which had averaged eleven daily since the first of the month) decreased to three on the ninth and to six on the following day. The Marines reported that total resupply was down to thirty-two and fifty-three tons on these respective dates. Concern moreover deepened at Khe Sanh with the fall of the outlying Lang Vei camp to a communist tank and infantry assault on February 7.[13]

During the siege of Khe Sanh, two notable incidents occurred to demonstrate the valorous conduct of airlifter crews. On February 5 a Tuy Hoa-based C–130E landed at Khe Sanh with ammunition aboard. The aircraft commander, Lt. Col. Howard M. Dallman, was an experienced pilot who was admired for his personal qualities by the younger officers serving under him. Upon landing, his aircraft came under heavy machine-gun fire which ignited some wooden ammunition boxes in the cargo compartment. Flames completely spread across the interior of the plane. While the crew fought the fire with hand extinguishers, Dallman backed the aircraft to the end of the runway thus minimizing possible damage to the base from a detonation. The crew managed to put the fire out but the stationary aircraft received further hits, several of which destroyed a main landing-gear tire. The crew quickly unloaded the ammunition and taxied to the parking ramp for tire change. A new tire was installed using an extemporized jacking rig while suppressive air strikes slowed but did not halt the mortar fire. A round detonated directly in front of the plane, showering it with debris and knocking out one engine. While Dallman prepared the aircraft for a three-engine takeoff, the copilot succeeded in restarting the damaged engine. Although low on fuel and still receiving fresh hits, the crew managed a successful takeoff. Dallman received the Air Force Cross for his role in the incident, the highest award thus far to an airlifter in Vietnam.[14]

Another Tuy Hoa Hercules C–130E also received mortar damage after landing on February 11. Two passengers were killed and the loadmaster was seriously injured. The aircrew, assisted by two members of an Air Force detachment at Khe Sanh, fought the fire with hand extinguishers. One airman was temporarily blinded by the chemicals. With the blaze out, the plane still remained utterly unflyable. Its tires were blown, the engines were damaged by shrapnel, and the hydraulic systems were badly damaged. The aircrew, joined by a repairman from Da Nang, went to work. One mechanic worked out on the tail assembly in darkness using only a flashlight. On the second day, another mortar round hit the aircraft starting a new fire. After two days on the ground, the battered Hercules lifted off. Ground crewmen at Da Nang afterwards added up over 242 bullet and shrapnel holes, "before they stopped counting." The aircraft's crew, commanded by Capt. Edwin Jenks, was nominated for Silver Stars.[15]

No Air Force transports were destroyed in more than a hundred landings during the first eleven days of February. On the other hand, disaster came on February 10 to a Marine KC–130 while it attempted a

TACTICAL AIRLIFT

landing with a load of fuel bladders. Ground fire penetrated the cockpit and cargo compartment as the plane descended on final approach. One of the fuel bags spilled its contents and a fire erupted in the rear. Several explosions occurred during the landing roll, and, as the aircraft came to a stop well down the runway, it became engulfed in flames. Rescuers saved several crewmen but two died as well as four passengers.[16]

During late January and the first weeks of February, alternative delivery methods had come under consideration. MACV alerted commands that Caribous might be utilized at Khe Sanh if the runway became unusable by the heavier transports. A proposal by the airlift control center and the Seventh Air Force operations staff to start Hercules night landings at Khe Sanh was overruled by the Marine base commander. Airdrops remained an obvious alternative. Although the Seventh Air Force indicated that drops were feasible, the difficult weather at the site made questionable a major drop effort using the customary visual methods. A possible solution lay in blind drops guided by the Marine ground radars at the camp or from Dong Ha. The method had been developed the previous year but it remained unproven and appeared to lack the required accuracy.[17]

The idea of using Marine ground controlled approach at Khe Sanh for guiding drops was original and this equipment had never before been tried for this purpose. The method was suggested by two experienced airlifters, Majs. Myles A. Rohrlick and Henry B. Van Gieson III, of the 834th Air Division. Rohrlick had first raised the idea soon after reporting to the division in late 1967, and the following January he received permission to arrange test drops at Khe Sanh. Several Hercules test missions were attempted in good weather. On February 4 the airlift control center advised the Marines that ground controlled drops could provide satisfactory accuracy and reliability. Meanwhile, the 834th developed similar procedures for C–123 drops using ground controlled approach equipment. Basically, navigators would adjust the cargo release point according to the prevailing winds and by stopwatch timing from a precise ground controlled fix one-half mile from the end of the runway.[18]

C–130 landings at Khe Sanh halted on February 12 by order of the Seventh Air Force. Thereafter landings by C–123s increased. In the five days starting with the twelfth, they made fifty-three landings and delivered a very creditable but inadequate daily average of forty-eight tons. Simultaneously, McLaughlin visited the III Marine Amphibious Force (III MAF) staff at Da Nang, and they reached a decision to resupply Khe Sanh using both C–123s and C–130s. Further, airlandings by the Providers were to continue, backed up as necessary by Caribous, the latter being used only for the delivery of passengers and nondroppable cargo and for medical evacuations. For bulk tonnage deliveries of ammunition, rations, and construction materials, C–130 container delivery and the low-altitude parachute extraction were to be the primary systems. Responding to an inquiry from Seventh Air Force four days later, the III MAF reaffirmed a daily supply requirement at Khe Sanh of 235 tons (18 tons for day-to-day consumption and the remainder for stock buildup for the remainder of the month). This amount, which was equivalent to sixteen C–130 loads, remained a loosely applied daily goal for the duration of the siege.[19]

The C–130 container drops, which began on February 13, coincided with the completion of repairs to the Khe Sanh ground controlled approach facility. The drop zone was situated to the west, just outside the main perimeter of the camp, in deference to the Marines' wish to avoid the complete closing of the airstrip during drops or injury to personnel and equipment from descending loads. The small size of the drop zone (three hundred square yards) made accuracy critical, especially in the final seconds of flight.

The new procedures called for the aircraft to enter the ground controlled approach pattern at several thousands of feet altitude. The aircrew then flew the headings and altitudes provided by the ground control operators. Upon reaching a drop altitude during the descent the pilot leveled off and continued to fly the furnished headings. When exactly over the runway threshold the navigator started his doppler computer-tracker, which commenced measuring actual movement over the ground. The pilot thereafter flew heading information from the doppler steering indicator, which compensated for measured flight-level wind and unintended variations in steering. The navigator computed time and distance to the exact release point, measuring by stopwatch and doppler from the ground controlled fix. Two drops were performed on the thirteenth while the aircrews remained slightly below the cloud overcast in order to make visual identification of the drop zone. In debriefings that followed they reported that blind drops were entirely feasible. Over the next two days, twelve more ground-guided drops were made during marginal visual conditions. Acceptance of the system was immediate; indeed it seemed that clouds were now an advantage in protecting aircrews from enemy fire.[20]

The new method verified the system's usefulness. During adverse weather conditions on the sixteenth, twelve container-drop sorties were scheduled for the day. The first crews arrived to find Khe Sanh obscured. They were, however, cleared by a senior officer from the 834th, who was aboard one of the aircraft to drop blind. The aircraft entered the ground controlled pattern but coordination was ragged since some of the aircrews had not flown in the earlier trials. At length, six loads were released and impacted on the average sixty yards from the desired point. After a midday break to allow recovery of loads on the ground, the aircrews made two more successful drops. Improved weather during midafternoon permitted five Provider landings (although thirteen had been scheduled) while four C–130 LAPES deliveries were performed. For the day the airlift system delivered 169 tons. Bad weather during the next few days totally prevented landings and the use of other delivery systems but, when deliveries resumed on the seventeenth, eight container deliveries were accomplished. Ten deliveries were made on the tenth.[21]

The vulnerability of the ground controlled system was brought home on the nineteenth when enemy shells damaged the Marine electronic unit and killed three men. Weather permitted a few visual drops by lining up on the camp's tacan station. The next day, another radar system at Khe Sanh was tried for positioning drop aircraft above the runway's threshold. The first load landed two thousand yards beyond the intended point, apparently because of inaccurate radar information. The second was successful, however, prompting the mission coordinator at Da Nang to launch the remaining supply aircraft. Eight other Hercules dropped their loads accurately.[22]

The weather improved sufficiently on the twentieth to permit C-123 landings. These averaged three daily to the end of the month, generally receiving heavy fire while over Khe Sanh. Air Force personnel at Da Nang meantime assured that only nondroppable cargo was carried by the 123s. Marine KC-130s also made occasional landings up to the twenty-second of February; enemy fire damaged two of these aircraft on that date. Air Force C-130s resumed landings four days later and of the two aircraft landing on that day one received fifty-seven hits and departed without offloading its cargo. A total of fifteen C-130s landed during the last four days of the month whereupon their landings again ceased for the duration of the siege. The Air Force mission commander at Khe Sanh predicted that continued landings would soon result in loss of a transport. Marine officers appreciated the landings because of their benefits to troop morale and the simplified cargo handling. Starting on the twenty-fifth, C-123s joined in the airdrops but they averaged three-ton payloads compared with an average of fourteen tons for the C-130s. This disadvantage discouraged the wider use of the C-123s.[23]

Supply levels held up satisfactorily at Khe Sanh; stockage on February 23 equated to sixteen days for rations and the principal ammunition types. More than half of the ammunition was stored at the firing positions and the remainder was placed inside bulldozed trenches twelve feet deep. Stocks of jet fuel appeared low (down to a one-day reserve on the twenty-sixth) but this was not critical since helicopters now refueled almost exclusively at Dong Ha, having been forced from the Khe Sanh revetments by the continuous shelling. With improved weather permitting C-130 deliveries above two hundred tons during the last three days of the month, munitions and fuel stockage improved.[24]

Khe Sanh continued to receive heavy fire, and daily two or three transports received some kind of damage, usually while on the ground during loading. Aircraft employing drop and LAPES were not immune to ground fire. Now enemy trenches appeared near the perimeter, the closest being thirty-five yards away. Despite these omens the airlifters took confidence in the resolution of their most pressing problem of having converted the difficult weather from an adversary to a friend.[25]

Air Force personnel stationed at Khe Sanh included aerial port, combat control, aeromedical evacuation, weather observation, and aircraft maintenance teams. These men shared the miseries of the Marine garrison enduring dirt, rats, chill, and shelling. Tasks which normally took one hour often became all-day projects in the primitive and dangerous environment at the camp. Air Force personnel served two-week tours at Khe Sanh. Most were enlisted men whose personal courage and resourcefulness earned unfailing praise from their officers.[26]

A mission commander represented the 834th Air Division at Khe Sanh. He supervised the Air Force detachment and acted as coordinator between the Common Service Airlift System and the Marines. Generally he was a lieutenant colonel and also a tactical airlift pilot on temporary assignment from his squadron. He lived in his "office"—a bunker fashioned by Air Force personnel using scrounged materials—and moved about the base in a much damaged jeep. Each officer was required to submit a detailed report to the 834th upon the conclusion of his tour at Khe Sanh.[27]

The aerial port mobility team was drawn from the 8th and 15th Aerial Port Squadrons. They worked mainly with the airlanded aircraft assisting in offloading, clearing loads from the ramp, loading casualties, preparing pallets for backhaul, and helping load and unload supply helicopters. Exposure to enemy fire was common since shelling often coincided with the presence on the ground of the transports. Shrapnel caused repeated damage to their equipment. Rough usage further contributed to the breakdowns of forklifts. On occasions all forklifts were out of commission. This prompted a suggestion that a forklift mechanic and spare parts be kept at Khe Sanh. A special problem was the storage of empty pallets awaiting return to the main air bases. The pallets made excellent bunker roofs and too often disappeared from the flight line despite the presence of a Marine guard.[28]

Several aircraft mechanics at Khe Sanh handled the frequent routine tire changes, but for more complex tasks repair teams with the appropriate equipment flew in from Da Nang. Air Force aeromedics prepared casualties for fixed-wing evacuation. Generally litters were simply placed on the aircraft floor thus minimizing ground time. The air transports lifted out a total of 306 patients, 138 of them litter cases.[29]

The role of the combat control team varied. They guided aircrews while taxiing and assisted the Marine control tower in directing air traffic. Other team members worked in the drop zone laying out panel markers and placing smoke signals to assist incoming aircrews.[30]

The decision to curtail landings at Khe Sanh probably prevented the loss of several aircraft and their crews. Load recovery within the drop zone, however, presented serious problems, constituting a major factor limiting the volume of resupply. Typically, five or six planes made drops during morning raids, releasing their loads at intervals of about twenty-five minutes each. Drops thereupon ceased for several hours while the cargo was picked up. Airdrops resumed in the afternoon and continued until, upon the judgment of a Marine "shore party" officer, they were halted. Since the drop zone was abandoned to the enemy each night, it was important to assure that all loads had been retrieved before dark. Each morning, the Marines swept the drop zone for fresh communist mines and snipers.

The work of retrieval was often harassed by communist shelling and recoilless rifle fire. The drop zone soon gained the reputation as the most dangerous place at Khe Sanh. Because of forklift breakdowns in the rough ground, cargo was sometimes recovered by disassembling the containers on the spot and loading individual boxes of ammunition or rations into trucks. An accurately delivered container required about forty-five minutes to recover; pallets landing in nearby trees or minefields added hours to the effort. Almost daily, loaded transports at Da Nang were canceled while still on the ground when the Marines declared their recovery capability saturated. On a number of occasions, C–130s carried loads back to Da Nang without dropping. Each afternoon, Air Force personnel at Khe Sanh found themselves urging the Marine drop-zone officer to permit a few more airdrops. And upon prodding from the Seventh Air Force, the Marines in late February asserted that efforts were being made to improve load recovery, but they remained unwilling to establish a drop zone inside the perimeter.[31]

The Marines were also responsible for recovering parachutes and rigging materials from the drop zone. Of approximately fifteen hundred chutes retrieved after a month's drops, sixty percent were found suitable for reuse after repairs. The in-country stocks of parachutes and rigging remained sufficient during this stand.[32]

At Da Nang, Army riggers worked in a tent area surrounded by earthworks. Rigged loads were moved to the aerial port ramp and kept ready for loading. Aircraft could be refueled and reloaded for Khe Sanh in forty minutes. But ramp congestion remained a problem, and until very late in the Khe Sanh campaign drop aircraft shared the crowded south ramp with other C–130s. As one means of reducing congestion, planes requiring only refueling were directed to Chu Lai. Another helpful measure was the use of Cam Ranh Bay and Bien Hoa as loading points for some of the container-drop missions. Missions loading at the southern points landed at Da Nang for a second container load before returning to their home base after the second drop.[33]

The cruel weather of February abated by the following month. Allied strike aircraft, now unrestricted by cloud cover, pounded the communist trenches and firing positions. Their heavy firepower promised an early end to the campaign, but for the airlifters the improved weather meant an end to the protective overcast which had shielded them from communist gunners.

Three C–123s went down in early March. Mortar fragments claimed one aircraft during lift-off at Khe Sanh on March 1. With one engine out, the pilot forced his plane to the ground to avoid an uncontrolled crash. Communist mortars completed its destruction. All on board survived, although six men were injured. Five days later, an inbound 123 received ground fire several miles to the east, spiraled to the ground, and exploded. The crew had been unable to use evasive tactics customary to Khe Sanh. Ordinarily, crews stayed at a safe altitude as long as possible, descending quickly and intercepting the standard landing slope in the final thirty seconds. In this incident, the crew had broken off its first landing attempt to avoid an unannounced Vietnamese Air Force light aircraft. The C–123 was hit shortly thereafter, while maneuvering at low altitude. The tragedy cost the lives of all forty-nine on board. Later the same afternoon, mortar fire damaged the empennage of a taxiing C–123 necessitating major repair to the aircraft; further shelling totally destroyed the plane the next day. The three destroyed aircraft belonged to the 311th Squadron. The squadron ready room at Da Nang acquired a grim atmosphere as crews waited for the next Khe Sanh run. On March 7, to equalize the risks, the four squadrons of the 315th Wing contributed planes and crews to the Da Nang detachment. The wing commander meanwhile gained assurances that C–123 loads would consist only of medicines, sensitive fuzes, and other items too fragile for airdrops.[34]

The disappearance of protective clouds forced new arrangements for coordinated fire suppression. The mission coordinator at Khe Sanh arranged locally for a forward air controller to circle east of the runway whenever a transport approached. He reported that enemy fire noticeably decreased whenever this tactic was employed. Apparently reacting to hits on two Hercules and the C–123 losses on March 6, the Seventh Air Force on the same day directed that forward air control and fighter aircraft should furnish escort for all transports if the weather permitted. Fighters scheduled specifically for this purpose were armed with appropriate ordnance. The directive further spelled out details of coordination. Rendezvous was to be to the east of Khe Sanh and during the run-in fighters were to fly racetrack patterns paralleling the transport flightpath. Fragmentation and machinegun ordnance was to be judiciously expended when the transports were within fifteen hundred feet of the ground. Finally, forward air controllers were to guide fighters against any known gun positions. Airlift crews reported the next day that the fighter efforts were

U.S. Army and Air Force riggers load cargo on a C–123 for paradrop to troops at Khe Sanh, March 6, 1968.

Maj. Jimmy Dennis pilots a C–130 to the paradrop zone at Khe Sanh, March 1968.

Air Force and Navy jets put down a line of defensive fire to protect a C–130 departing from Khe Sanh. Enemy forces were spotted along the mountainside near the base.

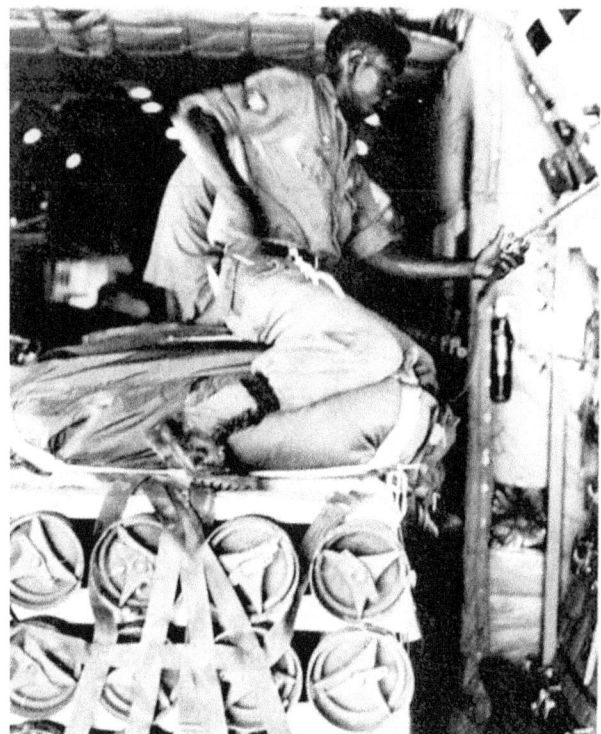

An Army rigger aboard a USAF C-130 attaches a static line to a hook-up cable, getting ready for a cargo drop to the Marines under siege, March 6, 1968.

Supplies are dropped into the beleaguered outpost of Khe Sanh.

Marine crews move quickly to recover cargo dropped by transport aircraft from Da Nang, March 1968.

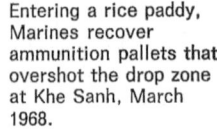

Entering a rice paddy, Marines recover ammunition pallets that overshot the drop zone at Khe Sanh, March 1968.

The trailing hook of the C–130 cargo load catches on the arresting cable stretched across the Khe Sanh runway. The technique, called the Ground Proximity Extraction System, was used successfully at Khe Sanh to decrease the aircrafts' exposure to enemy fire and ensure accurate cargo deliveries.

"excellent." Also tested were smoke screens laid down by fighters on either side of the run-in path. Transport crews agreed that the tactic was worthwhile, although the smoke sometimes made it difficult to sight the drop zone. For the remainder of the siege the effects of enemy ground fire receded as a result of intelligent use of fighter escort, smoke, cloud cover, and evasive tactics.[35]

During the last stages of the Khe Sanh stand, LAPES missions were limited by shortages of rigging items. In-country stocks became temporarily exhausted on March 3 and efforts were made to recover used components. Unfortunately, ten sets of LAPES electrical components awaiting airlift out of Khe Sanh (half the in-country supply) were destroyed in a mortar attack on March 8. The following day, the Marines requested tests of C–130 modular platform drops as a substitute for delivering outsize items. The 834th Air Division rejected the idea because of the limited size of the drop zone, and instead pressed for Army procurement of additional LAPES units. Although some parachute extraction equipment arrived from the offshore 315th Air Division, LAPES missions were seldom more than two in number daily.[36]

With little protection from communist shells, Marine teams broke down the eight-ton LAPES loads at the west end of the runway. Shrapnel littered the area, damaging trucks and forklifts. The LAPES sleds themselves proved destructive to the planking. Two events confirmed the hazards of receiving the heavy and fast-moving LAPES platforms. On February 21 a LAPES C–130 inadvertently hit the ground tearing off its rear ramp. The load extracted early and broke apart, killing one man and injuring another. Three weeks later, a load platform extracted without its deceleration parachute. The mass careened beyond the end of the runway hitting a bunker and killing a man. This event followed by one week a misdirected container drop wherein several bundles landed on bunkers and caused five casualties. The LAPES deliveries, however, were clearly more dangerous and at least three subsequent extractions took place without parachute braking, although there were no further serious injuries.[37]

An alternative to LAPES was the ground proximity extraction system developed in the early 1960s. When discontinued in mid-decade, GPES was determined to be inferior to LAPES because of the need to preposition heavy ground equipment. The ground proximity extraction system seemed well suited for Khe Sanh. The loads came to rest at an exact spot thus simplifying recovery, reducing damage to surfacing, and practically eliminating the chance of an uncontrolled runaway. Operations officers of the 834th Air Division proposed to PACAF on March 5 that GPES ground arresting gear stored in the United States be moved to Vietnam. By midmonth nine sets were airlifted to Vietnam. At Khe Sanh a combat control team detachment, assisted by Marines and naval engineer personnel, installed the arresting cable and twister equipment across the final one thousand feet of runway. Meanwhile, the 374th Wing aircrews flew practice GPES missions in Okinawa.

The first ground proximity extraction system combat delivery took place at Khe Sanh on March 30, performed by a crew of the 374th Wing. The Marines reported that the load included a crate of eggs of which only two were broken. During a second attempt two days later, one of the moorings pulled from the ground but the load extracted without damage. Thirteen additional GPES deliveries, mainly of construction materials, followed the next week. Loads averaged just under ten tons, all but one undamaged. Several pilots had difficulty flying the airborne hook into the ground cable, and twice loads were hauled back to the base after a series of unsuccessful passes. The proximity extraction system used the same platforms procured for heavy-equipment drops, platforms that were amply available in Vietnam. The conclusion that GPES was superior to LAPES for conditions at Khe Sanh was clear-cut, and this notion was shared by General McLaughlin as well as the airlift mission commander on the scene.[38]

A rash of inaccurate container drops in early March gained quick attention. On the seventh, four loads landed four hundred yards or more from the intended point and each was retrieved only with great difficulty. A few days earlier, two loads descended too far from the drop zone to be recovered. The 834th admonished its aircrews that this kind of performance was unsatisfactory and crewmen were expected to use professional judgment, aborting when accuracy was uncertain. To reduce drop-altitude errors, an Air Force weatherman arrived at Khe Sanh to furnish current barometric observations so that pilots could set their altimeters. Checks were made of ground controlled approach threshold fixes to determine their exactness. Through visual reference with the ground, it was established that ground control was in error by 250 yards. Other crewmen made checks and one in three reported similar discrepancies. Aircrews continued to use the radar information for lining up on the run-in. However, they cross-checked their information and shifted to visual methods for the actual releases whenever possible. It was later determined that the TPQ–10 Marine radar system gave more reliable information than the ground controlled approach equipment.[39]

The March inaccuracy proved temporary. McLaughlin reported that during the siege the C–130 had an average circular error of 95 yards when dropping visually and 133 yards when using the blind technique. The C–123s averaged 70 yards. Of the more than six hundred container drops, all but three loads were recovered. The rate of damage was ten percent for ammunition and five percent for rations.[40]

Most missions maintained delayed orbits near Hue while aircrews waited for clearance to approach Khe Sanh. The improved weather picture meant that airspace about the camp, once largely the preserve of the airlifters, was now crowded with strike aircraft and helicopters. Transport crews reported longer delays and several near-collisions. Procedures for coordinating artillery, strike aircraft, helicopters, and transports were tightened and centralized at the Marine fire support coordination center at Khe Sanh. When cleared in, airlift crews began primary radio contact with ground control approach. To reduce the intervals between aircraft, a second ground unit was installed at the site. But problems reappeared on March 27 when the Army took control of several sectors in preparation for 1st Cavalry Division operation. More than half of the scheduled airlift missions on that day could not be completed, and two days later all morning container delivery missions returned to Da Nang without making drops. As a remedy, corridors were designated for the transports along with new arrangements for advising on friendly artillery fire. The new system won the approval of transport crews, and references to the airspace control problem thereafter vanished from the daily reports from Da Nang.[41]

For the full month of March, Air Force transports delivered over fifty-one hundred tons. Stockage levels increased or held steady.[42] The course of the battle meanwhile clearly changed in favor of the allies. Shelling of the airstrip declined after the second. Communist infantry action and close-in digging also slowed, apparently discouraged by allied air and artillery firepower. The air link was now fully developed, assuring that the garrison could wait out the situation indefinitely. The Marines reported that enemy forces appeared to be relocating toward Laos.[43]

Plans for major ground operations, designed to destroy enemy forces and reopen road communications to Khe Sanh, took form in late January. Operation Pegasus called for Marine units near Dong Ha to attack westward while units of the 1st Cavalry Division assaulted by air along the flanks of Highway 9 and to the west.* The forward staging base for the assaults and resupply was to be at Ca Lu, located about halfway between Dong Ha and Khe Sanh on Highway 9. On March 20 construction of a new airstrip, known as LZ Stud, began at Ca Lu. Six days later, air buildup began with a flight of Caribous. An Army fire support site was set up at Ca Lu, and work continued toward improving the Stud airstrip for Provider use.[44] As a precaution against the disruption of the overland supply lines to Ca Lu by weather or the enemy, preparations were made for possible emergency air resupply. The objective was a capacity for delivering 360

---

* The 1st Cavalry Division was now based at Camp Evans, about midway between Quang Tri and Hue.

tons to Ca Lu daily by air, 260 tons in an all-weather airdrop, and one hundred tons through Provider landings. Loads were to be prerigged at Da Nang, Cam Ranh, and Bien Hoa, and additional drop-qualified Hercules crews were sent to Vietnam.[45]

The Pegasus assaults began April 1 and subsequent operations were brisk, though troubled by poor weather conditions most mornings. Stud remained a pivotal logistics point throughout the venture and, although preparations for airdrops proved unnecessary, the efforts of transports were substantial. Caribou pilots shuttled to Ca Lu, overcoming poor visibility and low ceilings. Providers joined the traffic into Stud on April 7 after completion of an extended runway. A Vietnamese airborne company helicoptered into the Khe Sanh perimeter during the first week and Highway 9 was opened to Khe Sanh by the eleventh. C–123 and C–130 airdrops continued at a reduced level of one hundred tons daily through April 8. The Khe Sanh runway reopened for Hercules use on the following day.[46]

The C–130 landings were as difficult as ever. Aircrews contended daily with enemy shelling, poor weather, and heavy Army helicopter traffic. Deliveries during the period were primarily construction materials, and stocks of consumables were allowed to decline to avoid a major backhaul effort after the battle. Pegasus officially ended on April 15. The cavalry withdrew to prepare for a planned thrust into the A Shau Valley.[47]

The Marine logistics support area at Khe Sanh closed in late April and its supply functions were absorbed by a new facility at Stud. The latter lay beyond the range of communist artillery in Laos, but it could support allied units in the northwest region with artillery fire and heliborne resupply. Transportation into Stud was to be primarily by road. A Seventh Air Force proposal to upgrade Stud for Hercules landings was overruled in the belief that helicopters and airdrop capabilities represented a sufficient backup. The runway at Khe Sanh was allowed to deteriorate, and the combat base itself was dismantled in early July and evacuated.[48]

Through their stand at Khe Sanh, the allies pinned down in combat substantial North Vietnamese forces through the Tet period and inflicted heavy casualties.[49] On the other hand, the air resupply venture never deteriorated into desperation. Khe Sanh occupied only a fraction of the total airlift work performed by the Common Service Airlift System during the period, although the Khe Sanh effort claimed highest priority. Supply levels never slipped to dangerous lows and, indeed, at times the Air Force appeared determined to haul more cargo than the Marines needed. Statistical data was carefully recorded and accurately conveyed the magnitude of the airlift effort. Air Force deliveries to Khe Sanh between January 21 and April 8 were as follows:[50]

	Completed Missions	Total Tonnage	Average Payload
C–130 landings	273	3,558	13.2
C–130 CDS	496		
LAPES	52	7,826	14.3
GPES	15		
C–123 landings	179	739	4.1
C–123 drops	105	294	2.3
C–7A landings	8	13	1.8
Total	1,128	12,430	

These achievements rested on the efforts of numerous supporting agencies, including the whole apparatus of the Common Service Airlift System with its aerial port, maintenance, communications, and control activities. Essential were the contributions of the U.S. Army riggers at Da Nang, Cam Ranh Bay, and Bien Hoa; the Marine radar operators at Khe Sanh; the Marine drop-zone recovery parties; the construction battalion men who repeatedly restored the battered Khe Sanh strip to functional condition; and the controllers and strike pilots who furnished escort and fire suppression. With Marine helicopter and KC–130 crews joining in air supply activities, the total endeavor became a multiservice enterprise. Distractions growing from separate outlooks appeared wholly absent in a common purpose.

The activities of the Marine airlifters, controlled apart from the Common Service Airlift System, brought to the surface several difficult questions. The Marine KC–130s were especially useful for lifting fuel bladders. In addition to his normal duties, the tactical airlift officer at Da Nang for a time also administered KC–130 operations, making up their daily itineraries, and even writing performance ratings on some of the pilots. Since the KC aircraft were unable to deliver palletized loads by the speed offload method, the tactical airlift officer generally tried to use them for missions elsewhere than Khe Sanh. Marine pilots were highly experienced and able but were less practiced than their Air Force counterparts in assault landings. The Da Nang tactical airlift officer's unusual and temporary role conceded that the III Marine Amphibious Force headquarters was the only agency for apportioning tasks between the Air Force and Marine Hercules units. The arrangement worked in 1968 because no overall shortage of aircraft prevailed.[51]

The organizational separation of the cargo helicopter arm from the common service airlift presented no serious handicap to efficiency. The capabilities of the helicopter and fixed-wing transports were meshed in complementary pattern, albeit without a formal allocations process. The agency directing fuel supply for the region, for example, was an office in the III Marine Amphibious Force logistics section. The logistics officers easily reallocated tasks as the CH–53s assisted and finally replaced the KC–130s in hauling fuel to the Khe Sanh airstrip. When necessary the fuels officers came to the tactical airlift officer for Air Force help. The conjecture remains attractive that a larger force of CH–53s, Air Force or Marine, might have replaced the C–130s in all airdrops except during the most unfavorable weather. This would have ended the problem of recovering loads at the drop zone and thwarted the enemy's concentration of fire along the fixed-wing approach path. That the Common Service Airlift System lacked a transport helicopter arm was a result of decisions dating back more than a decade. The point gave strength to later Air Force contentions in behalf of the development of vertical-flight craft as eventual replacements for the C–123 and Caribou.[52]

Officially, in addition to the three destroyed C–123s, twenty-six Air Force transports (eighteen C–130s and eight C–123s) received battle damage during the siege, although the data appears incomplete. No known surface-to-air missile firings were directed against transport aircraft although the Khe Sanh approach routes lay within the range of launch sites north of the demilitarized zone. On April 1 a Marine strike pilot observed a missile firing seven miles northwest of Khe Sanh, but this was the only reported incident. Captured in the battle area were enemy 37-mm and 57-mm guns with ammunition caches for both types.[53]

Although transport crews fully knew the hazards of the Khe Sanh missions, flight refusals were nonexistent. They were proud to be selected for the drop missions and accepted extensions of in-country tours without complaint. C–130 crews landing at Khe Sanh learned the positions of enemy guns mainly by experience or word of mouth from others. Those Air Force personnel on the ground at Khe Sanh, as well as the crews landing during the siege, were entitled to wear the Navy Presidential Unit Citation, a distinction awarded to the 26th Marines.

Ultimately, the success of the Khe Sanh resupply was a product of ingenuity. A foremost innovation was the use of ground radar for guiding airdrops, supplemented with the airborne doppler for the necessary offset capability. The idea of trying the nearly forgotten GPES and the speed with which it was revived can be credited to the existing staff system. Lesser examples of improvisation and resourcefulness among air and ground crewmen were every day commonplaces. The established Common Service Airlift System procedures and the standing doctrines for tactics and techniques were well understood by the airlifters. That room for imaginativeness remained and that individuals were encouraged in its use spoke well for the American military system.

XIII. Tet and the Battles of 1968

The 1968 communist Tet offensive, probably triggered by a recent pattern of defeat represented a major turning point in enemy strategy. The communists had little hope of igniting a general uprising, but apparently expected the widespread attacks to weaken Saigon's authority and sap America's will. Although surprised by the extent and timing of the attacks, the allies in a few days dislodged communist units from most of their gains, with Viet Cong losses in men and weapons adding up to a serious military defeat for the communists.[1]

The initial countrywide attacks momentarily disrupted the airlift system, although Air Force transports continued to make deliveries of troops and supplies to hard-pressed and isolated garrisons. By the fourth day of the offensive, February 3, the airlift system had regained its previous sortie level, but requirements for airlift steadily increased as units exhausted their supplies and surface lines of communication remained cut. The transportation situation was most critical in the northern provinces where the airlifters supported allied forces engaged at Khe Sanh and Hue, and in the eastern demilitarized zone where winter monsoon conditions made aerial transport extremely difficult. To assert that airlift saved the allies during Tet would be an exaggeration, but it is clear that the speed of the allied recovery during February was made possible by air transport.

The airlift system continued at forced volume into the summer of 1968, as intense fighting continued and the number of allied battalions to be supported increased. Two extraordinary episodes highlighted airlift operations. Air resupply of the 1st Cavalry Division's Operation Delaware (the air invasion of the A Shau Valley) succeeded despite conditions at least as difficult as those recently faced at Khe Sanh. And soon afterwards air evacuation of the Kham Duc camp, under threat of imminent communist capture, produced the Common Service Airlift System's only Medal of Honor winner, Lt. Col. Joe M. Jackson. Another late-year airlift activity was the redeployment by air of the 1st Cavalry Division, shifted from the north to the border areas about Saigon.

TACTICAL AIRLIFT

Lt. Col. Joe M. Jackson receives the Medal of Honor from President Lyndon B. Johnson at a White House ceremony, January 16, 1969. The airlifter was commended for his valor during the air evacuation of Kham Duc, 1968.

Early into the lunar New Year—a half hour past midnight on January 30, 1968—communist units launched scattered attacks against government posts in Nha Trang. These soon swelled into a concerted attempt to seize the city. Before dawn, bitter fighting erupted in a half-dozen other cities from Ban Me Thuot north to Da Nang. The night was clear, and C–130 crews could look down on the firefights in the towns and on the perimeters of bases. The airfields at Nha Trang, Kontum, Ban Me Thuot, Pleiku, and Da Nang—all customary stopping points for airlift transports—were shelled and attacked by infantry fire. Transport crews of necessity delayed landing during attacks, either orbiting until things quieted or proceeding to other destinations.

Heavy fighting continued after daylight with allied units counter-attacking at many points. Most fields soon reopened for the airlifters, but crews landing at Nha Trang could watch nearby allied air and helicopter strikes against communist positions inside the city. Communists held the radio and police stations at Qui Nhon most of the day but, despite sniper fire, the airfield remained open to receive Vietnamese and Korean troop reinforcements. At Ban Me Thuot, the communists temporarily held the civil airport and probed the military airfield further east. The C–130 bases —Tan Son Nhut, Cam Ranh Bay, and Tuy Hoa—were largely untouched, and the entire southern half of the republic remained quiet. It later appeared that the January 30 attacks had been mistakenly launched twenty-four hours earlier than intended.[2]

The full countrywide offensive opened in darkness the night of January 30/31. For the C–130B airlifters at Tan Son Nhut, the night was one of peril. Multibattalion communist assaults against the air base began shortly after midnight and one enemy battalion penetrated several hundred yards inside the base perimeter bunker line. Small arms harassed the C–130 parking ramp and fire from the roof of a nearby textile mill prevented landings and takeoffs. Helicopters, gunships, and fighter planes pounded communist forces on the airfield perimeter and in the textile mill. Those aircrewmen not flying had been summoned to the base the previous afternoon, but six officers were inadvertently left sleeping in upper floors of their hotel. They were awakened by the sound of grenades and automatic weapons when the communists occupied the hotel's ground floor, but the intruders never penetrated to the upper levels.

The airlift control center at Tan Son Nhut was flooded by emergency situation reports coming from all parts of the country, while hard pressed amid the local fighting to remain on the air. Transports returning to Tan Son Nhut were diverted to other points. Two C–130s landed at Vung Tau, where the local detachment was unaware of the crisis at Saigon. After refueling, the planes took two hundred Vietnamese marines aboard and headed for Saigon. They arrived at dawn to learn that the field was still closed, but after some discussion they were allowed to land. The marines disembarked and immediately joined the battle. Later that day another five hundred troops were airlifted from Vung Tau to Tan Son Nhut. In all, twenty-six transports landed at Tan Son Nhut on January 31, eleven of them from Vung Tau.

Except for a few aircraft, all C–130Bs were flown from Tan Son Nhut to Cam Ranh during the morning of the thirty-first, and for the next several days the detachment operated from Cam Ranh. The C–123s of the 19th Squadron also were evacuated from Tan Son Nhut on the thirty-first, although many squadron personnel were left behind in scattered downtown billets unable to get to the airfields. Extra crewmen were flown in from the Phan Rang squadrons to help with the evacuation. The aircraft flew missions out of Phan Rang for three days before returning to Saigon.[3]

The night attacks of January 30/31 raged at hundreds of provincial and district centers. Fighting flared up again at Qui Nhon, Nha Trang, and the other points attacked the night before. The most successful communist attack was at Hue, where eight regular battalions infiltrated and captured

TACTICAL AIRLIFT

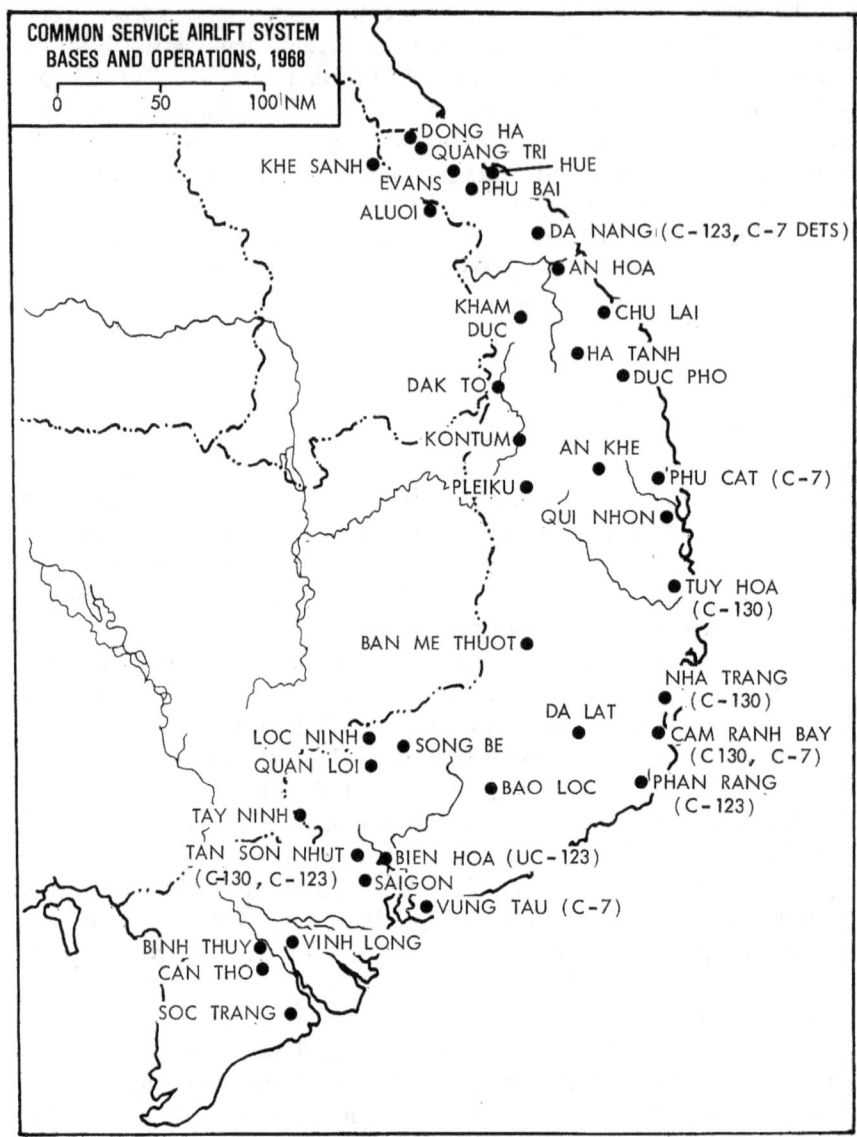

much of the city including the Imperial Citadel. Many airfields, including Bien Hoa, were attacked and forced to close for much of the night. Da Nang was pounded by heavy mortar and rocket fire, and pitched battles were fought at Kontum and Ban Me Thuot. C–130 crews attempting to fly night missions soon saw that useful operations were impossible and returned to Cam Ranh. Mission activity through the thirty-first was greatly curtailed; 625 sorties were flown, against a daily average of over eleven hundred for the previous thirty days. Moreover, many of the sorties flown were unproductive because of intermittent airfield closings during actual or anticipated attacks. The day's missions to Khe Sanh, however, were unaffected by the crisis.[4]

Of several emergency airlifts in the first hours, the most noteworthy was the resupply and reinforcement of the hard-pressed Vietnamese defenders of Ban Me Thuot. The communist forces held numerous strongpoints, threatened both the civil and military airfields, and surrounded the local military headquarters. Late in the afternoon of the thirty-first, C–123s began emergency resupply missions to the Ban Me Thuot military field, and continued into early evening. Oil was burned in oil drums to thwart the dusk. Eleven C–123s and two Caribous touched down with over sixty tons before landings were halted. Shortly after midnight, an emergency troop lift began into the city's civil airfield, near the heavy fighting. Five C–123K crews picked up troops of the 23d Ranger Battalion at Bao Loc, itself under fire. In miserable weather they transported more than three hundred troops to Ban Me Thuot by dawn on February 1. Despite automatic-weapons fire and occasional mortaring of the landing strip, all aircraft survived, but one was hit fifteen times, another thirteen. The headlamps of vehicles placed along the runway provided field lighting. Emergency troop movement directly into battle by night was unprecedented in Vietnam, and earned a message of congratulations from General Westmoreland. Equally meaningful was the admiration of the Army operations officer at Nha Trang, who said of the Air Force, "I'll tell you they'd do anything."[5]

Heavy fighting continued at many points during the first day of February, although it was clear that the Saigon government would survive the onslaught. Reactions of the Vietnamese people to the conflict were pivotal, and most were bitter toward the communists for starting the nightmare. Westmoreland at midday prescribed that counterattacks be made during the expected enemy withdrawals.[6]

For the airlift system, conditions remained difficult but were stabilizing, permitting a total of 887 sorties during the day. Aircraft maintenance work had been disrupted by the evacuations from Tan Son Nhut and by a virtual halt of night labor as Vietnamese civilians failed to show up for aerial port and base housekeeping jobs. Typical of the personnel reaction was that of the control element and aerial port staffs at Qui Nhon. Although fatigued from two sleepless nights in bunkers, they promptly manned their posts around the clock. Airstrips were again open, but flying crews were careful to assure themselves that conditions were safe before landing. It thus appeared that the Common Service Airlift System had weathered the enemy's blows. After hundreds of landings at places under intermittent attack, not a single transport had been lost. The air transport emergency had only begun, however, since reserve stocks of munitions and fuel used in the early battles were beginning to require replenishment at many locations.[7]

U.S. Army logisticians surveying the badly dislocated countrywide transportation system at midday, February 1, found that inland road movements in the II Corps area had been blocked by Viet Cong units since the start of the offensive. A convoy from Qui Nhon for Dak To, starting out earlier that day, was stopped by rifle and mortar fire only a few miles out of town. The roads from Cam Ranh Bay to Da Lat and Ban Me Thuot were officially closed. Heavy fighting continued at Da Lat, Ban Me Thuot, and Kontum, forcing airfields at all three cities to close. The detonation of eight hundred tons of munitions at Qui Nhon on January 31, and another one thousand tons the next day, necessitated temporary realignment of in-country supply routes as well as offshore replenishment airlifts. In the Saigon region all major highways, including the links to Tay Ninh, Phuoc Vinh, and Loc Ninh, were closed by enemy sabotage and roadblocks. Convoys caught at outlying points two days earlier still waited for engineers to clear the way. Truck movements within the delta also were at a standstill since the Vietnamese drivers, fearing reprisals, stayed away from work. River barges which normally served the region were held up at Vung Tau. Rail movements countrywide were entirely stopped. Several priority airlifts provided stopgap transportation, delivering ammunition to Dak To, jet fuel to Song Be, and Phuoc Vinh, and a combat essential airlift was readied for Can Tho. For the next several days, emergency and combat-essential movements monopolized all airlift capability and routine requests were pushed aside.[8]

Two C-123s of the 315th Wing executed a classic night airdrop resupply on February 2 at Kontum. The city had been critically short of ammunition since the previous day although Army helicopters did manage several deliveries. The drop zone was a compound, 75 by 150 yards, at the northwest edge of the town. Helicopter and C-47 gunships intermittently sprayed communist positions and the enemy replied with tracers. As Provider crews circled, the defenders fired a short-duration white-phosphorous grenade, establishing the target location with relation to nearby fires. The airlift crews quickly maneuvered into low-level patterns, and successfully dropped over five tons of munitions inside the darkened perimeter.[9]

Within the II Corps highlands region the transportation picture improved slowly, although road traffic was plagued by daily ambushes, landmines, and sabotage. Airlift transports averaged over thirty landings daily at Pleiku during the first week of February. And, since road travel to Dak To was at a standstill, C–130s lifted in sixteen loads of munitions from Qui Nhon and Cam Ranh in two days. The Dak To strip remained in use by the Hercules until February 3 when a ten-foot crater reduced usable length by 750 feet. Landings thereafter were mainly by Caribous, although several C–130s landed on the fourth, touching down just past the damaged point. At Ban Me Thuot the Hercules averaged eight landings daily, mainly into the military airfield while, in a maximum single-day effort, C–123 Providers hauled twenty-five loads into the civil strip, beginning at first light February 3 and continuing until dark. At battered Kontum most landings were by U.S. and Australian Caribous, until normal operations resumed on February 7. C–123s and C–130s lifted over one thousand men into the battle at Da Lat from February 2–9. Fighting ended at Kontum on February 4, at Ban Me Thuot on the sixth, and at Da Lat on the tenth. By February 11, road convoy activity in the region was described as normal.[10]

Within the III Corps area road clearance was slower, necessitating dependence on fixed-wing and helicopter airlift for resupply of areas usually reached by road convoy. There were numerous requests for ammunition lifts to various base camps and forward airstrips. And frequent emergency resupply lifts of jet fuel to Song Be continued through February 4, C–130 landings at that 101st Division airhead averaging sixteen daily for the first five days of the month. In one tactical emergency lift on February 2, five hundred troops and over one hundred tons of equipment of the 101st Division were moved in seventeen sorties from Song Be to Tan Son Nhut and the Saigon fighting. Road closings also necessitated airlift shuttles between Tan Son Nhut and the Bien Hoa depot, hauling aircraft spare parts for the Vietnamese Air Force. The first convoy for Tay Ninh, consisting of 141 trucks, departed early on February 3. Halted several times by firefights and roadblocks, the convoy finally arrived back at Long Binh after five days, completing a mission normally requiring only a day. Convoys from Saigon to other destinations gradually resumed, although they were frequently delayed by the need for extra security and road repairs.[11]

Emergency airlift was especially important in the IV Corps delta region where petroleum stocks were relatively low and where reliance on surface transportation had been nearly total. During the first fifteen days of Tet, Hercules and Provider aircraft lifted over thirty thousand tons of cargo in the corps area. This tonnage included jet fuel and 2.75-inch rockets, primarily for Army aviation operations. Airlift focal points were the main Army aviation centers of Soc Trang, Can Tho, and Vinh Long, and the Air Force installation at Binh Thuy near Can Tho. All except Binh Thuy had been attacked heavily on the first day of Tet. At Soc Trang C–130 deliveries of jet fuel began on January 31 when stocks were depleted. The 130s hauled in thirty thousand gallons that day, followed by

TACTICAL AIRLIFT

twenty-six thousand gallons the next, to meet an anticipated consumption of thirty-two thousand gallons daily. Shortages of storage and handling equipment prevented a still greater effort. C-130s also began delivering munitions to the defenders of Can Tho on February 1, hauling them from Cam Ranh to Binh Thuy. Mishandling at Binh Thuy, however, apparently caused some emergency deliveries to be issued to the wrong units, and the confusion was compounded by the experience of 5th Special Forces Group in initiating emergency requests for air delivery into the delta.

Since the C-130 Hercules landed only at Soc Trang and Binh Thuy, operations elsewhere in the delta depended heavily on the C-123 Providers. The 123s flew eight sorties daily into Can Tho, Vinh Long, and several other strips not ordinarily visited by 123s. Especially dramatic was a night emergency resupply into Vinh Long on February 2. Request for the flight was made by friendly forces although they held only the northwest corner of the strip. A Provider was quickly loaded for a five-ton munitions and rations drop. While it was en route the defenders recaptured the rest of the airfield, and it was decided to attempt a landing. Protected by two gunships, the plane made a precision approach by the light of airdropped flares, landed, unloaded its cargo, and was airborne again within five minutes.

In addition to the C-123s and C-130s, other aircraft hauled supplies into the delta region. Three Chinooks bore nearly the entire burden of resupplying some seventy artillery sites, and three Air Force Caribous each averaged seven sorties daily through February 14. U.S. Army fixed-wing Otters delivered to smaller airstrips. Airlift remained absolutely vital in the delta region until February 14 when the heavy fighting near Can Tho from the north resumed.[12]

Other events also swelled the countrywide demand for airlift. Heavy usage of U.S. Army aircraft in the early crisis quickly led to numerous requests for airlifts of spare parts. Three C-123s were allocated for parts deliveries from Tan Son Nhut to various aviation units. Deliveries started February 1 and by the evening of the third the Providers had hauled sixty tons of Army parts. One C-123 was later placed under daily operational control of the Qui Nhon airlift control element to shuttle repair parts to Army aviation units in the northern half of the country. Vietnamese forces likewise needed supplies, so MACV on February 11 granted Vietnamese and American forces equal priority for emergency air resupply.

The Common Service Airlift System flew more than one thousand sorties on February 3, approximately the pre-Tet rate. Tonnage airlifted on that date exceeded the late-1967 daily average of thirty-six hundred tons and thereafter remained generally well above this amount. Despite the fast recovery much routine cargo was left unmoved, intensifying the use of priority requests among those competing for service. Over the first nine days of Tet, priority movements accounted for over one thousand sorties lifting ten thousand tons, more than ten times the normal rate. As early as February 2, the airlift control center was unable to schedule enough aircraft to meet all priority requests. Two days later, General Westmoreland recognized the "serious strain on our overloaded airlift assets," and directed that resortation of surface transportation take equal priority with the destruction of enemy forces. Expansion of American ground forces in Vietnam, the imminent confrontation at Khe Sanh, and the clear communist capability for fresh attacks—all reinforce the conclusion that an expansion of the Common Services Airlift System was needed.[13]

The events of Tet intensified the already dangerous situation in the northern provinces, which as early as January 1968 required the presence of the 1st Cavalry Division and a brigade of the 101st Division. Marine intelligence reports in February placed enemy strength in the demilitarized zone and Quang Tri Province at fifty thousand combat troops, including thirty-two North Vietnamese infantry battalions. Tet attacks against Quang Tri and other towns were repulsed by February 2, except for Hue where the communists won world attention by holding out until February 25. Communist forces, however, blocked Highway 1 and the river mouths into Hue and Dong Ha, choking transportation from Da Nang to the north. Substituting for surface transportation amid chronic drizzle and low ceilings, the airlift became badly overloaded. Most affected was transportation support for the 1st Cavalry Division at Camp Evans, with four battalions engaged about Quang Tri, and two (eventually four) committed to isolating Hue on the west and north. Two hundred helicopters were based at Evans, with the main supply line running down from Dong Ha, now itself accessible only by air. Evans as yet had no runway capable of accepting C–130s, but in a four-day effort, February 4–7, Air Force C–130s in twenty-six airdrop sorties delivered over 350 tons of supplies, mainly ammunition, to Evans. A five-man Air Force combat control team parachuted in on the first day and controlled the later drops. Most of these sorties came from Cam Ranh, thus by-passing busy Da Nang and Dong Ha, although some ships landed at Da Nang to refuel and pick up second loads.[14]

The Evans missions were at least as difficult as those at Khe Sanh. Ceilings were below one thousand feet throughout the period, with scattered cloud cover down to five hundred feet. Crews used ground controlled approaches to line up, located panels on the ground visually, and used stopwatch timing to determine release points. The run-in path lay along Route 1 and the coastal railroad which formed an excellent visual refer-

TACTICAL AIRLIFT

ence for the drop zone, which lay between the road and railway. In order to release cargos visually, crews flew just below the clouds, in many cases releasing loads from well below the normal five hundred to six hundred feet. Hostile fire was severe. One crew—Lt. Col. Virgil H. Rizer, Maj. Billy R. Gibson, and Maj. Eugene Hartman—flew five drop sorties, taking hits on three, losing an engine just before drop on one, and on another using all fuel from three internal tanks. Slightly improved weather on the third day of the airlift allowed normal run-in and drop altitudes and, although ground fire seemed more intense, no hits were received. The 1st Cavalry Division commander later wrote of the "tremendous job" done by the aircrews during the Evans drops, and described the strange sight of parachutes descending out of the clouds. Caribou and Provider landings at Evans, virtually halted since January 31, resumed on February 13 and 19 respectively.[15]

Common Service Airlift System C–130s also made over one thousand landings during February at Phu Bai. Cargos included aviation fuels, munitions, military equipment, rice, and relief supplies needed by allied forces engaged in the Hue battle. Return flights lifted out allied dead and wounded, and many civilian refugees. Transport crewmen, used to the impoverished Vietnamese seen about Tuy Hoa, Cam Ranh, and the forward airstrips, were impressed by the well-dressed, urbane appearance of many Hue evacuees. Meanwhile, more than 350 airlift sorties landed at Quang Tri and Dong Ha, supporting allied forces in the eastern DMZ. In one ten-day period C–130s made nearly one hundred sorties bringing in munitions from Qui Nhon. By delivering from Qui Nhon and points south, the C–130s helped reduce congestion at overburdened Da

Members of the 82nd Airborne Division board a MAC C–141 at Pope AFB, North Carolina, for deployment to Southeast Asia, February 1968.

Courtesy: U.S. Army
UH–1D helicopter belonging to the 82nd is loaded onto a C–133, bound for Vietnam.

Nang. The sustained effort in the northern provinces claimed one C–130. It was destroyed while attempting to land at Phu Bai in light rain on the night of March 2, and six passengers were fatally injured.[16]

During the second week of February men and equipment for a new Headquarters MACV, Forward, were hauled from Tan Son Nhut to Phu Bai, and a twenty-three-sortie tactical emergency lift hauled a battalion of the 101st Airborne Division north from Song Be. The division's advance headquarters flew to Quang Tri on the fourteenth, and moved to a new camp west of Hue several days later. C–130s also assisted in moving Vietnamese marines from Tan Son Nhut to Phu Bai on the fourteenth, to replace depleted Vietnamese paratroop units. The biggest troop movement in February was the air and sea shift of the remainder of First Brigade of the 101st Division to Phu Bai. To accomplish this shift, C–130s made 129 sorties from Bien Hoa and Song Be the week February 17–23. Most of these sorties lifted vehicles, equipment, and supplies; the actual hauling of troops amounting to only twenty percent of the airlift. The departures from Song Be brought caustic comment from aircrews who had just finished lifting the brigade and massive supplies into that airhead. During the month of February there were well over two hundred C–130 hauls to Phu Bai from Song Be, Bien Hoa, and Tan Son Nhut. These long hauls, averaging more than an hour's flying time, were a drain on airlift capability, but served a secondary purpose by making aircraft from the southern bases available for further work in the north during the remainder of each crew's twelve-hour mission day.[17]

Aware that substantial North Vietnamese forces were still uncommitted, President Johnson on February 12 approved an accelerated air movement from North Carolina to Vietnam of a brigade of the 82d Airborne Division. This long-range move by MAC airlift began on the fourteenth, the President in person bidding the troops farewell. The flights terminated at Chu Lai, but one newly arrived battalion flew on, in forty-seven sorties, to Phu Bai. Also augmenting the allied forces in I Corps were six additional U.S. Marine battalions, deployed late in the month from outside Vietnam.[18]

Airlift capabilities in the north were now clearly saturated. Only tactical emergency and emergency resupply priority deliveries could be assured. Positioning a Hercules detachment at Da Nang was considered but ruled out because of the danger of shelling. Instead, a nineteen-man maintenance team was stationed at Da Nang, along with Hercules spare parts and equipment. To reduce landing and takeoff delays, sometimes exceeding an hour, additional radar approach control equipment was brought in and installed. Aerial port mobility teams were sent to Quang Tri and Phu Bai, and a new airlift control element also was established at Phu Bai. Preparations for possible airdrops in the DMZ region, however, proved unnecessary.[19]

For the full month of February, Seventh Air Force reported that thirty-six thousand tons of cargo had been airlifted to points in the I Corps area, a fifty percent increase in tonnage from the average of the previous nine months. This amounted to one-third of the countrywide workload. River access to Hue and Dong Ha reopened intermittently during the month, allowing sixty-eight thousand tons of cargo to move by water from Da Nang to other points in I Corps. In addition, Marine Corps CH–53s moved forty-three hundred tons between the coast bases. On March 1, however, restoration of Highway 1 to Phu Bai and Dong Ha brought to an end the critical transportation problem.[20]

Several circumstances made immediate buildup of in-country airlift capacity difficult. Expansions of the past twelve months had absorbed more unused ramp and billeting space at South Vietnamese bases and strained existing aerial port and traffic control facilities. Offshore flying hours of C–130 wings were close to the limit consistent with safety, even though most training and overwater airlift flights had been dropped. Moreover, the *Pueblo* incident in January 1968 required 315th Air Division support for nearly two hundred Air Force planes newly sent to South Korea. And sixteen TAC C–130s and crews were moved from Forbes Air Force Base, Kans., and Sewart Air Force Base to Japan to work in Korea under MAC control. To restore airlift capability in Vietnam, CINCPAC on February 2 requested more planes. As a result, two more TAC squadrons for use by the 315th Air Division arrived at Tachikawa, Japan, February 7–9.[21]

Sixteen C–130Es and twenty-five crews from Tachikawa moved to Cam Ranh Bay the second week in February. General McLaughlin briefed the new crewmen, stressing the need for mission safety despite the importance of every operational delivery. The TAC crewmen began in-country missions on February 11. Although many had recently completed full tours in the Far East, all flew initially with instructors from the assigned Pacific wings. Especially welcome in Vietnam were the fresh aircraft—clean and free of the many malfunctions common among veteran aircraft in Vietnam. The newer TAC ships were intermingled with the 314th E–models at Cam Ranh, and were flown by either TAC or 314th Wing crews. Aircraft were rotated from Tachikawa, with sixteen kept at Cam Ranh at all times; crews cycled for fifteen-day tours in Vietnam. The Sewart–Forbes squadron moved to Clark Air Base on February 15 and now flew under 315th Air Division Control. Ten days later, an eight-plane detachment, primarily from Langley, began flying from Nha Trang as the 315th Air Division's Task Force Bravo. This raised the total C–130 airlift fleet in Vietnam to ninety-six.[22]

C–123 missions increased from thirty-eight daily to forty-nine, each mission averaging seven planes. This increase was made possible by a decision to convert UC–123 spray aircraft of the 12th Air Commando Squadron to full-time transport work. Removal of spray equipment from all sixteen of the Ranch Hand aircraft began February 8 and required roughly fourteen man-hours per plane. Following the conversion, flights from Bien Hoa were for airlift exclusively. The shift to airlift usage presented no special problem, except for the temporary need for loadmasters from other units. The 12th Squadron returned to spray duties on March 20, having averaged over seventy sorties daily during its airlift stint.[23]

Several expedients were devised to ease problems of airfield saturation. The enlarged C–130 capability was used as much as possible at night to minimize daytime traffic. Aerial ports also received additional handling equipment and more than two hundred airmen were assigned temporarily to aerial ports during the month. Even so, the Seventh Air Force warned that more were needed to avoid "airlift system degradation." To minimize abuses of the priorities system, the MACV combat operations center and the traffic management agency were frequently asked to sort out "Combat Essential" requests and assign priorities within priorities. The glut of priority requests persisted, however, and was finally overcome only by tighter MACV review and a decision to stick to some scheduled itineraries regardless of priority requests. This gave shippers some assurance of delivery when using routine priority.[24]

The Common Service Airlift System transport fleet survived the Tet offensive with modest losses. During February, eighty-four transports were hit by ground fire (forty-two C–130, thirty-three C–123, nine C–7A), more than double the total for the previous month. But the communists shot down only one ship, a C–130 hit during takeoff from Song Be on February 28. Crew and passengers escaped the burning wreckage ahead of the explosion. Shellings damaged eighteen C–130s and C–123s on the ground at Bien Hoa and Tan Son Nhut. The single most destructive shelling at Tan Son Nhut on the eighteenth damaged nine transports and destroyed one C–130. At month's end, even with fifteen transports out of service for repairs of battle damage, and despite the loss of three C–130s (including the accidental loss at Hue), replacement C–130s maintained airlift strength.[25]

The speedy recovery and expansion of the airlift system enabled it to move impressive tonnage. Compared to 3,740 tons-per-day in January, airlift transports hauled 3,880 in February, and 4,470 in March. But overall efficiency declined, reflecting the dislocations of the period, bad weather in the north, and overuse of facilities. One indication of the effects of maintenance, aerial port, and traffic delays was the number of sorties flown per C–130. This declined from 5.75 in January to 4.93 in February and 4.77 in March. Tonnage lifted per C–130 Hercules dropped thirteen percent in February. Addition of a fifth airlift C–123 squadron enabled the airlift system to increase overall lift capacity, but efficiency during early spring suffered.[26]

The airlift system recovered from the initial Tet attacks much sooner than did land and water transport, and was crucial to the early allied countrywide recovery. Air transport was most indispensable in I Corps, sustaining the fighting at Hue and Quang Tri (as well as Khe Sanh) while ground movements were at a standstill. Petroleum deliveries from Tan Son Nhut to helicopter refueling points were especially vital due to disruption of commercial truck delivery. The airlifters also moved over thirty-four hundred refugees during the recovery period. General Westmoreland in April complimented the airlifters for their service during Tet. He specifically cited air movement of combat units, and the ability of air transport to function when surface lines of communication were disrupted. Summarizing airlift professionalism, he stated: "The classical role of tactical airlift has been admirably performed in its truest sense."[27]

TET OFFENSIVE, 1968

Courtesy: U.S. Army

(1)

(2)

Courtesy: U.S. Army

Tan Son Nhut Air Base endured a mortar and rocket attack on February 18, 1968. Among the ruins were (1) a C–45 aircraft and (2) a warehouse at the 8th Aerial Port. At right (below) a second aerial port building suffered slight damage. Left, firemen battle the blaze of a Vietnamese C–47 aircraft.

Courtesy: U.S. ArmyCourtesy: U.S. Army

TACTICAL AIRLIFT

The A Shau Valley lies along the Laotian border slightly below the latitude of Hue. Heavily forested slopes rise two thousand feet on either side of the four-mile-wide floor. Tall grass and light forest cover the low ground, and a loose surface road traverses the twenty-mile length, passing close to the old airfields at A Luoi, Ta Bat, and A Shau. For the communists, the A Shau Valley represented an avenue into South Vietnam from Laos, affording twenty miles of easy going toward Hue and Da Nang. Since the fall of the old A Shau camp in 1966, communist use of the valley had been almost unchallenged. In early 1968 the allies detected fresh road construction, troop activity at the old airfield sites, and a camouflaged network of 37-mm antiaircraft weapons. One officer called the A Shau, "the enemy's Cam Ranh Bay."[28]

At Westmoreland's direction, planners at III Marine Amphibious Force and MACV during 1967 studied concepts for returning to the valley. These studies at year's end resulted in OPlan York II, a proposed four-brigade air invasion primarily using the 1st Cavalry Division. A critical planning concern was the ability of combat engineers quickly to prepare C–130 airfields at A Luoi and A Shau to avoid the exclusive reliance on helicopter and airdrop resupply of 1,175 tons daily. Although canceled in favor of Pegasus, OPlan York II was the predecessor of Delaware.[29]

In late March 1968, Westmoreland realized that rapid success of Pegasus would permit a venture into A Shau. April seemed a suitable month since it was a period of transition between the low visibilities of the winter monsoon and the heavy rainfall of summer. Under the Delaware plan developed by the Army, two cavalry brigades would land by helicopter in the valley. They would be supported by a brigade of the 101st Division attacking westward from Hue and by South Vietnamese units operating both in and to the east of the valley.

All movements and resupply into the valley were to be by air. The possibility of opening a road from Hue was overruled, since major units would not remain after the initial operation. The estimated daily resupply requirement for the troops scheduled to enter the valley was 462 tons, of which 293 tons would be ammunition. Part of this total was to be provided by U.S. Army and Marine helicopters operating from Camp Evans. The 1st Brigade, scheduled to land by helicopter at A Luoi, was to receive 220 tons daily to be supplied by Air Force C–130 airdrops starting the second day of the operation. An engineer battalion and heavy construction equipment were to be lifted by helicopter to A Luoi on the second day, to begin airstrip rehabilitation. The A Luoi strip was to be ready for Caribou landings after two-day's work, and for C-123s after three. A daily capability to receive 140 tons was prescribed. There was apparently no intention to further improve the strip for C-130s.[30]

The 834th Air Division seemed in excellent shape to undertake a fresh major airdrop. Recent drops at Khe Sanh and Camp Evans had made C-130 crews expert in contending with the difficult conditions in the northern provinces. Also well practiced were the riggers of the 109th Company at Cam Ranh, Da Nang, and Bien Hoa. Col. William T. Phillips, director of the airlift control center, on April 17 alerted the 315th Air Division that C-130 drops would probably begin on April 20 and would last two or three weeks. Already present in Vietnam were sufficient C-130s and aircrewmen trained in container delivery of cargo. An additional loadmaster, however, was needed for each of the fourteen designated drop crews.[31]

Cavalry helicopters reconnoitered the valley daily during mid-April, while airstrikes hit known positions. Heavy antiaircraft fire near A Luoi ruled out opening the campaign in that sector. Instead, on D-day, April 19, the 3d Brigade of the 1st Cavalry Division launched an attack at the northwest end of the valley. Severe ground fire destroyed eleven helicopters that day and damaged twelve others. Solid overcast down to three hundred feet made tactical air operations hazardous. For four days the weather and enemy fire slowed the attack and not until April 23 were the desired fire bases in place to support the assault at A Luoi. Favored by temporarily improved weather, the first landings of the 1st Brigade near A Luoi were executed without difficulty on April 24. The following day the brigade landed at and seized the old airstrip.[32]

An Air Force combat control team, led by Maj. Donald R. Strobaugh of the 2d Aerial Port Group and Lt. Col. Richard F. Button, C-130 mission commander, landed at A Luoi by UH-1 helicopter in early morning, April 26. Also on board was Capt. Robert F. Mullen, tactical airlift officer with the 1st Cavalry Division. A CH-47 Chinook arrived soon afterward with the team's vital radio jeep. The Air Force party had attempted to reach A Luoi the previous afternoon, but their CH-47 had been forced by heavy weather to turn back to Camp Evans. The Army had made the Chinooks available reluctantly, since every available chopper was needed urgently for ammunition resupply. And unfortunately two Chinooks were lost to enemy fire in the valley on the twenty-sixth. Ground control equipment to enable C-130 drops in bad weather was left behind in favor of urgent resupply loads. As a substitute, Major Strobaugh and his

TACTICAL AIRLIFT

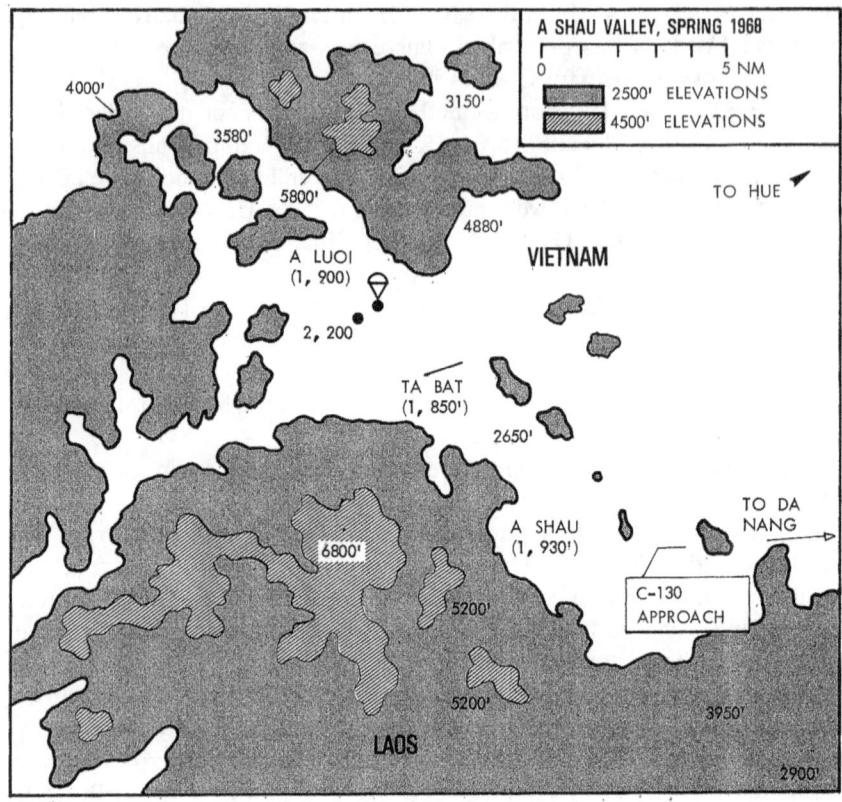

assistants quickly set up ground panels for visual drops about three hundred yards from the old dirt runway. Another possible drop-zone site had been ruled out the previous evening because of man-high elephant grass.[33]

Twelve C–130s, three A–models and five E–models from Cam Ranh, and four B–models loading at Bien Hoa, were scheduled to make drops on the morning of the twenty-sixth. The eight crews arrived at the line expecting a day of routine itineraries. Briefings were given to groups of two or three crews. Navigators received photographs of the old A Luoi airstrip with a diagram of the designated drop zone overprinted. The planes were to orbit west of the Hue tactical air navigation station, awaiting clearance for single-ship runs. The planes were to approach from the northwest, fly down the center of the valley, and depart with a climbing right-hand turn. Ground navigation aids would not be available except for the light-weight radar beacon usually operated by combat control teams. F–4s were to establish fire-suppression corridors and silence the heavy-caliber fire expected from the ridges. Takeoff times were spaced between 0630 and 0830 to assure arrival at appropriate intervals. The Cam Ranh ships were to drop first. All crews loaded and departed on schedule, navigating independently up the coast. Upon arrival at the orbit point, they made radio contact with the combat control team on the ground at A Luoi.[34]

The first, an E-model from Cam Ranh, reported in to the combat control team at about 0830. To the aircrew above it appeared that the cloud cover was solid from eight thousand feet down. Cleared by the control team to attempt a drop, the crew entered the soup on instruments and descended into the valley. Navigation was entirely without outside assistance. Descending cautiously, the crew broke out under the clouds only five hundred feet above the valley floor; the drop-zone panels quickly came into view less than two miles ahead. Captain Mullen watched as the ship approached and intermittently vanished into the clouds. Over the drop zone the ship made the usual container delivery pullup and reentered the clouds. A few seconds later a rain of chutes began spilling out of the overcast, a "fantastic" sight to Mullen. Soon afterward he heard the pilot advising the second crew, then orbiting aloft, that things had been "kind of sticky but you can press right on through."[35]

The operation soon fell into pattern. Each plane upon arriving at Hue entered the holding stack at a specified altitude above the clouds. As soon as one ship completed its drop and reported clear of the area, the control team cleared the next to enter the valley. The third and fourth C-130s in were E-models, commanded by Maj. Billy R. Gibson and Lt. Col. Nelson W. Kimmey. Both encountered rainshowers and ragged low ceilings, and both depended for guidance wholly on their navigators, Capt. Richard W. Jones and Capt. Ronald L. Selberg. Neither crew had difficulty spotting the drop zone after breaking through the clouds since the target was well marked with panels and smoke. The first plane broke out of the overcast too late to drop and circled at treetop level back up the valley for a second run. The second plane emerged on course for a successful drop on the first pass. During the run-in, Gibson's crew could hear hostile fire exploding overhead and shrapnel hitting the ship. Kimmey's crew was unaware of fire, but counted ten bullet holes in the plane after landing. The orbiting crews listened carefully for reports of ground fire, and commented with rancor on the absence of strike aircraft which had been prevented by the overcast from giving promised fire suppression. The crews, however, gave little thought to aborting the drops, appreciating the urgency of the mission and realizing that the weather afforded some protection from enemy fire.[36]

Shortly after noon, each of the twelve transports had completed a drop. Two had already made their second drops and several had landed at Da Nang for refueling and reloading. During the next two hours, six more missions were completed, four by aircraft reloading at Da Nang, one by a fresh A-model crew, and one by Major Gibson's crew, the first to recycle through Cam Ranh. Weather conditions in the valley during Gibson's second sortie were even worse than during the morning flight. The crew released from only three hundred feet, accurately and without apparent damage to loads. Thus, in twenty drop sorties, over 270 tons (mostly munitions) had been delivered. Seven planes had been hit by ground fire. One C–130B, flown by Lt. Col. William Coleman, was heavily damaged with multiple hits through the wing fuel tanks. On the ground at A Luoi, Army officers were profuse in their appreciation. The supply situation was getting tight with some 105-mm firing positions out of ammunition. The heavy weather stopped helicopter deliveries at midmorning, but the C–130s continued to get in. The combat control team relayed an Army request for an unplanned rations drop and the requested items were dropped in the afternoon missions.[37]

Disaster intervened on the twenty-first drop of the day. At about three in the afternoon, Strobaugh and Mullen watched from the ground as a C–130B approached. The run-in path appeared identical to that of the earlier ships, except that the ship broke through the overcast farther south than most. Fighter support was still absent. The Hercules began taking 37-mm and .50-caliber fire, and its radio transmissions were silenced. As it approached the drop zone the crew attempted unsuccessfully to jettison the load. As the plane crossed the drop zone, struggling to hold altitude, holes could be seen in both wings. One engine streamed smoke or fuel while smoke trailed from the fuselage, apparently from fire in the ammunition-laden cargo compartment. Maj. Lilburn R. Stow, an experienced and highly regarded pilot, guided the stricken aircraft into a descending turn, attempting an emergency landing at the A Luoi strip. The craft smashed into trees, the resulting explosions killing the six crewmembers and the two airman photographers on board. The day's drops ended with the crash, and several transports already airborne were directed to return home with their loads. It had been, in the words of one navigator, "a bad day for the C–130s."[38]

The abysmal weather in the valley continued on April 27, the second day of the drops. It prevented helicopter resupply as well as the installation of ground control approach equipment, and thwarted fire-suppression air strikes. Drops resumed at nine in the morning. Major Gibson reported weather similar to that of the previous day with ragged ceilings well under 1,000 feet. The drop zone was moved almost beside the end of the runway, and by day's end seventeen more drops had been completed. Weather improved slightly the third day, allowing resumption of helicopter traffic and progress toward ground control installation. Fifteen C–130 drops were completed during the day. Procedures by now had become standard. Each crew began a steep descent from about 6,000 feet ten miles out, leveled off at drop altitude (usually 500 feet) about four miles out, and made a normal visual release at slow (130 knots) airspeed. Errors for the

Capt. Ross E. Kramer, an aircraft commander who managed to fly his battered C–130 to Da Nang Air Base on 29 April 1968.

fifty-two drops averaged under one hundred yards, remarkable in view of the dismal weather and enemy fire.[39]

Flying an aircraft blind into a valley lined by high terrain required considerable confidence in the navigator and his radar and doppler equipment. Near the drop zone, elevations higher than flight altitude lay within a mile of the run-in path. Upon starting the descent the doppler computer was checked against information from the Hue tactical air navigation center, but navigation during the run-in depended mainly on the navigator's APN–59 radar, which could clearly show the hills on either side of the valley floor. By steering the aircraft a proper distance from the right-hand side of the valley the navigator could guarantee a safe and moderately accurate run-in path. The doppler confirmed the heading and gave distance-to-go. Crews kept radio altimeters operating as a check on terrain clearance. Navigators made little effort to pick up radar beacon signals, preferring to concentrate on keeping the mountains in view on the scope. After visual release of the cargo the navigator immediately resumed radar navigation for the departure.[40]

During the morning of April 29, the fourth day of the drops, vicious enemy fire nearly claimed a second victim, a C–130E flown by a TAC crew commanded by Capt. Ross E. Kramer. This was the crew's fourth mission into the valley. Warned to expect antiaircraft fire, the crew noticed as they approached the drop zone that cloud cover was incomplete and that ridge lines previously obscured were now visible from the air. Fighter escort aircraft were present but remained inactive well above the transport. Six miles from drop the crew saw a hail of tracers and began evasive maneuvers, but continued the run-in. Five miles from the drop zone they were hit by 37-mm shells, at four miles by .50-caliber fire, and at three miles by a projectile that exploded beneath the crew compartment. At two miles one engine was hit and was immediately feathered. Then a second engine lost oil pressure requiring shutdown. Captain Kramer decided to jettison the load. The crew managed to restart one of the lost engines and began a laborious climb, spiraling upward above A Luoi. At a safe altitude the crew steered for Da Nang. Safely on the ground, the crew discovered that seven feet of horizontal stabilizer were missing. The crew returned to Cam Ranh as passengers that afternoon and reported that the ride in the stricken C–130 had been "real terrifying." The battered aircraft remained at Da Nang for repair, serving for several months as a sightseeing attraction. Kramer's load landed well short of the drop zone and the cargo was recovered by a South Vietnamese unit.[41]

The drops resumed at A Luoi soon after this near disaster. To avoid the communist guns, pilots now spiraled down from almost directly overhead, exploiting breaks in the cloud cover or, when necessary, descending blind. The navigator's radar was of limited help during such maneuvers since it blanked during extended turns, so the doppler computer became all-important. Several crews broke out well off centerline during the day. This made it necessary to maneuver the heavily loaded planes at low level to get into position to drop, while the control team on the ground tried to give steering instructions and to help the crews line up. By day's end the crews had completed a total of twenty-two successful drops.[42]

Also on the twenty-ninth, helicopters succeeded in completing several delayed lifts into A Luoi, hauling in the cavalry division's command post and the division's 8th Engineer Battalion. CH–54 Flying Cranes, operating with limited fuel in order to clear high terrain along the route from

Camp Evans, delivered heavy construction equipment needed for airstrip restoration at A Luoi. The ground control approach equipment was installed, but awaited flight check under visual conditions.

Army personnel labored to retrieve the containers at the drop zone. Some were lifted by hand into Russian-built trucks captured in the valley, and moved to a collection point. Distribution to field units and artillery positions was by helicopter. Sometimes the helicopters picked up loads immediately at the spot of parachute landing. Except for occasional shelling of A Luoi, the enemy did not interfere with drop-zone activity. More dangerous were the descending containers. One crushed the combat control team's bunker, but fortunately nobody was inside. Another landed next to the control team's jeep, the parachute breaking off the jeep's radio antenna. The control team warned construction engineers when ships were arriving so they could avoid falling containers. The only attempted fuel drop resulted in a spectacular explosion on impact.[43]

The C–130s completed twenty-seven drops on April 30, the highest single-day drop effort. Drops averaged sixteen daily the next four days. Techniques changed only slightly. Fighter escort was provided whenever weather permitted, the fighters sharing radio frequencies with the transports. The ground control unit assisted the plane crews in lining up but, as before, all releases were made visually. A single C–7 Caribou landed successfully at A Luoi shortly before noon on May 2. Several other C–7s and C–123s arrived in the early afternoon prepared to land. Simultaneously, a thunderstorm rolled into the valley from the west, closing the strip and creating confusion as the smaller aircraft became mixed with the C–130s in the orbit pattern. Finally all planes left the area without delivering their loads, a fiasco according to one of the pilots present. The final drops were made on May 4, the date on which the first C–130 landed at A Luoi.[44]

The A Shau drops were more demanding than those at Khe Sanh, more dangerous for the aircrews, and required greater navigation skills. In nine days the C–130s in 165 drops released twenty-three hundred tons of cargo, including rations and two thousand tons of munitions. Deliveries were thus well above the forecast 220-ton requirement. The 380 tons dropped on April 30 exceeded the single-day airdrop maximum at Khe Sanh of 225 tons on March 18. All but one percent of the tonnage dropped was recovered with negligible damage. Except for seven loads dropped using modular heavy-equipment platforms, all drops were by container delivery system. Ground proximity extraction system equipment at one time planned for A Luoi was not used. The delays in ground control approach equipment installation were unfortunate, precluding use of blind-drop methods and increasing exposure to ground fire. In addition to the C–130B destroyed April 26, four aircraft received major battle damage during the drops.[45]

TACTICAL AIRLIFT

Among those witnessing the drops of the first days was Maj. Gen. John J. Tolson III, commanding general of the 1st Cavalry Division. General Tolson later expressed thanks and admiration to the C–130 crews on behalf of the division, for "one of the most magnificent displays of courage and airmanship that I have ever seen." But his suggestion that individual crewmen receive suitable awards for valor was not systematically pursued and later recommendations that some of the men be awarded the Silver Star were not approved. The A Luoi airdrops, however, confirmed not only the versatility of the C–130 force but also the extraordinary devotion to duty among its aircrewmen.[46]

The around-the-clock work of filling bomb craters and reconstructing the A Luoi strip began on April 29. A 1,500-foot segment was inspected and pronounced ready for Caribou landings at noon May 1 and for C–123s later in the day. Work continued to lengthen the segment to accommodate C–130s and on May 4 six C–123Ks, two Caribous, and two C–130 Hercules landed on the completed 2,900-foot strip. They lifted in 55 tons to supplement 165 tons airdropped by fourteen C–130s.[47]

The first C–130 landed at midday bringing in a ten-ton forklift and several passengers. The crew had tried to get in earlier in the day, but air traffic delays necessitated a return to Da Nang for refueling. After the second takeoff from Da Nang the pilot, Maj. Robert L. Deal, landed with little delay. The A Luoi strip, Deal reported, was the softest he had ever used, very dusty and still marred by chuckholes, apparently having been used by the communists as a roadway.[48]

Nineteen C–123s landed on May 5 and eighteen C–130s on the sixth, the latter delivering over 250 tons of cargo. The irregular high terrain complicated landings and approaches, especially to the north where elevations rose two thousand feet above field level only two miles from the airstrip. Enemy fire became a decreasing consideration since cavalry units combed the region well. (Major Strobaugh noted that the cavalry brigade was determined to beat the tally of other units in the valley in capturing 37-mm weapons.) None of the transports landing at A Luoi was hit, but rainstorms turned the red dust of A Luoi into mud, closing the airstrip from midday on May 7 until the morning of the ninth.[49]

Offloading at A Luoi was done by an Air Force aerial port team under 1st Lt. William J. Endres. The team arrived with the first C–130s, bringing in two adverse-terrain forklifts of a type introduced into Vietnam only a few months earlier. The work was hard and the life dusty with only a nearby pond for cleaning off dirt and sweat. The diet was C–rations

An Air Force Caribou takes off from A Luoi after delivering supplies, May 4, 1968.

supplemented by an occasional hot meal brought in by cavalry helicopters.[50]

Withdrawal began on May 10 when a Vietnamese battalion moved out by C–130 to Quang Tri. American logistics elements began leaving the following day. A total of twenty-eight C–130s had landed at A Luoi before rains in the afternoon of May 11 again closed the strip. And although fixed-wing landings were scheduled for the next few days, all further withdrawals were by helicopter. The aerial port team itself left by helicopter. Lieutenant Endres was told to destroy the forklifts, but instead he arranged for Army help in dismantling them into parcels suitable for CH–54 lift. The only piece of equipment left behind was the combat control team's radio jeep which had been totally destroyed.[51]

In all, airlift transports made 113 landings at A Luoi during Delaware, including 57 by C–130 and 26 by C–123. The C–130s delivered an average of 13 tons per sortie, the C–123s 4 tons, and the Caribous 2. Fixed-wing transports landed a total of 650 tons and flew out slightly more than two hundred tons.[52]

Allied officers judged Delaware a tactical and strategic success. They claimed 850 enemy killed and considerable weaponry captured including twenty-five hundred individual and ninety-three crew-served weapons of which twelve were 37-mm. The most notable weapons caches were found in the immediate vicinity of A Luoi. Costs to the cavalry division included the loss of twenty helicopters, damaged beyond recovery, and the loss of sixty-three lives. However, sightings of truck activity in the valley less than

TACTICAL AIRLIFT

a week after allied withdrawal confirmed that the interdiction would not be lasting. During Delaware, aircrews struggled with difficult weather using procedures for radar traffic control and instrument flight still in infancy. This led two pilots to conclude that the campaign showed the need for an "instrument-flight combat capability," including self-contained radar and doppler systems.[53]

The Air Force transport achievements at A Luoi reflected the evolution, since the early sixties, in utilizing fixed-wing aircraft in airmobile warfare. The success of fixed-wing transport in Delaware suggested that the capabilities of tactical airlift were understood by both air and ground officers and that neither conceptual nor organizational barriers now hindered its full exploitation. Moreover, the use of the American airhead at A Luoi, not only for resupply of the cavalry brigade but also for support of a Vietnamese regiment operating to the south, led the senior U.S. advisor on

Ammunition is loaded aboard a USAF C–7A Caribou for support of Operation Delaware in the A Shau Valley, 4 May 1968.

the scene to conclude that the Vietnamese were capable of mobile offensive operations deep in enemy territory "if they are provided the necessary aerial lift and resupply support." Delaware, however, revealed problems in transporting the combat control team with its equipment, the ground controlled approach unit, and aerial port equipment. These difficulties underlined the need for better planning and encouraged the view that the Common Service Airlift System needed its own helicopters for these purposes. Also important was the realization that low- and slow-flying transports were vulnerable at airdrop altitudes. And finally, the indispensable contributions made by the airlift system to the campaign, especially the spectacular performance of the airdrop C–130s, restored the occasionally tarnished reputation of airlifters among ground force personnel.[54]

Ten miles from the Laotian border, the camp at Kham Duc served as a base for allied reconnaissance teams and a training site for Vietnamese Civilian Irregular Defense Group troops. This border region southeast of Da Nang was among the most rugged in Vietnam and was nearly uninhabited except for the Vietnamese military dependents living in the Kham Duc village. The camp, village, and airstrip were situated in a mile-wide bowl, enclosed by hills rising abruptly to heights of two thousand feet. One Air Force airlifter described the setting as "a beautiful spot, absolutely lovely." C–130 crews had for years landed at the six thousand-foot asphalt strip. The C–130s began frequent landings in April 1968, bringing in American engineers and construction materials to improve the airstrip for sustained and heavy C–130 use. Hercules pilots detested the difficult landings at Kham Duc made dangerous by both weather and terrain, stacks of equipment beside the runway, and considerable enemy fire from the nearby high ground. Nevertheless, the C–130s lifted in some four hundred tons of cargo in the four weeks to May 8, and C–124 Globemasters delivered two twenty-ton bulldozers, too large for the Hercules.[55]

To counter obvious communist preparations for attack and to compensate for the loss of an important position several miles to the south, C–130s on May 10 hauled American infantry and artillery reinforcements to Kham Duc. Communist shells harassed the eleven C–130 landings, injuring several crewmen. C–130s, C–123s, and Caribous continued the buildup the next day, and by the evening of the eleventh, nearly fifteen hundred troops were landed including nine hundred Americans. General Westmoreland, however, reviewed the situation that evening and determined that the camp lacked the importance and the defensibility of Khe Sanh. So shortly after midnight he decided to pull out. The ensuing air

TACTICAL AIRLIFT

evacuation in the presence of a strong enemy was without plan and without precedent in American experience.[56]

Intense communist fire early on May 12 drove away the Chinooks and dashed expectations of uneventful withdrawal. General McLaughlin at 0820 was ordered by Seventh Air Force to start an all-out effort to evacuate Kham Duc. The 834th Air Division immediately dispatched two C–130s to the camp and flew others to Da Nang to await developments. Several 130s were rigged for container delivery, and crews were briefed for possible drops at Kham Duc. Meanwhile, the communists captured all hill posts and now ringed the entire Kham Duc camp with close-in firepower. American airstrikes, however, broke the backs of several infantry assaults.[57]

Army and Marine helicopters managed a few pickups during the morning but a downed Chinook blocked the runway for fixed-wing landings until dragged away at 1000. A C–130 flown by Lt. Col. Daryl D. Cole landed immediately and civilians, streaming from ditches alongside the runway, quickly filled the aircraft. As Cole began the takeoff down the cratered and shrapnel-littered strip, mortars burst on all sides flattening a tire. The crew aborted the takeoff, offloaded the passengers, and began stripping away the ruined tire. After two hours on the ground, and with fuel now streaming from holes in the wings, Cole finally managed a successful takeoff. The only passengers now were three members of an Air Force combat control team, whose radio equipment had been destroyed. Cole landed on a foamed runway at Cam Ranh. This exploit earned him the Mackay Trophy for 1968.[58]

At about 1100, while Colonel Cole was still on the ground, Maj. Ray D. Shelton brought in his C–123. The crew took aboard seventy persons including forty-four American engineers. Despite automatic-weapons fire and a dozen mortar detonations near the ship, Shelton got off safely. Meanwhile, three C–130 crews arrived over Kham Duc but were told by the airlift control center not to try landings. At 1230 another Hercules gave up a landing attempt because of the hostile fire. By 1520, with the communists now inside the camp's wire perimeter, only 145 persons had been lifted out by the one C–123 and fifteen helicopter sorties. But orbiting nearby were more than a dozen transports, a control C–130, and a C–130 carrying General McLaughlin.[59]

Hercules landings resumed about 1525. Maj. Bernard L. Bucher made a steep approach from the south and landed despite numerous hits. More than one hundred disorganized and panicky persons, mostly civilian dependents, crowded aboard. Either unaware of or disregarding the concentration of enemy forces to the north, Bucher made his takeoff in that direction. Tracer fire intercepted the plane crossing the north boundary. The stricken craft turned slightly and tumbled into a ravine where it crashed and burned. No one survived. Crewmen on later aircraft reported that the troops were shattered, indeed hysterical, after watching their families die.[60]

Landing behind Bucher was a C–130E flown by Lt. Col. William Boyd, Jr. Enemy troops were firing small arms so Boyd made an initial go-around just before touchdown. He loaded some hundred persons aboard, took off to the south, and banked after lift-off so the plane would be masked by the rolling terrain. The plane landed safely at Chu Lai despite dense interior smoke and numerous bullet holes. For this flight Boyd received the Air Force Cross.[61]

Next in was a C–130A commanded by Lt. Col. John R. Delmore, spiraling down from directly overhead. The flight mechanic, TSgt. John K. McCall, watched the scene of smoke, detonations, and aircraft. Bullets hitting the ship sounded like sledgehammers. Smoke curled through the cockpit floor, and bullet holes appeared overhead, "like a can opener." With all hydraulics gone, and almost out of control, the ship smashed into the runway. The wreckage came to rest beside the strip, the nose pressed into the earth. The five-man crew scrambled out unhurt but helpless. American soldiers guided the five to shelter and soon afterwards placed them aboard a Marine helicopter.[62]

Destruction of two 130s within minutes did nothing to inspire confidence in the orbiting transport crews. But they persisted and, for a short period after 1600, three C–130s managed to get in and out with full loads: an A-model flown by Lt. Col. Franklin B. Montgomery, a B-model piloted by Maj. Norman K. Jensen, and an E-model commanded by Lt. Col. James L. Wallace. Colonel Wallace described his experience in detail. During his approach he was aware of tracers but tried to disregard them and concentrate on landing procedures. He crossed the field at right angles, making a 270-degree turn at maximum rate of descent with power off and gear and flaps down. Touching down, he made a maximum-effort stop. More than a hundred Vietnamese scrambled aboard in such a near-panic that the loadmaster had to rescue a woman and baby trampled in the rush. A dozen or so Americans also appeared and were taken aboard. Shelling and enemy fire persisted so Wallace, like Montgomery and Jensen, took off southward. Although the controllers overhead did not realize it, these three C–130s had withdrawn the last defenders.[63]

The final evacuation was made possible by close-in air strikes. Fighters flew beside each approaching transport laying down a barrage during the run-in and providing a barrier of fire on both sides of the runway while the transports loaded. Helicopters timed their pickups to take advantage of the fire laid down for the C–130s. A downed air controller pilot, Capt. Phillip B. Smotherman, stayed on the radio on the ground until leaving on one of the last 130s. He and several airborne air controllers linked the C–130 control ship and an Army control helicopter with the helicopters, fighters, and transports.[64]

Then, just when things seemed to be going well, a near tragedy occurred. A C–130, flown by a TAC crew commanded by Lt. Col. Jay Van Cleeff, prepared to land at Kham Duc to pick up evacuees. Aboard was a three-man combat control team which already had been airlifted out of Kham Duc once earlier in the evacuation. But now the airlift control center inexplicably ordered that the team be relanded and left at the camp. Van Cleeff protested that the camp was almost completely evacuated, but the control center insisted that the control team be returned and left.

Obediently Van Cleeff landed his aircraft, and the three controllers scurried from the ship toward the burning and exploding camp. Van Cleeff waited patiently for two minutes for passengers waiting to be evacuated, and when none appeared he slammed the throttles open and took off. He dutifully notified the control ship that they had taken off empty, and was shocked to hear the control ship then report to General McLaughlin that evacuation of Kham Duc was complete. His crew immediately and vehemently disabused the commander. Kham Duc, they insisted, was not evacuated because they had, as ordered, just deposited a combat control team in the camp. There was a moment of stunned radio silence as the reality sunk in: Kham Duc was now in enemy hands—except for three American combat controllers.[65]

Meanwhile, Maj. John W. Gallagher, Jr., and the other two controllers ran through the camp and took shelter in a culvert next to the runway. They could see communist troops moving about so they began firing at them with their M–16 rifles. A C–123 approached from the south and touched down under fire from all directions. But not sighting the stranded men, the pilot, Lt. Col. Alfred J. Jeannotte, Jr., took off. Once airborne, he spotted the control team but dared not land because of low fuel. Jeannotte received the Air Force Cross for his actions.[66]

Next to land was another C–123, piloted by Lt. Col. Joe M. Jackson and Maj. Jesse W. Campbell. Their approach into the inferno was from eight thousand feet, sideslipping for maximum descent, with power back, landing gear and flaps full down, dropping "like a rock." Seconds after touchdown, the pilots braked the ship to a halt, took aboard the marooned controllers, and were rolling again. Communist troops fired savagely from the wrecked C–130 beside the runway with tracer and mortar fire that never abated. As the aircraft regained the air one of the rescued men recalled: "We were dead, and all of a sudden we were alive." General McLaughlin, who had witnessed the event from overhead, approved nominations for the Medal of Honor for both pilots. Colonel Jackson received the decoration in a White House ceremony in January 1969, the only airlifter so honored in the Southeast Asia war. Major Campbell received the Air Force Cross, and the rest of the crew were awarded Silver Stars.[67]

The dramatic rescue did not quite end the drama of Kham Duc. Another fiasco was in the making when the airlift control center, apparently unable to learn from past mistakes, ordered yet another plane to land another combat control party to search the camp for survivors. The plane's crew had witnessed Colonel Jackson's exploit but nevertheless was preparing to obey. However, the order was rescinded just before the aircraft landed.

Following the evacuation, air strikes demolished the remains of the camp, and helicopters picked up a few survivors from the hill posts over the next week. Although the evacuation of Kham Duc involved some eighteen hundred military and civilians, only 259 were lost and more than half of these were victims of the crash of Major Bucher's C–130. The U.S. Army lost twenty-five men. Two Chinooks, two Marine CH–46s, and two C–130s were destroyed. But Air Force transports brought out over five hundred persons, nearly all in the final minutes when speed was essential and only the indispensable C–130s could do the job.[68]

The events of May 12 tested morale and discipline and motivated many acts of individual valor and selfless cooperation among men of different services and nationalities. The ability of the Seventh Air Force to mass transport and strike aircraft in an emergency was proven, but the blunders with the combat control teams demonstrated that command and control during battle was not perfect. Aircrew dedication and persistence despite early disasters, however, assured Kham Duc of an honorable place in the history and tradition of the U.S. troop carrier arm.

As the convulsions of Tet subsided, America's leaders reconsidered the nation's strategy and goals. With the curtailment of bombing in North Vietnam came reappraisals of the American role in the South. Under Gen. Creighton W. Abrams, Jr., USA, who replaced General Westmoreland in early summer, MACV planners deemphasized major search-and-destroy activities, relying instead on smaller unit operations. On the question of keeping American troops in the highlands, the Air Force took the position that, despite the losses at Khe Sanh, A Luoi, and Kham Duc, the Air Force stood ready to provide airlift forces wherever needed.[69]

Airlift remained an important asset for the allies although missions now seldom had the urgency of those earlier in the year. In the northern provinces road and water transport recovered their former capacities, although airlifters still regularly supplied Dong Ha, Quang Tri, and Camp Evans. C–130s hauled a mechanized brigade from Da Nang to Quang Tri in July and many a soldier boarded a mud-spattered C–130 only a few steps from the silver C–141 that had carried him from Colorado. In the highlands of II Corps, C–130s flew 150 sorties to lift an airborne

TACTICAL AIRLIFT

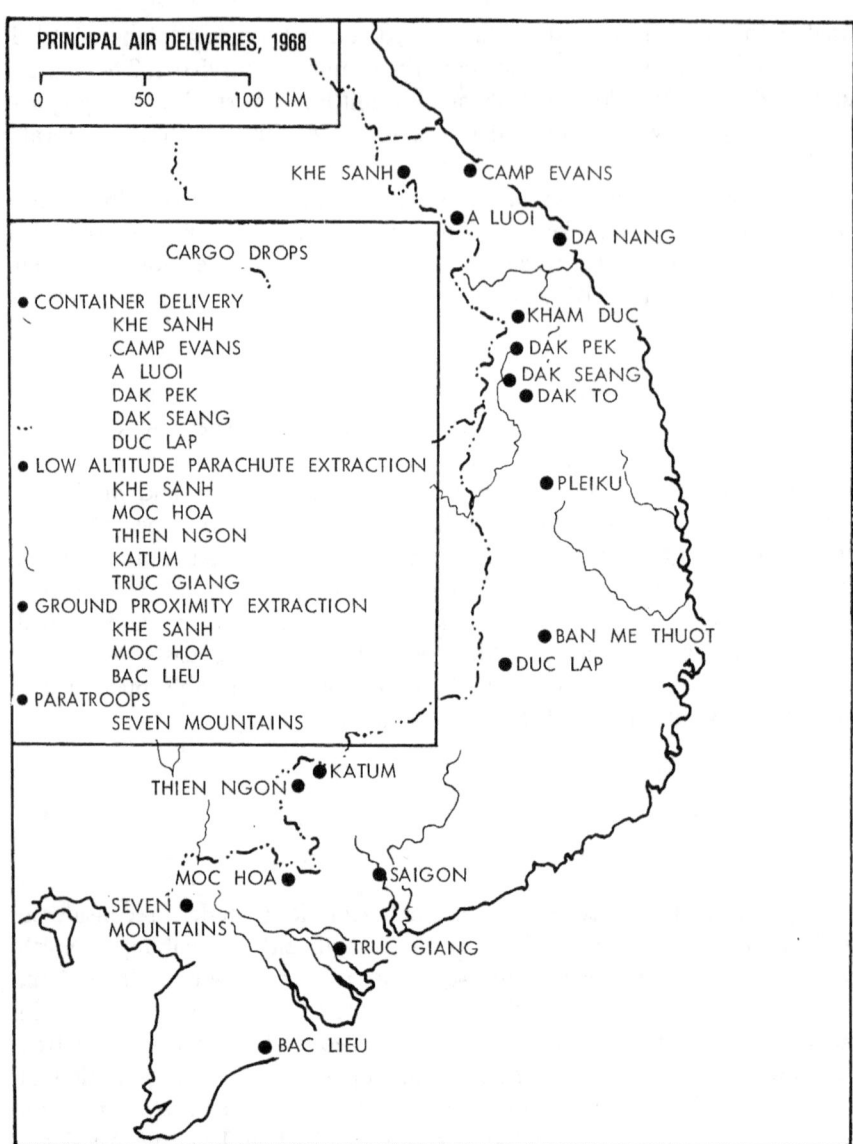

brigade to Dak To in May. The aircraft also made drops at the Dak Pek and Dak Seang camps for several weeks in June and delivered supplies to Ban Me Thuot during fighting at Duc Lap in August. The airlifters helped to cope with extensive communist attacks in May and a "third offensive" in August. The May attacks again necessitated moving the 123s and 130s away from Tan Son Nhut. A highlight of August was the airlift resupply of Katum, the camp developed in Operation Junction City. Activity increased in the delta, reflecting the increased number of American troops in that region, necessitating nearly a hundred air deliveries at five separate delta locations. The year's principal parachute assault took place on November 17 in the Seven Mountains area of southwestern Vietnam. Eight C–130s took the Vietnamese jumpers aboard at Nha Trang, and the expertly conducted venture again demonstrated the Common Service Airlift System's readiness for paratroop assault operation.[70]

Perhaps the most impressive unit movement of the war was Operation Liberty Canyon. In 437 lifts over two weeks beginning October 28, C–130s hauled eleven thousand five hundred men of 1st Cavalry Division and thirty-four hundred tons of cargo from the northern provinces to Song Be, Quan Loi, and Tay Ninh, new base camps northwest of Saigon. Eight extra C–130s, accompanied by extra maintenance men, were flown to Vietnam for the operation. Detachments for C–130 maintenance, airlift control, and aerial port activities were based temporarily at Camp Evans, a principal loading point. Cavalry helicopters were flown to the new bases, refueling at two or three points en route. Much heavy materiel went by water as far as Saigon for transshipment by air or road. The move placed the cavalry in the region promising the season's best weather. In leapfrogging the cavalry division more than three hundred miles, the C–130s showed their ability to expand the reach of the Army's air mobile forces.[71]

Studies for possible future operations into the Laos Panhandle also included concepts for the combined employment of airlift and airmobile forces. OPlan Full Cry, initially developed in 1966, envisioned seizure of an airhead in the Bolovens Plateau. Then C–130s would make some sixty resupply landings daily to sustain operations of the 1st Cavalry Division. The 1968 concepts for Operation El Paso entailed American and South Vietnamese overland penetrations westward from Khe Sanh. One option, however, prescribed a brigade paratroop assault as a means of conserving helicopter strength. Engineer troops would complete a C–130 airstrip inside Laos by the fourth day, and a second airfield would be readied to receive C–123s. Both airfields would have a fire support area with five-day stockage, and both would receive more than half their resupply by fixed-wing transport. The MACV feasibility study for El Paso was completed in June and reflected Westmoreland's conviction that such a venture was feasible and could be effective. Late-year diplomatic and political decisions, however, pointed toward American withdrawal and made such planning for the moment academic.[72]

Expectations of peace talks forecast the decline of the airlift system as well as the overall military effort in Vietnam. The monthly airlift workload reached a peak of 138,000 tons in March 1968 and then declined by five percent by year's end. C–130 sorties in Vietnam reached a maximum of 14,300 in March while C–123 sorties peaked at 9,500 in October. Until closure of the Nha Trang task force in April, the number of C–130s actually in Vietnam held at the February peak of ninety-six ships. One of the three C–130 squadrons temporarily assigned in Vietnam returned to TAC during the spring, and a second followed in August. Remaining were twelve permanently assigned offshore squadrons plus a single rotational squadron now manned from the 516th Wing at Dyess Air Force Base, Texas. The controversial issue of basing C–130s in Vietnam finally died out, reflecting the expectation that the U.S. war role would now diminish. At year's end only seventy-two C–130s were still in Vietnam.[73]

Despite the decline in activity, General McLaughlin and the 834th Air Division staff continued to work for managerial efficiency. Improving communications was a constant goal, and new facilities included teletype and telephone nets linking the airlift control center with control elements through UHF, VHF, and HF radio equipment in each control element. The airlift control center building at Tan Son Nhut was occupied just five days before Tet, providing additional communications equipment and a badly needed larger command post. The airlift control element network expanded to sixteen fixed detachments, and a mobile control element package of collapsible buildings was tested at forward sites. McLaughlin also directed that a preliminary mission schedule be published daily at midday, permitting aerial port detachments to recommend final changes based on the latest load information. McLaughlin's program for efficiency improved tonnage delivered per flying hour. In December 1968, tonnage delivered was fifteen percent above tonnage at the start of the year, and preliminary installations of automated scheduling and information flow promised further improvements in the future.[74]

At odds with this encouraging picture were the convictions of one C–130 crewman, apparently an officer, who wrote to a member of the U.S. House of Representatives charging the Combined Service Airlift System with mismanagement and serious inefficiency. The writer asserted that many missions were flown unnecessarily, that particular loads were repeatedly transshipped simply to raise tonnage totals, and that insufficient time was allowed for proper aircraft maintenance. The strongest criticism was directed toward the use of flying hour totals as basic managerial yardsticks in airlift squadrons and wings. This, he maintained, encouraged unnecessary flying. The writer's contentions reflected less extreme feelings often voiced by other crewmen, resentful whenever their efforts seemed wastefully employed. The 834th Air Division replied in an October message to PACAF denying the allegations and pointing out that crewmembers often failed to understand the importance of loads, such as construction materials, to ground units. The incident passed, but the fallibility of the flying hour yardstick and the danger that it could become an end in itself had been exposed. It also suggested that higher commanders needed to see for themselves conditions at the basic operating level. In this case, one individual felt it necessary to choose an irregular channel to expose shortcomings, hardly indicative of reform or of a climate of openness and self-examination within the Air Force.[75]

Eleven C–130 and five C–123 transports were destroyed during the Tet offensive and its aftermath. Ten of these were lost to enemy action, six in landing accidents. The total was equivalent to more than ten percent of the overall airlift capacity in Vietnam. Losses declined markedly in the second half of the year; two C–123s were lost in accidents, and a C–130 went down near Bao Loc, apparently the victim of enemy fire. Communist attacks on parked aircraft at Tan Son Nhut on March 21 and at Tuy Hoa on July 29 damaged nine airlift C–130s. All told, through June 1968, thirty-eight C–130s and an equal number of C–123s had been destroyed in airlift work in South Vietnam and Thailand. A total of 134 C–130 and C–123 crewmen had been killed or listed as missing. However, since few individuals flew more than a thousand sorties, and since aircraft losses averaged only one per thirteen thousand sorties, a man's chances of surviving a year's flying were good.[76]

But communist introduction of heavier antiaircraft weaponry in early 1968 held serious implications for the future. Now added to the 12.7-mm heavy machinegun was a Soviet 14.5-mm weapon, mounted on a two-wheeled carriage and served by a crew of five. Allied troops also captured 23-mm weapons near Hue in spring 1968. These were mounted like the 14.5-mm and fired projectiles designed to detonate and fragment on contact with aircraft. The 37-mm guns at Khe Sanh, in the A Shau Valley, and apparently near Kontum, raised the altitude of effective ground fire to above eight thousand feet. The communists had not yet used portable surface-to-air missiles (SAMs), but their potential effect on transport and helicopter operations was ominous. The U.S. Army decided against sending its own Redeye missiles to Southeast Asia lest the communists use captured or copied weapons against allied aircraft.[77]

For air and ground crews the stresses of 1968 intensified the strain of airlift duty. In the months after Tet, nearly all C–130 crewmen scheduled to return to the United States were held in their units well beyond normal departure dates. Undermanning, and therefore overwork, nevertheless persisted. At year's end, for example, the 463d Wing had only 175 qualified crews against an authorization of 256. Unsatisfactory living conditions also faced the C–123 detachments at Da Nang and Bien Hoa while the poor facilities for rest at Cam Ranh, coupled with considerable C–130 night flying, jeopardized operational safety. Morale nevertheless remained high, buoyed by the knowledge that, despite much "trashhauling," the overall job

TACTICAL AIRLIFT

was one worth doing. One relaxation was the inevitable off-duty gathering, at which were bawled lines such as these to tune of "Wabash Cannonball":

> Our planes aren't supersonic, in fact they hardly fly
> With jets and props and great big wings they're grappling for the sky
> With pilots and their grandsons, sitting side by side
> You can bet your sweet petunia, this will be a ride.
>
> Listen to the rattle, the rumble, and the roar
> As she rolls down the AM–2, they didn't close the door
> The crew is falling out the back and rolling on the ground
> But what the hell bartender, set up another round.[78]

For their role in the first five months of 1968, the men of the 834th Air Division and its assigned units earned the Air Force Presidential Unit Citation.[79] The airlifts at Khe Sanh, into the A Shau Valley, Kham Duc, and the countrywide effort during Tet, together were a culmination of decades of preparation in TAC and the development of the Combined Services Airlift System since 1961. In meeting these challenges, while maintaining countrywide air logistics service, the airlift system vindicated the Air Force's concepts of theater airlift operations under centralized management and control. Occasional mistakes were painful as in the case of the senseless marooning of the combat control team in Kham Duc and the absence of ground controlled approach equipment at A Luoi. But the valor of the airlifters in overcoming such mistakes confirmed the real measure of the men.

XIV. The Air Force Caribous

In early 1966 the Army and Air Force chiefs of staff agreed to transfer the Army Caribou force to the Air Force. This set in motion an eight-month changeover cycle. Both services cooperated wholeheartedly in the conversion, the Army Caribou companies in Vietnam phasing in Air Force air and ground crewmen while continuing daily missions. Six Air Force Caribou squadrons were established on January 1, 1967, all under the 483d Troop Carrier Wing in Vietnam.

In its first year of Caribou operations the Air Force generally surpassed prior Army performance, and most ground force users approved of the changeover. In managing its Caribou force the Air Force abandoned rigid doctrines of centralized control in favor of a "dedicated" arrangement, whereby each of several ground force users prescribed daily aircraft itineraries subject only to emergency MACV diversions. Air Force officers, however, never entirely lost hope of integrating the C–7A Caribous (formerly CV–2Bs) into the common service system for allocation and scheduling.

The Caribou, once viewed by the Air Force as a rival of and inferior to the C–123, proved an able vehicle in many roles. It proved invaluable for administrative courier work and emergency deliveries in weather and hostile fire all but prohibitive for other craft. The C–7s were especially valuable in resupplying Special Forces camps, a role largely relinquished by the C–123s. Air Force Caribou pilots admired both the reliability and the handling qualities of the aircraft and found satisfaction in the diverse missions. Having by 1968 accepted both the dedicated usage concept and the Caribou itself, the Air Force supported proposals for further C–7A procurement.

The six U.S. Army Caribou companies in Vietnam in 1966 operated from ten locations, most of them well known to Air Force airlifters. Each company was authorized sixteen ships (equal to an Air Force squadron), and each flew about ten missions daily. Each user command was responsible for scheduling and mission control and thus managed its own Caribou airlift for passenger, mail, medium cargo, and battlefield resupply. Principal users were the 1st Cavalry Division, the Special Forces, U.S. Army, Vietnam, headquarters, and corps-level American headquarters (III Marine Amphibious Force, I and II Field Force, Vietnam, and IV Corps senior advisor). Each was assigned between five and ten mission aircraft daily. Unlike the small Australian Caribou detachment at Vung Tau, only a token number of U.S. Army Caribous served within the common service system scheduled by the airlift control center.[1]

TACTICAL AIRLIFT

In some eighty thousand Caribou flying hours during 1962–65, the Army lost only four ships in accidents (enemy action destroyed a fifth ship). In February 1966, the first month of full six-company Army operation, flying hours averaged 2.5 daily per aircraft, slightly higher than programmed. Payloads averaged 1.7 tons per cargo-haul sortie.[2]

The Caribou transition was made without difficulty. Under Red Leaf, the joint basic plan of June 8, 1966, the Army kept responsibility for operational control and mission activity continued "without disruption to the Army tactical capability." The Air Force operated a training facility for pilots and airmen specialists at Fort Benning, Georgia, assisted by the Army. Graduates entered Caribou companies in Vietnam as replacements for Army personnel rotated out. Aircraft and equipment were transferred on December 31, 1966. Army personnel, however, did not shift to the Air Force.[3]

Aircrew training at Fort Benning began in May 1966 under the newly designated 449th Combat Crew Training Squadron, a component of the Sewart-based 442d Wing. Army instructors gave a concentrated three-week course for Air Force members designated for duty as instructors. The first student class entered in June, and by year's end nine classes, each approximately sixteen crews, had gone through overlapping four-week courses. Maintenance training began at Benning in August and was given by an Air Training Command team. Both programs moved from Benning to Sewart in December. Flying training was expanded to sixty hours per student (fifty hours had been standard) to overcome weaknesses in shortfield heavyweight operations and in low-level mapreading evident among the early graduates reaching Vietnam.[4]

The first Air Force Caribou pilots joined the 17th Aviation Company at Camp Holloway near Pleiku in late July, ready to begin in-country checkouts. The company moved almost immediately to An Khe where the men occupied tents erected over bare mud. The Air Force pilots learned the life of Army aviators, receiving orientation training in the use of infantry weapons and serving in self-defense platoons. These platoons were supposed to defend the living area and reinforce the outer perimeter if summoned. Air Force crewmen joined the unit at Dong Ba Thin (near Cam Ranh) on August 15 and shared the Army life of ancient tents, shaving out of helmets, and chasing rodents. By September Air Force crewmen were funneling into all the Caribou locations. They flew side by side with Army counterparts, the newly arrived pilots flying a half-dozen missions with an instructor, followed by a flight check. Air Force crewmen flew in the various tactical operations, and several earned decorations for landing the Army aircraft at isolated locations under enemy fire or in heavy weather. Gradually, Air Force members became the majority in each unit. The Army's Caribou crewmen regretted the loss of the Caribou and its mission, but men from both services agreed that the changeover was harmonious.[5]

The Air Force approved six new troop carrier squadrons in Vietnam, each with sixteen C–7 Caribous and twenty-four aircrews. The manning authorization was 1,555 spaces for the Caribou force, replacing 1,443 Army personnel. The 483d Troop Carrier Wing was activated at Cam Ranh on October 15, 1966, a nucleus of headquarters personnel arrived during the month, and Col. Paul J. Mascot assumed command on November 4. The staff set to work to develop the maintenance, support, and communications facilities and prepared plans to shift the squadrons to permanent sites. Bases were selected to take advantage of existing facilities, to gain logistic efficiency by reducing the number of operating sites, and to satisfy the Army that the aircraft remained near enough to be responsive. Withdrawal of Caribou units from the delta and from the cavalry division site at An Khe was especially controversial. A ruling by Secretary of Defense McNamara that the squadrons should be positioned at Air Force, not Army bases, paved the way for two C–7A squadrons each at Cam Ranh, Phu Cat, and Vung Tau.[6]

Logistic planners envisioned that heavy maintenance would be performed at the main support base at Cam Ranh. Supply functions also were to be concentrated at Cam Ranh with only sufficient spare parts and maintenance equipment at the other locations for flight-line maintenance and the replacement of defective parts. The Seventh Air Force director of maintenance surveyed the Caribou fleet in July 1966 and informed General Momyer that serious maintenance problems existed. A backlog of 250,000 man-hours of modification work was due, and aircraft had evidently been flown without proper maintenance. Cannibalization was an accepted way of life, documentation of completed work was often neglected, and aircraft were badly corroded in inaccessible places. Such conditions existed in Air Force airlift units in the early years but had been alleviated. The increasing number of Air Force maintenance men in the aviation companies was, in the opinion of the Seventh Air Force, raising standards toward those of the Air Force. Nevertheless, preparations were made to send an Air Force Logistics Command team to Cam Ranh in January to catch up on modification work and make major inspections.[7]

A series of major accidents, three of them fatal, plagued the changeover months. The most serious was the October 4 crash of two Air Force pilots into a hillside at An Khe during a ground controlled approach. Twelve persons died in the episode. During the first week of December alone, Air Force pilots were involved in four separate landing accidents. These mishaps were of urgent concern to Colonel Mascot who felt that the foremost problem was one of attitude. He shared the opinion of Air Force members of the Caribou units that the safe practices standard in Air Force units were being neglected, and pilots were accepting minimally airworthy aircraft for flight. In mid-December General Momyer, with Army concurrence, directed Colonel Mascot to assume control of the checkouts of Air

The U.S. Air Force took over the Army's Caribou operations on January 1, 1967. Here, prior to the transfer, USAF crews train with their Army counterparts at Vung Tau.

Courtesy: U.S. Army

From the "crow's nest" of a Caribou, the crew chief tells the pilot the way is clear to taxi for take off.

Courtesy: U.S. Army

An Army officer briefs Army and Air Force personnel on the transfer of the Caribous, September 1966.

USAF Lt. Col. John F. Yelton is briefed on the Caribou mission by Army Maj. Maynard A. Austin, commander of the 57th Aviation Company at Vung Tau. In the background is one of the Caribous.

Courtesy: U.S. Army

Force personnel in the Caribou companies. Even before this action, Mascot had directed his flight examiners to recheck pilots qualified under Army criteria. The most highly qualified pilots in each squadron were accordingly sought out to institute rechecks of the others. Checkouts for newcomers were also tightened to include a mandatory period of copilot duty. Only officers whose total flying experience was at least 750 hours were deemed eligible for first-pilot status. On December 11 Colonel Mascot directed all crews to review proper landing techniques, methods of computing landing roll and maximum safe weight, and insisted that each squadron commander designate assume aggressive supervision over Air Force crewmen during the final weeks prior to turnover.[8]

Other actions, too, occupied the Seventh Air Force, the 834th Air Division, and the 483d staffs in preparation for the Caribou assumption. New aerial port detachments were planned for points where heavy Caribou traffic was likely and other ports were expanded. Airlift control element detachments were planned for four additional locations, for a total of eleven. Airstrips to be used by Caribous were surveyed and tactical air navigation equipment was installed in Caribou cockpits. Safe weather operating minimums were carefully reviewed in view of the Army's practice of flying in conditions well below those officially specified for Air Force C–123s. Complicating the resolution of these and other matters was the inexperience of the 483d Wing staff of which not a single key member was qualified to fly the Caribou before arriving in Vietnam. Colonel Mascot consequently recommended that cadres should be formed at a base in the United States, before again creating new units in a theater of operations.[9]

A special problem was the lack of facilities at the new base at Phu Cat, where the only improvement was the three thousand-foot laterite strip used for hauling in construction items. During December the wing arranged for temporary barracks, messing and workspace tents, and for a surfaced parking ramp. Constant rain during late December hampered erection of the tent area, but the squadron movement from An Khe nevertheless began December 23. The second squadron moved from Qui Nhon soon afterwards. The shifts to Cam Ranh, where construction was ample, were less of a problem. Squadron aircraft arrived at the new location on January 1, and unit equipment was moved in by C–130 and LST. A change-of-command ceremony at Cam Ranh officially activated the wing's new squadrons. Fittingly, rain drove the ceremony inside a maintenance hangar.[10]

TACTICAL AIRLIFT

The Caribou transfer rekindled the troublesome issue of operational control. Should the planes be employed as part of the common service system or should they be allocated for mission control by specified users as hitherto? General Momyer in July reaffirmed the intention, expressed earlier by his predecessor, to bring the Caribous under airlift control center scheduling and control following their transfer to the Air Force. Ground force users strenuously objected. According to II Field Force, Vietnam, immediately available Caribous filled a gap in the airlift system and were "the sole factor preventing a state of near-constant tactical emergency." The 1st Infantry Division held that without the ready Caribous, helicopters would have to be diverted from combat tasks.[11]

In the April agreement between the Army and Air Force chiefs of staff, the Air Force agreed that in cases of operational need Caribous and C–123s might be "attached to the subordinate tactical echelons of the field army (corps, division, or subordinate commander) as determined by the appropriate commander." This confirmed long-standing roles agreements (Joints Chiefs of Staff Publication 2, 1959) and in May became part of the formal Army staff position on Caribou employment in Vietnam. General Westmoreland soon afterwards informally indicated that the agreement accorded closely with his own views. General McConnell on August 12 made clear his intention to compromise: "We anticipate that 1st Cavalry Division and possibly other Army units in Vietnam will validate requirements for attachments . . . with varying frequency over an extended period of time."[12]

General Momyer in October assured the ground force commands that no changes in employment procedures would be made in the first thirty days of Air Force ownership. Any subsequent changes would be gradual and would be made only after full study. Momyer envisioned that eventually most of the Caribous would be nominally integrated into the Common Service Airlift System but assigned on a daily basis to regional direct air support centers for usage outside the centralized request and priority systems. This appeared logical since the air support centers were collocated with the Army's corps-level tactical operations centers where most Caribou missions were apportioned. Momyer informed Westmoreland on October 31 that the Seventh Air Force would work to increase Caribou workload capacity, thereby permitting continuation of all present tasks while providing a surplus presumably for employment within the airlift system. The Director of Operations, United States Air Force, on December 5 advised PACAF that changes in usage should be made only after careful evaluation and after weighing the Army's need for responsiveness. Subsequently the Air Force late in the year approved a jointly developed manual for tactical airlift doctrine (AFM 2–50/FM 100–27, January 1, 1967). The manual described transport management from centralized control, as used with the C–130s and C–123s in Vietnam, to various arrangements for attaching transports to air support centers or to Army units.[13] Air Force approval of this manual confirmed acceptance of the concept that the Caribous would not be fully integrated into the Common Service Airlift System.

Meanwhile, General Westmoreland in November made a decision to assign the Caribou force not in "attached" status but rather in "direct support" of ground force echelons, leaving operational control nominally with the Seventh Air Force. Command and control arrangements followed those described in Joint Chiefs of Staff Publications 1 and 2 wherein a "supported force" commander indicated in detail the missions he wished fulfilled and a "supporting force" commander took action to meet these missions. Mission assignment procedures for use in January were designed to accord with General Momyer's October assurances and were patterned on those previously practiced by the Army.[14] 483rd Wing OpOrd 67–1, December 23, 1966, listed January airframe assignments based on the December MACV apportionment. The sixty mission aircraft desired were: ten each for the 1st Cavalry Division, I Field Force, Vietnam, and II Field Force, Vietnam; seven for Special Forces; four each for III Marine Amphibious Force and IV Corps senior advisor; five for Military Assistance Command, Vietnam; six for U.S. Army, Vietnam; two each for Military Assistance Command, Thailand, and U.S. Agency for International Development.

The operation order stated that each user would furnish mission itineraries to the airlift control center each afternoon for forwarding to the 483d Wing command post. The wing would then assign missions to particular squadrons and publish a daily assignment order. Users could make changes to itineraries at any time, ordinarily through the airlift control center and the wing command post. Certain officers held authority to make diversions in the field using a prescribed code word. A Caribou scheduling officer at the control center was in communication with the Caribou users, and a liaison officer from the 483d Wing coordinated activities with Army transportation officers at Tan Son Nhut. The 483d Wing command post was to monitor missions, communicating with aircrews directly or through airlift control elements, squadron command posts, and mission commanders in the field. Aircrews were to seek opportune loads at control elements or aerial port detachments only when a designated user was unable to provide a load. There were, however, several exceptions to these arrangements. Most significant was that the 537th Squadron at Phu Cat was designated to support exclusively 1st Cavalry Division. There was also to be direct mission coordination between the division and the squadron.[15]

Under this arrangement the airlift control center did not direct mission scheduling and control. This was in clear contradiction with past Air Force doctrines of centralization. The Air Force, however, could take satisfaction in retaining at least nominal operational control, and the ability of MACV to change allocations or direct emergency diversions was un-

TACTICAL AIRLIFT

questioned. Further, the Air Force anticipated bringing some of the Caribous into the common service system. Personal visits by Colonel Mascot to each of the user commands allayed misgivings among the ground force commanders.[16]

Although the Caribou squadrons were consolidated at three principal home bases, detachments of ships and crews still remained at six other points to provide a ready response to local needs. Activities at each outlying location were centralized under an onsite mission commander who was a senior officer from the squadron manning the detachment. The alignment of squadrons and detachments was subject to variations in detail over the next two years, but was initially:[17]

Unit	Home Base	Formerly	Operate Det at
457th TCS	Cam Ranh Bay	134th Avn Co (Can Tho)	Bangkok (2 acft)
458th TCS	Cam Ranh Bay	135th Avn Co (Dong Ba Thin)	Nha Trang (4 acft)
459th TCS	Phu Cat	92d Avn Co (Qui Nhon)	Da Nang (5 acft) Pleiku (4 acft)
535th TCS	Vung Tau	57th Avn Co (Vung Tau)	—
536th TCS	Vung Tau	61st Avn Co (Vung Tau)	Can Tho (2 acft)
537th TCS	Phu Cat	19th Avn Co (An Khe)	An Khe

As expected, the new units faced varied problems during shakedown. The maintenance crews labored to improve the condition of the force though hampered by heavy flying schedules and the necessity of adapting to the new facilities. The high frequency radio and hotline land communications of the wing command post proved extremely inadequate, allowing only limited monitoring of flight. Foul weather at the coastal bases complicated both maintenance and flying. Cam Ranh logged over nine inches of rainfall during January, and during one five-day period wind velocity remained steadily above thirty knots.[18]

Even with such handicaps, early achievements were creditable. Caribou flying hours for January exceeded slightly the December total and

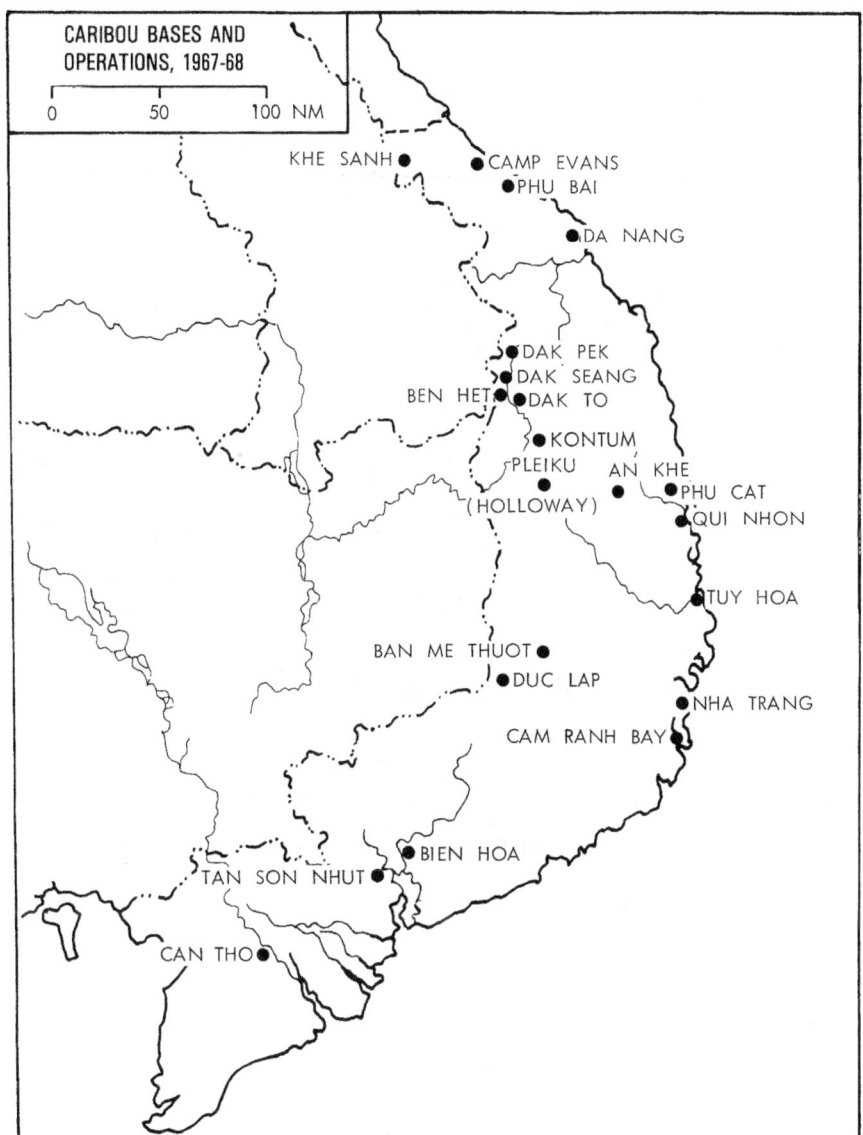

during February and March surpassed the 1966 monthly average by nine percent. Airlifted tonnage the first three months bettered the average 1966 performance by ten percent and the trend appeared clearly upward. Use of payload and space capacity was at least as effective as that of the Australian Caribou force operated under control center direction. Performance data was meticulously collected to counter the Army chief of staff's contention that the Air Force would be unable to match the Army's performance with the Caribous in Vietnam.[19]

At Cam Ranh Bay, Caribou mechanic Sgt. William T. Brown (right) discusses the C-7A engine with USAF Academy Cadet James D. Haas.

Despite a promising beginning, interservice acrimony soon appeared. On May 2, 1967, drawing from comments provided by II Field Force, Vietnam, the U.S. Army, Vietnam, advised Westmoreland and the Army staff that the shift to Air Force Caribou operation had necessitated increased use of Chinooks for movements to forward areas. Air Force Caribou pilots were unfamiliar with ground force problems, the Army stated, and "support and dependability" had suffered. Also, the Air Force's more stringent criteria for crew duty time, aircraft flying hours, and airfield safety had resulted in cancellation of some missions. The Army's message conceded that responsiveness, flexiblity, and support had been "good to excellent," but failed to point out that in contrast to the unfavorable comments from II Field Force, Vietnam, those prepared by I Field Force, Vietnam, had been unequivocal in praise of the new arrangement.[20]

General Momyer responded promptly, sending messages to West-

AIR FORCE CARIBOUS

Lt. Gen. William W. Momyer, Seventh Air Force commander, in October 1967.

moreland on May 8 and subsequently to PACAF and the Air Staff. The texts crisply answered the unfavorable comments. The inference that the Caribou transfer had resulted in a shift from tactical to logistical roles and had reduced airlift support to forward areas was false, Momyer insisted, since it was the user who determined itineraries not the Air Force. Momyer also pointed out that the alleged reduction of airlift support was in conflict with tonnage and flying hour data. The strong response muted criticism. Although individual Army officers occasionally grumbled over Air Force Caribou service (especially over the crew duty-time restrictions), official complaints were stilled.[21]

Modest steps to bring the Caribou force into the Common Service Airlift System were taken at mid-April. The 834th Air Division shifted responsibility for apportioning and monitoring C-7 missions from the 483d Wing to the airlift control center. This shift made available the superior communications and workspace of the control center while eliminating the wing level of operational control. Also the action made it possible to meet some Caribou mission requests by substituting fewer C-123 or C-130 sorties. The concept of the dedicated user remained unchanged, however. The airlift control center had no latitude in making up Caribou itineraries and as before was obliged to assign aircraft in designated numbers. General Westmoreland resisted suggestions for further integration of

Caribous into the airlift system. He informed CINCPAC on May 16 that there was "effective utilization" under existing arrangements and that a contingency plan was in existence in case the C-7s were needed to augment the common airlift system in some future situation. Colonel Mascot agreed. Appreciating ground force feelings on the subject, he judged that further shifts into the airlift system should be delayed for at least a year.[22]

Nevertheless, the 834th Division encouraged aerial port and control element detachments to take advantage of any lift capacity afforded by transiting Caribous. By late summer 1967, eighteen percent of the cargo lifted by the C-7s was classed as opportune. The C-7A liaison office at Tan Son Nhut became in effect an airlift control element, aerial port, and maintenance detachment, handling several dozen Caribous landing there each day. As early as the spring of 1967, Caribous were sometimes available over and above the sixty-ship allocation. This permitted some scheduling within the airlift system. Beginning toward the end of 1967, one of the Caribous allotted daily to MACV was designated for regular employment within the system, and by mid-1968 all five ships dedicated for MACV were customarily assigned to the Common Service Airlift System though only on a day-by-day basis. When still more Caribous were needed, the airlift control center or the traffic management agency sometimes asked dedicated users to relinquish aircraft or alternatively requested MACV to direct diversions.[23]

The 459th Squadron detachment at Da Nang undertook many of the tasks formerly performed by the C-123s. Missions from Da Nang included runs to Civilian Irregular Defense Group camps, resupplying the camp garrisons and U.S. infantry and artillery units operating nearby. One Caribou flew to Da Nang from Phu Cat each morning, hauling men and spare parts, and remained for a full day's flying in the northern region. The Special Forces units at Da Nang in March 1968 expressed thanks, "with the greatest sincerity," for the long hours, the seven-day week, and the bad weather flying by the 483d Wing, "the lifeline to our camps without which we could not survive."[24]

The four-ship detachment at Pleiku supported Special Forces camps in the region and flew a daily passenger circuit linking Pleiku with Holloway, Qui Nhon, Tuy Hoa, and Cam Ranh. The Cam Ranh squadrons took over the Pleiku duty in mid-1967 and the 459th Squadron shifted its emphasis to the coastal provinces north of Qui Nhon, using planes from Phu Cat. Special Forces resupply dominated the work of the Nha Trang and Can Tho detachments along with tasks for the regional corps-level commands. A communist mortar and sapper attack at Can Tho on the night of December 20/21, 1967, damaged two C-7s and eleven other American aircraft. This triggered an immediate reappraisal of dispersal arrangements. Caribous were withdrawn from Pleiku, Nha Trang, and Can Tho (although aircrew and maintenance personnel stayed) and thereafter took off from

Cam Ranh and Vung Tau each morning. Midday crew changes permitted a longer workday without breaking crew-hour rules. To cover emergency needs at the former sites, several ships and crews were kept on nightly alert at the home bases.[25]

The 537th Squadron, based at Phu Cat, had a distinctive mission. The full capability was dedicated to the 1st Cavalry Division. Relationships between the cavalry division and the squadron were excellent. The division set itineraries and came to regard the squadron as its own. Activities of the 537th Squadron fell into five categories. First, one or two ships were designated each day for FM radio relay work to link command posts with units in active field operations. The ships carried communications relay equipment operated by Army technicians and ordinarily stayed on ground alert, flying whenever required. The ground alert system was changed late in 1967, and the communications ships were used in airlift tasks subject to thirty-six-hour notice for relay work. A second regular mission task was aeromedical evacuation, both emergency evacuations and scheduled flights to lift patients to the Qui Nhon hospitals. Caribou flight mechanics received basic instruction in aeromedical practices although Air Force aeromedical specialists were sometimes carried. A third task, and the most common, consisted of routine courier and logistics flights linking An Khe with brigade and battalion locations. Fourth, the squadron made daily flights between An Khe and Tan Son Nhut hauling parts from Army aircraft. And fifth were battalion movements, roughly one per week, shifting units to new field locations or exchanging two units at opposite points.

Following the shift of the cavalry division to the northern provinces in early 1968, the 537th averaged fourteen round trips daily, linking the northern bases (Evans and Phu Bai) with the logistics sources at An Khe and Qui Nhon. Many such flights were between hard-surface fields capable of receiving C–130s. This wasted the Caribous' unique capabilities and forfeited the superior efficiency of the larger transports. The Air Force, however, chose to overlook this misuse to avoid any suggestion that the C–130s be incorporated in the dedicated user system. When the cavalry moved to the south in late 1968, the Vung Tau and Cam Ranh squadrons took over the duties of the 537th Squadron.[26]

The Caribou, in contrast with other transports, had poor cargo-handling characteristics. The plane's pallet and tiedown system was cumbersome in comparison with the pallet-handling system used with the C–130. Moreover, operative forklifts were unavailable at many remote sites necessitating loading and offloading by hand. Trucks sometimes damaged aircraft fuselages during cargo transfer. Ground forces sometimes failed to meet incoming aircraft and aircrews themselves had to offload. But tightened procedures and the Air Force practice of recording time on the ground helped to keep the Army people on their toes. By 1968 an Army load control supervisor nearly always met each incoming ship. Army personnel generally did the air terminal work but the Air Force was sometimes involved at the major fields. Helicopter shipments were handled separately and were usually loaded at another part of the airstrip.[27]

Total lift tonnage climbed steadily. Caribous lifted 183,000 tons in 1966, 224,000 tons in 1967, and 261,000 tons in 1968. These increases paralleled similar statistical gains by the Army's Chinooks. Shortages of Caribous, however, brought the number available for duty daily below an average of fifty in early 1968. Regular reexamination of aircraft allocations therefore became important. In June 1967, MACV decreed an "inviolate" minimum of twenty-nine mission aircraft with remaining allocations in order of priority to a total of sixty.[28] This C–7A service data for January 1968 illustrates the allocations breakdown, average payloads, and the extent of passenger service:[29]

User	Aircraft Daily	Sorties	Average Payload	Passengers (Percent of Total Payloads)
5th SF	8.0	1,910	3.02	56
1st Cav Div	8.0	1,236	2.29	85
III MAF	5.0	646	2.85	39
I FFV	6.0	998	2.02	69
II FFV	7.8	1,769	2.43	76
IV Corps	3.4	575	2.98	70
MACV	2.0	313	1.74	61
USARV	3.1	528	1.73	74
CORDS (AID)	1.9	342	1.61	25
834th AD	1.1	139	2.10	40
MACTHAI	2.0	141	1.66	76
Total/Average	49.0	8,597	2.59	67

Appraisals of Air Force Caribou operations were generally favorable. At a suggestion from the service chiefs of staff General McLaughlin and Maj. Gen. Robert R. Williams, U.S. Army aviation officer, appointed a joint field survey team to examine all aspects of Caribou operations. The team reported that rapport between airlifters and users was excellent, the only significant point of contention being the Air Force's crew-duty time restrictions. Army officers commented that Air Force transport crews left tasks unfinished because of the twelve-hour crew-duty rule, and contrasted such episodes with the reputation for perseverance of Army helicopter crews. Air Force leaders, convinced that crew fatigue caused accidents, continued to control tightly any duty extensions beyond a thirteenth hour. With this one exception, Army officers praised Air Force Caribou service. After reviewing the team's data, McLaughlin and Williams concluded in April 1968 "that the Air Force operation of C–7A aircraft has been effective and has resulted in a high degree of satisfaction and mutual regard."[30]

The dedicated user idea, however, was still controversial. Ground force officers were generally satisfied with Caribou scheduling and control arrangements, but officers of the 834th Air Division felt that more of the C–7s should be placed in the common user system, citing the tonnage accomplishments of the C–7s so employed in late 1968. Both General Moore and General McLaughlin, however, agreed that the Army had a valid need for some unscheduled airlift support similar to that provided by C–47 support aircraft at most Air Force bases. To force the Army to meet this need with its own aircraft, Moore reasoned, "would not advance any Air Force cause." Several years later, General Moore restated this view. He suggested, however, that the Air Force assure that ground forces use dedicated transport properly, and not as a substitute for the more efficient common service airlift. In their 1968 study, McLaughlin and Williams agreed that the dedicated system afforded the ground force commander a degree of reliability, responsiveness, and convenience beyond that offered by the common service system. It was irrefutable, however, that as long as airlift was scarce (and in 1968 numerous requests for common service airlift had to be turned down each day) any substantial diversion of aircraft to a separate dedicated user system had its price. McLaughlin, therefore, although supporting the arrangement which had evolved in Vietnam, advised caution in basing future doctrine on the Southeast Asia experience.[31]

For the C–7 aircrews, flying in Vietnam was both hard work and high adventure. The simplicity of the aircraft, and the primitive and remote airstrips often used, made a pilot's tour a memorable experience in "good, old-fashioned, seat-of-the-pants flying." All acknowledged that the aircraft itself required no outstanding flying ability, but felt that the challenge of mission and environment was more than enough. Special Forces resupply work required top skills in shortfield and rough-field work and in airdrops. Crews flying for cavalry and infantry divisions shared congested airheads with helicopters, faced hazards from friendly artillery fire, and were forced to make difficult landings at unimproved strips. Few sorties were free from concern over terrain or weather or both. And the possibility of hostile ground fire was ever present, a danger intensified by the Caribou's slow airspeed and sluggish climb performance.[32]

The Caribous sometimes flew in weather prohibitive even for helicopters. The planes were fully instrumented and many of their pilots were veterans of years of instrument flying, reflecting the emphasis on all-weather flight in the peacetime Air Force. Operating out of Phu Cat, for example, the C–7 crews took advantage of the excellent radar control facility there, which assured traffic separation and safe navigation during takeoff and landing. Confidence in the Air Force ground controlled approach at Phu Cat was high, but a 1966 accident at An Khe reduced confidence in the Army ground control there and for a time caused disagreements with the cavalry over safety measures. The new tactical air navigation equipment served as a check on ground controlled approach reliability although shortages of spare parts kept many tacan sets out of commission. The Caribou's nose radar also was helpful in foul weather flying, showing shorelines, terrain features, and precipitation clouds. When penetrating clouds, crews obtained advice on other traffic from ground radar sites. In occasional emergency situations, crews flew beneath ceilings as low as three hundred feet. More typically, however, crews stayed under low ceilings by flying offshore, avoiding the dangers at low level of terrain and enemy fire.

Before landing at remote strips, crews inspected carefully the condition of the runway, noted any obstructions, and assured themselves that friendly forces were present. For shortfield landings in insecure areas, crews flew directly overhead at three thousand feet, slowing to about one hundred knots. Then, with gear and flaps down, the pilot began a tight descending spiral holding airspeed just above stall-warning. At the runway threshold, power was further reduced and the nose raised. Caribou landing gear was designed to withstand vertical impact at fourteen feet-per-second, roughly thirty percent greater than other transports. After touchdown, brakes were pumped in one-second applications for maximum effect, and heavy reverse power was applied after assuring that pitch of both props was reversed to avoid loss of control from unequal forces. When departing, crews stayed close to the airstrip perimeter in a circling climb.[33]

The preferred tactic for avoiding enemy fire during a flight was to stay three thousand feet or more above the terrain. If lower flight was necessary, protection could be gained by flying at treetop level or along ground contours. Crews flying under clouds were urged to stay close to the overcast, ready to climb quickly into protective cover if fired upon. The 483d Wing enjoined its aircrews to be aware of the battle situation on the ground, and distributed diagrams showing sectors of high threat.[34] These measures held down hits to two or three a week. Only two Caribous were actually destroyed by enemy fire during the first two years of Air Force operation. The first was lost on December 13, 1967, when a single round cut a fuel manifold causing the plane to run out of fuel. The pilot, Capt. Kenneth L. Crisman, made a wheels-up landing in a rice paddy near Binh Thuy, without injuries to personnel. The second ship went down near the border northwest of Saigon on August 26, 1968. The crew reported hits by ground fire before the plane crashed and exploded. A third C–7 was destroyed by enemy shells on the ground at Vung Tau on April 23, 1968.[35]

Air Force officers hoped to achieve a safety record with the Caribous superior to the Army's. Initial success was remarkable; the Air Force had no accidents, either major or minor, during the first three months of 1967. This compared with eight accidents the previous quarter and twenty-seven during all of 1966. For the rest of 1967 and 1968 the 834th Air Division reported ten major Caribou accidents, equal to a two-year rate of 4.5 accidents per one hundred thousand flying hours. This was only slightly above the Air Force worldwide rate for all aircraft types.[36]

Holding down the accident rate was the strong remedial program begun by Colonel Mascot in December 1966. Examiners monitored each squadron's flying practices, administered check flights to pilots without notice, and identified the weaker pilots for remedial training. The C–7's vulnerability to helicopter wash, the value of practicing ground controlled approaches, and the dangers of using shortfield techniques unnecessarily were emphasized. Supervisors stressed crew coordination techniques; pilots and flight engineers were apportioned tasks during takeoffs and approaches, backing one another against the possibility of mistake. The wing acted to standardize cockpit arrangements among all assigned C–7s, and coordinated with Special Forces to improve camp airstrip markings. Crews were instructed to report hazards by telephone to wing headquarters, in addition to filing formal written reports. Schedulers assigned the most experienced pilots to the more demanding missions, and attempted to keep integral crews together. A list of especially difficult fields, where pilots were allowed to land only after special briefings, was published. Most important was the continual preaching by safety, operations, and examining officers, and by commanders that mission expediency was no excuse for an accident.[37]

Each aircrew consisted of an aircraft commander, a copilot, and a flight engineer. The large numbers of crewmen leaving after completing twelve-month tours late in 1967 produced temporary shortages, reducing crew levels to well below the authorized ratio of 1.5 crews per aircraft. Compounding the shortage was an increase in the daily flying rate from 2.5 to 3.0 hours per aircraft. To offset the attrition, the departures of some men were delayed and the arrival dates of some replacements moved up. The newcomer pilots proved competent, all were graduates of the Sewart school, and were capable of serving as copilots after a short checkout. Individuals with fifteen hundred hours of total flying experience and 120 hours in the C–7 were eligible for upgrading to aircraft commander. A total of 750 hours was required for first-pilot designation, which allowed an individual to make landings without an instructor on board. Nearly half the newcomers were recent graduates of undergraduate pilot training serving their first cockpit tours (127 in April 1968). Most other newcomers were veterans with at least five years of peacetime flying experience. At one point over fifty of the pilots were lieutenant colonels. Two were fighter aces of World War II, and six were Ph.D.'s.[38]

TACTICAL AIRLIFT

There was a chronic shortage of flight engineers because of the undesirability of the job. Caribou flight engineers doubled as loadmasters which entailed hot and dirty stevedore tasks. Proposals to add loadmasters as fourth crewmembers had been disapproved apparently because of the additional manpower required. Even though one of the pilots usually pitched in to help the engineer offload when ground personnel were absent, volunteers for tour extensions among flight engineers were rare. Several expedients brought temporary relief. These included use of temporary-duty engineers from the United States, some of them back in Vietnam only a few months after completing full tours in Southeast Asia. Since the simplicity of Caribou systems reduced the need for a skilled engineer, the 483d Wing late in 1968 began studying the feasibility of substituting loadmasters for engineers.[39]

Air Force success in maintaining the Caribous was most impressive. In the first months of 1967, extraordinary efforts were made to raise the force to Air Force standards after long, hard use with little preventive maintenance. Contract teams from the Air Force Logistics Command joined 483d Wing and base maintenance personnel in standardizing the planes, completing overdue modifications, repairing corrosion damage, and in some cases (according to an officer in the 834th directorate of materiel) practically rebuilding certain planes. Operational-ready rates steadily climbed from the seventy-one percent reported by the Army in December 1966 to a peak of eighty-six percent during July, August, and September 1967. Flying hours also increased from eight thousand hours monthly in early 1967 to over ten thousand hours monthly during 1968. These increases were achieved by hard work, and with manpower increases. During August 1967, for example, each man of the 537th Squadron's flight-line section worked an average of ninety-two overtime hours. The drop in experience during late-year turnover was a serious concern since incoming maintenance men went through only a seven-day orientation on the Caribou at Sewart Air Force Base. But the newcomers met the challenge. One veteran officer, commander of the Nha Trang detachment temporarily during 1968, declared that maintenance on the C–7 was "the best I've seen in the Air Force."[40]

The 483d Consolidated Maintenance Squadron, organized in January 1967 at Cam Ranh, performed most field maintenance for all six C–7A squadrons. Each squadron retained its own flight-line (crewchief) sections, but intermediate tasks were centralized in one squadron at Phu Cat and one at Vung Tau. Small maintenance teams worked at the detachment locations sometimes helped by specialists from local base personnel. Depot-level maintenance and corrosion control processing were done out of Vietnam. Parts supplies were stocked primarily at the Cam Ranh base supply office, with lesser supplies at Vung Tau and Phu Cat. Parts shortages were frequently overcome by cannibalization; in March 1968 for example the wing cannibalized 327 items. The Caribou's basic reliability held down parts problems except for certain engine and landing-gear components vulnerable to operations on dirt strips.[41]

Health and welfare conditions, though marginal by Air Force criteria, were well above Army standards. By the end of 1968 most officers lived in air-conditioned billets, and most enlisted men had hot-water showers and indoor latrines. Like other airlifters the men of the Caribou units were generous with their spare time, ingenuity, and funds, contributing to various schools, orphanages, and welfare programs. Although these projects touched only a few among the destitute Vietnamese population, they were undertaken in the spirit of humanity and were enormously satisfying to those who participated.[42]

For most members of the 483d Wing, Caribou duty was unlike any past or likely future job. Nothing else in the Air Force quite resembled either the C-7 or its mission. A special bond of common experience therefore linked the Caribou airmen, even though they were scattered at several locations in Vietnam. A frequent meeting place was the flight line at Tan Son Nhut where the men learned unofficially what was going on in the other units. Accounts of hairy missions and wild parties were part of Caribou lore, and memorable personalities included Lt. Col. James F. Akin, Jr., commander of the 535th Squadron, who mounted a machinegun in the rear of a "Bou" to answer enemy fire, and Lt. Col. Paul A. Whelan, ordered briefly home from Caribou duty to receive his Ph.D. degree in history as a result of a letter his son wrote to President Johnson.

Caribou roles in the larger search-and-destroy ground operations were modest. The aircraft's use was usually limited to single-ship administrative or high-priority airlift between base camps and forward operating locations. The C-7 was far inferior to the C-130 in payload capacity, and was rarely used for brigade movements or large-scale resupply. Occasionally, however, the Caribous performed tactical tasks for which they were especially suited, landing at points inaccessible to larger transports or making airdrops into small drop zones.

In a notable emergency lift the night of May 4/5, 1967, the Caribous joined Chinooks in hauling reinforcements to a fifteen hundred-foot strip thirty miles east of Bien Hoa. Surmounting thunderstorms, sporadic enemy fire, and unfamiliarity with the airstrip, six C-7s made twenty-eight landings by the light of portable lamps installed by combat control teams. Together the Caribous and Chinooks landed an entire battalion by dawn. Later in the summer the Caribous began a continuing flight to the allied base at Khe Sanh, at that time closed to C–130s and C–123s. The 459th Squadron daily hauled in petroleum supplies and foodstuffs and took back passengers, casualties, and parachute materials recovered from C–130 airdrops.[43]

Missions into the allied Special Forces camps at Dak Pek and Dak Seang, located in the mountainous area north of Dak To, were especially difficult. At Dak Pek rugged terrain forced steep final approaches at treetop level. To overcome severe downdrafts, pilots learned to add power generously when reaching the approach end of the runway. Takeoffs with heavy loads were extremely hazardous. The sod-and-gravel strip sloped upward to the north and gave poor braking action when wet. Runway length was fourteen hundred feet, barely adequate in view of the field's two thousand-foot elevation. Approaches to Dak Seang were somewhat less difficult, but the narrow and unpaved strip was tricky in crosswinds. Proximity of enemy troops to both camps added to the hazards. Three times during June 1967 the 483rd wing made one-day emergency shuttles into Dak Pek, for a total of over two hundred sorties. The missions on June 10 began at midday. Five crews were diverted from scheduled itinerary and five others took off from home bases. By nightfall seventy-seven C–7 sorties had lifted in over five hundred troops and thirty tons of cargo. American infantry commanders praised the "proficiency and courage" of the C–7 crews in the marginal-weather Dak Pek buildup.[44]

To make an airdrop a pilot would increase power and raise the ship's nose when passing over the drop zone. Simultaneously, cargo-handlers in the rear cut the load-restraining rig and shoved the bundles rearward. These bundles were usually mounted on four-foot-square wood pallets each holding about two thousand pounds. Several pallets, each connected to its own cluster of descent parachutes, could be released in a single pass. Release was usually from about four hundred feet with occasional free-fall drops from much lower. Procedures for dropping through overcasts using ground radar guidance, and for the Army extraction method, were provided but seldom practiced. Fewer than one percent of C–7 sorties were airdrops, and cargo dropped averaged only two hundred tons monthly. An exceptional series of fifty-six drops at Ha Thanh (west of Quang Ngai), however, helped save that camp during the enemy's August 1968 third offensive.[45]

For the Caribou airlifters the battle at Duc Lap in August 1968 was the climactic event of the period. Allied air power—strike aircraft, helicopters, and Caribous—made possible the survival of the South Vietnamese defenders. Use of the C–7s for airdrops in this desperate situation, in preference to costly and less maneuverable larger transports, established a pattern for similar operations.

Prompted by allied troop movements, the communists at mid-summer halted preparations for an attack on Ban Me Thuot to concentrate on a new target, a border camp to the west at Duc Lap, garrisoned by several half-strength Vietnamese irregular companies and American Special Forces advisors. Three rings of barbed wire surrounded the camp, enclosing two hills and numerous strong points. The surrounding terrain was hilly and heavily forested. The camp's airstrip was normally suitable for Caribou landings, and had been kept open by constant repairs. But the strip lay outside the defense perimeter and was therefore unusable during the communist attack. Stocks of food and munitions were at normal levels at the outset of the August siege, except for ammunition for the camp's lone 105-mm howitzer. Water supplies were also tight.

Shortly before the initial assaults on Duc Lap, the communists dug trenches undetected, reaching within two hundred yards of the camp's perimeter. Communist shelling, sappers, and infantry attacks began after midnight August 23 and soon involved four thousand troops of the 1st North Vietnamese Division. Bridge destruction made access to the encircled camp possible only by air throughout the battle.[46]

U.S. Army helicopters made four resupply deliveries into Duc Lap on August 23, hauling mainly munitions from Ban Me Thuot. The helicopters also brought in Vietnamese reinforcements after communist infantry temporarily captured the northern half of the camp. C–123s and C–130s meanwhile lifted other units to Ban Me Thuot, in readiness to reinforce Duc Lap.[47]

Caribou resupply drops by the 457th and 458th Squadrons began on the twenty-fourth. A major difficulty, however, was the small size of the remaining friendly zone, roughly seventy-five yards square. The first drops were made by a crew under Capt. David M. Rogers flying his final day in Vietnam prior to reassignment. Captain Rogers flew through heavy tracer fire, made a series of turns and evasive maneuvers, and leveled off at three hundred feet only during the final fifteen seconds of the drop. Two separate runs were necessary because of the short drop zone, but all but one bundle landed inside the compound. Returning to Ban Me Thuot, the crew discovered that battle damage was minor and took aboard a second load. On the second mission they encountered heavier ground fire, but again made a successful delivery. A third mission later in the day, by Maj. James L. Montgomery and his crew, also was a success. In the three sorties the Caribous delivered six tons of 105- and 81-mm ammunition and fuzes. Two helicopters also made deliveries during the day, bringing in small arms and artillery ammunition.

Late that afternoon the 458th Squadron alert crew at Cam Ranh Bay, commanded by Maj. George C. Finck, was called out for an emergency drop. Major Finck's crew flew to Nha Trang to load and took aboard two Special Forces riggers to help over the drop zone. Finck took off in darkness and steered for the glowing sky over Duc Lap. The compound was lit by flares and displayed a single steady light for identification. Enemy fire was heavy but inaccurate over the drop zone, and the darkened Caribou showed neither lights nor engine exhaust flame. Although the aircrew was told that both passes had been successful, the 5th Special Forces Group later reported that the bundles in fact failed to land inside the compound. This flight is believed to have been the first operational C-7 night drop.

At noon on August 25, Special Forces personnel at Duc Lap reported to Nha Trang that prospects for the camp's survival were "doubtful." All materiel resupply on that critical day was by Caribou drops, the helicopters being entirely occupied in airlifting troops. Maj. Hunter F. Hackney and his crew, from the 458th Squadron, loaded cargo at Nha Trang but landed at Ban Me Thuot without dropping the load after learning that fighting at Duc Lap was too heavy to permit the troops to retrieve the supplies. Hackney took off again at midafternoon, orbited east of Duc Lap, and turned toward the camp immediately after heavy air strikes, hopeful that enemy gunners would have been driven under cover. The hope was mistaken—ground fire began two miles from release. The ship received hundreds of hits but managed to complete an accurate first pass. Making the second pass from a different direction in hopes of a safer approach, Major Hackney found enemy fire equally vicious but again made a satisfactory drop. Landing at Ban Me Thuot, the crew discovered fuel leaks from all cells (in spite of "self-sealing" tanks) along the entire length of both wings. Hackney and his crew changed to another aircraft and made a second drop sortie, this time rigging the load to permit quick release of all four pallets in a single pass. The fresh ship approached Duc Lap from still a different angle, received substantial damage, but survived. During the day two other crews also took off from Ban Me Thuot. They were commanded by Lt. Col. Elbert L. Mott and Maj. Charles J. Bishop, both from the 457th Squadron. The four sorties by Hackney, Bishop, and Mott succeeded in delivering over eight tons of water, rations, munitions, and medical supplies. Two other Caribou drops during the day originated from Pleiku. All sorties were unescorted. Crews flew at treetop level until just prior to cargo release then popped up to about three hundred feet, the minimum altitude for the parachute to open.

Missions on August 26 originated from Ban Me Thuot and Nha Trang and followed the pattern of the previous day. During three days, August 24–26, Duc Lap received a total of forty-three tons of supplies, twenty-six tons in thirteen Caribou drops, and nineteen tons by helicopter, retrieved by armed ground parties just outside the inner wire. Chinooks thereafter took over the heavier resupply effort, shuttling from Ban Me Thuot. Bitter fighting by the allied reinforcing units finally ended the threat to the camp. The campaign officially ended on September 10 and Caribou landing resumed at Duc Lap about five days later. The allies claimed a clear victory, having captured over 140 enemy weapons including 56 crew-served guns. Enemy casualties numbered about eight hundred compared to

140 allied dead. Eleven allied helicopters were destroyed during the fight. Majors Hackney and Finck were awarded Air Force Crosses for their missions.[48]

The Duc Lap campaign again confirmed the allies' ability to maintain garrisons in remote regions despite enemy concentrations. Moreover, prospects for future Vietnamization of the war effort were heightened by the South Vietnamese infantry's success in bitter fighting and by the successful use of the C–7, a ·relatively simple ship seemingly well suited for future Vietnamese ownership and operations. The Caribou's ability to penetrate enemy fire nearly prohibitive for helicopters and heavier transports, and to deliver cargo successfully into a minuscule drop zone, foretold its use in future situations of similar difficulty.[49]

The successive commanders of 483d Wing, Cols. Paul J. Mascot, William H. Mason, and Wilbert Turk, as well as most subordinate officers, judged that the Caribou force performed well in Vietnam. The C–7 was able to do many of the same jobs as Chinooks or the larger transports and often at less cost. General McLaughlin cited the Caribou's ruggedness, its ease of maintenance, and its maneuverability at slow approach speeds, as being especially valuable in conditions of limited visibility. The craft's weaknesses, in McLaughlin's view, were its marginal single-engine performance when heavily loaded, its incompatibility with other cargo-handling systems, and its instability in turbulence.[50]

The Air Force appraisal of the Caribou had changed drastically since the early 1960s. Prior to 1966 the air commands in Hawaii and Saigon had opposed expansion of the Caribou force in Vietnam, contending that added airlift requirements should be met by C–123s or by airdrops. Prompted by Air Force headquarters, and with the questions of ownership and control near settlement, both PACAF and the Seventh Air Force in June 1966 gave support for expanding the Caribou force in Vietnam from six squadrons to nine, a proposal strongly favored by the Army, MACV, and CINCPAC. Although the Secretary of Defense late in the year disapproved purchase of the additional aircraft needed for the expansion, the idea persisted, to reappear in 1968. The McLaughlin–Williams study early in the year recommended a three-squadron expansion and General Momyer in June urged additional capability of the sort provided by Caribous. Lack of money, however, caused McConnell and the Joint Chiefs of Staff to withdraw proposals for Caribou purchases in order to use the funds to develop next-generation aircraft.[51]

Air Force support for the Caribous, and for the dedicated usage concept itself, was unquestionably strengthened by the desire to comply with strong Army desires while preserving Air Force tactical airlift authority. At the same time, the obvious usefulness of the C-7 in Vietnam and its growing combat record gradually lessened reservations toward the Caribou among Air Force leaders. Although prospects for further procurement appeared dim, prevailing Air Force programs promised retention of the Caribous in the active force through the year 1977. As the year 1968 ended, the larger history of the Air Force Caribous in Vietnam lay yet ahead.

Part Three:
Other Applications

XV. The Auxiliary Roles

Versatility made the transport airplanes useful in numerous auxiliary roles in Southeast Asia. Some of these were specialized airlifts, medical evacuation, civic action hauling, overwater transport, and air logistics service in Thailand. Others, which required only slight changes to the basic planes, included flareship work, leaflet operations, and explosive, incendiary, or chemical drops. Ships and crews of the 315th and 834th Air Divisions flew these missions as part of the theater airlift effort. Other applications of transport planes included gunship, spray, command and control, rescue, and reconnaissance roles, all of which required major aircraft modifications and were performed by special units dedicated to these purposes. These activities are not included in this study. Auxiliary applications, including the use of transports and helicopters in irregular warfare activities, reduced the number of ships, crews, and flying hours available for the primary mission of tactical airlift in South Vietnam.

The four-engine transports of the 315th Air Division continued to perform the overwater airlift role which had been their principal activity before 1965. The ability of the C–130 Hercules and C–124 Globemaster to carry fifteen-ton payloads well over fifteen hundred miles nonstop, allowed rapid deliveries from the Philippines, Okinawa, and Japan to the major bases in Vietnam. Cargo fell into five principal categories: (1) offshore-procured items, such as jungle boots from Korea and electrical gear from Japan and Taiwan, (2) U.S. Army and Marine equipment from Okinawa, (3) support materiel for Air Force units, (4) explosive ordnance moved by air from the Philippines because of seaport and storage limitations in Vietnam, and (5) items transloaded from offshore strategic airlift because of airfield limitations in Vietnam. Airlift thus supplemented surface shipping, helped overcome severe seaport bottlenecks during the American buildup, and cut down delivery and handling time for essential parts and equipment. Although responsibilities within Vietnam rapidly increased for the offshore transports, the overwater workload (cargo and passengers) also increased until late 1966:[1]

TACTICAL AIRLIFT

	Airlift to and from SEA (tons)	All Overwater Airlift (tons)	Overwater tonnage as % of overall workload
Jul–Sep 1965	13,000	21,000	34
Jul–Sep 1966	25,000	40,000	21
Jul–Sep 1967	18,000	28,600	12.6
Jul–Sep 1968	12,600	31,200	10.2
Jul–Sep 1969	8,800	21,500	9.7
Jul–Sep 1970	6,500	11,500	7.8

Among the C–130 units most active in overwater airlift was the 314th Wing at Ching Chuan Kang Air Base, Taiwan, whose C–130Es were used extensively in overwater work. The wing in early 1967 rotated a dozen aircrews through the main airlift terminals (Clark, Tan Son Nhut, and Bangkok), supplying fresh crews for aircraft in transit, thus preventing mission interruptions for crew rest. By contrast, the 463d Wing, based in the Philippines, devoted its efforts almost exclusively to work within Vietnam.[2]

The 315th Air Division's readiness to make short-notice unit movements to Vietnam was evident on the morning of May 14, 1967, when the division abruptly learned that the 3d Battalion, 4th Marines, was to be airlifted from Okinawa direct to Dong Ha. The 315th diverted C–130s from all wings to Naha to be loaded and launched by mission control of the 374th Wing. Forty-eight hours after first notification, forty-nine C–130s had deposited 1,230 marines and 320 tons of equipment at Dong Ha. The Air Force aerial port detachment at Dong Ha, which avoided bottlenecks despite very limited ground parking space, was especially commended.[3]

For routine control of its mission aircraft, the 315th Air Division operated a command center at Tachikawa and control detachments at Clark, Tan Son Nhut, Cam Ranh Bay, as well as at Bangkok and U Tapao in Thailand. Each troop carrier wing also had its own command post. These command elements were linked by voice radio and telephone hotlines, though both proved troublesome and unreliable. Daily mission activities for the 315th were assigned by the Western Pacific Transportation Office at Tachikawa, acting as an agent for CINCPAC. A high-level Joint Transportation Board, formed in August 1966 and chaired by the Pacific Command J–4 (Logistics), supervised both airlift and sealift activities.[4]

In effect there were two separate airlift systems, one serving CINCPAC for offshore tasks under WTO and 315th Air Division, the other serving MACV within Vietnam under the Traffic Management Agency and the 834th Air Division. Both systems depended heavily on the same force of C–130s. This arrangement produced two sets of procedures, regulations, and agencies, although this duplication apparently did not

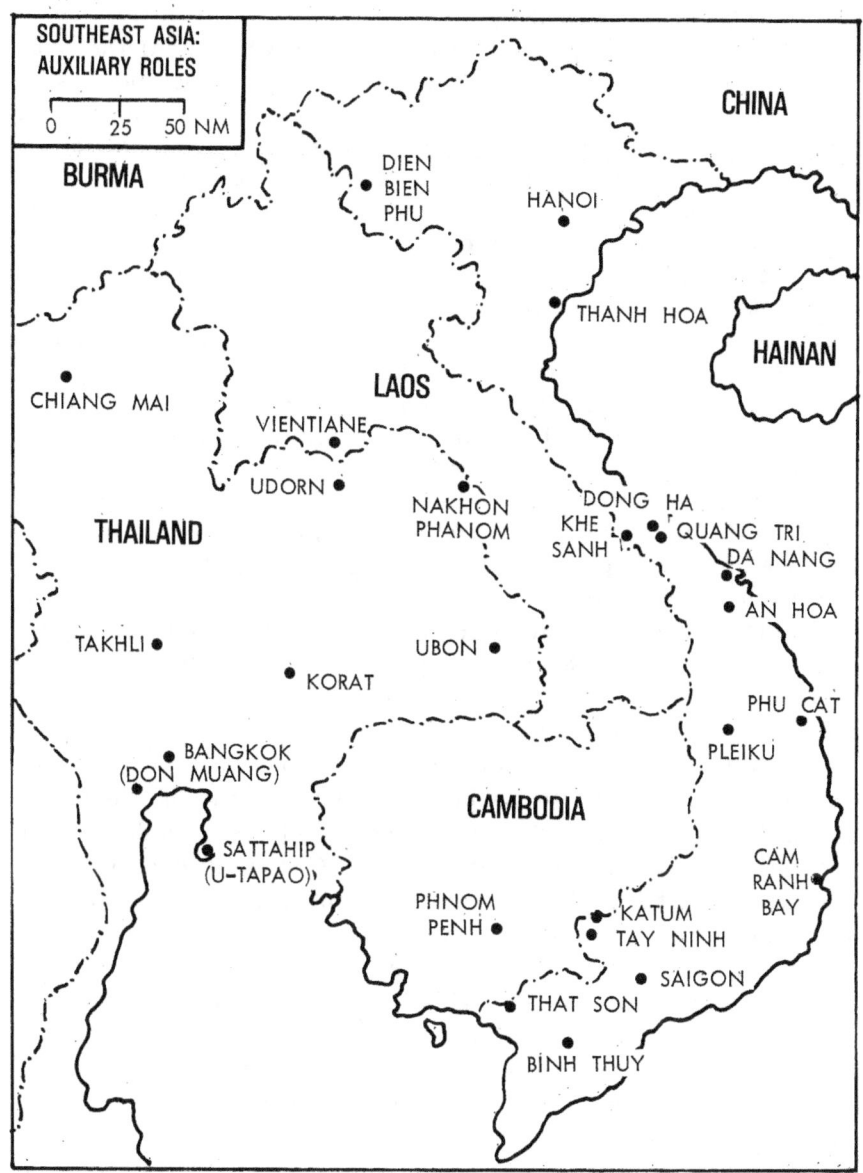

harm mission safety and efficiency. Earlier proposals had sought to head off the dual arrangement by shifting the 315th Air Division to a location closer to Southeast Asia or raising its status to numbered air force level. An early and aggressive effort by the 315th might have cemented its claim as airlift manager in Vietnam, thus exploiting its expertise and unifying the Far East airlift effort. Instead, as the mission of the C–130 force shifted increasingly to in-country work, the need for the existence of 315th Air Division became questionable.[5]

The Air Force Inspector General, Lt. Gen. Glen W. Martin, after visiting the Pacific in March 1966, concluded that although the existing system was satisfactory, "a clean line of airlift command" might prove necessary as the workload increased in the future. In a spring 1967 analysis of the mission and organization of the 315th Division, the PACAF plans staff recommended a major reorganization. The study called for inactivation of the 315th, transfer of its functions to a new directorate of airlift and an airlift control center in PACAF headquarters in Hawaii. The C–130 wings would be under the appropriate geographical air forces (the Fifth and Thirteenth Air Forces) for logistical and administrative matters; the Western Pacific Transportation Office would move to Hawaii; and the role of the 834th Air Division in Vietnam would remain essentially unchanged. Although the study group examined other possibilities, including assigning the 834th Air Division the 315th role, monetary and post-hostility considerations determined the final recommendation.[6]

Col. Charles W. Howe, 315th Air Division commander, disagreed with the PACAF proposal. He opposed fragmentation of airlift resources among numbered air forces whose concerns were much broader than airlift. General Momyer agreed, further citing the necessity of preserving the excellent rapport with other services that prevailed under the existing system. Early-1968 uncertainties in Northeast Asia caused General McConnell to rule out immediate reorganization, but with a further decline in C–130 overwater activities during the spring, McConnell in May 1968 gave his approval. CINCPAC approved in July, and two months later a formal PACAF directive established a timetable to accomplish the main recommendations of the study group. The PACAF airlift directorate was activated November 1, 1968, starting the transition that culminated in the inactivation of the 315th Air Division in April 1969. The demise of the 315th ended its eighteen-year continuous regime as the Pacific theater airlift command, and was an acknowledgement of the impossibility of managing the vast effort in Vietnam from overseas.[7]

Col. Robert D. Brown, who commanded 315th division in its last seven months, became the Assistant Deputy Chief of Staff/Operations for Airlift, PACAF. About one hundred men of the 315th moved to Hawaii to staff the new facilities under Brown and the Western Pacific Transportation Office. Tachikawa became a regional airlift control center similar to those in Thailand and the Philippines. All were under the airlift control center in Hawaii. The Joint Transportation Board continued to oversee intratheater surface and air transportation activities, its role strengthened by the addition of a working-level secretariat in early 1971.[8]

The overwater work of the Pacific-based transports, however, was small in comparison with that of Military Airlift Command.* By 1968 MAC military and contract transports were hauling 150,000 passengers and 45,000 tons of cargo monthly to and from Southeast Asia. At first MAC transports to Vietnam landed regularly only at Tan Son Nhut, necessitating considerable transshipment within Vietnam by the Common Service Airlift System. New airports opened at Da Nang and Cam Ranh in January 1966, and later at Pleiku, Bien Hoa, and Phu Cat, reducing the need for redistribution. Major unit movements by MAC aircraft from the United States usually required further airlifts to operating areas by in-country transports. Introduction of the C–5 Galaxy transport in the summer of 1970 created new problems of in-country distribution, since C–5 deliveries were massive and initially the planes could land only at Cam Ranh Bay. Eventually, however, C–5s could unload at Tan Son Nhut and elsewhere.[9]

The interisland use of MAC transports in the western Pacific raised the issue of possible duplication of effort. General Martin, in 1966, judged that activities of the Pacific transport forces and MAC were complementary and that coordination was good. The overlapping routings, Martin concluded, gave a useful flexibility in apportioning tasks. To permit greater use of theater C–130s in Vietnam, MAC in September 1966 increased its interisland hauling in the western Pacific by an amount equal to the work of two C–130 squadrons. Shortly afterwards, CINCPAC directed all subordinate commands to stop making requests directly to MAC, instead to forward all airlift requirements to WTO for apportionment of tasks between MAC and the theater transports. Also in 1966, contract transports took over airlifts of American troops from Vietnam to offshore cities for five-day rest and recuperation visits. This R&R program, first authorized in April 1962, had been exclusively served by 315th Air Division C–130s and Air Force C–54s and C–118s.[10]

The critical need for C–130 lift in Vietnam during 1968 brought further measures to reduce use of these planes in overwater work. On February 13 CINCPAC directed subordinate commands to limit airlift requests to direct support for operations in Korea and Vietnam. On April 5 the Deputy Secretary of Defense ordered the use of C–130s for overwater flights discontinued. MAC gradually undertook this workload and opened numerous new routes in the western Pacific during the next twelve months.[11]

The possible use of MAC transports for shipments between points in Vietnam was studied by the Seventh Air Force in early 1968. The Joint

---

* The Military Air Transport Service became the Military Airlift Command on January 1, 1966. At the same time, the 22d Troop Carrier Squadron became the 22d Military Airlift Squadron and its parent 1503d Transport Group became the 65th Military Airlift Group.

Transportation Board concluded that MAC help was not then needed but that plans should be developed for the future. On one occasion in 1968, MAC turboprop C–133s hauled electronic vans too large for C–130s from Phan Rang to Phu Bai for further movement by truck to final destination. By the time he left Vietnam in early 1969, McLaughlin had the authority to schedule thirty-ton-payload C–141s landing at Tan Son Nhut for a second in-country stop. This afforded a valuable reserve capability to reduce backlogs.[12]

The concept of using MAC aircraft regularly for in-country work again surfaced in early 1970. Traffic management officers evaluated how scheduled MAC service between the major Vietnam bases could supplement a reduced tactical airlift force. Such action, however, would require additional in-country support and would take C–141s from necessary tasks elsewhere. Further negotiations led to an Air Force decision in November 1970 that up to forty-two C–141s should be made available for Vietnam to meet temporary abnormal demands. These planes were used in early 1971 during the Lam Son 719 campaign. MAC C–141s hauled over six hundred tons in twelve sorties on February 22–23 and flew another thirty-seven sorties from March 7 to 9. Most missions were flown between Cam Ranh, Tan Son Nhut, and Da Nang. In addition, MAC C–133s made some fifteen hauls of outsize items during the first week of March. These included M–47 tanks, self-propelled howitzers, and helicopter maintenance vans, hauled from Pleiku, Saigon, and Phu Cat to Hue. Assessments of the limited effort were favorable, and in early April the Joint Chiefs of Staff gave continuing authorization for use of up to eleven MAC aircraft for short-term emergency duty.[13]

The contribution of the sixteen Japan-based C–124 Globemasters continued invaluable. "Old Shaky," as the Globemaster was nicknamed, could carry many items not transportable in the C–130, and some other cargo far more efficiently. A C–124, for example, could load eight assembled drop tanks for fighter aircraft, a C–130 only two. Nearly all the C–124 flying was done under 315th Air Division operational control. During the first half of 1968 the 124s hauled six hundred tons of cargo too large for the C–130s each month. This included 250 tons to and from Southeast Asia and 137 tons moved upon special requests between points within Vietnam. A news photo showing a gigantic C–124 on the ground at the primitive forward strip at Song Be appeared widely in 1968.[14]

Despite strenuous opposition from the WTO and CINCPAC, the Japan-based C–124 squadron was deactivated in early 1969 for budgetary reasons and its planes withdrawn from Japan, leaving only a single active C–124 Pacific squadron at Hickam Air Force Base, Hawaii. This unit too was deactivated in December 1969, leaving oversized cargo requirements to be filled by diverted U.S.-based C–133s and Air National Guard C–124s crossing the Pacific. The unsatisfactory arrangement ended when four C-124s were assigned to the 20th Operations Squadron, the Clark Air Base unit which operated the aeromedical C-118s. The 20th flew its first operational C-124 mission on April 1, 1970, and thereafter performed unscheduled operations as ordered by the Hawaii airlift command center. C-124 activity included troop lifts for exercises, hauls of outsize communications vans, and vegetable runs from Taiwan to Vietnam. The C-124s were again withdrawn on November 1, 1971, outsize needs to be met by C-5s in transit and Reserve forces C-124s. During its nineteen-month existence, the C-124 squadron at Clark flew without accidents and hauled six thousand tons of cargo in forty-five hundred flying hours. This accomplishment was noteworthy in view of the advanced age of "Shaky," severe parts shortages, and frequent operations in the difficult environment of Vietnam.[15]

For the Pacific C-130 crews, overwater tasks were undemanding and a welcome change from the difficult short sorties in Vietnam. Crewmen relished the modern paved runways, the ample base facilities, and the comfortable overnight accommodations encountered on overwater missions. The long-range flights at high altitude were less fatiguing for both crewmen and aircraft than was the demanding work in Vietnam. After the 1968 crunch, the 130s returned to occasional overwater work although still primarily preoccupied with work in Vietnam. Although lifts to and from Southeast Asia were typical, humanitarian missions were flown occasionally to places stricken by disasters, including the Marianas (July 1969), Pakistan (December 1970 and June 1971), and Malaysia (January 1971). The Pacific C-130Es began weekly flights to the Indian Ocean base at Diego Garcia in July 1971 despite strong protests from the Seventh Air Force, concerned by the loss of "tactical transport flying hours."[16]

The use of the strategic transports for airlifts within Vietnam, and the converse use of theater transports for overwater work, showed that the distinction between strategic and tactical airlift arms, never absolute, remained vague. Although MAC and PACAF aerial ports were consolidated at most points, separate maintenance, command post, and billeting activities existed at many Pacific bases. And, although workable arrangements for coordination had been worked out for the Southeast Asia war, the situation fueled the long-standing controversy over the organizational separation of U.S. military airlift activities.

Until late 1963 most night flareship work in Vietnam was done by Farm Gate and Vietnamese Air Force C-47s, primarily to illuminate outposts under attack. The load capacity of the C-123 Provider, however,

Strategic transports in Southeast Asia were assigned to the Military Air Transport Service, which became the Military Airlift Command in 1966.

C-124 Globemaster delivers a CH-34 helicopter at Da Nang.

USAF C-135 Stratolifter at Da Nang.

C-141 Starlifter on the flight line at Tan Son Nhut.

Interior view of the C-5 Galazy shows its huge cargo capacity, Cam Ranh Bay, 1971.

Air Force C–123s, C–47s, and C–130s supported tactical missions as night flareships.

Arc lamps mounted under a C–123 provide a constant light source with a two-mile diameter, when the aircraft flies at 12,000 feet altitude.

A Vietnamese C–47 Skytrain ready to take off for a flare-drop mission, Tan Son Nhut, 1967.

made it useful as a flareship, and with increasing enemy night action the 315th Group took over roughly half the overall flare activity. One ship stayed airborne through the hours of darkness while two others were on ground alert. During the first half of 1964 the C–123s flew 258 flare missions (roughly two percent of all C–123 sorties), dispensing three times the number of flares released by the Vietnamese C–47s. Farm Gate by this time had nearly withdrawn from flare work.

C–123 crews tried out new techniques and tested Mark–24 flares in hopes of cutting down the high percentage of duds. Accompanying each mission was a Vietnamese navigator, often sleepy from a day's C–47 flying, who talked with ground outposts by FM radio. A point-and-talk translation sheet was used for communication within the cockpit. Serving as flare handlers in the rear were personnel from the Vietnamese airborne brigade and various U.S. Air Force ground personnel. The latter were volunteers who undertook the nighttime alert and flying duties in addition to their daytime work. Their rewards included personal satisfaction, a chance to cool off, medals, and good performance ratings; there was no flying pay.[17]

C–123 flare work further increased in 1965, reaching a high of 243 sorties in November. Ten ships were scheduled each night for air and ground alert duty, three each at Da Nang and Nha Trang, and four at Tan Son Nhut. Flareships served in many of the year's ground battles and furnished light for one night helicopter assault west of Da Nang. The arrival in Vietnam of the 4th Air Commando Squadron, equipped with AC–47 gunships, promised relief from flare work for the C–123s. MACV in early 1966 pressed the Seventh Air Force to "return airlift aircraft to their prime role." Consequently, regular use of C–123s as flareships ended at Tan Son Nhut in February 1966, and at Da Nang and Nha Trang five months later.[18]

The C–130As of 315th Air Division began flying flareship missions in January 1965. Project Blind Bat used the C–130s with strike aircraft for night interdiction work, primarily in the Laotian panhandle. The Blind Bat force gradually acquired sophisticated equipment, including an automatic flare dispenser and the light-amplifying starlight scope to visually sight enemy trucks. Aircrews rotated from C–130A squadrons outside of Vietnam served periods of temporary duty up to 179 days at Da Nang and after March 1966 at Ubon, Thailand, where the force reached six ships and twelve crews. During 1967 and 1968, Blind Bat flying hours accounted for one-third of the flying done by airlift C–130As in Vietnam. Project Blind Bat ended on June 15, 1970, its role taken over by newer systems. During the project seventy-five hundred missions were flown and almost eight hundred thousand flares were dropped. Two ships and crews were lost to enemy fire.[19]

Transport aircraft for interdiction work also were organized and manned outside the theater airlift organization. The C–123s of the 606th Air Commando Squadron at Nakhon Phanom, Thailand (the Candlestick force), improvised techniques for hunter-killer work with strike aircraft, using the starlight scope and incendiary markers against enemy truck traffic in Laos. In late 1968 two other C–123s were equipped with sensors and a bombet-drop capability and became Project Black Spot. The twelve-ship Candlestick unit was disbanded in June 1971, while Black Spot remained limited to two ships. The fixed-wing gunship evolved from the flareship and cut significantly into the inventory of transport craft. By late 1969, seven AC–130A and twenty-eight AC–119 gunships were serving in Southeast Asia. The Air Force AC–47s were phased out by year's end, many shifted to the VNAF. General Momyer, now commanding TAC, recommended against converting already overworked airlift C–130Es to gunships. TAC's viewpoint and budgetary considerations limited the number of E-models converted to gunships to six, which were sent to Ubon in late 1971 to join twelve AC–130As.[20]

Proposed chemical warfare applications for airlift aircraft were most imaginative. Prominent among them was the Ranch Hand aerial spray project for jungle defoliation and crop destruction in South Vietnam to expose the enemy's trail network in Laos. The UC–123 consistently proved its sturdiness in this role and on several occasions in 1968 demonstrated its adaptability for reconversion on short notice to airlift work. Three other chemical-dispensing ventures were less profitable. Project Commando Lava, it was hoped, would close roadways to the enemy by inducing heavy mud during rainy seasons. This hope was expressed by Ambassador William H. Sullivan in Laos who speculated that "chelation may prove better than escalation—make mud, not war!" During 1967 the 374th Wing C–130s dropped 120 tons of soil destabilization compound in twenty-eight sorties in and about the A Shau Valley. The planes were hit frequently by enemy fire during their runs at two hundred-foot altitudes, despite friendly fighter support. But poststrike reconnaissance revealed that the communists continued to use the target roadways, covering over the muddy places with gravel or bamboo matting. Another chemical scheme was an attempt during the siege of Khe Sanh to dissipate cloud cover by sodium chloride seeding. A C–123 crew of the 309th Squadron flew fifteen sorties, seeding along the landing and airdrop approach path. This attempt grew from earlier iodide seedings to induce rainfall over infiltration routes in North Vietnam and Laos. Unfortunately, results at Khe Sanh were completely unsuccessful. A third chemical warfare project in 1968 used C–123s and C–130s to drop tear gas to block enemy infiltration. The chemicals were carried and dropped in fifty-five-gallon drums with explosive detonators to release the gas at ground level. Dispersal proved uneven and the desired effects were never attained.[21]

Transport aircraft also served as bombers on several occasions. The

Transport aircraft were converted to gunships for interdiction work.

AC–47 Dragonship crewmen tend their miniguns, firing at targets on the ground, November 1967.

USAF AC–119 "Shadow" gunship in flight over Nha Trang Air Base, January 1969.

Sgt. John E. Bradley checks the miniguns on an AC–119 prior to a combat mission, Binh Thuy Air Base, February 1969.

Chemical warfare applications included conversion of C–123 aircraft for aerial spray work in Operation Ranch Hand. Here, a C–123 is seen under the Ranch Hand sign at Nha Trang, January 1969.

In support of the Boi Loi woods-burning mission, C–123s line up to take off from Tan Son Nhut, March 31, 1965.

Royal Laotian Air Force (RLAF) in early 1965 devised a method of dropping 260-pound fragmentation bombs from C–47s to attack enemy positions and trucks, often in conjunction with flareship missions. Communist transports also dropped bombs in Laos. Especially dramatic were attacks by American C–130s against the Thanh Hoa railroad bridge in North Vietnam. On two successive nights in May 1966, TAC dispatched two ships in an attempt to place float mines upstream of the bridge. The planes approached from the sea by moonlight at treetop level, supported by diversionary airstrikes and electronic countermeasures. In the attack of May 20, the C–130 crew released its mines and returned to base, but on the following night the mine-carrying plane crashed near the target, apparently downed by enemy fire. In both cases the bridge, which had survived numerous attacks by allied strike aircraft, was untouched. The project consequently was abandoned.[22]

During 1962 both Farm Gate and Mule Train experimented with transports as napalm bombers. The C–123 proved far more suitable than the C–47 for this use due to its greater load capacity and its rear-opening ramp. The bombing method finally devised utilized a C–123 carrying nine wood pallets each holding three fifty-five-gallon drums filled with a mix of gasoline and napalm. The entire load could be dropped in five seconds making a pattern of flames on the ground twelve hundred feet long. The attacking crew would make a descending run-in, pull up, and add power as low as fifty feet over the target. Drops were made on several occasions against suspected enemy targets, and napalm-carrying 123s sometimes orbited over rail and vehicle convoys to deter ambushes. PACAF officers were aware of the vulnerability of transports in close-in attacks, and airlift leaders were not enthusiastic about diverting limited airlift capabilities. Officials also questioned whether psychologically the Saigon regime could claim local loyalties after subjecting a region to heavy napalm attacks. The method was abandoned after 1962.[23]

Formations of transports also were used occasionally in area attacks to burn out forested areas used by the enemy. On March 31, 1965, twenty-four C–123s, each carrying twenty-four fifty-five-gallon drums of fuel, burned part of the Boi Loi woods northwest of Saigon. Defoliation sorties and leaflet warnings preceded the mission. Strike aircraft fed the blaze, and smoke reached to eight thousand feet. Australian Caribous flew similar missions. MACV's interest in the project quickened in 1967, and in early 1968 the MACV science adviser reexamined the forest-burning idea.[24]

Under Project Banish Beach, Air Force C–130s flew seventeen forest-burn missions from April 7 to August 14, 1968, for a total of 227 sorties. Targets were suspected enemy camps, supply caches, and rocket launch sites. Most attacks were in the region north of Saigon, although targets near Nha Trang, Kontum, and Da Nang also were hit. Each C–130 carried sixty-four drums of fuel, loaded in fours on standard cargo-drop pallets.

AUXILIARY ROLES

Smoke grenades were attached to several of the drums to assure ignition. The load from each ship covered approximately one hundred by two hundred yards, creating a burn area comparable to that devastated by a B–52 but at far less cost. The fuel drums were released from about thirty-five hundred feet, each ship aiming visually and by stopwatch timing. Consequently, this procedure produced inaccurate results, and ground coverage was incomplete.[25]

Neither the 834th Air Division nor the Seventh Air Force was enthusiastic over the results of Banish Beach. None of the burn missions produced clearcut military advantages, although secondary explosions were sometimes seen and a prisoner reported that one strike killed many troops. Each mission disrupted normal airlift activity for much of a day, increasing cargo backlogs and consuming transport flying hours. General Momyer in July stated to General Abrams his opposition to continuing the fire missions and Momyer's successor, Gen. George S. Brown, in September, turned down proposals for further attacks. Banish Beach was formally terminated in January 1969.[26]

Project Commando Scarf in 1969 used C–130Bs to drop small antipersonnel mines in southern Laos. The XM–41 gravel mines were designed for placement by helicopters and fighters, but the communists countered with sweeps and a warning system that reduced the effectiveness of gravel below the costs of fighter delivery. The C–130s represented a means of dispensing the remaining stocks of gravel at minimum cost. The 463d Wing Commando Scarf task force consisted of three C–130Bs, four aircrews, and thirty-one maintenance men, all stationed at Udorn, Thailand. Mine loadings at Nakhon Phanom were performed by a team from the 2d Aerial Port Group. Operations began on June 29, 1969, and ended after one hundred missions in thirty-two days dispensed twelve hundred tons of gravel. Later Commando Scarf projects also involved use of C–130Bs in Laos. In December 1970, for example, the 130s flew eleven missions out of Ubon, dispensing CDU–10 noisemakers. Although successful, Commando Scarf efforts were a minor contribution to the overall interdiction campaign.[27]

By far the most significant use of the C–130s as bombers was during Project Commando Vault. General Momyer in February 1968 recognized the need for an explosive device capable of blasting out helicopter landing zones in jungle areas. Air Force Systems Command and the U.S. Army soon developed methods for dropping five-ton M–121 bombs from C–130s and CH–54 Flying Crane helicopters. A C–130 could carry two M–121s using standard platforms fitted to the dual rails. Each bomb was individually extracted from the plane by parachute, and each was stabilized in descent by additional chutes. A crew from the 463d Wing made four test drops in Vietnam in October 1968, guided to the release points by the Air Force MSQ–77 radar sites at Pleiku and Hue. Wing aircrews, guided by

393

Marine Corps radars, made two additional drops in December in support of ground operations southwest of Da Nang. Releases were from seven thousand feet, and accuracy was about one hundred yards. The CH–54 also was tested in Vietnam, but the C–130 was superior, especially in its ability to reach targets anywhere in Southeast Asia from a single loading base. It was clear from the 1968 drops that the M–121 could clear an area about two hundred feet in diameter—sufficient for one or two helicopters—and that the C–130 had a potential for dropping even larger bombs.[28]

Commando Vault drops resumed in March 1969 and a 15,000-pound weapon, the BLU–82, was first used on March 23, 1970. The BLU–82 consisted of an ordinary steel propane tank filled with a slurry explosive. Each bomb rested on a cradle attached to a standard heavy-drop platform. Parachutes extracted and stabilized the bomb. A detonating rod ignited the bomb four feet above the ground, blasting a clearing about 260 feet in diameter. The blast also could incapacitate and demoralize troops over several hundred yards.[29]

Crews from the 463d Wing dropped over two hundred M–121 and 250 BLU–82 bombs. Twenty bombs were dropped in Cambodia during the 1970 campaign and twenty-five were exploded in support of Lam Son 719 the next year. The C–130E wing at Ching Chuan Kang Air Base took over Commando Vault duties in late 1971 and dropped a total of 116 BLU–82s by the 1973 cease-fire. Most drops preceded helicopter assaults, sometimes preparatory to construction of an artillery firebase. Several bombs were detonated in southern Laos during the winter of 1970–71, clearing vegetation from supply trails and demolishing enemy truck parks and caches. At least eleven bombs during Lam Son 719 struck tactical targets. One BLU–82 was dropped in early 1970, mainly for psychological effect, near the intersection of two trails used by the enemy west of Long Tieng in northern Laos. Missions against enemy troops became more frequent in late 1972 and included attacks against 130-mm artillery positions north of Hue. Techniques for these drops were unchanged, but the greater threat of enemy fire necessitated cautious selection of routes and altitudes.[30]

Lavish precautions prevented bombing in the vicinity of friendly forces. Before every drop an airborne forward air controller inspected the target area, and until late 1969 target map coordinates were validated by preliminary fighter strikes with radar guidance. Radar beacon transmitters, installed in the C–130 bombers, improved radar tracking from the ground. All missions were approved by MACV operations or a higher authority and streamlined channels made possible drops within twenty-four hours of a field commander's request. Accuracy depended on close adherence by the aircrew to prescribed altitude, speed, and heading; impact errors averaged a satisfactory 197 feet. Flying techniques were not demanding, except overcoming the change in aircraft balance at the instant of release.[31]

Appraisals of Commando Vault were uniformly favorable. The effectiveness of the method far outweighing the modest diversion of C-130s from airlift duties. A bonus payoff came in 1972 when the techniques of ground radar direction developed during Commando Vault were used in high-altitude resupply drops. Moreover, the ability of the transport force to deliver large bombs was an airmobile warfare capability of both immediate and future value.

A peripheral 314th Wing responsibility, which until 1969 claimed considerable energy, was the airborne battlefield command and control center mission. Controllers in control center planes coordinated allied air strikes using information supplied by forward air controllers, flareships, ground observers, sensors, and reconnaissance. C-130Es serving as control centers were modified with an elaborate electronics package and twelve crew positions inside the cargo compartment. A single control aircraft was stationed at Da Nang in September 1965. The control center detachment moved to Udorn in 1967 and expanded to six planes, keeping two of them at all times airborne over Laos. For the airlifters the one-week cycles at Udorn were a restful and welcome change from the far more demanding work in Vietnam until a new 7th Airborne Command and Control Squadron took over the responsibility at Udorn in early 1969.[32]

Other additional duties, however, were assigned the airlifters. In mid-1969 the airlift wings began providing temporary-duty aircrews to Cam Ranh Bay for C-130 reconnaissance missions over Laos, and two standard C-130s were loaned to the same project in April 1970. In 1972 the C-130 reconnaissance force moved to Thailand, now requiring five planes and crews from the 374th Wing. The control center squadron took over these responsibilities the next year. Three C-130Bs were temporarily assigned to the 7th Squadron in 1971 to relay information from unattended ground sensors. The 7th Squadron moved to Korat in April 1972, and by early 1973 twelve C-130Es were stationed there, eight for control center and sensor relay, and four for reconnaissance.[33]

Transport airplanes were used in attack roles to a considerable extent in Southeast Asia, ranging from the actual delivery of ordnance to other direct contributions to effective air strikes. Airlifters at crew and squadron level revealed resourcefulness and flexibility in these enterprises, but their commanders, concerned with providing badly needed air transport, saw them as diversions. The Air Force was imaginative and undoctrinaire in using transport planes for a number of unusual tasks yet was sufficiently strong minded to drop these efforts when they outlived their usefulness.

TACTICAL AIRLIFT

The primary means of transporting casualties during the Korean War was by air. Army and Air Force helicopters moved patients from the battlefield to forward hospitals, and transports of the 315th Air Division evacuated more than three hundred thousand patients to hospitals in Korea and Japan. Roles agreements in 1952 and 1957 confirmed the Air Force's responsibility for evacuating patients to points outside the combat zone and from airheads during airborne operations. The latter task overlapped with the Army's responsibility for evacuations within the combat zone, and disputes over aeromedical roles marred joint exercises of the late 1950s. During Exercise Swift Strike in 1961, the Air Force established an aeromedical evacuation apparatus consisting of a control center, control teams for six field locations, a large casualty care facility, and teams of medical flight personnel. It was expected that troop carrier aircraft would move casualties back from the airheads, but the aeromedical apparatus remained inactive because the Army helicopters hauled persons injured in the jumps to nearby hospitals. The Air Force was, however, given an opportunity to display its own aeromedical concepts in the Indian River exercises of 1964. Air Force CH–3 and H–21 helicopters were used in medical evacuations and other battlefield tasks, and the apparatus of aeromedical control, casualty handling, and flight teams was expanded.[34]

The medical evacuation system in Vietnam up to 1964 had little resemblance to those set up for the joint exercise. In practice Vietnamese Air Force H–34s were primarily responsible for battlefield evacuation, supposedly freeing the U.S. Army helicopters for assault work. Mule Train C–123s often hauled sick and wounded patients on return flights from outlying locations and performed occasional emergency evacuations, keeping one C–123 on twenty-four-hour ground alert at Tan Son Nhut for this purpose. Two airmen manned the aeromedical evacuation control center (AECC) at Tan Son Nhut, received evacuation requests, and coordinated patient movements with the hospitals at Tan Son Nhut and Nha Trang. Late in 1962 the 123s began scheduled weekly runs between the two hospitals, and personnel of the evacuation control center often served as medical crewmen on in-country flights.[35]

C–130s based out of the country moved patients from Vietnam to Clark Air Base on regular flights, and in May 1962 a once-a-week schedule was begun, connecting with the C–123 Nha Trang-Saigon run. The C–130 aeromedical route extended into Thailand, and a second aeromedical control center was established at Don Muang. Medical crewmen from the 9th Aeromedical Evacuation Squadron in Japan accompanied the C–130 missions, and in 1963 detachments of the 9th Squadron were opened at Clark Field, Tan Son Nhut, and Bangkok. Statistics kept by the squadron show that roughly two hundred patients were moved each month in or from Southeast Asia during 1963 and 1964. Of these, less than forty percent were battle casualties.[36]

AUXILIARY ROLES

Overwater evacuation work increased sharply in 1965. Generally, patients requiring hospitalization for thirty days or more were moved to offshore hospitals; others were sometimes evacuated to keep an empty bed reserve of fifty percent in Vietnam. Military Airlift Command transports carried the more serious cases from Clark to the United States and in 1966 began making patient pickups in Vietnam. This permitted theater C-130s to be phased out of overwater evacuation.[37]

Supplementing the C-130s in aeromedical activities prior to 1966, and the MAC transports thereafter, were the propeller-driven C-118s of the 6485th Operations Squadron based at Tachikawa. Although slower than the C-130s and less suitable for landings at forward sites, the 118s were permanently modified for use as aeromedical craft and operated between the major bases. The 6485th Squadron expanded from four to seven ships in 1966 and moved to Clark in early 1968. The C-118s began limited in-country work in January 1968. Aircraft and crews were assigned for three-day cycles at Cam Ranh Bay and flew to some fourteen Vietnamese airfields. The planes also carried patients on return flights to Clark. The unit, renamed the 20th Operations Squadron, again operating exclusively from Clark, converted in 1972 to the C-9 Nightingale jet (the military version of the commercial DC-9). The first operational C-9 mission landed at Tan Son Nhut and Da Nang on March 15, 1972.[38]

Within Vietnam after 1965 nearly all battlefield evacuations were made by U.S. Army UH-1 Iroquois (better known as "Huey") helicopters. Each Huey had a capacity of six litter patients, and many of the planes were marked as medical vehicles and assigned to air ambulance companies. A battlefield casualty was usually airlifted to a thirty-bed clearing station located at the brigade airhead or base camp. From there serious cases were moved rearward by helicopter or occasionally by fixed-wing transport. Sometimes, helicopters on medical authority lifted casualties directly from battlefield to hospital, bypassing the brigade station. Air Force helicopters participated in battlefield evacuations whenever required, and air rescue H-43s were particularly valuable because of their two hundred-foot cable hoist which facilitated extractions at jungle locations.[39]

Air Force transports frequently hauled patients between hospitals in Vietnam, often shifting individuals to pickup points for oversea evacuation. To treat U.S. forces in Vietnam, there were by 1966 seven four hundred-bed field or evacuation hospitals, three sixty-bed surgical hospitals, a Navy hospital at Da Nang, and a convalescent center and an Air Force hospital at Cam Ranh Bay. Surgical hospitals were expanded to six by early 1968; field and evacuation hospitals to twelve. All American hospitals, except for a few near Saigon, were located at C-130 airstrips including Pleiku, Qui Nhon, Tuy Hoa, Nha Trang, Phu Bai, Quang Tri, and An Khe. During June 1967 the 834th Air Division moved over seven thousand patients between points in Vietnam, three thousand by C-130, two thousand by

The aeromedical evacuation system in Southeast Asia transported patients from the battlefields to in-country treatment facilities and staging areas and then to hospitals in the Philippines and U.S.

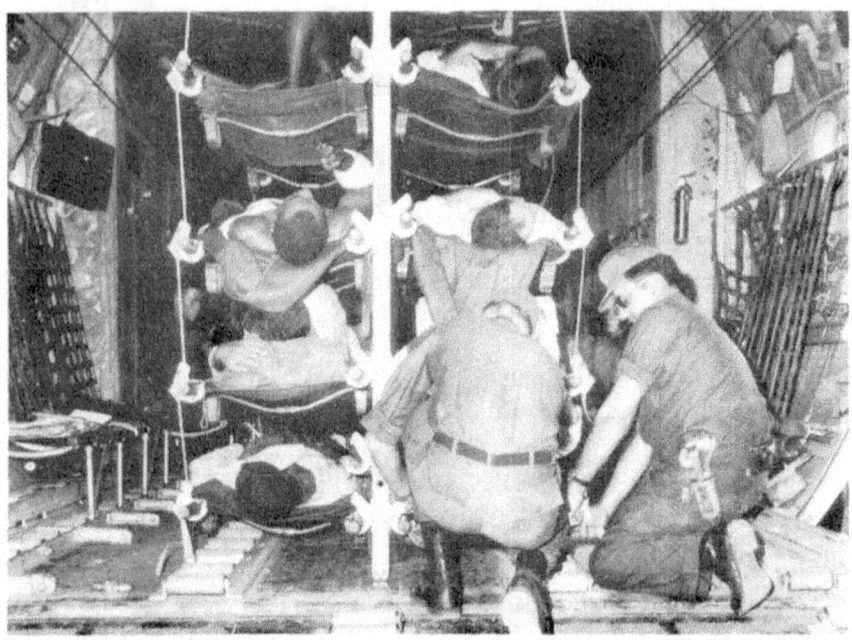

Aboard a C–130, patients on stanchions are secured in place by Capt. Nicholas J. Perrotto (right), a flight nurse, and A1C Stanley M. Danna. The wounded men are being evacuated to an in-country location.

Transferring patients to a C–141 for the trip to the States, 1967.

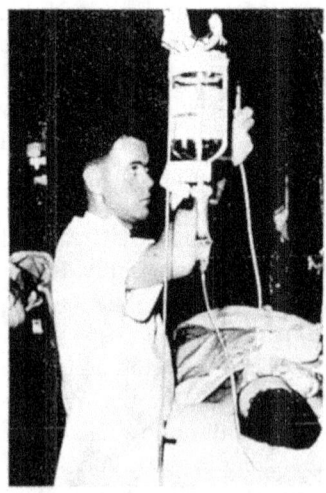

Aboard the C–141, SSgt. Billy E. Neeley prepares an intravenous bottle for a U.S. serviceman.

C–123, and two thousand by C–7. The Air Force was especially busy in I Corps, flying from Chu Lai, Phu Bai, and Dong Ha to better equipped medical facilities at Da Nang. Regularly scheduled medical flights were instituted in 1967, with one twice-weekly circuit linking the northern bases with Cam Ranh, another the highlands airfields with Saigon. By 1968 the twice-weekly missions had become twice-daily. These scheduled medical runs optimized use of transport capacity and reduced aeromedical emergency disruptions of other airlift activities.[40]

A new 903d Aeromedical Evacuation Squadron was organized at Tan Son Nhut on July 8, 1966, under the 9th Aeromedical Evacuation Group in Japan. The squadron manned the AECC with instructions "to work closely with the 7th Air Force ALCC to provide an integrated, immediately responsive in-country aeromedical evacuation system." The 903d included detachments at Cam Ranh, Nha Trang, Qui Nhon, and Da Nang, and soon added detachments at Pleiku and Vung Tau. Each detachment included two male flight nurses and up to ten aeromedical evacuation technicians. Female flight nurses, previously used only on overwater missions, were assigned in Vietnam beginning in late 1967. Besides providing medical flight crews, the aeromedical detachments operated control elements that coordinated patient and aircraft movements with the local hospitals, airlift control elements, and the aeromedical evacuation control center. The Air Force after mid-1966 also operated casualty staging flights at five major airfields. Each functioned as part of the local Air Force medical facility, caring for patients near the flight line while awaiting airlift out of Vietnam. Most had beds for one hundred or more patients; few patients stayed longer than twenty-four hours.[41]

The number of flight nurses, medical technicians, and administrators assigned to the PACAF aeromedical system reached three hundred by mid-1967. The five-fold expansion over three years, coupled with the twelve-month duty cycle in Vietnam, was responsible for low experience levels. Fewer than half of the flight nurses arriving in Vietnam had previous training in flight medicine. Training was on a person-to-person basis within the squadrons and detachments. Newcomers flew missions with experienced individuals until they acquired the necessary knowledge and self-confidence. Many medical technicians, whose duties included the loading of patients and who assisted the flight nurses in flight, also arrived untrained. Supply shortages too were occasionally a problem, although rarely a critical one.[42] The 903d Aeromedical Evacuation Flight was transferred to Phu Cat from Pope Air Force Base in February 1967 and assigned to the 903d Squadron. The 903d Flight was a self-contained unit of mobile teams to provide patient care at forward airstrips. The unit's personnel had diverse flight and ground medical skills and sufficient equipment for four twenty-five-bed forward facilities. Teams were sent to Khe Sanh in April 1967, to Dong Ha in May 1967, and again to Khe Sanh in early 1968.

TACTICAL AIRLIFT

During the battle at Dak To during the fall of 1967, a mobile close support force from the 903d Flight received patients brought to the fixed-wing airstrip by Army helicopters. The group worked with Army personnel to schedule patient transfers out and coordinated numerous C-130 evacuations. Although the joint service concept advanced no further after 1968, the existence of the mobile forces indicated the Air Force's willingness to undertake greater aeromedical roles in the blurred area left by existing agreements with the army.[43] Monthly M6 reports from the 9th Aeromedical Evacuation Squadron and the 9th Aeromedical Evacuation Group show the following patients evacuated by PACAF aircraft:

	Month Ending 25 July 1965	Month Ending 25 June 1967	June 1969
Intra-Vietnam	190	7,023	9,087
From Vietnam	607	2,259	224
Intra-Thailand	11	175	176
From Thailand	41	239	9
Non-Southeast Asia	629	1,703	598
Principal Destinations within Vietnam			
Nha Trang	76	121	
Da Nang	102	1,364	
Saigon	11	213	
Qui Nhon	0	2,707	
Cam Ranh Bay	0	1,688	

The 903d Squadron treated and moved over ten thousand patients during the thirty days after Tet 1968 and earned the Air Force Presidential Unit Citation. Patient flow gradually returned to normal, and by June 1969 the Air Force aeromedical effort reached its maturity. Of the 9,000 patients hauled within Vietnam in that month, 5,900 were moved by C-130, 1,100 by C-123, 300 by Caribou, and 1,700 by C-118. Hostile action injuries made up thirty-seven percent of the cases. Two-thirds of the missions were scheduled, a higher ratio than formerly. One principal C-130 schedule linked Cam Ranh Bay and Tan Son Nhut with Vung Tau, Binh Thuy, and Bien Hoa; another reached north from Da Nang to Quang Tri, Dong Ha, and Hue. C-123 and C-7 schedules generally reached the smaller fields. Operations were reduced as American casualties declined after 1969. 903d personnel were consolidated at Cam Ranh Bay in mid-1970, and two years later the squadron was phased out. Remaining aeromedical activities were directed by the 9th Group, now at Clark.[44]

Future theater aeromedical operations were spelled out in a revised AFM 3-4, September 22, 1971. The document plainly reflected the system in Vietnam and envisioned the aeromedical evacuation control center as the central element in a system extending to casualty staging operations at

AUXILIARY ROLES

forward airfields. The manual asserted that scheduled aeromedical missions should begin as early as possible. Specialized aircraft like the C-9 and the standard tactical airlift planes would both retain aeromedical roles. Division of responsibility between the strategic airlift force and the Army was not resolved.[45]

American counterinsurgency from the Kennedy years was conducted in the belief that long-term pacification of a nation must rest on strong programs of economic, social, and political improvement. Even while sending American troops to Vietnam, President Johnson gave lip service to this "other war" and urged expansion of Saigon's nation-building efforts. Revolutionary Development Program teams, comprising over thirty thousand persons in late 1966, were trained to introduce health, education, and construction programs at the "riceroots" level. The nation-building efforts of several American civilian agencies—the Agency for International Development, the CIA, and the U.S. Information Agency—were placed in 1967 under a high-ranking MACV deputy for civil operations and revolutionary (rural) development support (CORDS). In hauling personnel, supplies, and equipment for this "other war," air transport was vital, linking the Vietnamese government to its provinces and villages. Such duties accorded with the Air Force's long-held view, as stated by General LeMay to the Joint Chiefs of Staff in February 1962, that "the air transport net provides the vital link immediately; roads and railroads can follow on a practical and economic basis as the viability of the country is achieved."[46]

Air America, Inc., furnished considerable transport services within Vietnam under contracts funded by the American civilian agencies. In late 1965 the Air America fleet at Saigon consisted of over fifty aircraft including two dozen twin-engine C-45s, C-46s, and C-47s. Monthly lift capacity was 1,650 tons supplemented by another one hundred tons lifted monthly for AID by Air Force transports. To meet forecast AID requirements of thirty-five hundred tons monthly, MACV and AID reached agreement in February 1966 to increase the common service airlift tonnage to eighteen hundred per month. Although occasional acrimony marred the resulting cooperative effort (AID complained over shipping delays, the Air Force over AID failures to provide the agreed tonnages), the partnership was generally successful. During 1967 and 1968, Air America hauled most of the passengers and twenty-five hundred tons of cargo monthly for CORDS, while common service C-130s and C-123s hauled fifteen hundred tons of cargo monthly, and the Caribous 450 tons. The military stepped up its efforts during a 1967 strike of Vietnamese Air America

Air America headquarters, Udorn Air Base, Thailand.

employees and during the dislocations of the 1968 Tet offensive. Both the Air Force and the Joint Chiefs of Staff favored this increased Air Force participation and looked ahead to a "single airlift system under military control." CORDS successfully opposed such integration, viewing the Air America effort as an evolution toward a large, all-Vietnamese civil aviation establishment.[47]

CORDS' air operations division scheduled the multiengine transports of Air America and two Caribou missions daily. AID personnel manned passenger-booking and cargo-handling offices at Tan Son Nhut and small operations offices in each corps area. A MACV group in 1970 questioned duplication in routings between the common service system and Air America and existence of two separate aerial port systems. But it acknowledged that CORDS' association with future civil aviation in Vietnam justified organizational separation.[48]

Other civil air carriers provided airlift for American construction and engineering contractors in Vietnam. The largest carrier was Continental Air Services, Inc., which began in early 1966 and by 1968 was providing several firms with one hundred hours of flying monthly using four C–47s and six smaller craft. One firm, Pacific Architects and Engineers, Inc., operated two Caribous for its own needs, and Page Communication Engineers, Inc., contracted with Air Vietnam for C–47 and light aircraft service. All contractors justified their private airlift arrangements by expressing dissatisfaction with the common service system. Transportation delays, even though justified by military needs, meant lost time and money to the contractor. Military spokesmen acknowledged that such delays were not unusual, but both MACV and the Air Force opposed unsuccessfully the proliferation of airlift systems as simply a matter of contractor "convenience."[49]

The Vietnamese national airline, Air Vietnam, by late 1965 had thirteen C–47s, four C–46s, and some four-engine craft. The airline depended heavily on foreign technicians and its pilot force was largely detailed from the Vietnamese Air Force. Several agreements in late 1968 pointed toward an eventual Air Vietnam takeover of Air America and other contract carriers. These agreements included consolidation of some of Continental Air Services and Air Vietnam facilities and a contract for technical assistance by Pan American Airways to Air Vietnam. AID, meanwhile, administered numerous communications and construction projects at airports throughout South Vietnam to improve the future Vietnamese civil air structure and to gain immediate military benefits. Although the vast expansion of the Vietnamese Air Force transport arm after 1969 obscured the slower improvement in civil aviation, prospects by 1973 were excellent for a vigorous peacetime civil air arm.[50]

Both the usefulness and limitations of air transport were demonstrated at An Hoa twenty miles southwest of Da Nang. High-grade coal deposits, and plans for irrigation, electric power, and the manufacture of fertilizer, promised to make An Hoa an economic hub. The U.S. Marines came to An Hoa in late 1965 to assist in local defense and to rebuild and reopen the road to Da Nang. The communists nevertheless were able to continue harassing road traffic necessitating prolonged dependence on airlift. C–123s routinely brought supplies from Da Nang and hauled back loads of coal. Airstrip improvements later opened the field for C–130s. Vietnamese engineers estimated in mid-1966 that the seven hundred-ton monthly airlift to An Hoa would expand to fifteen hundred tons the following year. Aircrewmen, though, saw the large An Hoa airlift as extremely wasteful since the field was only a short distance from Da Nang. The strip's pierced-metal surface was destructive to C–130 tires, the nuisance threat of hostile ground fire was constant, and friendly air strikes and naval gunfire often caused long delays before landing. Thus airlift seemed a costly and temporary means of sustaining local defense and limited economic growth, while awaiting secure land lines of communication.[51]

The common service airlift also benefited the civilian population. Deliveries to Special Forces camps meant supplies for the local civilians and occasional trips to outside points. Montagnards in isolated regions were encouraged to improve airstrips by hand labor to gain the benefits of C–7 service. Airdrops of food, airlifts of refugees, and emergency medical shipments aided localities stricken by natural or war-associated catastrophes. During the general flooding of late 1964, despite heavy clouds and wet landing surfaces, the C–123 squadron at Da Nang alone hauled more than two thousand tons of cargo and thirteen hundred passengers in over six hundred relief flights. C–130s also assisted in the relief effort while helicopters hauled emergency supplies from the U.S.S. *Princeton* offshore.[52] Also noteworthy was the tradition among airlift men of organizing programs on behalf of local schools and orphanages, and of associating directly with the Vietnamese people. One Air Force colonel described the daily passenger run between Da Nang and Tan Son Nhut in 1964:

> I watched our [airlift] crews at work, and the way they handled themselves in helping people, reassuring children and ancient old peasant couples, laughing and joking, sweating and cursing, but acknowledging the human dignity of the individual all the while, made me realize that they were some of Mr. Lodge's best possible ambassadorial representatives.[53]

Transport aircraft were easily adapted to disperse psychological warfare leaflets. Farm Gate C–47s stopped dropping leaflets after a 1962 crash, but in August 1965 the first of several C–47s arrived at Nha Trang specifically for in-country leaflet and the loudspeaker work. C–130As of the 315th Air Division began leaflet missions against North Vietnam in July 1965. The leaflets were released at high altitudes from off shore or over Laos with the hope that the wind drift would get them to populated

TACTICAL AIRLIFT

Three airmen in a C–47 Skytrain load surrender leaflets into the aircraft's distribution chute, 1966.

regions. The frequency of leaflet missions increased from eight in 1965 to six in the month of February 1968. Missions against North Vietnam were stopped from November 1968 through 1971 but continued elsewhere in Southeast Asia. Miniradios were added to the leaflet drops in 1971, and in 1972 the drops over North Vietnam were resumed. Communist denunciations of this psychological warfare suggested it was well worth the effort since three missions per month required only thirty-eight flying hours.[54]

Several courier airlifts, some of them instituted by the Air Force, also were added to transport activities outside the common service airlift. When the R&R leave began in 1962, several C–54s were stationed at Tan Son Nhut to service the program, and during 1963 and 1964 the detachment moved an average of five hundred R&R troops monthly. By mid-1964, four C–54s, a VC–123,* a VC–47, and several U–3B aircraft at Tan Son Nhut made up a fleet of special mission aircraft for use outside the theater airlift system. Also at Tan Son Nhut in 1964 were two seven-passenger jet T–39s primarily for use of the ambassador. Six more T–39s were added in the summer of 1965. These were fast film couriers used to link reconnaissance aircraft bases in Thailand with the intelligence center at

---

* The VC designation derived from the customary passenger, the very important person, or VIP.

AUXILIARY ROLES

Saigon. The T-39s also hauled special passengers and made occasional flights to offshore points. Air Force U-3s supplemented the photointelligence effort by delivering finished films to smaller sites in Vietnam. The flight operations section of the Seventh Air Force scheduled all missions for the Tan Son Nhut courier ships. Two other C-47s, also at Tan Son Nhut, were assigned to the Air Force Advisory Group. Moreover, Air Force units stationed in South Vietnam possessed some twenty other base support C-47s, for administrative tasks and special airlifts. In December 1965 some of these craft were managed by the materiel control center of the 2d Air Division, primarily to move parts for grounded aircraft. The fifteen base support C-47s assigned to Thai bases were directed by a small control center at Udorn under the Seventh/Thirteenth Air Force.[55]

The other American services also operated airlift enterprises. A MACV priority air transportation system at Saigon flew passengers about Vietnam (seven thousand in the month of July 1968) using a fleet of Army helicopters and utility aircraft assigned to the 210th Combat Aviation Battalion. The Naval Support Activity, Saigon, operated six transports (primarily modernized C-47s designated C-117s) and two helicopters. Their workload in 1967 was four thousand passengers and two hundred tons in some months, linking Da Nang with Saigon and various naval operating sites. The III Marine Amphibious Force controlled several C-117s (the Marine version of the C-47) operated from Da Nang and Chu Lai, and airlift sorties by KC-130s exceeded five hundred monthly in the summer of 1967. Also some fifteen shore-based C-1A and C-2A transports mostly from the Philippines made deliveries to carriers off the coast of Southeast Asia, and naval helicopters redistributed loads to smaller vessels.[56]

The Air Force tolerated the other services' airlift activities without protest. It felt that these relatively small systems were not likely to "duplicate or supplant current Air Force airlift operations." But the Air Force disapproved of the costly contract in-country efforts. In October 1968, MACV made an accounting comparison which included fuel, maintenance, parts, and labor. The results supported the Air Force's preference for centralization:[57]

Typical Monthly Accomplishments/Costs

	Tonnage (includes passengers)	Cost	Cost per ton
Common Service Airlift System (C-123 & C-130)	118,560	$4,732,425	$ 39.7
Dedicated C-7A	15,722	1,396,500	88.5
Naval Forces, Vietnam	535	75,588	146.0
III Marine Amphibious Force (excludes KC-130)	309	72,700	234.0
AID/CORDS	7,379	1,015,470	137.0
Continental Air Services	639	276,000	433.0

TACTICAL AIRLIFT

The allied air and ground forces of Joint Task Force 116 that entered upcountry Thailand in May 1962 depended heavily upon air transport as a logistics link to the principal sea and airport at Bangkok. Operating in Thailand during the deployment were two Australian C–130s, several British transports, three Bristol freighters of the New Zealand Air Force, and four U.S. Air Force C–123s. The C–123 detachment was part of a squadron from TAC, which arrived in Thailand on June 11. The 123s were expected to remain, at least until arrival of a Caribou company recently ordered to Thailand from the United States.[58]

The C–123s operated from Bangkok's Don Muang Airport under mission control of the joint task force headquarters and its Air Force component command. Most missions were between Don Muang and the principal upcountry bases (Takhli, Korat, Chiang Mai, Ubon, and Udorn), each with ample runways of at least seven thousand feet. Only Don Muang had ground controlled approach, VHF omnirange, and tacan equipment, but each of the other fields possessed at least a control tower with VHF radio and a low frequency radio beacon. The main operating problems were the traffic and parking congestion at Don Muang and the limited fuel supplies at the upcountry bases.[59]

The diplomatic settlement at Geneva in July paved the way for withdrawal of the allied force. Looking to the possibility of future buildups in northern Thailand, however, and seeking to reduce dependence on airlift, the Americans acted to improve roads and rail lines across Thailand and increase stocks of military equipment. At Nakhon Phanom, in extreme northeast Thailand, a six thousand-foot airfield was constructed capable of receiving major troop units. Planners realized that another and larger buildup would require use of Air Force four-engine transports for cross-Thailand lift.[60]

The Air Force transports remained at Don Muang despite the withdrawal of the joint task force. Their number was reduced to two 123s by early 1963 but increased to five in July 1964. Aircraft and crews were rotated from units in Vietnam for two-week tours. Ground crewmen found the routine difficult since most maintenance work was done at night to prepare the ships for morning missions, and flight-line noise made daytime rest difficult. For the aircrews, however, duty in Thailand was a pleasure. Most flying was done in the daytime, and the long runways, flat terrain, and absence of enemy fire made the missions easy. The 123s made daily runs to the American depot at Korat and regularly visited some eight other upcountry fields. Crews particularly enjoyed the custom of hauling ice cream back from Korat to treat the Thai children waiting in line at Bangkok for the return of the "Good Humor" ship. Exceptions to the relaxed effort were missions into the tempoary strip at Nakhon Phanom in support of the large construction effort. One ship was destroyed while attempting a landing at an upcountry strip, mistaken for Roi Et. Thai scheduling and mis-

AUXILIARY ROLES

sion control at Don Muang were entirely separate from activities in South Vietnam.[61]

The expansion of U.S. Air Force strike aircraft in Thailand during and after 1965 greatly increased cross-Thailand transportation requirements. The C-123 detachment at Don Muang, now grown to six aircraft was, in September 1965, replaced by four C-130Bs from Mactan Isle Airfield in the Philippines. C-130As took over in early 1966 and were in turn replaced by C-130Es from Ching Chuan Kang in September 1967. Compared to a daily flying rate of 4.4 hours daily per plane for the A– and B–models, the six C-130Es in June 1968 logged 7.8 hours daily per plane. Monthly airlifted tonnage rose from sixteen hundred tons (including three thousand passengers) in late 1965 to more than five thousand tons per month three years later. C-124s passing through Thailand sometimes made one or two in-country flights to haul cargo too big for the C-130s. Improvements in road, rail, and pipeline communications meanwhile made an increase in air transport unnecessary, and the airlift role became primarily to move men, mail, spare parts, and emergency munitions, where speed was important.[62]

Reorganized in April 1965, the Don Muang Transport movement control was reestablished as Detachment 4, 315th Air Division, and included a maintenance staff as well as control personnel. Aircraft itineraries generally followed the monthly schedules set up by the 315th Air Division, with movement control publishing supplementary daily orders as necessary. Since the heavy flying rate made it difficult to cope with emergencies, additional C-130s were sometimes brought in for temporary needs. The C-130 operation in Thailand was therefore a project of the 315th Air Division, wholly distinct from the control or surveillance of the 834th Air Division in Vietnam.[63]

A new aerial port squadron was established in Thailand in April 1965 and was designated the 6th Aerial Port Squadron in July. It replaced the former detachment of the 8th Squadron. The port workload at Don Muang was mainly to prepare cargo and passengers newly arrived in Bangkok for further airlift to upcountry destinations. Detachments of the parent unit functioned upcountry. The busiest (in order of activity) were the detachments at Korat, Udorn, Ubon, Takhli, and Nakhon Phanom. Growing pains in the Thailand port system resembled those experienced in Vietnam and were caused by the inexperience of newly assigned personnel, frequent breakdown of materiel-handling equipment, shortages of protected storage space, and unreliable radios which made exchange of traffic information difficult. By mid-1966, however, the worst of these headaches had been surmounted.[64]

Like the C-123 crewmen earlier, C-130 aircrews found the Bangkok shuttle a welcome change from the more difficult flying in Vietnam. Nearly all loadings were passengers or palletized cargo, relatively easy

409

work for the loadmasters. The rigors of field or tactical operations were seldom experienced. Passenger missions were usually round-robin circuits linking Don Muang and the upcountry bases. An aircrew's seventeen-day cycle at Don Muang usually involved more flying than did a duty cycle in Vietnam. However, most crewmen felt more than compensated by the opportunities for sightseeing and shopping in Bangkok, the excellent arrangements for hotel billeting, transportation, and the regularity of missions flow.

A detachment of U.S. Army aircraft, mostly U–21s, also operated from Don Muang managed by the airlift support branch of the Military Assistance Command, Thailand. Two Army Caribous began working with the detachment in 1964, rotating from companies in Vietnam. When the Air Force took over the Caribous in 1967, it continued the Don Muang shuttle. Caribou missions usually flew one of three preplanned routes to U.S. Special Forces detachments that were inaccessible to the C–130s. After a reorganization in 1971, the Army flight detachment included seven U–21s and two UH–1 helicopters, now managed by the Army Support Command, Thailand. Given the small scale of the Army detachment's capability (less than ten percent of the C–130 tonnage workload), the separation of the Army and the Caribou transports from activities was in practice a harmless deviation from the principle of centralized management.[65]

Transportation patterns shifted away from Don Muang in 1970, reducing irritation at the large American presence at Bangkok and easing air traffic congestion. The C–130s moved to U–Tapao on the Gulf of Thailand in May 1970, and the main terminal of the 6th Aerial Port Squadron followed in July, leaving only a port detachment at Don Muang. MAC began airlifting directly to U–Tapao, and by year's end most of the depot storage activities formerly at Bangkok had been moved. Scheduling of the C–130s was thereafter done by the airlift control center at U–Tapao, functioning under the PACAF airlift directorate. A Thai decision to allow direct entry of American personnel into the upcountry bases in late 1971 promised to reduce the C–130 trans-Thailand workload and permit withdrawal of the C–130 detachment from U–Tapao. For the next several months, two C–130s flew daily in Thailand, taking off each morning from Tan Son Nhut. Several 130s returned to U–Tapao in late April 1972 to meet fresh transport needs resulting from the resumed bombing of North Vietnam. And in 1973 the enlarged U–Tapao force became the sole C–130 airlift contingent in Southeast Asia, with mission responsibilities in Thailand, Cambodia, and South Vietnam.[66]

The Air Force trans-Thailand effort was only a side endeavor to the much larger and more challenging operation in Vietnam. Thailand missions, mainly to major airfields with no threat of enemy fire, resembled the operations of a civilian airline. The crews from the Pacific adapted easily and attained impressive flying hour and workload statistics. The rotational system, the same as that used for South Vietnam, provided a flexible and reliable airlift force for service in Thailand.

In an effort to get "more flags" in Vietnam, President Johnson in late 1964 approached SEATO members and other Asian governments seeking greater third-country involvements. The responses from America's allies included troop units from Korea, Australia, Thailand, and the Philippines. Air transport was a particularly desirable form of third-country assistance, with proven usefulness and political acceptability.[67]

Proposals to place Chinese nationalist pilots in Vietnamese Air Force C-47 cockpits were vetoed by America in 1962 lest this justify increased Chinese communist intervention. Two Chinese nationalist C-46s with uniformed aircrews flew to Vietnam in November 1965 and thereafter operated as China Airlines, primarily for the Agency for International Development. Other proposals for placing Chinese pilots in Vietnamese squadrons and plans for deploying a Chinese C-46 or C-119 squadron were discussed. But, although the Chinese were believed willing, all such ventures were overruled for political reasons. Through much of the war, however, Chinese pilots served in cockpits of Air Vietnam C-47s and unconventional warfare C-123s.[68]

There were also several proposals to place a Philippine air transport squadron in Vietnam. None reached fruition, usually because of political difficulties but in one case because the Americans were unable to provide the planes. A two thousand-man Philippine civic action group came to Tay Ninh in late 1966 and flew troop rotation and logistics flights to their homeland.[69]

The Royal Thai Air Force (RTAF) in September 1964 sent a seventeen-man task force to Vietnam. It was assigned to work and fly as part of the Vietnamese C-47 units at Tan Son Nhut. The Thai pilots, navigators, and maintenance men served with the regular crews, not as advisors or instructors. Although the project continued until 1971, none of the Thais was allowed to serve as a first pilot or an aircraft commander. The Thais resented alleged Vietnamese attitudes of superiority and criticized loose Vietnamese Air Force flying practices. One Thai asserted that Vietnamese flight criteria "did not come up to Thai-U.S. standards," citing a lack of safety criteria, neglect of checklists, and generally poor pilot practices.[70]

During 1966 the Thais proposed that Thai air and ground crews serve with the U.S. Air Force C-123s in Vietnam. The idea seemed feasible since Thai transport crews had operated under the 315th Air Division in

TACTICAL AIRLIFT

Japan since the Korean War and the Royal Thai Air Force had operated eight C–123s since 1964. As finally agreed, two of the 315th Group's C–123s were given Thai markings and returned to Vietnam in July 1966 with a detachment of twenty Thai crewmen. This Royal Thai Air Force Victory Flight thereafter served as part of the 19th Air Commando Squadron.

The Americans scheduled and maintained the Thai-marked 123s integrally with the rest of the C–123s, and all the planes were U.S. owned. Crews usually were of combined nationality, an American pilot and flight engineer usually flying with a Thai copilot and loadmaster. The Thai crewmen were trained in the C–123B before reaching Vietnam but needed C–123K checkouts upon arrival. Each new pilot was assigned an American instructor and a fully qualified Thai as interpreter. The Americans found the Thais quick to learn and unfailingly cheerful. Language problems, however, were severe and hindered use of the Thais as first pilots. Under arrangements begun in 1970, qualified Thai pilots served as aircraft commanders, and some were upgraded to C–123 instructors. At least one U.S. Air Force crewman accompanied all flights, as much for political as operational reasons. Victory Flight strength in 1970 reached forty-five men —thirteen pilots, nine other officers, and twenty-three enlisted mechanics and loadmasters. Thai-Vietnam Air Force frictions seemed wholly absent. Upon inactivation of the 19th Squadron in early 1971, the Victory Flight became part of VNAF's 421st Transport Squadron, which was also equipped with C–123s. Victory Flight and the copilots and mechanics still serving with the Vietnamese C–47 unit returned to Thailand late in the year.[71]

The Royal Australian Air Force (RAAF) in 1963 had two air transport squadrons, one equipped with C–47s, the other with C–130s. The Pacific Command planned to send the C–47 squadron to Vietnam, to be controlled by the Southeast Asia Airlift System. The Australians, however, pointed out that their C–47 unit was converting to Caribous, which they called Wallabies, and that aircrew resources were too limited to permit them to go. On May 29, 1964, the U.S. embassy at Canberra informed Washington that the Australians planned to send six Wallabies with crews to Vietnam during the summer, if the Americans would provide logistics and airfield services. MACV agreed that the Australian aircraft would operate under the airlift system thus freeing additional U.S. Army Caribous for direct support of the corps areas. Six Wallabies flew into Vung Tau in August 1964, thereafter contributing four planes daily to the airlift system.[72]

The Wallabies became valuable to the common service system by making deliveries to delta airstrips inaccessible to the Air Force C–123s. Australian planes during one period rotated to Nha Trang and Da Nang for forward resupply work with the Special Forces. Equipped with rever-

RAAF crews leave their aircraft upon arrival at Tan Son Nhut to aid in the airlift support effort, 10 August 1964.

sible props, the Wallabies could operate into strips as short as five hundred feet. The seventy-three-man Australian detachment was skilled and hard working. One American C-123 squadron commander wrote that one RAAF ship did the work of two U.S. Army Caribous, and Col. Charles W. Borders, of the 315th Group, termed the Australian ships, "the best maintained machines in Vietnam." Spare parts were drawn from the U.S. Army stocks at Vung Tau or brought by weekly RAAF C-130 flights from Australia. Monthly tonnage and flying hour totals rose steadily.[73]

The arrival of Australian infantry units in 1965 and 1966 introduced an Australian UH-1 helicopter squadron and triggered proposals to assign both the Wallabies and UH-1s directly to the Australian army task force. The helicopters were used in this way but the Wallabies, redesignated No. 35 Squadron on June 1, 1966, remained under MACV and common service airlift operational control, though with priority to support the Australian force. The issue came up again in 1969 when Australian aircrews reported that the common service missions often "wasted time, tramping . . . around the Delta looking for work." In November the RAAF commander in Vietnam expressed satisfaction that Squadron 35 had begun part-time direct support of the Australian army, and by 1970 such support rose to seventy-five percent of the squadron's total activity.[74]

TACTICAL AIRLIFT

An Australian UH–1D helicopter used to support the 2nd Royal Australian Army Regiment, Vietnam, 1970.

The Wallaby unit was reduced to four ships (from seven authorized) in June 1971 and withdrew completely in February 1972. The Australians reported that, since their arrival in Vietnam in 1964, the Wallabies had lifted forty-five thousand tons of cargo and nearly seven hundred thousand passengers. The Wallabies attained better incommission and payload statistics than the U.S. Air Force C–7s. This was attributed by Australian officers to skilled maintenance and unit pride. The Americans noted, however, that all Australian ships operated from one location (Vung Tau), that the Australian ships were less encumbered with avionics, and that the Australian crews were less bound by crew-duty day rules.[75]

C–130s from both the RAAF and the Royal New Zealand Air Force were used to transport their nation's ground forces and thereafter operated routinely on long hauls between their homelands and Vietnam. Australian C–130s mainly entered at Phan Rang and Vung Tau, bringing in spare parts and evacuating casualties. U.S. Air Force exchange officers assigned to the Australian units found their two-year tours satisfying, due to the Australian practice of allowing aircrews considerable initiative and responsibility. Chartered jet airliners of Qantas Airlines made weekly passenger trips into Tan Son Nhut, linking there with feeder U.S. Air Force and Wallaby schedules. Australian aerial port units at Vung Tau, Phan Rang, and Tan Son Nhut served both the Wallaby and the overwater flights. The Australian ports worked closely with the American ports and often booked space-available American passengers and cargo for RAAF flights.[76]

AUXILIARY ROLES

Troops of the Korean Tiger Division board a USAF C–130 at Qui Nhon Air Base for airlift to Phan Rang, where they became base security guards.

An especially welcome contribution to the "more flags" policy was that of the Republic of Korea which reached twenty-two infantry battalions by the end of 1966. American officers therefore regarded the Korean desire to send air units to Vietnam as an expression of national pride. Early proposals were for either a Korean C–123 unit similar to the Victory Flight or for an independent Korean unit. Two Korean C–46 transports were sent to Tan Son Nhut on July 29, 1967, with air and ground crews, to provide in-country transport for Korean forces. The Republic of Korea Support Group, Vietnam, thereafter flew twice-weekly shuttles between Saigon, Vung Tau, Nha Trang, and Qui Nhon, along with numerous unscheduled missions. In its first year the unit carried eight hundred passengers and fifteen tons of cargo each month, hauling non-Korean passengers when space permitted.[77]

The Korean air force received four C–54s in July 1966, primarily for missions between Korea and Southeast Asia. The inaugural flight landed at Saigon on September 19 and thereafter the C–54s made about six trips monthly, frequently landing at Clark Air Base. Northbound flights often carried medical patients. Some missions made several stops in Vietnam thus providing in-country transport. Transports of the 315th Air Divi-

415

TACTICAL AIRLIFT

sion also made numerous trips between Vietnam and Korea, evacuating 1,350 Korean patients by the end of 1967. C-130s also made weekly passenger trips to Korea for a special leave program for Korean troops volunteering to extend tours in Vietnam. Most unit and cargo movements, however, were by sea.[78]

The Korean army operated nine UH-1 helicopters and three fixed-wing utility craft in Vietnam for administrative and liaison tasks. The Americans provided another ten C-54s in early 1970, and a three-ship detachment arrived at Tan Son Nhut, replacing the older C-46s for in-country missions. All Korean air force missions were outside common service scheduling and control.[79]

The significance of the third-country airlifts was as much political as military, serving to reinforce the alliance's appearance of solidarity. Conflicts among the allies over airlift roles were negligible, and the successful mixing of Thai, American, and South Vietnamese crewmen in C-123 cockpits verified the ability of airmen of different nationalities to work and fly together. The most important military contribution was that of the Australian Caribous, which enabled the Common Service Airlift System to land at otherwise inaccessible airstrips.

XVI. Airlift in Irregular Warfare

The ability of the transport airplane to fly over hostile territory and to overcome barriers of terrain and distance made it invaluable in irregular warfare. Airlift forces supported Civilian Irregular Defense Groups in South Vietnam, government counterinsurgency forces in Thailand, covert reconnaissance patrols in parts of Laos and Cambodia, and South Vietnamese agent teams in North Vietnam. In most of these situations, helicopters were superior to fixed-wing transports since helicopters could more readily land and pick up personnel. So the long neglected transport helicopter came into its own in special air warfare. The communists too apparently engaged in unconventional airlift, to the extent allied command of the air permitted.

The Civilian Irregular Defense Group program continued to grow, comprising seventy remote camps by 1967. Plans to phase out U.S. Special Forces advisors were dropped upon the entry of American ground forces into the war. Information from CIDG patrols often brought American units into remote regions for search-and-destroy operations. Meanwhile Air Force crews increased their substantial contribution to CIDG resupply, and tonnages lifted on behalf of the system almost doubled between 1965 and 1968.[1]

The U.S. Army Special Forces continued to furnish all materiel and transportation for the CIDG program thus assuring honest administration, good CIDG troop morale, and American leverage. Under support agreements negotiated in early 1966, Special Forces requisitioned munitions and fuel from the 1st Logistical Command in Vietnam. Most clothing and troop-issue items were brought from the Special Forces depot on Okinawa, mainly by sea; CIDG rations were generally procured in Vietnam. In-country distribution was from the Special Forces logistical support center at Nha Trang to the four forward supply points at Da Nang, Pleiku, Bien Hoa, and Can Tho. A fifth supply point was opened at Ban Me Thuot in early 1967. By 1968 considerable materiel entered the system at the supply points, either from overseas or from the 1st Logistical Command. Each supply point preserved a fifteen-day stock of items, and the support center

TACTICAL AIRLIFT

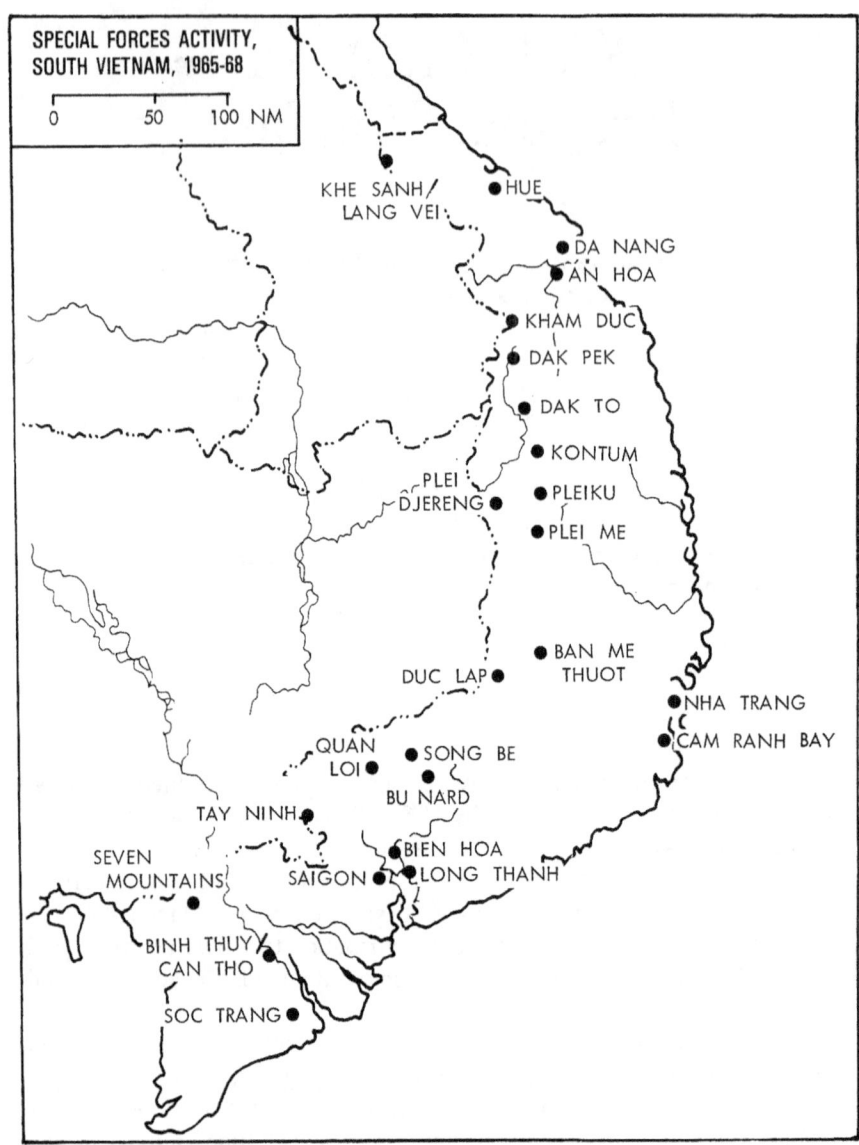

maintained a forty-five-day stock. Prerigged loads were kept ready for emergency airlift pickups at Nha Trang and the forward supply points. Routine requisitions were delivered in one to two weeks. CIDG camps supported from Bien Hoa came under an automatic requisitioning system, wherein daily stock level reports triggered resupply.[2]

The network used several transportation modes. Most shipments from Nha Trang to the forward supply points were by C–130, C–123, or by water. Shorter haul distribution from supply points to camps was by

C-123, Caribou, helicopter, utility aircraft, or in some cases by truck. In the three months ending in July 1968, for example, seventy-one percent of the cargo shipped by the logistical supply center (about ten thousand tons) was airlifted, twenty-five percent was moved by LST, and the remainder by road convoy. During the same period, ninety percent of the distribution from the forward supply points to camps (about seventeen thousand tons) was by air. The interaction of the various modes was most clear-cut in the delta where C-130s delivered daily from Nha Trang to the Binh Thuy Air Base at Can Tho. The Can Tho supply point in September 1966 (a period of flooding) shipped a daily average of 17.5 tons to camps, 6.5 tons by C-123, 6.5 by Australian and U.S. Army Caribou, 0.5 tons by helicopter, and three tons by surface transport. Among the Common Service Airlift System aircraft the C-123s were the major transports countrywide. In the spring of 1966 the C-123s lifted for Special Forces a daily average of seventy-one tons, compared to forty-three tons for the C-130s, and the Australian Caribous' five tons.[3]

Aircraft were assigned in several ways. Transfer of the 310th Squadron to Nha Trang in April 1965 made the old C-123 rotational arrangement unnecessary. Subsequently the squadron provided four ships daily for Special Forces scheduling. C-130 and additional C-123 service was arranged by normal common service request procedures, with itineraries specified by the control center. Caribou use steadily increased to a daily authorization for seven flyable ships in the summer of 1966. Later, under Air Force Caribou ownership, the logistical support center and each forward supply point were allocated one or more Caribous daily, and additional C-7s were usually available from those allocated to corps-level user commands. U.S. Marine helicopters worked for Special Forces out of Da Nang, and Army choppers and U-1As assisted from the other supply points. Although the 5th Special Forces Group was dissatisfied with the small number of helicopters thus made available, the helicopter contribution was valuable since in most cases the alternative was airdrops.[4]

The 5th Special Forces Group repeatedly declared its satisfaction with Air Force transport in quarterly reports but complaints were frequent at operational levels. One officer, commanding a forward supply point site in 1966–67, stated that of all his problems the biggest was getting supplies to CIDG camps by air. Irritants grew from the limited flying hours established, aircrew duty time restriction, the absence of forklifts at some camps (necessitating hand offloading), and problems in radio communications between aircrews and the camps. During the fall of 1966, four separate camps in the northern provinces reported food shortages among CIDG troops due to unsatisfactory resupply. The reporting officers appreciated that weather had been difficult but charged that C-123 crews were careless in handling items, in some cases allowing livestock to be crushed, and that there was pilferage, apparently on the ground at Da Nang. In 1967 the Air

Force control element commander at Binh Thuy described wide dissatisfaction among Special Forces personnel with late-arriving Air Force transports, lost cargo, and inaccurate airdrops. Aircrews sometimes returned to their home base after failing to land at the intended camp and their loads often became lost in the aerial port system, while the 834th Air Division counted the tonnage as delivered. Air Force officers down to squadron level took strong action to make improvements. They met frequently with Special Forces personnel, thus preventing such complaints from becoming general.[5]

Resupply drops to CIDG camps decreased to seven tons daily, mainly by C–123s and C–7s. Helicopters were much preferred since there was no necessity for rigging and recovering parachutes, and personnel could be evacuated on return flights. Further, inaccurate drops, although not frequent, occasionally landed on CIDG personnel or structures and required laborious efforts to recover. C–130s rarely dropped to camps except during major construction projects but made numerous low-altitude extractions for Special Forces in late 1968. The emerging techniques for ground-directed drops promised future improvements in accuracy and in bad-weather drops.[6]

In addition to its resupply role, air transport was able to reinforce camps in emergencies. Usually Air Force transports carried troops to nearby C–130 fields for helicopter lift into the camp proper or its immediate environs. This is how reinforcements entered the fights at Plei Me (1965), A Shau (1966), Kham Duc and Duc Lap (1968). Fixed-wing craft directly reinforced camps only when the reaction was early. Mobile strike forces were organized within the CIDG apparatus in 1964 and 1965. Three two hundred-man strike force companies served at supply point bases and at Nha Trang. Mobile strike force companies frequently were flown to CIDG camps for local sweeps. Twice in 1967, several hundred Special Forces and other CIDG troops parachuted into locations chosen for new CIDG camps—at Bu Nard on April 2, and near Duc Lap on October 5. On May 13, 1967, three companies from Nha Trang jumped from six C–130s into the Seven Mountains region of southernmost Vietnam not far from a somewhat larger operation in the following year.[7]

During and after 1969 the CIDG camps were successfully converted to Regional Forces status with Vietnamese rangers taking over the U.S. Special Forces advisory role. As each camp converted, its logistics support became a Vietnamese responsibility. U.S. Air Force airlift remained significant, however. In mid-1970, half the seventy-six camps still remained in the CIDG program, resupplied from Nha Trang and the forward supply points. But squadron inactivations reduced the C–123 role. In May 1970, of 402 Common Service Airlift System sorties for Special Forces, C–7s flew 234, C–130s 137, and C–123s only 31.[8]

By early 1971 the Vietnamese had taken over most camp resupply

IRREGULAR WARFARE

duties, using both helicopters and fixed-wing transports and relying on trucks to the extent permitted by the existing roadnet. In some cases, shipments were trucked as far forward as possible for short-haul helicopter shuttle into the camps proper. A regional Vietnamese area logistics command processed all resupply requests. When ground transport was impractical the request was passed to the Vietnamese movement control center in Saigon. Then if the Vietnam Air Force was unable to make the delivery, the request went to MACV and the Common Service Airlift System. The Americans insisted that Vietnamese resources be first exhausted, but recognized that since the Vietnamese lacked C–7s and C–130s some U.S. Air Force involvement was justified. Although the scaled-down Air Force role continued, Defense Secretary Melvin R. Laird reported to the White House in February 1971 that Vietnamization of the CIDG camps had been successfully completed and that the Vietnamese had assumed full responsibility for these camps and their missions.[9]

Stirrings of internal insurgency, primarily in the northeastern section of the country, were of growing concern to the government of Thailand. Ethnic and language differences, along with the presence of forty-thousand refugees who came from Indochina in 1954, heightened the communist-fed discontent with the Thai regime. Insurgent groups periodically entered villages, mixing propaganda and intimidation to win recruits and passive support. During early 1962 a task force of the Directorate of Plans, U.S. Air Force, looked into the situation and concluded that "an aggressive program, undertaken immediately, can prevent the development of problems similar to those now existing in Laos and South Vietnam." The group recommended a number of police and civic action measures, most of them requiring a nationwide air transport system. Consequently, the group recommended that the Royal Thai Air Force's C–47s be replaced by C–123s.[10]

The Air Force paper reached Bangkok in April 1962 and reinforced the embassy's earlier conclusion that the Thai government's greatest need was for "light transport for access to remote areas." Airlift thus became prominent in the Thai counterinsurgency programs encouraged by the Americans in the next years. By 1965 the Thais had activated a dozen hundred-man rural development teams, each with expertise in medicine, construction, and agriculture. The RTAF meanwhile organized several composite squadrons for counterinsurgency work, using C–47s and utility aircraft to haul intelligence and civic action teams. The RTAF received eight C–123s from active U.S. Air Force service and organized them in a single squadron based at Don Muang. The Thais also had by late 1964 a total of seventeen H–34 helicopters intended for counterguerrilla work, but all at Don Muang and judged by the Americans "probably the most ineffective unit in RTAF." The Thai border patrol police also had an airlift section that included C–47s and helicopters.[11]

In 1966 the 606th Air Commando Squadron was sent to Nakhon Phanom. This was a composite unit designed to augment and train the Thais in counterinsurgency work. The 606th had C–123s, UH–1Fs, and utility transports (U–6s, later replaced by U–10s), along with strike aircraft. U.S. Air Force helicopter units occasionally joined the 606th for lift tasks in Thailand. These units were based in north Thailand but with primary missions in Laos.[12]

U.S. Air Force missions in Thailand were varied. Crews lifted medical teams to villages, delivered medical supplies for local distribution, and made emergency patient evacuations. Helicopters carried VHF radios to villages for use in informing police of communist activity. 606th personnel helped local residents build strips for the U–10s, and periodically returned to survey field conditions. U–10 pilots flew daily circuits to check ground panels that signaled local security conditions. 606th training teams served at the main Thai air bases. Ships hauled civil engineer equipment and performed lift tasks for American units.

The Americans also joined in offensive troop missions. The C–123s of the 606th, for example, in early November 1966 flew twenty-one missions, each nine hundred miles, to a site identified for a new government camp and paradropped troops and cargo. The C–123s flew frequent flareship missions supporting police or army sweeps. The Air Force helicopters also flew several troop-assault missions, including an extended operation in easternmost Thailand during July and August 1966. On December 21, 1966, five CH–3s and ten UH–1s joined in a simultaneous assault that netted a number of prisoners. Royal Thai helicopters had been scheduled to join, but failed to show up. The success of these and similar operations was questionable, however, since prisoners usually professed their loyalty to the regime.[13]

Both the U.S. Congress and the Office of the Secretary of Defense were convinced that the Thais should shoulder their own internal security tasks. The UH–1s of the 606th Squadron in January 1967 accordingly were transferred to Vietnam, and the C–123s and U–10s were gradually reassigned to flareship, leaflet, and forward air control duties in Laos. Direct airlift support of Thai counterinsurgency operations was "virtually terminated" in January 1968, and the 606th Air Commando Squadron was inactivated in June 1971.[14]

Thai airlift forces however continued to grow, reflecting the usefulness of air transport in counterinsurgency. The C–123 squadron reached its authorized sixteen-ship strength in 1971, while a second squadron operated with C–47s. Planners periodically reexamined the ability of the transport fleet to supply division-scale Thai forces in remote regions. Thai helicopters were divided between the army and the air force. The army ships were used for troop assaults and supply, while the air force craft primarily worked in rescue, medical evacuation, and general transport roles.[15]

Although Thailand in 1972 did not seem ripe for revolution, it was clear that the several government programs had at best only slowed the growth of the insurgency. Communist units steadily improved in weaponry and tactics and expanded (by allied estimates) to ten thousand troops. Allied aircraft met increasing fire in Thailand. A U.S. CH-3 was downed near Ubon in August 1970 with loss of four crewmen, and American aircraft took hits on at least four occasions in 1971 near Nakhon Phanom. During one two-week operation against an insurgent area, seven Thai helicopters were hit. Armed formations in the countryside and in the urban political infrastructure seemed to be on the increase, fed by infiltration, supplies, and propaganda broadcasts from Laos and North Vietnam. The American embassy in Bangkok, reviewing the state of affairs in 1972, concluded that although the gradual improvement in Thai weaponry (such as that in airlift forces) was helpful, the defeat of insurgent military forces must be achieved by "small infantry-type units, both military and police," capable of both continuous patrolling and intensive fighting.[16]

Past Southeast Asian warfare—Burma during the second World War and in the counterinsurgency campaigns in Malaya—was characterized by reconnaissance teams operating in enemy territory. Such forces became increasingly important in allied strategy after 1964, penetrating areas used by the communists in South Vietnam and in adjacent Laos and Cambodia. Accordingly, highly trained mobile guerrilla force units were created for this purpose within the CIDG structure. In addition, several ten-man American–Vietnamese teams were organized separately as Project Delta in 1964. These teams were trained for infiltration by parachute or helicopter and equipped for five days of operations without resupply. A parachute-qualified battalion also was trained as a delta reaction force. Projects Omega and Sigma followed similar patterns in 1966.[17]

Infiltration teams were usually placed by U.S. Army or Vietnamese Air Force helicopter, fixed-wing transports being seldom used. Common service transports shifted patrol forces and their supplies from home bases to the advanced staging points. C-130s in a late-1967 odyssey hauled the delta reaction force to An Hoa in September in eighteen sorties, then to Nha Trang for recuperation, then to Kontum in late November in twenty-four C-130 lifts, to Plei Djereng four weeks later, and finally back to Nha

Trang in January.[18] Teams in the field were sometimes supplied by Caribou paradrop. During operations near Can Tho in June 1967, C-7 Caribous made deliveries of fresh water, clothing, and other materiel to teams every four days, dropping supplies from three hundred feet in the morning or at evening twilight. Caribou drops supplied Operation Blackjack 34 in July near Quan Loi. Techniques also were developed to make small, emergency deliveries from aircraft, using empty shell casings as containers.[19]

Two American officers at Pleiku invented a new method for resupplying teams by A-1E strike aircraft. Col. Eugene P. Deatrick, Jr., commander of the 1st Air Commando Squadron (equipped with A-1s), and Lt. Col. Eleazar Parmly IV, USA, the local Special Forces commander, realized that A-1 supply drops in twilight could be made to look like air strikes. Canisters ordinarily used for napalm delivery were packed with supplies, fitted with personnel parachutes, and mounted externally on the A-1s. Every A-1 could carry eight canisters each holding up to five hundred pounds for release at slow airspeed, in level flight, from altitudes between fifty and three hundred feet. The delivery aircraft covered their role by making strafing passes in the vicinity after dropping.[20]

The first actual deliveries by this method took place in early November 1966 in hill country west of Pleiku. Of eighty-eight containers dropped in five days, eighty-six were successfully recovered. Apprised of the new technique, the Seventh Air Force congratulated the 1st Squadron on its initiative but turned thumbs down on further experiments with aircraft configuration. Another supply container (the MA-6) was already certified for use by A-1s, the staff pointed out, and was in limited use by the Vietnamese Air Force.[21]

The A-1 activity remained a closely held secret, with only ten or twelve pilots checked out in the technique. The 5th Special Forces Group praised the "exceptional accuracy" of deliveries during Blackjack 31 in early 1967, when all ninety-six containers dropped were recovered. Results during Blackjack 41 were less satisfactory. A-1s were sent to Can Tho for the venture, but parachute failures caused several ammunition loads to blow up. Army officers complained that the numerous small containers complicated recovery (twenty-seven napalm canisters were needed to equal three packages from a single C-7), but Special Forces officers wanted A-1 deliveries increased to cover all Vietnam. Some Air Force officers at Pleiku, however, argued that the A-1s should be restricted to their air strike role. Although the napalm canisters received official Air Force certification in August 1967, the frequency of usage thereafter declined.[22]

Evidence of heavy communist logistical activity led to joint American–South Vietnamese planning for cross-border patrol penetrations into southern Laos in early 1964. The concept agreed upon called for night infiltrations by parachute, resupply by unmarked VNAF aircraft, and withdrawal by helicopter. Vietnamese Special Forces trained the teams at Nha Trang using Vietnamese C–47s and H–34s. During the last week of June, five eight-man teams jumped from Vietnamese transports into the region of Laos adjacent to Vietnam. The results of this Leaping Lena jump were "most disappointing with little intelligence gained," according to American officers.[23]

More extensive operations into Laos began in 1965 under Project Prairie Fire (originally called Shining Brass), with a specially recruited force of Nungs. Patrols launched from border camps, primarily Khe Sanh, A Shau, Kham Duc, and Kontum, were landed and withdrawn usually by the Vietnamese Air Force's 219th Helicopter Squadron's H–34s. During 1967 over 250 individual operations penetrated as far as twelve miles into Laos. Similar operations into Cambodia began in 1967 under Project Daniel Boone. Fourteen Vietnamese and U.S. Army helicopters were lost in cross-border operations during 1967.[24]

Cross-border infiltration work by the Air Force's 20th Helicopter Squadron was the result of an agreement which acknowledged that Air Force helicopters had a role in "special air warfare." With much of its strength based in northern Thailand in early 1966, the 20th in Vietnam made only routine lifts. An exception was a temporary mission at Kontum in January 1967, where CH–3s assisted in transporting patrol teams being staged from that point. The squadron acquired fifteen UH–1s in June 1967 and reopened its detachment at Kontum, shifting it soon afterwards to Ban Me Thuot. Each of the UH–1s was equipped with armored self-sealing fuel tanks and door-mounted, hand-operated machineguns. Some ships were further modified to carry rockets and 7.62-mm miniguns. These Air Force Hueys joined Vietnamese Air Force and Army choppers as troop carriers and gunships for reconnaissance forces, both in-country and cross-border.[25]

Rapport between members of 20th Squadron and the Special Forces was excellent. Mission assignment was by a command element of the MACV Studies and Observations Group (SOG): four gunships, one command vehicle, an emergency recovery craft, and one plane carrying the reconnaissance team. The force flew in loose formation, the gunships to either side and slightly to the rear. Teamwork was vital as were fast execution and measures to avoid detection. Withdrawals were similar except that secrecy was not essential, and the gunships orbited the landing zone prior to pickup to attract and suppress enemy fire. Night infiltration and pickup missions were extremely dangerous and were performed only in emergencies, when possible aided by flareship illumination. Technical developments included the "McGuire Rig" consisting of triple ropes, each with trapeze wrist locks, and a sling arrangement to lift teams out of jungle areas. Protective equipment too was effective. This was proven when two persons

Medal of Honor recipient Capt. James P. Fleming, of the 20th Helicopter Squadron.

received only superficial injuries when their ballistic helmets deflected enemy rifle bullets.[26]

In addition to infiltration work, the Ban Me Thuot detachment moved a number of companies and platoons in South Vietnam and fought as gunships in the 1968 battles of Ban Me Thuot and Duc Lap. At the height of the Duc Lap fight, UH–1s of the 20th Squadron landed a force of soldiers in the camp, distributed reconnaissance photography, and defended the base at Nha Trang.[27]

The detachment at Ban Me Thuot found living conditions primitive and at one time half the encampment was stricken with gastrointestinal sickness. To compound its problems, the squadron began receiving replacement pilots with inadequate training. Supply difficulties, however, were eased by parts assistance from the Army and increased cannibalization. During 1967–68 the 20th Squadron lost five UH–1s, four of them by enemy fire, and earned numerous individual awards for heroism, including six Silver Stars and eleven Purple Hearts in the second half of 1968 alone. Six crewmen earned the Air Force Cross during 1967–68, and 1st Lt. James P. Fleming received the Medal of Honor for rescuing a six-man team under close-in enemy fire on November 26, 1968. The squadron earned the Presidential Unit Citation in 1967 and multiple Air Force Outstanding Unit Awards.[28]

Cross-border helicopter activity reached a maximum in 1969 and early 1970. The number of transport and gunship choppers used in infiltration work daily averaged forty-eight: eleven Vietnamese Air Force, seven

IRREGULAR WARFARE

Thai troops and U.S. Army Special Forces advisors board a USAF CH-3E after completing a mission in June 1968.

U.S. Air Force, and the rest from the U.S. Army. Most missions supported small teams whose role was to obtain intelligence and locate targets for air strikes. Platoon-size units occasionally entered Laos and (after early 1970) Cambodia. Most missions were launched from border bases in Vietnam, though sometimes from Ubon or Nakhon Phanom in Thailand.[29]

HELICOPTER PERFORMANCE, BASIC MISSION*

	Takeoff Weight	Fuel Weight	Payload	Cruise Speed (knots)	Range[a] (NM)	Cargo[b] Space (CF)
CH-3C	22,050	4,308	5,000 (25 pax)[c]	113	372	1,014
CH-34A	12,600	1,840	3,000 (16–18 pax)	82	247	368
CH-47A	33,000	4,036	10,367 (33 pax)	102	200	1,472
CH-53C	42,000	8,136	8,000	133	448	1,462
UH-1F	7,494	1,592	2,000 (10 pax)	100	289	140

   a. NM—nautical mile
   b. CF—cubic feet
   c. pax—passenger

---

* Aeronautical Systems Division, Air Force System Command, *USAF Standard Aircraft/Missile Characteristics* (Brown Book), as of 1976. Data for CH-34A is from John W. R. Taylor, ed, *Jane's All the World's Aircraft, 1964–1965* (New York: McGraw-Hill, n.d.).

TACTICAL AIRLIFT

The missions from Thailand were secondary responsibilities of a detachment of the 20th Squadron at Udorn and the 21st Special Operations Squadron based at Nakhon Phanom. The 21st flew CH–3 helicopters until 1970 and thereafter the larger CH–53s. Distances to the Prairie Fire and Cambodian operating areas were great, and each Thai-launched mission meant two crossings of the enemy's main panhandle infiltration corridors. The high altitudes needed to assure safety from ground fire during these crossings were hard on engines, so crewmen often criticized Prairie Fire missions from Thailand, except when weather obviously prevented takeoff from Vietnam. The CH–53s generally operated in pairs with one staying high at the landing zone ready for emergency rescue. Crews used steep approaches and relatively high speeds for the final approach. Forward air controllers often coordinated fire suppression and helped to find the landing zone. Escort fighters accompanied most missions, with propeller-driven A–1Es preferred to jet fighters because of their slower speed, superior maneuverability, and greater endurance. Some CH–53s had miniguns for self-protection. Precautionary tactics held CH–53 losses in the Prairie Fire region to a single ship downed in February 1971.[30]

In contrast, the 20th Squadron fell upon difficult times.* The squadron lost five UH–1s in the first four months of 1969, all to ground fire. Further losses and sagging maintenance forced the unit to cease cross-border work from August to December, and upon the political decision to cease use of American craft for troop lifts in Cambodia on July 1, 1970, permanently ended this activity. The UH–1s continued gunship support for the Vietnamese H–34s, making occasional emergency pickups when H–34 crews could not. During the summer of 1971, the 20th made several eight-ship flights to Kontum and Da Nang, temporarily serving troop carriers. During 1972 American helicopters flew only occasional infiltration missions, and those only upon special requests.[31]

The unconventional warfare operations in Southeast Asia confirmed the superiority of the helicopter over parachute drops in most team infiltration and supply tasks, and the advantages of the helicopter for troop removal was indisputable. Contrasted with overland travel, the ease of movement by helicopter multiplied the efficiency of combat teams and vastly reduced troop hardships. Unconventional helicopter duties among the Air Force, the U.S. Army, and the Vietnamese Air Force, were reasonably well coordinated, and the distinguished work of the 20th and 21st Squadrons in Southeast Asia strengthened the Air Force's entitlement to future special air operations roles.

---

*The 20th Helicopter Squadron was renamed the 20th Special Operations Squadron in August 1968.

In the summer of 1964 a project was initiated to improve air transport capabilities. Six specially equipped C–123s arrived at Nha Trang for Project Duck Hook. Seven Chinese and three Vietnamese aircrews meanwhile completed special flying training at Hurlburt Field. The course stressed low-level navigation and bad-weather drops. Although the project made improvements, the Duck Hook C–123s faced inordinate operational difficulties. The communists lacked radar for night intercepts but their increased antiaircraft net sharply limited possible routes. The mountainous terrain over much of the north allowed missions only on moonlit and relatively clear nights. Consequently, of five resupply missions authorized for October, only one was completed by late the next month.[32]

Penetrations of the north were not frequent. Early activity was confined to high-altitude leaflet operations and routine airlift work. The first reinforcement-resupply mission to North Vietnam took place on December 25, 1966. Seven more resupply missions to the north were completed in the first three months of 1967, followed by only ten more through the end of 1968. Completion rate was one sortie in three. Only three teams of six scheduled were inserted in September and October 1967. One C–130 was lost with eleven persons on board while on a drop mission on December 29, 1967; another was victim to mortar fire a month earlier.[33]

These personnel spent considerable effort in developing and demonstrating the skyhook surface-to-air recovery system. The man to be picked up raised a gas balloon and donned a special harness. A cabling rig cushioned acceleration during the snatch, then towed the man aloft while hoisting him aboard. No actual combat pickups or rescues were made.[34]

The Combat Spear force was initially organized as a detachment of the 314th Wing, and its aircraft were flown periodically to Ching Chuan Kang Air Base for heavy maintenance. The detachment became the 15th Air Commando Squadron on March 15, 1968, under the 14th Air Commando Wing at Nha Trang. The Duck Hook C–123s continued to operate from Nha Trang, completing thirty resupply missions in the north during 1966–68, occasionally with U.S. Air Force markings and crews. The Duck Hook element merged into the 15th Squadron in late 1968, although it retained a separate commander. The Vietnamese Air Force C–47s ceased unconventional warfare work after failing to complete any of the twelve missions scheduled in the first three months of 1966.[35]

Most Combat Spear and Duck Hook missions were routine deliveries to border-area airfields such as Khe Sanh and Nakhom Phanom. Such missions provided transport for personnel and supplies to support cross-border operations. Combat Spear and Duck Hook in 1967 listed twenty-five thousand passengers and fifty-four hundred tons of cargo, and use of these unconventional warfare transports in ordinary airlift work of this magnitude inevitably made their organizational separation from the common service system questionable. This controversy diminished after July

TACTICAL AIRLIFT

1968 when the MACV SOG began moving nonpriority materiel through the established aerial port system. Concern at Seventh Air Force, over Combat Spear's and Duck Hook's lack of normal Air Force supervision of flying safety and similar matters, also diminished in 1968. This was due to the creation of a new agency in the 14th Wing charged with the entire unconventional warfare force, including the helicopters of the 20th Squadron.[36]

Strike aircraft also on occasions resupplied agent teams in areas of heavy antiaircraft defenses. Vietnamese A-1s began such work in April 1966 and completed five resupply missions during the year into the southern provinces of North Vietnam. Completion rates were low primarily because of difficulties caused by weather—only three of thirty-two scheduled missions were completed in 1968. Air Force F-4s based at Da Nang supplied the Red River Delta area, completing fifteen missions during 1966-68, roughly one of every five attempted. The difficulties encountered are exemplified by one plan that called for two F-4s to deliver from fifty feet above the ground, flying in twilight at three hundred fifty knots. Nearby air strikes were designed to disguise the resupply. Occasionally, forward air controller aircraft made small deliveries to teams operating just above the DMZ, using rocket-pod casings as containers.[37]

The belief that Vietnamese Air Force helicopter crews lacked skills in night, instrument, and low-level flying discouraged attempts to penetrate North Vietnam by helicopter. Vietnamese H-34s operated successfully into southern Laos, however, and in late 1965 two Vietnamese Air Force crews from Khe Sanh flew Team Romeo into North Vietnam just north of the DMZ. Air Force CH-3s resupplied the team using low-level contour flight techniques. In June 1966 the CH-3s of the 20th Helicopter Squadron landed their first team in the same area.

Authority to fly from Thailand in January 1967 made possible penetrations further north. During 1967 the 20th Squadron's Pony Express CH-3s completed eight of thirty-seven scheduled missions from Nakhon Phanom into North Vietnam. Penetration missions were ordinarily screened by strike aircraft and sometimes included refueling stops inside Laos. Resupply deliveries could be parachuted, free-dropped, or lowered by cable. Most resupply aborts resulted from failures to make contact with teams. The first successful team recovery in September 1967 boosted the morale of all team members and led to a program of short-duration infiltrations in 1968. The UH-1s assigned to the 20th Squadron lacked the necessary range and altitude capabilities and were therefore not used for missions against North Vietnam.[38]

Air Force clandestine missions into North Vietnam, both by helicopter and fixed-wing aircraft, ceased with the bombing halt of November 1, 1968. The four C-123s and four C-130s at Nha Trang thereafter flew occasional insertion and resupply drops into Laos and Cambodia, along with leaflet operations and routine airland missions.* C–123s made eleven supply drops in northeast Cambodia in June 1970 in conjunction with the departure of friendly forces from that region. Retention of the unconventional warfare transports in Vietnam was periodically reviewed. MACV preferred to retain them in case of resumed operations to the north, but both the 123s and 130s were withdrawn from clandestine operations on March 31, 1972.[39]

The use of unconventional warfare transports achieved high drama in the 1970 attempt to rescue American prisoners at Son Tay, North Vietnam. Two Air Force C–130s were sent from the United States to act as navigation pathfinders, leading formations of helicopters and A–1 strike aircraft to Son Tay. Both 130s had specially installed, forward-looking infrared navigation equipment. Each crew had three navigators—one for the normal radar, doppler, and computational work, the second for visual fixes, and the third to work the infrared gear. The task force, trained at Eglin Air Force Base, working out techniques to operate the C–130s in formation with the slower rescue helicopters.

The rescue force took off from Thailand shortly before midnight on November 20, 1970, with six helicopters behind the designated C–130. The formation crossed into North Vietnam one thousand feet above the ground, using terrain for masking as much as possible. Rivers served as radar and infrared checkpoints. Navigation was expert; the lead C–130 delivered the formation to the planned point three miles west of the objective, on course and within two minutes of the scheduled time. At this point the leader pulled up and ahead and released illuminator flares over the target area in front of the choppers. The second C–130 delivered the A–1s immediately behind the helicopter force and joined the first leader overhead, dropping markers during the assault. Both ships remained until the last helicopter left, whereupon both returned to orbits in Laos to broadcast homing radio signals.[40]

On the whole allied unconventional warfare efforts against North Vietnam were disappointing. The importance of air transport in these operations, however, was unquestioned since agent teams were completely dependent on airlift for mobility and survival. The missions into North Vietnam confirmed the ability of transports to penetrate enemy territory without heavy losses by using darkness and electronic aids. The successful use of the Pony Express helicopters against North Vietnam was also an innovation that deserves inclusion in future unconventional warfare doctrine. The organizational question, however, remained unanswered. Duck Hook, Combat Spear, and Pony Express aircraft performed many conventional airlift tasks, but it nevertheless was clear that these units needed

---

* The 15th Squadron became the 90th Special Operations Squadron, effective October 31, 1970.

TACTICAL AIRLIFT

rigorous special training and that their special capabilities required proper exploitation.

Allied dominance in the air severely limited the communists' ability to utilize their air transport forces. It seemed probable that the North Vietnamese would undertake clandestine airlift efforts wherever feasible in view of communist covert movements on the ground. Evidence of covert enemy airlift was widespread, although the lack of captured wreckage or other incontrovertible proof made American intelligence officers cautious in confirming its actuality. The exact dimensions of communist airlift ventures therefore remained obscure.

Communist airlift activity in Laos was extensive. Operations, both visible and covert, dated back to the shifting cold war confrontations of the early 1960s. In December 1960 Soviet IL–14 transports began deliveries into Vientiane to support the existing coalition neutralist regime. When rightist opponents seized the Vientiane airfield, Soviet ships began airdrops to leftist forces withdrawing to the north. By April 1961 the Soviets were landing twenty tons of supplies daily, hauled from Hanoi to Pathet Lao forces in the Plain of Jars. Paradrops to units in other areas also continued. The United States made diplomatic protests but took no direct action against the Soviet transports. The cease-fire in the spring of 1961 ended the immediate confrontation, but the Soviet transport fleet, numbering eighteen LI–2 and nine IL–14 craft, remained in North Vietnam.* In late 1962, apparently in a gesture of accommodation, the Soviets gave the Laotian coalition regime ten transport planes. These ships were for a time flown by Russian pilots and were used on behalf of all factions, including the Pathet Lao, the anti-communists, and occasionally to transport American personnel.[41]

Eight light transports owned by the Hanoi regime supplemented the Soviet ships in semicovert deliveries into Laos. During 1962, Russian and North Vietnamese transports regularly landed at unpaved strips and made airdrops to deliver munitions, clothing and other equipment to Pathet Lao troops. American officers became increasingly aware in 1963 of activity in the southern panhandle region where the communists were developing supply depots, improving airstrips and increasing the frequency of air de-

---

* Both the LI–2 and IL–14 had two engines. The LI–2 could carry sixty-six hundred pounds of cargo a distance of 305 nautical miles and return; the IL–14 could carry eighty-one hundred pounds. The AN–2 Colt was a single-engine, utility biplane that could land in 550 feet.

IRREGULAR WARFARE

liveries. The thirty-six hundred-foot laterite airfield at Tchepone appeared to be a focal point, close to the South Vietnamese border and defended by North Vietnamese antiaircraft forces. CINCPAC reported to the Joint Chiefs of Staff in September 1963 that as many as four communist aircraft had landed at Tchepone in one day, apparently from North Vietnam.[42]

Allied ground patrols and airstrikes forced an end to the operations into Tchepone in 1964. Enemy flights continued elsewhere in Laos, how-

TACTICAL AIRLIFT

ever. During the summer wet season of 1965 the North Vietnamese averaged several landings and drops daily into northeast Laos, flying twenty-five twin-engine craft recently received from the Soviets. The allies for diplomatic reasons for a time decided against attacking the communist transports. But allied fire in January 1968 brought down two modified AN-2s attempting to bomb an allied radar site in Samneua Province. The dead crewmen were found to be Vietnamese.[43]

By mid-1968 the North Vietnamese had sixty-six fixed-wing transports, mostly LI-2s, IL-14s, and AN-2s, as well as three dozen helicopters. Deliveries to the Plain of Jars were regular after communist reoccupation of that region in late 1969. Clandestine helicopter unescorted night missions into the Laos panhandle increased. Allied personnel periodically sighted unidentified helicopters, believed to be MI-4s and MI-6s, apparently delivering antiaircraft weapons and supplies. On one occasion in 1970 an allied observer near Saravane watched twenty armed troops debark from a darkened helicopter, having been guided by persons on the ground to what appeared a regularly used landing zone. A C-130A gunship crew claimed destruction of an enemy helicopter in May 1969, after the chopper put down in a clearing. A few weeks later, allied strike aircraft hit an apparent landing zone after sighting two helicopters on the ground.[44]

The communists also used air transport into Cambodia whenever possible to further the war effort in South Vietnam. Viet Cong and North Vietnamese officers used the courier flights of the International Control Commission to travel between Hanoi and Phnom Penh. Civil airlines and communist Chinese diplomatic flights were similarly used. During 1968 the Americans confirmed that the communists were again operating military transports into the regions of Cambodia adjoining Vietnam. At least some of these flights apparently originated in North Vietnam. On three occasions communist-marked, fixed-wing transports were observed at the hard-surfaced Memot strip north of Tay Ninh, and in one case crewmen were offloading cargo into trucks while North Vietnamese soldiers stood guard. AN-2 aircraft with North Vietnamese pilots also were sighted at the Snuol and Le Rolland strips located along the border directly above Saigon. One North Vietnamese soldier captured in South Vietnam said that his forty-man platoon had made a six-hour flight from North Vietnam to Cambodia during the 1969 Tet period and that his entire six hundred-man infiltration group had been briefed and prepared for an air trip. Helicopters also operated into the Cambodian border airstrips, transporting personnel from Phnom Penh and possibly senior officers of units moving overland through Laos.[45]

Enemy air deliveries apparently reached also into the highlands region of South Vietnam. During the spring of 1962, fixed-wing craft (probably AN-2s) made airdrops west and north of Pleiku, flying at night at low altitudes to avoid radar surveillance and intercept. On several nights, allied radars detected as many as a dozen aircraft entering Vietnam from Cambodia, whose government had for months complained of unauthorized communist overflights. All this activity appeared to be an extension of the traffic through Tchepone. Although no communist aircraft were destroyed, the radar tracks, radio intercepts, and sightings by American aircrews confirmed that covert flights were being made. The Americans surmised that the unidentified aircrewmen monitored allied frequencies and that they navigated visually, taking advantage of full moon periods and the radio beacons at Pleiku and Ban Me Thuot.[46]

Although increased allied radar and intercept capabilities apparently forced a gradual reduction of the intrusions during and after 1962, there were sporadic reports of occasional helicopter and light-aircraft penetrations from Cambodia. U.S. Special Forces near the border across from Memot observed flights, and a U.S. Army battalion commander and a helicopter crew sighted an MI-6 in Pleiku Province in April 1969. Clouding assessments of such evidence were the illegal (but not insurgent) flights of opium smugglers from Laos. A variety of aircraft served in the opium traffic, including light twin-engine cabin monoplanes made by Beechcraft. Press reports of airdrops near Quang Ngai in 1963 were apparently without foundation, as were multiple accounts of communist helicopter activity just south of the DMZ in June 1968. Clandestine drops, however, were observed on the South Vietnamese island of Phu Quoc in late 1962.[47]

Especially controversial were numerous reports of communist missions into insurgent regions of Thailand. Local villagers and tribesmen described helicopter landings at sites marked by bonfires or signal lights. Thais also told of watching helicopters land in cleared spaces or hovering to deliver cargo by rope to recipients on the ground.

Marks resembling helicopter landing-gear prints were discovered in soft ground at one suspected landing zone. Intercepted radio communications gave further confirmation of insurgent activity, and one band was detected near Korat after villagers reported helicopter activity. Air deliveries from Laos were made exclusively at night and were mainly limited to the northern and eastern parts of the country. Certain hill and cave regions apparently received regular weekly service, and some insurgent groups seemingly were supplied both by surface and air.[48]

Convinced that the reports were genuine, Thai officials authorized attacks on unidentified craft and offered monetary rewards. U.S. Air Force intelligence officers, however, remained skeptical, noting that despite great effort the allies had never made a successful interception. Many "unidentified" radar tracks upon investigation proved to be friendly, while those that remained unexplained doubtless included some opium-smuggling flights. The Americans nevertheless shored up night intercept capabilities, using helicopters of the 20th Squadron as practice targets. Air Force aircraft at

The air supply network to U.S. Army Special Forces camps employed several different modes:

USAF C-123 lands at a camp near Plei Djereng 1966.

Army UH-1C transports supplies from a central distribution point to a mountaintop at Nui Ba Den.

Anticipating a paradrop, A1C Gary W. Harwell stakes out fluorescent patches to mark the drop zone for an incoming C-130. Airman Harwell is an Air Force combat controller, working with the Army Special Forces near Bu Dop, 1967.

A low altitude parachute extraction delivery over Bu Dop.

Aerial view of a Special Forces camp.

Courtesy: U.S. Army

Nakhon Phanom spent many hours investigating unidentified radar tracks, many of which appeared "in the nature of logistic flights." But the Air Force remained officially unconvinced. This conservative attitude had the benefit of discouraging indiscriminate fire against unidentified aircraft, although on at least two occasions Thai forces mistakenly fired on low-flying U.S. Air Force craft.[49]

North Vietnamese airborne warfare suggested Soviet tutelage. Troopers of the North Vietnamese 305th Airborne Division, located near Hanoi, made numerous practice jumps between 1962 and 1967, jumping from AN-2s, LI-2s, and IL-14s. Each IL-14 could carry twenty-four troopers. Jump zones were marked with panels or lights, and practice missions were often at night, in part to avoid the possibility of intercept by American fighters. For battalion and regimental exercises each transport made several trips. Equipment up to 12.7-mm antiaircraft guns and 82-mm mortars could be parachuted. But, except for a single allied intelligence report that indicated that a paratroop unit jumped in Laos in 1961, the communists apparently made no combat use of their paratroop capability.[50]

The communists also used airlift in conventional ways. Soviet transports hauled weapons into North Vietnam through most of the war, and by late 1966 the Defense Intelligence Agency estimated that the Russian air bridge numbered over a hundred transports. The Soviets operated to Hanoi either directly or by way of the airfield at Nanning in south China. Chinese and North Vietnamese transports also operated from Nanning, Kunming, and other points, hauling supplies into North Vietnam and to fields in northern Laos. By late 1968, Chinese transports flew as far south as Luang Prabang, delivering matériel for distribution by truck to Laotian and Thai insurgents. After the 1973 cease-fire the communists rebuilt the airfield at Khe Sanh for their own use and in the decisive 1975 campaign used transports, helicopters, and civil airliners to fly troops, munitions, and maps to the south.[51]

Communist fixed-wing and helicopter transports apparently were active in Southeast Asia wherever tactical and political considerations permitted, and doubtless some of these activities remained undiscovered by the allies. To one U.S. Air Force officer the ability of the North Vietnamese helicopter pilots to penetrate at low-level at night in the mountains meant that "they had to be good." Unquestionably the communists, like the allies, fully appreciated the usefulness of air transport for supporting units engaged in guerrilla tactics.[52]

XVII. The War for Laos

The mountainous and primitive country of Laos occupied a crucial location separating North Vietnam and China from the non-communist states of Southeast Asia. The North Vietnamese were vitally interested in southern Laos as an avenue for moving men and materiel to South Vietnam and Cambodia. Hanoi, therefore (like Moscow and Peking), gave materiel and diplomatic support to the Pathet Lao insurgent movement, as increasingly North Vietnamese combat units carried on the war against Vientiane. The allies, for their part, supported the non-communist Laotian coalition with training and materiel, Thai ground troops, and American air power. The result was a rough military equilibrium that lasted for more than a decade.

Given the scarcity of roadways in Laos capable of long-haul truck travel, virtually the entire allied military effort depended on air transport. Airlift provided tactical flexibility, freedom from road lines of communication, and enabled the allies to reinforce or withdraw units at will. Transport airplanes moved and supplied government forces throughout the country and wholly sustained the Meo population, source of the allies' most effective fighters. Campaigns followed the calendar. The communists held the initiative in dry seasons, moving and supplying overland. The allies usually regained ground during the wet summers, their air transport and firepower only marginally affected by the season.

Air transport in Laos was primarily by civilian contract, mainly with Air America, Inc. Air Force equipment and expertise were provided, but with the rarest exceptions civilian crewmen flew all fixed-wing transport missions in Laos. U.S. Air Force transport helicopters and crews, however, regularly flew missions in Laos, augmenting the helicopter forces of Air America and the Laotian government. Late in the war, Air Force helicopters frequently lifted Laotian troops in tactical missions similar to airmobile operations by U.S. Army helicopters in South Vietnam.

During the late fifties the Pathet Lao movement gradually gained strength, nurtured by technical, materiel, and advisory assistance from the communist states. U.S. Air Force airlift units based in Japan and Okinawa stood ready to send American forces and materiel into north Thailand or Laos. There was a modest American assistance program for Laos to de-

TACTICAL AIRLIFT

velop roads and airfields, valuable in case of future military operations as well as for the internal political and economic development of the nation. Some dozen airfields were improved, and in some cases the runways were extended and surfaced. Extensive rehabilitation of Wattay Airfield, Vientiane, began in 1958, and a small Royal Laotian Air Force and several civil airlines operated into these fields.[1]

U.S. Air Force transports seldom entered Laos. The most noteworthy exception was Operation Boostershot, an American attempt to influence voters living in remote regions. Two C–130 Hercules flew from Japan to Bangkok on March 31, 1958, each carrying a bulldozer rigged for airdrop. From Bangkok the two planes made a total of seven drops inside Laos, delivering the bulldozers, air compressors, and other equipment. The 130s returned to Ashiya on April 3 as planned but remaining at Bangkok were several C–119 Flying Boxcars, also from Japan. As a result of general satisfaction with Boostershot, the 119s shifted to Vientiane for continued operations.

The ensuing C–119 missions in Laos were seldom easy, whether landing at Seno, Pakse, or other semiprepared strips, or making drops in the mountains of the north. The rugged and undeveloped geography made navigation difficult, and afternoon cloud buildups and smoke from agricultural burning added to the difficulties. Crews hauled rice, vehicles, petroleum products, cement, and other items. Drop zones were usually small, often surrounded by homes, and sometimes crowded with onlookers. Takeoffs and landings from Vientiane were a problem for 119s loaded to the safe limit permitted by the 3,900-foot runway. The pierced steel planking surface was harsh on tires, prohibiting hard braking and demanding reliance on prop reversal when stopping. Crews wore civilian clothes, stayed in Vientiane's very primitive hotel, and endured mosquitoes and temperatures constantly over one hundred degrees. Boostershot was extended several times, ending finally on April 27. Of eleven hundred tons delivered during the operation, three hundred tons were airdropped in seventy-two sorties—seven by C–130s, sixty-three by C–119s, and two by C–123s which joined in the final days. The entire effort was accident free and gave the American crews a taste of future operating problems in Southeast Asia. Although the effort failed to prevent communist gains during the May elections, it exemplified the enormous potential for air transport in Laos.[2]

Another isolated venture was the airdrop of machinery for airstrip construction at Phong Saly in extreme northern Laos. A 315th Air Division C–130 flew to Udorn to be rigged and loaded. In its first drop sortie, April 26, 1960, two trucks and a D–4 bulldozer were dropped successfully. An attempt three days later to drop a second dozer failed when only one of the five descent parachutes opened properly. The dozer was demolished on impact.[3]

In the second half of 1960 the Americans increased direct materiel assistance to the royalist forces under Phoumi Nosavan, who headed a faction opposed to inclusion of Pathet Lao in the Vientiane coalition government. Shipments reached Bangkok by sea and air while further movements into Laos were by truck or airlift. Substantial deliveries were made by contract C–46s and C–47s to the royalist base at Savannakhet. Successive political crises culminated in the outbreak of overt civil war in December 1960. The civilian transports carried royalist paratroops to jump zones near Vientiane in operations leading to the flight of the neutralist Kong Le forces northward. Air resupply continued on behalf of Phoumi's forces, which were pursuing the departing neutralists. An American officer, Maj. Eleazar Parmly IV, USA, accompanied one royalist unit marching into the mountain country, totally supplied by air. Parmly's column received supplies every Friday, with the narrow mountainside road sometimes the only available drop zone. The C–47s dropped many items without benefit of parachutes, including bags of rice and elephant-skin containers filled with water. Soviet transports, meanwhile, supplied the withdrawing neutralists and the Pathet Lao forces in and about the Plain of Jars.[4]

The C–46s and most of the C–47s belonged to the fleet of Air America, Inc., a firm owned by the CIA. Air America was a direct descendant of Civil Air Transport, Inc. and was organizationally linked to Air Asia, Ltd., which operated large maintenance facilities on Taiwan and leased aircraft to Air America. Like Civil Air Transport, Air America flew over much of the Far East, its operations including overt contract work for MATS in the Pacific. Some fifteen Air America C–46s and C–47s lifted approximately one thousand tons monthly into Laos, principally from Bangkok.[5]

Eager to avoid a communist takeover, President Kennedy in early March 1961 authorized use of U.S. Air Force C–130s for deliveries to Vientiane in case of "urgent delivery requirements." This had been requested by CINCPAC to avoid transshipping across Thailand. The President also approved Joint Chiefs of Staff recommendations that the Air Force provide four C–130s for operation by civilian crews under contract with the CIA. Accordingly four civilian crews were trained in early April, and four aircraft moved to Takhli for CIA scheduling. C–130s hauled a Thai artillery unit and equipment to Seno in the third week of April, and six Air Force C–130s landed at Wattay on the 26th, bringing in parachutes and varied military supplies. The lifts to Wattay continued for several weeks with C–124s supplanting the C–130s.[6]

President Kennedy also approved expansion of the American program to convert two hundred thousand Meo tribesmen into an independent anticommunist force. The Meos inhabited the highlands of northeast Laos, had little loyalty to either Vientiane or the Pathet Lao. Under their acknowledged leader, Lt. Col. Vang Pao, and rallied by CIA field officers and U.S.

Army Special Forces teams, the Meos quickly became an effective force responsive to CIA command. By May 1961 the CIA had equipped some five thousand Meo fighting men and had established a logistics pipeline entirely separate from that supporting other government forces. Vang Pao meanwhile cemented the loyalty of widespread Meo villages northeast of the plain, visiting them by light aircraft and arranging for air delivery of food and arms.[7]

The development of a network of short airstrips to support the Meos in the northeast was largely the work of Air Force Maj. Harry C. (Heinie) Aderholt. Aderholt was assigned in 1959–1960 to command the small Air Force unconventional warfare unit stationed in Okinawa, with an added role as senior air advisor on Southeast Asia for the CIA. Aderholt went to Vientiane in early 1960 to organize single-engine U–10 aircraft operations. He began by arranging U–10 service to distant Phong Saly, where the six hundred-foot airstrip had two twenty-degree turns and was carved into a hillside at elevation of six thousand feet. Working with Colonel Vang Pao, Aderholt criss-crossed much of Laos by U–10, surveying and arranging improvements at short airstrips left by the French, and establishing what became known as "Lima Sites." The resulting airlift service to the Lima Sites by U–10s and other single-engine craft, flown by contract pilots, supplied the CIA-sponsored guerrilla movement in the communist rear.[8]

From April 1961 until the Geneva settlement of 1962, the Americans had an overt, uniformed Military Assistance and Advisory Group in Laos, including Air Force members assigned to work with the fledgling Royal Laotian Air Force. Aderholt brought 1st Lt. Lawrence Ropka, Jr., and two other officers from his Okinawa unit to manage contract airlift activities. The three officers, assisted by several enlisted men, organized evening scheduling meetings, arranged for maps and intelligence services, and developed a rudimentary flight-monitoring system. A small traffic management control center included U.S. Army and CIA representatives. Although mission control was minimal once the transports left the Vientiane area, the expiring MAAG noted in its 1962 final report that the control center had improved ground-handling operations, aircraft utilization, and mission reliability. Air America meanwhile established flight-following locations and installed radio beacons at five Laotian airfields. Monthly lift totals surpassed seventeen hundred tons of cargo and six thousand passengers, including Laotian battalions moving to and from training centers in Thailand.[9] Airlift capacity increased in early 1962 when Air America added C–123s. TAC crews ferried the C–123s to the Pacific, Air Force instructors checked out the contract crews, and the Air Force Mule Train detachment at Clark contributed periodic maintenance assistance.[10]

At the time of the Geneva settlement, the North Vietnamese presence in Laos (by American estimates) was twelve battalions with another three thousand men serving in Pathet Lao units. The Declaration on the Neutrality of Laos in July 1962 called for the neutralization of Laos and the withdrawal of foreign troops. A shaky cease-fire ensued but the allies continued to use the contract airlift fleet. Contracts formerly between Air America and the Air Force were consolidated with others managed by the Agency for International Development. AID also contracted with the American firm of Bird and Sons for airlift by C–46 and smaller fixed-wing craft to support "National Development Projects" in Laos. Much of the hauling consisted of civil and refugee relief flights, especially on behalf of the scattered Meo. Missions into the northeast region were controversial since the Americans considered the Meos to be refugees while the communists saw them as bandits. Both Bird and Sons and Air America hauled troops and munitions, supporting the Meo guerrilla army and the scattered royalist and neutralist forces. The prime minister of Laos, Prince Souvanna Phouma, U.S. Ambassador William H. Sullivan, and most other Americans agreed that the United States should eventually stop such flights but the weakness of the Royal Laotian Air Force airlift arm precluded an immediate shift.[11]

When fighting resumed in 1963 the contract airlifters directly, and sometimes decisively, influenced events. Following communist victories over neutralist forces on the Plain of Jars in April, contract and Royal Laotian Air Force transports made airdrops and landed on impromptu grass strips, delivering weapons and ammunition from Vientiane, north Thailand, and Bangkok. Two royalist battalions entered the battle area and the combined anti-communist forces clung to positions on the plain's western edge. During 1964 the North Vietnamese and Pathet Lao pushed government forces off the plain and captured much equipment. A second communist drive threatened to reach the Mekong River at the country's waist. Air America transports vigorously supported the defensive operations and took on the additional role of hauling aviation munitions to Vientiane for air strikes by Royal Laotian T–28s. Meanwhile, the communists opened a systematic campaign against the Meos. The defenders were usually able to hold off attacks long enough for helicopters and light transports to shuttle the families to the next Lima Site. The fighting men could then fade into the night, forming again elsewhere, and often reoccupying the original site soon afterwards.[12]

Another important airlift contribution was in day-by-day logistical supply. In this role the transports served as part of the overall theater transportation system, supporting the formal Military Assistance Program

TACTICAL AIRLIFT

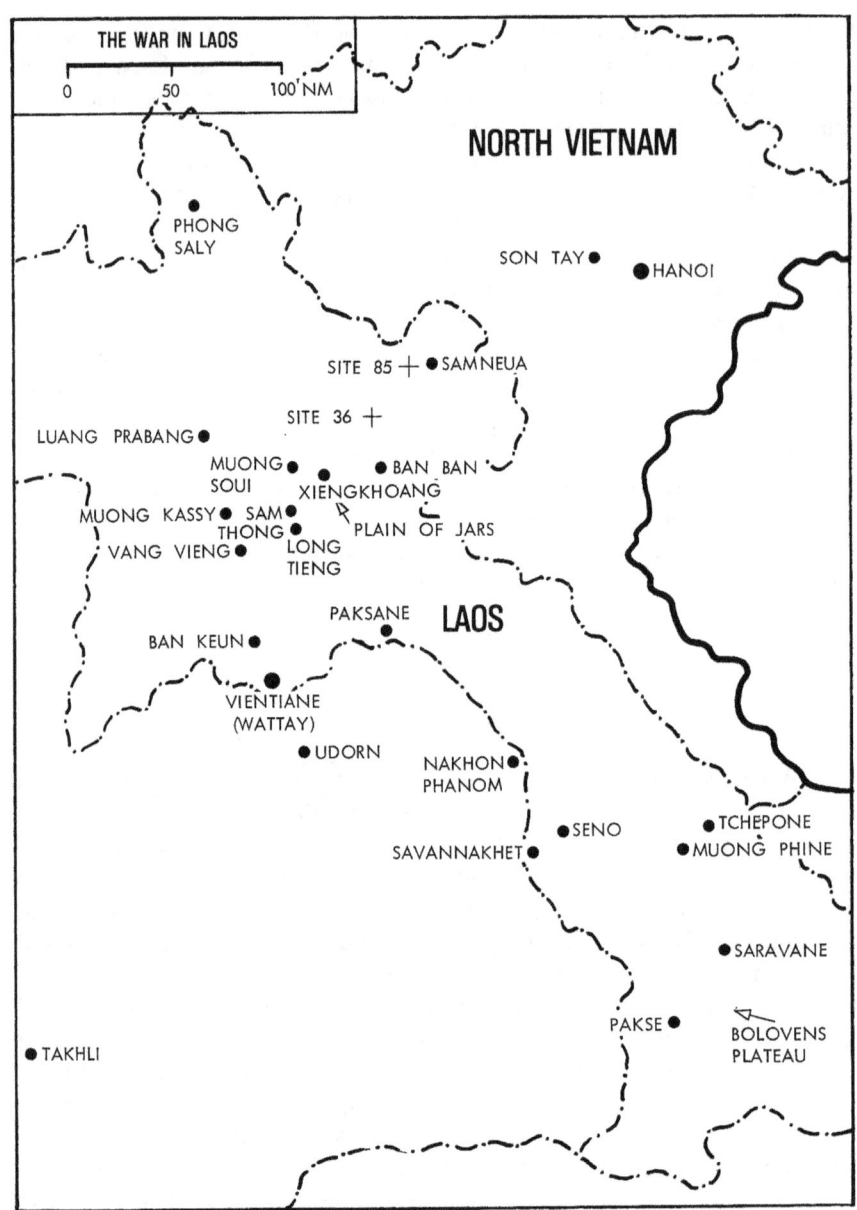

and Vientiane's regular forces. Materiel was shipped by sea to either Bangkok or Sattahip. Transport across Thailand was generally by surface, sometimes augmented by fixed-wing airlift, to the helicopter depot just outside Udorn. From Udorn materiel moved into Laos either by air to the several main Laotian airfields or by truck to the Mekong barge crossings near Vientiane, Pakse, and Savannakhet. For transport inside Laos the

Laotian government had five military truck companies, Army-operated barges, the Royal Laotian airlift arm, and funds for contract airlift. The American administration of the military assistance program was under the Deputy Chief, Joint U.S. Military Advisory Group (or "Dep Chief"), set up in late 1962 at Bangkok and moved to Udorn in late 1971.

There was an entirely separate logistics pipeline for the Meos. Materials were channeled from a depot on Okinawa to upcountry Thailand, either by surface through the Thai seaports or directly by air to Takhli. Nearly all shipments from Thailand into Laos were carried by multiengine contract airlift, arriving at one of the main fields for redistribution by contract light transports and helicopters. Thus the Meo supply chain was directly from the Americans to the users, avoiding the diversions and losses likely in Laotian government channels. Materiel airlifted under these programs into and inside Laos was double the tonnage entering the country by surface transports.[13]

The network of semi-improved airfields in Laos gave considerable scope for the twin-engine contract transports. A dozen main strips established the basic route structure. Paved runways existed from the earlier improvement program at Vientiane, Pakse, Seno, and Xiangkhoang in the Plain of Jars. Most of the other strips were surfaced with laterite or gravel and could be used in the winter dry season. At Paksane and Vang Vieng the allies benefited from earlier Russian improvement projects. Typical of Laotian airfields was Luang Prabang where the runway had "many rough spots, chuck holes, and loose rocks on the surface." The runway was only fifty feet wide and (as at many fields) nearby high terrain complicated landing approaches and departures. A new installation at Long Tieng southwest of the Plain of Jars became a main redistribution point. Although U.S. Air Force officers were impressed by the effectiveness of C–123s in forward fieldwork in Laos, the Caribou was superior for landings on soft surfaces. Consequently five U.S. Army Caribous were contracted to Air America.[14]

After 1965 the Laotian contract airlift carried approximately sixteen thousand passengers and six thousand tons of cargo monthly, about one-tenth the Air Force workload in South Vietnam. The contract force consisted of ships and crews of Air America and Continental Air Services, Inc. It comprised over ninety craft, including twenty-nine fixed-wing medium transports. AID and the Military Assistance Program had separate contracts for services, but aircraft were freely used for all purposes. This assured operational flexibility, although apportionment of costs among the CIA, AID, and the military became a bureaucratic nightmare. C–46s usually flew scheduled passenger circuits inside Laos, while C–123s hauled bulk cargo, and the Caribous made most of the airdrops.[15]

A small Air America staff at Udorn made up the daily mission schedules, and a communications net throughout Laos helped to monitor flights.

Sometimes crews operated without fixed itineraries, flying from point to point, hauling people and cargo wherever needed. Certain officers in Laos carried identifier cards that authorized them to make on-the-spot movement requests. For urgent resupply needs a radio call to Udorn often resulted in delivery of items the same day. The system was efficient in terms of managerial overhead and in results, and seldom did a plane fly without a useful load. Major Aderholt later warmly praised the simplified control system and the willingness of Air America to allow its pilots leeway in interpreting airfield criteria, operating rules, and maintenance standards. This flexibility went far beyond that allowed Air Force transport pilots in Southeast Asia, but was justifiable in view of the daily changing situation.[16]

A force of single-engine utility aircraft operated into strips inaccessible to the larger twin-engine transports. The U–10 Helio Courier and the Swiss-built Pilatus Porter were especially useful. Both were all-metal craft with fixed landing gear. The U–10 was rated to carry four persons including crew, the Porter eight. Both had limited internal cargo space, but both could readily operate into 600-foot strips. Late in the war Air America acquired a turboprop version of the Porter, built in the United States by Fairchild. Continental Air Services also had a twin-engine version of a single-engine German Dornier craft. The light transports were economical substitutes for helicopters. One Air Force officer termed the Porter "the real backbone of the resupply effort emanating from the main airfields in northern Laos."[17]

Most of the contract pilots were Americans, veterans of years of flying in Indochina. These men knew the terrain, airfields, and operating conditions in Laos, and were skilled in the techniques of low-level navigation, marginal weather operations, and forward field operations. They were highly informal and accustomed to getting things done. Some lived the life of suburbia, settling their families in Vientiane or Thailand. Others preferred more riproaring ways between missions. Salaries and allowances were excellent. One CIA inspector reported that "a common topic of conversation among pilots is how and where to invest their fairly substantial savings."[18]

Air America operated a large aircraft service complex at Udorn, maintaining the contract fleets (including C–123s and Caribous), as well as Royal Laotian and certain U.S. Air Force craft. Many Asians were ground crewmen, flight mechanics, and supervisors. Workers were glad to work double shifts for extra pay, and personnel turnover was slight. Middle-level supervision was especially good. The result was highly satisfactory aircraft maintenance. Incommission and flying hour rates for the contracted C–123s, for example, surpassed comparable Air Force performance. Overall costs were not excessive; the contract transport bill for

CONTRACT AIRLIFT FLEETS FOR LAOS*

	June 1966			February 1969		
	Air America	Continental Air	Total	Air America	Continental Air	Total
Medium Fixed-Wing						
C-46	4	5	9	4	6	10
C-47	2	4	6	1	4	5
C-123	9		9	8		8
C-7	5		5	6		6
Total			29			29
Light Fixed-Wing						
U-10	12	3	15	9	3	12
Pilatus Porter		9	9	9	7	16
Volpar/Beechcraft				2		2
Dornier					5	5
Total			24			35
Rotary Wing						
H-34	21		21	22		22
UH-1				7		7
Total			21			29

Note: Of the above, all C-123s, all except one C-7, and a few U-10s were supplied by the U.S. Air Force and U.S. Army to Air America.

* Report, Deputy Chief, Joint United States Military Advisory Group, Thailand, Historical Summary for June 1966-April 1968.

fiscal 1970 was $26 million. AID paid $380 for each C-123 flying hour, which included a $186 fee to the Air Force.[19]

The reasons for employing the contract system were reviewed in early 1966. Ambassador Sullivan favored expanding the contract fleets. But PACAF countered that Air Force planes and crews could greatly increase lift capability into Laos at lower cost. Ambassador Sullivan strongly disagreed, and urged that the military continue to contract transports for "our Rube Goldberg fleets." CINCPAC supported Sullivan's judgment and recommended the addition of several more Caribous and C-123s to the contract force.[20]

Assessments of the contract airlift system by military professionals were favorable. A Joint Staff study group reviewed arrangements in Laos in 1969, determined that CIA efforts were satisfactory, and recommended that the contract system continue without change. Lt. Col. William B. Foster, assistant air attaché at Vientiane in late 1970 and 1971, substantially agreed. Air America personnel were well motivated, in Foster's view, and responded with little urging to awkward working hours and difficult flying situations. Col. Robert S. Ferrari, U.S. Army deputy chief at

TACTICAL AIRLIFT

Bangkok, reported in 1968 that his relations with Air America were "excellent and fruitful" and speculated that the contract idea might provide "an answer to the requirement of flexible support in counter-insurgency situations in general, and not only in Laos."[21]

To a considerable degree the contract force was an extension of the U.S. Air Force, employing many former military airmen and borrowing its larger aircraft from the American military. Like the predominantly military airlift effort in Vietnam, the contract operation in Laos reflected the United States' inclination and ability to use air transport in military operations.

The link between the U.S. Air Force and the contract airlift was most apparent in the use of C–130s in the Laotian war. C–130 flights into Vientiane and the C–130 loan arrangement in 1961 had been of brief duration, and for several years the appearance of a Hercules inside Laos was exceptional. In June 1965 the CIA and the U.S. Embassy recommended that C–130s be used for deliveries from Thailand to Laos, relieving the C–123s and C–46s from this work. A single Hercules could make three or four deliveries in a single day, while a slower C–123 could make the trip only twice and with less than half the payload. C–130 missions began later in the year with Air America flying Air Force planes.[22]

In actuality C–130 usage was as originally stated: to transport military cargo. At first missions were exclusively between Takhli and Long Tieng on behalf of the CIA logistics pipeline. Subsequently the 130s landed at Vientiane, Luang Prabang, Sam Thong (near Long Tieng), and at fields in the extreme northwest. Occasional flights reached to the panhandle fields at Pakse, Savannakhet, and Saravane. Missions between Udorn and Luang Prabang to support the military assistance pipeline became significant in 1969. The part-time C–130 project became full-time in 1967 when at least one of the two ships at Takhli flew into Laos every day. Meanwhile the smaller transports ceased missions from Takhli but continued hauling from Udorn as well as within Laos.

The C–130s belonged to E–Flight, established in late 1961 within the 21st Troop Carrier Squadron on Okinawa. Air Force crewmen assigned to E–Flight ferried the ships between Okinawa and Thailand. An aircraft's tour at Takhli varied from a single day to the maximum permitted by maintenance needs. A few 374th Wing maintenance men performed flight-line maintenance tasks at Takhli each evening when the planes reverted to the Air Force. Heavy maintenance, including one hundred-hour periodic inspections, was done at Naha. Unlike other 315th Air Division C–130s, the four or five E–Flight ships were not camouflaged because in some circles camouflage implied a combat role.

The E–Flight ships were identical in internal configuration to the standard airlift A–models except that dual rails and 463L aluminum pallets were not used. Instead skate-wheel rollers were installed on the cargo-compartment floor over which cheap wood pallets could be moved. The smaller pallets made handling easier at locations without forklifts and eliminated the need to recover pallets. Offloading was often performed by taxiing the ship gently forward while pushing the pallets rearward one by one. Bundles sometimes broke apart during this operation, but without serious damage to the cargo. Loads were diverse, usually including fuel in fifty-five-gallon drums, munitions, or rice. Airdrops were infrequent, most often made when heavy rains temporarily closed one of the usual landing fields. To discharge cargo, the wood pallets, guided by a floor center-slot, were pushed to the rear over the rollers. Releases were from five hundred feet or lower, using inexpensive parachutes procured in the Far East. Air America used a standard five-man crew (including navigator) for all flights and added a second loadmaster for drops and some other missions. Jet fuel was available only at bases in Thailand, since the Laotian fields stocked only aviation gasoline.

Each member of E–Flight was selected from the 374th Wing early in his Far East tour. The flight functioned largely outside squadron control, the flight commander and operations officer exerting direct supervisory authority. E–Flight aircraft and crews flew cargo missions over the western Pacific and often made deliveries at intermediate points during ferry missions to and from Takhli. While in Thailand the Air Force crewmen assisted in loadings and briefings, and flew occasional night airlift missions between bases in Thailand. Many crewmembers were qualified instructors and helped to requalify the Air America crews. E–Flight crewmen periodically flew other 374th aircraft in normal missions, including shuttle duty at Cam Ranh Bay. The uncamouflaged aircraft, however, were scheduled and used entirely separately from the other 374th Wing planes. E–Flight supervisory crewmen occasionally traveled into Laos by lighter transport, surveying and approving airfields prior to C–130 usage.

The C–130 shuttles to Long Tieng supplied a local population of perhaps forty thousand. Access was entirely by airlift. The mile-long asphalt strip was ringed by mountains, with several near-vertical cliffs rising immediately at the northwest end of the runway. Because of the cliffs, all landings were to the northwest and all takeoffs to the southeast. The C–130s offloaded in a paved area at the northwest end, carved out among the cliffs. Meo and Laotian cargo handlers picked up the bundles using forklifts and muscle power, and repackaged them for C–123, helicopter, or light-transport loading. Persistent effort resulted in an efficient operation capable of clearing a fifteen-ton C–130 load out of Long Tieng only a few hours after delivery. Helicopters landed and unloaded in an area on the opposite side of the runway, keeping well clear of fixed-wing traffic. Sometimes ordnance hauled in by C–130 was immediately loaded on T–28 strike aircraft for use the same day. A considerable amount of airlift tonnage consisted of food for the Meo population to supplement the local livestock. This occasioned the quip that Meo children thought rice grew, not in the ground, but in silver airplanes.[23]

The possibility of using U.S. Air Force crews routinely for C–130 missions into Laos was reexamined on several occasions. In October 1969 the U.S. Ambassador to Laos, G. McMurtrie Godley, requested that Air Force crews be authorized to fly missions to selected destinations in Laos. The crews would carry military identifications but on no occasion would remain overnight in Laos. Ambassador Godley repeated the recommendation in late 1971 in an effort to reduce costs. The Air Staff opposed the use of unmarked aircraft flown by Air Force crews but supported the standing policy which allowed for use of U.S. crews in Air Force-marked ships in emergencies when Air America crews were unavailable. The Air Force permitted its ground crewmen to go into Laos to repair aircraft with documents identifying them as Air America employees, but only if the embassy ruled the area secure. (At that time ninety percent of C–130 missions into Laos landed at "secure" sites.) At any insecure site, Air Force personnel were required to wear uniforms and carry military identification.[24]

E–Flight crews flew missions into Laos only on the rarest occasions. During February 4–8, 1970, with all Air America crews occupied in flying evacuation missions from the Plain of Jars, Air Force crews flew twenty-two sorties from Thailand to operating bases in Laos, hauling in 307 tons. Again, during April 22–30, 1970, after the loss of a C–130 with its contract aircrew on a hillside near Long Tieng (the only transport C–130 lost in Laos), an Air Force crew shuttled daily in and out of Long Tieng. On these occasions uncamouflaged E–Flight ships were used, with miniature Air Force insignia. Crewmen wore Air Force flight suits with inconspicuous insignia and carried Air Force and Geneva Convention identification cards. Subsequently, the Seventh/Thirteenth Air Force staff wrote a detailed plan for using Air Force C–130s and crews in Laos in emergencies.[25]

Air America flew 170 C–130 hours per month in late 1970, and 270 hours each month during much of 1971. The number of flying hours thereafter declined because of increased fuel and operating costs. Charges for the C–130 were approximately $1,000 per flying hour, roughly triple C–123 costs. Upon deactivation of the A–model wing on Okinawa in the spring of 1971, responsibility for Laos activities shifted to the E–model wing at Ching Chuan Kang. On May 31, 1971, one of the Ching Chuan Kang squadrons was redesignated the 21st and included a special flight to replace the old E–Flight. The E–model ships were left uncamouflaged but were painted gray to retard corrosion.[26]

Also available to augment Air America were the Vietnam-based C–123s of the 315th Wing. In planning for the possible evacuation of Vientiane in 1964, for example, the wing was prepared to move C–123s to Vientiane, and to arrive twelve hours after MACV received the request.[27] C–123 task forces were sent to Udorn on two occasions in response to ambassadorial requests for assistance.

Six 315th Wing aircraft moved to Udorn on March 18, 1970, with maintenance men and equipment. The force arrived from Tan Son Nhut, Da Nang, and Phan Rang within twelve hours of first notice and crews attended briefings the following day. These included a presentation on operating conditions inside Laos by Air America's chief pilot. The primary mission was to evacuate Long Tieng in case of an emergency and secondarily to fly supplies. After a reassessment of needs, three planes were returned to Vietnam on the twentieth. The others, however, made seven supply missions to Laos on that date followed by ten more on the twenty-first. At least two of these sorties were to the Muong Kassy airstrip, west of Long Tieng, used by T–28 strike aircraft. The aircraft and crews remained at Udorn for another five days, available in case of emergency. All returned to Phan Rang on the twenty-seventh.[28]

Two planes and three crews were sent to Udorn on September 15, 1970, to move a backlog of munitions beyond the capability of the Air America 123s. In 109 sorties over nine days of operations (starting on September 16), the 315th Wing element hauled 375 tons from Udorn into Laos. The C–123s showed the standard Air Force markings and were flown and maintained overtly by Air Force crewmen. Missions were flown in daytime only, and all landing approaches were visual. Eight other sorties were canceled, three because of weather and five because of maintenance problems.[29]

The occasional airlifts into Laos by Air Force C–130 and C–123 aircrews were of limited significance. They did, however, demonstrate a capacity for a much larger contribution if called upon. Far more important was the sustained Air Force role in furnishing and maintaining the C–130s used daily in Laos, an activity that recalled the C–119 loans at the time of Dien Bien Phu. The Air Force stood willing and able to begin overt airlift operations into Laos, but was reluctant to expose its personnel to capture without the legal protection afforded military combatants.

The airlift capabilities of the Royal Laotian Air Force developed slowly, held back by Laotian inexperience in technical matters, political factionalism, rivalry with the ground forces, and the higher priority given to strike aircraft units. During the late fifties the Laotians had several C–47s, flown primarily by French pilots. Missions included occasional hauls of military units, spare parts runs, and passenger and supply lifts for the ground forces. By April 1961, shortly after the opening of the military assistance group, the number of Americans assigned to work with the

Laotian Air Force reached eighty-nine. The Royal Laotian Air Force itself then consisted of just 447 men, only 49 of them flyers. Despite the large American presence, the Laotian C–47s lagged well behind Air America in flying hour rates.[30]

Soviet advisory efforts were scarcely more profitable. Soviet instructors flew with Laotian crewmen in nine LI–2 twin-engine transports given to Laos in late 1962. An RLAF officer later recalled:

> The Russians had no training program at all. All they did was fly with us. The Russians and the Lao could not understand each other. They had only one interpreter. The Russians only stayed six months. Afterwards, one LI–2 crashed in the Plain of Jars; the others stopped flying because of parts . . . .[31]

A new program for training Laotian crews in the C–47 began at Udorn in July 1964, as a part of Project Water Pump. Instructors from the Air Force Special Air Warfare Center at Hurlburt gave upgrade and refresher instruction, training nineteen Laotian pilots and fifty-nine maintenance men during the ten-month effort. Progress was hampered by language differences and by troubles in keeping the airplanes flyable. Student aptitude varied, ranging from a colonel, "too set in his ways to improve much" to one cadet, "the shining star of the group." Training missions included dirt field landings and night operations. The Americans at one point reported that the instructors were "saving the aircraft on about 8 out of 10 landings."[32]

Other conditions hampered effective use of the C–47s. Rivalry with the ground force-dominated general staff produced an unsuccessful Royal Laotian Air Force revolt, resulting in the exile of the RLAF chief in 1966. The episode increased the general staff's mistrust of the RLAF, aggravated by the air force's independent dealings with the Americans. Factionalism within the Royal Laotian Air Force also was strong, with the airlifters remaining aloof from the air strike arm. The C–47s thus remained as much an instrument of internal politics as for military operations against the communists. The absence of a centralized allocations and scheduling system led American attaché officers to judge that the transports were often misused. A single air transport command did come briefly into existence, but operational command was returned to regional commanders in early 1968. More grievously, the American officers became aware that the C–47s were probably used for corrupt purposes, ranging from vastly profitable traffic in opium and gold to the private sale of passenger seats.[33]

By late 1968 the RLAF had sixteen C–47s and twenty-six crews. The monthly workload averaged seven hundred tons of cargo and passengers (including that lifted by a force of nine helicopters), up from four hundred tons in 1966. Plans for further expansion (and disappointments with the Laotian-operated training program at Savannakhet) resulted in a fresh American upgrade program at Udorn, begun in early 1969. Ambassador

Sullivan insisted that the instructors should again be drawn from the Hurlburt unit (now called the Special Operations Force), believing that one-year assignees from the general Air Force would be "middle-aged, straight-and-level" (and presumably, poorly motivated) flyers. Laotian instructors gradually replaced the Hurlburt people, and in December 1971 the program was returned to Savannakhet as an RLAF effort monitored by the U.S. Air Force.[34]

The Laotian air arm was expanded to thirty-four C–47s in late 1970 (including nine AC–47 gunships), and its contributions became more significant. Almost daily three or four ships made passenger and cargo flights scheduled by the ground force transportation staff at Vientiane. One or more C–47s also worked each day under the army's regional transportation offices at Savannakhet, Pakse, and Luang Prabang. A few missions operated out of Long Tieng in support of Vang Pao's forces. Flights from the main bases usually were to outlying places such as Saravane, Vang Vieng, and Seno. The transport C–47s also performed some flareship work.[35]

From 1967 on the RLAF C–47s were organized in composite squadrons, each including gunships, T–28s, helicopters, and light aircraft; most of the transports belonged to the squadrons at Vientiane and Savannakhet. In effect each squadron was a miniature air force, largely responsive to regional control. C–47s flew an average of thirty-three hours monthly. Spare parts were stocked at the Royal Laotian Air Force supply depot at Vientiane (moved from Savannakhet in late 1969). The Laotians also undertook certain periodic maintenance tasks, although in 1972 some phase inspections and heavy maintenance were still performed by contract in Thailand. Incongruities remained however. One Air Force crew had to fly a plane to Da Nang to have a "spirit" removed. Still, the RLAF C–47 arm made undeniable progress, possibly sufficient for the requirements for a low-grade insurgency situation. But to undertake the work of the contract fleets remained an impossibility given the existing level of hostilities.[36]

The distances separating the upcountry locations in Laos from the Thailand logistics bases (Takhli, Udorn, and Bangkok) ruled out any substantial use of helicopters for the bulk hauling performed by the fixed-wing transports. Neither were there sufficient helicopters on hand until late in the war to encourage major troop-assault operations of the sort practiced in Vietnam. Important rotary-wing roles remained, however, for team infiltrations and retrieval, local supply redistribution, aeromedical evacuation, liaison hauls, and search-and-rescue. Transport helicopter operations

TACTICAL AIRLIFT

in Laos included those of Air America, the Royal Laotian Air Force, and the U.S. military services, predominantly the Air Force.

H–34s deployed in early 1961 had been nominally furnished to the Royal Laotian Air Force, but were instead flown, maintained, and controlled by Air America. Although limited in payload and passenger capacity, these versatile craft were well suited for the several main missions in Laos. Air America operated a modest-sized H–34 fleet throughout the war, its strength reaching twenty-one aircraft in early 1972. Supported by an excellent maintenance facility at Udorn, the contract helicopters averaged an impressive 120 hours monthly flight time. Air America flew a few UH–1s late in the war and in late 1972 acquired eight CH–47C Chinooks from U.S. Army. In addition a small U.S. Army UH–1 detachment at Udorn hauled Army attaché and advisory personnel about Thailand and Laos.[37]

There was never a vigorous RLAF helicopter arm, although Souvanna and his military leaders wanted a significant force capable of directly supporting Laotian ground forces. Ambassador Sullivan agreed that Laotian helicopters could "facilitate military operations in the difficult and often trackless terrain of Laos." In 1965 the RLAF controlled and operated only two H–34s. U.S. Army instructors produced a few Laotian pilots and maintenance men and the RLAF slowly absorbed more H–34s, basing them in Laos. The limiting factor was Laotian maintenance capability. Despite heavy reliance on contract maintenance, flying rates were about half those of Air America. One unappreciative Air America mechanic judged a Laotian H–34, "a flying accident going somewhere to happen." The Laotians built a force of twelve H–34s in 1968 and seventeen in 1972. Laotian crews also briefly operated UH–1s in early 1972, using the UH–1s as gunships during dry seasons and for transport during the wet-season offensives. Royal Laotian Air Force craft received more than their share of hostile fire but the Laotian helicopter arm made few significant contributions.[38]

U.S. Air Force helicopters in Laos augmented and eventually exceeded the efforts of Air America and the Royal Laotian Air Force. A detachment of two CH–3Cs from the 20th Helicopter Squadron in Vietnam arrived in Nakhon Phanom in February 1966. After several realignments during the spring, the detachment (known as the Pony Express) was established at Udorn in May 1968 and soon added several UH–1s from the parent unit.[39]

Although the CH–3s were originally sent to Nakhon Phanom to support counterinsurgency programs in Thailand, missions into Laos soon predominated. Pony Express joined the contract helicopters in supporting the Vang Pao forces and various refugee and civic action lifts. The CH–3s lifted ordnance disposal teams to towns mistakenly struck by allied aircraft, backed up Air Force rescue helicopters, and hauled investigators to remote crash sites. One crew lifted out a damaged A-1E after removing its engine and outer wings. A high-priority role was hauling to and from several isolated radar and communications sites. Each of four tacan stations, for example, required three tons of petroleum products, parts, food, and water each week. One station routinely sustained was Lima Site 85, atop a 5,600-foot mountain defended by Vang Pao's forces in the Samneua region of northeast Laos. During installation of heavy radar in late 1967, Pony Express lifted in over 150 tons, assisted by U.S. Army CH-47 Chinooks. One CH-3 went down while approaching Site 85 in December 1967, possibly a victim of enemy fire. Three months later the station fell to the communists, and construction of a new tacan station near Samneua commenced in July 1968. Pony Express contributed seventy flying hours to the construction effort, again aided by Chinook sorties.[40]

The most challenging Pony Express tasks, however, were infiltrations for the Roadwatch program, augmenting the Air America H-34s. Roadwatch teams operated along the length of the eastern panhandle, gathering intelligence and harassing the communists. Pony Express also flew missions from north Thailand for teams operating in North Vietnam and in the region of Laos adjacent to South Vietnam. In 1966 Pony Express logged 315 infiltration sorties.[41]

A second CH-3 unit arrived in north Thailand in December 1967. The 21st Helicopter Squadron had been activated the previous summer at Shaw Air Force Base, S.C., and had completed unit training prior to moving overseas. The squadron arrived at Nakhon Phanom with CH-3Es (armed craft, with improved engines over the earlier CH-3Cs). The squadron's intended mission was part of a larger project to inhibit communist use of the panhandle. Early missions placed seismic sensor devices in the panhandle trails and did some roadwatch infiltration. The 21st began Prairie Fire missions in late 1968, inserting and withdrawing teams in the panhandle on behalf of Military Assistance Command Studies and Observations Group. In a reorganization in the summer of 1969, the 21st Helicopter Squadron absorbed the remaining CH-3s of Pony Express, while the UH-1s of the 20th returned to Vietnam. The change permitted a small savings in manpower and left the 21st Squadron with an authorized strength of fifteen CH-3s. The 21st also inherited all the old Pony Express roles including tacan site support, night reconnaissance of the base perimeter, and the insertion and withdrawal of special teams seeking information on downed aircrews.[42]

The need for heavy-lift capability beyond that of the CH-3 became increasingly evident. During 1967 U.S. Army Chinooks and Marine CH-53s were sent to north Thailand from Vietnam on ten occasions for a total of ninety-six days. CH-54 Flying Cranes were flown from Da Nang on several subsequent occasions to lift artillery, damaged aircraft, generators, and other items in Laos. To meet such needs, the Seventh/Thir-

455

teenth Air Force in early 1968 requested that several heavy-lift choppers be permanently based at Udorn. MACV, however, was unwilling to spare these craft from Vietnam and instead recommended that the Air Force procure its own CH–53s. The Secretary of Defense on April 20, 1968, approved the procurement of twelve CH–53s for this purpose. The first CH–53C joined the 21st Helicopter Squadron in August 1970, beginning a changeover period not completed until December 1971. The CH–53s thus became the Air Force's first heavy-cargo helicopter, with twice the power of the CH–3E and three times the latter's load-carrying capacity.[43]

Hostile fire became an increasing concern and required that crews practice precautionary tactics. Prior to 1969, Air Force transport helicopter losses in Laos to enemy fire totaled only three CH–53s and one UH–1. Of the fifteen crewmen, all but one were rescued. During 1969, communist fire brought down and destroyed six CH–3s in Laos, and a seventh was apparently destroyed by enemy troops after a forced landing. Fortunately, thanks to the practice of operating in pairs, all crews but one were rescued. Meanwhile, the circles on situation maps denoting antiaircraft danger areas began to overlap. Constant reappraisals of tactics, better guns, and introduction of the CH–53s, however, reversed the trend of losses. Through 1973 the Air Force lost a total of eleven CH–3s in Laos, and six elsewhere in Southeast Asia. All but three were lost as a result of enemy action. Enemy fire claimed only two CH–53s, both in early 1971 in Laos—one near Long Tieng, the other near South Vietnam during Lam Son 719.[44]

Hair-raising missions were commonplace. One two-ship team pickup, on December 29, 1967, earned Silver Star recommendations for two Pony Express aircraft commanders, Majs. James S. Villotti and Kyron V. Hall. Protected by armored vests, the pilots of the first plane received nondisabling injuries from enemy bullets, while three other crewmen replied with automatic weapons from side and rear exits. The first helicopter lifted out with twenty-nine passengers; the second completed the evacuation moments later, packing thirty-four men into space rated for twenty-five. A forward air controller later counted twenty-two enemy dead about the landing zone.[45]

Both the 20th and the 21st Helicopter Squadrons had maintenance troubles. Excessive use regularly pushed the CH–3s to the limits of airframe, engine, and transmission tolerance. Sand and grit got into critical parts, engines were damaged by foreign objects when operating at forward points, and metal fatigue cracks appeared. The new CH–53s increased spare parts difficulties and, despite frequent cannibalization, parts shortages regularly kept ten to twenty percent of these craft on the ground. Pilots warmly praised the efforts of inexperienced maintenance men and supervisors, but several pilots stated they were more concerned by the danger of mechanical failure than by the threat of hostile fire.[46]

The necessity of replacing all Southeast Asia personnel every twelve months strained the Air Force's thin reservoir of experienced helicopter pilots, especially in the later years of the war. One expedient was to train experienced fixed-wing pilots in rotary-wing flying, in many cases selecting older officers who had not flown in recent years. Such individuals, after graduating from the helicopter school at Sheppard Air Force Base, Tex., went through tactical training in the CH–53 at Shaw. After reaching Nakhon Phanom, each individual received further checkout and upgrade training under squadron instructors. Of thirty-nine pilots assigned to the 21st Helicopter Squadron in mid-1970, only ten had previous rotary-wing experience. Twelve were lieutenant colonels although only one lieutenant colonel was authorized. To balance these personnel deficiencies were the excellent flying characteristics of the CH–53 and the craft's large margin of engine power. In another measure, taken largely in response to congressional pressure, the Air Force abandoned its policy that helicopter pilots should first be rated in fixed-wing aircraft. Beginning in late 1970, candidates without fixed-wing ratings entered a 190-flying hour helicopter training program conducted by U.S. Army.[47]

Along with its many other responsibilities the 21st Squadron increasingly made tactical troop lifts, hauling Meo and Laotian battalions in airmobile assault and reinforcement operations. Indeed, in the later years of the war, the history of the whole allied airlift effort in Laos, including contract, Royal Laotian Air Force, and U.S. Air Force helicopter and fixed-wing arms, became increasingly involved in the campaigns on the ground.

The Air Force and Air America helicopter units collaborated in several major efforts in early 1969 in reaction to the communist dry-season offensive. During January 10–15, 1969, the 20th Squadron lifted over five thousand persons, cut off by enemy forces near Samneua, in a total of 539 sorties. Each morning, 20th crews hauled drums of helicopter fuel into the region for refueling during the rest of the day. Precipitous terrain and early morning fog hampered the effort, already made difficult by the 4,700 foot ground elevation at the pickup point. A similar joint helicopter evacuation in March preceded the fall of Site 36, the main Meo staging point north of the Plain of Jars.[48]

Allied defeats continued into early summer of 1969 and were climaxed with the evacuation and loss of Muong Soui. A helicopter task force assembled at Long Tieng on June 27 for the Muong Soui evacuation —ten from 20th and 21st Squadrons, three HH–53s from the Air Force air rescue unit in north Thailand, and eleven Air America H–34s. With-

TACTICAL AIRLIFT

drawal of a 350-man Thai unit began that afternoon and was completed in two hours, after which evacuation of Laotian troops and families began. One 21st Squadron CH–3 was shot down, but crews and passengers stood off enemy troops with rifles and grenades until picked up by an Air America H–34. The evacuation continued the next day, at all times plagued by difficult weather. Air attaché officers praised

> the aircrews of the unarmed and vulnerable helicopters who time and time again descended into the enemy-controlled area at minimum altitude and airspeed, crammed their burdens into the overgrossed machines, and staggered out of the area to the Long Tieng sanctuary. These deeds should not go unnoted to the men of the Air Force helicopter units and their comrades of Air America, Inc. . . .[49]

The pattern of defeat gave little hope for the future of Laos. Ambassador Sullivan, leaving the country in March 1969, realized that the Meo forces were being depleted and that the next dry season was likely to bring the communists major successes. Soon afterwards, plans and policy officers of the Joint Staff concluded that only political considerations could prevent the communists from eventually overrunning most of Laos. A pessimistic State-Defense-CIA paper was sent to President Nixon in August, describing American options for Laos. The paper saw a ray of hope in the effectiveness of "fixed-wing and helicopter airlift" and cited the enemy's difficulty in reacting to surprise assaults in his rear.[50]

The success of Operation About Face seemed to verify this airlift effectiveness. About Face was Vang Pao's late summer 1969 offensive which recovered Muong Soui and the Plain of Jars and captured much enemy materiel. Supplied by air, some Meo forces advanced nearly to the border of North Vietnam. Unfortunately the gains of About Face proved temporary. The communist dry season offensive began in December 1969 and soon swept into the Plain of Jars, threatening thousands of civilians in encircled positions immediately northwest of the plain. Again Air Force helicopters joined with Air America in massive evacuations in horrid weather. Ten planes and crews of the 21st Helicopter Squadron flew to Long Tieng on January 4, 1970, for daily operations about Muong Soui. Upon completion of the effort on January 15, the 21st Squadron had lifted over four thousand refugees, along with livestock and personal possessions, from their encircled locations to temporary safety at Muong Soui.[51]

The war's most dramatic fixed-wing transport effort soon followed. Under continuing communist military pressure, Laotian officials decided to evacuate all civilians from the southern Plain of Jars, moving them farther to the south. Air America and Continental Air Services ships lifted out over thirteen thousand of these refugees from Lat Sen airfield in the southern plain during February 4–10. Reporters witnessed the flights and described and photographed the loadings of the impoverished people into the silver C–130s, C–123s, and C–7s. At the dusty boarding locations, officials guided the refugees aboard while pilots kept their engines running. Most flights landed at Vientiane and Ban Keun airfield north of Vientiane. The Ambassador reported that the evacuation was "accomplished with all the elan we normally associate with such humanitarian efforts."[52]

The exodus came none too soon. The Xiengkhoang airfield in the plain fell on February 21, Muong Soui three days later. Air America transports managed to evacuate some refugees and most of the equipment used to support the RLAF T–28s at Muong Soui, despite heavy ground fire. Irregular and regular forces withdrew from Muong Soui and the plain in disorder and occupied hill positions in front of Long Tieng—the socalled Vang Pao line. Frightened refugees streamed out of Long Tieng by foot, and others clustered just outside the airfield perimeter begging for air transporation out. C–123s, Caribous, and helicopters continued to land and take off in the smoke and haze at Long Tieng, amid increasing danger of midair collisions, lifting out families of officials along with many villagers. The Air Force physician assigned to the Long Tieng hospital arranged for evacuation of his eighty patients in an Air America C–123. Nearby Sam Thong airfield and base were abandoned after Air America on March 17 lifted out all wounded and American personnel. All aircraft and most American equipment and personnel were evacuated from Long Tieng the next day although most individuals continued to commute each day for work.

Meanwhile transports and helicopters brought in reinforcements. Over three hundred Thai troops landed on March 18, with the base already under shellfire and the enemy reported close in. An American officer at Long Tieng watched the Thais arrive with full field gear and steel helmets, with crewcuts and wearing uniforms without insignia. The contrast with the ragtag and long-haired Meos was marked. Despite nearly prohibitive weather on the nineteenth, over five hundred Laotian and irregular troops arrived at Long Tieng from other military regions. One battalion was lifted in after an all-night march to reach their boarding strip. More reinforcements arrived on the twentieth, and most of them were repositioned to hill defensive positions by Air America and Air Force helicopters.

With visibility again borderline at Long Tieng, and with enemy troops reported a mile from the approach end of the runway, Air America transports delayed takeoffs at Vientiane on the morning of March 21. Reassured by radio from Long Tieng, and by a report that landings could be made by touching down at midfield, the C–123s took off at midmorning. Maj. John C. Pratt, an Air Force officer assigned to the Seventh Air Force, described the scene on landing at Long Tieng on the twenty-first:

> Prior to landing, all we could see until directly in the LT Valley were murky mountain peaks obscured by the haze and occasionally blotted out by thick columns of brown smoke from ground fires. Often, black burnt particles, some as large as pieces of carbon paper, flew by the

Courtesy: Vance Mitchell

Long Tieng, Laos, January 16, 1972. The city is under siege and intensive fighting is underway on top of Skyline Ridge, the high terrain on the left.

Courtesy: Vance Mitchell

Nighttime firing of tracers by a USAF AC–119K, in support of an outpost north of the Plain of Jars, Laos, January 1972.

Courtesy: Vance Mitchell

Left side of an AC–119K gunship used for air strikes over Laos. The long gun barrels are 20-mm cannon. Four windows house 7.62-mm miniguns.

aircraft. Visibility was about one mile or less with the air-to-air visibility effectively zero. As we broke out over the runway, the hills to either side appeared deserted, with no sign of any activity. Aircraft suddenly appeared from almost all sides, some landing, some taking off—helicopters, C-123s, Caribous, O-1s, T-28s, Porters, and an occasional C-130 . . . .[53]

Heavy rains on March 23 helped clear away the persistent cloud cover and disrupted communist resupply movements from the plain to the battle area. The allied buildup about Long Tieng now included thirty-four hundred irregular, Laotian, and Thai troops. Allied air strikes were intensified, favored by the improved visibility. On March 30 the ambassador reported that the formerly "grave" situation at Long Tieng was "brighter." One by one, defensive positions were retaken, and on March 31 Vang Pao forces reoccupied Sam Thong.[54]

Allied helicopters again were in the forefront of Pao's counteroffensive, Operation Leapfrog. Leapfrog began August 18, 1970, with the insertion of five hundred government troops at the rim of the Plain of Jars by Air Force and contract helicopters. A climax for the 21st Squadron occurred in the last week of November with the unit lifting nearly two thousand troops and equipment from Long Tieng to a landing zone near Ban Ban, well east of the plain. Compared with the successes of About Face, however, those of Leapfrog were small and no more permanent. The enemy reclaimed the initiative in early-year pushes against Long Tieng in 1971 and 1972. In both campaigns, allied helicopter and fixed-wing transport forces again provided Long Tieng's only transportation link to the outside.[55]

Although the northern campaigns appeared more critical for the survival of the Vientiane regime, allied initiatives in the southern part of the country represented a threat to communist control of the trails. In these southern campaigns, the allies frequently used their helicopter forces for tactical airmobile assaults. One early effort, on March 25, 1969, against a hill area in the upper panhandle, resulted in near-disaster. Ten Air Force and eight Air America helicopters successfully inserted the two hundred-man assault force, but strong enemy reaction necessitated an unplanned withdrawal. Air America choppers picked up seven hundred troops, but the eight Air Force CH-3s met heavy fire. Five were hit, two lost engines, and one pilot was wounded. The withdrawal was stopped and the helicopters returned home empty. CH-3s and H-34s completed the evacuation the next day, with fire support by A-1 strike aircraft.[56]

During the second half of 1969, Air Force and Air America craft flew numerous troop lifts in support of allied offensives in the central panhandle. The allies captured Muong Phine and neared Tchepone, located square amid the enemy's logistics arteries. Most heliborne assaults were successful but on October 6 enemy fire downed two CH-3s attempting to land near Muong Phine, entering what later appeared an enemy trap. One

TACTICAL AIRLIFT

of the pilots, Maj. Philip J. Conran, was nominated for the Medal of Honor for his role in the six-hour firefight which followed. Conran removed the machineguns from the downed choppers and led the fifty-odd friendly troops in forming a defensive perimeter. HH–53s later rescued all personnel.[57]

The 21st Helicopter Squadron continued to operate in the panhandle during and after 1970, now utilizing the substantial troop capacity of the CH–53s. On February 16, 1971, the squadron's largest effort to that date took place when eight CH–53s and six CH–3s shuttled over fifteen hundred troops and equipment to a landing zone near Muong Phine. The effort was part of Operation Desert Rat and coincided with Lam Son 719.[58] On June 15–16, 1972, eight CH–53s lifted nearly two thousand troops to jumpoff positions on the western Bolovens Plateau. Further lifts followed and in mid-October the 21st executed a two thousand-man assault near Saravane. Resistance was sometimes hot. On the second shuttle of the Saravane mission, six of the seven choppers were hit. Although technically successful, the Bolovens assaults failed to win the initiative permanently, and by the end of 1972 the allies had retired to the western extremity of the plateau, no longer challenging the trail sectors.[59]

Meanwhile, allied officials preparing fresh offensives northeast of the Plain of Jars for the 1972 rainy season were told that "mobility will be the key here, and mobility means CH–53 support." Air Force and Air America helicopters in August opened another Vang Pao operation, aimed at inserting a 2,400-man task force into the northern plain in the enemy's rear. But plagued by bad weather and rules prohibiting use of the CH–53s without escort, the helicopter force managed to deploy only half the intended assault force. Communist artillery and tank action forced a halt to further insertions. Survivors of the assault force made their way overland to safety over several weeks. Vang Pao nevertheless persisted in aggressive operations during the fall, and the 21st Squadron lifted a total of three thousand troops in several other tactical ventures. The last major combat air assault took place on January 20, 1973, when seven CH–53s and two Air America Chinooks transported over one thousand troops to reopen the Vientiane-Luang Prabang highway. Four helicopters were hit, but the isolation of Luang Prabang was broken prior to the February cease-fire.[60]

The tactics used for assault operations developed from those used in infiltration penetrations. Crews constantly sought refinements in order to stay ahead of the enemy's growing fire capabilities. Nine-ship formations, for example, flew in elements of two or three for safety and flexibility when operating in marginal weather. Some 21st Squadron craft were equipped with 7.62-mm miniguns, primarily for use in laying down suppressive fire during the final approach to the landing zone. Ideas on ways to cut down time on the ground at the landing zone also were tried. In late 1972 the jet-propelled A–7 aircraft largely replaced the A–1 for escort and fire-suppression work with the helicopters. The early A-7 missions were carefully planned and critiqued. A-1 pilots experienced in escort work rode in the helicopter formation in order to advise the A-7 pilots by radio. Customarily, the A-7s worked slightly in front of the helicopter elements, and made passes over the landing zone several minutes ahead of the choppers.[61]

Early planning for the larger assault operations involved CIA officers in Laos and the embassy staff in Vientiane, including the air attaché. CIA operations and intelligence staffs refined plans and coordinated informally with the special activities division of the Seventh/Thirteenth Air Force. Messages requesting employment of Air Force helicopters were passed along the military chain of command, via the Saigon and Hawaii staffs, to the Joint Chiefs of Staff and the Secretary of Defense. Generally multibattalion lifts required specific mission approval, although blanket authority to use a specified number of helicopters daily in support of a continuing ground operation was sometimes given.[62]

The Laotian cease-fire of February 22, 1973, left the future of that country uncertain. The communists controlled vast territory and were unhampered in their use of the panhandle trails for movements south. The confrontation in the Plain of Jars region became static, with only occasional minor clashes. The United States continued to view Laos as an important buffer, protecting the non-communist countries of Southeast Asia from Communist China and North Vietnam. The Americans therefore continued a modest military assistance program, administered by a defense attaché office in Vientiane and the subordinate deputy chief agency of Udorn. The latter managed the former dual logistics pipeline, unified since July 1, 1972, under Department of Defense funding.

With the cease-fire the CH-53s and most other Air Force aircraft ended missions within Laos. The CH-53s remained at Nakhon Phanom, however, ready to evacuate Americans from Laos and Cambodia or to assist in locating missing personnel. Contract airlift operations in Laos continued. Meanwhile, the airlift arm of the Royal Laotian Air Force assisted Laotian ground forces in protecting and policing those regions nominally under government control. Expansion just before the cease-fire brought the H-34 force to twenty-six ships, and in June 1973 RLAF received six C-123s. The presence of the transports, and the fact that forty-five airfields in Laos had runways of twenty-five hundred feet or more, promised that airlift would play a large role in the country's reconstruction, whatever its government.[63]

Events in Laos in 1975 were less turbulent than those in South Vietnam and Cambodia but no less conclusive. The Agency for International Development closed the last American sites outside of Vientiane during the spring, and the contract transport firms (Continental Air Services and Birdair, Inc.) withdrew most of their remaining personnel and aircraft from Laos and north Thailand. The Air Force thereafter provided a single C–130 for operation by Birdair crewmen, making daily trips to Vientiane. The coalition regime, nominally under Souvanna Phouma, proved unable to halt spreading left-wing violence. The Birdair C–130 crew on May 31 reported that armed Pathet Lao soldiers had threatened to seize the aircraft since it had been "stolen from Vietnam." Plans for a final American evacuation went through several evolutions during the summer, but growing communist dominance in Vientiane made it clear that only a quick-snatch helicopter effort was feasible. Communist takeover seemed complete in December 1975, with the dissolution of the coalition regime and the proclamation of the People's Democratic Republic of Laos. But no American emergency evacuation followed.[64]

The communist assumption of power in Laos made the long years of American intervention futile. The final outcome, however, did not detract from the essentially constructive contribution of airlift in the conflict. For more than a decade the Americans used air transport resourcefully and at modest cost as a central element in a strategy that prolonged military equilibrium in a situation otherwise favorable to the communists. Airlift flew over enemy forces and barriers of terrain to deploy and sustain units ranging from teams to multibattalions. The contract system worked, providing effective and responsive airlift, avoiding further commitments for the already strained Air Force airlift force, and making a larger American military presence unnecessary. The Air Force airlift contribution was a significant one. The Air Force provided transport aircraft and technical assistance to the contractors, actively operated a rotary-wing force, and trained and advised the Royal Laotian Air Force transport arm. Satisfaction with Air Force performance in these roles was general. The reasons for the failure of allied policy for the Mountain Kingdom must be sought elsewhere.

Part Four:
The Years of Withdrawal, 1969-1975

XVIII. The Airlift System, 1969-1971

In his news conference of June 19, 1969, President Nixon made public his explicit orders for General Abrams—"They are very simply this: he is to conduct the war with a minimum of American casualties." In the same month the President announced an initial reduction of U.S. troop strength in Vietnam to 524,500 by the end of August—down 25,000 from the previous peak. The nation's new strategy soon became clear—progressive American withdrawal coupled with early "Vietnamization" of former American war roles. A strong Vietnamization program appeared to offer, not only a way of facilitating American withdrawal, but also a stimulus to the communists in the hitherto disappointing Paris negotiations. Meanwhile, reduced casualty lists would help the administration counter the antiwar movement at home. The fundamental political goal remained essentially unchanged—to preserve South Vietnam from forceful communist takeover.[1]

In South Vietnam the intensity of fighting remained low. The communists, after their heavy losses of 1968, returned to a strategy of protracted conflict. Major allied incursions into Cambodia (1970) and Laos (1971) punctuated the otherwise formless conflict. Allied pacification efforts meanwhile apparently made headway, and numerous roads once unsafe were opened to full use. American ground forces ceased combat operations, except for defensive responsibilities, on July 1, 1971. This completed Phase I of the Vietnamization program. By March of 1972 only two U.S. brigades remained in Vietnam, deployed for security about Da Nang and Saigon.[2]

For the Air Force airlift system in Vietnam, the period was one of comparative stability. The high-volume countrywide airlift effort declined gradually, roughly in proportion to the pace of U.S. ground force withdrawal. Established patterns of management produced a high order of efficiency, safety, and control. The long-awaited experiment with computer scheduling yielded disappointing results, but blind and high-altitude airdrop capabilities improved significantly. Doctrinal conflicts with the Army subsided as both services acquiesced in the established division of roles. Some units became involved in activities to strengthen and expand the Vietnamese air transport arm. Airlift and aerial port units scaled downward, especially after 1970.

TACTICAL AIRLIFT

The workload of the in-country C–123 and C–130 fleets steadily declined from a peak cargo effort of 82,500 tons in 1969, 38,000 in 1970, and 20,000 in 1971. Direct combat activities also decreased markedly. In 1969 the 834th Air Division made over sixty unit movements each month; in 1971 these fell to below twenty monthly. Petroleum deliveries, which once represented twenty percent of total cargo tonnage, dropped to less than ten percent, and ammunition lifts declined similarly. Passenger moves, however, increased relatively. In-country C–130s hauled an alltime peak of 217,000 persons in July 1970, while the C–123s peaked at 99,000 the previous month. By early 1972, passenger movements accounted for fifty-three percent of the total C–130 workload (by tonnage), in comparison with thirty-one percent three years earlier. In-country C–130 flying hours and total sorties at the end of the period approximated the level of the summer of 1965.[3]

Air cargo shipments declined in relation to surface transport. In 1969 air cargo tonnages made up five percent of the countrywide transportation workload, while in 1970 this figure was down to three percent. The MACV logistics section favored this shift in emphasis, believing that the use of roads and waterways encouraged restoration of peacetime economic and social patterns. Accordingly, units were directed in July 1970 to exercise "maximum discipline in the use of airlift." The MACV traffic management agency continued as the focal point for daily assignment of both the common service sealift and airlift systems, while the Army support commands at Saigon, Cam Ranh Bay, Qui Nhon, and Da Nang remained the centers of distribution within the logistics "islands." Vietnamese military trucking and coastal shipping capacities slowly expanded, and both approached self-sufficiency by March 1972. Airlift self-sufficiency within the countrywide transportation system also was an important goal in Vietnamization planning.[4]

Brig. Gen. John H. Herring, Jr., who replaced General McLaughlin in June 1969, commanded the 834th Air Division through most of the period. General Herring's military career included troop carrier duty during World War II and Korea, Air Staff responsibilities for airlift support of Arctic construction, command of the 483d Troop Carrier Wing in Japan, and command duty in Military Airlift Command. Herring commanded the 834th until June 1971 when he relinquished the position to Brig. Gen. John H. Germeraad.

The organizational frame for management under the 834th—its airlift control centers and command posts, and the apparatus of airlift control element detachments, combat control teams, mission commanders, and liaison officers—carried over from previous years. The countrywide network of fixed control element detachments reached its fullest growth with the addition of two detachments in March 1969, making a total of eighteen. During late summer 1970, many control elements were administratively combined with local aerial port detachments, permitting consolidation of some facilities and functions. Retrenchment began with deactivation of four control elements in the second half of 1970. The prototype mobile control element unit, tested in 1968, was located at Tay Ninh through 1969 and functioned identically to the fixed units. Two improved mobile units arrived in Vietnam in June 1970 and were placed at Song Be and Phuoc Vinh to support the 1st Cavalry Division. One of the mobile units was sent to Khe Sanh during the 1971 Laos incursion. Except for numerous minor malfunctions resulting from the hot and dusty conditions at the forward sites, airlift control elements satisfactorily fulfilled their intended purpose. Particularly popular with all personnel was the control element's trenching machine, which was able to fill nine hundred sandbags per hour. All three mobile airlift control elements were removed from Vietnam field service during early 1971.[5]

Mission commanders and combat control teams continued to be sent to forward airfields without control elements. During the Cambodian operation in the spring of 1970, as many as seven mission commanders were simultaneously at border airstrips; and during the Laos incursion mission commanders served at Quang Tri, Dong Ha, and Khe Sanh. During both operations an overall forward area coordinator with rank of colonel moved among the forward bases, seeking out difficulties and coordinating airlift activities. Tactical airlift liaison officers remained with ground forces down to the independent brigade level and worked closely with logistics staff personnel.[6]

The 834th Division tried various managerial reforms to improve efficiency. In early 1969 a new schedule was prepared for each twelve hours of operations, replacing the single twenty-four-hour schedule. Night itineraries thus were based on more recent port information, and payloads for night missions in March improved nearly ten percent over those of three months earlier. Schedules for passenger missions were closely analyzed and improved from sixty-eight percent completed on time in March 1969 to seventy-three percent in May 1970. Published schedules were used for certain cargo missions in mid-1970 and the results were good. Port planning improved since shippers felt assured that priority cargo would move, and transshipments were reduced. Late in 1970, C–130s assigned to passenger circuits were reconfigured to carry two cargo pallets. This reduced passenger seating to sixty-seven but improved overall payloads since the number of troops was declining.[7]

In 1967 an anticipated need for an automatic airlift data processing system led to design studies and procurement of certain components the following year. One contractor estimated that automation could improve the performance of the 1967 in-country airlift force by fourteen thousand tons per month or alternatively permit force reductions that would cut monthly costs from $7 million to $6 million. As finally conceived, system hardware for the computerized airlift management system consisted of two International Business Machines (IBM) small-scale computers and cathode ray tube display devices in the control center, linked by cable with an IBM 360/50 large-scale computer at Seventh Air Force headquarters. AUTODIN (automatic digital network) and portable UYA–7 radio equipment afforded digital data flow from control element and field locations to the computers. Information entered the computers in several ways. Reports of mission progress could be introduced by card at any of the computers, by AUTODIN message at the 360/50 computer, or by light pen and keyboards at the airlift control element displays. Flight information received at the airlift control center by UYA–7 or voice communications was displayed on the cathode ray tube and entered by technicians. Information on cargo awaiting movement (including departure and destination airfields, item description, priority, and notification when items were outloaded) was transmitted by aerial ports to the control center by radio or landline for manual entry into the management system data base. Cargo backlog reports were periodically transmitted to ports for checks on accuracy.

The airlift management system in theory thus seemed capable of computer scheduling, in effect combining known variables such as aircraft and airfield characteristics with input information on aircraft location and cargo awaiting movement. The system could print schedules in daily fragmentary order format and could transmit the order to field units by AUTODIN. Automatic flight-following displays were intended to replace the manual displays formerly maintained for control center duty officers. A controller could select for presentation data giving the progress of any particular mission. A special capability provided a listing of divertible aircraft available for emergency use.

In actuality the airlift management system proved a dismal disappointment. The Seventh Air Force and the 834th Air Division approved final contractor design specifications in May 1969. Testing continued at Hawaii, along with a training program for 834th personnel, pending completion of computer installation at Tan Son Nhut in the spring of 1970. Air Force operation of the airlift management system began July 1, 1970, although contractors continued technical assistance. A first try at a full-scale mission scheduling on August 22 uncovered numerous unsolved problems and made it clear that substantial modifications were required. Computer schedules (paralleling the manually prepared schedules) were attempted every few days thereafter, invariably disclosing fresh troubles requiring laborious debugging. Eventually it became an inescapable conclusion that the complexity of airlift management and prevailing limitations of information made automatic scheduling impractical without substantial human intervention.

A modification was therefore introduced that allowed an essentially manually developed schedule to be entered into the computers for processing. Largely on this basis, an acceptable computer schedule for C–7s was produced on December 26, 1970, for C–123s the following month, and for C–130s in May 1971. Computer flight-following efforts, attempted in April 1971, encountered gross problems resulting from delays in data inputs and the system's inability to accept all significant information. The airlift management system was abandoned on August 31, 1971, essentially a step in the overall drawdown of the airlift effort in Vietnam.

To General Germeraad the experiment was "overly ambitious," especially since the airlift effort was scaling down. He felt that the system was too sophisticated to provide the necessary responsiveness. Good marks went only to the digital communications, which proved trouble-free, whether jeep-mounted for a combat control team or used by mobile control element in a "suitcase" model at an aerial port site.

A serious scheduling handicap was the lack of expertise in airlift management among those Air Force officers working with contract personnel in developing the project. In many cases, officers learned the airlift system at the same time they learned about the airlift management system, a condition worsened by the twelve-month duty tour. An automatic schedule satisfactory for actual use, without substantial manual change by knowledgeable scheduling officers, was never produced. And the computer's schedule was never superior in utilization of aircraft, in responsiveness, or in speed to the manually developed schedule under the old techniques. Intelligent guesswork by experienced schedulers and controllers could keep the system going even though available information was fragmentary; the same function performed by computers led to unworkable solutions. Accordingly, the limited use of the airlift management system (chiefly to convert a manually prepared schedule into proper format and disseminate it) scarcely justified the costs of the project.[8]

The chain of events leading to the closing out of 834th Air Division headquarters began in early 1971. On General Herring's recommendation the 834th maintenance and materiel management responsibilities ended, and the in-country C–130 detachments reverted to their wing. This realignment, along with the fast-declining airlift workload, led to the conclusion that the remaining functions of the 834th could be merged into the Seventh Air Force headquarters. A proposal to combine the airlift control center with the Seventh Air Force's tactical air control center, however,

TACTICAL AIRLIFT

was successfully opposed by 834th officers, reflecting the long-held view among airlifters that a separate airlift control and communications system was essential.

Under the reorganization proposed by the Seventh Air Force on September 16, and effected on December 1, 1971, the airlift control center preserved its separate existence, becoming a division of a new Seventh Air Force directorate of airlift under the operations deputate. Other divisions were set up for aerial port and special requirement matters. Units formerly assigned to the 834th (the 315th and 483d Wings, and the 2d Aerial Port Group) were placed directly under the Seventh Air Force. General Germeraad became head of the new directorate, and its personnel were drawn from the 834th and from the old six-man airlift division within the Seventh Air Force. A headquarters manpower saving of sixty persons was achieved. Airlift operations were unaffected. Routine mission requirements continued to flow from MACV's traffic management agency, while the MACV combat operations center proceeded to exercise approval authority for emergency requests. In the inactivation ceremony held December 1 at Tan Son Nhut, the 834th Air Division received its second Presidential Unit Citation, earned during the spring 1970 Cambodian campaign.[9]

The permanently assigned airlift force in the western Pacific reached its maximum upon designation of a thirteenth C-130 squadron to replace the temporary duty unit at Ching Chuan Kang left from 1968. Including the six C-7 and four C-123 squadrons based in Vietnam, the total force numbered twenty-three squadrons. Over the next several years, decisions on force cuts generally were based on MACV estimates of maximum in-country needs. For example, MACV in November 1970 determined upon a surge requirement for sixty-eight C-130s or equivalents. This equated to 689 C-130 loads, the number needed to move a Vietnamese division from the Saigon area to Da Nang in five days. To help meet such requirements the Joint Chiefs and CINCPAC envisioned use of Military Airlift Command C-141s, either to assist in the unit moves or to replace C-130s for other in-country tasks. Further, the Joint Chiefs of Staff for a time designated certain C-130 squadrons in the United States for fast augmentation of the Pacific force if needed.

Inactivations of C-130A and C-130B units began in late 1969. Aircraft were returned to the United States for assignment to the Air National Guard and the Air Force Reserve, and personnel were used as

472

fillers for the remaining squadrons.* As a result, at the outset of the Easter offensive, March 31, 1972, there were on hand the four E-model squadrons of 374th Tactical Airlift Wing (the 21st, 50th, 345th, and 776th), and the 774th Squadron at Clark.[10]

C-130s kept in Vietnam rose or declined every few weeks to meet changing requirements. The number ranged from a high of sixty-four in December 1969 to a low of twenty-nine in December 1971. The old detachment at Tuy Hoa was closed down in February 1969, because of concern for possible rocket attacks and the availability of better protection at Cam Ranh. The B-models at Tan Son Nhut and the A-models at Cam Ranh changed places between May 1969 and early 1970, thus simplifying logistics by bringing together similar models. The A-models ended in-country shuttle operations on December 28, 1970, the B-models on October 25, 1971. The E-models operated from both Cam Ranh and Tan Son Nhut after March 1970, until Cam Ranh was closed in February 1972. Strength at Tan Son Nhut on March 31, 1972, was twenty-four C-130Es.[11]

C-123 unit inactivations began in July 1970.† The last squadron, the 310th, moved to Tan Son Nhut in January 1972, and served thereafter as a U.S.-controlled contingency force capable of making pickups at fields where C-130s could not land. The final Air Force C-123K missions in Vietnam took place on June 14, 1972, and the last plane was turned over to the Vietnamese Air Force five days later.[12]

For most airlifters the job after 1972 was a little different than before. Flying became somewhat more routine, reflecting the decline in forward area work. Sorties lengthened, operations into the larger airfields increased, and night work decreased. A proposal to cease routine night operations to reduce aerial port and control element manning was rejected in recognition of the C-130's past effectiveness in night work. The 834th attempted to encourage aircrews to trust the civil air traffic control system and to use

---

* C-130 unit inactivations were: 915th Tactical Airlift Squadron (TAS) (C-130A), Tachikawa, December 15, 1969; 817th TAS (C-130A), Naha, June 15, 1970; 29th TAS (C-130B), Clark, September 30, 1970; 41st TAS (C-130A), Naha, February 28, 1971; 35th TAS (C-130A), Naha, March 31, 1971; 21st TAS (C-130A), Naha, May 31, 1971 (squadron designation moved to CCK to replace the 346th TAS); 374th Tactical Airlift Wing (TAW) (C-130A), Naha, May 31, 1971 (wing designation moved to CCK to replace the 314th TAW); 772d TAS (C-130B), Clark, June 15, 1971; 463d TAW (C-130B), Clark, December 31, 1971 (774th TAS placed under 405th Tactical Fighter Wing). The 374th Wing and 21st Squadron designations in the Pacific were retained in recognition of the lineage of these units, both of which have served in the southwest Pacific during World War II and in the Korean War.

† C-123 unit inactivations were: 309th TAS, Phan Rang, July 1970; 12th Special Operations Squadron (spray unit), July 1970; 19th TAS, Tan Son Nhut, May 1971; 311th TAS, Phan Rang and Tan Son Nhut, September 1971; 315th TAW, Phan Rang, March 31, 1972. The 315th Special Operations Wing became the 315th TAW on January 1, 1970; the four airlift squadrons were also redesignated.

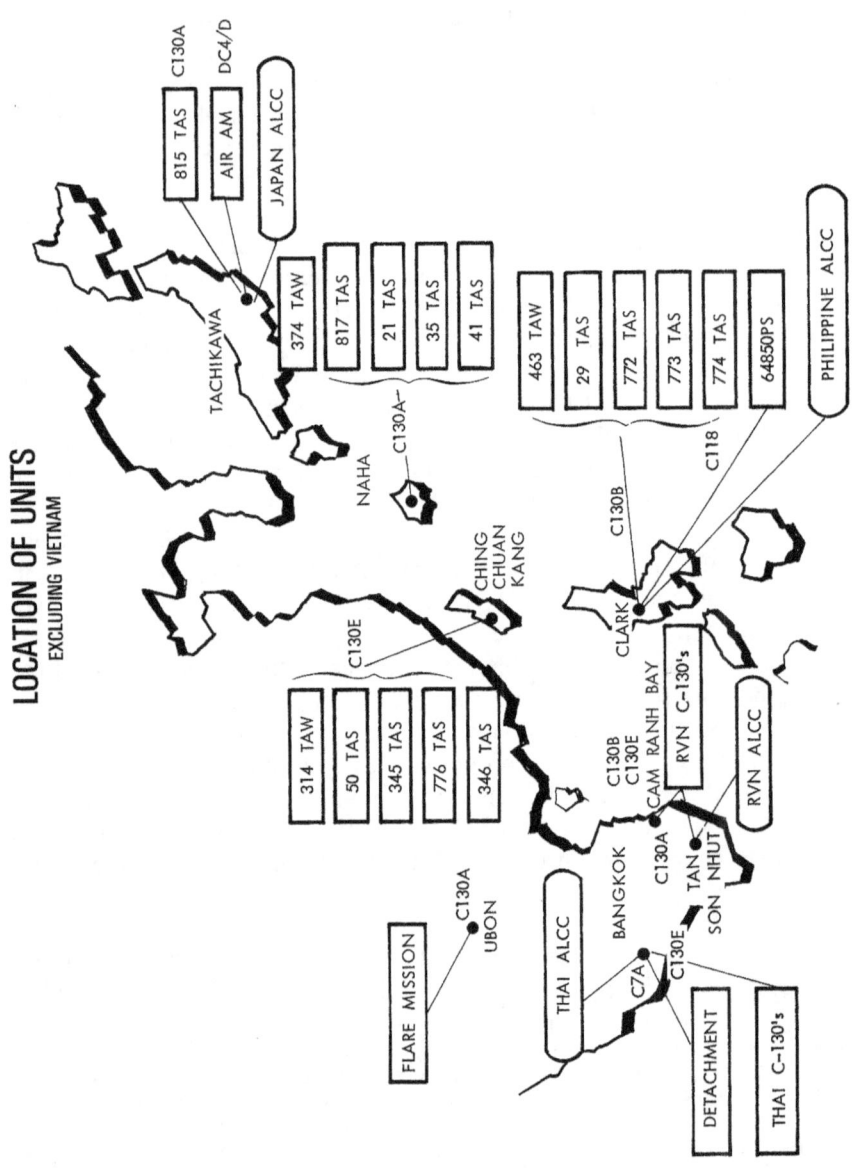

AIRLIFT SYSTEM, 1969–1971

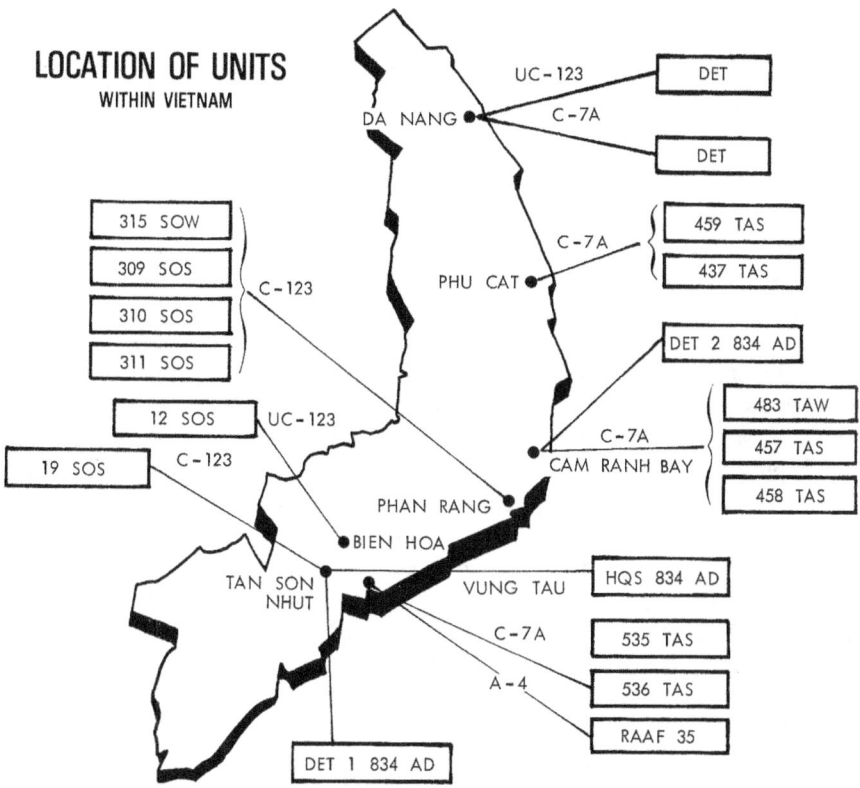

LOCATION OF UNITS WITHIN VIETNAM

instrument flight procedures when flying in clouds and in darkness, thus getting away from informal practice of the past. Most pilots, however, felt that this would not assure clearance from the many other aircraft not using the same procedures, and suspected that ground agencies might not have late warning information on friendly and enemy firing.[13]

Prior to 1968, three serious operating problems defied effective solution, all requiring better coordination between the U.S. Army and the Air Force in the field. First, flying officers of both services testified to the danger of midair collision near forward airstrips. This was the result of uncontrolled flying, incompatible radio equipment, and the absence of commonly accepted procedures for Army helicopter and Air Force transport operations at shared airheads. A midair collision between a Caribou and a Chinook near Camp Evans on October 3, 1968, cost twenty-five lives and tragically illustrated the problem. Second, physical conditions at forward airstrips were sometimes unnecessarily dangerous. Hazards included bunkers or other obstacles near runways and taxi areas, uncontrolled vehicle and pedestrian traffic, and landing surfaces needing improvement. Third, a better system for warning transport crews of firing by friendly artillery was needed. The destruction of an Air Force Caribou by a 155-mm shell while landing at Ha Thanh in August 1967 highlighted this problem.[14]

A joint study group proposed by the 834th Air Division to address these conditions first met on August 15, 1968. The committee met through September with representation from the 834th and the U.S. Army at the full colonel level. Both General McLaughlin and General Williams, aviation officer of the United States Army, Vietnam, attended committee meetings on October 15 and 17, which resulted in agreement to form a standing joint air operations group with working groups for air traffic control, airfield facilities, and artillery warning.[15]

The air traffic control working group laid out traffic patterns for use at each forward strip, to be published and distributed to transport and helicopter crews. In most cases, helicopter and fixed-wing patterns were on opposite sides of each field, with fixed-wing traffic above one thousand feet, helicopters at or below five hundred feet. When departing, fixed-wing craft were to climb out on runway heading until they reached one thousand feet. The working group also spelled out radio frequencies for direct talk between helicopter and transport crews and prepared an "educational" briefing for presentation to crews of both services. The group also drafted a new MACV directive, published in April 1969, clarifying the relation between the Air Force combat control teams and the Army's tactical air traffic control teams which would ordinarily replace the combat control teams no later than the tenth day of any operation.[16] Meanwhile, the airfield facilities working group monitored and reported on airstrip conditions, following the pattern of the old MACV airfield evaluation committee.[17]

The artillery warning working group attempted to establish direct radio communications between transport crews and the Army's artillery warning control centers. There were two major problems however. Many C-130s lacked the FM radio equipment needed for such communication. The warning centers were very numerous, each covering only a small region, so that a transport crossed center boundaries every few minutes. Nevertheless, the group distributed to airlift crews maps showing warning center areas, call signs, and frequencies. Further measures sought improved coordination between artillery warning control centers and the tactical air control system radar control sites and airfields. Meanwhile the former system, whereby crews received information on heavy caliber fire from tactical air control sites, airstrip tower personnel, and combat control teams, sufficed to avoid disaster.[18]

General Herring continued General McLaughlin's interest in the joint air operation group, whose membership was broadened to include the Marines, Navy, and Air America. The existence of the joint group was formalized by MACV Directive 95–15, May 1, 1969. The lack of such an agency had been a flaw in U.S. joint operational doctrine, one magnified by postwar incompatibilities in technique and equipment, so the joint air operations group idea seemed destined to find an important place in prewar doctrine.[19]

Airstrip deterioration became an increasing problem after withdrawal of U.S. Army infantry and engineer units from some regions. Subgrade failures, matting slippages and ruptures, and the effects of flooding added up to widespread difficulties, only slightly compensated for by reductions in traffic. The work of the airfield survey division of the 834th Air Division thus became especially important, along with on-the-spot reports on airstrip conditions by tactical airlift officers and aircrews, which provided a daily flow of information to transport aircrews. It seemed likely that airfield conditions would severely limit airlift after full U.S. withdrawal since the Vietnamese Air Force was to operate C–119s. These required 3,500-foot hard runways and were far less adaptable for forward field operations than the American C–130s. Only twenty-six fields in South Vietnam met C–119 criteria, compared to fifty-six used by the C–130s in early 1970. By mid-1971, although five Vietnamese army airfield repair teams had been trained, a severe reduction was planned in the number of airfields to be maintained. General Herring meanwhile reported the capabilities for forward airfield construction and maintenance had been one of his greatest limiting factors. The outgoing 834th chief recommended that in the future engineering forces be assigned specifically for airfield maintenance and repair.[20]

Accidents became less frequent, reflecting the less rigorous mission. Through the entire period January 1969–March 1972, mishaps claimed only a single C–130 in Southeast Asia, a remarkable figure in comparison with the twenty lost in accidents during the previous four years. This achievement was blemished, however, by four C–130 crashes elsewhere in the western Pacific (three in Taiwan and one off Okinawa), in each case with the loss of all personnel on board. Seven airlift C–123s were lost in accidents in Vietnam during the same period. Three of these losses resulted from materiel failures and reflected the increasing age of the Provider force and corresponding maintenance problems. The others were attributable to aircrew or ground control mistakes. Two planes crashed into hills near Cam Ranh Bay within two days in November 1971, taking over 120 lives. Crew actions headed off countless hazardous situations. In one episode, a crew landed a malfunctioning C–130 gear-up at Cam Ranh with seventy-four passengers on board. The cumulative major accident rate for the C–123s during 1969–71 was 5.1 per 100,000 flying hours; for the C–130s it was 1.1. These compared with an Air Force-wde rate of 3.7 during fiscal 1970. The determination to achieve safety in flight was firmly stated in official manuals of the 834th Air Division and in a February 1971 letter from General Herring to all units after several recent accidents.[21]

Communist action against the airlift force achieved some successes in

TACTICAL AIRLIFT

Courtesy: U.S. Army
Site of an aircraft accident near Gia Nghia, Vietnam, on December 17, 1969. This C-123 attempted to land, but struck the runway 14 feet short.

1969. During the spring months, enemy ground fire brought down and destroyed three C-130s in border areas northwest of Saigon, and a C-123 near Bien Hoa. Other C-130s were destroyed by rocket fire in January on the ground at Tonle Cham near the Cambodian border, by suspected sabotage while in flight in October, and by 37-mm fire while doing flareship work over Laos in November. During the year, 111 C-130s and C-123s were hit while in flight. Phan Rang, the principal C-123 base, was shelled thirty-four times during 1969, disrupting crew rest and night maintenance. After 1969, until March 1972, no C-130s or C-123s were lost to enemy fire while in flight, and the number of ships hit declined to thirty-nine in 1970 and twenty-three in 1971. A single C-130 was destroyed by rocket fire on the ground at Da Nang on February 20, 1971, and four others were damaged in the episode.[22]

Aircrews continued to use precautionary techniques to reduce damage from enemy fire, while aircrew fortitude and skill held down aircraft losses. One crew made a three-engine emergency takeoff from Song Be at dusk on April 2, 1969, under small-arms fire from several hundred yards away, knowing that the ship would surely be destroyed if left overnight for engine repairs. A Silver Star recommendation was earned by 1st Lt. Jerry B. Clark

The wreckage of a C–130, which was shot down during take-off at Kham Duc, Vietnam, August 11, 1970.

for making a C–123 emergency landing after sustaining mortar damage of over one hundred holes during lift-off from Bu Dop on May 4, 1970. Two weeks later, the same recommendation honored Col. Ivan D. Johnson for landing a C–123 despite wounds and severe aircraft damage incurred during an airdrop mission.[23]

There was a chronic shortage of aircrews in the flying squadrons. Combat-ready crews in the three C–130 wings in June 1970 numbered 296 against an authorization for four hundred. Many new crew members arrived without proper training; the 314th Wing for example, during February and March 1969 received thirty unqualified loadmasters, all from the Military Airlift Command and most of them trained only in the C–141. Involuntary separations of certain Reserve officers cut into the pool of experience in the squadrons. Moreover, Air Force policy against assigning persons involuntarily for second tours in Southeast Asia made it difficult to exploit the substantial pool of Pacific C–130 veterans in the United States. The burden of upgrade training was most harsh in the 314th and 463d Wings where turnover was most rapid. Both wings organized combined training flights in 1971, concentrating instructor talent. The 314th Wing temporarily reimposed involuntary extensions of oversea tours. The tragic

TACTICAL AIRLIFT

loss of seventeen newly arrived navigators in the crash of a C–130 on Taiwan in October 1970 left the E–model wing hard-pressed for more than a year. Manning problems eased as the A– and B–model squadrons were inactivated, and their personnel became available as fillers.[24]

Manning was less critical in the C–123 squadrons, but there was renewed concern over the rising percentage of young pilots reporting to 315th Wing for their first line assignments. The wing in March 1969 forecast that within four months such pilots would comprise two-thirds of the wing's pilot strength, "seriously jeopardizing" the mission. A strong internal training program was instituted to upgrade copilots to aircraft commanders. Even so, qualified aircraft commanders often flew more than a hundred flying hours monthly, an extremely high number in view of the short sortie lengths and the demanding flying conditions. The burden of training in Vietnam was intensified by curtailment of assault (shortfield) landings at the school at England Air Force Base, La., due to airframe metal fatigue problems. Col. Kenneth T. Blood, Jr., commander of the 315th Wing during 1971, concluded that the situation demanded strong leadership by operations, safety, and standardization officers.[25]

Aircraft maintenance, too, suffered from the continuing heavy flying hour rates and the wearing conditions of usage. The advancing age of the C–130s and especially the C–123s added to the maintenance burden, while the chronic shortage of trained maintenance personnel continued. All this spelled long and hard work for the men of the support force, mitigated in part by improving work and living facilities. Incommission rates sagged. The C–123s averaged seventy-seven percent in commission in 1969, seventy-five percent in 1970, and seventy percent in 1971. Flying hours went from 3.9 per plane daily in 1969 to 3.0 hours two years later. In-country C–130 operational ready rates were above eighty percent through 1969, but declined to sixty-nine percent by June 1970. The C–130Bs and C–130Es faced a wing fatigue problem, first discovered in 1967, requiring their cycling to the United States for lengthy retrofit work by 1971. The elderly A–models, still plagued by fuel leaks and, in 1970, troubled with defective engine air ducting (discovered after a 1970 accident at Naha), were even more of a problem.[26]

Some of the overall statistical decline resulted from tighter maintenance standards, imposed by PACAF, which ended shortcuts in inspections and the practice of deferring minor repairs. The effects of the new policy were salutary but maintenance work increased appreciably. General Herring in October 1970 informed the Seventh Air Force that the airlift force had been long overcommitted and that mission schedules should be reduced. Extra C–130s were accordingly brought to Vietnam and the daily schedule cut down to use only eighty percent of the aircraft in-country instead of ninety.[27]

Sgt. Dannie B. Needham of the 377th Supply Squadron at Tan Son Nhut, checks a valve on a 6,000-gallon fuel bladder inside the C–130 aircraft.

Two major materiel problems afflicted the C–123 force; both caused major accidents, and both temporarily limited the force's effectiveness. Inspections following a fatal accident in August 1970 revealed widespread cracking in flap fittings, caused by metal fatigue. Interim repairs were made, but an additional failure in late 1971 brought prohibitions against landing at short airstrips pending installation of new fittings at all critical points. Even more alarming were cracks in nose landing-gear struts discovered in February 1971. Such cracks were responsible for loss of an aircraft the following month. The nose gear took great stress in the hard landings

TACTICAL AIRLIFT

necessitated by short fields, and bore much of the force of deceleration during the landing roll. Again interim remedies proved insufficient. Another accident in July triggered the decision to require a special preflight inspection prior to landing at any short or rough field. The series of materiel problems boded trouble ahead when, as planned, the Vietnamese took over the aging C–123s.[28]

The special circumstances confronting transport aircraft maintenance in Southeast Asia—offshore C–130 basing and the short tour lengths for personnel—produced several nonstandard arrangements. The C–130 wings in 1969 established centralized maintenance squadrons, replacing centralized branches in the 314th and 463d Wings and a decentralized squadron system in the 374th. Most participants agreed that a centralized organization permitted the best use of available talent. The arrangement at the in-country operating locations, mixing permanent supervisory cadres from the 834th with temporarily assigned work personnel from off shore, drew criticism from both groups. Additional permanent personnel were authorized in the spring of 1969, but any change to full permanent manning was ruled out by overall troop-reduction goals. In addition skill levels were low. Among the ninety-nine permanently assigned supervisors in the Tan Son Nhut detachment in August 1970, fifty-three had no previous C–130 experience. Among all units the short-tour policy limited overall experience and hurt continuity, but it made tolerable the severe demands on individuals. The 315th Wing materiel chief noted that after twelve months most men were tired from the continuous grind and were no longer fully productive.[29]

Maintenance men often were flown to outlying locations to recover aircraft grounded by malfunctions or battle damage. Two of these episodes became legendary. One C–130 spent six weeks on the ground at An Hoa, damaged repeatedly by periodic shelling. A maintenance team from Air Force Logistics Command, assisted by 314th Wing personnel, installed two new wings, four engines, and five props, to enable it to be flown out on March 22, 1969. New "quick save" procedures, featuring preassembled equipment kits and the presence of a maintenance expert in the airlift control center, helped in the recovery of another C–130 caught at Bu Dop on November 28, 1969. Jury-rigged repairs, completed in two days under continued shelling, permitted a three-engine takeoff and a successful landing at Tan Son Nhut even though the plane was riddled with more than a thousand shrapnel holes.[30]

The airlift wings experienced some of the racial tensions characterizing the nation's society and the whole military establishment. Colonel Blood described how casual remarks in 315th Wing were often interpreted in a racial context and how satisfaction of one request usually led to several more, approaching the unreasonable. Blood on one occasion took rapid action to head off a rumored march on the wing headquarters, but otherwise found it wise to move carefully while maintaining open dialogue with young blacks. At Ching Chuan Kang Air Base a series of racially related incidents in the summer of 1971 caused Col. Andrew P. Iosue, commanding the 374th Wing, to institute direct channels for complaints to himself. He insisted that subordinate unit commanders open communications with potential dissidents and make appearances at offbase trouble spots to tone down incidents. Racial difficulties appeared to be nonexistent among aircrew personnel. Aircrews also remained relatively uninvolved in illegal drug usage, and the crewmen found the antidrug inspections of aircraft and baggage an annoyance, especially upon returning to offshore bases after arduous duty in Vietnam.[31]

Billeting and messing facilities at the in-country bases gradually improved. Officers at Phan Rang lived in air-conditioned and landscaped quarters, enlisted men in two-story barracks. But water shortages caused some inconveniences when aircrews returning from missions late in the day were unable to shower. At Tan Son Nhut all C-130 crewmen at last received onbase billets. Crews nevertheless preferred duty at Cam Ranh Bay where the climate was better, the airspace less congested, and the long-awaited barracks on the west side comfortable.[32]

Morale in the airlift units continued to be buoyed by a widespread sense of responsibility and achievement. The Seventh Air Force inspector general reported in December 1969 that morale in the 315th Wing was exemplary and discipline problems nonexistent. Voluntary extensions of oversea tours among air and ground crewmen of 463d Wing were numerous, except among loadmasters. Matters were less satisfactory at Ching Chuan Kang where most men were separated from their families and where tour length had been raised to fifteen months (up from thirteen months in 1968). General Germeraad found that his own assignment was most rewarding, and was convinced that those at all levels of his command took pride in what they were doing. The 315th and the 463d Wings both received the Air Force Outstanding Unit Award (the 315th's fifth since 1962), for periods ending respectively in June 1969 and May 1971.[33]

Progress slowed both the low-altitude parachute and the ground proximity extraction cargo delivery methods, LAPES and GPES. LAPES capabilities declined in the Pacific C-130 wings, but twelve crews retained their qualifications for the 1528 LAPES technique, introduced in Vietnam in 1968, that permitted tandem extraction of two LAPES platforms, each bearing nine-ton loads. Operational LAPES sorties in Vietnam occurred in surges: five in February 1969, eleven in December, and eight in March

1970. The December missions delivered fuel to support Army helicopter operations at delta airstrips and, except for one load destroyed by fire, the effort was successful. The 1970 missions delivered fuel to a delta airstrip temporarily isolated by runway deterioration and mined highways. In both cases, Chinook helicopters retrieved the LAPES platforms and rigging items for reuse. Hardware shortages discouraged use of LAPES elsewhere however. Only forty-four sets were on hand in June 1969, against a requirement for sixty. The U.S. Army riggers left Vietnam in 1971, but Air Force riggers at Ching Chuan Kang could rig for LAPES in an emergency. By the summer of 1971 the number of qualified LAPES aircrews in the E–model wing was down to two, regarded as an instructor cadre available to train other crews.[34] The GPES method was abandoned entirely in Vietnam although the A–model wing flew occasional practice missions off shore. GPES equipment remaining in country was returned to supply channels in 1971 for disposition.[35]

Further testing and development of the extraction idea went on in the United States although U.S. Army interest appeared half-hearted. Joint tests of the 1528 LAPES commenced at Pope Air Force Base in January 1969. After four months, thirty-nine extraction deliveries had been made including successful deliveries of fuel and ammunition. Damage was insignificant except in the case of LAPES-delivered vehicles. Testing resumed in October using improved rigging methods. The final Air Force test report in early 1970 concluded that 1528 LAPES could significantly augment delivery systems, but the Army disagreed, contending that LAPES was unsuitable for Army use and should be given no further consideration. The two services agreed, however, in September 1970, that 1528 LAPES was suitable to augment other systems for delivery of bulk supplies and "selected" vehicles. Funding for procurement of hardware, an Army responsibility, was not forthcoming, reflecting general budgetary stringency. But in early 1972, after TAC recommended further testing, the Army redirected funds for another round of joint tests.[36]

Progress in all-weather parachute capabilities was more encouraging. The techniques for drops directed by ground radar, first tested in 1967, were codified in a Seventh Air Force operation order of July 1969. The techniques were for use by Air Force transport crews in conjunction with either Air Force MSQ–77 Skyspot or Marine TPQ–10 radars. Published tables gave ballistics data for various aircraft, parachute, and cargo-weight combinations. A joint operational evaluation of the ground radar air delivery system (GRADS) was made in Vietnam in January and February 1970 by aircrews of the 463d Wing and the 101st Airborne Division. The test included thirty-three drops, most of them in actual instrument conditions from altitudes between four thousand and seven thousand feet. Guidance was by Skyspot radar, using voice communications and procedures like those developed to deliver the BLU–82 weapon. Average circular error was under two hundred yards. Emergency supply deliveries to the 101st Division were made by the GRADS technique the following October and in January 1971. All bundles were recoverable in the October effort but only half in January. General Herring later in 1971 recommended that the GRADS method be refined, especially to be able to deliver smaller loads tailored to support eight-man patrols.

GRADS missions were flown at altitudes considerably above normal in order to assure line-of-sight contact between aircraft and radar station. Parachute systems for high-altitude releases were of two designs. The HALO (high-altitude, low-opening) type was best for load survivability. A standard parachute was used, rigged to descend in reefed condition for a predetermined time, controlled between twenty and sixty seconds. When the chute opened, the bundle descended at normal velocity. In contrast, a high-velocity rigging system was more accurate and less prone to malfunctions. A slotted parachute stabilized the load during descent and assured that the cushioned underside of the load hit the ground first. The rate of fall was not much slower than by free fall. Both the HALO and the high-velocity methods were applicable to the GRADS or to any other high-altitude technique designed to minimize exposure to ground fire.[37]

TAC also focused on development of the adverse-weather aerial delivery system, designed to allow C–130s to make blind drops without external assistance. AWADS ships carried a dual-frequency, forward-looking radar, affording the navigator improved electronic vision over that provided by the APN–59. The navigator positioned electronic crosshairs on his actual or an offset aiming point. The system included a digital computer that made ballistic calculations which provided steering and distance information to the computed release point. The computer also assisted in navigating to en route checkpoints. Subsystems automatically introduced flight information into the computer, including doppler-measured ground speed and drift. TAC planned that those C–130s not receiving the full AWADS would be modified with stationkeeping equipment to allow crews to trail an AWADS-equipped pathfinder.

AWADS crew training commenced in the C–130 wing at Little Rock Air Force Base, Ark., in late 1970, and by year's end over three hundred drops had been made. Tactical testing at Little Rock and Pope ended in June 1971 after having attained an acceptable median circular error of just over two hundred yards. Aborts because of equipment malfunctions were frequent however. Further testing in 1971 evaluated AWADS in polar regions and for drops from altitudes above five thousand feet. The higher altitudes afforded better radar vision without serious decline in impact accuracy. Prompted by General Herring's recommendation, the Seventh Air Force in June 1971 requested that PACAF consider assigning several

AWADS ships to the Pacific for use in resupply or BLU–82 drops. The aircraft were not sent in 1971, but TAC crews did demonstrate AWADS equipment during North Atlantic Treaty Organization maneuvers in October.[38]

Officers of the 834th Air Division and the 16th Special Operations Squadron (equipped with AC–130 gunships at Ubon, Thailand) joined in exploring a different approach to the all-weather airdrop problem. The gunships were equipped with loran precision navigation systems and acted as pathfinders for cargo-carrying C–130s. The drop plane or planes could fly close visual formation on the pathfinder or use their own limited radar station keeping capability to trail at several thousand feet. Another possibility was to use the gunship's infrared light to illuminate a darkened drop zone and equip the cargo carriers with simple infrared detectors. The Seventh Air Force in July 1971 authorized trials of these concepts on certain gunship missions. The wish to make fullest possible use of the gunships in interdiction work, however, resulted in a decision the following month to stop further trials and to regard the method as an emergency expedient only.[39]

Testing of the portable instrument tactical landing approach radar landing system (TALAR IV) was completed in 1969, and pilots expressed full confidence in the system's accuracy and reliability. A combat control team could set up and align the equipment at the approach end of an airstrip in less than one hour. 834th Air Division transports began to receive TALAR components in late 1970, and by April 1971 all C–7s and half the C–123 force were modified. Caribou crews made over eight hundred TALAR approaches to Cam Ranh Bay and reported excellent results. C–123 and C–130 crews began using TALAR later in the year. The 834th Division recognized, however, that an additional navigation aid was needed to guide the aircrew to the TALAR pickup point (ten to fifteen miles out), and recommended portable tactical air navigation equipment for this purpose. Although TALAR was not sent to forward airheads in Vietnam, it appeared applicable for future conflicts. Use of TALAR for positioning during airdrops was tested at the tactical airlift center in 1970.[40]

These and other technical developments since 1961 reflected the Air Force's determination to improve combat-zone capabilities of the tactical airlift force. The impetus came from the experiences and needs of the Southeast Asia war, reinforced by earlier competition with the Army over roles. A special system, whereby the Seventh Air Force and PACAF officially specified their needs in formal Southeast Asia operational requirement documents, helped assure responsive action in the stateside commands. But more sweeping advances, such as developing and procuring a new generation of transport craft with vertical takeoff and landing potentialities, rested on decisions of national military and budgetary policy.

The number of detachments and operating locations under the 2d Aerial Port Group and its three squadrons declined from forty-two in early 1969 to seven at the end of 1971. Port functions at many of the deactivating sites were turned over to Vietnamese Air Force terminal personnel, usually after a period of overlap. Upon inactivation of the 834th Air Division in late 1971, the 2d Aerial Port Group functioned directly under the Seventh Air Force, which included an aerial port division under its new directorate of airlift.[41]

The quest for efficiency was unceasing. Aerial port officers were instrumental in introducing the twelve-hour (rather than twenty-four hour) schedule in 1969. To win confidence among shippers and to reduce excessive use of high priorities, port officers stressed reforms designed to move routine cargo in reasonable time. The average backlog of overage cargo (on hand more than two days) declined from sixteen percent in 1969 to under ten percent in late 1971.[42]

The application of data automation to aerial port activity (like the airlift management system of which it was a part) proved disappointing. Port personnel prepared a separate data card for each loaded pallet awaiting movement, and each card required fifteen items of information. The chore was especially burdensome since the old cargo backlog reports were still required. Late in 1970 the four principal ports received punchcard equipment, housed in modernized and air-conditioned buildings. Port management thus became "fully mechanized." This resulted in marginal improvements to local documenting but none to overall traffic flow. Aerial port personnel viewed the decision to return to manual reporting in September 1971 with satisfaction. In contrast, the mechanization of reporting between the aerial ports in Vietnam and the out-of-country MAC system appeared worthwhile, because the relationship was less variable than that among the more dynamic in-country port operations.[43]

The installation of an exclusive aerial port radio net was more successful. Single-sideband, high-frequency radios were placed at thirty-eight sites during 1969–70, linking the port detachments, the parent squadrons, and the traffic managers at the control center. This net ended reliance on landline communications, which had proven hopeless for exchanging immediate load information. Another successful piece of equipment was the ten thousand-pound, diesel-powered, four-wheel drive adverse terrain forklift. A shipment of sixteen arrived in early 1970, in time for strenuous service during the Cambodian campaign and proving, according to General Herring, "the backbone of forward area operations." Moreover, the arrival

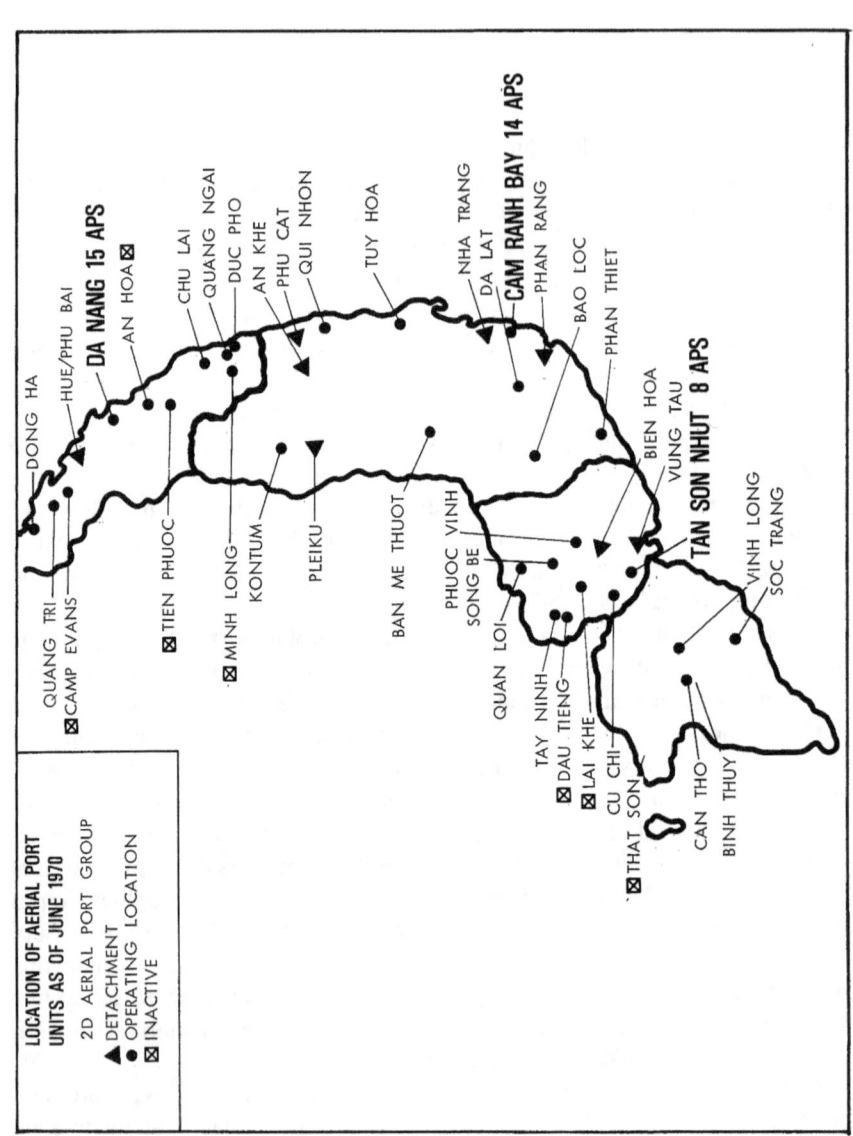

AIRLIFT SYSTEM, 1969–1971

U.S. military personnel board a commercial airliner at the Da Nang Aerial Port, for transportation back to the States, June 1970.

Aerial view of a C–5 Galaxy, with visor raised, preparing for off-loading at Cam Ranh Bay, September 1970. The new strategic transport had three times the cargo capacity of the C–141.

Searching for illicit materials, Mr. B. J. Lewis of the Department of Agriculture shows TSgt. Phillip Lewis what to look for when inspecting cargo bound for the U.S., July 1970.

of several dozen sets of shrapnel-resistant forklift tires in May 1970 increased forklift effectiveness. Whereas in the Cambodian campaign twenty-four tire changes had been required, the new foam-filled tires withstood a week of shelling at Kham Duc in July with only a single flat. Forklift maintenance, however, continued to be a chronic problem, requiring the assistance of logistic repair teams at Tan Son Nhut, Cam Ranh, and Da Nang. Although teams from the transportation squadrons attempted preventive and emergency maintenance at the outlying fields, incommission rates held barely above a marginally satisfactory seventy-five percent. The problems eased only upon the drawdown of equipment, which allowed retention of only the newer units.[44]

In-country port operations reflected the changing character of the war itself. Except during the Cambodian and Laotian incursions, aerial port mobility teams were seldom sent to active forward airheads. New tasks grew from programs against illicit drug traffic. Passengers, baggage, and cargo moving to destinations out of the country were searched carefully. In-country missions required less care, but aerial port and aircrew personnel habitually watched for evidence of drug shipments, the presence of explosive materials, or hijackers. Increased port efforts followed the introduction of the C–5A to the transpacific routes. The new strategic transport, with triple the payload capability of the C–141, first landed at Cam Ranh Bay on July 9, 1970. MAC opposed landing the C–5s at other points in Vietnam because of congestion and unsatisfactory facilities, so reshipments by C–130 out of Cam Ranh increased. Also, cargo arriving by C–5 (unlike C–141 loads) usually required repalletizing for C–130 loading.[45]

The men of the aerial port system followed the traditions established earlier. Some of the senior aerial port noncommissioned officers (NCOs) served second and even third tours in Southeast Asia, made necessary by Air Force-wide shortages in their career fields. On-the-job training was an unending way of life in all ports. Despite strenuous official emphasis on safety, accidents were frequent. During the spring of 1971, for example, the 2d Group reported sixty-three accidents, with six disabling injuries and one fatality. Instances of valor continued to accumulate. In 1969 the 15th Squadron alone was responsible for three such episodes. Five members of the 15th courageously rescued survivors from the wreckage of an Army craft downed at Kontum. One member of the squadron's Qui Nhon detachment was killed and three others wounded seriously while defending their positions during a night enemy penetration. Two NCOs were evacuated with wounds received during shelling at Tien Phuoc. Recognition for these and many other episodes of valor took the form of awards to individuals, repeated awards to squadrons by the National Defense Transportation Association, and a second award of the Air Force Presidential Unit Citation to the 2d Group and its squadrons as part of the 834th Air

Division, for action during the spring 1970 campaign. (The first award was for operations during the 1968 Tet offensive.)[46]

The history of the aerial port units during these years thus paralleled that of the whole airlift system. The period was one of declining workload, planned strength reductions, diminishing activity of a tactical nature, and moderate improvements in efficiency. The patterns of aerial port organization and operations developed in the earlier years changed only slightly. However, port activities again demonstrated that an effective theater airlift system depends not only on transport aircraft and aircrews, but on substantial and efficient maintenance, managerial, and aerial port functions.

(Frances Walter, Courtesy U.S. Air Force Art Collection)

Rescue—1969 Style.

XIX. The Campaigns of 1969-1971, Cambodia and the Panhandle

Combat airlift operations during and after 1969 were largely episodic, lacking the sustained and sometimes desperate character of 1968. The several emergency and forward area lifts, however, were valued contributions to the allied war effort and demonstrated the Air Force's continuing ability to undertake tactical missions.

Two major cross-border campaigns highlighted the ground war: the 1970 incursion into Cambodia and the 1971 venture into Laos. In both the Air Force airlifters sustained a high-volume effort, primarily hauling to airstrips in the border regions of South Vietnam. During the Cambodian campaign the transports landed at a number of forward fields, hauling in troops, equipment, and supplies. Further movement into Cambodia was primarily by helicopter. In 1971 the C-130s landed at the old Khe Sanh base, although disappointing delays in runway rehabilitation limited the extent of the Air Force contribution. Cargo drops and extractions were for emergency use only, because they involved too much cargo-handling effort at the receiving end for routine use in mobile ground operations.

Modest-scale airlift operations continued into Cambodia after the withdrawal of American troops from that country in mid-1970. Airlanded deliveries into Phnom Penh supplemented surface lines of communications, while airdrops intermittently supplied isolated units in the eastern half of the country. Domestic American opposition to participation in Cambodia accounted for the dominant Vietnamese role in the Cambodian lifts, and gave urgency to programs to strengthen the small Cambodian Air Force airlift arm.

Widespread communist attacks on the night of February 22/23, 1969, recalled the 1968 Tet offensive. Several emergency airlifts helped stop the enemy's bid, including a series of C-130 LAPES deliveries at the Tien Phuoc dirt airstrip south of Da Nang. The war's first C-130 night drop took place on the third night when an A-model crew under Capt. Curtis L. Messex released fifteen cargo bundles over the runway at besieged Ben Het west of Dak To.[1] Meanwhile, Air Force and Marine C-130 drops supported renewed ground operations in the A Shau Valley, and Air Force C-7s landed on the valley's fifteen hundred-foot clay runway at Ta Bat, opened by U.S. Army engineers on June 13, 1969.[2] Two months later, the C-130s spearheaded a new campaign shifting forces quickly into Bu Dop,

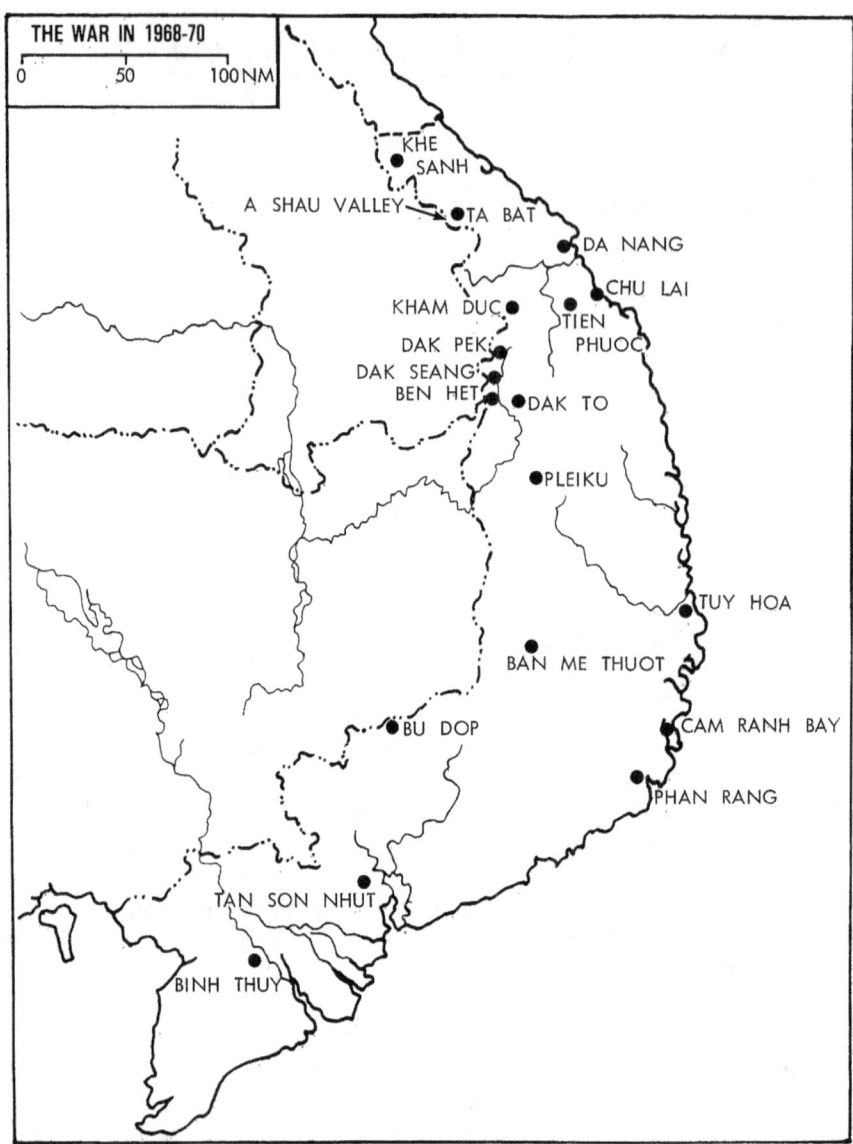

a twenty-four hundred-foot strip at the Cambodian fishhook. Deliveries of supplies and construction equipment continued through year's end, always threatened by enemy mortar fire. On three occasions, C–130s made successful three-engine takeoffs to avoid prolonged exposure on the ground at Bu Dop. Disaster struck on the fourth try, December 13, and the victim became the only C–130 lost in a major accident in Southeast Asia during 1969–71.[3]

The 1970 Cambodian campaign included intensive operations into border airstrips. A reminder of past search-and-destroy applications took place in the summer of 1970 when the allies returned to the historic Kham Duc airstrip. The object of this multibrigade operation was to interdict enemy communications and destroy forces in the mountainous border region. Allied heliborne units seized the airfield and nearby terrain on July 12, meeting no significant opposition. The airfield appeared untouched since the May 1968 evacuation, and some items of ordnance and construction equipment were found in salvageable condition. Runway rehabilitation began promptly, and on July 17, C-123s made twenty-seven landings on the available twenty-five hundred feet bringing in troops, equipment, and supplies. The strip meanwhile was lengthened to thirty-five hundred feet, permitting twelve C-130 landings the following day. The C-123s and C-130s thereafter continued daily deliveries of rations, ammunition, and large quantities of helicopter fuel. On the ground at Kham Duc were an Air Force mission commander, a combat control team, and a team from the 15th Aerial Port Squadron.

Crews landing at Kham Duc made steep, circling approaches and departures which minimized exposure to ground fire. Communist shellings occasionally delayed or prevented landings. Other traffic delays resulted from bunched arrivals, disabled aircraft on the runway, and the necessity of sharing airspace with helicopters and active artillery—conditions typical of forward area operations. The airstrip closed down on August 26 after withdrawal of most materiel, but the withdrawal was marred by the loss to enemy fire of a Chinook with thirty-one persons. In all, Air Force airlifters made 648 landings at Kham Duc—243 by C-130, 402 by C-123, and 3 by Caribou, bringing in over forty-three hundred troops and twenty-six hundred tons of cargo, mainly from Chu Lai. Overall results of the operation were intangible since allied ground troops made few major contacts with the enemy.[4]

The general decline in tactical activity was unmistakable. Most unit movements were routine, in many cases entailing troop and equipment lifts to major terminals for departure from Vietnam. Every six months the C-130s made some one hundred round trips between Saigon and Bangkok, rotating units of the Royal Thai volunteer force. Although a standing Seventh Air Force operation plan prescribed procedures for airborne assault operations, there were no actual paratroop operations. Frequent practice missions, however, assisted in training Vietnamese troopers. Bladderbird aerial tanker missions did not decline until 1971, the usefulness of the C-130 in the fuel-delivery role having won acceptance. Reducing the aircraft's wing tank fuel raised C-130 payloads by as much as ten thousand pounds over the previous standard twenty-six thousand-pound loading. The bladderbird missions were also valuable in allowing pilots to practice shortfield, heavyweight landing skills.[5]

Responsibilities for emergency supply drops generally shifted to the

A C-130 begins a sharp climb after take-off, in order to avoid enemy ground fire at Kham Duc, August 1970.

At Kham Duc, Vietnam, a combat control team backs its jeep onto a C-130 aircraft, August 11, 1970. The airstrip was closed on 26 August.

Combat controllers from the 8th Aerial Port coordinate air traffic at Kham Duc.

Air Force Caribous. C-123s flew a series of thirty-one drops at hard-pressed and isolated Dak Seang in April 1970, but thereafter C-123s and C-130s made only about ten drop sorties monthly countrywide. Aircrew proficiency declined through disuse, and in the summer of 1971 MACV decreed that only twenty percent of the C-130 crews in Vietnam needed to be drop qualified. The U.S. Army riggers were withdrawn in increments from Vietnam, reducing daily rigging capacity from 250 tons in 1969 to one hundred tons in late 1970. Additional riggers and equipment remained available on short notice from Okinawa. Upon its withdrawal in January 1972, the Army's 109th Quartermaster Company transferred parachutes and rigging materials to the Vietnamese Air Force's 90th Parachute Maintenance and Delivery Base Unit located at Tan Son Nhut. The latter unit thus acquired material sufficient to rig a total of six hundred tons of cargo.[6]

The reductions in tactical airlift paralleled the reduced use of ground forces in airmobile operations. U.S. Army helicopter airlift sorties, which had totaled 355,000 in May 1969, declined to 54,000 in February 1972. Helicopter losses in the 1971 Laos campaign raised new questions as to the role of airmobile forces in midintensity conflict. Plans to retain two airmobile divisions in the United States, however, made it clear that the airmobile idea remained very much alive and implied future roles for the fixed-wing transports much like those of Vietnam.[7]

Airlifters understood well the allied decision to enter Cambodia. Over past years, transport crews made countless landings and drops in border regions of Vietnam, supporting operations against communist forces sustained from Cambodian soil. Airlifters thus were well aware of the danger of hostile fire from across the border. The Cambodian incursion became the most sweeping allied offensive venture of the war to date, an exhilarating moment in a war which since 1968 had been formless.

The penetrations into Cambodia were along three fronts. Several divisions crossed on the right wing at the latitude of Pleiku and Ban Me Thuot. Over fifty South Vietnamese battalions entered on the left in the Mekong Delta country. Operations in the center stretched from Tay Ninh to Bu Dop and included the forested fishook sector. Penetrating the center sectors were five U.S. Army brigades, including most of 1st Cavalry Division, along with substantial Vietnamese forces. On all three fronts, surprise seemed complete, the enemy reportedly reacting as a "confused, milling crowd." Through the months of May and June, allied forces continued search-and-destroy operations in Cambodia, seizing sizable quantities of

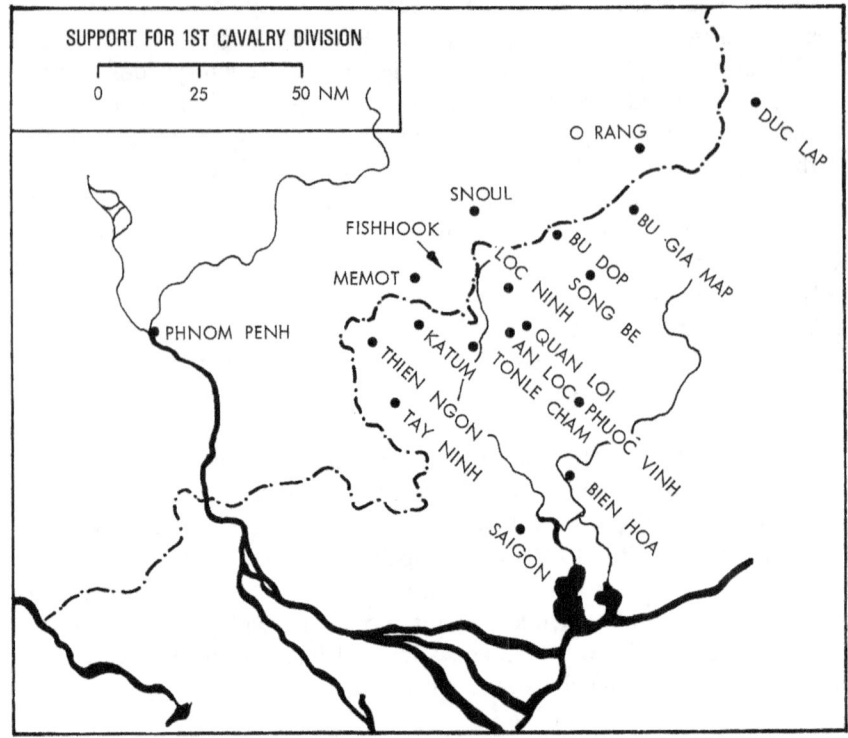

war materials at negligible cost in casualties. U.S. Army penetrations were limited to seventeen miles and ended upon withdrawal of the last American troops on June 30.[8]

The campaign presented a major challenge to allied logisticians. Lines of communications were stretched farther than in the past, extending from the ports and depots across Vietnam to the several sectors of operations. Truck convoys reached past the old road terminals to forward support bases near the border, and in some cases to units inside Cambodia. Consumption of munitions and petroleum products severely strained overall truck capacity, so air transport became an essential supplement for bulk deliveries to more than a dozen border airstrips.[9]

By far the heaviest use of Air Force airlift came in support of the 1st Cavalry Division and its attached forces. The cavalry first penetrated into the fishhook on May 1 with instructions to make "maximum use of forward airfields and fixed-wing airlift" for logistic support. During the first five days in the fishhook, the division's lines of communication from Saigon were both by air, as into Katum, and by road, as to Tay Ninh, Quan Loi, and Loc Ninh. Katum was for a time supplied by air exclusively. Helicopter refueling and rearming points were established at Katum, Loc Ninh, and between them at the Tonle Cham airstrip.

The division gradually shifted operations northeastward. After May 4, stocks were allowed to decrease at Katum and Tonle Cham and were instead built up at Loc Ninh and Bu Dop. Operations about O Rang after May 9 were supported from Bu Dop and Bu Gia Map, both used by helicopters for refueling and both primarily supplied by air. C–130s also delivered supplies to the all-weather Song Be field fifteen miles from the border, often diverted there because of rainfall at other strips. Redistribution from these airheads to units across the border was usually by CH–47 and CH–54.

Air deliveries for the cavalry consisted primarily of petroleum and ammunition. The division recorded that during the month of May C–130s made 329 petroleum-carrying sorties into Katum, 181 into Bu Dop, 325 into Song Be, and 90 into Bu Gia Map. The Air Force hauled into these four fields a total of 3.7 million gallons, nearly all the fuel for the cavalry's helicopters. Road movements of petroleum meanwhile exceeded six million gallons, most of it to the less advanced bases at Quan Loi, Tay Ninh, and Phuoc Vinh. Munitions shipments originated at the Army's Long Binh depot, near Bien Hoa. When loading space at Bien Hoa became saturated, a second loading point was set up at Long Thanh North airfield where an Air Force aerial port team palletized and loaded three hundred tons of munitions daily. Stocks were kept low at the border airstrips; in many cases, loads brought in by C–130 were immediately picked up by helicopter for delivery at firebases in Cambodia.[10]

For the aircrews, priority missions and lengthy extensions of crew-duty time became normal. The C–130 in-country fleet increased from fifty at the end of April to seventy a week later; the Tan Son Nhut element grew to twenty-nine ships, the largest number in more than a year. Air Force personnel on the ground at the border airfields—principally members of combat control and aerial port mobility teams—endured privations and hazards typical of field duty. One combat control team member, Sgt. Sidney E. Toups, became a celebrity for accepting the surrender of a dozen communists who appeared unexpectedly at the end of a dirt, border-area airstrip.[11]

Airfield improvement and repair work was critical to the activity. U.S. Army engineers, including those assigned to the cavalry division, early in the campaign worked on the Katum and Thien Ngon fields west of the fishhook. Although soon heavily occupied in highway repair and construction of forward facilities, the engineers labored over fifty thousand man-hours on the Bu Gia Map, Bu Dop, and Loc Ninh airstrips. Daily maintenance kept the fields open most of the time. Most difficult to keep up was the fair-weather-only laterite strip at Bu Gia Map, which required an average engineer effort of four platoon-hours daily. After each moderate rain the ramp and runway needed about three hours drying time before recompaction.[12]

TACTICAL AIRLIFT

Air Force transports made only a few deliveries inside Cambodia in the central sector. Suitable airstrips were not immediately at hand, nor were direct deliveries needed in view of the cavalry's shallow depth of penetration. Starting on May 23, Air Force C-7s landed at a sixteen hundred-foot strip at O Rang, lifting in over 250 tons of passengers, fuel, and dry cargo, in 169 sorties. Only moderate upgrading of the grassed strip had been required. Three C-130s of the 314th Wing made drops at a nearby fire support base on May 27, successfully delivering forty-four tons of ammunition.[13]

A special problem was the rearward transport of materiel captured by the cavalry in Cambodia. Generally, enemy items were hauled by truck and helicopter from Cambodia to collecting points at the forward support bases for lift-out by C-130s returning from supply missions. Weights were a matter of guesswork, and crews became wary about accepting doubtful loads. After one C-130 barely managed takeoff from Bu Gia Map, one pallet was discovered to weigh double the estimated amount—the pilot on this occasion had wisely declined to accept yet another additional pallet. Ground delays in loading the captured materiel were especially troublesome at Bu Gia Map where tight ramp space permitted only one plane on the ground at a time.[14]

Airlift operations supporting the northern front were less massive. Supply buildup and helicopter refueling facilities were established at Plei Djereng airfield ten miles from the border west of Pleiku. These facilities sustained two U.S. infantry brigades helicoptered into Cambodia on and after May 5. Stocking at Plei Djereng and resupply were principally by road, although C-7s, C-123s, and C-130s made over a hundred landings. On two occasions, with jet fuel running low, C-130 bladderbird deliveries were instituted. Operations west of Plei Djereng fell behind schedule, in part because the initial troop movement from An Khe (originally planned by C-130) was changed at the last minute to a road move. Further, the field proved too small for simultaneous fixed-wing and helicopter operations, and helicopter traffic frequently was halted temporarily to permit fixed-wing landings. The border airstrip at Duc Co served as a forward base supporting Vietnamese forces. Task units moved to Duc Co by C-130 and truck on May 4 and 5, commencing air assaults into Cambodia on the fifth. Air Force transports—mainly C-130s and C-7s—made eighty-four sorties into Duc Co, supplementing the predominantly landlines of communications. Vietnamese Air Force and U.S. Army helicopters joined in redistribution work out of Duc Co.[15]

A highlight of the Cambodian operation was the air evacuation of refugees from besieged points northeast of the country. Driven from the border areas, the communists acted quickly to seize most towns in the region; by mid-June only two government enclaves remained—at Ba Kev and at Boung Long, seventeen and thirty-two miles respectively from the

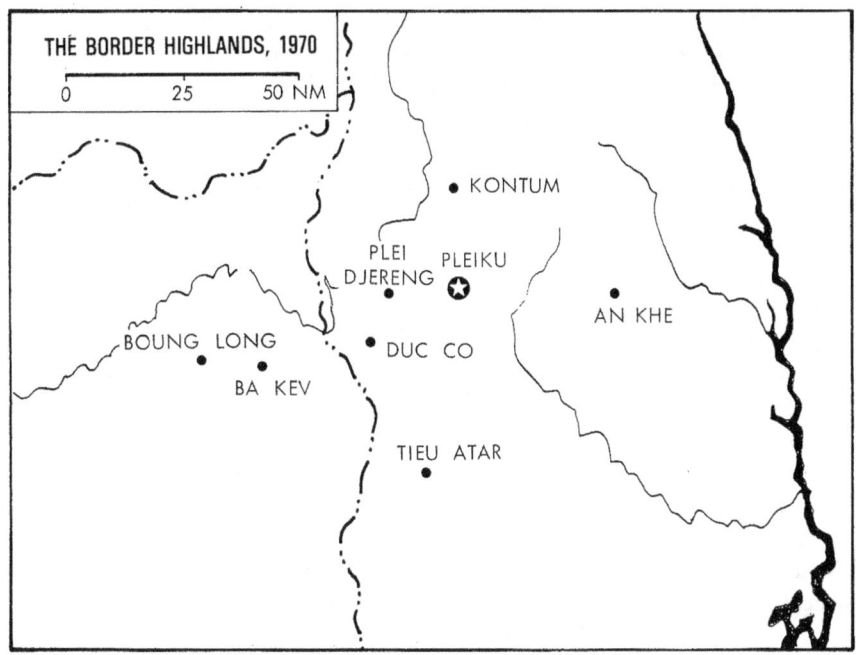

Vietnamese border. Allied teams had been lifted to both points and had helped organize resistance, supported by airdrops by Duck Hook C–123s. It appeared that both garrisons, although determined to resist, would soon be overcome. The troop units were capable of moving overland to safety, but evacuation of the local civilians remained a problem. A Vietnamese one-regiment relief force formed at Duc Co was moved from its coastal base in sixteen C–130 sorties. Relief force elements moved by helicopter from Duc Co to the two Cambodian strongpoints, while the main body proceeded westward by road.

The 834th Air Division learned of the evacuation plan on June 22. Since neither Ba Kev nor Boung Long airfield had been used previously by 834th aircraft, survey teams flew in by C–7 before dusk that evening. Both strips were of laterite, and both were more than thrity-three hundred feet in length. Based on the surveys, the decision was made to attempt the evacuation using C–123s rather than Caribous to take advantage of the 123's greater passenger capacity and the reliability promised by their auxiliary jets. C–7s were left on standby. On the morning of the twenty-third, after several hours of delay caused by rainfall and low visibility, C–7s lifted airlift mission commanders and combat control teams into the two evacuation points. Meanwhile three C–123s took off from home stations for the first pickups. The three landed and made safe departures, but it was clear that the rain-soaked laterite was too soft for further C–123 landings.

Accordingly the effort became entirely a C–7 one, and by nightfall Caribou crews had withdrawn 542 refugees from the two points.

Enemy fire prevented resumption of the airlift from Ba Kev the next morning, and the control team there was withdrawn by helicopter. The Boung Long evacuation continued, however, and by evening of the twenty-fourth another twenty-five hundred refugees had been lifted out to Pleiku. The communists nearly overran the camp during the night, and at dawn Capt. Palmer G. Arnold earned the Silver Star by flying out the last C–7 under small-arms fire. In all, the C–7s lifted out thirty-one hundred refugees in forty-five sorties, an average of sixty-nine passengers per load (twenty-four was the nominal maximum) without loss. In addition, Vietnamese Air Force C–47s and C–119s made landings at both Cambodian fields prior to the heavy rainfall. The garrison and the last two hundred civilians moved overland to Ba Kev by road on June 25 and by road and helicopter from Ba Kev to Duc Co. Most of the Cambodian troops, after reequipping and retraining, eventually returned to Cambodia.[16]

Supply for operations on the southern front was almost entirely a Vietnamese effort. American logisticians were pleased at the Vietnamese success in establishing forward supply bases and in sustaining high-volume supply. U.S. Air Force Caribous operated into the forward bases at Moc Hoa, Chau Doc, and four other border strips; C–123s made over two hundred landings at Moc Hoa. Air shipments included .50-caliber ammunition and repair parts for armored personnel carriers. Supply into the Parrot's Beak (west of Saigon) was by road from Saigon. Inside Cambodia the Parrot's Beak forces joined the Mekong River force at Neak Luong, where a ferry links the Saigon-Phnom Penh highway as it crosses the Mekong. A major forward base was developed at this point, and construction of an airfield for light aircraft was under way at mid-June.[17]

In summary, the Air Force airlift contribution to the Cambodian campaign was substantial. In the two months starting April 30, 834th Air Division transports delivered 75,000 passengers and 49,600 tons of cargo to twenty-two border airstrips. Of the combined passenger and cargo tonnage, C–130s delivered sixty-seven percent, C–123s twenty-two percent, and the Caribous eleven percent. Ninety percent was delivered to the ten airstrips along the fishhook and adjoining sectors, mainly for support of the 1st Cavalry Division. The division unreservedly praised the performance and élan of the Air Force airlifters.[18]

The supply effort had been launched with little advance notice and took advantage of the complex of remote area airstrips developed, and intermittently used, in previous years. Only a single transport (a Caribou) was lost. The airlift served two fundamental purposes—to extend lines of communications to the border points beyond highway limitations, and to add a capacity for fast emergency response. Only in rare instances, however, was airlift absolutely indispensable, since road communications were

Capt. Palmer G. Arnold receives the Silver Star from Vice President Spiro T. Agnew and Vice President Nguyen Cao Ky in flightline ceremonies at Tan Son Nhut. The C-7 Caribou pilot was honored for flying out the last group of Cambodian refugees under small-arms fire, June 25, 1970.

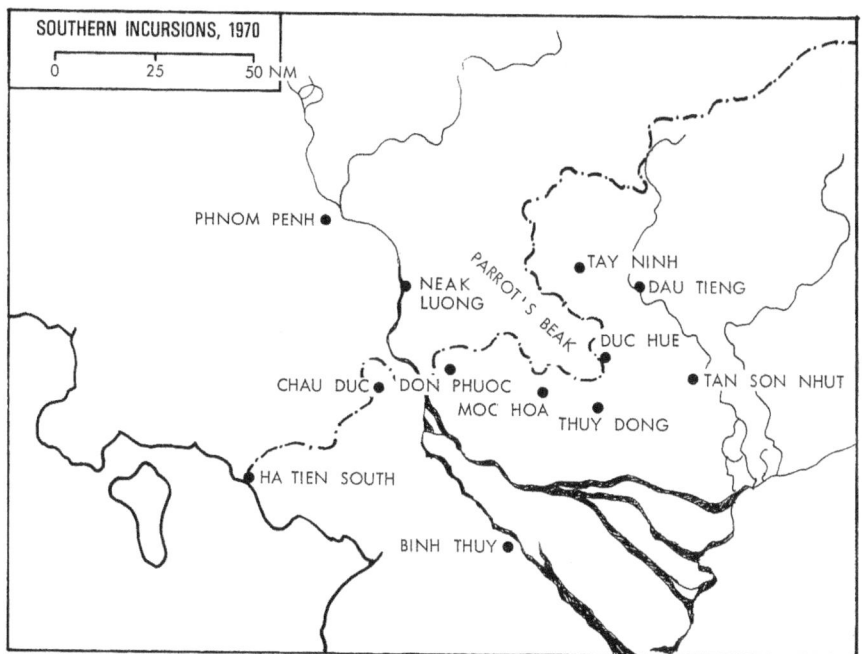

834th Air Division Support of Cambodian Operations, April 30–June 30, 1970

Border Airfield	Most Tons Delivered by:		Sector	Total Cargo & Pax Tonnage
1. Song Be	C–130		1st Cav Div	16,490
2. Bu Dop	C–130		1st Cav Div	12,965
3. Bu Gia Map	C–130		1st Cav Div	8,989
4. Katum	C–130		Fishhook	5,164
5. Loc Ninh	C–130		Fishhook	2,500
6. Thien Ngon	C–123		Fishhook	2,280
7. Tonle Cham	C–130		Fishhook	2,177
8. Quan Loi	C–130		Fishhook	1,644
9. Tay Ninh West	C–7		Parrot's Beak	1,506
10. Moc Hoa	C–123		Parrot's Beak	1,502
11. Ha Tien South	C–7		Southeast Cambodia	545
12. Don Phuoc	C–7		Mekong River	541
13. Duc Co	C–130		II Corps	518
14. Chau Doc	C–7		Mekong River	356
15. Dau Tieng	C–7		Parrot's Beak	325
16. Plei Djereng New	C–130		II Corps	304
17. Duc Lap	C–7		II Corps	211
18. An Loc	C–7		Fishhook	173
19. Duc Hue	C–7		Parrot's Beak	155
20. Minh Thanh	C–130		Fishhook	127
21. Tieu Atar	C–7		II Corps	109
22. Thuy Dong	C–7		Parrot's Beak	87
TOTAL SORTIES	C–7	3,786	Total	58,668
	C–130	3,287		
	C–123	2,570		

used at one time or another to all forward support bases. In supporting the cavalry division, as in past campaigns, the fixed-wing transports provided supplies to sustain air assaults and for forward redistribution by the Army helicopters and road vehicles.

By actions short of further direct intervention, Americans sought to head off a communist takeover in Cambodia. External assistance to Phnom Penh often relied heavily on air transport. During the spring 1970 campaign, for example, a South Vietnamese underground airline made nightly shipments to Phnom Penh. The first Vietnamese Air Force transports were loaded at Tan Son Nhut in darkness on May 1, taking aboard several thousand M2 carbines intended for local defense forces in Vietnam. A Vietnamese officer who had served previously at Phnom Penh briefed the others, describing the Pochentong airfield and its approaches. The transport landed after midnight, taking precautions to preserve secrecy. In subsequent weeks the C-119s and C-47s continued the lifts, hauling in uniforms, captured AK-47 rifles, ammunition, and ethnic Cambodian troops residing in Vietnam. Meanwhile, the Vietnamese civil transports by daytime hauled ethnic Vietnamese out of Phnom Penh at a rate reaching 250 persons daily. U.S. Air Force transports generally stayed away from Phnom Penh, except for occasional visits by aircraft of the Seventh Air Force flight operations branch. MACV on June 23 reached an oral agreement with Vietnamese officials to employ 834th Air Division transports for daily missions within Vietnam on behalf of the Vietnamese Air Force, and to compensate the Vietnamese Air Force for its continuing effort in Cambodia.[19]

The first substantial C-130 airlift into Pochentong resulted from a short-notice requirement by MACV on June 29, 1970. Over one hundred tons of combat equipment (including AK-47 ammunition) was to be flown in by the next evening—the deadline for removal of U.S. personnel from Cambodia. Within four hours a C-130 took off from Tan Son Nhut carrying a mission commander, a combat control team, and an aerial port mobility team. The first cargo-carrying C-130 landed at Pochentong later in the day. To keep the effort inconspicuous, each load was hauled away by truck before the next landing. The eighth cargo sortie, arriving the morning of the thirtieth, completed delivery of 110 tons; the ground teams returned to Vietnam by C-130 that afternoon.[20]

Most materiel entering Cambodia came from U.S. Army facilities in Vietnam by one of three surface routes: by road from Saigon, by road from the deep-water port of Kompong Som (formerly Sihanoukville), or by Mekong River vessel from Vietnam. Communist action against the two roads left the Mekong water route as the primary link, while airlift remained a useful supplement for movements of personnel, certain munitions, and urgently needed items.[21]

Through most of 1970, airlift into Cambodia remained almost entirely a Vietnamese task. Even those U.S. Air Force advisors serving with Vietnamese Air Force transport units were prohibited from accompanying the Phnom Penh runs. On most dates the Vietnamese Air Force scheduled four C-119 missions, delivering a monthly average of 470 tons to Phnom Penh through November. On November 15, 1970, MACV indicated that the Vietnamese C-119 arm was becoming badly strained by the effort and recommended that U.S. Air Force transports in South Vietnam be used "to reduce excessive backlogs and to provide emergency resupply." CINCPAC, the Joint Chiefs of Staff, and the Secretary of Defense authorized such lifts when the lift was requested by the American ambassador

TACTICAL AIRLIFT

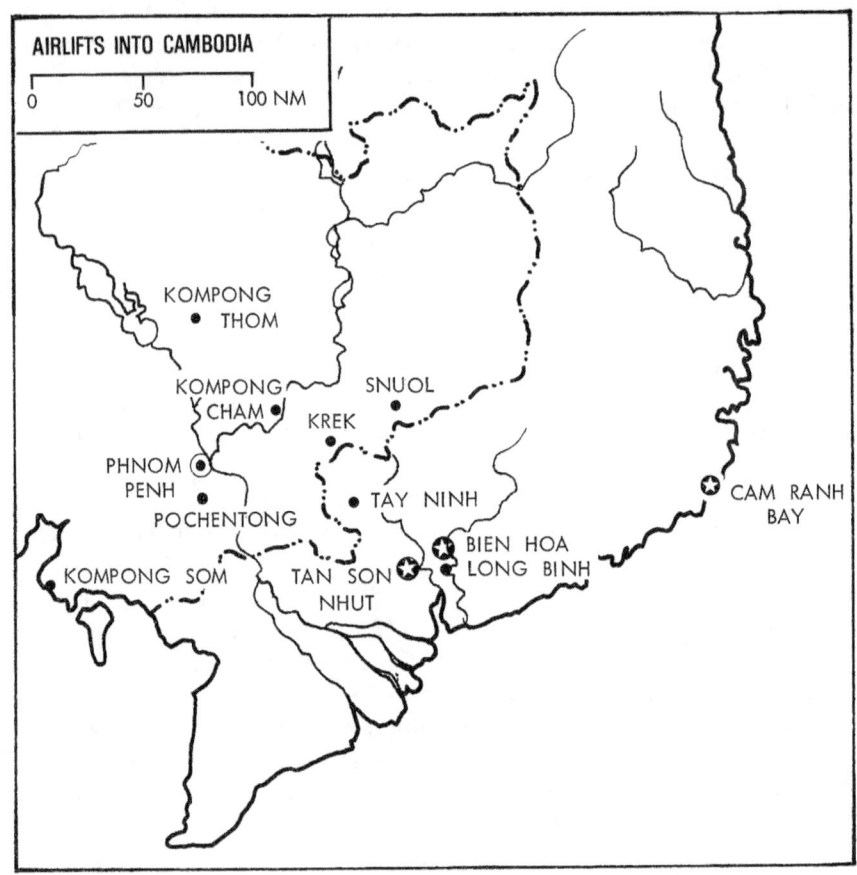

in Phnom Penh. Use of the C–130s was to be "judicious," thus preserving a "low U.S. profile."[22]

Under this proviso, C–130 cargo lifts into Phnom Penh averaged two daily during 1971, supplementing the Vietnamese Air Force effort. The U.S. Air Force contribution was heaviest in January while building up stocks in Phnom Penh prior to shifting logistics activities for the Laos campaign. Effort surged again during a period of heavy communist surface interdiction in the spring. During the nine months ending in October 1971, Vietnamese C–119s and C–123s made a total of 801 cargo sorties into Pochentong; the U.S. Air Force C–130s (and an occasional C–123) made 481. Vietnamese Air Force missions ceased after October 1971. U.S. Air Force cargo flights usually delivered munitions for the Cambodian Air Force, hauling from Cam Ranh Bay or Bien Hoa. C–130 bladderbirds delivered to the Cambodian capital for about two weeks in early 1972 to overcome a temporary shortage of fuel caused by convoy delays. Passenger missions roughly equaled cargo flights in frequency, with 130s shifting

Cambodian troops between Phnom Penh and training sites in Vietnam.[23]

For the C-130 aircrews the missions to Pochentong were not rigorous. The airfield had a 9,800-foot hard-surfaced runway suitable for heavy traffic, and with substantial parking and handling facilities. Crews entered Cambodia by prescribed international routes, made compulsory radio reports at specified points, and kept the airlift command center at Tan Son Nhut advised on mission progress. Flight altitudes were above the threat of ground fire except during the steep landing and departure patterns at Pochentong. No Air Force transports were lost in Cambodia. Cambodian aerial port personnel offloaded cargo at Pochentong and soon were efficiently getting the 130s turned around quickly.[24]

Occasional emergency and tactical airlifts sustained government forces fighting in the eastern half of the country. The garrison at Kompong Thom (seventy miles north of Phnom Penh) remained under pressure from several directions during summer 1970, with road access blocked by enemy forces. Single Air Force C-130s dropped loads of ammunition and equipment into the central marketplace on June 23 and 29. Vietnamese Air Force C-47s and the lone flyable Cambodian Air Force C-47 made further drops through August. Vietnamese Air Force crews, flying borrowed U.S. Army helicopters, periodically brought in reinforcements and supplies. On December 14, 1970, Vietnamese helicopters, C-119s, and C-47s, lifted South Vietnamese troops to seize the Kompong Cham airfield forty miles inside Cambodia, and the Vietnamese Air Force made over six hundred fixed-wing landings at Kompong Cham during the two-week operation. Enemy fire stopped Vietnamese C-119 drops in May 1971 near Snuol, contributing to a substantial allied defeat, but Vietnamese Air Force C-123s were successful in a similar situation in November near Krek, helping to gain tactical success on the ground. Vietnamese helicopter units, augmented by U.S. Army helicopters and crews (enjoined to keep ground time in Cambodia to a minimum), supported these and other South Vietnamese operations in Cambodia. U.S. Air Force C-130s made several series of drops in 1971, among them drops to still-pressed Kompong Thom in February, to a surrounded unit east of Phnom Penh in June, and to a relief column advancing toward Kompong Thom in November and December. In the final effort, one C-130 took fifty bullet holes and lost two engines before landing successfully at Pochentong. These and other airlift efforts were not enough to arrest the declining military situation in Cambodia, but were forerunners of more sustained operations in 1972 and after.[25]

The Cambodian Air Force was able to make only a small airlift contribution. When U.S. military assistance resumed in 1970 after a six-year break, the Khmer Air Force had eleven C-47s and several IL-14s and AN-2s. Nearly all craft needed major overhaul. The United States provided ten fresh C-47s during the summer, but most were destroyed in a communist shelling and sapper attack at Pochentong in January 1971. The Australians and the Americans furnished more C-47s, and some Cambodian C-47 crews were trained in Australia. The Cambodian transports hauled passengers, supplemented trucks for redistributing materiel from Phnom Penh, and made occasional drops to field units. U.S. officers judged the twelve-plane unit combat-ready in the summer of 1972. A separate light-transport squadron operated single-engine U-1As. By 1972 there was also a small helicopter force of seven UH-1s and ten pilots to supply isolated units and make medical evacuations. Future programming called for C-119s, for heavy-cargo drops.[26]

Airlift was the heart of contingency planning for Cambodia at the Seventh Air Force and the 834th Air Division. One analysis in late 1970 determined that 690 C-130 loads could move a Vietnamese division with most of its equipment to Phnom Penh. The U.S. Air Force C-130s in Vietnam, with moderate help from the Vietnam Air Force, could complete the shift in five days. Other possible moves, for example a move of forces to Kompong Som, also were studied for possible execution by the combined U.S.-Vietnam resources. The 834th continued to be responsible for hauling bulk petroleum to Phnom Penh in an emergency. There also were plans to evacuate noncombatants from Phnom Penh. Three options for evacuation were available: civil airlines, U.S. Air Force C-130s and C-123s, or U.S. military helicopters. Meanwhile the daily airlift to and from Phnom Penh preserved a basis for quickly expanding air lines of communications in the event of total blockage of surface routes.[27]

Allied proposals for major ground action against the Laotian panhandle in the past had encountered serious diplomatic and military objections. Denial of the port of Sihanoukville to the communists in 1970 meant that the panhandle lines of communications were more than ever crucial to the enemy. Urged by President Nguyen Van Thieu and U.S. Ambassador Ellsworth Bunker, General Abrams in December 1970 issued planning guidance for supporting of division-scale Vietnamese operations against the Tchepone region. The objective was to disrupt communist logistics corridors during the winter dry season, then withdraw when spring rains made truck movements difficult. The Joint Chiefs of Staff on January 19, 1971, approved the use of American planes in support of the Tchepone venture, with the proviso that U.S. personnel could not be employed on the ground in Laos.[28]

Headquarters XXIV Corps at Da Nang published the principal American operations order for Lam Son 719. U.S. Army units were to be

President Nguyen Van Thieu and Vice President Nguyen Cao Ky (background) in 1969.

responsible for clearing Highway 9 from Dong Ha to the Laotian border and were to provide artillery, helicopter, and logistics support for the Vietnamese assault force. A Vietnamese armored thrust was to penetrate about twelve miles into Laos along Route 9, flanked by heliborne assaults. Airmobile assaults into the Tchepone region were to follow, in turn followed by several weeks of search and blocking operations. The Americans were to provide aerial resupply from coastal bases, "as required" and rebuild the abandoned Khe Sanh airfield for landings by C–130s. General Abrams in December had planned that the old airfield at Tchepone would be renovated for C–123 and possibly C–130 use. But, although Vietnamese officials endorsed this intention, the XXIV Corps plan omitted the idea. Deception actions feigned airborne and surface threats to the southern provinces of North Vietnam, and parachutes were actually shipped from Saigon to further the illusion.[29]

General Herring and several 834th staff officers attended an initial XXIV Corps briefing on the planned operation on January 21. It was clear that the airlift role would be threefold: to haul combat forces and equipment from the Saigon area to the northern provinces during the preparatory phases, to land supplies at the Khe Sanh forward base through the duration of the operation, and to make airdrops inside Laos if needed. The MACV logistics section provided further details the next day. An all-Vietnamese contingency force, consisting of the airborne division and a marine brigade, were to be airlifted from Saigon to the Quang Tri and Dong Ha airfields. The planned movement of nearly ten thousand troops and eighteen hundred tons of cargo, equal to twenty-two C–130 loads, was to be executed in a five-day period starting January 31.

Planners at the 834th then turned to the technical questions. It soon became evident that the contingency force move would be only part of the immediate lift requirement. Starting on January 26, each day brought fresh and unexpected combat-essential mission requests, many to transport American personnel and equipment to northern points. On a single day, for example, the air division flew thirty-three combat-essential sorties to Quang Tri, including a twenty-eight-sortie cargo lift from Bien Hoa. On the thirtieth, thirty-nine lifts to Quang Tri included movement of a mechanized unit from Duc Pho. These unforeseen missions caused major adjustments in each day's schedule and made expansion of the in-country C–130 force necessary. Consequently, the force was increased on January 30 from forty-eight to fifty-seven planes—twenty-seven B–models at Cam Ranh and thirty E–models at Tan Son Nhut. The ratio of aircrews to planes was also increased (from 1.4 to 1.7 at Tan Son Nhut) to permit twenty-four-hour operations by the entire force. The in-country maintenance force was correspondingly augmented.[30]

An adequate airfield for the planned airlift force was a priority need. The airfield at Quang Tri had been in continuous use and had all necessary facilities including an Army ground controlled approach unit. A routine 834th Air Division survey group had concluded on January 19 that operating conditions there were satisfactory. An Air Force combat control team was sent on January 26, mainly to provide communications links to the airlift control center. The team began immediately two-shift, around-the-clock operations and continued until it withdrew four weeks later. The XXIV Corps forward command post became operational at Quang Tri on January 31; with the command post party came a tactical airlift officer who brought a radio jeep, later used to coordinate airlift matters with Da Nang and Khe Sanh.

The airfield at Dong Ha had been closed for months, but now was needed as an emergency backup for Quang Tri and to keep traffic moving during periods of bad weather. An 834th team surveyed the Dong Ha field, and Army engineers brought the strip to usable condition in a week of repair work. An Army ground controlled approach unit, temporary airfield lighting, a low-frequency beacon, tactical air navigation equipment, and a visual precision-landing light system were soon installed. A combat control team from the 8th Aerial Port Squadron arrived on February 1 to provide additional communications and traffic control service. Besides serving as a transshipment point, Dong Ha was the forward command post for the Vietnamese I Corps.

Numerous preparations reflected the know-how gained from past unit movements. Three six-man aerial port mobility teams were sent to Dong Ha, two of them later moving to Khe Sanh. Additional personnel and

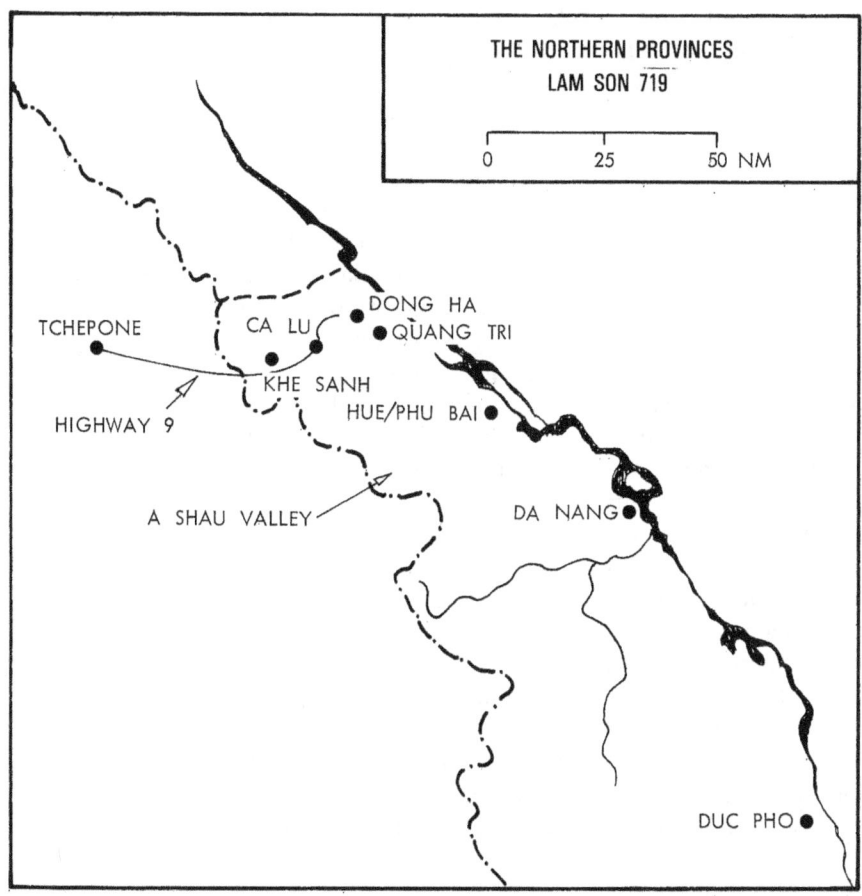

equipment augmented the port element at Quang Tri. On January 29, five-man C-130 maintenance teams took position at both Quang Tri and Dong Ha. Each was capable of tire changes and other quick maintenance tasks, and their efforts helped avert extensive maintenance delays at either point. Mission commanders from the 834th pool took position at both fields.[31]

The contingency force move began with 28 sorties on January 30, amassing a total of 203 sorties during the first six days. The largest unit moved was the 1st Airborne Division, which was marshaled and loaded at Tan Son Nhut under efficient Vietnamese direction. At Dong Ha the Vietnamese battalions moved directly to preselected assembly areas and immediately dug in.

In addition to moving the Vietnamese contingency force, 834th transports during the same six days flew an additional 245 sorties in support of U.S. forces to northern airfields, mainly from Bien Hoa.

The missions north went on around the clock. The relatively time-consuming round trips (well over an hour's flying each way) drained in-country airlift capability and necessitated reductions in service elsewhere. Most crews, however, were able to complete two round trips north with only a slight extension of the normal crew mission day. Air and ground crewmen shared the sense of urgency, recognizing that major ground battles were likely to be forthcoming. Presenting the greatest problem were the northeast monsoon wet conditions at the coastal northern fields, which challenged the skill and patience of crews and traffic controllers. Aircraft arriving in the north were cleared for airspace successively by control agencies at Da Nang, Hue, and Quang Tri, culminating in handoffs to either the Quang Tri or Dong Ha ground controlled approach. Prolonged orbits and go-arounds were frequent, with delays sometimes exceeding ninety minutes. Ground controlled approach at Dong Ha was troublesome, able to handle only one aircraft at a time and breaking down intermittently. Airspace corridors were specified and used, both for entry to the ground controlled pickup points and for departures after takeoff.

The contingency force move ended with 44 sorties on February 6 after a one-day standdown to await a decision on possible landings at Khe Sanh. In all the 247 contingency force sorties hauled 9,250 troops and seventeen hundred tons of cargo. The 834th Air Division calculated that its total activity in support of the U.S. and Vietnamese troop movements (from January 26 through February 6) included 592 C–130 and 12 C–123 lifts, nearly all into Quang Tri and Dong Ha. Only the traffic saturation at the northern points blemished the enterprise. The lifts north once again exemplified the superb qualities of the C–130 force for major airlanded combat unit hauls over significant distances.[32]

Lines of communications into the battle area were both by air and by surface. The old highway and water routes, which reached from Da Nang to the base support area facilities at Quang Tri, were supplemented by airlift as needed. As the American clearing forces pushed west from Quang Tri starting January 30, forward support area elements were established on January 30 at Ca Lu (the old LZ Stud), and on February 4 at Khe Sanh. Three-day stockages were planned at both fire support areas. Hauls on Route 9 were hampered by bad weather and the need to transload into smaller trucks at Ca Lu. The roadway west of Ca Lu was in marginal condition and was subject to enemy harassment. It could therefore accept one-way traffic only. Night convoys were instituted to increase the flow. Planners intended that the Khe Sanh airstrip be opened for C–130s on February 5 to receive forty to sixty C–130 landings bringing in five hundred tons daily (including fifty thousand gallons of jet fuel). Although the airstrip was not opened on schedule, the assaults into Laos commenced on February 8 with heliborne elements from Khe Sanh and an overland force crossing on Route 9.[33]

The delay in opening the Khe Sanh airstrip was agonizing to the airlifters. Aerial photographs in January indicated that several weeks would be required to repair the old 3,900-foot runway, but that a parallel shorter dirt strip capable of receiving C–130s could be fashioned more quickly. A preliminary engineer survey, conducted hours after the helicopter assaults on Khe Sanh on January 30, confirmed these conclusions. U.S. and Vietnamese army engineers the next day began work on both strips. On February 1 an 834th Air Division airfield survey officer arrived at Khe Sanh and remained for more than a month to monitor the engineering effort. The new assault strip was laid out just south of the old runway, and was pronounced complete on February 4 after around-the-clock efforts. The first C–130 landed at midafternoon with General Herring and a five-man combat control team on board. The plane became mired in seven-inch ruts and, although a safe takeoff was narrowly managed, it was clear that further use by C–130s was impossible. MACV the next day estimated that necessary compaction would delay airstrip readiness until February 9.[34]

The airstrip failure, along with the loss of eight tanker vehicles in an early-hour ambush on February 8, made the supply of jet fuel at Khe Sanh immediately critical. Army Chinooks and Marine CH–53s provided enough to permit continued helicopter operations in Laos. On February 8 alone the CH–53s made ninety-eight lifts to Khe Sanh, delivering over five hundred tons of cargo including fuel in five hundred-gallon blivet bags. Until the C–130 bladderbirds were able to land at Khe Sanh, Army logisticians officially reported, the Marines "made the difference between success and failure" in the petroleum situation. MACV reported on February 11 that the supply of jet fuel at Khe Sanh as of that date was "not a significant problem." The Marines thereafter continued to provide four or more Da Nang-based CH–53s for deliveries of petroleum, munitions, and airstrip matting to Khe Sanh; subsequently the 53s also joined in deliveries inside Laos.[35]

By continuing to operate into Quang Tri the C–130s partly compensated for their inability to get into Khe Sanh. On February 7 a twenty-sortie C–130 effort hauled in 250 tons of airfield matting from Bien Hoa, and thirty-eight sorties brought in nearly 500 tons from Da Nang on the ninth and tenth, much of it fuel destined for further movement to Khe Sanh. Army logisticians determined that, during the two weeks ending February 19, Air Force transports delivered 120,000 gallons of jet fuel and 800 tons of other cargo in ninety-five sorties from Da Nang to Quang Tri. The 130s thus supplemented surface transports to Quang Tri, freeing additional trucks for work on Route 9. Meanwhile, flights into Dong Ha were scaled down and night missions ended with completion of the contingency force move and removal of the combat team on February 11.[36]

Engineering work continued at Khe Sanh both on the old runway and the adjacent new assault strip. Despite intermittent rain, the engineers again compacted the assault strip using heavier roller equipment and on February 12 began surfacing with MX–19 aluminum matting. The matted assault strip opened on the fifteenth, receiving its first C–130 that afternoon. A second C–130 landed in late afternoon, hauling in an adverse-terrain forklift; a third aircraft was forced to return to Da Nang because of deteriorating weather. MACV reported to the Joint Chiefs the next day that "supply to the forward base at Khe Sanh had been on a knife edge," but that the opening of the airstrip promised relief within seventy-two hours. The Army ground controlled approach facility at Khe Sanh, however, was not yet operational, difficulties having been encountered in installation. Poor weather on the sixteenth, seventeenth, and eighteenth limited operations to a total of eighteen sorties, including delivery of Air Force ground controlled approach vans. On February 19 for the first time the C–130s began performing as originally intended. Forty sorties brought in over 350 tons on that date, including 57,000 gallons of jet fuel. Supply buildup was rapid and a two-day stockage was attained in previously critical 105- and 155-mm ammunition.[37]

For the remainder of February, C–130 deliveries into Khe Sanh averaged thirty-six daily. Munitions stocks at the Khe Sanh fire support area reached a three-day level on the twenty-first, despite temporary airstrip closure because of dust problems and an accident. Full-scale supply resumed on the twenty-second, and on that day General Abrams assured President Thieu that fifty C–130 sorties daily were dedicated to the supply of Khe Sanh. Four C–130Bs with 4,200-gallon bladder systems built up fuel stocks which reached 160,000 gallons on the twenty-third. Bladderbird deliveries were stopped temporarily three days later, existing storage capacity at Khe Sanh having been filled. The peak delivery occurred on the twenty-eighth when sixty-two sorties, twenty-seven from Tan Son Nhut and thirty-five from Da Nang, brought in 715 tons of cargo and 280 passengers. Truck deliveries from Quang Tri on that date totaled 815 tons.[38]

To sustain the heavy workload, an eleven-plane C–130B element took position at Da Nang on February 16. Planes and crews came from Cam Ranh Bay, accompanied by some ninety maintenance personnel and substantial quantities of equipment and parts, including spare engines and props. In forty-five days of operations at Da Nang, only four takeoffs were delayed for maintenance reasons. Col. Albert W. Jones, vice commander of the 834th, served as forward coordinator at Da Nang. Colonel Jones managed the scheduling and flight control of aircraft destined for Khe Sanh, keeping in communication with the airlift control center and the field tactical airlift officers and coordinating with aircrews, Army logisticians, and local traffic control agencies at Da Nang. A night rocket attack in the early hours of February 21 destroyed one C-130 and damaged others at Da Nang but only momentarily slowed the flow.

On the ground at Khe Sanh were an Air Force mission commander, the combat control team and the tactical airlift officer, a five-man aircraft maintenance team, and several cargo-handling teams principally from the 8th Aerial Port Squadron. Planes offloaded dry cargo with engines running; bladderbirds discharged at a double-reception point. In addition to the ground controller approach unit, the 1st Mobile Communications Group (based at Clark) provided a control tower and a tacan installation. Most officers concluded that this lavish package helped sustain the flow in instrument weather and headed off difficulties like those encountered earlier at Quang Tri and Dong Ha. Fog and ceilings below ground controlled approach minimums prevented early-morning landings on many dates and, although runways lights were installed, night landings were not attempted. Aircraft flew designated artillery-free corridors, approaching Khe Sanh from Hue and leaving at Quang Tri.[39]

The assaults and movements into Laos in the first few days were successful despite difficult weather and substantial helicopter losses. Strong enemy reaction came early and, as the penetrations reached their early objectives inside Laos, communist attacks by shelling, infantry, and tanks grew more violent. Small-arms fire against helicopters near landing zones became barrage-like. Difficulty in keeping Route 9 open necessitated exclusive reliance on helicopters for supplies from Khe Sanh to the nearly ten thousand troops now inside Laos. The airborne division—once envisioned as the spearhead for the assaults against Tchepone—was battered in heavy fighting, and its condition at the end of February was "worrisome." Communist troops overran a major artillery position, and the South Vietnamese withdrew from other insecure positions. Despite the toughness of the campaign, President Thieu (with American encouragement) appeared determined to go ahead with the delayed assaults against Tchepone.[40]

Heavy fighting continued during the first week of March. Enemy tanks appeared in greater numbers, and the presence of SA-2 surface-to-air missiles was confirmed. Sagging discipline and morale in the airborne division prompted the airlift of reinforcements from Saigon. The helicopter assaults into Tchepone on March 3-6 were nevertheless successful, although helicopter losses were heavy the first day. Ambassador Bunker and

TACTICAL AIRLIFT

General Abrams, in a message to Washington on the sixth, disagreed with press reports critical of the performance of South Vietnamese troops and commanders. The strong communist reaction, to the Saigon officials, was proof that the enemy understood "that we are after his jugular."[41]

The airlift effort into Khe Sanh reached its zenith during the first eight days of March, with C-130 landings averaging fifty-four daily and attaining a one-day high of seventy-eight on the second. During the second and third, seventy-three sorties from Tan Son Nhut lifted in nearly two thousand Vietnamese marines with their equipment. Cargo airlifted into Khe Sanh averaged 650 tons daily for the eight days, compared with 730 tons delivered daily by truck. Helicopters also lifted four hundred tons daily from Khe Sanh to Vietnamese tactical units.[42]

The original 3,900-foot runway at Khe Sanh, now renovated and covered with AM-2 aluminum matting after a month's engineer effort, received its first C-130 on March 1. Repairs had been slowed by the presence of unexploded shells, by difficulties in removing old torn AM-2 matting, and by use of the strip by helicopters. Now, with a matted parking apron, the Khe Sanh airfield was a substantial complex capable of handling a huge airlift effort. On March 6, however, undetected subgrade erosion made the first 700 feet of the new AM-2 strip unusable. Operations reverted to the MX-19 assault strip. On the ninth a C-130 landing gear failed, gouging 1,700 feet of surface from the center of the strip. No C-130s landed on the tenth, but landings resumed the next day using the portion of the AM-2 runway beyond the 700-foot failed segment. Fortunately the temporary airlift interruption produced no serious effect on the now ample supply stockages.[43]

For Air Force personnel Khe Sanh was no luxury spot. The men improvised wood flooring to cover the red mud beneath the canvas tents. But hot meals were usually available at the Army's field ration mess, and could be supplemented with canned C-rations. Over eight hundred shells hit Khe Sanh in the first two weeks of March, and the Air Force men, when off-duty, joined in the labor of filling sandbags. The maintenance men won plaudits for repairing the C-130, damaged on March 9 when it lifted off in darkness the same date. The mobile airlift control element arrived on March 8, its equipment loaded on fifteen C-130 pallets. Until it was removed on the twenty-fourth, control element personnel relieved the combat control team of mission-following tasks.[44]

The seventeen thousand South Vietnamese troops in Laos remained under sharp enemy pressure. Long forgotten was the idea of opening a C-123 strip at Tchepone, and the South Vietnamese in mid-March began pulling back. Ammunition and petroleum stocks at Khe Sanh were allowed to decline, with consequent reduction of the C-130 effort. Landings continued at reduced frequency, mostly using the MX-19 strip, its many damaged places now patched with a mixture of sand and epoxy cement.

The C-130 detachment at Da Nang was reduced to seven aircraft, and on March 28 withdrawal of materiel from Khe Sanh commenced.[45]

Although the C-130s made no supply drops in Laos, preparations had been extensive. Over 350 tons of ammunition, fuel, and rations were rigged at Da Nang for container drop by C-130. A platoon from the 109th Quartermaster Company remained at Da Nang, able to rig an additional fifty tons per day. Aircrew briefing materials had been prepared with instructions for use of a corridor along Route 9, safe from friendly artillery. The specific locations of drop zones were left to be specified later. Crews were to remain above forty-five hundred feet until starting fast descent eight miles from drop. An additional tacan station was placed near the Laotian border to assist drop crews in tracking the corridor when in clouds. Actual releases were to be performed visually. When the concentration of communist antiaircraft weaponry in Laos became apparent, 834th officers planned alternate tactics: penetrate at treetop level and pop up to drop altitude (six hundred feet) shortly before release. The feasibility of night drops was also studied. Officers of the Seventh Air Force later speculated that drops would have been used if the South Vietnamese had stayed much longer at Tchepone.[46]

Helicopter supply in Laos had been costly but not prohibitively so. U.S. Army-furnished data to MACV indicated that 118 Army helicopters were downed by hostile fire during Lam Son 719 inside Laos. Of these 48 had been recovered. Another 22 were downed in the northern region of South Vietnam, of which 10 were recovered. Seven Vietnamese Air Force choppers were lost in Laos, possibly some in accidents. Losses per sortie were thus double the rate normal for flying in Vietnam. Transport helicopters operated with more helicopter gunship support than usual, and when possible flew above four thousand feet to minimize the effect of ground fire. Comparisons between helicopter and fixed-wing losses were not possible since, although the C-130s faced antiaircraft fire in Laos only in several dozen heavy-bomb drops, they generally performed from safe altitudes. The "instant LZs" created in these detonations helped reduce helicopter losses, since the few natural landing zones were often defended by the enemy. Most helicopters flew to coastal bases for maintenance each evening, returning to Khe Sanh when weather lifted the next morning. The dedication of allied helicopter crews was beyond question.[47]

The Air Force airlift contribution during the supply phase, although delayed, was substantial. In effect, the C-130s provided an air link to Khe Sanh in partnership with the surface routes, but bypassing the ground transshipment points at Quang Tri and Da Lu. Especially constructive had been the 320 bladderbird sorties which hauled in 1.2 million of the 2.8 million gallons of fuel issued to users at Khe Sanh. Except for airstrip rehabilitation, technical support was more than adequate. The Air Force ground controlled approach and control facilities at Khe Sanh reduced the

Secretary of Defense Melvin Laird (left) talks with Gen. George S. Brown, commander of Seventh Air Force, and U.S. Ambassador to Vietnam Ellsworth Bunker at Tan Son Nhut, February 1970.

effects of difficult weather, while cargo handling and aircraft maintenance at Da Nang and Khe Sanh kept delays to a minimum. The massive airlift effort in support of Lam Son 719 drained capacity for other in-country tasks, but rising backlogs were held down by temporary use of MAC C-141s to lift cargo between main ports inside Vietnam. Without major exception the performance of the Air Force airlifters, including the ground echelons, was creditable.[48]

The C-130s also assisted in the withdrawal from Khe Sanh, performing eighty-two retrograde lifts between March 28 and the closure of the airfield on April 1. Several Air Force teams and their equipment were lifted out as were excess munitions and rations and much of the airfield matting. Leaving on the last of sixteen sorties on April 1 was the combat control team. Other lifts out of the northern provinces continued through the first week of April, including return of the airborne division and other Vietnamese forces from Quang Tri and Hue to Saigon area bases.[49]

Assessing Lam Son 719, allied officers estimated that the enemy had been hurt by heavy casualties and by temporary disruption of his Laotian lines of communications. On the other hand, the success of the North Vietnamese in containing and punishing the allied forces inside Laos was undeniable and promised lasting psychological effects.[50] The use of the C-130s for sustained deliveries as far forward as possible seemed to reflect past doctrine and suggested applications for future battlezones infested

CAMPAIGNS OF 1969–1971

with enemy guns and missiles. Dependence on airfield engineers had been crucial and the difficulties of opening Khe Sanh strengthened the case for low-altitude parachute extraction and for newer transports capable of operating with large payloads into relatively primitive strips.

For the rest of 1971, fighting in Vietnam remained light, although it was apparent that the North Vietnamese were determined to prevail in the south. Meanwhile, continuing communist warfare in Cambodia appeared intended to install a compliant government in Phnom Penh, one willing to allow the communists to use Cambodian territory to pursue the war in Vietnam. Secretary of Defense Laird in August 1971 issued guidance for shaping the remaining American forces in Vietnam, stating that tactical airlift should be, as much as possible, based offshore. In January 1972, Laird directed that the airlift force be reduced to sixty-nine thousand men by May 1, and reaffirmed that the chief mission of these forces was to ensure the success of Vietnamization. It thus appeared that the combat record of Air Force airlift in Vietnam was near its end.[51]

XX. The Caribou Force, 1969-1972

The reliable C–7 Caribous continued to crisscross the skies over South Vietnam each day. Tasks ranged from the routine to those of highest combat urgency. Most unusual were the airdrops at Ben Het and Dak Seang, besieged camps in the triborder highlands. Both camps had boundaries too small for drops by C–123s or C–130s. The C–7 crews faced vicious ground fire at both points, but continued operations until both garrisons were relieved.

The period from 1969 to 1972 was outwardly free of the controversies over roles which marked the earlier history of the Caribou in Vietnam. Air Force endorsement of the dedicated user idea was reserved, however, and criticisms of its desirability in Vietnam remained questionable. The basic arrangements for C–7 control, maintenance, and crew training were carried over from previous years, and efficiency steadily improved.

The men of the 483d Wing were drawn from all parts of the Air Force. Few had worked previously with the Caribou, but most found their twelve-month tours in Vietnam busy and rewarding. The experience was especially memorable for more than half the assigned pilots, for whom this assignment was the first line duty. The mission of Vietnamization made major inroads in operational activity starting in late 1971 and became the primary mission soon afterwards. The final Air Force Caribou squadron stood down in March 1972, a few days before the communist Easter offensive.

There were no substantial changes in the Southeast Asia Caribou force during the early 1970s. The six squadrons of 483d Tactical Airlift Wing were reduced to five in June 1970 and remained at that strength through most of the period.* The mission site at Bangkok remained open but the one at Da Nang closed in early 1970. New mission-staging detachments were activated at Bien Hoa, Tan Son Nhut, and Can Tho. These

---

* The 459th Tactical Airlift Squadron was inactivated at Phu Cat in June 1970. The 457th and 458th Squadrons remained at Cam Ranh Bay and were joined by the 535th and 536th from Vung Tau in the summer of 1970. The 537th remained active at Phu Cat.

improved service in the southern regions after the Vung Tau squadrons were transferred to Cam Ranh Bay in the summer of 1970. The wing's liaison and control detachments at Tan Son Nhut, Pleiku, and Nha Trang were closed early in the period and their functions were absorbed by the local airlift control elements.[1]

Mission scheduling and control remained largely under the "dedicated user" system, whereby MACV allocated aircraft daily to specified users. Users each day sent desired itineraries to the 834th Air Division's airlift control center for consolidation and publication of daily orders. The 483d Wing apportioned the missions among the squadrons. The control center followed the progress of the missions, and the 483d Wing monitored the flight by requiring crews to call in any difficulties or delays. Changes to scheduled itineraries required control center approval, except for those made for urgent humanitarian reasons. One or two aircraft and crews were kept in alert status at the main bases to meet emergencies or to replace ships down for maintenance. There were forty-nine missions scheduled daily through most of 1969, divided among the several dedicated users in roughly the same proportion as previously. The five missions specified for MACV use were scheduled at the airlift control center as part of the countrywide common service airlift system. Air Force officials liked this arrangement which assured that these Caribous would be used for tasks not suitable for the C–123s and C–130s.[2]

Although the Air Force outwardly accepted the dedicated user principle, internal criticisms of its working in Vietnam were widespread. One study undertaken by the Air Force office of operational analysis in the summer of 1969, indicated that three-fourths of the C–7 workload in Vietnam was between airfields at least twenty-five hundred feet long and therefore suitable for C–123s. A similar analysis by the Seventh Air Force and the 834th Air Division confirmed these findings. Col. Wilbert Turk, commander of the 483d Wing in 1969, reported many cases where missions scheduled by dedicated users duplicated C–130 or C–123 routings. Aircrews were intolerant of this misuse, believing that with only a little inconvenience and extra effort shippers could ready items for shipment under the common service system. Air Force Col. John M. Bennett, MACV director of transportation in 1969, confirmed that dedicated users often used the C–7s for nonessential cargo hauls or as personnel taxis. Bennett nevertheless saw validity in the Army's need for immediately responsive airlift in critical combat situations. He recommended that two-thirds of the fixed-wing shortfield force be kept under dedicated arrangements, with the remainder shifting into common service scheduling. PACAF took a position late in the year that improved scheduling and control of common service aircraft (for example, under the forthcoming airlift management system) could attain the same advantages as the dedicated user concept. The 834th meanwhile exacted commitments from users to attempt to reduce duplication with the common service system and to more fully exploit the shortfield capability of the C–7. In September 1969 the daily C–7 common service allocation was increased from five airframes to eleven.[3]

Army officers defended the dedicated user arrangement in Vietnam, citing the dependability and enthusiasm of the 483d Wing crews and alleging that the C–123s and C–130s of the common service airlift gave less satisfactory service. Furthermore, ground force officers noted, dedicated C–7 point-to-point service avoided the breakage and losses encountered when cargo was turned over to the aerial port system. Finally, assured mail and passenger service were desirable as morale builders. Data for January 1969 collected by the 483d Wing suggested that the dedicated user Caribous were in fact used with statistical efficiency. The eight daily missions dedicated to the cavalry division averaged 1.31 tons payload per sortie (space utilization was 55.3 percent), compared with 1.29 tons (and 51.2 percent) for the five daily common service. Again, dedicated aircraft in January 1970 carried payloads six percent larger than the eleven daily common service missions. This data, however, failed to negate the main Air Force contention that dedicated usage failed to exploit the shortfield and softfield capabilities of the C–7.[4]

Air Force officials at higher levels continued to give lipservice to the dedicated user idea, conscious of the political sensitivity of the issue. For example, the Air Staff through most of 1969 defended the dedicated role when pressing for purchase of additional Caribou aircraft to sustain the six-squadron force in Vietnam. Moreover, in later doctrinal statements, Air Force leaders showed their willingness under certain conditions to place aircraft larger than the Caribou in dedicated service. In Vietnam, Seventh Air Force officers worked toward the gradual reduction, but not the abolition, of dedicated user service. Withdrawals of U.S. Army units from Vietnam facilitated this policy, and at the end of 1970 C–7 common service missions stabilized at nineteen daily, after a brief rise to twenty-six in November. Common service missions further increased to twenty-four at mid-1971, more than half the total mission activity. Nevertheless distaste for dedicated activity remained strong. Col. Rodney H. Newbold, commander of the 483d Wing in 1971, criticized the "gross inefficiency," duplication, and cost of the dedicated system, and alleged that Army users lacked interest in properly screening loads.[5]

To improve Caribou use within the common service system the 834th Air Division introduced some ten scheduled missions in late 1970, with fixed itineraries, generally serving smaller installations. Scheduled C–7 service proved both reliable and efficient and by its regularity helped to hold down backlogs. The Caribous undertook some tasks earlier performed by helicopters, and increasingly served fields formerly used by C–123s which were now being shifted to the Vietnamese Air Force. Total activity stabi-

TACTICAL AIRLIFT

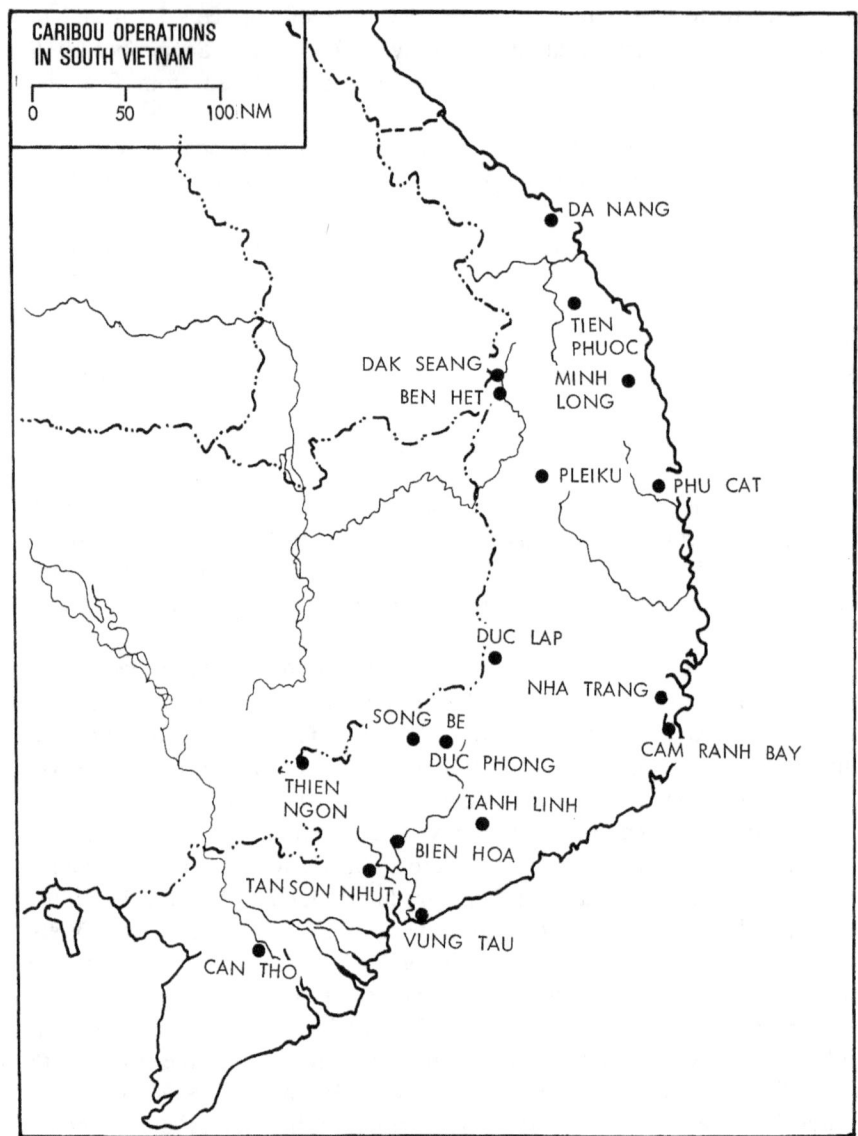

lized at forty-one missions daily after the reduction to five squadrons at mid-1970, but a weeklong test late in the year showed a capability of forty-eight. Two regularly scheduled medical evacuation missions were dropped in December, reflecting lower American casualties.

Supply drops to isolated camps averaged about fifty monthly through 1969 and most of 1970, with payloads averaging two tons. At Duc Lap in 1968 the slow-flying but agile Caribous had proven suitable for drops in an area of intense ground fire. The tradition of valor established at Duc

Lap was reinforced in 1969 and 1970 at Ben Het and Dak Seang where the Caribou aircrews met their greatest and most spectacular challenges of the war.[6]

The withdrawal of U.S. defense of the triborder area west of Dak To in early 1969 led to a test of South Vietnamese capabilities for independent ground combat. During most of May, more than five government battalions screened and searched sectors about the Ben Het camp—ground well forested and long familiar to the communists. Road convoys largely sustained the government's operations, the trucks delivering supplies as far as Dak To and Ben Het for further distribution to units by U.S. Army helicopters.[7]

Ben Het was long familiar to the Caribou airlifters. The camp was situated on a rise within communist artillery range of Laotian and Cambodian soil. The fixed-wing airstrip lay outside the defended perimeter and became unusable during periods of close-in enemy activity or shelling. At such times, air supply depended on drops inside the tight camp perimeter. On February 24, 1969, for example, the airlift command center diverted two C-7 crews to Pleiku for loading. The two crews made three successful drops into Ben Het, and a Hercules crew made a rare C-130 night drop. Renewed shellings in May periodically stopped landings and on the 12th damaged a C-7 on the ground. Transport crews landed only after forward air control pilots checked over the surrounding area and kept offload time to a minimum.[8]

Communist units in mid-May succeeded in cutting the roadway from Dak To, isolating the twelve hundred-man garrison inside the Ben Het camp. Despite heavy allied airstrikes the communists persisted in fire attacks. Their code name for the operation, "Dien Bien Phu," suggested their determination to overrun the camp. Caribou landings were halted on June 1 by shellings and deteriorating weather. Drops began on the third, using the ramp area of the airstrip as the drop zone. One or two C-7s operating singly made drops each morning and afternoon. Crewmen reported steady increases in enemy fire, and on June 13 two of the four Caribous making drops were hit and three crewmen were wounded. Shortly thereafter the airstrip became inaccessible to the defenders so the drop zone was shifted inside the compound to an area on the east side measuring only one hundred by two hundred yards. Although the need for an increasing volume of supply suggested the use of larger transports, the smallness of the drop zone and the need for tight maneuverability in the approach necessitated continued use of C-7s.

TACTICAL AIRLIFT

To hold down the increasing enemy fire (which now included 12.7-mm), allied A–1s, A–37s, and F–100s bombed and strafed prior to each drop. The A–1s also provided loose escort during each C–7 run-in, replying to fire with fire. Ships made drops singly at approximately fifteen-minute intervals. Coordination with fighters and controllers was impromptu. No effort was made, for example, to schedule and make good exact target times. After another week, eight C–7s had received battle damage while making a total of forty-two drops. Although all ships were repaired successfully at Pleiku, the need for tighter tactics was obvious.[9]

New tactics emerged from a meeting held at the Pleiku direct air support center on June 21. Present were Col. Leslie J. Greenwood, deputy for operations of the 483d Wing, and Maj. John H. Wigington of the 537th Squadron, his squadron commander, and officers from the several fighter and control units. Colonel Greenwood stated that unless the hazardous conditions at Ben Het improved he would not permit his crews to continue the drops. All agreed on details for a more systematic approach to the escort problem. Instead of dropping singly, up to six Caribous would make simultaneous run-ins, passing over the drop zone at intervals of fifteen seconds. This would permit the fullest concentration of suppressive fire. Air and artillery strikes would start twenty minutes prior to scheduled drop times. Then, immediately before the run-ins, A–1s would lay down smoke and ordnance on either side of the approach path. The A–1s would continue strafing during the Caribou run-ins, their relatively slow airspeed enabling them to stay close to the incoming transports.

The new procedures worked well, and in the final fifty-seven drops between June 21 and July 3, no Caribou received a hit. The methods were described to Seventh Air Force personnel in July and were later published as part of a tactics handbook. Major Wigington who flew eight drop sorties —five using the new tactics—felt that the ability of the A–1s to provide continuous strafing during the run-ins was pivotal. To Colonels Greenwood and Turk, the important lesson lay not so much in the specific tactics used but rather in the early systematic approach to the problem. Disciplined coordinated tactics in this case headed off any need for special heroism and sacrifice. In all, over two hundred tons of munitions and other supplies were dropped, mainly by crews of the 537th Squadron. On July 1 South Vietnamese forces cleared the road to Ben Het, in effect ending the siege.[10]

Allied intelligence in February and March 1970 again indicated increasing enemy activity in the triborder area. Despite these warnings, strong communist forces (including one of the regiments used at Ben Het in 1969) succeeded in moving through the region's well-forested valleys without opposition, to occupy well-bunkered positions around the Dak Seang camp. Tactical surprise was nearly complete. Only twelve hours before the initial attacks on April 1, Air Force C–7 transports had been landing at Dak Seang, lifting out ammunition believed needed at another camp. It soon became clear that the enemy had learned from the Ben Het fight and was exploiting the terrain to position antiaircraft guns along likely air supply corridors.[11]

483d Wing aircrews knew well the Dak Seang camp, having joined Army helicopters in routine supply and in periodic emergency reinforcements since the camp's construction in 1966. The camp lay in a north-south valley, sufficiently wide to permit Caribou drops from any direction. The camp was rectangular, roughly two hundred feet square, surrounded by a deep ditch and several wire barriers. Like at Ben Het the airstrip lay immediately outside the defended perimeter and became unusable during close-in attacks. Dak Seang lay within easy Caribou range from Pleiku, sixty miles to the south.

The garrison made a request for drops in the late morning of April 1, but Special Forces personnel at Pleiku and Nha Trang decided to wait, intending to use the crew and aircraft already scheduled for a practice drop the next day. By midafternoon, however, the perilous situation on the ground at Dak Seang became more apparent, and the Air Force tactical airlift officer made a call to the control center requesting immediate resupply. Two Caribou missions were diverted from scheduled itineraries to Pleiku for loading. Three drop sorties were made delivering flak vests, helmets, water, and medical supplies. The planes approached from the east and released from 300 feet at 110 knots, using the southern portion of the camp as a drop zone to avoid the structures to the north. The crews worked by radio with a forward air controller on the scene, but no strike aircraft were present specifically as escort for the drop planes. There was light ground fire against the planes, becoming heavy to the southwest immediately after drop; one aircraft received two hits. Although two of the three loads landed outside the camp perimeter, most items were recovered.[12]

Shelling and infantry probes increased during the night, and two Caribous were readied for launch the morning of April 2, loaded with ammunition. Again the transports approached from the east, while the onscene forward air controller coordinated suppressive fire and escort by strike aircraft. The first plane reported ground fire during a steep right-hand exiting turn after release; the second therefore departed to the left but was hit during the maneuver. The Caribou crashed five miles away, apparently trying to make Dak To; none of the three-man crew survived. The airlift control center therefore temporarily suspended further drops.

MACV, however, declared an immediate need for thirty tons of supplies for Dak Seang. Consequently, the control center in early afternoon directed all available C-7s with drop-qualified crews to divert to Pleiku. Within one hour, eighteen C-7s were en route to or at Pleiku. During the afternoon and early evening, eleven of these planes completed drops at Dak Seang. The crews used the tactics of Ben Het, making descending run-

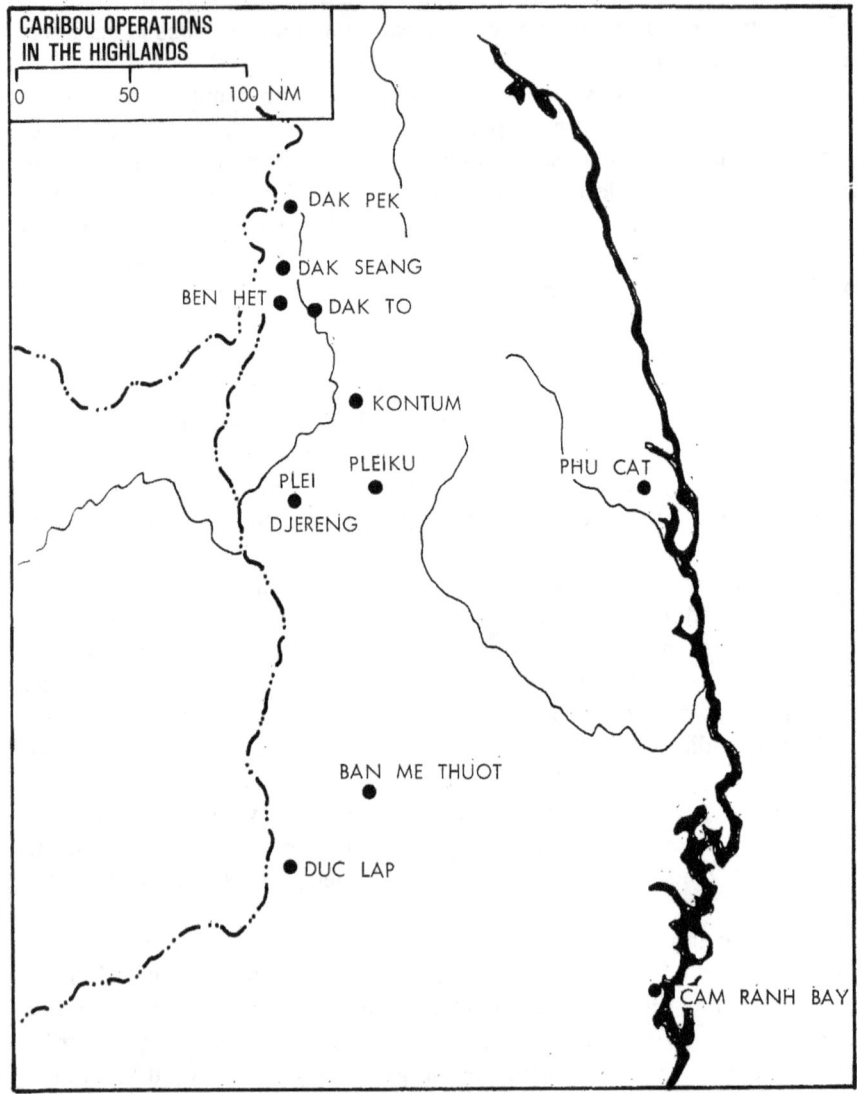

ins at intervals of about twenty seconds. Forward air controllers attempted to coordinate preparatory suppressive airstrikes, and slow-flying A–1Es flew close escort during the approaches. Despite these efforts, all drop planes drew fire and three were hit. The last four crews dropped in near-darkness, lining up on the light of the burning camp. The day's thirteen sorties dropped a total of twenty-three tons which were judged by the 483d Wing as eighty-eight percent recoverable. Bundles landing outside the perimeter could not be retrieved, however, and airstrikes were used to attempt their destruction.

USAF C–7B Caribou at Phu Cat Air Base.

The same tactic permitted thirty-one drops during the next two days, although fourteen aircraft were hit and one was forced to land at Dak To. All hits were received at low altitude and close to the camp. By this time most structures at Dak Seang had been leveled, so that the entire camp was now used as drop zone. Most runs were from either north or south, the crews attempting to use terrain to screen themselves from the enemy's view when nearing the entry points. From a C–130 overhead on April 4, General Herring watched preparatory fire suppression and a five-plane drop; three of the five Caribous were hit, one of them damaged seriously. A second five-plane drop was attempted later in the day during which the fourth aircraft received heavy fire and crashed two miles from the camp.

Matters improved little on the fifth. Seven Caribous, flying in formations of two, made drops; two were hit, and load recovery was a disheartening twenty-four percent. On the sixth, tactics were again changed. Single planes, approaching from a different direction, were scheduled at fifteen-minute intervals. Three planes made the morning drops supported by thirteen jet fighters for corridor suppression and four A–1s for close support. Damage from ground fire brought down one of the Caribous, the third lost in six days at Dak Seang. After a standdown through most of the day, one more three-plane flight took off from Pleiku in late afternoon when the camp defenders reported they were out of water and low on 105-mm ammunition. The first aircraft was hit just before release, causing an inaccurate drop; the second missed the camp because of a hung load; the third was told to abort because the fighters were low on fuel. Criticism of the drop crews was muted because of their obvious heroism, but it appeared that the crews had failed to fly down the centers of the prepared corridors.

TACTICAL AIRLIFT

The total failure of the afternoon drops nearly frustrated the air supply effort. Three planes and nine crewmen had been lost, and nineteen other aircraft had been hit. Furthermore, it appeared that the tactic of changing the direction of approach achieved little since the enemy entirely surrounded the camp.[13]

Alternative means of supply came under scrutiny at the 834th. Night drops by C-130 were tried at another mountainous location to test the feasibility of this method. The average impact error was 103 yards, and the idea was abandoned when the danger to camp personnel from the descending one-ton bundles was recognized. On the seventh, the 834th requested the 314th Wing to send a low-altitude parachute extraction crew to Vietnam "to provide an added option for current resupply operations at Dak Seang."[14]

The possibility of making night drops by Caribou, despite the area's forbidding terrain, had been suggested by one of the C-7 pilots. After careful discussion, Col. Roger P. Larivee, deputy commander for operations of the 483d Wing, authorized an attempt that night, arranging with Special Forces personnel that two minutes prior to scheduled drop time the garrison at Dak Seang would light fires or flares at each corner of the camp. The darkened plane approached from the south, passing over what was believed to be the camp without seeing lights. At that instant the identifying lights came on and the crew made an abrupt maneuver and released the load, but the bundles missed the camp. Nevertheless, night drops seemed feasible and in a meeting at Pleiku the next day tactics were devised for dropping by night using Air Force AC-119 gunships for protective cover and illumination.

The new procedures required radio contact between drop plane, gunship, and camp. The C-7 crew was to broadcast when five minutes out, and two minutes later the gunship was to turn on its spotlight, illuminating the camp for homing and release by the C-7 crew. In case of illuminator failure, camp personnel were to display flares. After midnight on April 7, three drops were made successfully using this method with no battle damage and with one hundred percent recovery. Six or more drops were made on each of the next five nights with negligible battle damage and close to one hundred percent recovery.

Technical difficulties during night drops were surprisingly minor. The use of the gunships for drop-zone illumination was wholly successful. Caribou copilots stayed glued to their instruments throughout the run to avoid possible confusion in sudden darkness when the illuminator was turned off. Special Forces troops, however, disliked stopping artillery fire during the run-in period because this left friendly patrols without fire support; tighter coordination minimized these periods of check-fire. An obvious recommendation was the use of infrared illuminators instead of visible lighting in the gunships and equipping the C-7s for infrared sighting. Another idea, apparently not tried, was the release of booby-trapped loads outside the perimeter to discourage recoveries by the communists.[15]

The possibility of drops at other triborder area camps was suggested on April 9, and a C-123 aircrew from the 315th Wing came to Pleiku to look over likely targets. Daylight C-123 drops commenced on April 13 at Dak Pek situated north of Dak Seang. Caribou drops at Dak Seang ended the same day when U.S. Army helicopters resumed supply deliveries. Simultaneously, most of the C-7s kept at Pleiku during the drops returned to Cam Ranh Bay. Allied heliborne assaults into and around the Dak Pek and Dak Seang camps further eased the pressure at both points, although night drops resumed at Dak Seang on April 22 at Special Forces request. The renewed Caribou drops continued at a rate of two or three nightly until April 2, the improved tactical situation now allowing recovery of bundles landing outside the perimeter. C-123s made daytime drops on May 7, and four days later Caribous resumed landing at Dak Seang, delivering twenty tons.[16]

The foremost lesson at Dak Seang once again was the ability of the airlifters to devise fresh tactics. Flexibility was important, both to conceive new methods and to execute them when unforeseen events broke down planned timetables. Colonel Larivee, who flew five daylight drop sorties at Dak Seang, wrote that in each case on-the-scene adjustments were necessary. The usefulness of the forward air controller for coordination was unquestionable. It was nevertheless clear that mission results improved in proportion to the time available for premission planning and coordination. This was especially so since, unlike the Ben Het campaign, transports, strike aircraft, and gunships operated from different bases.

Radio communications were less than ideal, especially in talking with camp personnel. No clear voice code existed for exchanging information likely to be valuable to the enemy, such as the planned times for drops or the condition of supply stockage in the camp. Messages between the camp and Pleiku had to be relayed by aircrews. Special Forces personnel at Pleiku in many cases guessed at what supplies were needed at Dak Seang, and were later praised by one officer present in the camp from their judgment. Rigging at Pleiku was done by U.S. Special Forces and Vietnamese personnel. These men constructed several hundred wood pallets and skidboards, working mostly at night. No parachute malfunctions or failures were confirmed.

The battle underlined the vulnerability of transports in dropping to besieged forces. Although the Caribou's slow airspeed aided accuracy in dropping, it also simplified aiming for communist gunners. Shoulder-held automatic weapons appeared responsible for three-fourths of the hits; the remainder were attributable to 12.7-mm machinegun fire. Most hits passed harmlessly through and out of the aircraft, but some caused fuel leaks and others produced serious damage to hydraulic systems and engines. The ability of the entrenched enemy to resist airstrikes was impressive. Colonel Larivee doubted that anything less than a series of B–52 strikes could have made the valley safe for daytime drops.[17]

For the Caribou force the Dak Seang drops were the war's best hour. Most of the early missions were flown by the 537th Squadron, based at Phu Cat and accustomed to working from Pleiku. Crews from the other squadrons joined the effort. The three downed crews were from the 537th, 457th, and 458th Squadrons respectively. At the peak, seven C–7s and crews along with fifteen maintenance personnel were staged nightly at Pleiku for the Dak Seang effort. Many individuals flew five or more drops; two pilots, Capt. Neil B. Crist and Karl T. Bame, flew ten or more. TSgt Franklin F. Godek was credited with eight missions. Between April 1 and May 1, Caribou crews made 127 drop sorties at Dak Seang, and released 240 tons of cargo with an overall recovery rate over ninety percent. The heartfelt comments by one Special Forces officer on the ground at Dak Seang, Capt. Paul Landers, sincerely praising the drop crews for the day and night drops, helped ease the pain of the losses.[18]

Flying operations in the early 1970s remained much the same as during the earlier period. The ruggedness and maneuverability of the Caribou enabled missions to reach the most primitive strip or the most isolated drop zone. Seat-of-the-pants flying skills thus remained important. A serious handicap, however, was the Caribou's limited altitude capability, which forced crews to share the lower flight levels with helicopter traffic. Long course deviations to avoid areas of artillery fire or bad weather were sometimes necessary because of the plane's inability to climb to safer altitudes. Low-level navigation in mountainous terrain remained difficult when outside tacan coverage. A number of landings and departures were at airspeeds too slow for safety in case of an engine loss. Several measures were helpful in reducing risks at crowded forward airfields. These included improved radio communication between Caribou and helicopter crews, conspicuous paint on helicopter rotors, and a ruling that a fixed-wing craft should climb out on runway heading until reaching one thousand feet altitude. Commanders continued to stress safety in this difficult flying environment, tempering the strong yen among aircrews for achievement with a realistic assessment of risk.[19]

Accident rates improved over the previously commendable record. For the three years (1969–71) only eight major accidents occurred, 2.6 per 100,000 flying hours, about half the former rate. Five of the eight resulted in aircraft destruction. All five occurred while landing—one in a crosswind attempt, two in emergency single-engine approaches, and two in normal attempts at forward strips. One aircraft, badly damaged in landing, was finally destroyed in an attempted helicopter recovery. No planes were destroyed in 1972, leaving the final tally of C–7s lost to operational causes at twelve. Twelve Caribou crewmen lost their lives in major accidents.[20]

The three transports and crews lost at Dak Seang were the last lost to enemy action during the war. Earlier communist ground fire brought down a plane near Plei Djereng on September 11, 1969, killing four crewmen, and downed another while it approached Tien Phuoc for a landing on December 26, 1969. On at least four occasions in 1969, aircraft hit by ground fire managed to land safely at forward airstrips where they were repaired. Various measures thereafter held hits to about four monthly. These included the old techniques of steep and tight approaches, the practice of staying at least three thousand feet above terrain when possible, and coordination to assure the presence of forward air controllers and fighters when landing or dropping in hot regions. Since acquiring the Caribous on January 1, 1967, the Air Force lost eight to enemy action, resulting in the deaths of eighteen crewmembers.[21]

The loss record was especially remarkable in view of the limited experience of the assigned C–7 pilots. During 1969, nearly two-thirds of the incoming pilot replacements had only recently completed undergraduate pilot training. But Colonel Turk, 483d Wing commander, considered these men "eager, intelligent, and trainable." By the summer of 1969, most new pilots advanced to aircraft commander status before the end of their twelve-month tours. Facilitating this advancement was Turk's policy relaxing the former fifteen hundred-hour flying requirement. The new pilots, inexperienced but properly guided and supervised, performed successfully. Upon completing flying school, few of them had volunteered for the unglamorous C–7, but most quickly appreciated their early opportunity to advance in responsibility. Individuals advancing to first-pilot status (after 750 total hours) had to demonstrate proficiency in shortfield work and drops and had to pass an extra flight check. At the heart of the flying program was a strong standardization and evaluation system, developed around carefully selected instructors and examiners. Local flying training was not slighted, even though this contributed to the chronic flying overload and the resulting overworked maintenance force. Most pilot assignees, both young and old, were graduates of the 4449th Combat Crew Training School, which moved from Sewart Air Force Base, Tenn., to Dyess Air Force Base, Tex., in late 1969. A few older pilots arrived in the Far East without this introduction to the Caribou but adapted to the C–7 Vietnam squadrons without serious difficulty.[22]

Continuing shortages of flight engineers meant overwork for those available. Studies by flight surgeons in early 1969 diagnosed fatigue as a significant problem among flight engineers, whose average age was near forty and

Col. Wilbert Turk (center), 483rd Tactical Airlift Wing commander, receives a visit from Gen. John P. McConnell, Air Force Chief of Staff, and Maj. Gen. Royal N. Baker, Seventh Air Force vice commander, at Cam Ranh Bay, November 1968.

who participated in heavy physical labor during loadings and offloadings. Fortunately, the simplicity of the Caribou made the duties of the flight engineer less critical than in other craft, and the use of loadmasters as engineers after rudimentary training proved successful. Medical technicians (already on flying status) meanwhile volunteered to accompany missions, helping in stevedoring, while pilots also often pitched in for the heavy work. By late 1969 the pipeline of replacement engineers had caught up to the need. Two veteran flight engineers received public recognition. TSgt Bobby D. Pennington, a graduate of the first Air Force Caribou class in 1966, by 1971 held twenty-seven Air Medals after several Vietnam tours in C–123s and C–7s. SSgt Jerry A. York served thirty-seven months in Vietnam, nearly all as a flight engineer with the 537th Squadron, participating in thousands of operational sorties.[23]

Maintenance effectiveness remained generally high despite the increasing age of the force and the hard usage. Operational-ready rates held at about eighty percent except for a decline during the winter of 1970–71 resulting from wet conditions on the ground at the coastal bases and an absence of maintenance hangars for protection from wind and rain. Flying hours held above ten thousand monthly until the first squadron inactivation and stabilized thereafter at slightly below nine thousand. Reorganizations within the 483d Consolidated Aircraft Maintenance Squadron followed the centralization of four squadrons at Cam Ranh and promised better use of skilled manpower, always a worthwhile goal in view of the turnover of personnel every twelve months. To ease higher than expected failure rates of engines, landing gear, and other systems, aircrews were instructed to "take care of the engines and aircraft, and they will take care of you." This meant, for example, that brakes and reverse pitch should be used gently during the landing roll and that taxiing should be slow. The Caribou remained essentially an easily maintained craft, requiring only twelve maintenance man-hours per flying hour.[24]

Living and work conditions were generally satisfactory at the Caribou squadron locations, and were further improved after the withdrawal from Vung Tau and the acquisition of space at Cam Ranh Bay formerly used by C-130 crews. Morale remained good in the Caribou units bolstered as in earlier times by the twelve-month tour and mission satisfaction. The 483d Wing and its squadrons received the Air Force Outstanding Unit Award for the fifteen-month period ending in October 1971, the wing's second such award in Vietnam.[25]

Squadron inactivations resumed with closure of the 537th Squadron at Phu Cat on August 31, 1971. The four remaining squadrons, all at Cam Ranh Bay, successively underwent standdown over the next nine months.*[26]

Individuals from each disbanding squadron were distributed among the remaining units. Aircraft from the 1971 inactivations were ferried to the United States for rework and assignment to the Air Force Reserve. Fifteen aircraft from the 537th Squadron left Cam Ranh Bay on September 14, 1971, each equipped with two extra 480-gallon fuel tanks, and flown by aircrewmen finishing their oversea tours. Two C-130s island-hopped the central Pacific with the C-7s hauling maintenance personnel and equipment. Twelve more Caribous left Cam Ranh on December 10. One ditched after engine failure east of Hawaii, but its crew was soon rescued by helicopters and a Coast Guard cutter. Aircraft left in Vietnam after the 1972 inactivations were kept for use in training Vietnamese crews and for eventual transfer to new Vietnamese Air Force squadrons.[27]

The rapid reduction of the Caribou force had little or no effect on the allied war effort, since highway travel was now safe in most regions. Colonel Newbold, 483d Wing commander, felt that sortie totals could have been cut back much earlier, since crews increasingly found themselves hauling to points accessible by safe roads. Each squadron, however, con-

---

* Total Caribou inactivations were: 459th TAS, June 1970; 537th TAS, August 1971; 536th TAS, October 1971; 535th TAS, January 1972; 458th TAS, March 1972; 457th TAS, May 1972 (flying standdown March 25, 1972); the 483d TAW and its maintenance squadrons were inactivated during April and May 1972.

tinued mission work full time up to its date of standdown. In February 1972, for example, forty C–7s remained in Vietnam—thirty-two assigned to the last two squadrons of the 483d Wing, and eight to the Vietnamese training program at Phu Cat. Each squadron flew eight missions daily, while Phu Cat provided considerable airlift capability as part of its training program.

Missions south were facilitated by an overnight stop at Tan Son Nhut after the operating site at Bien Hoa was closed in November 1971. Airlift tasks were shifted to the Vietnamese Air Force in several increments during March 1972, and the 483d Wing flew its last C–7 mission in Vietnam on March 25. The formal ceremony closing the wing and transferring Cam Ranh Bay to the Vietnamese took place May 15, 1972. Some eighty individuals from the 483d, nearly all of them maintenance personnel, remained for several months for duty with the new Vietnamese Air Force squadrons.[28]

The March standdown did not quite end Air Force C–7 missions in Vietnam. Aircraft and crews from the 457th Squadron were transferred to the 310th Tactical Airlift Squadron (a C–123 unit) under the 377th Air Base Wing (both at Tan Son Nhut) for use in special airlift tasks and in the Phu Cat training program. Some of the Caribous had been modified in late 1971 for tactical airborne communications relay work. These carried a package of additional radio equipment and wiring, with positions for three operators. On April 2, 1972, soon after the onset of the communist Easter offensive, the ships began around-the-clock airborne radio relay orbits out of Tan Son Nhut; six days later a similar twenty-four-hour orbit began at Da Nang. The effort made heavy demands on aircrews and ground crews, but continued until May 14. Subsequently, five planes served daily in the Vietnamese Air Force training program, and two were used for airlift missions between Saigon and the delta region. Air Force C–7 airlift work finally ended with the standdown of the 310th Squadron on October 31, 1972. The four C–7s still at Tan Son Nhut were shipped home by surface for duty with the Reserve.[29]

The ten-year history of the U.S. Caribous in Vietnam, six of them under Air Force ownership, permits conclusive assessments of the plane's qualities. Beyond question were the excellent shortfield and softfield qualities of the craft—C–7s could haul in useful payloads to places closed to larger craft. The demand for more and more Caribous by the Common Service Airlift System confirmed the usefulness of these unique capabilities, even in a system tuned to high-volume operations. The Caribous served as convenient administrative transports for passenger and low-volume cargo movements within the combat zone, and their reliability afforded dedicated users a much appreciated degree of responsiveness. Finally, the ability of the C–7 to make airdrops into confined drop zones smaller than those ordinarily used by the C–123s and C–130s proved pivotal on occasions, and the craft's durability, maneuverability, and its expendability in comparison with the larger transports encouraged its use in situations of heavy enemy fire.

Yet the very pilots who flew and were devoted to the "Bou" were critical of the craft's limited payload, slow airspeed, and low altitude capabilities. Early plans to use the Caribou in high-volume supply work in support of major airmobile operations were clearly unsound in view of the superior load capacity of the C–130 and the chronic air and ground congestion at forward airstrips. If Caribou procurement costs were low, the number of aircrew and ground crew personnel required was high in terms of payload accomplishments. The successful use of C–7s at Duc Lap, Ben Het, and Dak Seang required substantial fire suppression and escort by strike aircraft, while the Caribou's suitability in the face of the threat of surface-to-air missiles remained questionable.

By its simplicity, hardiness, and forward-airfield qualities, the Caribou appeared well suited for its future role with the Vietnamese Air Force either in reconstruction activities or in continued warfare. The withdrawal of the Caribous (and the C–123s) from the active Air Force, with no successors in immediate view, left a gap between the C–130s and the Army's helicopter transports. The Air Force viewed this condition as temporary, anticipating that next-generation transports would attain landing and takeoff capabilities approaching the vertical while preserving the payload of the C–123 or the C–130. Air Force doctrine bent grudgingly toward the dedicated user idea but avoided outright endorsements of its application in Vietnam. There was, however, little doubt that the Air Force looked with greater favor on the idea that a centralized theater airlift system was needed to control at least some shortfield (or rotary-wing) transport.[30]

XXI. The Easter Offensive— The Battle of An Loc

Allied officers in early 1972 realized that the communists were capable of major offensive action in several regions of South Vietnam. The most likely targets seemed to lie in the country's north and center. Large-scale attacks in the border provinces posing a threat to Saigon seemed improbable since the communist lines of communications in Cambodia were exposed to ground action by South Vietnamese forces. This changed in early March when the allies learned that three communist infantry divisions appeared to be concentrating against Tay Ninh.[1]

After an early feint against Tay Ninh, all three enemy divisions covertly moved out of the Cambodian fishhook region into the forested, rubber-producing country of Binh Long Province. One division seized Loc Ninh on April 7, and a second blocked Highway 13 south of the province capital An Loc. The final, and most difficult, task—the assault of An Loc itself—was given to the 9th Viet Cong Division, considered the elite of the three. The communists openly boasted that An Loc would become the seat of government for the liberated provinces, and captured documents indicated that its capture was to be followed by a drive southward along Highway 13 to Lai Khe and Saigon.[2]

The ensuing battle for An Loc was the most trying time of the war for Air Force C–130 crews. Conditions at An Loc were far more difficult than those at Khe Sanh four months earlier. The defenders at An Loc were Vietnamese, less reliable than the disciplined American marines at Khe Sanh. The only Americans on the ground were a few U.S. Army advisors. There was no Air Force detachment, no U.S. Marine bundle recovery team, no American ground controlled approach radar, and no airstrip within the defended perimeter. Moreover, the wall of communist fire over An Loc was formidable and included both medium-caliber antiaircraft shells and surface-to-air missiles. Prevented from making day or night drops from normal altitudes, the airlifters persisted in finding new drop methods. Temporary failures and tragedies occurred, but the airdrops eventually made the survival of the An Loc garrison possible, supplied entirely by air through three desperate months. The enemy thus failed by a narrow margin to gain a possibly crucial military, political, and psychological victory.

TACTICAL AIRLIFT

Maj. Gen. James F. Hollingsworth, USA, commander of the Third Regional Assistance Command, closely monitored the communist descent into Binh Long Province. On April 8 he warned General Abrams that without immediate action on the part of the South Vietnamese, "An Loc will fall, and it will be clear sailing into Lai Khe." Inside An Loc were the local garrison and the disorganized survivors of the defeats at Loc Ninh and the nearby rubber plantations. Two battalions of rangers arrived by road from the south just before the closure of Highway 13, and by midmonth U.S. Army helicopters had lifted to An Loc and nearby high ground two additional battalions and a paratroop brigade. Logistical staff work for the resupply was therefore predicated on a garrison of twenty thousand persons—half military and half civilians. The stated resupply objective was two hundred tons daily, including 140 tons of ammunition (mainly small-arms and 105-mm), 36 tons of rice and other rations, and 20 tons of water. Communist capture of the Quan Loi airstrip on April 5 eliminated any possibility of supplying An Loc by fixed-wing landings.[3]

The Vietnamese Air Force's 237th Helicopter Squadron, equipped with Chinooks, initially undertook resupply of An Loc assisted by UH-1s and U.S. Army Chinooks. During April 7-12, American and Vietnamese CH-47s made forty-two deliveries hauling in about 3.5 tons per sortie. Limited to a single landing zone within the defended perimeter, the helicopter crews had trouble avoiding the increasing communist fire. Despite fast offloading methods three U.S. craft received mortar damage, and on April 12 an enemy shell destroyed a Vietnamese Chinook. Furthermore, the presence immediately outside An Loc of a communist antiaircraft regiment, equipped with weapons up to 37-mm, confirmed the impracticality of substantial heliborne resupply. CH-47 deliveries therefore were halted for the remainder of the siege.[4]

The Chinook difficulties prompted an early Vietnamese army request to start airdrops. Vietnamese Air Force crews and transports, primarily C-123s, commenced drops on April 12. All drops were by daylight and all were troubled by enemy fire and the small size of the designated drop zone. The defended perimeter at the time consisted only of the southern part of An Loc, measuring about 1,094 by 766 yards. Crews approached from the south flying along Highway 13, sometimes in three-plane formations at seven hundred feet. Others released loads from five thousand feet or higher to avoid the hostile fire, using guesswork or makeshift sighting devices. Lacking delayed parachute-opening devices, loads drifted with hopeless inaccuracy during the prolonged descent from the higher altitudes. Overall

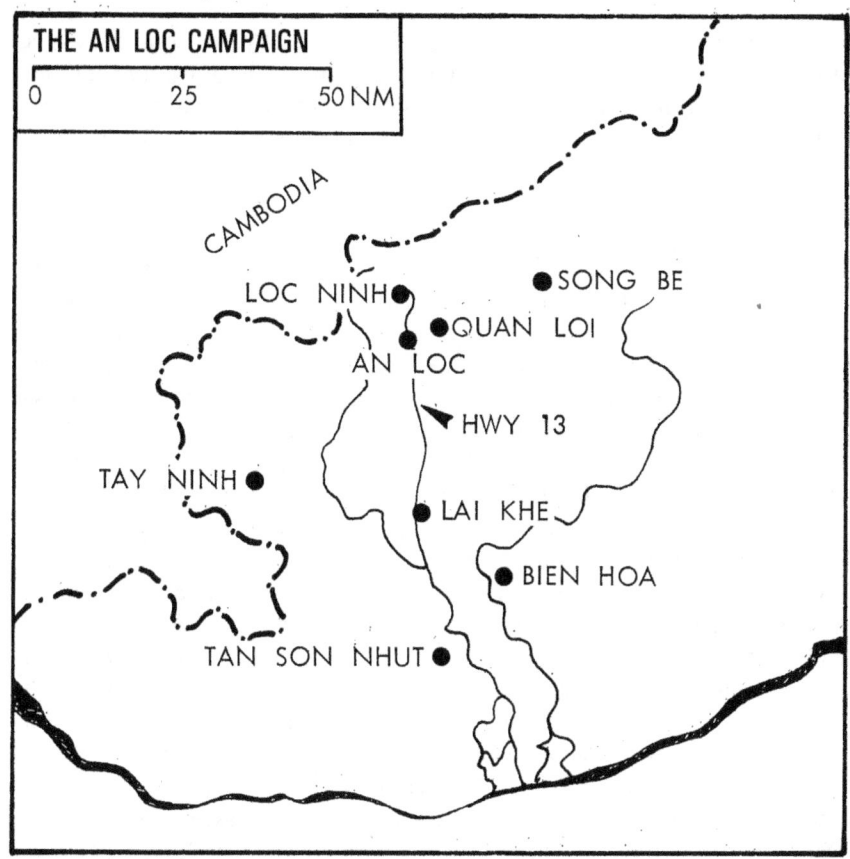

results were unsatisfactory—after twenty-seven C–123 and C–119 drops in the first three days only 34 tons of 135 dropped had been recovered. Most supplies landed outside the defended perimeter and were, when possible, destroyed by airstrikes. Six transports were hit by ground fire, and on April 15 a C–123 was downed, killing all on board including the squadron's commander. Another C–123 laden with ammunition exploded after hits on April 19. Col. Walter J. Ford, an Air Force advisor with the Vietnamese Air Force control center, praised the Vietnamese crews for persisting at An Loc to this point despite the hopelessness of their efforts. Colonel Ford sensed that Vietnamese pride prevented them from backing away before the Americans. The second C–123 loss, however, ended Vietnamese daytime low-level drops. A total of 195 tons had been dropped at An Loc in thirty-nine drop sorties.[5]

The disappointing early results brought the decision at MACV to begin U.S. Air Force C–130 drops. During the evening of April 14, three aircrews from the 374th Wing detachment at Tan Son Nhut received mission briefings, planned routes and tactics, and supervised loadings. The intended drop zone was a soccer field, measuring 219 yards square, located in the southern part of An Loc. The crews planned the now conventional descending run-in, leveling off two minutes from release at the standard container-drop altitude of six hundred feet. The approach was to be from the south along Highway 13. Each aircraft carried a full cargo load rigged for standard container delivery. Crews expected heavy ground fire.

The initial Hercules was commanded by Maj. Robert F. Wallace of the 776th Squadron. Major Wallace made the planned run-in, raising considerable tracer fire near the drop zone and taking damage in the rudder area, but releasing the load. After talking by radio with the airborne forward air controller on the scene, the second crew decided to approach from a different direction in the hope of taking the enemy by surprise. Heavy haze made it difficult to spot the soccer field, and the crew turned off for a second try. On the second run, thirty seconds from the release point, the enemy let loose, saturating the air over the drop zone using barrage techniques. Hits penetrated the cargo compartment and cracked the pilot's windscreen. Machine gun fire killed the flight engineer and wounded the navigator and copilot. The cargo (155-mm howitzer and 81-mm mortar ammunition) smoldered in intense heat from a ruptured hot-air line. The loadmasters jettisoned the ammunition and fought recurrent flames with hand extinguishers. With two engines out and the landing gear manually lowered, the crew nursed the plane back to Tan Son Nhut. For saving the aircraft and their wounded crewmates, Capt. William R. Caldwell and SSgt Charles L. Shaub, both of the 776th Squadron, earned Air Force Crosses. U.S. Army officers reported that, as could best be ascertained, of the twenty-six tons dropped by the two C-130s on April 15 nothing was recovered by the defenders.[6]

Reviewing the events of the day, Colonel Iosue, commander of the 374th Wing, called for a change in tactics. Majs. Edward N. Brya and Robert L. Highley, evaluation pilot and navigator respectively from the 374th, made plans accordingly for the next day's missions. Crews would make high-speed (250-knot) run-ins at treetop level, popping up about two minutes from An Loc to the six hundred-foot release altitude. Upon release crews planned immediate diving turns, returning to low level for departure. Navigators calculated six different approach paths, plotting an oval-shaped locus of computed release points about the target. Moreover Colonel Iosue, who previously had served as commander of the forward air controller parent unit in Vietnam, personally arranged for permission for aircraft crews to talk with forward air controllers on the ground before takeoff. This was an extremely important innovation, since before each run-in the on-the-scene controller was prepared to advise the C–130 crew as to what appeared the safest inbound and outbound headings. Several frequencies were identified for use, along with specific code words, in the belief that the enemy was intercepting radio talk.

Edward N. Brya, as a captain, at the controls of his aircraft.

Two ships—one of them flown by Iosue, Brya, and Highley—tried these methods on the sixteenth, receiving hits but not serious damage. Highley positively identified the intended drop zone, and both crews reported accurate releases; the Third Regional Assistance Command, however, listed all twenty-six tons as "probably lost." The disparity, it later appeared, may have resulted from erroneous map coordinates furnished the airlifters, indicating that the drop zone lay in a field east of, instead of west of, Highway 13. Highley later reported that a Vietnamese army officer clarified the matter two days later by drawing a hand sketch of the layout at An Loc.[7]

No missions were attempted on the seventeenth. On the eighteenth, communist fire defeated a final daylight low-level effort. Capt. Don B. Jensen and his crew began taking multiple hits at six hundred feet, just prior to release. With the right wing burning, with one engine out and another afire, and with communications gone, the crew jettisoned the load and steered away from An Loc, fighting for altitude. Jensen managed a crash landing in a marsh near Lai Khe. The crew helped one another from the wreckage and were picked up by Army helicopters. Thus, by evening of April 19 the allies had lost three transports (Jensen's C–130 and the two Vietnamese Air Force C–123s) in unsuccessful airdrops at An Loc.[8]

TACTICAL AIRLIFT

Whether or not a given load was recovered by friendly troops was often unknown even to Americans on the ground at An Loc. An American logistician estimated that only about twenty-five percent of the cargo dropped was received by the defenders. There appeared little hope of improvement using the old techniques. Accuracy was extremely difficult because of the need for strenuous evasive maneuvers in the final minutes, but precision was absolutely critical because of the small size of the soccer field drop zone. Even finding the soccer field presented problems in the short interval after pop up. Fortunately, navigators could easily recognize An Loc from a distance, since the town lay on a plateau surrounded by rubber trees.[9]

On the ground at An Loc the situation quickly became desperate. Two dozen communist tanks led major ground assaults into the city on April 13 and 15. Allied weapons proved effective against the enemy armor, but the communists firmly held the northern half of the city and continued pulverizing the remainder with heavy shells. The morale of the defenders also was lowered by the loss of parachuted supplies to the besiegers. One captured North Vietnamese officer reportedly asked for a can of fruit cocktail, saying he'd been eating it for days. To one American living in privation at An Loc, this information was "almost enough to make a grown man cry." Col. William Miller, USA, a senior American advisor on the ground at An Loc, reported on April 22: "Enemy enjoys observing no resupply; enemy enjoys lack of helicopters landing at this location. Come hell or high water, both should be accomplished."[10]

The goal of earlier ground radar-directed drop techniques was to improve capabilities for dropping in bad weather and at night. This ground radar air delivery system, using an MSQ–77 Skyspot ground radar and a beacon transponder in the drop ship, had been widely used to deliver BLU–82 bombs. To remain within radar line of sight of the ground station, ships ordinarily dropped from four thousand feet or higher. GRADS was more accurate than visual aiming from these higher altitudes, since the C–130 had no gyrostabilized sighting mechanism. Thus, GRADS appeared to offer the C–130 crews a method for releasing from altitudes above the ground-fire threat.

GRADS drops at An Loc began with two deliveries on the night of April 19/20. Crews released from eight thousand feet above the defenders, guided by the MSQ–77 mobile search radar at Bien Hoa. Major Brya flew one of the planes with Colonel Iosue on board. Disappointingly, the recipients on the ground reported that, of the twenty-six tons dropped, only two tons were recovered. C–130s of the 374th Wing made six more GRADS drops at An Loc in the next four days (through 23 April), some of them by daytime. During the eight missions, not a single C–130 was hit by ground fire, but the percentage of successful load recovery remained dismal. Many loads smashed into the ground while others broke apart during descent. Many other bundles descended far from the drop zone.

Part of the problem stemmed from unfamiliarity among the Vietnamese army's 90th Parachute Maintenance and Delivery Base Unit and their few American advisors with methods of rigging for high-altitude, low-opening drops. Technical manuals on the subject were nonexistent, and the lack of certain hardware items necessitated improvisations, some of them unsuccessful.

At the heart of matters, however, was the unreliability of the HALO delayed-opening mechanism. This incorporated a forty-second pyrotechnic timer designed to cause the parachute to open about six hundred feet above the ground. The timer actuated a cutter that severed a cord and allowed air to enter the skirt of the standard G–12D parachute. The skirt rig was locally developed, and it appeared that the restraining cord was too thin, often breaking soon after release thus causing premature parachute opening. When this happened, loads drifted downwind for as much as ten minutes with gross inaccuracy. In other cases, cutters failed to sever the cord and webbing at all. In an attempt to clear up the problem, a 374th Wing officer watched from a plane as a C–130 overhead made drops of dummy loads. Of eight bundles individually dropped, four opened prematurely, two not at all. It was plain that substantial technical improvement was mandatory, and the high-altitude drops were stopped after April 23.[11]

Beginning on the night of April 23/24, 374th Wing crews returned to container delivery system altitudes. Although realistic training in visual night drops had been nonexistent, darkness promised protection from the otherwise prohibitive curtain of fire. During the first two nights the blacked-out C–130s enjoyed some surprise, and U.S. advisors on the ground reported "possible recovery" by the Vietnamese of 120 of the 170 tons dropped. Major Brya advised crews to make run-ins at one thousand feet, descending to drop altitude shortly before release. Some crews flew lower, popping up in the final minutes. Crews often found the moonlight sufficient for visual orientation with the ground, and the fires at An Loc marked the town from a distance. Brya also coordinated with gunship liaison officers at Saigon, arranging tactics for fixed-wing gunship support. The AC–130 crews delivered near-continuous fire during the transport run-ins, hosing down known hot spots and replying to tracers. The communists nevertheless continued their barrage tactics, saturating the air over the drop zone, apparently getting warning of approaching transports from observers some distance out. The fourth C–130 over An Loc on the third night, April 25/26, crashed a mile from the drop zone after entering the wall of fire.

Two preceding C–130s that night also received hits, one of them sustaining severe damage.

The crash ended drops that night and weather forced cancellation of ten missions scheduled for the next, April 26/27. Planning meanwhile commenced for a ten-plane daylight standard-level (six hundred feet) mission. Each plane was to run in along a common patch at one-minute intervals supported by heavy suppressive airstrikes. Colonel Iosue thought the mission would be "plain suicide," a view shared among the forward air controller pilots familiar with conditions at An Loc. The plan therefore was abandoned. Two aircraft made daytime drops on the twenty-seventh and most of the cargo was recovered, but both planes received battle damage. Iosue remained reluctant to expose his crews to the daytime crucible, especially since the number of drop-qualified crews was small, necessitating that the same men be used repeatedly. Crewmen wore flak vests and helmets; loadmasters draped trash cans with heavy chain and climbed inside while over the drop zone. Seat armor—previously removed to save weight—was reinstalled. Meanwhile, a final Vietnamese Air Force C–123 high-altitude effort the night of April 27/28 resulted in the recovery of only 6 of 116 bundles dropped.

For the next seven days the Air Force C–130 force made night drops exclusively, thirty-seven drop sorties in all. U.S. advisors at An Loc reported that during the seven nights 35 tons were recovered, 96 tons "possibly recovered," and 350 tons "probably lost." They further reported that enemy barrages over the drop zone continued to increase in volume and intensity. More than half the night-drop C–130s took hits, and the loss of a third C–130 with all six crewmen on the night of May 3/4 forced a decision to terminate the night standard-level drops. To this point, in addition to the three C–130s destroyed, another thirty-eight had been hit by enemy fire at An Loc, twenty-six of them in the night drops since April 27.[12]

The disappointing results of the night effort were no reflection on the ingenuity of those engaged. Several expedients were devised to aid in spotting the soccer field drop zone. One relied on illumination by aerial flares, although this had the disadvantage of silhouetting the drop ships for enemy gunners. Devices to mark the drop zone included ignited cans of gasoline, portable runway lights, and markers placed by air. Transport crews, however, had trouble spotting all types of markers amid the fires and lights of An Loc. Good results were achieved by the use of the white-light searchlight carried by AC–130 and AC–119 gunships. When using this method the gunship crew orbited the battlefield, keeping oriented to the location of the soccer field and spotlighting it as the C–130 made its run-in. The light was customarily turned off just before the C–130 entered the cone of illumination, allowing the drop to be completed in darkness. For deception the gunship crews sometimes used the searchlight even when no drop was forthcoming. The method had been used at Dak Seang in 1970 and proved equally successful at An Loc. Use of the light, however, increased the danger of ground fire to both gunship and transport.[13]

Termination of the night drops coincided with rockbottom conditions on the ground at An Loc. Medical and sanitation conditions were horrible. One U.S. Army advisor, a major, arrived in An Loc on May 1 and reported that ammunition stocks were "highly critical" and that the food situation was "very dire." People were hungry and in some cases starving. Colonel Miller, interviewed three weeks later, expressed contempt for the early failure of air resupply. To Miller there was no explanation but "gross neglect on someone's part in the Air Force."[14] Another American advisor, an Army captain, made a quieter but equally telling commentary on the airdrop effort:

> Up through the 3rd or 4th of May, the (drop effort) was totally unacceptable and totally unsatisfactory, and as far as I'm concerned one of the real puzzling aspects of the entire operation is why it took the Air Force approximately 26 days to get with the program to do a job that their pilots are supposed to be trained to do on a routine basis. Our figures from the time the first drops started until 1 May indicated we only received 8 percent of the resupply.[15]

Colonel Miller also was unrestrained in criticizing the failure of the Vietnamese commanders to organize the bundle recovery effort. The problem grew from the communist habit of launching mortar attacks a few minutes after each airdrop. Miller felt that Vietnamese officers were unwilling to personally enforce discipline on the exposed drop zone. Loads landing anywhere inside the defended perimeter became fair game for any troops willing to risk "grab and run." Colonel Miller saw hospital patients with limbs missing struggling to recover food for themselves, only to receive additional wounds in the effort. On one occasion an American officer carrying C–rations was challenged at gunpoint, and at least once troops of the Vietnamese 5th Division fired on rangers and paratroops attempting to retrieve rations. Munitions were sometimes left above ground exposed to shelling. Darkness brought further problems in load recovery. Spotters were positioned to watch for descending bundles, and flashlights were placed on bundles just before release. But there was no way to stop the enemy shells.[16]

Unlike at Khe Sanh the Air Force sent no combat control team, no aerial port team, nor a mission commander to An Loc. Although a combat team was ready and eager to go, Colonel Iosue opposed subjecting the men to the confused and dangerous situation on the ground. While the team might have been of some assistance—marking the drop zone for the night missions and giving information on drop accuracy—Iosue remained firm. In effect, Air Force forward air controllers replaced the combat team for control, spotting, and coordination. Had the controller method failed, the combat team was available for landing by helicopter.[17]

The allies continued their efforts to make high-altitude rigging methods work, persisting even during the period of the night drops. Their approach was twofold—to augment the Vietnamese rigger force with Americans and to seek technical improvements. Parachute experts from TAC, from the Ching Chuan Kang aerial port at Taiwan, and from the U.S. Army's Okinawa-based 549th Quartermaster Company (Aerial Delivery), arrived at Tan Son Nhut to troubleshoot. On April 24, seventy additional men arrived from the 549th to join the Vietnamese in preparing chutes and loads. The work of packing and rigging was done at the east side of the Tan Son Nhut flight line, adjacent to a small aircraft loading area. Riggers worked shifts up to twenty hours under tightened supervision and inadequately protected from wet weather.

This activity led to an improved HALO system which was successfully tested in drops near Tan Son Nhut. This method, wherein the parachute descended in partly filled condition before the cutter activated, had been tried in the United States during all-weather delivery system tests and now proved workable at Tan Son Nhut, using heavier reefing lines and locally procured metal adapter rings. The new method appeared reliable for use with available fifty-second cutters and allowed release from nearly ten thousand feet. These and other modifications, along with more riggers, prompted a decision on May 3 to resume high-altitude, low-opening drops at An Loc.[18]

The resumption of HALO drops, again using ground radar guidance, met with partial success. Advisors at An Loc recorded that of sixteen bundles dropped on May 4 by two C–130s using the modified HALO method no parachutes opened prematurely and all loads but one landed within the drop zone. Rigging difficulties, however, were still encountered, and more than half the chutes failed to open fully, resulting in considerable destruction of cargo (although much was salvaged). On the next day, May 5, eleven C–130s made drops, each with eight-ton loads of ammunition, food, and medical supplies. Of eighty-eight bundles seventy-three landed in the drop zone. Fifteen chutes opened high, and once again more than half failed to open. Another twenty-one drops during the next two days yielded similar results. Over the four days, May 4–7, a total of 185 one-ton bundles were recovered.

The American Army advisors at An Loc kept a daily log of their activities and observations. Many entries described the abysmal conditions and criticized the conduct of the defenders. Standing out, however, were comments on the improved resupply. On the fourth: "today was a good day for C-130 resupply." The next day the number of chutes that failed to open was disappointing but "supplies recovered included mortar ammo, rice, small arms ammo, and C-rations (fruit and meat)." On the seventh: "resupply today was great. Only one pod landed outside the perimeter and it's in a place where the VC can't get it." One American officer on the ground at An Loc noted that the successful drops quickly restored confidence and morale, reversing the earlier "total frustration."[19]

Ballistics computation for the high-altitude drops required two steps. The navigator first calculated ballistics for the period of normal container descent which began upon parachute opening. This result was then combined with data for the period of free-fall reefed descent. The two vectors were plotted backwards from the desired point of impact, and the resultant was passed to the mobile search site operators. Wind information was taken from forecast data or doppler observations. Crews often made double passes, dropping only a few bundles on the first run and adjusting point of impact on the second. AC-130 gunship crews began providing wind information from their gunfiring computers for use in the ballistics calculations. Finally, enlargement of the defended perimeter permitted expansion of the drop zone and lessened the need for precision.[20]

Several measures were tried to overcome the continuing problem of parachutes that failed to open. First, on May 7, several rigging specialists discovered that the reefing lines in use were considerably shorter than the prescribed length. As a result, chutes were unable to gather air during reefed descent and were thus unlikely to open properly upon dereefing. Second, the riggers fitted a second timer and cutter to each bundle to improve the probability of proper cut. Finally, starting on May 8, twenty-foot slings were inserted between each chute and its load to allow a better chance for proper chute filling. The results of these measures were quickly evident—the incidence of unopened chutes dropped to five percent on May 10 and remained negligible thereafter.

The realization that the supply of fifty-second delay devices was approaching exhaustion was of concern. The use of double cutters on each bundle was therefore discontinued, but nevertheless on May 8 less than a two-day supply remained. A modest stock of thirty-second devices remained on hand but these would entail flying at a considerably lower (and more dangerous) altitude. Additional fifty-second and new sixty-second delay mechanisms were available only from fresh production and only after a wait of at least thirty-five days. Also disquieting was a Seventh Air Force report that on April 29 the communists had introduced and fired an SA-7 surface-to-air missile in Quang Tri Province. The possibility of SA-7s in the vicinity of An Loc made a return to low-level C-130 operations almost unthinkable.

TACTICAL AIRLIFT

Once again a fresh method was at hand to overcome these latest problems. A C–130 crew made the first "high-velocity" drop at An Loc on May 8, using thousand-pound bundles fitted to fifteen-foot slotted parachutes. These chutes were designed to stabilize descent at roughly one hundred feet-per-second, about four times the normal impact velocity with the G–12 parachutes. There was no low-opening phase and the need for a delay mechanism was entirely eliminated. Accuracy remained high because of the high-speed descent. It was essential, however, to use multiple layers of cardboard honeycomb packing material under each bundle to absorb much of the force of the greater impact.

In eleven high-velocity drop missions during May 8–10, sixty-nine tons were successfully delivered. Of 140 bundles 139 landed inside the drop zone and there were no parachute malfunctions. Although HALO missions continued at reduced frequency (twenty-one missions during May 8–14), the success of the high-velocity method made it clear that the resupply campaign would be won. Drops of both types were only temporarily interrupted during May 11 and 12 when the communists delivered their last major ground attack, once again preceded by heavy shelling and led by tanks. Although the enemy remained stubborn thereafter, later attacks were less intense than those of mid-May.

When drops resumed on the thirteenth, the suitability of the high-velocity method became still more apparent. Linear dispersion was excellent (a full load of sixteen bundles usually fell within an area 164 by 55 yards), facilitating load recovery. Two fifteen-foot chutes were now used, attached to a single two thousand-pound bundle. Descending loads were dangerous to those underneath. On one occasion, one thousand pounds of canned peaches crushed a parked jeep, and on several occasions loads of artillery munitions detonated on impact, usually after some kind of parachute malfunction. Small-arms ammunition proved able to survive partial parachute failure, and rice was indestructible if packed in cardboard. Drums of fuel usually broke, however, even under optimum conditions, and most medical supplies proved too fragile even for heavy packing. During May 13–17 the C–130s made seventy-four high-velocity drop sorties, and over nine hundred tons were successfully recovered of roughly one thousand tons dropped. Over ninety-five percent of the bundles landed within the boundaries of the drop zone, now over 1,640 yards square. Use of single twenty-two-foot slotted chutes with one-ton loads began on May 29, promising further improvement in reliability.[21]

Vietnamese Air Force helicopters operating from Lai Khe attempted periodic deliveries of light cargo and passengers to An Loc, and evacuation of casualties. Usually several UH–1s would make the attempt flying at low altitudes slightly east of Highway 19. A–1s and helicopter gunships gave close fire support. Upon reaching the landing zone, the transport helicopters climbed into an orbit circle then descending one by one to unload and pick up patients. These procedures totally failed to thwart enemy gunners, and their fire or marginal weather stopped most missions. Those that landed were usually mobbed by able-bodied men rushing to board. Colonel Miller blasted the Vietnamese officers for "criminal negligence" for remaining in their bunkers while the wounded died, helplessly awaiting evacuation on the landing zone. Medical evacuations became successful only after the return of discipline to An Loc in June.[22]

Radio communications with An Loc were satisfactory using both Vietnamese and U.S. advisory channels. Supply requirements were consolidated at Vietnamese divisional headquarters in An Loc, were passed to the III Corps logistics section at Lai Khe, and finally to Central Logistics Command in Saigon. Supplies from Vietnamese army depot stocks were trucked to Tan Son Nhut for rigging and loading; cargo manifests were simultaneously telephoned to Lai Khe for transmittal to An Loc. The supply cycle—from request to airdrop delivery—ordinarily took three days. One-day responsiveness could be attained if necessary and delays beyond four days were exceptional.

During the week ending May 24, An Loc requested 547 tons of supplies and 544 tons were actually delivered. Requirements thereafter stabilized, so that on most dates C–130s made four drop sorties at An Loc releasing sixty-four bundles. The composition of loads now differed substantially from that originally envisioned. The discovery of a satisfactory water source in An Loc early in the siege ended the need for water deliveries, while the destruction of most of the defenders' artillery pieces reduced munitions requirements. Deliveries of rice and small-arms ammunition were most frequent, while needs developed for antitank weapons and medical supplies.[23]

Confidence in the airlift among personnel at An Loc stimulated efforts to restore discipline and establish control over bundle recovery. Starting about mid-May the divisional logistics officer, a full colonel, was physically present on the primary drop zone during recoveries, supervising and listing materiel. When he was wounded, his deputy continued in this important role. Eventually the airborne brigade was given responsibility for all recovery. Gradual relief from enemy shelling was a blessing to the retrieval parties, and the time needed to break down and recover each bundle (according to one report) had been cut to less than two minutes. The absence of usable vehicles was a great handicap and led to efforts to shift points of impact closer to recipient units. This was partly successful, an indication of the accuracy and low dispersion of high-velocity GRADS drops.[24]

TACTICAL AIRLIFT

The development of man-portable surface-to-air missiles in the 1960s held crucial implication for the tactical airlift arm. In an arena such as Vietnam where there was no formal battle line, infantrymen armed with heat-seeking rockets might at small cost challenge the accustomed operational freedom of allied transports and helicopters in any or all regions. The tactical airlift center at Pope Air Force Base in 1967 undertook a study of possible countermeasures, identified the vulnerability of airlift planes, and recommended likely countermeasure such as the use of shielding and cooling devices to suppress engine heat. CINCPAC and the Joint Chiefs of Staff in 1968 took firm positions against export of U.S. Army Redeye missiles to most allied countries for fear that the technology might be used against friendly forces in Vietnam. Projects in the United States in 1971 examined possible C-130 evasive maneuvers when under SAM attack, and attempted to ascertain the infrared signature of the C-130. Thus, although aircrews and aircraft of the Seventh Air Force were in 1972 unprepared for the advent of SAMs in South Vietnam, a body of relevant knowledge had been amassed elsewhere in the U.S. military establishment.[25]

Several weeks after the first reported use of the SA-7 Strela in Quang Tri Province in early April, firings were detected in several other areas of Vietnam. By mid-June allied crews had reported a total of 145 launches. The allies quickly identified characteristics of the Soviet-made weapon—fifty-four inches in length, tube-launched, with infrared-seeker head, and carrying about two pounds of explosive. Speed was Mach 1.3 with an altitude capability to 10,000 feet. The Strela operator had to visually sight his target before launching. Introduction of the SA-7 posed a serious threat to low-flying and low-performance craft and prompted the allies to seek immediate countertactics. The U.S. Army on May 9 advised units of evasive techniques derived from tests using allied heat-seeking missiles. A multiservice meeting was held at Nellis Air Force Base, Nev., on May 11-12 with the conferees divided into groups, for fighters, forward air controllers, helicopters, and tactical transports. Accumulated knowledge formed the basis for recommended tactical airlift operations.[26]

SA-7 firings began at An Loc on May 11 and possibly accounted for the loss of two air controller aircraft. Late the next day an AC-130 gunship was damaged substantially by a Strela hit, and on the fourteenth a Strela downed an Air Force 0-2 forward air controller aircraft. Briefers warned C-130 drop crews to be alert for SAM firings and advised them, when sighting an oncoming missile, to eject flares and turn sharply into the missile path (thus using the aircraft wings to shield engine heat). C-130 drops continued from altitudes of ten thousand feet and above, so the earlier development of a high-altitude drop capability allowed resupply to continue at An Loc despite the SAM threat. Gunship operations were more

EASTER OFFENSIVE

seriously hindered because of the ineffectiveness of most gunship weaponry from ten thousand feet.

The Nellis tactics proved sound. One AC–130 crew reported that their flares successfully decoyed an SA–7. No airlift C–130s were hit by SA–7s, although four 374th Wing crews operating in Vietnam reported SAM attacks during May and June. Major Brya observed no excessive anxiety among C–130 crewmen over the new threat, noting that many individuals felt confidence in the prescribed countertactics. South Vietnamese troops captured several SA–7s in late May and gave some of these to the Americans for study. By late 1972, nineteen captured SA–7s were undergoing multiservice tests in the United States. The Air Force procured additional flare dispensers for installation on C–130 and other aircraft types and funded for prototype flare systems specifically designed for missile decoying. Investigations began, seeking new missile detection systems using doppler radar principles, in hopes of ending dependence on visual detection of oncoming missiles.[27]

Helicopters were even more vulnerable to SAM weapons than were fixed-wing aircraft. The U.S. Army promptly began to equip its UH–1s in Vietnam with scoop devices, designed to shield the hot metal of the engine and to diffuse exhaust gases upward. Vietnamese Air Force UH–1s received the same modification starting in August 1972. Soon afterwards Air Force planners decided to install flare dispensers on certain Vietnamese craft, including fixed-wing transports and CH–47s. Weight and size limitations ruled out the same modification for the Huey's. Helicopter crews quickly learned that the best defense against the SA–7 was to fly at altitudes below fifty feet, when possible along roads controlled by friendly forces. Vietnamese Air Force UH–1s were successful in breaking the lock of oncoming missiles by turning to face the SAM if given sufficient warning time; lock was usually broken when the engine tailpipe passed the forty-five-degree oblique. The CH–47, however, appeared to have too large an infrared profile for such tactics. Col. Thomas A. Barr, director of operations of the Air Force Advisory Group, concluded that the principal countermeasures were careful planning and "coordinated operations." Without preassault reconnaissance, and without substantial tactical air, artillery, and forward air controller support, Barr stated, airmobile operations in high-threat areas must be expected to result in "substantial losses."[28]

Strong communist forces remained around An Loc during June although hammered by allied tactical, B–52, and gunship aircraft. Enemy shelling of the battered city (which had totaled fifty thousand detonations in the thirty days ending May 24) fell off. South Vietnamese relief forces moved slowly toward An Loc along Highway 13, clearing the ground lines of communications and establishing firebases. C–130 ground radar air deliveries to the relief forces had begun on May 22 and encountered none of the problems which had bedeviled the drops at An Loc proper. During the first half of June, drops to the relief elements averaged about two daily and those to An Loc three or four daily, all by high-velocity GRADS.[29] The arrival at Ching Chuan Kang air base of ten C–130E aircraft from the United States, each equipped with the adverse-weather aerial delivery system, opened an alternative to GRADS guidance. The first AWADS drop at An Loc took place on June 20; others followed, but AWADS remained secondary to the GRADS method.[30]

An alternative to high-velocity rigging emerged from tests at Army laboratories in the United States. The new method employed an F–1B barometric device which actuated a cutter at a desired altitude during descent, causing a standard G–12D chute to deploy and release the smaller first-stage chute. The F–1B HALO system was instituted in part to conserve declining stocks of high-velocity rigging items and in part to reduce velocity when dropping munitions—descent speed using the G–12 was approximately twenty-six feet-per-second. Army and Air Force personnel tested the F–1B near Saigon in early June and the first operational drop took place on June 18 at An Loc. Reliability appeared little better than under the old HALO methods. Rigging malfunctions on June 22 and 23 resulted in detonations of munitions bundles on impact, while numerous high-opening parachutes spread cargo over wide areas. Fortunately, the area of allied control had expanded considerably since May, and most bundles were recovered.[31]

Vietnamese Air Force helicopters began bringing replacements to An Loc on June 11, and on June 13–14 U.S. Army helicopters hauled in fourteen hundred fresh troops. The defenders pushed slowly out of the ruins, and on June 18 the South Vietnamese command declared the siege at an end, although access by Highway 13 was still closed. After June, drops into An Loc were cut to about two daily. One plane usually used the high-velocity and one the F–1B HALO method. The F–1B proved less reliable than the fifty-second timer method but permitted drops from over ten thousand feet. Upon receipt of sixty-second cutters in August, use of the barometric cutters ended. High-velocity drops also ended in August when the supply of slotted parachutes was exhausted. The U.S. Army riggers returned to Okinawa on July 15, leaving six men as advisors and inspectors.[32]

The Vietnamese Air Force helicopters undertook more and more of the deliveries through the summer. MACV logistics officers studied alternatives to the drops, concerned over declining stocks of rigging items and

SUMMARY OF AN LOC SUPPLY, 1972*

Dates	Aircraft	Sorties	Tons Dropped	Tons Received
Preliminary Phase:				
Apr 7–12	US & VNAF CH–47	42		147
Apr 8–22	VNAF UH–1	11		5
Apr 7–18	VNAF C–123	39	195	195
Initial C–130 Phase:				
Apr 15–May 4	USAF C–130	6 day low-level		
		8 high-altitude		
		51 night low-level		
		65 total	845	47 confirmed
				231 possible
				278 total
High Altitude Phase:				
May 4–14	USAF C–130	82	622	515
May 15–27	USAF C–130	58	922	898
May 26–Jun 30	USAF C–130	98	1,568	1,440
Later Drops:				
June–Aug 31	VNAF C–123	33	195	
Jul–Sep	USAF C–130	190	2,790	2,690
Oct–Dec	USAF C–130	143	2,000	1,850
To Hwy 13, south DZs				
May 22–Jun 30	USAF C–130	56	896 est	
Jul–Aug	USAF C–130	12	168 est	
Jun–Aug 31	VNAF C–123	15	62	

TOTAL USAF C–130, April 15–June 30: 359 sorties; 4,853 tons dropped.

---

* Apps to AAR, 5th Inf Div, Binh Long Campaign, 1972 (for data to Jun 25): 7th AF, Airdrop Work Sheets (for June 25–30 and for DZ south of An Loc); hist, 374th TAW, Jul–Dec 72; rprt, Lt Col Allen R. Weeks, 7th AF, Combat Airdrop Report, Vietnam, Apr 15–Jul 15, 1972; Maj Paul T. Ringenbach, *Airlift to Besieged Areas, 7 Apr–31 Aug 72* (Project CHECO, Hickam AFB, Hawaii, 1973), p 55.

the $12,600 cost of each drop mission. Landings at Quan Loi were ruled out (despite South Vietnamese efforts to recapture the airfield) in view of the presence of SAMs and the likelihood that major runway repairs would be needed. General Hollingsworth felt that the continuing drops weakened South Vietnamese incentive to force open Highway 13, but he was overruled when he suggested a partial halt.[33]

As was typical in prolonged airdrop efforts, recovery of parachutes and rigging was a problem. During heavy fighting most chutes were left exposed to shelling and the elements. Many canopies were torn on buildings, wire, or litter, and others disappeared for impromptu uses by troops. Organized attempts to collect airdropped equipment began in late May. The Vietnamese central logistics command published a letter of instructions on the subject, and a joint American-Vietnamese team traveled to An Loc to emphasize the importance of recovery efforts. Only about ten percent of the items used in the first months at An Loc were recovered for reuse. Of those recovered by mid-July, more than a third were too badly damaged to use again and most of the rest required repairs.[34]

Although pressure against An Loc was slight during late 1972, communist forces remained in Binh Long Province and continued to threaten movements along Highway 13 and hold the Quan Loi airfield. The Air Force C–130s flew 190 drop missions at An Loc during July, August, and September, and another 143 missions during the last three months of the year. The airlift crews continued to report antiaircraft fire about An Loc, including airbursts at ten thousand feet, although no C–130s were damaged. Both sides maintained defensive positions in the region late in the year as the likelihood of an armistice agreement increased.[35]

The problems in the An Loc drop effort were new to the aircrews and riggers in Vietnam, but the solutions were soon found. Most successful was the ground radar air delivery system which achieved unsurpassed reliability and accuracy and avoided the problem of visual drop-zone identification. The technique had been tried before in Vietnam and found essentially trouble-free. The inherent limitations—the radius of coverage from the mobile search Skyspot locations, the need for precise map coordinates of the target, the need to protect the Skyspot site from enemy action, the need to use Skyspot for directing air strikes, and the occasional failures of radio and radar—had been insignificant at An Loc. The adverse-weather aerial delivery system proved a reliable backup, although in actuality the AWADS ships joined the An Loc effort after the verdict was assured.

The greatest difficulties were encountered in parachute rigging for the high-altitude drops. The high-velocity system proved the most accurate and reliable, but the need remained for some kind of high-altitude low-opening cargo requiring soft landings. The successive adaptation, first of locally skirted chutes, then of the reefed system, and finally of the F–1B method, met the immediate needs. A more significant lesson was that careful and correct rigging through prolonged training and supervision of rigger personnel was essential.

A meeting was held on May 31, 1972, at Eglin Air Force Base to examine problems brought to light during the spring campaign. Major Brya attended and gave a full briefing on recent developments in Vietnam as did Major Rohrlick, whose career in fashioning new air delivery methods dated back to the early 1960s. Major Rohrlick had gone to Tan Son Nhut from

TAC headquarters early in the An Loc campaign to troubleshoot. The Eglin discussions brought to light several cases of past liaison failures between the Pacific airlift units and the stateside development agencies. The group reviewed anti-SAM tactics and emphasized the importance of the forward air controller for on-the-scene coordination of drops. Among other technical points the group noted that—incredibly—most C–130s still lacked permanently installed FM radios, so crews had been unable to talk with persons on the ground at An Loc.[36]

Although the main danger at An Loc had been from conventional ground fire, the long-feared appearance of the surface-to-air missile held major implications for the future use of airlift forces. Sustained airlanded operations at objectives surrounded by SAM-equipped forces appeared out of the question, raising doubts as to the future of fixed-wing and helicopter airlift in major offensive operations. Also discouraging was the realization that newer SAMs with better altitude capabilities could easily nullify the latest drop methods, obliging the airlifters to resort to treetop penetrations and low-level drops without ground radar assistance. The answers seemed to lie in technical and tactical countermeasures yet to be developed. It was clear that henceforth planners must be cautious before using air transport in areas likely to contain small enemy units or guerrillas.

The An Loc campaign was a classic siege with the garrison supplied entirely by air, meriting comparison with Stalingrad, Imphal, Dien Bien Phu, and Khe Sanh. The failures of April were deeply troubling to the Air Force airlifters, pained by apparent failure of their craft and the loss of three C–130s and two full crews. No apology was needed for the courage and discipline of the crews who persisted in the April low-level drops despite the likelihood of battle damage on every mission. Only one man broke psychologically under the strain—a loadmaster with long past service in the often-hit spray C–123s. Colonel Iosue grounded the man without punitive action.[37] The professionalism of those who persisted in finding a better way was beyond question and resulted in the successful high-altitude drops of May. The development of high-altitude drops was the turning point of the campaign. Without the C–130 resupply, sustained under conditions all but impossible for helicopters, the garrison at An Loc could not have survived.

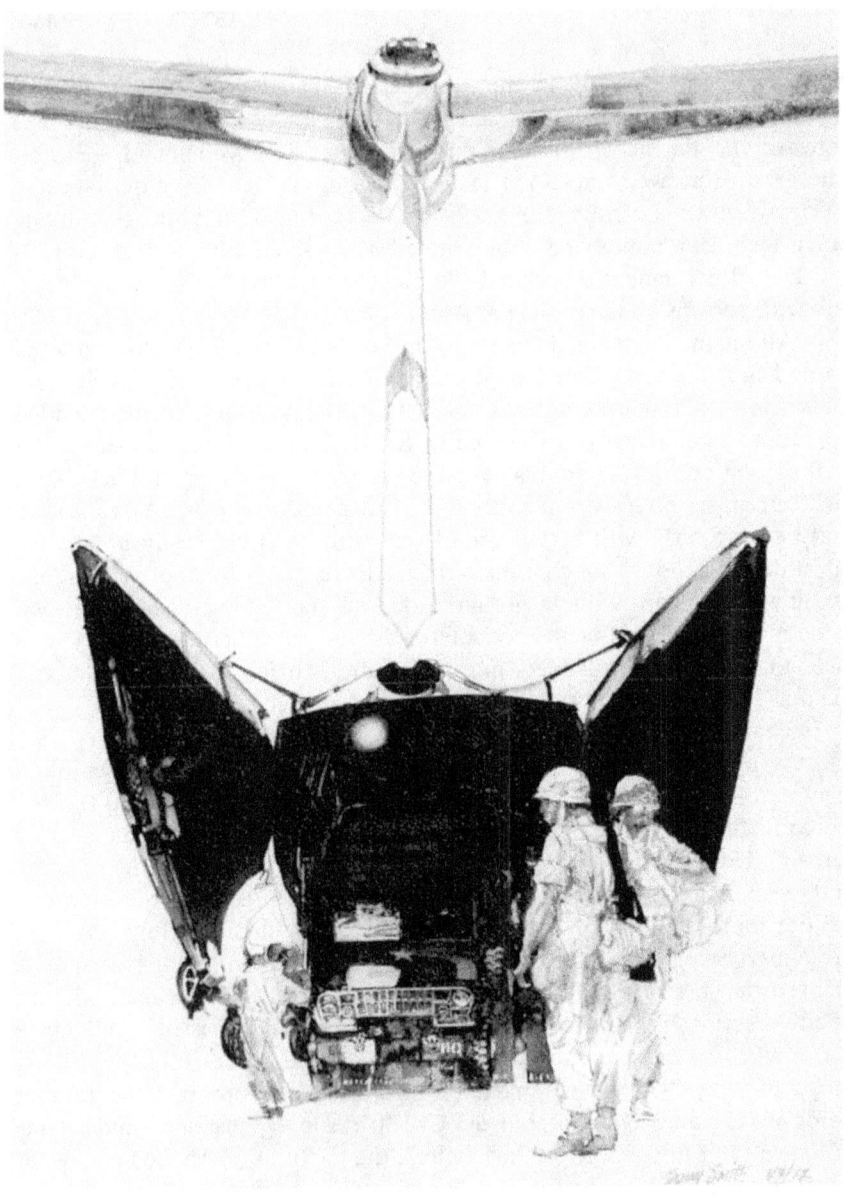

(Douglas D. Smith, Courtesy U.S. Air Force Art Collection)

C-141 Aircraft Unloading

XXII. The Easter Offensive— The Countrywide Response

The spring offensive in Binh Long Province was one of three main communist drives calculated to destroy South Vietnamese forces and together to bring down the Saigon government. The heaviest blows came in the far north where two North Vietnamese divisions began attacking southward from the demilitarized zone on the night of March 30, 1972. Another division moved against Hue from the A Shau Valley. In the central highlands, two communist divisions opened attacks on March 31 and soon swept over the old battlegrounds of Dak To, Kontum, and Pleiku. Meanwhile, in other regions, smaller forces stepped up guerrilla-like operations, menacing towns, bases, and lines of communications. Communist officers were told that Saigon "must be defeated while the U.S. is preoccupied with the elections and domestic problems."[1]

In their 1972 spring offensive the communists in part abandoned their customary tactics of camouflage and dispersion. Something resembling conventional ground warfare ensued, particularly in the northern region. Soviet and Chinese weapons were used in South Vietnam for the first time. These included the SA–7 antiaircraft missile, wire-guided missiles, bigger and more mobile artillery weapons, and new rockets (possibly up to 250–mm). Some 350 enemy tanks were in South Vietnam at the outset of the offensive and were backed by two hundred others in close reserve. No American infantry units were in active combat during the campaign.[2]

Allied air power, including a substantial air transport contribution, was unquestionably decisive in turning back the communist drives. A prolonged airlift to battered Kontum rivaled in significance and drama the An Loc resupply. Demanding night-landing techniques, airdrop methods lately worked out at An Loc, and adverse-weather aerial delivery system equipment were all used at Kontum. Throughout South Vietnam during the spring and early summer, allied airlifters made a maximum effort, moving countless units, hauling supplies, and lifting refugees. As the intensity of fighting eased in July, the airlifters gradually returned to former levels of activity, and U.S. withdrawal from Vietnam resumed.

TACTICAL AIRLIFT

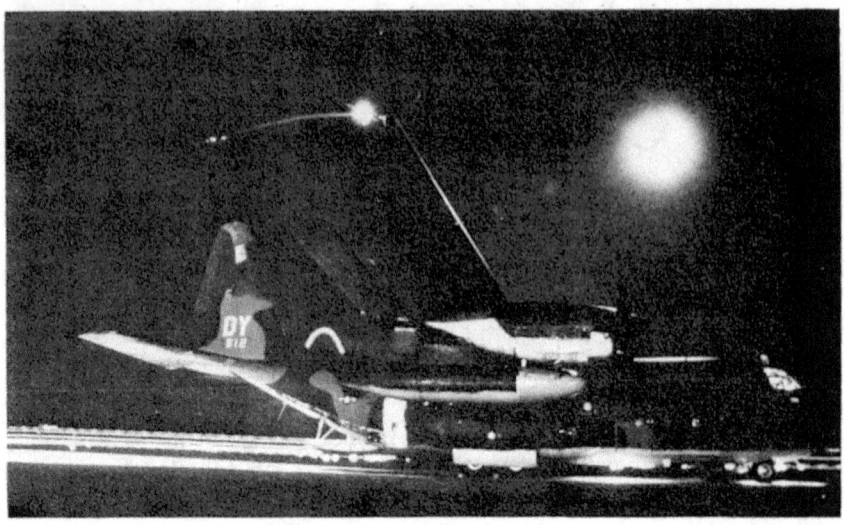

A C–130 makes a nighttime stop at Da Nang, 1972.

Air Force air transport forces in the Far East in March 1972 were awkwardly positioned for the new campaign. Recent planning anticipated that the Vietnamese Air Force would assume most in-country lift tasks. American activities therefore increasingly supported U.S. troop withdrawals and programs of Vietnamization. The 374th Tactical Airlift Wing with four C–130E squadrons at Ching Chuan Kang, Taiwan, maintained a twenty-four ship detachment at Tan Son Nhut for missions in South Vietnam and Thailand. The last C–130B squadron at Clark was scheduled for imminent inactivation. The last in-country C–123 and C–7 units were in the late stages of transfer to the Vietnamese Air Force. Col. Richard J. Downs, former vice commander of the 834th Air Division, on March 18 replaced General Germeraad as Director of Airlift, Seventh Air Force—the office which now fulfilled the functions once performed by the 834th. Also deep in the scaling-down process was the 2d Aerial Port Group, now operating ports at only six locations.[3] Vietnamese airlift units were heavily occupied with training and upgrade programs, although during the relatively quiet month of March Vietnamese Air Force transports performed eighty-five percent of the airlift required by Vietnamese military forces. The Air Force Advisory Group listed five Vietnamese transport squadrons as combat-ready. Two were equipped with C–123s, and one each with C–119s, C–47s, and C–7s.[4]

Indications of communist offensive preparations on several fronts, coupled with the withdrawal of American ground units from combat roles, made countrywide fixed-wing transport mobility vital. Units of the South Vietnamese general reserve were kept available for short-notice movements to active regions. The uncommitted reserve in late March consisted of two

THE COUNTRYWIDE RESPONSE

airborne brigades (with six battalions, one at Vung Tau and five at Saigon) and a Marine brigade. The third airborne brigade was already committed in Kontum Province, with three battalions operating in the ridges southwest of Dak To, and two Marine brigades operating in the northern provinces.[5]

Shifts of general reserve forces began on March 31. U.S. and Vietnamese Air Force transports commenced a thirty-six-hour effort, lifting troops and equipment of 3d Airborne Battalion along with a divisional command post from Tan Son Nhut to Kontum. Eight C–130s flew around the clock carrying 425 tons of troops and materiel north. Vietnamese Air Force C–123s meanwhile loaded and refueled on the opposite side of the Tan Son Nhut flight line. Trucks, jeeps, howitzers, ammunition, rations, and troops moved from a staging area by exact planeloads to the two loading sites. Ground times for the C–130s at Tan Son Nhut averaged one hour. Offloadings at Kontum were executed with minimum (fifteen-minute) ground time.[6]

The communists gained early successes in Quang Tri Province where weather and antiaircraft missilery minimized allied air superiority. General Abrams on April 1 reported that the situation in the north was "bad, and it is going to get worse," and he expected the Vietnamese to reinforce the region with Marines. Two battalions of marines and the Marine division headquarters moved north by air on April 4 followed by three ranger the general reserve. For the ranger deployment, U.S. and Vietnamese Air Force transports lifted four thousand men and over one hundred vehicles to Phu Bai on April 4–5, completing the lift in twenty-seven hours. The reinforcements allowed a measure of defense in depth along the northern front and were helpful in temporarily stalling the communist advance short of Dong Ha.[7]

During the first week the C–130s began hauling South Vietnamese units out of the delta region, delivering them to Bien Hoa to cope with the situation in Binh Long. Upon landing, troops shifted to trucks or helicopters for further movement toward An Loc. The C–130s made pickups at Can Tho, Quan Long, Xuan Loc, and other strips, fields shorter and rougher than most used in recent years. To head off accidents and as an aid in scheduling, Colonel Iosue reestablished the system of classifying pilots according to shortfield skills. As it turned out, the unit pickup flights gave valuable refresher training in shortfield techniques, soon to be tested under more demanding conditions at Kontum.[8]

Other pressing tasks included lifts of military supplies and equipment to Kontum, Phu Bai, Tay Ninh, and other hot spots. Tents, blankets, and other relief supplies for tens of thousands of refugees were flown to the northern provinces. Flights returning from the combat regions often carried refugees. During the first week of the offensive, U.S. Air Force transports groups from locations in III and IV Corps, newly designated as part of

561

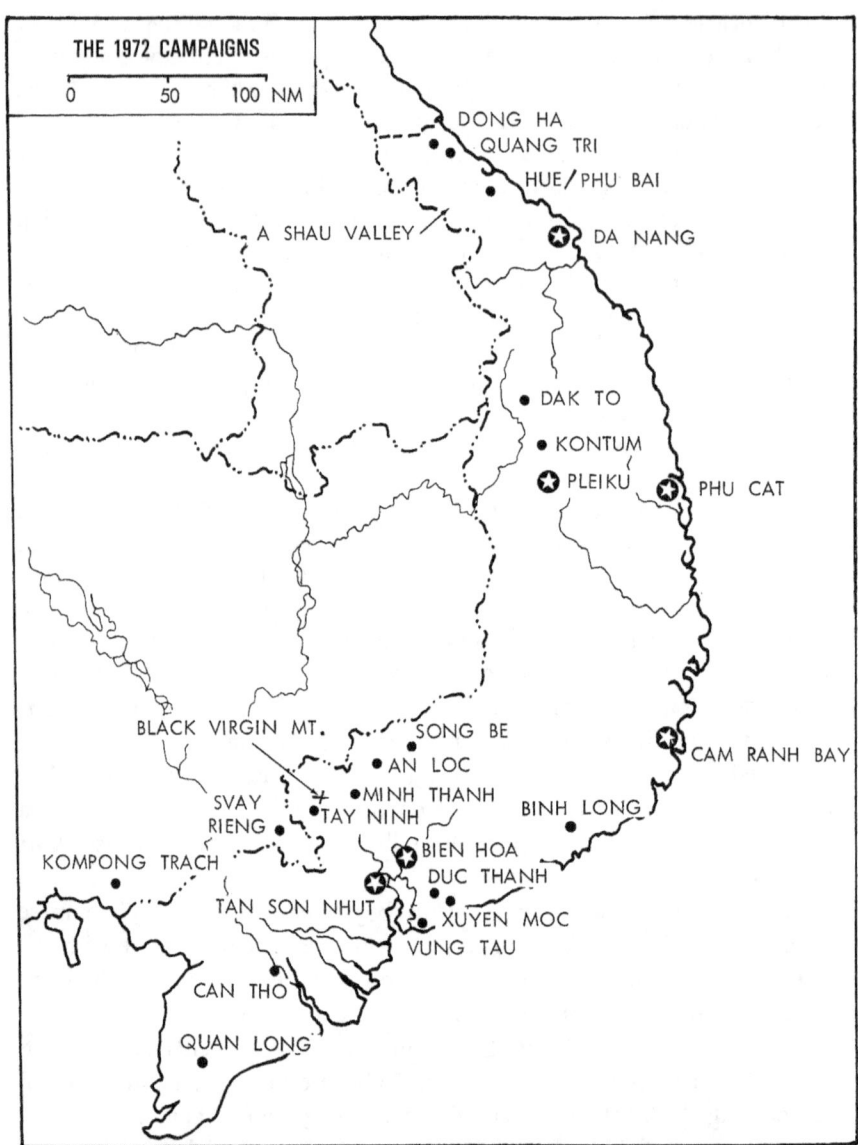

hauled sixteen thousand passengers and twenty-three hundred tons of cargo —twenty and fifty percent respectively above the recent weekly averages.[9]

An early decision to send additional 374th Wing transports, along with all available aircrews, into Vietnam made this surge of effort possible. The in-country C–130 force was quickly expanded to forty and soon afterwards to forty-four. Forty-four was the maximum number that could be accommodated at Tan Son Nhut, including twenty unsheltered aircraft. In-country aircrews rose from forty-three to sixty; maintenance strength

THE COUNTRYWIDE RESPONSE

increased from 260 to 370 men. All in-country aircraft were flown to the maximum, around the clock.[10]

At the end of the first week communist tanks and infantry were operating south of the Cua Viet River, apparently trying to effect a double envelopment of Quang Tri city. Pressures were building in the highlands country, particularly in the ridges north and east of Dak To. Meanwhile the situation in Binh Long was fast deteriorating. It was clear that a crisis lay ahead.[11]

The events in Vietnam meant plenty of overwater work for the C–130s based at Ching Chuan Kang and in the United States. Ships and crews from TAC supported the transpacific movements reinforcing tactical fighter units. The Joint Chiefs on April 5 directed the first such move, Constant Guard I, shifting two F–4 squadrons and additional F–105G and EB–66 craft to Thailand. Five C–130s of the Langley-based 316th Tactical Airlift Wing hauled support teams to Hickam and Guam, and later lifted the teams on to Thailand. Transports of the Military Airlift Command meanwhile moved other personnel and equipment to final destinations. Deployments under Constant Guard II and III were similarly supported by the other TAC C–130 wings. The Pacific-based C–130s meanwhile assisted in several unit movements from offshore bases to Vietnam, including shifts of Air Force and Marine air units. To facilitate these hauls the 374th Wing on April 6 opened a control element at Naha. The wing's 130s thereafter joined Marine KC–130s and MAC transports to link the Marine air units at Da Nang, Bien Hoa, and (after mid-May) Thailand, with their home bases at Iwakuni and on Okinawa. Daily C–130 service to Bien Hoa also supported Air Force strike and gunship aircraft assigned there from their main operating bases in Thailand.[12]

The most demanding tasks, however, were in-country missions to and from the regions of heavy fighting. During the second week of the offensive, Air Force transports in Vietnam hauled twenty-five thousand passengers and forty-three hundred tons of cargo, up substantially from the initial week. For the full month of April the 374th Wing flew 7,344 hours, up from 4,890 hours in March; 115 hours per plane, up from 76. Vietnamese Air Force transports lifted thirty-three hundred tons during April, up from nineteen hundred tons in March and roughly one-fourth of the C–130 workload. A highlight of this activity was the withdrawal of one of the airborne brigades from the highlands. Urgently needed for the An Loc relief effort, the brigade was lifted from Kontum during April 20–24.[13]

Conditions seemed more desperate in the northern provinces of South

TACTICAL AIRLIFT

Vietnam, where Vietnamese Air Force helicopters and transports labored in difficult weather to overcome the region's chronic transportation problems. Communist road interdiction intermittently isolated the region from Da Nang, intensifying the urgency of the airlift effort. The Vietnamese Air Force during April attempted airdrops at several fire support bases southwest of Hue and at Quang Tri city. The small size of the drop zones, difficult weather, and enemy fire, all contributed to disappointing results. Serious shortages of food, munitions, and fuel set the stage for the May 1 fall of Quang Tri and the disorganized retreat toward Hue.[14]

American and Vietnamese transports joined in supply drops to a South Vietnamese blocking force at Kompong Trach, in Cambodia, west of Tay Ninh. Vietnamese C–123s in late April achieved a bundle recovery rate of eighty percent although enemy ground fire steadily increased. An initial U.S. Air Force C–130 drop on April 24 was successful using daylight container-drop techniques. The ship however received eighty-six hits.* Enemy gunners were apparently concentrated along the highway used as a run-in guide by the drop crews. The Americans shifted to night drops, still using the normal container-drop altitude of six hundred feet, but five of the eight C–130s dropping at Kompong Trach during April received battle damage. Soon afterwards the South Vietnamese force withdrew, but its spirited action may have reduced enemy pressure in the delta provinces of South Vietnam.[15]

The few Air Force C–123s, C–7s, and C–130Bs still in the Far East made modest contributions to the action. The ten C–123s at Tan Son Nhut flew seventeen hundred airlift sorties during April, including numerous supply and refugee evacuation missions into and out of Song Be. The final Air Force Caribou squadron made 811 airlift sorties in April before being deactivated on May 1. Several C–7s and crews flew around-the-clock radio relay orbits out of Da Nang and Tan Son Nhut, linking tactical air control party personnel on the ground with direct air support centers. Meanwhile, the C–130Bs and crews of the Clark-based 774th Squadron undertook tasks within Thailand from a reopened operating location at U–Tapao. The Joint Chiefs of Staff in April approved a CINCPAC request to extend the tenure of the 774th in the Far East into the summer.[16]

Another asset was the Military Airlift Command's C–141 force, accustomed to operating in and out of Vietnam from off shore. The C–141s had been successfully used for shipments entirely within Vietnam during Lam Son 719 and procedures for such emergency usage subsequently had been codified. Beginning on April 21, 1972, MAC C–141s again began shuttling passengers and cargo between Tan Son Nhut and the other main in-country bases, principally Da Nang, Bien Hoa, and Pleiku. Planes and

---

* The crew hit on April 24 over Kompong Trach was the one shot down the next night at An Loc.

crews were based for one or more nights at Tan Son Nhut and performed two or more days of in-country work before departing for offshore destinations. This C–141 effort permitted the C–130s to concentrate on drops, unit hauls, and deliveries to forward locations. During the week beginning April 28, for example, the MAC transports flew 193 in-country sorties, lifting thirty-five hundred passengers and 1,630 tons of cargo, equal to twenty-five percent of the total Air Force in-country workload. The project lasted four weeks. Usually four C–141s worked in Vietnam daily although the effort expanded briefly to eight planes in late April. A highlight of the operation was the evacuation of 394 refugees in a single C–141 sortie from Pleiku to Saigon on April 30.[17]

Despite such help the stepped-up effort in Vietnam seriously strained the men of the 374th Wing. Many aircrewmen found themselves exceeding the thirty-day limitation of 120 flying hours. When not flying, crews found rest difficult in the severely crowded billets at Tan Son Nhut. Some slept in hallways, some enlisted aircrews and ground crews slept in the airplanes. The conditions prompted concern among flight surgeons of the Seventh Air Force and the 374th Wing. To meet the rising maintenance workload, men were sent to Ching Chuan Kang on temporary duty from other Pacific bases and individuals finishing Far East tours were invited to volunteer for extensions. The maintenance supervisors, Colonel Iosue felt, were especially overworked.[18]

The critical situations at An Loc, Kontum, and Quang Tri at the end of April made it apparent that the countrywide demand for more and more airlift would continue. Select TAC C–130 units in late April received preliminary notice to prepare for possible deployment to the Pacific. Upon direction by the Joint Chiefs of Staff, TAC in early May sent ten C–130s to the Pacific to replace aircraft out of service because of battle damage. In recommending further augmentations the Joint Chiefs on May 10 informed the Secretary of Defense that the Pacific force was already "committed at near-maximum level," and that the use of C–141s in Vietnam had strained MAC's capabilities elsewhere, forcing cancellation of most training. Two TAC C–130 squadrons during May 13–15, under Constant Guard IV, left for 179-day temporary duty tours with the 374th Wing at Ching Chuan Kang. One squadron was from the 316th Wing which sent fourteen planes to join two already in the Far East with Constant Guard III. The other was primarily from the 314th Wing at Little Rock, augmented from the 317th Wing at Pope to make up a sixteen-plane unit capable of all-weather cargo delivery. Each squadron included support personnel and forty aircrews. All aircraft flew the familiar transpacific route, and the last arrived on Taiwan on May 19. Two days later the first TAC planes and crews flew to Tan Son Nhut. Thereafter, the TAC force shared in all in-country work, including the critical effort at Kontum, and eventually took exclusive responsibility for all in-country drops.[19]

565

TACTICAL AIRLIFT

The fighting in the central highlands was at least as desperate as in Binh Long Province, and the contribution of the Air Force airlift nearly as crucial. Communist action in early April closed Highway 19, the main communication line to Pleiku from the coast. Battles north and west of Pleiku meanwhile sharply increased allied consumption of munitions and fuel, compounding resupply problems into and within the region. On April 16 John Paul Vann, senior American advisory official in the region, stated that stocks in the highlands were down to three days supply and that, although air shipments had recently begun, these appeared insufficient to sustain the necessary flow. The communist offensive gained momentum with the capture on April 24 of the town and airstrip at Dak To, long a focus for C–130 operations into the triborder area. On the same day communist units isolated Kontum by closing the roadway from Pleiku.

Numerous airlifts hauled munitions and equipment into Pleiku and Kontum airfields. The most noteworthy were the contributions of the C–130 bladderbird aerial tankers which exploited improvements in fuel carrying developed since early in the war. On April 17, three bladderbird 130s of the 374th Wing commenced a sustained lift of fuel into Pleiku. Each plane took off from Tan Son Nhut and each made four deliveries the first day, refilling three times at Cam Ranh. Thus Pleiku received twelve 4,500-gallon deliveries the first day. Three C–130s made a similar effort the next day, and on the nineteenth the effort expanded to four aircraft— three hauling jet fuel and one carrying aviation gasoline for reciprocating engines. Bladderbird operations direct into Kontum began with delivery of 9,000 gallons on the twenty-third followed by another 24,000 gallons the following day. Stocks had fallen to 4,000 gallons, against a daily consumption of 15,600.

A steady flow of transports continued into Kontum, many bringing in hard cargo and departing with the final units of the airborne brigade. Enemy shells periodically interrupted flight-line activity and surface-to-air firing harassed planes approaching or leaving the airfield, occasionally hitting one of them. An Air Vietnam transport was hit April 22 while on the ground, killing the stewardess and wounding several passengers, and shells damaged a bladderbird while offloading on the twenty-fourth. Air Force combat control teams and aerial port personnel labored daily to keep up the flow of ships and cargo.[20]

The five-day ordeal of one of the bladderbirds exemplified the hair-raising conditions at Kontum. The pilot, Lt. Col. Reed C. Mulkey, a member of the 50th Squadron and a veteran of the 1968 campaigns, attempted a hasty departure on the twenty-sixth while being shelled. A rocket detonated immediately in front of Colonel Mulkey's aircraft, flattening the landing gear tires, causing major fuel leaks, and silencing one of the engines. Mulkey and his crew parked the damaged plane and took shelter, later returning to Saigon aboard another aircraft. A three-man repair party from the 374th returned to inspect the damage and patched the ruptured fuel tank. While they worked, incoming rockets again began exploding. One holed a C–130 which had just landed, and another made a direct hit on a Vietnamese Air Force C–123 parked next to Mulkey's C–130. The C–123 started to burn and threatened to explode and take with it the adjacent C–130. U.S. Army and Air Force bystanders courageously extinguished the fire, initially with hand extinguishers, climbing inside and atop the burning hulk.

An eleven-man team arrived at Kontum at dusk April 30 to replace the engine and tires of Mulkey's plane. Working throughout the night with flashlights and into the morning, taking shelter during intermittent rocket attacks, the team completed their tasks at midday. Meanwhile, the men watched a Vietnamese Air Force C–123 barely get off with a load of refugees amid exploding rocket shells. Colonel Mulkey and his crew arrived soon afterwards to fly out the repaired bird. Fresh rocketings promptly ventilated both the relief plane and Mulkey's, but both got out successfully, Mulkey's aircraft with fresh fuel leaks. Colonel Mulkey lost an engine on the previously undamaged side during takeoff and made a three-engine landing at Pleiku.[21]

Despite the shellings, daylight airlift into Kontum went on. During the eight days prior to May 3, the C–130s made fifteen landings daily on the average, seven ships delivering munitions, five fuel, and three rice. During the same eight days, Vietnamese Air Force transports made a total of fifteen deliveries. On May 2 a C–130 lost several feet of wingtip in a collision with a helicopter at the crowded airhead but managed an emergency landing at Pleiku.* Yet another bladderbird received rocket damage the next day. These episodes finally forced the decision to stop daytime operations into Kontum even though the road from Pleiku remained closed.[22]

The start of night landings at Kontum in part negated the improving communist ability to hit individual aircraft on the ground. Deliveries continued at about the former frequency, the 130s hauling in supplies and departing with refugees. Twice the airlifters attempted to return to daytime

---
* This plane and Mulkey's underwent extensive repairs at Pleiku amid periodic shellings; both eventually survived. Transports landed at Pleiku through the campaign, although the reopening of Highway 19 to Pleiku from Qui Nhon on April 26 reduced the urgency of the air deliveries to Pleiku.

operations, but both times were forced to return to night work exclusively. In one instance the senior Air Force officer in the region overcame ground force objections to night deliveries by promising that all supply requirements would be met. The air of desperation intensified and communist tank and infantry attacks on May 14 depleted some items of the defenders' stock of munitions to nearly zero. Incoming rounds ignited the fuel storage area the next day. On the sixteenth, shells burned two Vietnamese C–123s and detonated the ammunition loaded in one of them. Later, all three C–123s immobilized at Kontum were bulldozed aside to make offloading space for other ships. On May 17 a C–130 crashed during a daylight takeoff try, apparently damaged by rockets and exploding ammunition. Only one crewman survived.[23]

C–130 landings, again exclusively in darkness and heavily reliant on fire suppression by AC–130 gunships, resumed the night of May 18/19 with some sixteen deliveries nightly. Rockets destroyed another C–123 on the twentieth, and surface-to-air fire forced some bladderbirds to divert to Pleiku. Despite considerable effort to keep the Kontum runway clear of shrapnel litter, a C–130 blew a tire landing after midnight on May 22. Rocket fire further damaged and finally destroyed the plane the next day. On the evening of the twenty-second, another damaged C–130 managed to take off from Kontum with one tire flat and made an emergency landing at Da Nang. Eight other 130s landed and unloaded that night, May 22/23, and thirty more during the next two nights. Cargo included a considerable quantity of 105-mm ammunition. Standard C–130s now delivered jet fuel in cylindrical containers, ending use of bladderbirds thus cutting down offload time on the ground at Kontum.

The dark approaches into the tight airhead called for maximum flying precision. Usable runway length was only about thirty-one hundred feet, close to the minimum for heavily loaded C–130s. To avoid ground fire from enemy-occupied areas of Kontum city, crews flew circling approaches down to three thousand feet, avoiding use of landing lights until the last possible moment. Portable lighting outlined the location of the runway. Colonel Iosue felt that the night landings at Kontum were "a dicey operation" and that the absence of accidents under these conditions was remarkable.

Shortly before dawn on May 25, enemy troops penetrated the airfield, establishing themselves at the east end of the runway. Soon afterwards a C–130 landed to pick up the Air Force ground team personnel and received small-arms fire from three directions while loading. Although damage was not serious, it was clear that C–130 landings must cease. Fighting continued throughout Kontum city, supplied temporarily only by U.S. and Vietnamese Air Force Chinooks, while the Americans quickly prepared to start C–130 drops.[24]

THE COUNTRYWIDE RESPONSE

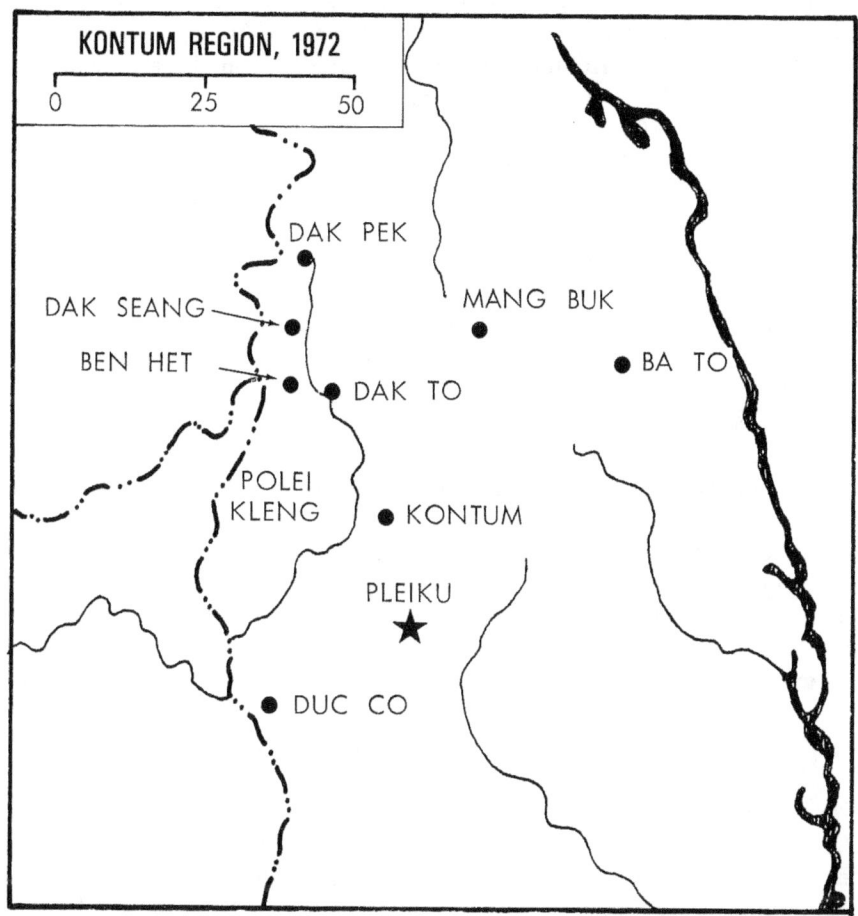

Important as a forerunner to the drops at Kontum was the recent series of drops sustaining isolated and hard-pressed camps to the north and west. In driving upon Dak To and Kontum the communists had swept around the garrisons at Ben Het, Dak Pek, and Mang Buk, places long familiar to the airlifters. At Ben Het communist fire stopped an allied attempt to evacuate the defenders by helicopters. Vietnamese Air Force supply drops missed the camp, but heavy gunship and tactical air support enabled the defenders to hang on. The U.S. Air Force began supply drops at Ben Het on May 13, successfully delivering fourteen of sixteen bundles under trying conditions. Ben Het, Dak Pek, and Mang Buk received a total of nineteen C–130 drops during May, twelve more during June. No camp received more than a single drop on any one date. Drops were performed using the high-altitude, low-opening and the high-velocity methods developed at An Loc, guided by ground radar from the mobile search site at

Pleiku. Loads averaged slightly over fifteen tons per mission. Accuracy was satisfactory, and no aircraft received hits from ground fire.[25]

Drops began at Kontum with a single mission on the afternoon of May 27. Since the communists held much of the city's eastern half, the drop zone was established near the river in the city's southwest corner. In four missions on the twenty-eighth, C-130 crews dropped sixty-four bundles of which fifty were retrieved. The 130s made three drops on the twenty-ninth, five on the thirtieth, and seven on the thirty-first. All used the ground radar high-velocity method, guided by the Pleiku mobile search radar. On June 2 government forces reclaimed much of the city, permitting use of a better drop zone in the northwest section. Load retrieval parties were enlarged to keep up with the increasing volume of delivery which totaled sixty-eight missions in the first seven days of June. On the eighth, II Corps logistics reported that drops "have been very accurate, and nearly all parachute bundles are impacting in the recovery area."

Landings resumed on the night of June 8/9, the danger from rockets and mortars having declined. Six C-130s made blacked-out, ground controlled approaches and landings that night. Only one aircraft was allowed on the ground at a time. Crews landed only after receiving assurances by radio that the field was not under attack. Reports of SA-7 firings on June 10 raised concern for the safety of the landing aircraft. To minimize this latest threat, South Vietnamese forces occupied the area east of the airstrip. During C-130 approaches, allied artillery fired into enemy-held sectors and detonated flare shells near the runway in hopes of distracting SA-7s. The only known SA-7 directed against a transport at Kontum was successfully avoided on June 13.

Daylight high-altitude drops continued, complementing the night landings. The last drop took place on June 14, a finale to forty-eight drop sorties flown since June 7. Crews had made their runs from the southeast, turning sharply immediately after release to avoid antiaircraft threat northwest of the city, and throughout the nineteen days of drops not a single C-130 received battle damage. The ground battle meanwhile continued to swing toward the allies. Effective enemy resistance in the city of Kontum ended on June 10, and the roadway from Pleiku to Kontum was reopened for convoys on June 30.[26]

The supply of Kontum once again exemplified the sometimes pivotal role of air transport in sustaining isolated ground forces. Unqualified plaudits went to the 374th Wing crews and to the TAC aircrews who performed most of the drops. The landings were executed under extreme hazards, demanding ultimate professionalism. The drops were easier, and most of them used techniques routine since the An Loc experience. In one aspect, however, the drops merited special attention: sixteen of the drops used the adverse-weather aerial delivery system, the Air Force's most recent answer to the chronic problem of all-weather delivery.

THE COUNTRYWIDE RESPONSE

The AWADS unit at Ching Chuan Kang Air Base, Taiwan (known officially as the 61st Tactical Airlift Squadron although consisting of ships and crews from both Little Rock and Pope) moved its initial contingent to Tan Son Nhut on May 21. Three days later, twenty crews and ten AWADS aircraft were on station in Vietnam. Each crew underwent a short in-country training routine consisting mainly of ground radar air delivery system checkouts, along with most of the in-country flying familiarization given all crews new to the theater. GRADS training included a three-mission cycle: crewmen first accompanied a drop mission as observers, then they themselves flew a drop with qualified crewmen on board, and finally made an unsupervised GRADS sortie. By May 31, nineteen of the squadron's crews had thus qualified. Meanwhile, the 61st Squadron had been designated the primary airdrop unit with the title of 374th Wing Airdrop Task Force. Besides flying all drop missions the task force was organized to do its own scheduling, briefing, and load inspections.[27]

Whereas the GRADS method had proven spectacularly successful at An Loc and in the early Kontum drops, the AWADS technique still remained unproven. The 61st had received its first all-weather drop ship only a year earlier, and many supposedly qualified crews had only the most limited experience with the system. All AWADS missions at Little Rock had been flown at the conventional container-drop or paratroop practice altitudes (i.e., under twelve hundred feet), altitudes close to suicidal by daylight at Kontum. Indeed the AWADS computer could accept altitudes only up to five thousand feet, but had been tested at higher altitudes by entering artificial values into the system. Nevertheless the desirability of trying AWADS in Vietnam seemed worthwhile, giving the system a stiff operational test and developing a backup for GRADS where mobile search was unavailable.[28]

The first AWADS drop took place on June 1 at Svay Rieng in the Cambodian Parrot's Beak. The pilot was Capt. Ronald G. Brundridge, the navigators Capts. David S. Dawson, Jr., and Calvin H. Chastain. Release was from ten thousand feet, cargo rigged for HALO, with thirty-second cutters. The crew used GRADS to check the AWADS solution, releasing four bundles, all of which landed within three hundred yards of the desired point. For the second pass, the crew introduced an offset correction; results were satisfactory except that cutter malfunctions caused a number of improper parachute openings.[29]

Two AWADS missions were flown at Kontum on June 3. The navigators aimed by placing their electronic crosshairs on returns from a radar beacon placed three hundred yards from the leading edge of the drop zone. The beacon was used because of concern that heavy rainshowers in the area would block natural radar returns. The hand-held, five-watt, ground beacon proved capable of avoiding the close-in scope saturation encountered when using beacons of higher output. The ground tactical situation dictated that the beacon be placed short of the drop zone, even though this prevented last-minute aiming adjustments. Nevertheless, all thirty-two bundles fell within the specified drop zone, generally within 328 yards of the desired point. Enemy fire, however, prevented recovery of half of the bundles. Releases were made from ten thousand feet above the ground. Capts. Brundridge and Dawson again were the navigators, while Capt. David A. Miles piloted the second.[30]

Beginning on June 7 and ending eight days later, C-130s made another fifteen AWADS sorties at Kontum. On all drops but one navigators used reflected radar returns to aim. A bridge south of town served for late computer update and navigators used a close-in river bend as the final offset aiming point. Often aircraft made two passes, correcting the offset distances after the first run. The drop zone measured 656 by 328 yards; the largest recorded impact error was 328 yards. All missions used high-velocity rigging, dropping from ten thousand feet. One drop, on June 12, was by a two-plane formation using electronic stationkeeping equipment, the trail aircraft dropping 5.4 seconds behind the AWADS-equipped leader. The result was spectacular, the second load landing on top of the leader's. The only problem with the stationkeeping equipment appeared to be that of flying in the leader's turbulent wake carrying a heavy cargo at slow airspeed. The Kontum AWADS drops were clearly successful, avoiding the delays typical in GRADS while the search site worked higher priority airstrikes. The average flying time for AWADS sorties at Kontum was 2.7 hours (taking off and landing at Tan Son Nhut) against an average of 4.7 hours for GRADS missions.[31]

The AWADS crews next shifted efforts to Svay Rieng again, and to Xuyen Moc (a coastal location east of Saigon) and Minh Thanh. For the Svay Rieng drops, approaches were made from the northeast near Tay Ninh with the main bridge at Svay Rieng as an excellent offset aiming point. Successful single missions took place at Dak Pek in late June and at Dak Seang in July. A second stationkeeping mission (on June 19 at Svay Rieng) yielded results as impressive as those a week earlier. The crews of Miles and Brundridge expertly made the first AWADS drop at An Loc on June 20. At another place, radar reflectors were parachuted in for use as offset aim points but enemy mortars destroyed the reflectors before they could be installed. By June 30, 61st Squadron crews had made a total of 387 drop sorties—70 AWADS, 3 stationkeeping, and 314 GRADS. Average impact error was 189 yards for AWADS and 121 yards for GRADS. The squadron also flew to some of the major fields in Vietnam, but AWADS planes were not used for shortfields or rough-field landings to avoid damaging AWADS components.³²

By far, most AWADS work during the summer was at An Loc where there were usually two drops daily. The run-in path was from the southwest, using the Black Virgin Mountain near Tay Ninh as the initial point. This axis maximized radar returns from a group of metal buildings still standing at the southeast edge of An Loc. These presented a marginal offset aiming point although they faded from radar view about forty seconds from release. As a result, AWADS impact errors were generally higher at An Loc than elsewhere.

Several procedures reduced the likelihood of gross errors. The squadron normally made GRADS drops at each new target before undertaking AWADS, allowing navigators to compare solutions with actual impacts. When first dropping by AWADS at a new location, crews verified approach paths, either by mobile search or visually. With increasing confidence in AWADS, however, these precautions gradually ended. An instructor accompanied each navigator's first AWADS mission to a particular drop zone. An AWADS-qualified crew was usually allowed the option of dropping by GRADS, provided there was no wait for mobile search.³³

Successful AWADS work depended not only on the skill of the individual navigator but also on the information available to him during mission preparation. Without up-to-date, expanded-scale maps and photographs, for example, selection of a suitable offset aiming point was guesswork. The 61st Sqaudron arrived in Vietnam without radar prediction or target intelligence personnel, since manning documents for the 314th Wing at Little Rock did not provide for these functions. Captain Dawson and several other aircrew personnel, assisted by intelligence specialists from PACAF, undertook to acquire and analyze target materials at Tan Son Nhut. In this work Dawson found his past experience in radar bombardment invaluable. Prompted by officers of the 61st, the Seventh Air Force requested that a targeting team be sent to the Pacific. As a result, an officer and three airmen arrived in early June and thereafter performed useful service.

In attempting to arrange for reconnaissance photography, Captain Dawson and the targeting team found it easier and more economical to reconnoiter prospective drop zones using an AWADS C–130 plane. Dawson himself flew several such missions, making hand-drawn sketches of radar returns for use in planning and briefing later missions. Unfortunately, the C–130s had no provision for scope cameras for use either in reconnaissance or for critiquing inaccurate drops. The need for effective target intelligence and for scope cameras had been long recognized by radar bombing units, and the experience in Vietnam induced the 61st Squadron to recommend strongly that these be provided.³⁴

Maintenance of the AWADS equipment presented no special difficul-

C–130 AIRDROP SORTIES, EASTER OFFENSIVE*

	Apr	May	Jun	Total
MR III:				
An Loc	44[a]	177	82	303
DZ's South of An Loc	—	18[a]	38	56
Duc Thanh	—	2	6	8
Xuyen Moc	—	2	8	10
Chi Linh	—	3	3	6
Minh Thanh	—	10	12	22
MR II:				
Kontum	—	20	116	136
Ben Het	—	4	3	7
Mang Buk	—	6	3	9
Dak Pek	—	9	6	15
LZ English	—	5	—	5
Gia Vuc	—	2	—	2
Cambodia:				
Kompong Trach	8[a]	—	—	8
Svay Rieng	—	6	5	11
TOTALS	52	264	282	598

a. Data corrected from sources cited in text.

* 374th TAW Tabulation, 1972.

ties. Seventeen AWADS maintenance specialists went with the 61st Squadron to Taiwan and most of them later were sent to Tan Son Nhut. A special kit of AWADS spare parts was made up from stocks at Little Rock and taken with the initial force. Parts consumption data was recorded for use in planning future requirements. The commander of the 61st deemed the quality of AWADS maintenance "overall satisfactory."[35]

Assessments of AWADS operations were generally favorable. AWADS was less accurate than the GRADS and more costly in terms of equipment, training, and necessary support. On the other hand, AWADS could be used in regions that could not be supplied by GRADS and was independent of enemy action against ground radar sites. AWADS also allowed evasive maneuvers not possible when under GRADS guidance. Aircrews of the 61st were ingenious in adapting the AWADS computer for high-altitude work and in overcoming weaknesses in intelligence and charting materials. It appeared that both the AWADS and its associated stationkeeping equipment had proven their reliability, and that both added valuable tactical capabilities.[36]

Although the battles at An Loc and Kontum claimed the most attention, the countrywide airlift effort was widespread. The critical situation in the northern provinces after the retreat from Quang Tri necessitated a shift of the airborne division. Allied transports on May 9 hauled the 2d Brigade, with three airborne battalions and an artillery battalion, to Phu Bai from the Saigon region, the unit having returned from the Kontum fight in the preceding fortnight. The 3d Brigade flew north on May 22 with three battalions and division headquarters, the units having reorganized and refitted near Saigon after the An Loc battle. The 1st Brigade remained in general reserve until late June, when it too moved north. Thus reinforced, the defenders of Hue contended for the initiative. On May 24 a Vietnamese marine brigade made a triphibious (land-sea-air) assault into Quang Tri Province, the airmobile units moving by Vietnamese Air Force and U.S. Marine helicopters. The airborne division meanwhile fought hard and steadily until the ruins of Quang Tri city were recaptured in August.[37]

The C-130s made airdrops at widespread points, generally supporting garrisons cut off from surface supply and under immediate pressure from enemy forces. During the first two days of May, C-130s flew five drops using the low-level container technique at Landing Zone English, located near the II Corps coast. Crews reported that the drops were accurate, but two aircraft were hit. The defenders withdrew overland the next night for further evacuation by sea. At Minh Thanh (lying between An Loc and Tay Ninh) the three hundred Regional Forces defenders reported on May 5 that supplies delivered by the Vietnamese Air Force had landed outside the minuscule (219 by 328 yards) drop zone and that foodstuffs were exhausted. U.S. Air Force C-130s made two GRADS sorties on the sixth, but the defenders reported that most bundles again fell outside the recovery area and that three men had been killed in retrieval forays. Two more C-130s tried drops the next afternoon. One crew reported that all bundles landed outside the drop zone while the other reported that results were unknown. The Minh Thanh garrison managed to survive supported by another nineteen C-130 high-altitude drops through June with slightly improved results.

More successful were a series of drops at Xuyen Moc and Duc Thanh, east and north of Vung Tau. The ground fire which deterred Vietnamese CH-47s and made drops at both points inaccurate was no problem for C-130 crews using high-altitude methods. A total of eighteen sorties supplied these points between May 21 and June 21.[38]

Flying time for the six-squadron Pacific C-130 force in June was up twenty-seven percent beyond the four-squadron total of April. Most missions directly supported combat operations, including numerous sorties that redistributed materiel brought to the main air terminals in Vietnam by C-5s and C-141s. Some flights assisted in American withdrawals. During June, for example, C-130s lifted over two thousand tons of cargo from Da

TACTICAL AIRLIFT

Nang for units relocating to bases in Thailand. The mission schedule for May 9 illustrated the work of the Tan Son Nhut 130s. Fifty-five missions were scheduled for launch in the twenty-four-hour period: sixteen drops (mainly at An Loc), thirty-four cargo and passenger airland circuits, one aeromedical evacuation, and four Commando Vault bombing missions.* The last Air Force C–123 sortie took place on June 14, and the last Provider was transferred to the Vietnamese Air Force on the twenty-ninth.[39]

The remarkable level of aircraft maintenance achieved in April was, if anything, surpassed in May and June. For the three months incommission rate for the war-aged C–130s averaged seventy-one percent, more than eight percentage points above the level of the previous quarter. This was accomplished despite an epidemic of leaking fuel cells which accounted for one-fourth of the out-of-commission aircraft time. Battle damage repairs during May were staggering; 374th Wing and a logistics repair team worked ninety-nine hundred man-hours to repair forty-one damaged planes (compared with 150 man-hours in April and thirty-three hundred in June). Cannibalizations climbed to a total of one hundred during May, nearly all at Tan Son Nhut. This was roughly double the rate for the previous four months. The accomplishments of the wing's maintenance crews and the TAC mechanics reflected both dedication and skill.[40]

The airlift managerial system during the spring campaign was austere compared to the apparatus of past years. Mission scheduling was manual, without computer assistance, at the airlift command center. High frequency radio and landline communications linked the command center to the remaining control element detachments at Tan Son Nhut, Bien Hoa, and Da Nang. Otherwise flight following depended on high frequency radio calls to the command center by flight crews. Airlift mission requests, both normal and emergency, passed through the transportation division of MACV logistics section which assigned priorities and passed them to the airlift control center for mission scheduling. The Seventh Air Force director of airlift, Colonel Downs, did much of the coordinaticn for the 374th Wing among Seventh Air Force and MACV agencies during the spring. He requested help from the 374th Wing, recognizing that his control center officers lacked the tactical airlift experience needed to provide leadership in the fast-changing campaigns at An Loc and Kontum. Colonel Iosue detached several highly qualified officers to the control center to work out new delivery methods and brief aircrews. Personnel assigned to the control center continued to perform the scheduling and flight-following roles. After the operations staffs of MACV and the Seventh Air Force were integrated on June 22, 1972, the airlift directorate was split and an airlift section was

---

* Air Force Commando Vault missions ended after five drops in April and eighteen in May.

created under the operational plans division. The airlift control center was placed under the command and control division, but in practice the airlift control center remained separate from the tactical air control center although both were under command and control.[41]

Like the transport force, the Air Force aerial port system in Vietnam at the start of the Easter offensive was enmeshed in programmed work reduction and withdrawal. At most locations, ports had been closed or shifted over to Vietnamese Air Force operation. The 2d Aerial Port Group remained in existence (its headquarters personnel reduced by fifty percent) under its commander, Col. Raymond H. Gaylor. Also still active were the three subordinate squadrons which operated ports at Tan Son Nhut, Cam Ranh Bay, and Da Nang, with detachments at Bien Hoa, Pleiku, and Can Tho. Personnel strength in field units was down seventy percent from the peak. Much of the equipment formerly assigned to all ports had been returned to supply channels.[42]

The truncated aerial port apparatus found itself hard pressed to meet the fast-moving situation of the first week, especially during the movement of the marines and rangers north. Colonel Gaylor himself stayed almost continuously in the aerial port command center of the airlift control center, supervising the major unit movements and the deployments of port mobility teams and combat control teams to outlying locations. Aerial port personnel continued to schedule, coordinate, and follow port activities around the clock amid severe pressure on the countrywide logistics system. Gaylor later wrote that the direct communications with ports and various agencies during the crisis wholly vindicated the existence of the aerial port command center.

High-volume aerial port activity was a consequence of the intensified countrywide airlift effort through April and May. Cargo handling rose dramatically from eighteen thousand tons in March, to forty-seven thousand tons in April, and fifty-one thousand in May. Air freight personnel worked straight twelve-hour workdays, with twelve hours between shifts, without break. Military Airlift Command deliveries at the major ports brought increased offloading and transshipment. The workload soared at Da Nang where C–5As now landed for the first time. Aerial port mobility teams were sent on more than one hundred occasions during the spring quarter to some twenty different outlying locations. Colonel Gaylor detected some decline in morale from overwork, and the 8th Aerial Port Squadron attributed a rising accident rate to individual fatigue. To sustain the effort, some seventy individuals due to leave Vietnam were held beyond their planned rotation dates. For the most part, these men recognized the important role being played by the airlift effort and accepted the tour extensions without bitterness.[43]

However materiel problems, chronic in the past, intensified. To meet shortages of cargo-handling equipment, some of the equipment turned in earlier was recalled from supply channels. Less easily solved was the problem of serious mechanical deterioration of available vehicles and forklifts, caused by heavy and continuous usage during May and June. Supervisors tried to remind personnel of the need for operator maintenance and preventive care but results were marginal. The consumption of chains, straps, and pallets soared, intensifying the usual shortages and necessitating pallet-retrieval visits by mobility teams to outlying sites. High-speed offloadings at Kontum and elsewhere made it necessary to repair three-fourths of the pallets used. Offshore ports also felt the pallet shortage, as the flow of cargo (and pallets) entering Vietnam far exceeded that leaving. The pallet repair facility on Taiwan raised its output, and additional pallets were sent from the United States, but shortages eased only with the decline in the critical in-country workload during the summer which allowed increased attention to pallet recovery and repair.[44]

The drops at An Loc and elsewhere created special problems, since the 8th Aerial Port Squadron at Tan Son Nhut had previously transferred away all air delivery personnel and nearly all rigging equipment and drop pallets. Colonel Gaylor quickly ordered air delivery specialists to Tan Son Nhut by air, primarily to prepare and load aircraft for drops. Personnel for the reborn aerial delivery section came from the Commando Vault section of the 15th Aerial Port Squadron and from the port at Ching Chuan Kang. Between April 11 and June 30, with rarely more than twelve men on hand, the section loaded up to seventeen aircraft each day for drops that totaled over nine thousand container bundles. Shortages of rigging items, along with changing drop methods, necessitated numerous improvisations.[45]

The failure of the communist spring offensive was evident by late June. In an article prepared for publication in a major U.S. newsweekly that month, President Nixon wrote that, both militarily and politically, Hanoi was losing its gamble. Not only had there been no uprising in South Vietnam, the President observed, but the streams of refugees away from the regions controlled by the communists made it clear that "Saigon, not Hanoi, speaks for the South Vietnamese people." The Joint Chiefs of Staff in July acknowledged that government casualties had been substantial (eighteen thousand killed, against an estimated eighty thousand enemy

THE COUNTRYWIDE RESPONSE

dead), that large quantities of military hardware had been lost, and that the domestic pacification programs had been disrupted in the areas of fighting. Nevertheless, they concluded, it was clear that any communist hope of gaining control of large portions of the population had failed. Further, the enemy appeared capable of major offensive efforts only in the northern provinces, and there only because of the relative ease of supply and reinforcement. During late summer, some North Vietnamese forces shifting into Cambodia increased pressure on routes into Phnom Penh and isolated certain towns and garrisons. Meanwhile in South Vietnam, communist units appeared to be breaking down into smaller, more flexible groups, possibly to resume guerrilla efforts.[46]

XXIII. The Advisory Role and the Vietnamese Air Force Airlift Arm

From the outset, allied officials asserted that air transport would be important to South Vietnam long after American withdrawal, whether used to continue counterinsurgency warfare or for peacetime nation-building. The Americans during the 1960s therefore nurtured a small but vigorous Vietnamese Air Force airlift arm, providing transports, equipment, crew training, and advisors. The U.S. Air Force's own airlift operation in South Vietnam, however, vastly overshadowed the activities of the two Vietnamese transport squadrons.

During 1969 and 1970, communist rigidity in the Paris peace talks indicated that the Americans were to find no way out of Vietnam. The Vietnamization of U.S. war roles accordingly became a primary aim. As part of a sweeping improvement and modernization program the Vietnamese Air Force gained three new transport forces, operating four different types of transports. A late-1972 decision to equip the Vietnamese with C–130s led to a last-minute conversion program during which the Vietnamese Air Force shifted easily to the more complex C–130 Hercules, a smooth transition which spoke well for past Vietnamization efforts.

The real health of the Vietnamese Air Force airlift arm was always questionable. Weaknesses glimpsed by the Dirty Thirty officers in 1962 were never entirely corrected. These included a reluctance to fly at night or during instrument conditions, a shortage of technical skills, a laissez-faire attitude to problems, and sharp divisions between officers and enlisted men. Most advisors tolerated these weaknesses, appreciating Vietnamese traditions and sensing that Americans could never entirely succeed in imposing their own businesslike methods. Meanwhile, the advisors witnessed numerous examples of fine performance and were uniformly impressed with the flying skills of Vietnamese pilots. The Vietnamese Air Force airlift arm did not equal the U.S. Air Force in maintenance skills, discipline, or modernity of equipment. But to meet the demands of medium-scale and prolonged counterinsurgency operations, the Vietnamese Air Force by 1973 appeared essentially self-sufficient in airlift.

Organized directly under MACV was the U.S. Air Force-manned Air Force Advisory Group, whose primary mission was to advise and assist the entire sixteen thousand-man Vietnamese Air Force to achieve combat readiness. Advisory group authorized strength in 1968 was nearly five hundred officers and men and grew to one thousand two years later. Most served as members of advisory teams at Vietnamese operating bases. Others worked at Vietnamese Air Force headquarters with Vietnamese officers in the directorates of materiel, operations, and personnel. The Americans were expected not to assume leadership themselves but instead to help the Vietnamese shoulder responsibilities at all levels. In the view of Brig. Gen. Albert W. Schinz, who commanded the advisory group during late 1965 and 1966, the outcome was superb comradeship and cooperation and "a real capable air force in a short time."[1]

Much evidence attested to the vigor of the Vietnamese Air Force airlift arm. At the start of 1965 the two veteran transport squadrons at Tan Son Nhut, with thirty-five C-47s and thirty-seven crews, were the only Vietnamese units officially listed in full (C-1) operational readiness. The old Dirty Thirty arrangement was temporarily revived in 1965-66 to permit transfers of Vietnamese transport pilots to other units. Twenty additional U.S. Air Force pilots were assigned to the Tan Son Nhut advisory team for duty with the C-47 squadrons. Unlike the original Dirty Thirty the Americans flew regularly as aircraft commanders, often with a second American as copilot. As in the earlier venture the Americans quickly recognized the flying ability and experience of the Vietnamese pilots and curtailed their advisory and instructional roles. Maj. Bruce Parker summed up the American experience:

> It was funny, when we got over there they were operating in a VFR [visual flight rules] environment, avoiding IFR [instrument flight rules] at all costs. We thought we'd probably go in there and show them how to operate IFR and just the opposite thing happened. We saw why they were operating in a VFR environment, and we turned to that as the best solution too. . . . I think they could probably operate their C-47s just as well as we could. . . . They're good pilots."[2]

A third C-47 squadron became active in 1967 but began conversion from airlift to gunship work the next year. Meanwhile, preparations began to convert one of the older squadrons to C-119 transports. Some crewmen were given C-119 training in the United States, and a U.S. Air Force team gave instruction to some two hundred maintenance men in Vietnam. Compared to the C-47 the C-119 had better payload and bulk-carrying capacities, better cargo-handling features, and superior airdrop qualities. Shortfield and rough-field capabilities were poor, however, which ruled out C-119 landings at many Special Forces camps. The squadron conversion was deemed complete in November 1968. Vietnamese Air Force passenger and cargo lift totals the following month amounted to double the monthly averages in 1967.[3]

Air Force Advisory Team 5 served with the transport squadrons at Tan Son Nhut. Most team members established good relations with their Vietnamese counterparts, especially with the younger officers, many of whom had received training in the United States. Most advisors agreed that an understanding and patient approach was essential in advisory work, along with a willingness to bend to local custom, food, and tradition. For example, Lt. Col. William B. Webb, a staff planning advisor with the airlift units, learned that much of the matting furnished to the Vietnamese to surface forward airstrips was being used for private patios and driveways. By quiet pressure, Colonel Webb saw to it that most of the matting was returned for the intended purpose. A more direct confrontation on the matter, he felt, would have spoiled the existing working relationship. He later discovered that some Vietnamese enlisted men were in the habit of sleeping overnight on the floors and desks of the plans office. Investigating, Colonel Webb and his Vietnamese counterpart found that many men lived in poverty off base, a situation inviting communist exploitation. Webb's report to the Seventh Air Force led to authorization to construct billets on base.[4]

The Air Force Advisory Team 5 advisors undertook only minor flying roles. American advisory pilots normally received an initial flight check and found the Vietnamese Air Force examiners as rigorous as those of the U.S. Air Force. After checkout most advisors flew only two or three times monthly, sometimes merely "watching the Vietnamese Air Force instructors instruct." The Americans pushed programs to upgrade copilots, overcoming habitual reluctance among the Vietnamese to give copilots opportunities in first-pilot tasks. As in the Dirty Thirty years, Vietnamese transport pilots were unenthusiastic over flying by formal instrument techniques preferring whenever possible to steer around clouds. Nevertheless Maj. Ronald T. Lanman, who served with Air Force Advisory Team 5 during 1970–71, judged that the C–119 crews were highly competent in flying true instrument approaches, sometimes necessary in the northern provinces. Few Vietnamese Air Force members had the kind of superdrive often seen among U.S. Air Force personnel in Southeast Asia, but most advisors were tolerant of this, appreciating that the war was a career-long matter for the Vietnamese.[5]

All trends seemed favorable. Flying rates consistently exceeded the programmed daily rates (raised to 2.5 hours per airframe in 1966). The flying safety record was acceptable; in the six years starting in 1965 the Vietnamese Air Force lost in accidents only seven transport C–47s and one C–119. The transports worked successfully with Vietnamese tactical air forces and artillery in occasional paratroop operations. The C–47s executed battalion-scale jumps in December 1966, April 1967, and August

The first C-119 transferred to the Vietnamese Air Force, delivered to VNAF Maj. Buie Huu The by USAF Lt. Col. Matthew A. Boonstra (center) and MSgt. Walter Kueck, 1968.

1967, albeit with generally indifferent tactical results on the ground. During the 1968 Tet offensive, according to a MACV study, leadership and combat effectiveness in the Vietnamese C-47 units had been "outstanding." Routinely, the Vietnamese Air Force transports linked the main airfields in South Vietnam and in the summer of 1970 began regular deliveries to Cambodia, allowing the U.S. Air Force to curtail airlift operations to that country.[6]

Operation Eagle Jump tested the competence of the Vietnamese airlifters in late 1970. The venture was designed to reinforce hard-pressed Cambodian forces fighting near Kompong Cham thirty miles inside Cambodia. The C-47s and C-119s were to land at Kompong Cham to deliver supplies to the Vietnamese 1st Airborne Brigade. Despite initial reservations among MACV officers, General Abrams approved the concept and gained CINCPAC authority to use American C-130s, C-123s, and Chinooks selectively, in case of emergencies "not now foreseen." CINCPAC specified that the bulk of the troops were to be moved by the Vietnamese Air Force, reflecting official policy limiting American actions in Cambodia.[7]

The Air Force Advisory Team 5 members learned of the impending Kompong Cham campaign some twenty-four hours before their Vietnamese counterparts. The Americans examined possible routes, flow rates,

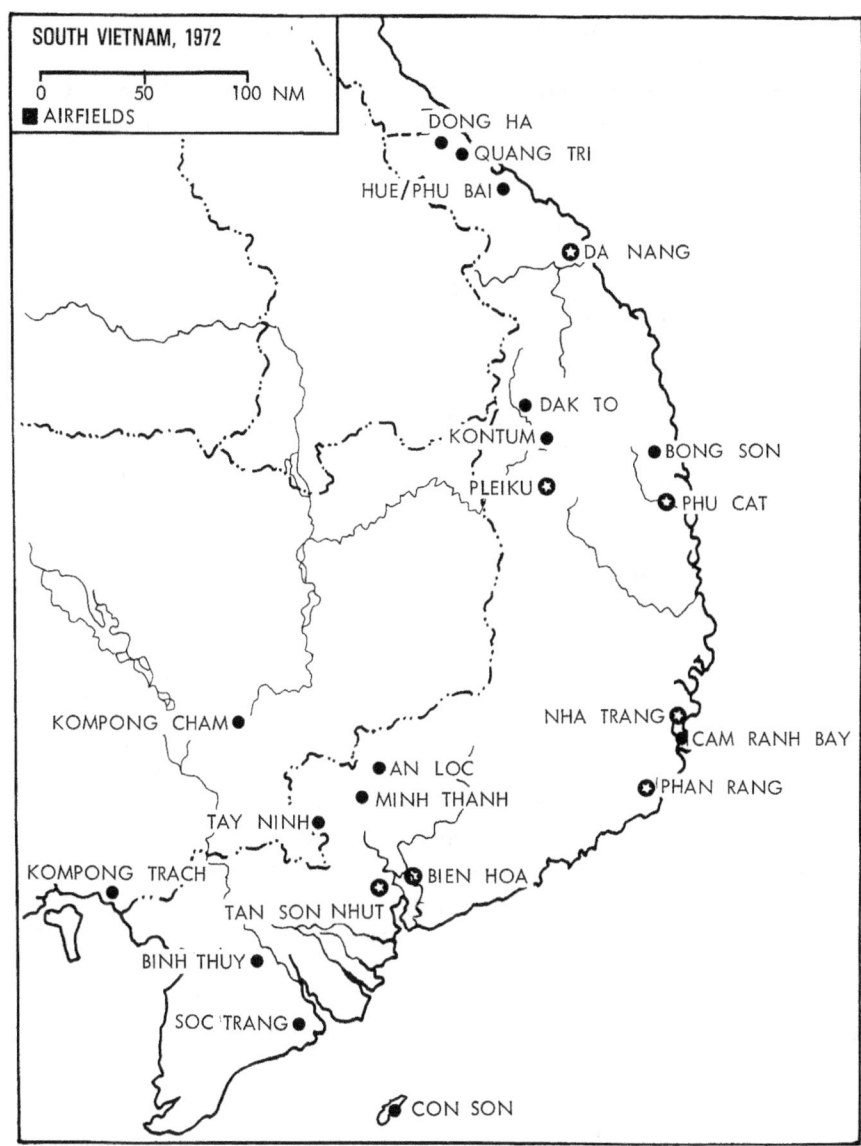

and other details. The Vietnamese received the resulting American concept paper with polite thanks but proceeded to disregard it. Rather pleased by this show of initiative, the Americans watched as the Vietnamese planning unfolded. Colonel Webb attended a meeting between airlift and paratroop officers, as well as the prelaunch briefing of aircrews. In both gatherings all talk was in Vietnamese, but to Webb the businesslike atmosphere was unmistakable. Confident in the competence of Vietnamese squadrons,

TACTICAL AIRLIFT

the advisors chuckled at the doubts expressed by an American officer from the 834th Air Division.

The advisors in the wing command post on December 14 were even more impressed as one crew after another called in to report on-time takeoffs. The mission status board gradually unfolded an impressive story. Meanwhile at Kompong Cham, Vietnamese Air Force helicopters made the initial landings, bringing in a small assault force from the closest sector of Vietnam. The fixed-wing transports soon followed, landing at twenty-minute intervals. The asphalt strip had no off-runway pavement for offloading so only one aircraft could be on the ground at a time. Approximately forty C-119s and C-47s landed the first day, delivering the brigade headquarters as mortar fire harassed the landings. The Americans at Saigon noticed that the aircrews donned flak vests for their second missions. Landings stopped at dusk since there was no lighting at the airhead. The airlift stream returned the next day, bringing in a second paratroop battalion and more artillery.

Each morning thereafter the transports resumed the Kompong Cham effort, hauling in fuel, munitions, rations, and wire. Considerable fuel was delivered, apparently to refuel helicopters. At Tan Son Nhut, American personnel from the 8th Aerial Port Squadron helped with loading, palletizing cargo, and operating forklifts; Vietnamese personnel tied down the loads inside the aircraft. In other activities, an aluminum-matting offloading ramp was laid down at Kompong Cham, and a C-119 required an engine change. Vietnamese personnel performed the switch in twenty-four hours, fashioning a steel A-frame from materials found nearby. Several ships received hits from enemy fire during the battle for Kompong Cham, and one pilot was wounded. Weather remained clear throughout the battle.

Assessments by the advisory personnel and the 834th Air Division were highly favorable. The Vietnamese Air Force transports hauled in 1,750 troops and nine hundred tons of cargo in 451 delivery sorties. During the withdrawal (completed on December 29) the transports lifted out fourteen hundred troops and 112 tons of supplies in 131 sorties. All missions were accident free. Vietnamese helicopters flew forty-five hundred sorties while a single U.S. Air Force C-130 made one landing. The airborne brigade succeeded in clearing the roadway to the west of Kompong Cham and claimed to have killed over two hundred of the enemy at a cost of twenty government dead. The operation appeared to verify that the Vietnamese Air Force air transport arm was ready for the substantial expansion ahead.[8]

PROGRAMMED AND ACTUAL VIETNAMESE AIR FORCE LEVELS*

	Posture Mid-1969 (20 sq)	April 1969 Program (40 sq by end of 1971)	Phase III Plan Revised 1971 (50 sq by mid-1973)	Unit Equipment January 7, 1972
Fixed-wing airlift:				
C–47	1 sq (16 acft)	1 sq (16 acft)	1 sq (16 acft)	1 sq (16 acft)
C–119	1 sq (16 acft)	1 sq (16 acft)	1 sq (16 acft)	1 sq (16 acft)
C–123	0	3 sq (48 acft)	3 sq (48 acft)	3 sq (48 acft)
C–7	0	0	3 sq (48 acft)	0
Gunships:				
AC–47	1 sq	2 sq	1 sq	1 sq
AC–119	0	0	1 sq	1 sq
Helicopters:				
UH–1H	4 sq	12 sq	16 sq	15 sq
H–34	1 sq	1 sq	0	0
CH–47	0	1 sq	2 sq	1 sq

* Elizabeth H. Hartsook, *The Administration Emphasizes Air Power, 1969* [The Air Force in Southeast Asia] (Washington, 1971), p 65; Fact Sheet, USAF, CRIMP, Jan 7, 1972.

Plans for manyfold expansion of the entire Vietnamese Air Force during and after 1969 reflected the American wish to make the South Vietnamese self-sufficient against both the North Vietnamese and the Viet Cong. From an overall Vietnamese Air Force strength of twenty squadrons, growth to fifty squadrons was envisioned by mid-1973. Most critical was the number of available pilots which was dependent on the output of training programs in the United States. In these years, 1969–71, Vietnamese Air Force pilot strength tripled, reaching twenty-five hundred.[9]

Expansion of the airlift force followed the buildup in helicopters and strike aircraft. Planning in 1969 called for activation of three C–123 squadrons in 1971 to increase Vietnamese Air Force lift capacity to 612

TACTICAL AIRLIFT

A VNAF C–123 comes in for a landing, 1972.

tons per day (against an accepted requirement for eight hundred). The Americans considered furnishing C–130s but rejected the idea because of costs, the need for retraining, the pressures likely from other countries also wishing C–130s, and the need for all C–130s in the U.S. Air Force inventory. On the other hand, independent studies by Air Force commands in Saigon, Hawaii, and Washington, all concluded that the Vietnamese Air Force needed the shortfield capabilities of the C–7 Caribou and that the simplicity of that craft favored successful Vietnamese operation. Accordingly, two twenty-four-plane C–7 squadrons were added to the plan in 1970. This was later changed to three squadrons each with sixteen aircraft.[10]

In earlier years the Vietnamese Air Force C–47 squadrons had been periodically tapped to provide crewmen for new strike units. A levy in 1970 for forty-eight C–47 pilots, needed for the future C–123 squadrons, signified the first regeneration of the airlift force itself. Forty-eight qualified pilots were selected, many of them recently upgraded from copilot status. All entered C–123 transition and combat crew training at Lockbourne Air Force Base, Ohio, in early and mid-1970. Future copilots were drawn directly from undergraduate pilot training in the United States and put through a C–123 copilot course at Lockbourne. Pilots and copilots completed training at Lockbourne in early 1971 then flew with the U.S. Air Force 315th Wing in Vietnam, acquiring further C–123 training and operational experience pending Vietnamese Air Force squadron activations later in the year.[11]

Direct association with the Vietnamese Air Force was a new experience for the 315th Wing. The wing formed a training flight in December 1970 to design and administer the activity, and the first Vietnamese train-

THE ADVISORY ROLE

Air Force TSgt. William Brazier (sixth from left) instructs VNAF students on the maintenance of the C–123 engine, Phan Rang Air Base, February 1971.

ees arrived at Phan Rang in early January. The eight pilots of the first group flew with the Americans an average of seventy-three hours in local transition and airlift missions, after which each successfully passed a flight check given by U.S. Air Force examiners. The main student difficulty lay in assault landings which had not been practiced at Lockbourne. Four of the initial eight copilot trainees failed check rides, necessitating extra training. Later groups began training at six-week intervals, and were generally weak in their knowledge of C–123K systems and operations. Ground training therefore was expanded and much of the material given earlier at Lockbourne was reemphasized. Language remained a handicap, especially in those phrases and concepts where the Vietnamese language lacked close equivalents in English. The navigator trainees were "sharp individuals" attaining proficiency ahead of schedule. The initial loadmaster and flight mechanic trainees later helped to overcome language comprehension problems among the later groups. Upon the conclusion of the program in late September 1971, the 315th Wing deemed a total of ninety-one pilots and copilots and seventy-six other aircrewmen "qualified."

C–123 maintenance training followed a slightly different pattern. Instructor cadres attended schools in the United States, returning to conduct courses in Vietnam assisted by a U.S. Air Force team. Early graduates of this program served with the Americans at Phan Rang during much of 1971. Results appeared good. American engine specialists, for example, repeatedly expressed satisfaction with the ability and motivation of the Vietnamese. A total of 152 mechanics earned qualification under the 315th Wing program.[12]

The C-123 activations were accomplished smoothly and on schedule. The 421st Transport Squadron, officially formed on April 1, 1971, received its sixteenth aircraft on May 8 from the inactivating U.S. Air Force 19th Squadron. The new unit initially undertook three missions daily formerly performed by the Americans. A second squadron was activated on July 1 and by September the two had forty-eight C-123s, enough to equip the third squadron which was officially activated December 1. The new units in September took over training responsibility for the final groups of aircrewmen, allowing U.S. Air Force training at Phan Rang to shift to the C-7. Several dozen aircrew and ground crew members from the inactivating U.S. Air Force squadrons stayed in Vietnam with the Vietnamese Air Force units through the end of the year. Air Force Advisory Team 5 members helped out where possible during the activations, for example, aiding the new squadrons in obtaining facilities at Tan Son Nhut.[13]

Activations of C-7 squadrons in 1972 followed similar patterns. Another forty-eight qualified pilots from the older squadrons were selected for training as C-7 aircraft commanders, while recent graduates of undergraduate pilot training became C-7 copilots. Two groups of pilot trainees underwent C-7 familiarization flying training at Dyess Air Force Base, Tex., during the summer of 1971, returning to Vietnam for combat readiness training at Phan Rang. Subsequent groups received all ground, familiarization, and combat readiness training at Phan Rang. The Phan Rang school used the facilities formerly used for the C-123 program, and received its first students in October 1971. The 483d Wing provided eight C-7 aircraft and most of the instructor pilots, with six instructor pilots from Dyess assisting during the first few months. After complaints by the early graduates, the American instructors were cautioned to avoid impatience in working with students. Students in the later groups were noticeably weaker than their predecessors in flying experience and English comprehension. The school shifted to Phu Cat in January 1972 and closed in late August. In all, 250 C-7 pilots and other aircrewmen went through the Phan Rang and Phu Cat program. All C-7 maintenance training was conducted in Vietnam, initially by a mobile training team from Dyess and later by Vietnamese Air Force instructors.

While waiting for squadron activations, early graduates served with the U.S. Air Force C-7 squadrons at Cam Ranh Bay. The first Vietnamese

Air Force squadron was formed at Phu Cat on March 1, 1972, immediately undertaking two daily missions from the Americans while continuing training flights. After two weeks Vietnamese Air Force missions were up to seven daily. Advisory group officers lauded the professionalism and morale of the squadron and certified that the squadron was operationally ready at the end of the first month. The later squadrons were activated at Phu Cat on May 1 and July 1 respectively, with one squadron shifting to Da Nang in July. A few U.S. Air Force pilots and maintenance men served temporarily in the Vietnamese Air Force squadrons after the activations.[14]

The dilution of experience accompanying the expansion increased problems in flying safety and maintenance. Pilot errors produced seven major transport accidents in the twelve months after November 1970. Five of these accidents occurred in takeoffs or landings usually in a training situation. Two ships crashed into hillsides while descending in marginal weather, costing thirty-two lives. The period followed more than a year of accident-free operation and caused the advisory group to press for tightened flying supervision. C–123 maintenance was handicapped by severe spare parts shortages and the absence of maintenance publications in the Vietnamese language. U.S. Air Force maintenance men helped bridge the first six months of each new squadron's existence.[15]

Fully committed to the ideal of centralized scheduling and control, the Americans as early as 1963 had pressed the Vietnamese to commit significant numbers of planes for use in the American-dominated common service system. Failing in this, apparently because of South Vietnamese nationalist feelings, the Americans instead urged that the Vietnamese create their own airlift control apparatus, simpler but patterned on the functioning of the 834th Air Division. A Vietnamese Air Force airlift control center accordingly was established in August 1968. The control center made up daily schedules but serious weaknesses in radio communications and the absence of control detachments in the field limited mission success. Consequently, the advisory group arranged that Vietnamese control element detachments might receive high frequency radios from departing American units, but by late 1972 the planned net of twenty-three control elements was still mostly on paper. Emergency mission diversions remained infrequent however. Aircrews spent their days flying the planned itineraries with little or no information from the airlift control center. Col. Walter J. Ford, who served with the Vietnamese Air Force airlift control center in 1971–72, reported that the twenty-man staff tried hard to make the system work, operating around the clock, and that their commander habitually put in twelve-hour workdays. Colonel Ford accompanied certain missions and observed that a useful load was invariably on board.[16]

The Vietnamese Air Force transports gradually took over several special roles formerly performed by the Americans. During 1971 the Vietnamese assumed resupply responsibilities for most Civilian Irregular Defense Group camps, except those requiring delivery by C–7. Late that year the Vietnamese Air Force began flying C–123 bladderbird missions, having received four fuel-carrying bladders from the Americans. The idea of converting C–123s into "poor man's gunships" faltered, in part because of the required training, costs, and the need for all aircraft for airlift. The C–119 and the C–123 had only rudimentary capabilities for carrying the fifteen thousand-pound BLU–82 bomb because of rigging and payload limitations. Aeromedical evacuation work was retarded by shortages of aeromedical technicians and equipment and the lack of pressurized transports. Requirements for patient shifts between hospitals were in any case small since Vietnamese regional hospitals did not specialize in particular types of cases.[17]

Other factors were favorable to the Vietnamese airlift. The average Vietnamese Air Force C–123 aircraft commander had over three thousand hours of flying experience, nearly twice the total typical among U.S. Air Force first pilots in Vietnam. During early 1973, Vietnamese transports lifted forty-two thousand passengers and seventeen hundred tons of cargo monthly, equivalent to eighty percent of the whole Vietnamese requirement and roughly triple the monthly workload two years before. On March 4–5, 1972, the C–123s hauled a two thousand-man airborne brigade with vehicles, artillery, and supplies, from Tan Son Nhut to Pleiku, completing the 150-sortie lift the second day. American advisors were delighted with the planning and execution evident in the effort, remindful of the earlier Kompong Cham lift by the older squadrons.[18]

Long-standing weaknesses of attitude—by American standards—remained not far below the surface. An example was the reluctance among Vietnamese Air Force crews to operate the C–123s into short, marginal airfields, as detected by Air Force Advisory Team Number 5 personnel in late 1971 and again by Col. Henry L. Baulch, the team's chief, in February 1972. Digging into the problem, Colonel Baulch encountered "an endless series of buck-passing" and a "don't-rock-the-boat" attitude among Vietnamese staff officers. Baulch concluded that Vietnamese Air Force commanders were satisfied that the C–123s were functioning successfully into the major fields and were unwilling to risk responsibility for accidents in forward field work. Stronger leadership was needed, in Colonel Baulch's view, to assure proper surveys of forward airfields, to emphasize shortfield training, and to press for necessary rework of flaps. Following up Baulch's comments the Air Force Advisory Group late in the month informed MACV that flap modifications were nearly complete, and that Vietnamese Air Force headquarters had directed a fresh program of shortfield training along with immediate use of U.S. Air Force airfield surveys. The suspicion remained, however, that without a close American presence shortfield operations would continue to be slighted in the future.[19]

Unlike the arrangement in the American services, all South Vietnamese military helicopter units were organized as part of the nation's air force. The nominal advisory responsibility therefore fell to the U.S. Air Force albeit with heavy reliance on the know-how and facilities of the U.S. Army. The members of the two American services cooperated without difficulty in this work, especially in field activities. Old rivalries over rotary-wing roles only occasionally appeared, and then only at the planning and policymaking level. The history of the Vietnamese Air Force transport helicopters, however, was marred by numerous cases of ineffective mission performance. Lacking the leavening of experience of the fixed-wing transport units, the discipline and skills of the Vietnamese helicopter units for most of the war remained questionable.

During the late 1950s the Vietnamese Air Force operated a handful of H–19 helicopters, primarily for liaison. Seeking to develop a troop-mobility capacity the Americans in early 1961 began providing H–34s, deemed superior to the H–19s in payload and ease of maintenance. A U.S. Air Force field training detachment in February 1963 undertook basic pilot and maintenance training in Vietnam. The materiel and training programs produced a force of seventy-six H–34s and 180 pilots at the end of 1964, organized in three squadrons with a fourth in training status. Ground force officers, however, frequently complained about failures in medical evacuation and emergency resupply tasks. There was a widespread feeling that Vietnamese H–34 crews would fly only in daytime and good weather and that their aircraft tended to go out of commission whenever dangerous missions loomed. The tough jobs thus went to the in-country helicopters of the U.S. Army. Air Force liaison officers serving with Vietnamese ground units confirmed the validity of these complaints. It therefore appeared that, in its regeneration through 1964, the Vietnamese Air Force helicopter arm had been pushed too fast.[20]

Expansion slowed after 1964 (the fifth H–34 squadron was activated only in April 1968), allowing closer attention to correcting past weaknesses. Advisory group officers pressed for a "vigorous flying safety program" and steadily reduced the accident rate from 116 per one hundred thousand flying hours (ten times the U.S. Air Force rate) in 1965 to 10 in early 1968. Successful mission accomplishments began to overcome criticisms. In a program started in 1966, Vietnamese H–34 pilots served temporary tours with U.S. Army UH–1 units in Vietnam, looking ahead to future Vietnamese conversion to UH–1s. The Americans urged greater employment of the H–34s in airmobile assaults, but the small number of ready choppers in any region discouraged such use. In 1968 two of the five squadrons were concentrated at Binh Thuy in order to facilitate assault operations, and U.S. Army officers were added to the Air Force Advisory Group as airmobile advisors. It appeared clear, however, that the three-year slowdown in expansion had resulted in a qualitative improvement of the helicopter force.[21]

Further and accelerated expansion soon followed. Four squadrons were added in late 1970, seven in 1971, and three more by February 1972, making a total of sixteen, all equipped with UH–1Hs. Each squadron had thirty-one aircraft including eight modified as gunships to escort the troop-carriers. Missions specified for the UH–1 force were (in order of priority): airmobile operations, medical evacuation, supply, and liaison. To fill the medium transport—lifting cargo, artillery, and downed aircraft—a single Chinook CH–47 squadron was activated in 1970, a second in 1972.[22]

Success in bringing the new squadrons to operational readiness depended heavily on the energies of aviators and mechanics of the U.S. Army, experienced in airmobile and UH–1 operations. Over fourteen hundred Vietnamese pilots went through basic helicopter pilot training at Army bases in the United States after 1969. Vietnamese Air Force pilots continued the ninety-day cycles with U.S. Army units in Vietnam, so that nearly all Vietnamese pilots flew at least one hundred hours with the Americans. Finally, to smooth the squadron activations, U.S. Army pilots served temporarily in the new units. The U.S. Air Force roles were less direct. The Air Force Advisory Group monitored training and operations of the new units with a vague directive to assist in "application of concepts and procedures." Air Force advisory teams with the Vietnamese helicopter units included U.S. Air Force rotary-wing pilots although they had little or no experience in assault operations. Overshadowing the Air Force contribution was the cooperative effect at cockpit level involving U.S. Army and Vietnamese Air Force flyers, resembling the arrangements that had proven successful in the C–123 and C–7 conversions.[23]

Vietnamese Air Force helicopters made a modest contribution to the Lam Son 719 venture into Laos, lifting over eight thousand troops and thirty-five hundred patients, although U.S. Army helicopters performed the main assaults. Airmobile work increased with the Vietnamese Air Force UH–1s lifting sixty thousand troops monthly in assaults in late 1971, three times the rate of 1969. A standard assault package included four gunships, ten troop-carriers, and one control plane. Tactics followed the American methods, including coordination with artillery and tactical air. Vietnamese Air Force medical evacuation sorties rose from 540 in May 1970 to thirty-one hundred in December 1971. Each squadron designated two choppers for "dustoff" (medevac) alert, and each alert crew included an aviation medical specialist. In emergencies any helicopter could be used for medevac.²⁴

Early in the conflict, U.S. Air Force officials took positions against assigning Vietnamese Air Force helicopters in direct support of specific ground units, fearing that this would create a framework for an "Army Air Corps." A nominal form of central control emerged. Under an early 1971 directive the Vietnamese Joint General Staff operations center issued flight orders each day to the air divisions. These were based on helicopter mission allocations by the several corps-level operations centers. Requests for supply required preliminary approval within the corps logistics section. The CH-47 Chinooks, however, by 1972 were scheduled in the Vietnamese Air Force airlift control center. Thus integrated into the nationwide airlift system, the Chinooks proved invaluable and they were always in demand. Tonnage lifted per CH-47 sortie was excellent. Vietnamese helicopter officers served in the airlift control center and there were no problems in meshing helicopter and fixed-wing capabilities at theater level. This centralized management was the arrangement that would probably have been used by the U.S. Air Force had the ban on a U.S. Air Force helicopter airlift arm been lifted.²⁵

Both the Americans and the Vietnamese worked hard to overcome the dilution of skill and experience resulting from the latest expansion. Weaknesses in night and instrument flying (often crucial in medevacs) led to tougher training programs. Inspection teams from the Seventh Air Force and PACAF investigated criticisms of Vietnamese Air Force helicopter maintenance. Six aircraft were selected at random and given hover checks. Only minor malfunctions were detected. Weaknesses doubtless remained however. One advisory team chief wrote that Vietnamese UH-1 pilots habitually overrevved engines and often reported weather at objective areas with undue pessimism. Rigorous tests of Vietnamese Air Force motivation and skill loomed in the campaign directly ahead.²⁶

The performance of the Vietnamese Air Force fixed-wing transports in the spring campaign was in most respects creditable. During April, May, and June 1972, the airlift force increased flying hours and sortie totals twenty-seven percent over the previous quarter. Airlifted cargo increased to thirty-two hundred tons per month, up eighty-six percent from the early-year rate. Vietnamese crews performed well in major unit movements and in making airlanded deliveries to numerous airfields. In the largest single aeromedical evacuation to date, Vietnamese Air Force transports on April 4 lifted 408 casualties from the overworked facility at Hue. Another highlight was the mission of May 28, when eleven transports lifted a parachute battalion from Tan Son Nhut to a drop zone near Quang Tri. The jump was accurate and the troopers quickly entered the battle beside the Marine forces.[27]

Vietnamese Air Force transport crews repeatedly showed their willingness to attempt missions against heavy enemy fire. Three C-123s were shot down during drops (at An Loc on April 15 and 19, and at Quang Tri on May 1) costing the lives of twelve crewmen. At least fifteen other Vietnamese transports received battle damage during April, and several C-123s were destroyed on the ground at Kontum in mid-May. Two crewmen died in the crash of a C-119 after engine failure in late May. The Vietnamese offered to join in the dangerous night effort to supply Kontum, but the Americans declined the offer, preferring to restrict the operation to C-130s.[28]

The losses, along with human fatigue and uncertainties over the course of the war, combined to test the morale of the Vietnamese Air Force crews. Colonel Baulch, still serving as Air Force Advisory Team 5 chief, in early May detected some erosion of spirit. He reported that crews tended to avoid the dangerous missions and shied away from fields likely to be mortared. Minor malfunctions or uncertain weather were sometimes given an exaggerated importance. Colonel Baulch spoke candidly with the Vietnamese air division commander and both agreed that the many newly trained crewmen lacked the confidence which came from experience. To help stiffen the younger crews, a senior Vietnamese officer was stationed at Pleiku where he monitored the highlands situation and made on-the-spot operational decisions. This and other supervisory reforms apparently paid dividends, and by the first week of June Colonel Baulch reported that Vietnamese Air Force resolve was improving.[29]

The low-level container delivery system airdrop technique learned from the Americans proved inadequate in the face of heavy enemy fire at Kompong Trach, An Loc, and Minh Thanh. Lacking satisfactory aiming and parachute rigging techniques, Vietnamese attempts at high-altitude releases were hopelessly inaccurate. Accordingly, during late April the Vietnamese Air Force relinquished nearly all airdrop work to the American C-130s.[30]

To equip the Vietnamese with high-altitude drop capability, Americans of the Tan Son Nhut C-130 detachment on May 13 started a fast training program. The object was to qualify six Vietnamese crews in GRADS drops, both HALO and high-velocity. Instruction included techniques of computation along with radio and radar procedures for working with the MSQ-77 mobile search ground site. Trainees accompanied U.S. Air Force C-130 missions, and each Vietnamese crew made several practice drops from Vietnamese Air Force aircraft. Early Vietnamese high-altitude drops had mixed success. After seven combat drops through June

5 the recovery rate was fifty-three percent. A serious handicap was a lack of airborne beacon transponders, necessitating use of the radar skin-tracking method, which reduced radar range and reliability. Ten beacon sets became available on June 10, and these were installed on drop ships before each mission. The Vietnamese Air Force C–123s and C–119s in September began a series of supply drops from above ten thousand feet. This demonstrated capability for high-altitude airdrops represented an asset in current operations as well as for the future.[31]

The spring battles were harsh on the Vietnamese Air Force helicopter force. Of the 628 UH–1s on hand during the spring quarter, 63 were destroyed and another 391 required significant "crash and battle damage" repair. The sight of a Vietnamese CH–47 slinghauling a UH–1 back to base became common and the existing supply of slings themselves became depleted from wear. Most damage was from enemy action; major accidents during the period totaled only eight. Vietnamese repair facilities became overwhelmed, necessitating major American assistance. Statistical indicators—sorties, flying hours, incommission rates, trooplift and cargo statistics—all declined sharply in April, thereafter recovering slowly. As of June 30, sixty-two UH–1s still required crash and battle damage repair.[32]

The most trying events took place at An Loc. Enemy shells were a constant reality but the men on the ground felt that helicopter crews often turned back in the face of only moderate fire or marginal weather. To minimize exposure, crews made passes and pushed out supplies twelve feet or so above the ground. One crew ruined a shipment of badly needed whole blood by tossing it out from fifty feet at high speed. Such tactics of course ruled out patient pickups but sometimes men clung to landing skids. The spectacle of undamaged helicopters passing over the assembled wounded, departing empty, was crushing to those on the ground. The chief U.S. Air Force advisor with the Vietnamese unit whose helicopters were involved agreed that the crews "lacked the aggressiveness to accomplish the mission with a sense of urgency." Vietnamese Air Force performance improved after an American army helicopter led a flight of four Vietnamese UH–1s into An Loc. Although the aircraft were swamped by the walking wounded and departed without litter cases, the episode helped stiffen resolve among Vietnamese crews. Vietnamese Air Force commanders began taking a stronger hand, in some cases disciplining aborting pilots. Later reports by the American advisors at An Loc noted that the Vietnamese crews at times "performed admirably." On one date (May 25), twenty-one UH–1s resupplied and reinforced nearby positions, evacuating two hundred wounded under enemy fire that shot down three aircraft.[33]

U.S. Army and Air Force officials tended to differ in their assessments of Vietnamese helicopter crews. At Pleiku, U.S. Air Force Col. Peter B. Van Brussel, Jr., praised the highlands-based UH–1 units for their conduct in the face of heavy losses. He judged that the squadrons emerged from the ordeal as hardened and professional, assault-capable units. The Air Force advisory group and the Air Staff compiled an impressive list of successful troop-lift, resupply, and medevac missions, holding that Vietnamese conduct under fire met "U.S. standards" and that "90 percent of the criticisms were unfounded." On the other hand, senior Army advisors in Vietnam deemed the Vietnamese Air Force crews unresponsive to ground commanders ("unwilling to postpone lunch to accomplish the mission"), inclined to abandon critical missions without notice, and guilty of "an underlying current of uncooperativeness." The ground force advisors made plain their feelings that the decision to place the helicopters in the Vietnamese Air Force had proven to be a mistake. Colonel Van Brussel acknowledged that vestiges of the old weaknesses remained—the inability and unwillingness to fly in instrument conditions, slowness in completing most tasks, and weak supervision.[34]

Despite these deficiencies, expansion of the Vietnamese Air Force continued. Under Project Enhance Plus in late 1972 the Vietnamese Air Force received nearly three hundred additional UH–1s to equip five new squadrons (making twenty-one). Three of these were transport-gunship units and two were medical evacuation and search and rescue squadrons. Third and fourth CH–47 squadrons were approved earlier for which some ninety UH–1 pilots entered transition training in the United States late in the year. The need for the new Chinook squadrons for forward supply was undoubted, but the readiness of the Vietnamese Air Force to undertake this final cycle of expansion in helicopters was at best questionable.[35]

Coexisting with the U.S. Air Force aerial port net throughout the war was a lesser chain of air terminals at thirteen bases including Tan Son Nhut, Da Nang, Nha Trang, Bien Hoa, and Binh Thuy. These were used principally by Vietnamese Air Force C–47s for passenger movements. At several of the thirteen locations, units shared facilities and workspace with the local U.S. Air Force port. Training and advising the Vietnamese terminal units, previously the responsibility of the Air Force Advisory Group, in April 1967 became the duty of the 2d Aerial Port Group under the 834th Air Division.[36]

Advisory group programs were largely limited to recordkeeping, planning, and safety, since the handloading methods used with the C–47 were totally different from the American system. Technical assistance activities increased with the introduction of C–119s which had floor conveyers that permitted use of cargo pallets. In late 1967 the 2d Aerial Port Group gave classes at six different bases, teaching palletizing, loading, and the maintenance and operation of heavy forklifts. A Vietnamese civilian employee translated the applicable technical orders into Vietnamese. During 1968 the Americans transferred pallets, nets, and forklifts to the Vietnamese Air Force for use with C-119s.[37]

The training effort under the 2d Group gradually expanded and became more systematic. Instruction at the transportation terminals after mid-1969 stressed safety, load planning, and care of the basic equipment, including standard and adverse-terrain forklifts. Most American instructors approached their task with enthusiasm, appreciating that successful Vietnamization of aerial ports could end the necessity for second and third tours in Vietnam by U.S. Air Force port personnel. Instructors reported problems stemming from the language difference, and several criticized the short working hours habitual among the Vietnamese. Although student enrollments were smaller than expected (apparently reflecting low Vietnamese Air Force priorities), by mid-1970 about two hundred individuals had been qualified as air freight specialists. A Vietnamese transportation school offering aerial port training opened soon afterwards, ending the American role in basic instruction.

A final cycle of U.S. Air Force instruction coincided with closures of the American ports and the assumptions of full local responsibility by each Vietnamese transportation terminal. Volunteers from the 2d Group formed a training team, moving from one terminal to another during the periods of changeovers. The first turnover took place at Soc Trang on March 1, 1971, and by year's end eight more ports became all-Vietnamese. At each location one or more American cargo specialists remained for three months after the official transfer. By mid-1972, at all points except Tan Son Nhut, Bien Hoa, and Da Nang, U.S. Air Force transports were onloaded and offloaded only by Vietnamese terminal personnel with only occasional American supervision. Not unexpectedly, the Vietnamese Air Force net was bedeviled by the same problems that had troubled the American ports in past years—forklift breakdown and shortages, undermanning, and shortages of skilled equipment repair personnel. These conditions, along with loose ramp supervision, contributed to frequent aircraft delays.[38]

The transportation terminal at Pleiku earned special praise during the critical 1972 battles in the highlands. The chief U.S. Air Force advisor in the region noted that the Vietnamese worked around the clock for two full weeks, sleeping in the port area when the workload permitted. "Sheer hard work and determination," according to the American officer, along with "imagination and originality" (in transferring fuel from aircraft to trucks), underlay the crucial air terminal contribution to the successful defense of Pleiku and Kontum. Other American advisors praised the efforts of Vietnamese port personnel at Tan Son Nhut (who took over from the U.S. Air Force on December 1, 1972) during the height of the late-year equipment deliveries, many of whom worked sixteen hours and more a day.[39]

Immediately before the 1973 cease-fire, Vietnamese Air Force port personnel totaled six hundred, sufficient to man twenty-two major and satellite air terminals. Port operations were planned to be daytime principally, with only a skeleton port apparatus on duty in darkness, with port personnel organized to augment local base defense forces at night. Only 430 Vietnamese airmen were actually assigned to the port system, however, and contractor personnel were employed to meet the shortage, to assist in further training, and to handle the few final U.S. Air Force transport movements.[40]

In developing the Vietnamese Air Force aerial port apparatus (as in other areas of Vietnamization), the U.S. Air Force created a scaled-down copy of the American model, one capable of functioning with somewhat less advanced equipment and techniques. In its training, materiel, and planning assistance to the Vietnamese terminal system, the Americans achieved all that could have been hoped. Air terminal work was not inherently complex so the general technical weakness of the Vietnamese Air Force was not critical. But whether or not the Americans had succeeded in instilling their own energetic habits—the aggressive leadership and initiative needed to overcome the inevitable day-to-day frictions which would otherwise build up to cripple aerial port system effectiveness—was doubtful.[41]

As fighting waned during the summer, the Vietnamese Air Force transport arm resumed progress toward full operational capability. C–123 and C–119 flying hour and incommission rates swung upward, and after June all airlift squadrons except the C–7 units functioned without American maintenance help. Activation of the third Caribou squadron on July 1 completed the planned force of eight transport squadrons. A series of accidents during the summer underlined the thin experience level. Pilot errors caused the destruction of two C–47s and a C–119 in takeoff and landing crashes, and four C–123s were damaged in ground-handling mishaps.[42]

The events of spring made it plain that the expanded Vietnamese airlift arm was still not capable of the volume of effort demanded in an all-out campaign. On May 29, acting on the initiative of the Air Force Advisory Group, MACV recommended to CINCPAC that the United States provide C–130s to replace all Vietnamese Air Force C–123s, C–119s, and C–47s. In justification MACV cited maintenance problems

THE ADVISORY ROLE

created by the age and diversity of the presently assigned aircraft. In the staff actions which followed, both the Seventh Air Force and PACAF supported the conversion of the Vietnamese Air Force to C-130s, while the Vietnamese again repeated their long-standing wish for these planes. The Air Staff, the Joint Chiefs, and the Office of the Secretary of Defense, however, all continued their opposition, citing the higher maintenance skills required, the likely delays in crew retraining, and the impact of taking C-130s from U.S. forces. Air Staff opposition began to waver, however, upon receiving further recommendations from the Seventh Air Force in late summer.

The question was abruptly settled on October 20, two days after the arrival in Saigon of Presidential Adviser Henry A. Kissinger, then working toward a cease-fire agreement. On the twentieth, Secretary of Defense Melvin R. Laird initiated Project Enhance Plus, stating that the President had directed that the South Vietnamese be provided materiel specified on a lengthy "shopping list." Included among the six hundred Enhance Plus aircraft were two squadrons of C-130s, each with sixteen aircraft.[43]

The Enhance Plus C-130s were A-models drawn from Air National Guard and Air Force Reserve units in the United States. Personnel from eighteen bases were recalled to prepare thirty-eight planes (including six spares) for movement across the Pacific. Air Force Reserve and Air National Guard aircrews flew the Pacific crossings, the first ships leaving California on October 29 by the central Pacific route. Some later crews flew via Alaska. The thirty-second plane reached Tan Son Nhut on November 6, four days ahead of the deadline. The successful mobilization and ferrying effort reflected well on Air Reserve Forces competence, as well as on the airworthiness of the elderly C-130As.[44]

Aircrew C-130 conversion training proceeded without accident despite pressures for haste, poor aircraft incommission rates, and the crowded flying environment about Tan Son Nhut. The first class, consisting of eight former C-123 crews, entered ground school on November 27, and flying training began two weeks later. Instructors were from a forty-six-man U.S. Air Force mobile training team which included volunteers from the C-130A Air Reserve Forces units. The E-model crewmen of the 374th Wing were not used in the transition program nor were the E-models used for orientation flights, in the belief that the cockpit differences between the E- and A-models might create confusion. The Vietnamese pilots and navigators proved high in motivation, excellent in English language skills, and possessed of vast flying experience. The American instructors thus quickly lost any doubts that the Vietnamese Air Force would be successful in operating the 130s. After attaining instructor qualification, members of the first class helped to train the later groups. The number of qualified crews reached thirty-two on February 24, 1973, ending the American role in training.[45]

601

Maintenance instruction took place simultaneously with aircrew training, drawing students from the C–123 and C–119 squadrons. Graduates numbered 312 by the first week of January, toward a goal of over four hundred. The American mobile training team chief reported that maintenance students "ranged from good to excellent" and that no major problems were encountered. Assisting in maintaining the C–130As during the first weeks were one hundred U.S. Air Force mechanics, sent from the United States for sixty-day tours. Civilian contract personnel joined subsequently, hired for long-term maintenance work beyond flightline tasks. Incommission rates declined drastically during December and January while awaiting spare parts.[46]

The November decision that the Vietnamese Air Force was to return all C–47s, C–119s, and C–123s to the U.S. Air Force was important. It assured that experienced aircrews and ground crews were available to man the C–130 units with a surplus of personnel for retraining to strike aircraft. Replying to the Vietnamese wish to keep some of the older aircraft, American officers repeatedly pointed out that the lift capacity of the two C–130 squadrons was more than double that of the five squadrons they replaced. Four of the five older squadrons ceased flying in November and December 1972, while a single C–123 squadron remained active to bridge the conversion period. Vietnamese Air Force and contract aircrews flew the C–47s, C–119s, and C–123s to Clark for renovation, storage, and (in many cases) for use by the air forces of other Asian allies. Unaffected by the Enhance Plus reprogramming was the Vietnamese Caribou force which afforded a capability for operating into very short and rough airfields.[47]

Events shortly before the January cease-fire indicated that the Vietnamese Air Force had made progress toward managing its C–130s both logistically and operationally. The first constructive airlift mission took place on January 6 as part of the crew-training program, linking Tan Son Nhut and Da Nang. Three days later, an all-Vietnamese crew flew a similar mission without American instructors. For the remainder of the month, three combined airlift and training missions were scheduled weekly. During the week of January 13, for example, Vietnamese Air Force 130s lifted eighty percent (115 tons) of the cargo air-shipped by the air logistics center at Bien Hoa.[48] Meanwhile C–130 airdrop training began. Major Robert L. Highley and several other members of the 374th Wing assisted in high-altitude GRADS instruction and accompanied several practice missions. Vietnamese crews made actual GRADS deliveries at An Loc on January 25 and 26. Major Highley felt that the Vietnamese pilots were outstanding but that weaknesses remained in parachute rigging, navigation, and other areas. Six Vietnamese Air Force crews were nevertheless deemed drop qualified, and two sets of MSQ–77 mobile search ground radar systems were transferred to the Vietnamese just before the cease-fire.[49]

THE ADVISORY ROLE

The mission of the Air Force Advisory Group ended on January 28, 1973. Advisory team roles had been minor in the C–130 conversions with stateside personnel dominating training and materiel assistance activities. In its official assessment of Enhance Plus, the advisory group concluded that a "great deal of training had been accomplished in record time," but that more time would have been useful. Without a doubt, Vietnamese proficiency in adapting to C–130s was a result of a decade of training and generally successful airlift operations. Upon leaving Vietnam the advisory group's director of operations, Colonel Barr, voiced the thoughts of numerous American officers after advisory duties with the Vietnamese Air Force. Colonel Barr wrote in January 1973, after nineteen months in Vietnam: "It had been a dynamic time and I'm certain when I reflect back on 31 years of active service, I will count this period as among the most challenging, interesting, and certainly rewarding. The Vietnamese have truly impressed me with their resiliency, energy, capability and potential."[50]

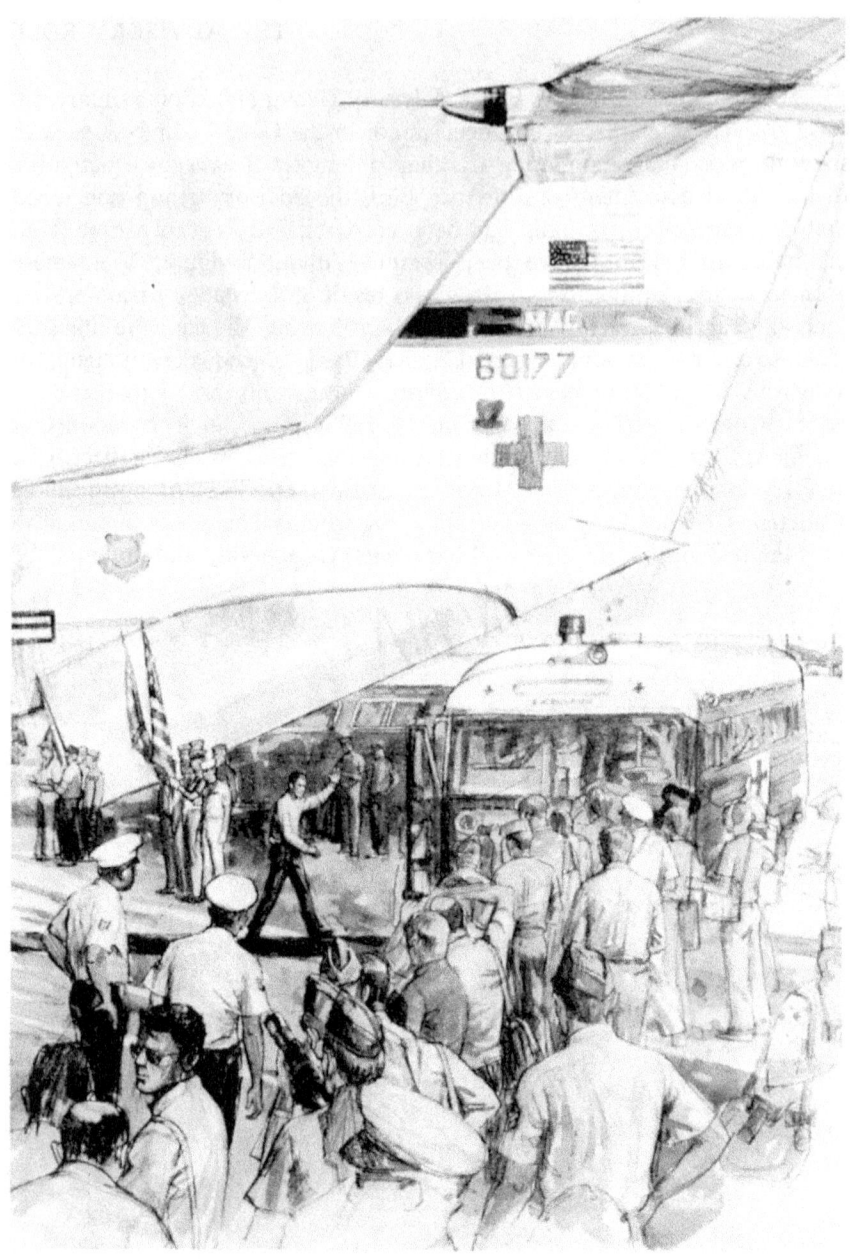

(Mazine McCaffrey, Courtesy U.S. Air Force Art Collection)

Operation Homecoming, Return of POWs, Clark AFB, 1973

XXIV. Return to Cold War in Southeast Asia

Most Americans welcomed the Paris agreements that resulted in a cease-fire in Vietnam. Although the cease-fire was short of full victory, it seemed enough that the killing had ended and that several hundred Americans imprisoned in North Vietnam would soon be free. The Air Force airlifters generally shared these feelings and were proud of their roles in attaining what appeared to be peace with honor.

For the airlifters the times were busy and exhilarating. C–130 crews on January 29, 1973, made the Air Force's first peaceful landings in North Vietnam in nearly two decades. In the weeks that followed, Hercules crewmen took part in the emotional prisoner-release ceremonies in Hanoi. Meanwhile, other C–130 missions in South Vietnam sped the release of communist personnel held by the allies, helping to assure that repatriations by the enemy would continue.

After the cease-fire the Pacific C–130 force continued its routine overwater airlifts and flights in Thailand. Most challenging was the air supply effort to Cambodia where intense fighting continued. C–130 crews each day landed with munitions and rice at the Phnom Penh airport and made drops to Cambodian garrisons isolated at other points. American bombing ceased in Cambodia in August 1973, but the airlift went on without a break. The survival of the Phnom Penh regime without question depended on the surface and air lines of communications through which American materiel flowed. Meanwhile, in widespread regions of South Vietnam the North Vietnamese army gained strength, now supplied and reinforced without interference by allied interdiction from the air.

Following the defeat of the communist spring invasion, the Americans returned to the policy of encouraging the South Vietnamese to rely as much as possible on their own transports. The 374th Wing in the early summer of 1972 briefly operated a ten-plane C–130 detachment from Nakhon Phanom, mainly to transport units from Vietnam to Thailand, and soon afterwards reduced the Tan Son Nhut C–130 force to twenty aircraft. A final tragedy took place on August 12 when enemy fire claimed a C–130 taking off from Soc Trang. Its forty-three passengers and crewmen became the war's last fatalities in Air Force C–130 operations.[1]

TACTICAL AIRLIFT

A potentially serious situation developed at Tan Son Nhut where the Vietnamese Air Force's newly acquired C–130s sat unprotected. Concerned by the possibility of shelling attacks, Gen. John W. Vogt, Jr., commander of the Seventh Air Force, on November 13 directed the 374th Wing detachment to give up its protected area. Despite the complete lack of forewarning, the detachment promptly flew out its aircraft and crews, and within twelve hours all but two of the Vietnamese planes were protected. The American 130s thereafter operated from Nakhon Phanom, continuing to fly missions in South Vietnam. A fourteen-man maintenance team and several aircrews remained at Tan Son Nhut. Shortages of spare parts and work facilities at Nakhon Phanom, however, soon forced a cut in the number of daily missions, compounding the loss of work capacity represented by the extra flying time to and from Nakhon Phanom. Meanwhile the Vietnamese Air Force's temporary preoccupation with retraining for the C–130s further decreased overall lift capability.[2]

To meet the rising backlogs, Military Airlift Command C–141s again undertook hauls between the major South Vietnamese airfields. The C–141 missions usually originated at Clark, landed and reloaded at Saigon, Da Nang, Nha Trang, and again at Saigon before returning to Clark. The C–141s lifted twenty-five hundred tons of cargo and seventy-seven hundred passengers in 250 such sorties during November and December.[3]

Airdrops remained the exclusive responsibility of AWADS ships and crews from TAC, now called the Easter Bunny force. All releases were from high altitude, rigged for either HALO or high-velocity descent; the incidence of parachute malfunctions (streamers and high-openers) remained troublesome—one bundle in six for HALO, one in ten for high velocity. AWADS releases gradually became more numerous than GRADS in preparation for closing the ground radar sites. An Loc remained a focus for drop activities along with several familiar highlands camps including Ben Het, Dak Seang, Duc Co, and Ba To, all of which yielded to the enemy during the fall. Extremely small drop zones, enemy pressure on camp perimeters, and parachute malfunctions all cut the effectiveness of the drops. After only 51 of 340 bundles released at Minh Thanh were recovered, the MACV logistics section wrote, "we appear to be supplying the besiegers rather than the besieged." Although results were unimpressive the airlifters in late-year operations refined the know-how in high altitude drops acquired in the difficult spring campaign. The Easter Bunny ships and crews left Tan Son Nhut with the other C–130s in November,* thereafter continuing the drops out of Takhli and later U–Tapao.[4]

---

* One of the two TAC C–130 squadrons returned to the United States in September 1972; the remaining unit rotated its personnel periodically from Langley and Pope. C–130Es of the 374th Wing replaced the B–models in the Klong rotation in July 1972.

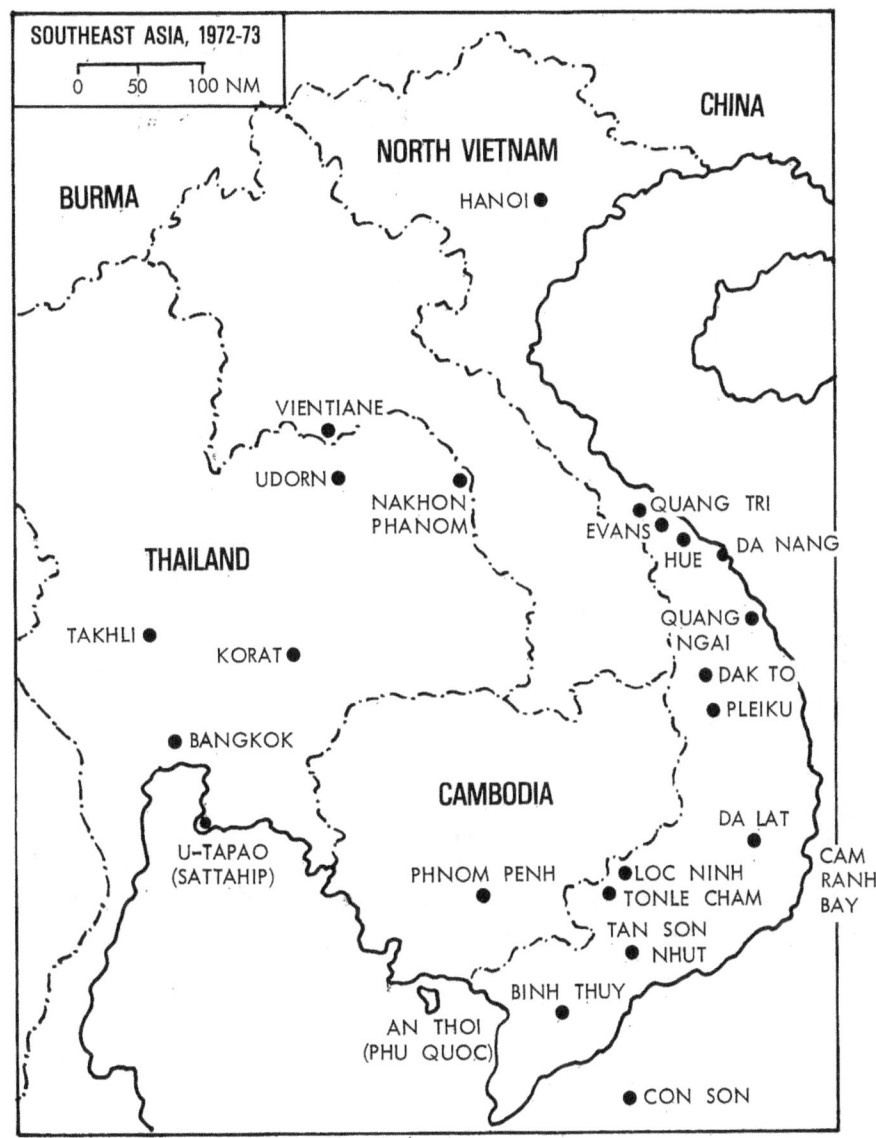

    The Nakhon Phanom and the Easter Bunny C–130s continued to operate under the scheduling and control of the Tan Son Nhut airlift control center. Another control center at U–Tapao managed the C–130s (called Klong) primarily used for lifts within Thailand. As in the past, aircrews and ground crews were rotated from Taiwan and remained in Thailand for cycles of up to twenty days.[5]

    A final incident of war, one remindful of countless episodes in the past, marked the final hours before the cease-fire. Caught on the ground at

TACTICAL AIRLIFT

Da Lat amid shellings and firefights, Capt. George P. Elwood's crew worked during lulls, making emergency repairs. A small battery taken from an O-2 FAC airplane finally provided starting power. With one engine shut down and the hydraulics pierced by shrapnel, Captain Elwood and his muddy crew made it back to Nakhon Phanom by nightfall. Elwood's plane was one of three C-130s that received battle damage that day, January 27. The Silver Stars awarded to each crewmember, and the annual award for heroism given by the Air Force Sergeants Association, were the last Air Force accolades earned for valor before the cease-fire.[6]

By the terms of the agreement initialed four days earlier in Paris, the cease-fire was to become effective in Vietnam the morning of January 28, 1973, Saigon time. American prisoners were to be released and the last 23,700 American troops withdrawn from Vietnam within sixty days. A four-party joint military commission (from the United States, North Vietnam, the Saigon regime, and the Viet Cong) was to oversee the cease-fire, exchanges, and withdrawals, supervised by an international commission from four nonbelligerent powers. President Nixon described the agreement as one "to end the war and bring peace with honor to Vietnam and Southeast Asia."[7]

During the evening of January 28 the American delegation in Paris officially requested MACV to furnish two C-130s the next day to land at Hanoi to pick up the communist delegations to the joint military commission. Assigned to fly the historic mission was Lt. Col. Philip J. Riede, commander of the 345th Squadron, with Col. Andrew P. Iosue, commander of the 374th. Chosen to pilot the second plane was Capt. Theodore C. Appelbaum. In their briefings at Saigon the crewmen were told to expect almost anything, and Colonel Riede admitted nervousness upon hearing the extent of antiaircraft and missile defenses located about Hanoi. U.S. Army and Vietnamese Air Force interpreters were to accompany both crews.

The two 130s took off from Tan Son Nhut on the morning of the twenty-ninth. Upon reaching Da Nang, both crews circled for nearly an hour waiting final clearance to communist territory. The planned flight route was mostly over water, but the new instructions called for westward flight to a point well inland, then northward to Hanoi. With strong reservations the crew set forth on the new routing. Back at the Tan Son Nhut airlift control center, General Vogt personally monitored the progress of the mission. Fifteen minutes before reaching Hanoi the crews established radio contact with Gia Lam airport and obtained landing instructions. Colonel Riede flew the arranged approach using the low frequency radio beacon and breaking out from the clouds at about three thousand feet. Before landing, the crewmen looked over Hanoi's bridge and bomb damage. The landings on the patched surface, of which six thousand feet were usable, were uneventful.

On the ground at the airport, buildings were in shambles from the recent bombings. Hundreds of civilians came to look at the Americans and their planes but kept their distance at the edge of the ramp. Conversations were cordial and an English-speaking official invited the crewmen to a small building for tea. The passengers meanwhile lined themselves into two contingents, each of about forty-five men. Each man carried a suitcase and a small container of personal possessions. Both planes took off shortly after noon, landing at Tan Son Nhut three hours later. The only hitch came midway in the flight when the Americans asked the communists to fill out visa forms. The senior communist officer at one point in the discussion told Colonel Iosue to return the ship to Hanoi, an instruction which the American ignored. After landing at Tan Son Nhut the communists stayed on the ships for another twenty-four hours, still disputing the use of the forms.[8]

374th Wing crews flew other missions to Hanoi during the next fortnight, still prior to the first prisoner release. One crew from the 345th Squadron, commanded by Captain Elwood (veteran of the recent episode at Da Lat), flew missions on three consecutive days, February 4–6. Three planes on the sixth and four on the seventh hauled a total of four hundred communist passengers south. Some of the communist teams, after processing at Saigon, were flown by C–130 to Hue, Da Nang, and Pleiku. The American crewmen were told to act in a "reserved but correct" manner toward the communists, avoiding breaches of courtesy. A product of these early flights to Hanoi was the accumulation of information on airfield conditions and flight procedures useful during the later prisoner-release missions.[9]

Planning for Operation Homecoming, the return of the Americans held by the communists, gave to the Military Airlift Command C–141s the coveted responsibility for bringing out men. The C–130s received the task of hauling recovery support teams to and from Hanoi. These teams were to administer the exchanges and provide initial care for the returnees.[10] On February 11, two C–130s of the 384th Wing flew from Ching Chuan Kang to Clark as primary and spare ships for the movement of the support team to Hanoi the next day. All crewmen were veterans of the earlier flights to North Vietnam. The mission commander for the venture was Colonel Riede, the pilot of the January 29 mission. Thirty-four passengers and crewmen were aboard during Colonel Riede's morning takeoff, February 12, along with aircraft support equipment and a radio jeep. The four-hour flight across the South China Sea to Da Nang and north to Hanoi was uneventful. Meanwhile, a second C–130 left Tan Son Nhut carrying members of the international commission to oversee the repatriations. This

Operation Homecoming gave USAF airlifters the responsibility of bringing the American POWs home.

C-141 at Clark Air Base, Philippines receives a red cross on its vertical stabilizer in preparation for the trip to Hanoi.

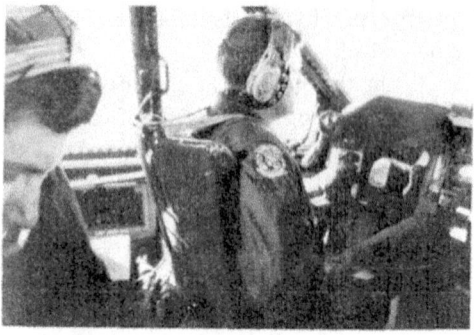

Maj. James E. Marrott at the controls of the first C-141 flown into Hanoi. Co-pilot John J. Shinoskie is in the foreground.

A jubilant ex-POW deplanes at Clark Air Base.

The Operation Homecoming command post at Scott Air Force Base, Illinois handled the MAC C-141 and C-9 flights.

C–130 arrived at Gia Lam airport about one hour before Colonel Riede and departed about the time of his arrival. Riede performed the now routine approach up the Red River to Gia Lam, navigating by airborne radar and the communist radio beacon.

The day was a highly emotional one for Riede's crewmen. 1st Lt. John W. Grillo was far more excited than on any of his previous four trips to Hanoi. On the ground at Gia Lam the crew met the airport manager, by now known to the Americans as "Fred," and went indoors for the customary tea. The first of three C–141s landed soon after Riede and repatriation began. Lt. Grillo was disheartened upon seeing the returnees because the injured were the first to appear. As the first returnee moved from the release desk, photographers and newsmen blocked his path to the waiting C–141. Seeing the awkward situation, one of the C–130 flight engineers quickly moved to clear the way, leading the former prisoner by the arm. Taking the cue, the other C–130 crewmen in the same way escorted each man to the waiting C–141. Grillo reported that those he guided were "pretty sharp in their thinking and all of them were feeling just great." Lt. Gen. William G. Moore, Jr., former commander of the 834th Air Division in Vietnam and in 1973 commander of the Thirteenth Air Force, later complimented the 374th Wing crewmen on their conduct: "I think it was most fitting that our returnees' first steps onto the road back were taken with the help of the airlifters. Over and over, returnees with whom I spoke expressed their deepest appreciation at having been greeted by a 'brother-in-arms' and, in those first few moments of freedom, welcomed home by their own kind."

A total of 116 Americans were released at Gia Lam that day and all were lifted to Clark by the 141s. Colonel Riede's crew carried the commissioners back to Saigon and flew on to Clark. With Riede during the memorable mission were four other pilots: Maj. Edward N. Brya, veteran of the An Loc drops, Elwood, Grillo, and Capt. Philip W. Ryan, Jr.[11]

Equally dramatic events took place on the same day at the communist-held airstrip at Loc Ninh in South Vietnam where twenty-seven Americans were scheduled to be released. An American airfield survey team had flown to Loc Ninh the day before aboard U.S. Army planes, and enlisted communist help in filling in holes and clearing away some of the old matting. Activities began on the twelfth with the arrival of U.S. Army helicopters, bringing communist and allied military observers. A trying day of bickering and delay ensued. At midafternoon an Air Force C–130 took off from Bien Hoa, carrying seventy-five communist prisoners scheduled for release and their South Vietnamese guards. The pilot was Maj. Bernard J. Clark, a member of 21st Squadron and a veteran of several tours in Southeast Asian airlift reaching back to the early Mule Train venture. Also aboard was an Air Force combat control team to control the planned flow of C–130s with communist prisoners into Loc Ninh.

TACTICAL AIRLIFT

Major Clark circled the Loc Ninh field, looking it over carefully before starting a tight approach and landing. Armed communist soldiers lined both sides of the runway. Clark kept his engines running during the entire three hours on the ground to avoid any difficulty in restarting. From the cockpit, Clark saw a truck arrive with the twenty-seven obviously excited Americans. Several of his crewmen and the control team crewmen walked over to talk to the prisoners. The reunion, preceding the official release, was memorable. Late in the day the twenty-seven men climbed into six U.S. Army helicopters and departed for Tan Son Nhut. Major Clark took aboard some eighty released South Vietnamese and headed for Bien Hoa. A second C–130, which had waited overhead throughout Clark's stay on the ground, landed at Loc Ninh with another load of communist prisoners and departed at dusk with repatriated South Vietnamese. Of the released Americans, all but one flew on to Clark that evening aboard a C–9 of the 20th Operations Squadron.[12]

One other C–130 participated in the first day of the releases. A single Hercules left Bien Hoa in midafternoon, carrying the first of the North Vietnamese scheduled for the repatriation at the Quang Tri steel bridge site. Because the old airstrips at Quang Tri and Dong Ha (both now in communist hands) were heavily cratered, the flow of C–130s was planned for Phu Bai where the prisoners were to reload into American CH–47s. Soon after the first landing at Phu Bai, however, communist officials at Quang Tri stated they were unready to receive returnees, thus ending the airlift operation for the day.[13]

The missions of February 12 began a massive airlift that moved most of the 26,500 enemy prisoners to exchange sites within South Vietnam. C–130 flights to Loc Ninh continued for a fortnight. Each day a two-man combat control team flew in with the first plane, along with a C–130 tire-change team and the mission commander, Maj. Richard Wieland. Aircraft unloaded at Loc Ninh with engines running, taking aboard South Vietnamese returnees before departing. Communist returnees generally ignored the American crewmen, and most discarded their prison clothing with gestures of contempt after landing. The releases at Quang Tri finally began on February 14, the 130s for several weeks landing at the quickly repaired strip at the former Camp Evans, guided in by an Air Force combat control team. When poor visibility and wet runway conditions prevented landings at Evans, crews diverted to Phu Bai and Da Nang. Meanwhile, C–130s also hauled substantial numbers of prisoners to Tay Ninh and Phu Cat for release. After the first few days of pickups at Bien Hoa, most loadings were at the An Thoi and Con Son Island airstrips.

The C–130 crews returned nightly to Thailand where a large chart showed the number of prisoners still awaiting movement. Aircrews and ground crews worked to exhaustion, appreciating that delays in the operation could interfere with the pace of releases by the communists. During the two weeks prior to the sixty-day deadline, even the AWADS ships and crews hauled prisoners. Upon movement of the last prisoners on the fifty-eighth day, the senior U.S. delegate to the joint military commission commended the 374th Wing to CINCPAC, citing the wing's "outstanding performance of duty in a variety of sensitive and demanding missions."[14]

Releases of Americans in Hanoi followed the pattern of the first day. Releases took place on February 18 and on seven dates in March, ending with the repatriation of the last sixty-seven men on the twenty-ninth. On each occasion two C–130s flew to Hanoi, one from Clark with the recovery support team, the other carrying the commissioners from Saigon. Colonel Riede accompanied most of the flights from Clark, but otherwise the opportunity was spread among numerous crews. Except for the low clouds and rain typical of Hanoi winters, the missions were free from problems. The C–130 crewmen continued to escort each released prisoner to C–141 planeside.[15]

Fighting declined only gradually in several regions of South Vietnam. The 374th Wing received its first SA–7 damage on January 29 when the missile passed through a C–130's fuselage at fifty-five hundred feet over the Mekong Delta, severing lines and starting fires but failing to detonate. A final instance of battle damage occurred on March 7 when a plane received .30-caliber hits while on a cargo mission. Besides the prisoner-of-war missions the C–130s were kept busy hauling American personnel and equipment from sites in South Vietnam to Thailand, Tan Son Nhut, or Da Nang for strategic airlift home. Airdrops in Vietnam ended with the cease-fire.[16]

All airlifters felt privileged to contribute to these early 1973 missions, especially the trips to Hanoi. Like most Americans, the airlifters felt the Operation Homecoming flights were a satisfying ending to the long years of war.

Air transport considerations were prominent in past air staff planning for postwar Southeast Asia. Of continuing concern, for example, was the ability of the Southeast Asia partners to keep up major airfields (such as Cam Ranh Bay) that would be needed in case of fast American reentry by air. One 1969 study in the plans directorate envisioned an American "residual force," to be kept in Thailand after any cease-fire in Vietnam, particularly if fighting continued in Laos. An essential part of such a residual force would be its airlift component, needed for logistical deliveries. The study group envisioned a rotational C–130 detachment at U–Tapao, an obvious crossroads of air and sea lines of communications.

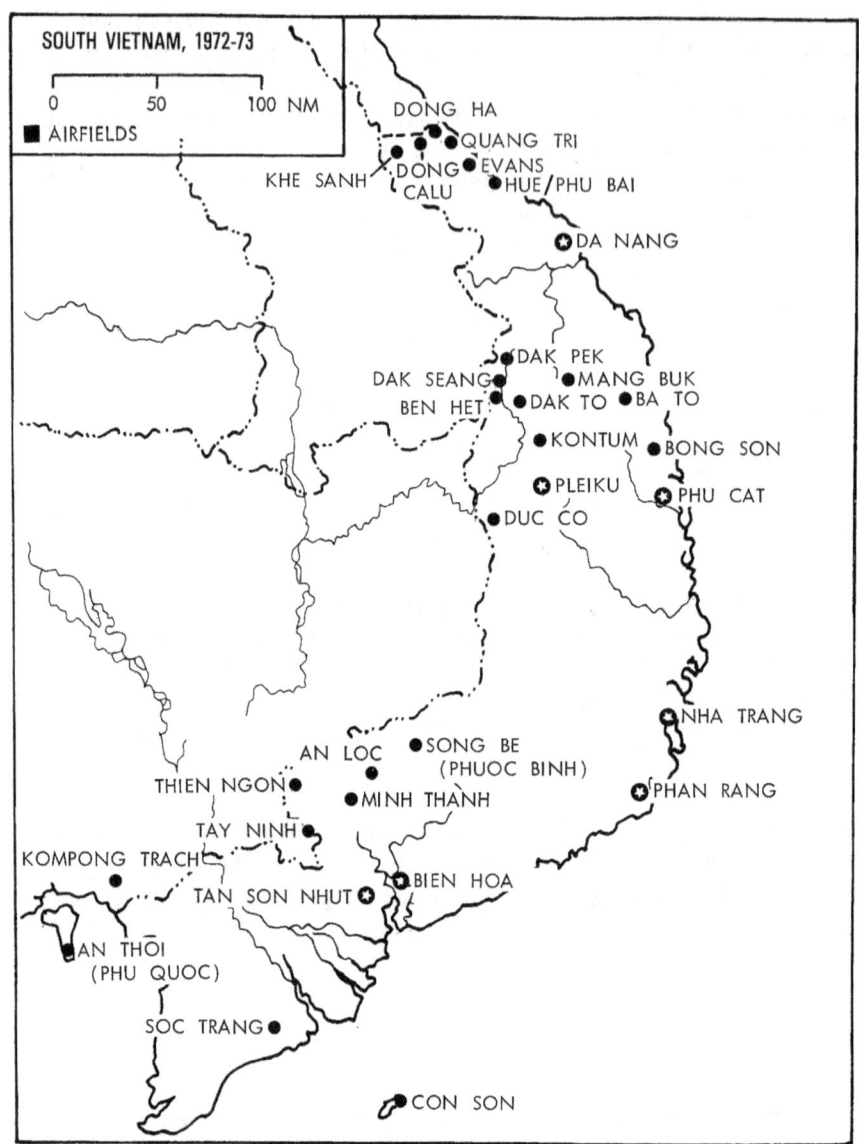

The 1969 paper closely foretold the arrangements actually made four years later, except that the expectation of continued fighting in Laos translated in 1973 to the campaigns in Cambodia.[17]

The cease-fire in Vietnam left unchanged the basic American goals for Southeast Asia—attainment of regional stability and deterrence of aggression, preferably under healthy non-communist regimes. Preservation of at least a token American military presence on the mainland appeared desirable to assure Hanoi's compliance with the Paris terms. SEATO members, however, were plainly disinterested in tightened cooperation within the alliance, and the foreign ministers of the Association of Southeast Asian Nations, meeting in Kuala Lumpur in February, inclined toward "neutralization" of the region, which would include eventual removal of U.S. bases.

The American regional posture thus depended on what was diplomatically feasible. Limited American forces remained in Thailand, along with substantial unused base facilities. Mobile forces and base areas remained in the Philippines and elsewhere in the western Pacific. The situation resembled that of Northeast Asia where units in South Korea were backed by forces and bases in Japan and Okinawa. Adm. Noel A. M. Gayler, USN, in October 1973 strongly defended this distribution of forces. In Admiral Gayler's view, this arrangement would discourage aggression, safeguard lines of communications and entry points, and provide strategic deterrence. The role of Air Force air transport in this strategy was crucial, linking the widespread forces in peacetime and affording a flexible capability in crisis for augmentation, lateral shifts, or withdrawal.[18]

The withdrawal from Vietnam brought command changes including several in airlift management. MACV headquarters was officially closed out on March 29, 1973, and replaced in effect by a new United States Support Activities Group (USSAG), located at Nakhon Phanom with responsibilities for planning and controlling operations in the event warfare resumed. The Seventh Air Force also moved to Nakhon Phanom and General Vogt became the first commander of the merged USSAG/Seventh Air Force headquarters. The Saigon airlift control center merged with the control center at U–Tapao on March 23, consolidating the scheduling, mission following, and control of all C–130s in Southeast Asia. The Pacific Transportation Management Agency, Thailand (at U–Tapao), had approval authority for Southeast Asia C–130 requests, but this function shifted to the USSAG in 1974. Within USSAG headquarters an operations support branch was responsible for airlift staff functions, while a transportation division in the logistics section monitored air and surface shipments. Some felt that the divisions of responsibility between U–Tapao and Nakhon Phanom contributed to confusion when information from Cambodia required last-minute changes in mission schedules.[19]

Force planning called for retention of three C–130 squadrons in the western Pacific thus returning to the level of 1961. The 374th Wing accordingly lost its fourth squadron on August 15, 1973. Late in the year the 374th headquarters and two squadrons moved from Taiwan to Clark, the third squadron to Kadena. Of the TAC rotational C–130s, only four AWADS aircraft remained, making up the Easter Bunny detachment at U–Tapao. Meanwhile, the Nakhon Phanom detachment made an interim shift to Takhli in late February before moving to U–Tapao in May 1973 to merge with the Klong force.[20] (A force of up to twelve special purpose C–130s remained at Korat. These planes were not used for airlift but were supported in part by temporary duty personnel from Ching Chuan Kang Air Base, Taiwan.)

C–130 missions out of U–Tapao included a growing number of flights in Cambodia, circuits linking bases still used by Americans in Thailand, flights into and out of South Vietnam, and occasional sorties in South Vietnam to support teams searching for missing Americans. Each Friday a 374th Wing C–130 flew between Saigon and Hanoi, hauling communist members of the joint military commission. The Americans provided this service in the belief that the flights could aid in getting information on Americans still listed as missing in action. The Hanoi flights continued weekly until the final 1975 collapse.[21] The U–Tapao C–130s met these commitments without difficulty, although maintenance and spare parts problems resulted in a threefold increase in cannibalizations in 1974. This reflected unsatisfactory work facilities at U–Tapao which was deemed "totally inadequate" by Thirteenth Air Force inspectors and labeled "criminal" by the 374th director of maintenance. Aircrew proficiency, flight safety, and morale, however, remained satisfactory.[22]

Several other airlift elements operated from Thai bases, all controlled separately from the C–130s. The Scatback unit, now operating seven T–39s and two C–118As from Nakhon Phanom, was scheduled directly by the USSAG operations support branch. Scatback continued to haul officials and high-priority cargo throughout the theater. The operations support branch also coordinated occasional mission requests for the CH–53s of the 21st Special Operations Squadron, still at Nakhon Phanom, whose primary mission was to be ready to evacuate Americans from Phnom Penh. Three C–47s at Udorn were scheduled by the Thirteenth Air Force advanced echelon at that base, mainly for intra-Thailand flights.[23]

An important aspect of airlift policy after the cease-fire concerned the air transport forces of the Southeast Asian allies, already recognized as valuable in overcoming poor surface communications. The conversion of the Vietnamese Air Force to C–130s made some fifty former Vietnamese C–123s surplus. These relatively simple craft were unlikely to pose problems for air forces accustomed to operating C–47s. Although the Air Staff and the Joint Chiefs of Staff recommended that the surplus 123s be given to the American Air Reserve Forces (replacing the C–130As given to the Vietnamese Air Force), the Secretary of Defense favored the CINCPAC view that the ships be transferred to the Asian allies. Eight C–123s were accordingly allocated to Cambodia, eight to Thailand, seven to Laos, and sixteen each to Korea and the Philippines.[24]

In view of the continued fighting in Cambodia, first priority in C–123 training and materiel went to the Khmer Air Force, which received its first five C–123Ks from Taiwan in April 1973. Teams from the Tactical Air Command soon afterwards started courses for airlift-experienced Cambodian air and ground crews, conducted in Thailand. U.S. Army instructors taught Khmer parachute rigger personnel. Three Khmer Air Force crews began C–123 air landings and airdrop missions in Cambodia in August. When the American instructors left in October, eight Khmer crews were qualified in C–123s, four as instructor crews, and more than a hundred men had completed training in various maintenance specialities. Subsequent C–123 contributions to the Khmer war effort stimulated planning for further Khmer Air Force expansion.[25]

The Royal Laotian Air Force likewise converted to C–123s easily. The Laotians received ten Providers, previously flown by Air America, in January 1973. These planes were delivered ahead of schedule in order to head off possible prohibitions under the expected cease-fire. Shortly after the cease-fire of February 22, 1973, Laotian crews began C–123 training at Udorn. The Royal Laotian Air Force also continued to operate fifteen C–47s and some twenty UH–34s. The contract airlift by Air America and Continental Air Services, Inc., was gradually scaled down, virtually ending by mid-1974. U.S. Army Maj. Gen. Richard G. Trefry, defense attaché at Vientiane, concluded in late 1974 that the C–123, C–47, and H–34 airlift force was the best feature of the Royal Laotian Air Force. Meanwhile, the continued activity of large North Vietnamese forces in Laos meant that prospects for the Provisional Government of National Union were not good.[26]

The Royal Thai Air Force already operated a sixteen-plane C–123 squadron so the additional Providers received in 1973 were absorbed without difficulty. Eight K–models arrived in the spring, two B–models later in the year. The American instructors from TAC, already working with the Cambodians, simultaneously assisted in upgrading Thai crews. Four other Royal Thai squadrons, equipped with C–47, utility, UH–1, and H–34 craft, provided further transport capacity. Another several dozen well-worn airlift craft were acquired by the Thais in 1975 from the defeated air forces of Cambodia, South Vietnam, and Laos. The Thai airlift force thus represented a significant force with which to fight internal insurgency, apparently on the increase.[27]

There was therefore three leading characteristics of American military policy for Southeast Asia after the cease-fire: the limited forward force in Thailand, plans for a possible reintroduction of U.S. forces, and the continuing military assistance program. In all three, consideration of the role of air transport was basic. Meanwhile, the weakening regimes in Saigon and Phnom Penh faced growing pressure from active communist operations. In South Vietnam the recently acquired C–130s offered a means for shifting forces and sustaining operations to meet regional threats, thus reducing the government's disadvantage in strategic defense. In Cambodia, American air transport operations sustained the regime's last thin hopes for survival.

The cease-fire left Vietnam still a divided and war-torn land. The communists controlled about a third of the land area, primarily in scattered enclaves and in the western border regions, containing perhaps five percent of the population. Sapper and guerrilla actions persisted, while the communist main force units were reequipped from the north. Government forces attempted to reduce some of the "liberated areas" and achieved some small territorial gains. A new cease-fire on June 15, 1973, only temporarily slowed the escalating level of fighting.[28]

The Vietnamese Air Force airlift arm met an early test during the communist siege of Tonle Cham, a border camp west of An Loc. Serious attacks began on February 26, 1973. The Vietnamese Air Force lost two helicopters in early attempts to rotate personnel and evacuate the wounded. The 250 defenders thereafter became entirely dependent on fixed-wing airdrops.

A C-123 squadron made the first drops, attempting to deliver supplies to a 164-yard square perimeter. Because of the SA-7 missile threat, releases were from ten thousand feet or higher. The Vietnamese-operated MSQ-77 mobile search radar at Bien Hoa was used for guidance, while navigators calculated wind and ballistics data and made corrections for impact errors after each pass. Steering instructions were transmitted as a series of tones in the pilots' headsets. Load recovery rates were at first unsatisfactory—roughly one bundle of every five dropped. Remedial measures included practice drops near Saigon to improve the pilots' ability to interpret the tone signals. Meanwhile, U.S. Army personnel undertook to repair and recalibrate the beacon transponders installed in the C-123s to aid tracking. The recovery rate climbed to fifty percent by July, but introduction of the C-130s to the Tonle Cham drops brought fresh troubles. The defenders retrieved not a single bundle from the first C-130 missions. Practice missions and beacon improvements proved helpful but troubles persisted with the high-altitude, low-opening, parachute-rigging system. Many chutes opened high (and drifted erratically) or not at all. American attaché officers in Saigon pressed for additional tests in the United States and urged the Vietnamese to apply the lessons learned. C-130 recovery rates gradually improved to fifty percent, and late in 1973 the Vietnamese Air Force acquired the high-velocity rigging system used successfully by the Americans the previous year.

RETURN TO COLD WAR

The air supply of Tonle Cham continued until the spring of 1974 when the garrison withdrew overland to An Loc. The effort indicated that, although the Americans had left the Vietnamese airlifters dubiously prepared to perform high-altitude drops, both air forces were resolute in overcoming technical and tactical problems. American officers in Saigon commended the Vietnamese forces "for an extremely difficult task that was well done."[29]

In managing and operating its airlift arm the Vietnamese Air Force was mainly on its own, since the American attaché office was neither conceived nor manned for close advisory roles.* Vietnamese Air Force officers at the airlift control center prepared daily orders for missions, for the most part reacting to the Army's Central Logistics Command mission requirements and to data received from the aerial ports. The Vietnamese aerial port system, which included detachments at twenty-two airfields, completed phaseout of contract port personnel in the spring of 1974. Supplementing the C–130s and C–7s was a squadron of C–119s, earlier intended for coastal patrol work but because of costs never equipped with the necessary surveillance radar. A small number of C–47s carried officials about the country.[30]

The two squadrons of C–130s were the backbone of the airlift force. To Col. Garvin McCurdy, U.S air attaché in Saigon during most of 1974, the C–130 force was "very professionally run," exhibiting the best safety record in the Vietnamese Air Force. In all of the Vietnamese Air Force, only the airlifters had an active aircrew evaluation program. The Vietnamese used their C–130s with care, appreciating their potential importance for shifting forces from one region to another. Colonel McCurdy noted that many times in the past the Vietnamese had seen "how troops can be deployed and redeployed, changing a losing ground situation into a winning one." For example, during fighting in the summer of 1974, an airborne brigade was shifted from Saigon in two days.[31]

A crucial test of Vietnamization lay in the ability of the Vietnamese Air Force to keep its C–130s flying. The A–models were not new airplanes and had had maintenance troubles during their long careers in PACAF. Incommission rates remained abysmal during the spring of 1973 due to leaky fuel cells, a rash of cracked wing fittings, lack of skilled mechanics, and (in the view of attaché officers) poor management of the maintenance work force. American instructors and technical experts who came to Vietnam to assist included teams from the Air Force Logistics Command to repair wing cracks. The overall incommission rate reached

---

* The U.S. Defense Attaché Office, Saigon, was activated January 28, 1973, with an initial manning of fifty military and twelve hundred Department of Defense civilian employees, plus contractor employees. Civilian strength was progressively reduced.

619

fifty percent (sixteen planes operationally ready) for the first time on June 20, 1973. During July the 130s hauled thirty thousand passengers and thirteen hundred tons of cargo. When added to the C–7 effort, the July accomplishments almost exactly equaled the work of the larger C–47, C–119, and C–123 force twelve months earlier.[32]

Maintenance problems nevertheless persisted, especially difficulties with the A-model fuel tanks. To Colonel McCurdy, "it seemed that people were forever on the inside of the blasted tanks trying to reseal them. They'd reseal them, put them back together, and the aircraft would fly for another little while, and begin to leak someplace else." During 1974 the number of C–130s available for flying each day gradually declined from thirteen or fourteen down to about eight. McCurdy felt that the problem was not so much weakness in basic skills but rather spare parts shortages, difficulties with depot contract assistance, and "those blasted leaks." Brig. Gen. Dung Dinh Linh, the Vietnamese Air Force's deputy chief of staff for materiel, agreed entirely with McCurdy's assessment.[33]

South Vietnam remained divided through 1974. Unhindered from the air since the cease-fire, the communists built and repaired roads and pipelines through southern Laos and western Vietnam, feeding in tanks, artillery, antiaircraft weaponry, and troops. A two-lane all-weather truck route reached from Quang Tri Province to Loc Ninh, paralleled by a gasoline pipeline and communications wires. The communists also repaired the old airfields at Dak To, Loc Ninh, Ca Lu, Dong Ha, and Khe Sanh, although there was no evidence of active airlift operations. The greatest effort was at Khe Sanh where a new 5,300-foot pierced-steel runway was built, and one of the older strips filled in to make a second runway of 3,700 feet. The Khe Sanh airfield thus appeared capable of handling all North Vietnamese transports and some jet fighters.[34]

Throughout South Vietnam the communists built up their antiaircraft capabilities, introducing radar-controlled guns and increasing the surface-to-air missile threat. Protected sites for SA–2 missile launchers were built near Khe Sanh and elsewhere in Quang Tri Province and about four of these sites were actually occupied most of the time. Even more important was the increase in the number of SA–7 man-portable weapons. During the first three months of 1974, SA–7s destroyed fourteen Vietnamese Air Force aircraft, including four helicopters. Firings totaled twenty-five and were most frequent in the southernmost regions. In the same period the Vietnamese Air Force lost fifteen craft (including five helicopters) to antiaircraft fire. The fixed-wing transports, flying mainly in safe areas or at high altitudes, avoided loss.[35]

With some three hundred thousand men in the south, their lines of communications unhampered, and in important respects better equipped than their opponents, the communists by mid-1974 were plainly capable of major offensive operations. While communist forces progressively recovered those bits of territory lost since the cease-fire, the government's strategic reserves found themselves increasingly on the defensive. Then came the further impact of funding cuts. The American Congress on October 8, 1974, appropriated $700 million for South Vietnamese defense for fiscal 1975, a figure well below past appropriations and much less than the billion-dollar authorization which had been used as a basis for spending since June. The effect, in the view of the Americans in Saigon, was devastating. The communist leadership also saw that henceforth Saigon must fight "a poor man's war."[36]

The long-term aim of gradual improvement in the Vietnamese Air Force accordingly was reversed. Forced to function with one-third its projected operating budget, the Vietnamese made drastic cuts in flying time and training, slashed contract assistance, and eliminated eleven of its sixty-six active squadrons. The airlifters received their share of the blows with the C-130 force losing flying time and contract maintenance funds. All C-7s were removed from active service. The latter decision was not surprising since the Caribous were difficult to maintain because of engine and corrosion problems, parts shortages, and some structural cracking. Furthermore, all missions suitable for the short-range Caribou could be shifted over to the CH-47s. But the absence of funds for proper storage care foreshadowed the rapid deterioration of the idle C-7s.[37]

All UH-1 and CH-47 squadrons were retained during the cutbacks although flying time was sharply reduced. Notions of large-scale heliborne assaults were a thing of the past, but the UH-1s were widely used to haul supplies and troops to isolated places, to fly ground officers to forward units, and for medical evacuations. The CH-47s continued valuable service, transporting artillery units and supplying camps and firebases. All helicopters were now controlled regionally by their respective corps. In-commission rates were generally below fifty percent due to troubles stemming from the complexity of transmission mechanisms and from problems in meshing Vietnamese Air Force needs to the logistics systems in the United States.[38]

Battles in Phuoc Long Province during the war's final winter exposed the government's military weakness. A key factor in the campaign was the Song Be airstrip, historically the C-130 airhead for allied operations in the region. Each of three C-130s landing on December 15, 1974, was met by mortar fire and all three were forced to take off without offloading. Two days later, again landing at Song Be at the insistence of the Joint General Staff because of the criticality of the battle situation, the Vietnamese Air Force lost a C-130 to shelling. Another 130 was destroyed on December 24, brought down by ground fire while attempting to land despite forward air controller and helicopter gunship support. Once again the Vietnamese Air Force had protested the staff directive to land, recommending that drops be started. Loss of the second C-130, along with communist capture of the nearby two-thousand-foot volcanic hill, ended hopes for using the Song Be airfield.

South Vietnamese troops were supplied thereafter by airdrops into the Phuoc Binh city stadium. Antiaircraft fire obliged release from ten thousand feet. Helicopters and light aircraft brought in supplies for the local population, often landing in the streets of Phuoc Binh. Only two hundred men were brought in as reinforcements, all by helicopter. It appeared that, with the airborne division already committed in the northern provinces, government reserves were too thin to react in strength. Phuoc Binh fell on the morning of January 7, 1975, the first provincial capital lost since 1972. Lt. Gen. Tran Van Minh, chief of the Vietnamese Air Force, later contrasted the defeat with the successful defense of An Loc three years earlier. Many circumstances were similar, General Minh noted, except for the greater strength of the attackers in 1975 and the absence in 1975 of B–52s and U.S. Air Force C–130s.[39]

The Phuoc Binh defeat destroyed confidence in the Vietnamese Air Force. It was clear that in a crisis the thirty Vietnamese C–130s could not match the 1968 performance by three times that number of U.S. Air Force craft. American military officers continued to do what was possible within the existing budget and legal limitations. The attaché office, for example, pressed the Joint Chiefs of Staff for better means of countering the SA–7, which in January claimed nine Vietnamese aircraft. Gen. David C. Jones, Air Force chief of staff, visited Vietnam in January to look into the sagging C–130 maintenance situation and other problems. Thereafter, the Vietnamese Air Force received higher priority for C–130 spare parts and Air Force units in the Pacific gave spares assistance. Congressman Paul N. McCloskey, Jr., visiting Vietnam with a fact-finding group in February, understood the hopelessness of the government's situation against the "tough, rigidly-disciplined" communists. McCloskey concluded that the regime would fall, even though it appeared that "95 percent of the Vietnamese people prefer not to live under a Communist government."[40]

The fighting in Cambodia shifted slowly but steadily in favor of the communists. A leopard-spot pattern prevailed; the communists dominated rural areas but the government held Phnom Penh and most of the provincial capitals. Preoccupied with preserving the land and water lines of communications against communist pressure, Cambodian government forces lacked initiative, depended heavily on American air power, and were barely capable of survival.

During 1972 most American deliveries of fuel and ammunition were brought into Cambodia by the Mekong River route through South Vietnam. Other materiel came through the port of Kompong Som for further movement overland to Phnom Penh and the interior. The U.S. Air Force C–130s in Vietnam made one or two lifts daily to Pochentong airfield at Phnom Penh, hauling munitions or rotating Cambodian army personnel to and from training in South Vietnam. The Klong 130s began regular deliveries to Phnom Penh from U–Tapao in June 1972 as part of an effort to shift Cambodian lines of communications away from South Vietnam. The Joint Chiefs of Staff discouraged plans requiring heavier use of airlift, concerned that such preparations would weaken Cambodian resolve in holding open surface communications. The airlift thus remained only a small supplement to surface modes of transportation, but the need to sustain Phnom Penh by air alone in an emergency was understood.[41]

The cease-fire of January 29, 1973, unilaterally announced by Phnom Penh, proved illusory. Communist military actions and renewed blockages of surface routes into the captial city soon brought a new crisis. The Secretary of Defense on April 7 authorized funding for C–130 petroleum deliveries, and two days later the Joint Chiefs directed CINCPAC to deliver six thousand gallons of jet fuel daily, an amount equivalent to one C–130 load. The first C–130 bladderbird landed with jet fuel at Pochentong on the tenth, followed by two more the next day. On the same date the Joint Chiefs increased petroleum deliveries to allow a buildup of reserve stocks and on the twelfth approved an initial lift of 826 tons of ammunition. For the next several weeks, three of four Klong C–130s shuttled between U–Tapao and Phnom Penh hauling munitions, rice, fuel, and general cargo. Missions were by daylight only, and just two aircraft were allowed on the ground at Pochentong at the same time.[42]

River convoys again reached Phnom Penh in May 1973. After a short scale-down period the C–130 force again expanded as part of an intensive logistics effort prior to and just after mid-August (666 sorties). Over eighty percent of the tonnage airlifted was munitions. Indeed, during the spring and summer, munitions airlifted to Cambodia were double the quantity delivered by surface.[43]

Although the missions to Phnom Penh were conducted without loss, the flights presented special problems for the aircrews. To provide traffic control among the many American aircraft flying over Cambodia, a C–130 airborne battlefield command and control center orbited around the clock. C–130 crews entering Cambodia checked in by radio with the center for traffic advisories and kept to predetermined flight altitudes, usually about thirteen thousand feet. When nearing Phnom Penh, crews called a U.S. Air Force combat control team on the ground at Pochentong to get clearance to begin descent. Crews spiraled downward from directly overhead attempting to remain within a few miles of the airfield center, thus staying clear of possible areas of fire. Descents were made visually, when necessary flying through breaks in cloud cover. Radio contact with the combat control team, the Pochentong tower, and other aircraft reduced the possibility of collision. Crewmembers stood at the rear exits, prepared to fire flare guns in event of SA–7 firing. When departing, crews spiraled upward until they passed ten thousand feet.

TACTICAL AIRLIFT

The 9,800-foot asphalt Pochentong runway was in good condition. Commercial airlines still used the runway and the bombed-out civilian terminal. The C–130 crews used shortfield landing techniques, turning from the runway at the offloading area midway down the runway while Cambodian soldiers stood guard. Most crews shut down engines during offloading since a second C–130 was usually available to provide a buddy-start if needed. The parking ramp was rough and occasionally caused damage to C–130 tires. The Cambodian aerial port workers were skilled in offloading by forklift while working under American supervisors.[44]

The 130s occasionally landed at other Cambodian fields including Kompong Som, Battambang, and Kompong Cham. One Klong crew landed at the dirt strip at Kompong Chhnang (forty miles north of Phnom Penh), dubbed "Kansas City" by the Americans, to pick up chutes and rigging left from recent airdrops. Active construction projects at Kompong Som, Battambang, and Pochentong, promised improved runway, taxi, and parking facilities.[45]

All C–130 airdrops were performed by Easter Bunny planes. Cambodian drops were first made in 1972 when the TAC crews supplied Cambodian and South Vietnamese troops trying to reopen the road through the Parrot's Beak. A late-1972 series of airdrops supplied Kompong Thom (where enemy shelling had closed the runway) and Takeo, thirty-five miles south of Phnom Penh. Drops resumed a week after the January cease-fire and steadily increased in volume. Over two thousand tons were dropped in July 1973 (139 sorties) of which three-fourths were munitions. Of the nineteen different drop zones, most lay within forty-five miles of the capital city. All missions used AWADS, while rigging for high-velocity descent increasingly predominated over HALO. Recoveries over ninety percent were consistently reported. Loads were released from eleven thousand feet or higher, well above any threat of ground fire. Although crews occasionally saw antiaircraft fire directed against themselves, no Easter Bunny plane was hit. Reports of five SA–7 missile firings during one evening in June 1973 confirmed the wisdom of staying at high altitudes.[46]

The number of drops each day was limited by the capacity of the U.S. Army rigger detachment at the Army depot near U–Tapao.* The arrival of more riggers in May 1973 raised daily sortie capability to six. The dedicated attitude of the Army riggers made a strong impression on aircrewmen visiting the facility. However, six percent of the bundles experienced parachute malfunctions, causing Easter Bunny supervisors to investigate the causes (with little success). Army personnel considered the

---

* Riggers were assigned to the support group of United States Military Assistance Command, Thailand, with assistance from 549th Quartermaster Company on Okinawa.

malfunction rate acceptable and one investigator after visiting a drop zone reported that most items landed in usable condition even after only partial parachute opening.[47]

The Easter Bunny force in 1973 consisted of four AWADS-equipped C-130s and four aircrews, all from the 317th Wing at Pope. At U-Tapao Easter Bunny remained distinct from the Klong. Each has its own supervisors, but both were under control of the U-Tapao airlift control center. Easter Bunny personnel rotated periodically from the United States, the newcomers receiving familiarization briefings and check flights after reaching Thailand. Emphasis lay on acquainting the navigators with the offset aiming points used with the different drop zones. Although most missions took place in the morning hours when weather conditions were best, crews if necessary made drops through solid overcasts, generally with excellent results. Morale stayed high and some airmen volunteered to extend the duration of their oversea tours. The Easter Bunny commander reported to the home unit after a five-day all-out effort in June:

> There is real excitement in watching a coordinated effort like we had: I wish those in the Wing who haven't experienced this mission could have watched the maintenance specialists, fuel trucks, flat beds, and fork lifts converge on our aircraft as the props were coasting down. Everyone was really spring loaded to the "hack the mission" position.[48]

The termination of American air strikes in Cambodia on August 15, 1973, had no immediate effect on the C-130 effort. The Joint Chiefs of Staff authorized continuation of the airlift, "except where serious risk to aircraft and crew is involved."[49] Both Klong and Easter Bunny operations continued at about the same scale of effort as before. Although the threat of communist antiaircraft and missile fire increased slightly, precautionary tactics averted any cases of battle damage. One Klong crew narrowly avoided an SA-7 at seven thousand feet near Phnom Penh in October by firing flares and making steep turns. The bombing halt in one minor respect aided the airlifters since it eased congestion of air traffic in Cambodian skies.[50]

Land routes into Phnom Penh (including the road from Kompong Som) were closed most of the time, leaving only the Mekong River and the airlift as lines of communications. Transportation volume surged during the year's last three months as stocks of weapons, munitions, fuel, and rice were built up. Cargo airlifted to Phnom Penh during this period approximated seven thousand tons monthly, nearly all of it munitions. This supplemented over forty-nine thousand tons of cargo delivered monthly by

TACTICAL AIRLIFT

Mekong convoys. C–130 landings at Phnom Penh averaged fourteen daily. A special airlift took place in October to alleviate rice shortages in the capital city caused by communist road blockages. The C–130s lifted thirty-three hundred tons of Cambodian-grown rice in 228 sorties from Battambang.[51]

During the winter dry season the communists reduced direct pressure on Phnom Penh, apparently in order to more completely isolate the government's provincial enclaves. One result was an increased requirement for C–130 drops to remote locations. In April 1974, cargo parachuted to Kompong Thom, Takeo, Kampot, and more than a dozen other isolated points, exceeded forty-six hundred tons. During one period C–130s hauled rice from Phnom Penh to be rigged for drops at U–Tapao and reloaded to be dropped at its destination. Despite seemingly satisfactory drop results, at least five bases being supplied by airdrop fell to the enemy. The five were Skoun, Romeas, Srang, Tram Khnar, and Vihear Suor.[52]

All loads were rigged for high-velocity descent and were released by AWADS from eleven thousand feet or higher. Poor AWADS incommission rates produced one imaginative expedient. A crew with inoperative AWADS would visually trail an AWADS-equipped leader, judging distance by radar, and judging timing from the instant of leader's release. Another aid, first used in September 1973, was the C–130 stationkeeping equipment which allowed standard C–130s to trail one mile behind an AWADS-equipped leader even in total cloud conditions. Joining the airdrop effort out of U–Tapao, between April and August 1974, were several unconventional warfare C–130s of the 1st Special Operations Squadron from Kadena. These ships had equipment which permitted independent drops from high altitude.[53]

Other measures were sought to improve efficiency and bundle recovery rates. To coordinate the several elements at U–Tapao—the airlift control center, the C–130 detachments, the 6th Aerial Port Squadron (which loaded the 130s), and the Army riggers—an Air Force officer on the scene was empowered to supervise airlift activities. To make sure that

COMMODITY MOVEMENTS INTO CAMBODIA*
JULY 1974
(SHORT TONS)

	Ammo	Rice	POL	Gen Cargo	Total
Airland	3	0	0	162	165
Airdrop	1,122	594	0	0	1,716
Mekong	13,515	18,026	19,855	12,633	64,029
Road	1,080	0	0	1,833	2,913
Total	15,720	18,620	19,855	14,628	68,823

* Hist, USSAG/7th AF, Jul–Sep 74, p 111.

RETURN TO COLD WAR

drops were not scheduled unnecessarily, American logistics personnel visited the several enclaves in Cambodia, inventorying weapons and ammunition. To cut cargo losses, aircrews began using dummy loads (drums of water) for initial spotting releases. RF-4 reconnaissance planes took photos of objective areas to aid C-130 crews in planning AWADS offset-aiming points and in visually identifying drop zones. Attempts to drop rice from high altitude without parachutes failed when the bags ruptured and the rice pulverized and mixed with dirt.[54]

Although the U.S. Air Force C-130 activity in Cambodia was publicly acknowledged, American officials remained concerned over the repercussions likely should a United States' crew be downed in Cambodia. Representatives of several American commands therefore met in Thailand in May 1974 to develop concepts for employing civilian aircrews. By a contract signed on August 28, 1974, the Birdair Division of Bird and Sons, Inc. agreed to provide five C-130 crews capable of making five delivery sorties into Cambodia daily, or as many as ten daily if necessary. The Air Force was to provide the C-130s and full maintenance support. Bird was an American firm with experience in Laos and South Vietnam in the early sixties. Birdair promptly hired retired Air Force C-130 crewmen and Reservists, most of whom needed only AWADS training. The first all-civilian drop mission took place on September 26, and on October 8, 1974, Birdair employees replaced the last Air Force aircrewmen for Cambodian flights. Ships flew without national markings. Aircraft were "government furnished" (not leased), thus making it legal to replace aircraft requiring maintenance. Henceforth, the U.S. Support Activities Group could use U.S. Air Force crews in Cambodia only in case of emergencies and then only with specific CINCPAC approval. This shift to contract aircrews had no apparent effect on the frequency or reliability of airlift service.[55]

Khmer Air Force (Cambodian) transports also flew supply missions. The eight C-123s acquired in 1973 proved especially valuable, landing at places not used by the American C-130s and making accurate drops from low altitude where not prevented by ground fire. The 123s flew daily circuits landing at Battambang, Kompong Chhnang, and Kompong Som, with supplies and personnel for Khmer Air Force T-28 units. Monthly C-123 sorties increased steadily, surpassing eight hundred for the first time in September 1974. In that month, munitions hauls alone totaled eleven hundred tons. Nearly one-fourth of this total was airdropped from low altitude with bundle recoveries approximating ninety-eight percent. The 123s provided the sole avenue of supply for Svay Rieng in late 1974, and were credited by CINCPAC as having been "instrumental in the survival of all other enclaves."[56]

Other Cambodian airlift capabilities were modest. The old C-47 squadron was weakened by transfers of pilots, declining maintenance, and accidents. Flareship, gunship, and airborne control tasks further reduced

TACTICAL AIRLIFT

the C–47 airlift workload which dropped from five hundred sorties a month in mid-1973 to below one hundred a month a year later. A few C–47s, based at the outlying fields, served local commanders in varied support tasks. The C–119s once intended for the Khmer Air Force were never received, in effect having been replaced by the C–123s. The AU–24s (light gunships with a secondary transport capability) were seldom used for airlift. Maintenance troubles plagued the helicopter force, preventing its use away from Pochentong. U.S. Army personnel in early 1974 ruled that most of the forty-three Cambodian airlift and gunship UH–1s were unsafe for flight and most were hauled to U–Tapao in U.S Air Force C–130s for repair by U.S. Army teams.[57]

Convinced that the C–123 was "the best possible all-around transport for the Khmer," blending good payload, box size, paradrop, and shortfield qualities, American officials in Phnom Penh pressed to enlarge the C–123 force. The idea of letting the Khmer Air Force take over the missions out of U–Tapao was especially attractive. Successive decisions in 1974 increased Khmer Air Force authorizations to twelve and later to eighteen C–123s. This expansion was expected to permit termination of the C–130 contract effort by June 30, 1975, and training programs were started at Udorn to supply the needed crews.[58]

The allied situation in Cambodia at the end of 1974 was discouraging. Late-year communist initiatives had been stronger than in previous years, reversing the small government gains of early summer. Cuts in American funding limited munitions expenditures and made it impossible to replace lost equipment. The Mekong was virtually the only surface line of communications into the country and the river had been permanently closed upstream of Phnom Penh. Admiral Gayler, CINCPAC, reported that a fresh enemy dry-season push would "probably pull the plug." However bleak the outlook, the continuing C–130 airlift provided important support and a last thin hope for survival.[59]

XXV. The 1975 Denouement

The events of the spring of 1975 left in wreckage the long American crusade in Indochina. The fall of Phnom Penh in mid-April closed out the slow allied decline in Cambodia which had been evident since at least 1971. More stunning was the grand collapse in South Vietnam climaxed by the dramatic helicopter evacuation from Saigon. The reasons for South Vietnamese defeat are controversial. Had inconsistency in American policy been crucial, or had the South Vietnamese themselves lost the will to resist?

Air transport remained at the center of events. American C–130 and DC–8 transports labored into the final hours in Cambodia, the predominantly civilian aircrews accelerating their efforts in the face of approaching defeat. Meanwhile in Vietnam, the Vietnamese Air Force airlift force proved too meager to exert the impact once exerted by a much larger American force. The Americans flew no troop-lift or drop missions in Vietnam in 1975, although C–130s and jet transports made relief flights, hauled in materiel from offshore, and evacuated large numbers of Americans and loyalist Vietnamese. The CH–53s of the 21st Special Operations Squadron helped to perform the final evacuation from Saigon and played the major airlift role in the American assault at Koh Tang Island, Cambodia, soon afterwards.

As 1975 opened, the Khmer Rouge tightened their stranglehold on routes linking Phnom Penh with the outside. Road traffic into the capital city was totally blocked, while a gauntlet of heavy-weapons fire challenged river convoys using the Mekong. Communist rockets regularly hit the Pochentong airfield, threatening the American contract airlift effort. It appeared that the government lacked the strength to keep the river open to traffic without fatally weakening the forces defending Phnom Penh. A last hope remained—that the city could survive until the summer when rainfall would hamper communist overland movement and help the river convoys by widening the Mekong.[1]

The Birdair C–130 crews began stepped-up deliveries to Pochentong on January 9. By midmonth missions had doubled; typically ten planes hauled munitions, two petroleum, and one general cargo. Although close to the maximum Birdair capability, the effort was well short of the forty sorties that would be required daily should surface routes become totally closed. Staff officers looked at several possibilities for increasing airlift capacity: using U.S. Air Force or Air Reserve Forces crews, providing additional C–130s from the United States, increasing the Birdair force, and using the low-altitude parachute extraction system for drops. Conditions meanwhile continued to worsen. Col. Douglas A. Roysdon, the U.S. air attaché at Phnom Penh, looked down from an orbiting C–47 as communist mines blew apart two tugs, setting adrift their tow barges. The remnants of the convoy of January 29 reached Phnom Penh battered and in small groups, the last vessels to reach the capital. American officials in Phnom Penh consequently requested "massive air resupply."[2]

Col. James I. Baginski was assigned to U–Tapao in early February to serve as supervisor of airlift in overall charge of the ensuing C–130 operation. Colonel Baginski had on-the-spot authority to waive aircraft and aircrew restrictions "without clear compromise of safety." He authorized increases in payload by stripping extra weight and obtained authority to permit three-engine takeoffs at Pochentong. Working close to the limit of fatigue, the five Birdair crews pushed their sortie average to thirteen daily at midmonth. Fearing a serious decline in Khmer morale as stocks declined, U.S. Ambassador John G. Dean on February 10 appealed to the state department for stronger action. Stressing that the next few weeks were to be critical, Ambassador Dean urged immediate resumption of U.S. Air Force deliveries to Cambodia.

Washington responded by authorizing increases in the Birdair force and use of additional C–130s from the 374th Wing. To bridge the period of Birdair buildup, the Air Force on February 12 signed contracts with two other American carriers. The new contracts called for a ten-day effort between U–Tapao and Pochentong, using three all-jet DC–8 civil transports, each with a forty-five-ton payload capacity. DC–8 missions began on February 15 and averaged 450 tons daily through February 26. On the twenty-seventh the DC–8s began operating from Tan Son Nhut under a new contract, hauling to Phnom Penh rice originally intended for water movement. Meanwhile, the Birdair C–130 flights from U–Tapao reached an average of twenty-six missions daily. On the twenty-eighth, combined C–130 and DC–8 flights into Cambodia (including C–130 drops) carried 1,087 tons, a figure that approximated recent daily consumption. Thus, although rice stocks in Phnom Penh declined during February (from twenty-three thousand tons to eighty-two hundred), airlift capacity roughly matched current need.[3]

Air deliveries averaged over twelve hundred tons daily during March. Birdair kept up the flow of munitions and general cargo from U–Tapao and added several C–130 bladderbirds to deliver motor and aviation fuels. Contract DC–8 increased by month's end to seven aircraft, provided by five different carriers: Airlift International, World Airways, Trans International Airways, Flying Tiger Lines, and Seaboard World. All landings were by daylight. Reporting on the precarious situation around Phnom Penh at mid-March U.S. Army Maj. Gen. John R. D. Cleland, Jr., a member of the Joint Staff, wrote that "the supply airlift operation is excellent" and meeting the essential military and civilian needs of Phnom Penh. Rice stocks in the capital held at about an eleven-day supply. Because of the belief that use of the contract transports to haul U.S. military passengers might compromise the "completely civilian character" of the airlift, Air Force-crewed Klong C–130s made five flights weekly into Phnom Penh starting on March 18, carrying embassy and airlift support personnel.[4]

Pochentong airfield remained the key to the airlift. Over twenty-five hundred shells fell on or near Pochentong during the first three months of the year. Artillery fire reached the field at least as early as March 6, although the communists seemed unable to observe and adjust their aim. To Colonel Roysdon, who visited the field daily from his air attaché office, it appeared that most shells landed harmlessly in unused areas. The Americans plotted each detonation and shifted offloadings to areas that appeared safest. Birdair 130s hauled in aluminum matting to strengthen ramps and sweeper equipment to clear away shrapnel debris. The shells damaged eight transports during March, none fatally, and caused interruptions equating to some 150 lost deliveries. Nine Cambodian aerial port workers were killed, several dozen others wounded. The threat of greater trouble was apparent, so Ambassador Dean made a special visit to the Cambodian head of state, stressing the "absolute necessity" of reducing the shelling. On the twenty-second, two aircraft (a C-130 and DC–8) received major damage. Both were removed after emergency repairs the same day, the DC–8 with over sixty shrapnel holes. Officials termed the resumption of landings two days later a "calculated risk."[5]

Air Force personnel on the ground at Pochentong included an officer supervisor, a combat control team, forklift repairmen, and maintenance men brought in as needed. The four-man combat control team talked with incoming crews by radio, advising if the field was under fire and assisting in ground operations. Until late in the siege the team members flew back to Thailand most evenings, thus holding down the number of Americans considered to be in Cambodia. A single American supervised the Cambodian civilian port crews. Colonel Roysdon judged the aerial port work satisfactory. The DC–8s were usually turned around in under twenty minutes despite a cumbersome side-door arrangement. C–130 turnarounds were even faster. Two Air Force mechanics had the hopeless task of keeping the seventeen elderly forklifts operative.[6]

Back at U–Tapao observers of flight-line activity were impressed. All Air Force members on station were ruled eligible for work supporting the airlift. Thus, many individuals of varied background found themselves

TACTICAL AIRLIFT

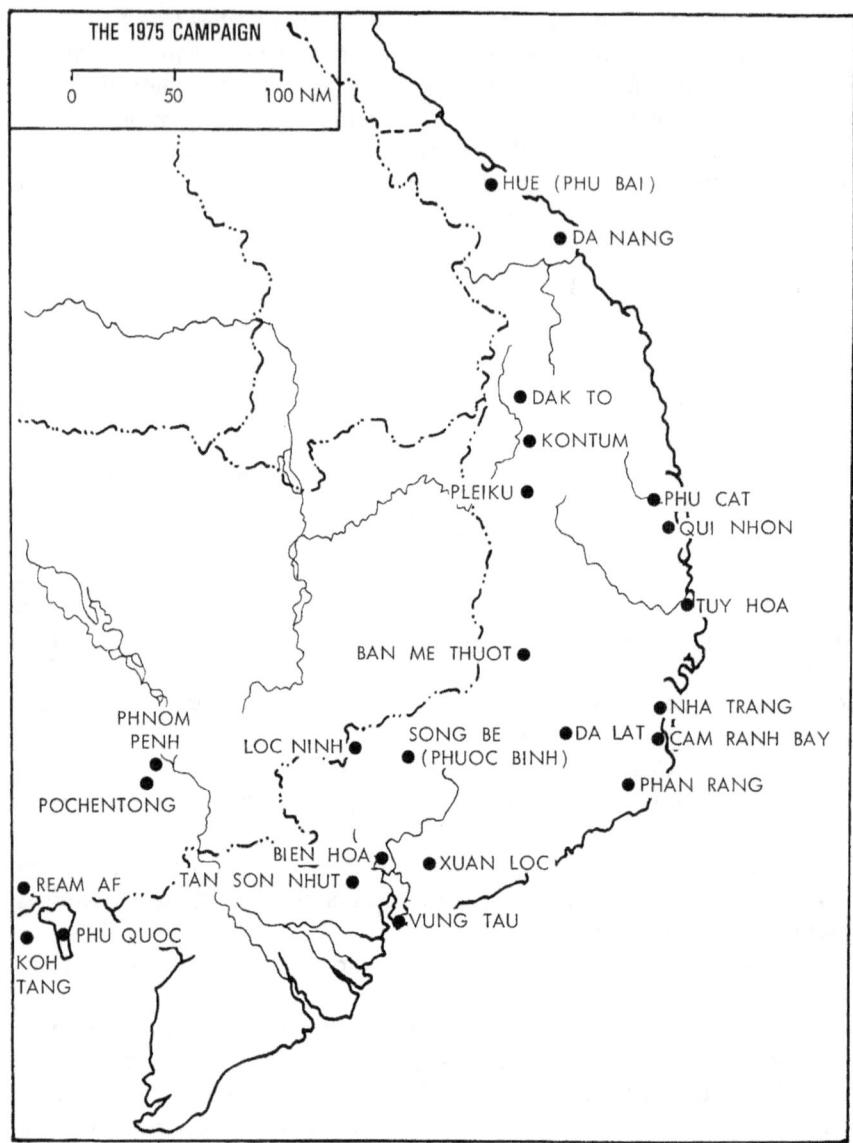

helping out in cargo handling, and some seventy airmen of the Strategic Air Command (men having previous experience with C–130s) joined the 374th Wing maintenance force. Motivation was superb. Maintenance men worked through the nights and aerial port personnel accompanied Birdair drop missions as extra loadmasters. Contract crews likewise won praise for their dedication, although their independence occasionally annoyed Air Force officials. DC–8 pilots frequently elected nonstandard flightpaths to Pochentong, and on one occasion threatened to stop flying unless the offloading site then used at Pochentong was shifted. Colonel Baginski and others at U-Tapao fully supported occasional decisions by Birdair crews to cancel landings because of hazardous circumstances on the ground.[7]

The defense of Phnom Penh slid downhill rapidly in early April, the defenders unable to stop the close-in rocket shellings of the city and airfield. Air Force and Birdair crews on April 3 began preliminary evacuations of Americans, certain Cambodians, and a few citizens of other countries, on return flights from Pochentong. Nearly a thousand persons including fifty-two orphan children were carried out, thus reducing requirements for the final heliborne exit. The 130s also hauled back to Thailand aircraft engines and other equipment deemed unusable in the last battles but worth salvaging. DC-8 and C-130 landings ended with the delivery of fourteen hundred tons at Pochentong on April 11.[8]

U.S. Marine helicopters picked up 276 evacuees in the Eagle Pull evacuation from Phnom Penh on April 12, 1975. Two air rescue HH-53s made the final landings at the city's soccer field, withdrawing members of the Marine ground security force that had landed earlier in the day. Air Force airlifters had no role in the evacuation except that nine CH-53s of the 21st Special Operations Squadron orbited just north of Phnom Penh in case of need.[9] Birdair resumed C-130 drops for five more days, April 13-17. The final fifty-five deliveries included rice from Saigon, dropped at a clearing just south of Pochentong and at several outlying enclaves. Cambodian Air Force C-123s worked into the final week, supplying isolated forces and dropping high-explosive bombs on enemy targets. Of the seventeen Cambodian C-123s, ten escaped to safety in Thailand.[10]

The air supply of Phnom Penh had been spectacular. During the final eight weeks of the siege, with the capital city wholly sustained by air, the American C-130s and DC-8s landed at Pochentong a daily average of eleven hundred tons.* Especially noteworthy was the contribution of the DC-8s, operated and maintained by civilians, which delivered high tonnages under difficult operating conditions. Air Force planes and crews stood ready either to expand the effort it needed or take over in the event of civilian crews refusing to fly. The airlift met the needs of the city and its defenders but was scarcely efficient, since it took fifty C-130s to carry the load of one river barge. During the same weeks, Birdair C-130 crews dropped another eighty-three tons per day to isolated garrisons elsewhere in Cambodia, using now routine high-altitude drop techniques.[11]

Cambodia fell to the communists not because of a failure of air trans-

---

* During February 15 through April 11, DC-8s landed 36,357 tons in 771 sorties. Birdair C-130s landed 15,667 tons in 1,198 sorties. By tonnage, thirty-two percent was munitions, forty-five percent rice, eighteen percent petroleum products, and the remainder general cargo. Birdair crews airdropped an additional 5,366 tons (seventy-one percent munitions, the remainder rice) in 361 sorties from February 19 through April 17.

port, but because of the general weakness of the government's land and air forces. Whether continuation of the old regime beyond 1973 was worth the air and surface supply which made its preservation possible remains unprovable.

Following the communist victory at Phuoc Binh, and convinced that the Americans could not again send forces to Vietnam, Hanoi on January 8, 1975, resolved to undertake major offensive operations in 1975, seeking final victory in 1976. Learning soon afterwards that the South Vietnamese airborne forces in the central highlands were being shifted to Da Nang, the Central Military Party Committee selected as a first objective the city of Ban Me Thuot. Intent on surprise, the communists waited until the final hours before the assault, March 10, to cut Route 14 linking Ban Me Thuot with Pleiku. Communist shelling, sapper, and infantry action meanwhile closed down the two Ban Me Thuot airfields, while other units shelled the airfields at Pleiku to preserve deception and hamper troop movements to Ban Me Thuot. The battlefield thus isolated by air and surface, well-prepared communist armor and infantry quickly rolled up the defenders of Ban Me Thuot, deeming their victory complete by noon, March 11.[12]

Immediate South Vietnamese efforts to recover Ban Me Thuot were ineffective. Reinforcements moved south from Pleiku by helicopters and trucks, but were defeated piecemeal by the North Vietnamese. Vietnamese Air Force helicopters paid for this effort heavily with at least four lost Chinooks. C–130s made high-altitude drops. Meanwhile, the North Vietnamese moved quickly to assure the isolation of Pleiku itself. Having already blocked Routes 19 and 21 as part of the deception effort before attacking Ban Me Thuot, the communists expected that the government's general reserve would move to Pleiku by air.[13]

When in past years communist forces cut the road lines of communications to the highlands, a stream of Air Force C–130s unfailingly operated into the Pleiku, Kontum, or Dak To airstrips, hauling in reinforcements, munitions, and fuel. On March 14 the deputy chief of the Vietnamese Air Force, Maj. Gen. Vo Xuan Lanh, flew to Pleiku to make plans for airlifting in materiel to support major ground operations. The readiness of the small number of maintenance-troubled Vietnamese Air Force C–130s to undertake large-scale operations, however, was doubtful. Whether or not President Thieu considered fighting at Pleiku supplied only by air is unclear. Vietnamese Air Force officers were neither consulted nor present at Cam Ranh Bay on the fourteenth when Thieu decided to withdraw from the highlands. The strength of the North Vietnamese in the interior and the need for the government's reserve forces elsewhere probably left no alternative. What was crucial was not the decision to pull out but rather the unplanned and chaotic nature of the exit.

The Vietnamese Air Force chief, General Tran Van Minh, attempted for several hours to get official authority to start an air evacuation. Though unsuccessful, General Minh nevertheless dispatched his eight flyable C–130s to Pleiku, supposedly to haul in spare parts and materiel. After landing, the 130s became part of the general pullout. In a three-day effort transports of the Vietnamese Air Force, Air America, the civilian airlines brought out a total of perhaps ten thousand persons. One Air America C–46 carried out 136 people, and three hundred persons crammed into one C–130. Families of Vietnamese Air Force personnel were among the first out, causing bitterness among Army people. One Army colonel blocked a taxiing C–130 with his jeep until he and his family were taken aboard. Intermittent shellfire hampered the loadings which became more and more disorderly. Uncontrolled crowds prevented landings after the seventeenth. Large quantities of military materiel remained behind. U.S. Air Force transports played no role. Meanwhile, harassed by the enemy, a twenty-mile convoy of troops and civilians moved overland along damaged Route 7 toward Tuy Hoa. Vietnamese Air Force helicopters made low-level dropoffs of food and water to the column, but roadside landings became impossible when panicked refugees attempted to board the helicopters.[14]

Organized resistance in the northern provinces collapsed soon afterwards, apparently hastened by decisions to move the airborne division to the southern part of the country and to shift the Marines from Hue for the defense of Da Nang. North Vietnamese forces meanwhile drove out of the interior against Hue and Highway 1, and streams of refugees and leaderless troops converged on Da Nang. Disorder took over the city. Thousands left aboard seagoing craft, while jet transports of World Airways and Birdair joined with C–46s and other elderly craft of Air America and Air Vietnam in carrying passengers from the air base. The hysteria matched that at Pleiku. An American reporter on March 27 watched contract aircrewmen fight off aggressive boarders in order to assist the young and the weak. An Air America official the same day reported that mobs had taken over the runway and had stripped one plane after landing. Colonel McCurdy in Saigon attempted to set up U.S. Air Force C–130 pickups, but his effort became academic when on March 29 communist shells and the disorder made landings impossible. A World Airways 727 transport that day made the last fixed-wing takeoff crammed with 330 persons, nearly all soldiers who ignobly forced their way aboard. One man became jammed in the landing-gear mechanism, preventing gear retraction, thus saving the lives of six others inside the wheel well. The Vietnamese Air Force made a final attempt to resume operations, launching twelve C–130s at midday but the crews arrived over Da Nang to find communist tanks at both ends of the runway.[15]

Early April brought a temporary lull. North Vietnamese units raced southward to exploit their advantage, while government forces tried to reorganize to defend their remaining territory. Colonel McCurdy in Saigon spent most of his time planning and coordinating airlift activities: the DC–8 missions to Phnom Penh, Air Force deliveries of war materiel from outside, and the early civilian evacuations from Saigon. Some twenty assorted transports were available for humanitarian flights within South Vietnam. These included seven Australian C–130s, three New Zealand Bristols, the domestic fleet of Air Vietnam, and several Birdair DC–6s. These craft hauled refugees and delivered food, relief, and medical supplies. Many flights reached to Phu Quoc Island to aid tens of thousands of refugees who had arrived by sea amid great suffering. A 374th Wing C–130 crew on March 31 carried from Da Lat a supply of U.S. owned nuclear fuel provided earlier for a South Vietnamese reactor. The lead-lined casks containing the radioactive material were transloaded into a C–141 at Clark.[16]

One by one the coastal towns and airfields fell to the communists: Phu Cat, Qui Nhon, Tuy Hoa, Nha Trang, Cam Ranh, and (on April 17) Phan Rang. Several dozen airplanes and considerable other Vietnamese Air Force materiel remained behind, partly because of shortages of air transport and partly because of the "family syndrome," a tendency among members of the Vietnamese Air Force to put concern for safety of family members above duty. Vietnamese Air Force UH–1s and CH–47s earned credit for lifting a parachute brigade into Phan Rang from isolated defensive positions above Nha Trang. Resistance was vigorous at Phan Rang, where nearly all supplies (including aviation gasoline and jet fuel) were brought in by C–130 and C–119, but a decision to begin withdrawing the paratroops contributed to the final unraveling.[17]

The communist campaign brought an increased threat of enemy anti-aircraft and missile fire. The SA–7s, with altitude capability to ten thousand feet, were especially numerous in the southern half of the republic. An improved version, reaching to fifteen thousand feet, was also in service. Another new problem was the larger, truck-borne SA–2. SA–2 launch crews followed the victorious forces into the newly captured areas and converged upon Saigon toward the finish. The airlift crews took precautions, remaining if possible at higher altitudes when over unsafe territory. Otherwise, communist gun and missile crews had little effect on the volume of airlift effort and brought down no C–130s during the campaign.[18]

With little more than the region immediate adjacent to Saigon still in government hands, the Vietnamese Air Force C–130s found their final

1975 DENOUEMENT

important roles as bombers, dropping drums of fuel and several varieties of explosive ordnance on enemy targets. During the final two weeks of April, the 130s dropped fifteen 15,000-pound BLU–82 bombs, all airlifted into Saigon in the final weeks by the U.S. Air Force. Targets were antiaircraft rocket, troop, and storage sites. Col. Philip L. Brewster, chief of the Air Force division in the Saigon defense attaché office, felt that the first BLU–82 drop at Xuan Loc produced a significant boost in Vietnamese Air Force morale. Assessments of damage were unreliable, but one detonation east of Saigon apparently killed over five hundred communist troops, and another reportedly eliminated an SA–2 missile launch site. Most releases were from twenty thousand feet or higher using ground radar guidance. General Minh called the Hercules force "my BC–130s."[19]

In summary, the Vietnamese Air Force transport fleet during the final weeks operated to the limit of its capability. General Minh afterwards spoke warmly of the tireless efforts of the C–130 air and ground crewmen, singling out the airdrops at Song Be, Ban Me Thuot, and southwest of Da Nang, along with several air movements of general reserve units. The Vietnamese Air Force chief also praised the centralized system that controlled the transport force, contrasting this arrangement with the fragmented use of the helicopters and strike aircraft. Colonel Brewster concluded that "the C–130 proved the Vietnamese Air Force's most effective and versatile weapons system."[20]

The main factor limiting the impact of air transport on events was the small size of the Vietnamese Air Force C–130 force. Having lost two aircraft at Song Be, and with a half-dozen others in major maintenance at Singapore, the Vietnamese began the campaign with twenty-four C–130s. Incommission rates remained low despite recent increases in spare parts supplies, partly because of the persisting fuel leak problem. There were never more than fourteen C–130s in commission. Roughly, eight were flown each day "to the limit of flying safety." Three or four C–119s supplemented the 130s on most days, and a few C–7s were returned to service from storage.[21]

Assessing the campaign soon afterwards, General Momyer voiced the opinion that the airlift force in Vietnam had been simply incapable of shouldering roles of the magnitude handled in 1968 and 1972. The former Seventh Air Force and TAC commander judged that the South Vietnamese had lost an important kind of mobility in stressing helicopters over fixed wing transports. The helicopters could neither operate in high-threat areas nor contribute to the requirement for shifts across regions. Momyer concluded:

> From a strategic viewpoint, it is better to have fewer ground forces and have a fully developed tactical airlift force than it is to have an inadequate tactical airlift force that is unable to move ground units as the combat threat unfolds.[22]

Vietnamese refugees aboard a C-141 en route to Clark Air Base from Saigon, April 17, 1975.

Although not disagreeing in principle, General Minh questioned whether additional C-130s could have changed the outcome much since few combat-effective forces were in any case available to be moved. Col. Le Minh Hoang, the youthful-appearing Vietnamese Air Force intelligence chief, agreed that the helicopters were almost helpless in hostile areas, and that many outposts became inaccessible because defenders were unable to secure landing zones. Colonel Hoang concluded that the "mobility balance" had shifted sides—allied forces had lost their heliborne mobility while North Vietnamese moved openly in trucks.[23]

Evacuations from Tan Son Nhut began during the first week of April, "thinning-out" the number of Americans and Vietnamese civilians eligible for any final exit. A few hundred persons departed each day aboard C-141s or C-130s. But the flow was stanched by redtape and the unwillingness of many Americans to leave behind Vietnamese dependents and friends, so many transports departed empty from Tan Son Nhut after unloading cargo. The Air Force also flew Operation Babylift, the airlift of some two thousand mixed-blood orphans, most of them destined for homes

A USAF airman carries refugee children from the C–141 at Clark.

in the United States. Unfortunately, the Babylift missions were marred by the crash of a C–5A after takeoff on April 4, killing 155 persons, most of them children.

Most of the five thousand Vietnamese refugees through April 19 departed openly aboard military or contract jet transports, but a few individuals formerly associated with intelligence activities came out semicovertly through the Air America terminal. A Seventh Air Force airlift contingent under Maj. Robert S. Delligatti coordinated flight-line and loading activities, and four Air Force officers helped man an evacuation control center that coordinated around the clock with Military Airlift Command and other outside commands. Finally, attaché, aerial port, and security police personnel formed an evacuation processing center which handled the paperwork and moved the evacuees to the flight line. Colonel McCurdy gave overall direction.[24]

Successive rulings in mid-April eliminated most of the legal and paperwork restrictions holding back the refugee flow. The C–130s of the 374th Wing, which had been used only occasionally in the evacuation, now joined the C–141s in a full-scale effort. On two days, April 21 and 22, sixty-four hundred persons left Tan Son Nhut for Clark Field aboard thirty-three C–141s and forty-one C–130s. Operations were around-the-clock, the 141s landing by day and the 130s generally by night. Typically each 130 spent about a half hour on the ground at Tan Son Nhut, keeping engines running. Passengers arrived by bus and boarded by the rear ramp.

The normal canvas seats were used. During the next three days, April 23–25, the 130s continued to fly twenty times daily to Clark, but the 141s flew fewer sorties than before, now operating direct from Saigon to Guam. Other C–141s and the contract carriers meanwhile moved those refugees already at Clark eastward to Guam and Wake. Meanwhile there was one final paradox, a 345th Squadron aircrew on April 25 flew a last mission to Hanoi, carrying delegates of the several powers from Saigon.[25]

The 374th Wing mobilized itself for the surge of evacuation, shifting all but the AWADS planes out of U–Tapao. A special flight-line coordination center expedited aircraft refueling and turnaround maintenance at Clark. Anticipating a further expansion of the evacuations, Pacific Command on April 25 requested additional C–130s and crews from the United States. Consequently, eighty hours later, the last of sixteen aircraft from Little Rock Air Force Base landed at Clark. Meanwhile, the evacuation processing center at Tan Son Nhut was barely able to preserve order among the expanding flow of humanity. Aircraft flow was less of a problem, although Col. Benjamin F. Ingram, Jr., chief of current operations of the Seventh Air Force's United States Support Activities Group, found command arrangements difficult. When changes to schedules or additional flights became necessary, for example, Ingram had to work with both PACAF (for the C–130s) and MAC (for the C–141s), a condition that slowed reaction times.[26]

Moreover hostile fire compelled respect. Nearly all aircrews reported tracer fire and airbursts with some bursts reaching to eighteen thousand feet. One C–130 crew, caught on the ground at Tan Son Nhut for four hours, watched as tracers reached toward other aircraft making landings, particularly those coming in with lights on. Some of the firing came from areas supposed to be friendly, and one crew reported fire from within Tan Son Nhut itself. Armed South Vietnamese troops in the loading area also were beginning to show hostility toward the Americans. To reduce the ground-fire threat crews made spiraling overhead descents from twenty thousand feet. 374th Wing aircrews meanwhile began to feel the effects of stress and overwork, the results of functioning with rest periods of only twelve hours between missions.[27]

The air of impending defeat increased. Birdair C–130 crews on the twenty-sixth began lifting "unserviceable" materiel from Bien Hoa and Tan Son Nhut to U–Tapao. President Thieu on the same date flew to Taiwan aboard an Air Force Scatback C–118. Two 374th Wing planes landed at Vung Tau on the twenty-seventh, bringing out 250 dependents of South Vietnamese marines after the marines gave assurances that the field would be defended. During the two days, April 26 and 27, twelve thousand persons left Tan Son Nhut for the Philippines aboard forty-six C–130 and twenty-eight C–141 flights. The intensifying enemy fire forced a painful decision to stop C–141 landings at Saigon at nightfall on the twenty-seventh.[28]

Events became desperate on April 28. The C–130s resumed daylight landings, although communist shells made the effort extremely risky. A Birdair C–130 crew reported that downtown Bien Hoa was in flames. One Air Force Hercules crew, having just landed at Tan Son Nhut, watched an attack by several North Vietnamese-piloted A–37s. Bombs destroyed several Vietnamese Air Force aircraft, including a CH–47 engaged in loading passengers. After the attack, one of the A–37s chased an Air Force C–130 to the coastline, threatening, but not firing on the helpless transport. Only eighteen of the planned fifty-eight C–130s landed on the twenty-eighth, carrying out thirty-five hundred passengers. Meanwhile, the North Vietnamese succeeded in positioning their 130-mm artillery within range of Tan Son Nhut, an action long planned by the communists in their timetable for the final week. The big guns opened up on the air base after midnight, April 29, catching three Air Force C–130s on the ground. Each had landed with a BLU–82 weapon, and each intended to pick up refugees. The detonations quickly destroyed one of the planes along with at least one Vietnamese Air Force C–130. The American aircrew scrambled to shelter and left shortly afterwards aboard one of the other planes.[29]

Despite the night's disastrous events, preparations continued to resume "maximum practicable C–130 evacuation lift" in the morning. Elements of drama marked the determination of Ambassador Graham A. Martin to attempt C–130 operations in hope of getting out as many refugees as possible before starting a final helicopter operation. Sixty C–130 sorties were scheduled for the twenty-ninth, to be covered by carrier fighter and electronic warfare aircraft. The C–130 stream began arriving at dawn. Ambassador Martin, after talking by satellite telephone with Lt. Gen. Brent Scowcroft at the White House, declared that the landings should commence if at all feasible. The field remained under intermittent shellfire and the runways were littered with debris. Police were controlling the crowds with difficulty and people were shooting at Vietnamese transports preparing to take off. Combat controllers spotted enemy 57-mm and at least one SA–7 firing, while the orbiting C–130s received airburst fire above twenty thousand feet. U.S. Army Maj. Gen. Homer D. Smith, Jr., chief of the defense attaché office and the senior American military officer on the scene, therefore informed Ambassador Martin that a C–130 evacuation was "just not in the cards." With regret Martin accepted the necessity of starting the helicopter evacuation, and the Air Force C–130s left Vietnamese skies for the last time.[30]

Directed to execute Option IV, Operation Frequent Wind, a first wave of thirty-six U.S. Marine and Air Force H–53 helicopters took off from vessels offshore in the early afternoon of April 29. Included were seven CH–53s of the 21st Special Operations Squadron and two air rescue

TACTICAL AIRLIFT

HH–53s which had flown to the carrier *Midway* the previous week. The H–53s shuttled between the main pickup points at Tan Son Nhut and at the downtown embassy and the ships offshore, and were joined by Marine H–46s and Air America UH–1s. Except for much confusion in timing the arrival of the Marine security force, the divided command arrangements caused no problems. Naval authorities retained control of aircraft over water while the Seventh Air Force's support activities group took control over land. Aircrews of the 21st reported that the flights were made difficult by random enemy fire, the onset of darkness, poor radio communications, and traffic congestion at the *Midway*. Although enemy fire was considerable (including SA–7s), none of the aircraft of the 21st was damaged. Any hope of resuming C–130 operations (a possibility raised briefly by the Joint Chiefs of Staff) proved impossible given the chaos on the Tan Son Nhut runways. Determined to get out as many Vietnamese as possible, Ambassador Martin allowed himself to leave only after direct White House order. Completing four round trips, the Air Force choppers lifted out 1,479 evacuees and 249 members of the Marine security force, roughly one-sixth of the overall total of 1,373 American evacuees, 6,442 non-Americans, and 989 of the Marine security force.[31]

Planning to evacuate Vietnamese Air Force aircraft had been minimal to avoid encouraging premature flight. Batteries were removed from aircraft between missions for the same reason. American officials resolved to take immediate custody of Vietnamese Air Force craft leaving the country and informed Vietnamese officials that in case of evacuation crews should fly to U–Tapao. On April 24 a Vietnamese Air Force C–130 made an unauthorized flight to Singapore where five others were undergoing overhaul. A C–47 escaped to Thailand on the evening of the twenty-eighth, and another landed at Clark. In the final disintegration of the twenty-ninth, more than two dozen transports came out, most of them crammed with refugees. Lockheed spokesmen stated that one C–130 carried 452 persons, including 32 in the crew-compartment space. Those C–130s left behind were unflyable because of damage, lack of parts, or lack of fuel. Some thirty UH-1 helicopters ditched alongside or landed on U.S. Navy vessels, others made it to a hastily prepared field just inside Thailand. The residual government of South Vietnam announced its unconditional surrender on April 30 and ordered South Vietnamese forces to stop firing. At U–Tapao the following day were 123 Vietnamese Air Force aircraft of all types, including 8 C–130s, 6 C–7As, and several C–47 and C–119 transports.[32]

A few loose ends remained from the evacuations. The Americans moved quickly to recover the former Vietnamese Air Force C–130s, flying the A–models out of Thailand and starting negotiations with the government of Singapore for the planes there. The CH–53s turned to the difficult task of lifting the former Vietnamese Air Force A–37s and F–5s from U–Tapao to the *Midway*. Meanwhile, the C–130s of the 374th Wing joined the jet transports in carrying the refugees still in the Philippines eastward, among them tens of thousands who had reached Subic Bay aboard navy vessels of the United States and South Vietnam.[33]

The strong American reaction to the Cambodian seizure of the U.S. vessel *Mayaguez* on May 12, 1975, proved satisfying to many Americans. For the 21st Special Operations Squadron, however, the episode was a bitter postscript to the war. Directed to form a helicopter assault force at U–Tapao, the squadron on May 13 launched all incommission CH–53s from Nakhon Phanom. Unfortunately bad luck quickly intervened. One chopper crashed en route to U–Tapao because of mechanical failure, killing the five-man crew and the eighteen Air Force security policemen aboard. The security police were being sent for possible duty as the infantry assault force. Joining the CH–53s at U–Tapao were air rescue HH–53s and a battalion of U.S. Marine troops which arrived from Okinawa aboard C–141s. Intelligence agencies in Washington and Hawaii estimated that over one hundred troops defended Koh Tang Island, including some equipped with heavy weapons. Marine officers planning the assault at U–Tapao later stated that information reaching them indicated that there were only twenty Cambodian irregulars on the island.[34]

The H–53s took off from U–Tapao before daybreak on May 15. Three HH–53s carried marines to the destroyer escort *Holt*, afloat close by the *Mayaguez*. The landings on the *Holt* proved uneventful and the Marine party quickly boarded the unoccupied *Mayaguez*. The main force consisted of five CH–53s and three HH–53s carrying 175 marines, briefed to assault two landing zones on Koh Tang, located thirty miles off the Cambodian mainland and a suspected location of the *Mayaguez* crewmen. Each of the five CHs of the 21st Squadron was assigned the unit's traditional call sign, Knife.

Knife 21 touched down on the beach at Koh Tang at about six in the morning. While the Marine assault troops debarked, the craft began to receive hits from nearby small-arms, rocket, and mortar fire. The pilot managed a single-engine takeoff, but the helicopter slipped into the ocean a short distance offshore. Knife 22, immediately behind, took numerous hits approaching the landing zone and turned back, later barely reaching the Thai coast, its troops still aboard. Knife 23 was hit while in the landing zone and attempted to leave with its marines, but the craft lost an engine and settled onto the beach. Knife 31 burst into flames while still inbound and thirteen men died inside the wreckage or at water's edge. Knife 32 managed to offload and leave safely, but upon reaching U–Tapao proved too badly damaged to take off again. The three HH–53s meanwhile made repeated attempts to approach the Koh Tang landing zones, and all three later in the morning managed to discharge their marines.

Word came at midmorning that the captain and thirty-nine crewmen of the *Mayaguez* had been rescued elsewhere. The objective at Koh Tang accordingly became withdrawal, but the desperate situation facing the some one hundred marines ashore meant that reinforcements had to precede any evacuation. Although all five CH–53s from the first wave were out of action, two fresh CHs joined three HHs in approaching Koh Tang with reinforcements at midday. Knife 52 took hits and was unable to deliver its troops but managed to get back to the Thai mainland although without hydraulic pressure. Braving automatic-weapons fire, Knife 51 landed nineteen marines and took off successfully with five wounded aboard. Knife 51, the last flyable CH–53, joined the HHs in several afternoon withdrawal flights and picked up the last twenty-nine marines from Koh Tang in darkness.[35]

Less dramatic was the role of the fixed-wing airlifters. Seven C–130s, including two AWADS craft, took position at U–Tapao on May 14, ready for BLU–82 bomb releases at Koh Tang. Five Hercules took off during the afternoon of the fifteenth, orbiting in the battle area in case they were needed. Four carried BLU–82s, one carried supplies rigged for airdrop. Crews were prepared to release from eight thousand feet, aiming by AWADS or by trailing an AWADS-equipped leader. One BLU–82 was released in late afternoon, landing about 109 yards from the intended position. The detonation apparently served to discourage movements of hostile troops. Capt. Ronald L. Edmiston was the AWADS operator for this first-ever AWADS release of a BLU–82. The other four C–130s returned to U–Tapao without dropping their bombs.[36]

The valor of the helicopter crewmen was generally praised after the operation. Two members of the 21st Squadron received Air Force Crosses: SSgt John D. Harston, flight mechanic, who led survivors from the wreckage of Knife 31 under direct fire, and 1st Lt. Richard C. Brims, pilot of Knife 51. A total of eighteen Americans died in the Koh Tang assault.

By acting strongly where the safety of its citizens was concerned, the United States regained some of its weakened credibility and pride. Otherwise, the decision to assault Koh Tang appeared in retrospect to have been a mistake although an understandable one given the information available at the time. The absence of preassault air strike and naval gunfire preparation, although unfortunate, had been unavoidable since the location of the *Mayaguez* crew was unknown. There seemed little justification, however, for the failure to provide the commanders at U–Tapao with accurate intelligence as to the defenses on Koh Tang, nor for an absence of slow-flying forward air control aircraft at the outset. Also controversial were the American air strikes against Ream airfield and other targets, executed after release of the crewmen to prevent Cambodian aircraft or reinforcements from reaching Koh Tang. The operation confirmed the hazards of helicopter assaults into hot landing zones without proper fire preparation and support.[37]

The defeats in Vietnam, Cambodia, and Laos left the future of other Southeast Asian countries cloudy: Malaysia, Indonesia, Singapore, Burma, and Thailand. These five governments remained anti-communist, although each joined in pledging the region's neutrality in mid-May and each recognized the new regime in Cambodia. Southeast Asian leaders appeared to want continued American military assistance and to prefer that American air and naval power remain in the Pacific, but at arm's length. Thailand remained the most exposed nation, and moved toward coexistence with its new and dangerous communist neighbors. The insurgency within Thailand continued to grow, now counting perhaps eight thousand armed communist fighting men. American radar operators at Nakhon Phanom, prior to closure of the base in late summer 1975, detected frequent helicopter and fixed-wing flights apparently supporting the Thai insurgents. Thai government forces now had over a hundred aircraft from the former Vietnamese, Cambodian, and Laotian air forces, including an airlift force of twelve 123Ks and several dozen other transports and helicopters.[38]

North Vietnam remained by far the region's strongest power. The North Vietnamese air transport arm had performed an important role in the 1975 campaign. Military and civilian transports hauled troops, supplies, and maps into the captured airfields of South Vietnam (including Phu Bai, Da Nang, and Kontum) and assisted in the final race to Saigon. A few days after the final victory, Vo Nguyen Giap and other Hanoi officials arrived by air at Tan Son Nhut to an emotional welcome by the communist officers already present. Helicopters and several kinds of multiengine transports flew over Saigon during the victory parade on May 15. The North Vietnamese put into their inventory fourteen former Vietnamese Air Force C–130s. Several former Vietnamese Air Force pilots were ordered to give flight instruction, and former Vietnamese mechanics and technicians were put to work on the captured Hercules. The C–130s were soon in regular service linking Saigon, Vientiane, and Hanoi, although only with outside assistance could the communists hope to overcome the maintenance troubles chronically afflicting the elderly A–models.[39]

The final episode of the war in Vietnam provided some satisfaction for U.S. Air Force airlifters. The performances of the C–130 and H–53 crews had been superb, while the campaigns again demonstrated the versatility of air transport. The collapse of American goals for Southeast Asia, however, was intensely personal for many airlifters, robbing of meaning the years of sacrifice. That the airlift arm emerged healthy and vigorous compensated only in part for the unsatisfactory ending of the drama.

XXVI. Reflections

The long history of air transport in Southeast Asia inevitably made a strong impact on the Air Force of the mid-1970s. Various technical lessons resulted in early improvements to existing airlift capabilities. More important was the war's effect on Air Force doctrine, an effect that promised to influence the nature of future tactical forces, roles, and organization. Finally, the end of the conflict made possible a backward look at the whole experience of tactical airlift in Southeast Asia—the manner of its employment, its overall contribution, and its costs in men and machines.

The Air Force midway in the war began Project Corona Harvest, a systematic effort to gather and evaluate evidence from Southeast Asia, looking to the development of future Air Force doctrine. Of primary interest to airlifters was a four-volume study treating the airlift system for the years 1965–68, researched by a team of officers from the Tactical Airlift Center. This material was refined into a single-volume report by a committee chaired by Col. Louis P. Lindsay, an officer with vast tactical airlift experience. After review by Air Force officers through four-star rank, a final report was issued in January 1973. These documents, validated by the reviewers' knowledge of events after 1968, fairly expressed the impact of the Southeast Asia War upon U.S. Air Force tactical airlift doctrine.[1]

The Corona Harvest reviewers addressed the touchy question of whether or not the theater airlift system required management and control separate from the strike aircraft force. Separation had in effect been the case in Southeast Asia where the Saigon airlift control center and its apparatus of airlift control elements and dedicated communications functioned largely independent of the tactical air control center. Although this contradicted the official view that theater airlift and strike forces required centralized control, the final Corona Harvest report concluded:

> The unique organizational management required and effected in Southeast Asia, in which control channels flow separately from the TACC and ALCC to the air component commander, should be fully recognized and provided for in revised doctrine as an authorized option.[2]

The Multi-Command Manual 3-4, published by TAC and the overseas commands, May 30, 1974, similarly affirmed that a separate airlift control center might be formed "when the allocated airlift force becomes too large for efficient direction from within the TACC."[3]

Even more controversial was the long-standing division of the nation's tactical and strategic airlift forces among separate commands. The Lindsay committee, after citing the duplications in control, aerial port, and support elements in Southeast Asia, in June 1970 voiced the unanimous recommendation "that steps be taken to achieve a single airlift command as soon as possible." Maj. Gen. Burl W. McLaughlin, former commander of the 834th and a member of the group immediately reviewing the Lindsay findings, termed the recommendation "just great." Others, including the commander of TAC, disagreed, feeling strongly that removal of the tactical transports from TAC and the overseas commands would diminish the "tactical" orientation of the force.[4]

The decision to endorse the Lindsay and McLaughlin view and include it in the final January 1973 report was a milestone. The report called for a "single organization for airlift" and led to a sweeping reassessment in Air Force headquarters during 1973. In the summer of 1974, Secretary of Defense James R. Schlesinger directed that "the worldwide airlift mission, roles, resources, and responsibilities" be consolidated under the Military Airlift Command. Behind this decision was the expectation that duplication would be ended and flexibility improved in meeting all needs. C–130 units in the United States transferred to the Military Airlift Command in late 1974, overseas units in early 1975. The wings and squadrons preserved their "tactical airlift" names, and an Air Force Airlift Center was opened at Pope Air Force Base to centralize development of tactics and equipment.[5]

The war strengthened the case for developing vertical flight transports. A 1969 memo by the Assistant Secretary of the Air Force for Research and Development, Alexander H. Flax, for example, made explicit the war's influence on thinking:

> Yet we do know from our experience in Southeast Asia, specifically in such situations as developed around Khe Sanh, a vertical or extremely short STOL logistics supply capability can be extremely important. In such situations, a V/STOL can provide far greater operational flexibility than available through the use of helicopters or STOL aircraft.[6]

The Corona Harvest reports asserted the need to develop two types of advanced tactical transports, one to replace the C–130 for large requirements, another to replace the C–123 and C–7 for feeder roles. During 1969 and 1970, Air Force policymakers pushed hard for the tilt-wing light intratheater transport (LIT), with five-ton payload capability in vertical flight. Because of the need for funds for the newer fighters and the B–1 bomber, Secretary of the Air Force Robert C. Seamans, Jr., and the Chief of Staff in March 1970 made what became a permanent decision to defer funding for the LIT. Meanwhile, the C–130 replacement—the advanced medium STOL transport (AMST)—was conceived as a low cost, medium payload, shortfield craft, powered by off-the-shelf jet engines. Vertical flight was not prescribed. Two firms received contracts in late 1972 to construct and test prototypes, and four years later both the Boeing YC–14 and McDonnell–Douglas YC–15 were flying at Edwards Air Force Base, Calif.[7]

Tight budgets forced difficult decisions in determining the size of the active duty force. Various staff and special study groups combed data from Southeast Asia seeking evidence useful in estimating future theater airlift requirements. Annually the Air Staff went through long staff procedures, justifying a substantial active tactical transport force and urging purchases to offset aircraft lost to attrition. Officials of the Office of the Secretary of Defense overruled or scaled down most such recommendations. The Air Force, for example, sought to meet its promise to provide "dedicated airlift support of the Army" by purchasing additional C–7s or related types.* Disapproval in 1971 of the Air Force request for four squadrons of "interim STOL" transports ended the idea of preserving this role in the active force. Meanwhile the helicopter and fixed-wing transport elements of the Special Operations Force (successor to the air commando force) were reduced and finally eliminated from active service. Any thrust to employ Air Force helicopters in battlefield assault and supply was wholly dormant, reflecting the standing roles agreement, fiscal stringency, and the Air Force's conviction (reinforced in the campaigns in Vietnam after 1970) that helicopters were highly vulnerable in battle areas. Only the sixteen-squadron C–130 force survived the regular reviews. Annual authorizations permitted procurement of small numbers of C–130Es and C–130Hs, preserving squadron strength and keeping open the Lockheed production line. The H–models, acquired after 1973, had a new type of turboprop engine for improved range, takeoff, and payload. Meanwhile the Air Reserve Forces expanded their tactical airlift strength. The Air National Guard and the Air Force Reserve at the start of 1976 had 254 C–130, 64 C–123, and 47 C–7 transports, all assigned to MAC in event of mobilization.[8]

Formal statements of doctrine, indicating how the C–130 and AMST fleet was to be used in the future, strongly reflected the Southeast Asia experience. These statements no longer emphasized parachute assault or the former mission of providing transoceanic transportation for ground and air strike forces. One 1969 paper envisioned for the future a continuation of all the basic roles performed in Vietnam: forward, lateral, and rearward

---

* Evaluated as possible alternatives to the Caribou were the deHavilland C–8 turboprop, a turboprop version of the C–123K, and a C–130 modified for better shortfield capability.

TACTICAL AIRLIFT

movements of ground combat units, high-volume air resupply of mobile ground forces, routine redistribution from strategic airheads or seaports, resupply to remote sites, logistics support of tactical air units, and aeromedical evacuation. The Multi-Command Manual 3–4 in 1974 defined the mission of tactical airlift similarly, quoting TAC planning documents:

> the immediate and responsive air movement and delivery of combat troops and supplies directly into objective areas through air landing, extraction, airdrop, or other delivery techniques; and the air logistic support of all theater forces . . . .[9]

Various technical developments from the Southeast Asia years gave promise of major influence on future battlezone methods. Considerable attention had focused on the extraction delivery methods. These had proven useful occasionally in Vietnam, but improvements lagged because of U.S. Army reluctance to provide funding. Army leaders held, with justification, that only in special and narrow circumstances were extractions superior to the established helicopter, shortfield transport, and airdrop delivery modes. Although tests of an improved low-altitude parachute extraction system continued in the early 1970s, it appeared that the future of the extraction systems would be limited. Clearly destined for wide future use, however, were the blind airdrop methods—ground radar and adverse-weather aerial delivery systems—both evolutions from the battles of 1968 and both proven in the later campaigns. GRADS and AWADS not only overcame the Air Force's long-standing weakness in all-weather dropping, but also permitted accurate drops from high altitude, helping to counter the portable surface-to-air missile. New projects in the mid-1970s sought improvements in the associated high-velocity parachute rigging method.[10]

In summary, the Corona Harvest reports verified that the Air Force fully appreciated the vast role of airlift within Southeast Asia. The formal expressions of doctrine, the continuing work in the high-altitude drop methods and low-altitude parachute extraction, and the orientation of the Air Reserve Forces, all confirmed that the Air Force remained committed to the tactical airlift concept. The commitment was less than absolute, however, since several trends in policy indicated a shift away from the extreme forward-delivery role. Among these were the decision against the vertical-flight LIT, the failure to replace the C–123s, C–7s, and transport helicopters in the active force, and the consolidation into MAC. The emergence of cheap, portable surface-to-air missilery, encountered in Southeast Asia in 1972 and thereafter, strengthened the contention (held by General Momyer and others) that C–130 or AMST landings forward of the division base could well prove too dangerous. Facing extreme fiscal stringency, the Air Force of the mid-1970s focused its priorities and powers of persuasion on behalf of the newer fighters and bombers, moving to assure the service's capabilities to perform its most basic missions.

REFLECTIONS

The American way of war in Vietnam reflected this nation's technical and aeronautic traditions. Through much of the conflict American troops fought offensively, seeking out communist forces and subjecting them to the killing power of tactical aircraft and artillery. Helicopters and tactical transports gave the infantryman mobility, staying power, and immunity from pressure on lines of communications. The expanding search-and-destroy operations battered communist main force units, by 1967 depriving them of widespread areas once safe. If the offensive approach, in failing to break communist resolve, appears in retrospect mistaken, to have kept American troops in defensive enclaves would have yielded the enemy a preposterous immunity akin to that which prevailed in the months prior to the 1975 collapse.

Within the offensive strategy, air transport played a central role. In versatility and capacity the C–130 and C–123 were far beyond the transports of earlier wars. The transport force in Vietnam was thus capable of sustaining large search-and-destroy operations by hauling units, their equipment, and large tonnages of supplies into forward airheads. With variations, the fixed-wing airstrip served as brigade headquarters, supply transshipment point, artillery firebase, and helicopter refueling and rearming point. Forward air control craft operated from the airhead, directing the firepower of tactical fighters based to the rear. From the perimeter of the airhead, airmobile and infantry operations projected outward over a thirty-mile radius.

Indeed, this widespread application of Air Force transports of aerial lines of communications for forward mobile ground operations represented the foremost development of the war for airlift use. Similar concepts had been glimpsed in Burma during World War II and in Indochina during the early 1950s. The French had used the "air-ground base" idea, albeit with transports of far less capacity, but finally overreached themselves at Dien Bien Phu. The Air Force C–47s and C–123s in Vietnam during the early 1960s occasionally worked in such ventures, although other usages took precedence. Meanwhile, in joint exercises in the United States, the Air Force and Army developed competing concepts of battlefield air mobility, setting the stage for doctrinal resolution in Vietnam. Upon the later introduction in Vietnam of major U.S. Army airmobile, airborne, and conventional infantry brigades in 1965, full-scale use of the C–130s as aerial lines of communications blossomed. The battle in the Ia Drang Valley in late 1965, Operations Birmingham and Junction City in III Corps, and the air invasion of the A Shau Valley in 1968, were but the high points in the

653

evolving partnership of Air Force transports and Army helicopters in combat-zone mobility and supply. Major offensive ventures became infrequent after 1968, but the incursions into Cambodia in 1970 and into Laos in 1971 were of greater dimension than any previous similar efforts. In both campaigns the fixed-wing transports hauled troop units and made sustained supply deliveries to airstrips at the fringes of South Vietnam. Extremely suggestive for the future was the increasing bladderbird role in the late years, where the C–130s hauled fuel to forward sites to refuel helicopters and forward air control aircraft.

One unmistakable trend was the lessened importance of parachute assaults. Of the many paratroop assaults by the French in the early 1950s, and by allied C–47s and C–123s a decade later, none was a significant tactical success. Indeed the Americans were on several occasions embarrassed by their failure to deliver the jumpers with precision. Even when missions were expertly performed, there seemed no way of forcing the elusive enemy to give battle. Parachute units were among the earliest American troop units in Vietnam, but after the inconsequential results of the Junction City operation of early 1967 the Americans made no further battalion jumps. In retrospect the parachute operations in Vietnam seemed an illogical attempt to turn back the clock, competing unsuccessfully with the more flexible technique of assault by helicopter. The applicability of paratroops in future conflicts thus appeared limited. It was not inconceivable, however, that in some situation paratroops might reach beyond the radius of helicopters to seize an objective suitable for use as a fixed-wing airhead to sustain regional airmobile operations.

Airlift was basic to allied offensive strategy in another though indirect way. The ready availability of the transport force to undertake short-notice emergency lifts permitted the Americans to concentrate forces in offensive roles. Since the transports if necessary could substitute for highway lines of communications, there was little risk in cutting down on road security forces. And since the transports could quickly shift units into threatened regions, defensive garrisons could be minimized. Again and again, for example, streams of C–130s reached into the highlands to overcome temporary road blockages. Again and again the transports carried reinforcing battalions to Da Nang or points north. In extreme conditions, parachute supply made possible the survival of hard-pressed isolated garrisons—Khe Sanh and An Loc were the most significant of many such endeavors. During the crises of 1968 and 1972 the air transport force helped to hold the nation together, flying emergency lifts of units and materiel between points wholly cut off from surface routes.

When not directly employed in military operations, the airlift force performed other useful services. Routinely the transports hauled personnel, mail, equipment, and supplies, supporting virtually every allied activity in Vietnam. Air shipments of spare parts cut down inventory costs and reduced losses and damage in transit; airlift of munitions avoided the chance of capture in road ambush. Deliveries of fresh foodstuffs benefited allied health and morale, and air movements of patients gave the allied fighting man fast access to professional medical care. Passenger circuits made possible face-to-face staff discussion. Routine deliveries to scores of Special Forces camps enabled local forces to detect and harass communist units in remote regions.

Unlike air strikes, airlift missions posed no threat to the safety of the civilian population. Indeed, Air Force transports made frequent and direct contributions to the welfare of the Vietnamese citizenry, including lifts of refugees and hauls on behalf of various civil programs. Such civic action missions remained secondary to the military activities, however, reflecting the fact that American forces were in Vietnam primarily to provide a shield for, not to engage in, local pacification. American civilian agencies active in Vietnam, including the CIA, AID, and contract construction firms, also used the military airlift system. All, however, preferred to rely on contract airlift service, criticizing the delays and interruptions met when military transports were diverted to higher priority tasks.

In its internal management of the airlift operation in Vietnam, the Air Force attained reasonable efficiency. Without question, examples of the misuse of airlift occurred daily. Airlift crewmen nicknamed themselves "the trash-haulers," reflecting the feeling that certain cargo was of little value, or that some sorties seemed pointless. Equally clear, however, was the resolve in the 834th Air Division and the higher commands to reduce these instances and to apply airlift to essential needs. Further, even when engaged in the most routine mission, every ship and crew remained available to shift to urgent and unexpected emergency tasks. Rigorous daily use of aerial port, maintenance, control, and operations facilities kept the system geared for high-volume effort in time of crisis.

Managerial weaknesses in the early airlift system were in most cases met aggressively. Early lack of attention to control and aerial port facilities was corrected by successive reorganizations which began in 1962 and culminated in the creation of the 834th Air Division in late 1966. Two new institutions—the tactical airlift liaison officer and the joint air operations group—represented attempts to strengthen cooperation at field level. The liaison officers provided airlift expertise to ground force users and the operations group coordinated artillery warning and other safety matters among the services. Other managerial innovations tried in Vietnam were the forward airlift control element package and the (disappointing) computerized airlift management system. As in past wars, the Air Force felt it wise to avoid taking sole responsibility for allocating airlift among competing requesters. Consequently, a theater-level board made monthly reallocations of transportation capabilities, and a jointly manned traffic management agency made daily rulings on priorities.

TACTICAL AIRLIFT

Several problems defied complete solution; none was crippling, but each claimed the frequent attention of the 834th Air Division's commanders and staff. First, under endless consideration, was the idea of basing the C-130s in Vietnam and Thailand to get away from the need to rotate aircraft and crews from abroad. In-country basing offered savings in maintenance costs, reductions in wasteful flying, and a single line of command authority. The rotational system gave some advantages, but one important reason for keeping the 130s out of the country—reduction of personnel spaces in Vietnam—was a result of poor planning. Had the duration and extent of the conflict been anticipated early, construction of facilities for C-130s in Vietnam could have yielded dividends. Second, the policy of assigning individuals for tours of only one year (somewhat longer for C-130 units based out of Vietnam) limited the level of experience and necessitated an endless cycle of replacement training. One byproduct was a broadening of experience within the Air Force which assured that a good percentage of the service's future leaders knew firsthand the problems and capabilities of theater airlift forces. Finally, a continuing drain on overall airlift capacity resulted from the inherent usefulness of the transport airplane for other roles—gunship, bombing, airborne control, psychological, and others. Although the obvious answer lay in buying more airplanes, periodic reconfigurations of the spray C-123s demonstrated that some special-use aircraft could be returned quickly to airlift work if needed.

The most common limitation on the effectiveness of air transport in Vietnam was the condition or availability of forward airstrips. In planning a forward operation, the location of the potential C-130 airhead was usually crucial, and engineering efforts to keep the strip in commission were essential. A stream of heavily loaded C-130s landing on a marginal or soft runway invariably produced some deterioration of the surfacing, in many cases causing serious concern for the continuation of the airlift. Strips covered with metal surfacing often proved destructive to C-130 tires, especially where the surface was torn or littered by shrapnel. The airlift commanders, dependent upon ground force combat engineers to build and maintain strips, would have preferred that this function be under their own command. Instead, to stay ahead of potential problems at forward sites, the 834th Air Division organized an energetic airfield survey program, meanwhile preserving close coordination with tactical airlift officers on airfield conditions. The dependence of the airlift force on the airfield engineers was exemplified by the serious delay in starting an aerial line of communications with Khe Sanh during Lam Son 719, one of several factors that slowed development of the allied offensive in Laos.

The aerial port effort suffered from serious weaknesses which were overcome by the hard work of thousands of meagerly rewarded port members. Aerial port inadequacies badly handicapped the airlift effort in the early war years, and chronic low priorities in equipment, facilities, and personnel were never satisfactorily surmounted. The relatively modern 463L family of handling equipment came into increasing use at the major ports in Vietnam, but major operations at forward airheads often depended on one or two patched-up forklifts. Amply proven was the need for an agency at theater level (such as the 2d Aerial Port Group) concerned exclusively with aerial port matters. Also demonstrated was the need for a vigorous effort during times of peace, conceivably by the Air Reserve Forces, to preserve combat-zone air terminal capabilities.

Prewar failures of the American services to agree on such matters as battlefield airspace control, aeromedical evacuation, and pathfinder roles, caused problems for transport crews operating to forward airfields in Vietnam. An example was the prewar divergency in radio equipment, such that Air Force transports flew in Vietnam without the FM radios needed for talk with U.S. Army aircraft and ground agencies. To the credit of the services, however, the interservice rivalry often evident in staff work in the early war years was firmly restrained after 1965 and its effects on strategy and policy became imperceptible. In operating the airlift system, Air Force commanders gave full energy to doing the best possible job under the division of roles established in 1966, striving to provide responsive and reliable service to ground force users. Despite what seemed compelling logic, the Air Force refrained from reopening the highly charged issue of an Air Force transport helicopter force. Above all, the tradition of wholehearted face-to-face cooperation in the field among officers of all services emerged intact from Vietnam.

In nurturing the air transport capabilities of the Southeast Asian allies, the Americans generally found a satisfactory balance between what was reasonably possible and what was needed. Results were generally good except where growth was too rapidly forced, for example, in the case of the early Vietnamese Air Force helicopter arm. In working with the allied air forces the U.S. Air Force showed its inclination to give first priority to strike aviation, using the transport arm in some cases as a school to permit later expansion of strike units. The twin-engine transports of the Laotian, Cambodian, Thai, and South Vietnamese air forces eventually became significant and valuable assets to their governments.

Whether the Americans closest to the Vietnamese were mistaken in their generally optimistic assessments of the Vietnamese Air Force airlift arm over the years requires comment. Most advisors were fully aware of the technical and human weaknesses of the Vietnamese—the lack of directness and determination in facing difficult tasks, the reluctance to fly on instruments and by night, the social chasm between officers and enlisted men, and the thin technical background of Vietnamese society. For many advisors these were outweighed by their recognition of the superior airmanship of the Vietnamese in many roles. Beyond question, for example, was the ability of Vietnamese airlift crews to perform routine deliveries including low-level airdrops. In the final test of 1975 the Vietnamese Air Force C–130s served with credit despite maintenance weaknesses and inadequate numbers.

The history of Air Force transport helicopters in Southeast Asia was both colorful and thought provoking. Troop-lift and supply missions in Laos appeared to contradict the 1966 interservice roles agreement but represented a sensible accommodation to the needs of the situation. Air Force chopper crewmen proved capable of performing the same roles as U.S. Army, U.S. Marine, and Air America crews, whether in covert infiltrations, in supply, or in large-scale troop movements. The South Vietnamese meanwhile used their CH–47 force as an integral part of the Vietnamese Air Force airlift system, an arrangement plainly reflecting the U.S. Air Force influence. Working against U.S. Air Force eagerness to acquire a future helicopter airlift arm was the problem of operating in an environment of heavy antiaircraft opposition, a reality reconfirmed at Koh Tang Island.

Among the foremost strengths of the Air Force airlift apparatus in Southeast Asia were the qualities of its principal aircraft—the C–130, the C–123, and the C–7—each of which proved safe, dependable, and often forgiving of human error. The durability, payload, and flying qualities of the C–130 made this aircraft a particularly remarkable one. The Hercules could land at relatively primitive strips with fifteen-ton payloads, offload palletized cargo rapidly, and move to the next task at healthy airspeeds. Moreover, a C–130 required only one or two refuelings in the course of a full mission day. Fewer than a hundred C–130s could thus do work equivalent to the capacities of fifteen hundred C–47s. The jet-modified C–123s possessed the same qualities in moderately different degree, while the ruggedness and simplicity of the once-unwanted Caribous enabled them to undertake tasks and venture into areas of enemy fire where their bigger brothers could not. Those who flew the Hercules, the Provider, and the Caribou in strenuous conditions in Vietnam spoke of their planes with warmth and admiration, a tribute to those who conceived, designed, and championed these three distinguished craft.

During the twelve years of operations, 1961–73, a total of 122 Air Force C–130, C–123, and C–7 transports were destroyed in Southeast Asia. Of the total, 40 were lost to enemy ground fire during missions and 17 to sapper or shelling attack while on the ground. The remainder were lost to "operational" causes—typically accidents associated with difficult conditions at forward airstrips. Nearly three-fourths of the losses took place before 1969. A total of 229 transport crewmen were killed or missing during missions in South Vietnam and Thailand (103 C–130 crewmen, 95 C–123, 31 C–7); 40 others were lost in nonairlift missions in North Vietnam and Laos. Some 30 crewmembers were killed in 38 Air Force helicopter losses, excluding rescue craft.[11]

REFLECTIONS

In the last analysis, the greatest asset of the Air Force airlift system in Southeast Asia rested in its people and the worldwide Air Force from which they came. Although fewer than half the pilots occupying transport cockpits had previous experience in tactical airlift work, the general competence in flying appeared beyond that of any past American wartime air force. Ingenuity and talent came forward when needed—from the 834th Air Division staff, from the transport squadrons and wings, and from the aerial port units. The contribution of the force of overworked maintenance crewmen was superb. These men, backed by the Air Force's internal logistics system, sustained a force of aging aircraft in rigorous use for more than a decade. Mistakes and bureaucratic inanities were not absent, but the working of the airlift system in Vietnam proved the human strengths of the professional United States Air Force. That the "trash-haulers" did all that was humanly possible in Southeast Asia, within the resources and support allotted, was beyond question.

Among those who served, a minority were direct volunteers for duty in Southeast Asia, and most did their duty with quiet satisfaction. Extreme personal valor was only occasionally called for. More typical was a sustained kind of heroism—unstinting effort, day after day, enduring withering heat, inadequate rest, and often intestinal sickness. Most airlifters returned to rewarding military or civilian careers and were able to regard the final defeat without overwhelming bitterness. Still, few would cease to remember the silent allied infantrymen sprawling exhausted inside the transport fuselages or the ugliness of the plastic bags in which the dead were returned. Neither would any airlifter forget the haunting beauty of the Vietnamese land nor his own transitory role in the long tragedy of her people.

Appendices

Appendix 1

2D AIR DIVISION ORGANIZATION
JULY 1963

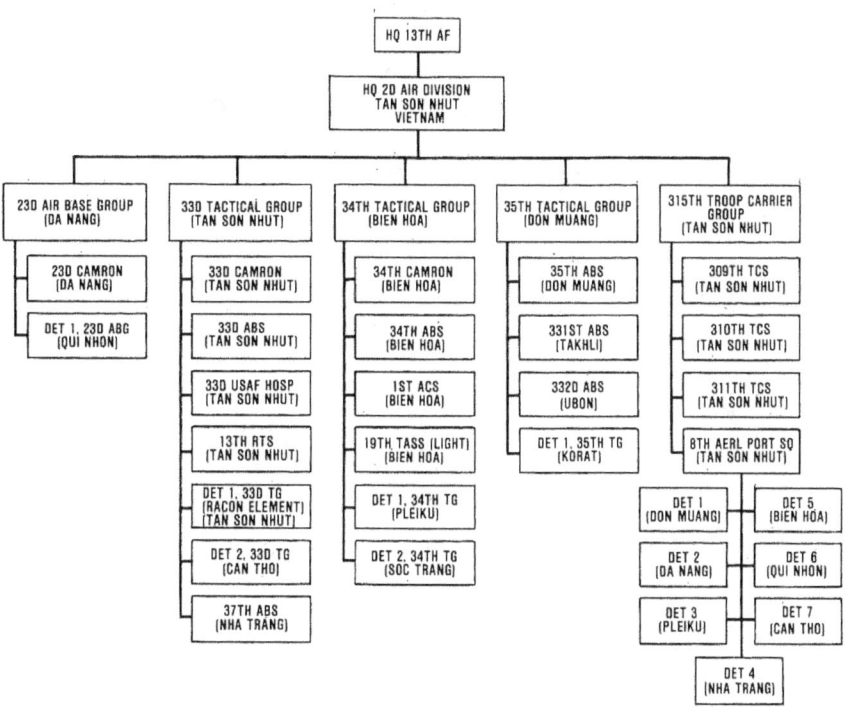

Appendix 2

315TH AIR DIVISION ORGANIZATION
JUNE 1964

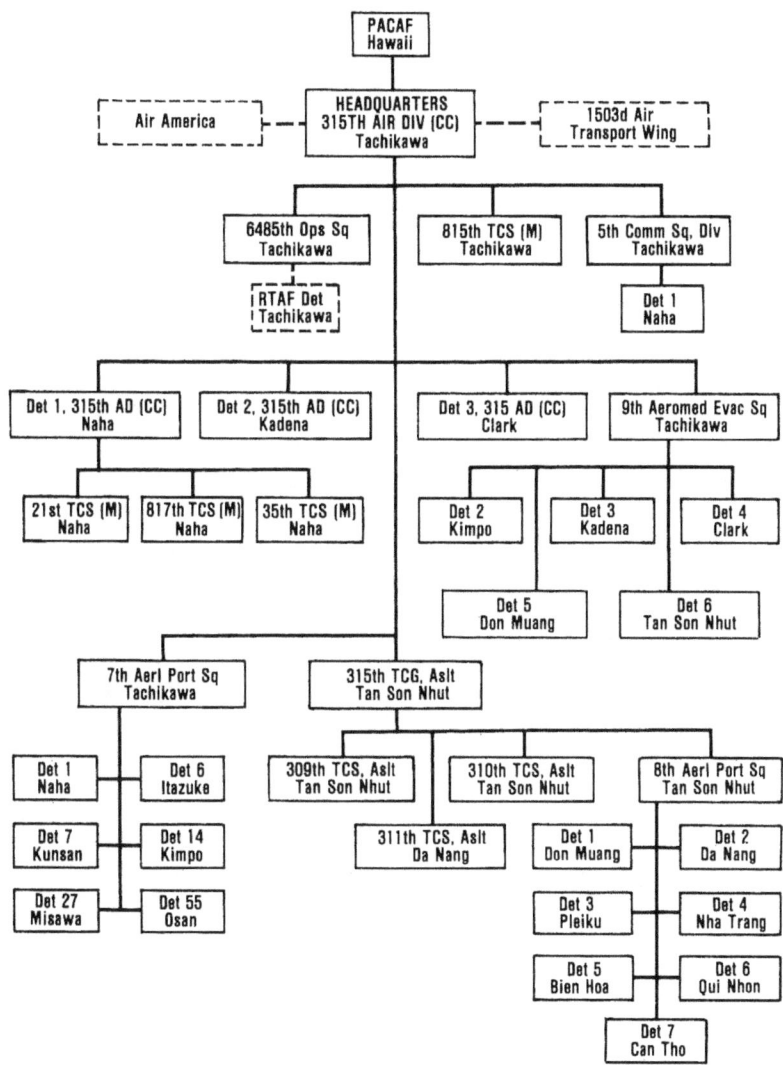

Appendix 3

**PACIFIC AIRLIFT ORGANIZATION
MARCH 1968**

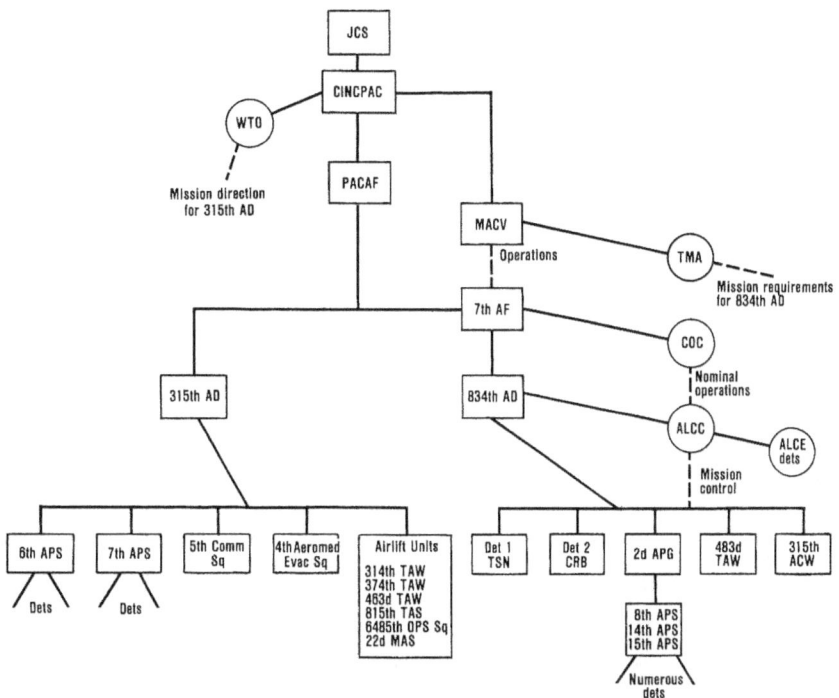

Appendix 4

Peak Theater Airlift Force Posture
March 31, 1968

834th Air Division, Tan Son Nhut:

315th Air Commando Wing, Phan Rang
 (4 sqs, C-123K and
 1 sq, UC-123 converted for airlift)

        309th ACS, Phan Rang
        310th ACS, Phan Rang
        311th ACS, Phan Rang
        19th ACS, Tan Son Nhut
        12th ACS, Defoliation, Bien Hoa
        315th CAMRON, Phan Rang (maintenance)

483d Tactical Airlift Wing, Cam Ranh Bay
 (6 sqs, C-7A)

        457th TAS, Cam Ranh Bay
        458th TAS, Cam Ranh Bay
        459th TAS, Phu Cat
        537th TAS, Phu Cat
        535th TAS, Vung Tau
        536th TAS, Vung Tau
        483d CAMRON, Cam Ranh Bay (maintenance)

Operational control of C-130 detachments
 (96 C-130 aircraft)

        Det 1, 834th AD, Tan Son Nhut (27 C-130B)
        Det 2, 834th AD, Cam Ranh Bay (23 C-130A, 28 C-130E)
        TF, 314th TAW, Tuy Hoa (10 C-130E)
        TF, Nha Trang (8 C-130E)

315th Air Division, Tachikawa:
374th Tactical Airlift Wing, Naha
 (4 sqs, C-130A)

        21st TAS, Naha
        35th TAS, Naha
        41st TAS, Naha
        817th TAS, Naha
        374th FMS, Naha (maintenance)

463d Tactical Airlift Wing, Mactan
 (4 sqs, C-130B)

        772d TAS, Mactan
        774th TAS, Mactan
        29th TAS, Clark
        773d TAS, Clark
        463d FMS, Mactan (maintenance)

314th Tactical Airlift Wing, CCK
  (3 sqs, C–130E)
    50th TAS, CCK
    345th TAS, CCK
    776th TAS, CCK
    314th FMS, CCK (maintenance)
    314th A&E Sq, CCK (maintenance)

315th Air Division
    815th TAS, Tachikawa (C–130A)
    22d MAS, Tachikawa (C–124)
    6485th Ops Sq, Clark (C–118)

315th Air Division operational control
  (3 rotational squadrons from TAC, C–130E)
    38th TAS (316th TAW, Langley), Tachikawa
    779th TAS (464th TAW, Pope), Tachikawa
    346th TAS (516th TAW, Dyess), Clark

Total Force: 28 sqs (15 C–130, 5 C–123, 6 C–7, 1 C–124, 1 C–118)

Appendix 5

*Theater Airlift Force Posture
March 31, 1972*

In South Vietnam, under Seventh Air Force, Tan Son Nhut:

483d Tactical Airlift Wing, Cam Ranh Bay
  (1 sq, C–7)

        457th TAS, 2 aircraft, standing down

377th Air Base Wing, Tan Son Nhut
  (1 sq, C–7/C–123/UC–123)

        310th TAS (14 C–7 at TSN and Phu Cat, 3 C–123 at TSN, 5 UC–123 at TSN)

Operational control of C–130 detachment
  (26 C–130E)

        Det 1, 374th TAW, Tan Son Nhut

Based outside Vietnam, under Thirteenth Air Force, Clark:
374th Tactical Airlift Wing, CCK
  (4 sqs, C–130E)

        21st TAS, CCK
        50th TAS, CCK
        345th TAS, CCK
        776th TAS, CCK

405th Fighter Wing, Clark
  (1 sq, C–130B, 1 sq, C–9/C–118)

        774th TAS, C–130B, Clark
        20th Ops Sq (2 C–9, 2 C–118 acft, Clark)

Appendix 6

Agreement Between Chief of Staff, U.S. Army and Chief of Staff, U.S. Air Force, 6 April 1966

The Chief of Staff, U.S. Army, and the Chief of Staff, U.S. Air Force, have reached an understanding on the control and employment of certain types of fixed and rotary wing aircraft and are individually and jointly agreed as follows:

a. The Chief of Staff, U.S. Army, agrees to relinquish all claims for CV–2 and CV–7 aircraft and for future fixed-wing aircraft designed for tactical airlift. These assets now in the Army inventory will be transferred to the Air Force. (CSA and CSAF agree that this does not apply to administrative mission support fixed wing aircraft.)

b. The Chief of Staff, U.S. Air Force, agrees:

(1) To relinquish all claims for helicopters and follow-on rotary wing aircraft which are designed and operated for intratheater movement, fire support, supply and resupply of Army Forces and those Air Force control elements assigned to DASC and subordinate thereto. (CSA and CSAF agree that this does not include rotary wing aircraft employed by Air Force SAW and SAR forces and rotary wing administrative mission support aircraft). (CSA and CSAF agree that the Army and Air Force jointly will continue to develop VTOL aircraft. Dependent upon evolution of this type aircraft, methods of employment and control will be matters for continuing joint consideration by the Army and Air Force).

(2) That, in cases of operational need, the CV–2, CV–7, and C–123 type aircraft performing supply, resupply, or troop-lift functions in the field army area, may be attached to the subordinate tactical echelons of the field army (corps, division, or subordinate commander), as determined by the appropriate joint/unified commander.

(3) To retain the CV–2 and CV–7 aircraft in the Air Force structure and to consult with the Chief of Staff, U.S. Army, prior to changing the force levels of, or replacing these aircraft.

(4) To consult with the Chief of Staff, U.S. Army, in order to arrive at take off, landing, and load carrying characteristics of follow-on fixed wing aircraft to meet the needs of the Army for supply, resupply, and troop movement functions.

c. The Chief of Staff, U.S. Army, and the Chief of Staff, U.S. Air Force, jointly agree:

(1) To revise all Service doctrinal statements, manuals, and other material in variance with the substance and spirit of this agreement.

(2) That the necessary actions resulting from this agreement will be completed by 1 January 1967.

J.P. McConnell, General, USAF Chief of Staff	Harold K. Johnson Chief of Staff General, USA

Appendix 7*

Workload, USAF Airlift Forces in Vietnam

Airlift C-123s in Vietnam

	Sorties	Flying Hours	Passengers	Cargo, tons
1962				
Jan	296	493	1,638	428
Feb	418	596	2,523	574
Mar	508	725	2,878	688
Apr	545	750	2,943	965
May	751	1,214	4,495	1,224
Jun	1,102	1,947	9,393	1,364
Jul	1,132	1,841	10,349	1,438
Aug	1,454	1,865	15,668	1,787
Sep	1,473	1,930	15,500	2,175
Oct	1,295	2,019	11,256	2,401
Nov	1,439	1,838	13,233	2,573
Dec	1,278	1,750	9,785	2,198
1963				
Jan	1,401	1,819	11,624	2,027
Feb	1,336	1,611	9,218	2,271
Mar	1,567	1,727	14,012	2,779
Apr	1,627	1,823	11,040	2,299
May	2,159	2,691	15,337	3,321
Jun	1,996	2,424	12,417	2,816
Jul	2,216	2,998	16,373	2,884
Aug	2,088	2,582	13,766	3,098
Sep	2,343	2,707	13,707	3,328
Oct	2,290	2,679	13,794	3,342
Nov	2,572	2,852	14,004	3,850
Dec	2,686	3,153	16,047	4,478

---

* Ops Rep-5 files at USAF comd cen; rprts, 315th AD, Airlift Accomplishments, CY 65 and CY 66; rprts, Mgt Analys Ofc, 834th AD, Tactical Airlift Performance Analysis, SEA, Dec 66, Dec 67, Dec 68, Dec 69, Dec 70, Dec 71; *Summary of Air Operations, Southeast Asia* (Hickam AFB, Hawaii, 1969–71); tabulations in 6492d Combat Cargo Gp, History of Airlift in SVN, Dec 61–Oct 62, Dec 17, 1962; monthly hist data rprts, TAFTS-P2, Oct–Dec 62; Donald F. Martin, *History of the War in Vietnam, October 1961–December 1963* (Project CHECO, Hickam AFB, Hawaii, 1964); rprt, PACAF comptroller, FY 64–65, in B. A. Whitaker and L. E. Paterson, *Assault Airlift Operations* (Project CHECO, Hickam AFB, Hawaii, 1967); hists, 315th TAW, 1969–72, 374th TAW, 1971–72, USSAG/7th AF, 1973; rprts, Airlift Sec, MACV (J-3), 1972; *Command Status Book*, 7th AF, Jun 72; Caribou data for late 1966 from USARV; *PACAF Tactical Airlift Summary*, Dec 69, Dec 70.

TACTICAL AIRLIFT

	Sorties	Flying Hours	Passengers	Cargo, tons
1964				
Jan	2,540	2,793	15,302	3,949
Feb	2,386	2,845	15,463	3,675
Mar	2,908	3,290	17,487	4,545
Apr	3,203	3,391	20,085	5,043
May	2,819	3,327	17,755	4,565
Jun	2,851	3,215	18,119	4,703
Jul	2,390	3,412	19,309	3,327
Aug	2,038	3,148	15,875	2,733
Sep	2,477	3,034	18,424	5,761
Oct	1,994	3,198	22,340	6,300
Nov	2,390	3,547	14,472	3,716
Dec	3,437	3,786	23,540	6,037
1965				
Jan	3,960	4,406	28,042	7,399
Feb	3,630	4,306	28,219	6,747
Mar	4,304	5,255	31,054	8,376
Apr	4,580	5,254	35,909	8,545
May	5,312	5,210	42,346	9,056
Jun	5,447	5,385	46,506	9,923
Jul	6,016	6,015	50,307	10,943
Aug	6,528	6,437	49,130	12,373
Sep	6,439	6,796	48,657	12,509
Oct	6,088	6,129	50,375	11,768
Nov	6,312	5,606	49,304	12,455
Dec	5,679	4,959	45,875	10,757
1966				
Jan	6,663	5,410	46,382	13,866
Feb	5,827	4,831	37,646	11,699
Mar	6,856	5,261	47,420	14,516
Apr	6,911	5,441	41,103	13,811
May	7,246	5,602	45,388	14,724
Jun	8,066	5,763	49,243	16,417
Jul	8,460	5,811	48,295	16,602
Aug	8,098	5,356	58,258	14,779
Sep	8,796	5,510	55,875	15,773
Oct	8,617	6,173	57,509	15,396
Nov	9,207	5,672	62,617	16,643
Dec	8,586	5,904	56,736	14,886
1967				
Jan	8,251	5,350	62,027	15,580
Feb	8,049	5,066	70,886	14,068
Mar	9,252	5,955	81,582	15,513
Apr	8,481	5,655	73,110	14,694
May	8,820	6,252	72,628	15,809
Jun	8,847	6,289	73,751	15,620
Jul	8,439	6,074	79,215	14,120
Aug	8,243	5,960	87,576	12,923
Sep	7,557	5,590	71,262	11,927
Oct	7,434	5,744	61,656	12,390
Nov	7,258	5,593	56,489	12,977
Dec	7,626	5,744	58,717	14,589

APPENDIX

	Sorties	Flying Hours	Passengers	Cargo, tons
1968				
Jan	7,727	6,091	79,149	11,804
Feb	8,600	6,975	84,287	12,178
Mar	9,305	7,557	97,898	13,097
Apr	7,243	5,702	85,665	9,317
May	7,972	6,051	83,890	10,641
Jun	8,143	5,988	89,806	12,194
Jul	8,831	6,072	95,773	14,477
Aug	9,121	6,323	89,279	16,760
Sep	8,602	5,948	84,028	15,966
Oct	9,551	6,767	95,383	16,639
Nov	9,263	6,271	90,019	16,004
Dec	8,869	6,104	91,265	14,382
1969				
Jan	8,680	6,182	85,379	14,182
Feb	7,972	5,563	77,382	13,065
Mar	9,426	6,612	94,052	15,159
Apr	8,988	6,335	96,404	14,651
May	9,707	6,629	96,062	16,686
Jun	9,020	6,356	91,859	14,949
Jul	8,864	6,516	96,639	14,782
Aug	8,777	6,578	89,685	14,339
Sep	8,080	6,375	78,400	13,585
Oct	8,367	6,376	80,998	13,610
Nov	8,521	6,454	85,168	13,441
Dec	8,630	6,472	74,545	13,981
1970				
Jan	8,483	6,772	74,946	13,234
Feb	8,392	6,468	77,616	12,990
Mar	8,249	6,698	85,757	13,417
Apr	8,514	6,305	83,409	13,613
May	9,452	6,595	92,055	14,046
Jun	8,422	6,223	99,869	13,207
Jul	7,382	5,110	90,039	11,889
Aug	6,819	4,797	75,444	10,306
Sep	6,184	4,436	74,761	9,690
Oct	5,843	4,542	69,836	8,376
Nov	5,986	4,869	76,394	9,404
Dec	5,923	4,851	70,966	8,748
1971				
Jan	5,648	4,631	60,632	8,299
Feb	4,887	4,233	57,829	7,521
Mar	5,437	4,927	51,989	9,256
Apr	4,093	3,882	41,182	6,708
May	3,412	2,999	37,942	5,069
Jun	3,346	3,088	33,155	4,543
Jul	2,879	2,947	36,249	3,295
Aug	2,871	2,865	30,138	4,071
Sep	1,750	1,760	18,369	2,298
Oct	1,456	1,594	12,020	2,215
Nov	1,278	1,509	11,380	1,945
Dec	1,515	1,573	14,895	2,195

TACTICAL AIRLIFT

	Sorties	Flying Hours	Passengers	Cargo, tons
1972				
Jan	1,042	—	11,295	2,650
Feb	679	—	—	—
Mar	801	—	10,380	750
Apr	731	—	6,600	859
May	686	—	7,652	939
Jun	283	281	—	—

In-country Airlift C–130s (TDY from Bases Outside Vietnam)

	Sorties	Flying Hours	Passengers	Cargo, tons
1965				
Jan–Jun (data not available)				
Jul	1,153	1,243	18,141	6,773
Aug	2,052	2,010	20,167	11,889
Sep	1,940	2,003	19,794	12,637
Oct	2,040	—	27,575	12,152
Nov	2,997	2,591	37,998	15,383
Dec	3,792	3,350	37,497	20,698
1966				
Jan	5,034	4,143	46,306	26,189
Feb	4,616	3,809	42,043	22,333
Mar	5,734	4,595	50,702	29,845
Apr	7,321	5,046	61,368	30,898
May	6,973	5,182	61,761	31,046
Jun	7,313	5,559	72,928	33,612
Jul	7,183	5,336	76,893	32,776
Aug	8,817	5,993	105,666	34,398
Sep	7,299	5,981	93,656	31,649
Oct	7,476	6,052	97,333	32,766
Nov	8,454	6,380	102,251	36,157
Dec	8,499	6,664	108,212	35,550
1967				
Jan	8,619	6,628	116,756	35,524
Feb	8,221	6,102	96,921	34,462
Mar	9,323	6,588	117,668	42,687
Apr	10,217	8,045	123,574	45,357
May	10,084	7,250	137,653	40,762
Jun	9,913	7,148	136,794	41,379
Jul	10,085	7,669	136,165	42,455
Aug	9,919	7,259	135,003	44,087
Sep	10,289	7,494	137,180	45,508
Oct	11,153	8,389	135,307	55,348
Nov	11,320	8,859	154,504	51,922
Dec	11,678	8,972	151,990	53,037
1968				
Jan	12,870	10,527	141,404	58,174
Feb	12,019	11,571	114,603	57,236
Mar	14,347	13,616	166,400	69,499
Apr	14,249	12,111	166,917	68,007
May	14,392	11,825	175,796	64,780
Jun	13,650	10,902	171,060	62,955
Jul	13,383	10,397	180,139	58,479

APPENDIX

	Sorties	Flying Hours	Passengers	Cargo, tons
Aug	13,618	10,573	186,789	59,239
Sep	13,424	10,897	194,922	58,584
Oct	13,429	10,889	193,386	56,777
Nov	13,509	10,543	188,065	57,129
Dec	13,775	10,124	200,819	57,050
1969				
Jan	12,849	9,820	193,652	54,120
Feb	11,484	8,749	176,942	48,799
Mar	11,748	9,240	196,182	47,075
Apr	11,316	8,768	195,184	45,164
May	11,279	8,722	200,005	43,118
Jun	9,868	8,020	193,879	35,313
Jul	9,883	8,624	210,737	35,059
Aug	10,196	8,262	199,249	37,789
Sep	10,252	8,187	173,804	39,974
Oct	10,789	8,590	180,272	40,626
Nov	10,982	8,704	190,458	40,479
Dec	11,674	9,188	201,474	44,299
1970				
Jan	10,071	8,473	208,422	34,273
Feb	8,719	7,453	159,836	30,287
Mar	10,397	8,578	195,869	38,412
Apr	9,675	7,722	178,166	34,419
May	11,670	9,159	180,967	46,475
Jun	10,013	8,310	208,885	34,322
Jul	9,166	8,003	217,636	28,742
Aug	8,055	7,112	209,970	21,342
Sep	7,204	6,531	195,779	17,794
Oct	5,819	5,754	167,574	11,682
Nov	5,839	5,859	148,157	14,789
Dec	6,714	6,846	149,444	17,682
1971				
Jan	6,432	7,068	128,407	17,728
Feb	6,853	8,100	115,635	22,308
Mar	8,025	8,806	108,049	32,081
Apr	6,315	6,696	131,963	19,730
May	5,864	5,866	134,355	15,639
Jun	4,653	4,797	115,845	12,552
Jul	4,668	4,934	114,482	11,645
Aug	4,471	4,733	111,212	10,575
Sep	4,185	4,409	100,138	11,537
Oct	4,049	4,263	103,898	9,639
Nov	3,880	4,121	94,701	10,015
Dec	3,429	3,862	82,310	9,325
1972				
Jan	2,803	3,232	66,553	7,295
Feb	2,240	2,634	52,061	6,052
Mar	1,883	2,010	44,014	3,639
Apr	4,032	4,927	57,265	14,423
May	4,010	4,720	55,136	19,789
Jun	3,465	4,673	52,915	17,056
Jul	2,349	2,888	44,623	8,011

TACTICAL AIRLIFT

	Sorties	Flying Hours	Passengers	Cargo, tons
Aug	2,463	2,820	47,167	8,573
Sep	2,399	2,861	56,080	7,062
Oct	1,899	2,180	44,051	5,927
Nov (TSN det only)	879	1,075	17,084	2,850

Thailand–Based C–130 Detachments Missions in Vietnam, Cambodia, and Thailand

	Sorties	Flying Hours	Passengers	Cargo, tons
1972				
Nov	2,219	2,900	36,878	6,341
Dec	2,825	4,046	48,543	5,800
1973				
Jan	3,085	4,799	66,159	7,132
Feb	3,073	4,175	36,890	8,944
Mar	3,014	4,418	39,356	7,933
Apr	1,824	2,255	9,170	7,531
May	2,029	2,018	9,134	8,601
Jun	1,048	1,037	7,501	2,031
Jul	1,679	1,596	7,275	8,129
Aug	2,370	3,081	7,440	13,501
Sep	1,825	2,493	7,077	9,011
Oct	2,479	2,963	7,637	14,627

C–130 Cargo Deliveries to Cambodia

	Airland Sorties	Airdrop Sorties	Total, tons
1973			
July	326	138	6,661
Aug	666	116	11,786
Sep	441	116	7,438
Oct	772	54	8,092
Nov	353	33	5,558
Dec	440	50	7,064
1974			
Jan	374	94	6,609
Feb	232	61	4,023
Mar	37	93	1,392
Apr–Jun total	115	833	11,737
Jul–Sep total	63	288	4,180

U.S. Army Caribou (1966) and C–7s of 483rd Wing

U.S. Army	Sorties	Flying Hours	Passengers	Cargo, tons
1966				
Jan	6,058	3,767	24,376	2,421
Feb	9,559	7,028	56,040	6,379
Mar	11,949	7,066	69,126	7,537
Apr	12,545	7,776	78,438	7,802
May	11,170	7,600	69,414	6,302

APPENDIX

	Sorties	Flying Hours	Passengers	Cargo, tons
Jun	12,689	8,026	58,231	6,206
Jul	10,695	7,283	76,919	8,416
Aug	10,881	7,360	82,193	9,015
Sep	10,131	7,141	63,987	8,245
Oct	10,168	7,285	73,942	7,266
Nov	13,204	6,932	66,732	7,852
Dec	9,499	6,451	60,843	5,791

U.S. Air Force

1967
Jan	10,222	6,661	74,301	6,340
Feb	12,451	7,545	82,239	7,400
Mar	13,590	8,250	93,010	8,022
Apr	13,846	8,169	98,499	8,410
May	13,916	8,373	100,458	8,402
Jun	13,193	8,378	94,132	7,700
Jul	13,423	8,576	94,827	8,202
Aug	13,691	8,766	92,362	8,653
Sep	13,274	8,667	86,743	8,307
Oct	13,242	8,967	87,969	8,232
Nov	12,312	8,693	85,640	7,994
Dec	12,668	8,818	85,016	7,903

1968
Jan	13,072	9,010	93,991	7,301
Feb	12,176	8,767	86,433	7,281
Mar	14,288	10,263	109,900	9,245
Apr	14,817	10,169	106,867	9,070
May	16,185	10,803	124,416	9,469
Jun	15,697	10,452	121,644	9,275
Jul	15,964	10,878	120,796	10,264
Aug	15,563	10,901	116,244	9,605
Sep	14,580	10,066	114,823	9,042
Oct	14,076	9,573	103,231	7,816
Nov	14,122	9,446	97,750	8,165
Dec	15,854	10,481	107,037	9,292

1969
Jan	15,858	10,506	109,120	9,157
Feb	14,678	9,807	93,452	8,793
Mar	16,327	11,170	106,897	9,576
Apr	15,699	10,625	104,030	9,005
May	15,864	10,781	96,214	8,851
Jun	14,235	10,152	89,877	7,646
Jul	14,493	10,653	94,285	7,779
Aug	15,575	11,229	90,964	8,913
Sep	12,354	9,304	71,628	7,304
Oct	14,374	10,565	79,307	8,031
Nov	13,437	9,815	69,831	7,511
Dec	14,630	10,430	70,470	8,340

1970
Jan	14,372	10,633	65,870	8,286
Feb	13,025	9,588	53,379	8,361
Mar	14,388	10,352	63,056	9,199

TACTICAL AIRLIFT

U.S. Air Force	Sorties	Flying Hours	Passengers	Cargo, tons
Apr	13,928	9,980	56,871	8,814
May	13,956	10,560	53,580	8,650
Jun	11,054	8,902	44,697	6,219
Jul	10,363	8,556	37,556	5,801
Aug	10,264	8,189	34,802	6,112
Sep	10,553	8,602	37,636	6,556
Oct	10,286	8,569	42,066	5,925
Nov	11,012	8,496	53,325	5,247
Dec	11,574	8,760	55,035	5,796
1971				
Jan	11,431	8,375	53,643	5,381
Feb	10,647	7,714	53,961	4,800
Mar	11,857	9,300	63,929	4,864
Apr	11,389	9,549	58,871	4,732
May	11,494	9,015	59,040	4,792
Jun	10,493	8,470	54,737	3,994
Jul	9,557	7,748	52,202	3,566
Aug	8,136	6,481	38,201	3,448
Sep	6,639	5,759	33,533	2,689
Oct	6,067	5,632	30,680	2,039
Nov	4,909	5,109	20,245	1,662
Dec	4,697	4,995	17,066	1,405
1972				
Jan	4,128	3,699	—	—
Feb	3,135	2,706	—	—
Mar	1,582	834	7,680	674
Apr	497	—	2,185	229
May	351	—	1,490	181
Jun	408	380	1,959	120
Jul	378	—	2,183	63
Aug	327	—	2,100	50
Sep	342	—	2,020	72
Oct	357	—	2,310	46

Workload, Combined Forces in Vietnam, 1965–1972
(Cargo Only, Monthly Average Tonnages)

	USAF C-123	USAF C-130	USAF C-7	VNAF C-47	VNAF C-119	VNAF C-123	VNAF copter Heli-	Australian Caribou	U.S. Army Caribou	U.S. Army Fixed-Wing U-1, U-6, U-21	U.S. Army and Marine Helicopter	USMC KC-130
Jan–Jun 65	8,341	—	—	500	—	—	—	604	—	—	—	—
Jul–Dec 65	11,801	13,255	—	350	—	—	—	615	—	—	—	—
Jan–Jun 66	14,172	28,987	—	—	—	—	—	702	6,108	—	—	—
Jul–Dec 66	15,680	33,883	—	232	—	—	—	455	7,764	—	—	—
Jan–Jun 67	15,214	40,028	7,712	238	—	—	—	478	—	—	52,000	—
Jul–Dec 67	13,155	48,726	8,215	201	—	—	—	298	—	—	86,000	—
Jan–Jun 68	11,538	63,442	8,607	—	—	—	—	396	—	—	90,000	—
Jul–Dec 68	15,705	57,876	9,031	—	—	—	—	620	—	—	97,000	—
Jan–Jun 69	14,782	45,598	8,838	47	641	—	185	706	—	448	112,828	2,731
Jul–Dec 69	13,956	39,704	7,980	34	448	—	194	705	—	445	102,138	2,469
Jan–Jun 70	12,418	36,365	8,255	42	565	—	488	669	—	416	128,269	1,789
Jul–Dec 70	9,735	18,672	5,906	51	937	—	617	498	—	454	83,147	884
Jan–Jun 71	6,899	20,006	4,760	183	778	—	993	452	—	138	54,304	268
Jul–Dec 71	2,670	10,456	2,469	32	444	973	2,458	225	—	—	49,241[a]	—
Jan–Jun 72	—	—	—	—	—	—	—	—	—	—	16,657[a]	—
Jul–Dec 72	—	—	—	—	—	—	—	—	—	—	8,175[a]	—

[a] U.S. Army helicopter only.

* Sources for 1965–1968: As given for App 1; *Transportation and Movement Control* (Joint Logistics Review Board Monograph 18, Washington, D.C., 1970). Sources for 1969–1972: *Summary of Air Operations, Southeast Asia* (Hickam AFB, Hawaii, 1969–71); rprts, PACAF, Tactical Airlift Summary, Dec 69, Dec 70; rprts, 834th AD, Tactical Airlift Performance and Accomplishments, Dec 69, Dec 70, Dec 71; hist, MACV, Jan 72–Mar 73, p B-50.

Appendix 9

Workload, PACAF Forces in Western Pacific, 1969–1972

	C–118 Flying Hours	C–124 Flying Hours	C–130 Flying Hours	C–118/C–124/C–130/ DC–6/DC–4 Worldwide Passenger and Cargo Tonnage (includes in-country shuttle)
1969				
Jan	577	1,510	19,835	93,749
Feb	477	1,354	17,914	86,200
Mar	489	1,517	19,193	88,946
Apr	482	—	18,999	84,880
May	499	—	19,333	83,637
Jun	511	—	18,065	73,174
Jul	595	—	18,934	76,313
Aug	493	—	17,994	76,355
Sep	538	—	17,744	75,831
Oct	518	—	17,614	77,489
Nov	495	—	17,788	78,114
Dec	514	—	17,963	82,639
1970				
Jan	501	—	16,874	72,348
Feb	241	—	15,166	59,623
Mar	262	19	17,547	73,918
Apr	185	137	15,321	66,889
May	209	223	16,507	79,465
Jun	224	291	15,143	70,803
Jul	162	323	14,842	64,263
Aug	202	168	13,128	53,445
Sep	201	234	12,455	49,477
Oct	140	261	12,271	41,443
Nov	180	283	11,790	41,193
Dec	217	298	11,801	44,122
1971				
Jan	228	267	11,672	39,765
Feb	204	259	11,747	43,077
Mar	244	256	12,742	—
Apr	209	277	10,545	—
May	236	278	9,916	—
Jun	237	150	8,532	—
Jul	215	290	8,697	—
Aug	155	262	8,815	—
Sep	153	259	8,062	—
Oct	167	208	8,276	—
Nov	192	0	7,119	—

Data from December 1971 on is for C–130s of the 374th Tactical Airlift Wing only.

1971	Flying Hours	Workload	1973	Flying Hours	Workload
Dec	5,595	—	Jan	6,979	—
			Feb	6,110	—
1972			Mar	6,796	—
Jan	5,703	17,750	Apr	4,722	—
Feb	5,169	13,624	May	4,868	—
Mar	4,890	10,467	Jun	3,493	—
Apr	7,344	23,643			
May	7,012	28,560			
Jun	9,744	28,380			
Jul	7,176	—			
Aug	7,875	—			
Sep	6,477	—			
Oct	6,924	—			
Nov	7,017	—			
Dec	6,029	—			

Appendix 10[*]

Workload, 315th Air Division, 1965–1968

	C-118 Flying Hours	C-124 Flying Hours	C-130 Flying Hours	315th Air Division Passenger and Cargo Tonnage (includes in-country shuttle)
1965				
Jan	152	1,035	4,335	6,081
Feb	157	953	4,609	5,774
Mar	229	1,265	5,608	8,531
Apr	180	1,260	7,712	9,505
May	149	1,151	8,716	9,497
Jun	291	1,376	7,469	11,386
Jul	340	1,303	8,804	17,053
Aug	351	1,283	8,741	19,564
Sep	362	1,237	10,171	23,186
Oct	449	1,255	11,236	25,335
Nov	412	1,212	11,532	31,383
Dec	334	1,289	13,486	37,380
1966				
Jan	—	1,495	13,719	41,936
Feb	—	1,371	14,691	47,047
Mar	—	1,492	15,761	46,450
Apr	—	1,482	15,891	56,521
May	—	1,527	17,149	62,753
Jun	—	1,474	16,902	55,811
Jul	—	1,525	18,525	57,115
Aug	—	1,526	18,957	64,999
Sep	—	1,554	19,026	58,946
Oct	—	1,607	18,613	55,858
Nov	—	1,548	18,735	63,333
Dec	—	1,609	18,648	59,402
1967				
Jan	657	1,452	18,271	61,510
Feb	638	1,205	18,261	66,540
Mar	689	1,436	18,756	77,500
Apr	680	1,431	18,993	68,914
May	731	1,519	20,916	72,450
Jun	686	1,409	18,625	69,697
Jul	718	1,401	18,745	74,203
Aug	708	1,358	18,301	75,097
Sep	702	1,314	18,510	76,060
Oct	746	1,367	18,471	87,348
Nov	742	1,320	18,617	82,800
Dec	711	1,368	18,454	84,137

[*] Rprts, 315th AD, Airlift Accomplishments, CY 65 and CY 66; *Commander's Review*, 315th AD, Jun 30, 1967, Dec 31, 1967, Jun 30, 1968, and Sep 30, 1968.

	C-118 Flying Hours	C-124 Flying Hours	C-130 Flying Hours	315th Air Division Passenger and Cargo Tonnage (includes in-country shuttle)
1968				
Jan	724	1,523	19,447	87,172
Feb	714	1,377	23,870	86,451
Mar	713	1,420	24,848	100,230
Apr	735	1,358	23,823	105,796
May	665	1,369	23,032	102,414
Jun	681	1,325	22,342	98,547
Jul	647	1,391	21,796	96,578
Aug	641	1,393	20,971	101,185
Sep	631	1,386	20,368	98,678

Appendix 11*

USAF Transports Lost in SEA (Excludes Rescue Aircraft)

	Accidents	AA Fire	Ground Attack	Total	Dollar Cost (millions)
During 1962–1973:					
C–130[a]	21	19	12	52	135.2
C–123[b]	32	14	4	50	33.3
C–7	12	7	1	20	16.0
CH–3	3	13	1	17	13.26
CH–53	0	2	0	2	4.59
UH–1 (gunship and slick)	6	13	0	19	6.94
During 1975:					
C–130	0	0	1	1	
CH–53	1	3	0	4	

[a] Excludes two HC–130s destroyed on ground in 1968. Excludes three C–130s destroyed by ground fire in North Vietnam and Laos in nonairlift activities before 1969.

[b] Excludes three C–123s and UC–123s lost in Laos in nonairlift activities before 1969. Includes three UC–123s lost in South Vietnam.

---

* USAF Management Summary, Southeast Asia, Feb 28, 1974.

Appendix 12*

Historic Theater Airlifts (Passengers and Cargo)

	Million Tons
USAF transports in Vietnam, 1962–1972	7
CBI Theater, World War II (40 percent to China, remainder to Burma)	1.75
USAF effort in Berlin airlift, 1948–1949	1.75
USAF effort in Korean War (mainly from Japan to Korea)	0.74

	Tons Per Day
USAF transports in Vietnam, January–December 1968	4,000
Peak effort in Western Europe, September 5–14, 1944	1,700
Peak effort to China, July 1945	2,200
Peak Allied effort to Berlin, late spring 1949	8,000
Deliveries to North Korea, November 1950	1,050

---

* Robert F. Futrell, *The United States Air Force in Korea, 1950–1953* (New York, 1961), p 522; Alfred Goldberg, ed, *A History of the United States Air Force, 1907–1957* (New Jersey, 1957), pp 82–83, 241. *Data is approximate.*

Appendix 12

Notes

Chapter I

The French War in Indochina

1. Department of Defense (*The Pentagon Papers*), *United States–Vietnam Relations, 1945–1967* (Washington, 1971), vol I, pt IV–A–2, pp 1–13. (Hereafter cited as *DOD Pentagon Papers*.)
2. FEAF Historical Study, *Far East Air Forces Support of French Indo-China Operations, 1 July 52–30 Sept 54*, Nov 1, 1954; rprt, Capts Robert Hickey and Robert Lloyd, FEAF Dir/Intel, subj: Visit to Saigon, Indochina, Mar 9, 1954; Rand, *A Translation from the French: Lessons of the War in Indochina,* Col V. J. Croizat, USMC, Ret, tr, vol II, also translated by Battelle Memorial Institute in 3 vols; rprt, Air Force Section, MAAG, Indo–China, subj: Activities Rprt for Jan 54, Feb 10, 1954.
3. Bernard B. Fall, *Street Without Joy: Indochina at War, 1946–54* (Harrisburg, Pa., 1961), pp 169–233.
4. Gen G. J. M. Chassin, French AF, "Lessons of the War in Indochina," *Interavia*, VII (Dec 52), 670–675; Fall, *Street Without Joy*, pp 61–63, 72, 77, 137–179; Rand, *Lessons of the War in Indochina*, II, 146–147, 168–172, 244–258; FEAF Hist Study, *Support of FIC Operations, 1952–54,* pp 15–16; Edgar O'Ballance, *The Indo–China War 1945–1954: A Study in Guerrilla Warfare* (London, 1964).
5. Rand, *Lessons of the War in Indochina*, II, 153–155, 166–167; Bernard B. Fall, *Hell in a Very Small Place: The Siege of Dien Bien Phu* (Philadelphia and New York, 1967), pp 8–34.
6. Hq USAF, *Summary of Mutual Defense Assistance: Program and Progress,* Nov 53 and Jul 54; Chassin, "Lessons of the War in Indochina," *Interavia*, VII (Dec 52), 670–675; FEAF Hist Study, *Support of FIC Operations, 1952–54*.
7. Msg TS–3011, Hq USAF (AFMMS-OT) to CINCUSAFE, 052020Z May 53; msg VO–025 Cdr, Cdr FEAF to CSAF (personal Twining to Weyland), 192353Z Jan 54, both in NA, RG 341, OPD 381; ltr, Brig Gen Albert Hewitt, AF Section, MAAG Indo–China, thru CSAF to Sec Def, subj: "Report of Fact Finding Group," Apr 6, 1954; Hq USAF, *Summary of Mutual Defense Assistance: Program and Progress*, Nov 52, Apr 53, and Dec 53.
8. Msg MG–728D, MAAG, Indo-China (Trapnell) to Sec Def, May 1, 1953; ltr, Brig Gen Albert Hewitt, AF Section, MAAG Indo–China, thru CSAF to Sec Def, subj: "Report of Fact Finding Group, 6 Apr 54"; rprt, Capts Robert Hickey and Robert Lloyd, FEAF Dir/Intell, Visit to Saigon, Indo–China, Mar 9, 1954.
9. Rand, *Lessons of the War in Indochina*, II, 299–305, 336, 384–385; Fall, *Hell in a Very Small Place,* pp 16–17; Hq USAF, *Summary of Mutual Defense Assistance: Program and Progress,* Nov 53.
10. FEAF Hist Study, *Support of FIC Operations, 1952–54,* pp 24–64; memo, JCS to Sec Def (JCS 1992/221), subj: Aid to French Airlift Capability in Indo–China, May 20, 1953; msg MG–747D2, MAAG, Indo–China (Trapnell) to Hq USAF, Mar 24, 1954; ltr, Maj J. F. Johnson to Cdr, 6410th Materiel Control Gp, subj: Trip Rprt of Maintenance Team to Indo–China, Aug 52; rprt, AF Sect, MAAG, Indo–China, subj: Monthly Activ Rprt for Jan 54, Feb 10, 1954.
11. Msg 382, Saigon to Sec State, Aug 15, 1952, in NA, RG 341, OPD 381; intvw, Dr. J. C. Hasdorff and Brig Gen Noel F. Parrish, with Gen O. P. Weyland, USAF, Ret, Nov 19, 1974.
12. Msg 1149, US Embassy, Saigon, to Sec State, Dec 5, 1952, in *DOD Pentagon Papers*, vol I, p A–25; JCS Historical

693

Study, *History of the Indochina Incident, 1940-1954,* 1955, reprinted 1971, pp 266-267; msg MG-3846-A, Ch MAAG Indo-China (Trapnell) to OSD, 140505Z Aug 52; memo, William C. Foster, Dep Sec Def, for JCS, subj: Requirement for Additional Transport Aircraft in Indo-China, Sep 12, 1952; msg TS-7978, Hq USAF (AFOOP-OC-T) to Ch MAAG, Fr and Cdr FEAF, 201558Z Sep 52.

13. Msg 1149, US Embassy, Saigon, to Sec State, Dec 5, 1952, in *DOD Pentagon Papers,* VIII, 538-539; msg 1286, Sec State to US Embassy, Saigon, 221821 Dec 52, in *DOD Pentagon Papers,* VIII, 540; JCS Hist Study, *Hist of the Indochina Incident,* pp 267-268, 307; msg TS-9673, Hq USAF (AFCVC) to CG FEAF, 242353Z Dec 52; msg MG-4090D, Ch MAAG Saigon to CG, 24th Air Depot Wg and 315AD, 222350Z Oct 52, in NA, RG 341, OPD 381; ltr, Capt L. E. Beckett to Cdr 6410 MCG, subj: Trip Report of Supply Team sent to Indo-China to Initiate Proj Sea Dog, n.d., (1952).

14. Hist, Dir/Opns, Hq USAF, Jan-Jun 53, pp 197, 201; msg TS-2925, Hq USAF (AFOOP-OC-T) to CG FEAF (personal White to Weyland), 302210Z Apr 53; msg VC 0459, Cdr FEAF (D/O RQMT) to Hq USAF, 130513Z Jul 53.

15. Note, Marshall Jean de Lattrede Tassigny, to CSA, subj: Memorandum on MDAP Materiel for Indo-China, Sep 20, 1951; memo, Dir/Plans, Hq USAF, for Gen Lee, subj: Aide Memoire of 12 Jan 52 from the French Ambassador, Feb 7, 1952; aide memoire, Fr Emb Washington, Jan 12, 1952, all in NA, RG 341, OPD 400.3295.

16. Hist, 315th AD, Jan-Jun 54, pp 1-3; intvw, author with Maj Gen Maurice F. Casey, Dir/Transp, Hq USAF, May 24, 1971.

17. Msg C-61640, CINC FE to Dept/Army (personal for Gen Collins), 261457Z Mar 53; msg C-61982, to Dept/Army (for G-3), 180825Z Apr 53; memo, Maj Gen Robert M. Lee, Dir/Plans, Hq USAF, for CSAF, subj: msg from Adm Radford, Apr 27, 1953, all in NA, RG 341, OPD 381; hist, 315th AD, Jan-Jun 53, pp 161-162; Robert F. Futrell, *The USAF in SEA: The Assistance and Combat Advisory Years* (comment edition, Off/AF History, 1972), p 18; MR, Mr. Douglas MacArthur II, Dept/State, ns, Apr 27, 1953; memo, Hon U. A. Johnson, Dept/State, to Sec State, subj: Flying Boxcars (C-119's) for Indochina, Apr 28, 1953, both in *DOD Pentagon Papers,* IX, 38-39; Mark W. Clark, *From the Danube to the Yalu* (New York, 1954), pp 319-322.

18. Msg TS-2937, Hq USAF (AFOOP-OC-T) to CG FEAF, 011325Z May 53; msg V-306-DO, CG FEAF to Hq USAF (personal Gen White from Gen Smart), 050605Z May 53; msg MG-769D, Ch MAAG Saigon to CSAF, 060430 May 53, all in NA, RG 341, OPD 381; FEAF Hist Study, *Support of FIC Operations, 1952-54,* pp 12-13, 42, 211; hist, Dir/Opns, Hq USAF, Jan-Jun 53, p 181; Hq USAF, *Summary of Mutual Assistance: Program and Progress,* Jun 53; JCS Historical Study, *Hist of the Indo-China Incident,* pp 307-309.

19. Hist, Dir/Plans, Hq USAF, Jul-Dec 53, pp 117-119; ltr, Maj Gen Charles Lauzin, Cdr, FAF-IC, to Sec State for Air, "Utilization of C-119's in Indo-China," n.d.; msg VC 0433 D/O, Cdr FEAF to Hq USAF (AFOOP), 300640Z Jun 53; msg VC 0453 D/O to Hq USAF (AFOOP), 090640Z Jul 53, all in NA, RG 341, OPD 381.

20. Msg CG-918-C, Cdr 315th AD to Cdr FEAF, Sep 8, 1953; rprt, Report of U.S. Joint Military Mission to Indo-China (O'Daniel Report), (JCS 1992/246), Nov 13, 1953; hist, 315th AD, Jan-Jun 54, pp 6-10; FEAF Hist Study, *Support of FIC Operations, 1952-54,* pp 208-210; 483rd TCWg, Oplan 4-53, Oct 9, 1953.

21. Hist, 483rd TCWg, Jul-Dec 53, pp 33-34; Hq USAF, *Summary of Mutual Defense Assistance: Program and Progress,* Nov 53 and Jan 54; FEAF Hist Study, *Support for FIC Operations,* pp 106-107; Casey intvw, May 24, 1971; intvw, author with Col Thomas A. Julian, Jun 8, 1971 (Julian was member of 483rd TCWg, and served at Cat Bi through much of Ironage); hist rprt, 315th AD, 315th AD Particip in French Indo-China, Sep 1, 1954, pp 3-4.

22. Msg, Sec State to US Embassy, Paris, and Saigon, 231817L Nov 53.

23. Lt Col Erskine B. Crew, USMC, "La Guerre d'Indochine," in *Marine Corps Gazette,* Apr, May, Jun 66; msg MG-1925A, Ch MAAG Indo-China (Trapnell) to CINCPAC, 010400Z Dec 53; Robert J. O'Neill, *General Giap: Politician and Strategist* (New York and

Washington, 1969), pp 121–144; Fall, *Hell in a Very Small Place*, pp 35, 50; O'Ballance, *The Indo–China War*, pp 170–171; Jules Roy, *The Battle of Dienbienphu* (New York and Evanston, 1965), pp 1–35, 143–147.

24. Ltr, Lt Col Hollis B. Tara, Dir/Opns, 483rd TCWg to Cdr, 483rd TCWg, subj: Statistical Data Ironage, 8 Mar 54; memo, Lt Col Faught, 315th AD, to Cdr, subj: Bulldozers Drops, 5 Jan 54; Casey intvw, May 24, 1971; Roy, *Battle of Dienbienphu*, pp 54–55; Fall, *Hell in a Very Small Place*, pp 16–17; ltr, Maj Gen C. L. Faught, Ret, to author, Nov 24, 1975.

25. Rprt, Capts Robert Hickey and Robert Lloyd, FEAF Dir/Intell, Visit to Saigon, Indochina, 9 Mar 54; Roy, *Battle of Dienbienphu*, pp 36–97; Fall, *Hell in a Very Small Place*, pp 53, 88–89, 96–99.

26. Msg MG–1934A, MAAG Indo–China to Cdr FEAF, 020425Z Dec 53; msg VC–0722 D/O–COD, Cdr FEAF to CINCFE, Tkyo, 050038Z Dec 53; ltr, Lt Col Hollis B. Tara, Dir/Opns, 483rd TCWg, subj: Statistical Data Ironage, 8 Mar 54; briefing text, Hq USAF, for Gen Twining, subj: US Aid for FAF of Indo–China, Mar 54.

27. Hist, 315th AD, Jan–Jun 54, pp 11–26; hist, 483rd TCWg, Jan–Jun 54, pp 32–39; ltr, Lt Col Hollis B. Tara, Dir/Opns, 483rd TCWg to Cdr, 483rd TCWg, subj: Statistical Data Ironage, 8 Mar 54; msg V–0025 Cdr, Cdr FEAF to CSAF (personal Weyland to Twining), 192358Z Jan 54; O'Ballance, *The Indo–China War*, pp 208–211; hist rprt, 315th AD, 315th AD Particip in French Indo–China, Sep 1, 1954, pp 14–17.

28. Msg MG 650-D-1, Cdr FEAF to Ch MAAG Saigon, Mar 18, 1954; memo CM–74–75, CJCS to Pres Spl Committee on Indochina, subj: Discussion with Gen Paul Ely, Mar 29, 1954, in *DOD Pentagon Papers*, IX, 277–279; Roy, *Battle of Dienbienphu*, p 195; Julian intvw, Jun 8, 1971; Casey intvw, May 24, 1971; Battelle Memorial Institute, *Lessons to be Drawn from the War in Indo–China* (3 vols, Columbus, n.d.), III, 148.

29. Intvw, author with Lt Col Benjamin N. Kraljev, Hq USAF, Jan 29, 1971 (Kraljev spent six months at Cat Bi and Tourane as a stand-by crewman, as a Second Lieutenant in 1954); Julian intvw, Jun 8, 1971; Casey intvw, May 24, 1971; hist, 483rd TCWg, Jan–Jun 54, pp 36–37; msg MG 2029D, Ch MAAG to Cdr 483rd TCWg, Dec 16, 1953; rprt, AF Sect MAAG Indochina, MDAP Monthly Activity Rprt, Mar 11, 1954; *DOD Pentagon Papers*, IX, 240–242; Weyland intvw, Nov 19, 1974.

30. Hist, 315th AD, Jan–Jun 54, pp 30–34, Jul–Dec 54, pp 39–47; hist, FEALOGFOR, Jan–Jun 54, pp 195–196; msg MG 21190, Ch MAAG to FEAF, Dec 30, 1953; Roy, *Battle of Dienbienphu*, p 98.

31. Rprt, Capts Robert Hickey and Robert Lloyd, FEAF Dir/Intell, Visit to Saigon, Indochina, 9 Mar 54; Julian intvw, Jun 8, 1971; intvw, author with Col Donald Pricer, USAF, Ret, Washington, DC, Oct 20, 1970 (Pricer was member of 62nd TCSq at Ashiya in 1953–54, visiting Cat Bi periodically, and became commander of the 483rd Wing Det at Tourane during summer 1954); Casey intvw, Mar 24, 1971; hist, 315th AD, Jan–Jun 54, pp 25, 31, 54, Jul–Dec 54, p 37; hist, 483rd TCWg, Jul–Dec 53, p 33, Jan–Jun 54, p 36.

32. FEAF Hist Study, *Support of FIC Operations, 1952–54*, pp 139–145; memo CSAFM 11–54, CSAF to JCS; subj: Steps the US Might Take . . . (JCS 1992/270), Jan 13, 1954; msg TS–7323, Hq USAF AFOOP-OC, to Cdr FEAF and Ch MAAG Indochina, 302339Z Jan 54; MRs, Brig Gen C. H. Bonesteel, US Army, Off Asst Sec Def (ISA); subj: Mtg of President's Spl Committee on Indochina, 29 Jan 54, 30 Jan 54, in *DOD Pentagon Papers*, IX, 240–242; Weyland intvw, Nov 19, 1974.

33. Ltr, Lt Col Kenneth F. Knox, USAF, Ret, to author, Oct 25, 1970; diary excerpts, Maj Kenneth F. Knox, 1954 (Knox was commander of the Do Son detachment): FEAF Hist Study, *Support for FIC Operations, 1952–54*, pp 108–114, 146–184, 188–197; paper, 6424th ADWg, subj: 6424th Air Depot Wing Support in FIC, 1954; Hq USAF, *Summary of Mutual Assistance: Program and Progress*, May 54, Jun 54; *DOD Pentagon Papers*, vol I, pt V–A–2, p 17; IX, 245, 277–279.

34. Study, Lt Col Courtney L. Faught, Dir/Opns and Tng, 315th AD, subj: Study of Lessons Learned in FIC Operations, Nov 15, 1954; Julian intvw, Jun 8, 1971; FEAF Hist Study, *Support for FIC Operations, 1952–54*, pp 87–88, 104–106; hist, 315th AD to Cdr FEAF,

subj: 315th AD Support in Indo–China, Apr 26, 1954; 483rd TCWg OPORD 16–54, Apr 12, 1954.

35. Roy, *Battle of Dienbienphu*, in full; Fall, *Hell in a Very Small Place*, pp 107–289; Gen Vo Nguyen Giap, Dien Bien Phu, (USAF Academy reprint 6-4397–12), pp 122–125.

36. Battelle Memorial Institute, *Lessons to be Drawn from the War in Indo-China*, I, 65–72, 120–126; III, 152; ltr, 315th AD OPROC to Cdr 315th AD, subj: High Altitude Delayed Parabundle Drops, May 28, 1954; hist, 483rd TCWg, Jan–Jun 54, pp 36–39, 55; hist, 315th AD, Jan–Jun 54, pp 13–24; Roy, *Battle of Dienbienphu*, p 93; Fall, *Hell in a Very Small Place*, pp 248–249, 327–377, 453; Julian intvw, Jun 8, 1971; Casey intvw, May 24, 1971.

37. Fall, *Hell in a Very Small Place*, pp 327–453; hist, 315th AD, Jan–Jun 54, p 26; *DOD Pentagon Papers*, vol I, p A–20.

38. Study, MACV J–5, Dien Bien Phu-Khe Sanh, Mar 68; memo, Maj Gen W. E. Dupuy, SACSA, for Dir/Joint Staff; subj: Comparison of the Khe Sanh Campaign Dien Bien Phu, Jan 31, 1968; Maj Fletcher K. Ware, US Army, "Perspective: Dien Bien Phu," in *Infantry*, May–Jun 65; "An Interview with Bernard Fall," in *Marine Corps Gazette*, Apr 67, pp 10–11.

39. Msg MG 1488-D-3, Ch MAAG Saigon to CINCFE, May 22, 1954; hist, 315th AD, Jan-Jun 54, pp 30–87; FEAF Hist Study, *Support for FIC Operations, 1952-54*, pp 102–103, 161; Casey intvw, May 24, 1971; Julian intvw, Jun 8, 1971; Pricer intvw, Oct 20, 1970.

40. Msg 560-C, 315th AD to FEAF (to Partridge from McCarty), June 10, 1954; msg A–6141, Cdr FEAF to CSAF, 010744Z Jul 54; hist, 315th AD, Jan–Jun 54, pp 49–50; memo, JCS to Sec Def, subj: Withdrawal of C-119 Acft and Supporting Personnel from Indo-China (JCS 1992/352), Jul 8, 1954; hist rprt, 315th AD, 315th AD Particip in Fr Indochina, Sep 1, 1954, p 15.

41. FEAF Hist Study, *Support for FIC Operations, 1952-54*, pp 150–151, 195–196; paper, 6424th ADWg, subj: 6424th Air Depot Wing Support in FIC, 1954; hist, 315th AD, Jan–Jun 54, pp 61–63; 483rd TCWg OPORD 28-54, Jun 25, 1954.

42. Hist, 315th AD, Jan–Jun 54, pp 64–77.

43. Memo, Col Frank G. Jamison, Dir/Plans and Policy, Dep/Opns, FEAF, to Maj Gen Jacob E. Smart, Dep/Opns, FEAF, subj: Clarification of Hanoi Evacuation, Jul 29, 1954; Kraljev intvw, Jan 29, 1971; FEAF Hist Study, *Support for FIC Operations, 1952-54*, pp 249–251, 270–274; hist, 315th AD, Jan–Jun 54, p 57; memo, Hq USAF, AFOPD-PL, for CSAF, subj: Status of Plans for Aid to French in Event they Evacuate the Tonkin Delta, June 24, 1954: *DOD Pentagon Papers*, vol II, pt IV-A-5, tab 1, pp 9–10.

Chapter II

The Troop Carrier Idea, 1954–1961

1. Wesley F. Craven and James L. Cate, eds, *The Army Air Forces in World War II* (Chicago, 1958), II, 446–460; III, 554–562; VI, pp 622–625; Col Samuel T. Moore, *Tactical Employment in the U.S. Army of Transport Aircraft and Gliders in World War II* (AAF Historical Office, 1946); Lt Gen Lewis H. Brereton, *The Brereton Diaries* (New York, 1946), pp 308–365; rprt, IX Troop Carrier Command, Supply by Air, Nov 20, 1944; Lt Col Robert L. Goerder, "The Progression of Tactical Air Transport and Its Role in South East Asia," (term paper, Georgetown Univ, pp 38–64); Riley Sunderland, "Burma: The Supply Problem," in Basil Liddell Hart and Barrie Pitt, eds, *History of the Second World War* (London, 1967), pp 1761–1792, 2577–2583; USAF Historical Study 75, *Air Supply in the Burma Campaigns* (RSI, Air University, 1957).

2. Robert Frank Futrell, *The United States Air Force in Korea, 1950-1953* (New York, 1961), pp 12-13, 73-74, 149-150, 148-327, 521-536; hist, 315th AD, Jan-Jun 51, pp 60-90, 109-115, 177-178, 222-226, Jul-Dec 51, pp 1-8, 206-217, Jan-Jun 52, pp 171-185, Jul-Dec 53, pp 1-17, 38, Jan-Jun 55, pp 27-36; Capt Annis G. Thompson, *The Greatest Airlift: The Story of Combat Cargo* (Tokyo, 1954); Lt Gen William H. Tunner, *Over the Hump* (New York, 1964); ltr, Maj Gen William H. Tunner, Cdr 315th AD, to CG FEAF, Jan 24, 1951.

3. AFM 1-9, Air Doctrine: Theater Airlift Operations, Jul 1, 1954; hist, 18th AF, Jul-Dec 53, I, 169; study, 18th AF, Concept of Troop Carrier Operations, 1955-58, 1953; Robert Frank Futrell, *Ideas, Concepts, Doctrine: A History of Basic Thinking in the USAF, 1907-1964* (Air Univ; second printing, 1974), pp 198-199.

4. Rprt, TAC, World Wide Troop Carrier Conference, 17-19 Jan 56; ltr, OPR-G, Hq 18th AF, to Cdr TAC, subj: A Concept of Operations for Tactical Air Power and Related Airfield Criteria Requirements Forecast, Jan 7, 1955; rprt, ODO, Hq 18th AF, Final Report, Exercise Sage Brush, 29 Dec 55; hist, 18th AF, Jan-Jun 54, pp 268-269; Jan-Jun 55, p 105; hist, TAC, Jan-Jun 60, p 7; *DOD Pentagon Papers,* vol I, pt II, p B-5.

5. Rprt, TAC, World Wide Troop Carrier Conference, 17-19 Jan 56, pp 92-93; study, Operations Analysis Directorate, TAC, A Review of Tactical Combat Airlift from 1956 to 1970, Aug 56, pp 2-22.

6. Rprt, Panel Report II of the Special Studies Project (Rockefeller Report), International Security—The Military Aspect, 1958; hist, TAC, Jul-Dec 58, pp 50-60, Jul-Dec 60, pp v-vi; James M. Gavin, *War and Peace in the Space Age* (New York, 1958), pp 92-179; draft memo CSARM, CSA (Taylor), subj: Army Requirements for Airlift, 1958; ltr, CSAF to CSA, May 13, 1958.

7. Rprt, TAC, World Wide Troop Carrier Conference, 17-19 Jan 56; hist, Dir/Plans, Jan-Jun 57, pp 140-141; prepared statement, Maj Gen C. L. Childre, Dir/Opns, Hq TAC, subj: Tactical Airlift Requirements and Capabilities, 1960; hist, TAC, Jul-Dec 59, pp 33-49, 338, Jan-Jun 60, pp 35, 68, Jul-Dec 61, pp 445-447; study, ACSC, Air University, Research Study 105b: Deployment Mobility of Composite Air Strike Force to the Far East, Mar 58; study, ACSC, Air University, Research Study 103b: Composite Air Strike Force in Southeast Asia, 1958.

8. Gavin, *War and Peace in the Space Age,* pp 227, 271-272; FM 57-35, Airmobile Operations, Nov 60 (supersedes FM 57-35, 10 Jun 58); Theodore H. White, "Tomorrow's Battlefield: An Interview with General Gavin," *Army Combat Forces Journal,* Mar 55; Maj Gen James M. Gavin, "Cavalry, And I Don't Mean Horses," in *Armor,* May 54, pp 19-22; Lt Gen John J. Tolson, *Airmobility, 1961-1971* (Dept/Army, Vietnam Studies, 1973), pp 3-14.

9. First Ind (ltr, Hq Army Ground Forces to AAF, subj: Air Transport of Airborne Assault Units, Jun 22, 1946), AAF to AGF, Aug 7, 1947; ltr, TORQ-D, TAC to Dir/Reqmts, Hq USAF, "Assault Transport Acft Requirement," Apr 17, 1952; draft USAF Hist Study 134, "Troop Carrier Aviation in USAF, 1945-1955," (RSI, Air University), pp 30-32; hist, TAC, Jul-Nov 50, pp 328, 39; Margaret C. Bagwell, *Case History of the C-123 Airplane (26 Apr 45-7 Sep 51)* (Hist Office, AMC, 1952); hist, Dir/Plans, Hq USAF, Jul-Dec 60, pp 51-52; hist, 464th TCWg, Jan-Jun 61, p 30; study, 18th AF, Fixed Wing Assault versus Heavy Drop, 1956; Col John H. Herring, "Should the Air Force Continue Development of Troop Carrier Type Aircraft"? (AWC Thesis, Air Univ, May 58), pp 88-90.

10. Memo, CSAF (Vandenberg) to CSA, subj: Army Organic Aircraft, Oct 12, 1950; draft USAF Hist Study 134, "Troop Carrier Aviation in USAF, 1945-1955," (RSI, Air University), pp 33-34; ltr, TCORQ, TAC, to Dir/Reqmts, Hq USAF, subj: Military Characteristics for Light Assault Cargo Helicopter, Feb 18, 1951; hist, TAC, Jul-Nov 50, pp 286, 311-312, Jul-Dec 51, V, 25, Jan-Jun 52, V, 29; Futrell, *USAF in Korea,* pp 533-543.

11. Study, 18th AF, Troop Carrier Concept for Employment of Assault Helicopters, [ca 1954]; rprt, DCS/Ops, Hq TAC, TAC Operational Plan for the H-21B Aircraft, Dec 15, 1954; stf study, 16th TCsq Test Project Board, Test Project T-3-52 (Test Drop), Sep 27, 1952 and Oct 30, 1952; stf study, Hq

USAF, Air Force Helicopter Program, 1954; 1st Ind (ltr, Hq 18th AF to Cdr TAC, subj: Activation Troop Carrier Squadron, Helicopter, Jan 7, 1952), TAC to 18th AF, Jan 15, 1952; hist, 18th AF, 1 Jan–30 Jun 1955, I, 158–160; hist, TAC, 1 Jul–31 Dec 1952, vol I; 1 Jul–31 Dec 1954, I, 14, 1 Jan–30 Jun 1955, I, 1; AFM 1–9, Jul 1, 1954, p 2.

12. Ltr, Maj Gen D. W. Hutchinson, DCS/Opns, TAC, to CSAF, subj: Provision of Airlift by Rotary-wing Assault Aircraft to the Army, Dec 27, 1954; memo, Gen Charles L. Bolte, Vice CSA, for CSAF, subj: Requirement for AF Support by Rotary-wing Aircraft, Feb 16, 1954; memo, CSAF, for CSA, subj: Provision of Airlift by Rotary-wing Assault Aircraft for the Army, Jan 17, 1955; Hq TAC to Cdr 18th AF, Apr 12, 1956, 1st Ind to Ltr, 18th AF to TAC, subj: Proposed Operational Concept for H–21B Aircraft, Mar 23, 1956; hist, TAC, Jan–Jun 55, V, 31–32; draft ms, Capt Stephen B. Webber, "Air Support for the Ground Forces: The Evolution of Roles and Missions for Army Aviation 1949–1967," 1974.

13. First Ind, (ltr, TODR–K, Hq 18th AF, to TAC, subj: Proposed Operational Concept for H–21B Aircraft, Mar 23, 1956), TAC to 18 AF, Apr 12, 1956; TAC Reg 20–14, Mission and Functions of Helicopter Squadrons, Aug 31, 1956; hist, 18th AF, Jan–Jun 56, p 128, Jan–Jun 55, pp 35, 52–53; hist, TAC, Jan–Jun 56, pp 29–30, Jan–Jun 57, p 10; hist, 315th AD, Jan–Jun 56, pp 3–4, 34–41, Jan–Jun 60, p 46.

14. Address by Maj Gen Chester E. McCarty, Cdr 18th AF, in rprt, TAC, World Wide Troop Carrier Conference, 17–19 Jan 56; ltr, Maj Gen Chester E. McCarty, Cdr 18th AF, to Maj Gen D. W. Hutchinson, DCS/Opns, Hq TAC, Mar 6, 1956.

15. Atch to ltr, Lt Gen J. K. Gerhart, DCS/Plans and Pol, to CSAF; subj: Army Aviation Requirements, Oct 17, 1960; hearings, Senate Subcommittee of the Committee on Appropriations, *DOD Appropriations for 1960*, 86th Congress, 1st Session, pp 74–75, 115–116, 961; memo, Col H. D. Edson, USA, Acting Dir/Army Avn, to Dep Dir/Materiel Programs, DCS/Materiel, Hq USAF, subj: Army Plan—Procurement of the AC–1 Fixed Wing Acft, 1960.

16. Gen Maxwell D. Taylor, *The Uncertain Trumpet* (New York, 1959), pp 178–180; FM 55–4, Transportation Movements in Theaters of Operations, Dec 59; FM 57–35, Airmobile Operations, Nov 60; rprt, Army Staff, Army Aviation Guidelines for the Development of Doctrine and Organization through 1961, Feb 14, 1957.

17. Ltr, Lt Gen J. K. Gerhart, DCS/Plans and Pol, to CSAF, subj: Army Aviation Requirements, Oct 17, 1960.

18. Minutes, 464th TCWg, Flying Safety Council Mtg, Sep 6, 1960; memo, 50th TCSq to Dir/Opns 314th TCWg, subj: Final Rprt of Exercise Swift Strike III, 2–23 Aug 63, Sep 3, 1963; memo, Gen Maxwell Taylor, CSA, to CSAF, subj: USCONARC–TAC Joint Airborne Operations Manual, Sep 24, 1958; memo, TPL, Hq TAC, to Dir/Plans, Hq TAC, subj: Joint Exercises, Jul 29, 1960; hist, TAC, Jan–Jun 57, pp 250, 333, 346, Jan–Jun 58, pp 47–48, Jan–Jun 60, pp 44–49, Jan–Jun 62, pp 515–518.

19. Hist, Dir/Plans, Hq USAF, Jan–Jun 60, p 182, Jul–Dec 60, p 113, Jan–Jun 61, pp 194–195; MR, Brig Gen Jerry Page, Dep Dir/Plans for War Plans, DCS/Plans and Pol, Hq USAF, and Brig Gen C. E. Hutchin, Dir/Strat Plans and Pol, Army Staff, subj: AF–Army Aviation Requirements and Capabilities, Feb 17, 1961; ltr, Lt Gen J. K. Gerhart, DCS/Plans and Pol, to AFCCS, subj: Army Aviation Expansion, Feb 6, 1961; ltrs, Lt Gen J. K. Gerhart, DCS/Plans and Pol, to CSAF, subj: Army Aviation Requirements, Oct 17, 1960 and Nov 14, 1960; ltr, Gen Thomas D. White, CSAF, to Gen George H. Decker, CSA, Oct 19, 1960.

20. SMAMA Historical Study 21, *C–130 Production and Support* (Sacramento AMA, Apr 58), pp 29–43, 59–60; rprt, JATB, 1953 Airborne Conference, Nov 53, pp 52, 137, 159–163; hist, 314th TCWg, Jul–Dec 59, p 12; hist, 18th AF, Jul–Dec 55, pp 38–46, 82, Jan–Jun 56, pp 13–16, 163–166, Jul–Dec 56, pp 52, 88–89, Jan–Jun 57, pp 82, 87.

21. SMAMA Hist Study 21, *C–130 Production and Support*, pp 44–46, 65–66; hist, TAC, 1958 through 1963; rprt, Air Provg Ground Cd, Employment and Suitability Test . . . of the C–130A Medium Troop Carrier/Transport Aircraft, Jul 9, 1957, pp 1–3.

22. Hist, 483rd TCWg, Jan–Jun 58, pp 10–18, Jul–Dec 58, pp 1–24, Jan–Jun

59, pp 1–46, Jan–Jun 60, pp 1–3, 56–63; hist, 315th AD, Jan–Jun 57, pp 17–20, Jul–Dec 57, pp 12–15; Jan–Jun 59, p 16, Jan–Jun 60, p 50; Jacob Van Staaveren, *Air Operations in the Taiwan Crisis of 1958* (USAF Hist Div Liaison Off, Nov 62), pp 21, 71–72.

23. Hist, 315th AD, Jul–Dec 57, pp 1–6; hist, PACAF, 1967, pp 80, 93; Lt Col B. A. Whitaker and Mr. L. E. Paterson, *Assault Airlift Operations*, (Hq PACAF, Proj CHECO, Feb 23, 1967), pp 7–8; WTO Instruction 4600.i, Common User Intra-theater Air Transportation, Sep 11, 1961.

24. Ltr, Gen Emmett O'Donnell, Cdr PACAF, to Gen Curtis E. LeMay, Vice CSAF, May 22, 1961; hist, Dir/Programs, Hq USAF, Jul–Dec 61, pp 24–27; hist, 315th AD, 1958 through 1962.

25. Hist, TAC, Jan–Jun 60, p 7; hist, 315th AD, 1958 to 1962.

26. Hist, TAC, Jan–Jun 60, pp 74–77; rprt, 50th TCSq, AU–15 CASF Participation, Jan 15, 1959; ltr, Hq 314th TCWg to Cdr, 839th AD, subj: Final Rprt of 19th AF Exercise 192-60 (Mobile Yoke), Jul 27, 1960.

27. Rprt, Off/Opns Analysis, Hq TAC, C–130 Aircrew Work Load Survey, Jan 62; hist, 314th TCWg, Jul–Dec 61, p 5, Jan–Jun 61, p 11; hist, TAC, Jan–Jun 61, pp 140–163, 173, 354–355, Jul–Dec 61, pp 149–154; Leverett G. Richards, *TAC: The Story of Tactical Air Command* (New York, 1961) ch 12.

28. *DOD Pentagon Papers*, vol I, pt II, pp B–8 and B–10; memo, JCS to Sec Def, subj: Studies with Respect to Possible US Action Regarding Indochina, May 26, 1954, and study, NCS Action no 1074A, Apr 5, 1954, both in *DOD Pentagon Papers*, vol IX, pt V–B–3, pp 310–311, 487–493; memo, JCS to Sec Def, subj: US Military Participation in Indo-China, May 20, 1954 (JCS 1992/316); memo, CSAF to JCS, subj: US Air Forces for Possible Military Courses of Action in Indochina, Apr 7, 1952; memo, Hq USAF, AFOOP–OP, for Maj Gen Ramey, subj: Initial Indo–China USAF Augmentation, Apr 6, 1954, all in NA, RG 341; msg V–DO–0215, Cdr FEAF to subord units, May 4, 1954.

29. Hist, Dir/Plans, Hq USAF, Jul–Dec 56, pp 141–142, Jan–Jun 58, p 86; memo, JCS to Sec Def, subj: US Policy in Event of a Renewal of Aggression in Vietnam, Sep 9, 1955 (JCS 1992/479); memo SM–582–56, JCS to CINCPAC, subj: Contingency Plan for US Military Participation in Event of Viet Minh Aggression in Vietnam, Jul 11, 1956 (JCS 1992/547); study, Joint Staff, Feasibility Study of Air Transportation Requirements of CINCPAC OPLAN 45-56, Feb 11, 1959 (JCS 2251/3).

30. Hist, Dir/Plans, Hq USAF, Jan–Jun 57, p 122, Jan–Jun 60, pp 66–67; AF Comments Memo 14–59, subj: CINCPAC OPLAN 32 (L)–59, Insurgency Phase—Laos, Aug 24, 1959; memo, J–4 Joint Staff, to JCS, subj: Transportation Requirements for Capabilities of Augmentation CINCPAC OPLAN 32 (L)–59; memo JCSM 716-61, JCS for Sec Def, subj: Concept of Use of SEATO Forces in South Vietnam, Oct 9, 1961; in *DOD Pentagon Papers*, vol XI, pt V–B–4, p 297; hist, CINCPAC, 1959, p 212.

31. Hist, 483rd TCWg, Jan–Jun 58, pp 10–18.

32. Hist, 315th AD, Jan–Jun 61, p 52; hist, CINCPAC, 1959, p 212, 1961, pp 62, 84–97; hist, TAC, Jan–Jun 61, pp 395–396.

33. Hist, 315th AD, Jan–Jun 61, p 46; hist, CINCPAC, 1961, pt II, pp 84–97; chronological study, JCS Hist Div, subj: Significant Events Concerning the Laotian Crisis, May 19, 1961; intvw, Lt Col Robert Zimmerman with Col Harry S. Coleman, Ret, 1975 (Coleman was sent as a "civilian employee" into Laos in 1961 to develop facilities at Vientiane and help the Laotian Air Force); msg, 315th AD to PACAF, 150710Z Dec 60.

34. *The Pentagon Papers as Published by the New York Times* (New York, 1971), p 89; memo of conversation, Dept/State, subj: Laos, 29 Apr 61, in *DOD Pentagon Papers*, vol XI, pt V–B–4, p 62.

35. Study, Joint Staff, Air and Sea Lift, Readiness and Posture of Laos, (JCS/1992/912), Feb 3, 1961; paper, JCS, subj: Defense of SEA, (JCS 2339/11), Aug 7, 1961; preliminary paper, Joint Staff J–5, subj: Assignment of Additional Army Forces to PACOM, (J–5 P815), Dec 15, 1961; msg, PACAF to CSAF, 050230Z Oct 61.

36. Charles H. Hildreth, *USAF Counterinsurgency Doctrines and Capabilities, 1961–1962* (Off/AF Hist), Feb 1964, pp 1–9; hist, Dir/Plans, Hq USAF, Jan–Jun 62, pp 255–258; *New York Times*,

Mar 29, 1961; memo, McGeorge Bundy, Sp Asst to President for Natl Security Affairs, NSAM-2, to Sec Def, subj: Development of Counterguerrilla Forces, Feb 3, 1961, in *DOD Pentagon Papers*, vol XI, pt V-B-4, bk 1, p 17.

37. Study, ASI, Air University, AU-411-62, The Role of Airpower in Guerrilla Warfare (World War II), Dec 62, pp 20-27, 65, 146-162, 198-208; study, Rand RB-3656-PR, Unconventional Warfare in the Mediterranean Theater, Jul 63; Monro MacCloskey, *Alert the Fifth Force* (New York, 1969); study, ASI, Air University, AU-411-62, Guerrilla Warfare and Airpower in Korea, 1950-1953, Jan 64; John H. Napier, III, "The Air Commandos in Vietnam, 5 Nov 61 to 7 Feb 65," (MA Thesis, Auburn Univ, 1967).

38. RAF, Ministry of Defence, *The Malayan Emergency, 1948-1960* (June 1970), pp 75-122, 150-153; study, ASI, Air University, AU-411-62, *The Accomplishments of Airpower in the Malayan Emergency (1948-1960)*; study, ASI, Air University, AU-411-62, *Guerrilla Warfare and Airpower in Algeria, 1954-1960*, Mar 65; study, Rand RM-3867, A Symposium on the Role of Airpower in Counterinsurgency and Unconventional Warfare, Mar 64.

39. Hildreth, *USAF Counterinsurgency . . . 1961-62*, pp 8-9; rprt, Dir/Opns, Hq USAF, Final Operational Concept, Jungle Jim, Apr 27, 1961; hist, Dir/Opns, Hq USAF, Jan-Jun 61, pp 213-214, 226-227; hist, TAC, Jan-Jun 61, pp 20-21, 272; intvw, Corona Harvest intvw no 219 with Brig Gen Benjamin H. King, Sep 4, 1969; intvw, 2nd AD historian with Lt Col Miles M. Doyle, Cdr Det 2, 1st ACGp, Feb 16, 1963; ltr, Col Robert L. Gleason, Hq Air Univ, to author, subj: Comments on Draft Historical Study, Dec 30, 1971 (Gleason was a member of Jungle Jim and a commander of the detachment in Vietnam in 1962); intvw, Dr. Thomas Belden with Gen Curtis E. LeMay, Ret, Mar 29, 1972.

40. Intvws, author and Maj Victor B. Anthony, Off/AF Hist, with Maj Roy H. Lynn, Sep 9, 1970, and with Maj James D. Carson, Sep 18, 1970 (both officers were members of Jungle Jim and the early detachment in Vietnam); hist, Special Air Warfare Center, Apr-Dec 62; King intvw, Sep 4, 1969.

41. Hildreth, *USAF Counterinsurgency . . . 1961-62*, pp 10-13; memo, JCS to Sec Def, subj: Presidential Requirement for Report on Sub-Limited Warfare, Jan 8, 1962 (JCS 1969/276).

42. MR, Col Edward G. Lansdale, Dep Asst to Sec Def/Spl Opns, subj: Pacification in Vietnam, Jul 15, 1958; *DOD Pentagon Papers*, vol II, pt IV-A-5, tab 3, p 59; rprt, Opns Coordinating Board, Rprt on SEA (NSC 5809), Jan 7, 1959, in *DOD Pentagon Papers*, vol X, pt V-B-3, pp 1166-1168; dispatch 278, US Embassy, Saigon, Mar 7, 1960, in *DOD Pentagon Papers*, vol X, pt V-B-3, p 1254.

43. Study, CINCPAC, Counterinsurgency Operations in South Vietnam and Laos, Apr 26, 1960; study, MACV, Military Assistance to SVN, 1960-63, 1964; msg, JCS to CINCPAC, Mar 24, 1960 (JCS 1992/791); *DOD Pentagon Papers*, vol II, pt IV-A-5, pp 34-35; pt IV-A-5, tab 1, pp 26-27; pt IV-A-5, tab 4, p 83.

44. Asst for Mutual Security, DCS/Materiel, Hq USAF, *Journal of Mutual Security*, May 1957 through Sep 1959; MR, CINCPAC, subj: Meeting Held at Independence Palace, Saigon, 29 Sep 61; ltr, Gen Emmett O'Donnell, Cdr PACAF, to CINCPAC, subj: Visit to SEA, Dec 12, 1961; Capt Mack D. Secord, "The Viet Nam Air Force," in *Air University Review*, Nov-Dec 63, pp 60-67.

45. McGeorge Bundy, The White House, NSAM-52, May 11, 1961; msg 72144, Hq USAF (XPD), to PACAF, for Col Yudkin, 201340Z May 61; *DOD Pentagon Papers*, vol II, pt IV-B-1, pp 43-46.

46. Memo, Eugene M. Zuckert, Sec AF, to Sec Def, subj: Experimental Command for Sub-Limited War, Sep 19, 1961; memo, Sec Def to Service Secretaries, subj: Experimental Command for Sub-Limited War, Sep 5, 1961; memo, Sec Def to JCS, subj: 4400th CCTS, Oct 3, 1961; *DOD Pentagon Papers*, vol II, pt IV-B-1, pp 84-85, 100-108; vol XI, pt IV-B-4, p 328; vol XII, pt V-B-4, p viii; Hildreth, *USAF Counterinsurgency . . . 1961-62*, pp 12-14.

47. Study, DOD, JCS, and Services, Summary of Lesser Courses of Action in South Vietnam, in JCS 2343/27, Oct 19, 1961; study, British Advisory Mission,

Saigon, Appreciation of Vietnam for Nov 61–Apr 62, Oct 27, 1961.

48. Rprt, Gen Taylor's Mission to South Vietnam, Nov 3, 1961; memo, Sec Def and Sec State, to President, subj: Actions with Respect to South Vietnam, Nov 11, 1961; NSAM–111, The White House to Sec State, Nov 25, 1961, also printed in, *DOD Pentagon Papers*, vol XI, pt V–B–4, p 149; hist, Dir/Plans, Hq USAF, Jul–Dec 61, pp 176–177; Gen Maxwell D. Taylor, *Swords and Plowshares* (New York, 1972); *DOD Pentagon Papers*, vol II, pt IV–B–1, pp 1–22, 79, 120–123; vol XI, pt V–B–4, pp 359, 400; Jacob Van Staaveren, *USAF Plans and Policies in South Vietnam, 1961–1963*, (USAF Hist Div Liaison Off, Jun 65), pp 9–13.

49. Memo, Sec Def to JCS and Service Secretaries, subj: South Vietnam, in JCS 2343/55, Dec 7, 1961; memo, Secretary, Joint Staff, to Control Div, Joint Staff, subj: South Vietnam, Nov 28, 1961; msg 70240, DCS/Plans and Prog, Hq USAF, to TAC, 122400 May 61; DJSM–374–67, subj: South Vietnam, Nov 14, 1961; talking paper, Hq USAF, subj: Current Situation, S. Vietnam, Nov 6, 1961; background paper, Hq USAF, subj: JCS 2343/43, Nov 27, 1961; rprt, J–3, Joint Staff, Project Beef-up Status Report, Nov 27, 1961 and Dec 5, 1961; hist, 346th TCSq, Dec 61.

50. Study, DOD, JCS, and Services, Summary of Lesser Courses of Action in South Vietnam, in JCS 2343/27, Oct 19, 1961; rprt, J–3, Joint Staff, Project Beef-up Status Report, Dec 12 and Dec 18, 1961.

51. Rprt, Gen Taylor's Mission to South Vietnam, Nov 3, 1961; rprt, J–3, Joint Staff, Project Beef-up Status Report, Nov 27, 1961; aide memoire, Ch MAAGV, to President, Diem, in JCS 2343/10, Aug 10, 1961; memo, Lt Gen B. Hamlett, DCS/Mil Opns, US Army, to Dir/Joint Staff, subj: Movement of US Army Helicopter Units for South Vietnam, Nov 15, 1961; msg 2042, Joint Staff to CINCPAC, Oct 30, 1961.

52. Background paper, Hq USAF, subj: Status of Air Force Actions, South Vietnam, Nov 29, 1961; talking paper, Hq USAF (AFOOP–DE), subj: Tactical Control Capability, South Vietnam, Nov 28, 1961; Van Staaveren, *Plans and Policies, 1961–63*, pp 16–20; Proj CHECO *Southeast Asia Report, October 1961–December 1963*, IV, 23–28; hist, 2nd ADVON, Nov 61–Oct 62, pp 1–15; hist, 13th AF, Jan–Jun 63, I, 1–11.

53. Record, CINCPAC, Sec Def Conference, Dec 19, 1961.

Chapter III

Farm Gate and The Air Commando Tradition

1. King intvw, Sep 4, 1969; memo, Brig Gen Edward G. Lansdale for Sec Def, subj: Vietnam—4400th CCTS, Oct 17, 1961; hist, 2nd ADVON, Nov 15, 1961–Oct 8, 1962, p 7; msg, CINCPAC to CSAF, 280335Z Oct 61; msg, PACAF to CSAF, (exclusive for Gerhart from O'Donnell), 100516Z Nov 61; intvw, Corona Harvest no 220, author with Maj Gen Edward G. Lansdale, Sep 9–10, 1969 (Lansdale accompanied the Taylor group).

2. Telephone intvw, author with Maj Richard C. Tegge, Charleston AFB, SC, Sep 25, 1970; form 5a records of Maj Richard C. Tegge; hist, TAC, 1 Jul–31 Dec 61, I, 62–64, 289, 496; hist, 2nd ADVON, Nov 15 1961–Oct 8, 1962, p 8; hist, Special Air Warfare Center (SAWC), Apr 27–Jul 31, 1962, pp 11–13.

3. Msg, PACAF to 13th AF, 042300Z Dec 61; msg, CINCPAC to PACAF and Chief, MAAG–V, 202238Z Dec 61; rprt, J–3, Joint Staff, Project Beef-up, Military Actions resulting from NSC Meeting 11 Nov 61, Nov 27, 1961; rprt, Hq USAF, Report of Air Force Study Group on Vietnam, May 64; hist, CINCPAC, 1961, pp 181–182.

4. Lynn intvw, Sep 9, 1970; Carson intvw, Sep 18, 1970; msg, PACAF to

13th AF, 042300Z Dec 61; rprt, J–3, Joint Staff, Project Beef-up Status, Dec 26, 1961; MACV Directive 62, subj: Operational Restrictions on US Aircraft in SVN, Nov 24, 1962; ltr, Gen Paul D. Harkins, Cdr MACV, to Ambassador Nolting, Apr 25, 1963 and atch; rprt, Hq USAF, Report of Air Force Study Group on Vietnam, May 64.

5. Msg, PACAF to 13th AF, 042339Z Dec 61; msg, CINCPAC to PACAF and Chief, MAAG–V, 202338Z Dec 61; talking paper, Air Staff, subj: Command and Control of Jungle Jim, file dated Nov 28, 1961; King intvw, Sep 4, 1969; diagram, Farm Gate Request System, in hist, SAWC, 27 Apr–31 Jul 62; hist, 2nd ADVON, 15 Nov–8 Oct 62, pp 130–131; book on Actions in SEA, 1961–64, Hq USAF, [ca 1965]; comments on ms, Col Robert L. Gleason, Dec 30, 1971.

6. Carson intvw, Sep 18, 1970; rprt, Capt Alton M. Smith, Farm Gate Tour Rprt, 1962; rprt, Capt James S. Young, 1st AAC, EOTR, 1963.

7. Msg 0290B, 2nd ADVON to Dep IG for Safety, et al, 111535Z Feb 62; msg 0292B, 2nd ADVON to Dep IG for Safety, et al, 120445Z Feb 62; hist, SAWC, Apr 27–Dec 31, 1962; comments on ms, Col R. L. Gleason, Dec 30, 1971.

8. Msg. 2–10372, TAC to PACAF, 200535Z Feb 62; msg 2–1160A, 13th AF to PACAF, 210800Z Feb 62; Carson intvw, Sep 18, 1970; Lynn intvw, Sep 9, 1970; rprt, Capt R. J. Nielsen, 1st ACS, EOTR, Sep 11, 1963.

9. Memo, Dr. Jacob A. Stockfisch, Off/Asst Sec Def, Comptroller, for Mr. Leon Gilgoff, AFABF, subj: Informal Discussion with AF Personnel on COIN Proposal, Jun 19, 1962; memo, Hon Eugene M. Zuckert, Sec AF, for Sec Def, subj: USAF COIN Capability, Aug 29, 1962; addendum, Off/Sec AF, Addendum to USAF COIN Force PGP, Aug 3, 1962; CSAF Policy Book, 1963; Hildreth, USAF Counterinsurgency . . . 1961–1962, pp 14–16, 29–30, 43–45.

10. Carson intvw, Sep 18, 1970; Lynn intvw, Sep 9, 1970; "The Air Commandos," in Airman, Sep 62; rprt, Tactics Board, 34th Tact Gp, C–47 Tactics, 1964; Tegge intvw, Sep 25 and 30, 1970; hist, SAWC, Apr 27–Dec 31, 1962, Jan–Jun 63; rprt, Lt Col Robert L. Gleason, Cdr Det 2A (Farm Gate), EOTR, 1962; Charles W. Gray, "Air Logistics Resupply," in hist, 2nd Air Div, Jul–Dec 64; comments on ms, Col R. L. Gleason, Dec 30, 1971.

11. Rprts, 1st Comb Applie Gp, HRT–2A Beacon, Jan 20, 1963; PFNS (Navigation Aids), Jan 20, 1963; HF Receiver (SARAH), Feb 20, 1963; In-flight Pickup System, Apr 20, 1963; Low Frequency Wilcox System, Apr 20, 1963; ILAS (TALAR), May 20 and Nov 20, 1963; DZ–IZ Locator System, Aug 20, 1963; Doyle intvw, Feb 16, 1963; briefing text, Brig Gen Gilbert L. Pritchard, Cdr SAWC, for Gen Sweeney, Nov 23, 1964; hist, SAWC, Apr 27–Dec 31, 1962, p 62; Jan 1–Jun 30, 1963, I, 261, Jan 1–Jun 30, 1964; I, 188.

12. Ltr, Capt Thomas H. O'Brien, ALO, Combined Studies Div, to Dep Dir JACC, 2nd Air Div, subj: Operation Hurricane II, June 6, 1963; ltr, Capt Thomas H. O'Brien, ALO, Combined Studies Div, to Dep Dir JAOC, 2nd Air Div, subj: Operation Hurricane III, Jul 1, 1963; rprt, Maj David E. Grange, Jr, Trip Report, Airborne Operation, Jun 3–5, 1963; MACV Duty Officer Log, Jun 26, 1963.

13. Msg 1953J, PACAF to Dir/Opns and Dir/Plans, Hq USAF, 292330Z Sep 62; msg 4682, J–5 MACV to CINCPAC, 071137Z Nov 62; JCS 2343/175, Dec 4, 1962; msg 63–772, JACC 2nd Air Div, to J–2 and J–3 MACV, 081600Z Feb 63; rprt, Asst CS/Ops PACAF, Draft Concept of Operations, Augmented Farm Gate, Jan 3, 1963.

14. Rprt, Det 1, 34th Tact Gp, Historical Data Rprt, Jul 1–Dec 31, 1963; msg 63A 23–146, 2nd Air Div to 13th AF, 230943Z Jan 63; hist, SAWC, Apr 27–Dec 31, 1962, p 179, Jan 1–Jun 30, 1963, I, 148; hist, 2nd Air Div, Jan 1–Jun 30, 1964, p 24; hist, 34th Tact Gp, Jul 1–Dec 31, 1964, pp 13–14; Lynn intvw, Sep 9, 1970.

15. Rprt to the President, Off/SecAF, Proj Farm Gate, Feb 62; msg PS–4628, Ch MAAGV to CINCPAC, 230441Z Dec 61; memo, Lt Col Robert L. Gleason, Cdr Det 2A, subj: Sect V, Psychological Warfare, [ca Mar 1, 1962]; msg, PACAF to DCS/Plans and Progr, Hq USAF (Exclusive for Gerhart from O'Donnell), 201010Z Feb 62; msg 3595, CJCS to CINCPAC, 121710Z Mar 62; Van Staaveren, Plans and Policies, 1961–63, pp 23–25.

16. Rprt, Lt Col Robert L. Gleason, Cdr Det 2A (Farm Gate), EOTR, 1962;

rprt, Hq PACAF, Alert Commitment in RVN, Jul 20, 1963; briefing text, Brig Gen Rollen H. Anthis, Cdr 2nd ADVON, for Sec Def, Jul 23, 1962; briefing text, 2nd ADVON, for Sec Def, May 6, 1963; rprt, Hq PACAF, Night Operational Activities, RVN, Apr 3, 1963; telephone intvw, author with Maj Robeson S. Moise, USAF Academy, Colo, Oct 6, 1970; King intvw, Sep 4, 1969; Carson intvw, Sep 18, 1970.

17. Ltr, Lt Gen James Ferguson, DCS/R&D, Hq USAF, to Maj Gen Joseph H. Moore, Cdr 2nd Air Div, Nov 12, 1964; msg 18669, MACV to CSAF, 290955Z Dec 64; ltr, 2nd Air Div to PACAF, 13th AF, subj: Development of New Tactics and Techniques, Jan 14, 1963; msg 3976, Ch MAAG-V to CINCPAC, 010829Z Sep 62; hist, 2nd Air Div, Jul 1–Dec 31, 1964, I, 62; Lt Col Jack S. Ballard, *The Air Force in SEA: Development and Employment of Fixed Wing Gunships* (Off/AF Hist, Jan 74).

18. Rprt, 2nd Air Div, Operational Test and Evaluation of U-10B in Vietnam, Jun 1, 1963; hist data rprts, 1st Air Cdo Sq, Jul–Dec 63, Jan–Jun 64, Jul–Dec 64; hist, SAWC, Jan–Jun 63, I, 147, 158–159, 180–185.

19. Carson intvw, Sep 18, 1970; Lynn intvw, Sep 9, 1970; telephone intvw, author with Maj Richard C. Tegge, Sep 30, 1970; CMSgt Edson T. Blair, "The Air Commandos," in *Airman*, Sep 62; Doyle intvw, Feb 16, 1963; intvw, 2nd Air Div Hist Off with Lt Col Charles E. Trumbo, Dir/Plans, 2nd Air Div, Jul 13, 1963.

20. Lynn intvw, Sep 9, 1970; Carson intvw, Sep 18, 1970; Tegge intvw, Sep 30, 1970; rprt, Capt Ronald R. Ellis, 1st AC Sq, EOTR, Jul 65; rprt, Maj Leland L. Johnson, 1st AC Sq, EOTR, Apr 65; rprt, 1st Lt Wells T. Jackson, 1st AC Sq, EOTR, [ca 1963]; rprt, 1st Lt Andrew W. Bianeur, 1st AC Sq, EOTR, Sep 10, 1963; rprt, Lt Col Garth L. Reynolds, DCO 34th Tact Gp, EOTR, Jun 65; hist, SAWC, Jan–Jun 64, p 197; msg CCR, 13AF to PACAF, 110557Z Mar 62.

21. EOTRs, 1st Lt Dale C. Holt, Sep 63; Capt Harry G. Rudolph, Oct 63; Capt Leland L. Johnson, Apr 65; 1st Lt Wells T. Jackson, 1963; Glenn E. Frick, Jul 20, 1963; Lt Col Doyle, Cdr Det 2A, Feb 6, 1963; Capt Ronald C. Ellis, Jul 65; Capt Richard C. St. John, Apr 18, 1963; Capt James L. Harper, Apr 18, 1963; Maj William W. McDannel, 1963 (all were Farm Gate crewmen or supervisors).

22. Rprt, Capt Robert C. Walker, Farm Gate Det, EOTR, Dec 15, 1962; rprt, Air Staff, Gen LeMay Visit to SVN, Apr 62; briefing text, 2nd ADVON, briefing for Lt Gen Moorman, Aug 62; Carson intvw, Sep 18, 1970; *PACAF Review*, Mar 62; CMSgt E. T. Blair, "The Air Commandos," in *Airman*, Sep 62.

23. Ltr, Col James G. Fussell, Asst DCS/Opns, 13th AF, to Cdr 13th AF, subj: Rprt of Staff Visit to 2nd Air Div, 1–6 Nov 62, Nov 9, 1962.

24. Ltr, Lt Gen Thomas S. Moorman, Vice Cdr PACAF, to Brig Gen Rollen H. Anthis, Cdr 2nd Air Div, Oct 23, 1962; ltr, Brig Gen Rollen H. Anthis, Cdr 2nd Air Div, to Lt Gen Thomas S. Moorman, Vice Cdr, PACAF, Nov 12, 1962; ltr, Brig Gen Rollen H. Anthis, Cdr 2nd ADVON, to Brig Gen Gilbert L. Pritchard, Cdr SAWC, Aug 4, 1962; msg 73-3A, 5th AF to 313rd Air Div, 300631Z Jan 63; msg 23-878, 2nd Air Div to 13th AF, 231355Z May 63; hist, 13th AF, Jan 1–30 Jun 1963, vol I, p III–149.

25. Rprt, Maj Thomas W. Riley, Det 2A, EOTR, Oct 8, 1962; rprt, Capt Harry G. Rudolph, 1st AC Sq, EOTR, 1963; memo, 1st CAGp, to Col Benjamin H. King, Cdr, 1st CAGp; subj: Debriefing of Maj Robert Gourtz, Dec 28, 1962; ltr, Vice Cdr, 2nd ADVON to 13th AF, subj: Items Relating to Activities in 2nd ADVON Area, Jun 10, 1962; hist, 13th AF, Jul 1–Dec 31, 1963, vol I, pp III–166 to III–168; Lynn intvw, Sep 9, 1970; Carson intvw, Sep 18, 1970.

26. Hist, SAWC, Jul 1–Dec 31, 1964; I, 40–41; Lt Col C. L. Glines, "The Most Meritorious Flight of the Year," *Airman*, May 65; Lynn intvw, Sep 9, 1970; Carson intvw, Sep 18, 1970.

27. Hist, SAWC, Apr 27–Dec 31, 1962, pp 67, 126–127, Jan 1–Jun 30, 1963, I, 63–64, 150–151, Jul 1–Dec 31, 1963, I, 6–8, 123; release, AF News Service, subj: Air Force Needs More Applicants for SAWC Duty, May 7, 1963; msg 11880, TAC to CSAF (XOPI), 222231Z Nov 63; msg 3-1-2902, TAC to PACAF, 291901Z Jan 63; rprt, Lt Col Miles M. Doyle, Cdr Det 2A, 1st Air Cdo Gp, EOTR, Feb 6, 1963.

28. Rprt, Capt Jack B. Harvey, 1st AC Sq, EOTR, Apr 65; rprt, Capt Ronald R. Ellis, 1st AC Sq, EOTR, Jul 65, Lynn intvw, Sep 9, 1970; msg 199G, 2nd Air Div to PACAF (for Gen Martin from Gen Henderson), Jul 5, 1963.

29. Hist, 13th AF, Jul 1–Dec 31, 1963, I, I–12; rprt, Lt Col Garth L. Reynolds, DCO/Opns, 34th Tact Gp, EOTR, Jun 65; rprt, 1st Lt Wells T. Jackson, 1st AC Sq, EOTR, [ca 1963]; rprt, 1st Lt Andrew W. Blancur, 1st AC Sq, EOTR, Sep 10, 1963; rprt, Capt Roy H. Lynn, 1st AC Sq, EOTR, 1963; Lynn intvw, Sep 9, 1970; Carson intvw, Sep 18, 1970.

30. Hist Data Rprt, 1st Air Cdo Sq, Jul–Dec 64; rprt, Lt Col Jack Robinson, Cdr 1st Air Cdo Sq, to Cdr, 34th Tact Gp, subj: Effect of Battle Damage, Living and Working Conditions on Flight Crew Performance, 1963; rprt, 34th Tact Gp, Summary Battle Damage, 1963, Dec 31, 1963; rprt, Lt Col Garry Oskamp, ALO Sp Forces, ALO Rprt for Sep 63, Oct 1, 1963.

31. Msg 68953, Dir/Plans, Hq USAF, to TAC, 052035Z Nov 63; Brig Gen Gilbert L. Pritchard, Cdr SAWC, "Commander's Appraisal," in Hist, SAWC, Jan 1–Jun 30, 1964; ltr, Col Earl J. Livesay, Dir/Ops, Hq SAWC, to Hq, 1st Spec Forces Gp (Airb), subj: Request for Doctrinal Information, May 7, 1964; hist, SAWC, Jul 1–Dec 31, 1963, I, 1, 5, 124–125, Jul 1–Dec 31, 1964, I, 1–2, 7–8, 126–127; rprt, Dir/Materiel, 9th AF, to Cdr, 9th AF, Materiel Activities rpt for week ending 22 Feb 63, Feb 25, 1963.

32. Ltr, Cdr C–47 Section to Cdr, 1st AC Sq, subj: Semi-annual Summary of C–47 Operations, Jul 10, 1964; rprt, Capt R. J. Nielsen, 1st AC Sq, EOTR, Sep 11, 1963; rprt, Capt Jack B. Harvey, 1st AC Sq, EOTR, Apr 65; rprt, Capt Ronald R. Ellis, 1st AC Sq, EOTR, Jul 65; rprt, Capt Leland L. Johnson, 1st AC Sq, Apr 65; intvw, 2nd Air Div, with Col William E. Betheu, Cdr 34th Tact Gp, [ca 1964]; hist, 34th Tact Gp, Jan 1–Jun 30, 1964.

Chapter IV

The Dirty Thirty and the Vietnamese Air Force Transport Arm

1. Hist, 13th AF, Jul–Dec 63, pp II–60 to II–62; Capt Mack D. Secord, "The Viet Nam Air Force," in *Air University Review*, Nov–Dec 63, pp 60–67; JCS 2099/367, subj: Vietnamese Air Force, Mar 25, 1954; briefing sheet, Hq USAF, Briefing for Gen Twining, subj: US Aid to FAF of Indochina, Mar 54; Hq USAF, *Summary of Mutual Defense Assistance: Program and Progress*, 1952 through 1954.

2. Asst for Mutual Security, DCS/Materiel, Hq USAF, *Journal of Mutual Security* and *Journal of Military Assistance*, 1957 through 1962.

3. MR, Col Edward G. Lansdale, Dep Asst to Sec Def, subj: Pacification in Vietnam, Jul 15, 1958; CSAF briefing book, Hq USAF, Apr 62; Asst for Mutual Security, DCS/Materiel, Hq USAF, *Summary of Mutual Defense Assistance: Program and Progress, Journal of Mutual Security*, and *Journal of Military Assistance*, 1952 through 1961; background book, PACAF, for Gen Moorman presentation before Congressional committee, [ca Jan 1963].

4. Record, CINCPAC, Record of Sec Def Conferences, Jan 15, 1962, Feb 19, 1962, Mar 21, 1962; info book, 2nd ADVON, Agenda and Information Book for Gen Anthis for Sec Def Conference, Feb 62.

5. Ltr, Lt Col Charles P. Barnett, USAF, Ret, to author, Oct 31, 1970, and attached questionnaire; info books, 2nd ADVON, Agenda and Information Books for Gen Anthis for Sec Def Conferences, Feb, Mar, and May 1962; Asst for Mutual Security, DCS/Materiel, Hq USAF, *Journal of Military Assistance*, Jun 62, p 179; ltr, Brig Gen Rollen H. Anthis, Cdr 2nd Air Div, to Hon Eugene M. Zuckert, Sec AF, Jan 9, 1963.

6. Questionnaire, Maj Robeson S. Moise, Sep 70; questionnaire, Lt Col Kenneth H. MacCammond, Oct 70; telephone conversation, author with Maj Robeson S. Moise, USAF Academy, Aug 26, 1970; intvw, author with Lt Col Harold L. Sweet, Sep 4, 1970; intvw, author with Maj Kendall G. Lorch, Aug 28, 1970; MSgt Gordon L. Poole, "Dirty Thirty," *Airman*, Oct 63; ltr, Lt Col Charles P. Barnett, USAF, Ret, to author, Oct 31, 1970.

7. Questionnaire, Maj Robeson S. Moise, Sep 70; questionnaire, Lt Col Kenneth H. MacCammond, Oct 70; telephone conversation, author with Maj Robeson S. Moise, USAF Academy, Oct 6, 1970; Sweet intvw, Sep 4, 1970; Lorch intvw, Aug 28, 1970; MSgt Gordon L. Poole, "Dirty Thirty," *Airman,* Oct 63; telephone conversation, author with Lt Col Harold L. Sweet, USAF, Ret, Washington, DC, Sep 9, 1970; hist, 13th AF, 1962, pp II–103 to II–106; ltr, Maj Charles P. Barnett, to author, Oct 31, 1970; information book, 2nd ADVON, Agenda and Information Book for Gen Anthis for Sec Def Conference, May 62; intvw, author with Maj Charles B. West, May 5, 1970; ltr, Capt Louis A. Klenkel, II ASOC to Dep Dir/II ASOC, subj: USAF Activities at Plateau Gi, Apr 30–May 8, 1963; msg 2913, Chief, MAAG, Vietnam, to CSAF, 180654Z Jul 62.

8. Pamphlet, Air Force Sect, MAAGV, Information to USAF Augmentation Pilots, 1963; discussion, author with Maj Sylvester Johnson, Washington, DC, Aug 25, 1970; hist, 13th AF, 1962, pp II–103 to II–106; questionnaire, Maj Robeson S. Moise, Sep 70; telephone conversation, author with Maj Robeson S. Moise, USAF Academy, Aug 26, 1970; Sweet intvw, Sep 4, 1970; Lorch intvw, Aug 28, 1970.

9. Questionnaire, Maj Robeson S. Moise, Sep 70; questionnaire, Lt Col Kenneth M. MacCammond, Oct 70; Sweet intvw, Sep 4, 1970; MSgt Gordon L. Poole, "Dirty Thirty," *Airman*, Oct 63; ltr, Brig Gen Rollen H. Anthis, Cdr 2nd Air Div, to Lt Gen Thomas S. Moorman, Vice Cdr PACAF, Nov 12, 1962; MR, Col Harvey E. Henderson, Dep Cdr, 2nd Air Div, subj: Visit by National War College Group, Mar 26, 1963; *Aviation Week and Space Technology*, Aug 20, 1962, p 75.

10. Sweet intvw, Sep 4, 1970, Lorch intvw, Aug 28, 1970; study, AF Advisory Group Intelligence Section, SVN Air Force, Jan 65; msg, 172D, 2nd Air Div to 13th AF (personal to Maddux from Moore), Apr 21, 1964; msg 188D, 2nd Air Div to PACAF (personal for Arnett from Moore), Apr 29, 1964.

11. Telephone conversation, author with Maj Kendall G. Lorch, Sep 24, 1970; Lorch intvw, Aug 28, 1970; Sweet intvw, Sep 4, 1970; msg 2286–63, PACAF to Dir/Plans, Hq USAF, 292019Z May 63; ltr, Maj Gen Rollen H. Anthis, Cdr 2nd Air Div, to MACV J–5, subj: Revised Phase-out of US Forces, Oct 1, 1963; msg, CINCPAC to JCS, 212109Z Oct 63.

12. Questionnaire, Lt Col Kenneth M. MacCammand, Oct 70; questionnaire, Maj Robeson S. Moise, Sep 70.

13. Rprt, Hq USAF, Report of CSAF Visit to SVN, Apr 16–21, 1962; msg 62–1395, 2nd ADVON to 13th AF (for Milton from Anthis), Apr 21, 1962; msg PFLDC 1132–62, PACAF to Hq USAF (AFXDC and AFSMS), 100636Z Aug 62; ltr, Hq MACV to CINCPAC, subj: Comprehensive Plan for SVN, Dec 7, 1962.

14. Background paper, Dir/Plans, Hq USAF, subj: Expansion of VNAF Fighter Squadrons, Nov 64; msg, CINCPAC to JCS, 172130Z Jun 64; msg 9820, JCS to CINCPAC, 091805Z May 63; CSAFM 101–63, CSAF to JCS, subj: Comprehensive Plan for SVN, Mar 4, 1963; msg 2CCR–64–271F, 2nd AD to PACAF (exclusive from Gen Moore to Gens Moorman and Maddux), subj: Expansion of VNAF Fighter Sqs, Jun 1, 1964.

15. Ltr, Brig Gen Robert F. Worden, Dep Dir/Plans, Hq USAF, to DCS/Plans and Progr, Hq USAF, subj: The Situation in South Vietnam, Dec 17, 1962, and atch; msg 1273, Chief, MAAG, Vietnam, to CINCPAC, 280753Z Aug 63; msg 64–226E, 2nd Air Div to CSAF *et al*, 152000Z May 64; rprt, Office/Sec AF, Rprt of AF Study Gp on Vietnam, May 64; draft ms, Warren A. Trest and Jay E. Hines, "Air Training Command's Support of Forces in SEA, 1961–73," Hq ATC, 1977, pp 168–175.

16. Memo, Col Winston P. Anderson, Dir/Opns, 2nd Air Div, to Cdr 2nd Air Div, subj: Memo for Gen Anthis, Apr 5, 1963; rprt, 13th AF Team, Staff Visit Rprt, RVN, 6–20 Jan 64; memo, CS/

MACV to Cdr, MACV, subj; Meeting with Secretary Thuan, Jun 12, 1963; hist, 2nd Air Div, Jul 1–Dec 31, 1964, III, 40–47; hist, Dir/Plans, Hq USAF, Jan 1–Jun 30, 1964, pp 219–221.

17. Talking paper, Hq USAF, subj: For General LeMay for Sec Def Rprt, Apr 62; rprt, Brig Gen Jack A. Gibbs, Dep Dir/Op Reqmts, Hq USAF, Rprt of Air Force Team's Orientation Team's Visit to SVN, May 25, 1962; rprt, Lt Col Bill A. Montgomery, ALO, I Corps, ALO Rprt for Sep 63, Oct 11, 1963; ltr, Lt Col Charles J. Chenault, Dep Dir/I ASOC, to AOC 2nd Air Div, Nov 13, 1963; msg C–165, Air Attache, Saigon, to CSAF, others, 310850Z Dec 63; background paper, PACAF, for Gen Moorman Presentation to Congressional committee, [ca Jan 1963].

18. Col Lyle D. Lutton, "The Southeast Asia Airlift System," unpub article, [ca Dec 1963]; ltr, Lt Col James F. Sunderman, Ch PIO Br, PACAF Off/Info, to 315th AD, subj: Article, The SEAAS, by Col Lutton, Dec 13, 1963; intvw, author with Lt Col Charles R. Blake, May 6, 1970 (Blake was a member of the USAF C–123 unit in Vietnam in 1962); msg CCR 007–S, 315th AD to PACAF, 250635Z Feb 63; ltr, MACV J–4 to Cdr PACOM, subj: US Airlift Resources RVN, Jun 11, 1963; msg 2CCR–63–312G, 2nd AD to PACAF, 13th AF, 182250Z Jul 63; ltr, Brig Gen Anthis, Cdr 2nd AD, to Maj Gen Glenn Martin, DCS/Plans and Ops, PACAF, Sep 2, 1963.

19. Intvw, author with Maj Charles W. Case, Maxwell AFB, Ala, May 5, 1970; intvw, author with Col Charles W. Borders, Nov 4, 1970; intvw, Maj Dean Gauche, with Col Thomas B. Kennedy, Feb 4, 1964 (Case, Borders, and Kennedy were, respectively, airlift center controller, operations officer, and commander of 315th Troop Carrier Group, the USAF C–123 unit in Vietnam).

Chapter V

Mule Train—The First Year

1. Hist, TAC, Jan 1–Jun 30, 1958, I, 70, Jul 1–Dec 31, 1958, I, 322–324, Jul 1–Dec 30, 1960, I, 343, I, 363–364; hist, 18th AF, Jan 1–Jun 30, 1956, I, 298–299, Jul 1–Dec 31, 1956, I, 24, 263, Jan 1–Jun 30, 1957, I, 103; hist, 464th TCWg, Jul 1–Dec 31, 1959, p 47, Jan 1–Jun 30, 1960, pp 28–29, Jul 1–Dec 31, 1960, pp 32, 49–54, Jan 1–Jun 30, 1961, pp 38–39, 61–62, Jul 1–Dec 31, 1961, pp 39, 61; ltr, 18th AF to Cdr TAC, subj: C–123 Aircraft Effective Analysis, Dec 13, 1956; ltr, Flying Safety Office, 464th TCWg to aircrews, subj: Aircraft Incident, Mar 18, 1960.

2. "C–123B Provider," Mar 20, 1961, in USAF Standard Aircraft/Missile Characteristics, vol II (Brown Book); fact sheet, Pope AFB, Factors and Standards Document, revised Oct 1, 1960.

3. Msg 5345, Dir/Opl Reqmts, Hq TAC, to Cdr AMD, May 31, 1956; Proving Ground Cd, Assault Field Suitability Test of the C–123H, Mar 58; 464th TCWg OPlan 1–62, Jan 19, 1962; hist, TAC, Jul 1–Dec 31, 1956, I, 103–104, Jan 1–Jun 30, 1957, I, 165; rprt, Air Proving Ground Cd, Operational Suitability Test of the C–123B Assault Transport Aircraft, Jan 5, 1956.

4. MR, Maj Charles Porter, 18th AF, subj: Gen McCarty's Comments, [ca 1955], in Supporting Documents to Hist, 18th AF, Jul–Dec 55; rprt, Acft Division, MAAMA, Weapon System Program and Status, C–123 Aircraft, Jun 30, 1959; hist, 18th AF, Jan–Jun 55, p 99, Jul–Dec 55, pp 29–30, 80.

5. Rprt, Air Proving Ground Cd, Operational Suitability Test of the C–123B Assault Transport Aircraft, Jan 5, 1956; rprt, Acft Division, MAAMA, Weapon System Program and Status, C–123 Aircraft, Jun 30, 1959; hist, TAC, semi-annual histories from 1956 through 1959; hist, 18th AF, semi-annual histories, 1954 through 1957.

6. Hist, 464th TCWg, Jan–Jun 60, pp

31–33, Jul–Dec 60, pp 23, 35–40, Jan–Jun 61, pp 47–48, 53–55, Jul–Dec 61, pp 53–56, 103–104; rprt, 464th TCWg, Exercise Swift Strike, Aug 28, 1961; hist, 345th TCSq, in Hist, 314th TCWg, Jan–Jun 60; hist, TAC, 1958 through 1962.

7. Rprt, 346th TCSq, Historical rprt for Dec 61, 1962; hist, 464th TCWg, Jul–Dec 61, pp 50–52; status book, PACAF, Cdr PACAF Book for Dec 61 Sec Def Meeting, Dec 61; West intvw, May 5, 1970; Kraljev intvw, Jan 29, 1971, (West and Kraljev were pilots with the Mule Train squadron, deploying in early 1962).

8. Rprts, 346th TCSq, Historical Rprt for Dec 61 and Jan 62, 1962; hist, 2nd Air Div, Jan–Jun 65, p 75; Kraljev intvw, Jan 29, 1971; West intvw, May 5, 1970; Blake intvw, May 6, 1970, (Blake was a 464th Wing navigator, deploying to the C–123 unit in Vietnam in May 1962).

9. Rprt, Joint Staff, Beef-up Rprt, Jan 3, 1962; hist, 13th AF, Jul–Dec 61, pp 86–87, 1962, p II–70; rprt, 346th TCSq, Historical Rprt for Jan 62, 1962; Kraljev intvw, Jan 29, 1971; Lt Col B. A. Whitaker and L. E. Paterson, *Assault Airlift Operations*, Hq PACAF, Proj CHECO, Feb 23, 1967, p 15.

10. Msg 9738M, Dir/Opns, PACAF to 13th AF, subj: Mule Train Concept of Opns, 081820Z Dec 61; record, CINCPAC, Sec Def Conference, Dec 16, 1961; Book on Actions in SEA, 1961–64, Hq USAF, [ca 1965]; testimony of Gen George H. Decker, CS, US Army, Jan 26, 1962; in Hearings before the Senate Committee on Armed Services, 87th Cong, 2d session, *Military Procurement Authorization, FY 1963*; status book, PACAF, Cdr Book for Dec 61 Sec Def Mtg, Dec 61.

11. Talking paper, PACAF, subj: Air Logistic System, in PACAF Book for Sec Def January Meeting, Jan 62.

12. Ltrs, Col L. J. Mantoux, Ret, to author, Dec 29, 1970 and Jan 27, 1971; hist study, 6492nd Combat Cargo Gp, Prov, *History of Airlift in South Vietnam from Dec 61–Oct 62*, Dec 17, 1962, pp 2–6; hist, 13th AF, Jul 1–Dec 31, 1963, I, II–90 to II–95; Robert F. Futrell, *The USAF in SEA: The Assistance and Combat Advisory Years, 1950–1965* (Comment ed, Off AF Hist, 1972), I, 170–178.

13. Intvw, author with Maj Hugh D. Perry, Pope AFB, Nov 3, 1970; West intvw, May 5, 1970; Kraljev intvw, Jan 29, 1971; rprt, 346th TCSq, hist rprt for Jan 62, 1962; briefing paper, 2nd ADVON, subj: Mule Train Operations, Feb 15, 1962; msg 2022A, 13th AF to PACAF, 161125Z Jan 62; talking paper, Dir/Plans, subj: Major Activities in SVN, Mar 22, 1962; rprts, Hq USAF, Status of Air Force Actions, SVN, Jan 12, Jan 19, and Feb 16, 1962. (Perry was a C–123 pilot with Mule Train, Sep 62–Jan 63).

14. Briefing paper, 2nd ADVON, subj: Mule Train Operations, Feb 15, 1962; West intvw, May 5, 1970; Kraljev intvw, Jan 29, 1971; intvw, author with Maj Bernard J. Clark, Pope AFB, Nov 4, 1970; *PACAF Review*, Mar 62; rprt, J–3 Joint Staff, Project Beef-up Status, Dec 12, 1961; rprt, ACTIV, Employment of CV–2, Feb 1–Jul 31, 1963, pp 45–47; CHECO Rprt, *October 1961–December 1963*, VI, 52; msg 976, PACAF to 13th AF, 302155Z Mar 63; memo, Maj Bob Roark, FAA Ln Off, to Col Evans, Dir/Current Opns, ACS/Opns, PACAF, subj: RVN Airfields for T–37 Operations, Feb 19, 1963; notes, PACAF, COIN Historical Project, Mar 17, 1964.

15. Asst for Mil Security, Hq USAF, *Journal of Military Assistance*, Mar 62; draft outline plan for the Establishment of QRF in SVN, atch to CSAFM 56–62, 1962; *PACAF Review*, Mar 62; Kraljev intvw, Jan 29, 1971; ltr, Lt Col Robert Ingalls, Dir/Combat Plans, 2nd ADVON, to Cdr 2nd ADVON, subj: Briefing of Marine Detachment at Soc Trang, Apr 18, 1962; msg 118, Cdr MACV to OSD/ARPA, 170215Z Mar 62; hist study, 6492nd CCG, *Airlift in SVN, Dec 61–Oct 62*, Dec 17, 1962, p 11; CHECO Rprt, *October 1961–December 1963*, VI, 36–37.

16. Perry intvw, Nov 3, 1970; West intvw, May 5, 1970; Clark intvw, Nov 4, 1970; Kraljev intvw, Jan 29, 1971; hist, TAFTS, p2, May 62.

17. Ltr, Dir/Opns, PACAF to PACAF agencies, subj: Rprt of Staff Visit, 10–20 Apr 62, Apr 25, 1962; hist, 464th TCWg, 1 Jan–30 Jun 62, p 46; rprt, 346th TCSq, historical rprt for Feb–Mar–Apr 62; msg S–21223A, 13th AF to PACAF, 121125Z Mar 62; Kraljev intvw, Jan 29, 1971.

18. Msg 62-0289B, 2nd ADVON to

TACTICAL AIRLIFT

Hq USAF, Dep IG for Flying Safety, et al, 111005Z Feb 62; msg 62–106, PACAF to TAC, 150300Z Mar 62; msg, 2–10519, Dir/Opns, TAC to CSAF, 202105Z Mar 62; talking paper, Dir/Plans, Hq USAF, subj: Major Air Force Activities in SVN, Mar 22, 1962; msg 62–0748C, 2nd ADVON to 13th AF, 311155Z Mar 62; msg 62–0992D, 2nd ADVON to PACAF, 251100Z Apr 62; msg 2–10813, Dir/Opns, TAC, to 9th AF, 042116Z May 62.

19. Rprt, Flying Safety Div, Dir/Aerospace Safety, Summary no 13–63, C–119 and C–123 Aircraft Accident Summary, 1962; msg 216A, 13th AF to Vice Cdr, PACAF, 090630Z May 62; msg 229, Vice Cdr, PACAF to 13th AF, Apr 28, 1962; msg 62–0960D, 2nd ADVON to Dep IG Safety, 220610Z Apr 62; Blake intvw, May 6, 1970; Kraljev intvw, Jan 29, 1971; West intvw, May 5, 1970; hist, 464th TCWg, 1 Jan–30 Jun 62, pp 55–56.

20. Rprt, Flying Safety Div, Dir/Aerospace Safety, Summary no 13–63, C–119 and C–123 Aircraft Accident Summary, 1962; msg 62–1064E, 2nd ADVON to Hq USAF, Dep IG for Safety, et al, 020920Z May 62; msg 0017E, Mule Train Det, 2nd ADVON, to OOAMA, 200410Z May 62; MSgt J. A. George, "Provider: Living Up to Its Name," in *Airman*, Mar 63; ltr, 2nd ADVON to 13th AF, subj: Items Relating to Activities in 2nd ADVON Area, Jun 10, 1962.

21. Rprt, Hq USAF, Status of Air Force Actions, SVN, Feb 16, 1962; ltr, Dir/Opns, PACAF to PACAF agencies, subj: Rprt of Staff Visit, 10–20 Apr 62; West intvw, May 5, 1970; Blake intvw, May 6, 1970; Kraljev intvw, Jan 29, 1971; msg 1–10057, Hq TAC to MAAMA, CSAF, 031647Z Feb 62; msg 62–2518, JOC, 2nd ADVON, to Maint Eng, Hq USAF, Feb 2, 1962; msg 1–1996–62, PACAF to Dir/Opns and Dir/Op Reqmts, Hq USAF, Dec 26, 1962.

22. Record, CINCPAC, Sec Def Conference, Feb 19, 1962; msg MAGCH–72, MACV to CINCPAC, 120711Z Mar 62; rprt, Brig Gen Jamie Gough, Dep Dir/Opl Forces, Hq USAF, Rprt of LeMay Visit to South Vietnam, Apr 62; msg 092 J-4, MACV to CINCPAC, 220841Z May 62.

23. Msg 2–1514A, 13th AF to 2nd ADVON, et al, 070452Z Jun 62; msg, CINCPAC to MACV, 082245Z Jun 62; hist, 2nd ADVON, Nov 61–Oct 62, pp 170–171; msg PFDOP 6043–62, PACAF to 13th AF, 020130Z Jun 62.

24. Ltr, Dir/Opns PACAF, to PACAF agencies, subj: Rprt of Staff Visit, 10–20 Apr 62, Apr 25, 1962; msg 62–1219C, PACAF to TAC (personal for Gen Disosway from Gen Hetherington), 102200Z Mar 62; msg 03–313, TAC to PACAF (personal from Gen Disosway for Gen Hetherington), 152055Z Mar 62; msg 3067, PACAF to Dir/Opns, Hq USAF, subj: Mule Train Rotation, May 10, 1962; hist, TAC, 1 Jan–30 Jun 62, I, 651–652; hist, 464th TCWg, 1 Jan–30 Jun 62, pp 50–51; hist, 464th CAM Sq, 1 Jan–30 Jun 62; TAC Programming Plan 129–62, Jun 20, 1962; West intvw, May 5, 1970.

25. Msg 62–1537G, 2nd ADVON to Dep IG for Safety, 190840Z Jul 62; msg 62–1589G, 2nd ADVON to Dep IG for Safety 020515Z Aug 62; msg, 2nd ADVON to Dep IG for Safety, 180955Z Jul 62; rprt, Flying Safety Div, Dir/Aerospace Safety, Summary no 13–63, C–119 and C–123 Aircraft Accident Summary, 1962; Blake intvw, May 6, 1970; Kraljev intvw, Jan 29, 1971.

26. Rprt, Flying Safety Div, Dir/Aerospace Safety, Summary no 13–63, C–119 and C–123 Aircraft Accident Summary, 1962; ltr, Dep Cdr, 13th AF to Cdr 13th AF, subj: Report of Staff Visit to 2nd Air Div, 1–6 Nov 62, Nov 9, 1962; Clark intvw, Nov 4, 1970; rprt, TAFTS-P2, Historical Data, Oct–Nov 62; msg 7–220R, 2nd Air Div to 13th AF, 191526Z Nov 62.

27. West intvw, May 5, 1970; ltr, Col William T. Daly, Cdr 464th TCWg, to Gen Walter C. Sweeney, Cdr TAC, subj: Trip Report, SEA, Aug 15, 1962; ltr, Col William T. Daly, Cdr 464th TCWg, to Maj Gen Richard T. Coiner, Cdr 5th AF, Oct 30, 1962; ltr, Col W. T. Daly, Cdr 464th TCWg, to Brig Gen R. H. Anthis, Cdr 2nd ADVON, Oct 29, 1962; Col Lyle D. Lutton, "The Southeast Asia Airlift System," unpub article, [ca Dec 1963].

28. Ltr, Dep Cdr, 13th AF to Cdr 13th AF; subj: Report of Staff Visit to 2nd Air Div, 1–6 Nov 62, Nov 9, 1962; ltr, Brig Gen Rollen H. Anthis, Cdr 2nd Air Div, to Lt Gen Thomas S. Moorman, Vice Cdr, PACAF, Nov 12, 1962; ltr, Col William T. Daly, Cdr 464th TCWg,

to Brig Gen Rollen H. Anthis, Cdr 2nd ADVON, Oct 29, 1962.

29. Hist, 464th TCWg, Jul–Dec 61, p 79, Jan–Jun 62, pp 45–54; hist, 346th TCSq, Jan–Feb–Mar 62; Perry intvw, Nov 3, 1970 (Perry was Mule Train pilot and former supply officer at Pope, Sep 62–Jan 63); ltr, Lt Col Floyd Shofner, Cdr Mule Train, to Brig Gen Anthis, Cdr, 2nd ADVON; subj: Mule Train Problem Areas, May 12, 1962; ltr, Col William T. Daly, Cdr, 464th TCWg, to Gen Sweeney, Cdr TAC, subj: Trip Rprt, SEA, Aug 15, 1962; West intvw, May 5, 1970; Kraljev intvw, Jan 29, 1971.

30. Perry intvw, Nov 3, 1970.

31. Hist, 2nd ADVON, 15 Nov 61–3 Oct 62, pp 67–70, 76–77, 184–195; Blake intvw, May 6, 1970; intvw, author with Maj Hugh D. Perry, Nov 4, 1970; Kraljev intvw, Jan 29, 1971; Clark intvw, Nov 4, 1970; West intvw, May 5, 1970; ltr, Dir/Opns PACAF, to PACAF agencies, subj: Rprt of Staff Visit, 10–20 Apr 62, Apr 25, 1962; hist, 464th TCWg, 1 Jan–30 Jun 62, p 45; msg 6–665A, 13th AF to PACAF, 130406Z Jun 62.

32. Rprt, Gen Emmett O'Donnell, Cdr PACAF, Summary, Air Posture, SVN, Apr 62; ltr, Dir/Opns PACAF, to PACAF agencies, subj: Report of Staff Visit, 10–20 Apr 62, Apr 25, 1962; Kraljev intvw, Jan 29, 1971; Blake intvw, May 6, 1970; Perry intvw, Nov 4, 1970; *Air Force Register*, Jan 1, 1962.

33. CSAFM 56–62, Feb 20, 1962; concept paper, Hq USAF, Concept for the Establishment of Quick Reaction Forces in SVN, 1962; Brig Gen Jamie Gough, Dep Dir/Opl Forces, Hq USAF, Rprt of LeMay Visit to SVN, Apr 62; LeMay intvw, Mar 29, 1972.

34. CSAM 64–62, Mar 1, 1962; brief, Dir/Plans, subj: JCS 2343/85 (Quick Reaction Forces in SVN), Mar 1, 1962; JCSM 70–62, subj: Draft Outline Plan for the Establishment of QRF in SVN, Mar 13, 1962; JCS 2343/85, Mar 5, 1962; ltr, Gen Curtis E. LeMay, CSAF to Sec Def, subj: Establishment of QRF in SVN, Apr 4, 1962; rprt, DCS/Plans and Programs, Hq USAF, Status Report, May 10, 1962; MR, Off/Sec AF, subj: Attached Rprt to the President, Mar 2, 1962; Brig Gen Jamie Gough, Dep Dir/Opl Forces, Hq USAF, Rprt of LeMay Visit to South Vietnam, Apr 62; msg 85592, Dir/Plans, Hq USAF, to PACAF (personal for O'Donnell), May 4, 1962; Van Staaveren, *Plans and Policies, 1961–63*, pp 22–23; msg 2256, Vice Cdr PACAF to USAF (personal for Gen Burchinal from Gen Moorman), 080415Z May 62; hist, 2nd ADVON, 15 Nov 61–8 Oct 62, pp 164–165.

35. Msg 62–0564C, 2nd ADVON to PACAF, 120630Z Mar 62; msg 21271A, 13th AF to PACAF, 220930Z Mar 62; Kraljev intvw, Jan 29, 1971.

36. Msg 21271A, 13th AF to PACAF, 220930Z Mar 62; ltr, Dir/Opns, PACAF, to PACAF agencies, subj: Rprt of Staff Visit, 10–20 Apr 62, Apr 25, 1962; rprt, Lt Col Howard E. Reaves, Cdr TAFTS-P2, EOTR, Aug 2, 1962.

37. CSAFM 56–62, Feb 20, 1962 and Atch.

38. Intvw, author with Lt Col Richard D. Kimball, Pope AFB, Nov 4, 1970; Clark intvw, Nov 4, 1970; bulletin, PACAF Tactics/Techniques, Bulletin 7, Troop Carrier/Transport Tactics in SEA, May 23, 1965; hist, 18th AF, 1951 through 1956; hist, 315th Air Div, 1 Jan–30 Jun 57, I, 44–45; rprt, Hq 18th AF, Troop Carrier Pathfinder Conference, May 21–24, 1952.

39. Blake intvw, May 6, 1970; Sweet intvw, Sep 4, 1970; ltrs, Maj E. R. McCutchan, ALO Abn Bde, to JOC ALO/FAC Div, 2nd ADVON, subj: Rprt of ALO Activities for Period Ending 3 Aug 62; *ibid.*, 24 Aug 62; ltr, Lt Col James Martin, ALO Abn Bde, to AOC 2nd Air Div, subj: Daily Activities Rprt, Jan 2, 1964; brief, Hq USAF, subj: Air Base Security in SVN, Aug 26, 1964.

40. Lorch intvw, Aug 28, 1970.

41. DJSM 150–62, subj: Bien Hoa Operation of 21 Jan 62, Feb 3, 1962; msg 62–30B, 2nd ADVON to PACAF (pass to Gen Anthis), 190030Z Feb 62; information book, 2nd ADVON, Book for Gen Anthis for Sec Def Conference, May 62.

42. Msg 62–0564C, 2nd ADVON to PACAF, 120630Z Mar 62; msg, US Embassy, Saigon, to Sec State, 100247Z Mar 62; information book, 2nd ADVON, Book for Gen Anthis for Sec Def Conf, Mar 62.

43. Msg PFOCC-S 62–113, quoted in msg 03–086, 13th AF to 2nd ADVON, 180605Z Mar 62.

44. Ltr, Lt Col C. J. Bowers, Dep Dir/JOC, 2nd ADVON, to Lt Col Mann,

Dep/Dir I ASOC, subj: Special Instructions for ALOs, Jul 62.

45. Blake intvw, May 6, 1970; questionnaire, Maj Robeson S. Moise, USAF Academy, to author, Sep 70; briefing text, Lt Col Earl Strong, 2nd ADVON, subj: Briefing for Lt Gen Moorman, Aug 24, 1962; *New York Times*, Jun 30, 1962.

46. Memo, US Army Section, MAAG, Vietnam for special distribution, subj: Lessons Learned, no 22, Sep 8, 1962; Blake intvw, May 6, 1970; ltr, Gen Walter C. Sweeney, Cdr TAC, to Adm Harry D. Felt, CINCPAC, Jul 25, 1962.

47. Ltr, Maj Eugene R. McCutchan, ALO Abn Bde, to 2nd ADVON JOC, ALO/FAC Sect, subj: Report of ALO Activities, Oct 1, 1962; msg 7–3744, 2nd ADVON JOC to MACV J–5 and J–3, subj: Headway Addenda to Opsum for 1600Z, Sep 18–25, 1962.

48. Ltr, Maj Eugene R. McCutchan, ALO Abn Bde, to 2nd ADVON JOC, subj: Report of Operations, Phase I and Phase II, Nov 28, 1962; msg 2138X, 2nd Air Div to PACAF, 13th AF (for Gens Martin and Milton from Gen Anthis), Nov 22, 1962; Sweet intvw, Sep 4, 1970; questionnaire, Lt Col Kenneth M. MacCammond, USAF, Los Angeles, to author, Oct 70.

49. AF Hq, JGS, and 2nd ADVON, Joint Ops Plan 62–2, Oct 17, 1962; Blake intvw, May 6, 1970; Clark intvw, Nov 4, 1970; rprt, 13th AF, Tactical Analysis of C–123B Aircraft in Republic of Vietnam, Apr 15, 1963; rprts, Air Staff, Status Rprts on LeMay Visit to SVN, Aug 16, Sep 17, Oct 15 and Oct 26, 1962; msg 339J, 2nd Air Div to PACAF, 13th AF (personal from Gen Anthis for Gens Moorman and Milton), 222350Z Oct 62; ltr, MACV to CINCPAC, subj: Comprehensive Plan for Vietnam, Dec 7, 1962; ltr, Lt Col C. J, Bowers to Lt Col Mann, I ASOC, Jul 25, 1962.

50. Rprt, 315th Air Div, Exercise Long Pass, 1961; rprt, 314th TCWg, Final rprt, Clear Lake, Jun 19, 1962; rprt, 314th TCWg, Operation Fraternidad, Sep 13, 1962; rprt, 18th AF, Concept of Troop Carrier Operations, 1955–58, [*ca* 1953]; text, U.S. Army Command and General Staff College, Airborne Operations, Mar 59; hist, 18th AF, 1 Jan–30 Jun 54, pp 201–202; 1 Jul–31 Dec 55, pp 25–27; hist, TAC, 1955 through 1962; AFM 1–9, Jul 1, 1954.

51. Msg 5–452A, 13th AF to PACAF, 040833Z May 62; ltr, Lt Col Floyd K. Shofner, Cdr Mule Train, to Brig Gen Rollen H. Anthis, Cdr 2nd ADVON, subj: Mule Train Problem Areas, May 12, 1962; hist study, 6492nd CCG, *Airlift in SVN, Dec 61–Oct 62*, Dec 17, 1962, p 9; West intvw, May 5, 1970; rprt, Lt Col Howard E. Reaves, Cdr TAFTS–2, EOTR, Aug 2, 1962.

52. Ltr, Dir/Opns, PACAF to PACAF agencies, subj: Rprt of Staff Visit, 10–20 Apr 62, Apr 25, 1962; ltr, Lt Col Floyd K. Shofner, Cdr Mule Train, to Brig Gen Rollen H. Anthis, Cdr 2nd ADVON, subj: Mule Train Problem Areas, May 12, 1962; rprt, Brig Gen Jamie Gough, Dep Dir/Opl Forces, Hq USAF, Rprt of LeMay Visit to South Vietnam, Apr 62; West intvw, May 5, 1970; Perry intvw, Nov 3, 1970; study, Air Cd and Staff College, Designated Study 7, vol I, Assault Airlift, Dec 15, 1967, p 3.

53. Ltr, Dir/Opns, PACAF to PACAF agencies, subj: Rprt of Staff Visit, 10–20 Apr 62, Apr 25, 1962; Brig Gen Jamie Gough, Dep Dir/Opl Forces, Rprt of LeMay Visit to South Vietnam, Apr 62; status rprts, Air Staff, CSAF Visit to SVN (Apr 62), July 1962 and Aug 16, 1962; msg 43–A, Cdr 13th AF to PACAF, 210455Z Apr 62; Julian intvw, Jun 8, 1971; Gen Anthis' comments reviewing author's ms, 1971.

54. Msg 72–A, 13th AF to PACAF (for Moorman from Milton), 260200Z May 62; msg A–098, AFCC (JTF–116) to PACAF (to Moorman from Milton), 290515Z May 62; msg 314, PACAF to 13th AF (to Milton from Moorman), May 29, 1962; hist, 13th AF, 1962, vol I, pp II–71; hist study, 6492nd CCG, *Airlift in SVN, Dec 61–Oct 62*, Dec 17, 1962, p 23.

55. Msg, CINCPAC to PACAF, 172108Z Sep 62; ltr, Lt Gen Thomas S. Moorman, Vice Cdr PACAF, to CINCPAC, subj: Proposed Establishment of a CCG (T/C) in SEA, Jul 6, 1962; msg, CINCPAC to MACV, 180418Z Jul 62; msg, MACV J–4 to CINCPAC, 230905Z Aug 62; hist, 315th AD, Jul 62–Dec 63, pp 5–6.

56. MACV Directive 42, Oct 11, 1962; and Incl, subj: US Military Airlift System in Southeast Asia; msg 335J, 2nd AD to PACAF and 13th AF (for Martin, Milton, from Anthis), 181900Z Oct 62; memo, 6492nd CCG (T/C) Provis, subj:

Responsibilities, Authorities, and Relationships of Certain Elements and Key Positions in the Proposed Airlift Org, [ca Sep 1962].

57. MACV Directive 42, Oct 11, 1962; ltr, Brig Gen Rollen H. Anthis, to Lt Gen Thomas S. Moorman, Vice Cdr PACAF, Nov 12, 1962; msg, CINCPAC to PACAF, 172108Z Sep 62; memos, Brig Gen Frank A. Osmanski, MACV J-4, to J-4 agencies, subj: Airlift, Apr 17, 1962; subj: J-4 Major Project no 6, JAAB, Jun 5, 1962, subj: Logistic Support of Future Opns, Sep 27, 1962.

58. PACAF SO G-92, Nov 19, 1962; hist, 315th TCGp, Dec 62; rprt, Dir/Opns, Hq USAF, Status rprt on LeMay Visit to SVN, Oct 25, 1962; memo, 6492nd Combat Cargo Group, subj: Responsibilities, Authorities, and Relationship of Certain Elements and Key Positions in the Proposed Airlift Organization, [ca Sep 1962]; ltr, Lt Gen Thomas S. Moorman, Vice Cdr PACAF, to 13th AF and 315th Air Div, subj: Operational and Support Responsibilities Applicable to 315th TCGp, Dec 12, 1962; MACV Directive 42, Oct 11, 1962, and Incl, subj: United States Military Airlift System in Southeast Asia.

59. Ltr, Col Lopez J. Mantoux, USAF, Ret, to author, Dec 29, 1970, Jan 27, 1971, Feb 15, 1971.

60. Ltr, Maj Bruce G. Gilbreth, 6492nd CCG, to Col L. J. Mantoux, Cdr CCG, subj: Rprt of Communications, 6492nd CCG, Nov 5, 1962; background paper, subj: Revised Airlift Reqmts for NCP, May 3, 1963.

61. Rprts, TAFTS-P2, Hist Data rprts, Oct, Nov, Dec 62; hist study, 6492d CCG, *Airlift in SVN, Dec 61–Oct 62*, Dec 17, 1962.

62. Final rprt, US Army Tactical Mobility Requirements Board, Aug 20, 1962, Robert F. Futrell, *Ideas, Concepts, Doctrine: A History of Basic Thinking in the USAF, 1907–64*, ASI, Air University, 1971, pp 745-748; Lt Gen John J. Tolson, USA, *Airmobility, 1961–1971*, (Vietnam Studies, Dept Army, 1973), pp 16-24; Alain E. Enthoven and K. Wayne Smith, *How Much is Enough? Shaping the Defense Program 1961–1969* (New York, 1971), pp 100-104.

63. Memo, Lt Gen Gabriel P. Disosway, for CSAF, subj: Comments on Report of Army Tactical Mobility Requirements Board, Aug 14, 1962, and atch, Comments and Recommendations of USAF Tactical Air Support Requirements Board, pp 1-24, 35-36; ltr, Gen Curtis E. LeMay, CSAF, to Sec AF, subj: Comments on Report of Army Tactical Mobility Requirements Board, Sep 15, 1962; memo, Robert S. McNamara, Sec Def, for Sec AF, Subj: Army Tactical Mobility, Nov 14, 1962; hist, Dir/Plans, Hq USAF, Jul–Dec 62, pp 39-41.

64. Ltr, Maj Gen Sam W. Agee, Dir/Opns, Hq USAF, to Sec AF, subj: Ranch Hand Aircraft, Mar 20, 1962; ltr, Brig Gen Robert F. Worden, Dep Dir/Plans, Hq USAF, to AFXDC, subj: The Situation in SVN, Dec 17, 1962; msg, Harkins, Saigon to Decker, Washington (SGN-206, eyes only), 151152Z Feb 62; rprt, Lt Gen Gabriel P. Disosway, DCS/Opns, and Maj Gen William W. Momyer, Dir/Opl Rqmts, Hq USAF, Trip Rprt, SVN, Dec 22, 1962; Brig Gen Jack A. Gibbs, Dep Dir/Opl Reqmts, Hq USAF, to CSAF, Report of Air Force Team's Orientation Visit to SVN, May 25, 1962; rprt, Air Force Group Orientation Visit (May–Jul 62), 1962; status book, PACAF, Cdr PACAF Book for Sec Def Mar 62 Mtg, Mar 1962.

65. Msg 2131K, 2nd Air Div, to 13th AF, PACAF, 211040Z Nov 62; Kennedy intvw, Feb 4, 1964; brief, Dir/Plans, subj: Actions Concerning South Vietnam, Feb 23, 1962; msg 3035, PACAF to CSAF (personal for Carpenter from Hetherington), Mar 9, 1962; rprt, Brig Gen Jack A. Gibbs, Dep Dir/Opl Reqmts, Hq USAF, Rprt of AF Team's Orientation Visit to SVN, May 25, 1962; briefing book, 2nd ADVON, for General LeMay, Apr 62; msg 62-1224, PACAF to CSAF, 220543Z Nov 62.

66. Msg 092, MACV J4 to CINCPAC (for Adm Felt), 220841Z May 62; msg, MACV to CINCPAC (for Adm Felt), 160414Z May 62; msg 2-197A, Cdr 15th AF to PACAF, 300521Z May 62; msg 4792, JCS to CINCSTRIKE, CSAF, 261337Z May 62.

67. Rprt, Dir/Army Avn, DCS/Mil Opns, Dept/Army, US Army Aviation Operations in South Vietnam, Oct 1, 1962; msg 14882, OSD (Sylvester) to CINCPAC, 292329Z May 62; msg A-350, AFCC, JTF-116 to PACAF, 171035Z Jun 62; ltr, Brig Gen Rollen H.

711

Anthis, Cdr 2nd ADVON, to Col Amos F. Riha, DCS/Opns, 13th AF, Sep 28, 1962 and atch.

68. Msg 284A, 13th AF to PACAF, 310945Z Jul 62; rprt, CDTC, RVNAF, Periodic Rprt, Aug 62; ltr, CINCPAC to Cdr, MACV, subj: Army Tests to be Conducted in South Vietnam, Sep 1, 1962; test plan, Army Tact Mobility Reqmts Board, Field Test of the AC-1 Caribou, Jun 6, 1962; JCS 2343/129, Jul 28, 1962; rprt, Dir/Army Avn, DCS/Mil Opns, Dept/Army, US Army Aviation Operations in South Vietnam, Oct 1, 1962; ltr, Brig Gen Rollen H. Anthis, Cdr 2nd ADVON, to Col Amos F. Riha, DCS/Opns, 13th AF, Sep 28, 1962, and atch; rprt, MAAG, Vietnam, Summary of US Army Aviation Support in SVN, Mar–Oct 62; msg 298A, 13th AF to PACAF, 060824Z Aug 62; rprt, Lt Gen Gabriel P. Disosway, DCS/Opns, and Maj Gen William W. Momyer, Dir/Opl Reqmts, Hq USAF, Trip Rprt, SVN, Dec 22, 1962.

69. Study, Mil Hist Div, G-3 USARPAC, subj: History of US Army Buildup and Operations in RVN, 1 Jan 61–30 Jan 63, pp 112–120.

70. CHECO Rprt, *October 1961–December 1963*, V, 15; hist, 315th Air Div, 1 Jan–30 Jun 62, I, 44–45, 51; ltr, Lt Col Ned M. Letts, Cdr 21st TCSq to 315th Air Div, subj: Report of CALSU Operation at Clark Air Base, 22 Dec 61 to 15 Jan 62, Jan 62; rprt, Lt Col George J. Nied, USAF, MCC Commander, Report (Barn Door), Detachment 11, Jan 62; record, CINCPAC, Sec Def Conference, Dec 16, 1961; msg 62–1041A, PFODC, PACAF, to Hq USAF, Jan 15, 1962; Van Staaveren, *Plans and Policies, 1961–63*, pp 20–21; CHECO Rprt, *Assault Airlift Operations*, Feb 23, 1967; hist, 13th AF, 1 Jul–31 Dec 61, pp 73–74.

71. Hist, 13th AF, 1962, pp I-3 to I-10; hist, CINCPAC, 1962, pp 213–215; Cd Post Log, Det 1, 315th AD, Deployment of US Forces to Thailand, May 62; hist, 315th AD, Jan–Jun 62, pp 48–54; rprt, Hq JTF-116, AAR, Dec 8, 1962; msg, CINCPAC to CINCPACFLT, 251925Z and 260040Z Jul 62.

72. Hist, Det 3, 315th AD, Jan–Jun 64, pp 6–11, Jul–Dec 64, pp 1–2; hist, Det 2, 6315th Opns Gp, Oct–Dec 64, pp 1–11; hist, 13th AF, 1962, pp III-157 to III-176; msg, CINCPAC to PACAF, 062249Z Oct 62; msg PFMDC 440, PACAF to CSAF for AFXPD, 292158Z Sep 62; msg MC J-4-928, MACV to CINCPAC, 271035Z Jun 62.

73. Monograph, MACV, Military Assistance to the RVN, 1960–63; rprt, SACSA, An Overview of the Vietnam War, 1960–63, Sep 63; memo, Roger Hilmann, Bur/Intell and Research, Dept/State, to Sec State, subj: The Situation and Short-term Prospects in SVN, Dec 3, 1962.

Chapter VI

The Airlift System, 1963–1964

1. MACV National Campaign Plan, Dec 15, 1962, and Logistics Annex; msg 2059-63, PACAF to Dir/Opns and Dir/Plans, Hq USAF, 011826Z Jan 63; msg 2007-63, PACAF to Dir/Plans, Hq USAF, 050128Z Jan 63; rprt, JCS Team, Rprt of Visit by JCS Team (Wheeler Visit), Jan 63; hist, Dir/Plans, Hq USAF, Jan–Jun 63, pt I, pp 179–180; Van Staaveren, *Plans and Policies, 1961–63*, p 29.

2. Ltr, 2nd AD to 13th AF, subj: National Campaign Plan, Jan 21, 1963; msg 0016, MACV J-4 to CINCPAC, 020824Z Jan 63; memo, JCSM-190-63, JCS to Sec Def, subj: SEA Situation Report, Apr 17, 1963; hist, 464th TCWg, Jan–Jun 63, p 20; msg 01908, 2nd AD to 13th AF, 040707Z Feb 63.

3. AFM 1-9, Theater Airlift Operations, Jul 1, 1954; ltr, Brig Gen Frank A. Osmanski, MACV J-4, to Col Byi Dinh Dam, JGS J-4, subj: Logistic Annex for Dien Hong Plan, Sep 18, 1963; rprt, Air Staff (Burchinall) group, Observations, SVN, Jan 16–30, 1963; briefing

book, MACV, Agenda Items for CINC-PAC Conference, Jul 12, 1963.

4. Quoted in Hist, MACV, 1964, p 151.

5. Msg 18-5, 315th AD to PACAF (personal Kershaw to Hetherington), 040258Z Jan 63; Kennedy intvw, Feb 4, 1964; notes, 2nd AD, Revised Airlift Reqmts for NCP, May 3, 1963; rprt, Maj Gen Krulak, Visit to Vietnam, Jun 25–Jul 1, 1963.

6. Rprt, Brig Gen Frank A. Osmanski, USA, MACV J-4, Rprt on Vietnam, Sep 26, 1963; hist, MACV 1964, pp 143–145; memo, Brig Gen C. A. Youngdale, USMC, MACV J-2, to C/S MACV, subj: J-2 Portions of US Mission Council Weekly Summary, Nov 8, 1963; ltr, Maj Gen Milton B. Adams, MACV J-5, to C/S MACV, subj: Trip Rprt, Jun 29, 1964; rprt, MACV Monthly Evaluation (Jul 64), Aug 15, 1964; msg, CINCPAC to MACV, 080120Z Feb 64; hist, 2nd AD, Jan–Jun 64, pp 102–103; comments, Robert F. Futrell on early ms, 1971.

7. Memo, MACV staff for Cdr MACV Notebook, subj: The Transportation System in RVN, Apr 65; briefing book, MACV, Agenda Items for CINCPAC Conf, Jul 12, 1963; MACV Qtrly Review, Jul–Sep 64; rprts, MACV J-3, Monthly Evaluations, (Mar, May, Jun, Jul 64).

8. Rprt, Brig Gen Frank A. Osmanski, USA, MACV J-4, Rprt on Vietnam, Sep 26, 1963; MR, Lt Col Franklin Rose, AFXPD, Dir/Plans, Hq USAF, subj: Improvement of US Logistics Support System in Vietnam, Dec 16, 1964; MACV Plan, Introduction and Employment of a US Army Logistical Command, Dec 21, 1964.

9. Borders intvw, Nov 4, 1970; Kennedy intvw, Feb 4, 1964; hist, 315th TCGp, Jan–Jun 63, pp 5–13; ltr, Lt Gen Thomas S. Moorman, Vice Cdr PACAF, to 13th AF and 315th AD, subj: Operational and Support Responsibilities Applicable to 315th Troop Carrier Group (Aslt), Feb 11, 1964; MACV Directive 87, Combined Movements System in RVN, Dec 9, 1963; ltr, Brig Gen Thomas R. Kennedy, Cdr 437th MAWg, to Maj Gen Robert N. Ginsburgh, Chief, Off/AF Hist, Feb 14, 1972.

10. Case intvw, May 5, 1970; hist, 2nd Air Div, 1 Jan–30 Jun 64, pp 97–98; Kennedy intvw, Feb 4, 1964; Kennedy, "Airlift in SEA," *Air University Review*, Jan–Feb 65, p 78.

11. Borders intvw, Nov 4, 1970; rprt, 1st Lt Donald L. Smith, EOTR, Jun 10, 1964; rprt, Capt Charles W. Case, EOTR, Jun 11, 1965; Case intvw, May 5, 1970; Kennedy, "Airlift in SEA," *Air University Review*, Jan–Feb 65.

12. Rprt, Airlift Staff Group, Rprt of USAF Airlift Staff Visit to PACOM Area, 11 Oct–10 Nov 65; 315th Air Div Manual 100–1A, Communications-Electronics Activities, Jan 1, 1965; ltr, Lt Col Bruce G. Gilbreth, Ch Comm-Electr, 315th Air Div, to Cdr 315th Air Div, subj: Staff Visit Report—Communications, Oct 5, 1964; rprt, Maj William W. Burnett, 311th Air Cdo Sq, EOTR, May 3, 1965; West intvw, May 5, 1970; Case intvw, May 5, 1970; Borders intvw, Nov 4, 1970; Perry intvw, Nov 3, 1970.

13. Rprt, Capt Carol L. Holley, 315th TCGp ALCC, EOTR, Mar 3, 1965; rprt, Capt Charles W. Case, EOTR, Jun 11, 1965; rprt, 1st Lt Donald L. Smith, EOTR, Jun 10, 1965; Kennedy intvw, Feb 4, 1964; Case intvw, May 5, 1970; briefing book, MACV, Agenda Items for CINCPAC Conference, Jul 12, 1963.

14. JCSM 190–63, subj: Air Augmentation, Mar 11, 1963; CSAFM 75–63, Feb 1, 1963; CSAM 52–63, Feb 1963; CSAM 86–63, Mar 5, 1963; msg, CINCPAC to JCS, 290023Z Jan 63; msg, CINCPAC to JCS, 230048Z Feb 63; msg 9270, JCS to CINCPAC *et al*, 280930Z Mar 63; msg 1151B, PACAF to CSAF (personal for Gen Carpenter from Col Pancake), 190657Z Feb 63; ltr, Gen Curtis E. LeMay, CSAF, to Adm Harry D. Felt, CINCPAC, Feb 28, 1963.

15. Msg 0009A, Cdr 2nd Air Div to PACAF, 100155Z Jan 63; MR, JAOC, 2nd Air Div, subj: Caribou Aircraft Allocated to SEAAS, Jun 26, 1963; rprt, 2nd Air Div, MACV Directives Relating to Control and Coordination of Air, 1963; ltr, MACV J-4 to CINCPAC, subj: US Airlift Resources, RVN, Jun 11, 1963; msg 176F, 2nd Air Div to Det 3, 6923rd RSM (for Anthis from Henderson), Jun 12, 1963; msg 5080–63, PACAF Dir/Opns to Dir/Plans, Hq USAF, Jun 19, 1963; msg, CINCPAC to MACV, 240411Z Jun 63; memo, JCS Dir/Opns for JCS, subj: SEA Situation Report, Jun 26, 1963; briefing book, MACV, Agenda Items for CINCPAC Conference, Jul 12, 1963.

16. Hist, 61st AV Co, 1963; ltr, Brig

Gen Rollen H. Anthis, Cdr 2nd AD, to Maj Gen Glen W. Martin, DCS/Plans and Opns, PACAF, Sep 2, 1963; MACV Directive 44, Task Organization and Management USMC/USA Aviation Resources in RVN, Jul 8, 1963.

17. Ltr, Col Donald Ross, Dir/Opns, 2nd AD, to MACV J-5, subj: Phase-out of US Forces, Oct 23, 1963 and atch; msg, CINCPAC to JCS, 212109Z Oct 63; rprt, ACTIV, Final Rpt on Employment of CV-2B Company in COIN Operations, Jan 23, 1965; rprt, US Army Sp Warfare Center, Rprts Concerning Aviation Activities in RVN, Dec 4, 1963; memo, Sec Def for Ch JCS, subj: Additional Support for RVN on an Accelerated Basis, Aug 7, 1964; msg, MACV to CINCPAC (to Adm Sharp from Gen Westmoreland), 161045Z Jul 64.

18. Intvw, Corona Harvest Intvw no 102, with Maj Robert N. Adams, USA, Jan 21, 1969; hist, 2nd AD, Jan-Jun 64, p 5; rprt, Army Sp Warfare Center, Rprt Concerning Aviation Activities in RVN, Dec 4, 1963; Kennedy intvw, Feb 4, 1964; Tolson, *Airmobility, 1961-71,* pp 44-47; Capt Arthur E. Dewey, "Caribou in Vietnam." *Army,* Aug 63; rprt, ACTIV, Final Rpt on Employment of CV-2B Company in COIN Operations, Jan 28, 1965.

19. Memo, Brig Gen Frank A. Osmanski, MACV J-4, to SJS, MACV, subj: Debriefing of Colonel Balthis, Oct 17, 1964; rprt, Gen Earle G. Wheeler, CSA, Visit to RVN, April 15-20, 1964; rprt, 1st Lt Donald L. Smith, EOTR, Jun 10, 1965; rprt, Sp Warfare Div, Dir/Plans, Hq USAF, Debriefing of Maj Alan G. Nelson, ALO, 9th Inf Div, Feb 15, 1965; rprt, Maj Gen Rollen H. Anthis, Debriefing Rprt, Dec 19, 1963.

20. Rprt, PACAF Manpower Team, Manpower Review and Analysis of 13th AF Activities, Jun 28, 1963; ltrs, Brig Gen Rollen H. Anthis, Cdr 2nd AD to Lt Gen Thomas S. Moorman, Vice Cdr PACAF, Mar 28, 1963 and Apr 18, 1963; CSAFM 183-63, Apr 4, 1963; memo, JCS (SM-492-63) to CSAF, subj: PCS Transfer of USAF Forces in RVN, Apr 12, 1963; ltr, Lt Gen Thomas S. Moorman, Vice Cdr PACAF, to Brig Gen Rollen H. Anthis, Cdr 2nd AD, Feb 11, 1963.

21. Ltr, Brig Gen Thomas B. Kennedy to Off/AF Hist, subj: draft hist study, USAF in SEA, T/C, Jan 11, 1972; hist, 309th TCSq, Jan-Jun 64; Kennedy intvw, Feb 4, 1964; *Airman,* Oct 64; rprt, Off/Sec AF, Rprt of AF Study Gp on Vietnam, May 64; rprt, Capt Francisco Machado, 315th ACGp, EOTR, Aug 10, 1965; rprt, Maj William W. Burnett, 311th ACGp, EOTR, May 3, 1965; ltr, 13th AF IG Team, Opns Member, to Dir/Opns, 13th AF, subj: Staff Visit Rprt, RVN, Jan 6-20, 1964, Jan 24, 1964.

22. Msg 3029, DCS/Plans and Opns, PACAF, to TAC, Feb 28, 1962; msg 63-0582D, to 13th AF, 270021Z Apr 63; msg 3-10797, Div/Airlift, Hq TAC, to Dir/Opns, Hq USAF, 162337Z May 63; rprt, Maj William W. Burnett, 311th ACSq, EOTR, May 3, 1965; rprt, Capt Robert L. Lee, 310th TCSq, EOTR, Nov 25, 1964; rprt, Dir/Plans, Hq USAF, Debriefing of Capt Walter E. Farron, 310th TCSq, Nov 25, 1964.

23. Msg 63-213G, 2nd Air Div to PACAF, 13th AF (for Gens Moorman, Martin, McElroy), 182250Z Jul 63; hist, 2nd Air Div, 1 Jan-30 Jun 64, ch 3, p 25; *ibid.,* 1 Jul-31 Dec 64, I, 66; Kimball intvw, Nov 4, 1970; Borders intvw, Nov 4, 1970; rprt, Maj William W. Burnett, 311th ACSq, EOTR, May 3, 1965; hist, 311th TCSq, Jul-Dec 64.

24. Msg PFCVC 009, PACAF to Dir/Plans, Hq USAF, 080501Z Jan 64; rprt, US Army Special Forces, Vietnam, Field Information Rprt, Apr 14, 1963; rprt, Intelligence Staff, 2nd AD, Offensive and Defensive Capabilities of the VC Against Aircraft, 1964; rprt, Opns Analysis Off, 2nd AD, COIN Lessons Learned, Jul-Dec 64, Jan 18, 1965; rprt, Hq USAF, Dir/Plans, Debriefing of 1st Lt R. E. Sepanski, 309th TCSq, Jan 65; rprt, Capt Robert L. Lee, 310th TCSq, EOTR, Nov 25, 1964; rprt, Opns Analysis Off, 2nd AD, COIN Lessons Learned, Jan-Jun 64, Jul 4, 1964; hist, 2nd AD, Jan-Jun 64, p 99.

25. West intvw, May 5, 1970; Duty Officer Log, MACV COC, Oct 24, 1963; MR, Lt Col W. P. Hall, Exec Off, 2nd Air Div, subj: C-123 Crash, Oct 24, 1964; rprt, MACV, Weekly USAF Air Activity Rprt, Oct 17-24, 1964; memo, MACV J-3 to C/S MACV, subj: Summary of Accomplishments, Oct 25-Nov 1, 1964; memo, MACV Section, JCC, for Gens Ty, Harkins, Don, subj: Weekly Resume, Oct 24-30, 1963.

26. Rprt, Dir/Aerospace Safety, Acft

Accident Summary, C–47, C–119, C–123, C–131, T–29, Jan 1–Dec 31, 1963; msg, 25896, Ch JUSMAAG, Bangkok, to CINCPAC, 171000Z Apr 63; msg 63D–011, 6010th Tact Gp to Hq USAF, 130844Z Apr 63; Blake intvw, May 6, 1970; West intvw, May 5, 1970.

27. Rprt, Dir/Aerospace Safety, Aircraft Accident Summary, T–29, C–131, T–39, C–47, C–119, C–123 for 1964; West intvw, May 5, 1970, hist, 315th Air Div, Jan 1–Jun 30, 1964, I, 44; citation, USAF Flying Safety Plaque to 315th TCGp, 1965; *The Air Division Advisor*, Tan Son Nhut AFB, Vietnam, Mar 10, 1965; Dir/Management Analysis, Hq USAF, *USAF Management Summaries, SEA*, Feb 1, 1965.

28. West intvw, May 5, 1970; rprt, Dir/Plans, Hq USAF, Debriefing of 1st Lt R. E. Sepanski, Jan 65; rprts, EOTR, Maj Leonard G. Hillebrandt, Mar 31, 1965, Capt Robert L. Lee, Nov 25, 1964, Lt Col Harry G. Howton, Sep 6, 1965, Maj William W. Burnett, May 3, 1965, Maj Carol D. Vickrey, Sep 1965, 1st Lt Donald L. Smith, Jun 10, 1965, Capt Charles W. Case, Jun 11, 1965, Capt Carol L. Holley, Mar 3, 1965, Capt Francisco Machado, Aug 10, 1965.

29. Rprt, SMSgt P. L. Spataro, 33rd CAM Sq, Jun 4, 1965; rprt, Maj Leonard G. Hillebrandt, EOTR, Mar 31, 1965; rprt, Lt Col Harry G. Howton, Cdr 311th TCSq, EOTR, Sep 6, 1965; rprt, Capt Robert L. Lee, 310th TCSq, EOTR, Nov 25, 1964; rprt, Maj William W. Burnett, 311th ACSq, EOTR, May 3, 1965; Borders intvw, Nov 4, 1970; MACV Directive 37–2, Administration of Special Pay, Subject to Hostile Fire, Mar 10, 1964.

30. Hist, 18th AF, Jan 1–Jun 30, 1955, pp 19, 133, Jul 1–Dec 31, 1956, p 80; hist, 315th Air Div, Jul 1–Dec 31, 1957, pp 4–5; hist, 464th TCWg, Jul 1–Dec 31, 1962, p 38; hist, 61st TCSq, Jul 1–Dec 31, 1958; West intvw, May 5, 1970; Clark intvw, Nov 4, 1970.

31. Rprts, EOTR, Maj William W. Burnett, 311th ACSq, May 3, 1965, Maj Leonard G. Hillebrandt, Da Nang, Mar 31, 1965; Borders intvw, Nov 4, 1970; West intvw, May 5, 1970; draft msg, Col Lyle D. Lutton, "The SEAAS," 1963; ltr, Lt Col Herman E. Luebbert to Col Lutton, Cdr, 315th TCGp, n.d. [ca 1963]; rprts, TAFTS–P2, Historical Data Rprts, monthly, Jan through May 63.

32. Hist, 315th TCGp, Jan 1–Jun 30, 1963, p 32; rprt, Div/Sp Warfare, Hq USAF, Debriefing of Col Harold E. Walker, Dir/Materiel, 2nd Air Div, Sep 15, 1964; briefing text, Col Harold E. Walker, Dir/Materiel, 2nd Air Div, Briefing for Gen Maddux, Aug 19, 1963.

33. Hist, SAWC, Jan–Jun 64, pp 48–50, 215, Jul–Dec 64, pp 15–18, 23, 97–99; hist, 464th TCWg, Jan–Jun 64, pp 2, 34–35; Charles H. Hildreth, *USAF Special Air Warfare: Doctrines and Capabilities, 1963*, USAF Hist Div Liaison Off, Aug 64, pp 9–12; briefing, Maj Gen Pritchard, Cdr SAWC, subj: How Goes It Briefing for Gen Sweeney, Nov 23, 1964.

34. Msg 117D, 2nd Air Div to PACAF, 5th AF (personal for Gens Martin, Kershaw, Milton, from Gen Anthis), 010230Z Apr 63; msg 6010, General Anthis to PACAF 13th AF, 2nd Air Div (for Gens Martin, McElroy, Henderson from Gen Anthis), Jun 63: msg 2001–63, PACAF to 2nd Air Div, 030552Z Jan 63; briefing text, Col Thomas B. Kennedy, 315th TCGp, subj: Visit of Gen Maddux, Aug 63, Aug 19, 1963; msg 117D, 2nd Air Div to PACAF *et al* (pers for Gen Martin from Gen Anthis) 050230Z Apr 63; ltr, Brig Gen Thomas B. Kennedy to author, Feb 4, 1972.

35. Ltr, Maj Eugene R. McCutchan, Abn Bde ALO, to JOC ALO/FAC Section, subj: Rprt of Operation, Jan 15, 1963; Perry intvw, Nov 3, 1970; Clark intvw, Nov 4, 1970; questionnaire, Lt Col Kenneth M. MacCammond, Oct 70; questionnaire, Maj Robeson S. Moise, Sep 70; rprt, TAFTS–P2, Historical Data, Jan 1963; hist, SAWC, Jan1–Jun30, 1963; I, 175–176; ltr, 57th Transportation Co to Cdr, 45th Transp Battn, subj: Evaluation of Helicopter Tactics and Techniques Rprt, Apr 9, 1963; MR, 2nd Air Div, subj: Meeting of Adm Felt and Pres Diem, Jan 9, 1963; telecon, MACV–PACOM, Jan 2, 1963; 2nd Air Div Off/Log, JOC, Jan 3, 1963.

36. Duty Officer's Log, MACV J–3 COC, Jan 2, 1963; Perry intvw, Nov 3, 1970; rprt, TAFTS–P2, Historical Data, Jan 1963; msg 009, ACAF to USAF (for Gen McKee from Gen O'Donnell) 040840Z Jan 63; msg 047, Vice Cdr PACAF to 2nd Air Div, 13th AF (exclusive for Gen Milton and Gen Anthis from Gen Moorman), 180245Z Jan 63; msg 0098A, 2nd Air Div to Dir/Plans,

Hq USAF (personal from Gen Dix to Gen Williams), 181145Z Jan 63; ltr, 45th Transp Battn to CG, US Army Support Gp, subj: Monthly Aircraft Rprt, Feb 4, 1963; msg 117D, 2nd Air Div to PACAF, 13th AF, 5th AF (personal for Gens Martin, Milton, Kershaw from Gen Anthis), 050230Z Apr 63; msg, PACAF to CSAF (for DCS/Opns, DCS/Plans and Progr), 041826Z Jan 63.

37. Ltr, Brig Gen Rollen H. Anthis, Cdr 2nd Air Div, to Cdr, MACV, subj: Duc Thang Heliborne Operation, Jan 2–16, 1963; MR, Col S. H. Nigro, subj: Visit by Adm Felt with Secretary Thuan, Jan 9, 1963; ltr, Dir/Plans, Hq USAF, to Dir/Opns Analysis, Hq USAF, subj: Analysis of Helicopter Incident in SVN, Feb 5, 1963; msg 0016A, 2nd Air Div to PACAF (for Gen Martin and Gen Milton from Gen Anthis), 041545Z Jan 63; CHECO Rprt, *October 1961–December 1963*, V, 28–33; *Washington Post*, Jan 7, 1963; msg 0010A, 2nd Air Div to PACAF, 13th AF (personal for Gen Henry from Gen Anthis), 031030Z Jan 63.

38. IR 2903011563, May 1, 1963.

39. Ltr, Maj Eugene R. McCutchan, ALO Abn Bde, to Dep Dir/JAOC, subj: Report of Operation, Mar 10, 1963; rprt, TAFTS–P2, Historical Data, Jan 63; CHECO Rprt, *October 1961–December 1963*, V, 60–64.

40. Ltr, Col Joe B. Lamb, USA, Advisor Abn Bde, to Cdr MACV, subj: Parachute Operations, Dec 4, 1963; ltr, Maj Hal G. Bowers, ALO III Corps, to Dep Dir/III ASOC, subj: After Action Rprt, Operation Phi Hoa II, Apr 5, 1963; hist, 13th AF, Jan1–Jun30, 1963, p II–54; msg, PACAF to SAFOI, 262009Z Mar 63.

41. Ltr, Capt Jack V. Cebe–Habersky, ALO 2nd Abn Battn, to JAOC–ALO/FAC, subj: After Action Rprt (10–14 Jun 63), Jun 1963; duty officer's log, MACV J–3 COC, Jun 11, 1963; ltr, Capt E. M. Robinson, ALO 5th Div, to III Corps ALO, subj: After Action Rprt, Jun 20, 1963; msg 5310, MACV J–3 to JCS *et al*, 132015Z Jun 63; memo, MACV Element, JOC, for Gens Ty and Harkins, subj: Weekly Resume, Jun 7–14, 1963, Jun 17, 1963; ltr, Col Joe B. Lamp, USA, Advisor Abn Bde, to Cdr MACV, subj: Parachute Operations, Dec 4, 1963.

42. Rprt, Maj Robert Butler, ALO 21st Div, subj: AAR, Oct 3, 1963; duty officer log, MACV COC, Sep 10, 1963; ltr, Capt Jack V. Cebe–Habersky, FAC Abn Bde, to ALO Abn Bde, subj: AAR, Cai Nuoc Parachute Drop, Sep 10, 1963; ltr, Lt Col James F. Martin, ALO Abn Bde, to AOC–ALO/FAC, 2nd AD, subj: AAR—Cai Nuoc, Sep 13, 1963; ltr, Col Thomas B. Kennedy, Dir/Air Transp, 2nd AD, to Cdr 2nd AD, subj: Joint Airborne Operations, Dec 4, 1963.

43. Duty Officer Log, MACV COC, Oct 20, 1963; ltr, Lt Col James F. Martin, ALO Abn Bde, to AOC—ALO/FAC, 2nd Air Div, subj: After Action Rprt, Oct 21, 1963; memo, MACV Element, JOC, for Gens Ty, Harkins, and Don, subj: Weekly Resume, Oct 24–30, 1963; rprt, Lt Col James F. Martin, ALO Rprt for Oct 63, Nov 4, 1963; ltr, Col Thomas B. Kennedy, Dir/Air Transp, 2nd Air Div, to Cdr, 2nd Air Div, subj: Joint Airborne Operations, Dec 4, 1963; West intvw, May 5, 1970.

44. Duty Officer Log, MACV COC, Oct 20, 1963; rprt, Lt Col James F. Martin, ALO Abn Bde, to AOC, Daily Activity Rprt, Nov 25, 1963; talking paper, Dir/Plans, Hq USAF, subj: Military Situation in RVN, Nov 30, 1963; memo, MACV Element, JOC, for Gens Harkins and Don, subj: Weekly Resume, Nov 21–27, 1963, Dec 2, 1963; ltr, Col Joe B. Lamb, USA, Advisor Abn Bde, to Cdr MACV, subj: Parachute Operations, Dec 4, 1963; ltr, Col Thomas B. Kennedy, Dir/Air Transport, 2nd Air Div, to Cdr, 2nd Air Div, subj: Joint Airborne Operations, Dec 4, 1963.

45. Rprts, Lt Col James F. Martin, ALO Abn Bde, Daily Activity Rprts, Nov 25 and 30, 1963; ltr, Maj Gen Tran Van Don, Ch JGS, RVNAF, to Col, Acting Cdr AF, subj: Deficiencies in Airborne Operations, Nov 28, 1963; ltr, Col Joe B. Lamb, USA, Advisor Abn Bde, to Cdr MACV, subj: Parachute Operations, Dec 4, 1963.

46. Ltr, Maj Gen Rollen H. Anthis, Cdr 2nd AD, to Cdr, 315th TCGp, subj: Airborne Operations, Nov 25, 1963; ltr, Col Thomas B. Kennedy, Dir/Air Transport, 2nd AD, to Cdr 2nd AD, subj: Joint Airborne Operations, Dec 4, 1963; ltr, Brig Gen Thomas B. Kennedy, Cdr 437th MAWg, to AFCHO, subj: Draft Hist Study, The AF in SEA, Tactical Airlift, Jan 11, 1972; Blake intvw, May 6, 1970 (Blake was lead navigator on the larger drop missions in 1962); ltr, Lt

Col James Martin, ALO Abn Bde, to 2nd AD AOC, subj: ALO Rprt for Feb, 64, Mar 10, 1964.

47. Msg 63M-1385, 2nd AD to Det 1, 7651st ACI Sq, 060015Z Dec 63; msg 2 AFTU-63A, 2nd AD to PACAF, subj: COIN Lessons Learned, Jan 10, 1964; RVN DOD, RVNAF High Cd, Directive 1455/TTL/P3/2, subj: Planning and Operating Procedures for Airborne Operations, Aug 20, 1964; ltr, Maj E. R. McCutchan, JAOC, to 2nd AD, Col Ross, subj: Orientation Trip to Singapore for Abn Bde Officers, May 3, 1963; ltr, Maj McCutchan, ALO Abn Bde, to 2nd AD JAOC, subj: ALO Activities for Jan 63.

48. Duty Officer Log, MACV COC, Apr 12 and 13, 1964; ltr, Lt Col James F. Martin, ALO Abn Bde, to AOC, subj: After Action Rprt, Apr 17, 1964; ltr, Maj Robert K. Butler, ALO 21st Div, to ALO IV Corps, subj: After Action Rprt, May 27, 1964; ltr, Capt Robert L. Paradis, FAC Abn Bde, to 2nd AOC, subj: After Action Rprt, Jul 23, 1964.

49. West intvw, May 5, 1970; rprt, Maj Gen Rollen H. Anthis, Debriefing Rprt, Dec 19, 1963; ltr, Lt Col James Martin, ALO Abn Bde, to AOC, subj: After Action Rprt, Feb 24, 1964; Borders intvw, Nov 4, 1970; ltr, Lt Col James F. Martin, ALO Abn Bde, to 2nd AD AOC, subj: ALO Rprt for Oct 63, Nov 4, 1963; MR, MACV J-03, subj: Daily Staff Conf, Aug 19, 1964; rprt, Capt Robert Lee, Nov 64; rprt, Abn Bde ALO, ALO Rprt for Sep 63, Oct 1, 1963; rprt, Hq US Army Sect, MAAG, Vietnam, Lessons Learned no 32, Eagle Flight Opns, Oct 19, 1963.

50. CSAFM 608-64, Jul 22, 1964; msg 3046, PACAF to 2nd Air Div (for Anthis from Martin), 200200Z Jun 63; hist, Dir/Plans, Hq USAF, Jul 1–Dec 31, 1964, p 328.

51. Rprts, Lt Col Bill A. Montgomery, ALO I Corps, to 2nd Air Div AOC, subj: ALO Rprts for Nov, Dec 63, Jan, Apr, May 64; daily msgs, I ASCC to 2nd Air Div ASCC, subj: CALO Rprts, Oct 24 through Dec 10, 1963; ltr, Col John W. Wohmer, USA, Sr Advisor, I Corps, to Lt Gen William C. Westmoreland, Dep Cdr, MACV, Apr 27, 1964; ltr, Capt Lorrell A. Kressin, ALO 1st Inf Div, to Sr ALO, subj: 3rd Regt Visit, Dec 20, 1962; duty officer log, MACV COC, Apr 24, 1964; Blake intvw, May 6, 1970; hist, 13th AF, Jul 1–Dec 31, 1963, Vol I, p III-155.

52. Duty officer log, MACV COC, Mar 14 and 15, 1964; ltr, Maj Clifton N. Conrad, USA, G-3 Advisor, III Corps, to Cdr MACV, subj: Combat After Action Rprt, Mar 18, 1964; ltr, Lt Col James F. Martin, ALO Abn Bde, to 2nd Air Div AOC, subj: After Action Rprt, Mar 19, 1964; ltr, Lt Col David Mallich, ALO III Corps, Dir/III ASOC, subj: After Action Rprt, Quyet Thang 33/64, Mar 21, 1964.

53. Ltr, Lt Col James F. Martin, ALO Abn Bde, to 2nd AOC, subj: After Action Rprt, May 1, 1964; rprt, Lt Col James F. Martin, ALO Abn Bde, ALO Rprt for May 64, Jun 3, 1964; ltr, Lt Col Kenneth L. Collings, Dep Dir/II ASOC, to II ASOC, subj: After Action Rprt, Op Quyet Thang 202, Jul 4, 1964.

54. Msg 64-223E, Cdr, 2nd Air Div, to Dir/Plans, Hq USAF, 131600Z May 64; memo, Brig Gen V. E. DePuy, USA, MACV J-3, to C/S MACV, subj: Summary of Accomplishments, Jul 4–11, 1964; memo, MACV Element, JOC, for Gens Ty and Harkins, subj: Weekly Resume, Jul 5–12, 1963; memo, Brig Gen Frank A. Osmanski, MACV J-4, to C/S, MACV, subj: US Mission Council Weekly Summary, Jul 18, 1964; memo, MACV J-3 to C/S MACV, subj: Summary of Accomplishments, 13–19 Jul 64, Jul 18, 1964; rprt, Lt Col Carleton N. Casteel, ALO Abn Bde, ALO Rprt for Aug 64, Sep 9, 1964.

55. Futrell, *The USAF in Korea, 1950–53*, pp 523–524; ltr, 3rd Aer Port Sq to 464th TCWg, subj: Final Report Exercise Swift Strike, Aug 25, 1961; hist, 18th AF, Jan–Jun 53, pp 169–173, Jul–Dec 53, p 269, Jan–Jun 54, p 203, Jan–Jun 56, p 217; rprt, Army Abn Center, Report of the Army Abn Conf, Feb 19–23, 1951; AFL 55-6 and Army Spec Reg 96-105-1, Opns: Memo of Understanding Relating to the Opn of AF Air Terminals, Jan 23, 1953; AFR 76-7 and AR 59-106, Air Transportation: Opn of AF Terminals, Sep 23, 1956.

56. PACAF SO C-8, Jan 24, 1962; PACAF SO C-38, Apr 18, 1962; PACAF SO G-44, May 10, 1962; ltr, Dir/Opns PACAF to PACAF Agencies, subj: Rprt of Staff Visit, 10–20 Apr 64, Apr 25, 1962.

57. Msg 62A-1032, 13th AF to 315th

TACTICAL AIRLIFT

Air Div, *et al*, 28–244Z Apr 62; West intvw, May 5, 1970; MSgt Gordon L. Poole, "Load Em, Move Em," *Airman*, Sep 63.

58. PACAF SO C–92, Nov 19, 1962; hist, 315th Air Div, 1 Jul 62–31 Dec 63; I, 6; hist, 13th AF, 1 Jul–31 Dec 63, I, 25, 142, 1 Jan–30 Jun 63, vol I, p III–156; msg 63B2294, DCS/Materiel, 13th AF, to PACAF, 260340Z Jun 63.

59. Kennedy, "Airlift in SEA," *Air University Review*, Jan–Feb 65; hist, 315th TCGp, 1 Jan–30 Jun 63, pp 35–42; Project CHECO Southeast Asia Report, *USAF Aerial Port Operations in RVN*, Aug 5, 1970, pp 5–6; rprt, MACV, Revised Airlift Reqmts for NCP, May 3, 1963; rprt, 13th AF Dir/Materiel, Facilities Programs Rprt, Jun 30, 1963; hist, 13th AF, 1 Jul–31 Dec 63, pp 12, 180; PACAF SO C–33, May 22, 1963.

60. Rprt, AF Flt Test Center, 463L Universal Cargo Handling System for C–130 Aircraft (techn rprt 62–27), Aug 62; ltr, 9th AF Dir/Airlift, to TAC, subj: TAC Project Officer's Rprt on Category II Test of Air Transportable Terminal, [ca Dec 1, 1963]; Capt William B. Holt, "An Analysis of the PACAF Problem Areas that Developed as a Result of the Implementation of the 463L Materials Handling System," (ACSC Thesis, Air University, Jun 66), pp 3–8; hist, TAC, 1 Jul–31 Dec 61, I, 637–640; policy books, Hq USAF, CSAF Policy Decks for 1962, 1963, and 1964; *Airman*, Dec 62.

61. Rprt, Maj William W. Burnett, 311th Air Cdo Sq, EOTR, May 3, 1965; hist, 2nd Air Div, 1 Jan–30 Jun 65, II, 19–20; rprt, Lt Col Harry G. Howton, Cdr 311th Air Cdo Sq, Sep 6, 1965; rprt, Opn Analysis Off, 2nd Air Div, COIN Lessons Learned, Jan–Jul 64, Jul 4, 1964.

62. Hist, 8th Aer Port Sq, Jul–Dec 64.

63. Hist, 13th AF, 1962, pp II–88 and III–175, Jan–Jun 63, pp III–142 to III–143, Jul–Dec 63, pp III–198 to III–199; Borders intvw, Nov 4, 1970; hist, Det 3, 315th AD, Jan–Jun 64, p 10; hist, Det 2, 6315th Opns Gp, Oct–Dec 64; study, Dir/Materiel, 2nd AD, SEA Munitions Logistics Study, 1964; rprt, Col H. E. Walker, 2nd AD, Dir/Materiel, EOTR, Aug 24, 1964; hist, 315th AD, Jul 62–Dec 63; brief, Hq USAF, subj: US Lodgment in SEA, Nov 23, 1964.

64. Msg 62A661, 13th AF to PACAF, 220535Z Mar 62; ltr, Lt Gen Thomas S. Moorman, Vice Cdr PACAF, to 13th AF, 315th Air Div, subj: Operational and Support Responsibilities Applicable to 315th Troop Carrier Group, Dec 12, 1962; msg 18–S, 315th Air Div to PACAF (personal Gen Kershaw to Gen Hetherington), 040258Z Jan 63; ltr, MACV J–4 to CINCPAC, subj: DOD Project Study, Traffic Management Overseas, Apr 30, 1964; msg 1328, 315th Air Div to units, 010350Z May 63; msg 312G, 2nd Air Div to PACAF, 13th AF (for Gens Moorman, Martin, McElroy), 182250Z Jul 63.

65. Hist, TAC, semi-annual histories, 1954 through 1964; rprt, Dir/Management Analysis, Hq TAC, TAC Response to Army Needs, Jul 31, 1963; hist, 314th TCWg, Jan–Jun 63, pp 11–12, 25, Jan–Jun 64, pp 22–23; Lt Col Richard E. Stanley, "Tactical Airlift Support: Army or Air Force," (AWC Thesis) Air Univ, Apr 65, pp 74–81; memo, Lt Col L. J. Cahill, Ch, Electr Div, TAC to TOCE, subj: All-Weather Drop Capability for Airborne Opns, Aug 22, 1961; rprt, Proj Close Look Opl Eval Rprt, Ph I, TAC Programming Plan 202–62, 1963.

66. Rprt, Project Close Look, Sewart AFB, Operational Evaluation Rprt, Phase I, 1963; ltr, 50th TCSq to Dir/Opns, 314TCWg, subj: Final Rprt of Exercise Swift Strike III, 2–23 Aug 63, Sep 3, 1963; rprt, 2nd Air Div, Operational Test and Evaluation of the YC–123H in the RVN, Jan 1, 1963; msg TAC to PACAF (personal for Gen O'Donnell from Gen Sweeney), 041510Z Feb 63; msg 0308C, 2nd Air Div to PACAF, 251025Z Mar 63; msg 06–63D–09, 2nd Air Div (AFTU), to 13th AF, PACAF, 130232Z Mar 63; msg 06–1782, TAC to PACAF and USAFE, 131801Z Jun 63; msg 06–1785, TAC to PACAF (personal for Gen Moorman from Gen Sweeney), 131812Z Jun 63.

67. Hist, TAC, 1 Jan–30 Jun 64, pp 457–458; ltr, 314th TCWg to 839th Air Div, 12th AF, TAC, subj: Final Rprt of 62nd TCSq and CAISU, 314th TCWg, Exercise Desert Strike, Jun 5, 1964; rprt, AF Force Mohave, Exercise Desert Strike Final Rprt, Jun 11, 1964; rprts, IG Safety, USAF, C–130 . . . Aircraft Accident Summary for 1963 (summary 9–64), and 1964 (summary 10–65).

68. Hist, 314th TCWg, 1 Jan–30 Jun

62, pp 16, 22; Col William G. Moore, Cdr 314th TCWg, Commander's Appraisal, in Hist 314th TCWg, 1 Jul–31 Dec 62; hist, 464th TCWg, 1 Jan–30 Jun 62, p vii; rprt, AF Flt Test Center, Proj Rough Road Alpha Rprt 63–8, Apr 63; memo, TACC, Hq TAC, to Dep/Materiel, Off/Opns Analysis, subj: Cdr's Decision, Dec 18, 1963.

69. Hist, 9th AF, Jul–Dec 64, pp 126–197; ltr, Lt Col James L. Blackburn, Cdr 4488th Test Sq (Helic), to ALTF Goldfire I, subj: Final Rprt for Helicopters, Goldfire I, 1964; ltr, 905th Air Div (Provis) to 314th TCWg, subj: Exercise Swift Strike III Final Rprt, Aug 27, 1963; CINCAFSTRIKE Plan, Airlift Test Plan for Composite Airlift Wing (Provis) (Swift Strike III), Jul 26, 1963; intvws, Corona Harvest, author with Maj Gen William G. Moore, May 4, 1970, and with Maj Gen Burl W. McLaughlin, Apr 20.

70. JCSM 162–64, subj: Testing of Army Tactical Mobility; CSAFM 408–64, May 22, 1964; CM 1356–64, subj: Army and Air Force Responsibilities Regarding the Use of Aerial Vehicles, May 13, 1964; Maj Gen E. L. Rowny, Off ACS/Force Development, Hq USA, at Assn of US Army, Nov 17, 1964, in Supplement to AF Policy Ltr for Cdrs, Jan 65; hist, Dir/Plans, Hq USAF, 1 Jan–30 Jun 63, pp 279–299, 1 Jul–31 Dec 63, p 314, 1 Jan–30 Jun 64, pp 258–260, 1 Jul–31 Dec 64, pp 260–262.

71. Ltr, Maj Charles J. O'Bier, Cdr MCC, Det 3, 315th Air Div, to Cdr, 315th Air Div, subj: MCC Commander's Rprt, Aug 31, 1964; rprt, PACAF, Lessons Learned, August 1964 Deployments, 1964; hist, TAC, 1 Jul–31 Dec 64, pp 557–560; hist; 315th Air Div, 1964 vol I, pp vii, 2; hist, 464th TCWg, 1 Jul–31 Dec 64, I, 37, 40–41; hist, 314th TCWg, 1 Jul–31 Dec 64, pp 11–12, hist, 463rd TCWg, 1 Jul–31 Dec 64, pp 103, 109–111, 137–139; hists, 345th, 346th and 347th TCSqs, in hist, 516th TCWg, 1 Jul–31 Dec 64 and 1 Jan–30 Jun 65.

72. Ltr, Maj Charles J. O'Bier, Cdr MCC, Det 3, 315th Air Div, to Cdr, 315th Air Div, subj: MCC Commander's Rprt, Aug 31, 1964; hist, 315th Air Div, 1964, I, 32–33; hist, Det 2, 6315th Opns Gp, 1 Oct–31 Dec 64, p 5; hist, Det 4, 315th Air Div, 1 Jul–31 Dec 64, pp 5–12.

73. Msg J–4 6227, MACV to CINCPAC, 170901Z Jul 64; msg J–3 6983, MACV to addressees, 271031Z Jul 64; msg J–3 9684, MACV to addressees, 141011Z Sep 64; Case intvw, May 5, 1970 (Case was staff officer in ALCC and Tan Son Nhut TMC during 1964–5); msg 00373, 315th AD to PACAF (pers from Gen Ellis for Gen Martin), 120830Z Mar 65; msg 7816; JCS to CINCPAC, 081949Z Aug 64; rprt, MACV, Monthly Evaluation (July 64), Aug 15, 1964; memo, MACV J–4 to MACV, subj: Signif Devel 5–11 Jul 64, Jul 11, 1964.

74. Memo, Off/Sec AF, subj: Report for President, Oct 16, 1964; hist, SAWC, Jul–Dec 64, p 72; PACAF SO G–114, Sep 18, 1964.

75. Hist, 2nd AD, Jan–Jun 65, p 93; memos, Brig Gen Frank A. Osmanski, MACV J–4 to C/S MACV, subj: US Mission Council Weekly Summary, Nov 16, 1964 and Nov 21, 1964; rprt, Lt Col Harry G. Howton, Cdr 311th ACSq, EOTR, Sep 6, 1965; mss, Kenneth Sams, "Civic Action Role of Air Power in RVN," (n.d.); hist, 311th TCSq, Jul–Dec 64.

76. Msg 25010, Dir/Opns, AFSTRIKE, to units, 092108Z Oct 64; msg 26566, Dir/Airlift, AFSTRIKE, to PACAF, *et al*, Dec 16, 1964; msg 00029, 314th TCWg to units, 181540Z Dec 64; 516th TCWg Frag Order 150–64 to CINCSTRIKE GPORD 150–64, Nov 25, 1964, hist, 463rd TCWg, 1 Jul–31 Dec 64, pp 62–63, 137–139; hist, 314th TCWg, 1 Jul–31 Dec 64, pp 11–12; hist, 516th TCWg, 1 Jul–31 Dec 64, p 35, hist, TAC, 1 Jul–31 Dec 64, p 571.

77. Rprt, MACV J–3, Military Analysis of the Counterinsurgency in Vietnam, 1963–4, Jan 26, 1965.

Chapter VII

Air Supply of Special Forces

1. MR, MAAG, Vietnam, subj: Meeting Held at Independence Palace, Saigon, Sep 29, 1961, atch to JCS 2343/26, Oct 19, 1961.
2. Rprt, Research Analysis Corp, U.S. Army Special Forces Operations under the CIDG Program in Vietnam, 1961–1964, RAC-T-477, Apr 66; study, Spl Opns Research Office, American Univ, *The U.S. Special Forces CIDG Mission in Vietnam*, Nov 64; Asst for Mutual Security, Hq USAF, *Journal of Mil Assistance*, Jun 62, p 178, Sep 62, p 155; Lt Col Walter P. Meyer, USA, "The Montagnards of Vietnam," *Infantry*, Mar–Apr 67 and May–Jun 67; rprt, Brig Gen Frank A. Osmanski, MACV J-4, Rprt on Vietnam, Sep 26, 1963; Col Francis J. Kelly, *U.S. Army Special Forces* (Vietnam Studies, Dept/Army, 1973) pp 19–35.
3. Kelly, *U.S. Army Special Forces*, pp 37–39; rprt, Off/Sec Def, Weekly Report to the President, Jul 10, 1962; Asst for Mutual Security, *Journal of Military Assistance*, Jun 62, p 178.
4. Rprt, RAC, Sp Forces under CIDG, 1961–4, Apr 66, pp 38–182; Carson intvw, Sep 18, 1970 (Carson was Farm Gate C-47 pilot in late 1962); draft hist study, MACV, US Special Forces and Operations, Jun 65.
5. Carson intvw, Sep 18, 1970; King intvw, Sep 4, 1969 (King was the initial Farm Gate commander); msg ODC 1-508, PACAF to 13th AF, subj: USAF Support of Special Forces in Vietnam, Mar 19, 1963; msg 62-335J, 2nd AD to PACAF, 13th AF, (Martin and Milton), 181900Z Oct 62.
6. Msg 62-307, 2nd Air Div to PACAF, 13th AF (personal for Moorman and Milton from Anthis) 140355Z Sep 62; msg 4443, J-3 MACV to CINCPAC, 251029Z Oct 62; msg 62-1888J, Dir/Opns, 2nd Air Div, to PACAF, 310257Z Oct 62; msg 62-1994J, Dir/Opns, 2nd Air Div to Dir/Opns and Dir/Plans, Hq USAF, 311330Z Oct 62; msg, CINCPAC to MACV, 022115Z Nov 62; msg 63-0010A, 2nd Air Div to 13th AF, PACAF (to Martin and Milton from Anthis), 101530Z Jan 63.
7. Ltr, CINCPAC to MACV, JCS, subj: CIDG Program in RVN, May 27, 1963; msg 393, US Embassy, Saigon to Sec State, 061300 Oct 62; rprts, Off/Sec Def, Weekly Report to President, Sep 4, 1962 and Sep 17, 1962.
8. Ltr, Capt Louis W. Gaylor, USA, Asst S-4, Logis Ops Center, USASF(P)V, to Cdr USASF(P)V, Attn: S-4, subj: Progress Report (Switchback), Jun 16, 1963.
9. Jacob Van Staaveren, *USAF Plans and Policies in South Vietnam, 1961–63*, (Off/AF Hist, Jun 65), p 102.
10. Rprt, Research Analysis Corp, U.S. Army Special Forces and Similar Internal Defense Advisory Opns in Mainland SEA, 1962–67, RAC TP-354, Jun 69, pp 117–123; Kelly, *U.S. Army Special Forces*, pp 57–58.
11. Ltrs, Lt Col Gary Oskamp, ALO Sp Forces, to 2nd Air Div (JAOC), subj: Monthly ALO Rprts, Mar 8, 1963 and Apr 1, 1963; ltr, Maj John R. Goodlett, Chief TMC, JAOC, to 2nd Air Div (ALO Section), subj: Monthly Airlift Opns Rprt, Mar 24, 1963.
12. Ltr, Capt Louis W. Gaylor, USA, Asst S-4, Logist Opns Center, USASF-(P)V, to Cdr USASF(P)V, subj: Semiannual Progress Rprt (Switchback), Jun 16, 1963; memo, PACAF OCO to Vice Cdr, PACAF, subj: Alert Commitment in RVN, Jul 20, 1963; ltr, Lt Col Gary Oskamp, ALO Sp Forces, to 2nd Air Div (JAOC), subj: Monthly ALO Rprt, Jun 1, 1963; memo, PACAF OCO TO CVC, subj: Alert Commitment, Jul 20, 1963.
13. Rprt, Dir/Plans, Hq USAF, Debriefing of Maj Horace W. Shewmaker, 315th TMC, Nha Trang and Qui Nhon, Feb 2, 1965; Kimball intvw, Nov 4, 1970; msg 63J-1260, 2nd Air Div to PACAF, 160818Z Sep 63; msg 6947-63, PACAF Dir/Opns, to Hq USAF, 180237Z Dec 63; rprt, Airlift Staff Group, Rprt of USAF Airlift Staff Visit to PACOM Area, 11 Oct–10 Nov 65; rprt, Capt James S. Young, 1st ACSq, EOTR, 1963.

NOTES

14. Hist, 2nd AD, Jul–Dec 64, p 97.
15. Rprt, Dir/Plans, Hq USAF, Debriefing of Maj Horace W. Shewmaker, 315th TMC, Nha Trang and Qui Nhon, Feb 2, 1965; Kimball intvw, Nov 4, 1970; West intvw, May 5, 1970; rprt, Lt Col Victor N. Curtis, ALO Sp Forces, EOTR, Jan 65.
16. Ltr, Lt Col Victor N. Curtis, ALO Sp Forces, to Dep Dir AOC, 2nd Air Div, subj: Monthly ALO Rprt, Dec 8, 1964; rprt, Dir/Plans, Hq USAF, Debriefing of 1st Lt R. E. Sepanski, 309th TCSq, Jan 65; rprt, Dir/Plans, Hq USAF, Debriefing of Capt Walter E. Herron, 310th TCSq, (rprt 64–11–4), Nov 25, 1964; rprt, Maj William W. Burnett, 311th ACSq, EOTR, May 3, 1965; *Journal of Military Assistance*, Mar 62, p 172; Lt John M. Chapman, "Flight to Gia Vuc," *Airman*, Apr 65, pp 46–47; Col Thomas B. Kennedy, "Airlift in Southeast Asia," *Air University Review*, Jan–Feb 65.
17. Rprt, Lt Col Victor N. Curtis, ALO, USASF, EOTR, Jan 65; ltr, Brig Gen Rollen H. Anthis, Cdr 2nd AD, to Maj Gen G. W. Martin, DCS P & O, PACAF, Sep 2, 1963; rprt, Lt Col Victor N. Curtis, ALO, to 2nd AD, Monthly ALO Report, Feb 4, 1964; hist, 13th AF, 1964, pp III–179 and III–180; Kimball intvw, Nov 4, 1970 (Kimball was 315th Group C–123 pilot in 1964–5); rprt, Dir/Plans, Hq USAF, Debriefing of Maj Horace W. Shewmaker, 315th TMC, Feb 2, 1965.
18. Ltr, Lt Col Garry Oskamp, ALO Sp Forces, to 2nd Air Div, subj: ALO Rprt for Dec 63, Jan 2, 1964; ltr, Brig Gen Frank A. Osmanski, USA, J–4 MACV, to Col Byi Dinh Dam, J–4 JGS, RVNAF, subj: Logistic Annex for Dien Hong Plan, Sep 18, 1963; ltr, Cdr, USASF(P)V, to Cdr MACV, subj: Parachute Delivery of Supplies and Equipment, Oct 21, 1963.
19. Msg 2–042A, Dir/Opns, 13th AF, to PACAF, 311150Z Jan 62; ltr, Col William T. Daly, Cdr 464th TCWg, to Gen Walter Sweeney, Cdr TAC, subj: Trip Report, SEA, Aug 15, 1962; ltr, Brig Gen Rollen H. Anthis, Cdr 2nd Air Div, to Lt Gen Thomas S. Moorman, Vice Cdr PACAF, Sep 27, 1962; msg 0081C, Cdr 2nd Air Div to Hq TAC, *et al* (for Martin and Milton), subj: Aircrew Training, Mar 7, 1963; rprt, Opns Analysis Off, 2nd Air Div, COIN Lessons Learned, Jul 4, 1964; ltr, Lt Col Victor N. Curtis, ALO Sp Forces, to Dep Dir/AOC, 2nd Air Div, subj: Monthly ALO Rprt, Sep 8, 1964; rprt, 13th AF, Tactical Analysis of C–123B Aircraft in RVN, Apr 15, 1963, pp 30–31; Perry intvw, Nov 3, 1970; Kimball intvw, Nov 4, 1970; Borders intvw, Nov 4, 1970; Blake intvw, May 6, 1970.
20. West intvw, May 5, 1970; Clark intvw, Nov 4, 1970; Kimball intvw, Nov 4, 1970; Perry intvw, Nov 3, 1970; Borders intvw, Nov 4, 1970.
21. PACAF Tactics and Techniques Bulletin no 7, Troop Carrier/Transport Tactics in SEA, May 23, 1965; rprt, 13th AF, Tactical Analysis of C–123B Aircraft in RVN, Apr 15, 1963, pp 30–31; rprt, Capt Robert L. Lee, 310th TCSq, EOTR, Nov 25, 1964; intvw, Project Corona Harvest, intvw no 26, Sep 27, 1967; photo article, "Resupply in the Pickle Barrel," *Air University Review*, Nov–Dec 63, pp 74–76; Col Thomas B. Kennedy, "Airlift in Southeast Asia," *Air University Review*, Jan–Feb 65; Perry intvw, Nov 3, 1970; West intvw, May 5, 1970; Blake intvw, May 6, 1970.
22. Ltrs, Lt Col Garry Oskamp, ALO Sp Forces, to Dep Dir AOD, 2nd Air Div, subj: ALO Rprts for Nov and Dec 63, Dec 2, 1963 and Jan 2, 1964; ltrs, Lt Col Victor N. Curtis, ALO Sp Forces, to Dep Dir AOC, 2nd Air Div, subj: Monthly ALO Rprts, Apr 6, 1964 and Jun 9, 1964; rprt, Opns Analysis Office, 2nd Air Div, COIN Lessons Learned, Jul 4, 1964; rprt, Capt Robert L. Lee, 310th TCSq, EOTR, Nov 25, 1964; intvw, Project Corona Harvest, intvw no 26, Sep 27, 1967; rprt, Dir/Plans, Hq USAF, Debriefing of Capt Walter E. Herron, 310th TCSq, Nov 25, 1964.
23. Ltrs, Lt Col Victor N. Curtis, ALO Sp Forces, to Dep Dir AOC, 2nd AD, Monthly ALO Reports, Sep 8, 1964 and Oct 8, 1964; Perry intvw, Nov 3, 1970; rprt, Capt Francisco Machado, Jr., 309th ACSq, EOTR, Aug 10, 1965; rprt, Maj William W. Burnett, 311th ACSq, EOTR, May 3, 1965; rprt, Maj Leonard G. Hillebrandt, EOTR, Mar 31, 1965.
24. Ltrs, Lt Col Victor N. Curtis, ALO Sp Forces, to Dep Dir AOC, 2nd Air Div, subj: Monthly ALO Rprts, Mar 9, Apr 6, and Nov 5, 1964; ltr, Gen Paul D. Harkins, Cdr MACV, to Maj Gen Tran Van Don, Ch JGS, RVNAF, Nov 6, 1963; rprt, Maj Thomas H.

721

TACTICAL AIRLIFT

Freudenthal, 315th TCGp, Feb 65; ltr, Capt Louis W. Gaylor, USA, Asst S-4, Logist Opns Center, USASF(P)V, to Cdr USASF(P)V, subj: Semi-annual Progress Rprt (Switchback), Jun 16, 1963.

25. Rprt, 2nd Air Div, Operational Test and Evaluation of the YC-123H in the RVN, Jun 1, 1963; rprts, 1st CAG, Project Summary and Rprt, Evaluation of YC-123H, Jan 21 and Feb 20, 1963; msg 63E-35, 2nd Air Div to 13th AF, 010947Z May 63; msg 55129A, 13th AF to PACAF, 071054Z Jun 63; Perry intvw, Nov 3, 1970.

26. Rprt, 2nd Air Div, Operational Test and Evaluation of the YC-123H in the RVN, Jun 1, 1963; rprt, JOEG, 2nd Air Div Test and Evaluation of YC-123H in RVN, Aug 26, 1963; MR, Lt Col Eugene B. Sterling, Div/Transport Forces, Dir/Opns, Hq USAF, subj: 2nd Air Div Test and Evaluation of the YC-123H in RVN, Dec 23, 1963; rprt, Brig Gen Frank A. Osmanski, J-4 MACV, Rprt on Vietnam, Sep 26, 1963; ltr, J-3 MACV to CSAF, subj: 2nd Air Div Test and Evaluation of YC-123H in RVN, Aug 26, 1963; msg 63-1210, 2nd Air Div to 13th AF (for Milton from Anthis), subj: YC-123H Procurement Requirement, Apr 5, 1963; msg 63-0293, 2nd Air Div to Hq USAF (personal from Hibner to Williams), 041055Z Mar 63.

27. Msg 74330, Dir/Opns, Hq USAF, to PACAF, 292137Z Mar 62; msg, CINCPAC to JCS, 230030Z Jun 62; msg 5607, JCS to CINCPAC, 081550Z Aug 62; msg 62-2671L, 2nd Air Div to 13th AF, 150921Z Dec 62; msg 30-63C-30, AFTU, 2nd Air Div to 13th AF and PACAF, 300905Z Mar 63; msg 5-613, PACAF to Dir/Plans, et al, Hq USAF, 030452Z Apr 63; rprt, Capt J. B. Mayo, Air Pvg Gd Cd, Test of a Decca Navigation System for the NATO Strike Fighter, Jan 60.

28. Rprt, JOEC-V, Evaluation of 2nd Air Div AFTU Operational Tests and Evaluation, TAPS in RVN, Oct 11, 1963; ltr, AFTU, 2nd Air Div, to 2nd Air Div, subj: TAPS Demonstration for General Smart, Sep 63; Blake intvw, May 6, 1970; Clark intvw, Nov 4, 1970; msg 103684, TAC Dir/Op Reqmts, to CSAF, 230018Z Oct 63; JCS 141/122-4 Aug 10, 1964.

29. Rprt, Dir/Plans, Hq USAF, Debriefing of 1st Lt R. E. Sepanski, 309th TCSq, (rprt no 65-2-4), Jan 65; hist, 2nd Air Div, 1 Jan-30 Jun 64, p 95; New Facilities Listing, in hist, 2nd Air Div, 1 Jul-31 Dec 64; rprt, Airlift Staff Group, Rprt of USAF Airlift Staff Visit to PACOM Area, 11 Oct-10 Nov 65.

30. Rprts, CDTC, Vietnam, Monthly Summaries of Activities, Aug 62 through Jun 63; JCSM 453-64, subj: Tactical Navigation, May 27, 1964; hist, 315th Air Div, 1 Jan-30 Jun 62, pp 42-43; hist, 13th AF, 1 Jan-30 Jun 63, p II-80; ltr, Lt Col Victor N. Curtis, ALO USASF-V, to Dep Dir/AOC, 2nd Air Div, subj: Monthly Activities Rprt, Sep 8, 1964; msg, 315th Air Div to PACAF, 100615 Jul 63; msg 63-976, PACAF to 13th AF, 302155Z Mar 63; msg 2-0272A; 13th AF to PACAF, 210220Z Mar 62.

31. Col Thomas B. Kennedy, "Airlift in Southeast Asia," *Air University Review*, Jan-Feb 65; msg 62-1395; 2nd ADVON to 13th AF (for Milton from Anthis), Apr 21, 1962; rprt, ACTIV, Employment of CV-2, 1 Feb-31 Jul 63, pp 13-14; address, Brig Gen George W. McLaughlin, Asst DCS/Opns Reqmts, Hq TAC, to Res Off Assn of Pennsylvania, Sep 27, 1969, in Supplement to AF Policy Ltr for Cdrs, 11-1969, Nov 69.

32. Hist, 18th AF, 1 Jan-30 Jun 53, I, 209, 220; rprt, Joint Airborne Troop Board, Proposed Concept for the Construction of Airfields and Airheads, Mar 14, 1952; rprt, Joint Airborne Troop Board, 1953 Airborne Conference, Nov 53; AFM 1-9, Theater Airlift Operations, Jul 1, 1954; hist, 315th Air Div, 1 Jul-31 Dec 51, I, 152; Philip H. Best, "Employment of Troop Carrier in an Adverse Situation as Might Occur in Europe," (AWC Thesis) Air University, Mar 1, 1953; study, DOD, JCS, Services, Summary of Lesser Courses of Action in SVN, atch to JCS 2343/27, Oct 19, 1961.

33. Rprt, ACTIV, Employment of CV-2, 1 Feb-31 Jul 63, pp 13-14; briefing book, MACV, Agenda Items for CINCPAC Conference, Jul 12, 1963; Lt Col Francis E. Torr, "The Air Force Civil Engineer's Role in Counterinsurgency," *Air University Review*, Jul-Aug 64.

34. Rprt, Capt Harry M. Kepner, 310th ACSq, EOTR, Aug 65; West intvw, May 5, 1970; Kimball intvw, Nov 4, 1970; hist, 2nd Air Div, p 97.

35. Briefing text, 2nd ADVON, subj: Briefings for Lt Gen Moorman, Aug 24-26, 1962; rprt, 13th AF, Tactical Analysis of C-123B Acft in RVN, Apr 15,

1963; briefing text, Col Thomas B. Kennedy, Cdr 315th TCGp, subj: Briefing for Gen Maddux, Aug 19, 1963; Kraljev intvw, Jan 29, 1971; rprt, 346th TCSq, Historical Rprt, Feb–Mar 62; msg, 2nd ADVON to PACAF (exclusive for Hetherington from Anthis), 051000Z Mar 62; hist, 2nd ADVON, 15 Nov 61–8 Oct 62, p 160.

36. Rprt, RAC, Special Forces Opns under CIDG, 1961–4, Apr 66, pp 173–177.

37. Kenneth Sams and Lt Col Bert B. Aton, *USAF Support of Special Forces in SEA* (Hq PACAF, Proj CHECO, Mar 10, 1969); pp 64–65.

38. Ltr, Lt Col Victor N. Curtis, ALO Sp Forces, to Dep Dir/AOC, 2nd Air Div, subj: Monthly ALO Rprt, Dec 8, 1964; rprt, MACV, Monthly Evaluation, Jun 64; hist, MACV, 1964, pp 56–57, 90; study, Sp Opns Research Off, American Univ, *Special Forces CIDG Mission in Vietnam*, Nov 64; rprt, RAC, Special Forces Opns under CIDG, 1961–4, Apr 66, pp 63–65, 120–131; rprt, RAC, Sp Forces and Similar Operations, 1962–7, Jun 69, pp 21, 85.

39. Msg 64–084C, Cdr 2nd Air Div, to PACAF, 13th AF, USAF (personal for Gens Martin and Maddux from Moore), subj: Sec Def Meeting, Mar 10, 1964; ltr, Col John H. Wohner, USA, Sr Advisor, I Corps, to Lt Gen William C. Westmoreland, Dep Cdr, MACV, Apr 27, 1964; msg 64–223E, 2nd Air Div to Dir/Plans, Hq USAF, et al (Gens Moorman and Maddux from Moore), subj: Visit of Sec Def to Vietnam, May 13, 1964; ltr, 5th Sp Forces Gp (Abn), to Cdrs, A, B, and C Dets, subj: Letter of Instructions no 7, the USASF/CIDG Program, Nov 3, 1964; ltr, Capt T. H. O'Brien, ALO Comb Studies Div, to Dep Dir AOC, 2nd Air Div, subj: Activity Rprt for Aug 63, Sep 1, 1963; rprt, MACV, Monthly Evaluation, Jun 64.

40. Rprt, ACTIV, Final Rprt on Employment of CV–2B Company in COIN Operations, Jan 28, 1965; rprt, CDTC, RVNAF, Periodic Rprt, Aug 62; msg RD 774, MACV to Off Sec Def, *et al* (for Godel), 201001Z Jun 62; rprt, RAND, Counterinsurgency and Air Power, Memo RM–3203–PR, Jun 62.

41. Rprt, Lt Col Garry Oskamp, ALO Sp Forces, to 2nd AD, Dep Dir AOC, Monthly ALO Report, Jul 1, 1963; ltr, Capt Louis W. Gaylor, Asst S–4, USASF(P)V, to Cdr USASF(P)V, subj: Semi-annual Progress Report (Switchback), Jun 16, 1963.

42. Rprt, Lt Col Victor N. Curtis, ALO Sp Forces, EOTR, Jan 65; ltr, Col John H. Spears, USA, Cdr 5th Sp Forces Gp, to Cdr MACV, subj: Army Aviation Support of Special Forces, Oct 27, 1964; ltrs, Lt Col Victor N. Curtis, ALO Sp Forces to Dep Dir AOC, 2nd Air Div, subj: Monthly ALO Rprts, Oct 8, Nov 5, and Dec 8, 1964; rprt, Dir/Plans, Hq USAF, Debriefing of Maj Horace W. Shewmaker, 315th TMC, Qui Nhon and Nha Trang, SVN, Feb 2, 1965.

43. Memo, Gen William C. Westmoreland, MACV, for Ambassador Maxwell D. Taylor, subj: Weekly Assessment of Military Activity for 20–26 Sep 64, Sep 28, 1964; Lt Col Walter P. Meyer, USA, "The Montagnards of Vietnam," *Infantry*, May–Jun 67; ltr, Maj Eugene R. McCutchan, ALO 23rd Inf Div, to Dep Dir/II ASOC, subj: After Action Rprt, Oct 2, 1964; rprt, RAC, Sp Forces and Similar Operations, 1962–7, Jun 69, pp 53, 86; hist, MACV, 1964, pp 122–124.

44. Ltr, Brig Gen Rollen H. Anthis, Cdr 2nd AD, to Brig Gen Gilbert L. Pritchard, Cdr SAWC, Nov 63; ltr, Col Pancake, Dir/Plans, Hq USAF, to Gen Burchinal, AFXDC, Hq USAF, subj: Report on South Vietnam, Mar 27, 1963; msg 2190K, 2nd AD to 13th AF (Gen Milton from Gen Ritchie), 300800Z Nov 62.

TACTICAL AIRLIFT

Chapter VIII

The Entry of the C-130, 1965-1966

1. Rprt, MACV J-3, Military Analysis of the COIN in Vietnam, 1963-4, Jan 26, 1965; hist, MACV, 1965, pp 1-5; study, DOD, United States-Vietnam Relations, 1945-1967 (hereafter cited as *Pentagon Papers*, GPO ed), 1971, vol III, pt IV-C-1, pp v-vii, a10-a16, 103.

2. Msg DOCOS 47, PACAF to CINCPAC, 315th AD, 072115Z Feb 65; msg, CINCPAC to COMUSMACV, 090514Z Feb 65; msg 2PDC 00107, 2nd AD to Hq USAF, 190249Z Feb 65; rprt, 315th AD, Airlift Accomplishments CY 65; *Washington Post*, Feb 10, 1965; memo, Philip F. Hilbert, Dep Under Secy to Mr. Perry, SAF IL, Feb 9, 1965.

3. Hist, Dir/Opns, Hq USAF, Jan-Jun 65, pp 44-45; msg DOCOS 114, PACAF to CHWTO, Feb 28, 1965; rprt, 315th AD, Airlift Accomplishments CY 65; hist, 315th AD, Jan-Jun 65, pp 23-24, viii; msg, PACAF to 5th AF, 13th AF, 315th AD, 072332Z Feb 65; msg DOCOS 83, PACAF to CINCPAC, 110435Z Feb 65.

4. JCSM 121-65, subj: Improved Security and Readiness Measures in RVN, Feb 20, 1965; hist, MACV, 1965, pp 29-37; Maxwell D. Taylor, *Swords and Plowshares*, New York, 1972, pp 324-325; *Pentagon Papers*, GPO ed, vol IV, pt IV-C-4, pp 6-8, pt IV-C-5, "Chronology."

5. Msg, CINCPAC to PACAF, MACV, WTO, 070135Z Mar 65; hist, CINCPAC, 1965, II, 452-453; monograph, Lt Col John J. Cahill, USMC, and Jack Shulimson, "History of U.S. Marine Corps Operations in Vietnam, Jan-Jun," 1969; *Pentagon Papers*, GOP ed, vol IV, pt IV-C-4, p 1; *New York Times*, Mar 9, 1965; ltr, Col L. M. Tannenbaum, DCS/Opns, 315th AD to 6315th Ops Gp, subj: Airlift of BLT, Mar 30, 1969.

6. Rprt, Gen Harold K. Johnson, CSAR, Survey of the Military Situation in Vietnam, Mar 14, 1965; hist, CINCPAC, 1965, II, 456-457, I, 37-40; *Pentagon Papers*, GPO ed, vol III, pt IV-C-1, pp v-vii, a10-a16, 103-116, vol IV, pt IV-C-5, pp 17-23; brief, XPDA, Hq USAF, US Deployments to RVN, Apr 15, 1965; memo, MACV J-5 to C/S MACV, subj: Proposal for Employing 173rd Abn Bde in RVN, Mar 19, 1965.

7. Memo, MACV J-3 to COMUSMACV, subj: Movement and Employment of 173rd Abn Bde, Apr 17, 1965; hist, 6315th Ops Gp, Jan-Jun 65, p 7; memo, MACV J-3 to C/S MACV, subj: April Historical Summary, May 21, 1965; *Washington Post*, May 5, 1965.

8. Memo, MACV J-3 to MACV, subj: May Historical Summary, Jun 16, 1965; rprt, 315th AD, Airlift Accomplishments CY 65; hist, 8th Aerial Port Sq, Jan-Jun 65; hist, 6315th Ops Gp, Jan-Jun 65, p 7; *New York Times*, May 6, 1965.

9. Msg 00373, 315th AD to PACAF (for Gen Martin), 120830Z Mar 65; rprt, Col Leon M. Tannenbaum, DCS/Ops, 315th AD, Comments on 315th TCGp Annual General Inspection, Jan 12, 1965; Case intvw, May 5, 1970, hist, 2nd AD, Jan-Jun 65, II, 29-68.

10. Msg CR 00373, 315th AD to PACAF (for Gen Martin), 120830Z Mar 65; fact sheet, MACV J-3, subj: Need for C-130 Airlift, Mar 11, 1965; msg DPL 51054, PACAF to CINCPAC (for Adm Sharp), 200505Z Mar 65.

11. Hist, 2nd AD, Jan-Jun 65, II, 29, 37, 45-46, 68; hist, 315th AD, Jan-Jun 65, p 17, Jul-Dec 65, pp 4-6; msg 01209, 315th AD to PACAF, 230422Z Jun 65; rprt, MACV Monthly Eval Rprts, May and Jun 65.

12. Ltr, Lt Col Hillary Perdue, Dir/Ops, 315th AC Gp, to 2nd AD, subj: Nov MONEVAL, Oct Supplement, Nov 4, 1965; msg 41377, MACV J-4 to CINCPAC, 221242Z Nov 65; msg DO 02390, 315th AD DCS/Ops, to PACAF, 290832Z Nov 65; msg DOCA 02549, Dir/Combat Ops, 315th AD, to Units, 150945Z Dec 65; msg 43575, MACV J-4 to CINCPAC, 130214Z Dec 65; msg FCR 08066, 315th ACGp to 315th AD, to Col Howe from Hannah, 290829Z Dec 65; intvw, author with Maj James C. Koehring, June 29, 1972; rprt, Airlift Staff Gp, Visit to PACOM Area, 11 Oct-10 Nov 65; hist, 315th AD, 1966, pp 41-42.

13. Hist, Det 5, 315th AD, Jan–Jun 66; hist, 463rd TCWg, Jul–Dec 66, p 3; paper, 315th AD, Concept of Opn for RVN C–130 Shuttle Opn, Oct 65; rprt, Airlift Staff Gp, Visit to PACOM Area, 11 Oct–10 Nov 65.

14. Msg MMA 17466, 315th AD to Det 5, 315th AD, 290555Z Dec 65; msg DO 00885, 315th AD to 463rd and 314th TCWgs, 020627Z Mar 66; msg 03857, 315th AD to PACAF, 140436Z Oct 66, hist, 374th TCWg, Aug–Dec 66; hist, 463rd TCWg, Jan–Jun 66, p 81; briefing rprt, Lt Col Abernathy, Cdr, 516th Rote Sq, 1965.

15. West intvw, May 5, 1970; intvw, author with Capt Leonard C. Lee, Apr 29, 1972; intvw, Corona Harvest with Maj Hall W. Smith, CH intvw no 10, n.d.; hist, 315th AD, Jul–Dec 65, I, 33, 1966, I, 46–48; rprt, Airlift Staff Gp, Visit to PACOM Area, 11 Oct–10 Nov 65; report of mission, Lt Col Robert W. Kinney, Nov 1, 1965; statements, Capt Marlon Banks, Capt P. L. Carr, Capt Donald A. Zaike, Maj Norman Urban, all atchd to Briefing Report, Lt Col Abernathy, Cdr 516th Rote Sq, Naha, 1965.

16. Briefing Report, Lt Col Abernathy, Cdr 516th Rote Sq, Naha, 1965; hist, 347th TCSq, Jul–Dec 65.

17. Memo, Maj William R. Dybvad, Dir/Safety, 315th AD, to Cdr, 315th AD, subj: Mission Safety 70 Council, Aug 5, 1966; Lee intvw, Apr 28, 1972; intvw, author with Maj Henry M. Davis, Apr 24, 1972; hist, 6315th Ops Gp, Jan–Aug 66; hist, 314th TCWg, Jan–Jun 66, pp 26–27, Jul–Dec 66, pp 13, 37, 48; intvw, author with Capt Lloyd J. Probst, May 8, 1972; rprt, Capt Charles W. Case, EOTR, Jun 11, 1965.

18. Rprt, Opns Analysis Office, Hq USAF, SEA Airlift Opns, May 66; memo, IG PACAF to 314th TCWg, subj: Memo of Safety Inspection, Jun 17, 1966; msg OC 17287, 315th AD to 463rd TCWg, 6315th Ops Gp, 160438Z Dec 65; msg DPO 07403, PACAF to ADCS/Pers, Hq USAF, 120139Z Feb 66; msg DO 00767, 463rd TCWg to Det 5, 315th AD, 130530Z Apr 66; msg DO 00110, 314th TCWg to 315th AD, 160350Z Apr 66; Clark intvw, Nov 4, 1970; hist, 315th AD, 1966, I, 46–49; hist, 463rd TCWg, Jan–Jun 66, pp 52–54, Jul–Dec 66, pp 12–13; hist, 314th TCWg, Jan–Jun 66, pp 10–11.

19. Clark intvw, Nov 4, 1970; West intvw, May 5, 1970; msg DOS 02430, 315th AD Dir/Spt Ops to units, 020708Z Dec 65; hist, 315th AD, Jul–Dec 65, p 31.

20. Msg GOC 02212, 6315th Ops Gp, to 315th AD, 060842Z Dec 65; msg 045, 839th AD to TAC, for DPL and DOAL, Sep 22, 1965; msg DPL 54505, PACAF to 2nd AD, 030212Z Dec 65; msg DOCO 34286, PACAF to 315th AD, *et al*, 262339Z Oct 65; hist, 315th AD, Jul–Dec 65, I, 31–33.

21. Ltr, Lt Gen William W. Momyer, Cdr 7th AF, to Gen Hunter Harris, Cdr PACAF, subj: Command and Control of In-country Airlift in SVN, Jul 10, 1966; background paper, Air Staff, Status of Deployments to SEA, Oct 2, 1965; brief, DCS/Plans and Ops, Hq USAF, subj: Change to Phase I Deployment Program, Apr 14, 1966; msg J-3 5710, JCS to CINCPAC, 302251Z Jun 66; msg 00599, 7th AF to PACAF, for Gen Hunter Harris, Sep 12, 1966; msg 45224, MACV J-3 to CINCPAC, 120110Z Oct 66; rprt, Col Arthur D. Thomas, 7th AF, EOTR, Oct 66.

22. Msg DOP 51048, PACAF to 7th AF, 170005Z Jul 66; msg 02110, CINCPACAF to 7th AF, pers for Momyer, 180835Z Oct 66; rprt, Lt Gen Glen W. Martin, IG USAF, Visit to PACOM Area to Evaluate Airlift, 27 Feb–12 Mar 66; ltr, Lt Gen Hewitt T. Wheless, Asst Vice CSAF, to CINCPACAF, subj: Airlift Organization in the Pacific, Oct 25, 1966; rprt, Opns Analysis Off, Hq USAF, 2nd Progress Rprt, Analysis of Airlift Opns in the Pacific, Jun 66; memo, Sec Def to JCS, subj: C–130 Deployment to SVN, Dec 5, 1966; JCSM-722-66, JCS to Sec Def, subj: C–130 Deployment to SVN, Nov 19, 1966; CM–1838–66, Gen Earle G. Wheeler, CJCS, for Dir/Joint Staff, subj: C–130 Deployment, Oct 17, 1966.

23. Rprt, Opns Analysis Office, Hq USAF, Analysis of SEA Airlift Opns, Sep 66; hist, 315th AD, 1966, I, 30–32; rprt, 834th AD, Tact Airlift Performance Analysis, Dec 66; rprt, 315th AD, PACAF Airlift System Accomplishments CY 66; Fact Book, MACV, Info for Senate Preparedness Subcom, Oct 66; rprt, II FFV, Operational Report for Qtrly Period ending 31 Jul 66, Aug 15, 1966; staff study sheet, MACV TMA,

725

subj: MACV Requirements for C-130 Aircraft, Oct 11, 1966.

24. Planning Document, MACV, Concept of Opns in RVN, Sep 1, 1965; memo, Gen William C. Westmoreland, MACV, to Sec Def, subj: Shopping List, Jul 20, 1965; listing, Shopping List Items, Jul 65; msg 50099, PACAF to CSAF, 310453Z Jul 65; msg DPL 51265, PACAF to CSAF, 030732Z Aug 65; hist, MACV, 1965, pp 37-45; *DOD Pentagon Papers,* bk 4, pt IV-C-5, "Chronology."

25. Hist, 6315th Opns Gp, Jul-Dec, p 2; hist, 315th AD, Jul-Dec 65, pp 12-16, xiii-xiv; hist, 463rd TCWg, Jan-Jun 66; hist, 314th TCWg, Jan-Jun 66, pp 1-3; Lee intvw, Apr 28, 1972 (Lee was a navigator with 314th TCWg in 1966).

26. Msg 01209, 315th AD DCS/Ops, to PACAF, 230422Z Jun 65; memo, Robert S. McNamara, Sec Def, for SAF, subj: Increase in Airlift Capabilities, Jul 26, 1965; hist, Dir/Opns, Hq USAF, Jul-Dec 65, pp 15-16; hist, 315th AD, 1966, I, 9-11.

27. Study, TAC, Tactical Airlift Study, Mar 23, 1966; hist, 315th AD, 1966, pp 34-38, 115-116; Borders intvw, Nov 4, 1970; hist, Dir/Opns, Hq USAF, Jul-Dec 66, pp 218-221; hist, 6315th Opns Gp, Jan-Aug 66, pp 4-2 to 4-3; hist, 374th TCWg, Aug-Dec 66, pp 42, 46.

28. Memo, Eugene M. Zuckert, SAF, to Sec Def, subj: Increase in Acft Utilization, Sep 30, 1965; draft ms, Capt Jackameit, TAC, "Advanced Flying Training in TAC in Support of SEA Operations, 1965-9," 1971; hist, 9th AF, Jul-Dec 65, I, 87-93; hist, 314th TCWg, Jul-Dec 65, p 14; hist, Dir/Opns, Hq USAF, Jul-Dec 65, pp 12-13.

29. Msg Dp 14746, 315th AD to PACAF, 140810Z Jun 66; msg DO 00302, 314th TCWg to PACAF, 120900Z Jul 66; msg DPMC, 315th AD to PACAF, 050415Z Aug 66; hist ISO, 314th TCWg, Jan-Jun 65, p 5, Jul-Dec 66, pp 2-10; hist, PACAF, 1966, pp 409-415.

30. Memo, MACV, subj: The Transportation System in RVN, Apr 65; briefing text, MACV J-4, Logistics Briefing, Oct 65; rprt, JLRB, Monograph 18, "Transportation and Movement Control, 1970," pp 109-121; hist, MACV, 1965, pp 104-108.

31. Msg 45412, MACV J-3 to CINCPAC, 130317Z Oct 66; rprt, MACV J-4, Logistical Review and Evaluation, Jul 66-Jan 67; briefing text, MACV, subj: US Logistics Posture, Jan 11, 1966; minutes, Mission Council Mtg held Jul 11, 1966; hist, MACV, 1965, pp 122-123, 1966, pp 294-296; hist, 2nd AD, Jan-Jun 65, I, 7-8.

32. Rprt, Opns Analysis Off, Hq USAF, Analysis of SEA Airlift Operations, Sep 66; rprt, JLRB, Monograph 18, "Transportation and Movement Control," 1970, pp 134-138; hist, MACV, 1965, pp 120-121, 1966, pp 296-299.

33. Msg DOP 51048, PACAF to 7th AF, 170005Z Jul 66; Fact Book, Hq MACV, Sec Def Visit to Vietnam, 10-14 Oct 66; planning document, MACV, Concept of Operations in the RVN, Sep 1, 1965.

34. Rprts, MACV, Monthly Evaluation Reports, Jan 65 through Dec 66; Fact Book, MACV, subj: Sec Def Visit to Vietnam, 10-14 Oct 66; rprt, USARV, Lessons Learned for Pd 1 Jan-30 Apr 66, Jul 1, 1966.

35. Rprt, Capt Charles W. Case, TMC/ALCC, 315th ACGp, EOTR, Jun 11, 1965; rprt, 1st Lt Donald L. Smith, TMC/ALCC, 315th ACgp, EOTR, Jun 10, 1965; rprt, Airlift Staff Gp, Report of USAF Airlift Staff Visit to PACOM Area, 11 Oct-10 Nov 65, pp 132-136; 1st Ind, PACAF DOCO to DOCC, Jul 6, 1965, to rprt, Capt Charles W. Case, EOTR, Jun 11, 1965.

36. MR, Lt Col Donald R. Hayes, J-4 TMA, subj: Minutes of JMTB Mtg (18 Jul), Jul 20, 1966; MR's, Col E. E. Robertson, MACV J-4, subj: Minutes of JMTB Mtgs (20 and 22 Jun 66), Jun 22, 1966; msg 10133, MACV J-4 to CINCPAC, 302345Z Mar 66.

37. Ltr, Col Jack W. Tooley, Cdr TMA-MACV, to Adj Gen, MACV, subj: Establishing TMA, MACV, Feb 7, 1966; ltr, Col L. M. Harris, USA, Adj Gen, MACV, to Cdr TMA-MACV, subj: Mission Letter for the TMA, MACV, Sep 23, 1965; TMA-MACV Pamphlet 10-1, Hq Traffic Management Agency, MACV, Organization and Functions, Mar 25, 1966; fact sheet, MACV J-4, subj: Traffic Management Agency (TMA), Mar 22, 1966.

38. Rprt, Opns Analysis Off, Hq USAF, Integration of Army CV-2 Aircraft into the USAF Inventory, Nov 66; hist, 315th ACGp, Jul-Dec 65, p 32; rprt, Lt Col Thomas M. Sadler, TALO, I FFV, Debriefing Rprt, Nov 10, 1966; ltr, Col George L. Hannah, Cdr 315th ACWg,

to subord cds, subj: Acft Operation in RVN, Mar 11, 1966.

39. Rprt, 1st Lt Donald L. Smith, TMC–ALCC, EOTR, Jun 10, 1965; hist, 315th ACGp, Jul–Dec 65, pp 30–31; hist, 315th ACWg, Jan–Jun 66, p 25; rprt, Airlift Study Gp, Rprt of Airlift Staff Visit to PACOM Area, 10 Oct–11 Nov 65.

40. Hist, 8th Aerial Port Sq, Jul–Dec 65, p 30, Jan–Jun 66, pp 75–76, Jul 66–Oct 67; hist, 315th TCGp, Jan–Jun 65, p 33; rprt, Lt Col Harry G. Howton, Cdr 311th TCSq, EOTR, Sep 6, 1965; ltr, Maj James F. Morgan, Cdr CCT, 8th Aer Port Sq, to TALC, subj: Comments on CCT Exper in VN, Oct 8, 1969.

41. Rprt, Lt Col Harry G. Howton, Cdr 311th TCSq, EOTR, Sep 6, 1965; rprt, Col Robert T. Simpson, Cdr 315th ACWg, Oct 28, 1966; Borders intvw, Nov 4, 1970; rprt, Capt Jimmie S. Rutledge, 19th ACSq, Aug 12, 1966; rprt, Capt Francisco Machado, 315th ACWg, EOTR, Aug 10, 1965; rprt, Col Robert J. Jones, Base Cdr, Nha Trang, EOTR, Apr 66; rprt, 315th AD Safety Survey Team, Safety Survey of 315th ACGp, 8–19 Feb 66, hist, 315th ACGp, Jan–Jun 65, pp 31–32, Jul–Dec 65, pp 33–35; ltr, Capt Robert M. Harkey, Dir/Telecomm, 315th AD, to Dir/Electron, PACAF, subj: AN/PRC-25 Radios for C-130 Interim FM Comm, Mar 8, 1966.

42. Probst intvw, May 8, 1972; West intvw, May 5, 1970; ltr, Capt William A. Barry to author, subj: Tactical Airlift Missions in Vietnam, May 72; rprt, Lt Gen Glen W. Martin, IG USAF, Visit to PACOM to Evaluate Airlift, 27 Feb–12 Mar 66; rprt, 315th ACWg, 315th ACWg Accomplishments, Jul 19, 1966; rprts, Opns Analysis Off, Hq USAF, SEA Airlift Opns, May 66 and Sep 66; rprt, 834th AD, Tactical Airlift Performance Analysis, Dec 66.

43. Rprts, PACAF, Airlift Reports for Apr and May 66; rprt, 315th ACWg, 315th ACWg Accomplishments, Jul 19, 1966; msg 06754, MACV J-4 to 2nd AD, 030832Z Mar 66; hist, 315th ACGp, Jul–Dec 65, pp 42–44.

44. Ltr, Lt Col Robert C. Ruby, ALO 1st Cav Div, to Brig Gen George B. Simler, Dep/Opns, 7th AF, subj: Airlift AAR on Opn Mosby, Apr 22, 1966; ltr, Col E. B. Roberts, USA, Cdr 1st Bde, 1st Air Cav Div, subj: Comb Opns AAR, Matador, Jan 30, 1966; msg AFXPDO 75269, Dir/Plans, Hq USAF, to PACAF (for Col Stanton), 092219Z Mar 66.

45. Paper, 7th AF, subj: Concept for SEA Airlift, Jul 31, 1966; memo, Maj Gen C. M. Dunn, ACS J-4, MACV, to J-3 MACV, subj: Airlift Organization and Operations, Aug 18, 1966; ltr, MACV J-3 to units, subj: Emergency Airlift Request System, Oct 25, 1966.

46. Msg 054356, PACAF to 7th AF, for Momyer, 062147Z Jul 66; ltr, Lt Gen William W. Momyer, Cdr 7th AF, to COMUSMACV, subj: Military Population in the Saigon Area, Jul 18, 1966; hist, Dir/Plans, Hq USAF, Jan–Jun 66, pp 262–264; ltr, Col Lester R. Ferriss, Vice Cdr, 315th AD, to 315th AD agencies, subj: Establishment of RVN Airlift Air Division, Jul 13, 1966; hist, 834th AD, 15 Oct 66–Jun 67, I, 1–7; Arne Ellermets, "The Influence of Vietnam on Tactical Doctrine," (ACSC Thesis), Air Univ, Jun 68, p 23.

47. Rprt, Opns Analysis Off, Hq USAF, Analysis of SEA Airlift Opns, 2nd Progress Rprt, May 66; Case intvw, May 5, 1970; rprt, 1st Lt Donald L. Smith, TMA–ALCC, EOTR, Jun 10, 1965; West intvw, May 5, 1970; rprt, Lt Gen Glen W. Martin, IG USAF, Visit to PACOM to Evaluate Airlift, 27 Feb–12 Mar 66; rprt, Airlift Staff Gp, Rprt of USAF Airlift Staff Visit to PACOM Area, 11 Oct–10 Nov 65; Koehring intvw, Jun 29, 1972; Capts Lowell W. Jones and Don A. Lindbo, "Tactical Airlift," *Air University Review*, XVIII (Sep–Oct 67), p 15.

48. Msg 2 DAT, 2nd AD to PACAF, 050323Z Oct 65; msg DPAMR 10955, PACAF to Asst DCS/Pers, Hq USAF, 092004Z Oct 65; hist, 315th AD, Jan–Jun 65, p 11, Jul–Dec 65, pp 22–23, 1966, pp 98–102; hist, 8th Aerial Port Sq, Jan–Jun 65 and Jul–Dec 65; rprt, Operations Analysis Office, Hq USAF, SEA Airlift Operations, May 66; rprt, Airlift Staff Gp, Rprt of USAF Airlift Staff Visit to PACOM Area, 11 Oct–10 Nov 65; Paul L. Peoples, "Aerial Port Problems in PACAF, 1963–66," (ACSC Thesis), Air University, Jun 67, pp 19–27; hist, 2nd Aer Port Gp, Jan–Jun 66, and Jul 66–Sep 67, pp 1–3.

49. Rprt, Airlift Staff Gp, Rprt of USAF Airlift Staff Visit to PACOM Area, 11 Oct–10 Nov 65; hist, 8th Aerial Port Sq, Jan–Jun 65, Jul–Dec 65, Jan–

Jun 66; hist, 14th Aerial Port Sq, Jan–Jun 66; hist, 315th AD, Jan–Jun 65, I, 38, 1966, I, 105–196; Ind, rprt, Brig Gen J. H. Thompson, DCS/Materiel, 7th AF, EOTR, Feb 28, 1967, PACAF, 1967.

50. Ltr, Gen William C. Westmoreland, Cdr MACV, to Lt Gen J. E. Engler, Dep CG USARV, Oct 10, 1966; rprt, MACV J–4, Monthly Hist Rprt, Sep 16, 1966; hist, 8th Aerial Port Sq, Jan–Jun 65, Jul–Dec 65, pp 17–29; intvw, Proj Corona Harvest with Lt Col Robert L. Jenkins, Maj Forrest H. Bennett, and Maj William Rios, CH intvw no 236, n.d.; Maj Arne Ellermets, "The Influence of Vietnam on Tactical Airlift Doctrine," (ACSC Thesis), Air Univ, 1968, p 50.

51. Hist, 8th Aerial Port Sq, Jan–Jun 65 and Jul–Dec 65, pp 14–15; msg GTR 111141, 315th ACGp to 315th AD, 150910Z Nov 65; rprt, Airlift Staff Gp, Rprt of USAF Airlift Staff Visit to PACOM Area, 11 Oct–10 Nov 65; Jenkins, Bennett and Rios intvw, n.d., rprt, Maj William W. Burnett, 311th ACSq, May 3, 1965; rprt, Col Harry Howton, Cdr 311th ACSq, Sep 6, 1965; Peoples, "Aerial Port Problems in PACAF, 1963–66," (ACSC Thesis), Air Univ, Jun 67, pp 12–14.

52. Ltr, Lt Gen Hewitt T. Wheless, Asst Vice CSAF, to Sec AF, subj: Proj NEW FOCUS, Jan 27, 1966; minutes, 315th AD, 463L Phasing Group Meeting, Tachikawa, 1–3 Dec 65; Jenkins, Bennett and Rios intvw, n.d.; Peoples, "Aerial Port Problems in PACAF, 1963–66," (ACSC Thesis), Air Univ, Jun 67, pp 4–10.

53. Hist, 8th Aerial Port Sq, Jul 66–Oct 67; 15th Aerial Port Sq, Jan–Jun 66, pp 142–147; Jenkins, Bennett and Rios intvw, n.d.

54. Jenkins, Bennett and Rios intvw, n.d.; hist, 8th Aerial Port Sq, Jul–Dec 65; PACAF Review, FY 67; hist, 315th AD, 1966, pp ix–x.

55. Background paper, Hq USAF, subj: C–123B Inventory, Apr 66; rprt, 834th AD, C–123 Total Tonnage Airlifted, n.d.; rprt, Opns Analysis Off, Hq USAF, Analysis of SEA Airlift Opns, Sep 66; hist, 315th TCGp, Jan–Jun 65, pp viii, x, 2; hist, 315th ACWg, Jul–Dec 66, p 27.

56. Rprt, Maj William W. Burnett, 311th ACSq, EOTR, May 3, 1965; rprt, Lt Col Harry G. Howton, Cdr, 311th ACSq, Sep 6, 1965; hist, 315th TCWg, Jan–Jun 65, p 3; hist, SAWC, Jul–Dec 65, pp 39–43; rprt, Off/TAC Hist, History, Advanced Flying Training in TAC in Support of SEA Opns, 1965–69, Jun 71, pp 144–161; rprt, 315th AD Survey Team, Safety Survey of 315th ACGp, 8–19 Feb 66; intvw, Proj Corona Harvest with Capt Perry G. Clark, CH intvw no 2, Aug 67.

57. Ltr, Col George L. Hannah, Cdr 315th ACGp, to Dir/Materiel, 2nd AD, subj: C–123 Maintenance, Jan 26, 1966; hist, 315th TCGp, Jan–Jun 65, pp 17–18; hist, 315th ACGp, Jul–Dec 65, pp 19, 38; ltr, Col George Budway, Cdr 6250th Comb Spt Gp, to Dir/Materiel, 7th AF, subj: C–123 Maintenance Program, Mar 11, 1966.

58. Rprt, Lt Col Hugh L. Baynes, Cdr 311th ACSq, Debriefing EOTR, Jul 5, 1966; rprt, Capt Jimmie S. Rutledge, 19th ACSq, EOTR, Aug 12, 1966; rprt, 315th AD Survey Team, Safety Survey of 315th ACGp, 8–19 Feb 66.

59. Msg DORQ 39819, PACAF, to 315th AD, 022328Z Aug 65; msg DO 32245, PACAF to AFRDQ, Hq USAF, 071954Z Dec 65; ltr, Lt Gen Hewitt T. Wheless, Asst Vice CSAF, to SAF–OS, subj: Use of C–123 Acft in Tactical Airlift Delivery Opns in Vietnam, Jan 18, 1966; hist, Dir/Opns, Hq USAF, Jul–Dec 65, pp 26–27; hist, 315th AD, Jul–Dec 65, I, 47–48; hist, 315th ACGp, Jul–Dec 65, pp 58–61.

60. Rprt, Capt Roger C. Woodbury, 19th ACSq, Debriefing EOTR, Jun 25, 1966; rprt, Lt Col Hugh L. Baynes, 311th ACSq, Debriefing EOTR, Jul 5, 1966; rprt, Capt Jimmie S. Rutledge, 19th ACSq, EOTR, Aug 12, 1966; rprt, Lt Col Harry G. Howton, Cdr, 311th ACSq, EOTR, Sep 6, 1965; rprt, Maj William W. Burnett, 311th ACSq, EOTR, May 3, 1965; rprt, Capt Harry M. Kepner, 310th ACSq, EOTR, Aug 65; rprt, Maj Carol D. Vickery, 309th ACSq, EOTR, Sep 65; Clark intvw, Aug 67; rprt, 315th AD Safety Team, Safety Survey of 315th ACGp, 8–19 Feb 66; hist, 315th ACGp, Jul–Dec 65, p 5; rprt, Airlift Staff Gp, Rprt of USAF Airlift Staff Visit to PACOM Area, 11 Oct–10 Nov 65.

61. Fact sheet, 7th AF, subj: USAF Combat/Operational Aircraft Losses, C–123/C–130, 1 Jan 65–31 Jul 66, 1966; rprt, Maj James R. McCarthy, 309th ACSq, Jul 19, 1966; rprt, IG Safety,

USAF, C-130 Aircraft Accident Summary for 1965 (summary 18-66), p 4; hist, 314th TCWg, Jan-Jun 65; hist, 6315th Opns Gp, Jan-Aug 66, pp 19-24; hist, 315th AD, Jan-Jun 65, pp x, 27-32, 1966, I, 54.

62. Daily Staff Journal, MACV J-313-1 COC, Oct 30, 1965; hist, 7th AF, 1 Jan 66-30 Jun 67, p ix; hist, 315th ACWg, Jan-Jun 66; hist, 6315th Ops Gp, Jul-Dec 65, pp 19-22.

63. Hist, 314th TCWg, Jul-Dec 66, pp 15-16; hist, 315th TCGp, Jan-Jun 65, pp 47-49; hist, 315th AD, Jan-Jun 65, I, 30-31; rprt, MACV, Monthly Evaluation Rprt, Jun 65; msg 0118, 309th ACSq to PACAF, 271120Z Dec 65.

64. Rprt, Col Robert T. Simpson, Cdr 315th ACWg, EOTR, Oct 28, 1966, p 2; rprt, Lt Col Hugh L. Baynes, Cdr, 311th ACSq, Debriefing EOTR, Jul 5, 1966; msg 00089, Cdr 6315th Ops Gp to 315th AD, 110730Z Jan 66; msg 10020, Cdr 315th AD to units, 280843Z Jan 66; msg 17323, Cdr 315th AD to units, 170750Z Dec 65; hist, 315th Ad 1966, I, 49-51.

65. Rprt, 315th AD Survey Team, Safety Survey of 315th ACGp, 8-19 Feb 66; Borders intvw, Nov 4, 1970; rprt, 834th AD, Tactical Airlift Performance Analysis, Dec 66; 1st Ind, (ltr, 315th AD, subj: 315th AD Safety Survey of 315th ACGp, 8-19 Feb 66), 315th ADWg to 315th AD, Mar 19, 1966.

66. Rprt, Hq II FFV, Opl Rprt for Qtrly Period ending 31 Jul 66, Aug 15, 1966; ltr, Maj Ernest L. Howell, Sr Controller, to Det 5, 315th AD, subj: Mission Cdr's Rprt on Op Birmingham, Apr 66; memo, Col William A. Knowlton, USA, Secy Joint Staff, MACV, to MACV agencies, subj: Command/Staff Action Memo no 66-53, Aug 15, 1966; directive no 95-9, MACV J-3, Joint Airborne/ Airmobile Air Strip Operation, May 9, 1966; unpublished manuscript, Lt Col Ray L. Bowers, SEA Journal, 1967-8, 1969; rprt, Col V. Froelich, EOTR, Aug 67.

67. Rprt, 315th AD, PACAF Airlift System Accomplishments CY 66; msg 00042, C-130 Mission Cdr, TSN to PACAF, 220730Z Dec 65; hist, 314th TCWg, Jan-Jun 66, p 28, Jul-Dec 66; hist, 315th AD, Jan-Jun 65, I, 21.

68. Msg 17422, Cdr 315th AD to PACAF, 241146Z Dec 65; msg 21644, MACV J-3 to CG III MAF, 241302Z Jun 66; rprt, Capt Marius F. Kempf, 19th ACSq, Sep 25, 1966; PACAF Tactics/Techniques Bulletin 7, Troop Carrier and Transport Tactics, SEA, May 23, 1965; PACAF Tactics/Techniques Bulletin 16, Evasive Tactics, 1965.

69. Ltr, 2nd Bde, 1st Cav Div, to CG, 1st Air Cav Div, subj: Combat Ops AAR, May 4, 1966; msg ALO 2004665, ALO 1st Cav Div to PACAF, 7th AF, 200345Z Apr 66; rprt, MACV, Monthly Evaluation, Jul 65; hist, 463rd TCWg, Jan-Jun 66, pp 44-45.

70. Rprts, USARV Army Opns Center, Operational Results as of 080400H and 140400H Jul 66; rprt, USARV AOC, Operational Summary, 17 Jun 66; hist, 314th TCWg, Jul-Dec 66.

Chapter IX

Search and Destroy

1. Rprts, MACV, Monthly Evaluation Reports, Jan through Dec 65; hist, 2nd AD, Jan-Jun 65, II, 25-28; *Pentagon Papers*, GPO ed, vol IV, pt IV-C-3, p 69; rprt, Col J. K. Woodyard, Dep Dir 2nd AD AOC, Phuoc Bien 13 Operation, 28-31 Dec 64; lecture presentation, Lt Col George MacGarrigle, USA, OCMH, Vietnam War, Mar 30, 1973.

2. Hist, 315th TCGp, Jan-Jun 65, pp 37-41; hist, 8th Aerial Port Sq, Jan-Jun 65; study, Ad Hoc Study Gp, JCS, subj: Intensification of the Mil Opns in VN and Appraisal, Jul 14, 1965; hist, 2nd AD, Jan-Jun 65, II, 68-69, Jul-Dec 65, II, 17-18; ltr, Col T. C. Mataxsis, Sr Advisor, II Corps, to Cdr, 2nd AD, subj: Exceptional Performance by 315th AD,

Aug 19, 1965; ltr, Gen William C. Westmoreland, Cdr, MACV, to CG, 2nd AD, subj: Ltr of Commendation, Jun 22, 1965; ltr, Maj William N. Ciccolo, USA, Dep Sr Adv, VN Abn Bde, to MACV, subj: Combat Ops AAR, Jul 26, 1965; rprt, Maj Robert McCutcheon to DDIH, 2nd AD, subj: After Action Report, Trung Doan 58, 1965; rprts, MACV, Monthly Evaluation Reports, Jan through Dec 65.

3. Rprt, MACV, Monthly Eval, Aug 65; msg DO–03131, 2nd AD to PACAF, subj: Summary of USAF Activities RVN, Aug 30, 1965; ltr, Lt Col Robert J. Craig, USA, Sr Advis, Sp Tact Zone 24, to MACV, subj: Comb Ops AAR, Dan Thang 4–7, Sep 13, 1965; ltr, 315th ACWg to 7th AF, subj: Recommendation for Pres Unit Citation, Jan 30, 1966; hist, 8th Aerial Port Sq, Jul–Dec 65.

4. Transcript, Questions and Answers at Mtg between Sec McNamara, Amb Taylor, COMUSMACV, and staffs, Jul 16, 1965; planning document, MACV, Concept of Opns in the RVN, Sep 1, 1965; MACV Directive 525–4, Tactics and Techniques for Employment of US Forces in RVN, Sep 17, 1965; msg 15182, MACV to CINCPAC, *et al,* 080700Z May 65; study, Ad Hoc Study Gp, JCS, subj: Intensification of the Mil Opns in VN, Concept and Appraisal, Jul 14, 1965; Fact Book MACV, MACV Responses to Questions by Sec Def, Jul 65; msg 22055, MACV to CINCPAC, 131515Z Jun 65; *Pentagon Papers,* GPO ed, vol V, pt IV–C–6(a), pp 13–17; Gen William C. Westmoreland, *A Soldier Reports* (New York, 1976), pp 130–150.

5. Msg VC 01537, PACAF to XPD, Hq USAF, 080400Z Jun 65; hist, Dir/Plans, Hq USAF, Jan–Jun 66, pp 6–7; msg 96668, CSAF to PACAF, McConnell to Harris, 132017Z Sep 65; JCSM–76–66, JCS to Sec Def, subj: Consequences of an Enclave Strategy, Feb 3, 1966; Gen James M. Gavin, "A Communication on Vietnam," *Harpers,* Feb 66; *Pentagon Papers,* GPO ed, vol IV, pt IV–C–5, Westmoreland, *A Soldier Reports,* pp 128–129.

6. Memos, Robert S. McNamara, Sec Def, for Sec Army and CJCS, subj: Army Airmobile Division, 19 Apr and 15 Jun 65; JCSM–205–65, JCS to Sec Def, subj: The Army's Proposal to Reorganize the 1st Cav Div as an Airmobile Div, Mar 20, 1965; hist, Dir/Plans,

Jan–Jun 65, pp 179–182, Jul–Dec 65, pp 149–150; Robert F. Futrell, *Ideas, Concepts, Doctrine: A History of Basic Thinking in the USAF 1907–1964,* (ASI), Air Univ, Jun 71, pp 739–759.

7. Study, MACV, Commander's Estimate of the Military Situation in VN, Mar 26, 1965; brief, Dir/Plans, Hq USAF, subj: Deployment of US/Allied Combat Forces to Vietnam, Mar 21, 1965; CSARM, C/S US Army, subj: Employment of a US Army Division in the Central Highlands of SVN, Mar 29, 1965; summary sheet, Mil History Br, MACV, subj: msg JCS 0936, Mar 16, 1965; *Pentagon Papers,* GPO ed, vol III, pt IV–C–1, pp v–vii, a10–a16, 103.

8. Msg VC–01537, PACAF to Dir/Plans, Hq USAF, 080400Z Jun 65; background paper, Hq USAF, subj: ALOC Within SVN, Mar 23, 1965; talking paper, Air Staff, subj: CSAM 163–165, Mar 30, 1965; brief, Lt Col C. W. Abbott, Dir/Plans, Hq USAF, subj: Comments on a Concept for Employment of Army Airmobile Div, May 4, 1965; memo, Maj Gen Arthur C. Agan, ACS/Plans and Ops, Hq USAF, to Vice CSAF, subj: Status of CSAF J–94–65, Air Lines of Communications, May 28, 1965; study, DCS/Logis, Dept/Army, A Systems Analysis: Air Line of Communications, Dec 64; ltr, J. A. Stockfisch, Rand, to author, Jan 28, 1975 (Stockfisch was analyst at OSD/Systems Analysis in 1965).

9. Msg 90300, Dep Dir/Plans/War Plans, Hq USAF, to PACAF, Jul 31, 1965; msg XPDX 81901, Ch Aerospace Doct Div, Hq USAF, to PACAF, 210214Z Jun 65; background paper, Dir/Plans, Hq USAF, subj: Working Conference on Deployments to SVN, Aug 1, 1965; msg 22055, MACV to CINCPAC, 131515Z Jun 65; *Pentagon Papers,* GPO ed, Vol IV, pt IV–C–5; Westmoreland, *A Soldier Reports,* pp 144–145.

10. Rprt, USARV, Battlefield Reports, A Summary of Lessons Learned, Jun 30, 1966; memo, MACV J–3 to MACV J–03, subj: July Historical Summary, Aug 27, 1965; *Pentagon Papers,* GPO ed, Vol IV, pt IV–C–5, pp 108–112.

11. Data Sheet, Dept/Army, subj: US Army Air Mobile Division, Jul 65.

12. Rprt, MACV, Monthly Evaluation, Aug 65; video tape, Lt Col John Stoner, Briefing from Vietnam, Apr 29, 1966; ltr,

315th ACWg to 7th AF, subj: Recommendation for Pres Unit Citation, Jun 30, 1966; Edward Hymoff, *The First Air Cavalry Division, Vietnam* (M. W. Lads: New York, NY, 1967), pp 6-12; Lt Gen John J. Tolson, *Airmobility: 1961-1971* (Dept/Army, Vietnam Studies, 1973), pp 67-72; preliminary draft ms, Lt Col George MacGarrigle, USA, "The War in Vietnam," n.d., OCMH.

13. Ltr, 1st Air Cav Div, to MACV, others, subj: Lessons Learned, 1 Oct-30 Nov 65, Jan 10, 1966; memo, Lt Gen J. H. Moore, Cdr, 2nd AD, to MACV, subj: Visit to 1st Air Cav Div, Nov 5, 1965, Nov 9, 1965; intvw, author with Col John R. Stoner, Aug 15, 1972; video tape, Lt Col John R. Stoner, Briefing from Vietnam, Apr 29, 1966; intvw, author with Lt Col Charles J. Corey, Aug 17, 1972; steno record, testimony of Gen Harold K. Johnson, USA, at Mil Airlift Subcomm, House Common Armed Services, Oct 22, 1965.

14. Ltr, Gen J. P. McConnell, CSAF, to CSAR, subj: USAF Support for Airmobile Division, Jul 19, 1965; brief, Col R. D. Lancaster, Dir/Plans, Hq USAF, subj: Analysis of Data Presented to CSAF by CSA on 13 Jul 65; msg 90300, Dep Dir/Plans/War Plans, Hq USAF, to PACAF, Jul 31, 1965; memo, Lt Gen K. K. Compton, DCS/Plans and Ops, Hq USAF, to Gen Blanchard, subj: 1st Cavalry Division (Air Mobile) Concept of Opns and Reqmts for USAF Support, Sep 14, 1965; steno record, testimony of Gen Harold K. Johnson, USA, at Mil Airlift Subcomm, House Common Armed Services, Oct 22, 1965; H. W. O. Kinnard, "A Victory in the Ia Drang: The Triumph of a Concept," *Army*, Sep 67, p 73.

15. Kinnard, "A Victory in the Ia Drang," *Army*, Sep 67; daily staff journal, MACV J-313-1 COC, dates in Oct 65; ltr, Maj Charlie A. Beckwith, Cdr, Det B52, 5th SF Gp, to Cdr 5th SF Gp, subj: Sequence of Events for Plei Me Opn for 20-28 Oct 65, Nov 15, 1965; article, "Success Story: CIDG in Camp Defense (Plei Me)," Atch to Report, 5th SF Gp, Qtrly Cd Report for Pd Ending 31 Dec 65.

16. Hist, 315th ACGp, Jul-Dec 65, p 21; rprt, PACAF, COIN Lessons Learned, Jun 29, 1966; daily staff journal, MACV, J-313-1 COC, 19-26 Oct 65; rprt, Col Archie R. Hyle, USA, Sr Advis STZ 24, subj: Combat Op AAR, 5 Dec 65; msg DOCA 21524, 315th ACGp to 315th AD, 240144Z Nov 65; memo, 1st Lt Peter R. Teasdale, QMC, USA, Air Movements Off, 5th SF Gp, to Cdr 5th SF Gp, subj: Support of Plei Me, Nov 65; Melvin F. Porter, *The Siege at Plei Me*, (Hq PACAF, Proj CHECO, Feb 24, 1966).

17. Kinnard, "A Victory in the Ia Drang," pp 71-91; daily staff journal, Div Tact Opns Center, 1st Air Cav Div, Oct 65; msg C-51324, PACAF to CSAF (for McConnell from Harris), 010500Z Dec 65; rprt, 1st Air Cav Div, Combat Ops AAR, Pleiku Campaign, Mar 4, 1966.

18. Daily staff journal, MACV J-313-1, COC, 26-28 Oct 65; Kinnard, "A Victory in the Ia Drang"; msgs, 1st Air Cav Div to CG FFV, subj: SITREPs, 220020Z, 222345Z, 232400Z, 250040Z, 252255Z, 272317Z, 282320Z, 292340Z Oct 65; Kenneth Sams, *Command and Control, 1965* (PACAF, Proj CHECO, 15 Dec 66), pp 31-33; msg DOPR, 2nd AD to PACAF, 281210Z Nov 65.

19. Col John R. Stoner, "The Closer the Better," *Air University Review*, Sep-Oct 67, pp 29-41; Corey intvw, Aug 17, 1972.

20. Stoner intvw, Aug 15, 1972; Corey intvw, Aug 17, 1972; hist, 8th Aerial Port Sq, Jul-Dec 65; rprt, 1st Air Cav Div, Comb Ops AAR, Pleiku Campaign, Mar 4, 1966; memo, Lt Gen J. H. Moore, Cdr 2nd AD, to MACV, subj: Visit to 1st Air Cav Div, 5 Nov 65; video tape, Lt Col John R. Stoner, Briefing from Vietnam, Apr 29, 1966; intvw, Corona Harvest with Col Kampe, USA, CH intvw no 101, n.d.

21. Rprt, 1st Air Cav Div, Comb Opns AAR, Pleiku Campaign, Mar 4, 1966; daily staff journals, 1st Air Cav Div Tact Opns Center, 28 Oct thru 10 Nov 65; Corey intvw, Aug 17, 1972.

22. Rprt, Maj Gen Harry W. O. Kinnard, Cdr, 1st Cav Div to DCS/Mil Ops, Dept/Army, Qtrly Cd Report for 2/FY 66, Feb 12, 1966; Kinnard, "A Victory in the Ia Drang"; rprt, 1st Air Cav Div, Comb Ops AAR, Pleiku Campaign, Mar 4, 1966; ltr, Maj William N. Ciccolo, USA, Sr Advis, VN Abn Bde, to MACV, subj: Combat Opns AAR, Dec 17, 1965.

23. Rprt, 1st Air Cav Div, Comb Ops AAR, Pleiku Campaign, Mar 4, 1966;

msg DOPR, 2nd Air Div to PACAF, 281210Z Nov 65; Kinnard, "A Victory in the Ia Drang," pp 78–91; msgs, MACV J–4 to CINCPAC, 151450Z Nov 65, 301955Z Oct 65, 011550Z Dec 65.

24. Msg C–51324, PACAF to CSAF, for McConnell from Harris, 010500Z Dec 65; hist, Dir/Plans, Hq USAF, Jan–Jun 66, pp 329–330; video tape, Lt Col John R. Stoner, Briefing from Vietnam, Apr 29, 1966.

25. Ltr, 1st Air Cav Div, to subord Cd and Staff officers, subj: Lessons Learned, no 2, Dec 9, 1965; ltr, 1st Air Cav Div to MACV, subj: Lessons Learned, 1 Oct–30 Nov 65, Jan 10, 1966; rprt, MACV Monthly Evaluation, Nov 65, Dec 31, 1965; Corey intvw, Aug 17, 1972; Stoner intvw, Aug 15, 1972; rprt, Maj Gen Harry W. O. Kinnard, Cdr 1st Cav Div, to DCS/Mil Ops, Dept/Army, Qtrly Cd Rprt for 2/FY 66, Feb 12, 1966; text statement, Ben Gilleas, Preparedness Subcomm, Senate Armed Forces Comm, Jan 12, 1966; rprt, Joint Army–AF Coordinating Team (NEW FOCUS), Trip to Vietnam, 25 Oct–12 Nov 65, Dec 65; rprt, Maj Gen H. A. Davis, AF Team Chief, Proj NEW FOCUS Visit to SVN, Nov 19, 1965; msg, 2nd AD to PACAF (personal Harris from Moore), 291200Z Nov 65.

26. Msg 12727, MACV to CINCPAC, Westmoreland sends, 020836Z Jul 65; brief, Col R. D. Lancaster, Dir/Plans, Hq USAF, subj: Analysis of Data Presented to CSAF by CSA on Jul 13, 1965.

27. Rprts, CG 173rd Abn Bde to MACV, Daily SITREPs for Oct 65; 173rd Abn Bde OPORD 25–65 (Iron Triangle), Oct 5, 1965; rprt, 173rd Abn Bde, to MACV, subj: Comb Opn AAR, Bde Opn 24–65, Oct 29, 1965; rprt, Brig Gen Ellis W. Williamson, Cdr, 173rd Abn Bde, Critique of the Iron Triangle Opn, Oct 25, 1965.

28. Hist, 19th ACSq, Jul–Dec 65, pp 25–30.

29. Hist, 6315th Ops Gp, Jul–Dec 65, pp 13–14; hist rprt, Maj Robert B. Carmichael and Lt Richard E. Eckert, USA, Opn New Life–65, n.d.; ltrs, Capt William A. Barry to author, subj: Tactical Airlift Missions in Vietnam, May 72 and Jun 17, 1972; rprt, 173rd Abn Bde, to MACV, Comb Opns AAR, New Life–65, Jan 26, 1966; briefing, 173rd Abn Bde S–3, for Sen Investigating Comm, Oct 66; msg ALFT 003, C–130 ALFT Bien Hoa, to 315th AD, 221200Z Nov 65; rprts, 173rd Abn Bde to CG 1st Inf Div, SITREPs for Nov and Dec 65 (daily).

30. Rprts, 173rd Abn Bde, SITREPs for Jan–Mar 66 (daily); rprt, 173rd Abn Bde, Qtrly Cd Rprt, Jan–Apr 66, Aug 28, 1966; rprt, 173rd Abn Bde, Comb Opn AAR, Silver City, 1966; ltr, 173rd Abn Bde, to MACV, subj: Comb Opns AAR, Marauder I, Jan 66; rprt, 173rd Abn Bde, Critique of Marauder and Crimp, Jan 24, 1966.

31. Rprt, Lt Col Harold S. Snow, Air Liaison Off, 173rd Abn Bde, AAR (Denver), Apr 28, 1966; rprt, PACAF, Airlift Rprt for Apr 66; ltr, Lt Col B. R. Cryer, Cdr 774th TCSq, to Cdr, Det 5, 315th AD, subj: Mission Cdr's Rprt Op Denver, Apr 66; ltr, Maj Ernest Howell, Acft Cdr, to Cdr, Det 5, 315th AD, subj: Mission Cdr's Rprt, May 66; briefing, 173rd Abn Bde S–3, for Senate Investigating Subcomm, Oct 66.

32. Rprt, 1st Bde, 1st Abn Div, Opl Rprt on Lessons Learned, 1 Jan–30 Apr 66, May 15, 1966; rprt, 1st Bde, 101st Abn Div, Comb Ops AAR, Van Buren, Mar 23, 1966; hist, 315th ACGp, Jul–Dec 65, p 22; hist, MACV, 1965, pp 166–167; study, 22nd Mil Hist Det, USA, subj: Vietnam Odyssey: The Story of the 1st Bde, 101st Abn Div, 28 Jul 65–31 Dec 66.

33. Rprts, USARV G–4, Daily Significant Logistical Activities, 7–26 Apr 66; intvw, Corona Harvest with Lt Col Wheaton, USA, CH intvw no 140, Jan 23, 1969; rprt, PACAF, Airlift Rprt for Apr 66.

34. Rprt, 1st Bde, 101st Abn Div, Comb Ops AAR, Op AUSTIN, Jun 5, 1966; daily staff journals, G–4, I FFV, dates in Apr 66; ltr, Lt Col O. M. Coats, Mission Cdr, to Det 5, 315th AD, subj: Mission Cdr Rprt, May 6, 1966; Wheaton intvw, Jan 23, 1969; rprts, PACAF, Airlift Rprts for Apr and May 66; rprts, USARV G–4, Daily Significant Logistical Activities, 1–18 May 66.

35. Ltr, Col William A. McLaughlin, Dir/Ops, 315th ACWg, to 7th AF, subj: May MONEVAL, Jun 6, 1966; ltr, Maj Peter T. DiCroce, Miss Cdr, to Det 5, 315th AD, subj: Miss Cdr Report for Op Hawthorne, 29 May–3 Jun, Jun 7, 1966; ltr, Maj Edward T. Yelton, Miss Cdr, to Det 5, 315th AD, subj: Miss Cdr Rprt for Op Cooper, 19–26 May, May 66; msg T–3908, CG I FFV to

MACV TMA, 260100Z May 66; rprt, 1st Bde, 101st Abn Div, Comb Ops AAR, John Paul Jones, Sep 28, 1966; hist study, 22nd Mil Hist Det "Vietnam Odyssey"; Wheaton intvw, Jan 23, 1969; daily operational summaries, Army Opns Center, USARV, 25 and 28 May 66; rprts, USARV G-4, Daily Significant Logistical Activities, 21–26 May 66.

36. Rprts, PACAF, Airlift Rprts for Apr and May 66; rprt, Lt Col Eugene R. McCutchan, ALO ARVN Abn Div, AAR, TACC-WRP, Apr 66; study, Mil Hist Br, MACV, The Mar–Jun 66 Political Crisis in SVN and its Effects on Mil Opns, 1966; daily operational summaries, Army Ops Center, USARV, 1–4 Apr 66; *Pentagon Papers*, GPO ed, vol VII, pt IV–C–9(b), pp ix–x; *The Pentagon Papers: The Defense Department History of US Decisionmaking on Vietnam*, Sen Michael Gravel, ed, (Boston, 1971), (hereafter cited as *Pentagon Papers*, Gravel ed), pp 288, 361–376.

37. Ltr, Lt Col Eugene R. McCutchan, ALO/FAC, ARVN Abn Div, to TACC WPP, subj: AAR Abn Air Tng Test, 3–5 Apr 66, Apr 7, 1966; hist, 315th ACGp, Jul–Dec 65, p 21; hist, 315th AD, Jul–Dec 65, vol I, p xi, 1966, vol I, chronology; hist, 8th Aerial Port Sq, Jan–Jun 66; memo, Maj James F. Morgan, OIC, CCT, to Cdr, 2nd APGp, subj: CCT Deployment at Vinh Long, Apr 15, 1966; ltr, Lt Col John C. Dunn, Miss Cdr, to Det 5, 315th AD, subj: Miss Cdr Rprt, Drop Mission, Apr 4, 1966, ARVN, n.d., ltr, Maj William N. Ciccolo, USA, Sr Staff Advis, VN Abn Bde, to MACV, subj: Comb Ops AAR, Free Way, Aug 17, 1965; rprt ICO, Col Francis E. Naughton, USA, Sr Advis, VN Abn Bde, Sr Advisor Monthly Evaluation, Jun 65; msg DO–03750, Sep 20, 1965; msg 00037, 314th TCWg to 9th AF, Sep 16, 1965; *Air Force Times*, Oct 20, 1965.

38. Msg 0695, CG FFV to MACV, 311200Z Jan 66; msg 40367, MACV J–3 to CG I FFV, 070202Z Sep 66.

39. Hist, 315th AD, Jul–Dec 65, I, 38; rprts, MACV, Monthly Evaluations, Nov 65, Dec 65, Apr 66; rprt, USARV, Lessons Learned for Pd 1 Jan–30 Apr 66, Jul 1, 1966; rprt, 1st Inf Div, Qtrly Cd Rprt, Dec 31, 1965; USARV OPORD 1–66 (Op Moon Light), Feb 9, 1966.

40. Msg 42887, MACV to III MAF, FFV, 1st Inf Div, 070002Z Dec 65.

41. Rprt, 1st Inf Div, Comb Ops AAR, Op Mastiff, 1966; rprt, 2nd Bde, 1st Inf Div, Comb Ops AAR, Mastiff, Mar 31, 1966; rprt, 3rd Bde, 1st Inf Div, Comb Ops AAR, Opn Crimp, Feb 15, 1966; rprt, MACV, Monthly Eval, Dec 65, Jan 31, 1966; ltr, Col William D. Brodbeck, USA, Cdr, 3rd Bde, 1st Inf Div to Cdr MACV, subj: Comb Ops AAR, Opn Crimp, Feb 15, 1966.

42. Rprts, USARV G-4, Daily Significant Logistical Activities, 17 Apr–16 May 66; ltr, Col William A. McLaughlin, Dir/Opns 315th ACGp, to 7th AF, subj: May MONEVAL, Jun 6, 1966; ltr, Maj Ernest L. Howell, Sr Controller, to Cdr, Det 5, 315th AD, subj: Msg Cdr Rprt Opn Birmingham, Apr 66; rprt, 1st Bde, 1st Inf Div, Comb Ops AAR, Birmingham, May 24, 1966; rprt, 1st Inf Div, Comb Opns AAR, Op Birmingham, May 66; rprt, 1st Inf Div, Opl Rprt, Lessons Learned, 1 May–31 Jul 66, Aug 15, 1966; rprt, 315th AD, PACAF Airlift System Accomplishments CY 66; *Pacific Stars and Stripes*, Apr 20, 1966; Kenneth Sams, *Operation Birmingham*, (PACAF, Proj CHECO, Jun 29, 1966), pp 1–16.

43. Rprt, 1st Inf Div, Comb Ops AAR, Opn Abilene, 1966; rprts, USARV G-4, Daily Logistical Activities, 30 Mar–10 Apr 66.

44. Ltr, Maj Robert A. Hutto, Miss Cdr, to Det 5, 315th AD, subj: Mission Cdr Rprt for Op El Paso on Jun 2, 1966; rprt, 3rd Bde, 1st Inf Div, Comb Ops AAR, El Paso I, Jun 26, 1966; rprt, 1st Inf Div, Comb Opns AAR, Op El Paso II/III, 1966; rprts, USARV G-4, Daily Logistical Activities, dates in Jun and Jul 66.

45. Study, USARV, Combat Service Support at Division/Separate Brigade Level, Dec 17, 1967; rprt, Maj Gen Shelton E. Lollis, USA, 1st Logistical Cd, Debriefing Report, Aug 11, 1967; intvw, Corona Harvest Project with Lt Col Douglas Huff, USA, Jan 24, 1969; fact sheet, 1st Air Cav Div, subj: The Division Support Command, 1966; briefing, 1st Logistical Cd, USARV G-4, and 1st Air Cav Div G-4, Briefings for Senate Preparedness Investigating Subcomm, Oct 1966; Maj Joseph Costa, USA, "The FSA," *Infantry*, Sep–Oct 68, pp 27–29.

46. Maj Gen Robert R. Ploger, USA, *U.S. Army Engineers, 1965–1970* (Dept/Army, Vietnam Studies, 1974), p 113; msg 4116, CG I FFV to MACV, 010946Z

Jun 66; msg 60009, CG II FFV to MACV, 011000Z Jun 66.

47. Memo, Eugene M. Zuckert, Sec Air Force, to Sec Def, subj: AF Capability to Construct Expedient AFs, May 26, 1965; talking paper, MACV, subj: Engineer Effort in Vietnam, Dec 21, 1965; rprt, JLRB, 1970, II, 264–267; briefing text, MACV Dir/Construction, subj: Construction in RVN, Oct 25, 1966.

48. Msg DPL 54505, PACAF to 2nd AD, 030212Z Dec 65; msg 44334, MACV J–4 to USARV, 190846Z Dec 65; msg 20225, MACV Dir/Construction to USARV, 7th AF, COMNAVFORV, 131514Z Jun 66; memo, MACV Dir/Construction to Ch, Hist Br, MACV, subj: Qtrly Hist Rprt, Aug 8, 1966; Planning Document, MACV, Concept of Operations in RVN, Sep 1, 1965.

49. Msg DPL 51247, PACAF Cd Center to Dir/Plans, Hq USAF, 172030Z Jul 65; background paper, Dir/Plans, Hq USAF, subj: JCS 2343/621-4, Jul 15, 1965; Discussion, author with Mr. Paul F. Carlton, Army Corps of Engineers, Aug 30, 1972; hist, Dir/Plans, Hq USAF, Jul–Dec 65, pp 181–182; memo, Stephen Ailes, Sec Army, to Sec Def, subj: Construction in SEA, Jun 12, 1965; Ploger, *U.S. Army Engineers, 1965–1970*, pp 110–115.

50. Rprt, 1st Cav Div, Opl Rprt on Lessons Learned, Aug 15, 1966; ltr, Lt Col Charles G. Olentine, Cdr 8th Engr Btn to CG 1st Cav Div, subj: AAR on Golf Course AF, Jul 11, 1966; rprt, PACAF, COIN Lessons Learned, Jun 29, 1966; ltr, Lt Col C. V. Comerford, Miss Cdr, to Det 5, 315th AD, subj: Weekly Activity Rprt, 22–28 May 66, May 29, 1966; rprt, UK Defense Attache, Saigon, Detailed Rprt no 18, Airstrip Construction Using T–17 Membrane, Dec 66; rprts, Daily Significant Logistical Activities, Apr 12 and Apr 28, 1966.

51. Memo, Maj Gen John Tillson, MACV J–3 to C/S MACV, subj: Airfield Upgrade Program, Oct 8, 1966; msg 30468, MACV Dir/Construction, to USARV, et al, 301640Z Aug 66; msgs, CG III MAF to MACV, 151334Z and 201316Z Sep 66; hist, MACV, 1966, pp 303–305.

52. Memo, MACV Dir/Construction to Ch, Hist Br, MACV, subj: Qtrly Hist Rprt, Aug 8, 1966; msg 1443, CG FFV to MACV J–3, 021135Z Mar 66; ltr, Lt Gen William W. Momyer, Cdr 7th AF, to COMUSMACV, subj: Runway Conditions at Cheo Reo, Jul 24, 1966; hist, MACV, 1966, pp 300–305.

53. Memo, Maj William R. Dybvad, Dir/Safety, 315th AD, to Cdr 315th AD, subj: Mission Safety 70 Council, Aug 5, 1966; rprt, Lt Col Thomas M. Sadler, TALO IFFV, Debriefing Report, Nov 10, 1966; ltr, CINCPAC to JCS, subj: Airfield Designator Codes in Vietnam, Sep 17, 1966; ltr, Lt Gen William W. Momyer, Cdr 7th AF to COMUSMACV, subj: Substandard Airfields, Oct 8, 1966.

54. MR, Lt Col G. L. Harman, USA, Secy MACV A/F Eval Committee, subj: MACV A/F Evaluation Committee, Sep 18, 1966; msg A–1018, CG I FFV to MACV, 270606Z Sep 66; msg A–0486, CG I FFV to MACV, 090035Z Sep 66; Fact Book, MACV, subj: Sec Def Visit to Vietnam, 1–14 Oct 66.

55. Hist, Dir/Plans, Hq USAF, Jul–Dec 65, pp 418–423; steno record, Subcomm on Airlift, House Comm on Armed Services, Hearings, Jan 19, 1966; msg, Brig Gen John Norton, USA, Saigon, to Brig Gen E. L. Mueller, ACSFOR, Dept/Army, 130745Z Nov 65.

56. Memo, Maj Gen Arthur C. Agan, ACS/Plans and Ops, Hq USAF, to Vice CSAF, subj: Status of CSAFM J–94–65, Air Lines of Communications, May 28, 1965; memo, Sec AF to Sec Def, subj: A Proposed Method for Clarifying AF and Army Aviation Functions and Use of Aerial Vehicles, Mar 18, 1965; paper, Air Staff, subj: DAF Comments on USSTRICOM Gold Fire I Report, Jan 10, 1965, Mar 65; 1st Ind, ltr, AFXDC, Hq USAF, subj: Helicopters in USAF SAW Force, Jan 4, 1965, Col Kenneth L. Temple, Asst Ch, Force Plans Div, Dep Dir/Plans for War Plans, Hq USAF, Jan 15, 1965.

57. Hist, Dir/Opns, Hq USAF, Jul–Dec 65, pp 13–14; hist, 2nd AD, Jan–Jun 65, p 67; msg MCOOM 04704, AFLC to WRAMA, 232151Z Sep 65; ltr, Col David T. Fleming, Dir/Air Transport, to MACV J–4, subj: SEA Airlift Capabilities, Jun 14, 1965; planning document, MACV, Concept of Operations in RVN, Sep 1, 1965.

58. Hist, Dir/Plans, Hq USAF, Jul–Dec 65, pp 124–125, 323–325, 415–416; talking paper, Hq USAF, subj: Air Force Helicopter ALOC Opns, Oct 20, 1965; memo, Cyrus Vance, Dep Sec Def, to

CJCS, Sep 15, 1965; memo, Gen J. P. McConnell, CSAF, to Dep Sec Def, subj: Helicopter Squadron (25 CH–3Cs), Sep 23, 1965; MR, Brig Gen Richard A. Yudkin, Dep Dir/Plans, subj: Use of Air Force Helicopters, Sep 21, 1965; msg 190154, Asst Vice CSAF to all major commands, 052110Z Oct 65.

59. Rprt, 7th AF Comptroller, Command Status, Sep 66; hist, 6250th Comb Spt Gp, Jul–Dec 65; hist, 20th Helic Sq, Sep–Dec 65, pp 1–4; chronology, WRAMA Hist Office, subj: CH–3C Pony Express, 1966; PACAF SO G-168, Oct 5, 1966; rprt, Airlift Br, 2nd AD, Hist Data Rcd, Jul–Dec 65; 7th AF Oplan 426–66 (Rev), 1966.

60. Hist, 14th ACWg, Jan–Jun 66, pp 86–103; msg DOPR-OA 05624, 2nd AD to 14th ACWg, 20th Helic Sq, et al, subj: Helic Support for USA, Mar 12, 1966; msg 12474, Cdr MACV to CG II FFV, 101337Z Apr 66; MR, Col E. B. Roberts, Secy Joint Staff, MACV, subj: COMUSMACV Visit to II Corps, Jun 12, 1966.

61. Hist, 7th AF, 1 Jan 66–30 Jun 67, p xxvi; Capt Donald W. Nelson, *The USAF Helicopter in SEA*, (PACAF, Proj CHECO, Dec 5, 1968), pp 23–26.

62. Hist, 315th ACGp, Jan–Jun 65, p 12; memo, Col Leroy M. Stanton, Dep Dir/Policy, Dir/Plans, Hq USAF, to AFAMA, subj: Army Air Transport, Oct 18, 1965; memo, Gen William C. Westmoreland, Cdr MACV, to Sec Def, subj: Shopping List of Items Designed to Facilitate and Accelerate Accomplishment of MACV Mission, Jul 20, 1965; memo, Brig Gen Richard A. Yudkin, Acting Dir/Plans, Hq USAF, to Gen Compton, AFXDC, subj: Caribou's (CV–2) for Air Mobile Division Support Package, Aug 12, 1965; memo, MACV J–3 to USARV, et al, subj: In-country Aircraft Inventory, Jan 16, 1966; White House Fact Sheet, Brig Gen G. P. Seneff, Dept/Army Aviation, Dept/Army (n.d., Dec 65); ltr, Maj Gen J. H. Moore, Cdr 7th AF, to COMUSMACV, subj: Airlift System, Apr 7, 1965; Air Staff Summary Sheet, Maj Gen Robert N. Smith, Dir/Plans, Hq USAF, subj: PCP-A-5-030, Aviation Requirement for the Combat Structure of the Army, Nov 3, 1965.

63. Ltrs, Maj Gen Richard A. Yudkin (Ret), to author, Sep 11 and Sep 22, 1972; ltr, Gen J. P. McConnell (Ret), to author, Oct 3, 1972; intvw, Maj Richard Clement and Dr. Charles Hildreth, with Gen J. P. McConnell, Nov 4, 1970; ltr, Vice CSAF to CSAR, subj: Air Force Fixed Wing/Army Rotary Wing Functions, Mar 9, 1966; msg AFXPDO 75269, Dir/Plans, Hq USAF, to PACAF, 092219Z Mar 66; memo, Cyrus Vance, Dep Sec Def, to CJCS, subj: Airborne DF and Tactical Airlift Functions for SEA, Mar 25, 1966.

64. Hist, 315th AD, 1966, I, 6–7.

65. MR, Brig Gen William V. McBride, OSAF, Apr 18, 1966; ltrs, Maj Gen Richard A. Yudkin (Ret), to author, Sep 11 and Sep 22, 1972; memo, Maj Gen Michael S. Davison, Actg ACS/Force Development, Dept/Army, to CSAR, subj: Intra-Theater Airlift Requirements Study, Mar 9, 1966; Tolson, *Airmobility, 1961–1971*, pp 104–108; testimony of Gen Harold Johnson, in Hearings before Committee of Armed Services, House, 89th Cong, 2nd Sess, *FY 1966 Supplemental Authorization for Vietnam*, pp 5217–5218.

Chapter X

The Airlift System in Growth, 1966–1967

1. Rprt, 834th AD Management Analysis Off, Tactical Airlift Performance Analysis, Jan 67; hist, 834th AD, 15 Oct 66–30 Jun 67, I, 99–103; Moore intvw, May 4, 1970.

2. Study, Maj Thomas J. Hosterman, TALC, Tactical Airlift Systems in the RVN, 26 Nov 66–7 Nov 67, TALC Study DCR-8002, Mar 15, 1968; study, Dir/Plans PACAF and Dir/Ops MAC,

PACOM Theater Airlift Study FY 68, Jun 30, 1967, pp 169–170; intvw, TSgt B. W. Pollica with Col William T. Phillips, ALCE Dir, 834th AD, Nov 1, 1968, rprt, Maj Gen Gordon M. Graham, Vice Cdr 7th AF, EOTR, Jul 67; rprt, J. M. Doughty, Mitre Corp Team, Analysis of 834th AD ALCC Operations and Problems, Seek Data II Rprt, Mar 68, pp 13–40, 53–72.

3. Msg, 315th AD to units, 060712Z Dec 67; hist, 834th AD, Jul 67–Jun 68, pp 80–82, hist, 315th AD, Jul–Dec 67, pp 41–46.

4. Hist, 2nd Aerial Port Gp, Jul 66–Sep 67, pp 8, 15–17, 29–31, Oct–Dec 67, pp 22–23; rprt, CCT Div, 2nd Aerial Port Gp, Hist Rprt, Jul 66–Sep 67; hist, 834th AD, 15 Oct–30 Jun 67, I, 76–78; ltr, Col George N. Blair, Dir/Opns, 834th AD, to 7th AF, subj: US Army Air Control Teams, Nov 30, 1966.

5. MR, Brig Gen Hugh E. Wild, Cdr 834th AD, subj: Visit of Lt Gen Edmundson, Vice CINCPACAF, Sep 7, 1967; msg 98786, Dir/Plans, Hq USAF to PACAF, 081757Z Mar 67; ltr, Col Elmer F. Hauser, Ch, Airlift Forces Div, Dir/Ops, Hq USAF, to Col Hugh E. Wild, Vice Cdr, 834th AD, Aug 8, 1967; hist, 834th AD, Jul 67–Jun 68, pp 23–24; Case intvw, May 5, 1970; Moore intvw, May 4, 1970; annotated comments, by Maj Gen William G. Moore, comments on draft Hist Study, USAF in SEA: Tactical Airlift, 1973.

6. Ltr, II FFV to Cdr MACV, subj: Evaluation of the Interim Emerg Request System, Dec 6, 1966; ltr, Col A. L. Hilpert, DCS/Plans, to MACV J–3, subj: Emerg Airlift Request System, Dec 66; hist, 834th AD, 15 Oct 66–30 Jun 67, p 59; ltr, Cdr 834th AD to 7th AF, subj: Emerg Airlift Request System, Jan 67; ltr, Lt Col John W. Matthews, AACO II CTZ DASC, to 7th AF, subj: Emerg Airlift Request System, Rprt for Pd ending Nov 25, 1966; ltr, Capt Frank K. Edmonson, FACO, 3rd Bde, 4th Inf Div, subj: Final Rprt—Emerg Airlift System, Nov 66; paper, MACV J–4, Eval of Comments on 7th AF Emerg Airlift Request System, n.d.

7. Ltr, Brig Gen J. H. Thompson, DCS/Materiel, 7th AF, to Cdr 834 AD, subj: 7th AF Emergency Airlift Missions, Feb 20, 1967; memo, Lt Gen William W. Momyer, Cdr 7th AF, to Brig Gen J. H. Thompson, subj: Emergency Airlift Requests, Feb 16, 1967; study, LTV Electrosystems, Inc, 834th AD Cost Reduction Summary Study, Oct 26, 1967.

8. Hist, 834th AD, 15 Oct 66–30 Jun 67, I, 56–62; ltr, Capt Frank K. Edmonson, FACO, 3rd Bde, 4th Inf Div, subj: Final Rprt, Emergency Airlift System, Nov 66; msg 66464, 7th AF to PACAF, 050704Z Oct 66; rprt, ACSC, Corona Harvest Proj, Designated Study 7, Assault Airlift, Dec 15, 1967.

9. Rprt, Lt Col Thomas M. Sadler, TALO IFFV, Debriefing Rprt, Nov 10, 1966; ltr, Lt Col John W. Matthews, AACO, III Corps DASC, to 7th AF, subj: Emergency Airlift Request System, Rprt for Pd ending Nov 25, 1966; ltr, Capt Richard H. Prater, AACO, 196th Light Inf Bde, to Dep Dir DASC, III CTZ, subj: Evaluation of Emergency Airlift Request System (n.d.), 1966; ltr, Capt Frank K. Edmonson, FACO, 3rd Bde, 4th Inf Div, subj: Final Rprt—Emergency Airlift System, Nov 66; rprt, Maj Joseph Marshall, AACO, 1st Inf Div, Rprt of Activities, Nov 29, 1966; Maj Arne Ellermets, The Influence of Vietnam on Tactical Airlift Doctrine, ACSC, Air Univ, Jun 68, pp 55–62.

10. Rprt, Brig Gen William G. Moore, Cdr 834th AD, EOTR, Nov 67; ltr, Col Hugh E. Wild, Vice Cdr 834th AD, to 7th AF, subj: Logistic and Admin Support of TALOs, Feb 1, 1967; msg 00029, Cdr 7th AF to PACAF, 090455Z Jan 67; msg 40952, PACAF Cd Center to 7th AF, 242000Z Dec 66; Adams intvw, Jan 21, 1969; intvw, Corona Harvest with Lt Col Henry B. Murphy, CH intvw no 119, Jan 22, 1969; rprt, Hq USAF, Rprt to SAF on SEA Action Items, Feb 21, 1967; ltr, Col George G. Loving, AFXDOD, Hq USAF, to Gen Yudkin, AFXDO, subj: Trip Rprt SEA, 10–19 Nov 67, Nov 21, 1967; paper, 834th AD, subj: Mobile Radio Communications Support for TALOs, Feb 1, 1967.

11. Rprt, MACV J–4 Logistical Review and Evaluation, 3rd and 4th Qtrs/FY 67; Fact Book, MACV J–4, Data for Sec Def Visit to RVN, Jul 67; rprt, JLRB, Monograph 18, Transportation and Movement Control, 1970, p A–50; rprt, JCS Study Gp, 1967 Year End Review of Vietnam, Jan 29, 1968; MR, MACV COC, subj: MACV Commander's Conference, Dec 3, 1967, Jan 2, 1968; rprt, Dr. Laurence E. Lynn, Dir/Eco-

nomics and Mobility Forces, OSD/Sys Analysis, subj: Trip Rprt, Aug 67; rprts, MACV J-4, LOGSUM, monthly.

12. MRs, Col Vernon O. Elmore, Chairm JMTB, subj: Minutes JMTB Mtgs, Jan 18, Mar 6 and Mar 22, 1967; msg 0274, MACV TMA to 2nd DTL, *et al,* 191600Z Oct 67; draft mss, Lt Gen Joseph M. Heiser, Logistic Support, Vietnam Monograph Series no 17, OCMH, Sep 3, 1971.

13. Rprt, Management Analysis Off, 834th AD, Tactical Airlift Performance Analysis, SEA, Dec 67; study, LTV Electrosystems, Inc, 834th AD Cost Reduction Summary Study, Oct 26, 1967; study, Dir/Plans, PACAF, and Dir/Opns, MAC, subj: PACOM Theater Airlift Study FY 68, Jun 30, 1967; hist, 315th AD, Jan–Jun 68, vol I, p xiv.

14. Hist, 834th Air Div, Jul 67–Jun 68, pp 10–12; 314th TAWg, Oct–Dec 67, pp 8–9, 17; rprt, MACV J-4, Monthly Hist Rprt, Jan 21, 1968.

15. Study, 834th AD, SEA/PACOM C–130 Airlift, Mar 8, 1967; staff summary sheet, Col A. L. Hilpert, DCS/Plans, 7th AF, subj: MACV CY 68 Reqmts, Mar 15, 1967; *DOD Pentagon Papers,* bk 5, pt IV-C-6(b); study, PACAF/MAC, Theater Airlift Study, FY 67, Jan 31, 1967; Moore intvw, May 4, 1970; msg 52146, PACAF to 7th AF, pers Ryan to Momyer, 251042Z Apr 67; msg C-52405, PACAF to 7th AF, *et al,* 200401Z Oct 67.

16. Hist, 315th ACWg, Jan–Sep 67, pp 1, 4, 19–20; rprt, 834th AD, SEA Airlift Statistics Summary, Dec 67; rprt, Maj Gen Gordon M. Graham, Vice Cdr, 7th AF, EOTR, Sep 67.

17. Rprt, 315th AD, PACAF C-130 Aircrew Manning Study, Apr 67; hist, 463rd TAWg, Oct–Dec 67, pp 4–6; hist, 314th TAWg, Oct–Dec 67, pp 19–20; hist, 374th TAWg, Jan–Jun, pp 4–5, Oct–Dec 67, pp 2–3; study, PACAF/MAC, PACOM Theater Airlift Study FY 68, Jun 30, 1967; rprt, 834th AD, SEA Airlift Statistics Summary, Dec 67; hist, 315th ACWg, Oct–Dec 67, pp 4–5.

18. Intvw, author with Maj Charlie J. Jennings, May 8, 1972; hist, 463rd TAWg, Jul–Sep 67, pp 13–14, Oct–Dec 67, pp 5–6; hist, 345th TASq, Jul–Sep 67, p 27; hist, 314th TCWg, Jul–Dec 66, pp 35–36; hist, 315th AD, Jul–Dec 67, pp 57–62.

19. Rprt, Brig Gen William G. Moore, EOTR, Nov 67; rprt, 7th AF, Analysis of 834th AD Maintenance Delays/Cancellations, 1968; ltr, Col Barney L. Johnson, Dir/Materiel, 834th AD, to DM, 7th AF, subj: Intratheater Airlift Deployment/Employment Logistics Policies, May 5, 1967; draft PACAF ltr 66-1, subj: C-130 Maintenance Management, Sep 15, 1967; hist, 834th AD, 15 Oct–30 Jun 67, pp 20–24; rprt, Col Robert L. Ventres, Cdr Det 2, 834th AD, CRB, Sep 67–Aug 68, EOTR, 1968.

20. Hist, 315th AD, Jan–Jun 67, pp 122–128, Jul–Dec 68, pp 176–177; hist, 834th AD, Jul 67–Jun 68, pp 40–42; msg DM 00347, 834th AD to 7th AF, 120948Z May 67; rprt, 7th AF, General Inspection of 834th AD, Tabs B and C, Nov 26, 1968.

21. Hist, 315th AD, Jan–Jun 67, pp 58–60.

22. Hist, 315th AD, Jul–Dec 67, I, 205, 211; rprt, Brig Gen William G. Moore, Cdr 834th AD, EOTR, Nov 67; hist, 463rd TCWg, Jan–Jun 67, pp 16–19; hist, 463rd TAWg, Jul–Sep 67, p 20; hist, 314th TAWg, Oct–Dec 67, pp 24–25, 38; hist, 374th TAWg, Oct–Dec 67, pp 15–16; hist, 315th ACWg, Jan–Sep 67, I, 30–35, Oct–Dec 67, pp 26–28; hist, 50th TCSq, Jan–Jun 67; hist, 345th TCSq, hist, 310th ACSq, Oct–Dec 67.

23. Rprt, MACV J-4, LOGSUM 8-67 for Jul 67, Aug 16, 1967; rprts, 834th AD Management Analysis Off, Tactical Airlift Performance Analysis, Jan 67 and Dec 67; briefing, 834th AD, subj: Tactical Airlift Briefing for Senate Preparedness Investigating Subcommittee, Oct 29, 1967; daily staff journal, G-3 Advis Sect, II Corps, Nov 26, 1967; msg ALCC 13967, 834th AD to CINCPAC, 261940Z Nov 66; hist, 19th ACSq, Jan–Sep 67.

24. Lee intvw, Apr 28, 1972; rprts, Management Analysis Off, 834th AD, Tactical Airlift Performance Analysis, Jan 67, Dec 67, Dec 68; rprt, 834th AD, SEA Airlift Statistics Summary, Dec 67; hist, 2nd Aerial Port Gp, Jul 66–Sep 67, pp 22–24, Oct–Dec 67, all qtrs, 1968.

25. Intvw, Corona Harvest with MSgt Donofry, CH intvw no 238, Jul 15, 1970; ltr, Col John D. Collins, Ch, Sys & Reqmts Div, Dir/Pers Planning, Hq USAF, to Dir/Opns, Hq USAF, subj: Lessons Learned in AF Opns, Oct 17, 1967; msg DTF/DP, 315th AD to 7th AF, PACAF, 110715Z Dec 67; hist, 14th

Aerial Port Sq, Jul 66–Sep 67, pp 10–11; hist, 2nd Aerial Port Gp, Jan–Mar 68, pp 6–9, Apr–Jun 68, pp 4–5, Jul–Sep 68, p 7; comments, Maj Gen William G. Moore, Comments on Draft ms, USAF in SEA, Tactical Airlift, 1973; rprt, Moore, EOTR, Nov 67, pp 11–14.

26. Hist, 2nd Aerial Port Gp, Jul 66–Sep 67, pp 1–2, 19–22, 41–42, Oct–Dec 67, pp 12–15, 22, Jan–Mar 68, pp 11–13; 834th AD Regul 23–3, 2nd Aerial Port Gp, Dec 7, 1968; study, Maj Thomas J. Hosterman, TALC, Tactical Airlift Systems in the Republic of Vietnam, 26 Nov 66–7 Nov 67, Mar 15, 1968, pp 17–19; rprt, Maj Gen Burl W. McLaughlin, Cdr 834th AD, EOTR, Jun 69, pp 5–17 to 5–19.

27. Rprt, Maj Gen Burl W. McLaughlin, Cdr 834th AD, EOTR, Jun 69, pp 5–3 to 5–4; rprt, Lt Col Jack T. Humphries, *USAF Aerial Port Opns in RVN*, (PACAF, Proj CHECO, Aug 5, 1970), pp 9–12; hist, 2nd Aerial Port Gp, Jul 66–Sep 67, pp 35–37, Oct–Dec 67, pp 39–40, Apr–Jun 68, pp 31–33; hists, 8th, 14th, and 15th Aerial Port Sqs, 1966 through 1968.

28. Rprt, Management Analysis Off, 834th AD, Tactical Airlift Performance Analysis, Jan 67, Dec 67, Dec 68; rprt, Brig Gen William G. Moore, EOTR, Nov 67, pp 4–7, 55; Moore intvw, May 4, 1970; ltr, Lt Gen William W. Momyer, Cdr 7th AF, to Gen Hunter Harris, Cdr PACAF, Dec 4, 1966; ltr, Gen Hunter Harris, Cdr PACAF, to Cdr 7th AF, Dec 18, 1966; rprt, Lt Col Jack T. Humphries, *USAF Aerial Port Operations in RVN*, (PACAF, Proj CHECO, Aug 5, 1970), p 19; rprt, Maj Gen Burl W. McLaughlin, Cdr 834th AD, EOTR, Jun 69, pp 5–3 to 5–5.

29. Hist, 2nd Aerial Port Gp, Apr–Jun 68, pp 23–27; ltr, Maj C. C. Breitenstein, Dir/Traffic, 315th AD to PACAF, subj: Recommended Programming Actions for 463L Materials Handling Equipment, Jun 13, 1968; rprt, Maj Gen Burl W. McLaughlin, Cdr 384th AD, Jun 69, pp 5–6 to 5–7; rprt, Lt Col Jack T. Humphries, *USAF Aerial Port Operations in RVN* (PACAF, Proj CHECO, Aug 5, 1970) pp 15–16.

30. MACV Dir 59–6, Air Transportation: 463L Pallet/Net/Tie Down Strap and Chain Recovery, Jun 17, 1967, Donofry intvw, Jul 15, 1970; hist, 7th AF, Jul–Dec 68, p 345; hist, 2nd Aerial Port Gp, Jul 66–Sep 67, pp 14–15, Oct–Dec 67, p 28, Jan–Mar 68, Oct–Dec 68, pp 26–28; rprt, Maj Gen Burl W. McLaughlin, Cdr 834th AD, EOTR, pp 5–12 to 5–15.

31. Rprt, Maj Gen Burl W. McLaughlin, Cdr 834th AD, EOTR, Jun 69, pp 5–10 to 5–12; msg 0098, 834th AD to 315 AD, 010221Z Aug 67; rprt, PACAF IG, Management Inspection Rprt, 9 Jan–17 Feb 67; hist, 2nd Aerial Port Gp, Oct–Dec 67, pp 28–31, Jul–Sep 68, pp 20–22, Oct–Dec 68, pp 25–26.

32. Draft ltr, Cdr 7th AF to COMUSMACV, subj: 7th Air Force Aerial Resupply Capability, Feb 67; rprt, II FFV, Monthly Eval for Mar 67, Apr 67; hist, 834th AD, 15 Oct 66–30 Jun 67, pp 65–66; Moore intvw, May 4, 1970; McLaughlin intvw, Apr 20, 1970; memo, MACV J–4 to Mil Hist Br, subj: Logistical Historical Activities, Feb 21, 1968; MACV Airdrop Resupply Plan 2–66, Jul 15, 1966; msgs MACV J–4 to USARV, 161230Z Feb 66 and 011516Z Jun 66.

33. Intvw, Corona Harvest with Capt R. H. Hoddinott, CH intvw no. 297, Apr 15, 1970; intvw, Corona Harvest with Lt Col John F. Ohlinger, CH intvw no 73, Dec 5, 1968; rprt, Brig Gen William G. Moore, Cdr 834th AD, EOTR, Nov 67, pp 14–16; hist, 2nd Aerial Port Gp, Jan–Mar 68, Apr–Jun 68, p 6; hists, 8th, 14th, and 15th Aerial Port Sqs, 1967 thru 1968.

34. Hist, 2nd Aerial Port Gp, Oct–Dec 67, pp 45–47; hist, AF Reserve, Aug–Dec 68, Jul–Dec 72.

35. Rprt, Col Leroy M. Stanton, Opns Analysis Standby Unit, Univ of North Carolina, Review and Analysis of USAF TALC, Apr 21, 1967; hist, TALC, Sep–Dec 66, pp 1–3; hist, TAWC, Jan–Jun 65, pp 14–16, Jan–Jun 66, pp 8–10, 25; rprt, TAWC, Test Projects, Monthly Activities Rprt, Aug 66.

36. Rprt, TAWC, Test Projects, Monthly Activities Rprt, Jul thru Dec 65; hist, 315th AD, 1966, I, 61–62; ltr, Lt Col Edmund B. Crandall, Dir/Spt Opns, 315th AD, to 315th ACWg, subj: Loadmaster Qualifications, Aug 11, 1966; msg DOOX 03745, 315th AD to 315th ACWg, 030720Z Aug 66; msg DPLP–CA 73276, 7th AF to PACAF, 315th AD, 210933Z Aug 66; rprt, Airlift Staff Gp, Report of USAF Airlift Staff Visit to PACOM Area, 11 Oct–10 Nov 65.

37. Rprts, TAWC, Test Projects, Monthly Activities Rprts, Jan thru Dec 65; hist, 315th AD, Jul–Dec 65, I, 33–34, 1966, I, 56–61; hist, 314th TCWg, Jan–Jun 66, p 33; hist, 315th TCGp, Jan–Jun 65, pp 20–22; msg OC–T, 315th AD to PACAF, 060306Z Jan 65; msg 44483, 8th Aerial Port Sq to TAC, 250900Z May 66; msg 44577, 8th Aerial Port Sq to TAC, 061606Z Jun 66.

38. Msg, 315th AD DCS/Opns, to TAC, 100845Z Jun 66; msg 43480, MACV J–3 to 7th AF, 290515Z Sep 66; ltr, Gen C. W. Abrams, Acting CSAR to Gen McConnell, CSAF, Aug 9, 1966; rprt, Maj Gen H. A. Davis, AF Team Chief, Proj NEW FOCUS Visit to SVN, Nov 19, 1965; msg, US Army CDC to Hq TAC, 291510Z Sep 66; ltr, Lt Col E. B. Crandall, Dir/Spt Ops, 315th AD, to 2nd Aerial Port Gp, subj: Support Equipment for PLADS and LAPES Training, Aug 11, 1966; msg 27375, USARV to 7th AF, 260357Z Apr 67.

39. Rprts, 1st Logistical Command, AARs, Airdrop Mission 44, 45, 47, 53, Jun 12, Jun 30, Jul 8, and Aug 30, 1967; rprt, Maj Gen William G. Moore, Cdr 834th AD, EOTR, Nov 67, pp 47–48; ltr, Brig Gen William G. Moore, Cdr 834th AD, to Cdr 7th AF, subj: Staff Action Items, Feb 22, 1967; rprt, Dir/Tactical Air Analysis Center, DCS/Opns, Hq 7th AF, The Application of Aerial Delivery Systems to Cargo Acft Opns in RVN (talking paper 67/1), Jan 12, 1967.

40. Rprts, TAWC, Test Projects, Monthly Activities Reports, Jun thru Dec 65; ltr, Cdrs TAC and AFSC, to CSAF, subj: Tactical Airlift-AWADS, Oct 13, 1966; msg 21019, MACV J–3 to 7th AF, 191203Z Jun 66; rprt, AF Test Unit, Vietnam, Evaluation of Red Chief (JRATA Proj 3T-754.0), Aug 31, 1965; Capt Marvin L. Payne, All-Weather Limitations of Tactical Assault Airlift (ACSC Thesis), Air Univ, Jun 1966, pp 30–31.

41. Ltr, Lt Gen Joseph R. Holzapple, DCS/R&D, to SAF R&D, subj: C–130 AWADS, Oct 4, 1967; memo, Alexander H. Flax, Asst Sec AF, R&D, to DCS/R&D, subj: C–130 AWADS, Oct 17, 1967; memo, J. S. Foster, DD R&D, subj: AWADS for C–130 Aircraft, Nov 22, 1967; msg 62953, Cdrs TAC, USAFE, PACAF, to CSAF, 252017Z Aug 67; ltr, Lt Gen William W. Momyer, Cdr 7th AF, to Hq USAF (RDQ), et al, subj: SEAOR 98, C–130 AWADS, Mar 27, 1967; ltr, Cdrs TAC, USAFE, PACAF, to CSAF, subj: Adverse Weather Delivery System—C–130 Aircraft, Feb 3, 1967; ltr, Cdrs TAC and AFSC, to CSAF, subj: Tactical Airlift—AWADS, Oct 13, 1966; SOR 216, Maj Gen Jack J. Catton, Dir/Opl Reqmts, Hq USAF, Aug 17, 1964 and revised Oct 12, 1965.

42. Ltr, Maj Gen Walter T. Kerwin, C/S MACV, to Cdr 7th AF, et al, subj: High Velocity Ground Radar Controlled Aerial Delivery System, Aug 26, 1967; rprt, TALC, TAC Test 66-184, Interim IFR/Night Aerial Delivery System, Final Rprt, Aug 67; ltr, Maj Richard D. Rosborough, Senior TALO, 5th SF Gp, to Dir/Opns, 834th AD, subj: Ground Radar Air Drop System (GRADS), Nov 24, 1967; msg DOO 18756, Dir/Opns 834th AD to PACAF, subj: AWADS Reqmt in SEA, Aug 25, 1967; rprt, TALC, Monthly Status Rprt, Jun 67; hist, 315th ACWg, Jul–Dec 66.

43. Msg DCOC 01739, 463rd TCWg to 315th AD, 141450Z Jun 67; rprts, Hq USAF, Rprt to Sec AF on SEA Action Items, Feb 21 and Mar 23, 1967; rprt, Brig Gen William G. Moore, Cdr 834th AD, EOTR, Nov 67; ltr, A. V. Petersons, Veh Equipmts Div, AF Flt Dynamics Lab, to WRAMA, subj: Reduced Inflation Pressure Investig for C–130 Acft, Sep 15, 1966; rprt, Dir/Construction, MACV Qtrly Hist Rprt, Apr 22, 1967; msg 26643, Cdr MACV to CINCPAC, JCS, 110242Z Aug 67; msg, DCS/Opns, 7th AF, to AFXOPHA, Hq USAF, 140300Z Nov 67.

44. Msg DOCO 34454, PACAF to Dir/Opl Reqmts, Hq USAF, 240746Z Oct 67; memo, Hugh E. Witt, Dep/Supply and Maintenance, to Mr. Charles, Off/SAF, subj: Meeting with Fairchild Hiller Personnel, Mar 8, 1967; ltr, Lt Gen Hewitt T. Wheless, Asst Vice CSAF to Sec AF, subj: Modification of C–123 Acft, Oct 26, 1967; hist, 315th ACWg, Jan–Sep 67, I, 20–21, 29; rprt, Brig Gen William G. Moore, Cdr 834th AD EOTR, Nov 67, pp 22–24.

45. Ltr, Col Charles W. Borders, DCS/Opns, 315th AD to PACAF (DORQ), subj: Bulk Fuel Delivery, May 27, 1966; memo, Brig Gen J. H. Thompson, DCS/Materiel, 7th AF, subj: Significant Logistic Events for 1966, Jan 9, 1967; memos, SAPOV/POL, MACV J–4 to Admin Off

J-4, subj: Hist Reports, Sep 20, 1965 and Dec 17, 1965; hist, 7th AF, 1 Jan 66–30 Jun 67, I, 82–83; rprt, MACV, Monthly Evaluation, Nov 65, Dec 31 1965; hist, 315th AD, Jul–Dec 65, I, 28–30, 1966, I, 42–44.

46. Rprt, USARV Aviation Section, Army Aviation in Vietnam, FY 69, 1969; memo, Stanley R. Resor, Sec Army, for Sec Def, subj: Operational Readiness of the CH-47 (Chinook), Feb 28, 1967; rprt, Laurence E. Lynn, Dir/Economics and Mobility Forces, Off Sec Def (Systems Analysis), subj: Trip Report, Aug 67; AFM 2–50 and Army Field Manual 100–27, US Army/USAF Doctrine for Tactical Airlift Operations, Jan 1, 1967.

47. Hist, 315th ACGp, Jul–Dec 65, pp 45–53; background paper, Hq USAF, subj: On-going Airlift Studies, Jun 19, 1966; hist, Dir/Studies and Analysis, Hq USAF, Jan–Jun 66; AFM 2–4, Tactical Air Force Operations: Tactical Airlift, Aug 10, 1966; rprt, Airlift Staff Gp, Report of USAF Airlift Staff Visit to PACOM Area, 11 Oct–10 Nov 65; rprt, AFXOP Study Gp, Hq USAF, Tactical Airlift Problems, 1966, pp 7–8.

Chapter XI

Junction City and the Battles of 1967

1. Rprt, 1st Inf Div, AAR, Opn Tulsa/Shenandoah, Mar 26, 1967; rprt, 1st Inf Div, AAF, Opn Attleboro, Apr 6, 1967; rprt, 196th Light Inf Bde, Comb Opns AAR (Attleboro), Dec 15, 1966; rprt, 1st Logistical Cd, Logistical Critique 1–67 (Opn Attleboro), Apr 29, 1967; Lawrence J. Hickey and Capt James G. Bruce, Operation Attleboro, PACAF, Proj CHECO, Apr 14, 1967.

2. Rprt, II VVF, Opl Report for Pd Ending 31 Jan 67, Feb 15, 1967; intvw, author with Lt Col Richard H. Prater, Nov 9, 1972; hist, 315th ACWg, Jul–Dec 66, pp 26, 44–45; hist, 8th Aer Port Sq, Jul 66–Oct 67; rprt, MACV, Monthly Eval, Nov 66.

3. Rprt, II FFV, Comb Opn AAR, Junction City, Aug 9, 1967; II FFV OPLAN 3-67, Junction City Alternate Phase 1 and 2, Feb 8, 1967; rprt, 1st Inf Div, AAR, Tucson, Mar 26, 1967; msg 08435, MACV J-3 to CINCPAC, 120730Z Mar 67.

4. Hist, 315th AD, 1966, p xxxi; memo, Maj Gen John C. F. Tillson, MACV J-3 to C/S MACV, subj: Abn Opns, Oct 8, 1966.

5. Rprt, MACV, Monthly Eval, Dec 66; hist, PACAF, 1966, p 139; ltr, Capt Charles T. Westphaling, Abn Div Advis Det, to Cdr MACV, subj: Qtrly Hist Rprt, Jan 19, 1967; ltr, Lt Gen William W. Momyer, Cdr 7th AF, to Gen John D. Ryan, Cdr PACAF, Jun 16, 1967.

6. 834th AD Opns Plan 476-67, Abn Opns, Jan 1, 1967; msg 03626, MACV J-4 to PACAF, 301005Z Jan 67.

7. Rprt, 173rd Abn Bde, Comb Opns AAR, Junction City (Abn Opn), n.d., 1967; Jennings intvw, May 8, 1972; Lee intvw, Apr 28, 1972; Moore intvw, May 4, 1970.

8. Intvw, author with Maj James T. Callaghan, Feb 8, 1972; rprt, 173rd Abn Bde, Comb Opns AAR, Junction City (Airborne Operation), n.d., 1967; rprt, II FFV, Comb Ops AAR, Junction City, Aug 9, 1967.

9. Lee intvw, Apr 28, 1972; Davis intvw, Apr 24, 1972; Koehring intvw, Jun 29, 1972; Jennings intvw, May 8, 1972; intvw, author with Maj John W. Frye, May 3, 1972; hist, 314th TCWg, Jan–Jun 67, p 4; msg, Det 6, 315th AD, CRB, to 374th TCWg, 231600Z Feb 67; ALOREP data extract.

10. Callaghan intvw, Feb 8, 1972; rprt, 173rd Abn Bde, Comb Ops AAR, Junction City (Airborne Operation), n.d., 1967.

11. Data Log, III Corps DASC, Feb 22, 1967; Lee intvw, Apr 28, 1972; Jennings intvw, May 8, 1972; Frye intvw, May 3, 1972; Koehring intvw, Jun 29, 1972; ALOREP data extract.

12. Moore intvw, May 4, 1970; hist, 2nd Aerial Port Gp, Jul 66–Sep 67, p 25; hist, 463rd TCWg, Jan–Jun 67, pp 9–10; memo, Lt Gen Harry J. Lemley, DCS/Mil Ops, Dept/Army, for Vice CSA, subj: Parachute Assault, Op Junction City, Mar 67; hist, 374th TCWg, Jan–Jun 67, p 9; Callaghan intvw, Feb 8, 1972; rprt, 173rd Abn Bde, Comb Ops AAR, Junction City (Airborne Operation) n.d., 1967; draft ms, Lt Gen John J. Tolson, USA, Airmobility in Vietnam: The Origin and Development of the US Army's Airmobile Concept in SEA, Oct 30, 1971.

13. Hist, MACV, 1967, p 390; rprt, II FFV, Comb Ops AAR, Junction City, Aug 9, 1967; rprt, 1st Inf Div, AAR, Junction City, May 8, 1967; rprt, 1st Bn, 503rd Regt, AAR, Junction City, Mar 18, 1967; rprt, 4th Bn, 503rd Regt, AAR, Junction City, Mar 17, 1967.

14. Msg, Det 6, 315th AD, CRB, to 374th TCWg, 231600Z Feb 67; rprt, 1st Logistical Command, Drop Mission 16–22 AAR, Apr 16, 1967; rprt, 196th Light Inf Bde, AAR, Junction City, May 4, 1967; ALOREP data extract, msg 20800, CG II FFV to MACV, 241545Z Feb 67; hist, 14th Aerial Port Sq, Jul 66–Sep 67.

15. Rprts, 1st Logistical Command, AAR, Airdrop Missions 16 through 22, Apr 16, 1967; ltr, Capt John E. Glagola to author, subj: Operation Junction City, Apr 72; intvw, author with Maj Jessie H. Burrow, May 9, 1972; Davis intvw, Apr 24, 1972; Koehring intvw, Jun 29, 1972; Frye intvw, May 3, 1972.

16. Msg, Det 6, 315th AD, CRB, to 374th TCWg, 231600Z Feb 67; daily journal, G–4, 1st Inf Div, Feb 23, 1967; hist, 35th TCSq, Jan–Jun 67; Moore intvw, May 4, 1970; rprts, 1st Logistical Command, Drop Missions 16–22 AAR, Apr 16, 1967; rprt, 173rd Abn Bde, Comb Opn AAR–Junction City I, Jun 15, 1967.

17. Rprt, 1st Logistical Command, Drop Missions 16–22 AAR, Apr 16, 1967; rprt, 196th Light Inf Bde, AAR Junction City, May 4, 1967; daily journal, G–4, 25th Inf Div, Tay Ninh, Feb 26, 1967; rprt, 1st Logistical Command, Logistical Critique 7–67, Operation Junction City, Phase I, Jun 30, 1967.

18. Rprt, 3rd Bde, 4th Inf Div, Comb Ops AAR (Junction City), May 12, 1967; rprt, 25th Inf Div Support Cd, AAR (Logistical) on Op Junction City I, Apr 6, 1967; rprt, 11th Armored Cav Regt, Comb Ops AAR—Op Junction City I, Apr 1, 1967; rprt, MACV, Monthly Evaluation, Feb 67, Mar 24, 1967; hist, 8th Aerial Port Sq, Jul 66–Sep 67, p 11; rprt, 1st Engr Bn, AAR, Junction City, May 2, 1967; msg 10957, MACV COC to NMCC 022255Z Apr 67.

19. Rprt, 1st Logistical Command, Logistical Critique 8–67, Op Junction City Phase II, 1967; msg 10957, MACV COC to NMCC, 022255Z Apr 67; rprt, 1st Inf Div, AAR, Junction City, May 8, 1967; rprt, II FFV, Comb Ops AAR, Junction City, Aug 9, 1967; rprt, 173rd Abn Bde, AAR, Junction City I and II, Jun 15, 1967; rprt, 1st Bde, 9th Inf Div, AAR, Junction City III/Diamond Head, May 29, 1967.

20. Rprt, 1st Engr Bn, Comb Opn AAR, Junction City, May 2, 1967; rprt, II FFV, Monthly Evaluation, Mar 67, Apr 20, 1967; rprt, II FFV, Comb Ops AAR, Junction City, Aug 9, 1967; rprt, 1st Inf Div, AAR, Junction City, May 8, 1967.

21. Daily journals, MACV COC, Mar 19, 1967 through Apr 2, 1967; msg 30154, II FFV to MACV, 060955Z Mar 67; msg 3–415, II FFV to MACV J–3, 140655Z Mar 67; rprts, 1st Logistical Command, AARs, Airdrop Missions 26–32 and 33–40, Apr 21, 1967; rprt, 196th Light Inf Bde, AAR Junction City, May 4, 1967; Maj Arne Ellermets, *The Influence of Vietnam on Tactical Airlift Doctrine*, (ACSC), Air Univ, Jun 68, p 64; hist, 2nd Aerial Port Gp, Jul 66–Oct 67; rprt, Brig Gen William G. Moore, EOTR, Nov 67; Moore intvw, May 4, 1970; hist rprt, CCT Division, 2nd Aerial Port Gp, Jul 66–Sep 67; rprt, Maj Gen Gordon M. Graham, Vice Cdr 7th AF, EOTR, Jul 67; daily journals, 25th Inf Div G–4, Feb 22–Mar 31, 1967.

22. Rprt, Maj Gen Shelton E. Lollis, Cdr 1st Logistical Command, Debriefing Rprt, Aug 11, 1967; msg 10957, MACV COC to NMCC, 022255Z Apr 67; rprt, 196th Light Inf Bde, AAR Junction City, May 4, 1967; rprt, II FFV, Comb Ops AAR, Junction City, Aug 9, 1967; Adm U. S. G. Sharp and Gen William C. Westmoreland, *Report on the War in Vietnam* (Washington, GPO, 1969), p 137.

23. Fact sheet, USARV G–4, Airdrop

Malfunctions Junction City, Feb 28, 1967; rprt, ICO, II FFV, Monthly Eval for Mar 67, Apr 20, 1967; rprt, 196th Light Inf Bde, AAR Junction City, May 4, 1967; rprt, 25th Inf Div Arty, Combat AAR (Junction City), Jun 8, 1967; bulletin, USARV, Combat Lessons Bulletin no 12, Jun 25, 1967.

24. Fact Books, 7th AF, Cdrs Opns Books, daily for Feb, Mar, Apr, and Dec 67; rprts, USARV G-3, USARDAY Daily Rprts, daily through 1966 and 1967; rprt, CAS Vietnam, FVS 17,194, May 21, 1968; msg 38937, MACV J-2 to CINCPAC, 301005Z Nov 68.

25. Ltr, Maj Thomas Sadler, TALO, 1st Cav Div, to ALO, subj: Airlift AAR, Apr 18, 1966; rprt, 1st Cav Div, AAR, Lincoln/Mosby, 1966; rprts, USARV G-4, Daily Logistical Activities, Mar through Aug 1966; msg 10049, 315th AD to 315th ACGp (Howe to Hannah), 030758A Mar 66; msg 315C 00019, 315th ACWg to NMCC, 130815Z Aug 66; rprt, 1st Cav Div, AAR (Paul Revere II), Jan 25, 1967; Lawrence J. Hickey, Operations Paul Revere/Sam Houston, (PACAF, Proj CHECO, Jul 27, 1967), pp 24-27.

26. Rprt, 1st Bde, 101st Abn Div, AAR, Opn Pickett, Feb 15, 1967; rprt, 1st Logistical Cd, Logist Critique 11-67, Opn Greeley, Dec 19, 1967; daily journals, MACV COC, dates in May, Jun, Jul 67; rprt, I FFV, Opl Rprt for Qtrly Pd ending 31 Jan 67, Mar 6, 1967.

27. Ltr, 299th Engr Bn to Cdr 937th Engr Gp, subj: AAR, Opn Greeley, Engr Support, Oct 31, 1967; ltr, Maj Howard E. Hobson, USA, G-2 Advisor, II CTZ, to DSA, II Corps, et al, subj: Indications of Impending Enemy Activity, Nov 3, 1967; hist, 315th AD, Jul-Dec 67, p xiv.

28. Rprt, 173rd Abn Bde, AAR, Battle of Dak To, Dec 10, 1967; hist, 315th AD, Jul-Dec 67, p xv; daily journal, MACV COC, dates in Nov 67; daily staff journal, G-3 Advis Sect, II CTZ, dates in Nov 67; daily staff journals, G-4 I FFV, Nov 11 and Nov 13, 1967; Adm U. S. G. Sharp and Gen William C. Westmoreland, Report on the War in Vietnam (Washington, GPO, 1969), p 139.

29. Daily staff journals, I FFV G-4, Oct 30 through Nov 20, 1967; rprt, 173rd Abn Bde, Comb Opns AAR, Battle of Dak To, Dec 10, 1967; C. William Thorndale, Battle for Dak To, (PACAF, Proj CHECO, Jun 21, 1968), p 7.

30. Daily staff journal, I FFV G-4, Oct 12, 1967; hist, 315th AD, Jul-Dec 67, I, 204-205; Adams intvw, Jan 21, 1969; unpubl ms, Lt Col Ray L. Bowers, SEA Journal, 1967-68 (AF/CHO, 1969).

31. Intvw, 7th AF, with Capt Keith Glenn, Nov 20, 1967; intvw, 7th AF, with Maj Joseph Madden, ALO, 1st Bde, 4th Inf Div, Nov 18, 1967; intvw, Corona Harvest with Capt Andrew Nichol, CH intvw no 41, n.d.; hist, 314th TAWg, Oct-Dec 67, pp 23-24; hist, 14th Aerial Port Sq, Oct-Dec 67; msgs, MACV COC to NMCC, CINCPAC, 102200Z Nov 67, 112200Z Nov 67, 150300Z Nov 67, 152200Z Nov 67, 230200Z Nov 67, 231000Z Nov 67; presentation, Maj Gen Peers, CG 4th Inf Div, Battle for Dak To, Dec 3, 1967.

32. Daily staff journal, I FFV G-4, Nov 15, 1967; hist, 7th AF, Jul-Dec 67, I, 192-193; rprt, I FFV, Oprl Report, Lessons Learned, Qtrly Pd ending 31 Jan 68, Feb 15, 1968; briefing, 1st Logistical Cd, Briefing for Gen H. K. Johnson, CSA, Logistical Support of Dak To, 1967; unpubl ms, Lt Col Ray L. Bowers, SEA Journal, 1967-68 (AF/CHO, 1969); C. William Thorndale, Battle for Dak To, (PACAF, Proj CHECO, Jun 21, 1968), p 8.

33. Daily staff journals, I FFV G-4, dates in Nov 67; rprt, Maj Gen Burl W. McLaughlin, Cdr 834th AD, EOTR, Jun 69; briefing, 1st Logistical Cd, Briefing for Gen H. K. Johnson, CSA, Logistical Support of Dak To, 1967; rprt, Col R. H. Goodell, USA, TMA, MACV, Debriefing Rprt, Jul 1, 1968, p 11; Adams intvw, Jan 21, 1969; intvw, Corona Harvest with Col Earl Acuff, USA, CH intvw no 133, Jan 23, 1969; remarks, Gen William C. Westmoreland, at Dak To, Dec 1, 1967; Adm U. S. G. Sharp and Gen William Westmoreland, Report on the War in Vietnam, (Washington, GPO, 1969), p 144.

34. Draft, Proposed Sec Nav Citation, for MARTS-152, Operation Hastings, 1966; Robert Shaplen, "Hastings and Prairie," New Yorker, Dec 17, 1966, p 172; hist, 311th ACSq, Jul-Dec 66.

35. Hist Summary, US Marine Corps Forces in Vietnam, Mar 65-Sep 67, 1967, vol I.

36. Msg 44069, MACV COC to CINCPAC, 031305Z Oct 66; msg 48971,

C/S MACV to USARV, III MAF, 100152Z Nov 66; 1st Logistical Cd OPLAN 4-67, Contingency Plan Oregon, Mar 5, 1967; msg 06009, MACV COC to USARV, et al, 191230Z Feb 67; study, 834th AD, Troop Movement Study, Apr 11, 1967.

37. Msg 11467, MACV COC to CG I FFV, et al, 061800Z Apr 67; msg 11570, Cdr MACV to CINCPAC, 071430Z Apr 67; Murphy intvw, Jan 22, 1969; Maj Arne Ellermets, The Influence of Vietnam on Tactical Airlift Doctrine, (ACSC), Air Univ, Jun 68, pp 70-71; hist, 463rd TCWg, Jan-Jun 67, pp 10-12.

38. Hist, 315th AD, Jan-Jun 67, p xiv; msg, CG, 196th Light Inf Bde to III MAF, 091210Z Apr 67; msg 12320, MACV COC to NMCC, CINCPAC, 132312Z Apr 67; rprt, MACV J-4, Monthly Hist Rprt, May 19, 1967.

39. PACAF Review FY 67, Memo, Dir/Construction MACV to Ch, Hist Br, MACV, subj: Qtrly Hist Rprt, Nov 24, 1966; hist, 315th AD, Jan-Jun 67, pp 65-72.

40. Cd Diary, Marine Aerial Refueler Sq 152, May and Jun 65; cd chronology, MARTS 152, Jul 65 through Feb 66, Jul 66, Jan 67; Vice Adm Edwin B. Hooper, *Mobility, Support, Endurance* (Naval Hist Div, Dept/Navy, 1972), pp 146-147; Capt H. T. King, USN, "Naval Log Support," *Naval Review* (US Naval Institute, 1969).

41. Hist, 14th ACWg, Jan-Jun 66, pp 90-91; ltr, Brig Gen Marion E. Carl, USMC, Board of Investig, to CG/Sr Advisor, I Corps, subj: Investig . . . the Defense of a Shau, Mar 8-13, and Apr 2, 1966; rprt, Det C-1, 5th SFGp, AAR, The Battle for a Shau, Mar 28, 1966; rprt, Det A-102, 5th SFGp, Monthly Opl Summary for May 65; staff journal, Det C-1, Mar 9 and 10, 1966; Kenneth Sams, *The Fall of a Shau*, (PACAF, Proj CHECO, Apr 18, 1966).

42. Hist Summary, US Marine Forces in Vietnam, Mar 65-Sep 67, 1967, vol I; rprt, III MAF, Monthly Eval Rprt for Apr 67, May 10, 1967; rprt, Marine Aerial Refueler Sq 152, Command Chronology, May through Aug 67; hist, 311th ACSq, Jan-Sep 67, p 9; rprt, III MAF, Command Chronology for Mar 67, May 8, 1967; Bernard C. Nalty, *Air Power and the Fight for Khe Sanh*, (AF/CHO, Washington, GPO, 1973), pp 3-9; Capt Moyers S. Shore, *The Battle for Khe Sanh*, USMC G-3 (Hist Br), 1969, pp 3-17.

43. Rprt, 3rd Marine Div, Command Chronology for Aug 67, Oct 5, 1967; rprt, MACV J-4, LOGSUM for Sep 67, Oct 15, 1967; hist, 463rd TCWg, Jul-Sep 67, pp 14-15; Hist Summary, US Marine Forces in Vietnam, Mar 65-Sep 67, vol I; ltr, Vice Adm Edwin B. Hooper, Dir/Naval Hist, to Brig Gen Brian S. Gunderson, Ch, AF/CHO, Sep 26, 1972; memo, Dir/Construction, MACV to Ch, Hist Div, MACV, subj: Qtrly Hist Rprt, Nov 24, 1966; rprt, Dir/Construction, MACV, Qtrly Hist Rprt, Jul 20, 1967; intvw, author with Lt Col Paul W. Amodt, Mar 27, 1973; Capt Moyers S. Shore, *The Battle for Khe Sanh*, USMC G-3 (Hist Br), 1969, pp 25-27.

44. Ltr, Capt J. V. Getchell, USARV, to Dept/Army, subj: Evaluation of LAPES, Jun 19, 1968; rprt, 1st Logistical Cd, AAR, Airdrop Missions 56 and 57, Sep 23, 1967 and Oct 20, 1967; msg, WTOB to Ch, WTO, 221620Z Aug 67; briefing, 834th AD, subj: Tactical Airlift, Oct 29, 1967; ltr, Lt Col Paul W. Amodt to author, Apr 72; hist, 315th AD, Jul-Dec 67, vol I, p xiii, 67; TSgt Bruce W. Pollica and TSgt Joe R. Rickey, *834th AD Tactical Airlift Support for Khe Sanh, 21 Jan-8 Apr 68*, (834th AD Hist Off, 1968), pp 7-8.

45. Hist, 315th AD, Jul-Dec 67, I, 2, 5, 206, 211-212; hist, 311th ACSq, Jan-Sep 67; rprt, MACV J-4, LOGSUM 10-67 for Sep 67, Oct 15, 1967; rprt, 1st Logistical Cd, AAR (Airdrop Mission 67-58), Nov 13, 1967; rprts, 1st Logistical Cd, AARs, Airdrop Missions 57 and 59, Oct 20 and Nov 13, 1967.

46. Rprts, 3rd Marine Div, Cd Chronology for Oct 67 and Dec 67, Dec 1, 1967 and Feb 5, 1968; rprt, MACV, Qtrly Evaluation for Dec 67, Feb 4, 1968; msg, 7th AF, Dir/ALCC to PACAF, subj: Special Report on Aerial Delivery, Oct 25, 1967; rprt, Dir/Construction MACV, Qtrly Hist Summary, Jan 21, 1968; rprt, 1st Logistical Cd, AAR (Airdrop Mission 67-64), Dec 27, 1967.

47. Msg, CG III MAF to COMUSMACV, 240120Z Mar 67; briefing, III MAF, for Sen Preparedness Subcomm Members, Nov 1, 1967; article, "Hai Van Pass," *Army*, Jun 69, pp 45-47; rprts, 3rd Mar Div, Command Chronology,

monthly, Aug through Dec 67; Vice Adm W. B. Hooper, *Mobility, Support, Endurance: A Story of Naval Opl Logistics in the Vietnam War, 1965–1968* (Naval Hist Div, GPO, 1972), pp 110–117.

48. Rprts, Dir/Construction, MACV, Qtrly Hist Summary, Oct 21, 1967 and Jan 21, 1968; Hist Summary, US Marine Corps Forces in Vietnam, Mar 65–Sep 67, 1967; briefing, III MAF, for Sen Preparedness Subcomm Members, Nov 1, 1967; ltr, Capt William A. Barry to author, subj: Tactical Airlift Missions in Vietnam, May 72.

49. Rprt, Col R. Goodell, USA, TMA-MACV, Debriefing Rprt, Jul 1, 1968; rprt, 1st Inf Div Support Cd, Combat AAR, Opn Portland, Sep 67; intvw, author with TSgt James F. Smith, Feb 22, 1973; ltr, 1st Avn Bn, 1st Inf Div, to CG 1st Inf Div, subj: AAR, Opn Shenandoah II, Dec 8, 1967; rprt, 1st Supply and Transportation Bn, 1st Inf Div, Annual Hist Supplement 1967, Mar 20, 1968; daily journals, MACV COC, dates in Oct and Nov 1967; hist, 19th ACSq, Oct–Dec 67.

50. Rprt, MACV, Qtrly Evaluation, Dec 67, Feb 4, 1968; rprt, II FFV, Opl Report Lessons Learned for Qtrly Pd ending 31 Jan 68, Feb 21, 1968; ltr, US Army Support Cd, Saigon, to CG 1st Logistical Cd, subj: AAR–Opn Yellowstone, Mar 11, 1968; msg 09257, Dir/Construction, MACV to USARV, et al, 191156Z Mar 67; unpubl ms, Lt Col Ray L. Bowers, SEA Journal, AF/CHO, 1969.

51. Rprt, 1st Bde, 101st Abn Div, Combat AAR, Opn San Angelo, Mar 9, 1968; rprt, I FFV, Opl Report Lessons Learned for Qtrly Pd ending 31 Jan 68, Jan 31, 1968; rprt, II FFV, Opl Report Lessons Learned for Qtrly Pd ending 31 Jan 68, Feb 21, 1968; rprt, 1st Bde, 101st Abn Div, Combat AAR, Opn Klamath Falls, Jan 27, 1968; msg 36379, MACV COC to CG III MAF, 051251Z Nov 67; daily journals, S–2, 1st Bde, 101st Abn Div, Jan 9–11, 1968; intvw, CHECO with Maj Robert G. Cox, TALO, 101st Abn Div, Mar 1, 1968; hist, 314th TAWg, Jan–Mar 68, pp 30–31; hist, 315th AD, I, 75–76; *Pentagon Papers*, GPO ed, vol V, pt IV–C–6(b), pp 218–223.

52. Msg, CC FMFPAC to CINCPACFLT, 230937Z Sep 67; memo, Hq USMC (ATA–12–GWG), Memo for the President, subj: Situation in the Area of the Vietnam DMZ, Sep 22, 1967; msg, CG FMFPAC to COMUSMACV, 191908Z Sep 67; msg 31663, MACV to CG FMFPAC, 260106Z Sep 67; CMCM 31–67, Commandant of Marine Corps for JCS, subj: The Situation in the DMZ, Sep 24, 1967; JCS paper, JCS, subj: Situation in the DMZ Area, Sep 29, 1967.

53. Memo, Gen Harold K. Johnson, CJCS, to Dep Sec Def, subj: Situation in the DMZ Area and Program 5 Accelerated Deployments, Sep 28, 1967; msg 33049, Cdr MACV to CINCPAC, 080307Z Oct 67; msg 32024, MACV COC to CG III MAF, I FFV, 290224Z Sep 67; daily journal, MACV, COC, Sep 14, 1967; rprt, 2nd Bde, 101st Abn Div, AAR (Offensive Opns 22 Jan–10 Mar 68), Mar 18, 1968; msg, CG III MAF to COMUSMACV, 241400Z Jan 68; msg, CG III MAF to COMUSMACV, 221414Z Jan 68; msg, III MAF to II FFV, 221416Z Jan 68; ltr, Maj Gen John J. Tolson, Cdr 1st Cav Div, to CG 7th AF, subj: Ltr of Appreciation, Feb 28, 1968.

54. Text, Opening Remarks of Gen Westmoreland to JCS, Nov 17, 1967; rprt, MACV, Qtrly Evaluation, Dec 67, Feb 4, 1968; *Pentagon Papers*, GPO ed, vol V, pt IV–C–6(c), pp 1–2; Adm U. S. G. Sharp and Gen William Westmoreland, *Report on the War in Vietnam*, (Washington, GPO, 1969), p 157; script, Speech by Gen Westmoreland before Natl Press Club, Nov 21, 1967; msgs 37083 and 41727, Cdr MACV to CINCPAC, JCS, 120100Z Nov 67 and 160113Z Dec 67.

55. Hist, 834th AD, Jul 67–Jun 68, p 14; fact sheet, 834th AD, subj: Biography, Maj Gen Burl W. McLaughlin, Aug 68.

NOTES

Chapter XII

The Khe Sanh Campaign

1. Rprt, 3rd Marine Div, Command Chronology for Jan 68; msg 16008, MACV J-2 to CJCS, 040737Z Jun 68; memo, Col George J. Keegan, DCS/Intelligence, 7th AF, to TACD, subj: Anticipated Enemy Action Against Khe Sanh, Dec 19, 1967; Capt Moyers S. Shore, USMC, *The Battle for Khe Sanh*, Hq USMC, G-3 (Hist Br), 1969, pp 29-30; draft ms, Bernard C. Nalty, *Air Power and the Fight for Khe Sanh*, Off/AF History, 1973, pp 17-20.

2. Study, MACV J-5, Strategic/Tactical Study, Dien Bien Phu-Khe Sanh, Mar 68; Maj Gen Burl W. McLaughlin, "Khe Sanh: Keeping an Outpost Alive," *Air University Review*, XX (Nov-Dec 68), p 59.

3. Memo, Maj Gen W. E. Dupuy, Off/SACSA, for Dir/Joint Staff, subj: Comparison of the Khe Sanh Campaign with Dien Bien Phu, Jan 31, 1968; paper, MACV J-5 Working Gp, Preliminary Conclusion, Dien Bien Phu/Khe Sanh, Feb 3, 1968; briefing, MACV Working Gp, Khe Sanh/Dien Bien Phu, Feb 69; Jacob Van Staaveren, *The Air Force in SEA: Efforts to Deescalate the War*, (Off/AF Hist, Jun 70); intvw, Corona Harvest, with Maj Gen Robert N. Ginsburgh, CH intvw no 481, Jun 3, 1971; Westmoreland, *A Soldier Reports*, p 338.

4. Memo, MACV J-4 to C/S MACV, subj: Khe Sanh Airlift, Jan 20, 1968; ALOREP data extract, for Jan 16-20, 1968, Shore, *Battle for Khe Sanh*, pp 31-32.

5. Memo, MACV J-4 to C/S MACV, subj: Khe Sanh Airlift, Jan 20, 1968; Lt Col Robert P. Guay, USMC, "The Khe Sanh Airlift—A VTOL Lesson," *Astronautics and Aeronautics*, Dec 69, p 47; rprt, Force Logistic Support Gp Alpha, FMFP, Cd Chronology, 1-31 Jan 68; rprt, III MAF, Cd Chronology, Jan 68.

6. Intvw, author with Lt Col Emmett A. Niblack, May 3, 1972 (Niblack was chief evaluation pilot with 311th Squadron, operating C-123s from Phan Rang and Da Nang during the Khe Sanh siege); McLaughlin, "Khe Sanh," *Air University Review*, Nov-Dec 68, p 59; unpubl ms, Lt Col Ray L. Bowers, SEA Journal, 1967-68, (AF/CHO, 1969).

7. Rprt, 3rd Marine Div, Command Chronology for Jan 68; hist, 374th TAWg, Jul-Oct 68, pp 69-73; rprt, III MAF, Jan 68; msg 02502, MACV to AIG 7051, 230615Z Jan 68; rprt, 1st Bn, 13th Marines, Comb Opns AAR, Opn Scotland, Apr 1, 1968; McLaughlin, "Khe Sanh," *Air University Review*, Nov-Dec 68, p 58; Shore, *Battle for Khe Sanh*, pp 42-47; Guay, "The Khe Sanh Airlift," *Astronautics and Aeronautics*, Dec 69, p 46.

8. Ltr, Maj John W. MacDonald, Ret, to author, May 6, 1972; rprts, HMM-364, HMM-262, HMM-164, Command Chronologies for Jan 68; msgs, MAG 36 to 1st MAWg, 211740Z and 231834Z Jan 68; rprts, HMH-463, SITREPS for 19-23 Jan 68; rprt, Marine Aerial Refueling Transport Sq 152, Command Chronology for 1-31 Jan 68; Guay, "The Khe Sanh Airlift," p 46-47; McLaughlin, "Khe Sanh," pp 58-59; ALOREP data extract, for Jan 68; *The Phan Rang Weekly*, Apr 17, 1968; daily airlift summary, Jan 21-Apr 8, 1968, Atch to Memo Maj Kenneth D. Stahl, 834th AD to DOC, subj: Tactical Airlift Support for Khe Sanh, 21 Jan-8 Apr 68, Apr 15, 1968. (Hereafter cited as Khe Sanh Daily Airlift Summary.)

9. Rprt, 3rd Marine Div, Command Chronology for Jan 68; rprt, 26th Marine Regiment, Command Chronology, Jan 1-31, 1968; ALOREP data extract, for Jan 24-31, 1968; Khe Sanh Daily Airlift Summary; TSgt Bruce W. Pollica and TSgt Joe R. Rickey, *834 AD Tactical Airlift Support for Khe Sanh, 21 Jan-8 Apr 1968* (834th AD Hist Off, 1969), p 20. (Hereafter cited as Pollica-Rickey, *Khe Sanh*.)

10. Intvw, author with TSgt John K. McCall, Apr 7, 1972 (McCall was a C-130 crewman with the 374th Wing which operated out of Cam Ranh Bay, and flew five sorties into Khe Sanh in late January and early February 1968); hist, 374th TAWg, Jul-Oct 68, p 70; Bowers, SEA Journal.

745

11. Bernard C. Nalty, *Air Power and the Fight for Khe Sanh* (Off/AF Hist, 1973), pp 43-44; msg, 7th AF DIS to 13th AF, subj: Khe Sanh Threat and Friendly OB, Mar 5, 1968; Probst intvw, May 8, 1972 (Probst was C-130B pilot, earning DFC for landing at Khe Sanh on Jan 24, 1968); Guay, "The Khe Sanh Airlift," p 46.

12. Memo, Col Ellis J. Wheless, Dir/ALCC, to DOCT and DOCC, subj: Aerial Resupply I Corps Area, Feb 4, 1968; msg, Dir/ALCC to Hq USAF Cd Post, 260730Z Feb 68; Ginsburgh intvw, Jun 3, 1971; Nalty, *Fight for Khe Sanh,* pp 16-17.

13. Warren A. Trest, *Khe Sanh (Operation Niagara), 22 Jan-31 Mar 68,* (PACAF, Proj CHECO, Sep 13, 1968); p 74; ALOREP data extract, for dates in Feb 68; msgs, III MAF COC to MACV, 100703Z and 110735Z Feb 68; rprt, Lt Col William R. Smith, Mission Cdr Rprt, Feb 21, 1968; rprt, 26th Marine Regt, Cd Chronology, 1-29 Feb 68; msg, Dir/ALCC, to III MAF, subj: Resupply Khe Sanh, Feb 11, 1968; Shore, *Battle for Khe Sanh,* pp 66-71.

14. Hist, 314th TAWg, Jan-Mar 68, pp 28-30; hist, 315th AD, Jan-Jun 68, pp 56-57; *Air Force Times*, Apr 3, 1968; information sheet, Sec AF/Off Information, subj: The Air Force Cross, Background Information, Mar 70; Ted R. Sturm, "Countdown to Eternity," *Airman*, May 70, pp 60-64.

15. Amodt intvw, Mar 27, 1973; hist, 314th TAWg, Jan-Mar 68, p 22; Capt Ken Kashiwahara, "Lifeline to Khe Sanh," *Airman*, Jul 68, p 7; Pollica-Rickey, *Khe Sanh,* pp 12-13.

16. Rprt, MARTSq 152, Cd Chronology, 1-29, Feb 68; rprt, 3rd Marine Div, Cd Chronology for Feb 68, Apr 7, 1968; daily situation rprt, USARV G-4, Feb 11, 1968; Shore, *Battle for Khe Sanh,* p 76.

17. Msg 02663, MACV J-3 to CG USARV, et al, 240858Z Jan 68; msg, Dir/ALCC, to III MAF, subj: Resupply Khe Sanh, Feb 11, 1968; 366th TFWg OPLAN 701-68, Aerial Drop and Resupply Support, Feb 10, 1968; msg 02561, MACV J-4 to USARV, 231241Z Jan 68.

18. Msg, 834th AD to 315th ACWg, 040906Z Feb 68; msg, Dir/ALCC to III MAF, 041206Z Feb 68; msg DOR, 834th AD to 315th AD, 240325Z Jan 68; intvw, author with Lt Col Myles A. Rohrlick, Jan 11, 1973; Kashiwahara, "Lifeline to Khe Sanh," p 6.

19. Pollica-Rickey, *Khe Sanh,* pp 22-24; staff summary sheet, Col William T. Phillips, ALCC, subj: Khe Sanh Resupply, Feb 18, 1968; Khe Sanh Daily Airlift Summary; msg, Dir/ALCC to III MAF, subj: Resupply Khe Sanh, Feb 11, 1968; msg, CG III MAF to 26th Marine Regt, 111258Z Feb 68; msg, CG III MAF to 7th AF, 161436Z Feb 68.

20. Staff summary sheet, Dir/Opns, 834th AD subj: IFR GCA/Doppler Aerial Delivery, Feb 15, 1968; hist, 314th TAWg, Jan-Mar 68, pp 25-29; Khe Sanh Daily Airlift Summary, McLaughlin, "Khe Sanh," p 60-61.

21. Staff summary sheet, Dir/ALCC, subj: Khe Sanh Resupply, Feb 18, 1968; intvw, author with Capt John D. Howder, Apr 14, 1972; msg, 7th AF to PACAF, 181020Z Feb 68; hist, 315th AD, Jan-Jun 68, I, 71; rprt, 7th AF, Khe Sanh Analysis: Air Logistic Support, Feb 21, 1968.

22. Ltrs, Maj Wayne K. Shanahan, Mission Coordinator, Da Nang, to Lt Col Kasarda, ALCC, subj: Khe Sanh Airland and Airdrop Opns Summary (Da Nang), Feb 19, 20, and 21, 1968; fact sheets, 7th AF, Khe Sanh Airlift Summary for Gen William Momyer, Feb 20 and 21, 1968; msg, 7th AF to CG III MAF, 090701Z Mar 68; study, Capt Anderson E. Hatfield, Opns Off, CCT, 8th Aerial Port Sq, subj: CCT Operations, Dec 68, pp 13-14; McLaughlin, "Khe Sanh," pp 61-63.

23. Ltr, Lt Col Paul W. Amodt to author, Apr 72; Guay, "The Khe Sanh Airlift," p 47; Khe Sanh Daily Airlift Summary; rprt, MARTSq 152, Cd Chronology, 1-29 Feb 68; msgs, Dir/ALCC to PACAF, 231315Z, 240915Z, 271113Z, 281157Z Feb 68, and 020315Z Mar 68; intvw, author with Lt Col Billy R. Gibson, Apr 21, 1972; Amodt intvw, Mar 27, 1973; rprt, Lt Col John F. Masters, Mission Cdr Report, 22 Feb-3 Mar 68; rprt, Lt Col Lewis H. Dunagan, Mission Cdr Khe Sanh Rprt, 2-17 Mar 68.

24. Rprt, Lt Col John F. Masters, Mission Cdr Rprt, Khe Sanh, 22 Feb-3 Mar 68; msgs, III MAF COC, to MACV J-4, 240247Z, 280611Z, 290233Z, 260555Z, 270217Z Feb 68, and 010207Z Mar 68; Shore, *Battle for Khe Sanh*, p 118; Guay, "The Khe Sanh Airlift," p 46.

25. Rprt, 26th Marine Regt, Cd Chronology, 1–29 Feb 68; rprt, FMFP, Opns of US Marine Forces in Vietnam, Feb 68.

26. Rprt, Lt Col Lewis H. Dunagan, Mission Cdr Rprt, Khe Sanh, 2–17 Mar 68; rprt, Lt Col Donald M. Davis, Mission Cdr Rprt, Khe Sanh, 16–31 Mar 68; rprt, Lt Col William R. Smith, Mission Cdr Rprt, Khe Sanh, Feb 21, 1968; *Newsweek*, Mar 18, 1968, pp 18–22.

27. Rprt, Lt Col William R. Smith, Mission Cdr Rprt, Khe Sanh, Feb 21, 1968; rprt, Lt Col John F. Masters, Mission Cdr Rprt, Khe Sanh, 22 Feb–3 Mar 68; rprt, Lt Col Lewis H. Dunagan, Mission Cdr Rprt, Khe Sanh, 2–17 Mar 68; rprt, Lt Col Donald M. Davis, Mission Cdr Rprt, Khe Sanh, 16–31 Mar 68; rprt, Lt Col Donald E. Girton, Mission Cdr Rprt, Khe Sanh, 31 Mar–12 Apr 68; rprt, Lt Col Paul W. Barker, Mission Cdr Rprt, Khe Sanh, 7 Apr–6 May 68.

28. Rprt, Maj Gen Burl W. McLaughlin, Cdr, 834th AD, EOTR, Nov 67–Jun 69, pp 1–23 to 1–24; McLaughlin, "Khe Sanh," p 65; rprt, Lt Col William R. Smith, Mission Cdr Rprt, Khe Sanh, Feb 21, 1968; rprt, Lt Col Lewis H. Dunagan, Mission Cdr Rprt, Khe Sanh, 2–17 Mar 68; rprt, Lt Col John F. Masters, Mission Cdr Rprt, Khe Sanh, 22 Feb–3 Mar 68; rprt, Lt Col Donald M. Davis, Mission Cdr Rprt, Khe Sanh, 16–31 Mar 68.

29. Pollica-Rickey, *Khe Sanh*, pp 44–45; McLaughlin, "Khe Sanh," pp 65–67; Capt Herbert M. Hamako, "Tactical Aeromedical Evacuation in Vietnam," *USAF Medical Service Digest*, XX (Nov 69), p 4.

30. Pollica-Rickey, *Khe Sanh*, pp 43–45; rprt, Lt Col William R. Smith, Mission Cdr Rprt, Khe Sanh, Feb 21, 1968; rprt, Lt Col Donald M. Davis, Mission Cdr Rprt, Khe Sanh, 16–31 Mar 68; hist, 2nd Aerial Port Gp, Apr–Jun 68; hist, 8th Aerial Port Sq, Jan–Mar 68; rprt, McLaughlin, EOTR, Jun 69, pp 6–16; McLaughlin, "Khe Sanh," p 65; Kashiwahara, "Lifeline to Khe Sanh," p 8; rprt, TAC, Activity Input to Proj Corona Harvest on Tactical Airlift in SEA, 1965–68, Dec 69, vol III, pp III–139 to III–140.

31. Ltrs, Maj Wayne K. Shanahan, Mission Coordinator, Da Nang, to Lt Col Kasarda, ALCC, subj: Khe Sanh Airland/Airdrop Opns, Da Nang, Feb 24 through Mar 15, 1968; rprt, Lt Col William R. Smith, Mission Cdr Rprt, Khe Sanh, Feb 21, 1968; msg 00163, 7th AF Liaison Off, MACV Fwd, to 7th AF, 030205Z Feb 68; msg, 26th Marine Regt to 3rd Marine Div, 151426Z Feb 68; msg, Dir/ALCC to III MAF, subj: Resupply of Khe Sanh, Feb 19, 1968; msg, Dir/ALCC to Hq USAF, 260730Z Feb 68; msg, Cdr, 7th AF to III MAF, 090701Z Mar 68; msg, Cdr III MAF to MACV, 101354Z Mar 68; intvw, Corona Harvest intvw no 95 with Col Milton N. Crawford, 834th AD, Feb 15, 1969.

32. Crawford intvw, Feb 15, 1969, pp 5–6; msg, 1st Log Cd to USARV, 060209Z Mar 68; msg, CG III MAF to MACV, 101354Z Mar 68; msg 07876, MACV J–4 to CINCPAC, 200443Z Mar 68; rprt, 3rd Marine Div, Cd Chronology for Mar 68.

33. Davis intvw, Apr 24, 1972; rprts, Maj Wayne K. Shanahan, Mission Coordinator, Da Nang, Mar 12 and 18, 1968; rprts, Maj Norman K. Jenson, Mission Coordinator, Apr 2 and 6, 1968; 366th TFW OPLAN 701-68, Aerial Drop and Resupply Support, Feb 10, 1968.

34. Msgs, Dir/ALCC, 7th AF to PACAF, 020946Z and 080730Z Mar 68; ltr, Lt Gen Bruce Palmer, Dep CG, to Lt Gen Arthur S. Collins, ACS/Force Devel Dept/Army, Apr 4, 1968; Shore, *Battle for Khe Sanh*, p 125; McLaughlin, "Khe Sanh," pp 64–65; *The Phan Rang Weekly*, Apr 17, 1968; rprt, Col Noble F. Greenhill, Cdr 315th TAWg, EOTR, Apr 30, 1971.

35. Rprt, Lt Col John F. Masters, Mission Cdr Report, Khe Sanh, 22 Feb–3 Mar 68; ltr, Maj Wayne K. Shanahan, Mission Coordinator, Da Nang, to Lt Col Kasarda, ALCC, subj: Khe Sanh Airland and Airdrop Opns, Da Nang, Mar 7, 1968; msg TACD, 7th AF TACC to 834th AD, units, 061245Z Mar 68; msg, Dir/ALCC to PACAF, *et al*, 071032Z Mar 68; ltr, Capt Anderson E. Hatfield, OIC, CCT 1, to Maj Barinowski, Ch, CCT Opns, 2nd Aer Port Gp, subj: Khe Sanh Suggestions and Observations, Mar 10, 1968.

36. Msg AVCA-GO-03-019, 1st Log Cd to III MAF, subj: Return of LAPES Electrical System Cables from Khe Sanh, Mar 6, 1968; msg, Dir/ALCC, 7th AF, to PACAF, 080730Z Mar 68; msg, III MAF to 834th AD, 091258Z

Mar 68; msg, 834th AD to 315th AD, subj: ARC LAPES Load Rigging Equipment, Mar 13, 1968; msg, 315th AD to 834th AD, 150625Z Mar 68.

37. Rprt, Capt Anderson E. Hatfield, Opns Off, CCT, 8th Aerial Port Sq, subj: CCT Operations, Dec 68; ltr, Maj Wayne K. Shanahan to Lt Col Kasarda, ALCC, subj: Khe Sanh Airland/Airdrop Opns, Da Nang, Mar 9, 1968; ltr, Maj Wayne K. Shanahan, Miss Coordinator, To Whom It May Concern, subj: Accident Statement Concerning the 57 Mission on 21 Feb 68; rprt, Lt Col William R. Smith, Mission Cdr Rprt, Khe Sanh, Feb 21, 1968; rprt, Lt Col Donald M. Davis, Mission Cdr Rprt, Khe Sanh, 16–30 Mar 68; rprt, Lt Col Lewis H. Dunagan, Mission Cdr Rprt, Khe Sanh, 2–17 Mar 68; hist, 374th TAWg, Jan–Mar 68, p 28; rprts, 26th Marine Regt, Cd Chronologies, Feb and Mar 68.

38. Rprt, Lt Col Donald E. Girton, Mission Cdr Rprt, Khe Sanh, 31 Mar–12 Apr 68; Phillips intvw, Nov 1, 1968; msg, Dir/Opns, 834th AD to PACAF, 052340Z Mar 68; msg DOALS, Dir/Airl, TAC, to 315th AD, 152158Z Mar 68; rprt, Capt Anderson E. Hatfield, Opns Off, CCT, 8th Aerial Port Sq, subj: CCT Operations, Dec 68, p 15; hist, 374th TAWg, Jul–Oct 68, p 71; rprt, FMFP, Opns of US Marine Forces Vietnam, Mar 68; McLaughlin, "Khe Sanh," p 64.

39. Rprt, Lt Col Lewis H. Dunagan, Mission Cdr Rprt, Khe Sanh, 2–17 Mar 68; rprt, Lt Col Donald M. Davis, Mission Cdr Rprt, Khe Sanh, 16–30 Mar 68; ltr, Maj Wayne K. Shanahan, Mission Cdr, Da Nang, to Lt Col Kasarda, ALCC, subj: Mission Cdr Rprt, Mar 18, 1968; ltrs, Maj Wayne K. Shanahan, Mission Coordinator, Da Nang, to Lt Col Kasarda, ALCC, subj: Khe Sanh Airland/Airdrop Opns, Da Nang, Feb 29, Mar 7, Mar 8, Mar 12, and Mar 13, 1968.

40. McLaughlin, "Khe Sanh," pp 62, 67; msg, CG III MAF to MACV, 101354Z Mar 68; ltr, Maj Wayne K. Shanahan, Mission Cdr, Da Nang, to Lt Col Kasarda, ALCC, subj: Khe Sanh Airland and Airdrop Opns (Da Nang), Feb 28, 1968; Cd Chronology, 26th Marine Regt, 1–29 Feb 68; msg DOC, 834th AD to Dets 1 and 2, 090740Z Mar 68; Davis intvw, Apr 24, 1972 (Davis was C–130A pilot making Khe Sanh drops).

41. Warren A. Trest, *Khe Sanh (Opn Niagara) 22 Jan–31 Mar 68* (Hq PACAF, Proj CHECO, Sep 13, 1968), pp 77–78; ltr, Maj Wayne K. Shanahan to Lt Col Kasarda, ALCC, subj: Khe Sanh Airland and Airdrop Opns (DN), Mar 1, 1968; ltr, Maj Paul E. Dahle, Ret, to author, Nov 25, 1972 (Dahle was C–130B navigator with missions into Khe Sanh); msg, III MAF to Cdr 7th AF, 310334Z Mar 68; ltrs, Maj Robert G. Archer, Mission Coord, Da Nang, to Lt Col Kasarda, ALCC, subj: Khe Sanh Airland and Airdrop Opns, Da Nang, Mar 27, Mar 28, 1968; ltr, Maj Norman K. Jensen, Mission Coord, Da Nang, to Lt Col Kasarda, ALCC, subj: Khe Sanh Airland and Airdrop Opns (DN), Apr 2, 1968.

42. Msg, CG III MAF to FMFP, 230619Z Mar 68; msgs, III MAF to MACV J–4, 020527Z, 090615Z, 150047Z, 290011Z Mar 68; rprt, 3rd Marine Div, Cd Chronology for Mar 68, p 22; rprt, FMFP, Opns of US Marine Forces Vietnam, p 82; Khe Sanh Daily Airlift Summary. Note: Data from MAG–36 (CH–46's) and HMH–463 (CH–53's) suggest that the stated helicopter tonnage figure is low. HMH–463 claimed delivery of 903 tons in support of Scotland during March, while daily SITREPs by the Sky Knight Group appear to indicate lifts of roughly 900 additional tons. These may include retrograde lifts, movements to nearby destinations such as Ca Lu, or lifts from the main base to the hill posts.

43. Rprt, MACV J–2, PERINTREP 3–68, 1–31 Mar 68; Shore, *Battle for Khe Sanh,* p 126; rprt, 3rd Marine Div, Cd Chronology for Mar 68, p 18; rprt, MACV, More Indications Air Strikes and Artillery Preempted Khe Sanh Attack, Apr 16, 1968; Westmoreland, *A Soldier Reports,* p 347.

44. Study 3–68, 31st Mil Hist Det, Operation Pegasus, May 68, p 12; Lt Gen John J. Tolson III, "Pegasus," *Army,* Dec 71, pp 10–19; msg, CG Provis CV, to CG III MAF, 310315Z Mar 68; rprt, MACV J–4, LOGSUM 4–68 for Mar 68, Apr 19, 1968.

45. Msg DOC, 834th AD to 315th AD, subj: Airdrop Qualified Crew Requirements, Mar 30, 1968; msg, III MAF to MACV, 011244Z Apr 68; msg, CG III MAF to COMUSMACV, 280600Z Mar 68; intvw, author with Maj Robert F. Mullen, Sep 20, 1973.

46. Mullen intvw, Sep 20, 1973 (Mul-

len was TALO with 1st Cavalry Division, at Stud during Pegasus); hist, 483rd TAWg, Mar–Jun 68; study 3-68, 31st Mil Hist Det, Opn Pegasus, May 68; hist, 315th ACWg, Apr–Jun 68, pp vii, 11-12, 20; rprt, FMFP, Opns of Marine Forces, Vietnam, Apr 68, pp 7-12, 64-65; Lt Gen John J. Tolson III, "Pegasus," *Army*, Dec 71, pp 10-19.

47. Rprt, Lt Col Zane G. Brewer, Mission Cdr Rprt, Khe Sanh, 12-26 Apr 68; Nalty, *Air Power and the Fight for Khe Sanh*, pp 100-102; rprt, Lt Col Donald E. Girton, Mission Cdr Rprt, Apr 14, 1968.

48. Memo, Dir/Construction MACV to Ch, Hist Br, SJS, subj: Qtrly Hist Summ, Jul 24, 1968; rprt, MACV J-4, LOGSUM 5-68 for Apr 68, May 20, 1968; Westmoreland, *A Soldier Reports*, pp 347-348; msgs, CG III MAF to COMUSMACV, 230403Z May 68 and 110156Z Jun 68; rprt, FMFP, Opns of US Marine Forces, Vietnam, Jun 68.

49. Nalty, *Air Power and the Fight for Khe Sanh*, pp 103; study, JGS, Study of VC Documents: VC Forces at B5 Front and Encircling Khe Sanh Base, Apr 27, 1968.

50. Khe Sanh Daily Airlift Summary.

51. Amodt intvw, Mar 27, 1973.

52. Amodt intvw, Mar 27, 1973; rprt, AFRDQ/AFSC/ANSER, Hq USAF, CFP/TDP for LIT, Aug 69; Guay, "The Khe Sanh Airlift," Dec 69.

53. Rprt, DCS/Plans and Ops, Hq USAF, Trends, Indicators, and Analyses, Jun 68; rprt, MACV, Qtrly Evaluation, Apr–Jun 68, p 11; fact sheet, MACV, subj: Khe Sanh Resupply Rprt, Apr 68; rprt, DIA, Defense Intelligence Digest, Sep 68; Khe Sanh Daily Airlift Summary.

Chapter XIII

Tet and the Battles of 1968

1. Study, Harold N. Sowers, WSEG Study 144, VC/NVA Opns and Activities in SVN for the First Six Months of 1968, Nov 68; rprt, MACV J-2, Intell Bulletin no 1-68 (Jan), Jan 1, 1968; msg, DODPEO to CINCPAC, 250636Z Feb 67; Don Oberdorfer, *Tet!* (Avon Book, New York, 1971), pp 59-93, 155-156; Westmoreland, *A Soldier Reports*, pp 310-334.

2. Oberdorfer, *Tet!*, pp 139-149; Gibson intvw, Apr 21, 1972; briefing text, Maj Angelo Theofanous, USA, G-2 Advisor, II CTZ, Briefing to Gen Hollas and Gen Smith, Apr 68; daily journals, US Advis Det, II CTZ, dates in Jan and Feb 68; draft rprt, US Advis Det, II CTZ, Tet Offensive, 1968; talking paper, Advisors II CTZ, subj: Tet Offensive AAR, Mar 21, 1968; unpubl ms, Bowers, SEA Journal.

3. Probst intvw, May 8, 1972; ltr, Maj Paul E. Dahle, Ret, to author, Nov 25, 1972; rprt, Col Joel C. Stevenson, Cdr, Det 1, 834th AD, [ca Jan 1969]; rprt, Lt Gen Fred C. Weyand, Cdr II FFV, Tet Offensive AAR, 31 Jan-18 Feb 68; rprt, Maj Gen Burl McLaughlin, EOTR, Jun 69; ALOREP data extract for 31 Jan-2 Feb 68; Maj A. W. Thompson and C. William Thorndale, *Air Response to the Tet Offensive, 30 Jan-29 Feb 68*, (PACAF, Proj CHECO, Aug 12, 1968), p 48; hist, 463rd TAWg, Jan–Mar 68, pp 11-12; hist, 315th AD, Jan–Jun 68, vol I, pp xiv, 77; hist, 315th ACWg, Jan–Mar 68, p 15; hist, 310th ACSq, Jan–Mar 68.

4. Daily journals, G-2/G-3 TOC, I FFV, Jan–Feb 68; Gibson intvw, Apr 21, 1972; unpubl ms, Bowers, SEA Journal, 1969.

5. Daily journals, G-2/G-3 TOC, I FFV, Feb 68; ALOREP data extract, Jan 31 and Feb 1, 1968; hist, 315th ACWg, Jan–Mar 68, pp 15-16; hist, 309th ACSq, Jan–Mar 68, p 2; hist, 310th ACSq, Jan–Mar 68; Acuff intvw, Jan 23, 1969; ltr, Gen William W. Momyer, Cdr, 7th AF, to 834th AD, subj: Ltr of Commendation, Feb 3, 1968.

6. Msg 03405, Cdr MACV to CG III MAF, *et al*, 010625Z Feb 68.

7. Ltr, Col Raymond O. Roush, Dir/

Materiel, 834th AD, to MA/DOO, 834th AD, subj: Feb TAPA Impacts, Mar 14, 1968; hist, 315th ACWg, Jan–Mar 68, p 26; unpubl ms, Bowers, SEA Journal, 1969: Thompson and Thorndale, *Air Response to the Tet Offensive* (PACAF, Proj CHECO, Aug 12, 1968), p 48.

8. Memo, Ch, P&O Div, USARV G–4, to USARV G–4, subj: Logistical Status as of 1 Feb 68 (as of 1100 hours), Feb 1, 1968; daily situation rprt, USARV G–4, Feb 2, 1968; memo, Dir/Transp, 1st Log Cd to ACS/SP&O, subj: Logistical Summary Rprt, Mar 4, 1968; msg 40419, CG USARV to COMUSMACV, subj: Logistics Summary 2–68, Mar 14, 1968; draft ms, MACV, Lessons Learned—VC/NVA Tet Offensive, 1968.

9. Rprt, USARV G–4, Daily Situation Rprt, Feb 2, 1968; duty officer log, USARV G–4, Feb 2, 1968; daily journals, G–2/G–3 TOC, I FFV, 30 Jan–1 Feb 68; hist, 315th ACWg, Jan–Mar 68, p 16; hist, 319th ACSq, Jan–Mar 68, p 3; hist, 310th ACSq, Jan–Mar 68, p 3; David R. Mets, *Tactical Airlift Operations*, (PACAF, Proj CHECO, Jun 20, 1969), pp 26–27.

10. Rprts, USARV G–4, Daily Situation Rprts, Feb 1–20, 1968; memo, Dir/Petroleum, 1st Log Cd, to SP&O, 1st Log Cd, subj: Log Summary Rprt, Mar 4, 1968; ALOREP data extract, 1–15 Feb 68, hist, MACV, 1968; pp 890–893; intvw, author with Lt Col Billy R. Gibson, Feb 22, 173.

11. Rprts, USARV G–4, Daily Situation Rprts, Feb 2–10, 1968; ALOREP data extract, 1–4 Feb 68; Thompson and Thorndale, *Air Response to the Tet Offensive*, (PACAF, Proj CHECO, Aug 12, 1968), p 50; rprt, MACV, Assessment of RVNAF as of 29 Feb 68, Mar 21, 1968; daily staff journals, G–4 II FFV, dates in Jan and Feb 68.

12. Rprt, Hq US Army Advisory Gp, IV CTZ, Historical Summary of the Viet Cong Tet Offensive IV CTZ, Apr 8, 1968; rprts, USARV G–4, Daily Situation Rprts, Feb 1 and 2, 1968; daily journals, S–4, 5th SFGp, Feb 1–4, 1968; ALOREP data extract; msg 36525, CG USARV to COMUSMACV, subj: Log Summ 1–68, Feb 14, 1968; msg WTOB, WTOB to WTO, 090915Z Apr 68; msg 200093, CG USARV to MACV, 020500Z Feb 68; hist, 18th ACSq, Jan–Mar 68, p 6; hist, 309th ACSq, Jan–Mar 68, p 3; hist, 310th ACSq, Jan–Mar 68.

13. Ltr, MACV J–4 to Dep CG USARV, subj: Allocation of Dedicated Airlift, Feb 20, 1968; ltr, Maj Delbert R. Brooks, USA, 9th Inf Div Advis Det, to Sr Advis, 9th Inf Div, subj: EOTR, Jun 17, 1968; rprt, USARV G–4, Daily Situation Rprt, Feb 3, 1968; msg 30168, Cdr MACV to Units, 041045Z Feb 68; msg 200093, CG USARV to MACV, 020500Z Feb 68; memo, Col R. H. Goodell, USA, Cdr TMA, to Brig Gen Henry A. Rasmussen, subj: Transportation Concept for Movement of Army Acft Repair Parts, Feb 11, 1968; rprt, MACV, Qtrly Eval, Jan–Mar 68, May 9, 1968; hist, MACV, 1968, II, 623; Thompson and Thorndale, *Air Response to the Tet Offensive*, (PACAF, Proj CHECO, Aug 12, 1968), pp 42–50; rprt, Proj CHECO SEA Digest, special issue, subj: Air Response to VC Tet Offensive, Feb 68, pp 17–20.

14. Ltr, Lt Col Paul W. Amodt to author, Apr 72; rprt, FMFP, Opns of US Marine Forces Vietnam, Feb 68, pp 78–103; rprt, MACV, Qtrly Eval, Jan–Mar 68, May 9, 1968.

15. Rprts, USARV G–4, Daily Situation Rprts, Feb 4–5, 1968; draft ms, Lt Gen John J. Tolson, "Airmobility in Vietnam: The Origin and Development of the US Army's Airmobile Concept in SEA," Oct 30, 1971, pp 284–286; Gibson intvws, Apr 21, 1972 and Feb 22, 1973; ALOREP data extract, 4–8 Feb 68.

16. Rprts, USARV G–4, Daily and Weekly Situation Rprts, dates in Feb 68; daily staff journals, Engr Sect, I FFV, Jan 30 and 31, 1968; ltr, Capt William A. Barry to author, subj: Tactical Airlift Missions in Vietnam, May 72; hist, 374th TAWg, Jan–Mar 68, pp 29–30; rprt, FMFP, Opns of US Marine Forces Vietnam, pp 41–42; ALOREP data extract, Feb 68; msg, III MAF to MACV, 181530Z Feb 68.

17. Study 2–68, 31st Mil Hist Det, Operation Hue City, Aug 68; rprt, USARV G–4, Daily Situation Rprt, Feb 3, 1968; ALOREP data extract, Feb 68; msg 04593, MACV COC to 7th AF, *et al*, 132312Z Feb 68; rprt, MACV, Qtrly Eval, Jan–Mar 68, May 9, 1968; daily staff journals, G–2/G–3 Sections, 101st Abn Div, dates in Feb 68; Cox intvw, Mar 1, 1968; daily journal source files, 101st Abn Div, dates in Feb 68.

18. Rprt, FMFP, Opns of US Marine Forces Vietnam, Feb 68; msg DM,

NOTES

PACAF to 7th AF, Dir/Materiel, 140500Z Feb 68; *Pentagon Papers*, GPO ed, vol V, pt IV-C-6(c), pp 2-9, vol VI, pt IV-C-7(b), p 149; JCS paper, JCS, subj: Emergency Reinforcement of COMUSMACV, Feb 11, 1968; ALOREP data extract, Feb 22-24, 1968.

19. Phillips intvw, Nov 1, 1968; rprt, Maj Gen Burl McLaughlin, EOTR, Jun 69; ltr, Lt Col Paul W. Amodt to author, Apr 72; hist, 14th Aer Port Sq, Jan-Mar 68; staff summary sheet, Dir/Opns, 834th AD, subj: Support of Airlift Forces in I CTZ, Mar 2, 1968.

20. Rprt, 7th AF, Dir/Tactical Analysis, Airlift Effort by Corps Area in SVN, DOA Note 68-4, 1968; rprt, FMFP, Opns of US Marine Forces Vietnam, Feb 68; hist, MACV, 1968, II, 619-620; article, "The Hai Van Pass," *Army*, Jun 69, pp 45-47.

21. Msg 9143, JCS to CINCSTRIKE, 040026Z Feb 68; msg 03614, Cdr MACV to CINCPAC, 040624Z Feb 68; ltr, Capt William A. Barry to author, subj: Vietnam Airlift, Jun 17, 1972; Howder intvw, Apr 14, 1972; hist, CINCPAC, 1968, IV, 123-131.

22. Howder intvw, Apr 14, 1972; msg, WTOB to Ch, WTO, 260945Z Feb 68; hist, TAC, Jan-Jun 68, pp 448-454; hist, 315th AD, Jan-Jun 68, p 62; unpubl ms, Bowers, SEA Journal, 1969.

23. Hist, 12th ACSq, Jan-Mar 68, pp 7-10; hist, 315th ACWg, Jan-Mar 68, p 14; rprt, Maj Gen Burl W. McLaughlin, Cdr 834th AD, EOTR, Jun 69.

24. Phillips intvw, Nov 1, 1968; msg, Dir/Opns, 7th AF, to CINCPACAF, 091130Z Feb 68; msg, 7th AF to PACAF, 211040Z Feb 68; Crawford intvw, Feb 15, 1969; Maj David R. Mets, *Tactical Airlift Operations*, p 28; Thompson and Thorndale, *Air Response to the Tet Offensive*, pp 52-53.

25. Staff summary sheet, Dir/Opns, 834th AD, subj: Support of Airlift Forces in I CTZ, Mar 2, 1968; rprt, PACAF Dir/Tact Eval, Summary Air Opns, SEA, Feb 68, pp 3-1 to 3-6, 5A-8; rprt, Management Analysis Off, 834th AD, Tactical Airlift Performance Analysis, Dec 68; memo, 7th AF, TACC for Gen Momyer, Feb 28, 1968; rprt, Col Joel C. Stevenson, Cdr, Det 1, 834th AD, EOTR, Jan 69; hist, 315th AD, Jan-Jun 68, vol I, p xvi; hist, 19th ACSq, Jan-Mar 68.

26. Study, Opns Analysis Off, Hq USAF, Transport Acft Utilization in VN, Jan 68, Jun 68; rprt, Management Analysis Off, 834th AD, Tactical Airlift Performance Analysis, Dec 68; rprt, Maj Gen Burl W. McLaughlin, Cdr 834th AD, EOTR, Jun 69.

27. Rprts, MACV J-4, LOGSUM 2-68 for Jan 68 and 3-68 for Feb 68, Feb 20 and Mar 20, 1968; hist, 7th AF, Jul-Dec 68, p 311; ltrs, Gen William C. Westmoreland, Cdr MACV, to Cdr 7th AF, subj: Commendation, Apr 4 and Apr 25, 1968.

28. Msg 07708, MACV J-2 to 5th SFGp, 181124Z Mar 68; msg 1142, MACV Combined Intell Sect, to AIG 7809, 200450Z Apr 68; rprt, FMFP, Opns of US Marine Forces Vietnam, Mar 68 and Apr 68; Lt Gen John J. Tolson, *Airmobility, 1961-1971* (Vietnam Studies, Dept/Army, 1973), p 192.

29. Msg, CG III MAF to COMUSMACV, 280906Z Jul 67; msg 41883, MACV COC to USARV, 171045Z Dec 67; msg, CG III MAF to COMUSMACV, 060758Z Feb 68; msg 06910, MACV COC to CG III MAF, 092005Z Mar 68.

30. PCV OPLAN 2-68, Apr 12, 1968; PCV OPLAN 3-68, Apr 16, 1968; 1st Cav Div OPLAN 5-68 (Delaware), Apr 16, 1968; study, 31st Mil Hist Det, Operation Delaware, Feb 69, pp 1-9; C. William Thorndale, Operation Delaware, (PACAF, Proj CHECO, Sep 2, 1968), pp 35-38; press memo, PCV, subj: Lt Gen Rosson's Press Brief Given at PCV on Morning of 17 May 68.

31. Msg, Col William Phillips, 834th AD to Col Pauley, 315th AD, Apr 18, 1968; msg DPMC, 315th AD to 314th TAWg, 180800Z Apr 68; hist, 315th AD, Jan-Jun 68, I, 33-34.

32. Daily staff journals, Fwd CP, 1st Cav Div, Apr 19 through 21, 1968; intvw, Capt J. A. Whitehorne with Maj Gen John J. Tolson, Cdr 1st Cav Div, May 27, 1968; intvw, Proj CHECO with Sgt Raymond Mills, USA, May 24, 1968; study 4-68, 31st Mil Hist Det, Operation Delaware, Feb 69, pp 16-19; C. William Thorndale, Operation Delaware, Feb 69, pp 1-29.

33. Intvw, Proj CHECO, with Capt Robert F. Mullen, TALO, 1st Cav Div, May 24, 1968; Mullen intvw, Sep 20, 1973; msg, PCV Tact Ops Center, to COMUSMACV, 260411Z Apr 68; hist, 2nd Aerial Port Gp, Apr-Jun 68; paper, Capt Anderson E. Hatfield, Opns Off,

751

CCT, 8th Aerial Port Sq, CCT Operations, Dec 68, pp 20–21; intvw, author with Col Donald R. Strobaugh, Mar 12, 1974.

34. Gibson intvw, Apr 21, 1972; intvw, author with Lt Col Nelson W. Kimmey, Mar 9, 1973.

35. Mullen intvw, May 24, 1968; Mullen intvw, Sep 20, 1973.

36. Gibson intvw, Apr 21, 1972; Kimmey intvw, Mar 9, 1973.

37. Gibson intvw, Apr 21, 1972; Mullen intvw, May 24, 1968; Mullen intvw, Sep 20, 1973; Probst intvw, May 8, 1972; intvw, author with Maj Alan L. Gropman, Apr 13, 1972; msg, CG 1st Air Cav Div to PCV COC, 260506Z Apr 68; ALOREP data extract.

38. Gropman intvw, Apr 13, 1972; Mullen intvw, Sep 20, 1973; Mullen ntvw, May 24, 1968; hist, 463rd TAWg, Apr–Jun 68, pp 16–18; Strobaugh intvw, Mar 12, 1974.

39. Msg, PCV TOC to COMUSMACV, 280350Z Apr 68; Gibson intvw, Apr 21, 1972; rprt, 1st Cav Div, SITREP no 118, 270001–272400 Apr 68; study 4–68, 31st Mil Hist Det, Operation Delaware, Feb 69; Mullen intvw, May 24, 1968; hist, 374th TAWg, Jul–Oct 68, pp 75–77; Gropman intvw, Apr 13, 1972; ALOREP data extract.

40. Gropman intvw, Apr 13, 1972; Gibson intvw, Apr 21, 1972; intvw, author with Lt Col Paul W. Arcari, Mar 14, 1973; intvw, author with Maj Stanley D. Berry, Mar 14, 1973.

41. Intvw, author with Capt Phillip A. Dibb, Mar 30, 1973; mission resume, C–130 Aircrew, atchd to 834th AD Memo for Gen William W. Momyer, May 3, 1968.

42. Intvw, author with Lt Col Ray F. Butts, Feb 9, 1973; Gropman intvw, Apr 13, 1972; Gibson intvw, Apr 13, 1972; ALOREP data extract.

43. Ltr, Capt William J. Endres to author, Mar 21, 1973; Mullen intvw, Sep 20, 1973; rprt, 1st Cav Div, SITREP no 120, 290001 to 292400 Apr 68; study 4–68, 31st Mil Hist Det, Operation Delaware, Feb 69; msg, PCV TOC to COMUSMACV, 290315Z Apr 68; Strobaugh intvw, Mar 12, 1974.

44. Gropman intvw, Apr 13, 1972; ltr, Capt William A. Barry to author, subj: Tactical Airlift Missions in Vietnam, May 72; ltr, Capt William A. Barry to author, subj: Vietnam Airlift, Jun 17, 1972; msg TFS, 315th AD TFA to 315th AD, 010836Z May 68; ALOREP data extract; study 4–68, 31st Mil Hist Det, Operation Delaware, Feb 69; rprt, CCT (8th Aer Port Sq), CCT Mission Rprt, A. Luoi, Apr 20–May 5, 1968.

45. Fact sheet, 7th AF, Summary of Major Emergency Aerial Resupply, Jan 10, 1969; staff summary sheet, Col Heath Bottomly, Dir/Plans, 7th AF, subj: Proposed Ltrs to Gen Ryan Recommending Changes to JCS Pub 2, Jul 14, 1968; memos, MACV J–4 to Mil Hist Br, subj: Logistical Historical Activities, May 21 and Jun 19, 1968; ALOREP data extract; Mullen intvw, Sep 20, 1973; McLaughlin intvw, Apr 20, 1970.

46. Ltr, Gen William W. Momyer, Cdr 7th AF, to 834th AD, subj: Commendation of C–130 Aircrews, May 9, 1968; hist, 345th TASq, Oct–Dec 68; hist, 314th TAWg, Jul–Sep 68, p 26.

47. Tolson intvw, May 27, 1968; memo, Dir/Construction, MACV, to Ch, Hist Br, subj: Qtrly Historical Summary, Jul 24, 1968; ALOREP data extract; study 4–68, 31st Mil Hist Det, Operation Delaware, Feb 69; Strobaugh intvw, Mar 12, 1974.

48. Hist, 374th TAWg, Jul–Oct 68, pp 75–77; intvw, author with Lt Col Robert L. Deal, Mar 23, 1973; ltr, Capt William J. Endres to author, Mar 21, 1973.

49. Msgs, CG 1st Air Cav Div to PCV COC, 240537Z and 270448Z Apr 68, 011730Z and 060641Z May 68; hist, 315th ACWg, Apr–Jun 68; hist, 309th ACSq, Apr–Jun 68, p 3; ALOREP data extract.

50. Ltr, Capt William J. Endres to author, Mar 21, 1973.

51. Msgs, PCV TOC to COMUSMACV, 110400Z and 160230Z May 68; msg, PCV TOC to CG III MAF, 130255Z May 68; study 4–68, 31st Mil Hist Det, Operation Delaware, Feb 69; hist, 2nd Aerial Port Gp, Apr–Jun 68, p 16; ltr, Capt William J. Endres, to author, Mar 21, 1968; Mullen intvw, Sep 20, 1973.

52. ALOREP data extract; study 4–68, 31st Mil Hist Det, Operation Delaware, Feb 69.

53. Rprts, 1st Cav Div, SITREPs nos 134–138, for successive dates, May 13 through May 17, 1968; rprt, FMFP, Operations of US Marine Forces, Vietnam, May 68; C. William Thorndale, Operation Delaware, Feb 69, pp 40–42;

Tolson intvw, May 27, 1968; rprt, 7th AF Dir/Intel, Weekly Air Intel Summary 68-22, Jun 1, 1968, pp 3-6; rprt, MACV J-2, PERINTREP, May 68; press memo, Hq PCV, subj: Lt Gen Rosson's Brief Given at Hq PCV on AM May 17, 1968; hist, MACV, 1968, I, 380.

54. Rprt, Maj Gen Burl W. McLaughlin, Cdr 834th AD, EOTR, Jun 69; rprt, Advisory Team 3, 3rd ARVN Regt, Combat AAR, Lam Son 216, May 31, 1968.

55. Gropman intvw, Apr 13, 1972 (Gropman was navigator with 463rd Wing, visiting Kham Duc on Apr 23, 1968); rprt, 26th Mil Hist Det, AAR, Upgrading Kham Duc Airfield, Jul 24, 1968; rprt, Co C, 5th SFGp, AAR, Battle of Kham Duc, May 31, 1968; memo, Dir/Constr, MACV to Ch, Hist Br, SJS, subj: Qtrly Hist Summ, Apr 20, 1968; rprt, Col R. H. Goodell, USA, Cdr TMA, Debriefing Report (EOTR), Jul 1, 1968, pp 5, 13.

56. Kenneth Sams and Maj A. W. Thompson, *Kham Duc* (PACAF, Proj CHECO, Jul 8, 1968), pp 8-9; Westmoreland, *A Soldier Reports*, p 360; ltr, Maj Paul E. Dahle, Ret, to author, Nov 25, 1972 (Dahle belonged to the C-130 squadron crew operating into Kham Duc, May 9-10, 1968); ALOREP data extract; rprt, MSF Co C, 5th SFGp, AAR Ngok Tavak FOB, May 16, 1968; press intvw, Lt Col Robert B. Nelson, Cdr 2/1, Americal Div, May, 1968.

57. Intvws, Proj CHECO with Lt Col Dave C. Hearell, Lt Col Charles Herrington, and Maj Ernest M. Wood, USA, May 17 and 28, 1968; rprt, Maj Gen Burl W. McLaughlin, Cdr 834th AD, EOTR, Jun 69; rprt, Co C, 5th SFGp, AAR, Battle of Kham Duc, May 31, 1968; press intvw, Brig Gen J. E. Glick, III MAF G-3, May, 1968.

58. Rprt, 8th Aerial Port Sq to 2nd Aerial Port Gp, CCT Mission Rprt, Kham Duc, May 68; hist, 374th TAWg, Jul-Oct 68, pp 77-81; intvw, 26th Mil Hist Det, with Capt Daniel Waldo, USA, 70th Engr Bn, May, 1968; intvw, Proj CHECO with Maj John W. Gallagher, Ch, CCT, May 17, 1968.

59. Ltr, Cdr 834th AD, ALCE, Da Nang, to ALCC, subj: Evacuation of Kham Duc, May 13, 1968; msg, CG III MAF to MACV, 131304Z May 68; ltr, Capt Robert M. Gatewood, 7th ACCSq to Cdr 834th AD, subj: Events of 12 May, May 15, 1968; Sams and Thompson, *Kham Duc*, pp 13-14.

60. Intvw, author with Lt Col James L. Wallace, Apr 3, 1972; Davis intvw, Apr 24, 1972; Gropman intvw, Apr 13, 1972; ltr, Cdr 834th AD, ALCE, Da Nang, to ALCC, subj: Evacuation of Kham Duc, May 13, 1968; rprt, Capt Robert Henderson, USA, Account of Kham Duc Battle, May 68; fact sheet, Sec AF/Off Info, subj: The Air Force Cross, Background Information (Bucher), Mar 70; hist, 463rd TAWg, Apr-Jun 68, pp 21-23.

61. Fact sheet, Sec AF/Off Info, subj: The Air Force Cross, Background Information (Boyd), Mar 70; Ted R. Sturm, "The Lucky Duc," *Airman*, Oct 70.

62. McCall intvw, Apr 7, 1972; hist, 21st TASq, Apr-Jun 68.

63. Wallace intvw, Apr 3, 1972; hist, 463rd TAWg, Apr-Jun 68, pp 22-23; hist, 374th TAWg, Apr-Jun 68, pp 19-21.

64. Intvws, Proj CHECO with Capt Phillip B. Smotherman, FAC, Americal Div, May 29, 1968, Lt Col Richard P. Schuman, ALO, Americal Div, May 28, 1968, Col James M. Fogle, Dep Dir I Corps DASC, and Maj James M. Mead, USMC Liaison Off, May 16, 1968; Wallace intvw, Apr 3, 1972; rprt, Proj CHECO, Debrief of Aircrews from Kham Duc (V-45), May 68; Sams and Thompson, *Kham Duc*, pp 21-32.

65. Gallagher intvw, May 17, 1968; ltr, Maj Edward Carr to author, Sep 4, 1970; statement, TSgt Morton J. Freedman, CCT member, May 68.

66. Ltr, Capt Robert M. Gatewood, 7th ACCS, to Cdr 834th AD, subj: Events of 12 May, May 15, 1968; statements, SSgt J. Lundie and TSgt M. K. Freedman, May 68; Ted R. Sturm, "Flight Check to Glory," *Airman*, Sep 69, pp 52-54; Bob Cutts, "On a Wing and a Prayer," *Pacific Stars and Stripes*, Aug 11, 1968; rprt, CCT, 8th APSq, Mission Report, Kham Duc, May 10-12, 1968.

67. Memo, Col John W. Pauly, Cdr 315th Spl Opns Wg, subj: Recommendation for Award of Medal of Honor, 1968; memo, Col William K. Bailey, Cdr 311th Spl Opns Sq, subj: Recommendation for Decoration, 1968; ltr, Capt Robert M. Gatewood, 7th ACCS, to Cdr

834th AD, subj: Events of 12 May, May 15, 1968; statement, TSgt Morton J. Freedman, CCT member, May 68; Flint Dupre, "Rescue at a Place Called Kham Duc," *Air Force*, Mar 69; Niblack intvw, May 3, 1972; Butts intvw, Feb 9, 1973; intvw, Proj CHECO with Lt Col Joe M. Jackson, ACSq Det Cdr, Da Nang, May 18, 1968; *Congressional Record*, Jan 16, 1969, pp S456–457.

68. Ltr, Maj Paul E. Dahle, to author, Nov 25, 1972; rprt, Co C, 5th SFGp, AAR, Battle of Kham Duc, May 31, 1968; msg, CG Americal Div, to Dep Dir DASC, Da Nang, 141227Z May 68; msg, Cdr 834th AD to units, 131100Z May 68; Sams and Thompson, *Kham Duc*, pp 1–2, 27–35; ltr, Lt Col Robert B. Nelson, Cdr 2/1st Infantry, Americal Div, to Cdr 834th AD, subj: Ltr of Appreciation, May 25, 1968; ltr, Brig Gen Burl W. McLaughlin, Cdr 834th AD, to Dets 1 and 2, 834th AD, and 315th ACWg, subj: Kham Duc Commendations, May 19, 1968.

69. Hist, MACV, 1968, I, 2, 26–30, 371; *DOD Pentagon Papers*, vol V, pt IV-C-6, pp 12–14, 26–27, 38–43.

70. Ohlinger intvw, Dec 5, 1968; paper, Capt Anderson E. Hatfield, CCT Opns Off, 8th Aer Port Sq, subj: CCT Operations, Dec 68; Gropman intvw, Apr 13, 1972; rprts, 3rd Marine Div, Cd Chronologies for May thru Dec 68; hist, 463rd TAWg, Jul–Oct 68, pp 15–16; ltr, Maj Paul E. Dahle, to author, Nov 25, 1972; hist, MACV, 1968, I, 132–133, 393, 387, 401.

71. Hist, 315th AD, Jul 68–Apr 69, pp 98–99; monograph, "The 1st Air Cav Div: Operation Liberty Canyon 1–69," 14th Mil Hist Det, 1st Air Cav Div, Jan 30, 1969.

72. Msg 48649, MACV J–5 to CINCPAC, 070855Z Nov 66; Oplan Full Cry, COMUSMACV, Jan 24, 1967; planning directive no 1–68, MACV, Project El Paso, Jan 29, 1968; study, MACV, Feasibility Study Supporting Oplan El Paso, Jun 7, 1968; Westmoreland, *A Soldier Reports*, pp 271–272.

73. Rprt, 834th AD Off/Management Analysis, Tactical Airlift Performance Analysis, Jun 68 and Dec 68; hist, TAC, Jan–Jun 68, pp 448–463; hist, 834th AD, Jul 67–Jun 68, pp 90–91; staff summary sheet, DCS/Plans, 7th AF, subj: C–130, Aug 9, 1968; hist, 315th AD, Jan–Jun 68, pp 48–52, Jul 68–Apr 69, pp xiv–xx.

74. Phillips intvw, Nov 1, 1968; rprt, Maj Gen Burl W. McLaughlin, Cdr 834th AD, EOTR, Jun 69, pp 2–2 to 2–13, 6–7 to 6–11, 6–23 to 6–25; McLaughlin intvw, Apr 20, 1970.

75. Msg, AFXOTZ, Hq USAF, to PACAF, subj: Congressional Investigation, 151536Z Oct 68; msg, 834th AD to PACAF, 170430Z Oct 68.

76. Rprt, Dir/Management Analysis, Hq USAF, USAF Management Summary: Southeast Asia, Jan 3, 1969.

77. Rprts, 7th AF Dir/Intell, Weekly Intellig Summaries, 68–17 and 68–37, Apr 2 and Sep 14, 1968; rprt, Management Analysis Off, 834th AD, Tactical Airlift Performance Analysis, Dec 68; brief, Dir/Opns, Hq USAF, subj: Red Eye Teams to Laos, Feb 19, 1968; PACAF Tactics/Techniques Bulletin 34, Evasive Tactics for Transport Aircraft, n.d.; rprt, MACV J–2, PERINTREP 3–68, 1–31 Mar 68; DIA, *Defense Intelligence Digest*, Sep 68, pp 26–27; Jac Weller, "The New and the Old in the Vietnamese War," *National Guardsman*, Sep 69, pp 2–7.

78. Davis intvw, Apr 24, 1972 (Davis was C–130A pilot based at Tachikawa, 1966–68); hist, 311th Sp Opns Sq, Oct–Dec 68; Ohlinger intvw, Dec 5, 1968 (Ohlinger was C–130 pilot and Mission Commander, 1966–68); Crawford intvw, Feb 15, 1969 (Crawford was Dep Dir/Opns, 834th AD in 1968); hist, 463rd TAWg, Nov–Dec 68, pp 7–8.

79. AFP 900–2, May 71; *The Vietnam Airlifter* (newspaper), 834th AD, Jan 70.

NOTES

Chapter XIV

The Air Force Caribous

1. Ltr, Lt Gen J. H. Moore, Cdr 7th AF, to COMUSMACV, subj: Reqmt for use of US Army Caribou CV–2B Acft in the SEA Cargo Airlift System, Mar 4, 1966; ltr, Lt Gen J. H. Moore, Cdr 2nd AD, to MACV, subj: Coord of CV–2B Staff Study, Mar 25 and Apr 7, 1966; ltr, MACV COC to units, subj: Army Aviation Allocations, Jul 20, 1966; rprt, Opns Analysis Off, Hq USAF, Analysis of SEA Airlift Opns, Sep 66, pp 32, 37, 39.

2. Memo, Maj Gen H. W. O. Kinnard, Acting ACS/Force, Dept/Army, to CSA, subj: Data Base on Performance of CV–2 Acft, Dec 28, 1966; rprt, Army Materiel Systems Analysis Agency, Analysis of Combat Damage on CV–2B Acft in Vietnam (Technical Memo no 35), Apr 69, pp 16–89; rprt, USARV Avn Section, Army Avn in Vietnam, FY 69, 1969.

3. Joint planning directive Red Leaf, Apr 27, 1966; joint basic plan Red Leaf, CV–2/7 Transfer (USA/USAF), Jun 8, 1966; rprt, Opns Analysis Off, Hq USAF, Integration of Army CV–2 Aircraft into the USAF Inventory, Nov 66, pp 10–13; memo, Maj Gen Harry W. O. Kinnard, Actg ACS/Force Developmt, Gen Staff, for CSA, subj: Transfer of Army CV–2/7 Mission and Resources to the Air Force, Jan 3, 1967.

4. Joint basic plan Red Leaf, CV–2/7 Transfer (USA/USAF), Jun 8, 1966, Annex A; memo, Brig Gen Robert R. Williams, Dept/Army AV, ACS/Force, for CSA, subj: Transfer of Army CV–2/7 Mission and Resources to the Air Force, Jun 3, 1966; rprt, Opns Analysis Off, Hq USAF, Integration of Army CV–2 Aircraft into the USAF Inventory, Nov 66, pp 15–16; rprt, 459th TCSq to 483rd TCWg, Hist Data Record, Jan–Mar 67, Apr 20, 1967, p 22; Capt William P. Jackameit, *Advanced Flying Training in TAC in Support of SEA Operations, 1965–1969* (Off/TAC Hist, Jun 71), pp 128–132, 137–143.

5. Rprt, 458th TCSq to 483rd TCWg, Hist Data Record, Jan–Mar 67, pp i–iii; rprt, 537th TCSq to 483rd TCWg, Hist Data Record, Jan–Mar 67, May 8, 1967, pp i–iv; rprt, Hq 483rd TCWg to Hist Off, 483rd TCWg, Hist Data Rcrd, Jan–Mar 67; hist, 834th AD, 15 Oct 66–Jun 67, I, 25–37; Army Unit Histories, 57th, 92nd, and 134th Aviation Companies, 1966; Army Unit Hist, 135th Av Co, Jun 65–Dec 66.

6. Ltr, Maj Gen Gordon M. Graham, Vice Cdr 7th AF, to Cdr 7th AF, subj: CV–2 Program, Oct 22, 1966; ltr, Col James J. Lannon, DCS/Plans, 7th AF, to MACV J–3, subj: Proposed CV–2 Beddown, Sep 5, 1966; msg DPL 54767, PACAF to CSAF (AFOAPDB), 310444Z Dec 66; hist, 834th AD, 15 Oct 66–Jun 67, pp 5–37; rprt, Opns Analysis Off, Hq USAF, Integration of Army CV–2 Acft into the USAF Inventory, Nov 66, pp 20–23.

7. Staff summ sheet, Col George A. Kemper, Ch, Maint Div, 7th AF, subj: CV–2 Modification Backlog, Jul 18, 1966; msg DMMA 101332, Dir/Maint, 7th AF to PACAF, subj: C–7A Acft, Dec 29, 1966; rprt, Col Paul J. Mascot, Cdr 483rd TCWg, Aug 15, 1967; hist, 834th AD, 15 Oct 66–Jun 67, pp 31–34; rprt, Opns Analysis Off, Hq USAF, Integration of Army CV–2 Acft into the USAF Inventory, Nov 66; rprt, 537th TCSq, Hist Data Record, Jan–Mar 67, May 8, 1967.

8. Rprt, Col Paul J. Mascot, Cdr 483rd TCWg, EOTR, Aug 15, 1967; ltr, Col Paul J. Mascot, Cdr 483rd TCWg to all Avn Companies, subj: Command Control and Supervision, Dec 11, 1966; Army Unit Hist, 135th Av Co, Jun 65–Dec 66; rprt, 537th TCSq to 483rd TCWg, Hist Data Record, Jan–Mar 67, May 8, 1967, pp vi–vii; MR, Col Paul J. Mascot, subj: Summary of Lessons Learned, May 29, 1967; ltr, Col Ralph E. Bullock, DC/Opns, 483rd TCWg, to Sr AF Officer, Avn Companies, subj: Theater Indoctrination for Newly Assigned Aircrews, Dec 66.

9. Ltr, Lt Col S. D. Mimms, Cdr AF Element, 92nd Av Co, to 6252nd Opns Sq, subj: Progress Rprt no 2, Sep 18, 1966; study, 7th AF, Concept of Operations for CV–2 Aircraft, Oct 66; MR,

Col Paul J. Mascot, Cdr 483rd TCWg, Summary of Lessons Learned, May 29, 1967; ltr, Maj Gen Gordon M. Graham, Vice Cdr 7th AF, to Cdr 7th AF, subj: CV–2 Program, Oct 22, 1966; rprt, Lt Col A. P. Mercogliano, Cdr 458th TCSq, EOTR, Jul 19, 1967.

10. Rprts, 459th TCSq, 537th TCSq, and 458th TCSq, to 483rd TCWg, Hist Data Rprts, Jan–Mar 67; rprt, 483rd TCWg to Cdr 834th AD, Hist Data Record, Jan–Mar 67.

11. Msg 054356, PACAF to 7th AF (for Momyer), 062147Z Jul 66; ltr, Lt Gen William Momyer, Cdr 7th AF, to Gen Hunter Harris, Cdr PACAF, subj: Command and Control of In-country Airlift in SVN, Jul 10, 1966; ltr, Brig Gen Richard T. Knowles, USA, C/S, II FFV, to Cdr MACV, subj: Airlift Organization and Operations, Aug 66; ltr, Col William K. Jones, Dir/COC to MACV J–3, subj: 7th AF Concept for SEA Airlift After Transfer of Army CV–2 Capability, Aug 20, 1966; 1st Ind (Ltr, MACV J–3 to units, subj: Airlift Organization and Operations, Aug 9, 1966), Brig Gen Richard J. Peters, C/S, USARV to Cdr MACV, Aug 19, 1966; hist, 834th AD, 15 Oct 66–Jun 67, I, 5–6; Lt Gen John J. Tolson, *Airmobility, 1961–1971* (Vietnam Studies, Dept/Army, 1973), pp 104–108.

12. Msg 02063, CINCPACAF to 7th AF (for Momyer), 220212Z Jul 66; msg AFCCS 86825, CSAF to CINCPACAF, 121506Z Aug 66; MR, Col E. B. Roberts, Secy Joint Staff MACV, subj: COMUSMACV Visit to II Corps, Jun 12, 1966; memo, Secy Gen Staff, US Army, for Heads of Army Staff Agencies, subj: Army Aviation Policy, May 4, 1966; text, Agreement between CSA and CSAF, Apr 6, 1966 (see Appendix).

13. Msg C–00724, Cdr 7th AF to COMUSMACV, subj: CV–2 Beddown and Concept of Operation, Oct 31, 1966; msg AFXOPF, Dir/Opns, Hq USAF, to PACAF, 051707Z Dec 66; rprt, Opns Analysis Off, Hq USAF, Integration of Army CV–2 Aircraft into the USAF Inventory, Nov 66, pp 14, 33–42; staff summary sheet, Col A. L. Hilpert, DCS/Plans, 7th AF, subj: CV–2 Beddown and Concept of Operations, Oct 28, 1966; ltr, Gen J. P. McConnell, CSAF, to Gen H. K. Johnson, CSA, Dec 8, 1966; AFM 2–50/FM 100–27, US Army/USAF Doctrine for Tactical Airlift Operations, Jan 1, 1967; annotated comments, Gen William W. Momyer, USAF, Ret, Comments on draft ms, USAF in SEA: Tactical Airlift, Oct 75.

14. Memo, Col Ralph E. Bullock, 483rd TCWg, to Brig Gen William Moore, Cdr 834th AD, subj: CV–2 Mission Assignment Procedures, Nov 18, 1966; memo, Col C. George Whitley, Ch, Aerospace Doctrine Div, Dir/Doct, Concepts, Objs, to Gen Yudkin, Dir/Doct, Concepts, Objs, subj: MACV Plan for CV–2 Employment, Dec 1, 1966; msg, COMUSMACV to USARV, 7th AF, *et al*, 230438Z Nov 66; JCS Publ 2, Unified Action Armed Forces (UNAAF), JCS, Nov 59, pp 43–45.

15. 483rd TCWg OPORD 67–1, Dec 23, 1966; pamphlet, 834th AD, subj: C–7A Mission Assignment Procedures 1 Jan 67, Dec 66.

16. MR, Col Paul J. Mascot, Cdr, 483rd TCWg, subj: Summary of Lessons Learned, May 29, 1967.

17. 483rd TCWg Operation Plan 67–1, Red Leaf, n.d.; 483rd TCWg OPORD 67–1, Dec 23, 1966.

18. Rprts, 459th TCSq and 535th TCSq, to 483rd TCWg, Hist Data Record, Jan–Mar 67; rprt, 483rd TCWg to Hist Off, 483rd TCWg, Hist Data Record, Jan–Mar 67; rprt, 483rd TCWg to 834th AD, Hist Data Record, Jan–Mar 67.

19. MR CS 452.1, Col William B. Caldwell, USA, Asst Secy to Gen Staff, subj: Data Base on Performance of CV–2s, Nov 17, 1966; rprts, MACV, Monthly Eval, Jan and Feb 67, Feb 25 and Mar 24, 1967; rprt, Brig Gen William G. Moore, Cdr 834th AD, Nov 67, p 18; study, Dir/Plans PACAF and Dir/Opns MAC, PACOM Theater Airlift Study FY 68, June 30, 1967; ltr, Col Paul J. Mascot, Cdr 483rd TCWg to units, subj: Airlift Accomplishments First Qtr 1967, Apr 4, 1967.

20. Memo, Lt Gen William W. Momyer, Cdr 7th AF, to DCS/Plans, subj: C–7A, Apr 22, 1967; draft msg AVFA–GD–T, I FFV to USARV (for Lt Gen Engler from Lt Gen Larsen), Mar 67; msg 30681, II FFV G–4 to USARV (for Lt Gen Engler), Mar 67; msg A–28956, CG USARV to Dept/Army, USARPAC, COMUSMACV, 020748Z May 67.

21. Ltr, Brig Gen William G. Moore, Cdr 834th AD, to Cdr 7th AF, subj: Fixed-Wing Cargo Airlift Support in

RVN, Apr 22, 1967; staff summary sheet, Col A. L. Hilpert, DCS/Plans, subj: Performance of the C-7A for Jan–Mar 67, May 6, 1967; msg 00304, 7th AF to COMUSMACV, subj: Performance of the C-7A (CV-2) for period Jan–Mar 67, May 8, 1967; msg 00402, 7th AF to PACAF, 151148Z Jun 67.

22. Msg 6362, COMUSMACV to CINCPAC, (Westmoreland to Sharp), 160319Z May 68; ltr, Col Paul J. Mascot, Cdr 843rd TCWg to Cdr 834th AD, subj: C-7A Capability Study, May 5, 1967; rprts, 457th TCSq and 535th TCSq to 483rd TCWg, Hist Data Record, Apr–Jun 67; rprt, 483rd TCWg to 834th AD, Hist Data Rcrd, Apr–Jun 67; hist, 834th AD, 15 Oct 66–Jun 67, I, 29–31; 834th AD OPLAN 500-67, Airlift Operations, Apr 12, 1967.

23. Rprt, MACV J-4, LOGSUM 1-68 for Dec 67, Jan 15, 1968; rprt, MACV J-4, Monthly Hist Report, Jun 17, 1967; MR, Maj Donald R. Hargrove, Opns Plans Officer, subj: C-7A Liaison Office, Aug 28, 1967; rprt, Maj Gen Burl W. McLaughlin, Cdr 834th AD, EOTR, Jun 69, pp 3-7 to 3-8; msg 00438, Dir/Opns, 834th AD to units, subj: C-7A Operations, Jul 67; msg 32562, MACV COC to USARV, et al, 040710Z Oct 67; msg 68-3, 834th AD to Dir/Opl Reqmts, Hq USAF (to Moore from McLaughlin), subj: C-7A Aircraft in SEA, Jan 19, 1968; rprt, Laurence E. Lynn, Dir/Economics and Mobility Forces, Off/Sec Def Systems Analysis, subj: Trip Report, Aug 67, pp 6–7.

24. Rprts, 459th TCSq to 483rd TCWg, Hist Data Record, Jan–Mar and Apr–Jun 67; hist, 459th TASq, Jan–Mar 68, pp 4–5, Oct–Dec 68, pp 5–6; ltr, Lt Col Daniel F. Scrungel, Cdr Co C, 5th SFGp, to Cdr 483rd TAWg, subj: Ltr of Appreciation, Mar 1, 1968.

25. Rprt, Col William H. Mason, Cdr 843rd TAWg, EOTR, Oct 68; memo, Col Alden G. Glauch, Dir/Opns, 483rd TAWg, to Cdr 843rd TAWg, subj: Reevaluation of C-7A Mission Site and Liaison Functions, Jul 23, 1968; ltr, Col William H. Mason, Cdr 483rd TAWg, to Cdr 5th SFGp and Sr Advis IV CTZ, et al, subj: C-7A Support of 5th TAWg, to Cdr 5th SFGp and IV Corps Sr Advisor, Dec 31, 1967; msg 68-3, 834th AD to Dir/Opl Reqmts, Hq USAF (from McLaughlin to Moore), subj: C-7A Aircraft in SEA, Jan 19, 1968; hist, 483rd TAWg, Oct–Dec 67, p 5, Jul–Sep 68; rprts, 459th TCSq and 536th TCSq, to 483rd TCWg, Hist Data Records, Jan–Mar 67; rprts, 457th TCSq and 459th TCSq, to 483rd TCWg, Hist Data Records, Apr–Jun 67; hist, 457th TASq, Oct–Dec 67; hist, 458th TASq, Jul–Sep 67, Oct–Dec 67, Jan–Mar 68, Oct–Dec 68; hist, 459th TASq, Jul–Sep 67, p 11.

26. Rprt, Lt Col Charles C. Smith, Cdr 537th TCSq, EOTR, Jul 3, 1967; ltr, Lt Col Gayle C. Wolf, Cdr 537th TASq to DCO, 483rd TCWg, subj: Project New Book, Aug 68; rprts, 537th TCSq to 483rd TCWg, Jan–Mar 67, Apr–Jun 67, Jul–Sep 67; hist, 537th TASq, Oct–Dec 67, pp 7–10, 25, Jan–Mar 68, pp 7–12, 16, Jul–Sep 68, p 6, Oct–Dec 68, p 7, 18; intvw, author with Lt Col Maurice V. Clegg, Mar 21, 1974 (Clegg was pilot with 537th, 1967-8).

27. Rprt, Lt Col A. P. Mercogliano, Cdr 458th TCSq, EOTR, Jul 19, 1967; rprts, 535th TCSq to 483rd TCWg, Hist Data Record, Jan–Mar and Apr–Jun 67; rprt, Hq Av Bn (F–W), Operational Report, Lessons Learned, May 10, 1966; study, Brig Gen Burl W. McLaughlin, Cdr 834th AD, and Maj Gen Robert R. Williams, USARV, subj: Review of C-7A Operations in Support of the Army, Apr 18, 1968; rprt, Col William H. Mason, Cdr 483rd TAWg, EOTR, Oct 68; hist, 2nd Aerial Port Gp, Jul 66–Sep 67, pp 13–14, 27–28; Clegg intvw, Mar 21, 1974.

28. Rprts, Management Analysis Off, 834th AD, Tactical Airlift Performance Analysis, SEA, Dec 67 and Dec 68; ltr, Maj Gen Robert R. Williams, Avn Off, USARV, to Col Edwin L. Powell, Jr, Dept/Army Avn, OASCFOR, Dept/Army, Jul 14, 1968; msg 68-3, 834th AD to AFRDG, Hq USAF, McLaughlin to Moore, subj: C-7A Acft in SEA, Jan 19, 1968; rprt, Col Paul J. Mascot, Cdr 483rd TAWg, EOTR, Aug 15, 1967; memo, MACV COC, to distribution, subj: Total C-7A Resource Priorities/Allocations, Jun 19, 1967; hist, 483rd TAWg, Jul–Sep 68, p 23, Apr–Jun 68, p 2.

29. Study, Brig Gen Burl W. McLaughlin, Cdr 834th AD, and Maj Gen Robert R. Williams, USA, USARV, subj: Review of Air Force C-7A Operations in Support of the Army, Apr 18, 1968.

30. Rprt, Maj Gen Burl W. McLaughlin, Cdr 834th AD, EOTR, Jun 69; rprt,

Col Paul J. Mascot, Cdr 483rd TCWg, EOTR, Aug 15, 1967; study, Brig Gen Burl W. McLaughlin, Cdr 834th AD, and Maj Gen Robert Williams, USA, USARV, subj: Review of Air Force C-7A Operations in Support of the Army, Apr 18, 1968; msg 01079, 483rd TAWg to 834th AD, subj: Favorable Comments from US Army Concerning USAF C-7A Operations, Sep 3, 1967; ltr, DC/Opns, 483rd TAWg to units, subj: Aircrew Flight Duty Time (Change to PACAFM 55-27), Apr 23, 1968; Crawford intvw, Feb 15, 1969; Huff intvw, Jan 24, 1969; Murphy intvw, Jan 22, 1969; intvw, Corona Harvest with Maj Marvin Myers, USA, CH intvw no 112, Jan 21, 1969.

31. Rprt, US Army Support Cd, CRB, Operational Report, Lessons Learned for Nov 67-Jan 68, Feb 10, 1968; Crawford intvw, Feb 15, 1969; study, Brig Gen Burl W. McLaughlin, Cdr 834th AD, and Maj Gen Robert R. Williams, USA, USARV, subj: Review of Air Force C-7A Operations in Support of the Army, Apr 18, 1968; rprt, Brig Gen William G. Moore, Cdr 834th AD, EOTR, Nov 67, pp 19-20; rprt, Maj Gen Burl W. McLaughlin, EOTR, Jun 69, pp 3-4 to 3-7; Moore intvw, May 4, 1970; McLaughlin intvw, Apr 20, 1970; msg 68-3, 834th AD to Dir/Opl Reqmts, Hq USAF (for Moore from McLaughlin), subj: C-7A Aircraft in SEA, Jan 19, 1968; ltr, Col Paul A. Whelan to author, Feb 25, 1974 (Whelan was a C-7 pilot assigned to line and staff duty in Vietnam 1967-68).

32. Rprt, 537th TCSq to 483rd TCWg, Hist Data Record, Jan-Mar 68; pamphlet, 483rd TAWg, C-7A Standardization Guide, 1968; *Air Force Times*, Sep 3, 1969, p 15.

33. 483rd TAWg Operations Bulletin no 3-68, Nov 15, 1968; 483rd TAWg Supplement 1 to PACAFM 55-27, Sep 1, 1968; rprt, 537th TCSq to 483rd TCWg, Hist Data Rprt, Jan-Mar 67; ltr, Col N. T. Lawrence, DC/Opns, 483rd TCWg, to Dir/Opns, 834th AD, subj: Radar Approach Facilities, May 24, 1967; Mullen intvw, Sep 20, 1973; pamphlet, 483rd TAWg, C-7A Standardization Guide, 1968; Clegg intvw, Mar 21, 1974; ltr, Whelan to author, Feb 25, 1974.

34. Intvw, Corona Harvest with Maj Harold C. O'Donovan, Apr 17, 1972; 483rd TCWg Operations Bulletin no 5, Apr 24, 1967; paper, 459th TASq, subj: Analysis of Hazardous Airfields in I Corps Area, RVN, 1967; rprt, 459th TCSq to 483rd TCWg, Hist Data Record, Jan-Mar 67; hist, 457th TASq, Jul-Sep 68.

35. Hist, 483rd TAWg, Oct-Dec 67, pp 15, 27-29, Jan-Mar 68, p 12, Apr-Jun 68, pp 17-19, Jul-Sep 68, pp 9-10, Oct-Dec 68, p 12; USAF management summary, Southeast Asia, Apr 26 and Aug 30, 1968.

36. Rprt, Col William H. Mason, Cdr 483rd TAWg, EOTR, Oct 68; rprt, 483rd TCWg to 483rd TCWg Hist Off, Hist Data Record, Jan-Mar 67; USAF management summary, Southeast Asia, Dec 29, 1967 and Jan 3, 1969; msg 68-3, 834th AD to Dir/Opl Reqmts, Hq USAF (for Moore from McLaughlin), subj: C-7A Aircraft in SEA, Jan 19, 1968; rprt, DOD, Annual Reports for FY 67 and FY 68.

37. Ltr, Lt Col Charles C. Smith, Cdr 537th TCSq, to DC/Opns, 483rd TCWg, subj: Crew Scheduling, Jun 24, 1967; ltr, Lt Col Henry A. Glover, Cdr 457th TCSq, to 483rd TCWg, subj: C-7A Aircraft Accident Progress Report, Feb 17, 1967; 483rd Operations Bulletins no 4 and 9, Apr 1 and Jul 17, 1967; 483rd TAWg Supplement 1 to PACAFM 55-27, Apr 6 and Sep 1, 1968; rprt, 483rd TCWg to 834th AD, Hist Data Record, Jul-Sep 67; rprt, Col V. W. Froehlich, Cdr 315th ACWg, EOTR, Aug 67; rprt, Col William H. Mason, Cdr 483rd TAWg, EOTR, Oct 68; rprt, Col Paul J. Mascot, Cdr 483rd TCWg, EOTR, Aug 15, 1967.

38. Hist, 483rd TAWg, Oct-Dec 67, pp 5-9, Jan-Mar 68, pp 8-9, Apr-Jun 68, pp 9, 21-22; rprts, 459th TAWg and 457th TASq to 483rd TAWg, Hist Data Record, Apr-Jun 67; rprt, 483rd TCWg to 834th AD, Hist Data Record, Jul-Sep 67; hist, 459th TASq, Jul-Sep 67, p 13; hist, 457th TASq, Jul-Sep 67, Oct-Dec 67, Jul-Sep 68, pp 16-17; ltr, Col George W. Kinney, Vice Cdr 834th AD, to Dir/Pers, 7th AF, subj: Critical Shortage in Aircrew Manning, Nov 30, 1967; memo, Lt Col Maynard E. Stogdill, Opns Off, 537th TASq, to DC/Opns, 483rd TAWg, subj: Upgrading Data for Newly Assigned Aircrew Members, Dec 12, 1967; hist, 7th AF, Jul-Dec 67, pp 163-164; rprt, Col Paul J. Moscot, Cdr 483rd TCWg, EOTR, Aug 15, 1967; Capt Robert P. Everett, "Vietnam Airlift is a Human Thing," *Airman*, (Oct 69).

39. Ltr, Col William H. Mason, Cdr 483rd TCWg, to 834th AD, subj: Aircrew Manning, Oct 22, 1967; ltr, Col Wilbert Turk, Cdr 843rd TAWg, to Maj Gen Burl W. McLaughlin, Cdr 834th AD, Oct 19, 1968; rprt, Col William H. Mason, Cdr 483rd TAWg, EOTR, Oct 68; hist, 7th AF, Jul–Dec 68, pp 366–368; hist, 483rd TAWg, Jul–Sep 68, pp 5–6, Oct–Dec 68, pp 9–16.

40. Intvw, TSgt B. W. Pollica with Lt Col Frederick F. Shriner, Asst Dir/Materiel, 834th AD, Sep 9, 1968; rprt, Col Paul J. Mascot, Cdr 483rd TCWg, EOTR, Aug 15, 1967; rprt, 535th TCSq to 483rd TCWg, Hist Data Record, Jan–Mar 67; rprt, 457th TCSq to 483rd TCWg, Hist Data Record, Apr–Jun 67; paper, 7th AF Dir/Materiel, subj: C–7A, 1967; O'Donovan intvw, Apr 17, 1972; rprts, Management Analysis Off, 834th AD, Tactical Airlift Performance Analysis, SEA, Dec 67 and Dec 68.

41. 483rd TAWg OPORD 68–1, Aug 1, 1967, Annex F; hist, 483rd TAWg, Oct–Dec 67, pp 17–19, Apr–Jun 68, p 38, Jul–Sep 68, pp 27–29; hist, 483rd CAMSq, to 483rd TAWg, subj: EOTR, Sep 19, 1967; O'Donovan intvw, Apr 17, 1972; rprt, Col Paul J. Mascot, Cdr 483rd TCWg, EOTR, Aug 15, 1967; rprt, Col William H. Mason, Cdr 483rd TAWg, EOTR, Oct 68.

42. Rprt, 7th AF, General Inspection of 834th AD, Nov 26, 1968; rprt, Col William H. Mason, Cdr 483rd TAWg, EOTR, Oct 68; Clegg intvw, Mar 21, 1974; all squadron histories, 483rd TAWg, 1967 through 1968.

43. Rprts, 535th TCSq and 536th TCSq, to 483rd TCWg, Hist Data Record, Apr–Jun 67; hist, 537th TASq, Jul–Sep 67, p 13; hist, 459th TASq, Jul–Sep 67, p 12, Oct–Dec 67, pp 9–10, Apr–Jun 68, p 9; hist, 483rd TAWg, Jul–Sep 68, pp 21–22; ltr, Lt Col James F. Akin, Mission Cdr, to Cdr 535th TCSq, subj: Ltr of Appreciation, May 5, 1967; msg 68–3, 834th AD, to Dir/Opl Rqmts, Hq USAF (for Moore from McLaughlin), subj: C–7A Aircraft in SEA, Jan 19, 1968; rprt, Maj Gen Burl W. McLaughlin, Cdr 834th AD, EOTR, Jun 69.

44. Msgs, CG I FFV to MACV COC 100409Z, 110245Z, and 130304Z Jun 68; hist, 457th TASq, Apr–Jun 68, pp 7–8; hist, 459th TASq, Apr–Jun 68, pp 9–10; ltr, Maj Williard H. Sinclair, Dir/Flying Safety, 7th AF, to 459th TCSq, subj: Operational Hazard Report, Apr 12, 1967; ltr, Col Lawrence L. Mowery, Cdr, 3/101st Div, to Cdr 483rd TAWg, subj: Ltr of Appreciation, Jun 22, 1968; paper, 459th TASq, subj: Analysis of Hazardous Airfields in II Corps Area, RVN, 1967; rprt, Col William H. Mason, Cdr 483rd TAWg, EOTR, Oct 68; Capt Robert P. Everett, "Vietnam Airlift is a Human Thing," *Airman*, (Oct 68), pp 8–9.

45. 483rd TAWg Operations Bulletin 3–68, Nov 15, 1968; 483rd TAWg Supplement 1 to PACAFM 55–27, Sep 1, 1968; ltr, Col N. T. Lawrence, DC/Opns, 483rd TCWg, to units, subj: C–7A SEA Airdrop Procedures, Aug 29, 1967; rprt, 834th AD, SEA Airlift Statistics Summary, Dec 67; rprt, Management Analysis Office, 834th AD, Tactical Airlift Performance Analysis, Dec 68.

46. Rprt, US Mil Advisory Det, 23rd Inf Div, Combat Opns AAR for Battle of Duc Lap, Oct 5, 1968; 21st Mil Hist Det, 5th SFGp, Combat AAR/Intvw Report, Battle of Duc Lap Sp Forces Camp, 23–28 Aug 68, Nov 27, 1968; rprt, Det A–239, 5th SFGp, Monthly Opl Summary for Aug 68; narrative, 21st Mil Hist Det, 5th SFGp, Account of Battle from Interviews (Duc Lap), 1968; msg 25155, MACV COC to CJCS, 270737Z Aug 68.

47. Briefing, G–3 I FFV, for Chairman JCS, Dep COMUSMACV, Mr. Colby, at Nha Trang, Nov 12, 1968; rprt, Det B–20, 5th SFGp, AAR–Opn Duc Lap, the 213th MSF Co, Aug 23 to Dec 11, 1968; rprt, USAF TACP, 23rd ARVN Div, AAR Battle for Duc Lap, RVN, 1968; rprt, 21st Mil Hist Det, 5th SFGp, AAR Intvw Rprt, Battle of Duc Lap Sp Forces Camp, 23–28 Aug 68.

48. Ltr, Lt Col Hunter F. Hackney to author, May 4, 1972; duty officer log, 5th SFGp S–3, Aug 23 through 27, 1968; O'Donovan intvw, Apr 17, 1972; rprt, 21st Mil Hist Det, 5th SFGp, Combat After Action Interview Rprt, Battle of Duc Lap Special Forces Camp, 23–28 Aug 68, Nov 27, 1968; fact sheet, Sec AF/Off Information, subj: The Air Force Cross, Background Information (Finck, Hackney), Mar 70; hist, 483rd TAWg, Jul–Sep 68, p 21; rprt, Col William H. Mason, Cdr 483rd TAWg, Oct 68; *7th AF News*, Sep 25, 1968.

49. Rprt, USAF TACP, 23rd ARVN Div, Comb Opns AAR on Battle of Duc Lap, 1968; rprt, I FFV, Qtrly Summary,

II CTZ, 3rd Qtr, CY 68, Oct 15, 1968; msgs 27327, 28099, and 30501, MACV COC to CJCS, 160915Z, 230656Z Sep, and 140724Z Oct 68; hist, MACV, I, 173–174.

50. Msg 68–3, 834th AD to Dir/Opl Reqmts, Hq USAF (for Moore from McLaughlin), subj: C–7A Aircraft in SEA, Jan 19, 1968.

51. Study, Brig Gen Burl W. McLaughlin, Cdr 834th AD, and Maj Gen Robert R. Williams, USA, USARV, subj: Review of Air Force C–7A Operations in Support of the Army, Apr 18, 1968; ltr, Lt Gen Bruce Palmer, USA, Dep CG USARV, to Cdr 7th AF, subj: Requirements for Additional STOL Tactical Aircraft, Jun 10, 1968; ltr, Gen William W. Momyer, Cdr 7th AF, to COMUSMACV, subj: Requirements for Additional STOL Tactical Airlift, Jun 15, 1968; memo, Lt Gen James V. Edmundson, Vice Cdr, 7th AF, to Cdr 7th AF, subj: Reqmt for Additional STOL Tactical Airlift, Sep 25, 1968; background paper, Dir/Plans, Hq USAF, subj: Three Airlift CV–2 Sqdns, Jul 66; Program Budget Decision no 421, Off/Sec Def, subj: CV–2 Aircraft, Dec 22, 1966; msg, JCS to CINCPAC, 072224Z Aug 68; msg, Cdr 7th AF to Cdr PACAF, 160210Z Aug 68; rprt, AFXOP Study Gp, Dir/Opns, Hq USAF, Tactical Airlift Problems, 1966.

Chapter XV

The Auxiliary Roles

1. Msg DOP 51048, PACAF to 7th AF, 170005Z Jul 66; rprt, PACAF, Airlift Rprt for May 66, RCS: AF–J–38; Borders intvw, Nov 4, 1970; rprts, 315th AD, Commander's Review, Jun 30 and Dec 31, 1966; rprt, Joint Logistics Review Board, Monograph no 2 (Ammunition), 1970, pp 123–141.

2. CINCPAC Instruction 4600.3B, Apr 3, 1967; hist, 315th AD, Jan–Jun 68, I, 59–62; study, 315th AD, PACAF C–130 Aircrew Manning, Apr 67; study, Hq PACAF and Hq MAC, Theater Airlift Study CY 67, Jan 31, 1967.

3. Hist, 463rd TCWg, Jan–Jun 67, pp 11–12; hist, 314th TCWg, Jan–Jun 67, p 5; hist, 374th TCWg, Jan–Jun 67, pp 18–19.

4. Rprt, Joint Logistics Review Board, Monograph no 18 (Transportation and Movement Control), 1970, pp 145–150; 315th AD Manual 20–3, Mission and Responsibilities, May 1, 1966; memo, Lt Col Bruce G. Gilbreth, Ch, Comm-Electr, 315th AD, to OC–SO, 315th AD, subj: Airlift Mission Monitoring System, Feb 25, 1965.

5. Msg DOP 02080, 315th AD to PACAF, 230658Z May 66; memo, Lt Gen Hewitt T. Wheless, Asst Vice CSAF to Air Staff agencies, subj: CSAF Decision, Airlift Organization in the PACOM Area, Oct 19, 1966; memo, Col Charles W. Lenfest, Asst Dep Dir/Plans for War Plans, Dir/Plans, Hq USAF, to AFXPDO, subj: PACAF Airlift Organization Structure, Sep 2, 1966; msg XPD 91625, Dir/Plans, Hq USAF, to PACAF (for Gen Vogt), 242232Z May 66; rprt, Airlift Staff Gp, Visit to PACOM Area, 11 Oct–10 Nov 65; telecon, Lt Col Stougger to Col Umpleby, CHWTO, 141013Z Nov 65; msg VC 57124, TAC to Hq USAF (XOP and XPD), 211940Z Sep 65.

6. Rprt, Lt Gen Glen W. Martin, IG USAF, Visit to PACOM to Evaluate Airlift, 27 Feb–12 Mar 66; study, Dir/Plans, Hq PACAF, Organization of 315th Air Division, DPLM 75153, May 16, 1967.

7. PACAF PAD 69–2, subj: PACOM Airlift Organization, Sep 24, 1968; ltr, Col Charles W. Howe, Cdr 315th AD, to CINCPACAF, subj: Org of PACAF Airlift System, Jun 12, 1967; msg 00403, 7th AF to PACAF, subj: Org of PACAF Airlift System, Jun 15, 1967; msg, CSAF to PACAF (for Ryan from McConnell), 042251Z Mar 67; msg, Dir/Plans, Hq PACAF, to 315th AD, *et al*, 110431Z May 68; hist, 315th AD, Jan–Jun 67, pp 10–26, Jul–Dec 67, pp 14–15, Jan–

Jun 68, pp 10–36, 241–242, Jul 68–Apr 69, pp 1–2, 17–23.

8. Hist, CINCPAC, 1969, I, 179, 1971, I, 305; hist, 315th AD, Jul 68–15 Apr 69, vol I, pp xxii; *The Airlifter* (315th AD), Jan 25, 1969; *Armed Forces Journal*, May 31, 1969, p 30.

9. JCSM–593–66, Memo for Sec Def, subj: Deployment of Troop Carrier Units, Sep 17, 1966; rprts, Dir/Management Analysis, Hq USAF, USAF Management Summary, SEA, Oct 12, 1970 and Apr 20, 1972; hist, 2nd Aer Port Gp, Apr–Jun 71, pp 15–16; rprt, Col Raymond Gaylor, Cdr 2nd Aer Port Gp, Jul 72, pp 34–36; hist, MACV, 1966, pp 292–294, 1967, pp 771–772, 1968, pp 669–670; rprt, Joint Logistics Review Bd, Monograph 18, Logistic Support in the Vietnam Era: Transportation and Movement Control, pp 93–99; rprt, MACV J–4, Logistical Historical Activities, Oct 21, 1967.

10. Rprt, Lt Gen Glen W. Martin, IG USAF, Visit to PACOM to Evaluate Airlift, 27 Feb–12 Mar 66; study, PACAF and MAC, Theater Airlift Study, CY 67, Jan 31, 1967; hist, MAC, FY 66, pp 531–533; hist, Dir/Opns Hq USAF, Jan–Jun 66, pp 20–22.

11. Memo, Paul H. Nitze, Sec Def, for Sec AF, SJCS, subj: Intra-theater Airlift Opns, Apr 5, 1968; msg AFCVC, Gen John D. Ryan, Vice CSAF, to PACAF, 301501Z Oct 68; hist, Dir/Opns, Hq USAF, Jan–Jun 68, pp 141–142, Jul–Dec 68, pp 185–186; hist, 315th AD, Jul 68, Apr 15, 1969, I, 71–75; hist, CINCPAC, 1968, IV, 106–107, 131–141; hist, MAC, FY 69, pp 174–181.

12. Rprt, Col R. H. Goodell, USA, Cdr TMA, MACV, Debriefing Rprt (EOTR), Jul 1, 1968, p 27; hist, 7th AF, Jan–Jun 68, I, 79; McLaughlin intvw, Apr 20, 1970.

13. Hist, 374th TCWg, Aug–Dec 66, pp 29–30; hist, 314th TCWg, Jan–Jun 66, p 51; memo, Col Oliver C. Doan, Asst DCS/Pers, PACAF, to C/S PACAF, subj: TDY Credit for C–130 Aircrews, Dec 8, 1966; Clark intvw, Nov 4, 1970.

14. Rprt, Opns Analysis Off, Hq USAF, Analysis of SEA Airlift Opns, Sep 66; memo, Eugene M. Zuckert, SAF, to Sec Def, subj: Inactivation of C–124 Sqdn at Hunter AFB, Aug 3, 1965; msg 00523, DCS/Opns, 315th AD to PACAF, 061435Z Apr 65; hist, 1503rd Air Tr Gp, qtrly, 1965; hist, CINCPAC, 1968, pp 176–177; hist, 315th AD, Jul 68–Apr 69, p 10; ltr 0311–68, Ch, WTO to CINCPAC J–4, subj: PACOM Theater Tactical Outsize Airlift Capability, 1968; study, PACAF and MAC, Theater Airlift Study CY 67, Jan 31, 1967.

15. Hist, 315th AD, Jul 68–15 Apr 69, I, 9–10; ltr, Col John R. Geyer, 405th Ftr Wg, to 13th AF, subj: Nomination for the USAF Flt Safety Plaque, Jan 12, 1972; hist, CINCPAC, 1969, I, 180–181, 1970, I, 210–211; rprt, Dir/Transp, 7th AF, Hist Data Record, Oct–Dec 71; hist, 20th Opns Sq, Jan–Mar 70 through Jan–Mar 71; hist, 463rd TAWg, Apr–Jun 71, pp 8–10, Jul–Dec 71, pp 3, 21, 24, 27.

16. Ltr, Philip F. Hilbert, Dep U/Secy (IA), Dept AF, for CSAF, subj: Tactical Airlift, Jan 11, 1972; rprts, PACAF, Tactical Airlift Summary, Dec 69, Dec 70, Feb 71; hist, CINCPAC, 1969, IV, 89–91, 1971, I, 314–315; hist, 374th TAWg, Jan–Mar 69, p 92; hists, 463rd TAWg, 1969 through 1971; hists, 314th TAWg, 1969 through 1970.

17. Rprt, Maj William W. Burnett, End of Tour, May 3, 1965; Kimball intvw, Nov 4, 1970; Borders intvw, Nov 4, 1970; hist, 315th TCGp, 1 Jul–31 Dec 63, p 3; Kennedy intvw, Feb 4, 1964; Hawkes, "AF in Vietnam Operation," *American Aviation*, (Apr 64), pp 16–21; *Air Force Times* (ltrs to editor), Mar 3, 1971.

18. Rprts, MACV, Monthly Evaluation, Feb through Jul 66; ltr, MACV J–4, to Cdr 2nd AD, subj: C–123 Flare Support Commitments, Feb 11, 1966; ltr, MACV J–4, to Cdr 7th AF, subj: C–123 Flare Support Commitments, Apr 5, 1966; rprt, Lt Col Hugh L. Baynes, Cdr 311th ACSq, Debriefing Report, Jul 5, 1966; ltr, Col George L. Hannah, Cdr 315th ACGp, to 315th AD, subj: UMD Change Request, Nov 16, 1965; ltr, Col William A. McLaughlin, Dir/Opns, 315th ACWg, to 7th AF, Dir/Airlift, subj: July MONEVAL Rprt, Aug 5, 1966; rprt, 315th AD, Significant Airlift Accomplishments for 1965; rprt, 315th ACWg, 315th ACWg Accomplishments, Jul 19, 1966.

19. Maj Victor B. Anthony, *The AF in Southeast Asia: Tactics and Techniques of Night Operations, 1961–1970* (Off/AF Hist, Mar 73), pp 36–43; msg DOP 50021, PACAF to 315th AD, *et al*, 152156Z Jan 65; msg DO 02405, DCS/

TACTICAL AIRLIFT

Opns, 315th AD to PACAF, 140624Z Jun 66; ltr, Maj Edward Orbock, Ch, Spl Opns Div, 315th AD, to Dir/Opns, 315th AD, subj: Special Operations Division, Sep 26, 1968; hist, 315th AD, Jul–Dec 65, I, 27, 1966, I, 65–69, Jan–Jun 67, I, 78–81, Jul–Dec 67, I, 101–111, Jan–Jun 68, I, 115–126, Jul 68–Apr 69, I, 159–164; hist, 6315th Opns Gp, Jan–Aug 66, pp 3–10; hist, 374th TAWg, 1966 through 1970.

20. Maj Victor B. Anthony, *The AF in Southeast Asia: Tactics and Techniques of Night Operations, 1961–1970* (Off/AF Hist, Mar 73), pp 81–89, 134, 148–176; memo, Brig Gen Richard Yudkin, Dir/Doctrine, Concepts, Obj, Hq USAF, to DCS/P&O, Hq USAF, subj: Provost Mohawk Project, Oct 7, 1966; ltr, Col A. L. Hilpert, DCS/Plans, 7th AF, to Distribution, subj: Operational Evaluations, Jun 24, 1967; msg 54642, PACAF to MACV, 150404Z Aug 67; hist, 7th AF, Jul–Dec 68, pp 4, 143–144, 152, 281–291; talking paper, 7th AF, subj: Reduction of C–123K Candlestick Force, Jun 19, 1971.

21. Rprts, MACV J–3, Historical Summary for Feb, Mar, and May 68; rprt, Capt Joseph L. Chestnut, 309th TCSq, Debriefing Rprt, May 65; JCS Paper, subj: Pop Eye Operation Plan, Dec 3, 1966; msg 7403, US Embassy, Vientiane, to Sec State, 291000Z May 67; msg 13288, Dir/Plans, 7th AF to MACV, 250220Z Jul 67; msg 13977, Dir/Plans, 7th AF, to MACV, 040345Z Aug 67; msg 14722, Dir/Plans, 7th AF, to MACV, 140230Z Aug 67; hist, 834th AD, 15 Oct 66–30 Jun 67, I, 42–47; hist, 463rd TAWg, Jul–Oct 68; hist, 309th ACSq, Jan–Mar 68, pp 4–5; Appendix, to Hist, 315th AD, Jul–Dec 67; Comments on ms, John F. Fuller, AWS, 1976.

22. Msg VC 03980, 2nd AD to PACAF, 281059Z May 66; msg DOCPD 043, PACAF to TAC, 110150Z Jun 66; *New York Times*, Mar 25, 1972; fact sheet, 7th AF, Sequence of Events, Opn Carolina Moon, 1966; msgs 01031 and 01068, Air Attache Vientiane to Hq USAF, *et al*, 081410Z and 151315Z Jan 65.

23. Msg 4675, MACV J–3 to CINCPAC, 070946Z Nov 62; msg 2–1964A, 13th AF, Dir/Opns to 2nd Air Div, 170256Z Nov 62; rprt, OSD, Weekly Rprt to President, Dec 4, 1962; Blake intvw, May 6, 1970; rprt, 2nd Air Div, Napalm Test Project, Nov 13, 1962; hist, 2nd ADVON, 15 Nov 61–8 Oct 62, pp 63, 154; rprt, 2nd Air Div, Farm Gate Tactics and Techniques, Jun 62.

24. Ltr, Col Charles W. Borders, Dir/Opns, 315th ACGp, to 2nd AD, subj: MONEVAL, Apr 2, 1965; memo, MACV J–3 to C/S MACV, subj: J–3 Historical Summary, Apr 21, 1967; rprt, Lt Col Joseph L. Pospisil, Off/Science Advisor, MACV, subj: Banish Beach, Mar 11, 1969; rprt, Maj R. I. Rivard, USMC, and D. A. Breslow, III MAF, Project Heartburn, Apr 68, pp B–1 through B–16; study, Maj Herschel E. Coulter, "US Airpower in COIN," (ACSC Thesis, Air University, 1967), pp 31–33; hist, 2nd AD, Jul–Dec 64, pp 65–66; hist, 315th TCGp, Jan–Jun 65, pp 35–37.

25. Rprt, Lt Col Joseph L. Pospisil, Off/Science Advisor, MACV, subj: Banish Beach, Mar 11, 1969; msg 13792, MACV COC to CINCPAC, 150257Z May 68; memo, MACV Off/Science Advisor, to W. G. McMillan, subj: Results of the C–130 Fire Mission, Apr 19, 1968; hist, 834th AD, Jul 67–Jun 68, pp 3–5; Gropman intvw, Apr 13, 1972.

26. Working paper 68/9, 7th AF, Dir/Tactical Analysis, subj: C–130 Burn Mission Operations, Jun 30, 1968; msg, Cdr 7th AF, to PACAF, CSAF, 140945Z Jul 68; MR, Gen George S. Brown, Cdr 7th AF, subj: Banish Beach, Sep 4, 1968; msg 1349, C/S MACV, to subord cds, 071213Z Jan 69.

27. Staff summ sheet, Brig Gen Walter T. Galligan, Dir/Opns Plans, 7th AF, subj: Disposal of Anti-Intrusion Mines, Oct 19, 1970; msg, Dir/Opns Plans, 7th AF, to US Embassy, Vientiane, 190645Z Nov 70; msg, CINCPAC to 7th AF, 290102Z May 71; hist, 463rd TAWg, Jul–Sep 69, pp 23–25, Jul–Dec 71, p 30; hist, 834th AD, Jul–Dec 70, p 20; hist, 8th Aer Port Sq, Jul–Sep 69.

28. Ltr, Gen William W. Momyer, Cdr 7th AF, to DCS/R&D, Hq USAF, *et al*, subj: SEAOR 168 (FY 68) (Weapon for Helicopter Landing Zone Construction), Feb 13, 1968; MR, Maj Harry E. Drennan, Dir/Opns, 7th AF, subj: 7 Dec III MAF G–3 Meeting, Dec 68; msg, 7th AF DCS/Opns, to Dir/Opns PACAF, 272346Z Dec 68; hist, 463rd TAWg, Jul–Oct 68, app XV; rprt, Maj Gen Burl W. McLaughlin, Cdr 834th AD, EOTR, Jun 69, pp 9–5 to 9–6; Col David R. Jones, "Combat Trap—Von

Clausewitz Revisited," *Air University Review,* Mar–Apr 70, pp 68–73; draft ms, Air Force Wpns Lab, AFSC, "Combat Trap," 1975.

29. 7th AF OPLAN DOLC 72-1, Commando Vault, Feb 11, 1972; rprt, Col Walter G. Lang, Cdr 2nd Aer Port Gp, EOTR, Jul 71, pp 31–32; hist, 834th AD, Jul 68–Jun 70, p 25, Jul–Dec 70, pp 18–19; rprt, Herring, EOTR, pp 78–85; Lt T. D. Boettcher, 7th AF, "Their Business is Booming," *Airman,* Sep 69, pp 26–27.

30. Rprt, Maj Gen John H. Herring, Cdr 834th AD, EOTR, Jun 71, pp 78–85; rprt, Col Andrew P. Iosue, Cdr 374th TAWg, EOTR, Jul 1, 1973; hist, 463rd TAWg, 1969 through 1971; hist, 374th TAWg, 1971 and 1972; rprt, Dir/Opns, 7/13th AF, Hist Rprt for 3rd Qtr/FY 71, Jul 2, 1971, p 4; rprt, Airl Sect, MACV J–3, DO Monthly Hist Rprt for Nov 72.

31. Memo, Col Ray Chapman, Dir/Opns, 834th AD to 7th AF (TACP), subj: Validation of Commando Vault Targets, Aug 11, 1969; hist, 834th AD, Jul–Nov 71, pp 21–23; hist, 374th TAWg, Jun–Sep 71, pp 31–34; *Air Force Times,* Aug 25, 1971; fact sheet, Col Thomas E. Newton, Ch, ALCC Div, 834th AD, subj: Commando Vault OPLAN 7th AF/DOLC 72-1, Feb 11, 1972; Melvin F. Porter, *Commando Vault* (PACAF, Proj CHECO, Oct 12, 1970).

32. Hist, 315th AD, Jul–Dec 65, I, 28, Jan–Jun 67, I, 74–77, Jul–Dec 67, I, 90–101, Jan–Jun 68, I, 102–108, Jul 68–Apr 69, I, 171–174; hist, 314th TCWg, Jul–Dec 66, Jan–Jun 67, p 5, Jul–Sep 67, p 10, Jan–Mar 68, p 11; Maj Robert M. Burch, *The ABCCC in SEA* (PACAF, Proj CHECO, Jan 15, 1969); rprt, TAC, Activity Input to Corona Harvest on Tactical Airlift in SEA, 1965–68, Dec 69, II, 11–12.

33. Hist, Dir/Opns, Hq USAF, Jul–Dec 72, pp 205–207; Maj Gen Dewitt R. Searles, Dep Cdr 7/13th AF, EOTR, Sep 9, 1972, pp 34–35; hist, USSAG, NKP, Jan–Mar 73, pp 52–56; hist, 314th TAWg, Apr–Jun 69, pp 19–20.

34. Futrell, *The United States Air Force in Korea, 1950–1953,* pp 543–554; hist, 315th AD, Jan–Jun 51, pp 100–106; ltr, Lt Col F. W. Thomas, Cdr 1st Aeromed Evac Gp, to 464th TCWg, subj: Final Mission Rprt, Swift Strike, Aug 24, 1961; hist, 1st AME Gp, 1957 through 1961, Jul–Dec 64, pp 5–7; ltr, Col P. C. Bullard, Cdr 1st AME Gp, to Hq TAC, subj: Mission Report, Indian River III, Oct 2, 1964.

35. Capt Herbert M. Hamako, "Tactical Aeromedical Evacuation in Vietnam," *USAF Medical Service Digest,* Nov 69, pp 1–3; Kimball intvw, Nov 4, 1970; Perry intvw, Nov 3, 1970; hist, 9th AME Sq, 1963 through 1964.

36. Hist, 9th AME Sq, 1962 through 1964; Capt Eric M. Solander, *Aeromedical Evacuation Operation in PACAF,* Dir/Inform, PACAF, Jun 30, 1967; *Stars and Stripes,* Feb 15, 1963.

37. Rprt, Off/Command Surgeon, MACV, Medical Year-end Wrap-up Rprt CY 67, Mar 10, 1968, pp 23–1 through 23–6; briefing text, MACV J–4, subj: Logistics, Oct 17, 1966; rprt, Airlift Staff Gp, Rprt of USAF Airlift Visit to PACOM Area, 11 Oct–10 Nov 65; hist, 9th AME Sq, Jan–Jun 66, p 7; hist, MAC, FY 66, pp 354–357; hist, MACV, 1968, II, 705–706.

38. Hist, 6485th Opns Sq, Apr 68 through Oct 69; hist, 20th Opns Sq, Oct 69 through Jun 73; rprt, Lt Gen Glen W. Martin, IG USAF, Visit to PACOM to Evaluate Airlift, 27 Feb–12 Mar 66, Tab 7; hist, 315th AD, 1966, pp 79–83.

39. DOD Directive 5160.22, subj: Clarification of Roles and Missions of the Departments of Army and the Air Force Regarding Use of Aircraft, Mar 18, 1957; rprt, MACV, Monthly Evaluation, Jan 67, Feb 25, 1967; rprt, Maj Gen Shelton E. Lollis, Cdr 1st Log Cd, subj: Debriefing Report, Aug 11, 1967, p 427; rprt, USARV, Battlefield Rprts, Lessons Learned Summary, Jun 30, 1966, pp 78–79; rprt, 173rd Abn Bde, Comb Opns AAR (Hump), Dec 19, 1965; rprt, 4th Inf Div, Comb Opns AAR (Paul Revere IV), Jan 28, 1967.

40. Rprts, MACV J–4, Logistical Review and Evaluation, Jul 66–Jan 67, and Jan–Mar 68; rprts, 9th AME Sq, Monthly Rprts of Aeromedical Evacuation, 1965 through 1967; Hamako, "Tactical Aeromedical Evacuation in Vietnam," *USAF Medical Service Digest,* Nov 69, pp 1–7; rprt, Off/Cd Surgeon, MACV, Medical Year-end Wrap-up Rprt CY 67, Mar 10, 1968.

41. Hist, 315th AD, 1966, pp 78–87, Jul–Dec 67, p xii; PACAF SO G–176, Jun 3, 1966; Solander, "Aeromedical Evacuation Opns in PACAF," Jun 30,

1967, pp 5–7, 16–17; ltr, Maj Robert R. Ryan, Cdr 903rd AME Sq, subj: Operational Concept and Communications Service, Mar 21, 1967; ltr, Col Ray L. Miller, USA, Cdr 44th Med Bde, to Cdr MACV, subj: Casualty Staging Facilities in RVN, Apr 8, 1967.

42. Capt Eric M. Solander, "Aeromedical Evacuation Operations in PACAF," Jun 30, 1967, pp 35–45; hist, 315th AD, 1966, I, 87–81.

43. Capt Eric M. Solander, "Aeromedical Evacuation," pp 7, 15–17, 38–39; rprt, TAC, Activity Input to Corona Harvest on Tactical Airlift in SEA, 1965–68, Dec 69, IV, 38b; fact sheet, Sec AF/Off Information, USAF Vietnam Battle Report, 7-4-69-156F; msg, CINCPAC to JCS, 262245Z Dec 66.

44. Rprt, 9th AME Gp, Monthly Rprt of AME (M6 rprt), Jun 69; hist, 9th AME Gp, FY 69, pp 1–16; paper, USARV, Submission to Army Green Book, summer 1972; rprts, 834th AD, Tact Airl Performance and Accomplishments, SEA, Jun 70 and Jun 71; hists, 9th AME Gp, FY 69 through FY 73.

45. AFM 3-4, Tactical Air Opns: Tactical Airlift, Sep 22, 1971, pp 5–13 to 5–15; rprt, Proj Corona Harvest, USAF Airlift Activities in Support of Opns in SEA, 1 Jan 65–31 Mar 68, Air University, Jan 73, p 39.

46. CSAFM 48–62, CSAF to JCS, subj: Concept for Employment of US Military Forces in Sub-limited War Opns, Feb 13, 1962; Air Staff summary sheet, AFXPDRA, subj: Pacification Plan for Long An Province, RVN, Jan 25, 1964; *DOD Pentagon Papers*, bk 3, pt IV-B-3, pp vii, viii, 76–78, bk 7, pt IV-C-9(b), pp ii, 40–41, bk VI, pt IV-C-8.

47. Memo, MACV J-3 to USARV, subj: In-country Aircraft Inventory, Jan 16, 1966; memo, R. W. Komer to Sec Def, subj: Support for Essential Civil Opns, May 7, 1966; msg XPDO 93162, Dir/Plans, Hq USAF, to PACAF, 021645Z Jun 66; JCS Paper, subj: USAID Airlift, Jun 25, 1966; rprt, Laurence E. Lynn, Dir/Economics and Mobility Forces, Off Sec Def (Sys Analysis), subj: Trip Report, Aug 67, pp 8–9; fact sheet, MACV J-45, subj: USAID/CORDS Airlift Opns, Sep 9, 1968; hist, 7th AF, Jan–Jun 68, I, 75–76.

48. Rprt, Col R. L. Hamilton, Chairman, MACV Ad Hoc Gp, Inquiry on Air America Inc in RVN, 1970.

49. Ltr, Col J. Smith, USA, Cdr, US Army Procurement Agency, Vietnam, to Cdr MACV (TMA), subj: Request for Acft Support, Vinnell Corp, Sep 13, 1967; Fact Book, MACV, COMUSMACV Back-up Book, Nov 67; msg 03703, OICC, RVN, to COMUSMACV, 050720Z Feb 68; memo, Col Ronald D. Bagley, Ch, Transp Div, MACV J-4, to Ch, Air Br, subj: Study on Airlift Reqmts, Jul 7, 1968.

50. Rprts, USAID, Saigon, USAID Contribution to Mission Weekly Activity Reports, Jan 11, Jan 25, Jan 31, and Mar 9, 1967; fact sheet, USAID, Civil Aviation, Vietnam, [ca Feb 1969]; fact sheet, MACV J-45, Contract Air Opns in RVN, Sep 25, 1968; hist, CINCPAC, 1968, 142–144; memo, MACV J-3 to USARV, et al, subj: In-country Acft Inventory, Jan 16, 1966; JCS Paper, subj: Expanded Use of Commercial Airlift in Vietnam, Jan 10, 1969.

51. Minutes, Mission Council Meeting held 1 Aug 66, pp 4–5; rprt, Lt Col Hugh L. Baynes, 311th ACSq, Debriefing Rprt, Jul 5, 1966; Lewis W. Walt, *Strange War, Strange Strategy: A General's Report on Vietnam* (New York: Funk and Wagnalls, 1970), pp 86–89.

52. Rprt, Lt Col Harry G. Howton, Cdr 311th TCSq, EOTR, Sep 6, 1965; ms, Kenneth Sams, "Civic Action Role of Air Power in RVN," 1965; msg Manila 11651, US Embassy, Manila to CSAF, 220211Z Dec 71; *The Vietnam Airlifter*, Jun 70 and Oct 71.

53. Rprt, Col Benjamin S. Preston, Jr., EOTR, Jul 64.

54. Hist, 2nd AD, Jul–Dec 65, pp 5–6, 24, 53–55; hists, 315th AD, 1966 through Apr 69; hist, 613th Opns Gp, Jul–Dec 65, pp 16–19, Jan–Aug 66, pp 10–11; hist, 374th TAWg, 1966 through 1972.

55. Intvw, J. Grainger with Maj William C. Johnson and Capt Ernest C. Cutler, 6220 ABSq, Opns Sect, Feb 7, 1963; fact sheet, MACV J-1, Spl Services and R and R, RVN, May 10, 1964; hist data record, 2nd AD, Dir/Materiel, Jul–Dec 65; background paper, ACS Programs and Resources, Hq USAF, subj: T–39s in Support of RVN, Apr 28, 1966; unpubl article, Capt R. L. Wing, "Courier Flying: Skill, Dedication, and Results," Sep 66; rprts, 7th AF Flight Opns, Unit Hist Rprts, FY 1–72 and FY 2–72.

56. Fact sheet, MACV, subj: The Transportation System in RVN, Apr 65;

rprt, Laurence E. Lynn, Dir/Economics and Mobility Forces, Off Sec Def (Sys Analysis), subj: Trip Rprt, Aug 67, pp 10–11; ltr, Brig Gen William E. Bryan, Dep C/S MACV, to CG USARV, subj: Aviation Support of Area Logistics Command Advisors, Nov 14, 1967; memo, Cdr Marine Refueler Transp Sq 152, to CG 1st MAWg, subj: Command Chronology, Nov 16, 1965; rprt, MACV J-3 to Hist Br, MACV, subj: Jul 68 Hist Summary, Aug 21, 1968; rprt, MACV J-4, LOGSUM 9-68 for Aug 68; Sep 22, 1968; rprts, MACV, Qtrly Evaluation, Dec 67 and Feb 68; Vice Adm Edwin B. Hooper, *Mobility, Support, Endurance: A Story of Naval Operational Logistics in the Vietnam War, 1965–1968* (Naval Hist Div, Dept/Navy, 1972), pp 146–147; fact sheet, US Marine Forces in Vietnam, Historical Summary, Mar 65–Sep 67, 1967, vol II.

57. Fact sheet, J-45 MACV, subj: Logistic Airlift Activity in RVN, Oct 21, 1968; brief, Dir/Opns, Hq USAF, subj: PCP/R:N-7-005, Rapid Response Airlift for SEA, May 1, 1967.

58. Ltr, Lt Gen J. L. Richardson, USA, Cdr, JTF-116, to CINCPAC, *et al*, subj: AAR, Dec 8, 1962; rprt, AF Comp Cd, JTF-116, Hist of the AFCC, JTF-116, Nov 25, 1962; msg 21553A, 13th AF to PACAF, 150850Z Jun 62; ltr, Col William T. Daly, Cdr 464th TCWg, to Gen Walter Sweeney, Cdr TAC, subj: Trip Rprt, SEA, Aug 15, 1962; background paper, Dir/Plans, Hq USAF, subj: US and Allied Military Forces Thailand, Jun 8, 1962.

59. Msg A-019, AFCC, JTF-116, to 13th AF, 211515Z May 62; msg 198E, 2nd ADVON to Dir/Opns, 13th AF, May 23, 1962; msg 1255E, 2nd ADVON to 13th AF, 290645Z May 62; msg 62A1647, 13th AF to JTF-116, 140935Z Jun 62; msg 62A1669, 13th AF to 315th Air Div and 1503rd ATWg, 160734Z Jun 62; ltr, IG 13th AF, to 6010th Tact Gp, subj: Accident Prevention Survey, 6010th Tact Gp, Nov 23, 1962; PACAF review, Mar 62.

60. Dir/Mil Assistance, OASD/ISA, *Journal of Military Assistance*, Jun 62, p 164, Sep 62, p 144, Mar 63, p 174; hist, Dir/Plans, Hq USAF, Jul–Dec 62, pp 133, 181–185, Jan–Jun 63, p 177; hist, CINCPAC, 1963, p 107.

61. Msg 1-257G, 2nd ADVON to PACAF (pers from Anthis to Moorman), 270805Z Jul 62; msg 150, 2nd AD to Hq USAF, *et al*, 021002Z Oct 65; Clark intvw, Nov 4, 1970; Perry intvw, Nov 3, 1970; West intvw, May 5, 1970; Borders intvw, Nov 4, 1970; Blake intvw, May 6, 1970.

62. Rprt, Airlift Staff Gp, Rprt or USAF Airlift Staff Visit to PACOM Area, 11 Oct–10 Nov 65; study, Hist Div, 13th AF, subj: The USAF Buildup in Thailand, I, 27–28; memo, Harold Brown, Sec AF, to Sec Def, subj: Thailand Construction Program, Jul 13, 1966; msg C-043, PACAF to CSAF (pers for McConnell from Harris), 100625Z Jul 66; msg, PACAF to Dir/Plans, Hq USAF, 232045Z Jul 66; commander's review, 315th AD, Sep 68, p A-4; hist, 374th TCWg, Jul–Sep 67, pp 8–9; hist, 315th AD, 1966, I, 49, msg, Dir/Tact Opns, 315th AD, to PACAF, 13th AF, 060238Z Dec 67.

63. Rprt, Airlift Staff Gp, Report of USAF Airlift Staff Visit to PACOM Area, 11 Oct–10 Nov 65; hist, CINCPAC, 1967, pp 862–863; hist, 315th AD, Jan–Jun 65, p 7, Jul–Dec 65, I, 6–7; hist, 315th TCGp, Jan–Jun 65, pp 3–5; rprt, Lt Gen Glen W. Martin, IG USAF, Visit to PACOM to Evaluate Airlift, Feb 27–Mar 12, 1966.

64. Hist, 6315th Aerial Port Sq, Apr–Aug 65; hist, 6th Aerial Port Sq, Jan–Jun 66; hist, 13th AF, 1965, II, 134; PACAF SO G-27, Apr 6, 1965; hist, 315th TCGp, Jan–Jun 63, pp 35–42.

65. Staff summ sheet, Col A. L. Hilpert, DCS/Plans, 7th AF, subj: C-7A Support for MACTHAI, Nov 6, 1966; ltr, Col Louis P. Lindsay, Dir/Opns, 834th AD, to 7th AF, Dir/Plans, subj: MACTHAI C-7A Support, Apr 25, 1967; msg 0143, CINCPAC to Cdr MACV, subj: JUSMAG Thailand Acft Reqmts, Mar 3, 1964; hist, 458th TASq, Jul–Sep 68; ltr, Col John I. Daniel, DCO/483rd TCWg, to Dir/Ops, 377th ABWg, subj: C-7 Opns, Feb 29, 1972; msg LG, 7/13th AF to 13th AF, 131100Z Mar 72; hist, MACTHAI, 1969, pp 31–32, 1970, pp 12–14, 1971, p 12; 483rd TCWg OPORD 70-5, Dec 1, 1970.

66. Hist, MACTHAI, 1970, pp 66–72; hist, CINCPAC, 1970, pp 347–349, 1971, pp 315–317; hist, 314th TAWg, Apr–Jun 70, pp 48–49, Oct–Dec 70, pp 26–27, 35, Jan–Mar 71, pp 14–15, 42–44, Apr–May 71, p 20; intvw, author with Maj William T. Posey, Hq USAF, Mar 29,

1974; intvw, author with Maj B. J. Clark, Hq USAF, Mar 29, 1964; hist, 374th TAWg, Jun–Sep 71, pp 34–35; msg, PACAF to 13th AF, 050222Z May 72.

67. Hist, MACV, 1965; p 354; msg JCS 002919, Joint Staff J–3, to CINCPAC, et al, 150201Z Dec 64; staff paper, Atch to JCSM 847–64, subj: Thai and Filipino Contributions to the War Effort in SVN, Oct 3, 1964; *DOD Pentagon Papers,* vol IV, pt IV–C–2–(c), p xvi.

68. Msg 62–339J, 2nd AD to PACAF, 13th AF (pers from Anthis for Moorman and Milton), 222350Z Oct 62; msg, CINCPAC to JCS, 230609Z Jan 63; msg 630010A, 2nd AD to 13th AF, PACAF (to Martin and Milton from Anthis), 101530Z Jan 63; msg 63–0037, PACAF to Dir/Plans, Hq USAF, 221845Z Jan 63; msg 131, Ch, MAG China, to CINCPAC, 040731Z Jan 66; msg 01180, C/S MACV to CINCPAC, 130334Z Jan 66; msg, CINCPAC to JCS, 290645Z Dec 66; daily staff journal, G–3 Advisory Sect, II CTZ, Oct 26 through Oct 28, 1967; hist, MACV, 1965, pp 73, 370–371, 1966, pp 79–87.

69. Fact sheet, MACV, Third Country Assistance to GVN, May 8, 1964; msg, US Embassy, Manila to Sec State, 301035Z Oct 64; atch to JCSM 847–64, subj: Thai and Filipino Contributions to the War Effort in SVN, Oct 3, 1964; memo, JCS to Sec Def (JCS 2343/484), subj: Philippine Assistance to SVN, Nov 3, 1964; hist, MACV, 1967, pp 277–280; msg 4193, US Embassy (Wilson) to Sec State, 061035Z Nov 67; hist, 463rd TAWg, Jan–Mar 68, pp 12–13.

70. James T. Bear, *The Employment of Air by the Thais and Koreans in SEA* (Hq PACAF, Proj CHECO, Oct 30, 1970), pp 4–7; hist, MACV, 1965, p 372; fact sheets, MACFWMAO, Hq MACV, subj: Thai Military Assistance to RVN, Mar 7 and Jun 6, 1966; msg 2CCR–00542, 2nd AD to CSAF, PACAF, 13th AF (pers for Harris and Maddux from Moore), 300557Z Oct 64.

71. Hist, 19th ACSq, 19th Sp Ops Sq, 19th TASq, Jul 66 through May 71; fact sheets, Free World Mil Assistance Off, MACV, subj: Thai Mil Assistance to RVN, Jan 11, Mar 7, and Jun 6, 1967; memos, FWMAO, MACV to SJS MACV, subj: Hist Summ for Apr–Jun 66 and Jul–Sep 66; background paper, MACTHAI, subj: RTAF Victory Flight, [ca 1970]; fact sheet, MACV J–5, subj: RTAF Victory Flight, Dec 8, 1971; hist, 834th AD, Jan–Jun 71, pp 70–71; hist, MACV, 1966, pp 98–99, 1970, pp VI–15 to VI–16, 1971, pp VI–5, G–17, G–18; hist, USMACTHAI, Annex B Hist CINCPAC, 1966, pp 152–153; Bear, *Employment of Air,* pp 4–12.

72. Ltr, Hq USAF AFXPDR (Yudkin) to AFXPD, subj: Assignment of Six Australian Caribou Acft to SVN, Jul 2, 1964; msg PFLDC 32G6–64, PACAF to AFXPD, Hq USAF, subj: Australian Aid to RVN, Jun 25, 1964; msg PFLDC, PACAF to CSAF (AFOD), 020446Z Apr 64; msg, CINCPAC to JCS, 272035Z Jun 63.

73. Borders intvw, Nov 4, 1970; rprt, Lt Col Harry G. Howton, Cdr 311th TCSq, EOTR, Sep 6, 1965; *Journal of Military Assistance,* Dec 64, p 179; hist, 2nd Air Div, 1 Jan–30 Jun 65, I, 94; ltrs, Cdr 2nd Air Div, to MACV J–3, subj: MONEVAL, Oct 2, Nov 3, 1964, and Jan 4, 1965.

74. Hist, 315th TCGp, Jan–Jun 65, pp 14–16; MR, Lt Col F. Ackerson, Asst Sec, Joint Staff MACV, subj: J–3 Briefing to COMUSMACV, subj: Australian Brigade, Mar 12, 1966; 834th AD OPLAN 520–67, Utilization of RAAF no 35 Sqdn, Vietnam, Jan 1, 1967; military working agreement, COMUSMACV and Ch, C/S Committee Australia, Nov 30, 1967; James T. Bear, *The RAAF in Southeast Asia,* (Hq PACAF, Proj CHECO, Sep 30, 1970), pp 29–40.

75. Article, "Royal Australian Air Force Caribous in Vietnam—1964 to 1972," *The Royal Air Force Quarterly,* summer 1972, pp 133–136; Bear, *RAAF,* pp 29–43; rprt, Australian Force Vietnam, Monthly Rprt for Nov 71, Dec 14, 1971; msg, Dir/Opns 834th AD to PACAF DOAL, 270237Z Dec 69; hist, MACV, 1971, p VI–5; msg DO–02310, 7th AF to AFXOPFH, Hq USAF, 091126Z Jun 67; rprt, Opns Analysis, Vice CSAF, Hq USAF, Analysis of SEA Airlift Opns, Sep 66.

76. Rprts, Exchange Officers Tour Reports, Maj Glen A. Bentz, Dec 18, 1968, Capt William M. Harley, Dec 12, 1969, Capt Jack L. Tinius, Apr 70, Capt James C. Bobick, Sep 70; hist, MACV, 1970, vol I, pp VI–14 to VI–15; Bear, *RAAF,* pp 40–43.

77. Msg XPD 84083, Dir/Plans, Hq USAF, to PACAF, 302135Z Jun 65; msg XPDO 78704, Asst Dep Dir/Policy, Dir/

Plans, Hq USAF, to PACAF, TAC, 102107Z Sep 65; memo, Maj Gen Gordon M. Graham, Vice Cdr 7th AF, to Cdr 7th AF, subj: Visit of Lt Gen Chang, Jan 25, 1967; msg 57426, COMUSKOREA to COMUSMACV, 061220Z Feb 67; msg 58861, COMUSKOREA to CINCPAC, 310130Z May 67; msg 25484, MACV to CINCPAC, 300229Z Aug 68; hist, 315th TCGp, Jan–Jun 65, p 11; hist, MACV, 1967, pp 261–263.

78. MR, MACV J–45, subj: Airlift Support for Spl ROKFV/Philcagv Lv Programs, Jan 8, 1968; Fact Book, MACV J–4, subj: Data for Sec Def Visit to RVN, Jul 67; hist, 14th Aerial Port Sq, Apr–Jun 68; hist, CINCPAC, 1966, pp 211–212; rprt, Hq US Forces, Korea, A Summary of Transportation of ROK Forces to Vietnam and their Continued Support, Sep 64–Dec 69.

79. Background paper, Dir/Plans, Hq USAF, subj: ROK Forces Participation in SVN, Mar 6, 1971; *Journal of Military Assistance*, Apr 70, pp 120–121, Sep 69, pp 111–113; hist, CINCPAC, 1969, II, 151–155, 1970, II, 341–343; hist, MACV, 1970, vol I, p VI–14, 1971, vol I, p VI–5.

Chapter XVI

Airlift in Irregular Warfare

1. Study, I FFV, Force Disposition Study, Apr 3, 1968, pp 2–4; rprt, 5th SFGp, Development of the CIDG Program, 1964–1968, Apr 22, 1968; study, 5th AFGp, Concept of Opns for the Role of Sp Forces in RVN, Apr 68; intvw, MACV with Lt Col C. E. Spragins, Dep Cdr, 5th SFGp, Aug 29, 1965; rprt, MACV, Monthly Eval Rprt, Apr 65; memo, MACV J–3 to MACV J–03, subj: J–3 Oct Hist Summary, Nov 29, 1965; Col Francis J. Kelly, *US Army Special Forces, 1961–1971*, (Dept/Army, Vietnam Studies, 1973), pp 77–90.

2. Rprt, 5th SFGp, Opl Rprt for Qtrly Period ending 31 Jul 67, Aug 15, 1967; rprt, 5th SFGp, Monthly Opl Summary for Oct 67, Nov 8, 1967; fact sheet, USARV G–4, subj: Logistical Support—5th SFGp (Airborne), Aug 26, 1968; Spragins intvw, Aug 29, 1965; rprt, 5th SFGp, Development of the CIDG Program, 1964–1968, Apr 22, 1968; study, 5th SFGp, Concept of Opns for the Role of Sp Forces in RVN, Apr 68.

3. Rprt, Det C–4, 5th SFGp, Monthly Opl Summary for Aug 66 and Jul 66; rprt, 5th SFGp, Opl Rprt for Period ending 31 Jul 68, Aug 31, 1968; rprts, PACAF, Airlift Rprts for May 66 and Apr 66, RCS: J–38.

4. Ltr, Col Francis J. Kelly, USA, Cdr 5th SFGp, to Cdr MACV, subj: Airlift Organization and Operations, Aug 18, 1966; msg, Brig Gen John Norton, USA, Saigon, to Brig Gen Edmund L. Mueller, ACS/For, Dept/Army, 130745Z Nov 65; rprt, 5th SFGp, Monthly Opl Summary (1–30 Nov 68), Dec 17, 1968; O'Donovan intvw, Apr 17, 1972; rprts, 5th SFGp, Opl Rprt for Qtrly Pd ending 31 Jul 67 and 31 Jan 68, Aug 15, 1967 and Feb 15, 1968; rprt, 5th SFGp, Opl Rprt for Qtrly Pd ending 30 Apr 68, May 15, 1968.

5. Intvw, author and Maj Ralph Rowley with Col Eugene P. Deatrick and Lt Col Eleazar Parmly IV, USA, Mar 9, 1972; ltr, Col Paul J. Mascot, Cdr 483rd TCWg, to Lt Col Robert W. Hassinger, Co D, 5th SFGp, Mar 2, 1967; rprt, 535th TCSq, to 483rd TCWg, Hist Data Rprt, Jan–Mar 67; intvw, Corona Harvest with Maj Ray E. Lucker, CH intvw no 193, Jun 30, 1971; hist, 834th AD, Jul 67–Jun 68, pp 82–87; rprt, Cdt C–1, 5th SFGp, Monthly Opl Summary for May 66; rprts, Det A–101, 5th SFGp, Monthly Reports for months through 1966; rprts, Det A–102, 5th SFGp, Monthly Opl Summaries, 31 Oct and 30 Nov 66; rprts, Det A–105, 5th SFGp, Monthly Opl Summaries, for Jul and Nov 66; rprt, Det A–106, 5th SFGp, Monthly Opl Summary for Sep 66.

6. Msgs DO, 7th AF to PACAF, 281157Z Feb 68 and 090820Z Mar 68;

intvw, Corona Harvest with Maj Lee Mize, USA, CH intvw no 43, 1968; daily journal, S-4, 5th SFGp, dates in Feb 68; rprt, 1st Log Cd, AAR (Airdrop Mission 63), Nov 13, 1967; rprt, 5th SFGp, Opl Rprt for Qtrly Pd ending 31 Jan 67, Feb 15, 1967; rprt, 5th SFGp, Opl Report—Lessons Learned for Pd ending 31 Jan 68, Feb 15, 1968; rprt, Det C-1, 5th SFGp, Monthly Opl Summary for Mar 66; rprt, Det A-109, 5th SFGp, Monthly Opl Summary for Oct 66; rprt, Det A-108, 5th SFGp, Monthly Opl Summary for May 66; rprt, Det A-425, 5th SFGp, Monthly Opl Summary for Oct 66.

7. Rprt, Research Analysis Corp, US Army Sp Forces and Similar Internal Defense Advisory Opns in Mainland SEA, 1962-67, Jun 69, pp 30-32, 87, 93; ltr, Capt B. L. Jervell, Adj 5th SFGp, to MACV J-3, subj: Employment of CIDG, Mike Force, MGF, and LRRP Projects, Apr 19, 1967; ltr, Col Francis J. Kelly, Cdr 5th SFGp, to CG 7th AF, subj: Airlift Support for Opn Harvest Moon, Apr 7, 1967; rprt, 5th SFGp, AAR, Blackjack 41C (Arrowhead), 1967; Probst intvw, May 8, 1972; rprts, 5th SFGp, Opl Rprts, Lessons Learned, Aug 15, Nov 15, 1967, and May 15, 1968.

8. Hist, MACV, 1969, pp IV-47 to IV-52, 1970, pp XIV-1 to XIV-4; Kelly, *US Army Special Forces, 1961-1971*, pp 151-159; msg, CG I FFV to Cdr 5th SFGp, 040216Z Dec 69; msg 25743, MACV to CINCPAC, 261250Z May 70.

9. Msg 47037, MACV J-3 to CG XXIV Corps, 101145Z Sep 70; ltr, Maj Gen W. G. Dolvin, C/S MACV to Lt Gen Nguyen Van Manh, C/S JGS, RVNAF, Sep 23, 1970; rprt, 5th SFGp, Monthly Cd Summary, Jan 9, 1971; msg, DSA Det, Da Nang to MACV, 080215Z Feb 71; memo, Melvin Laird, Sec Def, for Pres Asst for Natl Security Affairs, subj: Vietnamization of the Border Base Camps, Feb 25, 1971.

10. Msg, CINCPAC to JCS, 091331Z Mar 62; ltr, Col Frank R. Pancake, Asst Dep Dir For Policy, Dir/Plans, Hq USAF, to Air Staff agencies, subj: Appointment of Task Force, Mar 9, 1962; background paper, Dir/Plans, Hq USAF, Communist Encroachment—N.E. Thailand, Mar 10, 1962; Hq USAF, draft outline, Plan of Action, Thailand, Mar 62, and Atchmt, "Concept of Opns," Mar 16, 1962.

11. Hist, Dir/Plans, Hq USAF, Jan-Jun 62, pp 176-179; ltr, William P. Bundy, Actg Asst Sec Def, Memo to Sec AF, subj: Draft COIN Plan for Thailand, May 5, 1962; msg PFLDC 3081-62, PACAF to Dir/Plans, Hq USAF, 240110Z Mar 62; Dir/Military Assistance, OASD/ISA, *Journal of Military Assistance*, 1962 through 1965.

12. Msg XPDO 77994, Dep Dir/ Policy, Dir/Plans, Hq USAF, to PACAF, 222137Z Mar 66.

13. Hist, CINCPAC, 1967, pp 761-767; hists, 56th ACWg and 56th Spl Opns Wg, 1967 through 1968; hist, 634th CSGp, Apr-Dec 66, Jan-Apr 67; hists, 606th ACSq and 606th Spl Opns Sq, 1966 through 1968; hists, 20th Helic Sq and 20th Spl Opns Sq, 1966 through 1968; hists, 21st Helic Sq and 21st Spl Opns Sq, 1968.

14. Memo, Maj Rupert A. Leonard, Ch, Base Civic Act, 56th CSGp, to Dir/ Opns, 56th Sp Opns Wg, subj: Airlift Support for Civic Action, Jul 6, 1971; concept paper, US Embassy, Bangkok, subj: General Concept for US Support of COIN, May 23, 1972; Warren A. Trest, *Lucky Tiger Spec Air Opns*, (PACAF, Proj CHECO, May 31, 1967), pp 29-80; Warren A. Trest and TSgt Charles E. Garland, *Counterinsurgency in Thailand, 1966*, (PACAF, Proj CHECO, Nov 8, 1967), pp 20-28; TSgts E. H. Ashby and D. G. Francis, *Counterinsurgency in Thailand, Jan 67-Dec 68*, (PACAF, Proj CHECO, Mar 26, 1969), pp 28-44.

15. Memo, Col Paul B. McDaniel, USA, MACTHAI J-3, to C/S MACTHAI, subj: RTARF Use of Light Fixed-wing and Rotary-wing Acft, n.d. [ca 1972]; hist, MACTHAI, 1970, p 176, 1971, pp 93-96; Dir/Mil Asst, OASD/ ISA, *Journal of Military Assistance*, Feb 69 through Mar 72; memo, Col Dean C. Crane, Dir/Opns, Thai AFAG, subj: RTAF Airlift Capability, Aug 29, 1972; background paper, MACTHAI, subj: Airlift Support Options 9-10, n.d. [ca 1970].

16. Concept paper, US Embassy, Bangkok, subj: General Concept for US Support of Thai COIN, May 23, 1972; hist, MACTHAI, 1961, pp 38-40, 160-161, 1970, pp 36-37, 1971, p 8; Dir/Mil Assist, OASD/ISA, *Journal of Military Assistance*, Aug 70, p 131; TSgt Don Smith, *COIN in Thailand, 1969-70*, (PACAF, Proj CHECO, Jul 1, 1971);

Maj Edward B. Hanrahan, *An Overview of Insurgency and COIN in Thailand*, (PACAF, Proj CHECO, Feb 74).

17. Rprt, 5th SFGp, Opl Rprt for Qtrly Pd ending 31 Jan 67, Feb 15, 1967; Deatrick and Parmly intvw, Mar 9, 1972; ltr, Maj Howard D. Schulze, Asst AG, MACV COC, to Distr, subj: Capabilities and Employment of Project Delta, May 13, 1966; hist, MACV, 1965, pp 78–79; rprt, 5th SFGp, Development of the CIDG Program, 1964–1968, Apr 22, 1968; ltr, Capt B. L. Jervell, adj 5th SFGp, to MACV J–3, subj: Employment of CIDG, Mike Force, Mobile Guerrilla Force, and LRRP Projects, Apr 19, 1967; Kelly, *US Army Special Forces 1961–1971*, pp 134–148.

18. Rprts, Det B–52, 5th SFGp, AARs to OPORD 10–66, 12–66, and 13–66 (Ph II), Sep 13, Oct 8, and Dec 27, 1966; rprts, Det B–52 (Proj Delta), AARs to OPORD 7–67 (Samurai), 8–67 (Samurai II), and 8–67 (Samurai III), Aug 20, Nov 3, and Nov 5, 1967; rprt, Det B–52 (Proj Delta), AARs to OPORD 9–67 (Sultan) and 1–68 (Sultan II), Dec 29, 1967 and Jan 30, 1968; rprt, 10th Combat Avn Bn, Opl Rprt for Pd ending 31 Jul 66, Aug 9, 1966.

19. O'Donovan intvw, Apr 17, 1972; Mize intvw, 1968; rprt, 5th SFGp, AAR, Op Blackjack 34, 16–21 Jul 67; rprt, 5th SFGp, AAR, Blackjack 42, 1967; rprt, II Corps MSF Co, 5th SFGp, AAR, Op Brush (Blackjack 25A), 12 Dec 67–3 Jan 68, Jan 27, 1968.

20. Deatrick and Parmly intvw, Mar 9, 1972; intvw, Maj Ralph A. Rowley with Maj James R. Thyng, Feb 8, 1972; intvw, Maj Ralph A. Rowley with Col Eugene P. Deatrick, Feb 3, 1972; rprts, 5th SFGp, Opl Rprts for Qtrly Pd ending 31 Jan 67 and 31 Jul 68, Feb 15, 1967 and Aug 15, 1968; rprt, Det C–1, 5th SFGp, Monthly Opl Summary for Oct 66; rprt, Research Analysis Corp, US Army Special Forces and Similar Internal Defense Advisory Opns in Mainland SEA, 1962–67, Jun 69, pp 111–113, 123–124.

21. Hist, 14th ACWg, Nov–Dec 66, pp 18–19; rprt, 5th SFGp, Comb Op AAR, Blackjack 21, Nov 18, 1966; Deatrick and Parmly intvw, Mar 9, 1972; memo, Maj Burley O. Vandergriff, 1st ACSq, to Cdr 1st ACSq, subj: Sp Forces Aerial Resupply, Dec 27, 1966; MR, Brig Gen J. H. Thompson, DCS/Materiel, 7th AF, subj: Aerial Resupply using BLU–23/B Napalm Tanks, Nov 4, 1966; staff summary sheet, DCS/Plans, 7th AF, subj: Aerial Resupply Using BLU–23/B Napalm Tanks, Nov 9, 1966; staff summary sheet, DCS/Plans, 7th AF, subj: Certification and Availability of the MA–6 Drogue Deliverable Container, Nov 20, 1966; MR, 1st Lt Gary K. Wolf, Historian, 14th ACWg, subj: A–1 Resupply, [ca Dec 1966].

22. Ltr, Col Francis J. Kelly, Cdr 5th SFGp, to Cdr MACV, subj: USAF Support for Blackjack 31, Feb 26, 1967; rprts, 5th SFGp, AARs, Blackjack 41, Phase I and Phase II, 1967; rprt, 5th SFGp, Opl Rprt Lessons Learned for Qtrly Pd ending 31 Jul 68, Aug 15, 1968; hist, 14th ACWg, Jan–Mar 67, p 11.

23. Draft memo, JCS J–3, subj: Actions Relevant to South Vietnam, Jul 27, 1964; fact sheet, PACAF, subj: Crossborder Intelligence Operations, May 8, 1964; memo, MACV J–23, subj: Operation Delta, May 64; *Westmoreland, A Soldier Reports*, p 107.

24. Hist, CINCPAC, 1966, pp 629–635; rprt, Research Analysis Division, Sec AF/Off Info, DOD Report on Selected Air and Ground Operations in Cambodia and Laos, Sep 10, 1973; hist, AF Advisory Gp, Feb 67; hist, Dir/Plans, Hq USAF, Jul–Dec 67, pp 134–135; msg 19131, Cdr MACV to CINCPAC, 040923Z Jun 66; msg 08467, Cdr MACV to JCS, CINCPAC, 171008Z Mar 66; MR and encls, Maj Gen W. R. Peers, USA, Spl Asst for COIN and Spl Activity, Trip Report, 21 May–6 Jun 66; MR, Lt Col A. C. Wilhelm, Dir/Plans, Hq USAF, subj: Helicopters for 83rd SOG, Jun 10, 1966; ltr, Cdr MACV COC to Chief, AF Advisory Gp, subj: Aircraft Requirements, Nov 22, 1966; *Pentagon Papers*, Gravel ed, IV, 214, 535; ltr, Col John K. Singlaub, USA, Ch, SOG, MACV, to Maj Gen W. R. Peers, SACSA, JCS, Oct 11, 1966; hist, MACV, 1966, Annex M, 1967, Annex G, 1968, Annex F; Westmoreland, *A Soldier Reports*, p 107.

25. Memo, Col A. L. Hilpert, DCS/Plans, 7th AF, to MACV J–3, subj: Additional USAF Helicopter Support, Feb 10, 1967; msg AFCCS 86825, CSAF to CINCPACAF, 121506Z Aug 66; hist rprts, 20th Helic Sq, TSN Det, Feb and Mar 67; hist rprt, 20th Helic Sq, E-Flight, Jan–Mar 67; hist, 20th Helic Sq,

Jan–Mar 67; hist, 14th ACWg, Jan–Mar 67, pp 30–34, Apr–Jun 67, pp 29–34, Jul–Sep 67, pp 37–40; Capt Donald W. Nelson, *The USAF Helicopter in SEA*, (PACAF, Proj CHECO, Dec 5, 1968); paper, 20th Helic Sq, subj: Facts in SEA Helicopter Requirements and Employment, Apr 68.

26. Nelson, *Helicopter*, pp 27–31; ltr, Maj Alfred W. Paddock, USA, Det B–50, 5th SFGp, to 14th ACWg, subj: Ltr of Commendation, Jun 11, 1968.

27. Hist, 14th ACWg, Apr–Jun 68, pp 83–90; hist, 14th Spl Opns Wg, Jul–Sep 68, pp 43–48, Oct–Dec 68, pp 43–47; hist rprts, 20th Helic Sq, Jul–Sep 67, Oct–Dec 67, Jan–Mar 68, pp 3–10, Apr–Jun 68, pp 3–10; hist rprts, 20th Spl Opns Sq, Jul–Sep 68, pp 4–14, Oct–Dec 68, pp 1–10; paper, 20th Helic Sq, subj: Facts in SEA Helicopter Reqmts and Employment, Apr 68.

28. Rprt, Air Tng Cd, Activity Input to Corona Harvest, Aircrew Training, 1965–68, pp 51–73; hist, 20th Helic Sq and 20th Spl Opns Sq, 1967 through 1968; AFP 900–2, Jun 15, 1971; fact sheet, SAF/OI, The Air Force Cross, background information, Mar 1970; fact sheet, Raymond Fredette, AF/CHO, 1974.

29. Rprt, DOD, Rprt on Selected Air and Ground Opns in Cambodia and Laos, Sep 10, 1973; hist, CINCPAC, 1970, pp 213–235, 1971, pp 184–188; hist, MACV, 1969, Annex F, 1970, Annex B, 1971–72, Annex B.

30. Rprts, Maj Jerry J. Gilbert, 21st Sp Ops Sq, EOTR, Jul 71, draft EOTR, May 71; rprt, Lt Col James E. Cowan, Cdr 21st Sp Opns Sq, EOTR, Jul 13, 1971; rprt, Lt Col Robert B. Roberts, Opns Off, 21st Sp Opns Sq, EOTR, Oct 12, 1970; rprts, Capt David L. Hamann, Lt Col John F. Bird, Capt Roger J. Korenberg, 21st Sp Opns Sq, Mid-tour Reports, Jan 14, Jan 18, and Jun 15, 1971; rprt, Lt Col Roger S. Penney, 21st Sp Opns Sq, EOTR, 1970; 56th CSG Manual 55–2, vol I (A–1 Tactics Manual), vol III (CH–3/CH–53 Tactics Manual), Feb 15, 1971; msg DOZ, 56th Sp Opns Wg to Dir/Opns PACAF, 270700Z Nov 70; msg, 56th Sp Opns Wg to 7th AF, 110955Z Dec 70; hist, 21st Sp Opns Sq, monthly 1969 through 1972.

31. Hist, 21st Sp Opns Sq, monthly, 1969 through 1972; msg, 7th AF to Dir/Opns, PACAF, 200725Z Mar 70; rprt, Lt Col Meredith S. Sutton, Cdr, 20th Sp Opns Sq, EOTR, Mar 27, 1972; ltr, Col John F. Sadler, Ch, MACSOG, to Cdr, 7th AF, subj: 20th SOS Helicopter Support for MACSOG Activities, Jun 11, 1971.

32. Hist, MACV, 1964, Annex A, pp A–1 through II–9, II–20 to II–22; DF, Col Clyde R. Russell, Ch, SOG, to C/S MACV, subj: Consideration Expansion of 34A Opns, Nov 7, 1964; talking paper (TSO), JCS J–3, subj: Reprisal Actions NVN, Nov 30, 1964; hist, SAWC, Jan–Jun 64, pp 105–108; background paper, Hq USAF, XPD, subj: MACV Plan 34A–64, CAS Saigon Oplan Tiger, Apr 64.

33. Msg 00029, Det 1, 314th TCWg, to 7th AF, 290734Z Oct 66; hist, MACV, 1966, Annex M, pp 37–39, 43, 1967, Annex G, 1968, Annex F.

34. Hists, 14th Air Cdo Wg, 14th Sp Opns Wg, 15th Air Cdo Sq, 15th Sp Opns Sq, all quarters, 1968.

35. Hist, SAWC, Jan–Jun 66, p 28; intvw, Lt Col Douglas Huff, USA, CH intvw no 146, Jan 24, 1969; MR, Maj Gen W. R. Peers, USA, Spl Asst for COIN and Spl Activities, subj: trip report, 21 May–6 Jun 66; msg 2502, MACSOG to CINCPAC, 101011Z Jun 67; msg DOCO 30178, PACAF to 7th AF, 172255Z May 67; hist, MACV, 1967, Annex G, 1968, Annex F, 1966, Annex M.

36. Hist, 15th ACSq, Apr–Jun 68, p 5; hists, 15th Sp Opns Sq, Jul–Sep 68, p 7, Oct–Dec 68, p 5; hist, MACV, 1966, Annex M, pp 4, 37–39, 1967, Annex G, pp G–III–2–H–1, G–VI–1 to G–VI–7, 1968, Annex F, pp F–6, F–V–1 to F–V–3.

37. Hist, MACV, 1966, Annex M, Annex G, 1968, Annex F; msg 0133, MACSOG to CINCPAC, 200914Z Jan 66; msg 0318, MACV to CINCPAC, 171100Z Feb 66.

38. Msg SPLG–67–01740, 7th AF to Dep 7/13th AF, MACSOG, *et al*, 100100Z Feb 66; hist, MACV, 1964, Annex A, pp II–I–1 to II–I–3, 1966, Annex M, 1967, Annex G; hist, 20th Helic Sq, Udorn Det, Feb 67; hist, 20th Helic Sq, Jan–Mar 68; hist, 14th ACWg and 14th Sp Opns Wg, Jan–Mar 67 through Jul–Sep 68; msg MACSOG 1068, MACV to CINCPAC, 041235Z Nov 65; msg SOG 0318FM, MACV to CINCPAC, 171100Z Feb 66.

39. Hist, 15th Sp Opns Sq, 1969 through Sep 70; hist, 90th Sp Opns Sq, Oct 71 through Mar 72; hist, MACV 1969, Annex F, 1970, Annex B, 1971–72, Annex B; CSAFM E–37–70, CSAF for JCS, subj: PACAF UW–Configured C–130E Acft, May 21, 1970; CSAFM I–23–70, CSAF for JCS, Sep 23, 1970; hist, 7th AF, FY 72, pp 159–160; background paper, DCS/Prog and Opns, Hq USAF, subj: Combat Spear, Feb 3, 1973.

40. Rprt, Cdr, JCS Joint Contingency Task Group, The Son Tay POW Rescue Operation, Dec 18, 1970; study, William R. Karsteter, ARRS, subj: The Son Tay Raid, Annex to Hist, ARRS, FY 71; hist, Dir/Opns, Hq USAF, Jul–Dec 70, p 282; *Los Angeles Times*, Feb 2, 1971.

41. Msg 1396, Chief, PEO, Laos to CINCPAC, *et al*, 071520Z Apr 61; hist, Dir/Plans, Hq USAF, Jul–Dec 61, pp 184–185; study, RAC, *Case Study of US COIN Opns in Laos, 1955–1962*, RAC TM T–435, Sep 64; hist, 13th AF, 1962, pp I–50 and II–253; msg CX–71, US Embassy Vientiane to AFNIN, Hq USAF, 280935Z Apr 63.

42. IR 1–504,038, Aug 31, 1962; IR 1–501,599, Dec 19, 1962; IR 2222097764, Sep 17, 1964; ltr, CINCPAC to JCS, subj: Joint FAR/Nautralist Assault on Tchepone, Sep 11, 1963; memo, JCS J–3, subj: SEA Situation Report, May 8, 1963; msg J23–5649, MACV to CINCPAC, 280800Z Jun 63; msg J–4 63, US Embassy Vientiane to DIA, *et al*, 031310Z Jul 63; *Aviation Week and Space Technology*, Aug 20, 1962, p 76.

43. IR 2730017865, Apr 29, 1965; IR 1–887–0209–65, May 12, 1965; IR 0222160464, Nov 5, 1965; IR 311 04981–66, Apr 7, 1966; IR 2–856–0281–68, Mar 2, 1968; IR 1771–1408–68, Dec 24, 1968; IR 1–515–0172–69, Jul 15, 1969; rprt, 7th AF Dir/Intellig, Weekly Air Intellig Summary, 68–35, Aug 31, 1968, pp 3–8; msg DOP 30133, CINCPACAF to Dir/Opns, Hq USAF, 240400Z Apr 65; memo, Sec Def to CJCS, subj: Enemy Resupply Activity Northern Laos, Sep 24, 1965; hist, 13th AF, Jan–Jun 68, I, 159–160; Capt Edward Vallentiny, *The Fall of Site 85*, (PACAF, Proj CHECO, Aug 9, 1968), pp 12–13.

44. IR 1–515–0079–70, Sep 14, 1970; IR 1516–0640–69, Jun 2, 1969; IR 2730–0716–70, Dec 21, 1970; IR 6856–0106–69, Jul 31, 1969; IR 1775–0023–71, Jan 25, 1971; IR 2–727–0904–70, 1970; IR 6–818–0071–71, Apr 9, 1971; 13th AF Intellig Brief, Jun 12, 1969; *San Diego Union*, Mar 12, 1970; Maj William W. Lofgren and Maj Richard R. Sexton, *Air War in Northern Laos, 1 Apr–30 Nov 1971*, (Hq PACAF, Proj CHECO, Jun 22, 1973), p 71; Lt Col Jack S. Ballard, *The Air Force in Southeast Asia: Development and Employment of Fixed-wing Gunships, 1962–1971*, (Off/AF Hist, Jan 74), pp 152–153.

45. Study, Combined Intell Center, VN, subj: VC/NVA Use of Cambodia as a Source of Army and Ammo, May 15, 1968; ltr A–255, US Embassy Saigon to Dept State, subj: ICC Difficulties in Maintaining Airline to Hanoi, Nov 18, 1966; IR 6–026–1915–68, Apr 1, 1968; IR 1516–0426–69, Apr 19, 1969; IR 6–028–3711–68, Jul 27, 1968; IR 6–075–1356–68, Oct 27, 1968; IR 1776–0220–68, Sep 4, 1968; IR 6–075–0770–68, May 26, 1968; IR 1516–1769–69, Jan 4, 1970; IR 1516–0587–69, May 24, 1969; IR 1776–0051–70, Mar 17, 1970; Journal, *Defense Intelligence Digest* (DIA, Feb 71), pp 12–13.

46. Msg 2256, PACAF to AFCIN, Hq USAF, 220224Z Mar 62; msg C–41, US Air Att, Saigon to AFCIN, Hq USAF, 040902Z Apr 62; rprt, Off/Sec AF to Pres, subj: Enemy Air Activity in SVN, Apr 9, 1962; briefing, Gen Anthis for Sec Def, Jul 23, 1962; msg IDC 62–0322, 2nd ADVON to MACV, *et al*, 180400Z Apr 62; CHECO Rprt, October 1961–December 1963 (PACAF, Project CHECO), V, 76–81.

47. Rprt, Det B–52, 5th SFGp, AAR to OPORD 10–66, Sep 13, 1966; IR 6–045–4812–69, Apr 18, 1969; msg OCO–63–1000, PACAF to Hq USAF, 110035Z May 63; IR 3/501,083, Feb 8, 1962; hist, 7th AF, Jan–Jun 68, p 144; Alfred W. McCoy, C. B. Read, and L. P. Adams, *The Politics of Heroin in Southeast Asia* (New York, 1972), pp 160, 254–256.

48. IR 2895–0446–68, Nov 28, 1966; IR 311/08028–66, Jun 9, 1966; IR 1656–0103–66, Dec 23, 1966; IR 311/12606–67, Dec 67; IR 311–02648–68, Mar 15, 1968; IR 1–656–0113–70, Nov 3, 1970; IR 6–895–0170–71, Mar 19, 1971; IR 6–074–0055–69, Sep 25, 1969; IR 2–258–0006–70, Sep 23, 1970; msg, MACTHAI J–2 to CINCPAC, 020243Z Mar 72; msg, Det 3, Army Advis Gp to MACTHAI, 031115Z Mar 72.

49. Rprt, Col Edwin J. White, Cdr,

TACTICAL AIRLIFT

56th Sp Opns Wg, EOTR, Aug 69; msg, MACTHAI to US Embassy Bangkok, 270532Z Nov 68; hist, 7/13th AF, Jul–Dec 69, pp 18–19; msg, MACTHAI J-2 to CINCPAC, 020243Z Mar 72; ltr, Maj Gen Louis T. Seith, Dep Cdr, 7/13th AF, to US Embassy and MACTHAI J-3, subj: Evaluation of Unidentified Radar Tracks, Feb 17, 1969; msg, MACTHAI to DUA, 290320Z Apr 67; Warren A. Trest and TSgt Charles E. Garland, *Counterinsurgency in Thailand, 1966* (PACAF, Proj CHECO, Nov 8, 1967), pp 36–43; TSgts E. H. Ashby and D. G. Francis, *Counterinsurgency in Thailand, Jan 67–Dec 68* (PACAF, Proj CHECO, Mar 26, 1969), pp 21–27; IR 1–856–0138–68, Dec 26, 1968.

50. IR 3/470,553, Apr 6, 1961; IR 1516–0741–69, Jun 21, 1969; IR 1516–0306–69, Apr 7, 1969.

51. IR 2730007964, Apr 1, 1965; IR 1773–0042–66, Oct 6, 1966; IR 6–010–4115–66, DIA, Nov 8, 1966; IR 6–026–1773–68, Apr 26, 1968; IR 1773–0152–68, May 16, 1968; IR 2–730–0617–68, Sep 18, 1968; IR 1771–0052–69, Jan 30, 1969; *Washington Post*, May 30, 1976.

52. Comments on draft ms, XOOTZ, Spl Opns, Dir/Opns, Hq USAF, 1973.

Chapter XVII

The War for Laos

1. Study, Research Analysis Corp, Case Study of US COIN Operations in Laos, 1955–1962, Sep 64.

2. Rprt, 1st Lt Richard W. Kimball, Hist Off, 483rd TCWg, Operation Boostershot, 1958; 483rd TCWg, Opns Order 8-58, Mar 27, 1958; hist, 483rd TCWg, Jan–Jun 58, pp 10–18; hist, CINCPAC, 1959, p 203.

3. Hist, 315th AD, Jan–Jun 60, pp 64–65.

4. Deatrick and Parmly intvw, Mar 9, 1972; Arthur M. Schlesinger, Jr, *A Thousand Days* (New York, 1965; Fawcett Crest ed), pp 301–307; Peter Dale Scott, "Air America: Flying the US into Laos," in Nina S. Adams and Alfred W. McCoy, *Laos: War and Revolution* (New York, 1970), pp 313–315; draft ms, Maj Victor B. Anthony, *The USAF in SEA: The War in Northern Laos*, chapt 2 [ca 1974]; briefing sheet, Joint Staff, for JCS Meeting with State Dept, subj: Laos, Oct 27, 1960.

5. Scott, "Air America," pp 301–321; memo, John J. Czyzak, L/FE, Dept State, to Mr. Roger Hilsman, FE, subj: ICC Investigation of Air America, Apr 8, 1963; Final Rprt of the Select Committee to Study Governmental Operations w/Respect to Intelligence Activities, 94th Cong 2d Sess, Rprt no 94–755, *Foreign and Military Intelligence*, Apr 26, 1976, pp 205–251; intvw, Lt Col Robert Zimmerman with Lt Col Lawrence Ropka, Hq USAF, Dec 18, 1974; intvw, author with Col William Von Platen, San Juan Capistrano, Calif, May 10, 1975; Victor Marchetti and John D. Marks, *The CIA and the Cult of Intelligence* (New York, 1974), pp 137–142.

6. Memo, Hon Clark Clifford to the President, subj: Memo of Conference on 19 Jan 61 between Pres Eisenhower and Pres-elect Kennedy on the subject of Laos, Sep 29, 1967, *GPO Pentagon Papers*, bk 10, pp 1360–1362; Coleman intvw, 1975 (Coleman was sent as a "civilian" employee into Laos in 1961 to develop facilities at Vientiane and help the Laotian Air Force); msg, 315th AD to PACAF, 150710Z Dec 60; ltr, 315th AD to PACAF (PFESE), subj: Justification for 5th Comm Sq, Feb 27, 1962; *New York Times*, Apr 27 and 28, 1961; *Baltimore Sun*, Apr 27, 1961; hist, CINCPAC, 1961, part II, pp 77–78; study, JCS Hist Div, Chronological Summary of Significant Events Concerning the Laotian Crisis, May 19, 1961; Robert L. Kerby, "American Military Airlift during Laotian Civil War, 1958–1963," *Aerospace Historian*, Mar 1977 (Kerby was a participant in the 1961 Wattay missions).

7. Draft ms, Maj Victor B. Anthony,

The USAF in SEA: The War in Northern Laos, chapt 2 [ca 1974]; memo, Lansdale to Taylor, subj: Resources for Unconventional Warfare, Southeast Asia, Jul 61, *The Pentagon Papers as Published by The New York Times* (New York, 1971), p 135; John Lewallen, "The Reluctant Counterinsurgents," and D. Gareth Porter, "After Geneva: Subverting Laotian Neutrality," in Adams and McCoy, *Laos: War and Revolution,* pp 182–199, 360–363; Alfred W. McCoy, C. B. Read, and L. P. Adams, *The Politics of Heroin in Southeast Asia* (New York, 1972), pp 264–281.

8. Intvw, Corona Harvest intvw no 249, with Col Harry C. Aderholt, Mar 5, 1970, pp 115–125; McCoy, *et al, The Politics of Heroin,* pp 274–278.

9. Ropka intvw, Dec 18, 1974; rprt, JUSMAGTHAI, Final Report of MAAG, Laos, Nov 6, 1962; study, Research Analysis Corp, Case Study of US COIN Opns in Laos, 1955–62, Sep 64.

10. Msg DM 2-10459, TAC to AFODC, Hq USAF, 221900Z Aug 62; hist, 464th TCWg, Jan–Jun 62, p 62.

11. Memo, John J. Czyzak, L/FE, Dept State, to Mr. Roger Hilsman, FE, subj: ICC Investigation of Air America, Apr 8, 1963; Air Staff summary sheet, Maj L. A. Wilson, Hq USAF, subj: Airlift Services Outside the US by Air America, Inc, Jun 10, 1963; msgs, US Embassy Vientiane to Sec State, 020730Z May 63, 141025Z May 63, 060910Z Jul 63, 011310Z Aug 63; msg, Sec State to US Embassy Vientiane, 250155Z Jul 63.

12. Rprts, Asst for Mutual Security, DCS/S and L, Hq USAF, *Journal of Military Assistance,* Mar 63, p 167, Jun 63, pp 179–180, Mar 64, pp 139, 166–167, Jun 64, p 167; msg, US Embassy Vientiane to Sec State, 250615Z May 63; msgs CX–67 and CX–121, Air Attache Vientiane to CSAF, *et al,* 240412Z Apr 63 and 130955Z Jun 63; msg C–029, Air Attache Bangkok to CSAF, *et al,* 261022Z Apr 63; hist, CINCPAC, 1964, pp 259–263; Aderholt intvw, Mar 5, 1970; D. Gareth Porter, "After Geneva . . . ," in Adams and McCoy, *Laos: War and Revolution,* p 187.

13. Rprt, Col Robert S. Ferrari, DEPCHJUSMAGTHAI, EOTR, Jun 68, pp 198–199; paper, DEPCHJUSMAGTHAI, subj: Descriptions of RLG Force Structure and Capability, Oct 69; statement, Col Robert L. F. Tyrell, Air Attache Vientiane, for Symington Committee, 1969; study, Joint Staff, subj: Plan for Improvement of RLGAF, Nov 69; intvw, author with Col Austin Lemon, JCS/DOCSA, Jul 10, 1974.

14. SNIE 68-2-59, subj: The Situation in Laos, Sep 18, 1959, printed in *GPO Pentagon Papers,* bk X, pp 1242–1243; Deatrick and Parmly intvw, Mar 9, 1972; hist, CINCPAC, 1964, p 283; Directory of Useable Airfields in Laos, 2nd AD, Jul 1, 1962; Maj Gen Theodore R. Milton, "Air Power: Equalizer in SEA," *Air University Review,* Nov–Dec 63, pp 1–8; msg, 2d ADVON to PACAF, 051000Z Mar 62.

15. Rprt, DEPCHJUSMAGTHAI, Hist Summary for Jun 66–Apr 68; rprt, Col Robert S. Ferrari, DEPCHJUSMAGTHAI, EOTR, Jun 68, pp 203–215; intvw, author with Col Austin Lemon, Jul 16, 1974; Marchetti and Marks, *The CIA and the Cult of Intelligence,* pp 140–141.

16. Rprt, Col Robert S. Ferrari, DEPCHJUSMAGTHAI, EOTR, Jun 68; Aderholt intvw, Mar 5, 1970, pp 93–96; comments, Dir/Opns, Sp Opns (XOOTZ), Hq USAF, Comments on Bowers' draft ms, *The USAF in SEA: Tactical Airlift,* 1973; intvw, author with Lt Cols Marvin L. Jones and Lawrence Ropka, Hq USAF, and Col Austin Lemon, JCS, Oct 2, 1973.

17. Comments, Dir/Opns, Sp Opns (XOOTZ), Hq USAF, Comments on Bowers' draft ms, *The USAF in SEA: Tactical Airlift,* 1973.

18. Final Rprt of the Select Committee to Study Governmental Opns w/ Respect to Intelligence Activities, 94th Cong, 2d Sess, Rprt no 94–755, *Foreign and Military Intelligence,* Apr 26, 1976, p 231; article, Jack Anderson, "CIA Life in SEA," *Washington Post,* Feb 18, 1971; *Newsweek,* Apr 6, 1970.

19. Memo, John C. Bullitt, Asst Admin SEA, AID and Dept State, for Hon Townsend Hoopes, Actg Asst Sec Def (ISA), subj: Review of AF Rates for Bailed Acft in Laos, Jul 24, 1967; brief, AFXOXX, Hq USAF, subj: Support of Guerrilla Forces in Laos, Feb 22, 1972; intvw, author with Lt Col Marvin Jones, Sp Plans, Hq USAF, and Col William R. Foster, Eastern Div, Dir/Plans, Hq USAF, Jul 3, 1974; rprt, Subcommittee on US Security Agreements and Commitments Abroad of US Senate Comm on Foreign Relations, *Laos: April*

1971, Aug 3, 1971; Aderholt intvw, Mar 5, 1970.

20. Msg, CINCPAC to US Embassy Vientiane, 050116Z Feb 66; msg, US Embassy Vientiane to CINCPAC, 080240Z Feb 66; msg, CINCPAC to JCS, 152320Z Feb 66.

21. Rprt, Col Robert S. Ferrari, DEPCHJUSMAGTHAI, EOTR, Jun 68, p 215; Jones and Foster intvw, Jul 3, 1974; study, Joint Staff, subj: Plan for Improvement of RLGAF, Nov 69; comments, Dir/Opns, Sp Opns (XOOTZ), Hq USAF, comments on Bowers' draft ms, *The USAF in SEA: Tactical Airlift*, 1973; intvw, author with Col Austin Lemon, JCS, Oct 5, 1973.

22. Lemon intvw, Jul 16, 1974; msg, CINCPAC to MACV, MACTHAI, 131928Z Aug 65.

23. Jones, Ropka, and Lemon intvw, Oct 2, 1973; intvw, author with Lt Col Jones, Oct 5, 1973; Lemon intvw, Oct 5, 1973; Jones and Foster intvw, Jul 3, 1974; Lemon intvw, Jul 10, 1974; intvw, author with Col Lemon, Jul 17, 1974; intvw, author with Lt Col Raymond E. Hamilton, Dir/Intell, Hq USAF, Jul 8, 1974; intvw, author with Col Frank M. Hammock, Hq DSA, Oct 1, 1973; hist, 374th TAWg, 1967 through 1968; paper, DEPCHJUSMAGTHAI, subj: Descriptions of RLG Force Structure and Capabilities, Oct 69; Robert L. Kerby, "American Military Airlift during the Laotian Civil War, 1958-1963," *Aerospace Historian,* Mar 77, p 8.

24. Msg, Air Attache Vientiane to 7/13th AF, 040602Z Oct 69; msg DOSA, 7/13th AF to Air Attache Vientiane, 071138Z Oct 69; Fact Book, Off/Vietnamization, Hq USAF, Feb 70; Jones and Foster intvw, Jul 3, 1974; msg DOSA, 7/13th AF to Air Attache Vientiane, 160817Z May 69.

25. Fact Book, Off/Vietnamization, Hq USAF, Feb 70; paper, DEPCHJUSMAGTHAI, subj: Descriptions of RLG Force Structure and Capabilities, Oct 69; Lemon intvw, Jul 10, 1974; appendix VIII to Annex B, 7/13th AF Oplan 5K60L, Apr 1, 1971.

26. Hist, 21st TASq, Jul–Sep 70, pp 7–8, Oct–Dec 70, p 4, Jan–May 71, p 6; hist, 314th TAWg, Jan–Mar 71, p 1; rprt, Sp Activ, 7/13th AF, Hist Rprt, 3rd Qtr, FY 71, Apr 6, 1971; Jones and Foster intvw, Jul 3, 1974.

27. Msg, CINCPAC to US Embassy Vientiane, 232154Z Apr 64; msg, MACV to US Embassy Vientiane, 241130Z Apr 64.

28. Hist, 315th TAWg, Jan–Mar 70, pp 15–17; hist, 309th TASq, Jan–Mar 70, pp 6–7; rprt, Sp Activ, 7/13th AF (DOSA), Hist Rprt, 3rd Qtr, FY 70, Apr 4, 1970; Kenneth Sams, Lt Col John Schlight, and Maj J. C. Pratt, *Air Opns in Northern Laos, 1 Nov 69–1 Apr 70* (Proj CHECO, PACAF, May 5, 1970), p 18B.

29. Hist, 315th TAWg, Jul–Sep 70, p 24; msgs, 7/13th AF to Cdr 315th TAWg, 150811Z Sep 70 and 250816Z Sep 70; rprt, Sp Activ (DOZ), 7/13th AF, to Dir/Opns, 7/13th AF, Sp Activ Hist Rprt, 1st Qtr, FY 71, Oct 6, 1970.

30. Maj John C. Pratt, *The Royal Laotian Air Force, 1954–1970* (PACAF, Proj CHECO, Sep 15, 1970), pp 1–8; Capt Thomas R. Knox, "Waterpump, 1964–1965," *Aerospace Commentary,* (Air University), spring 1970; study, Research Analysis Corp, Case Study of US COIN Opns in Laos, 1955–1962, Sep 64; rprt, Asst for Mutual Security, Hq USAF, *Journal of Military Assistance* and *Journal of Mutual Security,* May 58, Dec 60, and Mar 62.

31. Lt Col Khouang, RLAF, quoted in Pratt, *The RLAF, 1954–1970*, p 10.

32. Msg 25026, Det 6, 1st ACWg, Udorn, to SAWC, 091000Z Nov 64; Knox, "Waterpump, 1964–1965"; hist, SAWC, Jan–Jun 64, pp 47–48; Jul–Dec 64, p 96; msg 20915, DEPCHJUSMAGTHAI to CINCPAC, 170915Z Nov 64.

33. Pratt, *The RLAF, 1954–1970*, pp 26, 34–40, 69–75, 142–149; rprt, DEPCHJUSMAGTHAI, Hist Summ for Jun 66–Apr 68, May 11, 1968; Warren A. Trest and SSgt Dale E. Hammons, *USAF Operations from Thailand, 1966* (PACAF, Proj CHECO, Oct 31, 1967), pp 31–54; IR 1-856-0001-68, Jan 5, 1968.

34. Msg, DEPCHJUSMAGTHAI to CINCPAC, 190320Z Dec 67; IR 1-856-0110-68, Oct 7, 1968; IR 1-856-0001-68, Jan 5, 1968; Pratt, *The RLAF, 1954–1970*, pp 77–79; msg, Amb Sullivan, Vientiane, to CSAS (for McConnell from Amb), Mar 1, 1969; study, Joint Staff, subj: Plan for Improvement of RLGAF, Nov 69.

35. Memo, Reqmts Div, AID, Vientiane, subj: RLAF C-47 Utilization, May 21, 1970; IR 6-856-0060-70, Mar 21,

1970; Jones and Foster intvw, Jul 3, 1974.

36. Rprt, PACAF Opns Assistance Team, Visit to DEPCHJUSMAGTHAI, 19 Nov 71, Feb 72; hist, Dir/Opns, Hq USAF, Jul–Dec 71, pp 121–123; study, Joint Staff, subj: Plan for Improvement of RLGAF, Nov 69.

37. Rprt, DEPCHJUSMAGTHAI, Hist Summ for Jun 66–Apr 68, May 11, 1968; Kenneth Sams, Maj John C. Pratt, C. William Thorndale, James T. Bear, *Air Support of COIN in Laos, Jul 68–Nov 69* (PACAF, Proj CHECO, Nov 10, 1969), pp 43–45; hist, CINCPAC, 1972, II, 447–448; memo, Kenneth Rush, Dep Sec Def, to Sec Army, Sec AF, subj: Helicopter Support for Forces in Laos, Jun 8, 1972; study, Research Analysis Corp, Case Study of US COIN Opns in Laos, 1955–1962, Sep 64.

38. Msg, US Embassy Vientiane, to Sec State, 290900Z Oct 65; study, Joint Staff, subj: Plan for Improvement of RLGAF, Nov 69; IR 1-856-0001-68, Jan 5, 1968; IR 6-856-0060-70, Mar 21, 1970; memo, Joe C. Williams, Proj 404, to Air Attache, Vientiane, subj: Staff Study Rprt, Jan 18, 1969; rprt, PACAF Opns Assistance Team, Visit to DEPCHJUSMAGTHAI, Nov 19, 1971, Feb 72; Aderholt intvw, Mar 5, 1974.

39. Hist, 14th ACWg, Jan–Jun 66, pp 93–94; hist, 14th Sp Opns Wg, Oct–Dec 68; rprt, Lt Col Lawrence R. Cummings, 20th Helic Sq, Debriefing Rprt, to 7th AF, Oct 3, 1966; msg 09720, MACV J-3 to CINCPAC, 280101Z Mar 66.

40. Memo, Col David C. Collins, Dep Cdr/Sp Air Opns, to 7th AF Dir/Opns, subj: Use of Helicopters in Support of SEA ITACS, Jun 26, 1968; msg, Dep Cdr 7/13th AF to 7th AF, subj: Helicopter Support, Feb 12, 1968; hist, 7th AF, Jul–Dec 68, p 286; hist, 14th ACWg, Jan–Jun 66, pp 93–97, Nov–Dec 66, pp 47–49, Oct–Dec 67, p 35, Jan–Mar 68; hist, 20th Helic Sq, Udorn Det, Feb, Mar, and May 67; hist, 20th Helic Sq, Apr–Jun 68 and Jul–Sep 68; Capt Edward Vallentiny, *The Fall of Site 85* (PACAF, Proj CHECO, Aug 9, 1968), pp 30, 36–38; Capt Donald W. Nelson, *The USAF Helicopter in SEA* (PACAF, Proj CHECO, Dec 5, 1968, pp 34–43; Capt Edward Vallentiny, *USAF Operations from Thailand, 1 Jan 67–1 Jul 68* (PACAF, Proj CHECO, Nov 20, 1968), pp 3–4.

41. Msg 01467, USAIRA Vientiane to 7/13th AF, 271330Z Sep 66; msg 00158, Dir/Opns, 7/13th AF to PACAF, Dir/Plans, Hq USAF, subj: Retention of US Manned Helos, Dec 1, 1966; hist, 14th ACWg, Jan–Jun 66, pp 93–94, Jul–Sep 66, pp 69–71, Nov–Dec 66, p 50, Apr–Jun 67, p 30; hist, 20th Helic Sq, Udorn Det, Jan, Feb, and May 67.

42. Draft rprt, Maj Jerry J. Gilbert, 21st Sp Opns Sq, EOTR, May 71; hist, 21st Helic Sq, in hist, 56th ACWg, 1968 through 1972; rprts, Sp Activities (DOSA), 7/13th AF, Qtrly, Jan–Mar 70 through Oct–Dec 71; msg, Dir/Opns PACAF to CSAF, 010515Z Jul 69.

43. Hist, 7/13th AF, Jul–Dec 69, pp 11–12, Jul–Dec 70, pp 25–26; MR, Lt Col Erwin J. Kaidy, Ch, Sp Activ Div, 7/13th AF, subj: CH-54 Activities, Feb 19, 1970; msg, US Embassy Vientiane to MACV, 111230Z Mar 70; msg, Dep Cdr, 7/13th AF to 7th AF, 270830Z Jan 68; msg, AFXDC, Hq USAF to PACAF, TAC, et al, 261713Z Jun 68; rprt, Maj Gen Dewitt R. Searles, Dep Cdr 7/13th AF, EOTR, Sep 9, 1972.

44. Rprt, Lt Col James E. Cowan, Cdr 21st Sp Opns Sq, EOTR, Jul 13, 1971; 56th CSGp Manual 55-2, vol III, CH-3/CH-53 Tactics Manual, Feb 15, 1971; rprt, Sp Activ Div, 7/13th AF, 3rd Qtr, FY 71, Apr 6, 1971; hist, 21st Sp Opns Sq, Dec 69; rprts, Dir/Management Analysis, Hq USAF, *USAF Management Summary: SEA, 1967 through 1973.*

45. Hist, 20th Helic Sq, Jan–Mar 68.

46. Hist, 21st Sp Opns Sq, 1969 through Jun 73; hist, 20th Helic Sq, Udorn Det, Jan 67 through Jun 67; hist, 20th Helic Sq, Oct–Dec 67 through Oct–Dec 68; rprt, Lt Col Lawrence R. Cummings, Cdr 20th Helic Sq, Debriefing Rprt, Oct 3, 1966; rprts, 21st Sp Opns Sq EOTRs, Capt Harold A. Brattland, Jul 28, 1970, Capt Edwin R. Albright, Jan 9, 1971, Capt Landon L. Kimbrough, Jan 25, 1971, Capt Alan D. York, n.d., [ca 1971].

47. *Armed Forces Management*, Jun 70, p 16; *Air Force Times*, Dec 24, 1969; statement, Gen John D. Ryan, CSAF, to Senate Armed Forces Comm, Mar 10, 1970, Supplement to AF Policy Ltr for Cdrs, 5-1970, May 70; rprt, Maj Charles J. Herrmann, 21st Sp Opns Sq, EOTR, n.d., [ca Aug 1969]; rprt, Lt Col William

B. Morey, 21st Sp Opns Sq, EOT Tactics Evaluation Rprt, Jul 6, 1970; draft rprt, Maj Jerry J. Gilbert, 21st Sp Opns Sq, Draft EOTR, May 71; draft ms, Warren A. Trest and Jay E. Hines, Air Training Command's Support of Forces in SEA, 1961–1973, (1977), pp 126–127.

48. Hist, 20th Sp Opns Sq, Jan–Mar 69, p 5; msg, Dep Cdr 7/13th AF to 20th Sp Opns Sq, Udorn Det, 170610Z Jan 69; rprt, Maj Gen Louis T. Seith, Dep Cdr 7/13th AF, EOTR, Jul 28, 1969, p 5; msg, Air Attache Laos to 7th AF, 180450Z Feb 69; Kenneth Sams, Maj John C. Pratt, C. W. Thorndale, and James T. Bear, *Air Support of Counterinsurgency in Laos, 1968–69* (Hq PACAF, Proj CHECO, Nov 10, 1969), p 140.

49. Quoted in Sams, Pratt, Thorndale, and Bear, *Air Support*, p 149.

50. Background paper, J–5 Joint Staff, Background Paper 63–69, subj: The Situation in Laos, Aug 2, 1969; rprt, State/Defense/CIA Coordinated Response, subj: Military Options in Laos, Aug 19, 1969; hist, MACV, 1969, p III–50.

51. Rprt, Sp Activ Div, 7/13th AF, Hist Rprt, Jul–Sep 69; hist, 7/13th AF, Jul–Dec 69, pp 38–88; hist, MACV, 1969, pp III–48 to III–52; hist, 20th Sp Opns Sq, Jan 70; Sams, Schlight, and Pratt, *Air Opns in Northern Laos, 1 Nov 69–1 Apr 70* (Hq PACAF, Proj CHECO, May 3, 1971), pp 44–46.

52. Memo, Col Robert L. F. Tyrell, Air Attache, to Reqmts Off (Mr. Newman), subj: Request for Logistics and Airlift Support—LS 108, Dec 16, 1969; hist, MACV, vol I, pp VI–84 to VI–91; Kenneth Sams, Lt Col John Schlight, and Maj John C. Pratt, *Air Operations in Northern Laos, 1 Nov 69–1 Apr 70* (Hq PACAF, Proj CHECO, May 5, 1970), pp 44–47, 53; *New York Times*, Feb 5, 7, and 14, 1970; *Washington Star*, Feb 6, 1970; *Time*, Feb 23, 1970.

53. Quoted in Sams, Schlight, and Pratt, *Air Opns in Northern Laos, 1 Nov 69–1 Apr 70* (Hq PACAF, Proj CHECO, May 3, 1971), pp 79–80.

54. Ltr, Col Edward W. Kenny, Ch, Current Opns, 7/13th AF, to DCS/Opns, 7/13th AF, subj: Info for EOTR, Feb 70, Mar 9, 1970; IR 6–856–0016–70; Field Intell Rprt FOV 19,477, Vientiane, subj: Long Tieng Sitrep, 1900 hrs, Mar 18, 1970; Field Intell Rprt FOV 20,467, Vientiane, subj: Long Tieng Sitrep, 0630 hrs, Mar 18, 1970; msg, Air Attache Vientiane to 7th AF, 181600Z Mar 70; hist, 7/13th AF, Jan–Jun 70, pp 18–19; Sams, Schlight, and Pratt, *Air Operations*, pp 65–95; *New York Times*, Feb 22 and 27, 1970; *Baltimore Sun*, Mar 19 and 21, 1970.

55. Melvin D. Porter and Lt Col H. D. Blount, *Air Operations in Northern Laos, 1 Nov 70–1 Apr 71* (Hq PACAF, Proj CHECO, May 3, 1971), p 14; hist, 21st Sp Opns Sq, Jan through Jun 70, Mar 71; Hamilton intvw, Jul 8, 1974; (Hamilton was intelligence officer at Vientiane during Aug 70–Feb 72); hist, 7/13th AF Jan–Jun 70, pp 23–25, Jul–Dec 70, pp 14–16; hist, 7th AF, FY 72, pp 53–54, 312–317.

56. Rprt, Maj Gen Louis T. Seith, Dep Cdr 7/13th AF, EOTR, Jul 28, 1969, pp 4–6; hist, 20th Sp Opns Sq, Jan–Mar 69, pp 7, 10; hist, 7/13th AF, Jan 68–Jun 69, I, 13–14; msg DOSA, 7/13th AF to PACAF, 300826Z Mar 69.

57. Hist, 21st Sp Opns Sq, Sep 69, Oct 69; hist, 20th Sp Opns Sq, Apr–Jun 69, pp 9–14; hist, 7/13th AF, Jan 68–Jun 69, I, 16–17, Jul–Dec 69, pp 13–16; msg DOSA, 7/13th AF to 7th AF, 191112Z Jun 69; msg, Air Attache Savannakhet to Air Attache Vientiane, 071025Z Jul 69; msg, Air Attache Vientiane to 7/13th AF, 101000Z Sep 69; msg, Air Attache Vientiane to JCS, DIA, 280135Z Sep 69; rprt, Sp Activ Div (DOSA), 7/13th AF, Hist Rprt, Jul–Sep 69.

58. Rprt, Maj Gen Dewitt Searles, Dep Cdr 7/13th AF, EOTR, Sep 72, pp 21–22; hist, 21st Sp Opns Sq, monthly, Sep 70 through Mar 71; hist, 7/13th AF, Jul–Dec 70, pp 22–24, 1971, pp 22–37; rprts, Sp Activ Div (DOSA), 7/13th AF, Hist, Rprt, 1st Qtr FY 71, Oct 6, 1970, 2nd Qtr FY 71, Jan 4, 1972.

59. Rprt, Maj Gen Dewitt Searles, Dep Cdr, 7/13th AF, Sep 9, 1972, pp 16–17, 23; 1st Lt Donald G. Kukle, et al, *The Bolovens Campaign, 28 Jul–28 Dec 71* (PACAF, Proj CHECO, May 8, 1974); unpubl ms, *The Air War in Laos, Jan 72–Feb 73* (Hq PACAF, Proj CHECO, 1973), pp 179–199; fact sheet, MACV Dir/Intell, subj: 1972 Laos Update, Dec 21, 1972; msg, 56th Sp Opns Wg to 7/13th AF, 170701Z Jun 72; msg, CINCPAC to MACV, 132225Z Jun 72; msg, 7/13th AF to 7th AF, 091440Z Oct 72; hist, 21st Sp Opns Sq,

Jun 72, Oct 72; rprts, Sp Activ Div, 7/13th AF, Hist Rprt 4th Qtr/FY 72, Jul–Sep 72, Dec 18, 1972, 2nd Qtr/FY 72, Jan 14, 1973.

60. Rprt, Maj Gen Dewitt Searles, Dep Cdr, 7/13th AF, EOTR, Sep 72, pp 11, 22; hist, 7/13th AF, 1972, pp 26–93; msg, 7/13th AF to 7th AF, 240927Z Aug 72; hist, 21st Sp Opns Sq, Mar 73.

61. Hist, 21st Sp Opns Sq, Sep 72 and Nov 72; talking paper, 7/13th AF, subj: A-7 as a SAR/Escort Acft, n.d., [ca 1972]; rprt, Lt Col James E. Cowan, Cdr, 21st Sp Opns Sq, Jul 13, 1971, pp 8–13; msgs, 7/13th AF to MAC Dir/Opns, Saigon, 080335Z Nov 72, 280929Z Nov 72.

62. Msg DO, 56th Sp Opns Sq to 7/13th AF, 020640Z Dec 70; msg, 7/13th AF to Hq USAF, 100500Z Dec 70; *The Air War in Laos, Jan 72–Feb 73*, pp 209–215; rprt, Sp Activ Div, 7/13th AF, Hist Rprt, Oct 1, 1972, Dec 18, 1972; rprt, Col Robert L. F. Tyrell, US Air Attache Vientiane, Jun 68–Aug 70, Sep 22, 1970.

63. Paper, JUSMAGTHAI, Recommended Security Assistance Program Objective Memo for Laos for FY 75–79, Aug 24, 1973; brief, Dir/Plans, Hq USAF, subj: Laos Airlift Reqmts (JCS 2344/188–1), Dec 12, 1972; JCSM–525–72, JCS to Sec Def, subj: Laos Airlift Reqmts, Dec 13, 1972; memo, G. Warren Nutter, Asst Sec Def, for CJCS, subj: Laos Airlift Reqmts, Nov 29, 1972; ltr, Maj Gen James A. Hill, Dir/Progr, Hq USAF, to multiple addressees, subj: USAF Decision Ltr D–73–13, CM–53 Helicopters, Mar 29, 1973; JCSM–113–73, JCS to Sec Def, subj: US Defense Attache Off, Vientiane, Laos, Mar 16, 1973; hist, USSAG/7th AF, Jan–Mar 74, pp 9–11, 125; hist, USSAG, Apr–Jun 73, pp 13–14.

64. Rprt, Col Robert A. Stefanik, USSAG/7th AF J–2, EOTR, Jun 30, 1975, pp 29–30; rprt, Maj Gen Richard G. Trefry, DEPCHJUSMAGTHAI, Def Attache Vientiane, EOTR, Feb 5, 1973–Dec 11, 1974; hist, USSAG/7th AF, Apr–Jun 75, pp x–xiii, 114–115; hist, PACAF, Jul 74–Dec 75, pp 125–126, 470–484; msg, PACAF to USSAG/7th AF, 240230Z May 75.

Chapter XVIII

The Airlift System, 1969–1971

1. News Conference of Jun 19, 1969, and Address to the Nation of Nov 3, 1969, both in *Public Papers of the Presidents, Richard Nixon, 1969* (GPO, 1971), pp 472, 901–909; memo, Melvin Laird, Sec Def, to CJCS, subj: Statement of Mission of US Forces in SEA, Jul 28, 1969.

2. Background paper 12–69, J–3 Joint Staff, subj: Military Situation in SEA, Jan 31, 1969; msg, JCS to CINCPAC, 211941Z Aug 70; Lansdale intvw, Sep 9–10, 1969, pp 101–104; hist, MACV, 1969, pp I-1 through II-13, III-116 through III-134, IV-10 to IV-15, 1971, pp I-1 through I-13, III-3 to III-5.

3. Rprt, Maj Gen John H. Herring, Jr, Cdr 834th AD, EOTR, Jun 71; hist, 834th AD, Jul–Dec 70, pp 12–13; rprts, 834th AD, Management Analysis Off, Tactical Airlift Performance and Accomplishments (TAPA), SEA, Jan 69 through Dec 71; rprts, PACAF, Tactical Airlift Summary, PACAF Rprt 55-2, Dec 69, Dec 70, Feb 71.

4. Rprt, Col Hubert N. Dean, USA, Ch, Transpt Div, MACV J–4, EOTR, Aug 71; USARV Reg 700-14, Airlift Challenge Program, Jun 30, 1969; msg 34583, MACV J–4 to CG USARV, *et al*, 130420Z Jul 70; fact sheet, MACV J–4, subj: Expansion of Military Highway Service within ARVN, Jan 13, 1971; fact sheet, MACV J–4, subj: Transportation, Functional Activities Brief, Mar 27, 1972; hist, MACV, 1969, pp IX-3 to IX-80, 1970, pp IX-4 to IX-19.

5. Ltr, Brig Gen John H. Herring, Cdr 834th AD, to 2nd Aer Port Gp, subj: ALCE/Port Branch Consolidation, Sep

TACTICAL AIRLIFT

21, 1970; ltr, Maj William A. Reese, Dir/Pers, 834th AD, to 7th AF Dir/Manpower & Org, subj: ALCE/Port Branch Consolidation, Aug 20, 1970; ltr, Col Robert T. Byerly, Dir/Ops, 834th AD, to Dir/Ops, 7th AF, subj: Evaluation of TALCEs and Suggested Improvements, Jun 20, 1971; rprt, Herring, EOTR, Jun 71, pp 50–53; hist, 834th AD, Jul–Dec 70, pp 8, 16, Jan–Jun 71, pp 67–68.

6. Ltr, Col William T. Hendricks, Dir/ALCC to 315th TAWg, subj: Mission Commanders, Aug 19, 1970; 834th AD Manual 55–1, Tactical Airlift Operations, Jul 1, 1971, pp 2–2 to 2–6; hist, 463rd TAWg, Jan–Mar 70, pp 25–26; rprt, Herring, EOTR, Jun 71, pp 31–38.

7. Ltr, Col Howard E. Bettis, Cdr, 2nd Aer Port Gp, to 8th Aer Port Sq, subj: Scheduled Cargo Service, Jul 70; rprt, Capt William J. Rohleder, Ch, Freight Br, 2nd Aer Port Gp, Trip Rprt, Jul 20, 1970; rprt, Maj Gen Burl W. McLaughlin, Cdr 834th AD, EOTR, Jun 69; rprt, Herring, EOTR, Jun 71, pp 23–28; rprt, Col Walter G. Lang, Cdr 2nd Aer Port Gp, Jul 71, p 26; rprt, Col Raymond H. Gaylor, Cdr 2nd Aer Port Gp, Jul 72, pp 36–37.

8. Rprt, Brig Gen John H. Germeraad, Cdr 834th AD, subj: User's Evaluation of the ALMS, Oct 31, 1971; hist, 834th AD, Jul 68–Jun 70, pp 87–90, Jul–Dec 70, pp 16–18, Jan–Jun 71, pp 65–67, Jul–Nov 71, pp 51–53; rprt, Herring, EOTR, Jun 71, pp 39–50; rprt, Germeraad, EOTR, Mar 72, pp 14–16, 37; rprt, McLaughlin, EOTR, Jun 69, pp 6–15 to 6–21; study, LTV Electrosystems, Inc, 834th AD TAL Cost Reduction Study, Oct 26, 1967.

9. Ltr, Gen John D. Lavelle, Cdr 7th AF, to Cdr PACAF, subj: Inactivation of the 834th AD, Sep 16, 1971; memo, Brig Gen John H. Herring, Cdr 834th AD, to Gen Clay, Cdr 7th AF, Feb 23, 1971; hist, 834th AD, Jul–Nov 71, pp x, 6–14; PACAF Sp Order G-272, Nov 16, 1971; rprt, Germeraad, EOTR, Mar 72, pp 17–20; hist, 7th AF, Jul–Dec 70, pp 120–121, Jan–Jun 71, pp 176–177, FY 72, pp 191–197; memo, Lt Col Thomas J. Lamb, Ch, Opns Plans Div, 834th AD, to Dir/ALCC, subj: Cd Post Consolidation, Jun 22, 1971.

10. Msg 62635, MACV to CINCPAC, 281253Z Nov 70; msg, CINCPAC to JCS, 150522Z Dec 70; ltr, Brig Gen John H. Herring, Cdr 834th AD to 7th AF, subj: Review of C–130 Airframe Reqmts, Nov 21, 1970; study, Opns Analysis Off, Hq USAF, subj: Use of C–141s for Unit Moves in RVN, Sep 70; ltr, Col Noble F. Greenhill, Cdr 374th TAWg, to Cdr 313th AD, subj: Retention of 374th TAWg Designation in PACAF, Jan 26, 1971; hist, MACV, 1970, vol II, pp IX–27 to IX–31; hist, CINCPAC, 1969, I, 181, 1970, I, 211–212, II, 344–347, 1971, I, 306–309.

11. Rprts, PACAF, Tactical Airlift Summary, Dec 69 and Dec 70; rprt, 834th AD, TAPA, Dec 71; msg, 7th AF to 834th AD, 131100Z Feb 69; hist, 834th AD, Jul 68–Jun 70, p 8, Jul–Dec 70, p 7, Jul–Nov 71, pp 26–27; rprt, Dir/Management Analysis, Hq USAF, USAF Management Summaries, SEA, Apr 72.

12. Hist, 311th Sp Ops Sq, Jul–Sep 69, pp 2–4; hist, 310th TASq, Apr–Jun 72, pp 1–15; hist, 315th Sp Ops Wg/315th TAWg, 1969 through Mar 72; hist, 834th AD, Jul 68–Jun 70, pp 6–8, Jan–Jun 71, pp 6–7, Jul–Nov 71, pp 4–5; rprt, Brig Gen John H. Germeraad, Cdr 834th AD, EOTR, Mar 72; rprt, Col Kenneth T. Blood, Cdr 315th TAWg, EOTR, Nov 26, 1971.

13. Ltr, Col David B. White, Cdr Det 1, 834th AD to Cdr 834th AD, subj: Test of C–130 In-country Opns Using IFR Flight Plans, Sep 14, 1970; hist, 41st TASq, Oct–Dec 70, pp 4–6; ltr, Lt Col Paul R. Zavitz, Asst Dep Ch, Opns, 315th TAWg, to Cdr 310th TASq, subj: Flight Plans, Jun 9, 1971; rprt, Col David B. White, Cdr Det 1, 834th AD, EOTR, Jul 71; 834th AD Manual 55–1, Tactical Airlift Opns, Jul 1, 1971, p 5–1.

14. Rprt, 7th AF, General Inspection of 834th AD, Nov 26, 1968; msg, Maj Gen Gordon F. Blood, 7th AF, to units, subj: Mid-air Collision, 161155Z Nov 68; msg DCO, 7th AF to MACV, 220515Z Mar 68; paper, Capt Anderson E. Hatfield, CCT Op Off, 8th Aerial Port Sq, subj: CCT Operations, Dec 68, pp 2–3; hist, 459th TASq, Jul–Sep 67; rprt, Brig Gen William G. Moore, Cdr 834th AD, EOTR, Nov 67, pp 44–51; Myers intvw, Jan 21, 1969; Crawford intvw, Feb 15, 1969.

15. Fact sheet, 834th AD, Tactical Air Control Joint Study Gp, Sep 68; ltr, Maj Gen Robert R. Williams, Av Off, USARV, to Maj Gen Burl W. McLaughlin, Cdr 834th AD, Oct 2, 1968; msg 35307, C/S MACV to USARV, subj:

Flying Safety, 140155Z Nov 68; MRs, Maj Robert L. Geasland, USAF, and Lt Col James R. Pierce, USA, subj: Minutes of the Joint Air Opns Committee Meeting, Sep 28 and Oct 17, 1968; MR, Maj Charles S. Shipman, subj: Minutes of the Joint Air Opns Gp Meeting, Oct 18 and 20, 1968.

16. MR, Joint Air Opns Gp, subj: Air Traffic Control, Oct 20, 1968; msg, Gen George S. Brown, Cdr 7th AF to Units, subj: Landing at Unsafe Fields, 191115Z Dec 68; MR, Maj Robert L. Geasland, Dir/Opns 834th AD, and Lt Col Louis C. Harris, USA, subj: JAOG Progress Report, Air Traffic Control, Nov 68; MACV Dir no 95-9, Airlift Operations at Airfields in RVN, Apr 29, 1969; rprt, Maj Gen Burl W. McLaughlin, Cdr 834th AD, EOTR, Jun 69, pp 7-4 to 7-9.

17. Rprt, Maj Gen Burl W. McLaughlin, EOTR, Jun 69, pp 7-14 to 7-23; ltr, Brig Gen Leo B. Jones, C/S USARV, to Units, subj: Airfield Opns, Nov 29, 1968; MR, Maj Leonard P. Ponte, USAF, subj: Minutes of Joint Air Opns Gp, Nov 14, 1968.

18. MR, Lt Col Martin M. Bretting, Chairman, Arty Warning Gp, subj: Meeting of Oct 21, 1968; msg 01827, Dir/Opns, 834th AD to Units, subj: Safeguarding Acft from Ground and Artillery Fire, Sep 16, 1967; staff summary sheet, TACC, 7th AF, subj: Artillery Coordination and Warning, Oct 28, 1968; rprt, Maj Gen Burl W. McLaughlin, Cdr 834th AD, EOTR, pp 7-1 to 7-27.

19. Rprt, Brig Gen Kelton M. Farris, Cdr 374th TAWg, EOTR, Jul 70, pp 6-7; ltr, Maj Gen Elias C. Townsend, C/S MACV, to CINCPAC, subj: JAOG, Sep 14, 1969; hist, 7th AF, Jan-Jun 69, pp 112-113; rprt, Herring, EOTR, Jun 71, pp 54-59; rprt, Maj Gen Allan M. Burdett, Jr, Avn Off, USARV and CG 1st Avn Bde, Senior Off Debriefing Rprt, Jan 6, 1970, p 8.

20. Rprt, Herring, EOTR, Jun 71, pp 60-67; rprt, Dir/Construction, MACV, Qtrly Hist Summary, Apr-Jun 70, Jul 24, 1970, p VI-2; msg, Dir/Ops, 834th AD to 483rd TAWg, 110815Z Mar 70; hist, 834th AD, Jul-Dec 70, pp 15-16.

21. Hist, 374th TAWg, Apr-Jun 70, pp 60-63; hist, 315th TAWg, Jan-Mar 70, p 36, Jan-Mar 71, pp 29-31, Oct-Dec 70, pp 31-32, Oct-Dec 69, pp 46-51; rprt, 315th Sp Opns Wg, Safety Summary, 1969; hist, 463rd TAWg, Apr-Jun 70, pp 29-33; hist, 314th TAWg, Jan-Mar 69, pp 52-53, Oct-Dec 69, pp 42-46, Oct-Dec 70, pp 45-48; ltr, Brig Gen John H. Herring, Cdr 834th AD, to Units, subj: Aircraft Accidents, Feb 27, 1971; rprts, 834th AD, TAPA, Jun 70, Dec 70, Nov 71.

22. Hist, 315th AD, Jul 68-Apr 69, I, 212-213; hist, 315th Sp Opns Wg, Jan-Mar 69, pp 13-14, 22, Apr-Jun 69, p 9, Jul-Sep 69, p 17, Oct-Dec 69, pp 27-28; hist, 463rd TAWg, Apr-Jun 69, p 13, Jan-Mar 71, pp 26-27; hist, 374th TAWg, Apr-Jun 69, p 45; hist, 21st TASq, Apr-Jun 69, pp 3-4; rprts, 834th AD, TAPA, Dec 69, Dec 70, Dec 71; rprts, Dir/Management Analysis, Hq USAF, USAF Management Summaries, SEA, 1969 through 1972.

23. Hist, 21st TASq, Apr-Jun 69, pp 4-5; hist, 315th TAWg, Apr-Jun 70, pp 8-10.

24. Rprts, PACAF, Tactical Airlift Summary, Jun 70, pp 8-5 to 8-7; hist, 314th TAWg, Apr-Jun 69, pp 25-26, Jan-Mar 69, pp 28-30, Jul-Sep 69, pp 11-13, Apr-Jun 70, pp 8, 20-21, Oct-Dec 70, pp 21-22, 32, Jan-Mar 71, pp 13-14; hist, 374th TAWg, Jul-Sep 69, p 63, Apr-Jun 70, pp 72-73, Apr-May 71, pp 27-28, Oct-Dec 71, pp 10-11; hist, 463rd TAWg, Jan-Mar 69, pp 4-5, Jul-Sep 69, pp 7-8, Oct-Dec 70, pp 11-12, Jan-Mar 71, pp 49-50, Jul-Dec 71, pp 11-13; rprt, Col Andrew P. Iosue, Cdr 374th TAWg, EOTR, Jul 1, 1973.

25. Rprt, Col Charles S. Reed, Cdr 315th TAWg, EOTR, May 1, 1971; hist, 315th Sp Opns Wg, Jan-Mar 69, pp 4-5, 10-11, Apr-Jun 69, app 3, Oct-Dec 69, pp 9, 22-23, Jul-Sep 70, p 6, Jan-Mar 71, p 16; msg, 315th Sp Opns Wg to 7th AF, 031130Z Mar 69; ltr, Brig Gen John H. Herring, Cdr 834th AD, to Cdr 7th AF, subj: Crew Integrity Program, Dec 10, 1970; rprt, Col Kenneth Blood, EOTR, Nov 26, 1971.

26. Rprts, 834th AD, Tactical Airlift Performance and Accomplishments, SEA, Dec 69, Dec 70, Dec 71; rprt, Col Thomas B. Krieger, DCM, 315th TAWg, EOTR, Aug 70, pp 2-9; memo, Harold Brown, Sec AF, to Asst Sec Def (SA), subj: C-130 Acft Fatigue and Corrosion Problems, Apr 25, 1968.

27. Ltr, Brig Gen John H. Herring, Cdr 834th AD to Cdr 7th AF, subj: C-130 Schedule Reliability, Oct 27, 1970; rprt, Herring, EOTR, Jun 71, pp

139–142; msg, Cdr 7th AF to PACAF, 270800Z Nov 70; hist, 834th AD, Jul–Dec 70, pp 28–32; hist, 314th TAWg, Oct–Dec 70, pp 73–74.

28. Hist, 315th TAWg, Jul–Sep 71, pp 47–51, Oct–Dec 70, pp 38–44, Jan–Mar 71, p 16, Apr–Jun 71, pp 41–42; study, Dir/Safety, 7th AF, subj: Flight Safety, 315th Wing, Jan–Aug 71, Sep 20, 1971, pp 5–8; rprt, Germeraad, EOTR, Mar 72, pp 4–6; rprt, Greene, EOTR, Oct 12, 1971, pp 6–7; rprt, Herring, EOTR, Jun 71, pp 149–150; rprt, Voyles, EOTR, Sep 14, 1971, pp 3–4; rprt, Blood, EOTR, Nov 26, 1971, pp 2–6.

29. Rprt, Col Julius P. Greene, Dir/Materiel, 834th AD, EOTR, Oct 12, 1971; hist, 7th AF, Jul–Dec 69, pp 204–205; rprt, Col J. J. Schneider, Cdr Det 2, 834th AD, Apr 68–May 69, EOTR, pp 11–13, 20; rprt, Krieger, EOTR, Aug 70; rprt, Col Valley J. Voyles, DCM, 315th TAWg, EOTR, Sep 14, 1971.

30. Hist, 314th TAWg, Jan–Mar 69, pp 43–44, Apr–Jun 69, pp 41–42; hist, 834th AD, Jul 68–Jun 70, pp 74–79; rprt, Col Julius P. Greene, Dir/Materiel, 834th AD, EOTR, Oct 12, 1971, pp 8–9; rprt, Col Henry J. Lupa, Dir/Materiel, 834th AD, EOTR, Dec 69; rprt, McLaughlin, EOTR, Jun 69, pp 4–5 to 4–6; rprt, Herring, EOTR, pp 155–159.

31. Clark intvw, Mar 29, 1974; rprt, Iosue, EOTR, Jul 1, 1973, pp 4–9; rprt, Blood, EOTR, Nov 71, pp 7–8; rprt, Maj Gen Donald S. Ross, Cdr 327th AD, EOTR, May 21, 1973, pp 4–5; hist, 374th TAWg, Jun–Sep 71, pp 125–130, Oct–Dec 72, pp 89–95, Apr–Jun 73, pp 119–123, Jul–Nov 73, pp 123–124.

32. Rprt, Lt Col Verus A. Yon, Cdr Det 1, 834th AD, EOTR, Jun 70; rprt, Col J. J. Schneider, Cdr Det 2, 834th AD, EOTR, May 69; rprt, Col David B. White, Cdr Det 1, 834th AD, EOTR, Jul 71, pp 5–7; rprt, Lt Col Edward J. Hughes, 463rd TAWg Liaison Off, Det 2, 834th AD, EOTR, Mar 10, 1971; hist, 311th Sp Opns Sq, Jan–Mar 69, pp 10–11, Jul–Sep 69, pp 17–19; hist, 41st TASq, Jan–Mar 70, p 7; hist, 21st TASq, Jan–Mar 69, p 4, Apr–Jun 69, p 3; hist, 374th TAWg, Jan–Mar 69, p 96, Apr–Jun 69, p 25, Jul–Sep 69, pp 19–22, Apr–Jun 70, pp 7, 29.

33. Rprt, Germeraad, EOTR, Mar 72, p 46; rprt, IG 7th AF, Inspection of 315th SOWg, Nov 12–Dec 6, 1969; hist, 463rd TAWg, Oct–Dec 69, pp 81–82, Jan–Mar 71, p 95, Apr–Jun 71, p 28; hist, 314th TAWg, Jan–Mar 69, pp 19–21, Apr–Jun 69, pp 20–21; hist, 834th AD, Jul–Nov 71, pp vii, 11–12.

34. Msg, 463rd TAWg to 315th AD, 030626Z Mar 69; msg DOOA, 7th AF to 13th AF, 281101Z Jun 69; MR, Lt Col Gerald B. Lane, Ch, Comb Opns, 834th AD, subj: TALAR IV, LAPES, CDS Update as of Jan 31, 1971; hist, 314th TAWg, Jan–Mar 69, pp 48–49, Apr–Jun 69, pp 49–55, Jul–Sep 69, pp 37–38; hist, 374th TAWg, Jun–Sep 71, pp 51–52; rprt, Col Walter G. Lang, Cdr 2nd Aer Port Gp, EOTR, Jul 71, pp 32–33; rprt, Herring, EOTR, Jun 71, pp 71–72.

35. Rprt, Lang, EOTR, Jul 71, p 37; msg, 834th AD to 315th AD, 200731Z Mar 69; msg, PACAF to 7th AF, 142159Z Apr 69.

36. Hist, Dir/Opns, Hq USAF, Jan–Jun 69, pp 193, 257–258, Jul–Dec 69, pp 163–165, Jan–Jun 70, pp 178–179, Jul–Dec 70, pp 143–144, Jul–Dec 72, pp 319–321.

37. Rprt, 834th AD, GRADS Report, Apr 70; 7th AF Opns Order 482-70, Emergency Airdrop Resupply, Jul 1, 1969; hist, 463rd TAWg, Jan–Mar 70, pp 50–53; rprt, Herring, EOTR, Jun 71, pp 75–77; rprt, Col W. S. Freesland, Jr, Cdr Det 2, 834th AD, EOTR, Jun 30, 1971.

38. Rprt, TALC, Monthly Status Report, May 71; rprt, TAWC, Final Rprt, TAC Test 71A-024, TAWC Proj 1126, AWADS High Alt Airdrop, Mar 72; Maj Jimmy D. Carver, 64th TAWg, "AWADS," *The Navigator*, vol XVIII, no 3, 1971; msg, Dir/Opns, 7th AF to PACAF, 240800Z Jun 71; ltr, Maj Gen John H. Herring, Cdr 834th AD, to Dir/Opns, 7th AF, subj: AWADS, Apr 23, 1971; hist, 314th TAWg, Jul–Sep 71, p 26, Oct–Dec 71, pp 26–30, Jan–Mar 72, p 28; hist, Dir/Opns, Hq USAF, Jan–Jun 71, p 309, Jul–Dec 71, pp 263–264, Jan–Jun 72, pp 290–292.

39. Msg DO, 7th AF to 8th TFWg, 090500Z Jul 71; msg, Asst DCS/Opns, 7th AF, to PACAF, 170200Z Aug 71; working paper, Maj William D. Nielson, 16th Sp Opns Sq, subj: Night/IFR Airdrops, n.d., [*ca* Jul 1971].

40. Rprts, TALC, Monthly Status Rprts, Mar 71 and May 71; memo, Maj Leonard W. James, Divis Reqmts Officer, 834th AD, for Col Chapman, subj: Trip Rprt, Nov 8, 1969; MR, Lt Col Gerald

R. Lane, Ch, Comb Opns, 834th AD, subj: TALAR IV, Jan 21, 1971; ltr, Col Robert T. Byerly, Dir/Opns, 834th AD to Cdr 834th AD, subj: TALAR IV, Apr 4, 1971; msg, 463rd TAWg to ASD, 060602Z Oct 71.

41. Hist, 834th AD, Jul–Nov 71, pp 9–14; hist, 2nd Aer Port Gp, Jan–Mar 69, pp 1–3, Jul–Sep 69, p 6, Oct–Dec 70, pp 6–7, Oct–Dec 71, p 34; ltr, Gen John D. Lavelle, Cdr 7th AF, to Cdr PACAF, subj: Inactivation of the 834th AD, Sep 16, 1971; ltr, Brig Gen Peter DeLonga, DCS/Materiel, 7th AF, to XP, 7th AF, subj: Realignment of Airlift Functions Under 7th AF, Sep 3, 1971.

42. Rprt, Col Robert Sunde, Cdr 2nd Aerial Port Gp, Lessons Learned (EOTR), Oct 6, 1969; rprt, Col Howard E. Bettis, Cdr 2nd Aer Port Gp, EOTR, Sep 70, pp 3–4; rprt, Col Walter G. Lang, Cdr 2nd Aer Port Gp, Jul 71, pp 21–24; rprt, Col Raymond H. Gaylor, Cdr 2nd Aer Port Gp, EOTR, Jul 72, pp 24, 56; rprt, Herring, EOTR, Jun 71, pp 110–111; rprts, 834th AD, TAPA, Dec 69, Jun 71, Dec 71; hist, 2nd Aer Port Gp, Jan–Mar 69, pp 12–14, 18–22, Apr–Jun 69, pp 13–14, Jul–Sep 69, p 9.

43. Rprt, Lang, EOTR, Jul 71, pp 41–42; rprt, Gaylor, EOTR, Jul 72, pp 20–23; rprt, Herring, EOTR, pp 116, 126–127; rprt, Bettis, EOTR, Sep 70, p 4; hist, 834th AD, Jul 68–Jun 70, p 49; hist, 2nd Aer Port Gp, Jul–Sep 69, pp 10–12, Oct–Dec 70, pp 29–30, Apr–Jun 71, pp 37–38, Jul–Sep 71, p 33; hist, 8th Aer Port Sq, Jul–Sep 69, pp 10–11, Oct–Dec 70.

44. Hist, 2nd Aer Port Gp, 1969 through 1971; rprt, Herring, EOTR, Jun 71, pp 105–108, 124; rprt, Col Robert Sunde, Cdr 2nd Aer Port Gp, Lessons Learned (EOTR), Oct 6, 1969; rprt, Col Walter G. Lang, Cdr 2nd Aer Port Gp, EOTR, Jul 71, pp 17, 33, 38–40; rprt, Bettis, EOTR, Sep 70, pp 3–6.

45. Hist, 2nd Aer Port Gp, 1969 through 1971; ltr, Brig Gen John W. Germeraad, Cdr 834th AD, to Cdr 7th AF, subj: Drug Traffic on In-country Airlift, Jun 15, 1971; intvw, Capt Joseph Ventolo with Capt Robert T. Mantor, 2nd Aer Port Gp, Jun 14, 1972; rprt, Gaylor, EOTR, Jul 72, pp 27–29.

46. Hist, 15th Aer Port Sq, Jan–Mar 69, p 9, Oct–Dec 69, p 10; *The Vietnam Airlifter* (834th AD publ), Mar 70, p 3; *Di Di Mau* (2nd Aer Port Gp publ), Jan 31, 1970; Mantor intvw, Jun 14, 1972; rprt, Gaylor, EOTR, Jul 72, pp 8–11, 12.

Chapter XIX

The Campaigns of 1969–1971, Cambodia and the Panhandle

1. Rprt, McLaughlin, EOTR, Jun 69, pp I-32 and I-33; rprt, Col Henry J. Lupa, Dir/Materiel, 834th AD, EOTR, Dec 69, pp 7–8; hist, 21st TASq, Jan–Mar 69, pp 4–5; msg, Det 2, 834th AD, to 834th AD, 250751Z Feb 69; hist, 14th Aer Port Sq, Jan–Mar 69, p 2.

2. Rprt, 9th Marines, 3rd Mar Div, Combat Opn After Action Report, Op Dewey Canyon, Apr 8, 1969; rprt, SSgt Trimple, CCT Mission Rprt, A Shau, Aug 28, 1969; news article, "Caribou Lands in A Shau," *The Screaming Eagle*, Jul 7, 1969; hist, MACV, 1969, p V-47; Brig Gen Edwin H. Simmons, USMC, "Marine Corps Opns in Vietnam, 1969–1972," Naval Institute *Proceedings*, May 73, pp 199–200.

3. Rprt, Col Charles G. Weber, Cdr Det 1, 834th AD, EOTR, Dec 69; hist, 374th TAWg, Oct–Dec 69, pp 31–33, 57–58; hist, 817th TASq, Oct–Dec 69, pp 4–5; hist, Oct–Dec 69, pp 3–6; *The Vietnam Airlifter*, Jan 70, p 4.

4. Rprt, Maj Ralph E. Jeffers, Mission Cdr's Rprt, Kham Duc, Aug 70; rprt, Lt Col Byron L. Webber, Mission Cdr Rprt, Aug 24, 1970; rprt, Lt Col Clifton P. Ohman, Mission Cdr Rprt, Aug 29, 1970; rprt, 15th Aer Port Sq, Monthly Status and Activ Rprt, Aug 4, 1970; hist, 315th TAWg, Jul–Sep 70, pp 22–24;

hist, 374th TAWg, Jul–Sep 70, pp 26–27; rprt, 834th AD, TAPA, Dec 70, p A–3a; rprt, 196th Inf Bde, AAR, Elk Canyon I, 1970.

5. Rprt, Col David B. White, Cdr Det 1, 834th AD, EOTR, Jul 71, pp 3, 7–9; rprt, Lt Col Verus A. Yon, Cdr Det 1, 834th AD, EOTR, 1970; 7th AF Oplan 706, Joint Abn Assault Opns, Aug 15, 1970; rprt, 834th AD, Tact Airlift Perf and Analysis, SEA, Dec 70, sect A–3c; hist, 834th AD, Jul–Dec 70, pp 19–20, Jan–Jun 71, p 19, Jul–Nov 71, pp 24–25.

6. Hist, 315th Sp Opns Wg, Oct–Dec 69, pp 3–5; rprt, Dir/Opns Support, DCS/Opns, 7th AF, Hist Data Rprt, Jul–Sep 71; 834th AD OPLAN 442–69, Airdrop Resupply, Apr 24, 1969; ltr, Maj Gen W. G. Dolvin, C/S MACV, to Lt Gen William J. McCaffrey, Dep CG USARV, Aug 6, 1970; MR, Lt Col Gerald B. Lane, Ch, Comb Opns, 834th AD, subj: TALAR IV, LAPES, CDS Update as of Jan 31, 1971; fact sheet, MACV, subj: MACV OPLAN J–199, Mar 29, 1972; rprts, 834th AD, TAPA, Dec 69, Dec 70, Jun 71.

7. Hist, Dir/Plans, Hq USAF, Jan–Jun 71, pp 261–262, Jul–Dec 71, pp 233–234; rprts, Hq PACAF, Summary Air Opns, SEA, May 69, Jun 69, Feb 72, May 72; memo, Stanley R. Reson, Sec Army, to Sec Def, subj: Formation of the TRICAP Div, Jan 15, 1971; msg, JCS to CINCPAC, 111353Z Aug 71; hist, MACV, 1971, vol I, pp VI–3 to VI–4; rprt, USARV Avn Sect, Army Aviation in Vietnam, FY 69, 1969, pp 33–50.

8. Rprt, 1st Cav Div (Airm), Comb Opns AAR (Cambodia Campaign), Jul 18, 1970; hist, MACV, 1970, vol III, Sect C; Maj D. I. Folkman and Maj P. D. Caine, *The Cambodian Campaign, 29 Apr–30 Jun 70* (Hq PACAF, Proj CHECO, Sep 1, 1970), pp 1–33.

9. Rprt, US Army Support Cd, Saigon, Opl Rprt, Lessons Learned, Pd Ending Jul 31, 1970, Aug 24, 1970; ltr, Cdr II FFV to Cdr MACV, subj: II FFV Cdr Evaluation Rprt, Cambodian Opns, Jul 31, 1970; hist, MACV, 1970, pp C–117 to C–128.

10. Ltr, Abn Div Advis Det to MACV, subj: Qtrly Hist Rprt, Apr–Jun 70, Jul 20, 1970; rprt, 1st Cav Div (Airm), Opl Rprt Lessons Learned, Pd Ending Jul 31, 1970, Aug 14, 1970; rprt, 1st Cav Div (Airm), Comb Ops AAR (Cambodia Campaign), Jul 18, 1970; Lt Gen John J. Tolson, *Airmobility, 1961–1971* (Dept Army Vietnam Studies, 1973), pp 218–233; rprt, Logis Readiness Center, 1st Log Cd, Summary of Activities 05066H to 060600H May 70; rprt, Col Howard E. Bettis, Cdr 2nd Aer Port Gp, EOTR, Nov 20, 1970; hist, 8th Aer Port Sq, Apr–Jun 70.

11. Rprt, Lt Col J. C. Bounds, Mission Cdr Rprt, DJAMAP, May 31, 1970; hist, 8th Aer Port Sq, Apr–Jun 70; rprt, Lt Col Verus A. Yon, Cdr Det 1, 834th AD, EOTR, 1970; rprt, Col Howard E. Bettis, Cdr 2nd Aer Port Gp, EOTR, Nov 20, 1970, p 7; *The Vietnam Airlifter,* Jun 70, p 6.

12. Rprt, Maj Dale, Mission Cdr Rprt, DJAMAP, Jun 10, 1970; rprt, Lt Col J. C. Bounds, Mission Cdr Rprt, DJAMAP, May 31, 1970; ltr, Cdr II FFV to Cdr MACV, subj: II FFV Cdr Eval Rprt—Cambodia Operations, Jul 31, 1970; rprt, 1st Cav Div (Airm), Comb Ops AAR (Cambodia Campaign), Jul 18, 1970, Annex G.

13. Rprt, 834th AD, Summary of Support for Cambodia Opns, Jun 4, 1970; rprt, Autom Systems Div, 834th AD, Summary of 834th AD Support for Cambodian Opns, Oct 2, 1970; hist, CINCPAC, 1970, II, 136–138; rprt, 1st Cav Div (Airm), Comb Opns AAR (Cambodia Campaign), Jul 18, 1970.

14. Hist, 41st TASq, Apr–Jun 70, pp 6–7; rprt, Maj Dale, Mission Cdr Rprt, DJAMAP, Jun 10, 1970; ltr, Cdr II FFV to Cdr MACV, subj: II FFV Cdr Eval Rprt—Cambodia Opns, Jul 31, 1970; intvw, Col Avery, MACV Mil Hist Br, with Maj Gen Raymond C. Conroy, MACV J–4, Jul 3, 1970.

15. Rprt, Autom Systems Div, 834th AD, Summary of 834th Support for Cambodian Opns, Oct 2, 1970; rprt, 4th Inf Div, Comb Opns AAR, Binh Tay I, Jul 21, 1970; rprt, 22nd Inf Div Advisory Det, Comb Opns AAR (Binh Tay I), Jun 13, 1970; rprt, 22nd Inf Div Advisory Det, Comb Opns AAR (Binh Tay II), Jun 19, 1970.

16. Rprt, MACV Advisory Team 22, AAR Binh Tay IV, Jun 28, 1970; msg 1229, CG I FFV to COMUSMACV, 211100Z Jun 70; hist, 483rd TAWg, Apr–Jun 70, p 10; hist, 834th AD, Jul 68–Jun 70, pp 32–33; rprt, Autom Systems Div, 934th AD, Summary of 834th AD Support for Cambodian Opns, Oct 2, 1970, pp 4–6; hist, MACV, 1970, Annex B, p

B-III-11; msg 30062, MACV to CINCPAC, 190145Z Jun 70; msg 30501, MACV to USARV, 210401Z Jun 70.

17. Msg, MACV to JCS, 190022Z Jun 70; hist, MACV, 1970, vol III, sect C, pp C57–C63, C93–C97, C108–C109; Conroy intvw, Jul 3, 1970; rprt, Autom Systems Div, 834th AD, Summary of 834th AD Support for Cambodian Opns, Oct 2, 1970; rprt, US Army Support Cd, Saigon, Opl Rprt Lessons Learned, Pd Ending 31 Jul 70, Aug 24, 1970.

18. Rprt, Automated Systems Div, 834th AD, Summary of 834th AD Support for Cambodian Opns, Oct 2, 1970; msg FCV 750, Maj Gen Casey, CG 1st Cav Div, to Brig Gen Herring, 834th AD, 181315Z May 70; rprt, 1st Cav Div (Airm), Comb Ops AAR (Cambodia Campaign), Jul 18, 1970; Lt Gen John J. Tolson, *Airmobility*, p 218.

19. Conroy intvw, Jul 3, 1970; memo, Col L. K. Nesselbush, USAF, Ch, Transp Div, MACV J-45, for Dir/ALCC, subj: Special VNAF Support Missions, Aug 25, 1970; hist, 7th AF, Jan–Jun 70, p 512; hist, MACV, 1970, vol III, pp C108–C128; hist, MACV, 1970, vol IV, p TSS–36.

20. Rprt, Maj Gen Raymond C. Conroy, USA, MACV J-4, EOTR, 1970; hist, Dir/Opns, Hq USAF, Jan–Jun 70, p 249; rprt, Autom Systems Div, 834th AD, Summary of 834th AD Support for Cambodian Opns, Oct 2, 1970, pp 3–4.

21. Rprt, Brig Gen Theodore C. Mataxis, Ch, MEDTC, EOTR, Feb 12, 1972; Conroy intvw, Jul 3, 1970; msg 0849, CJCS to CINCPAC, MACV, 152221Z Jun 70; rprt, CINCPAC/MACV Conf on Cambodia, May 71, Assessment of Enemy Situation, May 23, 1971; memo, JCS to Sec Def, subj: Review of Cambodia Plans and Programs, Aug 30, 1971.

22. JCSM 582–70, JCS to Sec Def, subj: Transportation of Cambodia MAP Equipment, Dec 23, 1970; hist, MACV, 1970, vol IV, p TSS–61; hist, 314th TAWg, Oct–Dec 70, p 27; rprt, Col Senour Hunt, Ch, AFAT 5, EOTR, Dec 30, 1970; fact sheet, MACV, subj: FWMAF Transportation Support of Khmer Republic, Mar 15, 1972; msg 60004, MACV J-45 to CINCPAC, 151524Z Nov 70; msg, CINCPAC to JCS, 191339Z Nov 70; msg, CINCPAC to MACV, 200441Z Jan 71.

23. Tabulation, 834th AD, Cambodian MAP Airlift FY 71, 1971; rprt, AFGP, VNAF Status Review, Dec 71; fact sheet, MACV J-4, subj: Transportation Functional Activities Brief, Mar 27, 1972; rprt, Brig Gen Theodore C. Mataxis, Ch MEDTC, EOTR, Feb 72; msg DO/LG, 7th AF to MACV, 312245Z Dec 71; fact sheet, 7th AF, subj: 7th AF Activities Supporting MEDTC and DRAF, May 71; intvw, author with Brig Gen Andrew P. Iosue, Hq USAF, Mar 25, 1975 (Iosue was Cdr, 374th TAWg, during period May 71–May 73).

24. Msg, 7th AF ALCC to units, 250810Z Jan 72; rprt, Brig Gen Theodore C. Mataxis, Ch, MEDTC, Feb 72.

25. Hist, 314th TAWg, Apr–Jun 70, pp 28–29; msgs, 7th AF to CJCS, 060340Z Aug 70 and 070407Z Aug 70; msg, CINCPAC to JCS, 261829Z Aug 70; rprt, RVNAF JGS J-3, Battlefield Experience Slip, Toan Thang 1/71, subj: Withdrawal from Seoul, Jul 71; rprt, Maj Gen Jack J. Wagstaff, Cdr TRAC, Debriefing Rprt, Dec 14, 1971; hist, 374th TAWg, Oct–Dec 71, pp 56–59; hist, 834th AD, Jul–Nov 71, pp 20–21.

26. Rprt, Asst for Mutual Security, DCS/S and L, Hq USAF, *Journal of Military Assistance*, Aug 70, pp 105–107, Apr 71, pp 110–114; msg, USDAO, Phnom Penh to JCS/DIA, 051140Z Feb 72; memo, atchd to JCSM 453–72, JCS to Sec Def, subj: Acft for Laos, Thailand, and Cambodia, Oct 20, 1972; hist, CINCPAC, 1970, II, 262–264, 1971, II, 380–387.

27. 7th AF OPLAN 5060B, Eagle Pull, Dec 15, 1971; background paper, Col James Cronin, 7th AF Dir/Plans, subj: Cambodian Planning, Dec 5, 1970; msg 34729, MACV to CINCPAC, 131340Z Jul 70; msg, MACV to USARV, 150300Z Jan 72.

28. Msg, JCS to CINCPAC, 211941Z Aug 70; msg 1475, JCS to CINCPAC, 192121Z Jan 71; msgs 15603 and 15808, Abrams, MACV to McCain, CINCPAC, 071130Z Dec 70 and 120952Z Dec 70; JCS 2344/132, JCS paper, subj: Operations, Laos, Aug 15, 1967; MR, Mil Hist Br, MACV, subj: Background Synopsis of Tiger Hound, Jul 11, 1966; Westmoreland, *A Soldier Reports*, pp 271–272, 314.

29. Hq XXIV Corps Opord Lam Son 719, Jan 23, 1971; Lt Gen John J. Tolson, *Airmobility*, pp 235–240; msg 15808, Abrams, MACV, to CINCPAC, 120952Z

Dec 70; msg, CG XXIV Corps to COMUSMACV, 021015Z Feb 71; msg, CG XXIV Corps to COMUSMACV, 031400Z Feb 71.

30. Intvw, Col John F. Loye and Maj G. St. Clair with Col Carlton E. Schutt, Dep Dir/Opns for Airlift, 834th AD, Mar 19, 1971; paper, 834th AD, subj: Lam Son 719 and Dewey Canyon II, 1971; hist, 314th TAWg, Jan–Mar 71, pp 17–18; hist, 463rd TAWg, Jan–Mar 71, p 34; worksheets, 834th AD, Lam Son 719 Mission Traffic by date, Jan–Feb 71; ltr, Lt Col Robert W. Taylor, Ch, Support Opns, 834th AD, to DOLS, 834th AD, subj: Lam Son 719, Mar 71.

31. Hist, 8th Aer Port Sq, Jan–Mar 71; ltr, Col Clayton J. Johnson, Cdr 8th Aer Port Sq, to 2nd Aer Port Gp, subj: Lam Son 719, Apr 3, 1971; Schutt intvw, Mar 19, 1971; memo, Capt Frederick L. Riggle, Airfield Survey Sect, 834th AD, to Dir/Opns, 834th AD, subj: Lam Son 719 Summary, Mar 71; rprt, TALO Div, 834th AD, subj: LS 719 Summary, 26 Jan–15 Mar 71, Mar 31, 1971; hist, MACV, 1971, vol II, p E20; rprt, Dep Dir/Materiel, 834th AD, subj: LS 719 Summary, Mar 30, 1971.

32. Hist, 834th AD, Jan–Jun 71, pp 29, 40–47; Schutt intvw, Mar 19, 1971; worksheets, 834th AD, Lam Son 719 Mission Traffic by date, Feb 71; Maj Ronald D. Merrell, *Tactical Airlift in SEA* (PACAF, Proj CHECO, Feb 15, 1972), pp 47–52; rprt, Col Arthur W. Pence, C/S 1st Avn Bde, AAR Lam Son 719, 12 Jan–28 Feb 71, Apr 1, 1971; ltr, Lt Col John A. Malcolm, Dir/Opns, Det 1, 834th AD, subj: Lam Son 719, Mar 31, 1971; rprt, White, EOTR, Jul 71, p 4.

33. XXIV Corps OPORD Lam Son 719, Jan 23, 1971; rprt, US Army Support Command, Da Nang, AAR, Lam Son 719, 1971; rprt, XXIV Corps, AAR Lam Son 719, May 14, 1971; msg, MACV to CINCPAC, 011210Z Feb 71; hist, MACV, 1971, vol II, pp E–15 to E–45.

34. Msgs, MACV to CINCPAC, 302225Z Jan 71, 01125Z Feb 71, 050755Z Feb 71; rprt, XXIV Corps, AAR Lam Son 719, Annex K, May 14, 1971; Schutt intvw, Mar 19, 1971.

35. Rprt, US Army Support Command, Da Nang, AAR Lam Son 719, 1971, p 46; rprt, XXIV Corps, AAR Lam Son 719, May 14, 1971, Annex N; msg, MACV to CINCPAC, 110745Z Feb 71; Brig Gen Edwin H. Simmons, USMC, "Marine Corps Opns in Vietnam, 1969–72," Naval Institute *Proceedings*, May 73, pp 217–218.

36. Rprt, US Army Support Command, Da Nang, AAR Lam Son 719, 1971, Annex G–1; worksheets, 834th AD, Lam Son 719 Mission Traffic by date, Feb 71.

37. Msgs, MACV to CINCPAC, 060645Z, 080840Z, 090950Z, 110745Z, 131530Z, 150615Z, 161140Z, 190153Z, and 200545Z Feb 71; worksheets, 834th AD, Lam Son 719 Mission Traffic by date, Feb 71; rprt, US Army Support Command, Da Nang, Lam Son 719, 1971, Annex H; msg, Vice Cdr 834th AD, Da Nang, to Cdr 834th AD, 151410Z Feb 71.

38. Msgs, MACV to CINCPAC, 210700Z, 211531Z, 221440Z, 231440Z, 251551Z, and 281540Z Feb 71; rprt, US Army Support Command, Da Nang, AAR Lam Son 719, 1971, Annex G–1; worksheets, 834th AD, Lam Son 719 Mission Traffic by date, Feb 71.

39. Ltr, Col Clayton J. Johnson, Cdr 8th Aer Port Sq to 2nd Aer Port Gp, subj: Lam Son 719, Apr 3, 1971; rprt, TALO Div, 834th AD, Lam Son 719 Summary, 26 Jan–15 Mar 71, TALOs, Mar 31, 1971; rprt, Dep Dir/Materiel, 834th AD to Dir/Opns, 834th AD, Lam Son 719 Summary, Mar 30, 1971; memo, A/F Survey Sect, 834th AD, to Dir/Opns 834th AD, Lam Son 719 Summary, Mar 71; ltr, Lt Col Robert W. Taylor, Ch, Support Opns, 834th AD to DOLS, 834th AD, subj: Lam Son 719, Mar 71; rprt, Lt Col Edward J. Hughes, 463rd TAWg Liaison Off, Det 2, 834th AD, EOTR, Mar 10, 1971; hist, 8th Aer Port Sq, Jan–Mar 71; hist, 834th AD, Jan–Jun 71, pp 29, 49–53; Schutt intvw, Mar 19, 1971; ltr, Col Albert W. Jones, Vice Cdr, 834th AD, to 7th AF DOAC, subj: Proj CHECO Rprt Lam Son 719, May 11, 1971.

40. Intvw, Ken Sams and Maj G. St. Clair with Maj Alan Winkenhofer, MACV J–3–06, Apr 4, 1971; Tolson, *Airmobility*, pp 240–242; msgs, MACV to CINCPAC, 161140Z and 260605Z Feb 71; msgs, MACV to CJCS, 141435Z, 251200Z, and 261400Z Feb 71; msg, XXIV Corps to MACV, 121144Z Feb 71.

41. Msgs, XXIV Corps (Sutherland) to COMUSMACV, 021420Z and 051155Z

Mar 71; msgs, MACV to CINCPAC, 081130Z and 041345Z Mar 71; msg, MACV to CJCS, 061010Z Mar 71.

42. Msg, XXIV Corps (Sutherland) to COMUSMACV, 111145Z Mar 71; msgs, MACV to CINCPAC, 121535Z and 130635Z Mar 71; worksheets, 834th AD, Lam Son 719 Mission Traffic by date, Mar 71; rprt, US Army Support Command, Da Nang, AAR Lam Son 719, 1971.

43. Rprt, XXIV Corps, AAR Lam Son 719, May 14, 1971, Annex K; Schutt intvw, Mar 19, 1971; intvw, Proj CHECO with Col George H. Howell, Dir/DASC, Quang Tri, Mar 10, 1971; msgs, MACV to CINCPAC, 010610Z and 091450Z Mar 71; msg, XXIV Corps to MACV, 111145Z Mar 71.

44. Ltr, Col Clayton J. Johnson, Cdr 8th Aer Port Sq, to 2nd Aer Port Gp, subj: Lam Son 719 (16 Mar–15 Apr 71), Apr 23, 1971; rprt, Lt Col John S. Hardwick, Ch Airlift Control Elms, 834th AD, Lam Son 719 Summary, Mar 25, 1971; rprt, Dep Dir/Materiel, 834th AD to Dir/Opns, 834th AD, subj: Lam Son 719 Summary, Mar 30, 1971; hist, 834th AD, Jan–Jun 71, p 50; *Air Force Times,* Apr 14, 1971, p 22.

45. Schutt intvw, Mar 19, 1971; worksheets, 834th AD, Lam Son 719 Mission Traffic by date, Mar 71; msgs, MACV to CINCPAC, 121535Z and 130635Z Mar 71; rprt, US Army Support Cd, Da Nang, AAR Lam Son 719, 1971.

46. Schutt intvw, Mar 19, 1971, briefing sheet, 834th AD, subj: Tabat-A Shau Aerial Resupply Corridor, n.d., [ca 1971]; rprt, 7th AF, Lam Son 719 Opns, Lessons Learned, May 9, 1971, p 17; ltr, Col Albert W. Jones, Vice Cdr 834th AD, to 7th AF DOAC, subj: Proj CHECO Rprt, Lam Son 719, 30 Jan–24 Mar 71, May 11, 1971; ltr, Lt Col Gerald R. Lane, Ch, Comb Opns, 834th AD, to Dir/Opns, 834th AD, subj: Lam Son 719 Summary, Mar 71.

47. Memo, Lt Col Fred E. Kelly, Inter-Svc Liaison Gp, DCO, Hq USAF, to AF/XOD, subj: Final Rprt—Airmobile Opns in Support of Op Lam Son 719, 8 Feb–6 Apr 71, n.d.; fact sheet, USARV, subj: Helicopters in AAA Environment, Mar 71; rprt, XXIV Corps, AAR Lam Son 719, May 14, 1971, Annex H; rprt, 101st Abn Div (Airm), Airmobile Opns in Support of Lam Son 719, 8 Feb–6 Apr 71, May 1, 1971; study, DCS/Intell, 7th AF, subj: Lam Son 719, 1971; msg, CG XXIV Corps to COMUSMACV, 281410Z Feb 71; msg, MACV J–3 to CINCPAC, 180710Z May 71.

48. Rprt, US Army Support Command, Da Nang, AAR, Lam Son 719, 1971, Annex G–1, pp 22–23.

49. Hist, 834th AD, Jan–Jun 71, pp 40–59.

50. Study, Bur Intell & Research, Dept/State, subj: Vietnam, The Communist Response to Lam Son 719, May 4, 1971; rprt, XXIV Corps, AAR Lam Son 719, May 14, 1971, pp 101–102; Tolson, *Airmobility,* pp 235–252.

51. Rprt, CINCPAC/MACV Conf on Cambodia, May 71, Assessment of Enemy Situation, May 23, 1971; JCS 2472/773–9, JCS Paper, subj: US Redeployment from the RVN, Mar 22, 1972; hist, MACV, 1971, vol I, pp II–2 and II–3; memo, Melvin Laird, Sec Def, to JCS, subj: US Force Planning, SEA, Aug 26, 1971; memo, Melvin Laird, Sec Def, to CJCS, subj: US Redeployments from the RVN, Feb 24, 1972.

Chapter XX

The Caribou Force, 1969–1972

1. Rprt, Col Wilbert Turk, Cdr 483rd TAWg, EOTR, Aug 18, 1969, p 12; msg DOS, 834th AD to 315th TAWg, *et al,* 180641Z Jun 70; rprt, 7th AF, Qtrly Rprt on 1970 Combined Campaign Plan, Jul–Sep 70; hist, 834th AD, Jul 68–Jun 70, pp 5–6, Jul–Dec 70, p 5; hist, 483rd TAWg, Qtrly, 1969 through 1970.

2. Rprt, Herring, EOTR, Jun 71; rprt, Turk, EOTR, Aug 18, 1961, pp 11–12; 483rd TAWg OPORD 70-5, Dec 1, 1970.

3. Position paper, PACAF, subj: Characteristics of Dedicated User Acft, Nov 69; rprt, Opns Analysis, Hq USAF, Short Airfield Utilization in SVN, Aug 69; summary paper, Analysis of Conclusions Reached in 834th AD/7th AF Analysis of C-7A Dedicated User Opns, Jan–Aug 69; rprt, Turk, EOTR, Aug 18, 1969; rprt, Col William A. Ulrich, Dep Cdr Materiel, 483rd TAWg, EOTR, Mar 6, 1970, p 3; rprt, Col Leslie J. Greenwood, DCO, 483rd TAWg, EOTR, Sep 14, 1969; rprt, Col John M. Bennett, MACV Dir/Transp, J-45, EOTR, Oct 69; hist, 834th AD, Jul 68–Jun 70, pp 16–17.

4. Tabulation, 483rd TAWg, Mission Data for Jan 69; rprt, MACV J-4, LOGSUM 1-70 for Jan 70; rprt, Greenwood, EOTR, Sep 14, 1969, pp 5–7; hist, 483rd TAWg, Jan–Mar 70.

5. Rprt, AFCVSB-P, Hq USAF, Rprt of Airlift Panel Mtg 69-11, May 23, 1969; msg 18216, MACV to 7th AF, 170850Z Apr 71; memo, Brig Gen Richard L. Ault, Dep Dir/Plans, Hq USAF, to Dir/Doct, Concepts, Obj, Hq USAF, subj: Dedicated Airlift Opns, May 27, 1970; hist, 483rd TAWg, Oct–Dec 70, pp 14–15; rprt, Herring, EOTR, Jun 71, p 93; rprt, Col Rodney H. Newbold, Cdr 483rd TAWg, EOTR, Feb 72.

6. Hist, 483rd TAWg, Qtrly, 1969 through 1971; ltr, 8th Aer Port Sq, to 2nd Aer Port Gp, subj: Monthly Activities, Nov 5, 1970, p 4; hist, 834th AD, Jul–Dec 70, p 13.

7. Rprt, I FFV, AAR, ARVN Op Dan Quyen, 24 Apr–5 Jun 69, Jun 24, 1969; Ernie S. Montagliani, *The Siege of Ben Het*, (PACAF, Proj CHECO, Oct 1, 1969), pp 1–16; hist, MACV, 1969, Annex H, pp 1–11.

8. Ltr and MR, Lt Col John H. Wigington to author, subj: Resupply Airdrop Support—Ben Het, Aug 1, 1974; ltr, Lt Col Henry L. Jones, TALO, I FFV, to Cdr 483rd TAWg, subj: Direct Combat Support for Ben Het Sp F Camp, Mar 2, 1969; rprt, McLaughlin, EOTR, Jun 69; hist, 457th TASq, Apr–Jun 69, p 9; hist, 483rd TAWg, Apr–Jun 69, p 14; Montagliani, *Siege of Ben Het*, pp 1–16.

9. Ltr and MR, Wigington to author, Aug 1, 1974; hist, MACV, 1969, pp IX–85 to IX–86, H–1 to H–3; rprt, Greenwood, EOTR, Sep 14, 1969, p 6; rprt, Turk, EOTR, Aug 18, 1969, p 16; MR, Lt Col John J. Trankovich, G–3 Air, I FFV, subj: Suppressive Fire Support for Caribou Acft on Ben Het Resupply Missions, Jun 21, 1969; study, Col Thomas M. Crawford, Jr, Tactical Air Support and the Battle of Ben Het, AWC Study 4029, May 70, pp 36–38.

10. MR, Lt Col John J. Trankovich, G–3 Air, I FFV, subj: Suppressive Fire Support for Caribou Acft on Ben Het Resupply Missions, Jun 21, 1969; ltr and MR, Wigington to author, Aug 1, 1974; article, "The Siege of Ben Het," *Air Force and Space Digest*, Aug 69, pp 48–49; rprt, Turk, EOTR, 18 Aug 69, p 16; rprt, Greenwood, EOTR, Sep 14, 1969, p 6; hist, 457th TASq, Apr–Jun 69, pp 8–9; hist, 4893rd TAWg, Apr–Jun 69, pp 14–15; study, Crawford, Tact Air Support and the Battle of Ben Het, AWC Study 4029, May 70, pp 36–38.

11. Rprt, Col Roger P. Larivee, Mission Cdr, Report of Dak Seang Aerial Resupply Opn, 1–12 Apr 70; Col J. F. Loye and Maj L. J. Johnson, *The Defense of Dak Seang*, (PACAF, Proj CHECO, Feb 15, 1971); rprt, 22nd Div Fwd Advis Team 24, AAR Battle of Dak Seang, May 30, 1970.

12. Rprt, Larivee, Dak Seang Aer Resupply Opn, 1–12 Apr 70; fact sheet, 483rd TAWg, subj: Dak Seang Air Resupply Opns, 1–10 Apr 70; hist, 537th TASq, Apr–Jun 70, p 4.

13. Briefing text, 7th AF, subj: Dak Seang Summary of 1 Apr and 2 Apr; msg, 483rd TAWg to JCS, 020310Z Apr 70; msg, II DASC to 7th AF, 081145Z Apr 70; hist, 537th TASq, Apr–Jun 70, pp 5–6; rprt, Larivee, Dak Seang Aer Resupply Opn, 1–12 Apr 70; fact sheet, 483rd TAWg, subj: Dak Seang Air Resupply Opns, 1–10 Apr 70.

14. Msg DO, 834th AD to 314th TAWg, 071010Z Apr 70; rprt, Lt Col Verus A. Yon, Cdr Det 1, 834th AD, EOTR, Jun 70.

15. Msg, Col Scott G. Smith, Pleiku, to 7th AF TACD, 091630Z Apr 70; hist, 537th TASq, Apr–Jun 70; Lt Col Jack S. Ballard, *The USAF in SEA: Development and Employment of Fixed-wing Gunships, 1962–1971*, (Off/AF Hist, Jan 74), pp 281–282; rprt, Larivee, Dak Seang Aer Resupply Opn, 1–12 Apr 71;

fact sheet, 483rd TAWg, subj: Dak Seang Air Resupply Opns, 1–10 Apr 1970.

16. Msg, Col Scott C. Smith, Pleiku, to 7th AF TACD, 091630Z Apr 70; draft msg, Col Scott G. Smith, Pleiku, to 7th AF, 151605Z Apr 70; hist, 537th TASq, Apr–Jun 70.

17. Memo, Col Roy L. DeRose, Dir/Intell-Sierra, to TACD, 7th AF, subj: Anti-aircraft Ground Fire History for the Combat Loss of a C-7A, 4 Apr 70, Apr 10, 1970; msg, Col Scott C. Smith, Pleiku, to 7th AF TACD, 091630Z Apr 70; rprt, Larivee, Dak Seang Aer Resupply Opn, 1–12 Apr 70.

18. Rprt, Herring, EOTR, Jun 71, pp 19–20, 72–74; rprt, 834th AD, Tact Airlift Performance & Analysis, SEA, Jun 70, pp A3a and A3b; msg, Col Scott G. Smith, Pleiku, to 7th AF TACD, 091630Z Apr 70; hist, 458th TASq, Apr–Jun 70, p 6; hist, 457th TASq, Apr–Jun 70, pp 4–5; rprt, Larivee, Dak Seang Aer Resupply Opn, 1–12 Apr 70; Loye and Johnson, *Defense of Dak Seang*, Feb 15, 1971.

19. Rprt, Greenwood, EOTR, Sep 14, 1969, p 7; rprt, Turk, EOTR, Aug 18, 1969, pp 3–7, 13–14.

20. Hist, 483rd TAWg, Qtrly, 1969 through 1971; rprt, 834th AD, TAPA, SEA, Dec 69, Dec 70, Nov 71; rprts, Dir/Management Analysis, Hq USAF, USAF Management Summaries, SEA, 1969 through 1971.

21. Hist, 483rd TAWg, Qtrly, 1969 through 1971, Jan 19, 1973, p 32; rprt, Turk, EOTR, Aug 18, 1969, p 8; rprt, Col Henry J. Lupa, Dir/Mat, 834th AD, Dec 69, pp 3–4; hist, 463rd TAWg, Jul–Sep 69, p 19; hist, 483rd TAWg, Qtrly, 1969 through 1971.

22. Hist, 483rd TAWg, Jul–Sep 69, pp 12–13; publication, *Tacfacts*, Jul 1, 1969; rprt, Turk, EOTR, pp 3–15; rprt, Greenwood, EOTR, pp 3–7.

23. Hist, 483rd TAWg, Oct–Dec 70, p 13, Jan–Mar 69, pp 22, 28, Jul–Sep 69, pp 10–11; *The Vietnam Airlifter*, Sep 71; rprt, Turk, EOTR, Aug 18, 1969, pp 7–11; rprt, Greenwood, EOTR, Sep 14, 1969, p 4; news release, SAFOI, Feature 6-6-69-132F, "Caribou Engineer Logs 3,000 Combat Missions," Jun 69.

24. Hists, 483rd TAWg, 1969 through 1971; rprt, Col William A. Ulrich, Dep Cdr Materiel, 483rd TAWg, EOTR, Mar 6, 1970; rprt, Col Julius P. Green, Dir/Materiel, 834th AD, EOTR, Oct 12, 1971; rprt, Turk, EOTR, Aug 18, 1969, pp 5–21; rprt, Herring, EOTR, Jun 71, pp 150–154; rprt, Col Alfred S. Hess, Dep Cdr Materiel, 483rd TAWg, EOTR, Feb 8, 1971; ltr, Ogden AMA to Dir/Mat, PACAF, subj: C-7A Landing Gear Malfunctions, Oct 2, 1969.

25. Rprt, Newbold, EOTR, Feb 72, pp 12–18; rprt, Turk, EOTR, Aug 18, 1969, pp 5, 11–12; hist, 483rd TAWg, Jan–Mar 69, pp 49–51, 58, Jan–Mar 70, p 31, Jan–Mar 71, p 24, Apr–May 72, p 11; hist, 457th TASq, Jan–Mar 69, pp 18–19.

26. Hist, 483rd TAWg, Qtrly, 1971 through 1972; hist, 7th AF, FY 72, pp 3–42; PACAF SO G-217, Aug 26, 1971.

27. Hist, 483rd TAWg, Jul–Sep 71, p 14, Oct–Dec 71, p 9; rprt, Dir/Opns Support, 7th AF, Hist Data Record, Jul–Sep 71; rprt, Dir/Transp, 7th AF Hist Data Record, Jul–Sep 71 and Oct–Dec 71; hist, 834th AD, Jul–Nov 71, pp 39–40; rprt, Brig Gen John H. Germeraad, Cdr 834th AD, EOTR, Mar 72, p 26.

28. Rprt, Newbold, EOTR, Feb 72, pp 2–4; memo, Brig Gen John H. Germeraad, Cdr 834th AD, to Gen Lavelle, Cdr 7th AF, subj: Elimination of Bien Hoa C-7 OL, Oct 29, 1971; ltr, Brig Gen John H. Germeraad, Dir/Airlift 7th AF, to AFGP, subj: USAF C-7A Airlift Resources vs Workload, Feb 7, 1972; hist, 834th AD, Jul–Nov 71, pp 45–46; 7th AF PAD 72-7-7, 457th TASq, Feb 22, 1972; 7th AF PAD 72-7-8, 458th TASq, Jan 21, 1972; hist, 483rd TAWg, Jan–Mar 72, p v, Apr–May 72, pp v, 9–10.

29. Ltr, Col John I. Daniel, DCO 483rd TAWg, to Dir/Opns, 377th ABWg, subj: C-7 Operations, Feb 29, 1972; msgs, Hq USAF (PRPL) to PACAF, 281541Z Sep 72; ltr, Brig Gen Eugene L. Hudson, ACS/Opns, 7th AF, to Dir/Opns, 377th ABWg, subj: C-7A Acft Available and Utilization, May 13, 1972; hist, 310th TAWg, Apr–Jun 72; hist, 834th AD, Jul–Nov 71, p 33.

30. Comments, Gen William Momyer, USAF Ret, Review of Tactical Airlift ms, 1975.

Chapter XXI

The Easter Offensive—The Battle of An Loc

1. Rprt, Off/Asst Sec Def (SA), Battle Prospects in the MR 2 Highlands, *SEA Analysis Rprt,* Nov–Jan 72, pp 7–16; msg, MACV to CINCPAC, 081155Z Mar 72; msg, CG XXIV Corps to all US Cds, MR1, 081545Z Jan 72; msg 19575, US Amb, Saigon (Bunker) to Sec State, 170948Z Dec 71; rprt, Comb Interdiction Coord Comm, Minutes Meeting of 25 Jan 72, Feb 2, 1972; ltr, Maj Gen George J. Keegan, ACS/Intell, Hq USAF, to Sec AF, subj: Items of Interest, Mar 6, 1972.

2. Hist, MACV, 1972–Mar 73, vol II, sect J; Maj John D. Howard, USA, "They Were Good Ol' Boys! An Infantryman Remembers An Loc and the Air Force," *Air University Review,* Jan–Feb 75, pp 26–31.

3. Rprt, USA Advisory Team 70, 5th ARVN Div Combat Assistance Team, AAR, Binh Long Campaign, 1972, Jul 20, 1972; tabulation, TRAC, subj: Major Movements of ARVN Forces to and from An Loc, 4 Apr–25 Jun 72; fact sheets, MACV, subj: Highlights of Ground Combat Activity, SEA, 140601H to 150600H, and 150601H to 160600H Apr 72; hist, MACV, 1972–Mar 73, vol II, pp J–5 to J–9; draft rprt, MACV TRAC, AAR Binh Long Campaign, 1972, sect 3, Sr Advisor's Eval, and Logistics Annex.

4. Rprt, CORDS MR–3, Annex J to Draft MACV TRAC AAR, Binh Long Campaign, 1972; draft rprt, MACV TRAC AAR Binh Long Campaign, 1972, Logis Annex; rprt, Advis Team 70, AAR Binh Long Campaign, Jul 20, 1972; debriefing statement, Capt Moffett, Dep Sr Advisor, 3rd Ranger Gp, An Loc, Apr 8–May 31, 1972; intvw, Maj Cash, MACV, with Capt Robert T. Hudson, USA, G–4, Coordinator, TRAC, May 24, 1972; Maj Paul Ringenbach, *Airlift to Besieged Areas, 7 Apr–31 Aug 72,* (Hq PACAF, Proj CHECO, Dec 7, 1973), pp 1–3; Maj Paul Ringenbach, Capt Peter J. Melly, *The Battle for An Loc, 5 Apr–26 Jun 72* (Hq PACAF, Proj CHECO, Jan 31, 1973), pp 26–27.

5. Intvw, author with Col Walter J. Ford, Apr 21, 1975 (Ford was 7th AF liaison officer with VNAF ALCC to Apr 72); Iosue intvw, Mar 27, 1975; msg, MACV to AIG 7870, 152000Z Apr 72; Ringenbach, *Airlift to Besieged Areas,* Dec 7, 1973, pp 1–5; Ringenbach and Melly, *The Battle for An Loc,* Jan 31, 1973, pp 26–28; fact sheet, AFGP, subj: Overview of VNAF Combat Airlift Opns, Apr–Oct 72, Oct 72, p 3; draft rprt, MACV TRAC, AAR Binh Long Campaign, 1972, Logistics and CORES MR–3 Annexes.

6. Hist, 776th TAWg, Apr–Jun 72; rprt, Col Richard J. Downs, Dir/Airlift, 7th AF, EOTR, Aug 3, 1972, p 2; "C–130 Resupply Missions to An Loc," Appendix 22 to Rprt, Advis Team 70, AAR, Binh Long Campaign, Jul 20, 1972; draft rprt, TRAC, AAR Binh Long Campaign, 1972, Logis.Annex; SSgt Dave Cole, "Agony of an Airlifter," *Airman,* Jan 73, pp 45–47; *Air Force Times,* Oct 18, 1972; TAC Press Release, OII–72–266–2 Nov 72.

7. Intvw, author with Maj Edward N. Brya, Apr 22, 1975; Iosue intvw, Mar 27, 1975; briefing, Maj Edward N. Brya, 374th TAWg, subj: C–130 Operations in Vietnam, May 31, 1972; Ringenbach, *Airlift to Besieged Areas,* Dec 7, 1973, pp 6–9, 12; hist, 374th TAWg, Jan–Jun 72, pp 42–43; rprt, Lt Col Allen R. Weeks, Airlift Sect, 7th AF Dir/Opns, Combat Airdrop Rprt, Vietnam, 15 Apr–15 Jul 72, pp 1–2; "C–130 Resupply Missions to An Loc," Appendix 22 to rprt, Advis Team 70, AAR, Binh Long Campaign, Jul 20, 1972.

8. Hist, 374th TAWg, Jan–Jun 72, pp 57–58; hist, 50th TASq, Apr–Jun 72, hist, 21st TASq, Apr–Jun 72, p 5; *Pacific Stars and Stripes,* Apr 22, 1972.

9. Intvw, Maj Cash, MACV, with Capt Robert T. Hudson, USA, G–4 Coordinator TRAC, May 24, 1972; Iosue intvw, Mar 27, 1975.

10. Fact sheets, MACV, Highlights of Ground Combat Activity in SEA, 110601H to 120600H and 130601H to 140600H Apr 72; MR, Howard H. Lange, US Embassy, Saigon, subj: Con-

versation with Binh Long Province Legislative Deputy, Saigon, Apr 20, 1972; hist, MACV, 1972–Mar 73, pp J–14 and J–15; Howard, USA, "Good Ol' Boys!," pp 26–31; Ringenbach and Melly, *The Battle for An Loc,* Jan 31, 1973, pp 16–26; TRAC, Debriefing of Maj Kenneth A. Ingram and Capt Moffett, Jun 72; debriefing statement, Capt Moffett, Dep Sr Advis for 3rd Ranger Gp, Apr 8–May 31, 1972.

11. PACAF Forms 20c, Airlift Sect, 7th AF, Airdrop Worksheets, 15–23 Apr 72; Brya intvw, Apr 22, 1975; rprt, Col Andrew P. Iosue, Cdr 374th TAWg, EOTR, Jul 1, 1973, p 12; rprt, US Advisory Det, 90th PMAD, Review of Airdrop Activity, 8 Apr–18 Jul 72; rprt, Lt Col Allen R. Weeks, Airl Sect, 7th AF Dir/Opns, Combat Airdrop Rprt, Vietnam, 15 Apr–15 Jul 72, pp 2–3 and Tab 2; Ringenbach, *Airlift to Besieged Areas,* Dec 7, 1973, pp 9–12, 23–25; fact sheet, Dir/Logistics, MACV, subj: Aerial Resupply Opns, Dec 21, 1972.

12. Brya intvw, Apr 22, 1975; Iosue intvw, Mar 27, 1975; briefing, Maj Edward N. Brya, 374th TAWg, subj: C–130 Opns in Vietnam, May 31, 1972; rprt, Col Richard Downs, Dir/Airlift, 7th AF, EOTR, Aug 3, 1972, p 2; PACAF Forms 20c, Airl Sect, 7th AF, Airdrop Worksheets, 24 Apr–4 May 72; hist, 374th TAWg, Jan–Jun 72, pp 46–48, 59; rprt, Advis Team 70, AAR Binh Long Campaign, Jul 20, 1972, pp 38–40 and Appendix 22; Ringenbach, *Airlift to Besieged Areas,* Dec 7, 1973, pp 13–21; tabulation, 374th TAWg, Acft Battle Damage, Apr–Jun 72.

13. Rprt, Col Harry G. Canham, 16th Sp Opns Sq and 8th TFWg, EOTR, Dec 72, pp 6–7; Brya intvw, Apr 22, 1975; hist, MACV, 1972–Mar 73, pp H–17 and B–40; rprt, Advis Team 70, AAR Binh Long Campaign, Jul 20, 1972, pp 38–40; rprt, Lt Col Allen R. Weeks, Airl Sect, 7th AF, Combat Airdrop Rprt, Vietnam, 15 Apr–15 Jul 72, Tab 1.

14. Intvw, Maj Cash, MACV, with Col William Miller, Sr Advisor to 5th Div, An Loc, May 24, 1972; debriefing statement, Maj Kenneth A. Ingram, 5th RVN Div Arty Advis, Jun 10, 1972.

15. Rprt, TRAC, Debriefing of Maj Kenneth A. Ingram and Capt Moffett, USA, Jun 72.

16. Miller intvw, May 24, 1972; rprt, TRAC, Debriefing of Maj Kenneth A. Ingram and Capt Moffett, USA, Jun 72; rprt, Advis Team 70, AAR Binh Long Campaign, Jul 20, 1972.

17. Iosue intvw, Mar 27, 1975; Byra intvw, Apr 22, 1975; briefing, Maj Edward N. Brya, 374th TAWg, subj: C–130 Opns in Vietnam, May 31, 1972.

18. Rprt, Col Richard J. Downs, Dir/Airl, 7th AF, EOTR, Aug 3, 1972, pp 3–5; fact sheet, Dir/Logistics MACV, subj: Aerial Resupply Opns, Dec 21, 1972; Ringenbach, *Airlift to Besieged Areas,* Dec 7, 1973, pp 26–28; rprt, Lt Col Allen R. Weeks, Airl Sect, 7th AF, Combat Airdrop Rprt, Vietnam, 15 Apr–15 Jul 72, pp 3–5.

19. Appendix 23, "C–130 Resupply Missions to An Loc, 4–14 May," to Rprt, Advis Team 70, AAR, Binh Long Campaign, Jul 20, 1972; PACAF Forms 20c, Airlift Sect, 7th AF, Airdrop Worksheets, daily 4–7 May 72; debriefing statement, Maj Kenneth A. Ingram, USA, 5th Div Arty Advisor, Jun 10, 1972; TRAC, Debriefing of Maj Kenneth A. Ingram and Capt Moffett, USA, Jun 72; daily log, US Advisors to 5th Div, 4–7 May 72.

20. Msg DO–235, 7th AF to TAC, 211020Z Jul 72; hist, 317th TAWg, Jul–Sep 72, pp 19–21; Brya intvw, Apr 22, 1975.

21. Ltr, the Div Comb Assistance Team, to CG TRAC, subj: Resupply Operations to An Loc during 4–27 May, May 30, 1972; draft rprt, TRAC, AAR, Binh Long Campaign, 1972, Logistics Annex; rprt, Advis Team 70, AAR Binh Long Campaign, Jul 20, 1972, Appendixes 23 and 24; rprt, Lt Col Allen R. Weeks, Airl Sect 7th AF, Combat Airdrop Rprt, Vietnam, 15 Apr–15 Jul 72; hist, MACV, 1972–Mar 73, p B–28; Ringenbach and Melly, *The Battle for An Loc,* Jan 31, 1973; Ringenbach, *Airlift to Besieged Areas,* Dec 7, 1973.

22. Miller intvw, May 24, 1972; daily logs, US Advisors to 5th ARVN Div, Apr and May 72; TRAC, Debriefing of Maj Kenneth A. Ingram and Capt Moffett, USA, Jun 72; debriefing statement, Maj Kenneth A. Ingram, USA, 5th Div Arty Advisor, Jun 10, 1972; rprt, Advis Team 70, AAR Binh Long Campaign, Jul 20, 1972, pp 27–28; memo, 3rd Ranger Gp Advis Team, to Sr Advis, III Corps Ranger Cd, subj: Activities Rprt, 8 Apr–20 May 72; rprt, Col Harold R. Fischer, Ch AFAT 3, EOTR, Aug 8,

1972; rprt, Col Arthur R. Burke, Ch, Det 4, AFAT 2, EOTR, Sep 30, 1972; rprt, Lt Col Louis J. Yost, Ch, AFAT 3, Monthly Unit Advisors Rprt, for Jun 72; hist, MACV, 1972–Mar 73, pp J–18 and J–19; Howard, "Good Ol' Boys!," *Air University Review*, pp 54–55.

23. Hudson intvw, May 24, 1972; rprt, Advis Team 70, AAR Binh Long Campaign, 1972, Jul 20, 1972, pp 28–30; draft rprt, MACV TRAC, AAR Binh Long Campaign, 1972, Sect 3, Sr Advisor's Eval, and Logistics Annex; ltr, 5th Div Comb Assistance Team, to CG TRAC, subj: Resupply Opns to An Loc during 4–27 May 72, May 30, 1972.

24. Howard, "Good Ol' Boys!," *Air University Review*, Jan–Feb 75, p 34; daily logs, US Advisors to 5th Div, An Loc, May 72; rprt, TRAC, Debriefing of Maj Kenneth A. Ingram and Capt Moffett, USA, Jun 72.

25. Rprt, Maj Gen Alton D. Slay DCS/Opns, 7th AF, 1972, pp 62–72; ltr, Lt Col Jack B. Shaw, DCR/Concepts Div, TALC, to DCS Concepts, Doctrine, and Rqmts, Aug 7, 1967; hist, CINCPAC, 1963, II, 15–18; ltr, Maj George E. Thompson, Dept/Aeronautics, USAF Academy, to Dr. W. L. Lehmann, Sec AF RD, subj: Optimal Evasive Maneuvers for C–130 Acft Against the SA–2 SAM, May 25, 1971; rprt, DCS/Rqmts, SOF, Monthly Status Rprt, Mar 71.

26. Msg, TFWC to TAC, 131540Z May 72; hist, 374th TAWg, Jan–Jun 72, pp 29–30; hist, MACV, 1972–Mar 73, p B–28; rprt, TRAC, PERINTREP, 10–72, May 14, 1972; rprt, Dir/Opl Intell, 7th AF, to 7th AF, Historical Data Rprt, Apr–Jun 72; msg, CG USARV to AIG 7485 (units), 090716Z May 72, Comments, Hq USAF Electr Warfare Center, Review of ms, (EW), Mar 11, 1976.

27. Hist rprt, Intell Sect, 374th TAWg, Jan–Jun 72, pp 6–15; rprt, Maj Gen Alton D. Slay, DCS/Opns, 7th AF, EOTR, 1972, pp 62–72; background paper, DCS/R&D, Hq USAF, subj: Summary of SA–7 Activity and Action Taken, n.d., [ca 1972]; hist, CINCPAC, 1972, II, 552–553; Brya intvw, Apr 22, 1975; msg, AF Sp Comm Center to AIG 8556, 132150Z May 72; ltr, Dir/Opns AFGP to Air Attache Phnom Penh, subj: Countermeasures Against the SA–7 Missile, Aug 10, 1972; Ringenbach and Melly, *The Battle for An Loc*, Jan 31, 1973, pp 46–49.

28. Staff summary sheet, Col Thomas A. Barr, Dir/Opns, AFCP, subj: Survivability of VNAF Helicopters, Jul 6, 1972; rprt, Col Thomas A. Barr, Dir/Opns, AFGP, EOTR, Jan 5, 1973; memo, Maj Gen Leslie W. Bray, Spl Assist for Vietnamization, Hq USAF, to CSAF, subj: Status of VNAF Infrared Countermeasures, May 5, 1973; Proposed Combat ROC, AFGP, Class V Modif ALC–29 Flare Dispensers for VNAF CH–47 Helicopters, Aug 14, 1972; hist, Off/Spl Asst for Vietnamization, Hq USAF, Jul–Dec 72, pp 34–38; *New York Times*, Jul 30, 1972; *Aviation Week and Space Technology*, Jul 17, 1972.

29. Intvw, MACV, with Maj Charles Brunick, USA, Arty Advisor, 21st Div, Lai Khe, May 25, 1972; msg 146–72, DIA to AIG 7011, 252334Z May 72; Appendix 18, "Major Movements of ARVN Forces to and from An Loc, 4 Apr–25 Jun 72," in Rprt, Advis Team 70, AAR Binh Long Campaign, Jul 20, 1972; hist, MACV, 1972–Mar 73, pp J–26 to J–30.

30. Rprt, Lt Col Allen R. Weeks, Airl Sect 7th AF, Combat Airdrop Rprt, Vietnam, 15 Apr–15 Jul 72.

31. Ringenbach, *Airlift to Besieged Areas*, Dec 7, 1973, pp 45–48; rprt, Lt Col Allen R. Weeks, Airl Sect 7th AF, Combat Airdrop Rprt, Vietnam, 15 Apr–15 Jul 72.

32. PACAF Forms 20c, Airl Sect 7th AF, Airdrop Worksheets, 22 May through 26 Jun 72; rprt, US Advisory Det, 90th PMAD, Review of Airdrop Activity, 8 Apr–18 Jul 72; fact sheet, MACV J–4, subj: An Loc Air Drops, Jul 11, 1972; staff summary sheet, MACV J–4, subj: An Loc Air Drops, Jul 72; staff summary sheet, Lt Col Allen R. Weeks, Dep Ch Airl Sect, 7th AF, subj: Supply of Air Items, Jul 13, 1972.

33. Fact sheet, MACV J–4, subj: An Loc Air Drops, Jul 11, 1972; draft memo, MACV J–4 to C/S MACV, subj: An Loc Air Drops, n.d., [ca Aug 1972]; MR, MACV J–4, subj: An Loc Air Drop, Jul 13, 1972; MR, MACV J–4, subj: Combat Airdrop Rprt, Aug 9, 1972; Ringenbach and Melly, *The Battle for An Loc*, Jan 31, 1973, p 52.

34. Fact sheet, Dir/Logistics, MACV,

NOTES

subj: Current Status of Aerial Delivery Items, Jul 29, 1972; rprt, US Advisory Det, 90th PMAD, Review of Airdrop Activity, 8 Apr–18 Jul 72; ltr, 5th Div Comb Assist Team, to CG TRAC, subj: Resupply Opns to An Loc during the pd 4–27 May 72, May 30, 1972; draft rprt, TRAC, AAR Binh Long Campaign, 1972, Logis Annex.

35. Hist, 374th TAWg, Jul–Sep 72, pp 32–33, Oct–Dec 72, pp 25–27; hist, MACV, 1972–Mar 73, pp J–26 through J–30.

36. Rprt, TAWC, Tactical Airlift Tactics Conference, 31 May–2 Jun 72; briefing, Maj Edward N. Brya, 374th TAWg, C–130 Opns in Vietnam, May 31, 1972; Brya intvw, Apr 22, 1975; ltr, Col R. E. Craycraft, DCS/Opns, 13th AF, to PACAF, subj: Position Paper on Tactical Airlift Tactics, May 24, 1972.

37. Iosue intvw, Mar 27, 1975.

Chapter XXII

The Easter Offensive—The Countrywide Response

1. Ltr, Maj Gen George J. Keegan, ACS/Intell, Hq USAF, to Sec AF, subj: Item of Interest, Mar 6, 1972.

2. Fact sheet, MACV Dir/Intell, subj: Enemy Armor Assessment, Aug 1, 1972; hist, 7th AF, FY 72, pp 57–60; IR 6-028-0513-72, Nov 2, 1972; hist, MACV, 1972–Mar 73, vol I, p A–5 to A–51.

3. Rprt, Col Raymond H. Gaylor, Cdr 2nd Aer Port Gp, EOTR, Jul 72; rprt, Col Richard J. Downs, Dir/Airlift, 7th AF, Aug 3, 1972.

4. Background paper, AFGP, MACV, subj: Overview of VNAF Combat Airlift Opns, 1 Apr–1 Oct 72, Oct 72; hist, 7th AF, FY 72, pp 343–345.

5. Msgs, MACV to JCS, 061357Z, 200814Z, and 260806Z Mar 72; hist, MACV, 1972–Mar 73, pp C–75, C–76; Brig Gen Edwin H. Simmons, USMC, Ret, "Marine Corps Opns in Vietnam, 1969–72," US Naval Institute, *Proceedings*, May 73, pp 220–223.

6. Fact sheet, MACV, subj: Highlights of Ground Combat Activity in SEA, 310601H to 010600H Apr 72, Apr 1, 1972; release 0294, 7th AF Dir/Inform, subj: USAF and VNAF Team Up, Apr 20, 1972; hist, 7th AF, FY 72, p 287; hist, MACV, I, 23; msg, MACV to JCS, 030930Z Apr 72.

7. Msgs, MACV (Abrams) to CJCS/CINCPAC, 011400Z and 051120Z Apr 72; hist, MACV, 1972–Mar 73, vol II, pts K and L; msgs, MACV to JCS, 030930Z and 101130Z Apr 72; Simmons, "Marine Corps Opns," *Proceedings*, May 73.

8. Iosue intvw, Mar 27, 1975; Brya intvw, Apr 22, 1975.

9. Msg, MACV (Abrams) to CJCS/CINCPAC, 031000Z Apr 72; hist, 345th TASq, Jan–Jun 72, p 12; hist, 776th TASq, Apr–Jun 72; briefing materials, Dir/Opns, Hq USAF, Apr 72.

10. Iosue intvw, Mar 27, 1975; briefing, Maj Edward N. Brya, 374th TAWg, subj: C–130 Opns in Vietnam, May 31, 1972; hist, 374th TAWg, Jan–Jun 72, pp 11–13; hist, 34th TASq, Jan–Jun 72, p 10; hist, 50th TASq, Apr–Jun 72; hist, 776th TASq, Apr–Jun 72.

11. Hist, MACV, 1972–Mar 73, vol II, Annex K and L.

12. Msg, 49th TFWg to 13th AF, 250350Z May 72; msg LOWC, 7th AF to TMO, Ubon, 150631Z Apr 72; msg, CG FMFPAC to CINCPAC, 260437Z May 72; msg 4638, FMFPAC to CINCPACFLT, 102225Z Jun 72; msg, 13th AF to 8th TFWg, 100730Z Apr 72; hist, 374th TAWg, Jan–Jun 72, pp 45–46; hist, 316th TAWg, Apr–Jun 72, pp v–vi, 11; hist, 317th TAWg, Apr–Jun 72, p 11; hist, 345th TASq, Jan–Jun 72, p 12; hist, Dir/Opns, Hq USAF, Jan–Jun 72, pp 438–439, 459–460.

13. Briefing, Maj Edward N. Brya, 374th TAWg, subj: C–130 Opns in Vietnam, May 31, 1972; hist, 374th TAWg, Jan–Jun 72, pp 26, 82–98; rprt, PACAF, Summary Air Opns SEA, May 72.

14. Background paper, AFGP, MACV,

subj: Overview of VNAF Combat Airlift Opns, 1 Apr–1 Oct 72; hist, MACV, 1972–Mar 73, vol II, pp L–12 to L–18.

15. Hist rprt, Intell Sect, 374th TAWg, Jan–Jun 72, p 10; Airl Sect 7th AF, Airdrop Worksheets, Apr 25–30, 1972; rprt, Lt Col Allen R. Weeks, Airl Sect, 7th AF, Dir/Opns, Combat Airdrop Report, Vietnam, 15 Apr–15 Jul 72; msg, MACV to JCS, 241551Z Apr 72.

16. Hist, 310th TASq, Apr–Jun 72; rprt, Airlift Sect, MACV J–3, Hist Data Rprt, Apr–Jun 72; briefing, 7th AF, subj: Airlift Operations, May 20, 1972; release 11–10–72–666, SAFOI, subj: Last TAS Leaves Vietnam, Oct 11, 1972.

17. Briefing, 7th AF, subj: Airlift Opns, May 20, 1972; briefing materials, Dir/Opns, Hq USAF, Apr 28–May 4, 1972; hist, 7th AF, FY 72, pp 341–344; releases 0367 and 0383, Dir/Inform, 7th AF, subj: C–141s Airlift Refugees, May 5, 1972, and Up-country Vietnam, New Sight and Sound, May 23, 1972.

18. Msg, 374th CS Gp to PACAF, 090615Z May 72; briefing, Maj Edward N. Brya, 374th TAWg, subj: C–130 Opns in Vietnam, May 31, 1972; Iosue intvw, Mar 27, 1975.

19. Msg, TAC/USAFRED to units, 120100Z May 72; Atch to JCSM 221–72, JCS to Sec Def, subj: US Force Augmentation in SEA, May 10, 1972; hist, 316th TAWg, Apr–Jun 72, pp 12–25; hist, 317th TAWg, Apr–Jun 72, pp 11–12; briefing materials, Dir/Opns, Hq USAF, Daily Cd Post Briefing for 13 May and 18 May 72; hist, 61st TASq, Apr–Jun 72; rprt, Lt Col Billie B. Mills, Cdr 61st TAWg, Documentation of 61st TASq AWADS Deployed Activities, Aug 72; msg, USCINCRED to AIR 933, 130001Z May 72; hist, Dir/Opns, Hq USAF, Jul–Dec 72, pp 267–268.

20. Fact sheets, MACV, subjs: Highlights of Ground Combat Activity in SEA, 180601H to 190600H and 240601H to 250600H Apr 72; ltr, John P. Vann, Sr Advis, II Corps and MR2, to Maj Gen Kang Won Chao, CG ROKFV Field Cd, Nha Trang, Apr 16, 1972; briefing, Maj Edward Brya, 374th TAWg, subj: C–130 Opns in Vietnam, May 31, 1972; rprt, Maj Gen Alton D. Slay, DCS/Opns, 7th AF, 1972, pp 42–49; releases 0334 and 0345, Dir/Inform, 7th AF, subj: C–130 Aerial Pipeline, Apr 27, 1972, and Hot Day at Kontum, May 2, 1972; Capt Peter A. W. Liebehen, *Kontum: Battle for the Central Highlands*, (Hq PACAF, Proj CHECO, Oct 27, 1972), p 30.

21. Msgs, 374th TAWg Det 1, to Dir/Opns 374th TAWg, 261445Z Apr 72 and 011800Z May 72; hist, 374th TAWg, Jan–Jun 72, pp 56–57; releases 0355 and 0409, Dir/Inform, 7th AF, subj: To Save an Aircraft, May 5, 1972, and One Step at a Time, Jun 12, 1972; *Air Force Times*, Jul 5, 1972, p 34.

22. Staff summary sheet, Col Thomas A. Barr, Dir/Opns, AFGP, subj: Kontum Airlift, 26 Apr–9 May, May 10, 1972; fact sheet, MACV, Highlights of Ground Combat Activity in SEA, 260601H to 270600H Apr 72, Apr 27, 1972; release C412, 7th AF Dir/Inform, subj: Teamwork Recovers Acft, May 30, 1972; Liebehen, *Kontum*, Oct 27, 1972, pp 30–31.

23. Rprt, Col Henry L. Baulch, Chief AFAT 5, Monthly Unit Advis Rprt, Jun 7, 1972; staff summary sheet, Col Thomas A. Barr, Dir/Opns, AFGP, subj: Kontum Airlift, 26 Apr–9 May 72, May 10, 1972; msgs, 374th TAWg Det 1, to JCS/NMCC, 181445Z and 190403Z May 72; hist, 21st TASq, Apr–Jun 72, p 7; hist, 50th TASq, Apr–Jun 72; hist, 345th TASq, Jan–Jun 72, p 11; Liebehen, *Kontum*, Oct 27, 1972, pp 42–46.

24. Msgs, 374th TAWg Det 1, to PACAF, 220335Z and 270400Z May 72; msgs, 374th TAWg Det 1, to AIG 913, 230030Z and 250340Z May 72; Iosue intvw, Mar 27, 1975; fact sheets, MACV, subj: Highlights of Ground Combat Activity in SEA, daily, 180601H to 190600H and 260601H to 270600H May 72; Liebehen, *Kontum*, Oct 27, 1972, pp 49–57.

25. PACAF Forms 20a, 7th AF, Airdrop Worksheets, May 14 through Jul 14, 1972; tabulation, 374th TAWg, subj: Drop Zones, Apr–Jun 72; rprt, Lt Col Allen R. Weeks, Airl Sect, 7th AF, Dir/Opns, Combat Airdrop Rprt, Vietnam, Apr 15–Jul 15, 1972; hist, 374th TAWg, Jan–Jun 72, pp 55–56; msg, 13th AF to 327th AD, 160745Z May 72; Ringenbach, *Airlift to Besieged Areas*, Dec 7, 1973, pp 40–41.

26. Intvw, author with Maj David S. Dawson, Nov 14, 1974; hist, 374th TAWg, Jan–Jun 72, pp 51–52; PACAF Forms 20a, 7th AF Airdrop Worksheets, daily for May and Jun 72; Liebenhen, *Kontum*, Oct 27, 1972, pp 57–82; hist,

MACV, 1972–Mar 73, vol II, pp K–24 to K–26; rprts, MACV, Highlights of Ground Combat Activity in SEA, 290601H to 300600H May 72, 080601H to 090600H and 120601H to 130600H Jun 72.

27. Rprt, Lt Col Billie B. Mills, Cdr 61st TASq, Monthly Activity Rprt for May 72, Jun 5, 1972; hist, 61st TASq, Apr–Jun 72; rprt, Lt Col Billie B. Mills, Cdr 61st TASq, Documentation of 61st TASq AWADS Deployed Activities, Aug 72.

28. Rprt, Lt Col Billie B. Mills, Cdr 61st TASq, Documentation of 61st TASq AWADS Deployed Activities, Aug 72; rprt, Lt Col Allen R. Weeks, Airl Sect, 7th AF, Dir/Opns, Combat Airdrop Rprt, Vietnam, 15 Apr–15 Jul 72, p 7 and appendix.

29. Dawson intvw, Nov 14, 1974; msg, Dir/Opns, 7th AF, to TAC, 070919Z Jun 72.

30. Msg, 7th AF Dir/Opns, to TAC, 070919Z Jun 72; rprt, Lt Col Billie B. Mills and Maj David S. Dawson, 61st TASq, Operational Combat Evaluation of the AWADS, Aug 72, p 5; rprt, Lt Col Billie B. Mills, Cdr 61st TASq, Documentation of 61st TASq Deployed Activities, Aug 72; rprt, Lt Col Allen R. Weeks, Airl Sect, 7th AF Dir/Opns, Combat Airdrop Rprt, Vietnam, 15 Apr–15 Jul 72, pp 7–8.

31. Msg, 61st TASq to 314th TAWg, 210420Z Jun 72; Dawson intvw, Nov 14, 1974; rprt, Lt Col Billie B. Mills and Maj David S. Dawson, 61st TASq, Operational Combat Evaluation of the AWADS, Aug 72, p 13; rprt, Lt Col Billie B. Mills, Cdr 61st TASq, Documentation of 61st TASq Deployed Activities, Aug 72.

32. Msg, Cdr 61st TASq to 314th TAWg, subj: 61st TASq Cdr Semi-monthly Rprt, Jul 14, 1972; hist, 61st TASq, Apr–Jun 72; rprt, Lt Col Billie B. Mills, Cdr 61st TASq, Documentation of 61st TASq Deployed Activities, Aug 72; rprt, Lt Col Billie B. Mills and Maj David S. Dawson, 61st TASq, Operational Combat Evaluation of the AWADS, Aug 72; Dawson intvw, Nov 14, 1974.

33. Dawson intvw, Nov 14, 1974.

34. Fact sheet, 314th TAWg, subj: AWADS Equipment, Jul 25, 1972; msg, DOLCO, 7th AF to 13th AF, 190400Z Jun 72; Dawson intvw, Nov 14, 1974; rprt, Lt Col Billie B. Mills, Cdr 61st TASq, Documentation of 61st TASq Deployed Activities, Aug 72, p 13 and Intell Support appendix; rprt, Lt Col Billie B. Mills and Maj David S. Dawson, 61st TASq, Opl Combat Evaluation of the AWADS, Aug 72, pp 6–7.

35. Msg, Cdr, 61st TASq to 314th TAWg, subj: 61st TASq Cdr Semi-monthly Rprt, Jul 14, 1972; rprt, Lt Col Billie B. Mills, Cdr 61st TASq, Documentation of 61st TASq Deployed Activities, Aug 72.

36. Rprt, Col Andrew P. Iosue, Cdr 374th TAWg, EOTR, Jul 1, 1973; pp 12–13; rprt, Col Richard J. Downs, Dir/Airl, 7th AF, Aug 3, 1972; Ringenbach, *Airlift to Besieged Areas,* Dec 7, 1973, pp 38–39.

37. Msgs, MACV to JCS, 080543Z, 151831Z, and 290005Z May 72, 270121Z, and 160442Z Jun 72; rprt, Maj Gen Alton D. Slay, DCS Opns, 7th AF, 1972, pp 26–42; hist, MACV, 1972–Mar 73, Annex L; hist, 7th AF, FY 72, pp 277–294; Maj Gen E. J. Miller, USMC, and Rear Adm W. D. Toole, USN, "Amphibious Forces: The Turning Point," US Naval Institute, *Proceedings,* Nov 74, pp 29–30.

38. Hist, 374th TAWg, Jan–Jun 72, pp 49–51; daily log, US Advisors to 5th ARVN Div, An Loc, May 5, 6, and 7, 1972; memo, MACV J-4 to MACV J-3, subj: Minh Thanh Airdrops, Aug 30, 1972; hist, MACV, 1972–Mar 72, I, 52, 59; Ringenbach, *Airlift to Besieged Areas,* Dec 7, 1973, pp 22, 42–44; draft rprt, MACV TRAC, AAR Binh Long Campaign, 1972.

39. Briefing, 7th AF, subj: Briefing for Gen O'Keefe on Airlift Opns, May 22, 1972; rprt, Airlift Sect, MACV J-3, Monthly Hist Rprt for Jun, Jul 4, 1972; hist, 310th TASq, Apr–Jun 72, pp 2–3; hist, 345th TASq, Jul–Sep 72, p 10; rprt, PACAF, Summary Air Opns SEA, May 72; rprt, Col Raymond H. Gaylor, Cdr 2nd Aer Port Gp, Jul 72; hist, 7th AF, FY 72, pp 157–158; hist, 374th TAWg, Jan–Jun 72, pp 26–27.

40. Iosue intvw, Mar 27, 1975; MR, 1st Lt Roy A. Hodges, Maint Analysis Off, 374th FMSq, subj: Battle Damage Sustained by 374th TAWg Acft, Sep 21, 1972; hist, 374th TAWg Jan–Jun 72, pp 82–98.

41. Posey intvw, Mar 29, 1974; rprt, Airlift Sect, MACV J-3, Monthly Hist Rprt for Jun 72, Jul 4, 1972; briefing,

7th AF, subj: Briefing for Gen O'Keefe on Airlift Opns, May 22, 1972; hist, 374th TAWg, Jul–Sep 72, p 22; rprt, Col Richard J. Downs, Dir/Airl, 7th AF, Aug 3, 1972, p 5; Iosue intvw, Mar 27, 1975.

42. Hist, 2nd Aer Port Gp, Apr–Jun 72; hist, 8th Aer Port Sq, Apr–Jun 72.

43. Rprt, Col Raymond H. Gaylor, Cdr 2nd Aer Port Gp, Jul 72, pp A-2 to A-11; hist, 2nd Aer Port Gp, Apr–Jun 72, pp 7–9; hist, 8th Aer Port Sq, Apr–Jun 72.

44. Msg, 15th Aer Port Sq to 8th Aer Port Sq, et al, 160545Z Jun 72; hist, 317th TAWg, Apr–Jun 72, p 34; hist, 2nd Aer Port Gp, Apr–Jun 72, pp 15–16; hist, 8th Aer Port Sq, Apr–Jun 72.

45. Ltr, Col William J. Norris, Dep Dir/Logis, MACV J-4, to Cdr 7th AF, subj: Quality Control of Aerial Delivery Parachute Packing/Rigging, Jun 21, 1972; rprt, Lt Col Billie B. Mills, Cdr 61st TASq, Documentation of 61st TASq AWADS Deployed Activities, Aug 72; rprt, Col Raymond H. Gaylor, Cdr 2nd Aer Port Gp, Jul 72, pp A-7 and A-8.

46. Off/Sec AF, AF Policy Letter for Cdrs, Jul 1, 1972; JCSM 327-72, JCS to Sec Def, subj: Situation in the RVN, Jul 14, 1972; hist, MACV, 1972–Mar 73, vol I, pp A-5, A-7, A-49, A-51.

Chapter XXIII

The Advisory Role and the Vietnamese Air Force Airlift Arm

1. Ltr, Maj Gen Albert W. Schinz, Ret, to author, May 23, 1972; hist, AF Advisory Gp, May 67, Mar 68; rprt, AF Advis Gp, VNAF Statistical Summary, Mar 68.

2. Rprt, Asst for Mut Security, DCS/S&L, Hq USAF, *Journal of Military Assistance*, Mar 65, p 185; hist, AF Advis Gp, 1965, Sep 66; ltr, Maj Gen Albert W. Schinz, Ret, to author, May 23, 1972; intvw, Corona Harvest, with Maj Bruce Parker, CH intvw no 62, Jun 19, 1968.

3. Hist, AF Advis Gp, Nov 66 through Nov 68; ltr, Brig Gen Albert W. Schinz, Ch, AF Advis Gp, MACV, to MACV, subj: Modernization of the VNAF, Oct 15, 1965; fact sheet, AF Advis Gp, subj: Status of VNAF, Summary of Questions and Answers, Oct 29, 1967; rprts, MACV J-3, RVNAF Regular Forces and Advisory Rprts, Apr–Jun and Oct–Dec 68, Aug 31, 1968 and Apr 2, 1969.

4. Intvw, author with Lt Col William B. Webb, JCS J-5, Lt Col Robert A. Erickson, OASD/Program Analysis and Eval, and Maj Ronald T. Lanman, AF/RDQSA, Hq USAF, Feb 14, 1974 (all three served with Advisory Team no 5 during 1970–71); rprt, Lt Col William B. Webb, DCS/Plans and Program Advisor, AFAT 5, EOTR, Jun 30, 1971; hist, AFGP, Apr–Jun 71, I, 1–5; hist, MACV, 1970, vol II, pp VII-71 to VII-73.

5. Rprt, Lt Col William B. Webb, DCS/Plans and Program Advisor, AFAT 5, EOTR, Jun 30, 1971; rprt, Col Harold E. Fischer, Ch, AFAT 3, EOTR, Aug 8, 1972; rprt, AFAT 5 to AFCP, Qtrly Hist Summary, Apr–Jun 71, Jul 15, 1971; study, 7th AF, Special Survey—I and M Program VNAF, Jul–Sep 71; rprt, Young, EOTR, Feb 15, 1971, p 40; ltr, Brig Gen Kendall S. Young, Ch, AFGP, to MACV, subj: Update of Periodic Assessment of the Sit in VN, May 27, 1970; Webb, Erickson, and Lanman intvw, Feb 14, 1974.

6. Rprts, Sr Advisor's Monthly Eval, Jan 65 through Dec 65; Parker intvw, Jun 19, 1968; rprt, MACV, Assessment of RVNAF Status as of 29 Feb 68, Mar 21, 1968; rprt, MACV, Monthly Eval, Aug and Dec 66; rprts, VN Abn Div Advis Det, Qtrly Hist Rprts, Jul 17, 1967 and Jan 17, 1968.

7. Msg 15785, MACV (Gen Abrams) to CINCPAC (Adm McCain), 111411Z Dec 70; msg, CINCPAC to MACV (Abrams), 121931Z Dec 70; ltr, Abn Div Advisory Det to MACV, subj: Qtrly Hist Rprt, Oct–Dec 70, Jan 71.

8. Webb, Erickson, and Lanman intvw, Feb 14, 1974; rprt, Col Roy D.

Broadway, Ch, AFAT 5, EOTR, Sep 71; rprt, Young, EOTR, Feb 15, 1971; hist, AFGP, Oct–Dec 70, p 43; hist, 8th Aer Port Sq, Oct–Dec 70; ltr, Abn Div Advisory Det, to MACV, subj: Qtrly Hist Rprt, Oct–Dec 71, Jan 71.

9. Hist, MACV, 1971, pp VIII–70; rprt, Brig Gen Kendall S. Young, Ch, AFGP, EOTR, Feb 15, 1971, pp 17–23; hist, Dir/Mil Assist and Sales, Hq USAF, 1969 through 1972; Capt D. L. DeBerry, *Vietnamization of the Air War, 1970–71*, (Hq PACAF, Proj CHECO, Oct 8, 1971), pp 11–20.

10. Elizabeth H. Hartsook, *The Air Force in Southeast Asia: The Administration Emphasizes Air Power, 1969*, (Off/AF Hist, Nov 71), pp 1–7, 54–85; hist, CINCPAC, 1969, III, 28–44, 1970, II, 117–122; msg, PACAF to Hq USAF (pers for Gen Ryan from Gen Nazarro), 140339Z Mar 70; rprt, Air Staff Task Group, Credible Crusade Final Rprt, Jan 9, 1970; staff summary sheet, Col Paul H. Wine, DCS/Plans, 7th AF, subj: VNAF Airlift Structure, Mar 13, 1970.

11. Joint Programmed Action Directive 71–106, AFGP, 7th AF, VNAF, Nov 30, 1970; msg XOP/SMS, Hq USAF to PACAF, 111513Z Dec 69; msg CPR, AFGP to PACAF Dir/Plans, 290720Z Dec 69; rprt, Col Senour Hunt, Ch, AFAT 5, EOTR, Dec 30, 1970; rprt, Opns Plans Div, AFGP, Input for Dir/Opns EOTR, Jul 71; hist, AFGP, Oct–Dec 70, p 26.

12. Rprts, 315th TAWg VNAF Training Flight, Summary of Strengths, Weaknesses, *et al*, Feb and Apr 4, 1971; hist, 315th TAWg VNAF Training Flight, Jan–Mar, Apr–Jun, and Jul–Sep 71; hist, 315th CAM Sq, Jan–Mar 71, pp 5–6, Apr–Jun 71, pp iv, 5–6; rprt, Col Charles S. Reed, Cdr 315th TAWg, EOTR, May 1, 1971; rprt, Brig Gen John Herring, Cdr, 834th AD, EOTR, Jun 71, pp 94–95; rprt, Col K. T. Blood, Cdr, 315th TAWg, EOTR, Nov 26, 1971; rprt, Capt G. K. Link, 315th TAWg, Nav Tng, Feb 13, 1971.

13. Rprts, Col Roy D. Broadway, Ch, AFAT 5, Monthly Unit Advisors Rprt (AFGP AC-U2), Feb 7 through Oct 7, 1971; hist, 19th TASq, Jan–May 71, pp vii, 3, 13; rprts, AFAT 5, Qtrly Hist Summary, Apr–Jun and Oct–Dec 71; ltr, Brig Gen James H. Watkins, Ch, AFGP, to 7th AF, subj: I and M Program Assistance at TSN, May 18, 1971; ltr, Brig Gen James H. Watkins, Ch, AFGP, to Cdr 834th AD, subj: VNAF Assumption of Airlift Missions, May 12, 1971; Webb, Erickson, and Lanman intvw, Feb 14, 1974.

14. 7th AF PAD 72-7-7, 457th TASq, Feb 22, 1972; 7th AF PAD 72-7-8, 458th TASq, Jan 21, 1972; hist, AFGP, Jul–Sep 71, pp 72, 77, Oct–Dec 71, p 11, and Jul–Sep 72, pp 22–23, 33; staff summary sheet, Lt Col Albert G. Rogers, Dep Dir/Opns, subj: C–7A Restricted Airfield Opns, Apr 5, 1972; hist, 483rd TAWg FOL and 377th ABWg—CCTS, Jan 1–Aug 24, 1972; rprt, Germeraad, EOTR, Mar 72, pp 29–31; hist, 483rd TAWg FOL, Sep–Dec 71.

15. Rprts, Col Roy D. Broadway, Ch, AFAT 5, Monthly Unit Advisor's Rprts, AFGP–AC–U2, May 7 through Aug 7, 1971; rprts, Col Henry L. Baulch, Ch, AFAT 5, Monthly Unit Advisor's Rprts, AFGP–AC–U2, Nov 7, 1971 through Mar 7, 1972; rprt, Maj Gen James H. Watkins, Ch, AFGP, Feb 71–May 72, p C–5; rprt, AF Advis Gp, MACV, Analysis of Major Acft Accident Experience in VNAF during CY 71, Jan 10, 1972; MR, Lt Col Thomas L. Bryant, Ch, Safety, AFGP, subj: Minutes of AFGP Semi-annual Flying Safety Conf, Sep 24, 1971.

16. Ltr, Maj Gen Robert R. Rowland, Ch, AFGP, to CDR VNAF, subj: VNAF C–47 Airlift, May 29, 1965; ltr, Maj Gen J. H. Moore, Cdr 7th AF, to COMUSMACV, subj: Airlift System, Apr 7, 1965; hists, AF Advis Gp, 1965 through 1968, Ford intvw, Apr 21, 1975; rprt, Brig Gen John H. Germeraad, Cdr 834th AD, EOTR, Mar 72, pp 27–32; ltr, Col William B. Griner, Dir/Opns, AF Advis Gp, to 7th AF, subj: Cd and Control of VNAF Airlift Acft, Sep 4, 1970; rprt, Col Senour Hunt, Ch, AFAT 5, EOTR, Dec 30, 1970, pp 3–4 to 3–5; memo, Col Walter J. Ford, ALCC Advisor, to AFAT 5, subj: VNAF Airlift Cd and Control, Feb 17, 1972.

17. Memo, Lt Col Gerald R. Lane, Ch, Combat Opns, 834th AD, subj: Commando Vault Airdrops from C–119 and C–123 Acft, Apr 14, 1971; fact sheet, AF Advis Gp, subj: Palletized Fixed-Wing Gunships (VNAF Combat ROC 35–70), Sep 70; staff summary sheet, Col Thomas A. Barr, Dir/Opns, AF Advis Gp, subj: Increased VNAF Airlift, Dec 13, 1971; hist, 310th TASq,

Jul–Sep 71, p 7; memo, Lt Col Albert G. Rogers, Dep Dir/Opns, AFGP, subj: Support for Expanded VNAF Aeromedical Evac Capability, Mar 26, 1972; AFGP Weekly Staff Digest, May 30–Jun 6, 1970, p 3.

18. Rprts, AF Advis Gp, VNAF Status Review, May 70, Dec 71, Dec 72; fact sheet, Col Raymond A. Boyd, Dir/Plans and Programs, AFAT, subj: VNAF Opns, Feb 9, 1972; rprt, Col Thomas A. Barr, Dir/Opns, AF Advis Gp, EOTR, Jan 5, 1973.

19. Rprt, AFAT 5, Qtrly Hist Summary, Jul–Sep 71, Oct 15, 1971; ltr, Maj Gen James H. Watkins, Ch, AFGP, to Maj Gen Jack C. Fuson, MACV J–4, subj: VNAF Short Field Capabilities, Feb 23, 1972; ltr, Col Henry L. Baulch, Ch, AFAT 5, to Dir/Opns, AFGP, subj: C–123 Type I Field Capability, Feb 2, 1972; rprts, Col Henry L. Baulch, Ch, AFAT 5, Monthly Unit Advisory Rprts, Mar 7 and Apr 7, 1972.

20. Rprts, Asst for Mutual Security, DCS/Materiel, Hq USAF, *Journal of Mutual Security*, Jul 58 through Mar 61; rprt, MACV J–3, Sr Advisor's Monthly Evaluation for Dec 64; ltr, Maj Edward M. Borinson, ALO 33rd Sp Zone, to ALO III Corps, subj: AAR, Nov 27, 1963; ltr, Capt Robert L. Paradis, FAC Abn Bde, to 2nd AD AOC, subj: ALO Rprt for Jul 64; ltr, Capt George E. Williamson, FAC, Abn Bde, 21st Inf Div, to 21st Div ALO, subj: Incident Rprt, Sep 3, 1964; ltr, Lt Col Earl Price, ALO 21st Div to IV Corps ALO, subj: Med Evac/Resupply Support, Nov 23, 1964; rprt, Capt Stanton R. Musser, ALO Abn Bde, 21st Inf Div, to ALO, 21st Div, subj: AAR, Nov 30, 1964; rprt, Sp Warfare Div, Dir/Plans, Hq USAF, Debriefing of Maj Alan G. Nelson, ALO 9th Inf Div, Feb 16, 1965; draft ms, Warren A. Trest and Jay E. Hines, "Air Tng Command's Spt of SEA, 1961–73," Hq ATC, 1977, pp 183–195.

21. Ltr, Brig Gen Albert W. Schinz, Ch, AF Advis Gp, MACV, to MACV, subj: Modernization of the VNAF, Oct 15, 1965; hists, AF Advis Gp, 1965 through Dec 68; rprt, MACV, Assessment of RVNAF, Feb 29 and Mar 21, 1968; rprts, AF Advis Gp, Monthly Eval Rprts, Feb and Sep 67; rprts, MACV, Monthly Eval, Nov 1965 through 1967; rprt, MACV J–3, RVNAF Regular Forces Advisory Rprt, 4th Qtr, CY 68, VNAF, Apr 2, 1969.

22. Rprts, AFGP, VNAF Status Review, May 70 and Dec 71; *Journal of Military Assistance*, Aug 70, p 140, Apr 71, p 154; JGS J–3 Directive no 310-19, Management and Employment of Helicopters, Feb 19, 1971; VNAF Plan 71–60, VNAF/USARV/AFGP, I & M Helicopter Activation Plan, Jul 7, 1971; rprt, Col Harold E. Fischer, Ch, AFAT 3, EOTR, Aug 8, 1972; ltr, Brig Gen Kendall S. Young, Ch, AFGP to MACV, subj: Assessment of the Situation, Aug 11, 1970; rprt, Col Franklin C. Davies, Dir/Opns, AFGP, EOTR, Jul 6, 1971.

23. Rprt, Col Harold E. Fischer, Ch, AFAT 3, EOTR, Aug 8, 1972; memo, Stanley R. Reson, Sec AR to Sec Def, subj: I & M of the VNAF, Apr 22, 1969; draft ms, 1st Avn Bde Info/Off, subj: 1st Avn Bde Opns, Jul 72; msg, CINCPACAF to CSAF (XPPE), 292223Z Aug 69; memo, Col Robert E. Grovert, Ch, Eval and Analysis Div, MACV J–3, to MACV J–3, subj: Eval of VNAF Helicopter Performance, Nov 19, 1970; rprt, AFAT 3, Qtrly Hist Summary, Jul–Sep 71; hist, AFGP, Jul–Sep 70, pp 68–69.

24. Rprt, Brig Gen Charles W. Carson, Ch, AF Advis Gp, EOTR, Aug 5, 1969; JGS J–3 Dir 310-19, Management and Employment of Helicopters, Feb 19, 1971; memo, Col Robert E. Grovert, Ch, Eval and Analysis Div, MACV J–3, subj: Eval of VNAF Helicopter Performance, Nov 19, 1970; msg, AF Advis Gp to Hq USAF (XOV), 130930Z May 71; memo, Lt Col Obie A. Smith, Dep Dir/Opns, AF Advis Gp, to Cdr, subj: Medevac/SAR, Oct 13, 1972; msg, 7th AF to CSAF, 271100Z Feb 71; study, AF Advis Gp, subj: VNAF Helicopter Capability, Jan 8, 1972, Tab B.

25. Ford intvw, Apr 21, 1975; memo, Col Richard A. Yudkin, Asst C/S Plans, Hq PACAF, for Gen Hetherington, subj: Force Objectives, Vietnam, 1962; JGS Dir 310-19, Management and Employment of Helicopters, Feb 19, 1971.

26. Memo, Col Robert E. Grovert, Ch, Eval and Analysis Div, MACV J–3, to MACV J–3, subj: Eval of VNAF Helicopter Performance, Nov 19, 1970; *Newsweek*, Mar 29, 1971; ltr, Robert Seamans, Sec AF, to Dep Sec Def, subj: VNAF UH–1H Maintenance, Apr 16,

1971; rprt, Maj Gen James H. Watkins, Ch, AF Advis Gp, EOTR, May 14, 1972; rprt, Col Harold R. Fischer, Ch, AFAT 3, EOTR, Aug 8, 1972; msg, AF Advis Gp to PACAF/CSAF, 190230Z May 71; fact sheet, Col Raymond A. Boyd, Dir/Plans and Programs, AF Advis Gp, subj: VNAF Opns, Feb 9, 1972.

27. Rprt, AF Advis Gp, VNAF Status Review, Aug 72, pp E-20 and E-21; hist, AF Advis Gp, Apr–Jun 72, p 17; article, translated from *Canh Thep* [magazine], "A Visit to an Aeromedical Division"; rprt, AFAT 5, Qtrly Hist Rprt, Apr–Jun 72, p 12.

28. Fact sheet, AF Advis Gp, MACV, subj: VNAF Combat Airlift Opns, Oct 7, 1972; rprt, Col Henry L. Baulch, Ch, AFAT 5, Monthly Unit Advis Rprt, Jun 7, 1972.

29. Rprts, Col Henry L. Baulch, Ch, AFAT 5, Monthly Unit Advis Rprt (U-2 Rprts), May 7 and Jun 7, 1972.

30. Rprt, AFAT 5, Qtrly Hist Rprt, Apr–Jun 72, p 12; fact sheet, AFGP; subj: VNAF Combat Airlift Opns, Oct 7, 1972.

31. MR, 7th AF, subj: VNAF Airdrops, Jun 7, 1972; memo, Maj J. D. Bryant, Transp Staff Off, AFGP, to Dir/Opns, AFGP, subj: VNAF Airdrops, Jun 14, 1972; memo, Col Thomas A. Barr, Dir/Opns, AFGP, to MACV J-45, subj: VNAF Airdrop Capabilities, Jun 22, 1972; msg 04438, Cdr MACV to Mr. Vann, SRAG, Pleiku, 131852Z May 72; Ringenbach, *Airlift to Besieged Areas,* Dec. 7, 1973, pp 36–37; rprt, AFAT 5, Qtrly Hist Summary, Apr–Jun 72; hist, AFGP, Apr–Jun 72, p 17; memo, Col T. A. Barr, Dir/Opns, AFGP, to Dir/Logis, subj: Radar Beacon, SST-181X, May 16, 1972; background paper, AF Advis Gp, subj: Overview of VNAF Combat Airlift Opns, 1 Apr–1 Oct 72, Oct 72.

32. Fact sheet, Off/Vietnamization, Hq USAF (XOV), subj: VNAF Helicopter Losses, 1 Apr–30 Jun 72, Jul 6, 1972; hist, AF Advis Gp, Apr–Jun 72, pp 32, 43, 71; rprt, AF Advis Gp, VNAF Status Review, Sep 72.

33. Miller intvw, May 24, 1972; daily logs, US Advisors to 5th ARVN Div, Apr and May 72; intvw, TRAC, Debriefing of Maj Kenneth A. Ingram and Capt Moffett, USA, Jun 1972; debriefing statement, Maj Kenneth A. Ingram, USA, 5th Div Arty Advisor, Jun 10, 1972; rprt, Advis Team 70, AAR Binh Long Campaign, Jul 20, 1972, pp 27–28; memo, 3rd Ranger Gp Advis Team, to Sr Advis, III Corps Ranger Cd, subj: Activities Rprt, Apr 8–May 20, 1972; rprt, Col Harold R. Fischer, Ch, AFAT 3, EOTR, Aug 8, 1972; rprt, Col Arthur R. Burke, Ch, Det 4, AFAT 2, EOTR, Sep 30, 1972; rprt, Lt Col Louis J. Yost, Ch, AFAT 3, Monthly Unit Advisors Rprt, for Jun 72; talking paper, Lt Col E. L. Carwile, Off/Vietnamization, Hq USAF, subj: VNAF Helicopter Aircrew Aggressiveness, Jul 6, 1972.

34. Rprt, Col Peter B. Van Brussel, Ch, AFAT 2, EOTR, Aug 14, 1972; rprt, Det 2, AFAT 2, Input for Qtrly Hist Rprt, Apr–Jun 72, Jul 6, 1972; talking paper, Lt Col E. L. Carwile, Off/Vietnamization (XOV), Hq USAF, subj: VNAF Helicopter Aircrew Aggressiveness, Jul 6, 1972, and atchd Fact Sheet, subj: VNAF Helicopter Operational Highlights, n.d.; rprt, Col Theodore C. Williams, USA, Sr Advis, 9th Inf Div, Debriefing Rprt, Jan 24, 1973; rprt, Col George A. Millener, USA, Sr Advis, 1st Inf Div, Debriefing Rprt, Feb 13, 1973; rprt, Maj Gen Howard H. Cooksey, Cdr 1st Regional Assist Cd, Debriefing Rprt, May 9, 1973.

35. Ltr, Col Peter B. Van Brussel, Ch, AFAT 2, to AF Advis Gp, subj: 2nd AD Instrument Flying Ability, Jun 10, 1972; rprt, Col P. B. Van Brussel, Ch, AFAT 2 Monthly Unit Advisory Rprt, Jul 4, 1972; rprt, Col Thomas A. Barr, Dir/Opns, AF Advis Gp, EOTR, Jan 5, 1973; msg, AF Advis Gp to PACAF, 040818Z Dec 72; hist, AF Advis Gp, Jul–Sep 72, pp 31–32, 63–64; rprt, AFAT 3, Qtrly Hist Summary, Jul–Sep 72, Oct 14, 1972; hist, Dir/Mil Assist and Sales, Hq USAF, Jul–Dec 72, p 79.

36. Ltr, Col John D. Rice, Dir/Materiel, AF Advisory Gp, MACV, to Cdr, 2nd Aerial Port Gp, subj: Transportation Advisory Support, May 26, 1966; hist, AF Advisory Gp, MACV, May, Jun, Aug 66; ltr, Col John D. Bigs, Dir/Materiel, AF Advisory Gp, to Cdr, 2nd Aerial Port Gp, subj: Transportation Advisory Support, May 26, 1966; ltr, Brig Gen Albert W. Schinz, Ch, AF Advisory Gp, to Cdr, 315th AD, subj: Proposed Ltr of Agreement, Oct 5, 1966.

37. Ltr, Col William E. Miller, Dir/Materiel, AF Advisory Gp, to 834th AD, subj: Memo of Agreement, Sep 28, 1967;

ltr, Dir/Opns, 2nd Aerial Port Gp, to 8th, 14th, and 15th Aerial Port Sqs, Oct 20, 1967; hist, AF Advisory Gp, Apr 67, Mar and Apr 68; hist, 2nd Aerial Port Gp, Jul 66–Sep 67, pp 40–41, Oct–Dec 67, pp 43–44, Apr–Jun 68, pp 35–36; hist, 8th Aerial Port Sq, Jan–Mar, and Apr–Jun 68; hist, 14th Aerial Port Sq, Jul–Sep 68, pp 9–10.

38. Hists, 2nd Aer Port Gp, Jul–Sep 69 through Oct–Dec 71; ltr, Maj Gen John H. Herring, Cdr 834th AD, to 483rd TAWg, et al, subj: Transfer of Aerial Port Operating Locations to the VNAF, Mar 20, 1971; rprt, 2nd Aer Port Gp and AFGP, Joint Rprt on Aerial Port Transfers, Jun 30, 1971; ltr, Maj Gen James H. Watkins, Ch, AFGP, to 7th AF, subj: VNAF Airlift Efficiency, Feb 24, 1972; rprt, Col Hubert N. Dean, Ch, Transp Div, MACV J-4, EOTR, Aug 71, pp 4–5; *Di Di Mau* [2nd Aer Port Gp publication], Feb 28, 1971; rprts, Gaylor, Long, and Bettis, EOTRs, Sep 70, Jul 71, and Jul 72.

39. Rprt, Col Peter B. Van Brussel, Ch, AFAT 2, EOTR, Aug 14, 1972, pp 16-5 and 16-6; rprt, Col Peter B. Van Brussel, Ch, AFAT 2, Monthly Unit Advis Rprt (U-2 Rprt), Apr 4, 1972; rprt, AFGP, Transportation Advisors Conf, Enhance II, Aug 3–4, 1972; rprt, Det 2, AFAT 2, Input for Qtrly Hist Rprt, Apr–Jun 72, Jul 6, 1972; rprt, Det 3, AFAT 2, Input for Qtrly Hist Rprt, Apr–Jun 72, Jul 12, 1972; rprt, Col Henry L. Baulch, Ch, AFAT 5, Monthly Unit Advisors Rprt, Dec 14, 1972.

40. Msg, AF Advis Gp to PACAF, 120800Z Jan 73.

41. Rprts, Col Henry L. Baulch, Ch, AFAT 5, Monthly Unit Advisors Rprt, Dec 14, 1972 and Jan 8, 1973.

42. Rprts, AF Advis Gp, VNAF Status Review, Sep and Oct 72; hist, AF Advis Gp, Jul–Sep 72, p 21; rprt, AFAT 5, Qtrly Hist Summary, Apr–Jun and Jul–Sep 72; hist, Dir/Mil Assist and Sales, Hq USAF, Jul–Dec 72, p 75.

43. Msg, MACV to CINCPAC, 290955A May 72; rprt, Col Raymond A. Boyd, Dir/Plans and Programs, AF Advis Gp, EOTR, Jul 14, 1972; Proposed Combat ROC, AF Advis Gp, subj: Modernization of Transport Fleet, Jun 24, 1972; background paper, DCS/S&L, Hq USAF, subj: C-130 for the VNAF, Mar 23, 1973; *Washington Post*, Oct 19 and 24, 1972; Capt Thomas DesBrisay, *VNAF Improvement and Modernization Program, Jul 71–Dec 73*, (Hq PACAF, Proj CHECO, 1975), pp 81–87.

44. Background paper, DCS/S&L, Hq USAF, subj: C-130 for VNAF, Mar 23, 1973; hist rprt, Gerald T. Cantwell, Hq AF Reserve, Operation Enhance Plus, Apr 73, I, 10–16; ltr, Lt Gen Harry E. Goldsworthy, DCS/S&L, Hq USAF, to Vice CSAF (Gen Wade), subj: Proj Enhance Plus, Oct 24, 1972; background paper, DCS/S&L, Hq USAF, subj: Enhance Plus Aircraft Movement Summary, Nov 15, 1972; hist, Dir/Opns, Hq USAF, Jul–Dec 72, pp 269–270.

45. Ltrs, Lt Col Fred G. Hyre, Ch, AFAT 5, to AFGP, subj: Spl Rprt on VNAF C-130 Flying Training Program, Dec 2, 15, and 22, 1972, and Jan 17, 1973; msg, PACAF to 7th AF, 040210Z Nov 72; ltr, Col Henry L. Baulch, Ch, AFAT 5, to AFGP, subj: VNAF C-130A Flying Training Program, Dec 20, 1972; rprt, AFGP, Enhance Plus AAR, Oct 26–Dec 21, 1972; Posey intvw, Mar 29, 1974 (Posey was assigned to MACV ALCC during Sep 72–Mar 73); hist, Off/Spl Asst for Vietnamization, Hq USAF, Jul–Dec 72, pp 25–26, 29; hist, Dir/Opns, Hq USAF, Jul–Dec 72, p 261, Jan–Jun 73, pp 221–222.

46. Ltr, Capt Darel M. Ray, Cdr/MTT, to AF Advis Gp, subj: Special Rprt, VNAF C-130A Maint Tng, Jan 4, 1973; background papers, Off/Vietnamization (XOV), Hq USAF, subj: VNAF Tng for Enhance Plus Acft, Dec 26, 1972 and Jan 9, 1973; rprts, Col Henry L. Baulch, Ch, AFAT 5, Monthly Unit Advisors Rprt, Dec 14, 1972 and Jan 8, 1973; msgs, AF Advis Gp to Hq USAF, 200817Z and 240901Z Dec 72.

47. Ltr, Gen Fred C. Weyand, Cdr MACV, to Gen Cao Van Vien, CJGS, Jan 14, 1973; ltrs, Maj Gen J. J. Jumper, Ch, AF Advis Gp, to Lt Gen Tran Van Minh, Cdr VNAF, Dec 9 and 31, 1972; background paper, DCS/S&L, Hq USAF, subj: C-130 for VNAF, Mar 23, 1973; msg T/LG, PACAF to CINCPAC, 040140Z Jan 73; rprt, Lt Gen William G. Moore, Jr, Cdr 13th AF, EOTR, Dec 28, 1973.

48. Ltr, Col Henry L. Baulch, Ch, AFAT 5 to AFGP, subj: VNAF C-130A Flying Training Program, Dec 20, 1972; ltr, Col Thomas A. Barr, Dir/Opns, AFGP to Cdr AFAT 5, subj: VNAF

C-130A Flying Training Program, Dec 25, 1972; msg, AFGP to CSAF, 270730Z Jan 73; rprts, AFGP, Staff Digest, Jan 6–12 and Jan 13–19, 1973.

49. Rprt, Maj Robert L. Highley, Aircrew Eval Sect, 374th TAWg, Trip Rprt, 13–29 Jan 73, Jan 30, 1973; rprt, Capt Harvey R. Elliott, 37th TASq, Acft Cdr's Rprt of VNAF Drop Training, Jan 73; hist, 374th TAWg, Oct–Dec 72, p 32, Jan–Mar 73, pp 47–48; Iosue intvw, Mar 27, 1975; ltr, Col Thomas A. Barr, Dir/Opns, AFGP, to Col Nguyen Van Ngoe, DCS/Opns, VNAF, subj: Seek Point Certification, Nov 29, 1972; msg, PACAF to AFGP, 190015Z Jan 73; msg, AFGP to CSAF, 270730Z Jan 73.

50. Rprt, Col Thomas A. Barr, Dir/Opns, AFGP, EOTR, Jan 5, 1973, p 13; rprt, AFGP, Enhance Plus AAR, Oct 26–Dec 21, 1972; hist, MACV, 1972–Mar 73, pp C–72 to C–74, H–17; JCSM–445–72, JCS to Sec Def, subj: US Advisors in the RVN, Oct 6, 1972.

Chapter XXIV

Return to Cold War in Southeast Asia

1. Hist, 374th TAWg, Jan–Jun 72, pp 3–4, 97, Jul–Sep 72, Oct–Dec 72; rprt, Airlift Sect, MACV J–3, Monthly Hist Rprt for Jul, Aug 4, 1972; msg MACDL–42, MACV to CINCPAC, 280121Z Jul 72.

2. Msg, Dir/Opns 7th AF to PACAF, 131130Z Nov 72; rprt, Col Andrew P. Iosue, Cdr 374th TAWg, EOTR, Jul 1, 1973, p 13; Iosue intvw, Mar 27, 1975; Clark intvw, Mar 29, 1974; hist, 374th TAWg, Oct–Dec 72, p 20, 24, 32; memo, Maj Gen C. M. Talbott, MACV Dir/Opns, to MACV Dir/Logistics, subj: Inadequate C–130 Airlift Support, Dec 7, 1972.

3. Rprts, Airlift Sect, MACV J–3, Monthly Hist Rprts for Nov and Dec, Dec 5, 1972 and Jan 4, 1973; memo, Maj Gen Jack C. Fuson, MACV, Dir/Logistics, to MACV Dir/Opns, subj: Inadequate C–130 Airlift Support, Dec 6, 1972; memo, Lt Col James E. Marshall, Ch, ALCC, for Maj Gen Jumper, subj: C–130A Planning Conf, Nov 27, 1972.

4. Ltr, Lt Col Daniel R. Parker, Sq Nav, 39th TASq, to Lt Col Jarmek, 317th TAWg, subj: Airdrop Ballistics, Sep 14, 1972; staff summary sheet, Col Thomas E. Newton, Ch, Airlift Sect, 7th AF, subj: Parachute Streamer Malfunctions during Aerial Delivery, Sep 7, 1972; memo, MACV Dir/Logistics to MACV Dir/Opns, subj: Minh Thanh Airdrops, Aug 30, 1972; hist, 374th TAWg, Jul–Sep 72, pp 33–37, Oct–Dec 72, p 24, 31; msg DO–227, Dir/Opns, 7th AF to PACAF, 300600Z Nov 72.

5. Hist, 316th TAWg, Oct–Dec 72, pp 7–9; ltr, Cdr 37th TASq to 316th TAWg, subj: Monthly Activity Rprt, Dec 72, Jan 6, 1973; rprt, Lt Col Arne Ellermets, Cdr 37th TASq, EOTR, Constant Guard IV, [ca Mar 1973]; hist, 374th TASq, Oct–Dec 72, pp 3–4; Posey intvw, Mar 29, 1974 (Posey was assigned to MACV ALCC at Tan Son Nhut in fall 1972, moving to Thailand in Mar 73).

6. Capt John B. Taylor, "Milk Run," *Airman,* Feb 75, pp 43–47.

7. *New York Times,* Jan 24, 1973; *Washington Post,* Jan 24, 1973; official text of agreement in Dept State *Bulletin,* no 1755, Feb 12, 1973.

8. Memo, Brig Gen H. P. Smith, ACS/Intell, Hq USAF, to CSAF, subj: C–130 Aircrew Debrief, Jan 30, 1973; Iosue intvw, Mar 27, 1975; Posey intvw, Mar 29, 1974; articles in CCK base newspaper, appended to Hist, 374th TAWg, Jan–Mar 73.

9. Msg, MACV J–3 to subord units, 311250Z Jan 73; fact sheet, US Delegation, FPJMC, subj: PRG and DRV Hanoi to Saigon Airlift for Feb 4, 1973; hist, 374th TAWg, Jan–Mar 73, pp 37–38; hist, 345th TASq, Jan–Mar 73, pp 9–10; hist, Intell Div, 374th TAWg, Jan–Mar 73, pp 9–10.

10. Rprt, Joint Homecoming Reception

Center, 13th AF, AAR, Opn Homecoming, Jun 6, 1973, pp 6–12.

11. Brya intvw, Apr 22, 1975; ltr, Lt Gen William G. Moore, Cdr 13th AF, to 374th TAWg, subj: Ltr of Appreciation, Apr 22, 1973; rprt, US Delegation, FPJMC, Final Rprt, Jun 73; intvw, Lt Col J. F. Ohlinger, 13th AF, with Col James R. Dennett, Feb 15, 1973; rprt, Col James R. Dennett, Team Chief, RST, 13th AF, 1973; rprt, 13th AF JHRC, Opn Homecoming, Jun 6, 1973, pp 15–16; articles in CCK base newspaper, appended to Hist, 374th TAWg, Jan–Mar 73.

12. Clark intvw, Mar 29, 1974; Posey intvw, Mar 29, 1974; MR, Lt Col Gordon L. Kremer, Sr Liaison Officer, Feb 11, 1973; ltr, Brig Gen Stan L. McClellan, C/S, USARV, to Ch, US Delegation, FPJMC, subj: Opn Homecoming, Ph 1, Feb 13, 1973; rprt, Maj Joseph G. De Santis, Acft Cdr, 20th Opns Sq, Mission Rprt, Feb 12, 1973; rprt, Opns Off, 9th AME Gp, Trip Rprt, Opn Homecoming, Feb 12, 1973.

13. Msg, Ch US Elm, FPJMC, Reg 1 Hue to Ch US Delegation, FPJMC, 101100Z Feb 73; MR, Maj Alonzo B. Method, Dy Off, FPJMC, Opns Br, subj: Bien Hoa POW's, Feb 12, 1973; rprt, Lt Col Robert L. Merrick, USA, Secy US Delegation, FPJMC, Reg 1 Hue, 15-Day Summary of Activities Rprt, X-day to X plus 15, Feb 14, 1973.

14. Clark intvw, Mar 29, 1974; hist, 345th TASq, Jan–Mar 73, pp 9–10; rprt, Lt Col Robert L. Merrick, USA, Secy US Elm, FPJMC, Reg 1 Hue, Fifteen-day Summary of Activities, X plus 16 to X plus 30, Feb 28, 1973; msg, Ch US Elm, FPJMC, Reg 1 Hue, to Ch US Elm, FPJMC, 141225Z Feb 73; MR, Maj Logan, FPJMC Opns, subj: Recap Movement of POW's to Camp Evans, 151010H Feb 73.

15. Rprt, 13th AF JHRC, Opn Homecoming, Jun 6, 1973; hist, 317th TAWg, Jan–Mar 73, pp 8–12; hist, 316th TAWg, Jan–Mar 73, pp 10–13; rprt, Maj Melvin F. Stutzman, 37th TASq, Mission Rprt, Mar 4–6, 1973; Clark and Posey intvws, Mar 29, 1974.

16. Hist, 374th TAWg, Jan–Mar 73, pp 28–29, 33–35; hist, USSAG, Apr–Jun 73, pp 133–134; staff summary sheet, Dir/Transp, Hq USAF, subj: Withdrawal of US Forces from Vietnam, Apr 5, 1973; msg, 7th AF to 56th SOWg TUOC/C–130 Opns, NKP, *et al*, 180400Z Jan 73; msg, MACV J–4 to Cdr 7th AF, *et al*, 140825Z Nov 72.

17. Study, Dir/Plans, Hq USAF, Study on USAF Post-Hostilities Posture in Thailand, Apr 25, 1969; ltr, Lt Gen A. J. Russell, Asst Vice CSAF, to Sec AF, subj: Reentry to SEA Bases, Dec 4, 1970; hist, Dir/Plans, Hq USAF, Jul–Dec 70, pp 81–82, 91–95, Jul–Dec 71, pp 255–256; JCSM 235–72, JCS to Sec Def, subj: Contingency Planning for the RVN, May 23, 1972.

18. Hist, CINCPAC, 1972, pp 591–594, 1973, pp 119–120, 125–128, 137–139, 653–664, 712–714; hist, Dir/Plans, Hq USAF, Jan–Jun 72, pp 102–103.

19. Msg, CINCPAC to MACV, 090215Z Dec 72; Posey intvw, Mar 29, 1974; hist, MACV, 1972–Mar 73, pp 137–139; hist, USSAG, Jan–Mar 73, pp 82–89, 96–97; rprt, Col Leo C. Wurschmidt, Ch, Maint, 374th TAWg, Trip Rprt, 374th TAW/FOL, May 11, 1974; rprt, Col Benjamin F. Ingram, Ch, Current Opns Div, USSAG/7th AF, Jun 30, 1975; hist, CINCPAC, 1974, pp 317–318.

20. Staff summary sheet, Dir/Programs, Hq USAF, subj: C–130 Contingency Planning, Aug 15, 1973; hist, CINCPAC, 1973, pp 343–347; msg 3635, JCS to CINCPAC, CSAF, 031938Z Aug 73; hist, 374th TAWg, Jan–Mar 73, pp 4–5, 23–24, 36–37, Jul–Nov 73, pp 2–18; background paper, Dir/Opns, Hq USAF, subj: Plans for SEA . . . , Nov 18, 1973.

21. Hist, USSAG/7th AF, Oct–Dec 74, p 53, Jan–Mar 75, pp 83–84; hists, 374th TAWg, Apr–Jun 73, pp 42–45, Jul–Nov 73, p 30, Nov 73–Mar 74, pp 7, 10, 18; Posey intvw, Mar 29, 1974; Capt Robert L. MacNaughton, "Do You Have Contact With Hanoi?" CCK newspaper, Jun 16, 1973.

22. Hist, 374th TAWg, Apr–Jun 74, chap 4, Nov 73–Mar 74, p 35; rprt, Col Leo C. Wurschmidt, Ch, Maint, 374th TAWg, Trip Rprt, 374th TAW/FOL, May 11, 1974; rprt, Lt Col Herschel E. Coulter, Dir/Supply and Svcs, 13th AF, Staff Assistance Visit, 374th TOL, U-Tapao, 8–14 Jun 74, Jun 20, 1974.

23. Hist, USSAG/7th AF, Jul–Sep 73 through Jan–Mar 75; rprt, Brig Gen James R. Hildreth, Cdr 13th AF, ADVON, EOTR, Jan 9, 1975; rprt, Col Benjamin F. Ingram, Ch, Current Opns Div, USSAG/7th AF, Jun 30, 1975;

hists, 21st SOSq, Apr 73 through Oct–Dec 74.

24. Hist, Dir/Plans, Hq USAF, Jan–Jun 73, p 170; hist, Dir/Mil Assist and Sales, Hq USAF, Jul–Dec 72, p 44, Jan–Jun 73, pp 102–103; JCSM 38–73, JCS to Sec Def, subj: C–123K Acft Disposition, Jan 23, 1973; background paper, Dir/Mil Assist and Sales, Hq USAF, subj: C–123K Allocation, Apr 18, 1973.

25. Fact sheet, Joint Staff, subj: C–123K Aircraft and Supporting AGE/Spares, Sep 28, 1973; fact sheet, Joint Staff, subj: FANK Aerial Delivery, Sep 28, 1973; hist, Dir/Mil Assist and Sales, Hq USAF, Jan–Jun 73, p 36, Jul–Dec 73, p 55; hist, CINCPAC, 1972, pp 396–401, 1973, pp 429–446.

26. Hist, Dir/Plans, Hq USAF, Jul–Dec 72, pp 177–178, Jan–Jun 74, pp 181–182; hist, USSAG/7th AF, Apr–Jun 74, p 6; hist, CINCPAC, 1973, pp 484–490, 1974, pp 417–421; rprt, Maj Gen Richard G. Trefry, Dep Ch JUSMAG Udorn and Def Attache Vientiane, 5 Feb 73–11 Dec 74, EOTR, Dec 11, 1974; msg, CINCPACFLT to AIG 286, 212141Z Feb 73.

27. Hist, Dir/Opns, Hq USAF, Jan–Jun 73, p 166; hist, CINCPAC, 1973, pp 523–525, 1975, pp 463–469; hist, USMACTHAI, JUSMACTHAI, 1973, p 144.

28. Hist, PACAF, Jul 74–Dec 75, pp 485–489.

29. Study, DAO, Saigon, Aerial Resupply, Tong Le Chan, Mar 73–Apr 74, 1974; Capt Thomas D. DesBrisay, *VNAF Improvement and Modernization Program, Jul 71–Dec 73,* Jan 1, 1975, p 88; hist, DAO Saigon, Jul–Sep 73, pp 160–161, Oct–Dec 73, pp 234–235, Jan–Mar 74, pp 181–182, Apr–Jun 74, pp 141–142; hist, USSAG/7th AF, Jul–Sep 73, pp 158–159; fact sheet, Brig Gen Ralph J. Maglione, Ch, Opns and Plans Div, subj: Aerial Resupply, Sep 20, 1973.

30. Hist, DAO Saigon, Oct–Dec 73, p 87, Apr–Jun 74, p 99; rprt, Col Garvin McCurdy, Air Attache, Saigon, Overview of the Working Environment in DAO Saigon and the VNAF in mid-September 1974, Sep 24, 1974, pp 15–48; intvw, author with Col Garvin McCurdy, Washington, DC, Jun 3, 1975.

31. McCurdy intvw, Jun 3, 1975; rprt, Col Garvin McCurdy, Air Attache, Saigon, Overview of the Working Environment in DAO Saigon and the VNAF in mid-September 1974, Sep 24, 1974; IR 1–502–0270–75, Jul 28, 1975; hist, DAO Saigon, Oct–Dec 74, pp 86–87.

32. Hist, DAO Saigon, Apr–Jun 73, pp 118–135, Jul–Sep 73, pp 75–76, Oct–Dec 73, pp 79–83, 85; Capt Thomas D. DesBrisay, *VNAF Improvement and Modernization Program, Jul 71–Dec 73,* Jan 1, 1975, pp 87–91; rprt, DAO, Qtrly Assessment of RVNAF, Jul 73; rprt, Lt Gen William G. Moore, Jr, Cdr 13th AF, EOTR, Dec 28, 1973; rprt, PACAF, Summary Air Opns SEA, Jul 73.

33. McCurdy intvw, Jun 3, 1975; memo, Col Ray L. Bowers, AFCHO, subj: Round-table Discussion with Lt Gen Tran Van Minh, Ch VNAF, Maj Gen Vo Xuan Lanh, Dep Ch VNAF, Brig Gen Dung Dinh Linh, VNAF DCS/Materiel, and Col Hoang, VNAF Dir/Intell, Hq USAF, Jul 16–17, 1975; IR 1–502–0210–75, Jul 22, 1975; IR 1–502–0211–75, Jul 22, 1975.

34. Gen Van Tien Dung, "Great Spring Victory," in Hanoi *Nhan Dan,* Apr 1, 1976, p 3, transl in FBIS-APA-76-110, Jun 7, 1976, p 1–4; hist, PACAF, Jul 74–Dec 75, pp 111–113, 485–491; hist, USSAG/7th AF, Jul–Sep 73, pp 64–65, Apr–Jun 74, pp 2–3, 115–116, Jul–Sep 74, p iv, Oct–Dec 74, pp v–vi; rprt, Comm on Foreign Relations, US Senate, subj: Vietnam: May 1974, Aug 5, 1974; rprt, DAO, Qtrly Assessment of RVNAF, Jul 73.

35. Hist, USSAG/7th AF, Apr–Jun 74, p 57, Jul–Sep 74, p 38, Oct–Dec 74, pp 28–30, Oct–Dec 73, p 87, Jan–Mar 74, p 45.

36. Rprt, Col Garvin McCurdy, Air Attache, Saigon, Overview of the Working Environment in DAO Saigon and the VNAF in mid-Sep 74, Sep 24, 1974, pp 15–32; rprt, Hon Paul N. McCloskey, Vietnam Factfinding Trip, Feb 24 to Mar 3, 1975, The North Vietnam-South Vietnam Confrontation, *Congressional Record,* Mar 14, 1975; Maynard Parker, "Vietnam: The War That Won't End," *Foreign Affairs,* Jan 75, pp 352–374; McCurdy intvw, Jun 3, 1975; hist, CINCPAC, 1974, pp 429–437; hist, DAO Saigon, Jan–Apr 75, pp 29–34; Van Tien Dung, "Great Spring Victory," p 5.

37. Hist, DAO Saigon, Jul–Sep 74, pp 53–55, Oct–Dec 74, pp 67–71, 125–126; McCurdy intvw, Jun 3, 1975.

38. Background paper, Maj R. E. Heverly, Off/Spl Asst Vietnamization (XOV), Hq USAF, subj: VNAF Heli-

copter Forces, Sep 19, 1973; hist, DAO Saigon, Apr–Jun 74, p 99, Oct–Dec 74, pp 88, 95–96; msg, CV/MM, AFLC to US Army Mat Cd, 202112Z Nov 73; rprt, Brig Gen Harry H. Hiestand, US Army, Cdr FRAC, Jan 25–Mar 23, 1973, Debriefing Rprt, May 11, 1973.

39. Msg, DAO Saigon to PACAF, 160618Z Jan 75; McCurdy intvw, Jun 3, 1975; memo, Bowers, Round-table Discussion with Minh, Lanh, Linh, and Hoang, Jul 16–17, 1975; *New York Times*, Dec 18, 1974–Jan 3, 6, 7, and 8, 1975.

40. Rprt, Hon Paul N. McCloskey, Vietnam Factfinding Trip, Feb 24 to Mar 3, 1975, The North Vietnam-South Vietnam Confrontation, *Congressional Record*; intvw, Capt DesBrisay with Mr. P. L. Tollestrup, Dep Ch, AF Div, DAO Saigon, Nov 24, 1973; msg, DAO Saigon to JCS/DIA, 310656Z Jan 75; hist, USSAG/7th AF, Jan–Mar 75, p 103; McCurdy intvw, Jun 3, 1975.

41. Study, DOD, Assessment of the Military Situation in Cambodia, Oct 72; msgs, CINCPAC to PACAF, 240516Z May 72 and 052351Z Apr 72; msg 3142, MEDTC Fwd, Phnom Penh, to CINCPAC, 230240Z May 72; msg 5039, JCS to CINCPAC, 140048Z Nov 72; hist, CINCPAC, 1972, pp 286–288, 338–339.

42. Hist, 374th TAWg, Apr–Jun 73, pp 14–15, 41–42; hist, 345th TASq, Apr–Jun 73, p 9; hist, USSAG, Apr–Jun 73, pp 131–132; msg, Ch, MEDTC, Phnom Penh, to CINCPAC, 151215Z Apr 73; msg 8158, JCS to CINCPAC, 211728Z Apr 73.

43. Fact sheet, Joint Staff, subj: Transportation Logistical Support of Cambodia, Sep 28, 1973; rprt, PACAF, Summary Air Opns SEA, Jul 23; rprt, Lt Gen William G. Moore, Cdr 13th AF, EOTR, Dec 28, 1973; hist, CINCPAC, 1973, pp 346, 350; hist, USSAG/7th AF, Jul–Sep 73, pp 28–29.

44. Clark intvw, Mar 29, 1974; hist, PACAF, Jul 73–Jun 74, pp 29–46; hist, 374th TAWg, Apr–Jun 73, p 42; SSgt Ben Langer, "Objective is to Deliver," Hist, 374th TAWg, Apr–Jun 73, p 30.

45. Posey intvw, Mar 29, 1974; SSgt Ben Langer, "U-Tapao FOL Aircrew Picks Up after Easter Bunny," Hist, 374th TAWg, Apr–Jun 73, p 31; fact sheet, Joint Staff, subj: Major Construction Projects in the Khmer Republic, Sep 26, 1973.

46. Fact sheet, Joint Staff, subj: C–130 Airdrops, Sep 28, 1973; daily mission worksheets, Airlift Sect, MACV J–3, PACAF Forms 20b, Nov 72 through Jan 73; hists, 374th TAWg, Jul–Sep 72 through Jul–Sep 73.

47. Ltrs, Mission Cdrs, 317th TAWg/AWADS Element, to Cdr 317th TAWg, subj: Weekly Rprt, 23–29 Apr 73 through 10–16 Jun 73; hist, USSAG/7th AF, Jul–Sep 73, pp 156–158; hist, PACAF, Jul 73–Jun 74, p 33; fact sheet, Lt Col J. C. Greenquist, JCS J–4, subj: Proj SCOOT, Airdrop of Supplies, 1973; hist, 374th TAWg, Apr–Jun 74; rprt, Col B. F. Ingram, USSAG, EOTR, Jun 30, 1975.

48. Ltr, Lt Col L. R. Fillmore, Mission Cdr, Det A, 317th TAWg, to Cdr 317th TAWg, subj: Weekly Rprt, Jun 24–30, 1973.

49. Msg CJCS sends, JCS to CINCPAC, 142330Z Aug 73; background paper, Capt R. A. Wiswell, Div/Pacific-East Asia, Dir/Plans, Hq USAF, subj: The Legality of USAF C–130 Support of Cambodia, Jan 13, 1975.

50. Rprt, Intell Div, 374th TAWg, Input for Wg Hist Rprt, 1 Oct–15 Nov 73; hist, USSAG/7th AF, Jul–Sep 73, pp 100–101.

51. Hist, USSAG/7th AF, Oct–Dec 73, pp 24–25, 118–119, 134–135, 138–141; fact sheet, Joint Staff, subj: Airlift of Rice from Battambang to P/P, Sep 28, 1973; hist, PACAF, Jul 73–Jun 74, pp 34–35.

52. Hist, USSAG/7th AF, Jan–Mar 74, pp 6–9, 126, 155–157, Apr–Jun 74, pp 112–113; hist, PACAF, Jul 73–Jun 74, pp 36–39; memo, Maj Gen Edward Bautz, USA, Actg Dir/Opns, to Dir/Joint Staff, subj: US Air Opns in Cambodia, Mar 12, 1974.

53. Hist, 374th TAWg, Apr–Jun 74; hist, PACAF, Jul 73–Jun 74, pp 31–32, 40; hist, USSAG/7th AF, Apr–Jun 74, pp 83–84, Jul–Sep 74, p 76; msg, U-Tapao SOA to USSAG/7th AF, 110620Z Apr 74.

54. Memo, Capt Donald A. Conklin, Asst Wg Nav, 374th TAWg, to Dir/Opns, 374th TAWg, subj: Qtrly Hist Rprt, Oct 25, 1973; hist, USSAG/7th AF, Apr–Jun 74, pp 85, 107–110, 115–116, Jul–Sep 74, p 26; Tony Koura, *The Cambodia Airlift, 1974–1975*, (PACAF, Oct 31, 1976), pp 21–23; msg, CINCPAC to JCS, 150714Z Apr 75.

55. Koura, *The Cambodia Airlift*, pp 6–16; hist, PACAF, Jul 73–Jun 74, pp 43–46; rprt, Col Benjamin F. Ingram, Ch, Current Opns Div, USSAG/7th AF, Jun 30, 1975; hist, USSAG/7th AF, Jul–Sep 74, pp 76–77, 102–103, Oct–Dec 74, pp 33–34, 52–53, 94–95; fact sheet, Dir/Pacific-East Asia, Dir/Plans, Hq USAF, subj: Bird Contracts, Mar 10, 1975.

56. Intvw, author and Dr. Elizabeth Hartsook, with Col Douglas A. Roysdon, Air Attache, Cambodia, Jul 74–Apr 75, May 28, 1975; msg J-832, CINCPAC to JCS/Sec Def, 040333Z Feb 75; hist, USSAG/7th AF, Jul–Sep 74, p 104; msg, Ch, MEDTC, Phnom Penh to Hq USAF, 020830Z Mar 73.

57. Hist, USSAG/7th AF, Oct–Dec 73, pp 9–11, Jan–Mar 74, p 8, Apr–Jun 74, pp 92, 105–106; msg, Ch, MEDTC, Phnom Penh, to CINCPAC, 180230Z Nov 74; fact sheets, KAF Air Opns, atch to Rprt, Maj Gen John R. D. Cleland, Vice Dir/Opns, JCS, Trip Rprt to SEA, 10–20 Mar, Mar 24, 1975; rprts, PACAF, Summary Air Opns SEA, May and Jul 73.

58. Hist, USSAG/7th AF, Jul–Sep 74, pp 77–78, 100–101, Oct–Dec 74, pp 53–54, 92–94, Jan–Mar 75, pp 168–169, 85, Apr–Jun 75, pp 132–133; msg 1881, Ch, MEDTC, Phnom Penh to Hq USAF, 020830Z Mar 73; rprt, Col Benjamin F. Ingram, Ch, Current Opns Div, USSAG/7th AF, EOTR, Jun 30, 1975; Koura, *The Cambodia Airlift*, pp 3–5.

59. Hist, CINCPAC, 1974, pp 328–330, 649–654; hist, USSAG/7th AF, Oct–Dec 74, pp vi–viii; hists, Intell Div, 374th TAWg, Nov 73–Mar 74 through Oct–Dec 74.

Chapter XXV

The 1975 Denouement

1. Koura, *The Cambodia Airlift*, pp 27–30; hist, USSAG/7th AF, Jan–Mar 75, pp viii–xi; rprt, Col Robert A. Stefanik, USAF, J-2 USSAG, EOTR, Jun 30, 1975, pp 22–24.

2. Koura, *The Cambodia Airlift*, pp 27–34; hist, USSAG/7th AF, Jan–Mar 75, pp 8–18; Roysdon intvw, May 28, 1975.

3. Koura, *The Cambodia Airlift*, pp 34–52; fact sheets, Atch to Rprt, Maj Gen John R. D. Cleland, Vice Dir/Opns, JCS, Trip Rprt, SEA, 10–20 Mar, Mar 24, 1975; ms, Zoe Hanisian and Kenneth L. Patchin, Off/MAC History, "Cambodian Resupply and Evacuation, A Chronology," Dec 15, 1975, pp 9–22; msgs, US Embassy, Phnom Penh, to Sec State, 100530Z and 230800Z Feb 75.

4. Koura, *The Cambodia Airlift*, pp 52–73; hist, USSAG/7th AF, Jan–Mar 75, pp 21–23, 174–175; rprt, Maj Gen John R. D. Cleland, USA, Vice Dir/Opns, JCS, Trip Rprt, SEA, 10–20 Mar, Mar 24, 1975; msg J4716, CINCPAC to JCS, 202243Z Mar 75.

5. Roysdon intvw, May 28, 1975; rprt, Col Benjamin F. Ingram, Ch, Current Opns Div, USSAG/7th AF, EOTR, Jun 30, 1975, pp 5–7, 35–36; rprt, Col Drury Callaghan, Ch, Cd and Control Div, USSAG/7th AF, EOTR, Jul 1, 1975; hist, USSAG/7th AF, Jan–Mar 75, pp 147–148; ms, Zoe Hanisian and Kenneth L. Patchin, Off/MAC History, "Cambodia Resupply and Evacuation, A Chronology," Dec 15, 1975; msg, US Embassy, Phnom Penh to Sec State, 111152Z Mar 75.

6. Roysdon intvw, Mar 28, 1975; msg, USSAG/7th AF DCS/Opns, to 374th TAWg and 6th Aer Port Sq, Det 6, 010625Z Mar 75; draft ltr, 22nd AF to MAC, subj: Recommendation for Award of PUC, [*ca* 1975]; fact sheet, Joint Staff, subj: Deadlined Forklifts in Khmer Air Force Inventory at Pochentong, Mar 75, atchd to Rprt, Maj Gen John R. D. Cleland, US Army, Vice Dir/Opns, JCS, Trip Rprt to SEA, 10–20 Mar, Mar 24, 1975.

7. Hist, 374th TAWg, Apr–Jun 75,

TACTICAL AIRLIFT

pp 31–32; rprt, Col Benjamin F. Ingram, Ch, Current Opns Div, USSAG/7th AF, EOTR, Jun 30, 1975, pp 12–15; draft ltr, 22nd AF to MAC, subj: Recommendation for Award of PUC, [ca 1975]; msg, PACAF to CINCPAC, 260455Z Feb 75; msg, PACAF to MAC J4/J3, 220325Z Mar 75; ltr, Robert E. Hiller, Asst for Opns Analysis, DCS/Plans and Opns, PACAF, to Lt Col Johnson, DOOS, USSAG/7th AF, subj: Contract Airlift Opns in Cambodia, Apr 29, 1975.

8. Hist, 374th TAWg, Apr–Jun 75, pp 27–29; Koura, *The Cambodia Airlift*, pp 63–69.

9. Hist, 21st Sp Opns Sq, Apr–Jun 75, p 19; hist, USSAG/7th AF, Apr–Jun 75, pp 37–53; Koura, *The Cambodia Airlift*, pp 85–97.

10. Hist, 374th TAWg, Apr–Jun 75, pp 29–32; hist, USSAG/7th AF, Jan–Mar 75, pp 98–101; Koura, *The Cambodia Airlift*, pp 60–78; msgs, 086378 and 088988, Sec State to US Embassy, Bangkok, 152314Z and 180238Z Apr 75; msg, US Embassy, Bangkok Sec State, 150628Z Apr 75; msg, AFSOA U–Tapao to USSAG/7th AF, 131100Z Apr 75.

11. Msg, USSAG/7th AF to CSAF, 170725Z Apr 75; msg, USSAG/7th AF to CINCPAC, 230530Z Apr 75; hist, USSAG/7th AF, Jan–Mar 75, p 20; statistic data in Koura, *The Cambodia Airlift*, pp 99–110.

12. Gen Van Tien Dung, "Great Spring Victory," transl in FBIS–APA–76–110, Jun 7, 1976, pp 6–32.

13. Dung, "Great Spring Victory," Jun 7, 1976, pp 32–43; McCurdy intvw, Jun 3, 1975; memo, Bowers, Round-table Discussion with Minh, Lanh, Linh, and Hoang, Jul 16–17, 1975.

14. IR 1–502–0183–75, Jun 25, 1975; IR 1–502–0103–75, May 21, 1975; hist, PACAF, Jul 74–Dec 75, pp 492–500; paper, Maj Gen H. D. Smith, USA, Def Attache Saigon, subj: The Final 45 Days in Vietnam, May 22, 1975; Dung, "Great Spring Victory," Jun 7, 1976, pp 45–47; memo, Bowers, Round-table Discussion with Minh, Lanh, Linh, and Hoang, Jul 16–17, 1975.

15. Msg, USSAG/7th AF, Dir/Opns, to CINCPAC, 251945Z Mar 75; msg, CINCPAC to USSAG/7th AF, 270843Z Mar 75; msg, USDAO Saigon to USSAG/7th AF, 300640Z Mar 75; Smith, The Final 45 Days, May 22, 1975; hist, PACAF, Jul 74–Dec 75, pp 501–504;

IR 1–502–0103–75, 212030Z May 75; *New York Times,* Mar 28, 1975.

16. McCurdy intvw, Jun 3, 1975; hist, USSAG/7th AF, Apr–Jun 75, pp viii–ix; Dung, "Great Spring Victory," Jun 7, 1975, p 64; Wayne G. Peterson, The Fall and Evacuation of South Vietnam, Mar–May 1975, (Off/PACAF Hist, Feb 1, 1977), preliminary ed, pp 115–124, 203–223.

17. IR 1–502–0278–75, Aug 75; hist, DAO Saigon, Apr–Jun 75, p 100; Smith, The Final 45 Days, May 22, 1975, pp 9–11; memo, Col Philip L. Brewster, Ch, AF Div, DAO Saigon, to Lt Col Piner, subj: Historical Documentation of RVN, May 75.

18. IR 1–502–0431–75, Dec 11, 1975; IR 1–502–0212–75, Jul 22, 1975; Dung, "Great Spring Victory," Jul 7, 1976, p 95; hist, USSAG/7th AF, Apr–Jun 75, pp 24–26, 111–113.

19. Memo, Col Philip L. Brewster, Ch, AF Div, DAO Saigon, to Lt Col Piner, subj: Historical Documentation of RVN, May 75; memo, Bowers, Round-table Discussion with Minh, Lanh, Linh, and Hoang, Jul 16–17, 1975; IR 1–502–0110–75, Jun 20, 1975; IR 1–502–0193–75, Jun 26, 1975; IR 1–502–0104–75, May 75; IR 1–502–0219–75, Jul 75; hist, USSAG/7th AF, Apr–Jun 75, pp 136–137.

20. Memo, Bowers, Round-table Discussion with Minh, Lanh, Linh, and Hoang, Jul 16–17, 1975; memo, Col Philip L. Brewster, Ch, AF Div, DAO Saigon, to Lt Col Piner, subj: Historical Documentation of RVN, May 75.

21. IR 1–502–0271–75, Jul 75; memo, Bowers, Round-table Discussion with Minh, Lanh, Linh, and Hoang, Jul 16–17, 1975; McCurdy intvw, Jun 3, 1975.

22. Memo, Gen William W. Momyer, USAF, Ret, to Gen Ellis, Vice CSAF, subj: Corona Harvest (USAF Opns in Defense of SVN, 1 Jul 71–30 Jun 72), Mar 27, 1975; comments on draft ms, Tactical Airlift, by Gen Momyer, 1975, p 430.

23. Memo, Bowers, Round-table Discussion with Minh, Lanh, Linh, and Hoang, Jul 16–17, 1975.

24. Hist, 374th TAWg, Apr–Jun 75, pp 34–43; hist, PACAF, Jul 74–Dec 75, pp 531–533; msgs, 15th AF Ops Center to JCS, 061135Z and 061655Z Apr 75; msgs, PACAF Opns Center to CINCPAC, 070440Z and 080741Z Apr 75; draft ms,

Lt Cols Thomas G. Tobin, Arthur E. Laehr, and John F. Hilgenberg, "Last Flight from Saigon," SEA Monograph Series (Air Univ, Jul 76), pp 29–65.

25. Msgs, PACAF to AIG 8296, 211510Z and 220630Z Apr 75; draft ms, Zoe Hanisian and Kenneth L. Patchin, Off/MAC History, "Vietnam Evacuation (Frequent Wind/New Life): A Chronology," Dec 31, 1975; ltr, Col Frederick C. Griswold, Cdr 604th Mil Airlift Support Sq, to Dir/Opns, 13th AF, subj: AAR (Operations Babylift and New Life), May 20, 1975; hist, 374th TAWg, Apr–Jun 75, pp 38–39; hist, 345th TASq, Apr–Jun 75.

26. Msg, USDAO, Saigon, to USSAG/7th AF, 260940Z Apr 75; msg, CINCPAC J-3 to JCS, 250251Z Apr 75; msg, OLC MAC Langley, to 314th TAWg, *et al*, 291756Z Apr 75; memo, Maj David L. Sweigart, Support Opns Br, USSAG/7th AF, to Dir/Opns, subj: Vietnam Evacuation AAR, n.d.; rprt, Col Benjamin F. Ingram, Ch, Current Opns Div, USSAG/7th AF, Jun 30, 1975, pp 64–65.

27. Msgs, Clark Opns Center to JCS/NMCC, 232251Z, 242306Z, 251430Z, 251930Z, 260130Z, 270030Z Apr 75.

28. Msg, PACAF to Proc Center, Bkk, 282200Z Apr 75; hist, 374th TAWg, Apr–Jun 75, p 40; rprt, 656th SOWg/Scatback, Hist Data Record, Apr–Jun 75; ltr, Col Frederick C. Griswold, Cdr 604th Mil Airlift Support Sq, to Dir/Opns, 13th AF, subj: AAR (Operations Babylift and New Life), May 20, 1975.

29. Hist, USSAG/7th AF, Apr–Jun 75, p 23; msg, Clark Opns Center, to MAC, 281733Z Apr 75; msgs, Clark Opns Center to JCS/NMCC, 290550Z and 290535Z Apr 75; Dung, "Great Spring Victory," transl in FBIS-APA-76-131, Jul 7, 1976; msg, COMIPAC to AIG 8724th, 282135Z Apr 75.

30. Msgs, Clark Opns Center to JCS/NMCC, 290614Z and 290745Z Apr 75; msg, 374th TAWg U-Tapao to 13th AF, 291131Z Apr 75; Smith, The Final 45 Days, May 22, 1975; Testimony of Amb Graham A. Martin, Jan 27, 1976, before Sen Subcommittee, on Investigations, Coll/Intl Relations, House, 94th Cong, 2nd Sess, GPO 1976, p 578; tape transcript, PACOM, NMCC, DAO, Blue Chip, 290100Z and 290128Z; msg, Cdr 7th Fleet to CTF-77, 282126Z Apr 75; msg, COMIPAC to AIG 8724th, 290550Z Apr 75.

31. Tape transcript, PACOM, NMCC, DAO, Blue Chip, 290725Z Apr 75; hist, 21st Sp Opns Sq, Apr–Jun 75, pp 4–6; hist, USSAG/7th AF, Apr–Jun 75, pp 56–84; hist, PACAF, Jul 74–Dec 75, pp 514–530; msg, USSAG/7th AF to CINCPAC J-3, 050400Z May 75.

32. IR 1-502-0270-75, Jul 28, 1975; IR 1-502-0285-75, Sep 18, 1975; memo, Bowers, Round-table Discussion with Minh, Lanh, Linh, and Hoang, Jul 16–17, 1975; McCurdy intvw, Jun 3, 1975; hist, PACAF, Jul 74–Dec 75, pp 533–543; *Air Force Times,* Sep 17, 1975.

33. Hist, 21st Sp Opns Sq, Apr–Jun 75, p 7; hist, 56th Sp Opns Wg, Apr–Jun 75, pp 22–24; msg, PACAF Opns Center to AIG 8296th, 292144Z Apr 75; hist, PACAF, Jul 74–Dec 75, pp 544–556; Wayne G. Peterson, The Fall and Evac of SVN, Mar–May 75, (Off/PACAF Hist, Feb 1, 1977), preliminary ed, pp 591–620.

34. Rprt, Comptroller General of the US, "The Seizure of the *Mayaguez*—A Case Study of Crisis Management," in 94th Cong, 2nd Sess, Subcomm on Intl Political and Military Affairs, Comm on Intl Relations, House, "Seiure of the *Mayaguez* . . . ," Part IV, GPO, 1976, pp 90–91; hist, 21st Sp Opns Sq, Apr–Jun 75.

35. Study, DCS/Plans and Opns, PACAF, subj: Assault on Koh Tang, Jun 23, 1975; msg, 56th Sp Opns Wg to PACAF, 191200Z May 75; hist, PACAF, Jul 74–Dec 75, pp 434–469; hist, USSAG/7th AF, Apr–Jun 75, pp 85–106; hist, 21st Sp Opns Sq, Apr–Jun 75.

36. Msg, 374th TAWg to PACAF, 201030Z May 75; rprt, Capt Douglas T. Way, Acft Cdr, AWADS/BLU-82 Pilot Rprt, May 19, 1975; hist, 374th TAWg, Apr–Jun 75, pp 43–47.

37. Rprt, Col Robert R. Reed, Ch, Opns Plans Div, USSAG/7th AF, EOTR, Jun 30, 1975; rprt, Lt Col John H. Denham, Cdr 21st Sp Opns Sq, EOTR, Jul 1, 1975; hist, 21st Sp Opns Sq, Apr–Jun 75; article, Capt John B. Taylor, "Air Mission Mayaguez," *Airman,* Feb 76, pp 39–47; msg 04075, Cdr MAC to All MAC, 161400Z May 75; rprt, Comptroller Gen, "Seizure of the *Mayaguez* . . . ," pp 92–104.

38. Hist, USSAG/7th AF, Jan–Mar

74, p 46, Apr–Jun 75, pp 107–109; hist, CINCPAC, 1975, pp 468–469, 625–668.

39. IR 1-502-0434-75, Dec 18, 1975; IR 1-502-0288-75, Nov 75; IR 1-502-0213-75, Jul 22, 1975; Dung, "Great Spring Victory," Jul 7, 1976, pp 60–61, 64–65, 123; hist, CINCPAC, 1975, p 115.

Chapter XXVI

Reflections

1. Rprt, Proj Corona Harvest, USAF Airlift Activities in Support of Opns in SEA, 1 Jan 65–31 Mar 68, Jan 73; eval rprt, Corona Harvest Airlift Rprt Preparation Committee, Col Louis P. Lindsay, Chairman, Eval of Airlift in Support of Opns in SEA, 1 Jan 65–31 Mar 68, Jun 70; rprt, TALC, Corona Harvest Activity Input, Tactical Airlift in SEA, 1 Jan 65–31 Mar 68, 4 vols, Dec 19, 1969.

2. Rprt, Proj Corona Harvest, USAF Airlift Activities in Support of Opns in SEA, 1 Jan 65–31 Mar 68, Jan 73, pp 3–4.

3. Multi-Command Manual 3-4, TAC, AAC, PACAF, USAFE, Tactical Air Opns: Tactical Airlift, May 30, 1974, vol I, p 3–1.

4. Eval rprt, Corona Harvest Airlift Rprt Preparation Committee, Col Louis P. Lindsay, Chairman, Eval of Airlift in Support of Opns in SEA, 1 Jan 65–31 Mar 68, Jun 70; MR, Lt Col Ray L. Bowers, AFCHO, subj: Gen Momyer Presentation to Airlift Symposium, Nov 6, 1971.

5. Rprt, Proj Corona Harvest, USAF Airlift Activities in Support of Opns in SEA, 1 Jan 65–31 Mar 68, Jan 73, p 4a; hist, Dir/Doctrine, Concepts, Objectives, Hq USAF, Jan–Jun 74, pp 51–52, 100; MAC/TAC Programming Plan 74-30, CONUS Airlift Consolidation, Sep 15, 1974; hist, MAC, Jul 74–Dec 75, pp 37, 42–49, 308–323; hist, 374th TAWg, Oct–Dec 74, pp 5–6.

6. Memo, Alexander H. Flax, Asst SAF (R&D), subj: LIT, Feb 14, 1969.

7. Concept Formulation Package/Technical Development Plan (CFP/TDP), AFRDQ, AFSC, ANSER, Hq USAF, Light Intra-theater Transport LIT, Aug 69; hist, Dir/Doctrine, Concepts, Objectives, Jul–Dec 69, pp 77–78, Jan–Jun 70, pp 83–85; hist, Dir/Opns Hq USAF, Jul–Dec 72, pp 307–308, Jan–Jun 73, pp 261–262; study, DCS/Plans, Hq TAC, Concept of Opns for a Tactical Medium STOL Transport Acft (MST), Jul 13, 1971; hist, MAC, Jul 74–Dec 75, pp 124–125, 333.

8. Hist, MAC, Jul 74–Dec 75, pp 65–67; rprt, Hq USAF–AFCVSB-P, Rprt of Airlift Panel Meeting 69-11, May 23, 1969; memo, Col K. R. Stow, Ch, Doctrine Div, Dir/Doctrine, Concepts, Objectives, Hq USAF, for Gen Yudkin and Col Junkerman, Dir/Doctrine, Concepts, Objectives, Hq USAF, subj: LIT Memo, Apr 15, 1969; hists, Dir/Plans, Hq USAF, 1969 through 1971; hists, Dir/Doctrine, Concepts, Objectives, Hq USAF, 1969 through 1971.

9. Multi-Command Manual 3-4, TAC, AAC, PACAF, USAFE, Tactical Air Opns: Tactical Airlift, May 30, 1974, pp 2–5; memo, Col Joseph E. Mestemaker, Dir/Plans, Hq USAF, to AFRDQRA, subj: Intra-theater Airlift Analysis by OASD(SA), Apr 9, 1969; study, DCS/Plans, Hq TAC, Concept of Opns for a Tactical Medium STOL Transport Acft (MST), Jul 13, 1971; CFP/TDP, AFRDQ, AFSC, ANSER, Hq USAF, Light Intra-theater Transport (LIT), Aug 69.

10. Hist, Dir/Opns, Hq USAF, Jul–Dec 72, pp 319–321, Jan–Jun 73, pp 265–266, 268–269; hist, 317th TAWg, Oct–Dec 72, pp 29–30; rprt, US Army Avn Systems Cd, Aerial Delivery Equipment Meeting, 11–15 Sep 72; rprt, PACAF, Tactical Airlift Tactics Conf, 8–11 Aug 72, CCK, Aug 72.

11. Rprt, Dir/Management Analysis, Hq USAF, Southeast Asia Review, Feb 28, 1974.

Glossary

A–1E Skyraider	Prop-driven, single-engine, land- or carrier-based multipurpose aircraft, developed to permit greater versatility as an attack bomber or utility aircraft. Two crewmembers. Formerly designated AD–5.
A–37	Modified version of Cessna's twin-engine T–37 pilot trainer. See T–37.
AC–47	C–47 transport converted into a gunship by adding the General Electric SUU–11A minigun. The AC–47 had several nicknames: Puff the Magic Dragon, Dragon Ship, and Spooky.
AC–119	C–119 modified into the AC–119G Shadow and AC–119K Stinger gunships.
AC–130	C–130 modified into the AC–130 gunship.
AN–2 Colt	Russian, single-engine, utility biplane for carrying passengers and cargo. Powered by a seven-cylinder, radial, air-cooled engine. Four-blade propeller. Specially designed for operation from small airfields—can land in 550 feet.
AU–24A Helio Stallion	General-utility, short-takeoff-and-landing, single-engine turboprop aircraft. Side-by-side seating for pilot and copilot and room for six to eight passengers. Passengers can be removed for carrying cargo. Numerous combinations of rockets, bombs, and flares can be carried on the five external stores stations. Has cabin mounting for side-firing gun. In Cambodia this plane was used mainly as a gunship and seldom for airlift.
AA	antiaircraft
AAC	Alaskan Air Command
AAF	Army Air Forces
A&E	armament and electronics
AAR	after-action report
ABG	air base group
abn	airborne
ABS	air base squadron
acft	aircraft
ACS	air commando squadron

TACTICAL AIRLIFT

ACS/	Assistant Chief of Staff for
ACSC	Air Command and Staff College
ACTIV	Army Concept Team in Vietnam
ACW	air commando wing
AD	air division
adm	admiral
ADVON	advanced echelon
AECC	aeromedical evacuation control center
aerl	aerial
aeromed	aeromedical
AF	Air Force
AFAT	Air Force advisory team
AFB	Air Force base
AFCC	Air Force communications center
AFM	Air Force manual
AFSC	Air Force Systems Command
AFTU-V	Air Force Test Unit—Vietnam (US)
AID	Agency for International Development (US)
AIG	address indicating group
ALCC	airlift control center
ALO	air liaison officer
ALOREP	airlift operational report
AmEmb	American Embassy
ammo	ammunition
AMST	advanced medium short-takeoff-and-landing transport
analys	analysis
AOC	air operations center
app	appendix
appln	application
APS	aerial port squadron

GLOSSARY

ARPA	Advanced Research Projects Agency. A separately organized research and development agency of the Department of Defense under the direction and supervision of the Director of Defense Research and Engineering.
ARVN	Army of the Republic of Vietnam
aslt	assault
atch	attachment
ATCO	air traffic coordinating office
Attleboro	A ground operation extending from September to November 1966. The area of operations included the northern three-quarters of Tay Ninh Province, the known location of the Central Office for South Vietnam (Viet Cong headquarters), headquarters of the National Front for the Liberation of South Vietnam, and the main base of the Viet Cong's 9th Division.
AU	Air University
AUTODIN	automatic digital network
AWADS	adverse-weather aerial delivery system
AWC	Air War College
B–26B Invader	Prop-driven, twin-engine, three-place, midwing, all-metal monoplane, light bombardment aircraft with tricycle landing gear. Three crewmembers.
B–26K Invader	Similar to B–26B aircraft except modified for special air warfare missions including photo-reconnaissance.
B–52 Stratofortress	All-weather, intercontinental, strategic heavy bomber powered by eight turbojet engines. Can deliver nuclear and nonnuclear bombs, air-to-surface missiles, and decoys. Its range is extended by inflight refueling.
B–57 Canberra	Wide-short, midwing, twin-jet bomber aircraft with retractable landing gear. Two crewmembers.
Boeing Model 727	Short/medium range commercial transport. Cantilever low-wing monoplane. Fuselage is semi-monocoque fail-safe structure. Has two turbofan engines mounted on the sides of the rear fuselage and a third at the base of the T–tail assembly. Basic accommodation for 163 passengers, maximum of 189 passengers. Three crewmembers.
Bristol Type 170	Prop-driven, twin-engine, cantilever high-wing monoplane designed as a freight or passenger transport. Used in Southeast Asia by the Royal New Zealand Air Force.
Banish Beach	C–130 pallets of fuel oil dropped to achieve area denial. They were ignited by smoke grenades.

TACTICAL AIRLIFT

Barn Door	Barn Door I was one increment in the establishment of a complete communications network for the Republic of Vietnam. In late 1961, Thirteenth Air Force ordered the establishment of a tactical air control system, which was completed in January 1962. Barn Door II involved the movement in early 1962 of a control and reporting post at Don Muang RTAFB, Thailand, to Ubon RTAFB, to provide radar coverage of the northwestern approaches to the Republic of Vietnam (a possible route for aerial resupply of the Viet Cong).
bde	brigade
Birmingham	Joint 1st Infantry Division and 25th ARVN Division operation in Tay Ninh Province during April–May 1966.
bk	book
Black Spot	NC–123s (modified C–123s) equipped with forward-looking radar, low-light-level television, forward-looking infrared, laser ranger, advanced navigation system, weapon-release computer, and dispensers for BLUs.
Blindbat	C–130 flareships used in Laos, from Ubon Royal Thai Air Force Base.
BLU	bomb, live unit
BLU–82	A 15,000-pound demolition bomb used to prepare landing zones for U.S. Army helicopters.
brig gen	brigadier general
C–1A Trader	General-utility transport trainer. Prop-driven, twin-engine, cantilever high-wing monoplane with retractable tricycle landing gear. Besides a crew of two, can carry up to nine passengers in backward-facing, easily removable seats. A "cage device" secures cargo in arrested carrier landings. Has navigational devices for all-weather operation.
C–2A	Cantilever high-wing monoplane of all-metal construction. Powered by two turboprop engines. Three crewmembers with side-by-side seating for pilot and copilot. Designed to deliver cargo to air groups deployed on carriers. Can be launched by catapult (using nose-tow gear) and can make arrested landings.
C–5A Galaxy	Large cargo transport aircraft powered by four turbofan engines, capable of very large payload and cargo volume, intercontinental range, forward-area airfield operations, and airdropping of troops and equipment.
C–7A Caribou	Prop-driven twin-engine, all-weather transport, designed for short-takeoff-and-landing in forward battle areas or unimproved strips. Three crewmembers. Can carry six thousand pounds of cargo, or thirty-one passengers, or twenty-five paratroops, or twenty litter patients.

GLOSSARY

C–8A	Twin-turboprop, short-takeoff-and-landing, cargo transport. This cantilever high-wing monoplane has a range of 1,320 nautical miles. Gross weight in conventional flight is thirty-eight thousand pounds, thirty-four thousand pounds for short-takeoff-and-landing. Cruising speed, 222 knots. Eight crewmembers, thirty-four passengers. Formerly designated CV–7A.
C–9A Nightingale	Twin-jet, low-wing, medium-sized, T–tail transport for domestic and intratheater aeromedical evacuation. Seven crewmembers. Thirty stretcher patients, or forty ambulatory patients, or a combination of both plus flight attendants.
C–45 Expeditor	Light, low-wing, prop-driven, twin-engine, cargo aircraft of all-metal construction. Two crewmembers, four passengers.
C–46 Commando	Twin-engine, prop-driven, low-midwing, all-metal, land monoplane. Two crewmembers, forty-two passengers.
C–47A Skytrain	Prop-driven, twin-engine, low-wing monoplane with retractable landing gear. Utilized as a cargo, ambulance, or troop transport. Two crewmembers, twenty-four passengers.
C–47D Skytrain	Has external cargo provisions and glider tow. Five crewmembers. Twenty-seven paratroops or twenty-four to twenty-six litters with two attendants.
C–54 Skymaster	Prop-driven, four-engine, low-wing monoplane with retractable tricycle landing gear. A long-range cargo, troop, or personnel transport. Six crewmembers.
C–117 Skytrain	Basically similar to the C–47 except for airline-type interior for use as a staff transport. Three crewmembers, twenty-one seats.
C–118A Liftmaster	Prop-driven, four-engine, long-range, low-wing monoplane equipped with fully retractable landing gear and pressurized cabin. Used as a cargo, personnel, ambulance, or staff transport. Five crewmembers. Seventy-nine troops or sixty-one litters. Air Force designation of DC–6A.
C–119C Flying Boxcar	Twin-boom, high-wing, land monoplane of all-metal construction having a conventional tricycle gear with a steerable nose gear. Its two reciprocating engines have constant-speed, four-bladed, reversible-pitch propellers. Five crewmembers, forty-two troops.
C–119F Flying Boxcar	Similar to C–119C except for engines, hydraulic landing gear, and flaps. Five crewmembers. Forty-two troops or thirty-five litter patients.
C–123 Provider	Prop-driven, two-engine, high-wing monoplane. Used to transport combat and other equipment for airborne assault troops, the resupply by air of advanced combat positions, evacuation of wounded, and air transportation of paratroops to the drop zone. Two crewmembers, sixty troops, or fifty litters plus four attendants. Also served as a

TACTICAL AIRLIFT

	forward air control/flareship. (The C–123K features two pod-mounted turbojets in addition to its piston engines.)
C–124 Globemaster	Low-wing monoplane powered by four reciprocating engines. Has clamshell cargo doors in front fuselage and loading elevator in center fuselage capable of transporting heavy ground-force and ordnance equipment in the main cabin. Five crewmembers, two hundred troops, or 127 litters plus twenty-five ambulatory patients.
C–130A Hercules	High-wing, all-metal construction, medium-range, land-based monoplane, for rapid transportation of personnel, cargo, or paratroops. Powered by four turboprop engines. Four crewmembers, ninety-two troops, or sixty-four paratroops, or seventy litters plus six attendants.
C–130B Hercules	Similar to C–130A except for engines and propellers. Has additional electronic equipment, more fuel and oil capacity, and increased weights. Four crew, ninety-two troops, or four crewmembers, seventy-four litters plus two attendants.
C–130E Hercules	Similar to C–130B except for increased fuel, weight, and load-carrying capacity. Five crewmembers. Ninety-two troops, or sixty-four paratroops, or seventy-four litters and two attendants.
C–130H Hercules	C–130E airframe equipped with new engines and new communication and navigation equipment. Intended for military assistance programs.
C–133A Cargomaster	High-wing monoplane powered by four turboprop engines. Has facilities for truckbed-height loading, an aft-loading door with integral ramp, and a forward side-loading door. Four crewmembers plus three relief ones.
C–141A Starlifter	All-metal, high-wing, full cantilever monoplane with a fuselage of semi-monocoque construction. Powered by four turboprop engines. Transports military and commercial cargo over long distances. Eight crewmembers. One hundred fifty-four troops, or 127 paratroops, or eighty litters with two attendants.
CH–3B	Twin-turbine, single main rotor, anti-tail rotor, passenger/cargo helicopter capable of operating from land or water. Provides rapid, direct-to-the-scene transportation for logistic support, drone recovery, and airlift operations. Has side-loading features. Antisubmarine warfare equipment removed. Three crewmembers, twenty-five passengers.
CH–3C	Similar to CH–3B but has a rear loading ramp. Three crewmembers, twenty-five passengers.
CH–3E	Similar to CH–3C but has a T58–GE–5 engine.
CH–21 Workhorse	All-metal, semi-monocoque-constructed helicopter for transport and cargo operations. Crew compartment in nose, side-by-side seating. Has three-blade, all-metal rotors ar-

GLOSSARY

	ranged in tandem and turning in opposite directions. Tricycle-type landing gear. Two crewmembers, sixteen passengers. Formerly designated H–21.
CH–34 Choctaw	Sikorsky Model S–58 helicopter equipped with a four-blade, main rotor and a tail rotor. Has two-wheel main landing gear and small tail wheel. Two crewmembers, eighteen passengers. Formerly designated H–34.
CH–46 Sea Knight	Twin-engine, rotary-wing aircraft used by the Marine Corps for troop and cargo movement. Tandem three-bladed motors. Three crewmembers. Seventeen troops, or fifteen litter patients with two attendants, or cargo.
CH–47A Chinook	Twin-engine, tandem-rotor, passenger/cargo helicopter having all-weather flight capabilities. Has quadricycle gear, dual controls, and rear-loading ramp. Three crewmembers. Thirty-three passengers.
CH–47B Chinook	Similar to CH–47A except for a modified rotor system which allows increased airspeeds.
CH–47C Chinook	Similar to CH–47B except for greater installed power, endurance, and payload.
CH–53A Seastallion	Twin-turbine assault helicopter employed primarily in moving cargo and equipment, and secondarily in transporting troops, in the amphibious assault and subsequent operations ashore. Six-blade main rotor. Three crewmembers.
CH–54A Tarhe Flying Crane	This helicopter has a heavy (twenty thousand-pound), cargo-lifting capacity, one main lifting rotor, tricycle gear, duel controls plus limited-authority controls for the aft-facing pilot during winch operations. Has single-point hoisting system plus four-point, load-leveling capability. The CH–54B can lift twenty-five thousand pounds.
CV–2 Caribou	See C–7A.
CV–7 Buffalo	Cargo, transport, fixed-wing aircraft with two turboprop engines. Range, 1,320 nautical miles. Gross weight, thirty-eight thousand pounds for conventional flight, or thirty-four thousand pounds for short-takeoff-and-landing. Cruising speed, 222 knots. Crew of three plus thirty-four passengers.
CAG	combat aviation group
CALSU	combat airlift support unit
CAMRON	consolidated aircraft maintenance squadron
capt	captain
CARP	computed air release point
cav	cavalry
CC	combat cargo

CCK	Ching Chuan Kang Air Base
CCT	combat control team
CCTG	combat crew training group
CCTS	combat crew training squadron
CDS	container delivery system
cen	center
ch	chief
CHECO	Contemporary Historical Evaluation of Counterinsurgency Operations (1962); Contemporary Historical Evaluation of Combat Operations (1965); Contemporary Historical Examination of Current Operations (1970)
CHWTO	Chief, Western Pacific Transportation Office
CIA	Central Intelligence Agency
CIDG	Civilian Irregular Defense Group (RVN)
CINCFE	Commander in Chief, Far East
CINCUSAFE	Commander in Chief, United States Air Force in Europe
CJCS	The Chairman, Joint Chiefs of Staff
COC	combat operations center
COIN	counterinsurgency
col	colonel
Combat Spear	C–130E support for the MACV studies and observations group.
comd	command
comdo	commando
comdr	commander
comm	communications
Commando Lava	Mudmaking program using United States Air Force aircraft to drop chemicals on selected infiltration routes. Began May 17, 1967.
Commando Scarf	C–130 munitions drops in Laos (special project).
Commando Vault	Employment of the M–121 (ten thousand-pound) bomb or the BLU–82 (fifteen thousand-pound) bomb, delivered by C–130 aircraft to create helicopter landing zones.

GLOSSARY

COMUSKOREA	Commander, United States Forces in Korea
COMUSMACV	Commander, United States Military Assistance Command, Vietnam
Cong	Congress of the United States
CORDS	Civil Operations and Revolutionary (Rural) Development Support
CRB	Cam Ranh Bay Air Base, South Vietnam
CRIMP	Consolidated RVNAF Improvement and Modernization Plan
C/S	chief of staff
CSA	Chief of Staff, United States Army
CSAF	Chief of Staff, United States Air Force
CSAFM	Chief of Staff Air Force memorandum
CSAS	Common Service Airlift System
CSD	combined studies division
CY	calendar year
DC–6A	See C–118A Liftmaster.
DC–8	Four-jet, swept-wing, civil airliner. The DC–8F is a turbofan-engined variant of the DC–8, designed basically as a combination cargo and passenger transport.
Dornier AG	German aircraft company. Among its productions are light, fixed-wing, single- and twin-engine utility transport aircraft.
DABIN	Data Base Inventory
Daniel Boone	MACV support of reconnaissance commando teams.
DAO	defense attaché office
DASC	direct air support center
DAST	deployed air strike team
DCS/	Deputy Chief of Staff for
DEPCHJUSMAGTHAI	Deputy Chief, Joint United States Military Advisory Group, Thailand
det	detachment
DIA	Defense Intelligence Agency

815

TACTICAL AIRLIFT

dir	director; directorate; directive
Dir/	Director of
div	division
DOLS	delayed-opening leaflet system
DZ	drop zone
EB–66B Destroyer	Light, sweptback, high-wing, tactical bomber equipped with tricycle landing gear and a steerable nosewheel. Powered by two jet engines. Modified to a special electronic configuration.
ed	edition, editor
El Paso	Major ground campaign in III Corps by the 1st Infantry Division and III Corps forces of the Army of the Republic of Vietnam. The operation took place during June–July 1966.
EOTR	end of tour report
est	estimate
evac	evacuation
F–4A Phantom	Twin-engine, carrier-based, all-weather, jet fighter. Carries missiles and special stores. Has tricycle landing gear. Two crewmembers.
F–4B Phantom	Modification of the F–4A embodying the J79–GE–8 engine. Two crewmembers.
F–4C Phantom	Air Force version of the F–4A but with different engine and different equipment. Two crewmembers.
F–4D Phantom	Similar to the F–4C but has improved avionics equipment for air-to-air and air-to-ground operations.
F–5 Freedom Fighter	All-metal, midwing, twin-engine, single-place, jet fighter. Has tricycle landing gear and steerable nose wheel. Nose is fitted with two M–39 20-mm cannon. Can carry sixty-two hundred pounds of ordnance. Has a range of four hundred miles and a speed of about nine hundred miles-per-hour.
F–100 Super Sabre	Supersonic, single-engine, turbojet-powered, tactical and air superiority fighter. Has a low, thin, swept wing and nose air intake. Employs air brake and drag chute. Can provide close support for ground forces and be refueled in flight. One crewmember.
F–105 Thunderchief	Supersonic, single-engine, turbojet-powered, all-weather, tactical fighter. Capable of close support for ground forces. Its range can be extended by inflight refueling.

GLOSSARY

FAA	Federal Aviation Administration
FAF	French Air Force
FEAF	Far East Air Forces (USAF) (1944–56)
FEALOGFOR	Far East Air Logistics Force (USAF)
FFV	Field Force, Vietnam
FIC	French Indochina
Fire Brigade	United States Air Force-Vietnamese Air Force air transport rapid alert capability for Army of the Republic of Vietnam airborne employment.
1st lt	first lieutenant
FM	frequency modulation
FMFPAC	Fleet Marine Force Pacific
FMS	field maintenance squadron
gen	general
gen	general (officer)
gp	group
GPES	ground proximity extraction system
GRADS	ground radar air delivery system
GVN	Government of Vietnam
H–19 helicopter	See UH–19 Chickasaw.
H–21 helicopter	See CH–21 Workhorse.
H–34 helicopter	See CH–34 Choctaw.
H–43 helicopter	See HH–43.
H–53 helicopter	Sikorsky S–65 helicopter designed to meet need for patrolling close to the North Vietnam border during aircraft attacks on North Vietnam targets, ready to dash in and pick up crews shot down over enemy-held territory. See CH–53A and HH–53B.
HC–47 Skytrain	The C–47 transport especially equipped for search and rescue missions, and with twice the normal fuel load, a stronger landing gear, and jet-assisted takeoff. Three crewmembers. Formerly designated SC–47.
HH–43 Huskie	Twin-rotor, single-engine helicopter designed for crash-rescue operations. Semi-monocoque-constructed fuselage.

TACTICAL AIRLIFT

	Rotors are intermeshing, counter-rotating rotors, each with two blades, mounted side-by-side. Has non-retractable, four-wheel-type, landing gear. Two crewmembers, three passengers. Formerly designated H–43.
HH–53B Super Jolly	Similar to CH–53A except reconfigured to accomplish Aerospace Rescue and Recovery Service combat crew recovery missions. Also armed with three 7.62-mm miniguns. Equipped with refueling probe for midair refueling. Six crewmembers.
HU–1D Iroquois	See UH–1D Iroquois.
HALO	high-altitude, low-opening
Hawk	U.S.-made, surface-to-air missile that can seek out and destroy attacking aircraft traveling at supersonic speeds at altitudes as low as one hundred feet and as high as thirty-six thousand feet. Has solid-propellant, two-stage, propulsion system, a homing device, and a conventional warhead. Length, seventeen feet; diameter, fourteen inches; span, four feet; weight about 1,279 pounds; speed, supersonic; warhead, high-explosive, blast-fragmentation. Missile and ground equipment can be airlifted by helicopter and medium-sized aircraft.
HF	high frequency
hist	history; historical
hosp	hospital
HQ	headquarters
hwy	highway
IL–12	Russian, prop-driven, two-engine, medium-range airliner. A low-wing cantilever monoplane. Oval fuselage is an all-metal, semi-monocoque structure. Tail unit is cantilever monoplane type with single fin and rudder. Crew of five, twenty-seven to thirty-two passengers.
IL–14	Russian airliner similar to the IL–12 but has a revised tail configuration, blunter wingtips, and some thrust augmentation. Crew of five. The IL–14P accommodates between eighteen and twenty-six passengers, the IL–14M between twenty-four and twenty-eight.
IBM	International Business Machines, Inc.
IFR	instrument flight rules
IG	inspector general
ind	indorsement
intvw	interview

GLOSSARY

IR	intelligence report; infrared
Iron Age	Overall program for United States Air Force materiel support of the French in Indochina (1953–54).
JU–52	Prop-driven, three-engine, low-wing, transport monoplane built in Germany by Junkers.
JAOC	joint air operations center
JCS	Joint Chiefs of Staff
JCSM	Joint Chiefs of Staff memorandum
JGS	Joint General Staff, Republic of Vietnam Armed Forces
JLRB	Joint Logistics Review Board
JOC	joint operations center
JOEG–V	Joint Operational Evaluation Group, Vietnam (MACV)
JRATA	Joint Research and Test Activity (MACV)
J–Staff	Joint Staff. Used in numerical combinations as J–1 (Personnel), J–2 (Intelligence), J–3 (Operations), J–4 (Logistics), J–5 (Plans), and J–6 (Communications and Electronics).
JTF	joint task force
Junction City	Massive two-and-a-half month sweep of War Zone C, aimed at opening the area for clearing operations which would eliminate this major enemy sanctuary. The plan was to root out the Central Office for South Vietnam (Viet Cong headquarters) and cripple the Viet Cong's 9th Division.
JUSMAAG	Joint United States Military Assistance Advisory Group
JUSMAG	Joint United States Military Advisory Group
JUSMAGTHAI	Joint United States Military Advisory Group, Thailand
KC–130F Hercules	Similar to C–130B. Tactical tanker/cargo/personnel/evacuation transport. Seven crewmembers.
L–19 aircraft	See O–1 Bird Dog.
LI–2	Russian twin-engine transport similar to the U.S. C–47. Can carry sixty-six hundred pounds of cargo 305 nautical miles and return.
LAPES	low-altitude parachute extraction system
Leaping Lena	Airdrops in mid-1964 by the Vietnamese Air Force of several small South Vietnamese information-gathering teams along selected areas of the Ho Chi Minh Trail.

819

TACTICAL AIRLIFT

LIT	light intratheater transport
LOGSUM	logistics summary
LOLEX	low-level inflight extraction
loran	Long-range electronic navigation system that uses a time divergence of pulse-type transmissions from two or more fixed stations. Also called long-range navigation.
LST	landing ship, tank
lt col	lieutenant colonel
lt gen	lieutenant general
ltr	letter
LZ	landing zone
MI–4	Russian single-rotor, general-purpose helicopter. All-metal semi-monocoque structure of pod-and-boom type, with nonretractable four-wheel landing gear. Military version carries up to fourteen troops or 3,525 pounds of freight. Crew of two on flight deck with under-fuselage gondola for observer in military version.
MI–6	Russian heavy general-purpose transport helicopter. Can accommodate up to 120 passengers. Maximum payload is 26,450 pounds. Maximum level speed, 186–217 miles-per-hour. Cruising speed, 155 miles-per-hour. Service ceiling, 14,750 feet. Maximum range, 650 miles.
M–121	A 10,000-pound demolition bomb used to prepare landing zones for U.S. Army helicopters.
MAAG	Military Assistance Advisory Group
MAAGV	Military Assistance Advisory Group, Vietnam
MAAMA	Middletown Air Materiel Area
MAC	Military Airlift Command
MACSOG	Military Assistance Command, Studies and Observations Group
MACTHAI	Military Assistance Command, Thailand
MACV	Military Assistance Command, Vietnam
MAF	Marine amphibious force
maj	major
maj gen	major general
MAS	military airlift squadron

GLOSSARY

MATS	Military Air Transport Service
MCAF	Marine Corps airfield; Marine Corps air facility
MCC	movement control center
MDAP	Mutual Defense Assistance Program
medevac	medical evacuation
memo	memorandum
mgt	management
mil	military
MONEVAL	monthly evaluation report
MR	memorandum for record; military region
msg	message
MSQ-77	MSQ-35 radar bomb scoring equipment modified for radar guidance of bombers.
mtg	meeting
Mule Train	Nickname of initial United States Air Force C-123 detachment in Vietnam.
NA	National Archives (of the United States)
NCO	noncommissioned officer
n.d.	no date
NM	nautical mile
NMCC	National Military Command Center
NSAM	national security action memorandum
O-1 Bird Dog	Single-engine, two-place tandem, closed-cabin, high-wing aircraft of conventional strut-braced, two-spar design. All-metal semi-monocoque fuselage with a fixed-pitch McCauley propeller. Twenty-four-volt electrical system. Two crewmembers. Formerly designated L-19.
OASD/ISA	Office of the Assistant Secretary of Defense, International Security Affairs
ofc	office
Omega	See Leaping Lena.
OOAMA	Ogden Air Materiel Area

TACTICAL AIRLIFT

opl	operational
OPlan	operation plan
OpOrd	operation order
ops	operations
OSD	Office of the Secretary of Defense
Pilatus PC–6 Porter	Swiss, single-engine, all-metal, general utility aircraft with fixed landing gear. Short-takeoff-and-landing characteristics permit operations from small airfields. Can carry loads up to eleven hundred pounds, or be rapidly converted from freighter to a five- to seven-passenger transport. One crewmember.
p	page (plural pp)
PACAF	Pacific Air Forces (USAF)
PACAFM	Pacific Air Forces manual
PACOM	Pacific Command (US)
pax	passenger(s)
Pegasus	Combined United States, Army of the Republic of Vietnam, and Australian air-ground operation whose objective was to relieve the pressure on Khe Sanh in April 1968.
PERINTREP	periodic intelligence report
PLADS	parachute low-altitude delivery system
POL	petroleum, oil, and lubricants
Prairie Fire	Formerly Shining Brass. Consisted of air-supported ground reconnaissance teams sent into enemy territory to select targets for air strikes and to make poststrike assessments of damage.
PSP	pierced steel planking
pt	part
RB–26 Invader	The B–26 modified for reconnaissance missions by changes in nose and installed equipment. Three crewmembers.
RF–4C Phantom	Similar to the F–4C but modified for photographic and/or electronic reconnaissance missions. Two crewmembers. See F–4A and F–4C.
RAAF	Royal Australian Air Force.
RAC	reconnaissance aircraft company; Riverine assault craft

GLOSSARY

RACON	radar beacon
RAF	Royal Air Force (United Kingdom)
Ranch Hand	Nickname of United States Air Force C–123 aerial spray detachment deployed to Vietnam in 1961–62 and applied to later defoliation and herbicide activity.
RAND	Research and Development (The RAND Corporation, Santa Monica, California)
R&R	rest and recuperation
Redeye (XMIM–43A)	U.S.-made, portable, surface-to-air missile using an infrared seeker and electromechanical guidance device to seek out and destroy low-flying enemy aircraft. The weapon is carried and launched by one man. Length, four feet; diameter, three inches; weight, twenty-nine pounds; speed, supersonic; warhead, high-explosive.
Red Leaf	An Air Force/Army agreement of April 6, 1966, whereby CV–2/C–7 assets and control were to pass from the Army to the Air Force on January 1, 1967.
ret	retired
Riverine	Waterway interdiction forces which operated mostly in the Mekong Delta and its associated waterways network.
RLAF	Royal Laotian Air Force
RM	RAND memorandum
ROC	required operational capability
ROK	Republic of Korea
rote	rotational
rprt	report
rqmt	requirement
RSI	Research Studies Institute
RTAF	Royal Thai Air Force
RTAFB	Royal Thai Air Force Base
RTS	reconnaissance technical squadron
RVN	Republic of Vietnam
RVNAF	Republic of Vietnam Armed Forces
SA–2 Guideline	Soviet-made, surface-to-air, Mach 3.5, radar-guided missile for medium- to high-altitude interception of subsonic nonmaneuverable aircraft. Length, 35.5 feet; diameter

TACTICAL AIRLIFT

	twenty-six inches; weight, three thousand pounds; slant range, thirty miles; and a ceiling of about sixty thousand feet. Truckborne.
SA–7 Strela	This Soviet-made, shoulder-fired, surface-to-air missile is fifty-four inches long, tube launched, with infrared seeker head. Carries two pounds of explosive and has a speed of Mach 1.3 with a ceiling of ten thousand feet (fifteen thousand for improved version). Strela operator has to visually sight his target before launching.
SC–47 aircraft	See HC–47 Skytrain.
SAC	Strategic Air Command
SACSA	Special Assistant for Counterinsurgency and Special Activities, Office of the Secretary of Defense
SAF	Secretary of the Air Force
SAM	surface-to-air missile
SAR	search and rescue
SAW	special air warfare
SAWC	Special Air Warfare Center (USAF)
SEA	Southeast Asia
SEAAS	Southeast Asia Airlift System
SEAOR	Southeast Asia operational requirement
SEATO	Southeast Asia Treaty Organization
sec	section
SECDEF	Secretary of Defense (US)
SECSTATE	Secretary of State (US)
sess	session
Shining Brass	United States-led South Vietnamese team and platoon probes into the Ho Chi Minh Trail with Army and Air Force helicopter and aircraft support. Began September 15, 1965. Renamed Prairie Fire on March 1, 1967.
SITREP	commander's situation report
SOG	Studies and Observations Group (MACV)
sq	squadron
starlight scope	An image intensifier using reflected light from the stars and moon to identify targets.
STOL	short-takeoff-and-landing

GLOSSARY

STRICOM	Strike Command (US)
subj	subject
SVN	South Vietnam
T–28 Trojan	Prop-driven, single-engine, low-wing, all-metal monoplane with retractable tricycle landing gear with steerable nose wheel. For primary pilot training. Two crewmembers. The T–28D version is an attack plane, capable of carrying a variety of ordnance on counterinsurgency missions.
T–37	All-metal, jet-powered, two-place, full-cantilever, low-wing monoplane primary trainer employing a retractable tricycle landing gear. Is completely equipped with flight instruments. Features side-by-side seating. Nose gear is equipped with power steering. Two crewmembers. See A–37.
T–39 Sabreliner	Swept, low-wing, twin-jet trainer aircraft. Engines are mounted on pylons on each side of fuselage just aft and above the wing trailing edge. Primary mission is flight training and maintenance of flying proficiency on multi-engine jet aircraft. Two crewmembers, four passengers.
TAC	Tactical Air Command
tacan	tactical air navigation
TACC	tactical air control center
TACP	tactical air control party
TACS	tactical air control system
TAFTS–P2	Tactical Air Force Transport Squadron-Provisional 2
Tailpipe	Collective call sign for combat control teams in Southeast Asia
TALAR	tactical landing approach radar
TALC	tactical airlift center
TALO	tactical airlift liaison officer
TAS	tactical airlift squadron
TASS	tactical air support squadron
TAW	tactical airlift wing
TAWC	Tactical Air Warfare Center (USAF)
TCG	troop carrier group
TCS	troop carrier squadron

TACTICAL AIRLIFT

TCW	troop carrier wing
TF	task force
TG	tactical group
TMA	Traffic Management Agency
tng	training
TRAC	Targets Research and Analysis Center
trnsp	transport, transportation
TSN	Tan Son Nhut Air Base, South Vietnam
U–1 Otter	Prop-driven, single-engine, short-range, high-wing, light utility aircraft. Has provisions for operating on wheels, wheel-skis, or floats. Features throwover control column, dual rudder controls, tailwheel powered steering, double-slotted wing flaps. Two crewmembers, eight passengers.
U–3A	Twin-engine, low-wing monoplane with tricycle landing gear. Used for administrative and light cargo purposes. Two crewmembers, three passengers.
U–3B	Same as U–3A except for engine. Used for administrative and light cargo purposes. Two crewmembers, three passengers.
U–6 Beaver	Single-engine, high-wing, all-metal monoplane. Has fixed landing gear, throwover controls, and dual rudder controls. For general utility missions. One crewmember, five passengers. Formerly designated L–20.
U–10 Helio Super Courier	Prop-driven, single-engine, light, short-takeoff-and-landing aircraft used for general utility missions. Two crewmembers, two passengers. Formerly designated L–28.
U–21 Ute	Two-engine, turbo-powered, unpressurized, cantilever low-wing utility aircraft. Has full feathering and reversing propellers, retractable tricycle landing gear and dual flight controls. Performs utility missions in the combat zone. Supports commanders and staff in command and control functions. Two crewmembers, ten troops.
UC–123	C–123 modified for Ranch Hand defoliation and herbicide operations. See C–123 and Ranch Hand.
UH–1A Iroquois	Used for transporting personnel and supplies. Has two-blade helicopter shaft driven by a gas turbine engine. Torque counteracted by a two-blade, tail rotor mounted on a tail boom. Has skid-type landing gear. Provisions for dual controls and internal ferry tank. One crewmember, five passengers. Formerly designated HU–1A.
UH–1B Iroquois	Used to transport personnel and supplies and as a gunship. Similar to UH–1A except for engine and wider rotor

GLOSSARY

	blade, copilot controls, provisions for armament, and capability to carry three litters. Two crewmembers, seven passengers. Formerly designated HU–1B.
UH–1D Iroquois	Similar to the UH–1B but has a single two-bladed forty-eight-inch main rotor and provision for two internal ferry tanks of 150 gallons each. One crewmember, eleven passengers or six litters. Formerly designated HU–1D.
UH–1F Iroquois	Similar to the UH–1B but has a single two-bladed forty-eight-inch main rotor, a single two-bladed tail rotor (eight and a half feet in diameter), and a modified tail boom. Uses skid landing gear. One crewmember, ten passengers.
UH–19 Chickasaw	All metal, semi-monocoque fuselage helicopter. Has one all-metal, three-blade, main rotor and an all-metal, two-blade, antitorque, tail rotor. Engine mounted in nose, quadricycle landing gear, side-by-side seating, external cargo sling, dual controls. Used for general utility operations. Two crewmembers, ten passengers. Formerly designated H–19.
UH–34 Seahorse	Similar to CH–34 Choctaw. Utility version. Two crewmembers, twelve passengers.
UHF	ultra high frequency
US	United States (of America)
USA	United States Army
USAF	United States Air Force
USAFE	United States Air Forces in Europe
USAFRED	United States Air Force Forces, Readiness Command
USARV	United States Army, Vietnam
USASF(P)V	United States Army Special Forces, Vietnam (Provisional)
USCINCRED	Commander in Chief, United States Readiness Command
USMC	United States Marine Corps
USN	United States Navy
USSAG	United States Support Activities Group
VC–47 Skytrain	The C–47 equipped for administrative operations. Three crewmembers. Twenty-eight passengers or cargo.
VC–123 Provider	The C–123 equipped for administrative operations.
Volpar/Beechcraft Model 18	Twin-engine, light, fixed-wing aircraft. Converts Beechcraft Model 18 to a tricycle landing-gear configuration, offering much slower approach speeds, greatly improved braking, and easier ground handling. Since all three

	wheels are completely retractable, cruising speed is increased.
VC	Viet Cong
VFR	visual flight rules
VHF	very high frequency
VIP	very important person
VNAF	Vietnamese Air Force
vol	volume
VSTOL	vertical- and/or short-takeoff-and-landing
VTOL	vertical-takeoff-and-landing
Water Pump	Nickname for Detachment 6, 1st Air Commando Wing (USAF), that deployed to Udorn Royal Thai Air Force Base in April 1964 for the purpose of training and providing logistic support for Thai and also Lao air force personnel.
wg	wing
WSEG	Weapons Systems Evaluation Group
WTO	Western Pacific Transportation Office
XM–41	An injurious gravel mine (and a variant mini-gravel mine, XM–41E1) were used to keep infiltrators on main trails, cause injury if they did not, and slow vehicles by blowing up tires and backing up traffic.
Z	Zulu Time (Greenwich Mean Time)

Bibliographic Note

Except for the early years source material proved more than ample. Indeed a major problem lay in overcoming the vastness of the collected records in order to complete the research in reasonable time. Enormously valuable in discovering and selecting the more valuable materials was the computerized Data Base Inventory (DABIN) system which catalogs by subject the substantial holdings of the Albert F. Simpson Historical Research Center at Maxwell Air Force Base, Ala. I was able to obtain, for example, a roughly chronological listing of some four thousand documents, all identified as dealing with tactical airlift in Southeast Asia during 1965–68. In most cases the title and originator of each document gave an idea as to its content and value. The DABIN printouts thus became a constantly available deskside reference for selecting material for each successive stage of research.

The records of the Secretary of the Air Force have been systematically retired each year to Washington National Records Center, Suitland, Md. Subject indexing and box references have been kept at the secretary's administrative offices. The collection includes numerous reports and correspondence, principally treating procurement and development matters, force level and basing questions, and doctrinal issues. Correspondence with officials of Office of Secretary of Defense and the Air Staff is abundant.

Also systematically retired at Suitland are the records of the Directorate of Plans, United States Air Force, through the early 1970s. Prominent in this collection are internal staff papers focusing on matters under Joint Chiefs of Staff (JCS) consideration, filed along with copies of the JCS papers themselves and varied background material. Numerous policy positions concerning U.S. force levels in Southeast Asia are here illuminated. Often found are details as to activities in the field and previous staff actions, included as background in considering related issues. Contending service positions are usually fully developed. Material concerning "Vietnam," "Southeast Asia," and "Airlift" is filed under these titles. An index converting keywords from titles into JCS paper numbers is available.

Another important collection at Suitland consists of the records of ground force units in Vietnam—brigades, field forces, and the U.S. Army Vietnam. These include quarterly "Operational Reports, Lessons Learned," after-action reports assembled following tactical operations, and the daily journals kept by the staff sections and command posts. Logistical data from the staff G–4s (Logistics) and from the reports of the 1st Logistical Command illuminate how airlift was applied in specific tactical and logistical situations. Frequently included are descriptions of difficulties, statements as to user satisfaction with Air Force lift, and statistical compilations of sorties and tonnages. Much material associated with the Army unit records is kept at the Army's Center of Military History in Washington, including an index of the records giving box numbers at Suitland. Comparable reports from U.S. Marine squadrons, regiments, divisions, and the marine amphibious force in Vietnam are available at the Marine Corps Historical Center.

Also at Suitland are the retired records of MACV headquarters. These are not well indexed but the filed shipping lists give an indication of the contents of most boxes. Especially valuable are those boxes, apparently assembled by the MACV historical office, containing much of the material collected during preparation of the annual MACV histories. Varied studies and reports abound. Considerable material from the former MACV historical office is kept at the Army's Military History Institute at Carlisle Barracks, Pa. Much of this duplicates the Suitland holdings, except for documents from 1972–73 not to be found at Suitland.

Much of the documentary material kept at the Simpson center at Maxwell consists of microfilm, and some of it is also available in printed form, machine-copied from the film. The documents were originally filmed in Southeast Asia by Project CHECO. The film may be approached either by using the DABIN or the printed lists showing the contents of each roll. Much of the microfilm is difficult to read, apparently because of conditions during photographing.

The three editions of the *Pentagon Papers* (*N.Y. Times*, Department of Defense, and Gravel) include excerpts from numerous official documents, along with narratives written by the project's authors. The twelve-volume Department of Defense edition is the most useful, but some parts omitted therein can be found in the others. An index to the Gravel edition has been commercially published.

An unusual primary source was the computer-stored information from the airlift operational report (ALOREP) airlift reporting system, instituted in 1966. Data from each Pacific airlift sortie was recorded by the aircrew for entry into the computerized system. Information included departure and destination bases, times, and the size and nature of loads. Retrieval is possible, for example, using the delivery base and desired dates, resulting in a sortie-by-sortie printout. The data appears to be nearly complete and is highly authoritative. The magnetic tapes, formerly available from the Air Force command center computer personnel, were returned to PACAF in about 1973.

BIBLIOGRAPHIC NOTE

Annual or semiannual narrative histories were produced during the war years by the Seventh Air Force, Pacific Air Forces, Tactical Air Command and its subordinate units, other zone of interior major commands, Pacific Command, Military Assistance Command, Vietnam, Military Assistance Command, Thailand, and the directorates of the Air Staff. More valuable are the histories of the various Pacific troop carrier wings and air divisions—the 314th, 315th, 374th, 463d, and 483d Wings, and the 315th and 834th Air Divisions. Squadron narratives are often appended to the wing histories. More important than the narrative histories themselves are the collections of supporting documents accompanying each periodic history. Taken together, the supporting documents constitute a substantial body of documentary material, all of it identified and selected by persons designated as historians. Thus, most of the material is of historical significance and can be easily scanned by the researcher. The existence of this long-established system for supporting documentation overcomes what would otherwise be a serious omission—the failure by units and field commands to retire official records. For purposes of this book, the documents supporting the 315th and 834th Air Division histories were enormously rich and seemed of exactly the correct volume.

Several hundred monographs have been prepared in Southeast Asia under Project CHECO, treating various aspects and campaigns of the Southeast Asia war. Several of these focus directly on the airlift effort, and many others give information secondarily on airlift activities. As in the case of the unit histories, the attending supporting documentation (often found in the CHECO microfilm collection mentioned above) is of extreme value. Especially distinguished in content and insight were studies on the 1972 campaigns by Maj. Paul T. Ringenbach, Capt. Peter A.W. Liebchen, and Capt. Peter J. Melly. Their earlier work vastly facilitated preparation of this volume. Also very helpful were studies on the final events in Cambodia and Vietnam, undertaken by historians at PACAF and MAC (Anthony Koura, Capt. Thomas D. DesBrisay, Wayne G. Peterson, Zoe Hanisian, and Kenneth L. Patchin).

Early drafts and interim publications by fellow Southeast Asia historians at the Office of Air Force History and the Army's Center of Military History provided valuable perspectives and background.

The activity inputs and reports of Project Corona Harvest, an internal Air Force review of its work in Southeast Asia, rest largely on the same source material likely to be used by the historian. Of special interest are the Corona Harvest recommendations which themselves conditioned Air Force doctrine and organization for the future.

TACTICAL AIRLIFT

The substantial collection of End of Tour reports and debriefings—kept at Maxwell and indexed under DABIN as well as separately—are rich sources of activities at numbered air force and lower levels. Many persons preparing these reports were candid and highly expressive in giving their perspectives, both as to their own job problems and toward the whole allied war effort. The oral history effort at Maxwell, originally under Project Corona Harvest and now affiliated with the Simpson center, has gathered taped interviews with numerous airlifters. Many of the interviews have been transcribed to written text, others are available only on tape. Interviews and End of Tour reports are available from both principal commanders of the 834th Air Division during 1966–69—Gen. William G. Moore, Jr., and Maj. Gen. Burl W. McLaughlin—whose outlooks are vital. The later commanders—Maj. Gen. John H. Herring, Jr., and Brig. Gen. John H. Germeraad—also wrote End of Tour reports.

I have myself made personal contact with about one hundred Southeast Asia airlift participants. Written résumés have been prepared for several dozen interviews, of which about half were tape recorded; many were by telephone, limiting conversations to unclassified matters. In some cases, written correspondence was exchanged, for example with former Chief of Staff Gen. John P. McConnell, and with Maj. Gen. Richard A. Yudkin, former staff officer to McConnell in matters of doctrine. The information from McConnell and Yudkin helped meet a scarcity of surviving documentation concerning negotiation of the pivotal 1966 Chiefs of Staff agreement on airlift roles and forces.

Most other interviews were intended to expand detail on specific operations, primarily the campaign in the Ia Drang Valley (1965), Junction City (1967), the Khe Sanh resupply (1968), the A Shau Valley invasion (1968), and the Kham Duc evacuation (1968). Very helpful was the insight of Lt. Gen. Andrew P. Iosue, who as a colonel commanded the Pacific C–130 wing in 1972, obtained by personal interview in 1975, and in Iosue's End of Tour report. Direct correspondence and interviews with participants were especially important in overcoming a scarcity of surviving written documentation from the early years in Vietnam, through about 1964. Large sections of the chapters on Farm Gate, Mule Train, and the Dirty Thirty ventures rest principally on these personal accounts.

In addition, several major figures in the events of this book have read and commented upon interim drafts. These included Maj. Gen. Rollen H. Anthis and Gen. William W. Momyer (commanders of 2d Air Division and the successor Seventh Air Force, respectively), Brig. Gen. Thomas B.

BIBLIOGRAPHIC NOTE

Kennedy (commander of the C-123 group in 1963-64), General William Moore, 834th Air Division commander in 1966-67, and General Iosue. A final personal input was the author's perspectives coming from service in the airlift system in 1967-68.

The U.S. Air Force biweekly management summaries provide a convenient and usually reliable fact-finding source. Numerous studies produced by students at Air University (kept at the university library) focus on Southeast Asia and airlift matters. A varied collection of reports and studies are available in the library of the Assistant Chief of Staff/Studies and Analyses, USAF. Numerous informative articles in the military professional journals focus on Southeast Asia; these are well indexed in the Air University's *Index to Military Periodicals*. Commercially published literature on the war is growing fast; the most perceptive, in my judgment, is Charles Bracelen Flood's *The War of the Innocents* (New York: McGraw-Hill Book Co, 1970). Finally, my debt is large to my colleagues for sharing their perspectives in numerous conversations as well as in rigorous critiques of many of my draft chapters.

Index *

A Luoi
    airfield construction and repair: 332–333, 339–340
    airlifts to and from: 332–334
    cargo delivery to: 136, 290, 333–340, *341*, 342–343

A Shau Valley
    airfields in: 332
    airlifts to and from: 90, 123–124, 135–136, 163, 333, 343, 425, 493
    combat operations in: 290, 314, 317, 332–343, 420, 559, 653
    mud-producing mission in: 389
    terrain features: 332, 340

About Face Operation: 458

Abrams, Creighton W., Jr., USA
    and An Loc campaign: 540
    becomes USMACV commander: 347
    and Cambodia campaign: 508–509
    and forest-burning missions: 393
    and Khe Sanh campaign: 514
    and Quang Tri campaign: 561
    and Vietnamese airlifts: 584
    and Vietnamese morale: 516
    and Vietnamization program: 467

Accident rates: 477, 532–533. *See also* Aircraft, lost and damaged

Adak Island: 49

Adams, Paul D., USA: 233

Aderholt, Harry C.: 442, 446

Advance Echelon (ADVON), 2d: 46, 49–50, 86, 91, 95–96, 101, 104–106, 141

Adverse-weather aerial delivery system. *See* Airlift, cargo delivery and handling

Advisors
    in Cambodia airlifts: 505
    mission: 3, 582, 598–599, 603
    number assigned: 582
    relations with Vietnamese: 74–75, 77–79, 80, 82, 103, 583, 591
    VNAF evaluated by: 581–582, 586, 597–599, 603

Aerial Port Group, 2d: 252–253, 256–258, 393, 472, 487–490, 560, 577, 598–599, 657

Aerial Port Squadrons
    6th: 409–411, 626
    7th: 138
    8th: 107, 138–140, 191, 194, 305, 409–410, *496*, 510, 515, 577–578, 586
    14th: 191
    15th: 191, 277, 305, 490, 495, 578
    6493d: 106, 138

Aerial port units and facilities: 106, *131*, 137–147, 153, 185, 191, 194, 209, 252–258, 271, 276, 287–289, 293, 305, 321, 328–329, 340–341, 343, 350, 385, 467, 469, 472–473, 487–491, 499, 505, 507, 510, 547, 560, 566, 577–578, 599–600, 619, 624, 633–634, 655–657. *See also* Ground crews

Aeromedical evacuation. *See* Casualties

Aeromedical Evacuation Flight, 903d: 309–400

Aeromedical Evacuation Group, 9th: 397, 400

---

* Numerals in italic indicate an illustration of the subject mentioned

TACTICAL AIRLIFT

Aeromedical Evacuation Squadrons
    9th: 396, 400
    903d: 397
Agee, Sam W.: 109
Agency for International Development
    aircraft assigned to: 359, 366, 410, 411, 445
    airlift use: 247, 443, 447, 463, 655
    cargo tonnages moved for: 401, 407
    civic actions by: 401
    and Farm Gate mission: 50
Agnew, Spiro T.: *503*
Air America, Inc.: 401, *402–403*, 404, 439–451, 454–462, 476, 617, 637, 641, 644
Air Asia, Ltd.: 441
Air Base Wing, 337th: 536
Air cavalry concept. *See* Airmobility concept
Air Commando Groups
    1st: 41*n*, 52
    315th: 187
Air Commando Squadrons
    1st: 63, 424
    4th: 388
    12th: 329
    15th: 439, 431*n*
    19th: 146, 218, 411
    309th: 187*n*, 195*n*, 248, 389
    310th: 187*n*, 195*n*, 197, 212, 248, 419, 473, 536
    311th: 187*n*, 248, 262, 290, 297
    317th: 128
    315th: 248*n*, 263, 307
Air Commando Wing, 14th: 236, 429–430
Aircrews: *156*
    in air commando units: 47, 59–60, 63, 65, 128, 196
    Army, relations with: 60
    Australian hat symbol: 56, 60, 196
    carelessness and recklessness: 124–125
    civic actions by: 371, 405, 408
    civilians in: 441, 627, 631
    clothing and footwear: 125
    combat injury potential: 64
    and combined crews: 49
    complaints against: 134, 159, 177–179, 190, 199, 204, 219
    complaints by: 60, 105, 120, 138, 177, 189, 350–351, 522
    composition: 369, 449
    crew-to-aircraft ratio: 123, 510
    decorations and awards: 64, 89, 125, 286, 301, 316–318, 340, 344–346, 352, 354, 375, 400, 426, 456, 462, 472, 478–479, 483, 490, 502, *503*, 534–535, 542, 608, 646
    double manning: 61–64
    flak suits use: 91
    flight conditions: 37, 52
    flight schedules: 59–60, 88, 153
    flying proficiency and methods: 63–64, 83–84, 88, 93–94, 123–124, 153–154, 195
    French: 7–11, 16

INDEX

  in French support: 17
  ground crews, relations with: 61, 126
  ground transportation for: 126, 177
  health status: 126
  living conditions: 17–18, 61–62, 69, 88, 94, 125–126, 154, 177, 182–183, 196, 351, 354, 371, 409–410, 426, 440, 446, 483, 535, 565
  Makay Trophy award: 63
  maps, reading and use: 97
  mess facilities: 17, 62, 88, 125, 153–154, 177–179, 196
  morale, motivation and discipline: 37, 41, 47, 59–60, 62, 64, 93–94, 108, 125–126, 166, 181, 184, 196, 301, 316, 340, 347, 351–352, 367, 371, 478–479, 483, 512, 535, 557, 616, 625, 647
  multiple drops by: 532
  number and task assignments: 84, 562
  personal and family life: 37, 181
  proficiency standards: 497
  recreation and welfare facilities: 57, 62, 154, 351
  rotation and tour lengths: 51, 92, 123, 154, 181–182, 195, 316, 329, 351, 388, 408–411, 479, 483, 534, 607, 625, 656
  shortages in: 125, 187, 195, 249, 351, 369, 479–480, 533
  Special Forces, relations with: 154, 159
  in spray missions: 45, 89–90
  team scheduling: 249
  training programs: 8–11, 34–37, 59, 63, 85, 97, 123, 184, 354, 357, 369, 479, 485–486, 521, 571
  water supply for: 62, 483
  work hours and conditions: 179, 199, 249, 284, 365–366, 369, 385, 409–410, 535, 565, 612–613, 642
Air divisions
  staff structure: 242
  2d: 50n, 57, 85, 107, 109, 116, 118, 121, 145, 159–160, 170, 179–180, 191, 196, 213, 215, 236, 406–407, 663
  315th: 10, 18–19, 21, 26–27, 35, 38, 86, 104–106, 111–114, 118, 141, 144–146, 163, 170–186, 196, 199, 228, 248–249, 259, 288–289, 311, 329, 333, 379–384, 388, 396, 405, 408–412, 414–415, 440, 448, 665, 687–688
  316th: 140n
  834th: 169, 191, 241, 245, 248–250, 252–253, 256, 271, 288, 302–303, 305, 311–312, 333–344, 350, 352, 357, 363–369, 379, 393, 397, 409–410, 420, 468–472, 476–477, 486–487, 490–491, 501–502, 505, 508–513, 517, 522–523, 530, 560, 586, 591, 655–656
Air Force Reserve: 29, 137–138, 258, 385, 472, 535–536, 601, 616, 632, 651, 657
Air Forces (*see also* Far East Air Forces; Pacific Air Forces)
  Fifth: 27, 35, 382
  Seventh: 180n, 190, 224, 230, 232, 235–236, 243, 250, 253, 256, 261–263, 302–303, 306–307, 314, 328–329, 344, 347, 357–359, 375, 383, 385, 388, 393, 399, 406–407, 424, 430, 450, 455, 463, 470–471, 480, 483–486, 495, 505, 508, 517, 522–523, 526, 549, 552, 565, 573, 576, 583, 595, 615, 641, 644
  Thirteenth: 47, 57, 81, 85, 90, 95, 101, 104, 107, 109, 382, 406–407, 450, 455, 463, 616
  Eighteenth: 26
Air National Guard: 384, 472, 601, 651

TACTICAL AIRLIFT

Air strike force. *See* Composite air strike force
Air strikes in airlift support: 57, 95, 124, 128–129, 133, 158, 197, 299, 301, 307, *308*, 311, 313, 319, 322, 333–339, 344, 347, 388, 405, 422, 428, 430, 461–463, 525–530, 533, 537, 545, 550, 569, 657
Air supply. *See* Airlifts
Air support operations center: 112
Air traffic control: *See* Command, control and coordination
Air traffic coordinating office: 104
Air transport. *See* Airlift; Parachute assaults
Air Vietnam: 42, 68, 88, 402–403, 411, 566, 637–638
Airborne Brigade, 173d: 171, 173–174, 205, 208, 216–219, *220*, 221, 223–224, 270–279, *280–281*, 282, 284–285
Airborne Command and Control Squadron, 7th: 395
Airborne divisions
    82d: *326*, 328
    101st: 209, 222–223, 284, 293, 323, 325, 327–328, 332, 484–485
Airborne assaults. *See* Airlift; Parachute assaults
Airborne units training: 174, 270–271, 274
Aircraft, fixed-wing (*see also* Airlift; *for component parts, see by name*)
    accident rates: 477, 532–533. *See also* lost and damaged, *below*
    airdrop facilities in: 84
    airlift missions. *See* Airlift
    allocations: 522–523
    altitude capabilities: 83, 90, 532, 537, 658
    armament: 58, 159
    armorplating: 90–91, 546
    Army, integration into airlift: 121–123, 144, 190–191, 203, 237–238, 353–363
    auxiliary uses: 379–415
    bombing missions: 58, 144, 169, 203, 347, 389–395, 410–411, 430, 576, 592, 605, 609, 639, 646, 656
    cloud-dissipating missions: 389
    command and control. *See* Airlift
    as command and control center: 395, 656
    courier missions: 406–407
        defoliation and crop destruction missions: 89, 389, *391*, 392, 656
    design, modification and flight performance: 19–20, 33, 83, 89, 159–160, 329, 367, 371, 375, 449, 469, 536, 650–651, 658
    enemy losses: 452
    evacuation of: 20–21, 644
    first combat losses: 50, 200
    flying time rates: 183–184, 195, 250–251, 263, 354, 360–361, 366, 369, 408–409, 446, 480, 534, 575, 583, 600, 620
    forest-burning missions: *391*, 392–393
    fuel capacities and consumption: 34, 213–214
    as gunships: 58, 388–389, *390*, 395, 426, *460*, 656
    insignia: 68, 76, 86, 627
    instrument flying aids: 9, 70, 87–88, 94, 112, 367, 475
    interdiction missions: 388–389
    jet-equipped: 263
    last losses: 533
    leaflet drops: 58, 405, *406*, 422, 429, 431
    light designs: 58

INDEX

lost and damaged: 17, 50, 58, 60, 64, 69, 72, 74, 83, 89–93, 122–125, 154, 160, 163, 169, 184, 197, *198*, 199–201, 250, *251*, 252, 270–271, 276, 285–286, 291, 300–304, 311, 316, 321, 326–327, 330, *331*, 336–339, 344, 347, 351, 354–355, 364, 368–369, 374, 388, 392, 408–409, 450, 455, 475–478, *479*, 480, 490, 494, 502, 507, 515, 525–535, 540–541, 543, 545–546, 552, 557, 564–568, 575, 583, 586, 596, 600, 605, 608, 613, 620–621, 633, 639, 641, 643, 658, 689
loudspeaker missions: 41, 58–59, 74, *405*, 406
maintenance and repair. *See* Maintenance and repair
mechanical and structural failures: 251, 480–482, 535, 596, 645
mine-dropping missions: 392–393
misuse alleged: 81, 522
mud-producing missions: 389
napalm assaults by: 17, 392
night strikes by: 73
in nuclear warfare: 27–28
number in service: 37, 61, 64, 83, 116, 126–127, 169, 174–176, 182–183, 196, 213, 250–251, 370, 480, 534, 576
payload capacities and averages: 28, 31–35, 58, 83, 95, 109, 111, 160, 179, 196, 207, 214, 217, 304, 354, 366, 371, 379, 384–385, 446, 469, 489–490, 495, 523–524, 536–537, 582, 602, 658
procurement: 651
in psywar missions: 50, 57–59, 73, 95, 656
range capabilities: 28, 34, 83, 111, 658
reconnaissance missions: 55, 58–59, 98, 333, 395, 423–432
reserve components, number in: 651
roles and missions controversy and agreements: 30, 32, 89–90, 93–94, 107–111, 114–115, 203, 212, 233, 236–238, 266, 359, 407–408, 467, 521, 657–658, 673–674
sensors use by: 389, 455
speed capabilities: 34–35, 83, 537, 658
spray missions: 45, 89–90
starlight scope use: 388–389
surplus, disposal of: 616–617
takeoff and landing capabilities and hazards: 34–35, 53, 83–84, 88, 90, 92–93, 109–110, 143, 160, 165, 180, 184, 196, 232, 297, 368, 371–372, 475–476, 481, 486, 532
takeoff weights: 34
tear-gas drop missions: 389
types. *See* Aircraft types
Aircraft, rotary-wing. *See* Helicopters
Aircraft types
   A–1 Skyraider: 55, 424, 428, 430–431, 455, 461–463, 526, 528–529, 550
   A–7 Corsair: 462–463
   A–37 Dragonfly: 526, 643–644
   AC–47 Dragonship: 388–389, *390*, 453, 587
   AC–119: 389, *390*, *460*, 530, 587
   AC–130: 389, 486, 545, 549, 552–553

TACTICAL AIRLIFT

Advanced medium STOL transport: 651
AN–2 Colt: 432*n*, 434, 438, 507
B–1 bomber: 650
B–26 Invader: 17–18, 41, 43, 57, 160
B–52 Stratofortress: 223, 622
B–57 Canberra: 144
Beechcraft: 435, 447
Bristol: 407–408, 638
C–1 Trader: 407–408
C–2: 407
C–5 Galaxy: 383, 385, *387*, *489*, 490, 575, 577, 641
C–7 Caribou: 31, 34, 45, 81, 109–110, 114*n*, 115–116, 121–122, 136, 144, 151, 154, 159, 161, 164–165, 190–191, 200, 203, 207–209, 212–218, 222–223, 228–233, 236–238, 242, 257, 263, 279, 284, 290–291, 299, 302, 313–316, 321, 323–326, 330, 332, 339–341, *342*, 343, 353–376, 399–401, 404–405, 407–410, 414, 419–421, 424, 445–447, 458–461, 471, 475, 486, 493, 495, 500–504, 521–537, 560, 564, 587–588, 590, 592, 600, 619–621, 639, 644, 640–651, 658
C–8 DeHavilland: 651
C–9 Nightingale: 397, 401, 612
C–45 Expediter: 7, *331*, 401
C–46 Commando: 21, 37, 52, 55, 401, 404, 410–411, 414–416, 441, 443–448, 637
C–47 Skytrain: *6*, 7–11, 16–21, 25, 34, 41–55, *56*, 57–64, 68–74, *76*, 78–82, 87–88, 95–103, 114*n*, 128, 132–137, 149–166, 177, 181, 187, 200, 252, 262, 270, 285, 322, *331*, 385, *387*, 392, 401, 404, *405*, 406–407, 410–414, 421–422, 425, 429, 441, 447, 451–453, 502, 505–508, 560, 582–588, 598–602, 616–617, 620, 627–628, 644, 653–654
C–54 Skymaster: 18–19, 35, 383, 406–407, 414–416
C–117 Skytrain: 406–408
C–118 Liftmaster: 383, 385, 497, 400, 616, 642
C–119 Flying Boxcar: 9, *12*, *14*, 16–21, 33–34, 37, 410–411, 440, 477, 502, 505–508, 541, 560, 582–583, *584*, 586–587, 592, 596–602, 620, 628, 638–639, 644
C–123 Provider: 29–46, 50, *56*, 58–65, 73, 80–99, *100*, 101–111, 114*n*, 115–129, *130–131*, 132–169, 174–181, *188*, 190–249, *250*, 251–263, *264*, 266, 270, *272–273*, 278–297, *298*, 299–316, 319–333, 339–351, 353, 357–358, 363–364, 372–375, 385, *387*, 388–392, 396, 399–401, 408–409, 411–416, 418–422, 429–431, *436*, 440, 442, 445–451, 458–461, 468–473, 477, *478*, 479–481, 486, 495, 497, 500–506, 509, 512, 516, 521–523, 531, 534–537, 541, 555, 557, 560–561, 564, 567–568, 576, 584, 587–592, 596–597, 600, 602, 616–619, 627, 629, 635, 647, 650–658
C–124 Globemaster: *13*, 18, 21–22, 34–45, 111, *112*, 113, 140–141, 144–145, 173, *193*, 343, 379, 384–385, *386*, 408–409, 441
C–130 Hercules: 24, 33–45, 109–128, 137–141, 143–146, 152–169, *170*, 171–177, *178*, 179–192, *193*, 195–197, *198*, 201–203, 209, *210–211*, 212–219, *220*, 221–224, *226*, 228–238, *240*, 242–249, *251*, 252, *255*, 259, *260*, 261–263, *265*, 266–279, *280–281*, 282–307, *308–310*, 311–316, 319–351, 357–358, 363–365, 371–372, 379–385, *387*, 388, 392–397, *398*, 400–401, 405–411, 416, 418–423, 430–431, 434, 440–441, 448, 451, 458, 461, 464, 468, 471–472, 476–

INDEX

        480, *481*, 482, 485–486, 490, 493–495, *496*, 497–518, 521–525, 529–530, 535–539, 542–557, *560*, 561–575, 581, 584–588, 596, 600, 603, 605–629, 631–647, 650–658

  C–133 Cargomaster: 223, *327*, 384
  C–135 Stratolifter: *254*, *386*
  C–141 Starlifter: *326*, 347, 384, *386*, *398*, 472, 479, 490, 518, 564–565, 575, 606, 609, *610*, 611, 613, 638, *640*, 641–645
  CV–2 Caribou. *See* C–7 Caribou, *above*
  CV–7 Buffalo: 237–238
  DC–8 commercial transport: 631–634, 638
  Dornier: 446–447
  EB–66: 563
  F–4 Phantom: 299, 334, 430, 563
  F–5 Tiger: 644
  F–100 Super Sabre: 113, 144, 526
  F–105: 252, 563
  IL–14: 432, 434, 438, 507
  Ju–52 transport: 6
  FC–130: 141, 172, 288, 290–291, 299, 301, 304, 315–316, 407–408, 563
  L–19: 133
  L–28: 58
  LI–2: 432, 434, 438, 452
  light intratheater transport: 650–652
  O–1 Bird Dog: *281*, 461
  O–2 forward air controller: 552, 608
  Pilatus Porter: 446–447, 461
  RB–26: 44
  RF–4: 627
  SC–47: 41, 43–44, 48–50, 62
  STOL transport: 651
  T–28 Trojan: 41, 44, 49, 57, 69, 80, 95, 105, 133, 137, *142*, 443, 450–451, 453, 459–461
  T–39 Sabreliner: 406, 616
  U–1 Otter: 324, 419, 508
  U–3 utility: 406–407
  U–6 Beaver: 422
  U–10 Helio Courier: 52, 55, 58–59, 422, 442, 446–447
  U–21 Ute: 409
  UC–123: 389
  VC–47: 406–407
  VC–123: 406–407
  Volpar: 447
  V/STOL transports: 650
  XC–123 Chase: 29
  XCG–20 glider: 29
  YC–14 Boeing: 651
  YC–115 McDonnell-Douglas: 651
  YC–123H Boeing: 159–160, 196
Airdrops. *See* Airlift
Airfields
  conditions at: 18, 20, 28, 53, 59, 62, 93, 112, 141, 146, 153–154, 162–163, 177, 179, 192, 197, 209, 214, 218–219, 222–223, 225, 293, 372, 407–408, 477, 500, 564

TACTICAL AIRLIFT

    congestion at: 196–197, 285–286, 306, 314, 326–327
    construction and repair: 17, 39, 42, 161–163, 192, 209, 214, 229–230, *231*, 232–233, 235, 242, 253, 263, *264*, 278–279, 285, 290–292, 297, *398*, 303, 313–315, 343, 408–409, 422, 440, 442, 477, 493, 495, 499, 509–510, 512–514, 516, 519, 586, 620, 624, 656
    defenses: 171–173
    enemy assaults on: 20, 200, 323. *See also site by name*
    enemy construction and repair: 620
    inspections and surveys of: 232, 656
  lighting systems: 53, 179, 228, 263, 321, 371, 510, 515
    locations: 88
    number in use: 163, 232
    runway materials: 230, *231*, 232, *264*, 514, 516
    safety and security measures at: 20, 53, 197
    Soviet construction: 445
    type classification: 232
    versatility: 653
Airlift (*see also* Aircrews; Aircraft; Ground crews; Helicopters; Parachute assaults; Pilots)
    aerial port teams and facilities: 106, *131*, 137–140, 153, 185, 191, 194, 209, 252–258, 271, 276, 287–289, 293, 305, 321, 328–329, 340–343, 350, 385, 467, 469, 472–473, 487–491, 499, 505, 507, 510, 547, 560, 566, 577–578, 599–600, 619, 624, 633–634, 655–657
    Agency for International Development use: 247, 443, 447, 463, 655
    air crews role in. *See* Air crews; Pilots
    Air Force Reserve in: 385
    Air force use, volume of: 247
    Air National Guard in: 384
    air strikes in support of: 57, 95, 124, 128–129, 133, 158, 197, 299, 301, 307, *308*, 311, 313, 319, 322, 333–339, 344, 347, 388, 405, 569, 657
    of air units: 27, 563
    aircraft and units assigned to: 33, 41, 43, 45–51, 63, 106–108. *See also* station by name
    airdrops use in. *See* cargo and handling, *below*
    Army aircraft integration into: 121–123, 144, 190–191, 203, 236–238, 353–363
    Army role in: 16, 122, 137, 209–213, 219, 247, 290, 324–344, 373, 409–410, 513, 680–681, 683
    of artillery: 218, 225, *227*
    autonomy for: 191
    blind drops: 485
    call signs use: 120, 243
    cargo delivery and handling: 29, 115, 135–140, 143, 151–154, 158, 170, 173, 185–186, 192, *193*, 194, 203–229, 239, 245, 253, *254–255*, 256–262, *268*, 270, 276, 294, 303, 365–366, 449, 545, 548–550, 554, 556, 568–574, 576, 596, 606, 618, 623–624, 626–627, 633, 652, 657
    cargo diversity: 379, 384–385, 440, 449, 455, 527, 654–655

INDEX

cargo extraction delivery: *142*, 143, 165, 217, 235, 259, *260–261*, 262, 291, 294, 300–303, *310*, 311–312, 316, 372, *437*, 449, 483–484, 493, 652
cargo tonnage predictions: 114, 117, 207, 228, 247, 297, 303, 332–333, 401, 407–408, 470, 472, 508, 510, 513, 540, 635
cargo tonnages moved by: 3, 20–21, 47, 89, 108, 112–113, 117, 122, 136, 138–140, 144, 151–152, 163, 171, 174, 181, 185–186, 191, 195, 213, 215, 219–222, 224, 228, 241, 246–248, 252, 262, 270, 276–279, 282–283, 288–289, 292, 299, 302–304, 313–315, 323–325, 328, 330, 336–343, 349–350, 361, 366, 372, 374, 380, 383–385, 401, 405, 407–409, 414, 417, 419, 429, 440–442, 445, 450–451, 455, 468–469, 495, 499–505, 513–516, 526, 528, 532, 540–541, 550–551, 555, 561–565, 570, 577, 583, 586, 592, 595, 606, 624–627, 632, 635n, 675–688, 691
casualty evacuation: 21, 35, 59, 62, 114, 205, 214, 269, 292, 305, 326, 365, 372, 396–397, *398*, 399–401, 414–416, 459, 524, 550–551, 576, 592–597, 646, 655
Central Intelligence Agency in: 441, 445, 447–448, 655. *See also* Air America
in civic actions: 59, 95, 164, 219, 385, 401, 404–407, 655
civil airlines in: 383, 401, *402–403*, 404, 439–451, 454–464, 476, *488–489*, 504–505, 617, 627, 631–635, 637, 641–642, 655
combat cargo group functions: 106
combat control teams in: 187, *188*, 243, *244–245*, 270, 274, 276–277, 279, 282, 286, 288–289, 305, 311, 315, 325, 333–336, 343–347, 371, 469–470, 473, 486, *496*, 499, 505, 510, 515–516, 518, 547, 566, 577, 611–612, 623 643
command, control and coordination in: 26–27, 31–32, 35, 49–50, 57, 86–87, 91, 98, 103–111, 114–121, 126, 137, 141, 144–146, 152–153, 158, 165, 169, 174–177, 180, 187–191, 209, 213–214, 228, 242–245, 259, 266–267, 270–271, 293, 300, 305, 313, 350, 353, 357–358, 363, 380–382, 385, 407–408, 412–414, 421, 425, 428, 445–446, 463, 468–469, 471–472, 512, 521–522, 531, 537, 576–577, 591, 595, 607, 615–616, 639, 641–642, 644, 649–650
commendations of: 241, 245–246, 259–261, 276–278, 282, 289, 304, 321, 326, 336, 340, 353, 362, 364–366, 372, 419, 424, 447–448, 458, 502, 532, 570
communications in: 108, 120, 138, 159, 189, 208, 212, 243, *244*, 245, 445, 487, 510, 515, 536, 564, 576. *See also* radio communications, *below*
Communist China role in: 438
complaints against: 181, 189–191, 237, 239, 278, 350–351, 362, 366, 419–420, 424, 522–523, 547
computers use in: 467, 470–471, 485, 655
concept proved: 87, 114–115, 146–147, 201, 203, 215, 224, 228–229, 315, 342–343, 349, 352, 370, 448, 647, 652
concept, service views on: 27–28, 30–32, 104, 151, 159, 215–216, 233, 358, 523
construction machinery lifts: 332, 339, 343, 440

843

TACTICAL AIRLIFT

    container delivery: 259, 277, 279, 291, 302–304, 306, 311–313, 333, 339, 344, 424, 430, 517, 542, 545, 564, 568, 575, 578, 596
    costs and cost reduction: 407–408, 446–447, 450, 470, 555
    data processing system in: 242, 469–470, 487
    decline in activities: 349–350, 467–468, 473, 480, 490–491, 495, 519, 523–524, 627–628
    dedicated user concept: 522–523, 537, 651
    deficiencies and failures in: 105–106, 177, 189, 194, 247, 277–278, 284, 304, 312, 330, 339, 350–351, 419, 529–530, 539–545, 548–550, 554, 564, 575, 597, 606, 618, 655, 659
    doctrine formulation: 25–27, 29–31, 39–40, 42, 86, 103–104, 179–180, 233, 266–267, 358–359, 649, 651–652. *See also* roles and missions, *below*
    drop altitudes and tactics: 54, 142–143, 154, 158, 160–161, 164–165, 217–218, 223, 271, 276–277, 326, 336, 368, 372, 424, 430, 449, 467, 483–485, 495, 507, 517, 526–531, 533, 539–540, 542–544, 557, 564, 624
    drop loads, size and weight: 54
    drop zones designations: 55, 97–98, 101–102, 132–134, 517, 546
    dual system: 380–381, 429–430
    duplications in: 122, 383, 407–408, 650
    efficiency improvement programs: 350, 469, 486–487, 523–524, 556–557
    electronic aids in: 55
    emergency and priority missions: 86, 106–107, 119–120, 186–187, 189, 209, 222–223, 327, 330, 371, 424, 446, 469, 485, 493, 495–497, 499, 505, 507, 591, 593, 654–655
    equipment shortages: 139, 578
    equipment used. *See by name*
    evaluation of: 22–23, 215–216, 649–650, 653–659
    facilities strained: 328–329
    first units assigned: 47
    flare illumination in: 58, 176, 204, 212–213, 243, 297, 385–386, *387*, 388–389, 422, 431, 486, 530, 546
    flare signals use in: 62, 98, 530
    flight conditions: 52–53, 275–277
    flight records system: 189
    floods, effect on: 97, 146, 405
    food supply by: 58, 146, 204, 417, 450, 540, 548, 550–551, 567, 605, 626–627, 632, 635, 655
    force requirements for future: 651
    forward air controllers in: 58–59, 275, 277, 279, 299, 307, 394, 422, 428, 514, 527–528, 531, 533, 542, 546–548, 557, 653
    forward distribution system: 229
    freefall delivery: 54
    French experience: 6, 9, *12–13*, 16, 18–20, 22, 40
    fuel deliveries: 214–215, 225, 228, *234*, 263, *265*, 266, 304, 315–316, 322–323, 326, 330, 372, 457, 468, *481*, 484, 495, 499–500, 506, 508, 513–514, 517, 550, 566–568, 592, 623, 626, 631, 654
    ground controlled approach in: 17, 52, 88, 161, 179, 200, 263, 299–304, 312–313, 325, 339, 343, 355, 368, 510, 512, 514–515, 517, 570

helicopters in. *See* Helicopters
historic airlifts: 691
hours and sorties flown: 3, 18–19, 49, 55, 59–63, 87, 89, 102, 108, 111–113, 145, 152, 169, 173–174, 183–184, 204–205, 212–215, 219, 222, 225, 228, 243, 245, 270, 279, 285, 289, 292–293, 297, 315, 320–321, 324–326, 329–330, 336, 339, 341, 347–350, 354, 366, 370, 372, 384–385, 407–408, 420, 440, 450–451, 468, 495–500, 506, 510–514, 516, 532, 550, 555–556, 563–565, 570, 572, 574–576, 586, 595, 606, 624, 632, 675–688
insignia used: 86
joint operations center role in: 62, 86, 89, 99, 103–104, 106–107, 120, 138, *188*, 476–477, 655
Korean experience: 26–27, 35, 47, 103, 247, 379, 691
landing zones, locating: 55
last missions: 473
liaison and liaison officers in: 27, 57–58, 101–102, 121–122, 134, 136, 153, 190–191, 237, 241, 245–246, 289, 359, 364, 469, 545, 593, 655
light aircraft in: 58
lines of communication in: 141
loadmasters role in: 126, 137–138, 158, *227*, 257, 333, 370, 449
logistics command, relation to: 117–118
Malaya experience: 40, 134, 149
management system: 469–471, 487, 576, 595, 655
maps use in: 134, 154
Marine Corps role in: 113–114, 141, 247, 288, 290–292, 295, 297–316, 332, 344–345, 419, 493, 513, 575, 635, 683
materiel lifts: 204, 214, 225, *240*, 285, 287, 292, 297, 301, 304, 322–326, 332, 339, *342*, 373, 443, 451, 468, 499, 502, 505–507, 513–514, 526–527, 540, 548, 550–551, 566–568 592, 605, 622–624, 626–627, 631, 636, 638–639, 655
medical supplies dropped: 204, 548, 550–551
by Military Airlift Command: 28, 35, 38, 49, 85, 91–92, 111, 114, 223, 288, 328, 383–384, *386,* 410–411, 441, 518, 563–565, 577, 606, 609, 641–642, 650
mission commanders role: 469, 511, 515, 547
mission defined: 32, 85–86, 116, 652
mobility provided by: 26–27
movement control in: 108, 112
navigation and navigators in: 25, 49, 52–53, 55, 84–85, 87–88, 97, 154, 158, 160–161, 179, 197, 262–263, 271, 275, 288, 304, 334, 338, 357, 368, 431, 486, 510, 515, 517, 532, 549, 572–573, 618
Navy role in: 247, 290, 406–408
night missions: 52–55, 58, 123, 204, 222, 285, 302, 322, 324, 329, 373–374, 425, 469, 473, 493, 504–505, 514, 517, 525, 530–531, 545–547, 559, 564, 567–568, 570
North Vietnam use: 432–438, 441, 647
nuclear fuel moves: 638
offensive strategy, role in: 653–654
organization structure and restructure: 103–106, 116, 146, 468–469, 472, 576–577, 650, 663–673

845

TACTICAL AIRLIFT

pallets use and misuse: 54, 122, 139, *142*, 192, *193*, 194, 256, *260*, 300, 305–306, *310*, 365, 372, 449, 469, 490, 499–500, 531, 578, 598
panel signals use: 54, *188*, 305, 325, 334–335, 422, *436*
in parachute assaults: 55, 57, 73, 96–103, 114–115, 128–129, *131*, 137, 269–292, 349, 423–432, 575, 583–584, 596, 651, 654
passengers moved: 22, *24*, 86, 89, 108, 113, 117, 122, 136, 164, 170–171, 185–186, 204, 228, 289, 299, 330, 344–347, 364, 366, 372, 383, 401, 405–407, 409–410, 414–416, 429, 442–443, 445, 450, 456–459, 468–469, *488–489*, 500–502, 506, 508, 561–562, 564–565, 567, 576, 583, 592, 598, 606, 609, 620, 631, 635, 637–638, *640*, 641–644, 655, 675–683
pathfinders in: 57, 98, 137–138, 141, 486
photos use in: 54–55, 169, 271, 334, 513, 573, 627
preflight preparations: 53–55
in prisoners repatriation: 605, 608–609, *610*, 611–613, 616
quick reaction concept: 95–103, 135
radar guidance in: 55, 87–88, 112, 141, 161, 179, 197, 243, 262, 302, 304, 312, 315–316, 328, 337, 342, 367, 372, 393–395, 476, 484–486, 544–545, 554, 556, 569–575, 596–597, 602, 618, 652
radio communication and equipment in: 41, 54–55, 60, 87–88, 102, 108, 112, *119*, 120, 123, 152, 159, 161, 177, 179, 189, 199–200, 204, 243–246, 263, 276–277, 313, 350, 360, 365, 380, 388, 409–410, 419, 442, 446, 470, 476, 487–490, 507, 510, 527, 530–532, 536, 542, 551, 556–557, 564, 570, 576, 591, 596, 623, 633, 657
rigging devices and services: 158–159, 257, 261, 306, 315, 333, 484, 531, 545, 548–549, 554, 556, 624–626, 652
roles and missions controversy and agreements: 30, 32, 89–90, 93–94, 107–111, 114–115, 203, 212, 233, 236–238, 266, 359, 396, 407–408, 467, 521, 657–658, 673–674
safety and security measures in: 70–71, 89–90, 93–94, 125, 179, 194, 199, 201, 284, 355, 357, 368–369, 475–477, 489–490, 532, 542, 546
in search-and-clear missions: 39–40, 95–103, 203–229, 239, 269–292, 313–314, 371–372, 421–432, 439–464, 493–508, 653
in search-and-rescue missions: 62, 345–347, 429–431
searchlights in: 546–547
smoke signals and screens use: 54–55, 98, 133, 159, 165, *188*, 212, 275–276, 305, 311, 335, 526
by Soviet Union: 432, 438, 441
for Special Forces Units: 50, 65–65, 115, 122, 125, *142*, 149–155, *156*, 157–166, 262–263, 290, 353, 364, 367, 372, 405, 409–410, 412–414, *436–437*, 655
supplies loss rate: 213
strike aircraft use in: 430
in tactical missions: 54, 57–58, 95, 98, 212, 216–229, 239, 243, 269–292. *See also by geographical location or station*
telephone service in: 120, 350, 380

INDEX

    teletype service in: 120, 189, 350
    terrain effect on: 3, 164, 295, 332, 340, 429, 449
    third nations role in: 410–416
    traffic control and management: 17, 32, 52, 92, 104, 186–187, *188*, 189, 199–200, 204, 253, 285–286, 473–476, 510
    training programs and exercises: 32–42, 51–53, 55, 58, 123, 158
    trooplifts: 209, *210–211*, 212, 216, 224, 236, 284–293, 317, 323, 325, *326*, 327–343, 347–349, 365, 371–373, 380, 383, 385, 420, 422, 443, 457, 461–463, 468, 495, 500, 505–513, 515–518, 540, 554, 561, 566, 569, 575, 577, 586, 592–595, 622, 638, 644–647, 653–654
    warning systems: 476
    water supplies lifts: 540, 551
    weather effect on: 54–55, 102, 119, 133, 135–136, 140–141, 144, 146, 182, 197, 222–223, 228, 231, 277, 284, 291, 295–296, 300–304, 307, 314, 330, 333, 335, 339–343, 360, 440, 451, 459–461, 501, 512, 514–515, 525, 546, 561, 564
    weighing facilities: 257
    World War II experience: 25–26 41, 47, 247, 295, 557, 653, 691
Airlift Center: 650
Airlift International: 632
Airmobile division organization: 208–209
Airmobility concept, service views on: 29–30, 101, 108–111, 121, 141, 143, 203, 207–209, 216, 267, 497, 653
Akin, James F., Jr.: 371
Algeria experience: 40
Aluminum matting: 230–232, 514, 516
Ambushes, by enemy: 4–5, 102, 117, 291, 322, 513
Amphibious assaults, airlift for: 141
Ammunition. *See* Materiel
An Hoa
    airfield construction and repair: 230
    airlifts to: 404–405, 423
    maintenance & repair at: 482
An Khe
    accidents at: 197, 199, 251, 355, 368
    aircraft lost at: 200
    aircraft and units assigned: 354
    airfield conditions at: 209, 500
    airfield construction and repair: 229, 231
    airlifts to and from: 208–209, 213, 222, 285, 365, 500
    cargo handling and delivery: 209, 259, *261*
    in casualty evacuation system: 397
    disarray at: 192
    enemy assaults on: 200, 208, 222
    mine clearing at: *198*
    troop units assigned: 209
An Loc
    accidents at: 197
    aircraft lost at: 540–541, 543, 545–546, 596
    airfield at: 542, 544
    airlifts to and from: 228, 504, 540–551, 554–557, 559, 561, 563, 571–574, 576, 578, 596–597, 602, 606, 654

conditions at: 539–540, 547–549, 551
enemy assaults on: 539–544, 546, 550, 552–554
helicopters at: 550–551
An Thoi: 612
Anderson, Winston P.: 81
Andrews, James L.: *244*
Anthis, Rollen H.: 46, *130*, *157*
and air crews proficiency: 106
and pilots in VNAF aircraft: 68–69
and aircraft capabilities: 91, 160
and airfields suitability: 163
and combat cargo organization: 107
on command and control: 90
and Dirty Thirty: 77, 79
and duplicated airlifts: 122
and Farm Gate mission: 50
on roles and missions: 107
and Special Forces aircraft: 151
and tactical airlift: 103, 128, 134
and training programs: 93
Antiaircraft measures and weapons
Allied: 434
defense against: 170, 622
enemy: 19–20, 31, 60, 64, 90–91, 124, 132–134, 158, 200, 204, 212, 218, 225, 252, 299, 301–304, 307, 316, 326, 330, 332–339, 343–345, 347, 351, 368, 373–374, 388, 392, 405, 423, 425–429, 455–456, 461–462, 478–479, 490, 495, 507, 515, 517, 525–533, 539–541, 543, 545–546, 549, 552–553, 556–557, 559, 561, 564–570, 575, 586, 596–597, 605, 613, 618, 620, 622–625, 631, 638, 642–644, 658
Ap Bac, battle at: 129–132
Applebaum, Theodore C.: 608
Armor assualts
enemy: 462, 515, 544, 550, 568, 636
South Vietnam: 509
Army of the Republic of Vietnam (ARVN)
airborne units: 314, 509–511, 515, 561, 563, 566, 575, 584, 592, 619, 637–638
airborne units operations: 55, *56*, 57, 96–99, *100*, 101–103, 128–129, *130–131*, 132–137, 204–205, 223, 585
arms and equipment supply to: 42
combat effectiveness: 343, 375, 525, 539
Eagle Flight force: 135
engineer units: 232
parachute assaults: 270, 349, 495, 575
pay scales: 98
personnel strength: 68
Ranger units: 212, 299, 321, 540, 561, 577
Special Forces units: 55, 57, 150, 164
Arnold, Henry H.: 63*n*
Arnold, Palmer G.: 502, *503*
Artillery fire assaults
Allied: 20, 196, 213, 269, 313, 509, 526
enemy: 19–20, 292, 297, 300, 343, 373, 462, 478, 490, 495, 507, 515–516, 525, 550, 554, 559, 566, 633, 636, 643

INDEX

Ashiya Air Base: 9, 11, 16, 19, 34, 440
Assassinations by enemy: 42
Association of Southeast Asian Nations: 615
Attleboro Operation: 245, 270
Austin, Maynard A., USA, *356*
Australian air and troop units: 173, 218, 353, 392, 407–408, 412, *413*, 414–416, 419, 638, 683
Aviation Companies
    1st: 110, 121–122
    17th: 209, 354
    61st: 121–122
    92d: 165
Aviation Week: 77
Awards. *See* Decorations and awards

Ba Kev: 501–502
Ba Ria: 132
Ba Tho: 606
Babylift Operation: 640–641
Bac Mai: 4
Baginski, James I.: 632, 635
Bame, Karl T.: 532
Ban Ban: 461
Ban Keun: 459
Ban Me Thuot: *89*, 150, 165
    aircraft and units assigned: 425
    airlifts to and from: 88, 92, 283, 321, 373–374, 426, 636, 639
    cargo delivery and handling, 284, 321, 323, 348, 374, 417
    disarray at: 192
    enemy assaults on: 282–283, 318–323, 372–373, 426, 636
    living conditions at: 426
    navigation and radio facilities: 263
Bangkok. *See* Don Muang Royal Thai Air Base
Banish Beach Project: 392–393
Bao Loc
    accidents at: 252
    aircraft lost at: 351
    airfield conditions: 293
    airlifts to and from: 50, 125, 321
    enemy assaults on: 321
    Bao Trai: 219
Barn Door Project: 111, 113
Barnett, Charles P.: 68–69, 71, 75
Barnett, Robert: 75
Barr, Thomas A.: 553, 603
    Base Aero-Terrestre: 5–6, 11
Battambang: 624, 626–627
Baulch, Henry L.: 592, 596
Belgian Air Force: 8*n*
Ben Het
    airfield at: 525
    airlifts to and from: 493, 521, 525, 537, 569, 574, 606
    cargo delivery to: 525

TACTICAL AIRLIFT

 enemy assaults on: 525–526, 569
 search-and-clear missions: 525
Bennett, John M.: 522
Berlin airlift: 28, 247, 691
Bien Hoa
 aerial port service at: 139, 577
 aircraft lost at: 478
 aircraft and units assigned: 44, 46–49, 116, 274, 521, 536, 563
 aircraft conditions at: 112
 airlifts to and from: 57–59, 88, 105, 114, 150, 205, 208n, 218–222, 224–225, 274, 279, 284, 293, 323, 328, 334, 383, 418, 506, 511, 513, 561, 563–564, 602, 611–612, 642
 base defenses: 173
 cargo handling: 151, 219, 252, 255, 270, 276, 306, 314–315, 333, 417, 510, 599
 in casualty evacuation system: 400
 communications at: 576
 defense force and missions: 55–57, 173
 enemy assaults on: 216, 320, 330, 643
 French defense of: 4
 living conditions: 62–63, 351
 maintenance service: 61
 parachute assaults on: 270
 passenger service: 598
 rigging service: 257
 troop units assigned: 216
Binh Hung: 59
Binh Long Province: 539–579
Binh Thuy: 323–324, 400, 419, 598
Birdair, Inc (Bird & Sons): 443, 463–464, 627, 631–633, 635, 637–638, 642–643
Birmingham Operation: 225, 226, 227–229, 269, 653
Bishop, Charles J.: 374
Black Spot Project: 389
Black Virgin Mountain: 573
Blackburn, Bill: 76
Blackjack Operations: 424
Blake, Charles R.: 102
Blind Bat Project: 388
Blood, Kenneth T., Jr.: 480, 482–483
Bo Tuc: 99–101
Boi Loi Woods: 391, 392
Bolovens Plateau: 349, 462
Bomb types: 393–394
Bombing missions: 58, 144, 169, 203, 347, 389–395, 410–411, 430, 576, 592, 605, 609, 639, 646, 656
 assessment of effects: 395
 helicopters in: 393–394
 against North Vietnam: 58, 144, 169, 203, 347, 389–395, 410, 430, 576, 592, 605, 609, 639, 646, 656
 by North Vietnam: 643
 safety measures in: 394
Bong Son: 223
Booby traps, Allied: 531
Boonstra, Matthew A.: 584

INDEX

Boostershot Operation: 440
Border surveillance: 115
Borders, Charles W.: 118, 412–414
Boung Long: 500–502
Boyd, William: 345
Bradley, John E.: *390*
Brandt, William H.: *56*
Brazier, William: *589*
Brewster, Philip L.: 639
Bridges
    air assaults on: 392
    enemy destruction: 295, 373
Brims, Richard C.: 646
Brodie, Bernard: 28
Brooks, Allison C.: 118
Brown, George S.: 393, *518*
Brown, Harold: 263, *264*
Brown, William T.: *362*
Brundridge, Ronald G.: 571–572
Brya, Edward N.: 542, *543*, 544–545, 553, 556, 611
Bu Dop
    accidents at: 494
    airfield construction and repair: 499
    airlifts to: 261–262, 292, *436–437*, 479, 493–494, 499, 504
    maintenance and repair at: 482
Bu Nard: 420
Bu Gia Map: 222–223, 499–500, 504
Bucher, Bernard L.: 344
Bunker, Ellsworth: 508, 515–516, *518*
Bunker, William: 72
Bunker systems, enemy: 297
Buon Blech: 283
Buon Chay: *157*
Buon Mi Ga: 154
Burke, Arleigh A.: 39
Burma, airlifts in: 26, 41, 47, 295, 653
Button, Richard F.: 333

Ca Lu: 313–314, 512, 620
Ca Mau Peninsula: 133–134
Calcutta: 35
Caldwell, William R.: 542
Call signs use: 120, 243
Cam Ranh Bay
    accidents at: 477
    aerial port service: 577
    aircraft lost at: 200
    aircraft and units assigned and withdrawn: 176, 180, 191, 248, 257, 274, 277, 319–320, 329, 355, 357, 360, 370, 395, 400, 473, 490, 510, 514, 521n, 522, 531, 535
    airfield construction and repair: 229, 248, 613

851

TACTICAL AIRLIFT

    airlifts to and from: 176, 324–325, 334–335, 364–365, 373, 383–384, 449, 490, 506, 566
    cargo handling: 185, 222, 252, 277–278, 283, 287, 306, 314–315, 333, 355, *489*
    in casualty evacuation system: 397, 399, 400
    command and control at: 380
    enemy assaults on: 638
    lighting system: 179
    living conditions: 179, 483
    maintenance and repair: 249–250, 355, *362*, 370, 490, 535
    recreation facilities: 351
    sabotage at: 200
    troop units assigned: 208n, 216
Cambodia
    air force of: 493, 507, 627, 629, 635, 657
    aircraft transferred to: 507–508, 616–617, 627, 629
    airfields in: 500
    airlifts to and from: 467, 469, 493–513, 564, 571–572, 574, 584–586, 605, 616, 623–628, 631, 654, 680
    armor actions: 509
    Army restricted role in: 508–509, 584
    bombing assaults in: 394, 605, 646
    border surveillance: 164
    casualties: 633
    civil airlines in: 505, 627, 631–633
    enemy airlifts to and from: 434–435
    enemy assaults in: 500, 519, 579, 622
    as enemy sanctuary: 215, 269, 282, 519, 539
    fall of: 635–636
    helicopter force of: 508
    helicopter operations in: 513
    lines of communication to: 498, 508, 512–513, 539, 623, 625, 629
    Mayaguez incident: 645–646
    morale status: 622, 632
    search-and-clear missions in: 423–432, 493–519
    surprise achieved in: 497
    training programs: 508, 617, 629
    water transport to: 622, 629, 631–632
Camouflage
    Allied use: 449–450
    enemy use: 19, 169, 295, 332, 559
Camp Evans: 313
    accident at: 475
    airlifts to and from: 332, 365, 612
    cargo handling: 325–326, 333, 347, 349
Camp Holloway: 214, 354, 364
Camp Zinn: 274–275
Campbell, Jesse W.: 346
Can Tho
    aerial port service: 139, 577
    aircraft and units assigned: 108, 364, 521
    airlifts to and from: 115, 163, 322–324, 364, 424, 561
    enemy assault on: 323–324, 364
Canadian Air Force: 97

INDEX

Candlestick force: 389
Cannibalization practices: 93, 176–177, 250, 355, 379, 456, 576, 616
Cap Saint Jacques (later Vung Tau): 38
Cargo delivery and handling: 29, 115, 135–140, 143, 151–154, 158, 170, 173, 185–186, 192–194, 203–229, 239, 245, 253, *254–255*, 256–262, 270, 276, 294, 303, 363–366, 449, 545, 548–550, 554, 556, 568–574, 576, 596, 606, 618, 623–624, 626–627, 633, 652, 657
Cargo diversity: 379, 384–385, 440, 449, 455, 527, 654–655
Cargo extraction delivery: *142*, 143, 165, 217, 235, 259, *260–261*, 262, 291, 294, 300–303, *310*, 311–312, 316, 372, *437*, 449, 483–484, 493, 652
Cargo-handling equipment: 139, 578. *See also by name*
Cargo tonnage predictions: 114, 117, 207, 228, 247, 297, 303, 332–333, 401, 407–408, 470, 472, 508, 510, 513, 540, 635
Cargo tonnages moved
  by helicopters: 246, 299, 328
  by truck transport: 117, 163, 186, 215, 224, 228, 246, 292, 499
  by water transport: 117, 140, 163, 186, 246–247, 292, 328, 625–626
Cargo-transport aircraft. *See* Aircraft, fixed-wing
Casey, Maurice F.: 9–11, 16–17
Casualties
  air evacuation of: 7, 21, 35, 59, 62, 114, 205, 214, 269, 292, 305, 326, 365, 372, 396–397, *398*, 399–401, 414–416, 459, 524, 550–551, 576, 592–597, 646, 655
  Air Force: 50, 72, 75, 124–125, 163, 197, 199–200, 225, 251–252, 271, 291, 301–302, 307, 311, 327, 336, 344–345, 347, 351, 355, 423, 429, 475, 477, 480, 490, 495, 525, 530, 533, 542, 546, 557, 645–646, 658
  Army: 81, 129, 136, 277, 344, 347, 375, 475
  Cambodian: 633
  civilians: 124–125, 344–345, 347
  doctrine on evacuation: 400–401
  enemy: 129, 150, 215, 270, 341, 374, 456, 518, 578, 586, 639
  evacuation by aircraft: 21, 35, 59, 62, 114, 205, 214, 269, 292, 305, 326, 365, 372, 396–397, *398*, 399–401, 414–416, 459, 524, 550–551, 576, 592–597, 646, 655
  evacuation by helicopters: 30, 396–401, 550–551
  last fatalities: 605
  Marine Corps: 290, 304, 646
  number evacuated: 400
  Republic of Vietnam: 50, 102, 129, 134–135, 150, 197, 375, 541, 566, 568, 575, 578, 586, 591, 596
Cat Bi: 4 10–11, 16–22
Cat Lai: 261–262
Catecka Tea Plantation: 207, 214, 284
Cavalry Division, 1st: 203, 207, 209, *210–211*, 212–216, 224, 231, 236, 284–285, 288, 293, 313, 317, 325–326, 332–333, 349, 353, 358–359, 365–366, 368, 469, 497–498, 502
Cease-fire agreement: 467, 581, 608, 615, 618, 644
Cebe-Habersky, Jack V.: 133
Cedar Falls Operation: 244
Censorship, by U.S. Air Force: 82
Central Highlands: *148*, 149, 203. *See also station by name*

853

TACTICAL AIRLIFT

   airlifts to: 282–285
   enemy airlifts to: 434
   enemy offensives in: 282–285, 559–566
Central Intelligence Agency
   in airlifts: 441, 445, 447–448, 655. *See also* Air America
   in civic actions: 401
   and Civilian Irregular Defense Groups: 150
   and Farm Gate mission: 49–50
   and Meo tribesmen: 442
   planning role: 463
Central Logistics Command, RVN: 551, 555, 619
Ceylon: 18*n*
Cha La: 252
Chains in cargo handling: 256
Chase Aircraft Company, Inc.: 29
Chastain, Calvin H.: 571
Chau Doc: 502, 504
Cheo Reo: 204, 223, 232, 283
Chi Linh: 574
Chiang Mai Royal Thai Air Base: 407–408
Chief of Naval Operations. *See* Burke, Arleigh A.
Chief of Staff, U.S. Air Force. *See* Jones, David C.; LeMay, Curtis E.; McConnell, John P.; White, Thomas D.
Chief of Staff, U.S. Army. *See* Decker, George H.; Johnson, Harold K.; Wheeler, Earle G.
China, Communist. *See* People's Republic of China
China, Nationalist. *See* Republic of China
China Airlines: 410–411
China-Burma-India Theater, airlifts in: 247, 691
Ching Chuan Kang
   accidents at: 199, 477, 480
   air craft and units assigned: 181–182, 185, 249, 394, 408–409, 429, 450, 472, 554, 560, 565, 571, 574, 607, 615
   airlifts to and from: 37, 379–380, 385, 563, 609
   cargo handling: 484
   living conditions: 483
   maintenance and repair: 578
   racial incidents: 483
Cholon district: 69
Chu Lai
   accidents at: 197
   airfield construction and repair: 299–230
   airlifts to and from: 236, 288–290, 306, 328, 407–408, 495
   in casualty evacuation system: 399
   enemy assaults on: 236, 288–289
Chu Pong Mountain: 215, 284
Civic actions: 59, 95, 164, 219, 371, 385, 401, 404–409, 410–411, 655
Civil Air Transport, Inc.: 10–11, 17, 19, 21, 441
Civil airlines
   aircraft available to: 401, 404, 445–447, 632
   airlifts by: 383, 401, 404, 439–451, 454–464, 476, 488–489, 504–505, 617, 627, 631–635, 637, 641–642, 655

cargo tonnages moved: 401, 407–408, 635n
enemy use: 434
passenger service: 401, 414
Civil Operations and Revolutionary Development Support: 401–402, 407–408
Civilian Irregular Defense Groups: 150–153, 159, 162–166, 204, 212, 215, 290, 292, 343, 364, 417–421, 423, 592
Civilians
  in aircrews: 441, 627, 631
  airlifts of. *See* Airlift, passengers moved
  casualties: 124–125, 344–345, 347
  employment of: 138–140, 151, 153, 158
  evacuation of: 141, 170, *171*
  as pilots: 7, 10, 17, 19, 446
  training programs: 441
Clark, Bernard J.: 611–612
Clark, Jerry B.: 478–479
Clark, Mark W.: 10
Clark Field
  airborne units assigned: 39
  aircraft evacuation to: 644
  aircraft and units assigned: 20–21, 37–39, 45, 49, 85, 87, 91, 112–113, 144, 146, 170, 182–183, 263, 329, 385, 473n, 560, 615
  airlifts to and from: 9, 17–19, 34–35, 37–39, 86, 114, 140, 144, 379, 407–408, 414, 564, 606, 609, 611, 613, 638, 641–643
  in casualty evacuation system: 396–397, 400
  command and control at: 380
  maintenance and repair: 61, 93, 112, 126, 256, 442, 602
  as staging base: 39
  as training center: 11, 16
Cleland, John R. D., USA: 633
Cloud-dissipating missions: 389
Coastal enclave plan: 206
Cole, Daryl D.: 344
Combat Applications Group, 1st: 52
Combat Aviation Battalion, 210th: 406–407
Combat Cargo Group, 6492d: 106
Combat control teams. *See* Airlift, combat control teams in
Combat Crew Training Squadron, 449th: 354
Combat Crew Training Group, 442d: 184
Combat Crew Training Squadron, 4400th: 41, 44–45, 47–52, 55, 58–59, 63, 149–152, 158–159, 385, 388, 392
Combat Crew Training Wings
  442d: 354
  410th: 195n
  4449th: 533
Combat Spear Project: 429–431
Command and control center, airborne: 395, 656
Command, control and coordination
  in airlift. *See* Airlift, command, control and coordination
  of helicopters: 30–31, 109, 135, 235–236
  in maintenance and repair: 248–249, 251, 370, 482, 535

TACTICAL AIRLIFT

Commander in Chief, Pacific Command. *See* Felt, Harry D.; Gayler, Noel A. M.; Radford, Arthur W.
Commando Lava Project: 389
Commando Scarf Project: 393
Commando Vault Project: 393–395, 576, 578
Common Service Airlift System (formerly Southeast Asia Airlift System): 295, 305, 314–316, 321, 324–325, 343, 358–359, 363, 364, 383, 407–408, 416, 522, 536
Communications operations and systems: 108, 120, 138, 159, 189, 208, 212, 243, 244, 245, 445, 487, 510, 515, 536, 564, 576
Composite air strike force: 28, 34
Computers in airlift: 467, 470–471, 485, 655
Con Son Island: 612
Conran, Philip J.: 462
Consolidated Maintenance Squadron, 483d: 370, 535
Constant Guard Projects: 563, 565
Construction machinery airlifts: 332, 339, 343, 440
Containerized cargo delivery: 259, 277, 279, 291, 302–304, 306, 311–313, 333, 339, 344, 424, 430, 517, 542, 545, 564, 568, 575, 578, 596
Continental Air Services, Inc.: 404, 407–408, 445–447, 458, 463, 617
Contract carriers. *See* Civil airlines
Contractors, construction: 230, 602
Convoy system: 214–215, 219, 282–284, 292–293, 512, 525
Cooper, Captain: 93
Corona Harvest Project: 649–652
Corps, XXIV: 508–510
Corps Tactical Zones
    I: 288, 300, 328, 330, 510
    II: 57, 209n, 223, 229, 246, 322, 347, 570, 575
    III: 209n, 221, 229, 323, 551, 561, 653
    IV: 323, 353, 359, 366, 561
Correspondents: 275, 458
Costello, Richard B.: *56*
Counterinsurgency missions. *See* Search-and-clear missions
Courier service: 406–407
Crisman, Kenneth L.: 368
Crist, Neil B.: 532
Crop destruction missions: 389, *391*, 392, 656
Cruz, Jesus M.: *254*
Cu Chi: 102, 224, 228, 293
Cua Viet River: 563
Cung Son: 162

Da Lat
    airlifts to and from: 8, 323, 638
    enemy assaults on: 322–323, 608
Da Nang (formerly Tourane): 20, *244*
    accidents at: 199
    aerial port service: 138–139, 577
    aircraft lost at: 478
    aircraft and units assigned: 73, 81, 87, 91–92, 97, 107, 110–111, 116, 122, 136, 172, 191, 248, 290, 307, 328, 388, 397, 412–414, 451, 514, 517, 521, 563, 591

INDEX

    airlifts to and from: 88, 90, 97, 105, 112, 115, 120, 137, 146, 150, 155, 159, 163, 171–173, 232, 290, 297, 300, 304, 306, 310, 325, 340, 344, 347, 364, 383–384, 405–408, 419, 428, 430, 472, 510, 512–514, 564, 575–576, 602, 608–609, 612–613, 637–639, 647, 654
    antiaircraft defenses: 170
    base defense: 171–172
    bombing assaults on: 394
    cargo handling and delivery: 139, 185, 252, 288, 297–299, 306, 314–315, 333, 335, *386,* 405, 417, 517–518, 599, 606
    in casualty evacuation system 399–400
    in civilians evacuation: 170
    command and control: 395
    communications: 536, 564, 576
    congestion at: 326–327
    enemy assaults on: 200, 223, 252, 293, 318, 320, 515
    fighter escort at: 57
    flareships at: 388
    forest-burning missions from: 392
    French defense: 4
    helicopters and units assigned: 236
    living conditions: 94, 125, 196, 351
    maintenance and repair: 126, 490, 514, 518
    mess facilities: 196
    passenger service: *489,* 598
    troop units assigned: 39
Dak Pek
    airfield hazards at: 372
    airlifts to and from: 162, 348, 372, 531, 569, 572, 574
    helicopter assaults on: 531
Dak Seang
    aircraft lost at: 533
    airfield at: 372, 527
    airlifts to and from: 348, 372, 497, 521, 525–532, 537, 547, 572, 606
    enemy assaults on: 526–530
    helicopter assaults on: 531
Dak To
    accidents at: 251, 285–286
    airfield construction and repair: 163, 285, 620
    airlifts to and from: 92, 204, 223, 269, 284–287, 348, 372, 636
    cargo delivery to: 322–323, 525
    in casualty evacuation system: 400
    congestion at: 285–286
    enemy assaults on: 252, 286, 292, 559, 563, 566, 569
    sabotage at: 200
Dallman, Howard M.: 301
Daly, William T.: 84, 93, 116
Dan Chi 4 Operation: 133–134
Daniel Boone Project: 425
Danna, Stanley M.: *398*
Data processing systems: 242, 469–470, 487

Dau Tieng: *272–273*
    accidents at: 197
    aircraft lost at: 252
    airfield conditions: 225
    airlifts to: 225, 504
    cargo handling and delivery: 270, *273*
    enemy assaults on: 270
    parachute assaults at: 271–274
Dawson, David S., Jr.: 571–573
Deal, Robert L.: 340
Dean, John G.: 632–633
Deane, John R., Jr., USA: 274–276
Deatrick, Eugene P., Jr., 424
Decca navigation system: 55, 160–161
Decker, George H.: 32, 85–86
Declaration on the Neutrality of Laos: 443
Decorations and awards
    to aircrews: 64, 89, 125, 286, 301, 316–318, 340, 344–346, 352, 354, 375, 400, 426, 456, 462, 472, 478–479, 483, 490, 502, *503*, 534–535, 542, 608, 646
    to ground crews: 195, 258
    Marine Corps: 316
Dedicated user concept: 522–523, 537, 651
Defense, Department of. *See* Laird, Melvin R.; McNamara, Robert S.
Defense Intelligence Agency: 438
Defoliation missions: 89, 389, *391*, 392, 656
DeHavilland Aircraft of Canada: 31
Delaware Operation: 317, 332–343
Delligatti, Robert S.: 641
Demilitarized Zone: 288, 291, 293, 325–326
Delmore, John R.: 345
Delta Project: 423
Democratic Republic of Vietnam. *See* North Vietnam
Demolition assaults, enemy: 291, 364, 373, 507, 618, 636
Dennis, Jimmy: *308*
Denver Operation: 219–221
Dependents evacuation. *See* Airlift, passengers moved
Deployed air strike teams: 57
Desert Rat Operation: 462
Diego Garcia: 385
Diem, Ngo Dinh
    and air base construction: 42
    and air units assignment: 44
    and airfields expansion: 161
    and arming Montagnards: 150
    and Dirty Thirty: 77
    and political crises: 42
    and priorities in RVNAF: 80
    and quick reaction units: 96
    and VNAF expansion: 80
Dien Bien Phu siege and battle: 6–7, 11, 16–20, 22–23, 37, 295–296, 557, 653
Dirty Thirty: 67–75, *76*, 77–80, 581
Disosway, Gabriel P.: 109, 241

Do Son: 4, *6*, 18, 21
Don Muang Air Base: *112*
    aerial port service: 138, 409–411
    aircraft and units assigned: 46, 91, 107, 110, 113, 408–409, 421, 440, 521
    airfield conditions: 407–408
    airlifts to and from: 35, 37, 65, 114, 407–408, 410–411, 440–444, 495
    in casualty evacuation system: 396
    command and control: 380, 408–410
    helicopters assigned: 422
    maintenance and repair: 256
    passenger service: 409–410
    as recreational area: 57
Don Phuoc: 136, 504
Dong Ba Thin: 354
Dong Ha: 90
    aerial port service: 380, 510
    aircraft lost at: 200
    aircraft and units assigned: 290
    airfield construction and repair: 230–231, 510, 620
    airlifts to and from: 292, 299, 380, 509, 511, 513–514, 612
    cargo delivery to: 289, 292, 326, 347, 380
    in casualty evacuation system: 399–400
    enemy assaults on: 292, 325, 561
    maintenance and repair: 511
Dong Xoai: 204
Doolittle, James H.: 63*n*
Dover, Richard D.: *255*
Dowell, Richard S.: 92–93
Downs, Richard J.: 560, 576
Drop altitudes and tactics. *See* Airlift, drop altitudes and tactics
Drop loads size and weight: 54
Drop zones, designating: 55, 97–98, 101–102, 132–134, 517, 546
Drug traffic, illicit: 483, 490
Duc Co
    airlifts to and from: 214, 284, 372–374, 420, 500–502, 504, 606
    enemy assaults on: 204–205, 215–216
Duc Hue: 504
Duc Lap
    airlifts to: 504, 524–525, 537
    enemy assaults on: 348, 372–375, 420, 426
Duc Pho: 510
Duc Thanh: 574–575
Duck Hook Project: 429–431, 501
Dunning, John A.: 95
Dyess Air Force Base: 144, 182, 350, 533, 590

Eagle Jump Operation: 584
Eagle Pull Project: 635
Easter Bunny force: 606, 615, 624–625
Easter offensive, enemy: 539–579, 605
Edmiston, Ronald L.: 646
Edwards Air Force Base: 84
E-Flight: 448–450

TACTICAL AIRLIFT

Eglin Air Force Base: 58, 235, 258, 431, 556–557
Eisenhower, Dwight D.: 11, 17
El Paso Operation: 228, 349
Electronic aids: 55
Elmendorf Air Force Base: 48–49
Elwood, George P.: 608–609
Emergency and priority missions. *See* Airlift, emergency and priority missions
Endres, William J.: 340–341
Engineer Battalions
    1st: 279
    8th: 229, 338
Engineer troops and operations: 278–279, 285, 290–291, 295, 332, 349, 493, 499, 510, 513–514, 519, 656. *See also* Airfields, construction and repair
Engines, aircraft
    design and performance: 33, 84, 196
    failures: 197
    jet additions: 196, 658
    turboprop: 651
Exchange Plus Project: 598, 601–603
Eniwetok staging base: 35, 37
England Air Force Base: 480
Exhaust flame dampeners: 41

463L cargo delivery system: 139, 192, 449, 657
Fairchild Engine and Aircraft Corporation: 29, 84
Fairchild-Hiller Aircraft Company: 196, 263, 446
Far East Air Forces: 8–9, 17–18, 35n
Far East Air Logistics Force: 18n
Far East Command. *See* Clark, Mark W.
Farm Gate Project: 44–65, 69, 73. *See also* Combat Crew Training Squadron, 4400th
Fast Fly Project: 183–184
Felt, Harry D., USN: (*see also Pacific Command*)
    and airlift units missions: 85
    and Army aircraft: 110
    and Army aircraft integration into airlift: 121
    and Special Forces aircraft: 151
Ferrari, Robert S., USA: 447–448
Field Forces, Vietnam
    I: 209n, 353, 359, 362, 366
    II: 181, 209n, 245, 353, 358–359, 362, 366
Field Maintenance Squadron, 642d: 18n
Field Maintenance Squadron, 542d: 18n
Fighter strikes. *See Airlifts*, air assaults in support of
Finck, George C.: 373–375
Flak suits: 91
Flare illumination: 58, 176, 204, 212–213, 243, 297, 385–386, *387*, 388–389, 422, 431, 486, 530, 546
Flare signals: 62, 69, 530
Flax, Alexander H.: 650
Fleming, David T.: *118*, 233–235
Fleming, James P.: 426
Flight Dynamics Laboratory: 263

INDEX

Flight engineers
    shortages: 370, 533–534
    training programs: 184, 369, 534
    work conditions: 249, 533–534
Flight mechanics. *See* Aircrews
Floods, effect on airlifts: 97, 146, 405
Flying Tiger Lines: 633
Food drops: 58, 146, 204, 417, 450, 540, 548, 550–551, 567, 605, 626–627, 632, 635, 655
Forbes Air Force Base: 183, 329
Ford, Walter J.: 541, 591
Forest-burning missions, *391*, 392–393
Forklifts in cargo handling: 256, 305–306, 340–341, 365, 487–490, 578, 633
Fort Benning: 110, 354
Fort Bragg: 151
Forward air controllers. *See* Airlift, forward air controllers in
Forward distribution system: 229
Forster, George M.: 105
Foster, William B.: 447
Foulois, Benjamin D.: 63*n*
France
    aircrew training and strength: 7–11, 16
    air superiority: 3
    Airborne Forces Command: 5
    aircraft deliveries to: 6–11, 16, 18
    aircraft lost and damaged: 8–9, 17, 19, 21
    aircraft strength: 6–8, 11, 20
    airlifts by: 6, 9, *12–13*, 16, 18–20, 22, 40
    Algeria experience: 40
    casualty evacuation by aircraft: 16, 19, 21, *22*, 23
    casualty evacuation by helicopter: 7
    civilian pilots use: 7, 10, 17, 19
    defense plan: 3–5
    engineer operations: 16
    ground crew strength: 7
    helicopter strength: 7
    helicopters use: 7
    hours and sorties flown: 16, 20–21
    instrumentation in aircraft: 9
    language barrier: 9
    lines of communication: 20
    maintenance and repair by: 7–9, 18
    military assistance to: 3, 6
    napalm assaults by: 17
    parachute assaults by: 5, 11, *14*, 19, 654
    patrols, ground: 5–6
    radio equipment: 9
    supply operations and systems: 5, 20
    tonnages delivered: 20–21
    training programs: 9–10, 67
Freefall delivery: 54
French Fort: 278–279
Frequent Wind Operation: 643

Fritz, Richard A.: *198*
Fuel
    airlifts of. *See* Airlift, fuel deliveries
    loss from enemy action: 286
    truck transport of: 117
Fuel tanks: 33
Futema Marine Corps Airfield: 288*n*

Gallagher, John W., Jr.: 346
Gavin, James M., USA: 29, 206
Gayler, Noel A. M., USN: 615, 629
Gaylor, Raymond H.: 577–578
Geneva accords: 3, 7, 37, 38*n*, 39, 42, 407–408, 442
Germeraad, John H.: 468, 471–472, 483, 560
Gia Lam air base: 4, 9–10, 22, 608, 611
Gia Nghia: 252, *478*
Gia Vuc: 125, 574
Giap, Vo Nguyen: 647
Gibson, Billy R.: 326, 335–336
Gleason, Robert L.: 50
Glenn, Joseph K.: 286, *287*
Glider operations: 25
Gliders, powered: 29
Godek, Franklin F.: 532
Godley, G. McMurtrie: 450
Gough, Jamie: 105
Graham, J. W.: 244
Grant, Joseph: *76*
Greenwood, Leslie J.: 526
Grillo, John W.: 611
Ground combat units. *See* Troop units
Ground controlled approach: 17, 52, 88, 161, 179, 200, 263, 299–304, 312–313, 325, 339, 343, 355, 368, 510, 512, 514–515, 517, 570
Ground crews (*see also* Aerial port units; Maintenance and repair)
    aircrews, relations with: 61, 126
    Asians in: 446, 449
    cadre system: 249–250
    decorations and awards: 195, 258
    in flare missions: 388
    French: 7
    living conditions: 94, 191, 480, 516
    mess facilities: 94, 340–341, 516
    morale, motivation and discipline: 61, 181, 195, 250, 253, 258, 305, 321, 388, 490, 576–577, 659
    number assigned: 563
    proficiency and resourcefulness: 84, 93, 138, 482
    promotions in: 194–195
    rotation and tour lengths: 177, 305, 482–483, 577–578, 607
    shortages in: 250, 577
    training programs: 34, 354, 370, 602
    work hours and conditions: 61, 126, 176–177, 183, 191, 250, 253, 270, 305, 340–341, 370, 408–409, 480, 482, 499, 548, 565, 567, 576–577, 612–613, 634, 659

INDEX

Ground radar air delivery system. *See* Airlift, radar guidance in
Ground transport. *See* Truck transport
Guam air bases: 49, 85, 563, 642
Guerrilla operations, enemy: 20–21, 64. *See also* Search-and-clear missions
Gunships
    fixed-wing aircraft: 58, 388–389, *390*, 395, 426, *460*, 656
    helicopters: 425–426, 428, 462, 517
Ha Thanh: 372, 476
Ha Tien: 504
Haas, James D.: *362*
Hackney, Hunter F.: 374–375
Haiphong: 4, *14*, 19, 37
Hall, Kyron V.: 456
Hampton, James: 151
Hannah, George L., Jr.: 187, 195
Hanoi
    airlifts to and from: 608–609, 613, 616, 642
    French defense of: 4
    in French supply system: 5
Harkins, Paul D., USA: 110, *111*, 129, 160
Harper's magazine: 206
Harris, Hunter, Jr.: *198*, 199, 215, *255*, 256
Harston, John D.: 646
Hartman, Eugene: 326
Harwell, Gary W.: *436*
Hawaii, airlifts from: 38
Hawk missile: 170
Heath, Donald R.: 8–9, 49, 77
Helicopter Flight, 8th: 29
Helicopter Squadrons
    20th: 235–236, 425–426, 428n, 454, 456–457
    21st: 455–458, 461–462
    219th: 425
Helicopter types
    CH–3 Sea King: 208, *225*, *227*, 233, *234*, 235–236, 396, 422–425, *427*, 428, 430, 454–458, 461–462
    CH–34 Choctaw: *386*, 427, 617
    CH–6 Sea Knight: 347
    CH–47 Chinook: 197, 208–209, 212–216, 233, *234*, 236, 257, 266, 324, 333, 344, 347, 371, 374, 427, 454–455, 484, 495, 499, 513, 540, 553, 555, 568, 575, 584, 587, 594–598, 612, 636, 638, 643, 658
    CH–53 Seastallion: 299, 316, 328, 427–428, 455–457, 462–463, 513, 616, 631, 635, 643–646
    CH–54 Flying Crane: 233, *234*, 338, 341, 393–394, 499
    H–19 Chickasaw: 29, 593
    H–21 Work Horse: 45, 98, 102, 129, 396
    H–34 Sea Horse: 37, 95, 396, 422, 425, 428, 430, 447, 454–457, 461, 463, 587
    H–46 troop carrier: 644
    H–53 Sikorsky: 643–647
    HH–53 Super Jolly Green Giant: 457, 462, 635, 644–646
    HU–1 Iroquois: 197
    MI–4: 434
    MI–6: 434–435

TACTICAL AIRLIFT

UH-1 Iroquois: 218, 236, 397, 409–410, 412–413, *414*, 415–416, 422, 425–430, *436*, 447, 454–456, 508, 540, 550, 553, 555, 587, 593–598, 628, 638, 644

Helicopters
    Air Force use: 25, 29–31, 233–236, 238, 316, 425, 651, 657–658
    in airlifts: 29, 102, 128–132, 135–137, 154–155, 207, 209, 212–213, 216–221, 225, 228–229, 35–236, 277, 282, 290–292, 295–316, 324, 332, 338–341, 344–347, 366, 371, 373–374, 406–407, 419, 423–432, *436*, 443, 453–461, 493–508, 513, 516, 531, 540, 550, 554, 568, 575, 616, 622, 631, 635, 638, 683
    Algeria experience: 40
    arming, opposition to: 135
    Army assignments to RVN: 45, 151
    Army strength: 31
    assault missions: 388, 422–432, 461–463, 515, 531
    Australian: 412, *413*, 414
    benefits proved: 428
    bombing missions: 393–394
    Cambodian use: 508
    cargo capacities: 427
    cargo diversity: 236
    cargo tonnages moved: 246, 299, 328
    in casualty evacuation: 30, 396–401, 550–551
    command and control: 30–31, 109, 135, 235–236
    design and characteristics: 30–31
    enemy use: 454
    flying time rates: 454
    formation and tactics: 462–463
    French use: 7, 40
    fuel capacity: 427
    fuel supply to: 263–266
    ground fire, vulnerability to: 31, 129, 135, 651
    ground forces employment: 25, 269
    as gunships: 425–426, 428, 462, 517
    Korean: 416
    Korean War experience: 29
    Laotion use: 454–457
    lost and damaged: 129, 236, 333, 341, 347, 423, 425–426, 428, 455–456, 458, 461–462, 495, 497, 515, 517, 540, 597, 618, 620, 636, 645
    maintenance and repair: 456
    Malaya experience: 40
    Marine Corps use: 45, 136, 172, 296–316
    mechanical weaknesses: 456
    mobility feature: 135
    navigation systems: 160–161
    payload capacities: 31, 214, 427
    pilots and crews training: 455, 457, 494
    pilots service in VNAF craft: 594
    radio communications: 161
    in roles and missions controversy and agreements: 30, 32, 89–90, 93–94, 107–111, 114–115, 203, 212, 233, 236–238, 266, 359, 407–408, 467, 521, 657–658, 673–674

    search-and-clear missions: 203–229, 239, 269–292, 423–432
    search-and-rescue missions: 535, 543
    shortages: 236
    sorties logged: 235–236, 457, 497
    speeds and ranges: 427
    in tactical air support: 215–216, 222–223, 269–292, 322
    takeoff weights: 427
    Thai use: 422
    traffic control: 286
    types. *See* Helicopter types
    units activated and assigned: 30–31
    VNAF use: 430, 586–587, 593–595, 597–598, 600, 621, 638, 657–658
Herring, John H., Jr.: 468
    and airfield construction and repair: 477
    and airlift missions reduction: 480
    and AWADS aircraft: 485–486
    and Cambodia operations: 509, 513
    and cargo delivery systems: 485
    at Dak Teang: 529
    and forklifts: 487
    and inactivations: 471
    and joint air operations: 476
    and safety measures: 477
Herschkorn, John A., Jr.: 71
Hetherington, Travis M.: 105
Hickam Air Force Base: 85, 140n, 382, 384, 563
Highley, Robert L.: 542–543, 602
Highway 1: 291–292, 325, 328, 637
Highway 7: 637
Highway 9: 290–291, 313–314, 508–509, 512–513, 515, 517
Highway 13: 539–540, 542–543, 554–556
Highway 14: 636
Highway 19: 204, 207–209, 214–215, 247, 550, 566, 567n, 636
Highway 21: 636
Hill 875: 287
Hirondelle Operation: 5n
Hoa, Father: 59
Hoa Binh Operation: 5n
Hoang, Le Minh, VNAF: 640
Hollingsworth, James F., USA: 540, 555
Holt, USS: 645
Homecoming Operation: 605, 608–609, *610*, 611–613
Hong Kong: 35, 57, 170
Honolulu conferences: 85
Hospitals, number and capacity: 397, 399
Hours and sorties flown. *See* Airlift, hours and sorties flown
Howe, Charles W.: 382
Howton, Harry: 123–125, 189
Howze, Hamilton H., USA: 108–109
Hue
    accidents at: 251
    airlifts to and from: 74, 88, 293, 317, 335, 512, 518, 564, 609, 637
    cargo delivery to: 330, 384

TACTICAL AIRLIFT

    in casualty evacuation system: 400
    enemy assaults on: 293, 319–320, 325–326, 559, 575
    radar facilities: 393
Hurlburt Field: 41, 45, 47–48, 55, 59, 63, 128, 146, 158, 195, 429
Hurricane III Operation: 57
Huu, Bule, VNAF: *584*

Ia Drang Valley: 213–215, 266, 284, 653
Imphal experience: 557
Inchon experience: 26
Indian River Exercises: 396
Indochina War: 3–23, 37–38
Infantry Brigade, 196th Light: 277–282, 288–289
Infantry Divisions
    Americal: 288–289
    1st: 208, 218, 224–226, *227*, 228–229, 278, 358
    4th: 284, 286
    25th: 224
Infantry Regiment, 503d: 274–282
Infiltrations. *See* Search-and-clear missions
Infrared devices: 431, 486, 530
Ingram, Benjamin F., Jr.: 642
Insignia: 68, 76, 86, 627
Instrument flying aids: 9, 70, 87–88, 94, 112, 367, 475
Intelligence estimates and reports
    Allied: 125, 132, 435–438, 455, 526
    enemy: 129
Interdiction missions: 388–389
International Business Machines: 470
International Control Commission: 434
Iosue, Andrew P.: 483, 542–547, 557, 561, 565, 576, 608–609
Iron Age Project: 11, 16, 19–21
Iron Triangle: 217–218
Iwakuni Air Base: 563

Jackson, Joe M.: 317, *318*, 346
Japan
    aircraft and units assigned: 34–35, 37, 170, 329, 384
    in airlift system: 18, 35, 379, 440
    in casualty evacuation system: 396
Jeannotte, Alfred J., Jr.: 346
Jenks, Edwin: 301
Jensen, Don B.: 543
Jensen, Norman K.: 345
Jet-assisted takeoff equipment: 41
Johnson, Andrew: 129
Johnson, Barney L., Jr.: 249
Johnson, Harold K.
    and airlift complaints: 190
    and airmobile concept: 207
    and Army aircraft integration into airlift: 237, 353, 358
    roles and missions agreement: 212, 673–674
Johnson, Ivan D.: 479

INDEX

Johnson, Lyndon B.: *210*
    and Allied participation: 410–411
    civic action program: 401
    and dependents evacuation: 170
    and Khe Sanh campaign: 300
    and limited objectives policy: 207
    and troop units commitments: 170, 173, 207–208, 328
Joint Chiefs of Staff (*see also* Taylor, Maxwell D.; Wheeler, Earle G.)
    and aircrews in French support: 17
    and Air Force helicopters: 235
    and airborne assaults: 98
    and aircraft tactical use: 101, 113
    and aircraft transfer to VNAF: 601
    and aircraft and units assignments: 10, 21, 44–45, 116, 122, 145, 180–181, 375, 472, 563–565
    and airfield construction: 162
    and airlift operations: 10, 206, 402, 463, 623, 644
    and airmobile concept: 207
    and Army aircraft integration into airlift: 237–238
    and Army aircraft and units: 121
    and Cambodia campaign: 508, 625
    casualty estimates: 578–579
    and civil airlines: 447
    and civilian aircrews: 441
    and crew-to-aircraft ratio: 123
    and defense against antiaircraft: 622
    and emergency airlifts: 505
    and enemy combat capability: 433
    on enemy offensive failure: 579
    and fuel deliveries: 623
    and Indochina as military objective: 37
    and Khe Sanh campaign: 296, 514
    and Laos campaign: 458
    and limited war: 42
    and Military Airlift Command use: 384, 472
    missiles policy: 552
    and navigation systems: 161
    and quick reaction units: 95, 97
    on roles and missions: 359
    and RVN training program: 42
    and search-and-clear missions: 40, 206
    and strike team concept: 57
    and surplus aircraft disposal: 616
    and training programs: 143
    and troop unit commitments: 37–38, 171–173
Joint exercises training: 140, 143–144
Joint General Staff, RVN: 223, 595, 621
Joint Military Transportation Board: 35, 380, 382
Joint Operations Center: 62, 86, 89, 99, 102–104, 106–107, 120, 138, *188*, 476–477, 655
Joint Task Force 116: 113, 407–408
Jones, Albert W.: 514
Jones, David C.: 622

Jones, Richard W.: 335
Junction City Operation: 269–282, 348, 653–654
Jungle Jim. *See* Combat Crew Training Squadron, 4400th

Kadena Air Base. *See* Okinawa
Kampot: 626
Karachi: 18n
Katum
    airfield conditions: 293
    airfield construction and repair: 278–279, 499
    airlifts to: 277–278, 293, 348, 498–499, 504
    parachute assaults at: 271, 274, 277
Kendig, Robert C.: *254*
Kennedy, John F.: *43*
    and air units commitment: 44, 47
    and civilian aircrews: 441
    and Farm Gate mission: 49
    and Laos airlifts: 441
    and limited war policy: 32, 42
    and Meo training: 441–442
    and quick reaction units: 95
    and search-and-clear forces: 40, 42–43, 53
    and Special Forces: 150
Kennedy, Thomas B.: 118, 134
Kernan, Pat: 71
Kershaw, Theodore G.: 117
Kham Duc: 163
    accidents at: 252
    aircraft lost at: 344–347, *479*
    airfield construction and repair: 343, 495
    airlifts to and from: 317, 343–347, 425, 495, *496*
    enemy assaults on: 343–346, 420, 490, 495
    terrain features: 343
Khe Sanh
    accidents at: 251, 291, 297, 311
    aerial port service: 510
    aircraft lost at: 200, 297, 300, 307, 316
    aircraft and units assigned: 469
    airfield construction and repair: 230–232, 290–291, 297, *298*, 300, 303, 314–315, 493, 509, 512–514, 516, 519, 620, 656
    airlifts to and from: 296–299, 372, 425, 430, 493, 510, 512–513, 516–518, 557
    cargo handling and delivery: 262, 290–291, 295, 302–306, *308–310*, 311–312, 314–317, 321, 330, 333, 339, 429, 509, 512, 514–516, 518, 654
    in casualty evacuation system: 399
    congestion at: 306, 314
    cloud-dissipating mission 389
    enemy airlifts from: 438
    enemy assaults on: 20, 269, 290–292, 295–316, 516
    ground crews assigned: 305
    maintenance and repair: 515–516, 518
    withdrawal from: 517–518
Khrushchev, Nikita S.: 40

INDEX

Kien Long: 135
Kimmey, Nelson W.: 335
Kimpo Air Base: 26
King, Benjamin H.: 41, 47–50
Kinnard, Harry W. O.: 213, 215–216
Kissinger, Henry A.: 28, 601
Knox, Kenneth F.: 18
Koh Tang Island: 631, 645–646, 658
Kompong Cham: 507, 584–586, 624
Kompong Chhnang: 624, 627
Kompong Som: 505, 508, 622, 624, 627
Kompong Thom: 507, 624, 626
Kompong Trach: 564, 574, 596
Kong Le forces: 441
Kontum: 72
    accidents at: 567
    aircraft lost at: 490, 596
    aircraft and units assigned: 425
    airfield construction and repair: 230, 253
    airlifts to and from: 177, 207, 212, 282, 284–285, 287–288, 322–323, 423, 425, 438, 559, 561, 563, 566, 570–572, 574, 596, 636, 647
    cargo handling: 578
    disarray at: 192
    enemy assaults on: 204, 207, 282, 284, 318–323, 599, 568–570
    forest-burning missions: 392
    maintenance and repair: 567
    navigation and radio facilities: 263
Korat Air Base
    accidents at: 197
    aerial port service: 409–410
    aircraft and units assigned: 110, 395, 616
    airlifts to: 407–409
    enemy airlifts to: 435
Korea. *See* Republic of Korea
Kraljev, Benjamin N., Jr.: 94
Kramer, Ross E.: *337*, 338
Krek: 507
Krulak, Victor H., USMC: *157*
Kuala Lumpur conference: 615
Kueck, Walter: *584*
Kung Kuan Air Base: 37, 182–184
Kunming: 438
Kwajalein staging base: 37
Ky, Nguyen Cao: 70–71, 75, 77–79, 128, *131*, 503

Lai Khe: 223, 225, 270, 539, 551
Laird, Melvin R.: *518*
    and aircraft transfer to VNAF: 601
    and aircraft and unit assignments: 565
    and airlift missions: 519
    and emergency airlifts: 505
    and fuel deliveries: 623
    and surplus aircraft disposal: 616

TACTICAL AIRLIFT

Loudspeaker use: 41, 58–59, 74, 405–406
Luang Prabang
    airfield at: 445
    airlifts to and from: 448, 453, 462
    Chinese Communist airlifts to: 438
    enemy assaults on: 9, 16
Lutton, Lyle D., Jr.: 81–82

MacCammond, Kenneth M.: 79
MacDonald, Theodore R.: *119*
Mack, Joseph F.: 286, *287*
Mackay Trophy awards: 63, 344
Mactan Isle Airfield: 181–183, 408–409
Maintenance and repair: 61, 93, 112, 126, *130*, 178, 249–250, 256, 355, *362*, 370, 412–414, 442, 448, 482, 490, 511, 514–518, 521, 526, 535, 567, 578, 602
    cannibalization in: 93, 176–177, 250, 355, 370, 456, 576, 616
    command and centralization: 248–249, 251, 370, 482, 535
    complaints against: 195, 250, 616
    deficiencies in: 61, 256, 355, 480, 578
    for and by French: 7–9, *14*, 17–18, 21
    helicopters: 456
    improvement program: 64, 126–128
    Laotian: 453
    Logistics Command role in: 355, 370, 482, 619
    man-hours vs. flying-hours: 184, 576
    parts delivery: 324
    parts shortages: 18, 93, 110, 126, 370–371, 385, 456, 591, 602, 606, 616, 620
    personnel. *See* Ground crews
    quality standards: 93, 370, 534
    simplifying program: 60–61
    by VNAF: 67–68, 74, 586, 590–591, 597, 619–620
Malaya experience: 40, 134, 149
Malaysia: 385
Malmstrom Air Force Base: 48
Management system: 469–471, 487, 576, 595, 655
Mang Buk: 162, 569, 574
Mantoux, Lopez J.: 86, 106–108
Maps, use in airlift: 97, 134, 154
Marauder Operation: 219–221
Mariana Islands: 385
Marrott, James E.: *610*
Martin, Glen W.: 135, 382–383
Martin, Graham A.: 643–644
Mascot, Paul J.: 355–357, 360, 364, 369, 375
Mason, William H.: 375
Mastiff Operation: 225, *227*, 236
Mataxis, Theodore C., USA: 204
Materiel lifts. *See* Airlift, materiel
Materiel losses
    allied: 286, 297, 322, 568, 579, 638
    enemy: 132, 341, 374, 458, 498, 500, 553
Mayaguez incident: 645–646

INDEX

McCall, John K.: 345
McCarty, Chester E.: 10–11, 21, 31, 84
McCloskey, Paul N., Jr.: 622
McConnell, John P.: *211, 287, 534*
    and Air Force helicopters: 233–235
    and aircraft and unit assignments: 375
    and airlift reorganization: 382
    and airmobile concept: 207, 215–216
    and Army aircraft integration into airlift: 237–239, 353, 358
    and limited objectives policy: 206–207
    roles and missions agreement: 212, 673–674
McCurdy, Garvin: 619–620, 637–638, 641
McGarr, Lionel C., USA: 45, 47–48, 58
McGovern, James: 19
McLaughlin, Burl W.: 294
    and aircraft and unit assignments: 375
    and airlift missions: 367
    and cargo delivery: 302, 312, 366, 384
    and Caribou performance: 375
    on command and control: 650
    efficiency improvement program: 350
    and Kham operation: 344, 346
    and mission safety: 329
    and safety measures: 476
McNamara, Robert S.: *43, 145*
    and air commando units: 52
    and Air Force helicopters: 235
    and aircraft capabilities: 91
    and aircraft and units assignments: 44–45, 84, 128, 145–146, 180–181, 237*n*, 375
    and airfield construction and repair: 162, 231
    and airlift missions: 85, 108–109, 233, 463
    and airmobile concept: 207
    and Army aircraft integration into airlift: 190, 237, 355
    and Civilian Irregular Defense Groups: 150, 164
    and coastal enclaves concept: 208
    and decision-making process: 32
    and dependents evacuation: 170
    on Farm Gate mission: 49, 55
    and helicopter units commitments: 45, 456
    and limited war policy: 43
    and psywar missions: 58
    and quick reaction units: 95
    and RVN as priority: 46
    and search-and-clear forces: 40
    and troop units commitments: 39, 248
    and USAF pilots in RVNAF aircraft: 68–69
    and Vietnamization program: 80
Mechanics: *See* Ground crews
Medal of Honor awards: 317–318, 346, 426, 462
Medical Air Evacuation Group, 6481st: 21
Medical personnel: 399
Medical supplies drops: 204, 548, 550–551
Mekong River and Delta

airfields in: 88, 162
airlifts to: 129, 136, 348–349, 561
combat actions in: 443, 502
flood conditions: 97
parachute assaults: 270
Membrane airfield fabric: 230–232
Memot airfield: 434
Meo forces: 439, 443–445, 449, 457–459
Mess facilities: 17, 62, 88, 94, 125, 153–154, 177–179, 196, 340–341, 516
Messex, Curtis L.: 493
Middle East crises: 28
Midway, USS: 644
Midway Island: 49
Miles, David A.: 572
Military Air Transport Service. *See* Military Airlift Command
Military Airlift Command: 28n
    air terminal detachments: 138
    aircraft and units assigned: 650–652
    airlifts by: 28, 35, 38, 49, 85, 91–92, 111, 114, 223, 288, 328, 383–384, *386*, 410–411, 441, 518, 563–565, 577, 606, 609, 641–642, 650
    and cargo-handling equipment: 256
    cargo tonnages and passengers moved: 140, 383–385
    casualties evacuation: 21, 397
Military Airlift Group, 65th: 383n
Military Airlift Squadron, 22d: 383n
Military Regions, II and III: 540, 543, 574
Miller, William: 544, 547, 551
Milton, Theodore R.: 47, *48*, 106
Minh, Tran Van, VNAF: 622, 637, 639–640
Minh Thanh: 270, 279, 572, 574–575, 596, 606
Minigua. *See* Aircraft, gunships
Mine clearing: *198*, 218
Mine-dropping missions: 392–393
Mining, by enemy: *198*, 322, 632
Missile systems
    American policy on: 200, 351, 552
    enemy use: 316, 351, 515, 539, 549, 552–553, 557, 559, 570, 613, 618, 620, 623–625, 638, 643–644
Mission commanders: 469, 511, 515, 547
Mission defined: 32, 85–86, 116, 652
Mobile Communications Group, 1st: 515
Mobile Group 100 (France): 5
Mobile Yoke Exercise: 37
Moc Hoa: 502, 504
Moise, Robeson S.: *76*, 77
Momyer, William W.: *198*
    and aircraft and unit assignments: 180, 190–191, 248
    and airlift reorganization: 382
    and Army aircraft integration into airlift: 358–359
    and cargo-handling equipment: 256, 261
    on command and control: 382
    and complaints about airlift: 362–363
    and forest-burning missions: 393

INDEX

and forward deliveries: 652
and gunships: 389
on helicopter vs. fixed-wing: 639
and liaison concept: 246
on maintenance and repair: 355
and mission control and priority: 245, 358
and safety measures: 355–357
Montagnards: 149, *157*, 165, 405
Montgomery, Franklin B.: 345
Montgomery, James L.: 373
Moore, Johnnie M.: *244*
Moore, Joseph H.: *198*, 236–237, 264
Moore, William G., Jr.: *272*
and aerial port service: 253
and aircraft and units assignments: 248
and airlift missions: 241, 243–245, 278, 367
and cargo-handling equipment: 253–261
and jet-equipped aircraft: 263
and liaison concept: 246
and maintenance control: 251
and parachute assaults: 271, 274–276
and prisoners repatriation: 611
and rigging service: 257
Moorman, Thomas S.: 90
Morale and discipline: 61, 181, 195, 250, 253, 258, 305, 321, 388, 490, 576–577, 659
aircrews. *See* Aircrews
ARVN: 98–99, 129, 515, 544, 547, 551, 637
Cambodian: 622, 632
Dirty Thirty pilots: 75, 77
Ground crews. *See* Ground crews
VNAF: 67, 81, 541, 593, 596–597, 600, 639
Mortar assaults, enemy: 251–252, 286, 289–290, 297, 300–301, 307, 311, 320–322, 344, 346, 364, 429, 479, 494, 540, 547, 570, 572, 586, 621
Mott, Elbert L.: 374
Movement control centers: 103
Mud-producing missions: 389
Mule Train Project: 45, 83–114, 120, 123, 126, 140, 151, 158, 163, 392
Mulkey, Reed C.: 566
Mullen, Robert F.: 333, 335–336
Munitions. *See* Airlift, materiel lifts
Muong Kassy: 451
Muong Phine: 461–462
Muong Soui: 457–459
Mutual Defense Assistance Program: 6
My Tho: 129

Na San: 6, 9
Naha Air Base. *See* Okinawa
Nakhon Phanom Air Base
aerial port service: 409–410
aircraft and units assigned: 124, 389, 393, 422, 463, 605–606, 615–616
airfield construction and repair: 408–409
airlifts to and from: 408–409, 427–430, 606, 616

875

TACTICAL AIRLIFT

    command and control at: 615
    helicopters assigned: 454–455, 616
Nanning: 438
Napalm assaults: 17, 392
National Defense Transportation Association: 258, 490
National Security Council: 44
Navarre, Henri E.: 10–11, 16
Navigation systems
    in airlift. *See* Airlift, navigation and navigators in
    in helicopters: 160–161
    mission assignment: 249
    training programs: 184
Neak Luong: 502
Needham, Dannie B.: 481
Neeley, Billy E.: *398*
Nellis Air Force Base: 552
Nets in cargo handling: 256
New Focus Projects: 212, 216
New Zealand air units: 407–408, 413–415, 638
Newbold, Rodney H.: 523, 535
Nha Trang: *210, 251*
    aerial port service: 138–139
    aircraft and units assigned: 8–9, 64, 69, 108, 116, 165, 176, 248, 274, 329, 364, 405, 412–414, 419, 429, 522
    airlifts to and from: 64–65, 88, 105, 114–115, 151–155, 163, 208–209, 212–213, 222, 349, 364, 374, 414–415, 418–420, 423, 429–430
    call sign: 120
    cargo handling: 138–139, 164, 185, 222, 252, 373–374, 417, 606
    in casualty evacuation system: 396–400
    communications at: 120
    enemy assaults on: 64, 200, 252, 318–319, 638
    flareships at: 388
    forest-burning missions: 392
    French defense: 4
    helicopters and units assigned: 236
    lighting system: 179
    living conditions: 179
    as logistics center: 140
    passenger service: 598
    runway conditions: 112
    strike aircraft at: 57
    as training center: 67
    troop units assigned: 209, 216
Nhon Co: *220,* 222–223
Nicholson, Raymond E.: 75, 78
Night missions
    in airlift. *See* Airlift, night missions
    by strike aircraft: 73
    by truck transport: 512
Nixon, Richard M.
    and aircraft transfer to VNAF: 601
    and cease-fire agreement: 608

INDEX

    on enemy offensive failure: 578
    and Laos campaign: 458
    and troop unit withdrawals: 467
    and Vietnamization program: 519
Normandy campaign experience: 25
North Atlantic Treaty Organization: 486
North Korea, airlifts to: 691
North Vietnam
    aircraft acquired by: 647
    aircraft and helicopter strength: 434
    airlifts by: 432–438, 441, 647
    airlifts to and from: 605, 608–609
    bombing assaults by: 643
    bombing offensive against: 144, 169, 203, 347, 392, 410–411, 430, 609
    casualties: 129, 150, 215, 270, 341, 374, 456, 518, 578, 586, 639
    cease-fire delegation flight: 608–609
    civil airlines use: 434
    combat effectiveness: 433, 518, 620–621
    demolition assaults by: 291, 364, 373, 507, 618, 636
    helicopter losses: 434
    materiel losses: 132, 341, 374, 458, 498, 500, 553
    military assistance to: 3, 559
    mining by, *198*, 322, 632
    missiles use. *See* Missile systems
    offensives by: 203–204, 212–221, 223, 373, 314, 317–325, 330, 351, 373, 457, 467, 473, 493, 521, 536, 539–557, 559–579, 605, 636
    peace talks: 349
    prisoners of war: *87*, 422, 434, 499, 544, 605
    propaganda campaigns: 42, 421, 559
    road construction and repair: 332, 389, 620
    road interdiction by: 322, 325, 405, 505, 507, 512, 525, 539–540, 554–555, 564, 566, 636, 654
    rocket assaults and systems: 297, 300, 320, 478, 515, 559, 567–568, 570, 631, 635
    ruses and deceptions: 159, 636
    search-and-clear missions in: 429–432
    south invaded by: 38, 169, 203
    supply operations and systems: 19–20, 169, 424, 439, 461, 463
    tactics: 132, 559, 579
    terrorism campaigns: 42
    training programs: 438
    troop strength estimates: 325
    truck transport by: 620, 295, 620
    victory celebration: 647
Norton, John, USA: 233
Nuclear fuel lift: 638
Nuclear warfare, aircraft in: 27–28
Nui Ba Den: *436*

O Rang: 499–500
O'Donnell, Emmett: *96*, 101
Offensive strategy, airlift role in: 653–654

Okinawa
　accidents at: 477
　aircraft and units assigned: 35, 39, 140, 144, 146, 170, 182–183, 195n, 448, 450,
　　　473n, 563, 615, 626
　airlifts from: 35, 38, 152, 164, 171–173, 379–380, 417, 445, 645
　maintenance and repair: 448
Omega Project: 423
One Buck Project: 144–146
On-the-job training: 490
Operations Group, 6315th: 170, 173, 182–183
Operations Squadron, 6485th: 397
Opium smuggling: 435, 452
Orly Field, France: 13
Osgood, Robert: 28
Osmanski, Frank A., USA: 106–107, 116, 122, 160

Pacific Air Forces
　and aircrews qualifications: 249
　and aircrews work conditions: 179
　and aircraft assignments: 522
　and aircraft transfer to VNAF: 601
　and aircraft and units assignments: 44–45, 141, 180, 248, 375, 382
　and airfield construction: 192
　airlift by: 85–86, 106, 685–686
　and airlift deficiencies: 105
　airlift directorate activated: 382
　and airlift reorganization: 382
　and airmobile concept: 207
　and Army aircraft integration into airlift: 358
　and cargo-handling equipment: 256
　and cargo targeting teams: 573
　and civil airlines: 447
　and civilian employees: 139
　and coastal enclaves plan: 206
　on command and control: 109
　and complaints about airlift: 350–351
　and criticism of VNAF: 595
　and defense against ground fire: 200
　and Farm Gate mission: 49
　FEAF merged into: 35n
　and flying time rates: 183
　and jet engine additions: 196
　and maintenance and repair: 61, 480
　and MATS as sole airlift: 114
　and napalm missions: 392
　and navigators assignments: 249
　and pallets use: 194
　and quick reaction units: 95
　and radar guidance systems: 262
　and tours length: 92
Pacific Architects and Engineers, Inc.: 404
Pacific Command (see also Felt, Harry D.; Gayler, Noel A. M.; Sharp, U. S. Grant)
　and Air Force helicopters: 235

INDEX

    and aircraft transfer to VNAF: 600–601
    and aircraft and units assignments: 45, 48, 174, 181, 329, 375, 384, 564
    and airlift operations: 117, 180, 380, 383, 441
    and airlift reorganization: 382
    and Army aircraft and units: 121
    and Australian units: 412–414
    and Cambodia campaign: 627
    cargo handling criticized: 138
    and civil airlines: 447
    and emergency airlifts: 505
    and enemy airlifts: 433
    on Farm Gate mission: 49
    and fuel deliveries: 623
    and Laos airlifts: 441
    and Military Airlift Command use: 114, 472
    and missiles use: 552
    and parachute assaults: 171
    and passenger airlifts: 642
    and psywar missions: 58
    and quick reaction units: 95
    and Special Forces aircraft: 151, 153
    and surplus aircraft disposal: 616
    and troop units commitments: 171–173
Pacific Transportation Management Agency: 615
Page Communication Engineers, Inc.: 402
Pakistan, airlifts to: 385
Paksane: 445
Pakse Air Base: 440, 444–445, 448, 453
Pallets use and misuse: *See* Airlift, pallets use and misuse
Panel signals use: 54, *188*, 305, 325, 334–355, 422, *436*
Parachute assaults: 128, 173, 218, *220*, 224, 244
    by Air Force teams: 223–224
    airlift for. *See* Airlift, parachute assaults
    with amphibious landings: 141
    ARVN in: 55, 57, 68, 73, 96–103, 128–129, *131*, 132–137, 270, 239, 495, 575, 583–584
    decline of: 26–27, 29, 115, 135, 651, 654
    by enemy: 438
    by French: 5, 11, *14*, 19, 654
    Korean War experience: 26
    VNAF role in: 55, 57, 68, 73, 96–103, 128–129, *131*, 132–137, 575, 583–584
    training programs: 495
    World War II experience: 25
Paris cease-fire agreements: 467, 581, 608, 615, 618, 644
Parker, Bruce: 582
Parmly, Eleazar, IV, USA: 424, 441
Parrot's Beak region: 133, 502, 571, 624
Partridge, Earle E.: *15, 22*
Passengers moved. *See* Airlift, passengers moved
Pathet Lao forces: 432, 439, 441, 443, 464
Pathfinders: 57, 98, 137–138, 141, 486
Patrols, ground: 164–165, 205
Peace negotiations: 349

TACTICAL AIRLIFT

Pegasus Operation: 313–314, 332
Pennington, Bobby D.: 534
People's Republic of China: 3, 438, 559
Perrott, Nicholas J.: *398*
Peterson, Charles L.: *198*
Petroleum products. *See* Fuel
Phan Rang
    aerial port service: 413–414
    aircraft and units assigned: 248, 319, 451, 473*n*
    airfield construction and repair: 229, 231
    airlifts to and from: 413, 638
    cargo handling: 185, 222, 248, 384
    enemy assaults on: 478, 638
    living and work conditions: 249, 483
    maintenance and repair: 250
Phan Thiet: 146, 220, 222, 265
Phi Hoa 5 Operation: 133–134
Philippines: 410–411. *See also* Clark Field
Philippines Air Lines: 61
Phillips, William T.: 333
Phnom Penh
    aircraft and units assigned: 628–629, 633
    airfield construction and repair: 624
    airlifts to and from: 493, 504–508, 605, 616, 622–623, 626, 632–633, 635, 638
    cargo handling: 624
    enemy assaults on: 507, 626, 631, 633, 635
    helicopters at: 628
    truck transport to: 625
    water transport to: 623
Phong Saly: 440, 442
Photography, use in airlift: 54–55, 169, 271, 334, 513, 573, 627
Phoumi Nosavan: 441
Phu Bai
    accidents at: 327
    airlifts to and from: 290, 292–293, 327–328, 365, 561, 575, 612, 647
    cargo delivery and handling: 292, 326, 328, 384, 561
    in casualty evacuation system: 397, 399
Phu Cat
    aircraft and units assigned: 355, 357, 360, 521*n*, 535, 591
    airfield construction and repair: 357
    airlifts to and from: 359, 364, 383–384, 536, 612
    in casualty evacuation system: 399
    enemy assaults on: 638
    living conditions: 357
    maintenance and repair: 370
Phu Loi: 225
Phu Quoc Island: 435, 638
Phu Tuc: *156*
Phuoc Long Province: 102, 621
Phuoc Vinh
    aircraft and units assigned: 469
    airlifts to and from: 204, 219, 225, 622
    cargo delivered to: 322, 499

INDEX

Pierced steel planking: 230, *231, 264*
Pilot Augmentation Group. *See* Dirty Thirty
Pilots (*see also* Aircrews)
    ages and grades: 184–185, 249, 369, 457
    civilian: 7, 10, 17, 19, 446
    Dirty Thirty: 67–80, 581
    flying safety concept: 70–71
    helicopter: 457
    Marine Corps: 315
    proficiency and experience: 369, 426, 446, 533, 659
    recreation facilities: 77
    relations with VNAF: 74–75, 591
    replacements: 71
    in Republic of China aircraft: 79
    Republic of China offer of: 411–414
    in VNAF aircraft: 67–80, 582–583, 591, 594
    in Thai aircraft: 79
    shortages: 238, 249
    survival kits for: 74
    training programs. *See* Training programs
    Vietnamese Air Force: 44, 67–69, 80–81, 411–412, 583, 586–587, 591–592, 600, 603, 619
Plain of Jars
    airlifts to and from: 458, 461
    allied airlifts from: 450
    combat actions in: 458, 462–463
    enemy airlifts to: 434, 441
    enemy assaults in: 9, 16, 443
Plei Djereng
    aircraft lost at: 533
    airlifts to: 284, 423, *436*, 504
    cargo handling: 500
Plei Me: 212–213, 230, 420
Pleiku
    accidents at: 197
    aerial port service: 138–139, 577
    aircraft lost at: 200
    aircraft and units assigned: 73, 81, 108, 110–111, 122, 209, 364, 522, 531
    airlifts to and from: 74, 88, 105, 204, 207, 213–214, 284, 288, 364, 374, 383–384, 502, 529, 532, 564–567, 592, 597–598, 609, 636–637
    call sign: 120
    cargo handling: 139, 163, 323, 417, 424, 525, 527, 599
    in casualty evacuation system: 397, 399
    enemy assaults on: 16, 200, 204–205, 207, 212–216, 223, 282–283, 318, 559, 566, 636
    maintenance and repair: 526, 567
    radar guidance from: 393, 569–570
    runway conditions: 112
    strike aircraft at: 57
Pleiku-An Khe-Ban Me Thuot triangle: 5
Pleiku Province: 435
Pochentong: 505–507
Pony Express Project: 430–431, 454

TACTICAL AIRLIFT

Pope Air Force Base
    aircraft and units assigned: 83, 85, 91–93, 123, 128, 146, 158, 182, 399, 565, 571, 606n, 625
    as Airlift Center: 650
    airlifts from: *326*
    developmental activity: 258–259, 484–485, 552
Prairie Fire Project: 425, 428, 455
Pratt, John C.: 459
Pratt & Whitney engines: 84
Prek Klok: 278–279
Pricer, Donald C.: 21
Princeton, USS: 405
Priority missions. *See* Airlift, emergency, emergency and priority missions
Prisoners of war
    American: 21
    enemy: 87, 434, 499, 544, 605
    repatriation: 605, 608–609, *610*, 611–613
Propaganda, enemy: 42, 421, 559
Propeller malfunctions: 184
Psychological warfare missions: 50, 57–59, 73, 95, 656. *See also* Leaflet drops; Loudspeaker use
Pueblo incident: 258, 329
Qantas Airlines: 414
Quan Loi
    airlifts to and from: 128, 270, 279, 349, 424, 498, 504, 555
    cargo handling: 499
    enemy assault on: 540
Quan Long: 561
Quang Ngai
    airfield construction and repair: 230
    in airlift system: 92, 136–137, 146, 204, 223
    enemy assaults on: 223
Quang Tri
    aircraft lost at: 596
    airfield construction and repair: 231, 292, 510
    airlifts to and from: 292–293, 327, 341, 347, 509–510, 512, 518, 596, 612
    cargo delivery and handling: 326, 328, 330, 347, 513, 564
    in casualty evacuation system: 397, 400
    conditions at: 564
    enemy airlifts reported: 435
    enemy assaults on: 325, 563, 575
    maintenance and repair: 511
Quang Tri Province: 325, 549, 575, 620
Quartermaster Companies
    109th: 257, 261, 277–279, 333, 497, 517
    549th: 548
Quartermaster School, USA: 259
Qui Nhon: *131*
    accidents at: 197, *198*
    aerial port service: 139
    aircraft and units assigned: 108, 116, 165, 175
    airlifts to and from: 74, 86, 88, 115, 174, 177, 204, 207–208, 212–213, 232, 326, 364–365, 414–415

INDEX

call sign: 120
cargo handling and delivery: 140, 185, 252, 324
in casualty evacuation system: 397–400
convoys to and from: 214
enemy assaults on: 222–223, 318–319, 322, 638
lighting system: 179
troop units assigned: 209
Quick reaction forces concept: 95–105, 135
Quyet Thang 33/64 Operation: 136
Racial relations: 482–483
Radar equipment and guidance. *See* Airlift, radar guidance in
Radford, Arthur W.: 10
Radio communications and equipment
in airlift. *See* Airlift, radio communications and equipment in
French: 9
in helicopters: 161
Railroads: 117, 185, 292, 408
Ranch Hand Project: 45–46, *391*
Ream: 646
Reconnaissance missions
aerial: 55, 58–59, 98, 333, 395, 423–432
enemy: 295
ground: 285
Recreation and welfare facilities: 57, 62, 77, 154, 351, 383, 406
Red Chief beacon transponder: 262
Red Horse squadrons: 230
Red Leaf plan: 354
Red River and Delta: 3–4, 20, 430
Redeye missile: 200
Regional Forces: 420, 575
Reporters. *See* Correspondents
Republic of China: 79, 411–414, 429, 691
Republic of Korea
air units contribution: 415–416
aircraft and units assigned: 7*n*, 329
airlifts in and to: 26–27, 35, 47, 103, 247, 379, 691
troop units in RVN: 214, 410–411
Republic of Vietnam (*see also* Ky, Nguyen Cao; Diem, Ngo Dinh; Thieu, Nguyen Van)
aircraft and units assigned: 10, 21, 25, 43–45, 47, 82–85, 111, 115–116, 122–123, 144–145, 180–182, 195, 204, 237, 247–248, 349–350, 353, 355, 375, 384, 472, 487, 499, 510, 523, 560, 562–565, 577, 656
aircraft and units withdrawn: 350, 472–473, 521–522, 535, 606*n*, 643–644
American goals and policy in: 32, 42–43, 206–207, 614–615, 617–618, 647
casualties: 50, 102, 129, 134–135, 150, 197, 375, 541, 566, 568, 575, 578, 586, 591, 596
cease-fire in: 467, 581, 608, 615, 618, 644
collapse of: 631, 637, 644
defense funding by U.S.: 621
invaded by North: 38, 169, 203
military assistance, extent of: 42
missions incidence: 38–39

883

morale status: 515–516
national elections: 269
number of U.S. aircraft in: 115, 329
peace talks: 349
psywar operations: 59
public attitude toward insurgency: 42
religious crises: 78
strategic hamlets plan: 95, 115
supply operations and systems: 502
terrain features: *148*, 149
transportation facilities: 468
troop units commitments and withdrawals: 37–39, 43, 78, 169–174, 207–208, 216, 248, 328, 407–409, 467, 523, 559, 608

Rescue missions. *See* Search-and-rescue missions
Rest and recuperation plan: 383, 406–407
Richards, William: 94
Rickenbacker, Edward V.: 63n
Riede, Philip J.: 608–609, 611, 613
Rigging devices and services: 158–159, 257, 261, 306, 315, 333, 484, 531, 545, 548–549, 554, 556, 624–626, 652
Rizer, Virgil H.: 326
Roads
    allied construction and repair: 290, 295, 408–409
    enemy construction and repair: 332, 389, 620
    interdiction by Allies: 389, 509
    interdiction by enemy: 322, 325, 405, 505, 507, 512, 525, 539–540, 554–555, 564, 566, 636, 654
    security of: 455, 467, 508–509, 654
    transportation by. *See* Truck transport
Roadwatch Project: 455
Rockefeller Report (1957): 28
Rocket assaults and systems, enemy: 297, 300, 320, 478, 515, 559, 567–568, 570, 631, 635
Rodenbough, Jacob H.: 78
Rogers, David M.: 373
Rohrlick, Myles A.: 302, 556–557
Roi Et Royal Thai Air Base: 408–409
Roles and missions controversy and agreement: 30, 32, 89–90, 93–94, 107–111, 114–115, 203, 212, 233, 236–238, 266, 359, 407–408, 467, 521, 657–658, 673–674
Romeas: 626
Ropka, Lawrence, Jr.: 442
Rotation and tour lengths
    aircrews: 51, 92, 123, 125, 154, 181–182, 195, 316, 329, 351, 388, 408–411, 479, 483, 534, 607, 625, 656
    ground crews: 177, 305, 482–483, 577–578, 607
    Tactical Air Command: 92
Royal Air Force: 40
Royal Laotian Air Force: 392
    aircraft and personnel strength: 452–453, 463

INDEX

airlift missions by: 451–453, 463
development: 451, 657
factionalism in: 452
helicopters use: 454–457
maintenance and repair: 453
Royal Thai Air Force units: 411–412
Roysdon, Douglas A.: 632–633
Ruses and deceptions
    allied: 271, 274, 509, 547
    enemy: 159, 636
Rusk, Dean: 44–45
Ryan, John D.: 248
Ryan, Philip W., Jr.: 611

Sabotage: 200, 322, 478
Sadler, Thomas M.: 245–246
Safety and security measures: 20, 53, 70–71, 93–94, 117, 125, 179, 194, 197, 199, 201, 284, 355, 357, 368–369, 394, 455, 475–477, 489–490, 508–509, 532, 542, 654
Sagebrush Exercise: 27
Saigon, conferences at: 151–152
Saigon area (*see also* Tan Son Nhut)
    aircraft lost at: 478
    airfields in: 9, *13*
    airlifts to and from: 74, 86, 88, 102, 105, 115, 119, 137, 150, 152, 163, 177, 223–224, 228, 285, 317, 319, 323, 384, 406–407, 414–415, 472, 495, 509, 515, 518, 536, 565, 613, 616, 631, 635, 638–639, *640*, 643
    cargo handling and tests: 139, 164, 185, 349, 551, 554, 606
    in casualty evacuation system: 396, 399–400
    defense forces and missions: 173
    enemy assaults in: 216, 293, 539
    forest-burning missions: 392
    in French supply system: 5
    French defense: 4
    in ground supply system: 117
    helicopters and units assigned: 135
    living conditions: 62, 69
Saigon International Airport: 96
Saigon-Phnom Penh road: 502
Saigon River area: 225
Sam Thong: 459–461
Samneua Province: 434, 455, 457
San Francisco, airlifts to: 35
Sandbags production: 469, 516
Sapper assaults. *See* Demolition assaults, enemy
Saravane: 21, 434, 448, 453, 462
Sattahip: 444
Savannakhet Air Base: 441, 444, 448, 453
Sawbuck I and II Projects: 91–93
Scales in cargo handling: 257
Schinz, Albert W.: 582
Schlesinger, James R.: 650

885

TACTICAL AIRLIFT

Scowcroft, Brent: 643
Seaboard World: 633
Sealift operations: *See* Water transport
Seamans, Robert C., Jr.: 650
Search-and-clear missions
    airlift in: 39–40, 95–103, 203–229, 239, 269–292, 313–314, 371–372, 421–432,
        439–464, 493–508, 653
    in Cambodia: 423–432, 493–519
    forces for: 40, 42–43, 53
    helicopters in: 203–229, 239, 269–292, 423–432
    in Laos: 423–432, 515–516
    Marine Corps in: 173
    in North Vietnam: 429–432
    training programs: 425
    tactics and equipment: 425–426, 428, 525
Search-and-rescue missions: 62, 345–347, 429–431, *492*, 535, 543
Searchlights use: 546–547
Secretary of the Air Force: *See* Zuckert, Eugene M.
Secretary of Defense. *See* Laird, Melvin R.; McNamara, Robert S.; Schlesinger,
    James R.
Secretary of State. *See* Kissinger, Henry A.; Rusk, Dean
Security measures. *See* Safety and security measures
Selberg, Ronald L.: 335
Senegalese troops: *14*
Seno air base
    airfield at: 445
    airlifts to and from: 6, 21, 38–39, 440–441, 453
Sensor devices: 389, 455
Seven Mountains: 349, 420
Sewart Air Force Base: 29, 37, 141, 143–144, 182, 184, 329, 354, 369, 533
Sharp, U. S. Grant, USN: 208, 216
Shaub, Charles L.: 542
Shaw Air Force Base: 455, 457
Shelton, Ray D.: 344
Sheppard Air Force Base: 457
Shewmaker, Horace W.: 121
Shining Brass Project: 425
Shinoskie, John J.: *610*
Shofner, Floyd K.: 84–85, 89–90, 104
Shoran. *See* Navigation systems and navigators
Sigma Project: 423
Sihanoukville. *See* Kompong Som
Silver City Operation: 219
Simpson, Robert T.: 199
Singapore: 644
Skoun: 626
Skyline Ridge: *460*
Slough, William J., *198*
Smart, Jacob E.: *155–156*, 161
Smith, Homer D., Jr., USA: 643
Smoke screens and signals: 54–55, 98, 133, 159, 165, *188*, 212, 275–276, 305, 311,
        335, 526
Smotherman, Philip B.: 345

886

INDEX

Snuol: 434, 507
Soc Trang: 57, 88, 323, 605
Son Tay prison camp: 431
Song Be
    aircraft lost at: 330, 621, 639
    aircraft and units assigned: 469, 639
    airfield construction and repair: 230
    airlifts to and from: 219, 293, 323, 327–328, 349, 499, 504, 564, 639
    cargo delivery to: 322–323, 349, 384
    enemy assaults on: 219–221, 621
Sorties flown. *See* Airlift, hours and sorties flown
Soui Da: 225, 279
Southeast Asia Airlift System (later Common Service Airlift System)
    activated: 106
    aircraft and units assigned: 144–145, 190
    Army aircraft integration into: 121, 236, 238
    cargo moved by: 186
    command and control by: 175, 187, 412–414
    expansion: 115, 169
    logistical demands on: 137
Southeast Asia Treaty Organization: 37–39, 410–411, 615
Souvanna Phouma: 443, 454
Soviet Union
    airfield construction: 445
    airlifts by: 432, 438, 441
    training programs: 438, 452
    weapons supply by: 559
Spare parts. *See* Maintenance and repair
Special Air Warfare Center: 52, 63, 128, 195*n*, 196
Special Forces: *157*
    advisory role: 417
    aircrews, relations with: 154, 159
    aircraft assigned to: 151, 165
    airlifts to. *See* Airlift, for Special Forces Units
    border surveillance mission: 164
    number of teams: 150
    personnel strength: 165
    supply system: 140, 151–152, 417–421
    training programs: 42, 53, 150
Special Forces Group, 5th: 164, 212, 324, 366, 374, 424
Special Operations Force: 651
Special Operations Squadrons
    1st: 626
    12th: 473*n*
    16th: 486
    20th: 385, 397, 428, 430, 435, 612
    21st: 428, 616, 631, 635, 643–645
    90th: 431*n*
Special Operations Wing, 315th: 473
Spraying equipment and missions: 45, 89–96
Srang: 626
Stalingrad experience: 295, 557
Starlight scope: 388–389

TACTICAL AIRLIFT

State, Department of. *See* Rusk, Dean
Stead Air Force Base: 37
Steel matting: 230, 232
Stoner, John R.: 214–215
Stow, Lilburn R.: 336
Strategic Air Command: 69, 634
Strategic hamlets plan: 95, 115
Strobaugh, Donald R.: 333, 336, 340
Sullivan, William H.: 389, 443, 447, 458, 454, 458–461
Supply operations and systems
    aircraft in. *See* Airlift
    enemy: 19–20, 169, 424, 439, 461, 463
    French: 5, 20
    Republic of Vietnam: 502
    Special Forces: 140, 151–152, 417–421
Survival kits: 74
Svay Rieng: 571–572, 574, 627
Sweeney, Walter C., Jr.: 77, 102
Sweet, Harold L.: 76, 79
Swift Strike Exercises: 138, 143, 396
Swivel Chair Project: 10
Systems Command: 262, 393
Ta Bet: 136, 493
Tacan. *See* Airlift, navigation and navigators in
Tachikawa Air Base: 35, 48, 140n, 170, 182–183, 256, 259, 329, 380, 382, 397, 473n
Tactical Air Command: 26
    and aerial port squadrons: 137–138
    aircraft and units assigned: 144, 146, 170, 181–182, 563, 565
    aircraft usage lengths: 183
    and airlift doctrine: 104, 179–180
    airlifts by: 18n
    and cargo delivery systems: 484, 486
    crews provided by: 107
    developmental activity: 258–259
    and Farm Gate permanency: 63
    formation tactics: 223
    and gunships: 389
    helicopters assigned to: 235
    and radar guidance: 262
    and takeoff and landing improvements: 143
    and tours length: 92
    training programs: 184
    and troop-carrier helicopters: 29
Tactical air control system: 86, 88, 107
Tactical Air Force Squadron, Provisional: 91
Tactical Air Warfare Center: 258
Tactical Airlift Center: 258–259
Tactical Airlift Squadrons
    19th: 473n, 590
    21st: 473
    29th: 473n
    35th: 473
    41st: 473

61st: 571–574
309th: 473
311th: 473
458th: 521n, 532, 535n
459th: 521n, 535n
457th: 521n, 532, 535n, 536
535th: 521n, 535n
536th: 521n, 535n
537th: 526, 532, 534–535
772d: 473n
774th: 573n, 564
816th: 473n
915th: 473n
Tactical Airlift Wings
   314th: 473n, 482, 500, 530, 573
   315th: 473, 480, 483, 531, 590
   316th: 563
   317th: 565, 625
   374th: 473, 482, 541, 553, 560–567, 570–571, 576, 601–602, 605–606, 609–616, 632, 634, 638, 641–644
   384th: 609
   405th: 473
   463d: 473n, 479, 483–484
Tactical landing approach radar: 55
Tactical Wing, 34th: 63–64
Taddiken, Captain: 93
Taiwan. *See* Ching Chuan Kang
Taiwan crisis: 28, 34
Takeo: 624, 626
Takhli Air Base
   aerial port service: 409
   aircraft and units assigned: 448, 616
   airlifts to and from: 407–408, 445, 448, 606
Tan Hiep: 129
Tan Son Nhut: *76, 145, 155–156, 178, 188, 193, 255*
   accidents at: 252
   aerial port service: 138–139, 243, 414–415, 577–578
   aircraft lost at: 351
   aircraft and units assigned: 20, 42, 46, 68, 73, 85, 87, 92, 97, 106–107, 110, 123, 126, 145–146, 174, 176, 191, 195n, 207, 271, 274, 277, 319, 348, 397, 399, 411–412, 414–416, 451, 473, 499, 510, 521–522, 536, 548, 560, 562, 565, 571, 574, 605–606
   airfield construction and repair: *231*, 242
   airlifts to and from: 88, 90, 92–93, 96, 102, 105, 112, 114, 116, 136, 146, 150–151, 153, 174, 177, 214, 218, 278, 319, 323, 327–328, 330, 365, 383–384, 410–411, 504–505, 511, 514, 516, 536, 561, 564–566, 576, 592, 596, 602, 608–609, 612–613, 632, 640–644
   cargo handling: 138–139, 143, 209, 252, *254*, 270, 497, 548, 586, 599
   in casualty evacuation system: 396, 400
   civil airlines at: 404, 641
   command and control: 380, 607, 615, 649

TACTICAL AIRLIFT

    communications at: 108, 120, 536, 564, 576
    computer facilities: 470
    courier service: 406–407
    enemy assaults on: 319, 330, *331*, 643
    flareships at: 388
    French defense: 4
    fuel deliveries: 266
    helicopters and units assigned: 235–236
    liaison at: 359, 364
    living conditions: 94, 196, 483, 565
    maintenance and repair: 126, 249–250, *481*, 482, 490, 576, 606
    mess facilities: 196
    passenger service: 405–407, 598
    rigging service: 257
    runway conditions: 112
    safety and security measures: 606
    work conditions: 126
Tanks, enemy strength: 559
Tannenbaum, Leon M.: 160
Task Force 116 (Joint): 113, 407–408
Task Force Bravo: 329
Task Force Oregon. *See* Infantry Divisions, Americal
Tay Ninh
    aircraft and units assigned: 469
    airlifts to and from: 56, 128, 133, 225, *226–227*, 228–229, 279, 288–289, 349, 498, 504, 612
    cargo delivery: 349, 498–499, 561
    enemy assaults on: 228–229, 539
    navigation and communications facilities: 263
    truck supply: 323
Tay Ninh Province
    airlifts in: 99, *130*, 132, 653
    cargo delivery: *281*
    enemy assaults in: 225–229, 270
    parachute assaults in: *281*
Taylor, Maxwell D., USA: *157*
    and air units assignment: 44
    and airlift concept: 31
    and Civilian Irregular Defense Groups: 164
    and helicopter units commitment: 45
    as Presidential advisor: 32
    and quick reaction units: 95
    and troop units commitment: 171
Tchepone: 433, 435, 461, 508–509, 515–516
Team Romeo: 430
Tear gas drops: 389
Technicians. *See* Ground crews
Tegge, Richard: 48
Telephone service: 120, 350, 380
Teletype service: 120, 189, 350
Terrain, effect on airlift: 3, 164, 295, 332, 340, 429, 449
Terrorism by enemy: 42

INDEX

Tet offensive: 314, 317–325, 330, 351, 584
Thailand (*see also individual stations in*)
    aerial port service: 138–139
    air force development: 657
    aircraft evacuation to: 644, 647
    aircraft operation by: 411–412, 647
    aircraft transferred to: 616–617
    aircraft and units assigned: 46, 65, 91, 110, 113, 144, 406–408, 421–423, 448, 563, 607, 612–613, 615
    airfields in: 39, 422
    airlifts to and from: 6, 21, 35, 37–39, 422, 430–431, 439, 448, 450, 564, 576, 605, 607, 613, 616, 635, 680
    cargo handling: 140
    in casualty evacuation system: 396
    enemy airlifts reported: 435–438
    enemy threat to: 421, 423
    helicopters assigned to: 39, 453–457
    pilots use: 412–414
    training programs: 617
    troop units commitments to: 39, 410–411, *427*, 495
    USAF pilots in aircraft of: 79
Thanh Hoa bridge: 392
Thien Ngon: 499, 504
Thieu, Nguyen Van
    and Cambodia campaign: 508
    flight to Taiwan: 642
    and Khe Sanh campaign: 514
    and Laos campaign: 515
    and Pleiku campaign: 636
Thompson, Robert G. K.: 44
Thuy Dong: 504
Tien Phuoc: 490, 493, 533
Tieu Atar: 504
Tires, damage to: 184, 222–223, 225, 230, 256, 263, 405, 440, 490, 624, 656
Tokyo International Airport: 22
Tolson, John J., III, USA: 340
Thomsett, Warren P.: 62
Tonkin Gulf incident: 144
Tonle Cham
    aircraft lost at: 478, 618
    airfield construction: 279
    airlifts to: 498–499, 504, 618–619
    enemy assault on: 252, 618
Tou Morong: 223
Toups, Sidney E.: 499
Tour length: *See* Rotation and tour lengths
Tourane (later Da Nang): 4, 18, 20–22, 37–38
Tra My: 154
Traffic control: 17, 32, 52, 92, 104, 186–187, *188*, 189, 199–200, 204, 253, 285–286, 473–476, 510. *See also* Airlift, command, control and coordination
Traffic Management Agency: 380
Trai Bi: 277–278

TACTICAL AIRLIFT

Training programs
    aircrews: 8–11, 34–37, 59, 63, 85, 97, 123, 184, 354, 357, 369, 479, 485–486, 521, 571
    airborne units: 174 270–271, 274
    in aircraft: 32–39, 41–42, 51–53, 55, 58, 123, 158
    by Australia: 508
    Cambodian crews: 508, 617, 629
    in cargo handling: 139–140, 259, 261, 485–486, 596–597, 617
    Chinese aircrews: 429
    civilian aircrews: 441
    computer operators: 470
    enemy airborne units: 438
    flight engineers: 184, 369, 534
    French: 7–11, 16, 67
    ground crews: 34, 354, 370, 602
    helicopter pilots and crews: 455, 457, 494
    joint exercises: 140, 143–144
    Laotian crews: 452–454, 617
    loadmasters: 184, 534
    medical personnel: 399
    Meo tribesmen: 441
    in navigation: 184
    on-the-job: 490
    in parachute assaults: 495
    pilots: 42, 48–49, 67–68, 73, 123, 153, 180, 354, *356*, 357, 369, 426, 429, 457, 480, 533, 560–561, 582–583, 587–590, 593–596, 601, 603
    search-and-clear forces: 425
    by Soviet Army: 438, 452
    Special Forces: 42, 53, 150
    Tactical Air Command: 184
    Thai crews: 617
    VNAF: 42, 48–49, 67–68, 73, 429, 535–536, 560, 582–583, 587–590, 593–594, 596–599, 601–603
Tram Khnar: 626
Trans International Airways: 632–633
Transport. *See* Truck transport; Water transport
Transport aircraft. *See* Aircraft, fixed-wing; Airlift
Transport Group, 1503d: 383*n*
Transport Wing, 1503d: 140*n*
Trefry, Richard G., USA: 617
Triphibious assault: 575
Troop Carrier Group, 315th: 107, 118–120, 123, 125–126, 138, 141, 151–153, 159–161, 174, 194, 232, 388, 411–412, 588
Troop Carrier Squadrons
    21st: 182–183, 448, 450, 473
    22d: 140*n*, 383*n*
    29th: 183
    35th: 182–183
    41st: 183
    50th: 183, 185, 473, 566
    210th: 123
    311th: 123, 307

345th: 183, 249, 473, 609, 642
346th: 84, 89, 93
457th: 360, 373–374
458th: 360, 373–374
459th: 360, 364, 372
535th: 360
536th: 360
537th: 359–360, 365, 370
772d: 183
773d: 183
774th: 183, 473
776th: 183, 286, 473, 542
777th: 91
815th: 182–183
816th: 19
817th: 182–183
Troop Carrier Wings
    314th: 144, 182–184, 200, 250–251, 271, 274n, 329, 380, 395, 429, 479
    315th: 21, 187n, 190, 236, 270, 322, 451
    374th: 183, 274n, 312, 389, 395, 448–449, 545
    436th: 182
    463d: 144, 182–183, 249, 251, 274n, 351, 380, 393–394
    464th: 83–84, 90, 116, 128, 182
    483d: 9–11, 16–17, 20–22, 34–35, 353, 355, 357, 359, 363–364, 368–372, 375,
        521, 523, 527–530, 535–536, 590
    516th: 144, 182, 350
Troop lifts. *See* Airlift, troop lifts
Truck transport
    cargo movement and delivery by: 152, 185, 207, 247, 285, 323, 419, 421, 444,
        468, 498–505, 512, 514, 551, 570
    cargo tonnage moved: 117, 163, 186, 215, 224, 228, 246, 292, 499
    convoy system: 214–215, 219, 282–284, 292–293, 512, 525
    enemy: 620
    enemy assaults on: 322, 325, 513
    enemy supply system: 295
    fuel supplies: 117
    night convoys: 512
    security of: 117
    troop movements by: 225
Truman, Harry S: 3
Tunner, William H.: 26
Turk, Wilbert: 375, 522, 526, 533, *534*
Tuy Hoa
    accidents at: 197
    aircraft lost at: 200, 351
    aircraft and units assigned: 200, 248, 301, 473
    airfield construction and repair: 253
    airlifts to and from: 222–223, 364
    cargo handling: 185, *254*
    in casualty evacuation system: 397
    enemy assaults on: 236, 638

TACTICAL AIRLIFT

U-Tapao Air Base
    aircraft evacuation to: 644
    aircraft and units assigned: 410–411, 613–616, 625, 642
    airlifts to and from: 564, 606, 616, 623, 626, 629, 632–634, 642, 644–646
    cargo handling: 633–634
    command and control at: 380, 607, 615
    helicopters at: 628
Ubon Air Base
    aerial port service: 409–410
    aircraft lost at: 423
    aircraft and units assigned: 388–389, 393, 486
    airlifts to and from: 407–408, 427
Udorn Air Base
    aerial port service: 409–410
    aircraft and units assigned: 39, 393, 406–407, 446, 451, 629
    airlifts to and from: 407–408, 428, 446, 448, 451
    command and control at: 395
    helicopters assigned: 454, 456, 616
    maintenance and repair: 454
    Marine troops airlift to: 113–114
    truck delivery to: 444
United States Army
    aircraft integration into airlift: 121–123, 144, 190–191, 203, 236–238, 353–363
    aircraft losses: 354
    aircraft strength: 31, 110–111, 237, 353
    and aircraft and units assigned: 31, 45, 81, 108–111, 353, 359
    airlift concept: 27–28, 30–32, 104, 151, 159, 215–216, 233, 358, 523
    airlifts by: 16, 122, 137, 209–213, 219, 247, 290, 324–344, 373, 409–410, 513, 680–681, 683. *See also* Helicopters, airlift missions
    and airmobility concept: 29–30, 101, 108–111, 121, 144, 143, 203, 207–209, **216**, 267, 497, 653
    Army Support Command, Thailand: 409–410
    and cargo delivery systems: 484
    casualties: 81, 129, 136, 277, 341, 347, 375, 475
    and command and control: 104
    helicopters in. *See* Helicopters
    logistics command activated: 117–118
    parachute assaults: 128, 173, 218, *220*, 224, 244
    psywar missions: 59
    and roles and missions: 108–111, 115
    search-and-clear missions: 173
    tactical air support of. *See* Airlift, air strikes in support of
    troop units commitments: 169, 171, 173–174
United States Army, Vietnam
    aircraft assigned to: 359, 366
    complaints about airlift: 362–363
    organization: 209n
United States Information Agency: 401
United States Marine Corps
    airlift role: *See* Airlift, Marine Corps role in
    casualties: 288–290, 293, 295–316
    combat operations: 288–290, 293, 295–316
    decorations and awards: 316

INDEX

    helicopters use: 45, 136, 172, 296–316
    in joint operations group: 476
    missile units commitment: 170
    pilots proficiency: 315
    search-and-clear missions: 173
    troop units commitments: 38–39, 169–172, 208, 328
    III Marine Amphibious Force: 302–303, 315–316, 332, 353, 359, 366, 406–407
    4th Marine Regiment: 380
    26th Marine Regiment: 296, 316
    152d Marine Aerial Refueler Squadron: 288n
United States Military Assistance Advisory Group, Vietnam: 42, 67. *See also* McGarr, Lionel C.
United States Military Assistance Command, Thailand: 359, 366
United States Military Assistance Command, Vietnam (*see also* Abrams, Creighton W., Jr.; Westmoreland, William C.)
    and aircrews proficiency: 497
    and Air Force helicopters use: 235–236
    aircraft allocation by: 522
    aircraft assigned to: 359, 366
    and aircraft transfer to VNAF: 600–601
    and aircraft and units assignments: 91, 111, 116, 121, 145, 151, 174, 180, 182, 366, 375, 431
    and airfield construction and repair: 230–233, 513
    and airlift operations: 50, 106, 110, 228, 288, 324, 388, 472, 606
    and An Loc campaign: 541
    and Army aircraft integration into airlift: 121–122, 237
    and Australian units: 412–414
    and bombing missions: 394
    and Cambodia campaign: 505, 509
    and cargo delivery systems: 259–261
    cargo tonnages predictions: 114n, 119, 181–182, 228, 247, 297, 401, 527
    and cease-fire delegation: 608
    and combat control teams: 243, 476
    and command and control: 106–107, 118, 135, 175, 359–360
    and contract carriers: 404
    and dual airlift system: 430
    and emergency and priority missions: 330, 472, 505
    enemy casualties estimates: 293
    and enemy motivation: 147
    and forest-burning missions: 392
    and fuel supply: 513
    and helicopters in Thailand: 456
    inactivated: 615
    and joint air operations group: 476–477
    and Khe Sanh campaign: 296, 302, 514
    and Laos airfields: 349
    and liaison in airlift: 190
    and missiles use: 200
    and night airlifts: 285
    and parachute assaults: 224, 270
    and priority transportation system: 406–407
    and psywar missions: 58
    and quick reaction units: 96

and radar guidance: 262–263
and safety measures: 199–200
and search-and-clear missions: 115, 206, 347
and Special Forces aircraft: 151
and transportation allocations system: 106–107
and truck transport: 247, 468
and water transport control: 117
United States Navy
    aircraft evacuation by: 644–645
    airlifts by: 247, 290, 406–408
    gunfire support by: 20, 405
    in joint operations group: 476
    Naval Forces, Vietnam: 407–408
    Naval Support Activity, Saigon: 406–407
    tactical air support by: *308*
United States Support Activities Group: 615–616, 627

Van Brussel, Peter B., Jr.: 597–598
Van Cleeff, Jay: 346
Van Gieson, Henry B., III: 302
Vance, Cyrus R.: 235, 238
Vang Pao: 441–442, 453–455, 458, 461–462
Vang Vieng: 445, 453
Vann, John Paul: 566
Vientiane
    aircraft and units assigned: 451
    airfield at: 445
    airlifts to and from: 21, 38, 39, 440, 443, 448, 459, 464
    truck delivery to: 444
Vientiane–Luang Prabang highway: 462
Viet Cong. *See* North Vietnam
Viet Minh: 3, 5
Vietnamese Air Force (VNAF)
    activation: 67
    aircrews: 72, 639
    air terminal units: 598
    air traffic control: 88
    aircraft evacuation from: 644–645
    aircraft flying time rates: 583, 600, 620
    aircraft lost and damaged: 72, 74, 583, 586, 591, 593, 596, 600, 620–621, 639, 643
    aircraft transferred to: 42, 473, 477, 535, 560, 576, 581, *584*, 587–588, 590, 600–601, 616
    aircraft varied uses by: 74
    aircraft vulnerability: 73
    airlift units in: 42
    airlifts by: 45, *56*, 68, 72, 74, 81–82, 247, 285, 385, 421, 430, 493–508, 536, 540, 550, 554–555, 560–561, 563, 567–570, 577, 583–586, 592–597, 600–603, 619–621, 631, 636–639, 657–658, 683
    American pilots in aircraft of: 67–80, 582–583, 591–594
    bombing missions: 639
    cargo handling: 599
    cargo tonnages moved: 247, 583, 586, 592, 595, 602, 619–620

    in casualty evacuation: 592–597
    combat effectiveness: 582, 584
    command and control in: 81–82, 591, 595
    criticism of: 598
    decline in activities: 621
    deficiencies in: 581, 595, 597
    equipment transferred to: 599
    evaluation by advisors: 581–582, 586, 597–599, 603
    flareships use: 58, 73, 81
    flight schedules: 74
    flying practices and habits: 70–71, 583, 592, 595
    ground crews: 639
    helicopters lost and damaged: 597, 618, 620, 636
    helicopters use: 430, 586–587, 593–595, 597–598, 600, 621, 638, 657–658
    hostility toward Americans: 642–643
    hours and sorties flown: 68, 586, 595, 600
    insignia: 68
    irregularities in: 583
    landing methods: 70, 72
    language barrier: 71–72, 74–75, 411–412, 452, 589, 591, 599
    living conditions: 583
    loudspeaker missions: 74
    maintenance and repair: 67–68, 74, 586, 590–591, 597, 619–620
    morale and discipline: 67, 81, 541, 593, 596–597, 600, 639
    navigation proficiency: 72–73
    organization and expansion: 67–68, 80, 587–588, 590–591, 593–594, 598, 657
    in parachute assaults: 55, 57, 68, 73, 96–103, 128–129, *131*, 132–137, 575, 583–584
    personnel strength: 68, 582
    pilots proficiency and experience: 44, 67, 69, 81, 411–412, 583, 586, 591–592, 600, 603, 619
    pilots strength: 68, 80, 587
    pilots training: 80
    ports operation by: 599–600
    psywar missions: 58, 73
    radio equipment use: 73, 591
    relations with Americans: 74–75, 77–79, 80, 82, 103, 583, 591
    in search-and-rescue missions: 81
    squadron mission conversion: 582–583
    training programs: 42, 48–49, 67–68, 73, 429, 535–536, 560, 582–583, 587–590, 593–594, 596, 599, 601–603
        1st Transport Group: 68
        43d Air Transport Group: 79
        90th Parachute Maintenance and Delivery Base Unit: 497
        237th Helicopter Squadron: 54
        421st Transport Squadron: 412–414, 590
Vietnamese Army. *See* Army of the Republic of Vietnam
Vietnamese Marine Corps: 223, 319, 327, 509, 516, 561, 575, 577, 596, 637
Vietnamese National Army: 5
Vietnamization program: 80, 375, 421, 519, 521, 560, *580*, 581, 619
Vihear Suor: 626
Villotti, James S.: 456
Vinh Long: 323–324

TACTICAL AIRLIFT

Vo Dat: 218–219
Vogt, John W., Jr.: 606, 608, 615
Vung Tau (formerly Cap Saint Jacques): *131*, 132, *356*
    aerial port service: 140, 413
    aircraft lost at: 368
    aircraft and units assigned: 111, 121–122, 176, 209, 355, 360, 412–414, 521n, 522, 561
    airlifts to and from: 88, 116, 208n, 224, 228, 319, 365, 413–415, 642
    in casualty evacuation system: 398–400
    defense measures: 173
    enemy assaults on: 216, 319, 322
    maintenance and repair: 370, 412–414
    sabotage at: 200
    troop units assignments: 208, 224

Wake Island: 85, 642
Wallace, James L.: 345
Wallace, Robert F.: 542
War and Peace in the Space Age (Gavin): 29
War Zone C: 270, 277–279, 282
War Zone D: 102, 219
Warning systems: 476
Water drops: 540, 551
Water Pump Project: 452
Water supply: 62, 483
Water transport
    cargo handling and delivery: 111, 115, 152, 185, 222, 328, 349, 357, 418–419, 444–445, 505
    cargo tonnages moved by: 117, 140, 163, 186, 246–247, 292, 328, 625–626
    command and control of: 117
    enemy action against: 322
    troop movements by: 173, 222
Wattay Airfield: 440–441
Weather, effect on airlift. *See* Airlift, weather effect on
Webb, William W.: 583, 585
Weighing facilities: 257
West, Charles: 94
Western Pacific Transportation Office: 35, 380, 382–384
Westmoreland, William C.: *155–156*. *See also* United States Military Assistance Command, Vietnam
    in A Shau Valley campaign: 136, 332
    and Air Force helicopters use: 236
    and aircraft and units assignments: 174, 180, 236, 248
    and airfield construction and repair: 232, 292
    and airfields serviceable: 263
    and airlift operations: 137, 225, 285, 288, 321, 330
    and airmobile concept: 207–208, 216
    and Army aircraft integration into airlift: 236, 358–359, 363–364
    becomes USMACV commander: 137
    and cargo delivery systems: 257–259
    on command and control: 359
    and complaints about airlift: 362
    on enemy capabilities: 293

INDEX

    and Kham Duc campaign: 343
    and Khe Sanh campaign: 296
    and Laos airfields: 349
    and parachute assaults: 224, 270
    and RVN airborne units: 223
    and search-and-clear missions: 182, 206, 213, 225, 269, 279, 288, 293
    and Tet offensive: 321
    and troop units commitments: 171–172, 206, 208
    and truck transport: 185
Weyland, Otto P.: 10, *15*, 18
Wheel assembly: 90
Wheeler, Earle G.: 81, 208, *211*, 237
Whelan, Paul A.: 371
White, Thomas D.: 32
White Horse, Yukon Territory: 49
Wieland, Richard: 612
Wigington, John H.: 526
Wild, Hugh E.: 241, 286
Williams, Robert R., USA: 366–367, 375, 476
Wingate, Orde C., British Army: 41*n*
Witherington, Wayne J.: 85, 104
Work hours and conditions. *See* Aircrews; Ground crews
World Airways: 632, 637
World War II experience: 25–26, 41, 47, 247, 295, 557, 653, 691
Wounded Warrior Operation: 22
Wright, Howard W.: 91
Wyrick, Carl: 94, 163

Xiangkhoang: 21, 445, 459
Xuan Loc: 561, 639
Xuyen Moc: 572, 574–575

Yeager, Charles E.: 63*n*
Yellowstone Operation: 293
Yelton, John F.: *356*
York, Jerry A.: 534
Yudkin, Richard A.: 237–238

Zuckert, Eugene M.: 43–44, 55, 95, 233

www.ingramcontent.com/pod-product-compliance
Lightning Source LLC
Chambersburg PA
CBHW082017300426
44117CB00015B/2257